The Definitive Guide to Drupal 7

Benjamin Melançon, Jacine Luisi, Károly Négyesi, Greg Anderson, Bojhan Somers, Stéphane Corlosquet, Stefan Freudenberg, Michelle Lauer, Ed Carlevale, Florian Lorétan, Dani Nordin, Ryan Szrama, Susan Stewart, Jake Strawn, Brian Travis, Dan Hakimzadeh, Amye Scavarda, Albert Albala, Allie Micka, Robert Douglass, Robin Monks, Roy Scholten, Peter Wolanin, Kay VanValkenburgh, Greg Stout, Kasey Qynn Dolin, Mike Gifford, Claudina Sarahe, Sam Boyer, and Forest Mars, with contributions from George Cassie, Mike Ryan, Nathaniel Catchpole, and Dmitri Gaskin

Apress®

The Definitive Guide to Drupal 7

ISBN-13 (pbk): 978-1-4302-3135-6

ISBN-13 (electronic): 978-1-4302-3136-3

President and Publisher: Paul Manning
Lead Editors: Ben Renow-Clarke and Matthew Moodie
Technical Reviewer: Richard Carter
Editorial Board: Steve Anglin, Mark Beckner, Ewan Buckingham, Gary Cornell, Jonathan Gennick, Jonathan Hassell, Michelle Lowman, James Markham, Matthew Moodie, Jeff Olson, Jeffrey Pepper, Frank Pohlmann, Douglas Pundick, Ben Renow-Clarke, Dominic Shakeshaft, Matt Wade, Tom Welsh
Coordinating Editor: Debra Kelly
Copy Editor: Mary Behr
Compositor: MacPS, LLC
Indexer: BIM Indexing & Proofreading Services
Artist: April Milne
Cover Designer: Anna Ishchenko

Distributed to the book trade worldwide by Springer Science+Business Media, LLC., 233 Spring Street, 6th Floor, New York, NY 10013. Phone 1-800-SPRINGER, fax (201) 348-4505, e-mail orders-ny@springer-sbm.com, or visit www.springeronline.com.

For information on translations, please e-mail rights@apress.com, or visit www.apress.com.

Apress and friends of ED books may be purchased in bulk for academic, corporate, or promotional use. eBook versions and licenses are also available for most titles. For more information, reference our Special Bulk Sales–eBook Licensing web page at www.apress.com/bulk-sales.

The source code for examples and projects shown in this book is available to readers at definitivedrupal.org and apress.com. You will need to answer questions pertaining to this book in order to successfully download the code.

Dedicated to the Drupal community.

Contents at a Glance

iv

Contents

Foreword

There are many Drupal books out there vying for your hard-earned money. From site building to theming to module development, there are books out there that specialize in whatever area of Drupal you might be interested in.

This book, on the other hand, is one of a kind. Its aim is to expose you to *all* facets of Drupal, in many cases from the very experts who helped author them. There is material here for literally all levels of Drupal experience and interest.

The book starts with introductory material about getting up and running quickly with a simple site and how to extend it with some of Drupal's most popular contributed modules. There are also chapters on how to make your Drupal site not look like a Drupal site with both beginning and advanced theming and jQuery for front-end development. You'll learn how to customize Drupal through module development, for use cases that go beyond what the vast library of contributed projects can do, as well as how to port Drupal 6 modules to Drupal 7 and how to add automated tests to ensure your code stays working. And for the übergeeks out there, there's information on utilizing Drupal from the command line and pairing it with Git, and managing server deployments and performance. There's even material about more wide-reaching topics that expand far beyond Drupal, such as project management, creating documentation for your web site, and user experience.

Found throughout are best practice recommendations and tales of battle directly from the field, from a truly all-star cast of some of the biggest, brightest, and most innovative minds in the Drupal community. As the co-maintainer or Drupal 7, I'm incredibly excited to see this enormous body of work come together. Bravo to Benjamin and the rest of the authoring team!

Angela Byron (webchick)
Drupal 7 Maintainer

About the Authors

■ **Benjamin Melançon**, as a co-founder and principal of Agaric (`agaric.com`), helps people create and use powerful web sites. He and Agaric look to work with companies and organizations that value openness and freedom and share a passion for creating collaborative networks that scale. Seeking the most power possible for all people over their own lives (as a working definition of justice and liberty), Benjamin lives to connect ideas, resources, and people.

■ **Albert Albala** began dabbling in Drupal in 2006, after completing a university undergraduate degree combining linguistics and computer science and. After two years with Joomla, he co-founded `Mediatribe.net`, a partnership offering Drupal consulting services. In 2009 he joined Koumbit, a Drupal-oriented not-for-profit collective in Montreal. Being part of a larger team has allowed him to concentrate on Simpletest and Features, two areas that are reinforcing the quality of Drupal sites as the platform matures. Albert's other activities include small-scale international development projects through Terre des jeunes.

■ **Greg Anderson** is one of the co-maintainers of drush, the Drupal shell. He also runs the Developer Technical Support Group in the Americas for Ricoh Corporation. Greg uses Drupal in both his work and in his personal life. He did the Drupal conversion of the web site for The Great Dickens Fair, where he and other performers bring the spirit of Christmas to life. He is assisting with another large migration of many web sites for The Society for Creative Anachronism, a historic recreation society where he and his wife run the children's program. He also works with a community school district support group and writes an environmental blog with his wife.

■ **Sam Boyer** led the Drupal project's migration from CVS to Git and continues to lead the efforts of the Drupal.org Git Team to expand Git-related features on `Drupal.org`. To that end, he is also a member of the d.o infrastructure team.

Sam's core contributions were light prior to D8, but he now devotes a fair bit of effort to a scattering of Drupal's lower-level, critical path systems. In contrib, he co-maintains Panels and CTools with merlinofchaos, and he leads maintainership of the Version Control API suite of modules.

■ **Ed Carlevale** is a long-time web developer at MIT, working in the area of energy and sustainability (`mitenergyclub.org`, `sustainability.mit.edu`). As the founder of the nascent MIT Drupal Group, he has hosted many Drupal events at MIT, including Dries Buytaert's State of Drupal (MIT World, 2009), Boston Design4Drupal Camp 2009 and 2010, and the monthly meetings of the Boston Drupal Group, led by Moshe Weitzman.

■ **George Cassie** has built a variety of sites and tools with Drupal, starting back in version 4.7. He currently works as a Client Advisor at Acquia with a focus on Drupal Gardens.

■ **Nathaniel Catchpole** has been using Drupal since version 4.5 and has been a regular contributor to Drupal core since 2006. He contributed more than 400 patches to the Drupal 7 release alongside extensive code profiling, and he maintains the entity cache and performance hacks contributed modules.

▓ **Stéphane Corlosquet** holds a master's degree specializing in Semantic Web from the Digital Enterprise Research Institute (DERI), Ireland. He currently works at the Mass General Institute for Neurodegenerative Disease (MIND), MGH, as a Software Engineer focusing on the Science Collaboration Framework, a Drupal-based distribution to build online communities of researchers in biomedecine.

Stéphane has contributed to Drupal 6 and is one of the top 30 contributors to Drupal 7 core. He maintains the RDF module in Drupal 7 and is a member of the Drupal security team. Since joining the community in 2005, he has been a speaker at many DrupalCons and DrupalCamps, mostly on the topic of RDF and Drupal. He co-authored "Produce and Consume Linked Data with Drupal!" which won the ISWC 2009 Best Semantic Web In Use Paper award.

Stéphane lives in the Boston area with his beloved wife, Diliny, new-born son, Kiran, and hyperactive dog, Maya.

▓ **Kasey Qynn Dolin** is an anthropologist with extensive experience studying (and organizing) the growth and survival of communities and not-for-profit projects. She received a BS in Anthropology, with minors in Latin American Studies (focus on Brazil) and International Studies from Virginia Commonwealth University. Her published works include "Candombléwords, Sounds, and Power in Jamaican Rastafari" and "Yorùbán Religious Survival in Brazilian Candomblé."

▓ **Robert Douglass** has worked with Drupal full-time since 2004. He wrote the first book that was published about Drupal (*Building Online Communities with Drupal, phpBB and Wordpress;* Apress, 2005) and has been the technical editor of all three editions of *Pro Drupal Development* (Apress, 2007). Through teaching and personal influences he has helped hundreds of people transition into careers as Drupal developers and service providers. In 2005 he led Drupal's involvement in the first Google Summer of Code program and has been active as a leader and mentor ever since.

Robert has been a member of the Drupal Association General Assembly since 2006 and has actively participated in many Association activities, including the organization of DrupalCons and DrupalCamps. In 2008 he co-founded the Drupal-Initiative, Germany's non-profit for the promotion of Drupal. After a two-year tenure as the Vice President of that organization, he helped coordinate the election of a new Board and handed over control in 2010.

In 2007 Robert founded and built goPHP5.org, an initiative to bring open source PHP projects and Webhosts together in order to speed the upgrade to PHP5. One result of this is that Drupal 7 relinquished PHP4 compatibility, allowing the core team to do things like add the PDO database drivers. Over 100 software projects and over 200 web hosts joined the movement and it received a lot of press.

Robert's largest code contributions to Drupal have come in the form of the Apache Solr module and the Memcache module, both of which began in 2007 and which he still maintains today. In addition to being a full-time consultant and Advisor for Acquia, Robert also serves on the advisory boards of Commerce Guys and ICanLocalize, where he helps with business, product, and marketing decisions.

▓ **Stefan Freudenberg** is a back-end developer with some experience in Linux system administration. Drawn into developing web sites with Drupal and into the community in late 2008, he has spent most of his commercial and volunteer activity on it. His debugging and profiling skills make him popular with his teams while arguing for simpler architecture and standards compliance is what he enjoys most but is not always as well received. Stefan is a principal at Agaric (agaric.com).

▓ **Dmitri Gaskin** is a Drupal contributor who is perhaps better known as dmitrig01. He started coding when he was 8 and started with Drupal when he was 11. Since then, Dmitri has become very familiar with Drupal, PHP, JavaScript, and jQuery. He maintains several modules (including Drush Make) but mostly works on Drupal core patches. Dmitri has talks at Drupalcon, Badcamp, and Google. When Dmitri isn't coding, he's writing music, listening to music, or attending the tenth grade.

▓ **Mike Gifford** founded OpenConcept Consulting Inc. in 1999. He has been particularly active in developing and extending open source content management systems to empower people to have more control over their own sites. Mike has been very active in building online campaigns for progressive organizations and politicians in both Canada and the United States.

Since 2005, OpenConcept (OC) has been developing exclusively on Drupal. The OC team has contributed a number of modules to the Drupal community and promotes the use of Drupal within the government and non-profit sectors.

Mike has been involved with accessibility issues since the early 1990s and is a strong advocate for standards-based design. Since 2009, he has contributed to the accessibility enhancements adopted by the Drupal community, including improvements in Drupal 7 core. Mike has presented at DrupalCamp Toronto & Montreal, most recently on OC's work on accessibility enhancements.

▨ **Dan Hakimzadeh** is an original co-founder of Agaric. Dan spends his time and energy building on this mystical phenomenon popularly called the Internet. He believes in the principles of free open source software and develops primarily using the Drupal content management framework.

▨ **Michelle Lauer** (aka miche on `drupal.org`) started her Drupal adventures in 2006 and quickly became known for her incredible sense of detail while possessing the ability to see the big picture. These innate skills allowed Michelle to cultivate her specialty of site architecture and multi-phased deployments. In addition to custom module development and theming, she develops and implements the strategy for complex content architecture from the end user experience to the manageability by web site administrators. Michelle's resume includes presentations at DrupalCon Paris, DrupalCon San Francisco, and DrupalCamp Montreal, as well as coordinator and curriculum author for DrupalCamp NH Training Day. Learn more about Michelle on `bymiche.com` and follow her on Twitter @bymiche.

▨ **Florian Loretan** started working with Drupal in 2005, a passion which turned into a full-time job two years later. As a Drupal developer, he has worked on many large social networking projects and has provided consulting services to many well-established web development agencies. His contributions include modules and themes as well as many core patches. Originally from Switzerland, Florian has also been an active member in many communities worldwide. He was a core organizer of the first Drupal Dev Days, a track chair for DrupalCon Copenhagen and he has participated in the organization of many other events. He has given presentations at DrupalCons, DrupalCamps and various local communities from Geneva to San Diego. Florian is a co-founder of Wunderkraut, a company providing Drupal coaching and consulting services for the European market. He occasionally writes on his personal blog at `happypixels.com`.

▨ **Jacine Luisi** is a front-end developer, specializing in Drupal theme development. She's been working on web sites since 2004 and has been working primarily with Drupal since 2007. She spends much of her free time working on markup- and CSS-related issues for Drupal core; she also works on contributed projects such as the Skinr module and the Sky theme. She currently resides in Rye Brook, NY.

▨ **Forest Mars** is a hypermedia architect who has been using Drupal since 2005—mainly in the space of media and business integration—and is extremely active in the Drupal community. As a member of the DrupalCon Paris 2009 team he built the infamous "Druplicon Road Trip" site. Some of his recent projects include architecting a video delivery platform for the world's largest television network and New York City's first civic engagement platform. In whatever time he has left over he gives talks on the Drupal API such as "Bongo for Mongo" and "The Horrible Truth about Drupal." He lives in New York without his two cats.

▨ **Allie Micka** has been an open source developer and advocate since 2001. She has worked on several open source applications, including three years of extensive development and participation in the Drupal project. Through her hosting and services work, she has provided active sponsorship and education in local communities and now works on education, infrastructure and open source development at Advantage Labs. Prior to this, Allie was the team manager of web development for a major online brokerage, which taught her to apply enterprise business strategies to sustainable community participation.

Robin Monks (robinmonks.com) is an avid open source contributor with over seven years experience within the Drupal community and is the founder of Podhurl Inc. He currently works on tools and services to expand the growth of the "Open Web."

Károly Négyesi spent the 1990s as a columnist and editor of Hungary's then-largest computing monthly, Chip Magazine. After that, he turned to web programming. His life and Drupal got hopelessly entangled in 2004. Since then he has become one of the most prolific core contributors with a brief stint of being the first leader of the security team. These days he is the senior software architect for Examiner.com, one of the biggest Drupal-based web sites. He is very intrigued about cognitive sciences and considers Orson Scott Card's *Ender's Game* as the Book.

Dani Nordin (tzk-design.com) is a user experience designer who switched from Wordpress to Drupal in 2008. Since then, she's been active as a voice in the Design for Drupal community and has spent entirely too much time looking for ways to make design for Drupal more efficient and effective. She speaks regularly at Boston Drupal events, including Boston's Design for Drupal Camp. Dani is currently writing *The Designer's Guide to Drupal*, to be released in 2011. You can find her most often on Twitter, where she goes by @danigrrl.

Mike Ryan has given much to the Drupal community since first contributing in 2003. He's behind the Migrate and Table Wizard modules, and he specializes in migrating data to Drupal as part of Cyrve. He was also the original author of the Pathauto module, the extremely popular Drupal module for automatically creating friendly URLs for pages and thus greatly improving SEO.

Claudina Sarahe began her career as a front-end developer for both Pop Art and The New Group in Portland, Oregon. In 2007, she left the West Coast and set up shop in New York, where she began work at the *Huffington Post*. She then went on to become one of the founding members of UNICEF Innovation. It was at UNICEF where her interest in open-source technology strategies developed. She further pursued this at Method, leading interactive development for clients such as Charlie Rose, PBS, Scholastic, and Count Me In. She lead the strategy and initial product development for Vestify, a crowdfunding web application for entrepreneurs powering the MassChallenge Global Start-Up Competition.

For the last three years and counting she has been working with Drupal and loves the code but above all, the community. She still loves front-end development and is excited about the HTML 5 initiative and overall rise in concern within the Drupal community around front-end issues, including usability and accessibility.

Claudina Sarahe has turned a lot of her focus to bettering collaboration between clients and technologists and to Drupal education for less advantaged and bi-lingual middle to high school students. She believes the philosophy and practices of open source offer great models for society as a whole to learn from. She is currently a principal at Agaric (agaric.com).

Amye Scavarda is a project manager. She's been involved with Drupal since October 2008 and in that time has realized how much there is to learn. She runs Function, a consulting company focusing on open source, and organizes community events in her spare time. She lives in Portland, OR and you'll find her online as @msamye on twitter and amye in IRC.

Roy Scholten is an interaction designer and has a small design studio, yoroy. He lives in the Netherlands and speaks Dutch, English, and German. He is the UX maintainer for Drupal 7. Before Drupal 7 reached beta, Roy made a Drupal 7 site using only core functionality with a custom theme that is CSS only. It's in Dutch at gaghilversum.nl.

Bojhan Somers is an interaction designer living and working in Amsterdam. He is passionate about designing complex (web) applications and physical things, and he is studying Interaction Design at Utrecht school of Arts. Bojhan is active as UX-Team Lead in the Drupal community, and he regularly speaks about open source, information architecture, and design on conferences. Bojhan has been involved with the Drupal community, helping form the UX team and taking a leading role in bringing user experience changes to the core software. He enjoys the challenges of designing in an open source environment.

▓ **Susan Stewart** is an eight year Drupal veteran with a passion for community engineering. As Drupal's Support Team lead and president of Drupal Indy Group, Susan is always looking for new ways to grow the community and turn passive consumers into active contributors. She works as a Drupal consultant in Indianapolis, Indiana.

▓ **Greg Stout** is Director of Technology at GlobalPost. Each month GlobalPost serves breaking and in-depth global international news to more than 6 million readers from its Drupal site.

A trained expert in user interface design and development, Greg has 16 years experience in web application development, web site development, product and project management, feature planning, specification, design, creation, and usability testing. He has worked on a number of high-profile commercial web sites including Sovereign Bank and Kinko's Print on demand B2B service.

Recently, Greg was part of the User Interface Development team at Ektron Inc., which produces the popular .N scalable web authoring and content management solution CMS400.NET. He holds a BA in Computer Graphics and Visual Effects from the Roy H. Park School of Communications at Ithaca College, Ithaca, NY.

▓ **Jake Strawn** has been working with the web since 1998. He started with a brief background in HTML/CSS, moving into PHP/MySQL and web application programming. After almost eight years of PHP/MySQL programming, he discovered Drupal and his life was changed forever, as complex tasks were made simple with a framework built for extensibility and efficiency. Jake has extensive experience with the Drupal framework with over 1600 commits to his name (drupal.org/user/159141). He has been a speaker at many Drupal events including DrupalCons and DrupalCamps. Jake works almost exclusively with Drupal 7 now and has invested hundreds of hours into learning and expanding on the new Drupal 7 APIs, including upgrading his 960 grid-system–based Omega base theme (drupal.org/project/omega), which promises to be one of the most powerful base themes in Drupal 7. Jake also recently relaunched his blog (himerus.com) on Drupal 7.

▓ **Ryan Szrama** got his start in web development through an online sales company based in Louisville, KY, his home of over 10 years. It was there that he nursed Ubercart through its infancy to its use on over 20,000 web sites as the Project Lead and community face of the project. Ryan joined Commerce Guys in 2009 and continued to lead Ubercart until switching gears into Drupal Commerce, a new initiative that empowers users to build e-commerce sites with the best new features Drupal 7 has to offer. He focuses most of his time developing the code base, growing the community of contributors to the project, and training new users online and at community events.

▓ **Brian Travis** has been disassembling technology since shortly after birth. Before computers came along, he was content with household appliances. An advocate of the "learn by making mistakes" school, Brian is never afraid of doing just that. He lives in beautiful New Hampshire.

▓ **Kay VanValkenburgh** is a Boston-based Drupal project director with a strong focus on training and mentorship. His latest venture is OwnSourcing, started in 2010 to develop hands-on training and project-specific documentation that help non-developers do great things with Drupal. Under the same aegis, Kay founded a mentorship program to help budding Drupal developers get their start (see ownsourcing.com/mentorship). Kay geeks out on usable software, how people learn, world languages, and competitive sailing.

▓ **Peter Wolanin**'s involvement with Drupal dates to late 2005 when a friend who had been a Howard Dean supporter involved him in a project to build a new web presence for the local Democratic party club. They started building the site using Drupal 4.7 beta. Peter soon became as much interested in the challenge of fixing bugs and adding features in Drupal core and contributed modules as actual site building. He became a noted contributor to Drupal 5, 6, and 7; a member of the Drupal documentation team; a member of the Drupal Security Team; and was elected a Permanent Member of the Drupal Association in 2010. Peter joined the Acquia engineering team in 2008, and enjoys the company of his stellar colleagues. Peter graduated from Princeton University, received a doctoral degree in Physics from the University of Michigan, and conducted post-doctoral and industrial research in Biophysics and Molecular Biology.

About the Technical Reviewer

Richard Carter is a seasoned web designer and front-end web developer with a focus on integrating designs into content management, e-commerce, and other software. He has worked with clients including Directgov, NHS Choices, and University College Dublin, and—most memorably—a Buddhist abbey.

Richard is author of four books (*MediaWiki Skins Design*, Packt Publishing, 2008; *Magento 1.3 Themes Design,* Packt Publishing, 2011; *Joomla! 1.5 Themes Cookbook*, Packt Publishing, 2010; and *Magento 1.4 Themes Design*, Packt Publishing, 2011) and has acted as a technical reviewer on *MediaWiki 1.1 Beginners Guide* (Packt Publishing, 2010) and *Inkscape 0.48 Essentials for Web Designers* (Packt Publishing, 2010).

Currently Creative Director at Peacock Carter Ltd, a web design agency based in the North East of England, Richard tweets (@RichardCarter) and blogs at earlgreyandbattenburg.co.uk.

Acknowledgments

Tremendous thanks to all the many people who reviewed or revised any portion of this book, including Susan Mildrum of LinioGroup.com (First Steps, Extending Your Site, Module Development), Diliny Corlosquet (Commerce), Moshe Weitzman (Drush, Page Rendering), Angela Byron (Scaling Drupal), Brian Gilbert, Eric Johnston, Daniel Kudwein (Contributing to the Community), Fox (The Other 90%), Rich Johnson (Deploy), Shreya Sanghani and Andrew Grice (Preface, Contributing to the Community), Amanda Miller Johnson (Introduction), Evelyn Melançon and Stephen Cataldo (Module Development), Matt Corks, Heidi Strohl, Christopher Gervais, Guillaume Boudrias, Shane Bill, Koumbit.org (Simpletest), Greg Knaddison, Ben Jeavons, and Nick Maloney (Security), Lin Clark, Oshani Seneviratne, Nick Maloney, Boris Mann for the analogy of RDFa and food for robots (Semantic), Benjamin Doherty (GIT), Reinhard Gloggengiesser (Site-specific Code, Distributions and Installation Profiles), and Boz Hogan (Building a Drupal 7 Site, Views). In addition, various authors put in significant work as reviewers also. In particular, Károly Négyesi acted as technical editor and a consistent push for quality on many chapters, especially in Part 4 on theming and Part 5 on module development. Stéphane Corlosquet and Albert Albala also put in review work on many chapters, joined by Dan Hakimzadeh, Amye Scavarda, Ed Carlevale, Dani Nordin, Peter Wolanin, and more.

Preface: Why Drupal?

By Benjamin Melançon

Drupal is a great content management system, a powerful framework for web applications, and a cutting edge social publishing platform. Above all, Drupal is more than software—it is a vibrant community of developers, designers, project managers, business innovators, technology strategists, user experience professionals, standards and accessibility advocates, and people who just mess around with stuff until they figure it out.

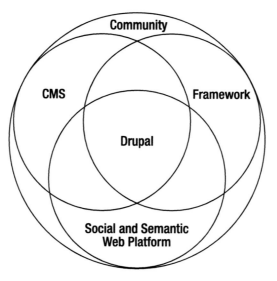

Figure 1. Drupal as the intersection of web content management system, application framework, and social and semantic publishing platform—encompassed by a diverse community

Drupal Is a CMS for Building Dynamic Web Sites

"The stuff that I am able to build with Drupal ... is just mind-blowing."

—Merlin Mann of 43folders.com

With Drupal, you get all the features of a powerful content management system, or CMS—user login and registration; definition of types of users and content; different levels of permissions; content creation, editing, categorization, and management; syndication and aggregation—out of the metaphorical box. In addition to this core functionality, there's an expanding universe of additional functionality available from the rising influx of community contributions.

The Views module (see Chapter 3) allows you to organize and display content in any number of ways. The Groups module (see Chapter 5) can be used to create online workgroups, discussion groups, and more. Drupal Commerce (see Chapter 25) allows you to configure full online stores. This is just a small sampling of the powerful extensions available to Drupal through contributed modules (see Chapter 4 for some more). From theming examples to make your site look better (see Chapters 15 and 16) to command line tools (Chapter 26) to powerful search (Chapter 31), if you want to build it in Drupal, it's very likely that someone already has—and has contributed the code or the instructions back to the community. If you want to go beyond functionality that anyone has contributed yet by writing your own modules (Chapters 18 to 24), there will be a lot of help out there for that, too. (See Chapter 9 for getting the most out of Drupal by participating in the community and Chapter 38 for contributing to this ecosystem yourself.)

Drupal is written in PHP with a great deal of JavaScript (mostly using the JQuery library) for the front-end experience, and it uses a database such as MariaDB/MySQL or PostgreSQL to store both content and configuration. Of course, by doing enough custom coding with these or other programming languages and databases, a developer can do anything a Drupal site can do. But why? Using Drupal saves site builders from reinventing the wheel, allowing a focus on achieving their goals. Drupal takes you where you drive it, without you having to build a car first.

> *"I needed a system that was able to take lots of different types of structured content and slice and dice it in different ways. [...] I had thought of a really cool way to organize my data and then I realized I would need to write a CMS on top of that, and I didn't want to spend the next eight years of my life writing it. And I found out a bunch of people had spent the last eight years of their life writing it, and it was called Drupal; so I was thrilled."*

—Jeff Eaton

Drupal Is an Application Framework

"Yes, Drupal is what you need it to be."

—Wim Mostrey

Drupal has become so solid at its core, so extensible, and so powerful for building different kinds of web sites that it is more than a CMS: it is a platform for developing serious web applications. Each major release includes better APIs (Application Programming Interfaces; how code talks to code) and other powerful features that take it beyond being a CMS.

Drupal is used as the basis for different types of applications, from smart phone and Facebook apps to web sites with complex business logic (nysenate.gov/mobile, data.gov.uk, zagat.com) to social media and retail-ready software as a service (buzzr.com). Drupal can also be found in such non-CMS roles as the front end for Java-based applications and the back end for AJAX or Flash-driven front ends.

Where this distinction between framework and CMS or other product can mean the most to you is the growth of distributions built on Drupal to solve specific use cases. Examples include OpenAtrium (openatrium.com) for team intranets, Drupal Commons (drupalcommons.com) for social business, OpenPublish (openpublishapp.com) for online publishers, and OpenScholar (scholar.harvard.edu) for personal academic and research web sites. (See Chapter 34 for more on distributions, including how to create your own.)

Drupal Is a Social and Semantic Web Platform

"If you have to be the center of the world, you will either succeed and own everything, or you will die."

—Sir Tim Berners-Lee

The ideal of the social and semantic web embraces a vision for a future where information isn't trapped in a single web site or company. Instead, your information and that which others share with you is under your control and available among multiple platforms and devices. Sites working together offer a way out of a dystopian world where control of connections among people and data is all or nothing. Drupal and its support for RDF (Resource Description Framework) help make this better future possible.

RDF helps label data in a way that computers can universally understand, so that they can do intelligent things with data from diverse sources. By building tools directly into Drupal that make it easy to share structured data, we are helping usher in the Semantic Web, the age of linked data, when web sites and other Internet-connected devices can automatically answer complex questions based on data shared all over the Internet.

Drupal Is a Community

Another reason to choose Drupal is this book—and many, many other books, videos, web sites, classes, and songs. (Well, maybe not the songs. Search at your own risk.) The large number of beginner-friendly and expert-ready resources growing up around Drupal are both an effect of and a contributor to its success and growth.

The top 10 Drupal shops in the world could switch to stone tablet technology tomorrow and there would still be an amazing array of contributors to carry development forward. Not many free software projects can say that, and, of course, no proprietary products can make such a claim. Of course, most Drupal companies are growing along with Drupal, not leaving the scene.

A Community at Critical Mass

With Drupal events happening all over the world several times a year, there is objective reason to believe that Drupal has achieved critical mass as a vibrant participatory project, but anecdotes are more fun. Drupal developer Matt Schlessman wrote about his first Drupal conference, DrupalCon San Francisco, in 2010:

> As I stepped off the plane, I wasn't sure what to expect. To date, I had been amazed by the energy of the Drupal community and the great things folks are doing with Drupal. But would the conference live up to all of the DrupalCon hype?
>
> I had my answer within minutes of hailing a taxi. As we merged onto the 101, the driver asked me why I was in town. Assuming he wouldn't be familiar with Drupal, I mentioned that I was in town for a convention.
>
> "Is it Drupalcon?" he asked. Indeed.
>
> "Do you work for a Drupal company?" Yes, Acquia.
>
> In the middle of the freeway, the cab driver turned around in his seat with excitement and exclaimed, "That's great! I have two Drupal Gardens sites! I love Drupal! And I love Dries!"
>
> Wow! The first five minutes. Unbelievable.

The number one reason to use Drupal is not the functionality, the extensibility, the power, the flexibility, or even anything related to the code. The number one reason to use Drupal is the breadth and depth of the community.

Drupal Is...

- ... a Belgian student who shared his college dorm intranet software with the world (buytaert.net).

- ... a community leader (webchick.net) who co-maintains the entire Drupal 7 release, welcomes and helps new contributors, routinely organizes essential initiatives for Drupal, makes a living consulting and training, and still manages to spend some time with her wife.

- ... thousands of people converging on Paris, San Francisco, Copenhagen, Chicago, London, or Denver from all over the world to see, show, share, meet, eat, talk, and dream Drupal (drupalcon.org).

- ... a 145-year-old liberal magazine now publishing online with a CMS that's "more in synch with our politics" (thenation.com).

- ... the campaign of the first Republican Senator from Massachusetts in 35 years (scottbrown.com).

- ... a web service for progressive political candidates (starswithstripes.org).

- ... the United States government (sba.gov and whitehouse.gov, among others).

- ... the online home of libertarian communism (libcom.org).

- ... the first U.S. automobile company to have an initial public stock offering in 50 years (teslamotors.com).

- ... an international association of interaction designers (IxDA.org).

- ... a couple of comedians (robinwilliams.com and chrisrock.com).

- ... the largest corporate participatory media site (examiner.com) and many small anti-corporate participatory media sites around the world (such as bolivia.indymedia.org and tc.indymedia.org).

- ... hundreds of thousands of sites of all sizes and purposes, including tens of thousands of sites hosted for free on Drupal 7 as a service (drupalgardens.com).

- ... thousands of people making their living doing Drupal, from a wizard (angrydonuts.com) making powerful tools (partly paid for by high-end web sites, but used by everyone) to a key employee (angrylittletree.com) at a high profile Drupal shop, to a worker cooperative focusing on the needs of community organizations (palantetech.com).

Drupal is all this and much, much more. Drupal is also, or could be, you.

What's New in Drupal 7

by Dani Nordin

Of course, every Drupal release is better than the last; otherwise, there'd be no point. However, a case can be made that Drupal 6 was a greater leap forward than any previous release, and that Drupal 7 is a still greater leap. The section highlights some of the more notable improvements.

Note This book is written to be as useful to people who never used Drupal before as to those who have used it before Drupal 7. This seemed like a good approach given that the Drupal community roughly doubles in size after every major release.

Easier to Use

An entirely revamped administrative interface makes routine tasks easier, with many improvements added specifically for site builders and content editors (Figure 2).

Administrative toolbar: Navigation for administrative tasks is now provided by a Toolbar located at the top of the browser window. Toolbar access can be set via User Roles, and only the functionality already permitted to that Role will be available from the toolbar.

Shortcuts drawer: Below the administrative toolbar is the Shortcuts drawer, which can be toggled open or closed. A Plus or Minus icon on every administrative screen adds or removes a shortcut from the drawer. Shortcuts can be as general (a link to the Blocks page) or as specific as you like (a link to a specific view while you're still refining it). Also, shortcuts can be saved as sets, making it possible to create one set of shortcuts for a Site Editor, another set for administrators, etc.

Contextual links: Contextual links are noted by a small wrench icon when you hover over various pieces of site content, such as blocks, views, menu lists, and teasers. They provide one-click navigation to editing screens related to that piece of content, greatly reducing the clicks-per-task for most routine Drupal tasks. As importantly, contextual links provide a useful cheat-sheet for Drupal newcomers who may not know the source of the content they're trying to edit. After you have made your edits and saved the block, view, or menu, the contextual link then returns you to the original screen. Drupal 7 is filled with many small touches like that, and, taken together, they significantly improve the Drupal experience. For more information on the User Experience principles in Drupal 7, see Chapter 32 in this book.

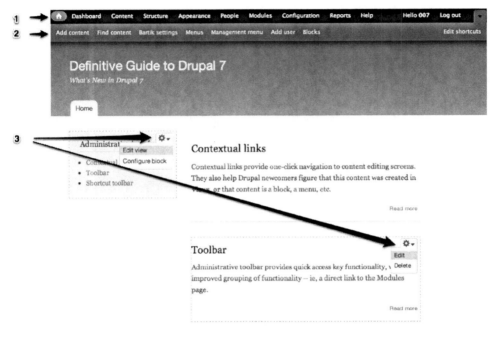

Figure 2. Improvements to Drupal 7's administrative interface include 1) administrative toolbar, 2) shortcuts drawer, and 3) contextual links.

Drupal's new admin interface includes a number of other enhancements to the content creation and curation process, including a new Dashboard with a simple and powerful drag-and-drop interface that can be customized by site administrators to include recent content, comments/content in need of moderation, or any other block available to your Drupal site (see Figure 3).

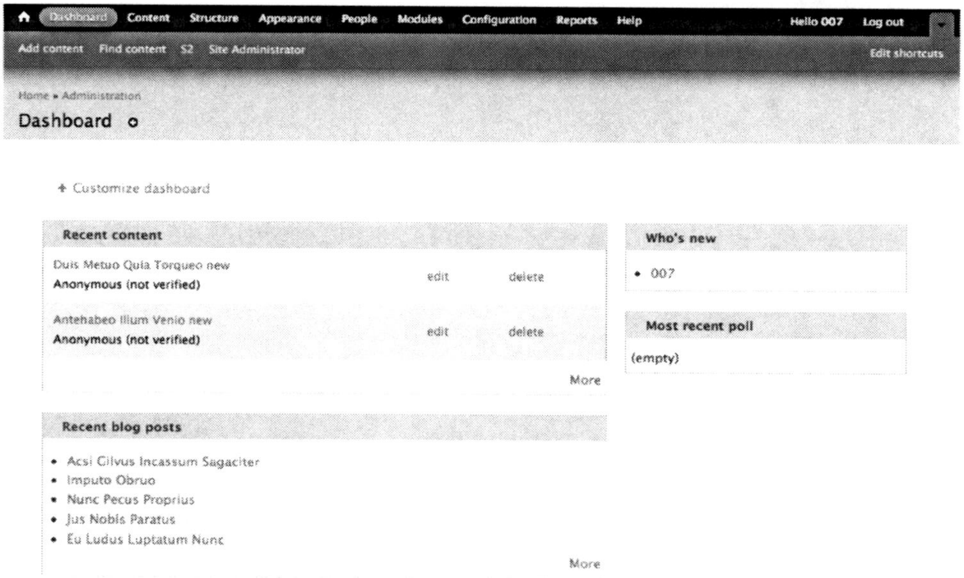

Figure 3. The Drupal Dashboard gives site users a customized view of the information they need to perform content or user maintenance. Administrators can customize the dashboard depending on what individual site editors need.

More Flexible

With Drupal 7, you can define your own content structure and add custom fields to content, users, comments, and more—without adding modules. In addition to creating custom text and list fields, you can upload images directly into Drupal fields and create custom Image Styles to automatically scale and crop your images.

You can also extend your site with some of the over 1,000 modules available for Drupal 7 at the time of this writing. Many module and theme maintainers took and fulfilled the D7CX pledge, meaning that more contrib modules were ready for the new version of Drupal on the date of its release than ever before.

Drupal 7 also now supports different types of databases, including MariaDB 5.1.44 and greater, MySQL 5.0.15 and greater, PostgreSQL 8.3 and greater, or SQLite 3.x. This gives you more flexibility and control over your site's data.

More Scalable

Your Drupal 7 site will be fast, responsive, and able handle huge amounts of traffic thanks to improved JavaScript and CSS optimization, better caching, and more. Drupal 7 also requires PHP 5.2.4 or greater to run, which leads to better performance, but may require checking with your web host before installing or upgrading.

Other Changes in 7

In addition to the changes previously listed, the following important changes have also been incorporated into Drupal 7.

Install Modules and Themes Through the User Interface

In Drupal 7, you can now install contributed modules and themes directly in the Drupal interface, either by providing a link to an external source or uploading the file directly (see Figure 4). Similarly, you can update modules and themes directly through the Drupal UI, a vast improvement over previous versions of Drupal.

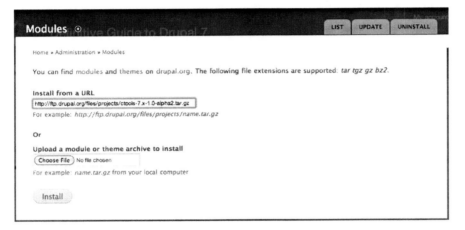

Figure 4. Installing a new module is easy through the Drupal interface.

New Core Themes and Enhancements

The new version of Drupal also includes several new default themes, including:

- Bartik: The Drupal 7 default theme, a clean, multi-region theme that allows easier customization of colors, regions, and CSS style settings (Figure 5).

- Seven: The Drupal 7 administration theme, a minimalist theme used in configuration overlays and administration pages.

- Stark: A completely empty theme that provides a way to look under the hood at Drupal's default markup. This is useful for module and theme developers who need to see the markup that Drupal is spitting out before they start working.

***Figure 5**. Bartik, Drupal 7's new default theme*

As good as the themes themselves are, what's important here is the explicit separation between web site theme and administrative theme, as Figure 6 indicates. Bartik is a sophisticated theme with 15 configurable regions. By contrast, Seven has only two regions, greatly simplifying the administrative interface.

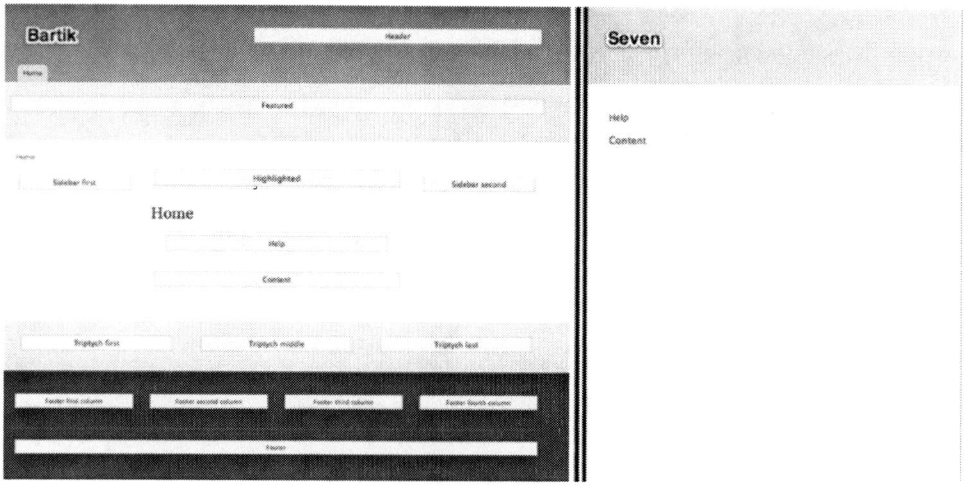

***Figure 6**. Content regions available in Bartik and Seven themes*

Enhancements to Content Entry and Organization

Drupal 7 includes many enhancements to the content entry screens, including a more intuitive interface, vertical tabs for key configuration areas, and the option to add summaries to content, which can be used in custom page views.

It also includes a revamped Taxonomy (content categorization) setup, which allows you to add images, descriptions, and fields to content categories, and even add links to them. This is useful for heavy-duty content sites and in theming, where a default image could be used to denote every piece of content in a specific category.

RDFa Support

RDFa provides a way to structure HTML output so that machines can tell the difference between calendar content, contact information, and other types of content. This not only provides built in SEO for your web site, it sets the stage for a host of other functional enhancements to your website.

For more information about RDFa, visit `w3.org/TR/xhtml-rdfa-scenarios/`.

Security and Testing Improvements

The release of Drupal 7 comes along with a variety of important security improvements, including:

- Password hashes are salted (meaning, passwords cannot be cracked with a look-up table).

- Unique key for `cron.php` to make Denial of Service attacks more difficult. *(Note: This means you can't run it just by going to* `example.com/cron.php` *like you might be used to.)*

- Permissions have normal, human-oriented names and descriptions.

- Filter permissions are on the main permissions page.

- Allows choosing between public and private files on a per filefield basis.

- The Test module (formerly Simpletest) is included in Drupal core. This module helps you write tests to make sure your site and modules work as they should, and test your site after you make changes. See Chapter 23 for more information.

This is only a smattering of the tremendous changes that were made in Drupal 7. If you'd like to see all of the changes, visit `drupal.org/about/new-in-drupal-7` and `drupal.org/drupal-7-released`.

How to Use This Book

Elwood: It's 106 miles to Chicago, we got a full tank of gas, half a pack of cigarettes, it's dark, and we're wearing sunglasses.

Jake: Hit it.

—*The Blues Brothers, 1980*

Welcome to the Definitive Guide to Drupal 7! Picking up this book suggests an interest in learning Drupal, a desire to make full use of Drupal 7's great new capabilities, or a commitment to continuous improvement in Drupal knowledge. Or, for the person who has never heard of Drupal, picking up this book indicates plain good luck—*fate* kind of luck. To that person, and others more hard-working than lucky, the authors say: Congratulations on a new hobby, career, passion, community.

This book accelerates people along the Drupal learning curve for the many dimensions of Drupal, such as:

- Building sites by choosing and configuring freely available extensions, called modules.

- Planning and sustaining Drupal projects.

- Creating themes to give your sites their own look and feel.

- Writing new modules that extend what Drupal and other modules can do.

- Getting help from and contributing back to the Drupal community.

Note What does that fifth point have to do with building stuff with Drupal? Everything. All the functionality, the flexibility, and the power of Drupal come from the community. Becoming part of this community as you begin to learn Drupal benefits you and benefits the community. See Chapters 9 and 38 for more.

Who Should Read This Book?

This book is for anyone serious about gaining a deep understanding of Drupal and doing great things with Drupal. It does not presume any specific prior curriculum. There are as many paths to Drupal as there are members of the community.

This book is intended to be the most comprehensive guide to getting sites done with Drupal—or likely any content management system. It goes well beyond the code to cover much other knowledge and skills and help make you effective.

The goal is to help you develop a solid set of skills to maneuver and mold Drupal—and more importantly, to promote the concept of developing in a manner which many have termed "The Drupal Way," which includes the following:

- planning for future upgrades, possible disasters, new client feature requests, etc. and building web sites that age gracefully.

- participating in the open source free software ecosystem that makes Drupal and other key projects possible—in Drupal, a remarkable community that encompasses administrators, developers, themers, and designers.

"Definitive" is quite a claim to make. Not everyone who works in Drupal is good at all of it, or even knows about all of it. Which is fantastic news for you, the reader and user of this book. Precisely because there are so many parts of Drupal, and no one is expert in all areas, there are many onramps and avenues to becoming a Drupal expert. This book helps you learn how to think about and approach Drupal with the aim of making your mark in the community.

This book will cover a lot of ground, from building sites to writing code to enhance Drupal's look or extend its functionality to managing all such projects. Throughout, it maintains a focus on engaging with and contributing back to the Drupal community. Giving back to Drupal is what makes Drupal possible, of course, but engagement with the community also provides we who work with Drupal the continuous learning we need to keep up and keep improving.

The *Definitive Guide to Drupal 7*, then, will not cover every detail of a vast and expanding universe of software. Instead, it will cover what is needed to do some real things, with a focus on building the knowledge and tools needed to figure everything else out.

Requirements

To work with Drupal, you will need the following:

- A working computer.

- At least intermittent Internet access.

Tip Readers whose computer is not set up to easily run a web server, PHP, and a database (those unsure can figure on an answer of no) can start right now downloading VirtualBox and a Drupal-ready VirtualBox image, as described at `drupal.org/project/quickstart`. See Appendices F through I for more ways to get set up to run Drupal, and also Chapter 12.

Approach and Philosophy

A reference book gives just the facts; a good teaching book tries to show how we come to develop knowledge in the first place. This book teaches.

If something is worth doing, there are probably three or a dozen ways to do it with Drupal. Given the limitations of time and space, the authors picked their favorite to write about. There's a whole Internet out there with most of the rest; if we wanted every possibility, we would not need a book. Nevertheless, this book's purpose is not to claim and deliver the one best solution, but to teach how to find and evaluate solutions. It aims to make you better at thinking about web site projects and Drupal development.

Although this book is written for cover-to-cover reading, it's not linear. A book about a project of and for the Internet and about a large, active community could hardly be linear. And a book meant to be of practical use must allow people to pick up where dictated by the projects they need to work on and their present skill levels. Many parts of the book can be taken as short sections that stand alone on how to do a particular task.

Above all, this book is about equipping, not about spoon-feeding facts. A powerful lesson of open source free software is that no human system or structure is static and unchangeable; everything changes. If, at some point, you don' think that a topic is covered adequately, refer to Chapter 9, which is about getting involved in and getting help from the community.

A Note on Jargon

Drupal 7 has made great strides in usability, in part by removing jargon from the administrative interface. (Interface? That's jargon for the thing you're looking at when you use a web site.) Nonetheless, that jargon will reappear in this book, because it is how Drupal thinks of things internally, and to be a great Drupal site builder, you need to know a bit about how Drupal thinks. So let's get a couple things out of the way.

A person using a web site is called a *user*. We are upgraded to *people* in parts of the Drupal 7 administrative interface, but when you see ourselves referred to as *users* from time to time, you shouldn't freak out—it's not a slur (although Drupal can be addictive). It's just a more precise and concise way of referring to a person using a web site.

A piece of content in a Drupal site is also called a *node*. Why not call it content all the time? Well, sometimes nodes aren't content; sometimes they're really better thought of as a piece of data or a container for more nodes (sorry, content).

There will be plenty of other jargon, and the authors will try to explain it better as it comes up, but the most important thing is that a word or phrase or even concept that does not make sense to you at first will not stop you. There is an entire book of context, and help of all kinds online, to keep you moving as you understand more and more of this complex conglomeration of people and software called Drupal.

You can go at your own pace, you can re-read sections and try things again, and you can go to the book forums (definitivedrupal.org/forums or dgd7.org/fora). There's one forum per chapter where you can ask questions of authors and other readers (if your question hasn't already been addressed).

Conventions

Locations of administration and other pages are described both with a Click ➤ Path and with a url/path (relative to the root of a Drupal site, for instance the path admin/content). For instance, the help topics are directly reached from the toolbar or administration menu, so we would instruct simply: Go to Administer ➤ Help (admin/help).

You can always skip clicking through the links and tabs and sublinks by entering the provided URL path directly (in the last example, for site example.com, the URL http://example.com/admin/people/permissions/roles would take you directly to the path).

When members of the Drupal community are mentioned, their drupal.org handles are frequently added in parenthesis, as this nickname (often also used on IRC) may be much better known among Drupalistas than their real name. For instance, when introducing the Drupal 7 co-maintainer (and all-around Drupal superstar) for the first time, we would write her name as Angela Byron (webchick).

In this book, the word "we" is generally used to include you, the reader, as well as the authors and anyone else who may be doing Drupal.

Beyond the Book

The companion site to this book is definitivedrupal.org (also reachable at dgd7.org). You can download code used in the book at dgd7.org/code. Also online you will find additional information on Drupal and the authors. The site supplements the book; it does not replace it. Let the authors know what was most helpful, what confused, and what can be improved upon. Share Drupal success stories and express frustrations, but keep discussion related to the book chapters, and take overall Drupal discussion to one of the many places introduced in Chapter 9 on participating in the community.

Where examples are used, the authors took every effort to make information in this book the best way to do the specific task. However, there's always another way to do a task in Drupal, Drupal is an always-evolving entity. This book strives to provide the knowledge and resources needed to come up with your own solutions, and you can also subscribe to dgd7.org/updates or e-mail your area of interest to news@definitivedrupal.org to learn when corrections are made to the text, new techniques are suggested, and new material is released.

The authors' goal is to accelerate you along the Drupal learning curve by covering all aspects of building web sites with Drupal: architecture and configuration; module development; front end development; running projects sustainably; and contributing to Drupal's code, documentation, and community.

How Drupal Works

by Dani Nordin

Before you can get started working with Drupal, there are a few basic things you should know. This chapter provides a broad overview of how Drupal works, and some basic terms and concepts you should know before you get started.

How Drupal Works

Drupal, much like systems such as WordPress (wordpress.org) or Expression Engine (expressionengine.com), is a Content Management System (CMS). It takes your content as individual pieces of information and gives you a framework for displaying that content in a way that makes sense to your site's audience.

What Drupal Really Does

The easiest way to think about Drupal is as a digital coin sorter. Your nodes are the coins, and content types are the different denominations (quarters, dimes, etc). In addition to content types, you can use taxonomy to organize the coins by the country of currency, color, condition, etc. Views are the mechanism that sorts the coins; they take your nodes and sort them out as Pages or Blocks according to size, shape, color, or whatever criteria you set. Themes and modules are like the coin wrappers and gears; they make sure that everything stays organized and keep the system running smoothly. See Figure 7.

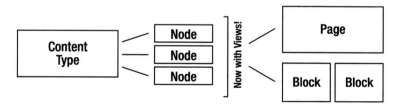

Figure 7. Graphical overview of how Drupal delivers content

Drupal differs from other content management systems in the following ways:

- It's incredibly flexible. Unlike WordPress, which is primarily focused as a blogging platform, Drupal sites can be built to handle almost any functionality that you need from corporate intranet to e-commerce to donor management, and more. You can even blog with it, if you really want to.

- Drupal's huge community of developers, designers, and themers means that even the least experienced site builder can get help breaking in and figuring out sticky issues. While IRC and drupal.org's Issue Queue can be immensely helpful (and are great places to start), even posting a question using the #Drupal tag on Twitter will often lead to offers of help and answers you may not have thought of. More information on getting help with Drupal can be found in Chapter 9.

Some Terms You Should Know

Node: An individual piece of content. This could be a news item, event listing, simple page, blog entry—you name it. Anything in your site that has a heading and a bit of text is a node. Nodes can also have custom fields, which are useful for all sorts of things.

Fields: Fields are one of the best things about creating content in Drupal. Using fields, you can attach images or files to content, create extra descriptors (like a date for an event, or a subheading for an article), or even reference other nodes.

Block: A standalone piece of reusable content (for example, a sidebar menu or callout box). Blocks can be created by a View (see below) or created by hand in Drupal's Blocks administration menu. The beauty of blocks is the flexibility of display; you can set up blocks to display based on any criteria that you set. This is especially helpful on home pages, for example, or for displaying a menu that's only relevant to a specific section of a website.

Content type: The type of node you're creating. One of Drupal's best features is its support of multiple content types, each of which can be sorted out and displayed by any number of criteria.

Taxonomy: Content categories. At its most basic level, you can think of taxonomy as tags for content (like blog entries). The true power of taxonomy, however, lies in organizing large quantities of content by what an audience might search for. For example, a recipe site can use taxonomy to organize recipes by several criteria type of recipe (dessert, dinner, etc.), ingredients (as tags), and custom indicators (vegetarian, vegan, gluten-free, low carb, etc.). In building the site, you could then use Views to allow users to search by or filter recipes by any one (or several) of these criteria.

Users, Roles and Permissions: Users are exactly what they sound like—users that have registered on your site. The key to working with users is roles; Drupal allows you to create unique roles for anything that might need to happen on your site and set permissions for each role depending on what that role might need to do. For example, if you're creating a magazine-type site with multiple authors, you might want to create a role called "author" that has permission to access, create, and edit their own content, but nobody else's. You might also create a role called editor that has access to edit, modify, and publish or unpublish the content of any of the authors.

Module: A plug-in that adds functionality to your site. Out of the box, Drupal provides a strong framework, but the point of the framework is to add functionality to it using modules. `drupal.org/project/modules` has a list of all the modules that have been contributed by the Drupal community, sorted by most popular. At the very least, every Drupal installation should use Views, Pathauto, and Token. Pathauto and Token help you create automatic URL aliases for your content; you'll learn more about Views in Chapter 3 as well as Chapter 8 and elsewhere in the book.

View: An organized list of individual pieces of content that you create within the site, using the Views module. You'll dive a bit deeper into Views in Chapter 3.

Theme: The templates that control the look and feel of a Drupal site. Drupal core comes with several themes that are very useful for site administration and prototyping; however, custom themes should *always* reside in your `sites/all/themes` folder and *not* in the core themes folder.

tpl.php: Individual PHP files that Drupal uses for template generation. Most Drupal themes will have, at the very least, a `tpl.php` for blocks, nodes, and pages. Once you get the hang of working with `tpl.php`, you can create custom templates for anything from a specific piece of content or specific content types to the output of a specific view.

Drupal Core: The actual Drupal project files, as downloaded from `drupal.org`. Anything that exists *outside* your `/sites` folder is considered core.

For other theming-specific definitions, check out Chapters 15 and 16.

Planning a Drupal Project: Designing from the Content Out

Since so much of the power in Drupal is based on the ability to create different types of content and sort it into manageable chunks, the importance of creating an effective content strategy and information architecture BEFORE YOU START DEVELOPING cannot be understated. Drupal is, at its core, a content curation and display engine, so taking time to understand the types and format of your site's intended content, as well as the site's functionality, is essential to success with Drupal.

What follows is a brief overview of the planning of a typical Drupal site. A more comprehensive overview can be found in Chapter 10.

Phase 1: Discovery

The discovery phase of any creative project sets up important information about the project's business objectives, audience, and functional requirements. This is where you work with the client to determine who they are, who their audience is, and what types of things that audience might need to do. At this stage, you're focusing mostly on the client's perspective and objectives; in the phases following, you'll be able to research and confirm or amend these perspectives.

While it's often tempting to dive right in and start building, putting enough time and attention into the discovery phase is essential to avoiding headaches down the road. Ask any Drupaller who's ever had to redo huge sections of a site because the project requirements changed.

During the discovery phase, you're looking to answer the following questions:

- Who is the client? What do they do?

- Who is the primary contact on the client's project team?

- Who are the other decision makers (if any) on the client side? How will feedback be handled?

- What are the primary business objectives surrounding this project? In other words, why are we doing this?

- What is the client's understanding of their primary audience for this project? Secondary audience? What is their understanding of this audience's needs?

- What is the primary message that the audience needs to get from this project?

- What financial, staff, and content resources are being made available for this project?

- What deadlines are you trying to meet with this project?

Phase 2: Information Architecture and Functional Requirements

While the discovery phase sets up the client's objectives and perceptions of their audience, the second phase focuses on gaining a deeper understanding of the site's intended users; it works on making sure that the user experience of the site matches the client's business objectives with the intended audience's needs.

The tangible deliverables of this phase may vary from team to team, but they often include things like:

- User profiles or stories.

- An outline, or matrix of functional requirements.

- Site wireframes.

- Paper or digital prototypes.

- Content strategy documents, including a breakdown of site content, content types, and categories. This may also include a breakdown of the site's user roles (editor, member, etc.) and what content they have permission to access, edit, etc.

The goal of this phase, which can take anywhere from a couple of days to a few months, is for the client and the development team to get on the same page regarding who the site's users are and what they're there for. Additionally, and most importantly, the goal is to identify areas of the project where budget or project scope might need tweaking and head off any confusion that might occur down the road.

Phase 3: Development Implementation

Once functional and content requirements have been established and approvals have been given, the team can begin to install and configure Drupal. In some teams, this installation/configuration process begins in the information architecture process, after functional requirements have been established. The benefit of this approach is that the team can build a working prototype of the site early in the process that can then be iterated. The downside is the potential for some aspects of the project to require re-doing later in the process, as new needs are uncovered.

During development, the site's functionality is developed and iterated. Modules are chosen (more on that in Chapter 4) and implemented, custom functionality is developed, and user roles and permissions are set, along with content types, taxonomy, etc. During this phase, designers can begin working on look and feel issues, and content editors can (and should) begin adding content to the site, with guidance from the project lead.

Phase 4: Design and Theme Implementation

A Drupal site's theme controls the look and feel of the site. While it is possible to implement visual design in a Drupal site at the same time that functionality is being implemented, it's not recommended. The development phase of a Drupal site is an important time to iron out functionality and usability issues; adding visual elements (even simple ones) during this phase causes many clients to focus on aesthetics too early in the project.

Another important distinction to be made is that between visual design and theming. While many themers can design and vice versa, visual design is the act of creating a set of visual standards that will control the way the site looks. This could involve something as simple as picking out colors and font choices for the site, and creating some standards for laying out type, boxes, etc. It often involves creating visual mockups in a program such as Fireworks or Photoshop.

Theming, however, is the process of implementing those visual standards across the site's template files, using HTML, CSS, and PHP. While theming can (and sometimes does) happen without design, design is what truly brings the message home to the client's audience. When well thought out and implemented by talented themers, a site's design is often an important factor in whether the site meets the client's business objectives.

Phase 5: Staging, Testing, and Launch

Once the site's functionality has been implemented, and the visual design has been integrated into the site's theme, it's time to get the site ready for the world to see. While a more comprehensive overview of this can be found in Chapter 13, the basic idea is as follows:

1. Back up the site's database and files.
2. Establish a staging URL (best as a subdomain of the actual URL, such as staging.newsite.com) and move the site files and database to that URL.
3. Test.
4. Test.
5. Test.
6. When you've tested the heck out of it, and fixed any issues that arise, move or copy the site files and database to the live (also called "production") URL.
7. Test.
8. Test.
9. Test.
10. Rejoice!

Now that you have an idea of what you're doing, it's time to set up a development environment and install Drupal for the first time. See Appendices F through I for installation instructions on various operating systems: Windows, Ubuntu (including as a virtual machine on non-Linux computers), Mac OS X, and (the easiest way to get started) a cross-platform Drupal stack installer.

PART I

■■■

Getting Started

Chapter 1 takes you through building a Drupal site from planning to giving people the privilege of posting pages and other content, with lots of key Drupal concepts covered and tips given along the way. Building this site is continued in Chapters 8 and 33.

Chapter 2 introduces two essential tools in the life of any Drupalista: Drush, the Drupal Shell that makes many tasks in Drupal much faster and easier; and Git, a distributed version control system that allows you to experiment freely with your code—and to collaborate with people around the world.

■ ■ ■

## CHAPTER 1

Building a Drupal 7 Site

by Benjamin Melançon, Dan Hakimzadeh, and Dani Nordin

> *"Ok, we can do this the hard way or we can do this the Drupal way."*

> —Forest Mars (kombucha)

This book will accelerate you along Drupal's learning curve by covering all aspects of building web sites with Drupal 7: architecture and configuration; module development; front end development; running projects sustainably; and contributing to Drupal's code, documentation, and community.

What better way to get started than to build a complete site in the first chapter? You'll go from zero to sixty miles per hour (or one hundred kilometers per hour, as the case may be) in 27 pages. In later chapters, you'll add turbochargers with dynamic pages using Views, racing stripes with theming, and cup holders with JQuery; you'll also perform some fancy maneuvers with Commerce and much more.

Throughout the book, we'll try to guide you to the Drupal way of doing things. There's never only one way to reach a goal, but some approaches ignore or even work against Drupal's offerings. The Drupal way, by contrast, is any way that builds on Drupal's strengths. (Chapter 8 covers one of those strengths—an active and helpful community that can keep you on course.)

The site you'll build in this chapter will allow users to easily create and categorize content. The scenario is not hypothetical. This book needs a website, and you are going to create it! You will:

- Use a basic approach to planning a site.

- Install Drupal 7.

- Configure Drupal core to provide a collaboration-oriented site that accepts content and comments from authors and visitors.

- Give the site and its front page a mix of static (semi-permanent) content and fresh updates.

- Give authors and visitors different levels of access for adding and editing content.

This is just the first chapter, so buckle up!

Planning: Setting Parameters and Knowing Where You're Going

Before embarking on any project, you should have some idea what it entails, if only to set some parameters on what you're getting into. The key to delivering happiness is setting expectations. (See Chapter 9 for more on planning and management with an agile approach.)

Discovery: Why Should This Site Be Built?

When starting a project, the first thing to figure out is not *how* to do it but *why*. All implementation answers should flow from an understanding of the project's purpose. The process of discovering this purpose is the *discovery phase* of a project, which is defined in this book's introduction and discussed further in Chapter 9.

■**Tip** Though obvious, the critically important discovery phase is sometimes given too little attention. Even a website built only for yourself should begin by you defining your goals. Skipping this step can mean repeating all the other phases as the understanding of needs changes and new needs are discovered late in the process.

Asking the site initiators (the authors) about their goals for the site reveals that they want people to learn more about *The Definitive Guide to Drupal 7* and they want the site to aid conversation and collaboration among multiple authors, readers, and interested Drupalistas.

Overall, the DefinitiveDrupal.org web site (hereafter referred to as the DGD7 site) should complement the book's goals, which include the following:

- Give people of diverse skill backgrounds onramps to going great places with Drupal.

- Help people learn how to learn more on their own.

- Encourage those interested in the Drupal software to participate in the community that makes the software possible.

For the book to meet its goals, it helps if people buy it, so all web site visitors must be able to see basic information about the book, selected and bonus content, and book buying information. Authors need to be able to add, edit, and arrange this information. People must be able to suggest ideas for inclusion in the book or future editions. Later, readers of the book must be able to comment on or ask questions about particular chapters. (These more structured forms of interaction are more sustainable for the authors than a contact form or site-wide forum.) The site must be able to be extended with new features as well as new content, and visitors must be able to sign up to receive updates when important new information about Drupal is added.

▧**Tip** Another question the builders of a site should ask early on is where the resources will come from. Who is going to pay for this project—in time, resources, and money? Everyone involved needs to have a sense of what can be accomplished with funding and what can only be achieved with volunteered time.

Information Architecture: Exactly What Will You Build?

Once the purpose of a project is well understood, it's time to move onto the next step, *information architecture*. Discovery is *why*. Information architecture is *what*. This phase is sometimes also called *specifications* or *site architecture*. Typically, information architecture consists of writing functional requirements and drawing wireframes.

Functional requirements consist of every individual thing the site must do and how each will fit together, stated as clearly and succinctly as possible. *Wireframes* are quick sketches of where links, forms, features, menus, content, and anything else should be on key pages or sections of the site. Together, functional requirements and wireframes show precisely what the site must do.

With the grounding of the broad goals established in the discovery phase, you can ask the site initiators what they want in the site. You must filter requests based on the already established goals. With the DGD7 site, requests range from a paragraph-by-paragraph annotation tool to making the whole web site look like a book. This is where you must learn—and employ—the most important technique of web development: saying no.

▧**Tip** In web development, the question "What do you need?" often comes back as something like "I need a fully 3D pony leaping around the screen and every click on him adds another cup of hot chocolate to the shopping cart and I need it by Tuesday." It's your job to say no and to help people prioritize their ideas to be in line with their goals and resources.

As Drupal developers, it is very tempting to say yes to everything, because pretty much everything is possible with Drupal. The missing word is *eventually*. For the sake of everyone's happiness, it is best to help site initiators keep their vision in mind and build web site features that achieve this vision first. Requirements need to fit into a strategy for what the site's initiators want to accomplish. Explain that time and resources are finite: yes, nearly everything is possible with Drupal, but not all at once. Given the overall goal, what are the most important parts of the site? Which have priority?

With this in mind, we can produce a list of functional requirements for the book site:

- Visitors shall see a prominent mission statement on the front page of the site.

- The authors shall be able to edit and rearrange a public table of contents with optional chapter summaries.

- The authors shall be able to post resources that relate to their chapters and are connected to their chapter summary in the table of contents.

- Registered visitors shall be able to comment on individual resources associated with a chapter.

- Registered users should be able to share suggestions for the book such as tips or warnings, anecdotes about Drupal, or concepts that should be covered.

- The most recent participant-contributed posts and comments should be visible in a side column on every page on the site.

- Authors and other participants shall be able to categorize content to create linkages and organization throughout the site.

- After publication, readers shall be able to register and participate in discussions (grouped by chapter), discover new material, and give feedback.

Functional requirements are frequently more specific than these, but we'll break down these broader ones as we implement each feature. (Note that not all of these features will be built in this chapter.)

With the functional requirements complete, it's time to use wireframes to suggest a basic visual structure for the data on the website (see Figure 1–1). This is an important part of the initial development stage because it lays out the requirements visually, shows how they relate to each other, and helps develop the user interface for the site. If nothing else, wireframes help keep you honest about what will fit on a given page.

Figure 1–1. Napkin sketch wireframe. Chapter 9 has resources for making slick-looking wireframes, but wireframes can be simple hand-drawn sketches, too.

Exercising the discipline to do wireframes as a first and separate step helps ensure that you do not prematurely close off your options. It is too easy with Drupal to slip from planning *what* must be done to planning *how* to do it—or even to starting to configure it. Drupal can be (and often is) used as a rapid prototyping tool, but the separation of phases should be adhered to—no site building yet. Indeed, at the information architecture stage, the use of Drupal to build the site should not yet be a foregone conclusion.

■**Tip** The authors love Drupal, but even they can admit that using Drupal for a one-page site is like setting up a catapult to hand someone a mango.

Design

When creating a design, remember that Drupal web sites are dynamic. A Drupal design (or, when implemented, *theme*), acknowledges that every page will have regions, such as header, left sidebar, main content, footer, and so on. A quick glance at the requirements shows that the site needs a sidebar for displaying the most recently added posts and comments (requirement #6). So this region (the sidebar) that contains the recent comments list will need to expand when there are more or longer comment titles. This is why functionality should be defined first; the dynamic areas of a site specified by the functional requirements should be reflected in the wireframes on which the design then builds.

For the DGD7 web site, it makes sense to create a professional, easy-to-read design that is consistent with the Apress style. Theming is covered in Chapters 15 and 16; what is important to note here is that the design you make with a graphics program is *not* a theme. It is a drawing of what the site should look like after it is built and then themed.

Drupal separates appearance from functionality, and the design phase does not need to take place in this order. Building the site first and designing directly before or even as part of the theming phase may be the way to go (this is the order in the introduction). Regardless of when the design is made, the site should be built based on its functional requirements and wireframes before it is themed (see Figure 1–2).

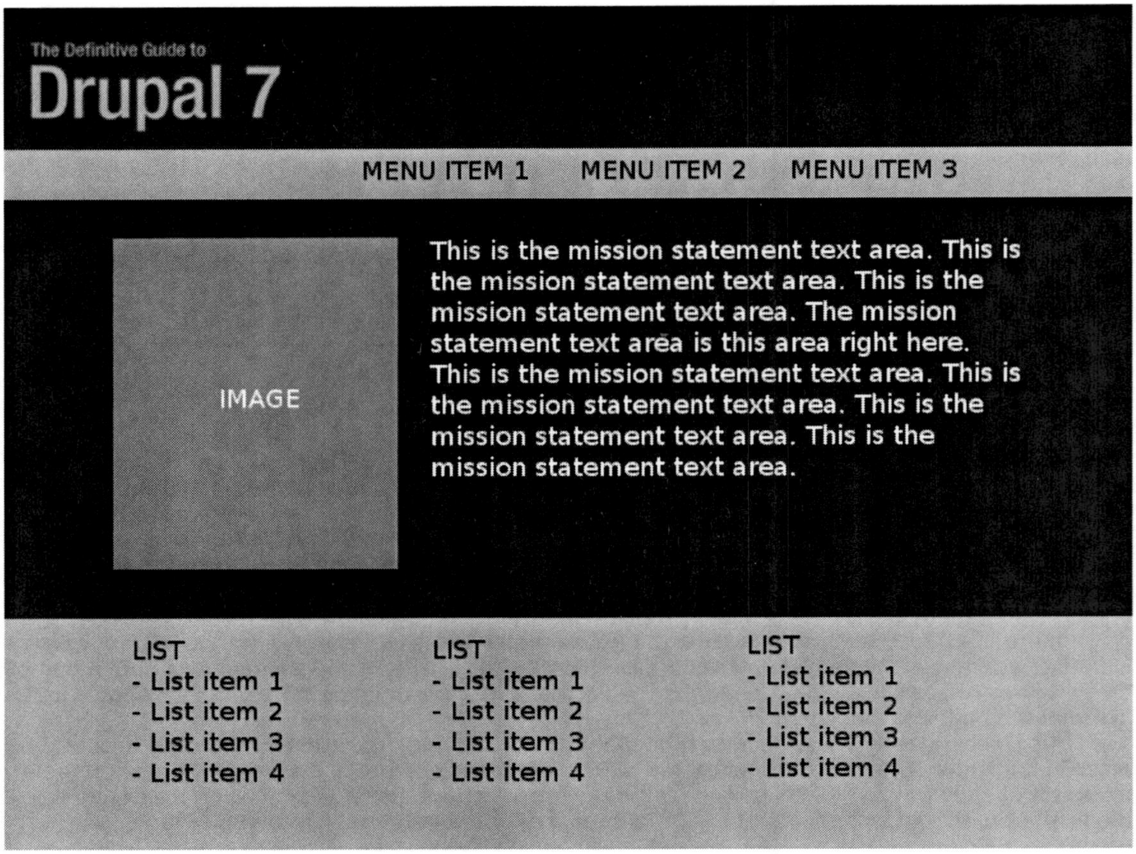

The Definitive Guide to

Drupal 7

MENU ITEM 1   MENU ITEM 2   MENU ITEM 3

IMAGE

This is the mission statement text area. This is the mission statement text area. This is the mission statement text area. The mission statement text area is this area right here. This is the mission statement text area. This is the mission statement text area. This is the mission statement text area. This is the mission statement text area.

LIST
- List item 1
- List item 2
- List item 3
- List item 4

LIST
- List item 1
- List item 2
- List item 3
- List item 4

LIST
- List item 1
- List item 2
- List item 3
- List item 4

Figure 1–2. *A mock-up of the DGD7 home page. It is not a working site, or even HTML; it is only a design, a picture. (The home page has a special arrangement and places recent comments below the main content, rather than in a sidebar.)*

■**Note** Design is typically the third step in a project's life-cycle, but thanks to the separation of appearance from content and functionality in Drupal, it can be worked on in parallel with implementing a site's functionality.

Implementation

Now the rubber hits the road. The implementation phase is covered in the balance of this chapter. It includes installing and configuring Drupal to fulfill the plan of the previous phases. After implementation, the remaining phases of site building are commonly broken into the following three:

- *Content staging:* the writing and uploading of content, which is usually the site initiator's responsibility (with coaching from the site builders).

- *Quality assurance:* the testing of the site, which should be done by both the site builders and the site initiator.

- *Deployment and launch:* putting the site or service out in the world for its intended audience and users.

The post-implementation phases are covered more extensively in later chapters (deployment and launch specifically in Chapter 12).

■**Tip** Large projects can be done in iterations of these same basic steps, from discovery to deployment. As you add features to a web site, you will follow these steps over and over again.

Installing Drupal

To begin building any Drupal website, you first need to install Drupal. Many different combinations of operating systems (Linux, Windows, Mac OS X), web servers (Apache, IIS, Nginx), and databases (MariaDB/MySQL, PostgreSQL, SQLite) support Drupal. Appendices F through I cover getting set up with a web server and database on several operating systems. Let's move on to the fun stuff.

Putting the Files in Place

Drupal core is hosted as a project on Drupal.org along with thousands of related contributed projects. While Drupal.org highlights direct download links, you can also download Drupal from its project page at http://drupal.org/project/drupal (see Figure 1–3). Like every other project, it has recommended releases, and that's where you can download the latest stable release of Drupal 7.

Figure 1–3. Drupal's project page

Where you put your files is determined by your chosen web server setup (see `dgd7.org/install`). Wherever you unpack your Drupal files, the location where you see `index.php` and `.htaccess` is what we refer to as the Drupal root or web root directory.

■**Tip** It is good practice to create a directory for the project (in this case, `dgd7`) and put Drupal core into it as a subdirectory (such as `dgd7/web`). This makes it easy to put everything related to a project—including things that should not be accessible from the web—in version control together (see Chapter 2).

Then go to your Drupal root directory and create a copy of the `sites/default/default.settings.php` file as `sites/default/settings.php` (copy, don't move) and change the permissions of the new `settings.php` file to make it writable by Drupal. Also, create the `sites/default/files` directory at this time and make it writeable by the web server. OS-specific installation instructions are covered in Appendices F through I; see `dgd7.org/install` for more resources.

■**Tip** Don't be deterred by any difficulties in getting set up. Really. Installing can be the hardest part. Take the remaining 800 pages of the book as proof that it is possible, and don't give up.

Drupal's Automatic Installer

Now load up your Drupal root directory in your browser (the exact address will be different depending on your local hosting environment). For the recommended Ubuntu instructions, the DGD7 web site will be at `http://dgd7.localhost`; for a WAMP, MAMP, or a standard LAMP setup, it might be `http://localhost/dgd7/web`. You will automatically be redirected to `install.php`, Drupal's automatic installer.

Choose the standard installation profile. (The minimal installation profile doesn't even create the administrator role for you.) Click through the language page; it won't offer any options unless you first get files as described at `drupal.org/localize` (or, better, begin with the localization-ready distribution of Drupal, `drupal.org/project/l10n_install`).

Enter in your database settings on the next screen (the values you provided when creating the database). Alternatively, you can choose SQLite and tell Drupal to use a directory that is writeable by your web server, and Drupal will create an SQLite database for you. (The authors don't currently recommend SQLite for a site headed for an important production deployment, but it's great for getting started easily.) Submit the form and Drupal will install itself!

When installation is done (it may take a couple of minutes), you will be able fill in some basic site details and create a username and e-mail address with credentials suitable for the administrative user (called the site maintenance account).

■**Caution** The first user created in the installation process is given permission to do everything on the site, forever. Therefore, it is advised that you do *not* use this site maintenance account as your own personal account. The site might be just on your computer now, but when you move it online, you'll want to preserve the user accounts. See Chapter 6 on Drupal security for more information, including advice on strong passwords and dealing with Drupal's unique e-mail address per account requirement.

Congratulations, you now have a Drupal site! And it's...completely empty. There is no content at all yet, and Drupal 7 is nice enough to tell you that your home page is empty because there is no front page content (see Figure 1–4). (Front page content means, sensibly enough, content that is marked as "promoted to front page.") Before we start creating content, however, let's take a look at the Administration menu.

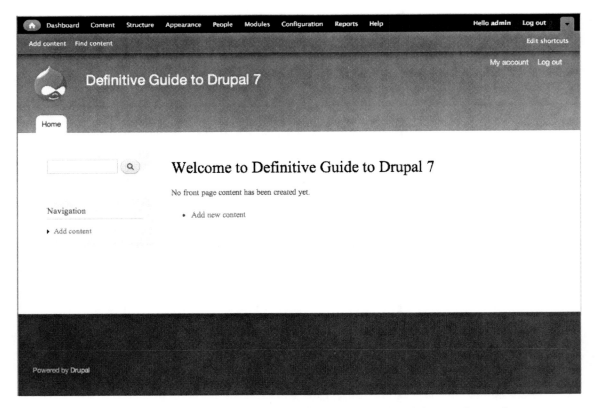

Figure 1–4. Your new, empty home page, including the Drupal toolbar and shortcut bar at the top

Drupal's Administration Menu

Drupal's Administration menu (see Figure 1–5) gives you access to administer every aspect of your Drupal site. The standard installation profile installs the Toolbar module that puts the main sections of the Administration menu at the top of every page of your site. From the toolbar you can do the following:

- Find and add content.
- Build things that affect the site's structure.
- Add and enable themes to change the site's appearance.
- Manage which people can log into your site and what they can do.
- Extend your site's functionality by adding and enabling modules.
- Change default settings and the configuration of everything.
- See reports regarding the status of different things on your site.
- Get help on all of these topics and tasks.

Figure 1–5. Drupal 7's Administration menu in the toolbar, with the shortcut bar beneath it

Other modules can add links to the Administration menu. Indeed, the Dashboard module, also included in Drupal core and enabled by the standard installation profile, provides a configurable overview of what's happening on your site and adds the dashboard link to the toolbar.

The Shortcut module adds a hideable bar beneath the toolbar that holds bookmarks to any pages you want to make instantly accessible. You can make multiple sets of shortcut links at *Administration ➤ Configuration ➤* User interface ➤ Shortcuts (admin/config/user-interface/shortcut). Administrators can set which shortcut set a user sees in the user's Shortcuts tab (user/7/shortcuts, for instance, for the user with ID number 7). Alternatively, you can give all people in a role permission to choose their own shortcut set at Administration ➤ People ➤ Permissions (admin/people/permissions) with the "Select any shortcut set" permission. (Roles and setting permissions will be covered later in this chapter.) The shortcut bar is visible to users in roles with the "Use the administration toolbar" permission; if they can't see the toolbar, they can't use shortcuts.

■**Tip** Like all core modules, the shortcut bar has additional documentation in the built-in help (admin/help/shortcut) and online at http://drupal.org/documentation/modules/shortcut.

Appearance: Changing a Core Theme's Color Scheme

Using themes, you can quickly and easily change the overall look and feel of a Drupal website. The design aspect of the DGD7 web site plan calls for the site to have a clean, professional appearance and use the black and yellow color scheme of Apress books. You can see the themes available for your site, currently only core, at Administer ➤ Appearance (admin/appearance). These themes—and more importantly, how to make your own—are described in Chapter 15.

■**Tip** Many, many more themes are available for Drupal for free. Browse drupal.org/project/themes and filter by compatibility with 7.x. One of these, Corolla (drupal.org/project/corolla), was built for inclusion in Drupal 7 core (but wasn't considered sufficiently vetted in time to be included in the core download).

The new default theme for Drupal 7, Bartik, features integration with the Color module. This makes it possible to change the color scheme without touching any code (see Figure 1–6). By following the Settings link, you can select a new color scheme. Choose **Slate**, a subdued and neutral color scheme (which was the intended default for Bartik before the Drupal community demanded blue).

Slate won't have the yellow called for in the design, but it will be clean and won't be a distraction. In Chapter 15, you'll learn how to create themes. For now, the Bartik theme provides a layout and regions consistent with the wireframes so you can move on to building the website.

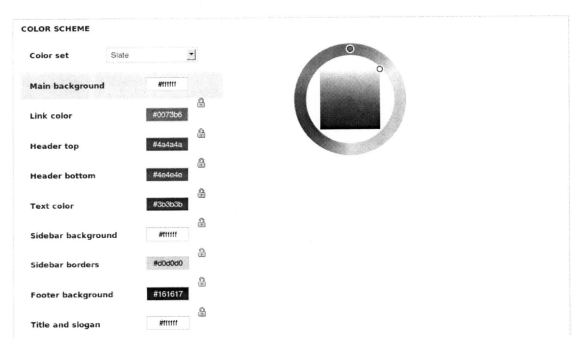

Figure 1–6. Selecting a different color scheme in Bartik's theme settings

---

▓**Caution** Trying to create your own color scheme though the Color module's tempting user interface (UI) is a really good way to make your site look unprofessional. Unless you are sure of what you're doing—or you just don't care—stick with a pre-set color scheme.

Extending Functionality with Modules

Modules can be used to extend Drupal's features and functionality. Core modules are those included with the main download of Drupal, and you can turn on their functionality without installing additional software. Contributed modules—thousands of them—are available on Drupal.org (see Chapter 4). Later in the book you'll even learn how to create your own modules. For now, enabling core modules is a good place to begin. You can do this at the Administration ➤ Modules page (admin/modules).

Allowing People to Register and Log In with OpenID

Enable the OpenID module by selecting the checkbox next to it and submitting the form with the Save configuration button at the bottom (see Figure 1–7).

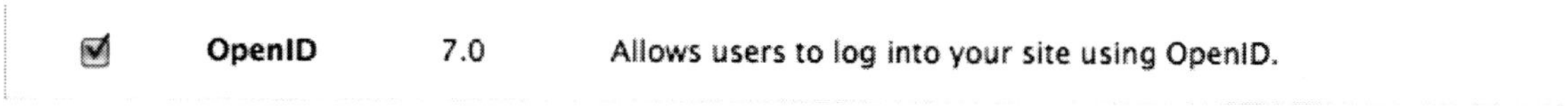

☑   **OpenID**   7.0   Allows users to log into your site using OpenID.

Figure 1–7. The OpenID module row in the form at `admin/modules`

■**Note** You will find core modules in alphabetical order (by their system name, which may not be the same as their displayed name) under Core on the modules administration page. As more contributed modules are added to this page, using your browser's in-page search capability (often available with Control+F or Command+F) can be the fastest way to find the module you are looking for.

No configuration is needed for OpenID—people will be able to register and log in using their OpenID accounts now. (OpenID is a decentralized standard for authenticating users, allowing users to log on to different services with the same digital identity. Anyone with a Google, Yahoo, LiveJournal, Wordpress.com, MayFirst.org, or AOL.com account has an OpenID; dedicated OpenID providers such as MyOpenID.com and Yiid.com offer free sign-up. See openid.net for more information. You can host your own OpenID, too, and there's a Drupal module for that at drupal.org/project/openid_provider.)

■**Caution** When taking your site online, you will want to set up an anti-spam module (see Chapter 4 for a brief introduction to options such as Captcha, Mollom, and Antispam) or turn off user self-registration (which Drupal has enabled by default, though accounts need to be approved by an administrator). When a CAPTCHA is used, a text riddle or an image that has an audio fallback is preferred for accessibility reasons.

Disabling Unneeded Modules

Introductions to Drupal are mostly all about enabling modules to unleash new functionality, but it can be good to know when to disable a module instead. Disabling unneeded modules reduces the complexity of the site for you, the site builder, and improves the site's performance and scalability. We'll disable two modules, Color and Overlay.

You have already used the Color module to set Bartik's color scheme and you don't need it any more. Banish the temptation! The Overlay module makes it too easy to lose your work (see note). Disable these two modules by unchecking the boxes next to their module names at Administration ➤ Modules (`admin/modules`). Submit the form with the Save configuration button at the bottom.

▓**Note** Why disable Overlay? If a user of your site types a thousand-word post into an Add content form (such as node/add/page) in Overlay and clicks the "More information about text formats" link before submitting, everything typed is gone forever. Without Overlay, a good browser like Firefox typically preserves whatever data has been entered into a tab. Accidentally click a link? Pressing a back button brings you back to what you've written. Close a tab? Control+Shift+T brings it back—with any data you've typed into it. With Overlay, a single misclick will lose your administrative form changes or an unsubmitted post. (There is a proposed fix for this behavior; see drupal.org/node/655388. If an issue is marked fixed for Drupal 7, you can know the fix will be included in the next point release of Drupal 7 after that date.) If you're using Overlay, at the very least you should disable the administration theme (which uses Overlay) when creating and editing content; see the bottom of the Administration ➤ Appearance (admin/appearance) page for this option. Overlay can also be disabled for individual users on their user Edit forms (such as user/86/edit).

Creating Content Types and Adding Content

As a world-class content management system, Drupal naturally does quite well at managing content. Every piece of content on your Drupal site will belong to one of several content types, and you can create as many of your own content types as you need. Content types make it easy for site editors to update content that you, as a site builder, have made sure will end up displaying in the right way and in the right place.

All content has a title, a creation date, and an author (a user on the site), among other qualities. The content type determines if a piece of content will have a body (main text) field, if it allows comments, and what its default settings are. Most wonderfully, a content type can have any number of fields including text and number fields, file and image fields, listing and option fields, and categories. The particular bundle of fields that you configure for a content type is available to all posts of that content type.

Creating the Suggestion Content Type

For this site, registered users should be able to leave suggestions for concepts to cover in subsequent editions of the book. For this, we'll be creating a new content type called Suggestion and giving registered users permission to create content of this type. To enable people to categorize their suggestions (as a tip, a warning, an anecdote, a module suggestion, etc.), we'll also be creating a taxonomy vocabulary and attaching it to this content type. (This will all be explained below!)

To create the Suggestion content type, click on Structure in the administration toolbar, then select Content types. In the screen that follows, click + Add content type.

▓**Note** This book will typically direct you to pages by the breadcrumb trail followed in parenthesis by the relative path you could enter directly in your browser's address bar. For example, Administration ➤ Structure ➤ Content types ➤ Add content type (admin/structure/types/add).

Name your new content type Suggestion and add a quick description in the description field. Descriptions are displayed on the Add content page (node/add) and help site editors and users decide if a given content type is the one they want to use. Farther down this form, in the Submission form settings, you can enter an explanation or submission guidelines, which will be shown at the top of the content adding and editing forms. You can always return later to edit anything here. There are no other settings you need to change, and you will be adding fields, so go ahead and press the Save and Add Fields button.

Note For the Suggestion content type, you left comments enabled; this is the default when creating a new content type when the Comment module is enabled. For some content types, such as a news or event listing, you might want to disable comments, which can be done in the Comment settings tab in the vertical tabs at the bottom of the content type add/edit form.

Drupal now takes you to the Manage fields tab for your content type, where you can edit fields, delete fields, re-order fields, and add new and existing fields (see Figure 1–8). (Drupal lets you share fields across content types.) At this point, your content type only has two fields, a title and a body. Although the body field is created by default, you can delete it. The title field is not fully using the field system and is always required.

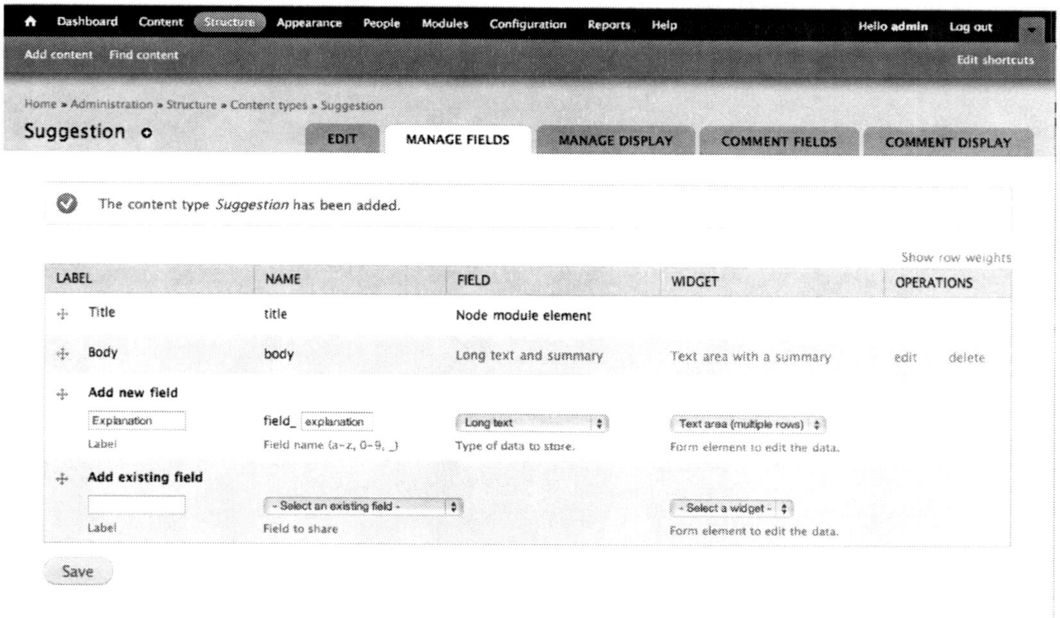

Figure 1–8. Add a new field to your content type. This field is called Explanation with the machine name field_explanation (the field_ part is automatically prefixed for you).

To enable users to explain how their suggestion fits into the book, make a new field called Explanation. Under the Add new field section, give your new field a label, field name (a machine-readable name), and choose the long text data type. The field label will show up next to the field on the edit form; the field name will identify the field within Drupal. Using the *long text* data type allows users to submit paragraphs; the *text* data type is for a single line of input.

▓**Tip** Field names are an important part of working in Drupal. Note that they can't be changed once they're set. Pick field names that are both descriptive and short, as exercising the full flexibility of custom theming will make use of these field names. You'll learn theming in Chapters 15 and 16.

Click Save field settings on the next page, as the long text field type has no settings. (You wouldn't be the only one who thinks Drupal ought to skip an unnecessary page here, but currently the issue to fix it is marked for Drupal 8; drupal.org/node/552604.)

On the *next* page you can configure some settings (see Figure 1–9). You can make it a required field, which will prevent suggestion authors from publishing the suggestion if the field isn't filled out. Add some help text to explain that you want the field to be an explanation. Set the rows to only three to try to convey that the explanation should be short. Set text processing to plain text, since this field is not about presentation. (Both plain text and filtered text will, by default, strip out potentially malicious script tags from published content.) Keep the Number of values at one (unless you think people should be able to submit multiple explanations for one suggestion!), and press Save settings. Your new content type is good to go.

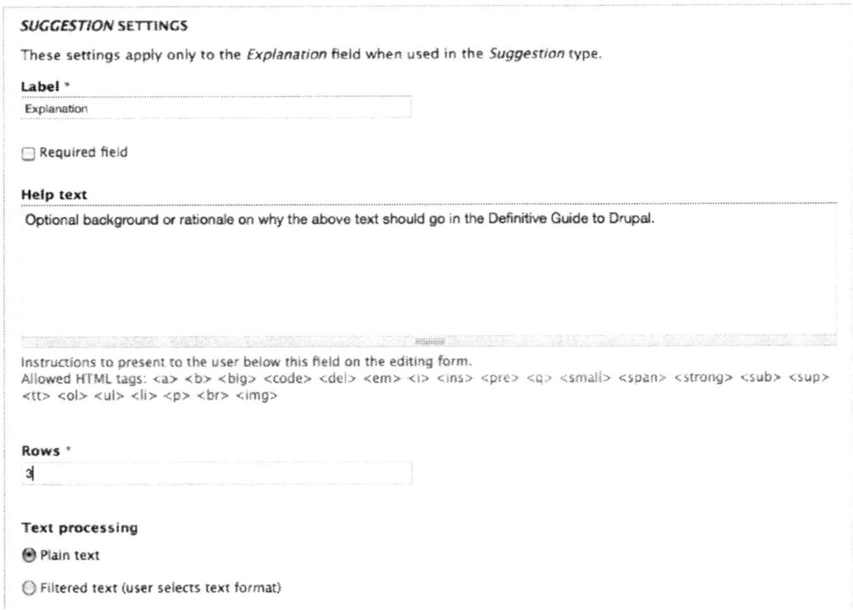

SUGGESTION SETTINGS

These settings apply only to the *Explanation* field when used in the *Suggestion* type.

Label *

Explanation

☐ Required field

Help text

Optional background or rationale on why the above text should go in the Definitive Guide to Drupal.

Instructions to present to the user below this field on the editing form.
Allowed HTML tags: <a> <b> <big> <code> <del> <em> <i> <ins> <pre> <q> <small> <span> <strong> <sub> <sup> <tt> <ol> <ul> <li> <p>
 <img>

Rows *

3

Text processing

◉ Plain text

○ Filtered text (user selects text format)

Figure 1–9. Configure settings for a long text field

Creating Content

This book is focused on site building, not using Drupal sites, but you still need to create content sometimes!

Adding a Page with a Human-Readable URL and a Link from the Main Menu

Don't let the long heading fool you; this is a simple task. To fulfill the requirement of a page where people can get information about buying the book, you can create a static page linked from the main menu. You can use the basic page content type provided by Drupal's standard installation profile. Begin by going to Add content ➤ Basic page (node/add/page).

■**New in 7** The Add content link (formerly Create content in Drupal 6) is available from the shortcut bar beneath the toolbar and from the content administration page, as well as the Navigation menu.

Give the new page a title like Buying the Definitive Guide to Drupal 7 and in the body put in an a link to the book. Powell's and Amazon provided cut-and-paste affiliate links. To embed an image into the text and do other special formatting you will need to change the body field's text format to Full HTML.

Next, in the nifty vertical tabs at the bottom of the form, go to Menu settings and check "Provide a menu" link (see Figure 1–10). Provide a title (the text of the link), a description (the tool-tip people will see if they hover their mouse over it), and a "heavy" (positive) weight to put it toward the right side of the selected <Main menu>, and you are in business.

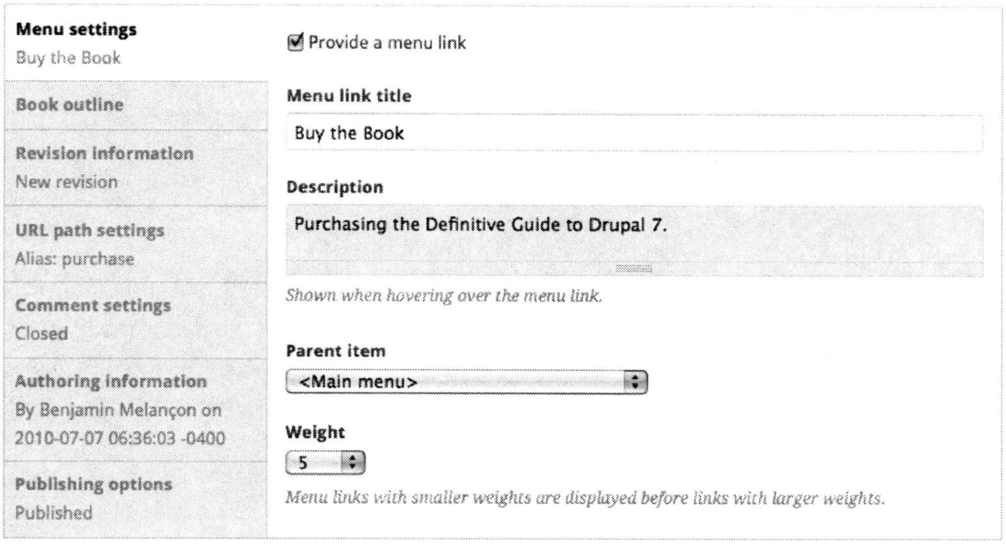

Menu settings	☑ Provide a menu link
Buy the Book	
Book outline	**Menu link title**
	Buy the Book
Revision information	
New revision	**Description**
	Purchasing the Definitive Guide to Drupal 7.
URL path settings	
Alias: purchase	
	Shown when hovering over the menu link.
Comment settings	
Closed	**Parent item**
	<Main menu>
Authoring information	
By Benjamin Melançon on	**Weight**
2010-07-07 06:36:03 -0400	5
Publishing options	
Published	*Menu links with smaller weights are displayed before links with larger weights.*

Figure 1–10. Adding a menu link for a basic page

Add a human-friendly URL for the post (which people will see instead of "node/1", for instance, in their browser's address bar) at the URL path settings tab. Make the URL alias purchase. (Figure 1–10 shows the summary where this has already been done.)

■**Note** You may notice in Figure 1–10 that Revision information indicated "New revision." This doesn't mean anything when you first create a piece of content, but it's best practice to have your content types set to create new revisions by default. See Chapter 4 for a description of using the Content Type Overview module to set this and other settings for every content type at once.

Save the new content, and see your link appear to the right of Home in the main menu bar.

Adding a Post and Promoting It to the Front Page

The web site plan calls for the front page to have a brief introduction to the book, which stays above any other posts put on the front page. You can do this in Drupal from the Administration menu: add content as a basic page. Write in what you want for the title and the body. Under Publishing options, check the two unchecked-by-default options: "Promoted to front page" and "Sticky at top of lists" (see Figure 1–11). You now have content that's been promoted to your front page. "Sticky at top of lists" means that the post will "stick" to the top of listing pages, such as the default front page, as new content is added (normally the newest post is displayed first).

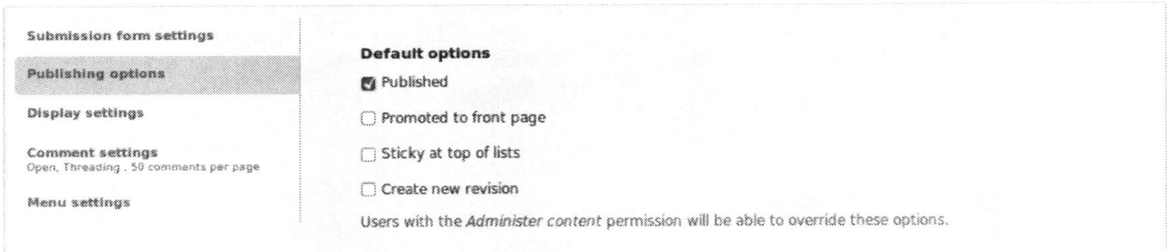

Figure 1–11. The publishing options of a default basic page

■**Note** A common beginning Drupal question is "Where's my content?" because the front page remains blank even after you create content if it is not promoted to front page. In the standard installation profile, the Basic page content type is not set to be promoted to the front page by default. You can always see all the content on a Drupal website by going to Content in the Administration menu (admin/content).

Blocks: Creating a Mission Statement

Blocks are pieces of information that can be displayed in the regions of your theme. Blocks can take many forms. Usually they are dynamic lists of information or menus. Drupal 7 provides some default blocks; you can find them on the blocks page at Administration ➤ Structure ➤ Blocks (admin/structure/block). The blocks page shows all the available blocks and all the regions they can be placed in. If you have multiple themes enabled, you can configure blocks for each enabled theme (and you can always configure blocks for the administration theme, which does not have to be enabled to be used).

The third requirement for the website is for the front page of the site to have a prominent mission statement. To add this, you can create a custom mission statement block. Again, go to Administration ➤ Structure ➤ Blocks and this time Add block. In the block description field, write "Mission statement" (this is not shown to site visitors). Leave the block title blank. In the block body, write the mission statement (see Figure 1–12).

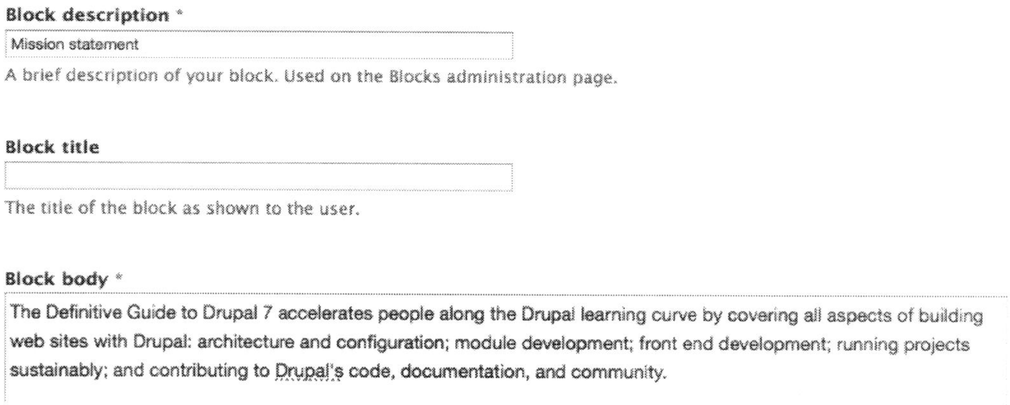

Block description *

Mission statement

A brief description of your block. Used on the Blocks administration page.

Block title

The title of the block as shown to the user.

Block body *

The Definitive Guide to Drupal 7 accelerates people along the Drupal learning curve by covering all aspects of building web sites with Drupal: architecture and configuration; module development; front end development; running projects sustainably; and contributing to Drupal's code, documentation, and community.

Figure 1–12. The custom block add/edit form at (for adding a new block) admin/structure/block/add

---

▓**New in 7** All prior versions of Drupal since version 4.0 in 2002 had a configuration setting mission statement field under site information. Drupal 7 drops this special-case region for this more flexible approach.

Move farther down the form to Region settings and place this new block in the Highlighted region; Bartik provides this region for mission statement-like content and it will work nicely. Under Visibility settings, go to the Pages vertical tab and set "Show block on specific pages" to "Only the listed pages" and type <front> in the text area (see Figure 1–13).

▓ **Tip** Region names can differ between themes, so if you change themes you might have to respecify the correct region for your blocks.

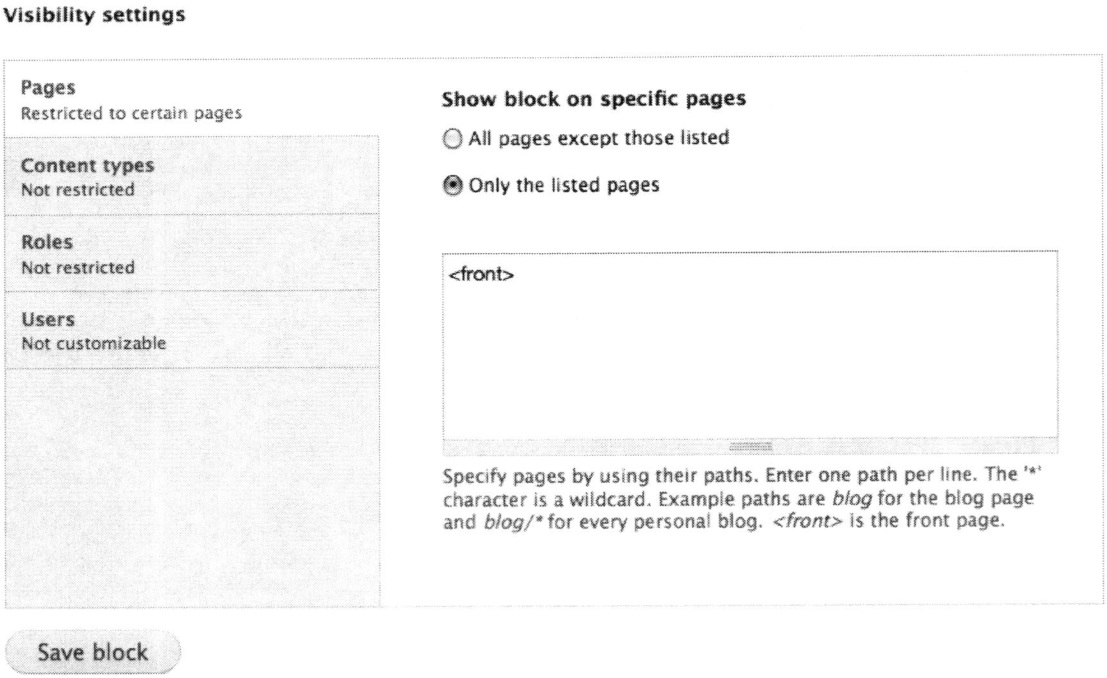

Visibility settings

Pages Restricted to certain pages	**Show block on specific pages** ○ All pages except those listed ◉ Only the listed pages
Content types Not restricted	
Roles Not restricted	<front>
Users Not customizable	

Specify pages by using their paths. Enter one path per line. The '*' character is a wildcard. Example paths are *blog* for the blog page and *blog/** for every personal blog. *<front>* is the front page.

(Save block)

Figure 1–13. *Visibility settings for the mission statement block*

Finally, submit the form with the Save block button.

▓**Tip** Drupal will let you set visibility settings not just for specific pages, but for content types and user roles as well. This is helpful when you only want to show a list of recent blog entries, for example, on all the blog pages but not anywhere else on the site.

One of the DGD7 web site requirements is that the most recent participant-contributed posts and comments should be visible in a side column on every page on the site (see Figure 1–14). Dragging the Recent content and Recent comments blocks to the Sidebar first region (or selecting the region in the drop-down selection for each), and saving the page is all you have to do to check that requirement off as complete (see Figure 1–15).

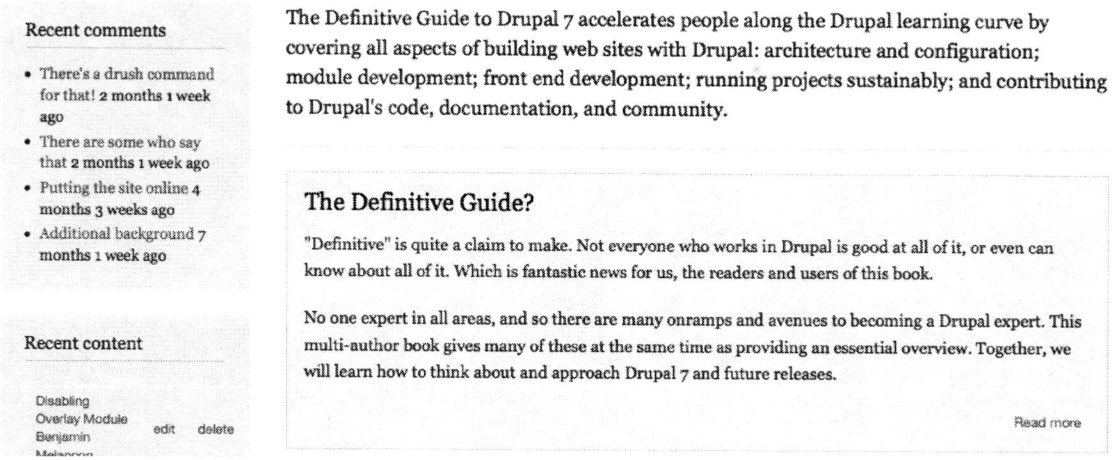

Recent comments

- There's a drush command for that! 2 months 1 week ago
- There are some who say that 2 months 1 week ago
- Putting the site online 4 months 3 weeks ago
- Additional background 7 months 1 week ago

Recent content

Disabling Overlay Module Benjamin Melançon   edit delete

The Definitive Guide to Drupal 7 accelerates people along the Drupal learning curve by covering all aspects of building web sites with Drupal: architecture and configuration; module development; front end development; running projects sustainably; and contributing to Drupal's code, documentation, and community.

The Definitive Guide?

"Definitive" is quite a claim to make. Not everyone who works in Drupal is good at all of it, or even can know about all of it. Which is fantastic news for us, the readers and users of this book.

No one expert in all areas, and so there are many onramps and avenues to becoming a Drupal expert. This multi-author book gives many of these at the same time as providing an essential overview. Together, we will learn how to think about and approach Drupal 7 and future releases.

Read more

Figure 1–14. The home page contains the recent comments, Mission Statement block, and the first piece of content.

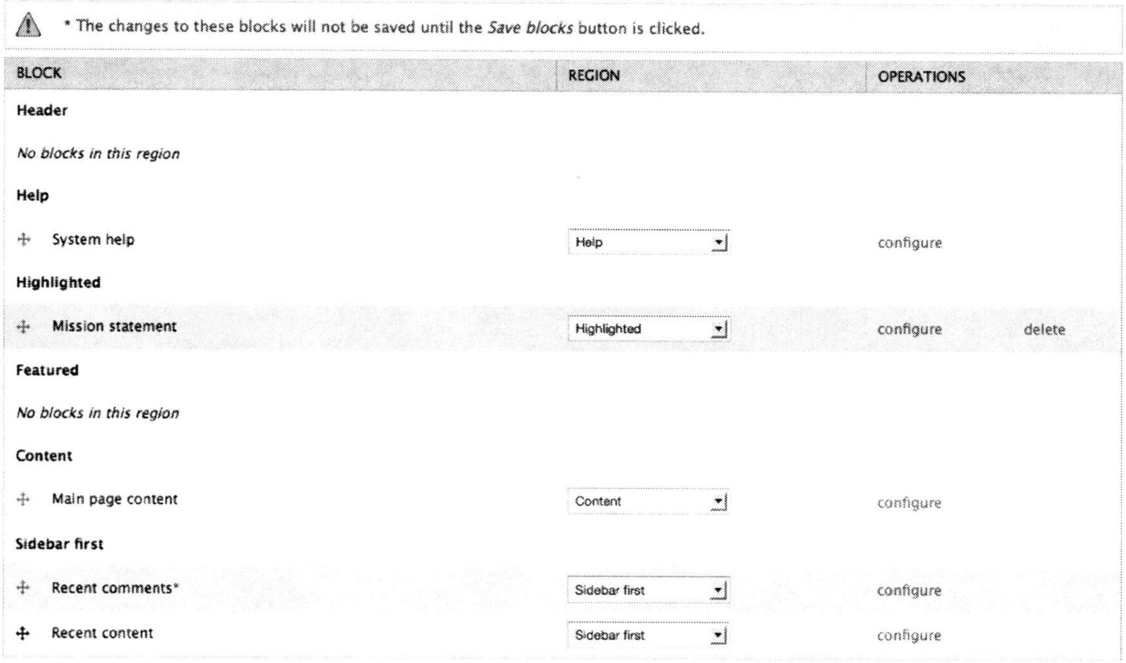

⚠   * The changes to these blocks will not be saved until the *Save blocks* button is clicked.

BLOCK	REGION	OPERATIONS	
Header			
No blocks in this region			
Help			
✛ System help	Help ▾	configure	
Highlighted			
✛ Mission statement	Highlighted ▾	configure	delete
Featured			
No blocks in this region			
Content			
✛ Main page content	Content ▾	configure	
Sidebar first			
✛ Recent comments*	Sidebar first ▾	configure	
✛ Recent content	Sidebar first ▾	configure	

Figure 1–15. The block administration page with the Recent comments block enabled for the Sidebar first region but the form not yet saved

---

■**Caution** Custom blocks can be deleted, but there is no undo. Be certain you are not mistakenly deleting a block when you really want to disable it temporarily or only for a particular theme. The delete link is out in the open; to disable a block, change the block's region to None or Disabled.

Taxonomy: Categorizing Content

Drupal allows you to easily classify content using the core Taxonomy module. You can define your own vocabularies (groups of taxonomy terms) and add terms to each vocabulary. Vocabularies can be flat or hierarchical, can allow single or multiple selection, and can also be "free tagging" (meaning that you can add new terms on the fly when creating or editing content). Each vocabulary can then be attached to one or more content types; in this way, nodes on your site can be grouped into categories, tagged, or otherwise classified in any way you choose.

■**Tip** A major use of applying taxonomy terms to content is that content with a given term can then be listed together. Drupal core provides this by default at the path `taxonomy/term/8`, where 8 is the taxonomy term ID. (This is the path you go to when you click on a term on a piece of content—it will list that piece of content and any others that have that term. You can use taxonomy to show content in many more ways (see Chapter 3 on the most important of these, Views). For example, you could make events that are listed by format and topic, or album listings that are sorted by music genre.

Let's go back to the requirement that registered users shall be able to share suggestions for the book such as tips or warnings, anecdotes about Drupal, or concepts that should be covered. You've already created the Suggestion content type; now you need to allow it to be categorized.

For organizing all the different types of suggestions the authors will accept for the book, go to Administration ➤ Structure ➤ Taxonomy (`admin/structure/taxonomy`). Next, create a new vocabulary by clicking + Add vocabulary. Enter a name that is logical; in this case `Book element`. Click the edit link next to the automatically generated machine name to shorten it to `element`, as shown in Figure 1–16. In the optional description text field, used for the administrative interface only, put in something like `Content or concepts in, or suggested for, the book`.

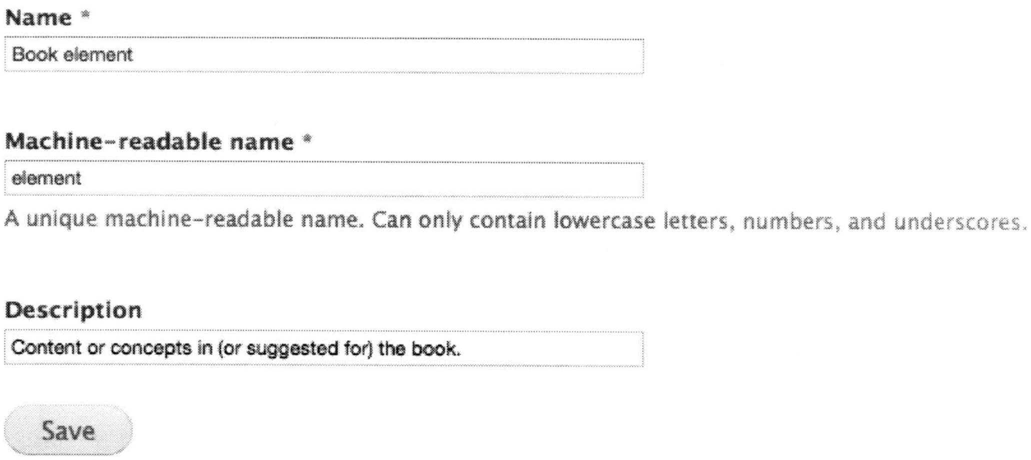

Name *

Book element

Machine-readable name *

element

A unique machine-readable name. Can only contain lowercase letters, numbers, and underscores.

Description

Content or concepts in (or suggested for) the book.

Save

Figure 1–16. Using Taxonomy module to add a Book element vocabulary

Now you can add taxonomy terms to this vocabulary by pressing the + Add term link. Add the following terms:

- Tip
- Note
- Gotcha
- Caution
- Reality
- New in Drupal 7
- Concept
- Anecdote

Next, create another vocabulary called Status and add these terms to it:

- Don't waste pixels on it
- If there's room
- Slated to go in
- Already in the book

Now you need to add a field to your Suggestion content type for each vocabulary. The option for people adding suggestions to select these associated taxonomy terms will then show up right near the title and body fields.

Go to Administration ➤ Structure ➤ Content types, and click on the Manage fields link for your Suggestion content type. Under Add new field, enter Book element for your new field's label, enter element for the field name, and select term reference for the data type. This last selection will bring up options in the last column; select "check boxes/radio buttons" for the form element, as shown in Figure 1–17. Click Save.

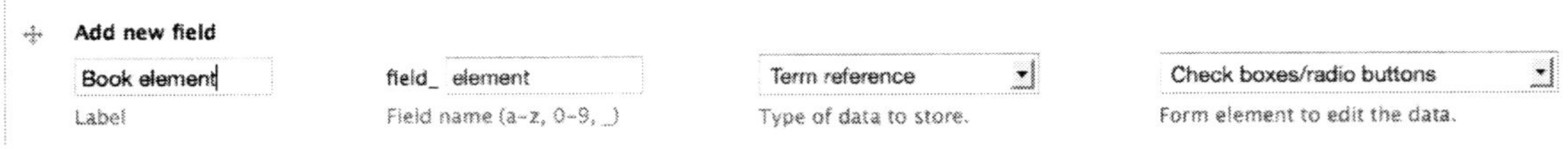

┼ **Add new field**			
Book element	field_ element	Term reference ▾	Check boxes/radio buttons ▾
Label	Field name (a–z, 0–9, _)	Type of data to store.	Form element to edit the data.

Figure 1–17. *Adding a vocabulary to a content type with term reference field*

▓**Note** If a "Check boxes/radio buttons" field has a Number of values limit of only one value, it will be radio buttons. If it can have two or more or unlimited values, it will be checkboxes.

On the configuration page you are brought to after saving, choose the vocabulary called Book elements and click Save field settings. On the next screen, checkmark Required field and save the page.

▓**Tip** New in Drupal 7, the same vocabulary can be attached to the same content type twice by adding a new field that references the same vocabulary. This allows, for instance, a Location vocabulary to be used as both the origin and destination of a product content type.

Follow the same steps used to add the Book element field to add a Status term reference field for the Status vocabulary to the Suggestion content type. This time, make the field optional by leaving the Required field checkbox unchecked.

With this done, you can test it out by clicking Add content (in the default shortcut bar) and then choosing Suggestion. You'll see the text field for the title and text areas for the body and explanation, followed by the radio buttons for the taxonomy terms. Cool!

You can adjust the order of these fields by returning to the content type's field management page at Administration ➤ Structure ➤ Content types ➤ Manage ➤ Suggestion ➤ Fields (`admin/structure/types/manage/suggestion/fields`). Drag the fields up and down using the cross icon. This affects the field order on Suggestion add and edit forms (the order of fields when displaying can be changed independently at the Display fields tab). Don't forget to click Save.

Now, registered users of DGD7 can add suggestions and classify them, too. Or can they? Nothing in Drupal is finished until you have configured permissions.

Users, Roles, and Permissions

Every visitor to your site is considered a *user* by Drupal. Users on your site can be assigned permissions via *roles*. Drupal supports multiple roles, and each user can be assigned to one or more of these roles.

▨**Note** Drupal 7 tries to be polite and uses "people" for its administration section, but the term "user" is more correct for a person who uses the site. You will add *users* and configure *user settings*.

A standard installation of Drupal starts out with the following three roles:

- *Anonymous user:* any visitor to your web site who is not logged in.

- *Authenticated user:* any visitor to your web site who *is* logged in.

- *Administrator:* a role that automatically receives all permissions when a new module is enabled.

The first two roles cannot be deleted; they are needed for Drupal's functioning. The administrator role can be deleted, but you really shouldn't. If you do delete it or you install Drupal with the minimal installation profile, you can choose which role will be the administrator role at Administration ➤ Configuration ➤ People ➤ Account settings (`admin/config/people/accounts`).

The more interesting thing about roles is you can create any number of your own custom roles. Each role can be assigned specific permissions that control what the users in that role can or can't do on the site. For example, if you have content editors who should be able to add or edit content, but shouldn't be able to handle other administrative tasks, you would create a role called "editor" and assign appropriate permissions to it.

▨**Tip** Giving a permission to the authenticated user role means all other roles receive it. Note, however, that giving a permission to the anonymous user role does *not* mean that the authenticated role or any other role has that permission. The anonymous user role is entirely separate from the authenticated user role. All other roles require that a user be logged in to have it, however, so they inherit the permissions given to the authenticated user role.

On the DGD7 web site, all registered, or authenticated, users should be able to submit suggestions and edit or delete their own suggestions, but they shouldn't be able to edit or delete someone else's suggestion or add other types of content. Authors should be able to add any type of content and edit chapter content. Let's go ahead and do that for book authors.

First you'll need to add an author role. This can be done at Administration ➤ People ➤ Permissions ➤ Roles (`admin/people/permissions/roles`). On the People administration page, Permissions is the tab farthest to the right and Roles is in the next level of tabs below it (after you click the Permissions tab). In the text field beneath the existing roles type author and press the **Add role** button, as shown in Figure 1–18.

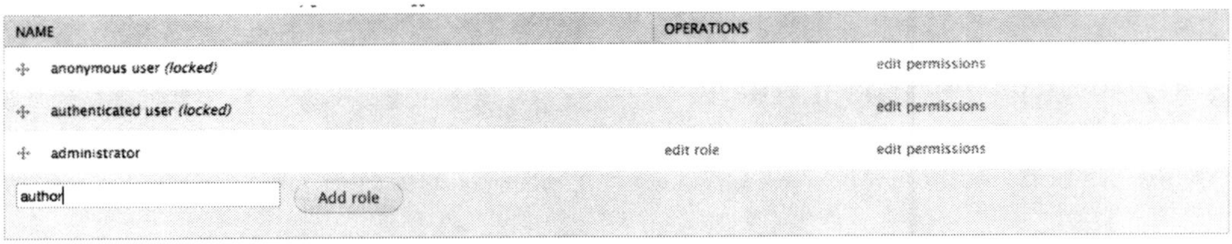

NAME		OPERATIONS
✛ anonymous user *(locked)*		edit permissions
✛ authenticated user *(locked)*		edit permissions
✛ administrator	edit role	edit permissions
author	Add role	

Figure 1–18. The roles administration screen. You can have many roles on your site.

Next, you assign permissions to the role that tell Drupal what users with that role can and can't do on the site. So that your site has users to have roles assigned to them, you will need to allow anonymous users to sign up, configured at admin/config/people/accounts, or you will need to add users yourself, at admin/people/create.

For Suggestions on the DGD7 website, registered or authenticated users should be able to submit suggestions, but the Status field should be reserved for the book's authors when filtering through the suggestions. Chapter 8 introduces the Field Permissions module for even more fine-grained permissions— making the Status vocabulary field you just created available only to authors and administrators.

To assign permissions, you can click the Edit permissions link next to your newly created role to edit the permissions for that role, or you can edit the permissions for every role at once by clicking back to the Permissions tab. Checking the appropriate boxes in the user role columns will grant role-specific permissions. This will allow all users in the author role to take the actions specified, when they are logged in. Users can have any number of roles, and permissions aggregate across the roles they have.

To finish the Suggestion requirement, scroll down to the Taxonomy section and give authors the ability to edit and delete terms from Status. Authors will also need the following permissions:

- Access the content overview page.
- Create new Basic page content.
- Edit own Basic page content.
- Edit any Basic page content.
- Create new Suggestion content.
- Edit own Suggestion content.
- Edit any Suggestion content.
- Use the administration pages and help.
- Use the administration toolbar.

Once the author role permissions are configured, you can assign users to that role. Clicking on People in the Administration menu will show you a list of users that have registered on the site. You can create accounts for people with the + Add user link. While creating a new user account, you can select roles for that user and ask Drupal to e-mail the person that their account has been created. (Note that people can't use your site and likely can't get e-mail from it until it is online, of course; see Chapter 12.)

■**Tip** You can add or remove a role from many existing users at once by checking the chosen people and using the appropriate option from the Update options drop-down menu. See Figure 1–19.

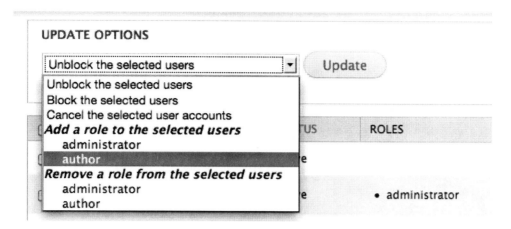

Figure 1–19. *Easily change or add roles for multiple users simultaneously on the People page under the Administration menu*

Time for a Celebratory Beverage

Congratulations, you have just built a web site using Drupal 7! It might be overwhelming to think that you have only scratched the surface—you have not yet added a single contributed module to Drupal's core functionality—but there's nothing to be worried about. The best way to learn Drupal is to get it installed and start playing around with it. That's what Chapter 1 was all about.

You planned a web site and built it. Specifically, you:

- Installed Drupal 7 locally and configured a core theme.

- Created new content types and taxonomy vocabularies to categorize them.

- Configured blocks and created a custom block to serve as a mission statement.

- Enabled and disabled selected core modules.

- Created a role and configured permissions to give authors and visitors different levels of access to adding and editing content.

In the next chapter we'll cover some essential tools for doing work with Drupal at a high level, Drush and Git. (The important matter of good tools is continued in Chapter 12, which covers setting up your development environment). In Chapter 3, you will move beyond Drupal core with the extremely powerful and versatile Views project. Chapter 4 provides a survey of some contributed extensions (called modules) available for Drupal 7 and some advice on choosing which ones to use. With this new knowledge, building the DGD7 site continues in earnest in Chapter 8.

■**Note** See additional material and ask question questions about this chapter at dgd7.org/firstsite.

■ ■ ■

## CHAPTER 2

Essential Tools: Drush and Git

by Dani Nordin and Benjamin Melançon

> *"There is no knowledge that is not power."*

> —Ralph Waldo Emerson

Whether building sites, developing themes or modules, or trying to make a Drupal distribution that can drive your car, Drush (the Drupal shell) and Git (the open source version control system) will help you get where you are going quickly and safely. This chapter will give you a brief overview of Drush and Git and then it will help you get started with these powerful tools. If you are already familiar with Drush, or want to go deeper into all of the things that you can do with it, check out Chapter 26, "Drush."

Drush is easy to explain. It lets you perform all manner of repetitive Drupal tasks much, much faster. Need to upgrade your code? Use `drush up`. Need to download a new module? Use `drush dl MODULE_NAME`. Drush does the rest of the work—usually within a minute or two (see Figure 2–1).

Git may be a little harder to explain. The short explanation is that if you are not using version control, you need to. If you are the pesky type of person that expects reasons for doing things, here's a slightly longer explanation: have you ever wanted an undo or rewind button for life? That's version control. The best way to perform backups of your work is with a properly configured version control system (VCS), which you use constantly to record changes to a file or set of files over time so that you can revert to or compare specific versions later.

Like most developers, we made our first sites without version control. And like most developers, we have a tale or two of minor catastrophes, from the change that broke a site in Internet Explorer to the deleting of three days' work. But you get the benefit of our experience, and we're going to make you start off doing it right. Before we get into that, however, we need to set up some foundations. You need to install Drush and Git.

■ **Tip** You can also use Git to track changes for non-Drupal projects, even folders with only one file in them.

```
Dani-Nordins-MacBook-Pro:~ Dani$ cd Dropbox/MAMP/drupal7
Dani-Nordins-MacBook-Pro:drupal7 Dani$ drush up
Refreshing update status information ...
Done.
Update information last refreshed: Fri, 01/21/2011 - 17:40

Update status information on all installed and enabled Drupal projects:
Name        Installed      Proposed       Status
            version        version
Backup      7.x-2.0        7.x-2.0        Up to date
and
Migrate
Drupal      7.0            7.0            Up to date
core
Chaos       7.x-1.0-alph   7.x-1.0-alph   Up to date
tool        a2             a2
suite
Pathauto    7.x-1.0-alph   7.x-1.0-beta   Update available
            a2             1
Token       7.x-1.0-alph   7.x-1.0-beta   Update available
            a3             1
Views       7.x-3.0-alph   7.x-3.0-alph   Up to date
            a1             a1
Wysiwyg     7.x-2.0        7.x-2.0        Up to date
Boron       7.x-1.0-beta   7.x-1.0-beta   Up to date
(HTML5      1              1
base
theme)
NineSixt    7.x-1.x-dev    7.x-1.x-dev    Update available
y (960
Grid
System)


Code updates will be made to the following projects: Pathauto [pathauto-7.x-1.0-beta1], To
ken [token-7.x-1.0-beta1], NineSixty (960 Grid System) [ninesixty-7.x-1.x-dev]
```

Figure 2–1. Upgrading Drupal with the drush up *command. Total time? About 30 seconds. Manually? 15 minutes to a couple of hours, depending on how many modules need to be upgraded.*

A Beginner's Guide to Installing Drush

Installing and using Drush—a command line tool that lets you do things on your Drupal site like update modules via two word commands—is a no-brainer. But even hard-core Drupal users have been late to experience the benefits of Drush because they put off the little bit of up-front work that would make their lives easier. For people new to Drupal, or those of us raised with a love of pixels and a distaste for the command line, the idea of installing Drush can be overwhelming.

This section provides a simple guide to installing Drush.

THINGS TO KNOW BEFORE YOU GET STARTED

- You're going to use the command line now.

- On Mac OSX or Ubuntu, you can open Terminal to reach the command line. If you're developing in Windows, see Appendix F on setting up a Windows development environment for instructions, or you could consider setting up a virtual machine running Ubuntu for your Drupal development environment (discussed in Appendix G).

- For this exercise, you're going to focus on local development. When working on sites that are staged on a remote host, you'll want to also install Drush and Git on the host servers and log into those servers on the command line. If you're on Mac OSX, Panic's Coda (www.panic.com/coda/) includes a Terminal editor that will let you do this automatically. If you're developing locally, you'll still have to use Terminal.

- Whether you're installing Drush locally or remotely, be ABSOLUTELY SURE to put Drush outside your web root (i.e. where your Drupal installation is stored). Putting a site with Drush inside it on a remote server could make it very easy for attackers to break into your Drupal site.

Once you have Drush installed (covered next), you'll be able to run many Drush commands from within folders containing the Drupal site root. Once you're on the command line, using the command cd /path/to/drupal will get you there (where '/path/to/drupal' is replaced with the path to your Drupal site in your file system). Then you can execute Drush commands using drush commandname. (If you run Drush commands from your Drupal folder, drush targets the default site on your installation (the one in sites/default); if you're running several sites on the same installation, navigate to your site directory [cd /path/to/drupal/sites/example.com] or add [-l http://example.com] to your drush command.) The following is an example of downloading and enabling the Date module using Drush. The first command, cd Dropbox/MAMP/dgd7, navigates you to the Drupal site's folder; the path will differ on your system:

```
Last login: Fri Jan 21 17:40:08 on ttys000
Dani-Nordins-MacBook-Pro:~ Dani$ cd Dropbox/MAMP/dgd7
Dani-Nordins-MacBook-Pro:dgd7 Dani$ drush dl date
Project date (7.x-1.0-alpha2) downloaded to                        [success]
/Users/Dani/Dropbox/MAMP/dgd7/sites/all/modules/date.
Project date contains 6 modules: date_views, date_tools, date_repeat, date_popup
, date_api, date.
Dani-Nordins-MacBook-Pro:dgd7 Dani$ drush pm-enable date
The following extensions will be enabled: date_api, date
Do you really want to continue? (y/n): y
date was enabled successfully.                        [ok]
date_api was enabled successfully.                    [ok]
Dani-Nordins-MacBook-Pro:dgd7 Dani$ █
```

The three steps that follow are adapted from a blog post by Laura Scott and used with permission; these steps walk you through the process of installing Drush. She installed Drush on Mac OS X, which the authors also develop in, and the instructions will work on any Unix-like system. If you're on Windows, see Appendix F to get started with a Windows development environment for Drupal or Appendix G to run Ubuntu Linux in a virtual machine (you can also consider using Cygwin to mimic the UNIX environment).

1. Download Drush

Get Drush at `drupal.org/project/drush`. Drush works for every version of Drupal, so just find the latest version and download it (see Figure 2–2). (Drush may be the last project you need to download manually!)

Put the tarball into your working folder, which, ideally, is a folder in your home directory. We created a working folder called dev in our home directory.

Double-click on the tarball to open it up. When you go into the drush folder, you'll see a number of files, including the README.txt file. Read it!

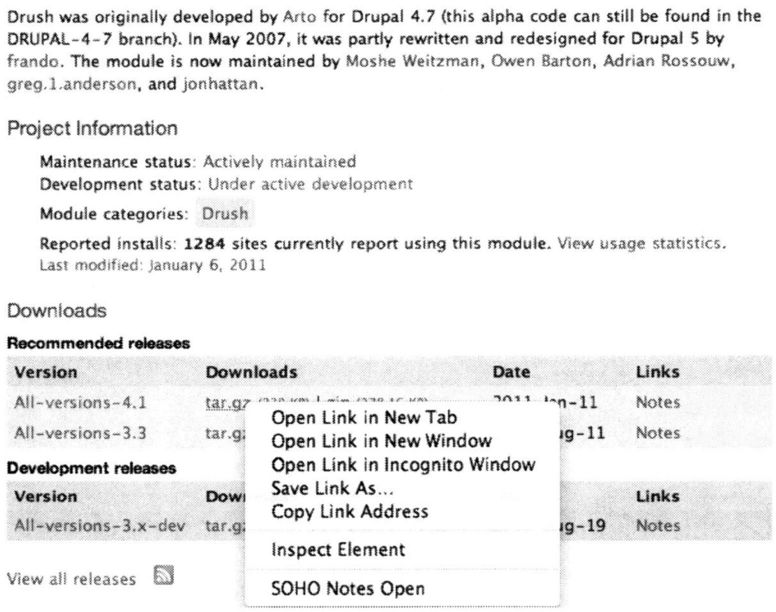

Drush was originally developed by Arto for Drupal 4.7 (this alpha code can still be found in the DRUPAL-4-7 branch). In May 2007, it was partly rewritten and redesigned for Drupal 5 by frando. The module is now maintained by Moshe Weitzman, Owen Barton, Adrian Rossouw, greg.1.anderson, and jonhattan.

Project Information

Maintenance status: Actively maintained
Development status: Under active development

Module categories: Drush

Reported installs: **1284** sites currently report using this module. View usage statistics.
Last modified: January 6, 2011

Downloads

Recommended releases

Version	Downloads	Date	Links
All-versions-4.1	tar.gz	2011-Jan-11	Notes
All-versions-3.3	tar.g:	g-11	Notes

Development releases

Version	Dow		Links
All-versions-3.x-dev	tar.g:	g-19	Notes

Open Link in New Tab
Open Link in New Window
Open Link in Incognito Window
Save Link As...
Copy Link Address

Inspect Element

SOHO Notes Open

View all releases

Figure 2–2. *The Drush project page. The latest version under "Recommended releases" is the one you want.*

If you're already comfortable with the command line, you can also do this via Terminal by copying the link to the tar.gz on the project page, then typing the following into Terminal from the home folder (see Figure 2–3). Note that comments are surrounded by **.

```
wget http://ftp.drupal.org/files/projects/drush-7.x-4.4.tar.gz
     ;** downloads the Drush tarball - replace what's after wget with the current link **
tar xzf drush-7.x-4.4.tar.gz
     ;** unpacks the tarball into your folder **
rm drush-7.x-4.4.tar.gz
     ;** removes the original tarball **
```

```
Dani-Nordins-MacBook-Pro:~ Dani$ wget http://ftp.drupal.org/files/projects/drush
-All-versions-4.1.tar.gz
--2011-01-21 18:22:52--  http://ftp.drupal.org/files/projects/drush-All-versions
-4.1.tar.gz
Resolving ftp.drupal.org... 64.50.233.100, 64.50.236.52
Connecting to ftp.drupal.org|64.50.233.100|:80... connected.
HTTP request sent, awaiting response... 200 OK
Length: 243711 (238K) [application/x-gzip]
Saving to: `drush-All-versions-4.1.tar.gz'

100%[======================================>] 243,711      973K/s   in 0.2s

2011-01-21 18:22:52 (973 KB/s) - `drush-All-versions-4.1.tar.gz' saved [243711/2
43711]

Dani-Nordins-MacBook-Pro:~ Dani$ tar xzf drush-All-versions-4.1.tar.gz
Dani-Nordins-MacBook-Pro:~ Dani$ rm drush-All-versions-4.1.tar.gz
Dani-Nordins-MacBook-Pro:~ Dani$ ▊
```

Figure 2–3. Installing Drush via the command line. This is highly useful when you have to install Drush on multiple servers, or for a new project.

2. Make Drush Executable

Now you venture into the command line. We hope that doesn't vex you, because Drush *is* a command line tool.

Open your Terminal. This opens up to your home directory, which corresponds to the Finder folder that bears your Mac username.

The path to your drush will depend upon where you put it.

You will want to type the command chmod u+x /path/to/drush/drush (replacing "/path/to/" with the actual path where you placed Drush). So in our case, with Drush residing in the dev folder, it's

```
chmod u+x dev/drush/drush
```

Now that you've made Drush executable, you want to set things up so you actually can execute the drush command outside of the actual Drush folder (such as in the working folder for the site you're building).

3. Create an Alias

This part may seem a bit mysterious, but it's really quite simple. You will be adding to your bash profile file the path to the drush command so that you can run the drush command from anywhere in your filesystem.

A handy UNIX shortcut to your home folder is "~" (the tilde character). You can use that in any path designation.

Find your bash profile file using the Terminal in your home directory.

If you're not there, go ahead and enter on the command line:

```
cd ~
```

The bash profile files are hidden from normal view, so to see what files you have in your home directory, enter this command:

```
ls -a
```

You'll get a list of all the files in that folder, similar to that in Figure 2–4. The hidden files start with a dot (.), so look for one of these files:

```
.profile
.bash_aliases
.bashrc
.bash_profile
```

```
Dani-Nordins-MacBook-Pro:~ Dani$ cd ~
Dani-Nordins-MacBook-Pro:~ Dani$ ls -a
.                       .drush              Documents
..                      .freemind           Downloads
.AB64CF89               .gem                Dropbox
.CFUserTextEncoding     .gitconfig          FontExplorer X
.DS_Store               .hAWabAzAr          Library
.Trash                  .htaccess           Movies
.adobe                  .realobjects        Music
.bash_history           .rnd                Pictures
.bash_profile           .ssh                Public
.crash_report_checksum  .subversion         Sites
.crash_report_frames    .viminfo            drush
.crash_report_preview   .wdswlock           drush-backups
.cups                   Applications        qtm-blog
.dropbox                Desktop
Dani-Nordins-MacBook-Pro:~ Dani$ ▐
```

Figure 2–4. Use the ls command to list the files in your home folder.

Your bash profile can have any of these four names. If you don't see any of these in your home folder, create one using the nano editor (the really simple, old school text editor that comes with UNIX); nano will create the file if it doesn't find one with that name.

Any one will do, so just pick an existing file. (We picked .bash_profile.)

To edit the file, enter nano [filename]. For us, that means

```
nano .bash_profile
```

This takes you into the editor. You might be looking at one or two lines of code. Cursor down to the end of the file; make sure you're on a new line, and add:

```
alias drush='/path/to/drush/drush'
```

Replace the "/path/to/" part with the actual path—but this time it needs to be relative to the system root. Remember that shortcut to the home directory? Now is a time to use it (see Figure 2–5).

```
alias drush='~/dev/drush/drush'
```

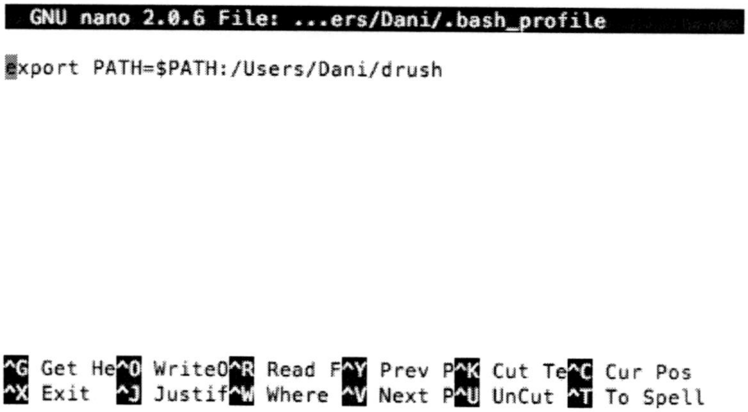

```
 GNU nano 2.0.6 File: ...ers/Dani/.bash_profile
export PATH=$PATH:/Users/Dani/drush




^G Get He^O WriteO^R Read F^Y Prev P^K Cut Te^C Cur Pos
^X Exit  ^J Justif^W Where ^V Next P^U UnCut ^T To Spell
```

Figure 2–5. *Another recommended approach to having the drush command at your fingertips: Add the path to the Drush folder to your shell's path, also done in a file such as .bash_profile or .profile.*

Save the file using <control>-x, y(es), <enter>. Now you're back at your Terminal prompt.
Now all you need to do is reload the updated bash profile using source [filename]. In my case:

```
source .bash_profile
```

4. Test

Yes, we said it was three steps. But this is testing, an everpresent understood additional step. To test, type:

```
drush
```

You should get a long list of available Drush commands. You're done! (Or rather, now you can get started!) See Figure 2–6 for details.

```
Dani-Nordins-MacBook-Pro:~ Dani$ cd Dropbox/MAMP/dgd7
Dani-Nordins-MacBook-Pro:dgd7 Dani$ drush
Execute a drush command. Run `drush help [command]` to view command-specific
help.  Run `drush topic` to read even more documentation.

Global options (see `drush topic` for the full list):
 -r <path>, --root=<path>               Drupal root directory to use
                                        (default: current directory)
 -l http://example.com,                 URI of the drupal site to use (only
 --uri=http://example.com               needed in multisite environments)
 -v, --verbose                          Display extra information about the
                                        command.
 -d, --debug                            Display even more information,
                                        including internal messages.
 -y, --yes                              Assume 'yes' as answer to all
                                        prompts
 -n, --no                               Assume 'no' as answer to all prompts
 -s, --simulate                         Simulate all relevant actions (don't
                                        actually change the system)
 -p, --pipe                             Emit a compact representation of the
                                        command for scripting.
 -h, --help                             This help system.
 --version                              Show drush version.
 --php                                  The absolute path to your PHP
                                        intepreter, if not 'php' in the
                                        path.


Core drush commands: (core)
 cache-clear (cc)       Clear a specific cache, or all drupal caches.
 core-cli (cli)         Enter a new shell optimized for drush use.
 core-cron (cron)       Run all cron hooks in all active modules for specified
                        site.
 core-rsync (rsync)     Rsync the Drupal tree to/from another server using ssh.
 core-status (status,   Provides a birds-eye view of the current Drupal
 st)                    installation, if any.
 core-topic (topic)     Read detailed documentation on a given topic.
 drupal-directory       Return path to a given module/theme directory.
 (dd)
 help                   Print this help message. See `drush help help` for more
                        options.
 image-flush            Flush all derived images for a given style.
 php-eval (eval, ev)    Evaluate arbitrary php code after bootstrapping Drupal
```

Figure 2–6. *Success!*

Now that you've got Drush installed, you can do all sorts of things that would take a long time through the Drupal interface. First, make sure you have a working Drupal installation on your system and navigate to it: cd /path/to/drupal. Now, need to install a module? Type drush dl projectname. (Note that for Drush, the project name is the name of the folder containing the module or group of modules, not the human-readable module name. For example, if you want to install X-ray module, use its machine name xray.) Need to update your code? Type drush up. Be sure to check out Chapter 26 to see all the great things that Drush is capable of (and how you can extend it to do even more).

Git: Development Grease

Continually backing up your work is an essential practice for any web developer. Whether your workflow is based on downloading and installing modules, building custom themes, or writing code, putting everything in version control lets you focus on progress. You don't need to worry about taking the wrong route because you can always go back.

Version control is development grease. It makes everything run smoothly and helps you get in the zone. Chapter 14 discusses how to use version control (also called revision control) in achieving a state of optimal productivity.

Why Git?

There are many different version control systems for you to choose from. This book will focus on Git. Why? Because it's free, it's easy(ish) to use once you know a few basics, and Drupal.org has moved over to using it. This last part means that, once you get the hang of Git, contributing code to the community will be much easier. (And while getting the hang of Git—which will be a lifelong learning process—you can ask the Drupal community for help.)

■ **Note** If you do choose another VCS, we highly recommend you make it a modern one—a distributed version control system, or DVCS. Bazaar and Mecurial are both ones that were considered by Drupal.org (the infrastructure team uses Bazaar) but the Drupal community had already voted for Git with its feet. In other words, many more people were already using Git.

Installing Git

To install Git, the first thing you'll need to do is grab the installer. You can find the Git software at git-scm.com. Download the installer appropriate to your OS, indicated by the handy icons on the right side of the page (see Figure 2–7).

■ **Tip** If you're using a UNIX-like OS with a package manager, you can use that to install Git; feel free to skip this section. For instance, on Debian or Ubuntu, sudo apt-get install git will take care of it for you. If you're on Mac OS X and you want to enjoy the goodness of a package manager, set up Homebrew (mxcl.github.com/homebrew), the latest and greatest apt-get clone for Mac. If you're on Windows see Git for Windows (code.google.com/p/msysgit), or Cygwin will help you create a UNIX-like environment on your machine that will help you to use the command line effectively.

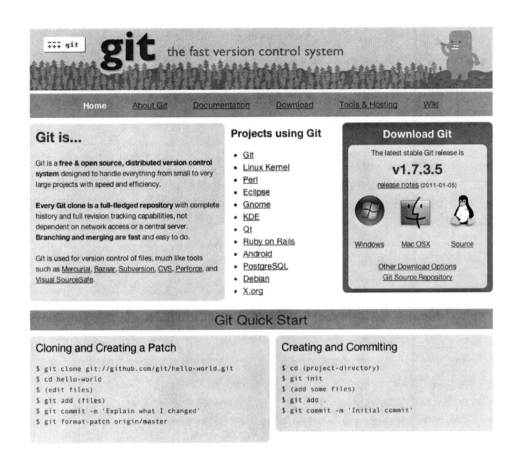

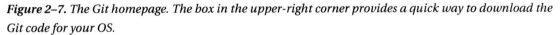

Figure 2–7. The Git homepage. The box in the upper-right corner provides a quick way to download the Git code for your OS.

Follow the instructions on the website to install the Git software. Git is a command-line program, which means that you won't find it in your Applications folder. To access it, you have to go into Terminal. (The Windows installer adds an icon to your start menu, which launches a Git terminal for you.) Once you're in there, just type git. You should see a handy list of commands, much like you did when you typed drush previously (see Figure 2–8).

```
Last login: Fri Jan 21 10:48:55 on console
Dani-Nordins-MacBook-Pro:~ Dani$ git
usage: git [--version] [--exec-path[=<path>]] [--html-path]
           [-p|--paginate|--no-pager] [--no-replace-objects]
           [--bare] [--git-dir=<path>] [--work-tree=<path>]
           [-c name=value] [--help]
           <command> [<args>]

The most commonly used git commands are:
   add        Add file contents to the index
   bisect     Find by binary search the change that introduced a bug
   branch     List, create, or delete branches
   checkout   Checkout a branch or paths to the working tree
   clone      Clone a repository into a new directory
   commit     Record changes to the repository
   diff       Show changes between commits, commit and working tree, etc
   fetch      Download objects and refs from another repository
   grep       Print lines matching a pattern
   init       Create an empty git repository or reinitialize an existing one
   log        Show commit logs
   merge      Join two or more development histories together
   mv         Move or rename a file, a directory, or a symlink
   pull       Fetch from and merge with another repository or a local branch
   push       Update remote refs along with associated objects
   rebase     Forward-port local commits to the updated upstream head
   reset      Reset current HEAD to the specified state
   rm         Remove files from the working tree and from the index
   show       Show various types of objects
   status     Show the working tree status
   tag        Create, list, delete or verify a tag object signed with GPG

See 'git help <command>' for more information on a specific command.
Dani-Nordins-MacBook-Pro:~ Dani$ ▉
```

Figure 2–8. The git home screen within Terminal

▒ **Note** If the command `git` doesn't work after installing, try quitting Terminal (File > Quit in most operating systems, or Cmd+Q on the Mac) and re-opening the program.

Working with Git

Git is primarily a command line tool and is very easy to use on the command line. We recommend learning Git on the command-line first, before trying the visual tools. Knowing the command-line gives you a common vocabulary with other Drupal git users. The basic steps to get started are discussed in the following sections. It is possible, however, to find some clients that will create a GUI for you. See drupal.org/node/777182 for some examples, including SmartGit and (for Mac OS X only, proprietary) Tower (git-tower.com).

▒ **Tip** See dgd7.org/git for common Git commands and useful tricks.

Bonus One-time Step: Identify Yourself

To properly identify yourself for every commit in case you share your code later, you should use these two commands:

```
git config --global user.name "Your Name"
git config --global user.email you@example.com
```

You will only have to do this once.

Creating a Repository

In order to start using Git, the first thing you need to do is create a repository. This repository should be in your project folder. You create the repository with the command git init. (You can navigate to the folder using the command cd). This only needs to be done once per project.

We'll go over some of the additional commands here in a moment; but say you were starting with the DGD7 web site project you created in Chapter 1, you would use these commands in succession to create your repository:

```
cd ~/code/dgd7
git init
```

This creates a new .git folder in your Drupal project (see Figure 2–9), which will store all of your code versions.

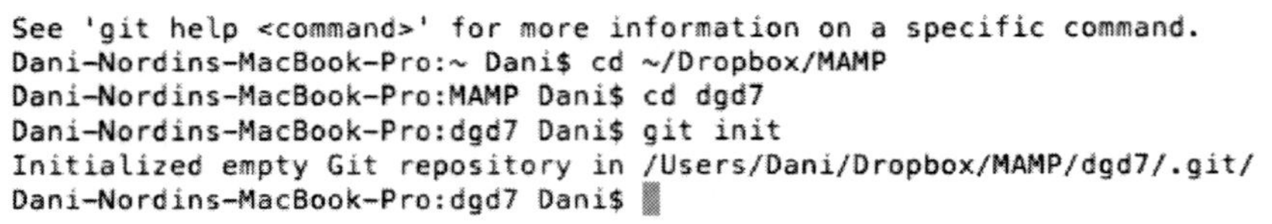

```
See 'git help <command>' for more information on a specific command.
Dani-Nordins-MacBook-Pro:~ Dani$ cd ~/Dropbox/MAMP
Dani-Nordins-MacBook-Pro:MAMP Dani$ cd dgd7
Dani-Nordins-MacBook-Pro:dgd7 Dani$ git init
Initialized empty Git repository in /Users/Dani/Dropbox/MAMP/dgd7/.git/
Dani-Nordins-MacBook-Pro:dgd7 Dani$ ▉
```

Figure 2–9. Creating your Git repository

While developing, it's important to put your code in the repository as early and often as possible. We recommend committing each time you make a change to your project, such as adding a module, updating the CSS on a site theme, or changing functionality in code. Once you've created a repository, all the files that you are working with are considered the working copy of that repository. It can be clean (all your changes are committed) or changed. Currently, with no files committed, it is considered in a changed state.

The first step to committing your code is to add it to "stage." The stage temporarily holds your changes until you commit them. To add your changes to stage, use the command git add . from within your working copy of the site project. The final period is important—it tells Git to prepare to add everything that's changed in your code in that directory (and any directory nested below it) to the repository. You can see what you are about to commit (and what's still not staged for committing) with git status (see Figure 2–10).

```
Dani-Nordins-MacBook-Pro:dgd7 Dani$ git add .
Dani-Nordins-MacBook-Pro:dgd7 Dani$ git status
# On branch master
#
# Initial commit
#
# Changes to be committed:
#   (use "git rm --cached <file>..." to unstage)
#
#       new file:   .htaccess
#       new file:   CHANGELOG.txt
#       new file:   COPYRIGHT.txt
#       new file:   INSTALL.mysql.txt
#       new file:   INSTALL.pgsql.txt
#       new file:   INSTALL.sqlite.txt
#       new file:   INSTALL.txt
#       new file:   LICENSE.txt
#       new file:   MAINTAINERS.txt
#       new file:   README.txt
#       new file:   UPGRADE.txt
#       new file:   authorize.php
#       new file:   cron.php
#       new file:   includes/actions.inc
#       new file:   includes/ajax.inc
#       new file:   includes/archiver.inc
#       new file:   includes/authorize.inc
#       new file:   includes/batch.inc
#       new file:   includes/batch.queue.inc
```

Figure 2–10. Adding your DGD7 site code to stage and viewing the status

Next, you actually commit your code to the repository. This is done using the command git commit (see Figure 2–11). No path name is needed here; Git will commit everything that you just added. You can also add a message to your commit by using -m "Message goes here" where "Message goes here" is the text of your message. The message should inform anyone who downloads your code what they're downloading (e.g., "Initial build of DGD7 demo site"). In practice, the act of adding and committing code would happen in succession, like so:

```
git add .
git status
git commit -m "Added photo of kittens to the theme header per client request."
```

```
Dani-Nordins-MacBook-Pro:dgd7 Dani$ git commit -m "Initial commit of files for DGD7 demo site"
[master (root-commit) dd5c5d4] Initial commit of files for DGD7 demo site
 2052 files changed, 461943 insertions(+), 0 deletions(-)
 create mode 100644 .htaccess
 create mode 100644 CHANGELOG.txt
 create mode 100644 COPYRIGHT.txt
 create mode 100644 INSTALL.mysql.txt
 create mode 100644 INSTALL.pgsql.txt
 create mode 100644 INSTALL.sqlite.txt
 create mode 100644 INSTALL.txt
 create mode 100644 LICENSE.txt
 create mode 100644 MAINTAINERS.txt
 create mode 100644 README.txt
 create mode 100644 UPGRADE.txt
 create mode 100644 authorize.php
 create mode 100644 cron.php
 create mode 100644 includes/actions.inc
 create mode 100644 includes/ajax.inc
 create mode 100644 includes/archiver.inc
 create mode 100644 includes/authorize.inc
 create mode 100644 includes/batch.inc
 create mode 100644 includes/batch.queue.inc
 create mode 100644 includes/bootstrap.inc
 create mode 100644 includes/cache-install.inc
 create mode 100644 includes/cache.inc
 create mode 100644 includes/common.inc
 create mode 100644 includes/database/database.inc
 create mode 100644 includes/database/log.inc
 create mode 100644 includes/database/mysql/database.inc
 create mode 100644 includes/database/mysql/install.inc
 create mode 100644 includes/database/mysql/query.inc
 create mode 100644 includes/database/mysql/schema.inc
 create mode 100644 includes/database/pgsql/database.inc
 create mode 100644 includes/database/pgsql/install.inc
 create mode 100644 includes/database/pgsql/query.inc
 create mode 100644 includes/database/pgsql/schema.inc
 create mode 100644 includes/database/pgsql/select.inc
 create mode 100644 includes/database/prefetch.inc
```

Figure 2–11. Committing your DGD7 code for the first time

This will commit any code in your site that has changed since the last time you committed. It's worth noting that if you're adding code for the first time, the process might take some time; Git will be copying every file and piece of code to stage.

Ideally, you commit constantly (see Chapter 14). At the very least commit after you've made any major change to your site's files (for example, after downloading a module or theme) or periodically while writing custom modules for your site.

What to Do When Things Go Wrong—Throwing Away Changes and Reverting in Git

There are many ways to fix your mistakes in Git while you're developing. If, while you're developing, you realize that you don't want to save what you just did at all, and you haven't yet committed your changes, you can use the following command:

```
git reset --hard HEAD
```

▧ **Caution** This command will throw away everything you did since your most recent commit.

If you don't want to replace all of your code, but retrieve just one file, you can use the following command:

```
git checkout -- path/to/filename.php
```

This command will restore filename.php to the last committed revision. If you've already committed your code, you can use this command

```
git revert HEAD
```

to return your code to the last committed revision. If you want to go back one further (i.e. the next-to-last revision), you can amend it to

```
git revert HEAD^.
```

Other Useful Git Commands

Now that you have the lay of the land, here are some other Git commands that you might find useful:

- `git status` shows what you're about to commit.

- `git log` provides a list of what you've committed. Variations of this command, such as `git log --pretty=oneline`, are a lot more practical. And `git log --pretty=oneline -n5` gives you the last 5 commits, useful when you have hundreds. Also, ":q" might have to be typed in order to get back to the command line after viewing the log.

- `git checkout mymodule.info` lets you check out (i.e., download) a specific file or revision.

For a full list of Git commands, type `man git` into Terminal.

Database Backup Tools

While Git will help you keep your files and code backed up via version control, it is also important to back up your database regularly. This is vitally important for a site being used by other people, such as clients. Since much of Drupal websites (including content) resides in the database, not backing up could have serious consequences if things go wrong.

The Drupal Git Backup Drush script, available at github.com/scor/dgb, can be used to easily export the database tables you care about and commit them to version control. This is covered more in Chapter 12.

If the setup is too much for you—heck, even if you do nothing else in this chapter—please install the Backup and Migrate module (drupal.org/project/backup_migrate), which will allow you to easily and regularly back up your entire database into a folder that you set up in the configuration settings.

Another way of backing up your database using Drush directly is the command

```
drush sql-dump > /path/to/filename.sql
```

This will create a backup of your database file in the location of your choosing. One thing that Drush doesn't do automatically, however, is empty the cache tables; this can cause the database backups to be overly large, which will fill up your repository quickly. The Drupal Git Backup script addresses this, and Chapter 26 explains how to exclude selected tables from export. Another approach is to simply clear your cache using the command `drush cc all` before making a database backup. This command will clear all of the database cache tables.

Summary

We hope that this chapter has given you a quick overview of how important (and how easy!) it is to keep your code in version control and your database backed up during development. By setting up a few key processes up front, you can save yourself hours of headaches down the line; ask anyone who has ever taken their programming down the wrong path or dealt with a crashed site. You'll thank us later.

■ **Note** Get the essential updates to the tools and tips we missed as people correct us at dgd7.org/essential.

PART II

Site Building Foundations

Chapter 3 takes you on a journey of thorough understanding for the most important contributed project Drupal has: Views. Most if not all sites you build will rely on the Views module for the powerful ways it provides to list, filter, and sort content.

Chapter 4 introduces many other modules (bundles of functionality) available from the Drupal community that you may want to use and, more important, how to find and evaluate modules to meet your site-building needs.

Chapter 5 gives a tour of the Organic Groups suite of modules, which can give people the power to organize content and themselves on your site. This chapter includes an extended cameo by Panels, another powerhouse module for displaying content, especially in concert with Views.

Chapter 6 teaches security practices and provides ways to keep your site secure, from configuration to evaluating and even writing code.

Chapter 7 follows up on the security chapter with several approaches to keeping Drupal core and contributed modules up-to-date.

Chapter 8 continues the site build begun in the first chapter by configuring Fields, Views, and chosen contributed modules to showcase authors, present a table of contents, connect authors and resources to chapters, and allow visitors to participate. It gives a taste of how far you can go in Drupal without writing any code.

CHAPTER 3

■ ■ ■

Building Dynamic Pages Using Views

by Michelle Lauer and Greg Stout

Views changed my life. If you have built dynamic web sites for any period of time, you know that there are two main tasks that you perform over and over. You create content and store it in a database and then requests nuggets of that content to build stuff for your web pages. The latter requesting often requires complex formulas where the slightest typo will return you the wrong items or, more likely, nothing at all.

The Views module allows you to easily specify the criteria for displaying a subset of content, even combining multiple content types. It also allows you to massage the format in which the data is displayed. As new content is added to your web site, the resulting View is dynamically updated to reflect the new content. It helps you to do all of this—without asking you to write a single line of code; thank you, Earl! Views changed my life; and it's about to change yours.

What Are Views?

The name Views comes from database terminology. A database view is a complex stored query that you use like a table in the database. When you request items from a database view, you get the things that you need in exactly the way you need them.

Drupal Views work in a similar manner but they let you use a graphical user interface to create the database query. When you create a Drupal View, the module writes the queries for you so you don't have to know anything about database administration.

The Views module was envisioned/created and is maintained by Earl Miles (merlinofchaos on drupal.org). All downloadable versions, documentation, and the issue queue can be found on its project page at drupal.org/project/views.

> This tool is essentially a smart query builder that, given enough configuration, can build the proper query, execute it, and display the results.
>
> Among other things, Views can be used to generate reports, create summaries, and display collections of images and other content.
>
> —*Excerpted from* drupal.org/project/views

Like Drupal itself, the Views module offers powerful functionality right out of the box. With only a few clicks, you can put a block on your home page that lists your site's most recent content. A few more clicks and you can turn that block into a tabbed menu, so that the first tab shows your site's most popular content, the second tab shows recent comments, and a third lists new members.

The Views Module provides the dynamo in a dynamic web site. It makes your work—in building the site and especially in maintaining it—easier and more powerful. One could easily write a book only about Views and not run out of interesting things to do.

For all these reasons, the essential thing to learn in this chapter is not what you can do with Views or how to do it, but how to do it in a way that makes it easier for you to maintain your site—and pass on that responsibility to the next person. In other words, it is the process, the tags, the descriptions, and the naming conventions that I want you to really learn. Once this is ingrained, you will be able to visualize and use Views to build almost anything.

Examples of Views Usage

The following are just a few examples of common usages of Views:

- The five most recent press releases

- Upcoming events

- All posts written by a specific person, like a blog

- A monthly archive of content

- List of content for administrative purposes (see Figure 3–1)

Post date ▲	Published	Title	Type
Sun, 01/10/2010 - 12:38	Yes	Gemino Magna Pala	Basic page
Tue, 01/12/2010 - 15:36	Yes	Exputo Mos Si Sit	Basic page
Sun, 01/17/2010 - 18:07	Yes	Jus Mos Nibh	Basic page
Mon, 01/18/2010 - 13:40	Yes	Et Humo Ibidem Lobortis	Basic page
Wed, 01/20/2010 - 06:15	Yes	Aliquam Camur Irure Tum	Article
Sat, 01/23/2010 - 11:50	Yes	Eum Ibidem Melior Vel	Basic page
Mon, 01/25/2010 - 12:24	Yes	Exputo Feugiat Pala	Article

Figure 3–1. An example list of content for administrative purposes

You really can display any type of content and also bring in related content as well. If it's in the database, you can use the Views module to display it.

The most common display types for Views are pages and blocks. With pages, you assign your output to a URL of its own, and with a block, your output can be placed in any region on any page in your site.

Download, Enable, and Configure Permissions for the Views Module(s)

To begin developing with Views, you need to download the module and enable it by following the standard procedure for downloading a module.

Download

In your web browser, go to `drupal.org/project/views`. When you scroll down to the Downloads section, you see a table titled "Recommend releases" shown in green. Click on the download link for the format that you want (tar.gz or zip) that accompanies the version of Drupal that you have installed, like 7.x-3.x.

Unpack the compressed files and put them in your contributed modules directory. For most developers, this is at `sites/all/modules/contrib` or simply `sites/all/modules` so that you can find all of the Views files in `sites/all/modules/contrib/views` or `sites/all/modules/views`. (Drush, covered in Chapter 2, can download and place the files for you.)

Enable

On your web site, make sure you are logged in as a user with permission to administer modules or as a user with the Administrator role (or user/1). Use the administrative menu at the top and click Modules (`admin/modules`).

Scroll down to the Views fieldset. You will see three modules: Views, Views exporter, and Views UI. Underneath the description of the Views module, you will notice that CTools is a required module for Views to work. If you already have the CTools module downloaded and enabled on your site, the text noting the dependency will say "enabled." If you have CTools downloaded, but not enabled, the text will say "disabled." And lastly, if you have not downloaded CTools, the text will say "missing." Drupal will not allow you to enable a module if all dependencies are not present in your site files.

If you haven't already done so, please download the CTools module from its project page at `drupal.org/project/ctools`. Unpack the compressed files and put the `ctools` folder in your contributed modules directory. For most developers, this is at `/sites/all/modules` so that you can find all of the CTools files in `sites/all/modules/ctools`.

■ **Note** CTools (Chaos Tools Suite) is a module that provides helper code for other modules.

In your browser, go back to the Modules page (`admin/modules`) and click Refresh. Scroll down to the Views fieldset. The text noting the CTools dependency should say "disabled." Since all required files are available, you may now enable Views. Check the checkboxes for Views and Views UI, then Save configuration (see Figure 3–2).

■ **Note** We will be discussing the Views exporter module later in this chapter.

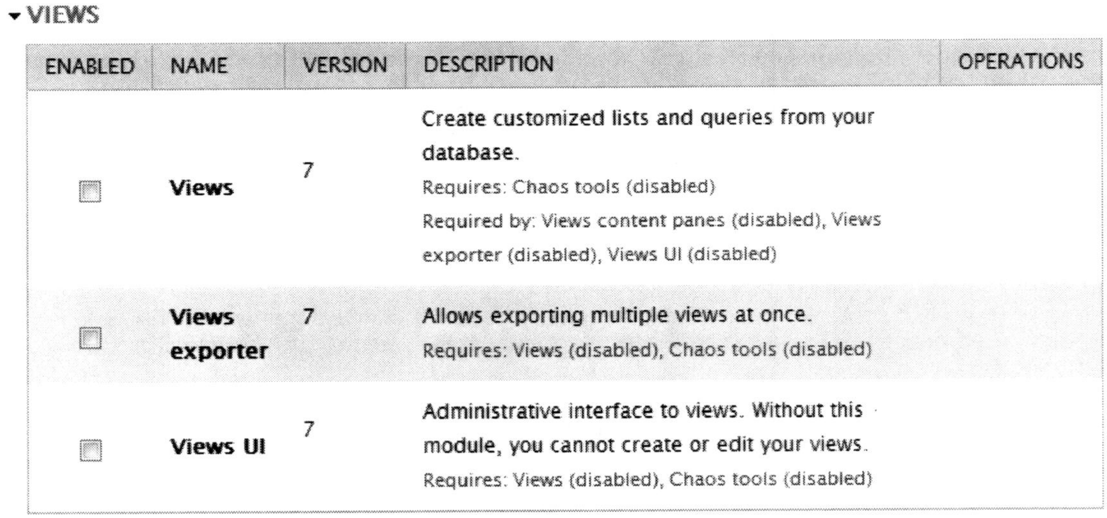

▾ VIEWS

ENABLED	NAME	VERSION	DESCRIPTION	OPERATIONS
☐	**Views**	7	Create customized lists and queries from your database. Requires: Chaos tools (disabled) Required by: Views content panes (disabled), Views exporter (disabled), Views UI (disabled)	
☐	**Views exporter**	7	Allows exporting multiple views at once. Requires: Views (disabled), Chaos tools (disabled)	
☐	**Views UI**	7	Administrative interface to views. Without this module, you cannot create or edit your views. Requires: Views (disabled), Chaos tools (disabled)	

Figure 3–2. Modules list administration page. The needed modules have been downloaded but not yet enabled.

Drupal knows that the Views module needs another module enabled and prompts you.

```
You must enable the Chaos tools module to install Views UI.  Would you like to continue with
the above?
Please "Continue".
```

Configure Permissions

One of the features that Drupal offers is the ability to grant permissions to different roles, as covered in Chapters 1 and 8. Most modules have associated permissions that need to be granted to roles in order to interact with them. Users of your web site will either have the role of Anonymous User or Authenticated User and will possibly have additional roles assigned to them.

▓ **Tip** After enabling any module, it is best to configure the permissions right away. Waiting until the end of development often leads to an overwhelming permissions audit.

Go to the Administrative menu at the top and click People. Once on this page, click the Permissions tab. Scroll down to the bottom and find the Views section. There are two permissions for the *Views* module, "Administer views" and "Access all views".

■ **Note** You may also use the Permissions link for Views on the module administration page. This will take you directly to the Views section on the permissions page.

"Administer views" grants access to the Views administration pages allowing users the ability to create, edit and delete Views. Only give this permission to roles assigned to users that are appropriate and trained to use them properly. Most "Administer" permissions are only given to the Administrator role.

"Bypass views access control" is another permission that should be used sparingly. For a specific View, you can specify which roles can see the results. Selecting the "Access all views" permission for a role will override that setting. We recommend only granting this permission to roles assigned to users that are appropriate and are trained properly to use them properly, like your site administrator.

Confirm that neither checkbox is selected for Authenticated User and Anonymous User roles. Confirm that both checkboxes are selected for Administrator role. If you made any changes, click Save permissions.

■ **Tip** During development, make sure you check your web pages as different users to confirm they are having the correct user experience as defined by the permission settings. Try having three different browsers open, each demonstrating a different Role, such as Administrator in Firefox, Authenticated user in Chrome, and Anonymous user in Internet Explorer. You need a different brand of browser for each role because your browser shares among its open windows/tabs the user account you are logged in with.

Congratulations! You have now successfully downloaded and configured permissions for the Views modules. You are now ready to administer Views.

The Views Administration Page

Using the Administration menu, click Structure and then on that page, click Views (admin/structure/views). This is the Views list page where all Views in your web site are listed.

Advanced Help Module

If you have not yet installed and enabled the Advanced Help module, you will see a status message at the top of the page (see Figure 3–3).

The Advanced Help module will provide some additional information explaining the options while you build your Views. You may choose to download it at drupal.org/project/advanced_help or click Hide this message.

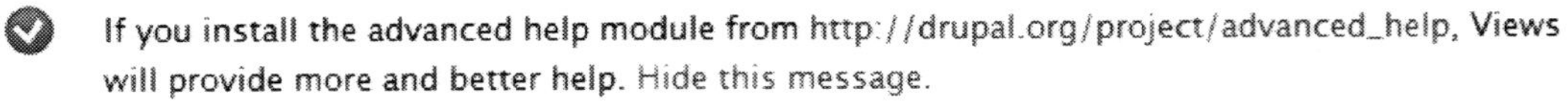

✓ If you install the advanced help module from http://drupal.org/project/advanced_help, Views will provide more and better help. Hide this message.

Figure 3–3. Advanced Help status message

Action Links

Beneath the status message, you will see Add new view and Import. We will be discussing using those later in this chapter.

Change Which Available Views Are Listed

By default, all available Views display on this page. Although it may not be necessary now, if your site has a lot of views, sorting and filtering them makes this administration page much more manageable. You can sort the table of views by clicking the columns heading of View Name, Tag, and Path. Click once to sort first to last and again for the reverse.

You can also enable a set of additional filters by clicking the Settings tab, checking the box next to "Show filters on the list of views," and clicking Save configuration.

Above the table you will see a Search box for finding a view by name and the drop-down filters shown in Table 3–1.

Table 3–1. Filtering Controls

Filter	
Tags	What extra classification (similar to metadata) has been added to this View to make it easier to find related Views?
Displays	Does this View display as a full page with its own URL, a feed, or as a block that can be placed on any page in your web site?
Types	Is the View display about content that is nodes, users, files, etc.?
Storage	Is the View stored in the database, in code only, or in the database overriding code (more on this later)?
Status	Is the View enabled or disabled?

Any filter selection is automatically applied to the list but you can click "Reset" to return the list display to its default settings (see Figure 3–4).

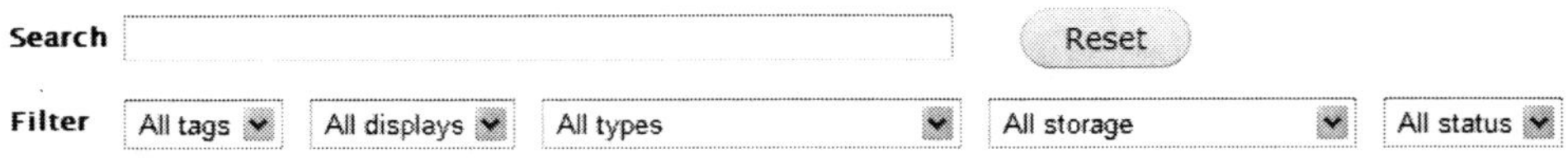

Search [   ] (Reset)

Filter [All tags ▾] [All displays ▾] [All types ▾] [All storage ▾] [All status ▾]

Figure 3–4. Refine the list of available Views

Available Views

The Views module comes with several default Views that you may choose to enable and use in your site. Other modules in your site may also define Views that could appear in the listing. By the end of this chapter, you'll be creating your own Views.

Elements of a View Listing

For each View listed, there is a lot of information provided. The following elements are mapped in Figure 3–5 and relate directly to how you can refine which Views are displayed in the list:

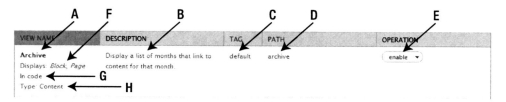

Figure 3–5. *Elements of a View listing*

A. What is the name of the View?

- This is the human readable name of the View.

- You can hover over this label to see the machine name.

B. What is the description?

- The description only appears in the administrative list. This is useful when looking at all the available Views and determining what each one does.

- Optional

C. What are the tags?

- Tags are metadata for Views. They are additional information that helps you categorize your Views and find them easier on the list page. An example would be to tag all Views about company information including employees and departments as "internal."

D. What is the path?

- This is used only for display types of pages.

- If your View is set to display as a page, you are required to enter a path. This is the URL where you find the display of your View on your web site. Drupal only needs the part after your domain name. For example, if your View is to display at http://www.example.com/archive, you would only see archive shown here.

E. Is it enabled or disabled?

- This is the ability to change that setting.

- When a module defines a View, it is often an optional feature that you may toggle on and off. Some modules will create a View with the initial state as disabled, allowing you to decide whether or not you want to you use it. If this is the case, you are provided with a link to enable it. Once enabled, you may then disable it if you choose not to use it.

- Also under this menu you will find clone and export (discussed later).

▨ **Tip** The word that is displayed is the action you want to take, not the current state. If Enable is displayed, it means that the View is disabled; you may click Enable to enable it.

F. What displays are used?

- When you create a View, you can select in what format you would like content to be displayed in. Do you want a page, a block, or something else? A single View may have several displays created. For example, a View of press releases may have a block that shows the title of the most recent five and a page that shows all teasers for press releases in a single month.

G. What is the storage format? There are three possibilities for storage format.

- In code means that the code for the View is stored in a module file. Any module may define any number of Views.

- Database overriding code means that a module originally defined the View, but you have modified it and saved a copy in the database. It is the copy in the database that is currently being used on the site.

- In database means that you created the View using administrative interface and the code is stored only in the database.

H. What type of View is it?

- This describes the type of content you want to display in your View. Options include content, user, comment, term, file, etc.

The Default Views

The main page for administering Views (`admin/structure/views`) displays a list of all Views available. Table 3–2 lists the Views that are defined by the Views module. Other contributed modules may define additional default Views. A default View is stored in code whereas when you create a View using the administrative interface, its definition is stored in the database. Because your web site may be set up differently, you probably have additional Views in your list.

Table 3–2. *Views Defined By the Views Module*

View	Definition
Archive	Displays a list of months that link to content for that month.
Backlinks	Displays a list of nodes that link to the node, using the search backlinks table.
Front page	Emulates the default Drupal front page; you may set the default home page path to this view to make it your front page.
Glossary	A list of all content, by letter.
Recent comments	Contains a block and a page to list recent comments; the block will automatically link to the page, which displays the comment body as well as a link to the node.
Taxonomy term	A view to emulate Drupal core's handling of taxonomy/term; it also emulates Views 1's handling by having two possible feeds.
Tracker	Shows all new activity on system.

Deconstructing a View

The Views module is a very powerful module with many configuration options. Looking at all of these options for the first time can be very intimidating. We will explain all of them but will highlight the ones that are the most important to know when you are getting started.

Let's look at a default View and inspect all of its elements. On the Views administration page, locate the default View named Front page. Locate the operations column on the far right and click Enable. Now that you have enabled the View, the operations link has changed to Edit.

This small menu of option allows you to perform a series of different actions with the chosen View.

- *Edit*: You may edit this View and save your revised version. If this View was stored in code, you will be making an active copy of its definition and saving it in the database. You will always have the option to revert to that original version that is stored in code.

- *Disable*: If the View you are working with is stored in code and you no longer want to use it, you may disable it. If you disable it, the View's displays are no longer visible on your web site. That means blocks or pages may disappear.

- *Clone*: As mentioned, you can edit and save a View that is stored in code. If you prefer to make a View that is similar to an existing View, you can clone it. This makes an exact copy of the View so that you may rename it and make as many changes as you would like. Rather saving over a View that is stored in the database or overriding a View in code, cloning allows you to create a brand new View that is identical to an existing one. You can then edit the new View without affecting the original.

- *Export*: If you are interested in the code that creates a View, you may export it. Clicking this will take you to a page where you may copy the code and place it in your module (more on this later).

■ **Tip** If your new cloned View uses a page display, be careful to not use the same identical path as the original View.

For the Front page View, click Edit, as shown in Figure 3–6.

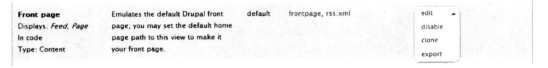

Front page	Emulates the default Drupal front	default	frontpage, rss.xml	edit ▲
Displays: *Feed, Page*	page; you may set the default home			disable
In code	page path to this view to make it			clone
Type: Content	your front page.			export

Figure 3–6. *An enabled View in the listing and its operations menu*

Display Types

Clicking Edit brings you to the configuration page for a specific View. In this case, you should be looking at the Front page View. The first item to notice is the horizontal navigation for each display in the View. When you first edit a View, you are shown the first display available, indicated by its dark highlight (see Figure 3–7).

Displays

Page	Feed	✚Add		edit name and description ▲
				analyze
▾ **Page details**				clone
				export
Display name: Page				

Figure 3–7. *Displays with Page active (left) and the operations menu(right) of a View*

This Front page View has two displays; Page and Feed. If you wanted to, you could use the +Add button to add a new display (more on this later).

On the right of the display bar is another menu of operations. Clone and Export have identical functionality to the same items on the Views list. In addition, you find the following:

- *Edit name and description*: This opens a dialog that allows you to edit the human-readable name for the view and the View description which you'll use to describe the purpose of the View (see Figure 3–8)

  You can also create or look up an existing View tag; these can be incredibly helpful. As you use Views more and more you will create dozens and dozens for every project. Using a tag will help you to organize and manage the Views in your project. While this is not required, I highly suggest you take advantage of it.

- *Analyze*: The Analyze button will look to see if you have any settings that are in conflict with each other or report any other relevant development information.

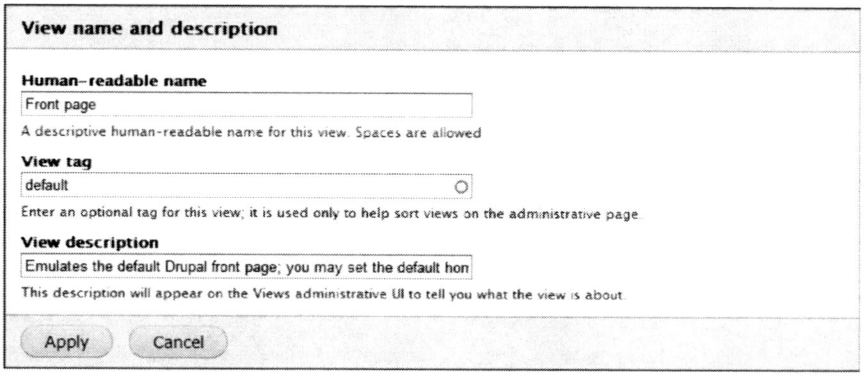

View name and description

Human-readable name

Front page

A descriptive human-readable name for this view. Spaces are allowed

View tag

default

Enter an optional tag for this view; it is used only to help sort views on the administrative page.

View description

Emulates the default Drupal front page; you may set the default hon

This description will appear on the Views administrative UI to tell you what the view is about.

Apply   Cancel

Figure 3–8. *The Edit name and Description Dialog*

Views Configuration Detail

Now we come to the heart of defining a View. Get comfortable, because you will spend a large portion of your development career creating, editing, tweaking, and massaging you Views using this interface (see Figure 3–9). While it might seem a little daunting at first, you will quickly learn your way around the interface. Each grouping of functionality, designated by the black headers, controls one aspect of your View. You'll use these to set what content is to be displayed and how it will be displayed, as well as setting metadata and providing functional controls like a pager.

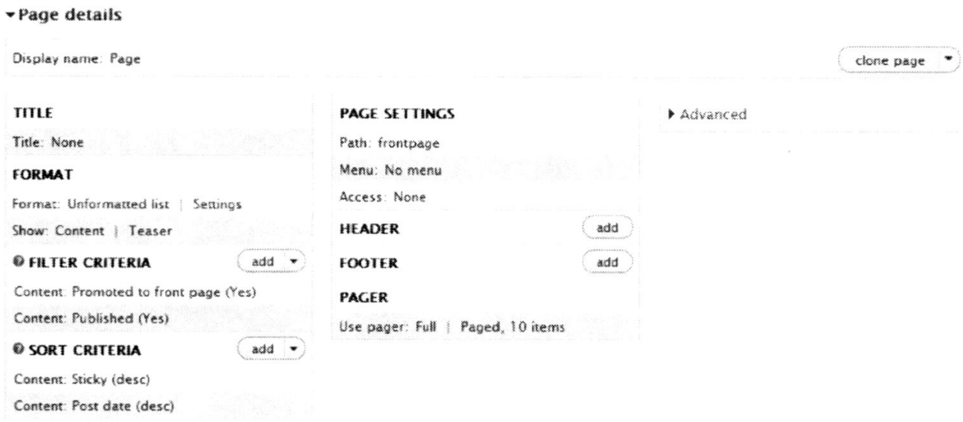

▼Page details

Display name: Page   clone page ▼

TITLE   **PAGE SETTINGS**   ▶ Advanced

Title: None   Path: frontpage

FORMAT   Menu: No menu

Format: Unformatted list | Settings   Access: None

Show: Content | Teaser   **HEADER**   add

⊗ **FILTER CRITERIA**   add ▼   **FOOTER**   add

Content: Promoted to front page (Yes)   **PAGER**

Content: Published (Yes)   Use pager: Full | Paged, 10 items

⊗ **SORT CRITERIA**   add ▼

Content: Sticky (desc)

Content: Post date (desc)

Figure 3–9. *View details with the advanced section expanded*

We will briefly discuss all the options for the Page display for the Front page View, then we'll circle back around and give much more detail about the pivotal players in creating a View.

Display Name

The first item that you can edit is the display name. To edit, click the text "Page." Clicking the current setting will open a modal dialog that allows you to edit the information for the specific display.

- *Name*: The same of the display of the View you are editing. When you create a new display, this name field is prefilled with the type of display you just created. It's important that you edit this field to distinguish between several displays of the same type. For example, you could have a View that has a block that displays the five most recent posts and another block that displays five random posts. When you created each of these block displays, Views would pre-fill the name of the display as "block" for both of them. It's a good idea to change the name to something more descriptive, like "Block: 5 recent" and "Block: 5 random."

- *Description*: A human-readable description of the view display.

Title

The title appears in different places depending on the display type. If the display type is a page, the title will become the page title, both the H1 tag and in the metadata. If the display type is a block, the title will appear as the block title above the content output. Click the current title to open the modal dialog with the following settings, as shown in Figure 3–10:

- *For menu:* This drop-down controls whether the title you enter here is applied to only this display if you choose "This page (override)," or all displays if you choose "All displays (except overridden)."

- The text field for the Title.

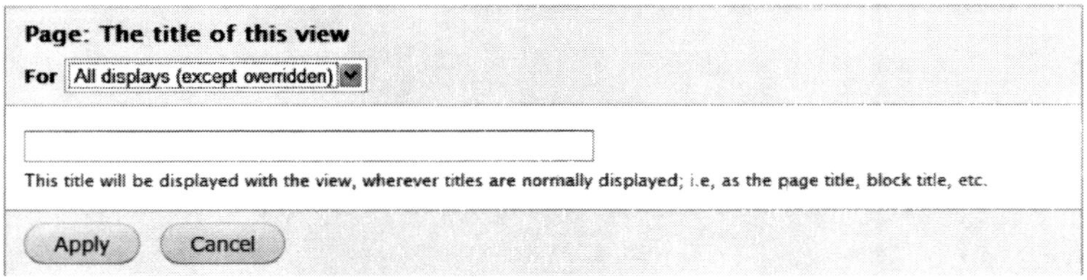

Figure 3–10. Display title dialog, an example modal dialog

Format

What kind of HTML markup do you want the results of the View to use? Options include a list, table, grid, or unformatted, which wraps each result in a div tag. Other contributed modules can add additional ways to display the results.

- *Settings*: Allows you to add a custom CSS class to each row's output container.

- *Show*: Do you want to display the content or teaser as a whole pre-formatted chunk or select specific fields to display?

- Based on your first choice, you will have options after the "|" symbol (pronounced as "pipe") to specify the formatted chunk options or options for how the fields are grouped or arranged. If you choose fields, a whole new section labeled Fields will appear that lets you add and configure field specific settings.

Fields

This grouping is hidden if Content is selected as the Show option, but appears if you select to display your results as fields. Here you would select fields from a catalog of available options provided by Drupal.

Filter Criteria

So as not to display all possible content, limit the result set based on specified criteria. By default you'll see that "Content: Published (Yes)" is set as a filter. This is a gift from the wise programmatic forefathers of development who have added this for you, as if to say, "May you never know the shame of creating a View that shows the world your unpublished content." Know that if you seek to remove it, their eyes are upon you.

Sort Criteria

In what order should the results be shown? By default you'll see that "Content: Post date (desc)" is set as a sort. This will put your content in reverse chronology (also known as blog order) where the most recent content is at the top.

Display Settings

These setting will vary to reflect the display type you are currently editing. In our example it will be a page.

- *Path*: This is the URL where this View will display its content. In this example, it's `http://www.example.com/frontpage`.

- *Menu*: Create a menu item that will bring users to your View. You can also make tabs and other options.

- *Access*: Do you want to only allow users with certain permissions or roles to see the content? "None" means that there are no special restrictions.

Header

Is there any content you would like to display above the Views results?

Footer

Is there any content you would like to display below the Views results?

Pager

- *Use pager*: If you decide to display 10 results, yet your View produces 35 results, you can tell Drupal to automatically paginate it. After 10 results, there will be a pager to take you to the next page with another 10 results. This is a great solution if you have a lot of content that is making your page too long to be usable.

- *More link* (only appears for blocks and attachments): Creates a link to a page with more results. If you have a block that only displays five results and a page that displays all results, you can let Drupal create a link on the block to the page.

Contextual Filters

If you would like to create dynamic pages that use the URL to make decisions about what content is displayed, you can specify that here. This section used to be called Arguments.

Relationships

If there is content that you want to display that is related to the actual result but not a part of it, you may join to it and display it using a relationship.

If you are scratching your head at that description, I hear you. Relationships are a hard concept to grasp but once you do, you'll find them rewarding, just like real relationships. We'll cover this in detail later.

No Results Behavior

If there are no results, would you like to display any text to the user? This setting used to be called Empty text.

Exposed Forms

- *Exposed form in block*: If you have set filters to be exposed, would you like to render them in a separate block rather than with the View results? Filters and how to expose them will be discussed later in this chapter.

- *Exposed form style*: Allows more configurations for the exposed filters including labels.

Other

- *Machine Name*: This field lets you define a machine-friendly name, one without spaces or special characters.

- *Comment*: A block where you can enter notes or message about this View.

- *Display Status*: Just as you could enable or disable a whole View, you can enable or disable a display within a View.

- *Use AJAX*: Do you want paging, table sorting, and exposed filters to load content on the fly without a page refresh?

- *Hide attachments in summary*: Hide attachments when displaying a contextual filter summary.

- *Use grouping*: Do you want to allow Views to group results together based on a certain field? If you also specify a sort order, the results will be grouped first then sorted.

- *Query settings*:

    - Disable SQL rewriting: Do you want to disable the fact that results are tested to make sure the user has permission to see them? This skips `node_access` checks and any other implementation of `hook_query_alter()`. In most cases, it's not recommended to change this setting.

    - Distinct: Do you want to ensure that there are no duplicate results? By selecting Distinct, if your View results had the same node several times, this setting would remove it.

      An example of when you don't want multiple instances of a node would be if you had a View that displayed all nodes with file attachments. Because this is a multi-value field, the node would show up for every attachment.

      An example of when you want multiple instances of a node would be if your View grouped nodes by taxonomy terms and your nodes are tagged with several terms, you would want it to display in all appropriate groups.

    - *Use Slave Server*: This is a performance option. This will make the query attempt to connect to a slave server if available.

- *Caching*: Do you want to cache the results of this View so they are delivered faster? Note that if content is updated, it won't be immediately updated in the View. Cache would only be cleared at the interval you set here. For Views where the content is changing often, like a list of the most recent posts on a very active site, you might not want to cache your results. However, if your View displays content that doesn't change that often, caching is a good idea. Even short intervals of caching can dramatically improve site performance.

- *Link display*: If you are using the More link, to which display would you like it to go to? For example, if your block uses the More link and you also have several Page displays in your View, to which page would you like the More link to go to?

- *CSS class*: Do you want to add a CSS class to the wrapper `div` so you can apply styling?

- *Theme*: This is not a setting, but rather information to help you create templates so you can customize the output of the View further. Click on it to see the template information available to you. Note that these templates need to be saved in code to be functional and are not used in this administrative interface.

Overriding: A Views Concept

Many settings can be overridden for a particular display. Before we go any further, it's important to understand the concept of a settings override.

When you create a View for the first time, the settings you configure for the first display will get inherited by subsequent View displays. In other words, when you add additional displays, like Pages or Blocks, all the settings that they can have in common with the first display will be set the same. This makes developing related displays very efficient but you also have the option to override any of these settings for an individual display.

Understanding when a setting has been overridden is important to building consistent Views and there are clear visual cues for identifying overrides. When a setting on a view configuration has been overridden a broken link icon will be displayed to the left of the setting, as shown in Figure 3–11.

TITLE

 Title: New Title

Figure 3–11. The broken link icon indicates this title has been overridden.

Understanding What Type of Content Will Be Output: Views Filters

No matter which display you are editing, there are three columns of configuration options. To understand the type of content that will be displayed, look at the Filters section in the first column. A filter reduces the content that will be displayed to match your criteria. The Front page View has two (2) filters.

Click Content: Promoted to front page, as shown in Figure 3–12.

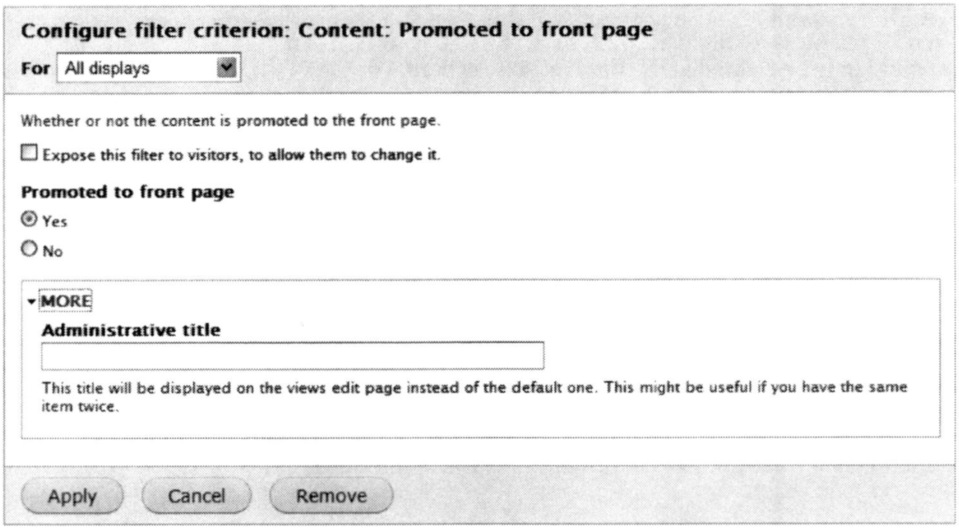

Configure filter criterion: Content: Promoted to front page

For All displays

Whether or not the content is promoted to the front page.

☐ Expose this filter to visitors, to allow them to change it.

Promoted to front page

◉ Yes

○ No

▾ **MORE**

Administrative title

This title will be displayed on the views edit page instead of the default one. This might be useful if you have the same item twice.

(Apply) (Cancel) (Remove)

Figure 3–12. Configuring a filter

The title of this dialog tells you a lot: "Configure filter criterion: Content: Promoted to front page".

- *Configure filter criterion* tells you that you are working with filters as opposed to another grouping of configurations, like fields or sort criteria.

- *Content: Promoted to front page* is the name of the filter. "Content" refers to the type of filter and "Promoted to front page" is the specific one.

- *For All Displays* drop-down tells you that this display uses the same setting as all other displays that have not been overridden.

You have the option to expose a filter. This will allow the web site visitor to determine the value of the filter. This will be discussed in more detail later.

This particular filter has two (2) values for you to choose from, either Yes or No. Think of this filter as asking you a question. Do you want to only show content that has been promoted to the front page? Yes or No? In this case, the answer is Yes.

Below, the configuration options are three (3) buttons:

- *Apply*: This will set the configuration with the option selected. Note that it doesn't actually save the View.

- *Cancel*: This will exit you out of this configuration setting. Even if you changed something, it will not set those changes.

- *Remove*: If you no longer want this filter as part of your View, it will remove it completely.

All filter configurations are composed of the following parts:

- A descriptive title.

- Option to expose the filter and if set, those configurations.

- The actual settings.

- Buttons to set or cancel the filter configuration and remove the filter.

Looking at the three (3) columns again, click "Content: Published." This configuration block is set up just like the previous one. It asks the question: Do you want to only show content that has been published? Yes or No?

░ **Tip** It is extremely important that unless you have another intention, you include a filter for the published state. While managing your site's content, you may choose to unpublish a node because you do not want your visitors to see it. In order to keep this content hidden, you must filter the View to only show published content. A published state filter is provided as a default filter for each new View you create. Remove it with extreme caution.

Click Cancel to exit out of this configuration dialog.

Advanced Filter Criteria Groups: Combining Sorts with Logical Operators

The Views module has the ability to build logical combinations of filters to achieve more complex groups of content. For example, you might want a block of all stories that

- have more than ten comments, **or**

- that received a comment in the past hour.

Having either of these conditions met keeps the content in a block very fresh. However, if you added both the Comment count filter and the Last comment time filter you would instead get a block with stories that had gotten ten comments **and** the one last within the last hour. That would be a very different group of items that what you wanted. Instead, you need to specify that items need to meet the first **or** the second criteria as opposed to both.

On the right of the Filter Criteria section, open the option list and select And/Or.

You will see the dialog "Page: Rearrange filter criteria," as shown in Figure 3–13. You can set the standard For option to say whether this filter change will apply to just this display or all displays in the View. By default, all of the filters you have specified will be included in one filter logic group and the operator is set to And. This configuration will make the filters have the same effect as filters do by default, meaning all content must pass each filter to be included in the results for the view.

In the current example (Front page View), if you change the Operator to Or, you will get a list of content that is published OR promoted to the front page. This will include any unpublished content in your Views output, so use logical operators with caution.

Clicking "Create new filter group" will create another operator box; if you had many more filters, you could use the small arrow next to each filter to drag them into more logical groups, potentially creating combinations where the same filter is used in multiple filter groups.

■ **Tip** Remember, each grouping in an Or logical group works autonomously from the other groups; for example, ((A and B) or (C and D)). You will need to add multiple Content: Published Yes filters to your Filter Criteria and one to each group so that each requires its content to be published.

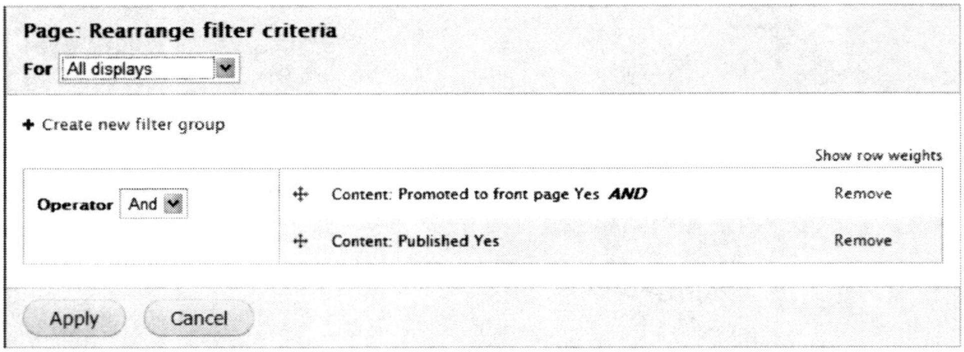

Figure 3–13. Configuring an And/Or filter group

▓ **Tip** You most likely noticed the More toggle at the bottom of each filter. If you open it, you'll see a field called Administrative title. This allows you to give each filter a customized name. You'll most likely only use this if you have multiple copies of the same filter as you might for use in logical groups.

Understanding the Order in Which Content Will Be Output: Views Sort Criteria

To understand in what order content will be displayed, look at the Sort criteria section in the first column. Multiple sort criteria allow you to be very granular with this setting. The Front page Views has two (2) sort criteria.

Click Content: Sticky. This particular filter has two (2) values for you to choose from: Sort ascending or Sort descending. Think of this filter as asking you a question. Do you want content that is marked as sticky to rise to the top or sink to the bottom of your results? In this case, the answer is Sort descending. All content marked as sticky will be at the top of the page.

Looking at the three (3) columns again, click Content: Post date under Sort Criteria. This configuration block is set up just like the previous one. It asks the question: Do you want the most recent content displayed first or the oldest content displayed first? If you would like what is considered Blog Chronology where the most recently posted content is the top, you would chose Sort descending.

Because there are two (2) sort criteria, the first one is called and sorts the results. Where there are results with the same sort weight, the next sort criteria is called. You can have as many sort criteria as you want for a very granular result order.

In the current example, the results would first show all posts as sticky at the top. Then it would go through the sticky posts and sort them to make sure the most recent are at the top and also go through all posts not marked as sticky to sort those to make sure the most recent posts are listed first.

Click Cancel to exit out of this configuration dialog.

Understanding What Pieces of Content Will Be Output: Views Format Settings

You have already figured out what type of content will display and the order in which it will be displayed. But what will it look like? What pieces of the content will display? In the first column, the Format box allows you to configure several elements. The Front page View displays its results as content teasers with a container div. Under Settings, you can see that no extra CSS classes are set (see Figure 3–14).

FORMAT

Format: Unformatted list | Settings

Show: Content | Teaser

Figure 3–14. Format settings configuration box

When editing or creating a View, the first item you should look at is the Show setting. Yes, it's the second one in the list, but has more of an impact on what the results will look like.

You may click the word link Content to change the Show setting. If you click the Teaser, you change the settings for the selected Show style.

Configuration Options for Format Settings

When you click the current value for Show setting, Content, you see all available options. The Views module provides two options: Fields and Content. Other contributed modules may provide additional options that would display here. Examples include displaying results as points on a map, a slide show, or as customizable HTML.

To see the settings for Content Show setting, click Teaser. The select box for View Mode is currently set as Teaser. This means the shortened version of the content displays with a linked title and a Read More link. If your theme uses a custom template for teasers, your Teaser may look different than described.

In addition to the Show setting, you may also configure the Format of the whole View, as described in Table 3–3.

Table 3–3. Configuration Options

Option	Description
Grid	A Grid puts all of the content of a View into a box and you choose how many boxes you want in a row or a column.
HTML List	You have the option of either an ordered list (numerical) or an unordered list (bullets).
Jump Menu	If you put content titles in a jump menu, when you select that title, you will automatically be directed to that content.
Table	A table puts the resulting fields into a table that resembles a spreadsheet. You can allow the column headers to act as sort links.
Unformatted	A simple div with a customizable CSS class goes around each class.

Creating a Basic View

Let's dive right in and create the first View. For this example, it is assumed that you already have content in your web site. Near the top of the Views administration page (admin/structure/views), find the link that says Add new view and click it.

The Goal

You want to create a page that has teasers that lead to all articles authored by a specific person and a block that shows the five most recent titles for those articles, linked to the actual content. You also want a more link to take the user to the main page for all articles.

Systematic Approach

When I create a View, I follow the same pattern each time. I ask myself a series of questions that correspond to a different configuration box. This ensures that I get the results that I expect and that I don't miss a step.

If I am creating a new View, the wizard has an initial window that allows me to answer some of these questions. The answers I type in will prepopulate some of the configuration boxes on the primary editing page.

If I already have a View and I am adding an additional Display to it, I follow all of the following steps:

1. *Create the display*: Should this be a block or a page or something else?

2. *Name*: When I look at the displays, what name should appear to help me understand which one I am editing? When I want to place a block somewhere in the site using other administrative interfaces, what name would make sense?

3. *Title*: What should the title be? What should the web site users see as the title of this content?

4. *Filters*: What type of content do I want to display?

5. *Fields or Show Content/Teaser*: What parts of the content do I want to display?

6. *Format*: Do I want the results to display as a table or a list?

7. *Sort*: In what order should the results be?

8. *Contextual Filters/Relationships*: Do I need to use parts of the URL in order to further customize the result set? Do I need to pull in related data? Contextual Filters and Relationships are discussed in a later section.

Set Up the Basics for Your Views

Thanks to the wizard, you can configure much of your Views on the Add new view screen. Let's do that! Use the Administration menu and go to Structure ➤ Views (`admin/structure/views`) and click Add new view.

It is important to think about the Views you will need on your site and create a naming convention that will facilitate managing them. Consider including the site section or content type in your view name.

For this example, name your View "articles by {author name}." Mine is named "articles by bob." The machine name is automatically generated from the name you type.

Check the Description box to display the field where you can enter your Views description. The description should be something similar to "Show articles written by {author_name}."

The next section of the wizard helps you articulate the type of content that you want to display. From start to finish, you want to show "Content" of type "Article" tagged with "___" sorted by "Newest first."

You can see that Create a page was checked by default and that much of the information for the page is now filled in for you by using your title.

The Page title and Path have been prefilled using the {author_name} you used in the title. In this example, I'm choosing a fictitious Bob, so my page title becomes "Articles by Bob" and my path "articles-by-bob."

The Display format settings also look good with the defaults: an unformatted list of teasers with links (allow users to add comments, etc.) without comments.

Items per page can be left at 10.

You could add a menu here or include an RSS feed, but let's wait.

Check the Create a block box. You can accept the default settings for now but change the Block title to "Articles by Bob."

If your settings look like those in Figure 3–15, you're ready. Click "Continue & edit" to create you first view.

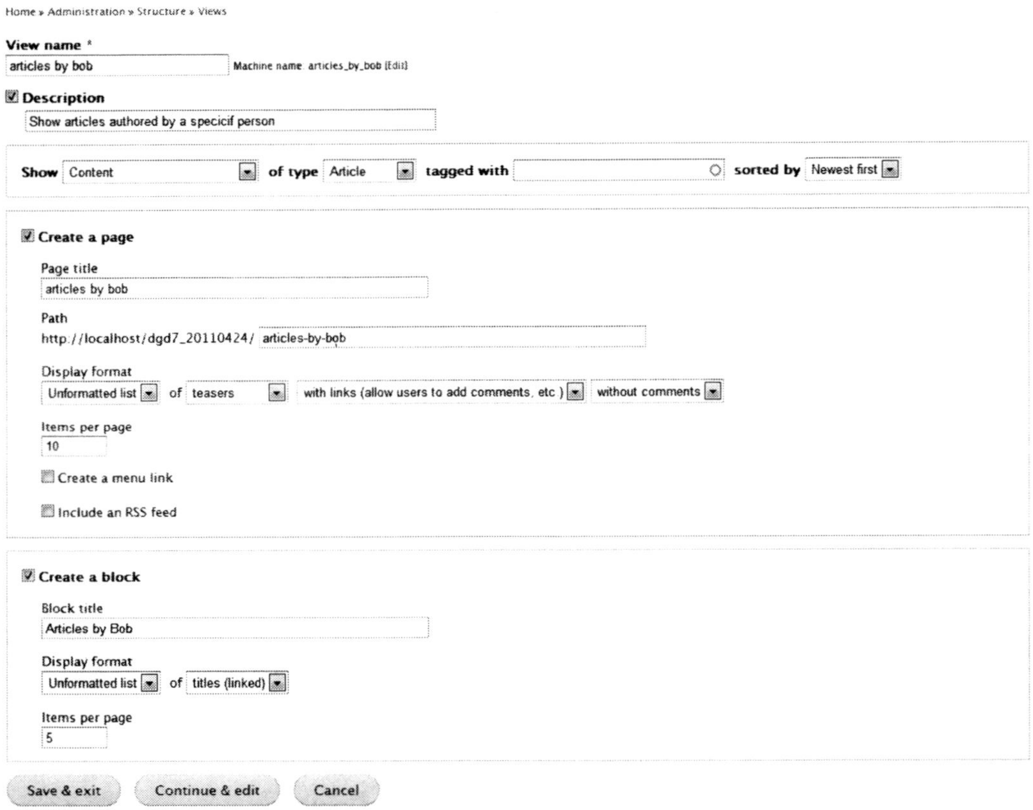

Figure 3–15. *Add New View wizard*

Other types of Views will be discussed later in this chapter. Click Continue & Edit.

▨ **Tip** While creating/editing, it's important to periodically save your View. Also note that if you are creating/editing on a production site, when you save the View, it will be available to your users. To avoid this, read the "Exporting to Code" section later in this chapter.

You are now looking at the main page for editing a View.

■ **Tip** The URL is `admin/structure/views/edit/articles_by_bob`. To edit any View, you can find it in the listing on the Views administration page or just replace `articles_by_bob` with the machine name of the View you want to edit.

Define the Administrative Information

As mentioned, if your View has multiple displays, it can be difficult to decipher which one does what. Fortunately, Views allows you to set an administrative name for each display. It is important that you use a name that is meaningful so other developers can easily edit the View you created.

For this example, next to Display name, click the active link Page. When the dialog opens, change this to "Page: by {author_name}" where you replace {author_name} with the username you chose earlier. Remember, I chose "Bob." You can repeat the same text for Description. Click Apply and the Save your View. You might need to scroll up to see the Save button.

Notice how the Page display buttons at the top now reflect the name you entered.

Define the Title

When you set a display for your View (either as a page or a block), you want a title to appear above the results so that the user knows what the content is about.

In the Title box, you can see Title: Articles by {author_name}. This title will be displayed with the View wherever titles are normally displayed: as the page title, block title, etc. If you want to change it, click the linked title and then click Apply.

Define What Type of Content You Want to Display

You are going to jump over a configuration box so that you can specify Filter Criteria. Unless you are creating a View for site administrators, you always want your first filter to be Content: Published. This will ensure that you don't inadvertently display hidden content. This filter is added by default, but always check for it.

Now, you want to make sure you only display nodes authored by a specific person. Click Add in the Filters Criteria section. Select User from the Filter select box and select the User: Name filter from the list. Click "Add and Configure filter criteria."

In the new dialog, select the operator to be "Is one of." For the Usernames auto complete, just start typing a username of a person who has authored Articles on your site, like Bob. Apply.

■ **Note** In the previous example, you selected and configured one filter at a time. When adding filters, you may select several filters from different filter groups. After you click Add, you will be guided to configure each one. Doing it this way can be a time-saver because there are significantly less clicks!

You have successfully set the filters! Now your result set will only display published article nodes authored by a certain person, as shown in Figure 3–16.

❷ FILTER CRITERIA (add | ▼)

Content: Published (Yes)

User: Name (= Bob)

Figure 3–16. Filters selected for Articles by Author Name View

Define What Elements of the Content You Want to Display

Now you can go back to the Format configuration box. As you can see, this section has been prepopulated with your selections in the wizard. Show is set to Content | Teaser, which is both the type and the way you want your content to display. If you had chosen fields as the display format in the wizard, you would now need to start adding and configuring fields to a Fields configuration box.

Define Format Settings

You have already set the row settings to be Content | Teaser. Now you can confirm the HTML markup around each result. For results that are either Content | Teaser or Content | Full Content, I like to choose Unformatted as the style. This means each result will have a `div` around it, as opposed to being in a list or table. This is the default setting, but you may also specify a CSS class to go on that row div. This can be helpful when you are theming/styling your web pages. In the Format section, click Settings next to Unformatted list to enter in a CSS class.

Additionally, if you want several Views to look the same, you may add a CSS class to the entire View. This can be specified by clicking the active link None for CSS Class in the Other section in the third column under the Advanced header.

Define the Order in Which You Want Your Content to Display

Consistent with many listings of content, you want your View to display the results with the most recently posted article at the top and the older articles at the bottom.

You can see that Sort Criteria is set to Content: Post date (desc), which is exactly what you want, so again you move on.

Define the Number of Results

In the middle column, click the active link for Use Pager: Full. This is where you set what kind of pager style you want or if you only want to display a fixed amount of results. Click Cancel to exit the modal window.

Click "Paged, 10 items" to change the number of items to display. I think 10 will be too few so let's have 15 items per page.

There are quite a few options to explore under Exposed Options. These are the settings for what to display to the user, including allowing the user to determine how many items to display per page.

Click Apply to save the change for number of items to display per page.

Add a Menu

Let's add a menu for your page so it will appear in the site's main navigation. Under Page settings, next to Menu, click No Menu to open the modal dialog. Choose Normal menu entry. Enter the title "Articles by {author_name}" for the title. Also select Main Menu in the Menu drop-down. Click Apply.

■ **Note** We will discuss Menu Tabs in a later exercise.

Define Advanced Settings

In the Advanced Settings box, you are going to leave Use AJAX as "no" because this is the main content for the page. If you choose to change this setting to "yes," the subsequent paged pages will not be indexed by search engines since the HTML is never printed in the source code, but rather created on the fly.

You won't be using the Grouping or Query settings on this View, so you can skip those configurations in this step.

Views Caching can be very useful for sites with a lot of traffic. If you choose to do a time-based cache of either the query or the results, the data is not generated each time someone visits the page. This can save some processing resources on high-traffic sites, but it also means that the most up-to-date results only get displayed after the cache expiration. So, for highly dynamic or time-sensitive content, I don't recommend setting up caching, but for content that doesn't change that frequently, caching can be useful.

■ **Tip** If you decide to use Views caching, during development, you may want to clear Views cache periodically to see the changes rather than waiting for the set expiration. To clear Views cache, click the tab at the top that says Tools and click the Clear Views' Cache button at the top.

Preview Your Work

The Views module allows you to preview the settings you just configured without leaving the Views interface. If you scroll down to just below all of the configuration boxes, you will notice the Auto Preview area. It demonstrates the display that you are currently editing; assuming the user you selected has authored some content, you should have a nice preview.

Dynamically Editing Your View

One of the nifty features in Views is the ability to edit your View results in the auto preview area. Once you have set up some display options so your view is displaying content, it can sometime be easier to make editing decisions that are based on the actual content.

For instance, now that I see my Title, "Articles by Bob" I just don't like it. The "by Bob" simply has too much alliteration for me to take it seriously and I want to change it. I'm going to make that change right here in the preview area.

Above my title I'm going to click on the Gear icon. I'll see a small menu appear with the item Edit Title, so I'll click that item (see Figure 3–17).

Figure 3–17. Preview area Edit menu

The same dialog opens that would appear if I clicked the link next to Title in the main settings area. I make my change and click Apply.

Wow, that was great. In fact, if you'd rather work by just tweaking what you see in the preview area, you can actually collapse the main setting area by click the "Page: By {author_name} details" name at the very top of the dialog, just below the display buttons. Don't forget to save your view when you are done!

Admire Your View

At the start, you assigned a path to your page display. Go to that page in your browser. If you followed my suggestion, it should be something like `http://example.com/articles-by-author_name`. Also, if you created a normal menu item in the main menu for this page, you can go to any page and click the link in your navigation bar.

Congrats! But there is more....

Add More Features

As I mentioned in the goal of this exercise, you also want a block that shows the five most recent titles for those articles, linked to the actual nodes.

For each display, follow the steps outlined in the systematic approach. Although many of these settings won't need to be changed, it is important to adhere to the process and check your work.

Create Another Display

You already created your block using the wizard; if you needed another, you could easily create it by editing your view and clicking the + Add button at the top left. You can also clone an existing display.

Since you have your block, click the Block button at the top left to see that display's settings.

Define Administrative Information

For ease of usability while administering Views, update the Name in the Display name to be "Block: titles only" or something else meaningful.

Override the Format

For your block, you want to display only the content titles. This means you need to have it set to show fields, so that you can choose exactly what fields to show (with the title considered a field by Views for this purpose). Formerly, the Show setting was called Row Style.

Look at the Show line in Format box. It has a broken link next to it. This means that it is using your overridden format and you can see that it is set to Fields.

If you click Fields, you can see the scope for this configuration is set to "This block (override)." Click Cancel to exit out of this modal window.

Edit Fields

You need to confirm that you have the fields you want and that they are outputting the markup you need for both semantic quality and styling.

If you look in the Fields section, you can see that when you created the block in the wizard, it added Content : Title by default.

1. Click Content : Title to open the field configuration dialog.

2. Configure the options as described below (I am only noting the ones that need to be changed).

3. Confirm that "Link this field to the original piece of content" is checked.

One thing you want to change is the HTML markup that is being output. Currently all the titles are simply being output in div tags but you want to indicate that they are headings to your readers and to search engines.

1. Click on Style Settings to expand the setting box.

2. Check the box "Wrap field in HTML" and more settings will appear. From the HTML element box, select H2.

3. Check the "Create a CSS class" box and enter "title" in the field that appears.

You settings should now look like those in Figure 3–18.

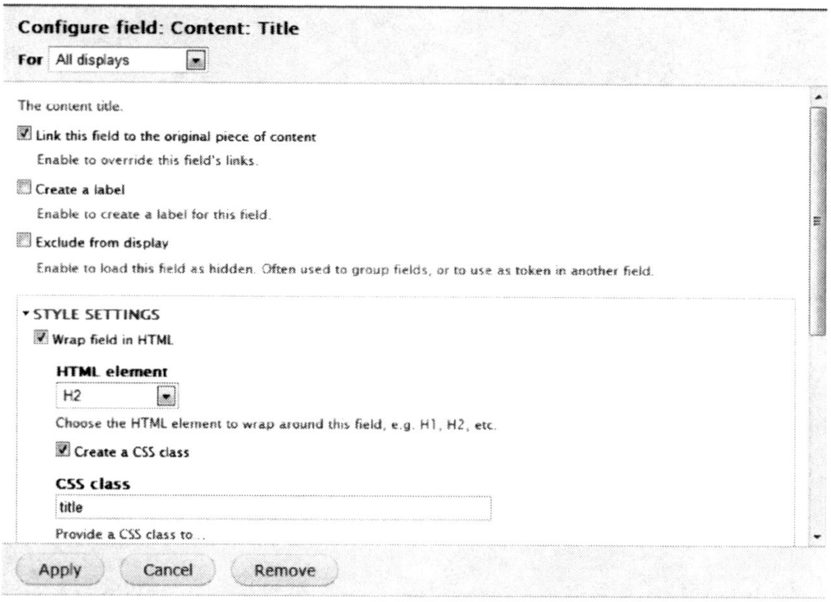

Configure field: Content: Title

For All displays ▼

The content title.

☑ **Link this field to the original piece of content**
 Enable to override this field's links.

☐ **Create a label**
 Enable to create a label for this field.

☐ **Exclude from display**
 Enable to load this field as hidden. Often used to group fields, or to use as token in another field.

▼ STYLE SETTINGS
 ☑ Wrap field in HTML

 HTML element
 H2 ▼
 Choose the HTML element to wrap around this field, e.g. H1, H2, etc.
 ☑ Create a CSS class

 CSS class
 title
 Provide a CSS class to …

(Apply)   (Cancel)   (Remove)

Figure 3–18. Title field Style Settings

4. Click Apply and scroll up to Save your View.

Add a More Link

It would be a nice touch to add a More link to your block display so a user won't have to do a lot of paging to see all the items.

In the Pager Settings box, click the link "More Link: No." The first thing you want to do is change the For setting so that your link only appears on this display. Set the drop-down to "This block (override)." Click the checkbox for Create More Link. Click Apply and check out your work in the Auto preview area.

Save the View.

You can test your More link in the preview area. Note that if you have less content than your block is set to display, a More link will not appear.

▓ **Note** The wildly astute in our audience might say, "How did my More link know to link to the Page view?" Since it's the only page in this View, it's likely to share the block's criteria and so that's where Views linked it. You might also then say, "That's a lame answer because what happens if I have more than one page in my View?" Ah yes, if you have more than one Page, a new item will appear in the Block's Options section called "Link display: [page name]". Clicking the name will open a dialog where you can designate which page should be your destination for things like summary links, RSS feed links, More links, and so on.

Place the Block

Once you save your View, your block will appear in the list of disabled blocks on the Block Administration page. Enable the block as you would any other. For more information on placing blocks, please refer to Chapters 1 or 8.

Extend a View

There are other configurations you can make to the View you created to increase usability. Let's start with the basic View you created showing articles by a specific author.

Handling the Use Case of Zero Results

Sometimes we create Views with the anticipation of content in the future. It is conceivable that, as a developer, we knew we needed to show all articles by {author_name} even though those articles hadn't been written yet. If our View goes to the production site before the content is created, we need to account for that when users navigate to the page.

For the Page display, in the right column, click Add for No Results Behavior. Check Global: Text area and then Add and Configure.

For the administrative label, type "default". Enter in your default no results text, something similar to "There are no articles available yet. Check back soon as we are updating content frequently." Apply.

If you want to check to see this is working as expected, you can change one of your filters to something that you know will product zero results and look at the Auto Preview area.

Because you didn't change the For setting, your message was applied to both the Page and the Block display—twice the work accomplished in one shot.

One Page, Multiple Displays to Highlight First Result

The page you previously created shows 15 teasers with a pager. This is a great way to show all the content. However, in another area of the site, you might want to highlight the most recent node.

Let's make a page where you display the most recent article as a full node and the following 14 nodes in a table below it.

To accomplish this, follow these steps:

1. Add a new page display.

2. Update the Display name to "Page: Highlight".

3. Add a Path "highlights" under Page Settings where this View will display. Add a normal menu item in the Main Menu so you can easily find it.

4. Under Format, change the Show setting to display full content; make sure you set "For" to "This page (override)."

5. Override "Use pager" and set it to "Display a specified number of items" and set this to 1 for only this display

---

░ **Tip** When you went to add the page title, you saw the error message "Display 'Page' uses a path but the path is undefined." Don't worry; this is the first display you have created without using the wizard and you just need to set a path for the display before it lets you save it.

Look at the Auto Preview area to see if the results are as you expect.
Now, you need to add the table below that highlighted node.

6. Add a new attachment display.

7. Update the administrative name to "Attach: table to highlight".

8. Override the Show Style to use fields. You don't need to make any other further configurations.

9. Click Add in the Fields menu. In the Content group, select Content: Post Date, and Add. Change the Date Format to whatever you want it to be. Apply.

10. Experiment with adding two other fields.

11. Override the Format from Unformatted to Table.

    The Table style option dialog is pretty fancy. You are probably hoping for guidance but just take a look and read the text. You'll quickly see that it's powerful but not hard or confusing. You can accept the defaults or make all kind of changes; it's up to you.

12. Override the number of items to display under Pager to display 14 with an offset of 1. This means that the first result will not display, but the subsequent 14 will. This is exactly what you want since you are going to use the full display for the first node.

13. Override the More link in Pager to create a More link.

14. In order to attach this table to the full node page display, click on the link in Attach to: Not defined in the Attachment Settings box. Select Page: Highlight and Apply. Click Before under Attachment position and change this to After. Apply.

15. Save your View and go to Page: Highlights. You can now see your awesome table view below the Contents.

Using Tabs for Unique Displays

You can create a page that has several tabs so your users don't have to leave the page to see a lot of content.

Let's create a new View that has a primary page that shows all Article nodes, a tab for all Event nodes, and a tab for Blog nodes (see Table 3–4).

Table 3–4. Creating a New View Using Tabs for Unique Displays

+Add new View	
Add new Page Display:	
Display name	Name = Page: landing
Title	Title = Content
Filter Criteria	Content: Published = Yes Content: Type = Article

Fields	Content: Title
	   –Element Class = H2
	   –Remove Label
	   –Link this field to its content

Sort Criteria	Content: Post Date = Sort Descending
Pager	Use Pager = Display all items
Format	Style = HTML List –List Type = Unordered List

Page Settings	Path = content
	Menu =Normal Menu Item
	   –Title = Content
	   –Menu = Main Menu

+Add new View

Add new Page Display:

Display name	Name = Page: Articles
Title	Title = Articles

Page Settings	Path = content/articles
	Menu = Default Menu Tab
	  –Title = Articles
	    –Parent Menu Item = Already Exists

Add new Page Display:

Display name	Name = Page: Blog
Title	Title = Blog
Override – Filter Criteria	Content: Type = blog
Page Settings	Path = content/blog Menu = Menu Tab –Title = Blog

Add new Page Display:

Display name	Name = Page: Events
Title	Title = Events
Override –Filter Criteria	Content: Type = event
Page Settings	Path = content/events Menu = Menu Tab –Title = Events

---

Save your View and go to a page where you can see your main menu. Click on the Content link you created, as shown in Figure 3–19.

Figure 3–19. *A View with tabs*

Cloning and Making Administrative Tables Using Exposed Filters

There are often cases where you want a group of your administrators to be able to see content lists and be able to filter them to get an exact result set of their choice. The Views module provides this functionality with exposed filters. By exposing filters, you allow the user to set the conditions.

Let's create a new View for administrators (see Table 3–5)that shows all content in table format, but is filterable and sortable, as shown in Figure 3–20.

Table 3–5. *Creating a New View for Administrators*

Add New View:	
Add Page Display:	
Title	Title = All Content
Filters	Content: Published –EXPOSE –Published = <Any> –Options = Yes Content: Type –EXPOSE –Unlock Operator = Yes –Optional = Yes –Force Single = No Content: Post Date –EXPOSE –Operator = Is Between –Unlock Operator = Yes –Optional = Yes

---

Add New View:

Fields	Content: Post Date Content: Published Content: Title –Link this field to its Content Content: Type
Pager	Use Pager = Display all items Access = Role –Administrator

Format	Format = Table
	  –Make sure all columns are sortable
	  –Set Post Date as Default Sort, Descending

Header	Global: Text Area –Use the filters below to refine what displays in the list.

Page Settings	Path = administer/content
	Menu = Normal Menu Item
	  –Title = Content
	  –Menu = Navigation

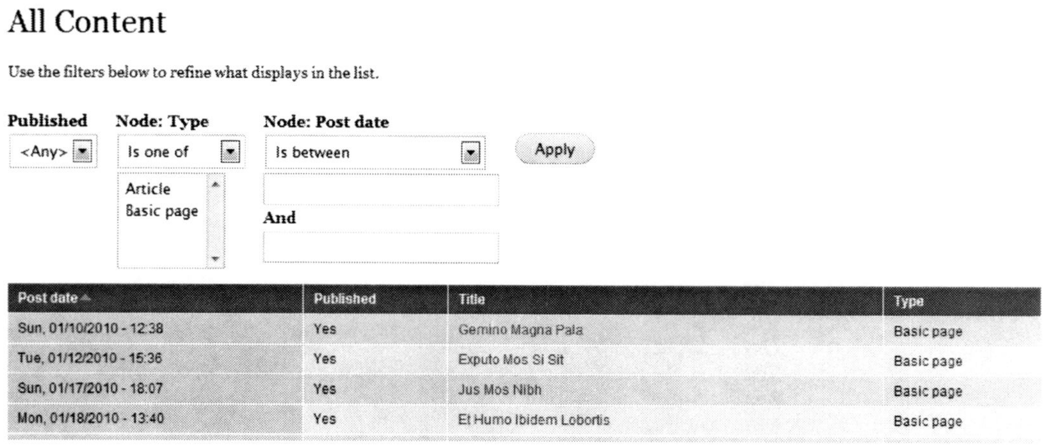

All Content

Use the filters below to refine what displays in the list.

Published **Node: Type** **Node: Post date**

`<Any>` ▾   Is one of ▾   Is between ▾   [Apply]

Article
Basic page

And

Post date ▲	Published	Title	Type
Sun, 01/10/2010 - 12:38	Yes	Gemino Magna Pala	Basic page
Tue, 01/12/2010 - 15:36	Yes	Exputo Mos Si Sit	Basic page
Sun, 01/17/2010 - 18:07	Yes	Jus Mos Nibh	Basic page
Mon, 01/18/2010 - 13:40	Yes	Et Humo Ibidem Lobortis	Basic page

Figure 3–20. A View with exposed filters

Advanced Views Implementations

We have discussed how to create Views where we set criteria and even where the user sets criteria, but we can also create a View where a variable is passed in that will determine what the results are. Additionally, we are able to pull information that is related to the result to display alongside it.

In this section, we discuss the only configuration boxes left: Contextual Filters and Relationships.

Contextual Filters

Contextual filters are input that usually come from the URL, often called arguments. A typical use of an argument might be to reduce a View to a single node, a single user, or nodes with a given taxonomy term. It is like a filter, but rather than setting the value in a form, it is coming from the URL.

Similar to the View created earlier in this chapter, let's create a View where each user with at least one blog node gets their own page and these pages are created dynamically so that you never need to explicitly filter on username (see Table 3–6). You'll also create a menu and a block.

Table 3–6. Creating a View with Contextual Filters

Create a new node View	
Add new Page display	
Title	Title = Blogs
Format	Show = Content | Teaser
Filters	Content: Published = Yes Content: Type = Blog
Sort Criteria	Content: Post Date = Sort Descending

Page Settings	Path = blog
	Menu = Normal Menu Entry
	  –Title = Blog
	  –Menu = Main Menu

Contextual filters	User: Name
	  –When the filter value is NOT in the URL = Show "Display all
	    results for the specified field"
	  –Override Title = Blogs by %1
	  –Specify validation settings = Basic Validation, Display contents of "No
	    results found"
	  –More Section:
	  –Case = Capitalize each word
	  –Case in path = lowercase
	  –Transform spaces to dashes in the URL = Yes

Add new Block display	
Override Contextual Filters	User: Name -Action to take if argument is not present = Display a summary -Sort order = Ascending

■ **Tip** The contributed module Pathauto (`drupal.org/project/pathauto`) allows you to specify patterns for URL aliases so that they are automatically created. These aliases are user and SEO friendly. In this example, you should set Pathauto for blog node to use the pattern `blog/[user]/[title]` so that this page URL follows the Views you are creating.

Place your block on pages with a path of "blog/*" so that it is on all blog pages, both Views and nodes. Go to your main page and click the Blog link in your Main Menu.

Relationships

The Relationship configuration allows you to bring in content that is related to the content you are displaying, but not stored in the same area of the database. Once you create a relationship, you then need to associate it with either a field or contextual filter.

For this example, you want to display who created the node and who edited/revised the node for each node result. Use the View you created in the Contextual Filters example and make some modifications. You'll pretend that instead of blog nodes, you have a View of wiki nodes (Table 3–7).

While you are building, look at the Live Preview area once you finish adding the new fields. Then look again after you associate the relationship with the username field.

Table 3–7. *Creating a View of Wiki Nodes*

Update the Page display

Format	Show = Fields

Fields	Content: Title
	  –Link this field to its Content
	  –Wrap field and label in HTML = H2
	User: Name
	  –Label = Created by
	  –More: Administrative title = Created by
	User: Name
	  –Label = Revised by
	  –More: Administrative title = Revised by
	Content: Body
	  –Remove the Label
	  –Formatter = Trimmed, 300

Relationships	Content Revision: User

Edit Fields	User: Name (the 2nd one you added with an
	  administrative title of Revised by)
	  –Relationship = revisions user

Format	Style = Grid –Number of columns = 3
Pager Settings	User pager = Paged output, full pager –Items per page = 9

You just assigned a relationship to a field. Before the relationship, it printed the author of the node. After the relationship, it printed the author of who saved it last (the revision), as shown in Figure 3–21. The reason you needed to use a Relationship to accomplish this is because of where the data for the node, the node revision history, and the user are stored in the database. You needed to relate the information.

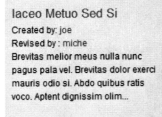

Figure 3–21. *A View using a relationship to display the username of the person who edited the node most recently*

▧ **Tip** Some contributed modules that you choose to install will require relationships in order to display the desired content. If you are having difficulty finding the filter or field in the available groups and know that is has to be there, it probably requires a relationship.

Other Modules

There are many modules that extend what you can accomplish with Views. Often, they will create Views for you to customize so most of the work is already done. This list is far from exhaustive, but some modules you should investigate include:

- Administration
    - Views Bulk Operations (VBO) – drupal.org/project/views_bulk_operations
- Maps
    - OpenLayers – drupal.org/project/openlayers
    - Gmap – drupal.org/project/gmap
- Calendars
    - Calendar – drupal.org/project/calendar
- Styles and Displays
    - jCarousel – drupal.org/project/jcarousel
    - Views Accordion – drupal.org/project/views_accordion
    - Views Infinite Scroll – drupal.org/project/views_infinite_scroll

Remember, that all modules are a continual work-in-progress and it is up to the members of the community to help strengthen them by reporting issues and testing patches.

Exporting to Code

You must, you must!! And I'll tell you why….

I mentioned during the exercises that it is important to save your Views periodically, but the catch was that it would display on your site even if you weren't ready. I suppose it really isn't that big of a catch for a new View since there is a configuration to change the Display Status in the Basic Settings box. But what if you are make changes to an existing View?

Additionally, if you are initially making your View in a development environment, how do you get your View to display on the production server? Do you have click 100 times to replicate it?

Of course not; you export your View to code!

Use your development environment to create, edit, and fine-tune your Views; export the final version; and copy the file to your production server. It is so easy and reduces human error from mis-clicking.

However, before you export the View, you need to create a module to keep the code. Based on what you learn in Chapter 22, create your module folder, .info, and .module files. Also, create a folder in your module named views. This is where you will put each export. In that folder, create an empty text file named articles_by_author.inc or whatever the name of your View is.

Open the .inc file that you just created and type the following code at the top:

```
<?php
//put export code here
$views[$view->name] = $view;
```

Go to the Views Administration page at /admin/structure/views and locate the View you want to export. Click Export in the Operations menu for that view on the right side of the View listing. This will take you to a page with lots of code. Copy all the code in the text area and paste it over the *one* middle line (//put export code here) in articles_by_author.inc.

For every View you want to export, you will need to create a file in your module's views folder and paste in the export code just like you did for this one.

The next step is to add some code to your module that tells the Views module to look in your module's views folder. In your module's .module file, add the following code, replacing "dgd7glue" with the name of your module:

```
/**
 * Implements hook_views_api().
 */
function dgd7glue_views_api() {
  return array(
    'api' => '3.0',
  );
}

/**
 * Implements hook_views_default_views().
 */
function dgd7glue_views_default_views() {
  $path = './' . drupal_get_path('module', 'dgd7glue') . '/views/*.inc';
  $views = array();
  foreach (glob($path) as $views_filename) {
    require_once($views_filename);
  }
  return $views;
}
```

Enable your module like you would any other module at `admin/modules`.

Just to make sure the Views module knows you added a View into code, you want to clear Views cache. Go to the Views Tools tab at `admin/structure/views/settings/advanced` and click Clear Views' Cache.

Go back to the Views listing page. Find the View you just exported. You will notice the words "Database overriding code" on the left. This means that Drupal knows you have this View in code, but it is using the version in the database. You want to use the code version you just added and delete the database version. Click Revert in the Operations menu for the View you just exported. It will confirm that you really want to. After you say, "Yes, I want to Revert my View!", it will redirect you back to the listing page. Notice how the words next to your View are now "In code."

Congratulations!

This greatest benefit of exporting Views into code is how easy you can make changes and transfer a View you created from one environment to another. Just don't forget to clear Views' cache.

Additional Resources

Because the Views module is popular, there are a lot of resources online and presentations at Drupal events. If you are looking for more help, check out these places:

- *Drupal Documentation pages*: These are updated by the community; although Views has matured over the years, the concepts and strategies have remained relative consistent.

  `drupal.org/documentation/modules/views`

- *Views Issue Queue*: Search through these issues to see if someone is discussing something similar. If you don't find it, you can create a support ticket.

  `drupal.org/project/issues/views`

- *Google*: There are so many blog posts, tutorials, and videos on Views online.

  `google.com/search?q=drupal+views`

- *Your local Drupal group*: Every region has monthly meetups and this is a great place to ask questions. Find you local group and join!

  `groups.drupal.org/groups`

- *Professional Training*: There are many professional paid training sessions to take you to the next level. See Chapter 9 for more ways to get involved in Drupal and get help, but never hesitate to play and experiment on your own (just work locally and not on a live site).

■ ■ ■

## CHAPTER 4

There's a Module for That

by Dani Nordin, Dan Hakimzadeh, and Benjamin Melançon

When building a Drupal site, "there's a module for that" can be the sweetest words you can hear. Modules are nicely packaged bits of code that extend what Drupal can do. With thousands of contributed modules, the odds are good that someone has written one that does something close to what you need. The main challenge, then, is two-fold:

1. Figuring out exactly what you need.

2. Finding the best module to accomplish that goal.

This chapter will start you off with some essential modules that will benefit many kinds of Drupal sites. Then we'll take on the creative challenge of finding the right modules for specific use cases. Once you find the module that fits your use case, it's important to learn how to evaluate the module's effectiveness and sometimes to compare it against several modules with similar functionality. Reporting bugs and requesting features usefully and respectfully is another learned art.

■ **Tip** Finding a module that does exactly what you need in one package is most often *not* what you want in Drupal. Many pieces each doing their part and working together well is the way Drupal is headed. Fields and views are a prime example. You don't want three specialized modules for a page of recipes, a list of sponsors, and a news and events section. You want Field and Views modules and friends, which you can configure to do all that and much more. (Features modules, and other modules that define their own views and create content types for you, try to provide the best of both worlds by packaging up this configuration work to have drop-in functionality, but you can modify or extend it if you need to using flexible, widely used tools.)

Modules for Drupal Are Constantly Evolving

There are many different ways to evaluate modules to use for Drupal. The folks at NodeOne did a series called "49 Modules You Should Know" (nodeone.se/blogg/49-modules-you-should-know), which provides a good way to think about it. NodeOne.se's recommendations are modules you should know, but not necessarily use, and certainly not on every site. Palantir has a more in-depth series called "Better Know a Module" (palantir.net/blog/series/14), which is the same idea. Drupalistas put out lists of top 10 or top 100 modules all the time, all of which are good ways of keeping up-to-date on what's available.

Fewer Modules Is Better

The Drupal community likes to brag about its thousands of contributed modules, but here's a very important fact: the more modules you install, the worse your web site will perform.

Performance and scalability expert Khalid Baheyeldin of `2bits.com` regularly gives presentations about helping Drupal sites serve two to three million page views a day, tens of millions of visitors a month, on a single server with none of the reverse proxy, caching, content delivery network, noSQL databases, or Drupal modifications that are often associated with scaling.

His first step, after making sure the server itself is tuned for serving Drupal and doesn't have extra stuff going on, is to remove all unnecessary modules. This means:

- Less code to load/execute.

- Less memory to consume.

- Fewer database queries.

More important than performance considerations, adding too many additional modules increases the complexity of your site, making it harder to develop and maintain. To prevent the code and conceptual overhead of unneeded module bloat, we don't necessarily recommend creating a list of "essential" modules. Every module should have a reason to be on a particular site. Nevertheless, as you continue to create web sites in Drupal, certain modules will prove to be consistently useful. This is one of the reasons it's helpful for people or teams working with Drupal to develop documentation on their workflow and process as soon as they start creating web sites; over time, these documents become essential to the efficiency of your team. Check out Chapter 11 for more info on creating project wikis.

How to Find and Choose a Module

The important thing to understand is this: **every module needs to be evaluated from the perspective of the site you are building.** This is one of the key reasons that appropriate site planning is such an important part of the Drupal development process; knowing the business objectives and required functionality for your site ahead of time makes it much easier to find the right module to suit your site's needs. Even powerhouse, super-useful modules—such as Views, an essential part of most sites to which Chapter 3 is devoted—could be left off of certain specialized projects.

In a few cases, some modules should be seen as either/or: two or more modules may do similar things, or in rare cases are completely incompatible, and you must choose between or among them.

While there's no magic formula for finding the right module for a specific project, the following tips can help weed out the less-than-helpful modules from the truly fantastic modules:

- *Filter by compatibility.* Drupal.org, as part of the recent redesign, allows you to filter modules by compatibility with versions of Drupal core at `drupal.org/project/modules` (see Figure 4-1). This should become a default behavior when searching for modules for a specific project. By filtering modules by the version of Drupal you're specifically working with, you can avoid filtering through hundreds of modules that aren't yet available for your version of Drupal core.

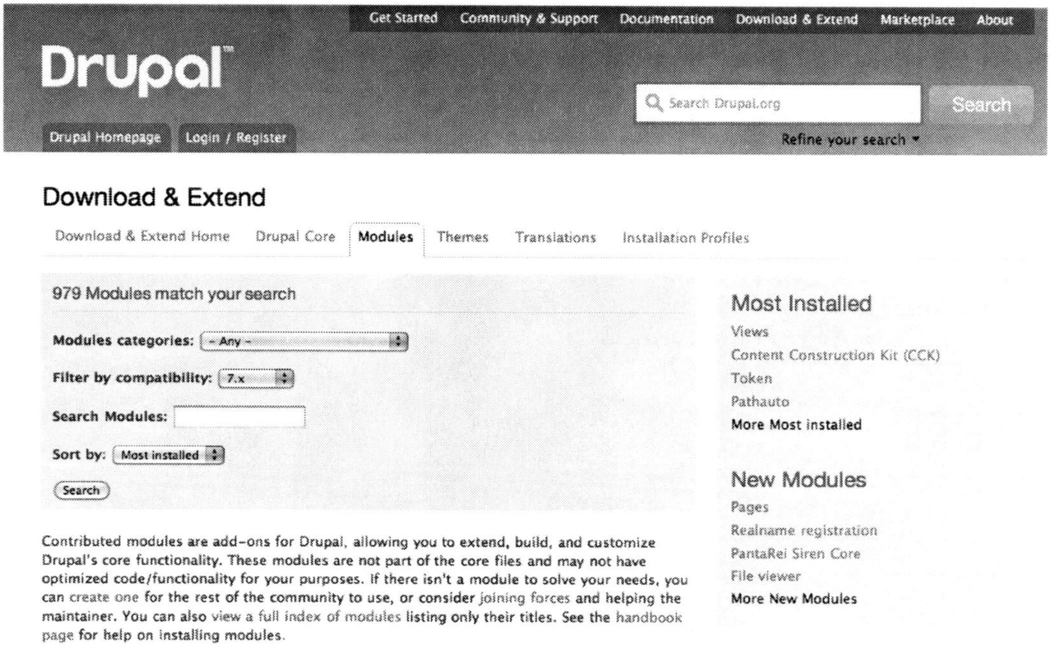

Figure 4-1. The Drupal.org modules page (drupal.org/project/modules) allows you to filter by category, popularity, or by compatibility with your version of Drupal.

■ **Note** At the time of this writing, the Drupal "Most installed" sort includes *all* versions of Drupal in determining ranking even when you are filtering by compatibility. Therefore, you are not necessarily seeing the most popular modules *for Drupal 7* but a module that may be of little use in Drupal 7, was very popular in Drupal 6, and happens to have a Drupal 7 release. To see module popularity in a specific version, click the *View usage statistics* link in the Project information section of the module's project page, above the Downloads section. This link takes the form `drupal.org/project/usage/modulename`.

- *Find modules that are actively maintained.* Most modules on Drupal.org will include a Recommended Release and a date on which that release was made. You can also see the most recent date for which commits were made to that module. It is generally a good idea to choose modules that are listed as "Actively Maintained" and were updated within the last six months. While it's certainly possible to find a module that works perfectly well and hasn't been updated in a year or more, it's enough of a red flag that you want to look deeper into the module before using it on your site. See Figure 4-2 for an example of release information on the popular Views module. If you visit `drupal.org/project/views` now you will see there have been many releases since this screenshot was taken.

■ **Tip** You can also sort by "Last release" to get a view focused on better-maintained or simply more recent modules.

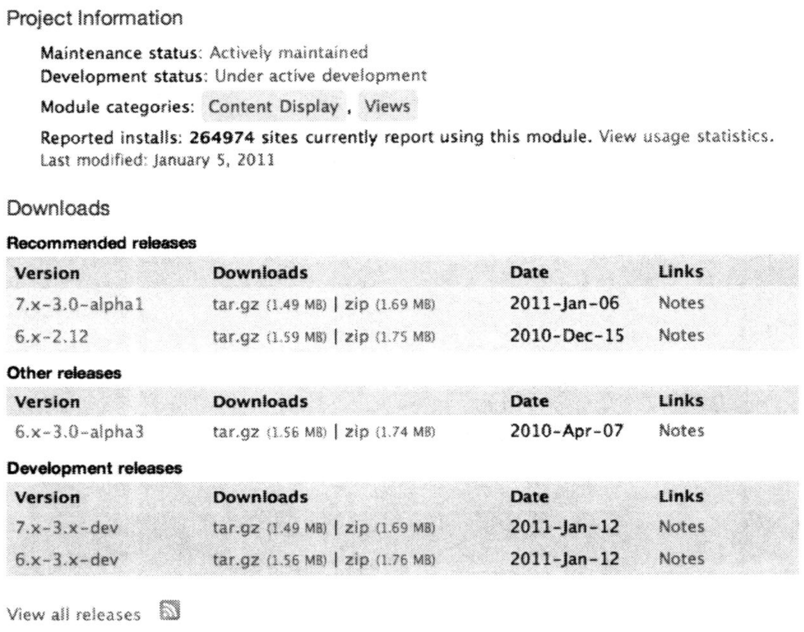

Project Information

Maintenance status: Actively maintained
Development status: Under active development

Module categories: Content Display , Views

Reported installs: **264974** sites currently report using this module. View usage statistics.
Last modified: January 5, 2011

Downloads

Recommended releases

Version	Downloads	Date	Links
7.x-3.0-alpha1	tar.gz (1.49 MB) | zip (1.69 MB)	2011-Jan-06	Notes
6.x-2.12	tar.gz (1.59 MB) | zip (1.75 MB)	2010-Dec-15	Notes

Other releases

Version	Downloads	Date	Links
6.x-3.0-alpha3	tar.gz (1.56 MB) | zip (1.74 MB)	2010-Apr-07	Notes

Development releases

Version	Downloads	Date	Links
7.x-3.x-dev	tar.gz (1.49 MB) | zip (1.69 MB)	2011-Jan-12	Notes
6.x-3.x-dev	tar.gz (1.56 MB) | zip (1.76 MB)	2011-Jan-12	Notes

View all releases 🔊

Figure 4-2. Release information for the Views module

- *Restrict your search to Full projects until you are desperate.* By default, developers' sandbox modules—which have no official release—are hidden from your searches at `drupal.org/project/modules`. You generally do not want to even try this unsupported code, but if you can find nothing else, and you're willing to contribute to its development somehow, you just may find some hidden gems among the sandbox projects.

- *As with all searches, try a mix of keywords.* If your first search doesn't bring you a good module, try again with fewer or different keywords. You can also take your search off Drupal.org to the general internet, to benefit from the wider array of language people may have used to talk about your hoped-for module. (And if you want to benefit everyone else, and quite likely yourself in a month or three, keep track of the words you searched for to find a module and post them with a link to the successful result.)

- *Ask for help. Ask for the module you need to be made!* When all else fails, including asking in Drupal support forums or IRC (see Chapter 9), post your dream module to the Contributed Modules Idea group at `groups.drupal.org/contributed-module-ideas`. (It is highly unlikely to be made just on your request, but it can be a start!)

What to Do When Something's Wrong with a Module

While all of these contributed modules can prove incredibly useful in improving the functionality of your Drupal site, occasionally you'll find that a module doesn't work exactly as you hoped, or worse—it breaks your site entirely. When that happens, the easiest thing to do is uninstall the module and find another one. But, the Drupal community gives you some additional options for making modules work better.

One key bit of help can be found in the Drupal.org issue queues. Often, entering error text or a description of the problem into the Drupal.org search field will uncover a wealth of information from the community about the problem you're facing. This may include a quick list of ways that others in the community have solved the problem, or it may include a patch that you can tack onto the module that fixes the issue. If you have the initiative to write a patch yourself, contributing patches for specific modules is a great way to give back to Drupal. For more information on patches, check out Chapter 38 on contributing to the community and `drupal.org/patch`.

Modules in Core

If you installed Drupal with the **standard** installation profile, the following modules are likely installed and enabled already in your Drupal installation:

- Block—allows you to create and manage blocks in your theme. Blocks are like widgets, or bits of functionality, that you can drop into a defined region on a page. The display of blocks in a region can be controlled based on the URL path the block should or shouldn't appear on, the type of content a user is viewing, the role of the user viewing the content, and the theme which is currently applied to your web site.

- Color—allows you to change the color of themes that support this option. End users can define a hexidecimal color code or a select a color from a color wheel that they would like to use in a specific region of their site. If your theme is not recolorable (or you are done recoloring it) you can disable Color module.

- Comment—allows visitors to post comments on any piece of content within the site. All content types can have comments enabled, and comments can have custom fields added to them.

- Contextual Links—controls links that help you more easily access actions related to page elements. By default, Drupal 7 will place an edit and delete link on each node and on each block. This provides fantastic usability for Contributed modules (and modules you make) and can define additional contextual links.

- Dashboard—enables an administrative Dashboard on your site. The admin dashboard offers a page in the administrative interface with a two-column layout on which blocks can be assigned to display "quick glance" information about the web site (e.g., recent comments and logged-in users).

- Database Logging—logs and records items into the database. This module provides a reporting screen in the administrative interface that lists all recent activity and errors on the site. Administrators can filter through these logged items and click through to see more details.

- Field SQL Storage, Field UI—allow you to create fields and attach them to content types, comments, and other entities on your site. Fields can be stored in different formats and formatted in different ways using the following optional core modules as well as the required Text module:

  - File

  - Options

  - List

  - Number

  - Image

- Help—displays help text. Using this module, other modules display information to users and especially site administrators explaining various settings or actions available in the Drupal user interface.

- Menu—allows site administrators to manage the site's navigation menus.

- Overlay—enables the administrative overlay. The overlay was an attempt to provide context to tasks by presenting administration screens (and optionally content creation/edit forms) in an overlay on the page. This module can be disabled without any loss of functionality.

- Path—allows users to create search engine-friendly URL's. Drupal by default uses a URL pattern of node/[node ID], such as node/123, for content. Path allows you to change this to whatever-path-you-want. (See the Pathauto module, discussed later in this chapter, to create path aliases automatically from node data such as the title.)

- RDF—attaches metadata to your content defining what items you write about are in the real world. For example, the module adds RDFa semantic markup indicating that the poster of a piece of content is its creator. This lets other sites or tools understand your content in ways that allow them to query or combine it in intelligent ways. See Chapter 28 on Drupal and the Semantic Web for much more about Drupal 7's new RDFa capabilities.

- Search—allows users to search site content. The search module provides a basic search form as a block and a search page with advanced search filters to allow users to find more relevant results.

- Shortcut—allows administrators to create helpful lists of shortcut links available through the administration toolbar. These links are presented in the expandable portion of the toolbar, which can be exposed by clicking on the gray tab on the far-right-hand corner of the toolbar.

- Taxonomy—gives the ability to categorize content using vocabularies, or groups of tags. You can create an unlimited number of vocabularies and add them to content and users in the same way you add fields. You have some options over how the vocabulary is presented—single select, multi-select, or free tagging.

- Toolbar—creates the admin menu at the top of the administrative interface. The toolbar offers quick links to administrative functions within Drupal.

- Update manager—handles updates to Drupal core and contributed modules and checks for available updates. You can download and update more modules from the Update Manager itself.

Additionally, the following modules are required by Drupal:

- Filter—formats content before displaying it.

- Node—controls site content.

- System—handles general site configuration for administrators.

- Text—defines simple text field types.

- User—manages the user recommendation and login system. Drupal provides still more modules in core that are not enabled by default in the Standard installation profile. You may consider enabling the following modules according to your site's functional requirements:

  - Aggregator—allows you to import RSS feeds into your Drupal site. The aggregated items are not stored as nodes.

  - Blog—enables multi-user blogs and sets up some standard options that blogs need, such as recent posts listings, etc., without the need for Views modules.

  - Book—allows you to create and organize content in an outline format.

  - Contact—creates a contact form on your Drupal site and assigns different recipients of e-mails based on the reasoning selected by an end user.

  - Content translation—allows you to translate content into different languages.

  - Forum—creates discussion forum-like functionality to facilitate organized conversations on the site.

  - Locale—allows you to translate user interface elements into different languages (or even different jargon). While it may seem that Content translation and Locale would provide all your site's translation needs, in fact they are just a start. Translation of content and interface is a very complicated space—and still in flux for Drupal 7 at the time of this writing, but we'll try to keep you up to date with contributed module resources at dgd7.org/translate.

  - Open ID—allows users to log into your Drupal web site using the Open ID online identity management service.

  - PHP filter—allows users to use PHP when creating content or custom blocks in the Drupal administrative interface. For security and maintainability reasons, use of this module is discouraged.

  - Poll—suitable for simple popularity polls, this module has not historically received much attention or work despite being in core.

- Profile—unless you are upgrading from Drupal 6 and had the Profile module enabled, you won't even see it in Drupal 7. It is deprecated in favor of Fields and contributed solutions such as Profile2.

- Syslog—this module can be used instead of the Database logging module to store Drupal's Watchdog log to the less resource intensive system log (at /var/log/syslog on Debian and Ubuntu systems).

- Testing—a developer-oriented module that allows module developers to run automated tests of custom code they write for Drupal.

- Tracker—stores information about site visits and changes to content, which are displayed to site administrators.

- Trigger—a simple workflow system that allows users to add actions or system responses to tasks completed on the site, such as sending an e-mail when someone comments on a post.

A quick look at the Modules screen of any Drupal installation (**Modules** from the administration menu, at path admin/modules) will show you all these modules that come pre-installed with Drupal. Now, let's start talking about rounding out Drupal's functionality with contributed modules.

Where to Store Contributed Modules

Before we start our deep dive into the world of Drupal's contributed modules, also referred to as contrib, we need to know where to put them. Contributed modules you download should go in sites/all/modules/contrib. Being in the all directory means they will be available for every site on a multisite installation (should you go that route). Being in the contrib directory (which you will have to create) establishes proper separation from any custom modules you may make, which can go in sites/all/modules/custom (which you would also have to create).

Contributed modules should *not* be placed anywhere outside of sites. Everything you add to Drupal beyond core or an installation profile should go in the sites folder. When you eventually update your Drupal installation—which is necessary to apply security updates and bug fixes (see Chapter 7)—having all non-core data in the sites folder allows you to back up just that folder, and replace everything else, without worrying about losing anything.

Site Building Essentials

All of the modules in this section are available on Drupal.org and can be found by going to the overall listing at drupal.org/project/modules. As we've already mentioned, not every module that we list here will be necessary for any given Drupal site; however, experience has shown that these are well maintained and useful modules to know about. Further, this is by no means a complete list, for any purpose. Thorough searching as described earlier is recommended when seeking particular functionality.

Technically, everything we list here is a project, not a module per se, and each module project may contain one or more modules. To go to a specific project page, use the project short name listed under each project name headline as drupal.org/project/*project_shortname*.

▨ **Tip** If you're using Drush, the command `drush dl project_shortname` will automatically download and unpack your module with short name *project_shortname* into the `sites/all/modules/contrib` folder if you create it first (and `sites/all/modules` if you do not create a `contrib` directory). If you still need to get started with Drush, see Chapter 2. For power tips, check out Chapter 26.

Views

Project: `views`

The Views module is a powerful tool for building custom displays of content. Think of it as a query builder—it allows you to, through a point-and-click interface, request content, users, and other data that you want to present on your site from Drupal's database. You can then, using Views "style plug-ins," display that content in some very interesting ways, such as a listing, slideshow, or a map.

The reasons and motivations behind using Views on a Drupal site are so extensive that Chapter 3 is devoted to it. While some sites—extremely simple sites, for example, or highly customized applications—can flourish without views, the great majority of web sites built on Drupal now use Views.

Views comes prepackaged with a number of "helper" modules. Of these, Views UI is the most important one—as it controls the user interface for Views. If you are working on a Drupal site and can't access any of your Views, check that Views UI is enabled.

Chaos Tools (Dependency)

Project: `ctools`

Chaos Tools, also known as CTools, is a developer-oriented module that provides a set of helpers for making difficult development tasks in Drupal easier. Some of these options include exporting Drupal configuration to code, building multistep forms, easier implementation, and management of AJAX requests. Views has a dependency on some of the helpers provided by CTools.

As described in Chapter 3, Views UI requires CTools to function. Modules included in the CTools package set the stage for a variety of interesting site building tools.

▨ **Note** All modules can be found at `drupal.org/project/project_shortname`, and this project short name is listed underneath each module project's human-readable name. For example, the CTools suite of modules is available at `drupal.org/project/ctools`. If you want to download a module with Drush, use the project short name in that command; for example, `drush dl ctools`.

Pathauto

Project: `pathauto`

Every page on your Drupal site has its own unique internal path. By default, Drupal shows this internal path in the browser" address bar. For example, your first node on a Drupal site would be at the path `node/1`. Pathauto allows you to automatically create human readable, search engine-friendly URLs for each of your nodes. You can also use Pathauto to set up automatic prefixes depending on content type or any other aspect of content that is understood by the Token module.

Using the content type machine name token and the title token, for example, would allow all blog entries to automatically have path aliases such as example.com/blog/blog-post-title. Pathauto is powered by tokens and depends on the Token module, covered next. See also Chapter 8 for more examples of Pathauto in use.

Token (Dependency)

Project: token

Token allows you to create simple placeholders for users, nodes, or other references, in different areas of your administrative interface. These placeholders are replaced by the value of that token when appropriate. In the example of creating search engine-friendly URL's with Pathauto, defining a default pattern for all posts of [node:content-type:name]/[node:title] and posting an article with the headline "Education is the path from cocky ignorance to miserable uncertainty" would create the URL example.com/article/education-path-cocky-ignorance-miserable-uncertainty.

▓ **Note** (By default, words like "a" and "the" that carry little meaning are excluded from Pathauto-created aliases, but you can configure this at *Administration* ➤ *Configuration* ➤ *Search and Metadata* ➤ *URL Aliases* ➤ *Settings* (admin/config/search/path/settings) under Strings to Remove. You can create Views to match Pathauto-generated content type prefixes (for instance, providing a view of all story content at the story path). See Chapter 33 for an example of creating hackable URLs.

Additional Field Types

Prior to Drupal 7, fields were handled through a module called the Content Construction Kit (CCK) and various add-on modules that would format fields for adding images, links, videos, and other types of data to content. This functionality has been rolled into Drupal 7 as the Fields and Fields UI modules.

Below is a listing of helpful modules that add custom field types to the Fields module:

- References (drupal.org/project/references) allows you to create references to users or nodes, which can then be displayed in the content doing the referencing. In time, it may be superseded by the Relation module (drupal.org/project/relation), a much more powerful—and more complex— way to relate any Drupal entity to any other entity. Block reference (drupal.org/project/blockreference) and View reference (drupal.org/project/viewreference), for their part, create fields that allow administrators to choose to display a specific block and view, respectively.

- Field Group (drupal.org/project/field_group) allows you to cluster fields into groups to create a more intuitive and streamlined content creation screen and display of content to end users. Useful for keeping address information together, for example, or project related information. You can display field groups as collapsed field sets, vertical tabs, or horizontal tabs.

- Link (drupal.org/project/link) provides storage and formatters for URLs with associated titles.

- Media (`drupal.org/project/media`) is much more than a field module, but it does provide formatters for different types of media, such as videos, images, and documents. It also implements a centralized storage space and system for managing various types of media on a Drupal site.

There are dozens of further fields available for download on Drupal.org. You can also create your own custom modules to implement new field types if one does not exist.

WYSIWYG

Project: `wysiwyg`

Drupal defaults to plain text and manual HTML input on content creation and edit forms. While this is often not a problem for developers or those experienced with HTML, site editors and users are often more comfortable with some form of WYSIWYG editor (think word processor) that will let them format text more easily. The WYSIWYG module allows you to do just that, choosing from many WYSIWYG editors including TinyMCE, CKEditor, and FCKeditor.

■ **Tip** Any WYSIWYG editor adds a lot of complexity, and none can fully deliver on the promise of "What You See Is What You Get"—which can lead to a lot of headaches working with content whose HTML markup is not as clean as it would be if it were entered by hand. Therefore, you are much better off if your site users are able to handle plain text content entry, assisted by Drupal's automatic paragraph tags and perhaps by an HTML markup aid such as BUEditor (`drupal.org/project/bueditor`).

In order to use WYSIWYG, you'll need to download an editor library and install it in your `sites/all/libraries` folder. See WYSIWYG module's `README.txt` file and its configuration page for more information.

We highly recommend downloading the WYSIWYG line breaks (`drupal.org/project/wysiwyg_linebreaks`) in addition to the WYSIWYG module. This add-on module helps fix some of the HTML oddness that WYSIWYG editors can cause.

Alternatives

If it is possible to avoid WYSIWYG, do so. The keep-it-simple approach will benefit users of mobile devices and keep the code in your content cleaner. For an alternative to full WYSIWYG controls, you can use the excellent BUEditor module (`bueditor`), which adds buttons for inserting HTML markup. Or you can use Markdown filter (`markdown`), which allows you to use markdown syntax in your edit fields. Markdown syntax is a very simple method of formatting that mimics old-school word processing applications. As an example, you add bold text to your content by surrounding the text with asterisks (e.g., *Bold text*), italics with underscores (e.g., _Italics_), and so on.

Webform

Project: `webform`

Drupal comes with Contact module available, which will allow any user on your site to send a quick e-mail either to configurable addresses (via a main contact form at path `contact`) or, if so configured, to a registered user on the site (at `user/[uid]/contact`). The limitation with this is that the form is very basic. All it collects is the user's name, e-mail address, and a brief comment. Furthermore, the submitted messages are not stored in the site database, so there is no reference point to go back to other than your e-mail account.

For many sites, this is not enough—some sites require more flexibility in building forms with any number of custom fields, flexible layout options, and reporting. The Webform module allows you to build customized forms that can be used to collect data. You can use Webforms to build contact forms, surveys, online applications, and so forth. The module comes with reporting out of the box and allows you to configure e-mail notifications that can be sent out upon each form submission.

AntiSpam or Mollom

Projects: `antispam, mollom`

One of the most important things in any site, at least a site that includes any kind of social interaction, is to protect the site from spam. Drupal's contributed modules have several ways of doing this. Two with an acceptable balance between preventing spam and not irritating users are AntiSpam and Mollom. Both modules require signing up for a spam detection web service, which is either free or paid depending on the number of requests sent.

Mollom is a service started by Drupal's founder, Dries Buytaert. It is free up to a limit of blocked spam messages per day. To use the Mollom module, create an account at `Mollom.com` and register your site. Then copy the public and private API keys to the Mollom settings page on your site (`admin/config/content/mollom/settings`).

▓ **Note** By default, Mollom blocks all form submissions if its service is not working. If you would rather deal with the occasional influx of spam than denying all form submissions when Mollom is down, change the When Mollom is down or unreachable setting to Accept all form submissions.

To use the AntiSpam module sign up for Akismet at `akismet.com`, which is free for most non-commercial sites. Akismet is the most widely used anti-spam service and was created and primarily used with the WordPress content management system. The configuration is very similar to that of Mollom—just copy the API keys to the Mollom settings page on your site (`admin/config/content/antispam/settings`).

By default, the module will e-mail users when a submission is blocked. To change this, select disable e-mail notifications under general options on the Antispam setting screen.

■ **Note** Instead of using an external spam-detecting service, the CAPTCHA suite of modules (drupal.org/project/captcha) allows you to plug in a wide range of CAPTCHAs (see drupal.org/project/captcha_pack), including simple math problems and configurable questions that can be tailored to your community. You can also extend it to use the reCAPTCHA service (drupal.org/project/recaptcha), which has the needed accessibility fallback of an audio CAPTCHA. A solution that avoids CAPTCHAs entirely, even as a fallback for spam detection, is the Hashcash module (drupal.org/project/hashcash), which relies on JavaScript and the hashcash algorithm to thwart spam submissions.

Other Modules That May Prove Useful

Now that you've gotten a rundown of some of the most useful Drupal modules, here's a truncated list of additional modules that may prove useful for your specific site plan. This list is by no means comprehensive; if you don't see a module that suits your needs here, a quick search on Drupal.org for modules is likely to result in at least something close to what you need.

Administrative Interface and Content Entry

The Drupal community offers a number of helpful modules that make administering your web site and managing content a better experience.

Workbench

Project: workbench

An all-new-for-Drupal-7 project, the Workbench suite of modules provides usability improvements for content creators and editors, including a customizable editorial workflow.

Environment Indicator

Project: environment_indicator

Environment indicator adds a colored strip to the side of your site to make the environment you're currently in (Development, Staging, Production, etc.) extremely clear. Though this is more of a developer module, it proves very useful if you don't appreciate entering content on the wrong version of a site.

Smart Crop

Project: smartcrop

Smart crop helps to better automate the cropping of photographs. It provides an image style that crops based on entropy, which produces a more effective result when cropping to a fixed shape. For example, it can reduce the likelihood of cutting off a person's head when cropping a profile picture to a square.

Content Type Overview

Project: content_type_overview

This extremely useful module gives you the ability to edit the settings for multiple content types from one place.

CONFIGURING AND USING A MODULE: CONTENT TYPE OVERVIEW

After obtaining the module via its page at drupal.org/project/content_type_overview or drush dl content_type_overview, enable it at the Modules administration page (admin/modules).

It's hard to know in which category a module will put itself on the administration page, so it is always easiest to find it by using our browser's within-page search (try the key combination ctrl f or command f) and typing the module's name (its official name, not its system name). In this case, Content Type Overview is alone under Administration.

We checkmark it and submit the modules page with the Save configuration button at the bottom. Drupal tells us, "The configuration options have been saved." We go back to the entry on the administration page in the hopes that the Content type overview module will have one of those nifty configuration links that Drupal 7 makes possible, but we are disappointed to see nothing at all in the Operations column. We make a mental note to file a patch to add the link to the .info file so that it will appear on the Modules page here, and this will be easier next time. (The issue is posted at drupal.org/node/1032930.)

When a module does not provide a link to its configuration page, you can go looking for it. We look in Configuration (admin/config) first, because that's the most common place for module configuration to be put.

Searching via ctrl f is again a good way to try to find the module, this time amid the other configuration.

It's under "Development", which seems a little odd for a configuration aid, but we should have stopped expecting everything to make perfect sense much earlier in our work with Drupal. We click the link there to get to `admin/config/development/content_type_overview`. We check off every content type on our site.

Home » Dashboard » Configuration » Development

Content type overview ⊙

Content types

☑ Article

☑ Chapter

☑ Basic page

☑ Point

☑ Profile

☑ Research question

☑ Simplenews newsletter

☑ Suggestion

Select the content types you want to include on the overview page.

☑ Shorten form labels

Enable this to shorten the form element labels. This makes it possible to display more widgets per screen.

(Save configuration)

Then we submit the form with the Save configuration button. Yay!

But now what? This is a too-common annoyance with Drupal. Couldn't we get some clue where we're supposed to go next? Are we supposed to be psychics?

All right. We know content types are under *Administer* ➤ *Structure* (`admin/structure`), let's look for the content types overview there. Hmm, no. Well, let's click on Content types (`admin/structure/types`). Mmm... aha! There, on the far right, a new tab, Overview.

Home » Dashboard » Structure

Content types ⊙

LIST   OVERVIEW

Let's go to that tab (`admin/structure/types/overview`). Wow. We have dozens of options for all the content types we chose, all in one place!

	CHAPTER	BASIC PAGE
Name	Chapter	Basic page
Machine name	book	page
Description	A summary or a list of headings for a c	Use <em>basic pages</em> for your

Submission form settings

Title field label	Chapter title	Title
Preview before submitting	○ Disabled ⦿ Optional ○ Required	○ Disabled ⦿ Optional ○ Required
Explanation or submission guidelines		
Submit again?	☑	☑

Publishing options

Default options	☑ Published ☐ Promoted to front page ☐ Sticky at top of lists ☑ Create new revision	☑ Published ☐ Promoted to front page ☐ Sticky at top of lists ☑ Create new revision

This is awesome. We can set the publishing options of Create new revision for every content type at once, along with all the other publishing options such as Promoted to front page and Published. Also from this page we can change any content type name, description, the label for the title field, whether or not the preview before submitted button is disable, optional, or required, the submission guidelines text, whether to Display author and date information, the Comment settings, Menu settings, and even contributed module settings such as the submit again option (see Chapter 21 for how that module was upgraded to Drupal 7).

We can see from the messages after we submit that it saves each content type individually, just as if we'd gone to all eight content types one by one.

Masquerade

Project: `masquerade`

Normally, testing user permissions when building a site requires you to log out of the site and log in as a different user. The Masquerade module allows users (who have the correct permissions set) to switch users without logging out.

Content Display

This group of modules will help you customize the way that your site looks and displays content.

Panels

Project: `panels`

Another Earl Miles (merlinofchaos) tour de force, Panels allows site administrators to create custom page layouts that can be used in multiple areas throughout the site. It also creates a drag-and-drop interface for managing content and block placement. While by no means essential to creating dynamic Drupal sites, many site builders base their entire site around the modules provided by the Panels project and the required Chaos Tools (`ctools`) project.

Code Filter

Project name: `codefilter`

This module is by no means essential for successfully developing a Drupal site, but it is key if you want to write about development and include code snippets! This module provides a simple way to add snippets of code and have it formatted nicely.

It does this by providing an input filter, which you must enable for one or more text formats before your newly enabled module will do anything for you.

1. Go to *Administration* ➤ *Configuration* ➤ *Content authoring* ➤ *Text formats* (`admin/config/content/formats`) and edit (to start) the Filtered HTML format.

2. In the list of Enabled filters, enable Code filter.

3. Under Filter processing order, put Code filter *after* "Limit allowed HTML tags."

4. Don't forget to Save configuration at the bottom of the form.

▦ **Tip** If you put the *Limit allowed HTML tags* filter after *Code filter*, it strips out the HTML that the code filter adds. As a rule, put *Limit allowed HTML tags* first and *Correct faulty and chopped off HTML* last.

Do the same for the Full HTML format, except you don't have to worry about the filter processing order because Full HTML does not limit allowed HTML tags by default.

Colorbox

project: `colorbox`
A Drupal 7-ready successor to popular Drupal 6 modules such as Lightbox2, JQuery Lightbox, Thickbox, and others, Colorbox helps you use JQuery to show images, videos, forms, and other content in an overlay in front of a web page.

Menus and Navigation

The next group of modules will help with the placement of custom navigation menus.

Menu block

Project: `menu_block`
This module allows you to create blocks from menus—starting at whatever level you want. For example: let's say that you have an About section on your site, with sub-items for Team, History, and The True Story. This module lets you create a custom sub-menu block that only appears on pages in the about section. This is just the beginning of the awesomeness you can have with this module.

Menu position

Project: `menu_position`
Menu position can tell the menu system that a page belongs in a certain place in the menu hierarchy, without having to create menu items for them. This is especially useful for making sure the menu system knows that all 12,000 blog posts "belong" beneath the Blog menu item (so the Blog menu item stays highlighted when any of them are viewed) without actually adding them as menu links. An overly large number of menu links can really slow down a site.

Community Building and Social Networking

While Drupal is a powerful option for many different types of sites, it's especially good for creating sites with a social component. The following modules are designed to help users build community on the web.

Comment notify

Project: `comment_notify`
Comment notify lets your site visitors—signed-in and anonymous—request to receive e-mail notifications about subsequent comments while they are leaving a comment themselves. (This module has been suggested to Drupal founder Dries Buytaert and is now in use on his blog, and it is being considered for inclusion in Drupal core. That's always a good sign.)
Comment notify requires the core Token module (`drupal.org/project/token`). If a required module is present but not enabled, Drupal will be prompt you to enable it, as shown in Figure 4-3.

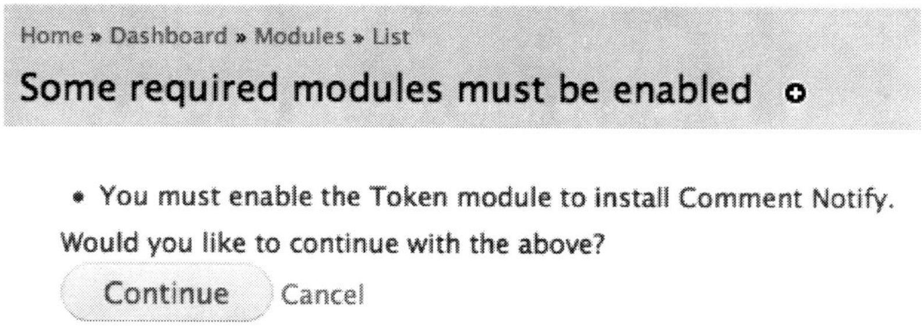

Home » Dashboard » Modules » List

Some required modules must be enabled ⊙

- You must enable the Token module to install Comment Notify.

Would you like to continue with the above?

Continue Cancel

Figure 4-3. Drupal prompting to enable the Token module, a dependency of the Comment notify module

When Comment notify is enabled, it starts working immediately. At *Administer* ➤ *Configuration* ➤ *People* ➤ *Comment notify* (admin/config/people/comment_notify), there is a settings page to configure which content types can have notifications, whether all comments or just replies to one's comments send notices, what the default settings are, and even the format for the messages.

Organic Groups

Project: og

Organic Groups provides a way to add social activity to Drupal by allowing users or administrators to create their own "groups" within a Drupal site. Each Group can set its own standards for membership and can contribute to the group using either the standard content types that you are using for your site or custom content types that you create. See Chapter 5 to get started using this suite of modules.

Rate

Project: rate

Rate provides an assortment of voting widgets for nodes and comments, which are added and arranged using Drupal 7's fields system.

Dependency: Voting API

Project: votingapi

Voting API gives modules a standardized set of functions and database schema for storing, retrieving, and tabulating votes. It is a well-established best practice for voting and rating modules. The Fivestar module (fivestar), a very popular module using Voting API in Drupal 6, also has a Drupal 7 version.

Userpoints

Project: `userpoints`

Userpoints gives you a way to give registered users "points" for doing certain things on your site; for example, posting comments or content.

Profile2

Project: `profile2`

This module is designed to allow users to create personal profiles on your site, which can be customized with Drupal's Field API. This is recommended over core's Profile module, which Drupal developers set out to convert to use Fields but ended up having to hide it instead.

Role Limits

Project: `role_limits`

Role limits allows you to set limits on how many users can inhabit a specific role. This is especially useful, for example, if you want to put a limit on how many members a specific group can have or how many users on the site can be given administrative or editor roles.

Paths, Search and 404 Errors

This next group of modules help control and expand Drupal's handling of search and 404 errors.

Apache Solr

Project: `apachesolr`

Apache Solr brings content search capabilities that far exceed Drupal's core search module, but it doesn't do this alone. Apache Solr is an integration module, meaning it makes Drupal work with an outside application. You don't need to write any code to use it, but it's a bit more complex to set up than most modules and is covered in Chapter 31.

Search 404

Project: `search404`

This module replaces the less-than-helpful File Not Found page with a search of your site using any keywords in the path that wasn't found.

■ **Caution** Performing searches instead of serving up a lightweight page when a path is not found can put immense strain on your server's resources. You should frequently check for 404 errors in your Drupal watchdog logs (at `admin/reports/dblog` if using the Database log module and your server's system log if using the Syslog module). If there are common incorrect 404 paths that should go to particular pages, you should set up redirects for those pages in your server configuration or, at the least, with the Redirect module (which provides a handy link on 404 pages to do this). If you regularly notice paths that aren't relevant to the site, you'll want to block them so that the significant amount of work done each time a path is searched for is not a drain on your hosting resources. The best way to do this hasn't been figured out yet, so see `dgd7.org/fast404` for the most up-to-date recommendations.

404 Navigation

Project: `navigation404`

This smallish module solves a simple but annoying problem that happens often in Drupal sites. 404 Navigation makes sure that Drupal keeps your site's navigation menus on "File not found" pages. 404 Navigation is not necessary if you set an alternate page for file not found, including if you use the Search 404 module.

Global Redirect

Project: `globalredirect`

Global redirect makes sure that when people visit a page on your site, they see your latest beautiful alias, not the Drupalish internal path or your second-to-last alias. Enable Global redirect, and it starts doing its work: There is a configuration page, but the defaults will work fine for you in almost all cases.

Note that Global redirect is not necessary to keep search engines from interpreting multiple paths as duplicate content (Drupal 7 adds a canonical link identifier), and it will not work with multilingual sites and some server setups.

Miscellany

If there weren't a few things that defied categorization, it wouldn't be Drupal: If you can imagine it, you can make a module out of it.

Bot

Project: `bot`

Bot module runs an IRC bot. For more about IRC, a central gathering place for Drupalistas real-time chat, and the Druplicon bot that is powered by this module, see Chapter 9.

OpenLayers

Project: openlayers

OpenLayers enables you to combine maps from various sources with data from your Drupal site to make amazing online maps.

The Beauty of It All

We could fill the rest of this book with useful modules and descriptions, but, as the world of modules is evolving, we recommend using Drupal.org and the multitudes of blogs out there. We've even built a special forum section on the companion web site to this book, listing many recommended modules and their descriptions, complete with links to many other web resources.

By now, hopefully you're realizing how easy it is to build powerful web sites with Drupal. Most of the heavy lifting has already been done for you, and there's a whole community out there that understands the value of sharing, meaning you will be able to achieve more, even if you're not a php developer. So the next time someone asks you if Drupal can do this, start searching and maybe you can say, "There's a module for that!"

■ **Tip** This chapter does not claim to list the best modules nor a module for every purpose, but given the title of the book and human nature there are going to be a *lot* of strong opinions about what was left out! Join the fun at dgd7.org/modules.

CHAPTER 5

■■■

Creating Community Web Sites with Organic Groups

by Ed Carlevale

Many aspects of Drupal will be recognized as revolutionary in the years to come, but the revolution, still largely undeveloped, has to do with the power buried within the Roles and Permissions settings. Most web platforms offer two or three roles, some variant on User, Member, Administrator, then call it a day. The exception is Facebook, of course, with its brilliant interface and variations on Friend categories. Facebook turns its Users into Administrators and its Visitors into Contributors, and that's a redivision of duties that both Marx and Wall Street would applaud.

Drupal can do the same and more... and it's the "and more" that causes the problems. Hundreds of options has a lot in common with none. Yet it is here that group-building in Drupal offers the most power, and revolutionary power at that, so we'll return to this idea after working through the basics involved in deploying the Organics Groups module.

The steps involved in getting Organic Groups up and running are, well, basic. Create a content type called Group and use it to create as many groups as you want on your site. Then create other content types such as Blog, Events, and Aggregator to create the content that you post into your groups. Then add Members and assign them appropriate roles—e.g., Group Manager, Administrator. One of the quirks of Organic Groups is that it works its magic mostly within the database. To show the relationships between Members and content and groups on your web site requires the help of other modules, primarily Views, which was introduced in Chapter 3, and Panels, which will be introduced here. Views selects and orders information from the database, and Panels allows you to position it on a page. Blocks and Regions can do the same, but they're dependent on your theme. Panels breaks you loose from your theme, so you can select and arrange content in more powerful and flexible ways.

The exercise in this chapter involves building a web site for senior citizens. As anyone who has tried to teach a parent the basics of a computer knows, the instructions have to be clear, the opportunities to ask questions abundant, and patience remains a virtue. The same is true for building a community-based web site. The essence of that effort is that you are trying to engage others in your group. Drupal's peculiar mix of power, simplicity, and quirkiness can present a barrier to newcomers. So an interface designed for simplicity is key, as are site resources such as how-to guides and videos.

The good news is that one of the best aspects of Drupal 7 has to do with improvements to Drupal's interface. What used to require ten clicks now requires one or two, and developing a web site no longer feels like commuting to work on a pogo stick.

Installing and Configuring Organic Groups

You'll start with a clean install of Drupal 7 and download and enable new contributed modules as you move through the chapter. The ones you need at the outset are Organic Groups and Views modules. Each of these in turn requires a helper module—the Entity module for Organic Groups and CTools for Views—so we'll download those as well. To install the modules, we'll use Drupal 7's new automated install feature (admin/modules/install) and add the currently recommended versions of each module:

- Organic Groups (drupal.org/project/og)

- Entity (drupal.org/project/entity)

- Views (drupal.org/project/views)

- CTools (drupal.org/project/ctools)

▨ **Note** Organic Groups for Drupal 7 was still in major development at the time of writing. This chapter will focus on the basic functionality that is likely to remain unchanged. The concluding section will touch on the functionality that is likely to evolve in future releases.

The Organic Groups project consists of seven modules (see Figure 5–1)—we'll be using all but the Migrate module in this chapter, so it is probably easiest to enable them all here at the outset.

ENABLED	NAME	VERSION	DESCRIPTION
☑	**Organic groups**	7.x-1.x-dev	API to allow associating content with groups. Requires: Entity API (disabled), List (enabled), Field (enabled), Field SQL storage (enabled), Options (enabled) Required by: Organic groups access control (disabled), Organic groups context (disabled), Organic groups UI (disabled), OG example (disabled), Organic groups field access (disabled), Organic groups migrate (disabled), Organic groups register (disabled)
☑	**Organic groups access control**	7.x-1.x-dev	Enable access control for private and public groups and group content. Requires: Organic groups (disabled), Entity API (disabled), List (enabled), Field (enabled), Field SQL storage (enabled), Options (enabled)
☑	**Organic groups context**	7.x-1.x-dev	Get a group from a viewed page. Requires: Organic groups (disabled), Entity API (disabled), List (enabled), Field (enabled), Field SQL storage (enabled), Options (enabled)
☑	**Organic groups field access**	7.x-1.x-dev	Provide field access based on group. Requires: Organic groups (disabled), Entity API (disabled), List (enabled), Field (enabled), Field SQL storage (enabled), Options (enabled)
☐	**Organic groups migrate**	7.x-1.x-dev	Migrate Organic groups data. Requires: Organic groups (disabled), Entity API (disabled), List (enabled), Field (enabled), Field SQL storage (enabled), Options (enabled), Chaos tools (disabled)
☑	**Organic groups register**	7.x-1.x-dev	Allow subscribing to groups during the user registration. Requires: Organic groups (disabled), Entity API (disabled), List (enabled), Field (enabled), Field SQL storage (enabled), Options (enabled)
☑	**Organic groups UI**	7.x-1.x-dev	Organic groups UI. Requires: Organic groups (disabled), Entity API (disabled), List (enabled), Field (enabled), Field SQL storage (enabled), Options (enabled) Required by: OG example (disabled)

Figure 5–1. The suite of Organic Groups modules

■ **Note** When you enable the OG access control module, you will be prompted to rebuild your permissions. Click yes so that the Drupal system can perform this update.

You also want to enable the OG Example module (see Figure 5–2). This is grouped in the Features section on the Modules page. In fact, you could enable the module through the Features UI (structure/features). But if you do it on the Modules page, we'll be prompted to enable the various helper modules that the example requires (see Figure 5–3).

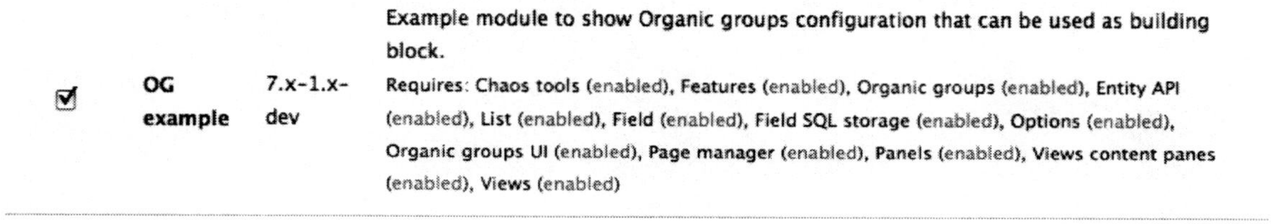

☑	**OG example**	7.x-1.x-dev	Example module to show Organic groups configuration that can be used as building block. Requires: Chaos tools (enabled), Features (enabled), Organic groups (enabled), Entity API (enabled), List (enabled), Field (enabled), Field SQL storage (enabled), Options (enabled), Organic groups UI (enabled), Page manager (enabled), Panels (enabled), Views content panes (enabled), Views (enabled)

Figure 5–2. OG Example module

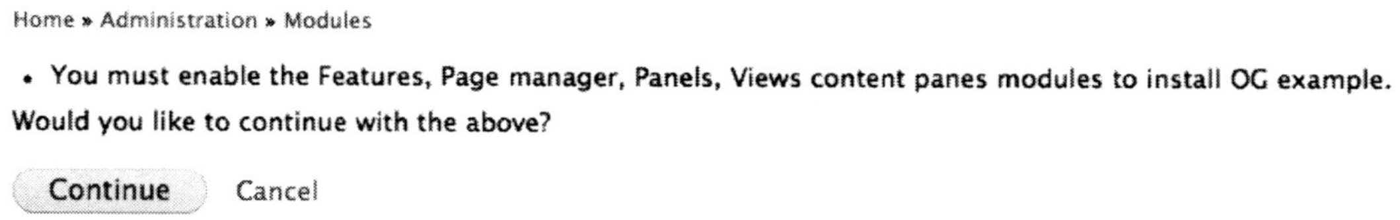

Home » Administration » Modules

• You must enable the Features, Page manager, Panels, Views content panes modules to install OG example. Would you like to continue with the above?

(Continue) Cancel

Figure 5–3. Helper modules required by the OG Example module

Group Content Types

By default, a Standard Drupal installation includes two content types: Article and Basic page. When the OG Example module is enabled, two more content types are added, Group and Post (see Figure 5–4).

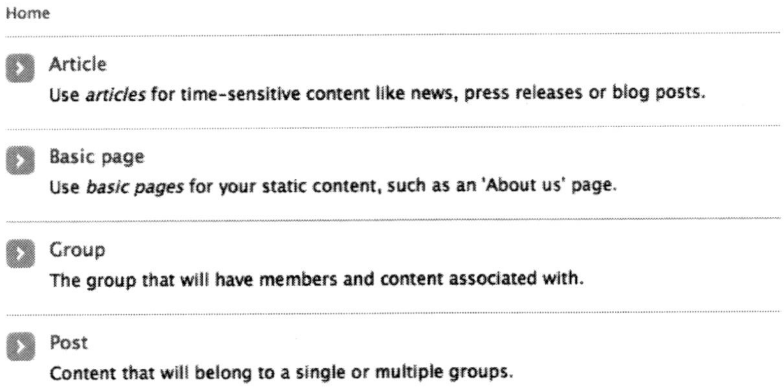

Home

▶ Article
Use *articles* for time-sensitive content like news, press releases or blog posts.

▶ Basic page
Use *basic pages* for your static content, such as an 'About us' page.

▶ Group
The group that will have members and content associated with.

▶ Post
Content that will belong to a single or multiple groups.

Figure 5–4. Two new content types, Group and Post, are added when the OG Example module is enabled.

We'll use the Group content type to create the groups for our site and the Post content type to create content that we'll post into our group. Let's open up the Group content type so that you can tweak some of its settings. Go to Structure ➤ Content types and select the Group content type (admin/structure/types/manage/group). Make the following changes:

- Change title field label to Group name.
- Description: "Create a new group."
- Publishing options: Uncheck 'Promoted to front page'
- Display settings: Uncheck this option.
- Comment settings: Closed.

The result should look close to Figure 5–5.

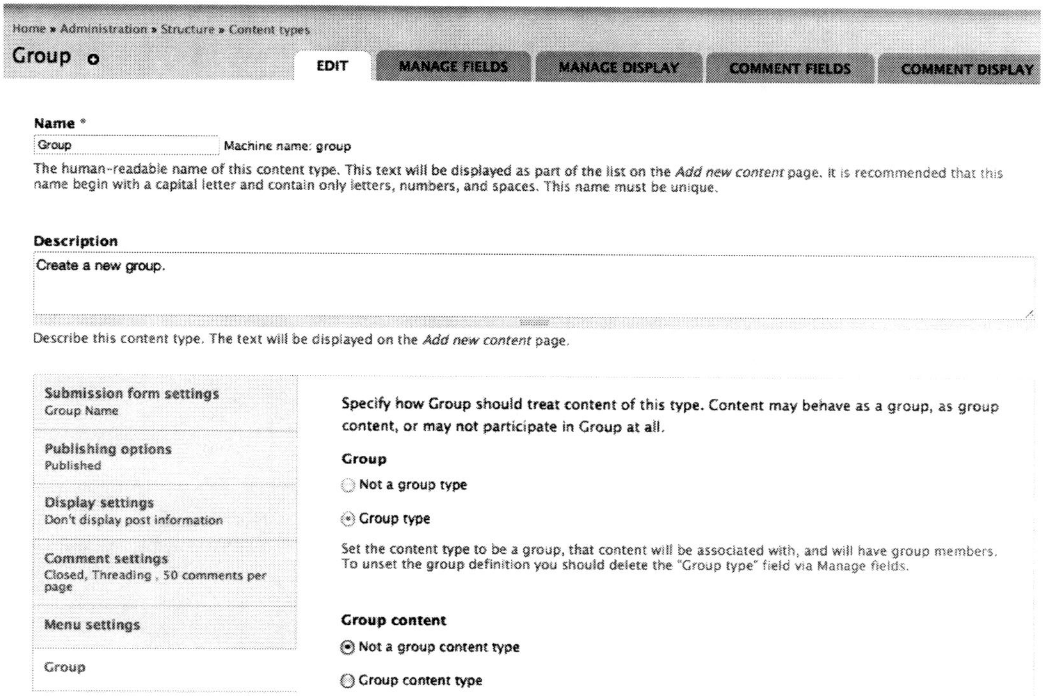

Figure 5–5. *Group content type*

Note the new vertical tab, Group, added to the form when the OG modules are enabled. This setting allows you to designate a content type as a group, group content, or neither. The nodes created with the Group content type should be groups, so the radio button is set to Group type. Save the modified form.

Next, open the Group content type again and this time, under the Manage Fields tab, change the body label from Body to Mission statement (see Figure 5–6). As any motivational speaker will tell you, defining a strong mission statement is the first step toward success in any endeavor. Even if you don't display the label for this field on our web site, knowing that this is what we're supposed to be doing here will help clarify our goals for each group added to the site. Click Edit and change the label from Body to Mission statement.

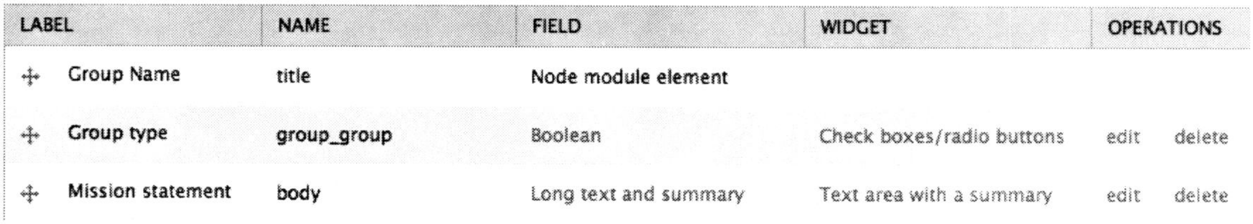

LABEL	NAME	FIELD	WIDGET	OPERATIONS	
⊹ Group Name	title	Node module element			
⊹ Group type	group_group	Boolean	Check boxes/radio buttons	edit	delete
⊹ Mission statement	body	Long text and summary	Text area with a summary	edit	delete

Figure 5–6. *Modifying field label for the Group content type*

Next, click the Manage Display tab to make one final adjustment. In order to allow visitors to the site to subscribe themselves to a group, you need to enable the Subscribe option. You do that by setting the format for the Group type to Group subscription (see Figure 5–7).

Then save the form.

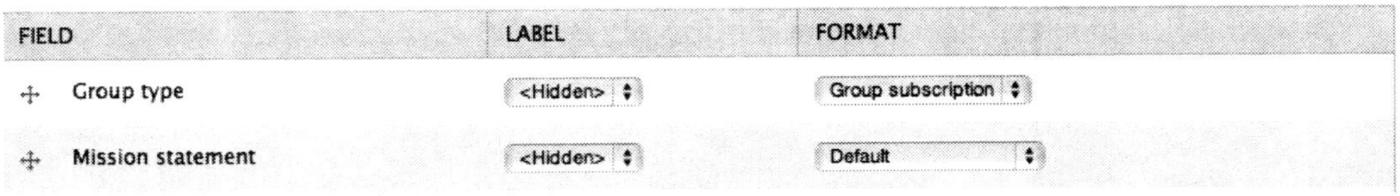

FIELD	LABEL	FORMAT
⊹ Group type	\<Hidden\> ⬦	Group subscription ⬦
⊹ Mission statement	\<Hidden\> ⬦	Default ⬦

Figure 5–7. The Manage Display tab. Subscriptions to groups are controlled by modifying the display of the group type field to be Group subscription. This places a Join link on every group page.

Creating Groups

Using the Group content type, we'll go ahead now and create some groups for the web site. Click Add content on the Shortcuts toolbar, which brings up the content types available on the site. Select Group (node/add/group). We'll add an iPad Users Group, fill in a Mission Statement, and save the form (see Figure 5–8).

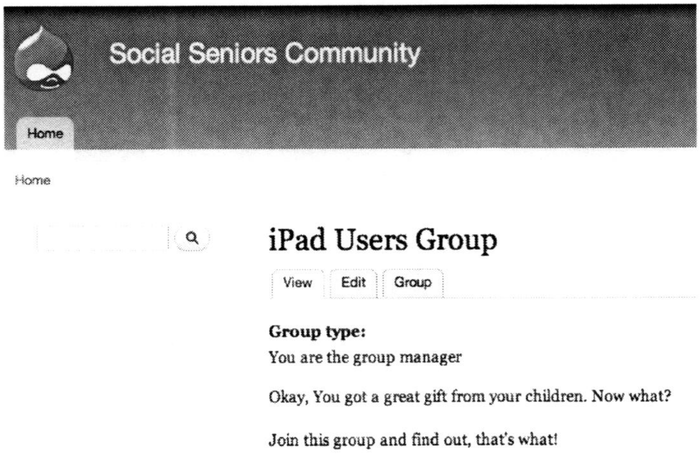

Figure 5–8. Home page for iPad Users Group

A new tab, Group, has been added to group home pages, visible to users with appropriate permissions, as indicated by the message "You are the group manager." Non-group members and administrators will see a link, "Request group membership." The Group tab allows the group manager to add Members and modify roles and permissions. We'll deal with those options later.

But basically, there's not a lot of design going on here, which is why help is needed from the Views and Panels modules.

Using Views with Organic Modules

Four views are included with the OG modules (see Figure 5–9), and they'll get you started.

VIEW NAME	DESCRIPTION	TAG	PATH	OPERATIONS
OG content None In code Type: Content	Show all content (nodes) of a group.	group		edit ▾
OG list Displays: *Feed, Page* In code Type: Content	Show active groups that are nodes	group	group-list, group-list/feed	edit ▾
OG members Display: *Block* In code Type: User	Newest group members.			edit ▾
User groups Display: *Page* In code Type: Content	Show groups of a user.	default	user-groups	edit ▾

Figure 5–9. *Four default views included with the OG modules*

OG List will be used as the groups landing page, so open that one and make some adjustments. Out of the box, the page view has a path (group-list) but no menu (see Figure 5–10), and you want to access this page from the Main menu. So add a menu item to the Main menu.

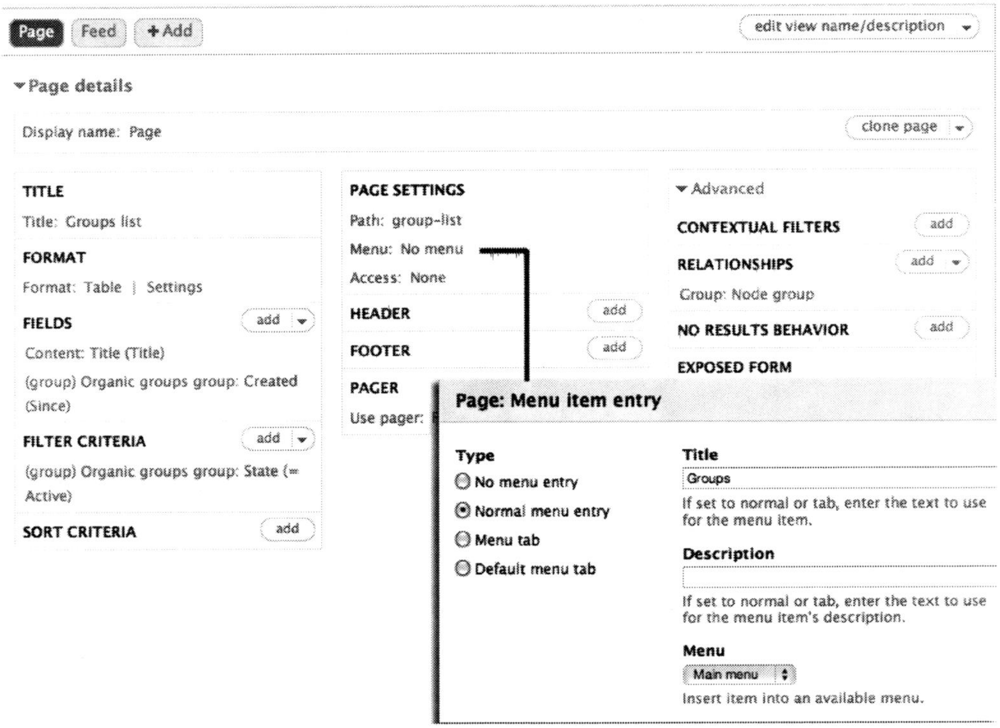

Figure 5–10. Group-list view

Click the menu link under the Page Settings and add a Menu item called Groups to the Main menu. Click and save the View. Now you have a Groups tab and a barebones Groups landing page (see Figure 5–11).

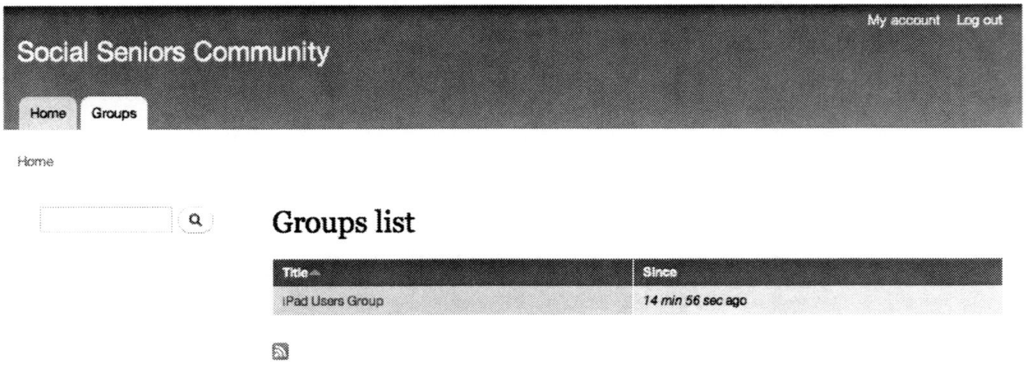

Figure 5–11. Groups landing page

The other views create blocks that show group members and group content, so you need to add some content and members to the group before those views can do anything.

Creating Group Content

In order to add some content to the groups, you need to create content types that can be used to create nodes that you post to the groups. You could simply use the Post content type that is included with the OG Example module. But instead, enable Drupal's own blog module (see Figure 5–12) by going to the Modules page (admin/modules).

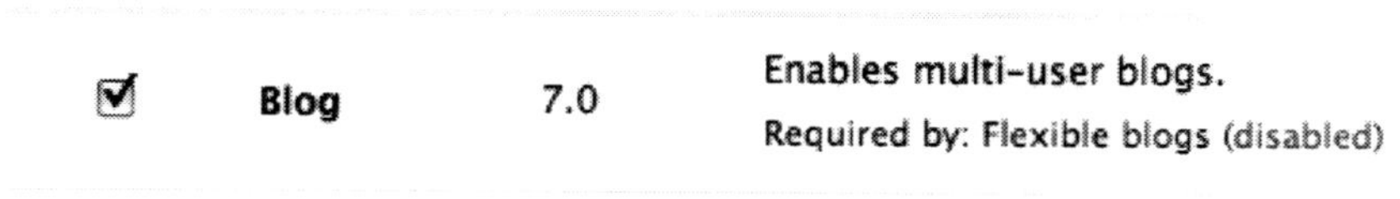

☑   **Blog**   7.0   **Enables multi-user blogs.**

Required by: Flexible blogs (disabled)

Figure 5–12. Enabling the Blog module

Once enabled, open the Blog content type (admin/structure/types/manage/blog) and designate this content type as a group content type (see Figure 5–13). This means that when you create content with this content type, you'll have the option to post that content into any of the groups on the site.

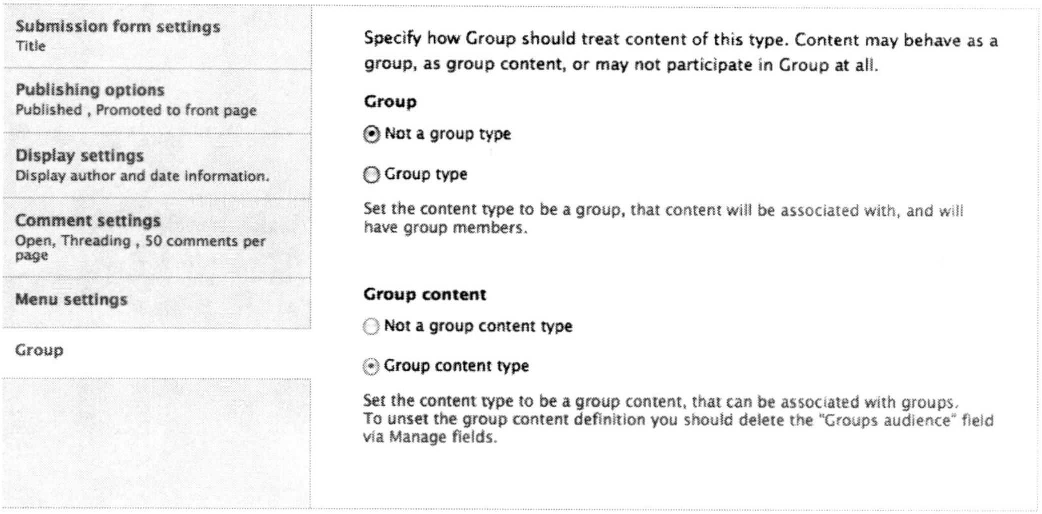

Submission form settings	Specify how Group should treat content of this type. Content may behave as a group, as group content, or may not participate in Group at all.
Title	
Publishing options	**Group**
Published , Promoted to front page	⦿ Not a group type
Display settings	○ Group type
Display author and date information.	Set the content type to be a group, that content will be associated with, and will have group members.
Comment settings	
Open, Threading , 50 comments per page	**Group content**
Menu settings	○ Not a group content type
	⦿ Group content type
Group	Set the content type to be a group content, that can be associated with groups. To unset the group content definition you should delete the "Groups audience" field via Manage fields.

Figure 5–13. Designating Blog entries as Group content

For some reason I imagine that Golfers are more likely to blog than iPad Beginners, so I created a new group (via node/add/group), the Tee-Birders Golfing Group, and created a blog entry (via node/add/blog) to post into the group (see Figure 5–14).

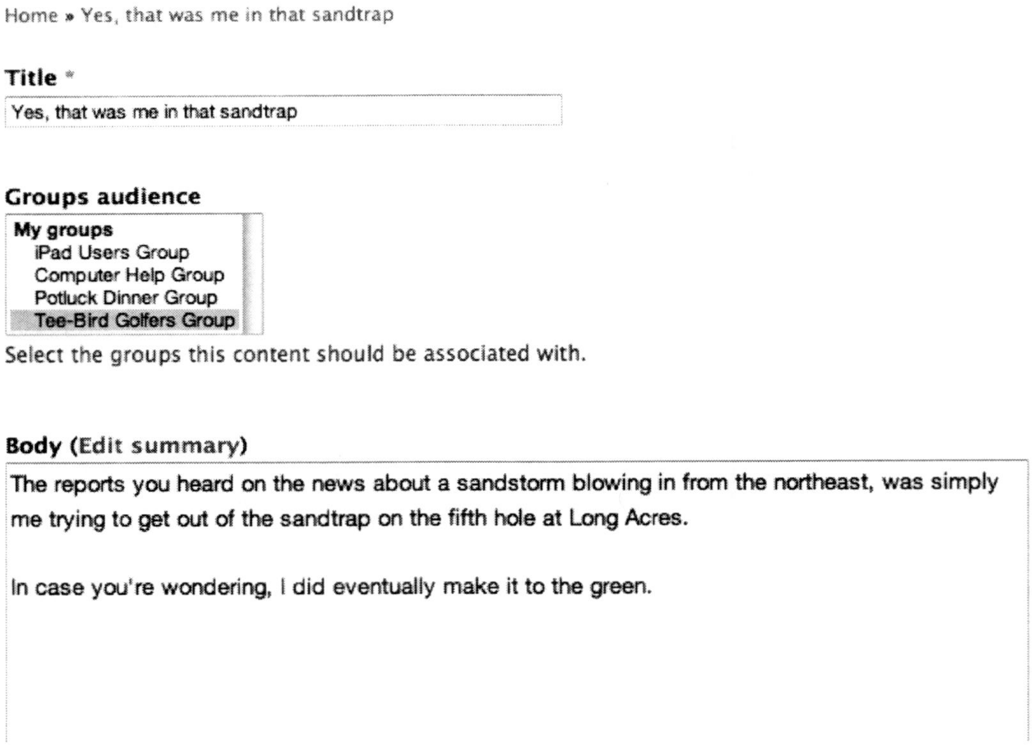

Home » Yes, that was me in that sandtrap

Title *

Yes, that was me in that sandtrap

Groups audience

My groups
iPad Users Group
Computer Help Group
Potluck Dinner Group
Tee-Bird Golfers Group

Select the groups this content should be associated with.

Body (Edit summary)

The reports you heard on the news about a sandstorm blowing in from the northeast, was simply me trying to get out of the sandtrap on the fifth hole at Long Acres.

In case you're wondering, I did eventually make it to the green.

Figure 5–14. When a content type has been designated as Group content, a Group audience pull-down menu is added to the node creation form, allowing users to post the content in one or more groups.

My account   Log out

Social Seniors Community

Home   Groups

Home

Yes, that was me in that sandtrap

View   Edit

Submitted by 007 on Thu, 04/28/2011 - 16:13
Groups audience:
Tee-Bird Golfers Group
The reports you heard on the news about a sandstorm blowing in from the northeast, was simply me trying to get out of the sandtrap on the fifth hole at Long Acres.

In case you're wondering, I did eventually make it to the green.

Figure 5–15. Blog post to the Tee-Birders Golfing Group

A group link is added to group content (see Figure 5–15). But both the group content and the group landing page (see Figure 5–16) still look a bit bare, so now you need to enable the Panels module to help with the layout.

Social Seniors Community

My account   Log out

Home   Groups

Home

🔍

The Tee-Birders Golfing Group

View   Edit   Group

You are the group manager

Golfing group for seniors who aren't afraid to go over a hundred. Outings, three times a week, on Tuesdays, Thursdays, and Sundays.

Figure 5–16. Home page for Tee-Birders Golfing Group

Getting Started with Panels

You already enabled Panels and its helper modules when you enabled the OG Example module. Now you need to enable the Panel itself. Go to Structure ➤ Pages (admin/structure/pages) and enable the Panel that controls the Node template (Figure 5–17).

TYPE	NAME	TITLE	PATH	STORAGE	OPERATIONS
System	node_edit	Node add/edit form	/node/%node/edit	In code	Edit Enable
System	**node_view**	**Node template**	**/node/%node**	**In code**	Edit Disable
System	term_view	Taxonomy term template	/taxonomy/term/%taxonomy_term	In code	Edit Enable
System	user_view	User profile template	/user/%user	In code	Edit Enable

Figure 5–17. Enabling the Panels example included in the OG modules

The enabled Panel immediately takes over the layout of your Group home page (see Figure 5–18). In addition to the Mission statement, the group home page is now showing three more group-related elements:

- Group content, displayed in teaser format
- Contextual links to add new content and post it into the current group
- A list of group members

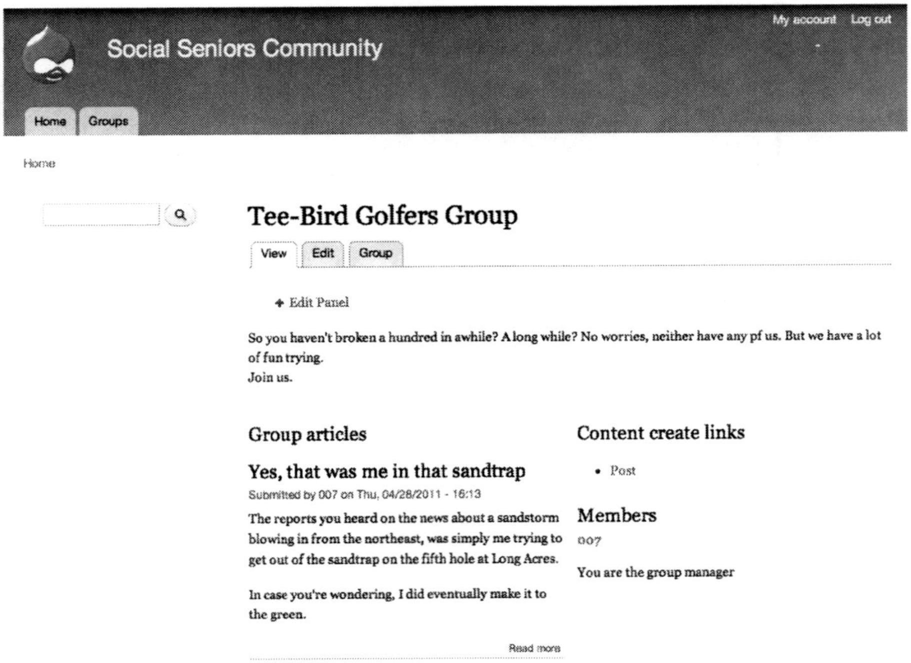

Figure 5–18. A group home page using the layout provided by Panels

If you click the Edit panel link, you're taken to the panel's administrative interface (see Figure 5–19). The vertical menu on the left provides links to different sections of the panels administrative interface.

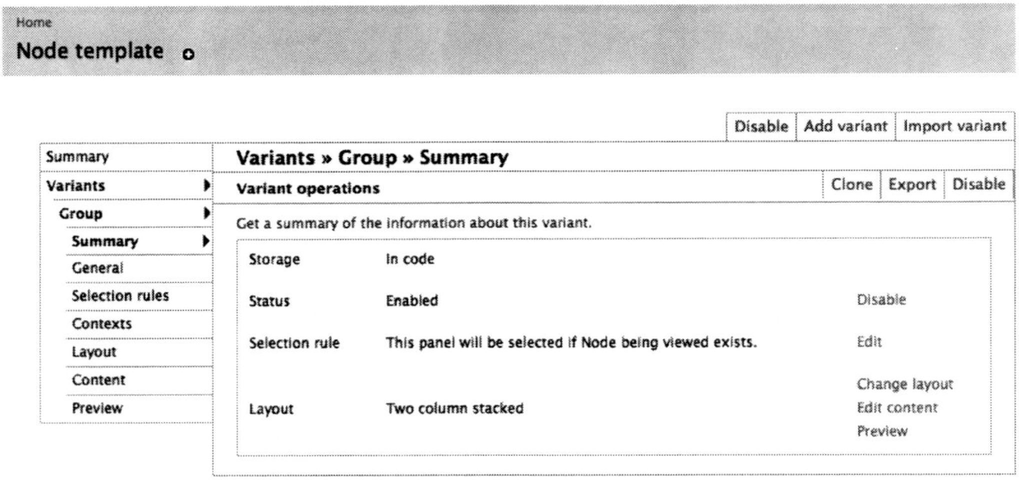

Figure 5–19. Summary of settings for OG Example panel

The key settings are Selection, which determines the conditions under which the panel becomes active, and Layout, which determines whether a 1, 2, or 3 column layout will be used, and what content will be displayed. The default settings for the OG Example panel include:

- **Selection**: The panel will become active for all Group nodes (see Figure 5–20).

- **Layout:** The 3-column layout is selected (see Figure 5–21).

- **Content:** (see Figure 5–22).

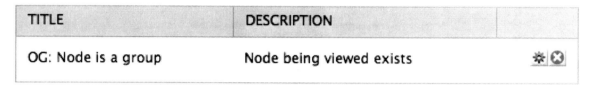

Figure 5–20. This shows the Selection settings. Panel will be used for all Group nodes.

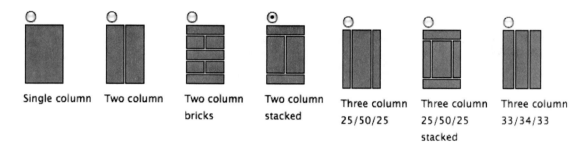

Figure 5–21. This shows the template layout. Two column stacked layout is selected.

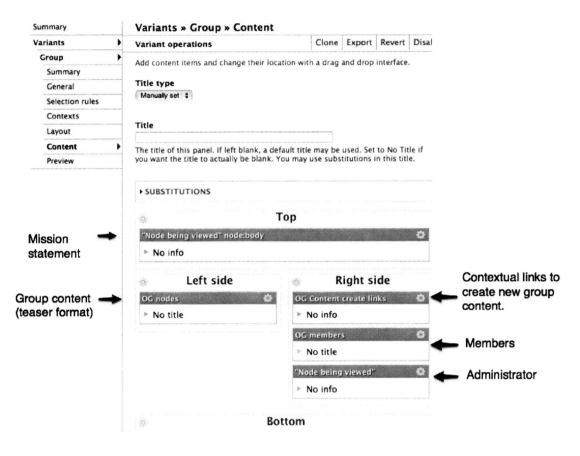

Figure 5–22. *Panel content*

A full discussion of Panels is beyond the scope of this chapter, but the head start provided by the OG Example panel serves as a useful introduction to this powerful module. More information, including videos and tutorials, is provided on the Panels 3 Documentation page (`drupal.org/node/496278`).

Members, Roles, and Permissions

For the most part, the functionality related to management of Group Members mirrors Drupal itself, except that the settings are available on a group-by-group basis. Once a new role is created (`admin/config/group/roles`, see Figure 5–23), then group-specific permissions can be set for that role (`admin/config/group/permissions`, see Figure 5–24).

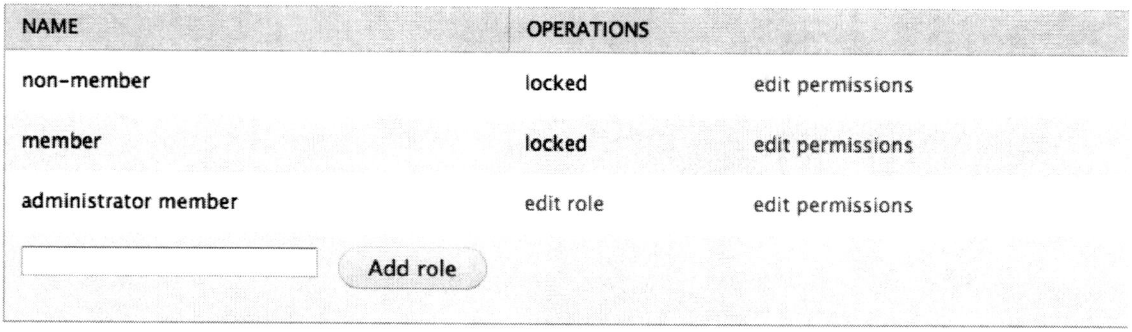

NAME	OPERATIONS	
non-member	locked	edit permissions
member	locked	edit permissions
administrator member	edit role	edit permissions

 Add role

Figure 5–23. Group-related Roles

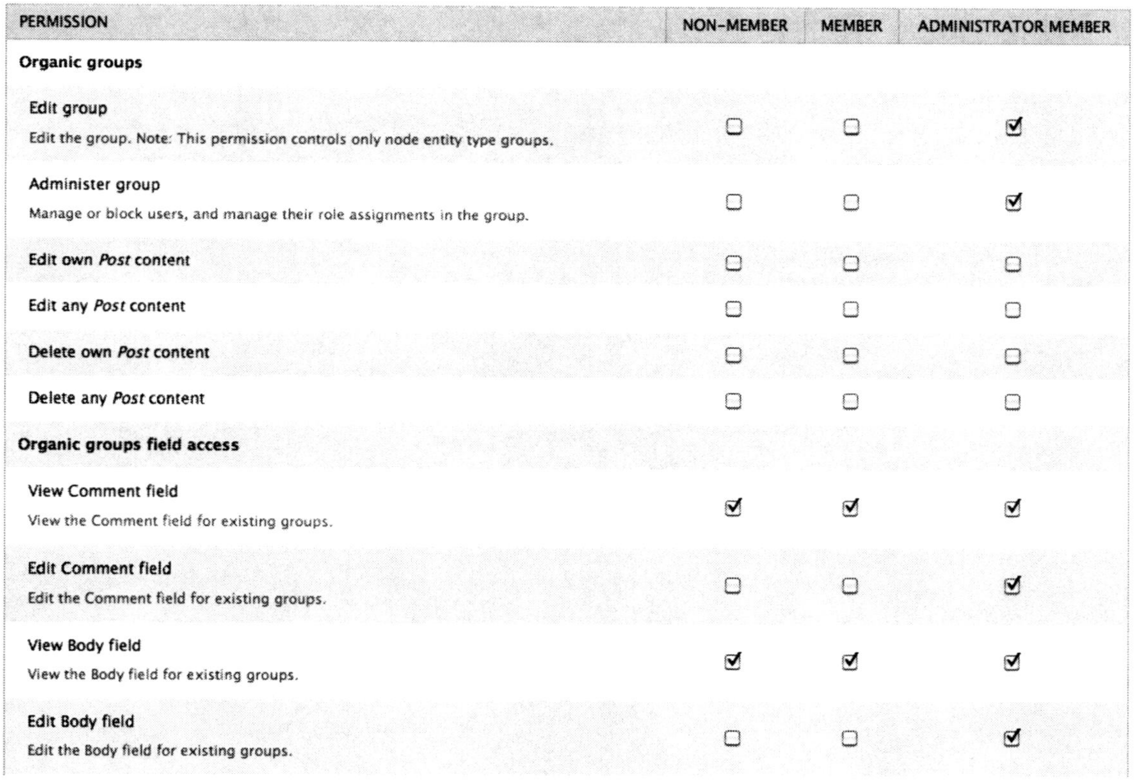

PERMISSION	NON-MEMBER	MEMBER	ADMINISTRATOR MEMBER
Organic groups			
Edit group Edit the group. Note: This permission controls only node entity type groups.	☐	☐	☑
Administer group Manage or block users, and manage their role assignments in the group.	☐	☐	☑
Edit own *Post* content	☐	☐	☐
Edit any *Post* content	☐	☐	☐
Delete own *Post* content	☐	☐	☐
Delete any *Post* content	☐	☐	☐
Organic groups field access			
View Comment field View the Comment field for existing groups.	☑	☑	☑
Edit Comment field Edit the Comment field for existing groups.	☐	☐	☑
View Body field View the Body field for existing groups.	☑	☑	☑
Edit Body field Edit the Body field for existing groups.	☐	☐	☑

Figure 5–24. Group-related Permissions

Still in active development, Organic Groups for Drupal 7 will continue to evolve, so following the module's issue queue is strongly recommended (drupal.org/project/og).

Summary

In this chapter I've covered the basics of building group-based web sites in Drupal 7, deploying the Organic Groups module on the backend to create Groups and Groups Content, and to establish relationships among groups, content, and users. Then I showed how to enable the Views and Panels modules to organize and position content on your pages. User experience is key to building successful member-driven web sites, and I touched on some of the key issues involved, including Roles and Permissions.

■ ■ ■

## CHAPTER 6

Security in Drupal

by Stéphane Corlosquet

"Security is a process, not a product. Products provide some protection, but the only way to effectively do business in an insecure world is to put processes in place that recognize the inherent insecurity in the products."

—Bruce Schneier

The Internet is rife with spammers and hackers threatening to deface or take down your site, ruin your brand, paralyze your community, or steal confidential data. Whether you are a site administrator, module developer, themer, system administrator, or user, you ought to bear security in mind when administering your site or writing code. You could put your own site or other people's sites at risk if you don't follow some simple rules and best practices. Fortunately, you are not alone in this situation, and the Drupal community has developed a solid process to help you avoid major headaches when dealing with security matters.

Setting Up a Secure Drupal Site

Let's start off with the good news: Drupal is configured to be secure out of the box! This is because it adopts fairly conservative settings by default. You will most likely want to change these settings to extend and tweak your site to your needs, and that's where you run the risk of opening some doors for unwanted visitors to damage your site. However, you're in good hands: with its improved user interface, Drupal 7 will often warn you when a setting could have an impact on security. Don't just rely on it, though; exercise common sense, and read on to know the common pitfalls of misconfigured Drupal sites.

Use Strong Passwords

This advice is true for any system using passwords for authentication: you must use a strong password (see Figure 6–1). Anyone who knows your password can log in and perform potentially damaging actions on the site. This is especially true for the user id 1 or any other account with elevated permissions.

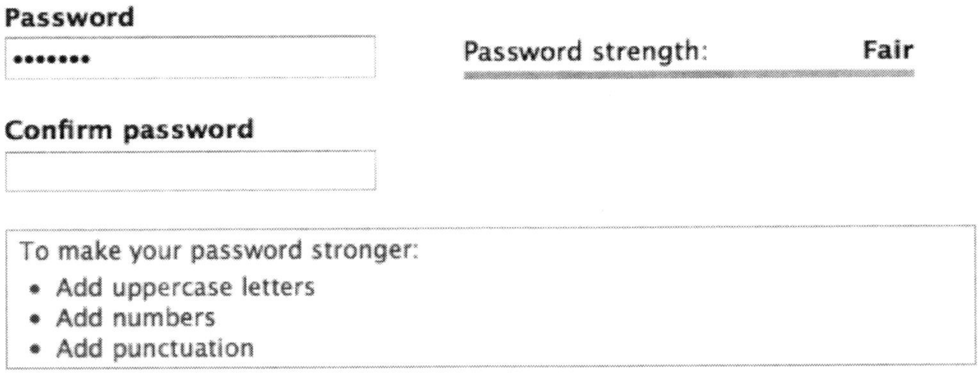

Password

| •••••• |

Password strength: **Fair**

Confirm password

| |

To make your password stronger:
- Add uppercase letters
- Add numbers
- Add punctuation

Figure 6–1. Use a strong password to keep your user account safe.

But what makes a password strong?

The article at `www.baekdal.com/tips/password-security-usability` demonstrates that having a three-common-word password is 10 times more secure than a regular one-word password. (Drupal passwords can contain spaces, by the way.)

It's also important to avoid sharing your password with anyone. Likewise, don't create accounts shared among users for site management and moderation purposes. If a group of users needs to perform similar actions on a site, create an account for each user and grant them the same role(s); this will make it easier to track who did what.

Your account will also be linked to an e-mail address. While you're at it, make sure you trust your e-mail provider and have a strong password there, too; if your e-mail account is compromised, your Drupal account password can be reset in a few seconds, defeating the effort you put into creating a strong password.

Reserve User 1 for Administration Purposes Only

The first user created during the installation process is given permission to do everything on the site, always. Therefore, it's considered best practice to reserve this user not as one's own personal account, but as a superuser or superadmin account. (Drupal requires account e-mail addresses to be unique, so if you have only one e-mail address, it's better to make the first account your own than to have an account with a broken e-mail address. Note, however, that some e-mail services allow you to use variant addresses: for instance, example@gmail.com will receive e-mail sent to example+site1@gmail.com, and Drupal will accept the latter as a separate address.)

▓ **Note** While sharing uid 1 password was sometimes necessary in Drupal 6 to run `update.php` without editing `settings.php`, it is no longer the case in Drupal 7 because the ability to run `update.php` is now role-based.

Be Cautious When Assigning Permissions

Each user can be given a set of roles, and each role includes a set of permissions. While some permissions are fairly benign, such as View published content, others can have dramatic consequences. Generally, permissions starting with "Administer" should only be granted to highly trusted users. Others, like Bypass content access control, can give the ability to view, edit, and delete any content: this can lead to information loss if granted to a careless user. Drupal 7 highlights these permissions with a warning indicating they should only be given to trusted users, as shown in Figure 6–2.

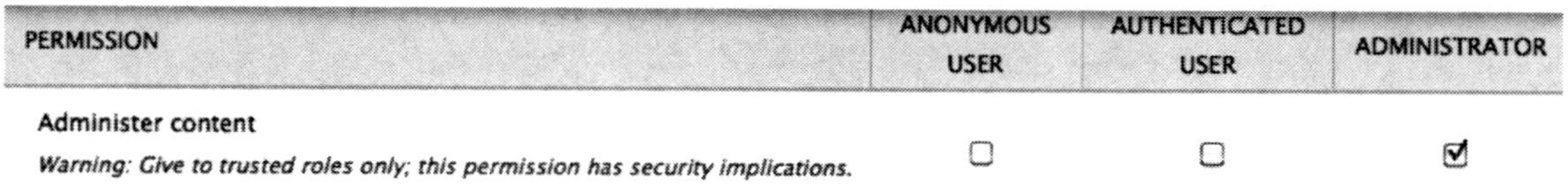

PERMISSION	ANONYMOUS USER	AUTHENTICATED USER	ADMINISTRATOR
Administer content *Warning: Give to trusted roles only; this permission has security implications.*	☐	☐	☑

Figure 6–2. Some permissions have security implications and should only be granted with care.

Beware that the Authenticated User role is given to any user able to log in to your site unless their account has been blocked. By default, Drupal is configured to require administrator approval for new accounts, but if you have changed this setting at admin/config/people/accounts to allow visitors to register accounts without approval, you should review what permissions the Authenticated User role has and ensure they are all safe. Failure to do so could lead to unintended consequences, like a flood of spam on existing nodes since the Post comments and Skip comment approval permissions are both granted to the Authenticated User by default.

Keep Text Formats Tight and Secure

User input is evil and should never be trusted. With the exception of a few places like the e-mail address where user data is validated on input, Drupal sanitizes user submitted data on output. This has the advantage of preserving user input data so that it can be escaped properly depending on which context it has to be rendered. See the excellent article by Steven Wittens on "Safe String Theory for the Web" at acko.net/blog/safe-string-theory-for-the-web for an in-depth explanation of this design choice. Thus, failure to escape any user submitted data can lead to the one of most common web application vulnerabilities: cross-site scripting (XSS)[1]. Drupal uses text formats when displaying a piece of content submitted by a user in a text field (e.g., the body of a node), for example. Each text format contains a set of filters that will escape content and make it safe for display in a given context. By default, the text formats Filtered HTML and Plain Text are safe, which is why they can be both used by anonymous users and authenticated users. Be cautious if you change the settings of these text formats; they can become unsafe if misconfigured. The Security Review module[2] makes it easy to check text format configurations.

---

[1] Wikipedia, "Cross-site scripting," http://en.wikipedia.org/wiki/Cross-site_scripting, 2011.

[2] http://drupal.org/project/security_review

Avoid Using the PHP Filter Module

Although it's handy to be able to write PHP code directly into your Drupal web interface without having to create a module, it's also very dangerous! All PHP code should live in the form of modules or themes. Writing PHP in Drupal's web interface is a bad idea for the following reasons:

- It's unfriendly to edit and debug (no syntax highlighting and no proper error reporting).

- It makes code reviews difficult and versioning impossible.

- A trusted user might inadvertently damage your site with malformed PHP code.

- If your site was to be compromised, a hacker could penetrate and damage your server using well-crafted PHP code. Keeping the PHP Filter module turned off (or even better, removing it entirely from the filesystem) could help contain such intrusion to the Drupal level only.

- In terms of performance, storing PHP code in the database will prevent any opcode caching mechanism from working on this piece of code

Note that some contributed modules might offer a functionality similar to that of the PHP Filter module; they will suffer from the same flaws noted previously. Also, be careful when using PHP snippets found on drupal.org or elsewhere: make sure you understand what they do and how they can affect your site. Many of these snippets have not been reviewed from a security standpoint and might expose your site to vulnerabilities. Code snippets are also generally less reliable than code found in a module.

Security Process

As a site administrator, security is not just something to consider when setting up your site. The Drupal core project maintainers can only go so far as to release software with no known security holes on the day of the release. However, that does not guarantee that there will never be any security problems in the future. Things evolve quickly on the Web, and new security vulnerabilities and techniques are discovered frequently. They might not be specific to Drupal and might impact any we6–based system.

The Drupal Security Team is a group of volunteers with an interest in keeping Drupal secure by helping both site administrators and developers understand how to avoid security issues on their site and in their code. The first goal of the Drupal Security Team is to help resolve security issues in Drupal core and contributed modules. All issues reported to the Security Team are first discussed privately with the reporter and the project maintainer until a solution is found and a fix is made to the code repository. The Security Team coordinates Security Advisories (SA) in release cycles, usually on Wednesdays. Each SA has a unique ID including its type and year. There are three types of advisories.

- Drupal Core security advisories (e.g., SA-CORE-2010-002) are the most important type of advisories as they concern every Drupal site. Updating is strongly recommended.

- Contributed projects security advisories (e.g., SA-CONTRI6–2010-015) are the highest volume type of advisories published by the Security Team. Each advisory refers to a particular contributed project (or sometimes several of them), and site maintainers should carefully evaluate whether any of the sites they maintain are affected and update them appropriately.

- Public service announcements (e.g., PSA-2011-001) aim at educating the community and contain general security-related information such as security policy changes, recent threats, or social engineering attacks that don't affect any particular module but are nonetheless relevant to site administrators and developers.

Security advisories and announcements are communicated publicly through the following channels:

- Drupal.org security announcements listings at drupal.org/security

- RSS feed for each listing:

    - Core: drupal.org/security/rss.xml

    - Contrib: drupal.org/security/contrib/rss.xml

    - Public service announcements: drupal.org/security/psa/rss.xml

- E-mail via the Security Announcements mailing list; all three types of announcements are included. You can subscribe in the "My newsletters" tab when editing your profile on drupal.org.

- Twitter: twitter.com/drupalsecurity

All security advisories include steps to resolve the security vulnerability at hand. In most cases, it will be a link to a security release for site administrators to update their site. In the rare case when project maintainers are not responsive or available to fix the issue, the Security Team might advise to turn off a particular module. PSAs include more general advice on security best practices.

Choosing Modules and Themes: How Secure Are Contributed Projects?

Each line of code in Drupal core goes through a rigorous peer review process before it is committed to the code base; even after being committed, this code is continuously audited by hundreds of contributors due to the nature of open source software. Several thousands of contributed projects are available for free on drupal.org. The Drupal community tries to find the right balance between keeping a low barrier of entry for new contributors and accepting code that is clean and secure, but a growing community and only a handful of volunteers monitoring this growth in terms of code quality makes the task very difficult. The consequence is a varied level of quality of code in the land of contributed projects. However, code found on Drupal.org is more likely to be of higher quality than code found elsewhere outside Drupal.org, since the community tends to scrutinize code on Drupal.org more than anywhere else.

As a site administrator looking at installing a module or a theme on your site, you are responsible for evaluating the quality of a project from a security standpoint. Neither the Drupal community nor the project maintainer can be held responsible for any damage done to your site, whether the damage is done during the installation or later on due to a security bug.

Assessing the value of a project is a somewhat subjective task. Each of the criteria in the next sections will not give you the complete picture when taken on its own; hopefully, by combining them you will be able to make an educated decision when choosing contributed projects for your site.

Project Home Page

A project home page includes a lot of useful information to assess the health of a project. These elements will help you in your evaluation. An example of contributed project page is drupal.org/project/views. Figures 6–3 and 6–4 contrast an abandoned project with a well-maintained project.

- *How reputable are the maintainers?* You can find the list of maintainers as well as their activity on the right-hand side of the project page. If you don't know a maintainer, look up his profile on drupal.org to see his participation in the community; he might maintain other modules that you might know or use. It's a good sign if the project in question has a reputable maintainer with fairly recent activity.

- *How active is the module development?* Is the module abandoned or seeking a new maintainer? This information is available on the project description page (see the example of an abandoned and obsolete module in Figure 6–3). Modules falling under these categories are not likely to receive any attention in the future and might contain security vulnerabilities. Although the Drupal Security Team will generally add a warning message on the description of projects that are abandoned and known to contain a security vulnerability, the absence of such message does not mean that an abandoned project is safe to use.

- *Popularity:* Check how many sites report using a project in the "Project Information" section shown in Figure 6–4. The more sites using a project, the more likely it has been reviewed and is trusted.

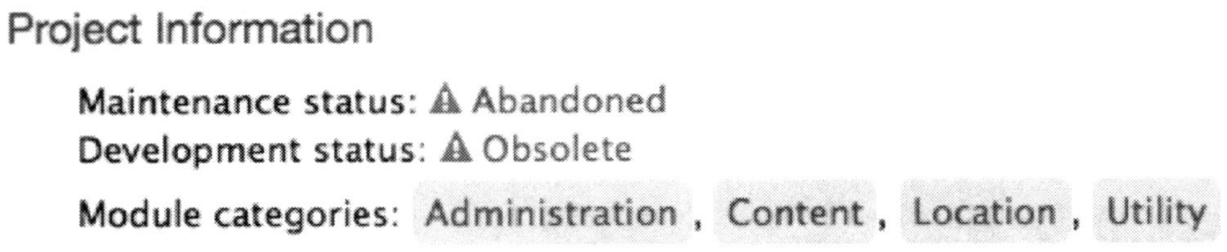

Project Information

Maintenance status: ⚠ Abandoned
Development status: ⚠ Obsolete

Module categories: Administration , Content , Location , Utility

Figure 6–3. The Project Information section of an abandoned project

Project Information

Maintenance status: Actively maintained
Development status: Under active development

Module categories: Content Display , Views

Reported installs: 271070 sites currently report using this module.
Last modified: January 18, 2011

Figure 6–4. The Project Information section of a well maintained project

- *Releases:* Avoid using development releases on production web sites. Pick a stable release if one is available for your Drupal version. Unstable, alpha, beta, or release candidate releases can contain security bugs, which are generally discussed publicly. If you make the decision to use such modules on your site, be sure to know what these bugs are and take the right measures to protect your site.

- *Does the project have known security bugs?* The issues block located on the right hand side of each project's home page shows some statistics on the issues and bug reports on the project (see Figure 6–5). Click on the number of open issues to view an exhaustive list of issues, as shown in Figure 6–6.

- *Check the issue queue to see what pending outstanding issues have been reported so far, and whether some of them have an impact on security.* Looking at the last updated column in the issue queue will give you a sense of how active a project development is (see Figure 6–6). Seeing issues with the status of Fixed is a strong indication of a well-maintained project. You might want to use the filters at the top of the list of issue to narrow down your search on a particular version of the module or on a particular type of issue, such as bug reports.

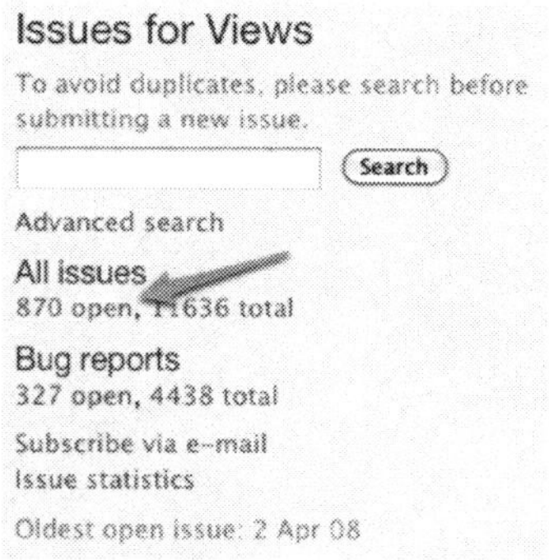

Issues for Views

To avoid duplicates, please search before submitting a new issue.

[   ] (Search)

Advanced search

All issues
870 open, 11636 total

Bug reports
327 open, 4438 total

Subscribe via e-mail
Issue statistics

Oldest open issue: 2 Apr 08

Figure 6–5. Click on the number of open issues to browse the issue queue

Summary	Status	Priority	Category	Version	Component	Replies	Last updated
exceedingly minor css syntax cleanup: extra semi-colon new	active	minor	bug reports	6.x–2.12	Miscellaneous	0	10 min 3 sec
Conditional Fields new	needs work	normal	feature requests	6.x–2.12	User interface	0	25 min 28 sec
Panel Field not working after upgrading Views 2.11 to the version of 2.12 new	active	normal	bug reports	6.x–2.12	Miscellaneous	2 2 new	41 min 47 sec
Better contextual link integration for blocks updated	active	normal	tasks	7.x–3.x–dev	User interface	4 1 new	1 hour 5 min
Problem making a seach in a view in a multilingual site new	active	normal	bug reports	6.x–2.8	Miscellaneous	1 1 new	1 hour 14 min

Figure 6–6. An active issue queue is the sign of a healthy module.

Security Code Reviews

What do you do if you've found a contributed project that matches your needs but you have doubts about its level of security? It might not have reached a stable release yet, or your department might require that any code be security reviewed prior to being used.

If you're a developer, the Coder[3] and the Secure Code Review[4] modules will be of great help at identifying pieces of code that do not comply with Drupal security standards. While these modules are quite good for a first pass at a security review, they can't guaranty that a module is secure, and they don't replace the eyes of a security expert.

If you would rather hire skilled consultants to do code reviews, several Drupal shops specialize in this area of expertise, most notably Drupal Scout (`drupalscout.com`) operated by Greg Knaddison and Ben Jeavons, both members of the Drupal Security Team.

Keep Your Code Base Current

Configuring Drupal properly is only the first step towards a secure Drupal site. Dynamic web applications like Drupal can't be left unmaintained on the Internet where new threats and exploits are discovered every day. It is a mistake to think that once you've built a site and pushed it to production, you can just leave it there and not worry about it. Just as you monitor your server performance or maintain your software stack, you will want to run the latest version of Drupal core and its contributed modules. Fortunately, the Drupal community has a very good infrastructure that helps site administrators know when they need to upgrade a given module.

Drupal core ships with the Update Manager module that will warn you when new security releases are available for your installed modules. You will see a red warning message in the administrative area encouraging you to update your modules. An e-mail notification is also configured by default. You can view the list of available updates at Admin ➤ Report ➤ Available updates (`admin/reports/updates`). Any security update will appear with a red background, as depicted in Figure 6–7.

---

[3] http://drupal.org/project/coder

[4] http://drupal.org/project/secure_code_review

Figure 6–7. *The Update Manager module shows available updates for installed modules and themes. It is strongly recommended that you update any module with a security update.*

Updating a module or theme is very easy with the tools available for Drupal. The core Update Manager module lets you to update any module via the web interface. You can also use Drush[5] or update the code manually by downloading the tarball from the project download links or via git. See Chapter 7 for more detailed information on how to update Drupal.

Writing Secure Code

Drupal offers great APIs for module and theme developers. As long as these APIs are used properly, writing secure code for Drupal is easy, even with little knowledge about security. There are, however, some basic rules to keep in mind. The first rule is to **use Drupal's APIs as much as possible and use them properly,** even if they do not seem to make sense; there is generally a reason for using them. Here are a couple of examples:

---

[5] Drupal, "Drush," http://drupal.org/project/drush, 2011.

- *When displaying a link*, it might be more intuitive to build the HTML string by concatenating the <a> and href elements, but this can introduce a cross-site scripting vulnerability if the input is not trusted. By using the link function l()[6], you save yourself some headaches since Drupal will take care of the proper escaping for you and will also filter for malicious protocols.

- *Form API*: You should never use data straight from the $_POST variable, but instead rely on the Form API validation and submit functions which prevent cross-site request forgeries[7].

- *Database API*: When writing SQL queries, it's tempting to use PHP variables directly in the SQL query. That can create a SQL injection[8], and it can be avoided with proper use of the Database API[9].

There are many more examples where the Drupal framework prevents security vulnerabilities. Here is a list of helpful resources for developers willing to learn more about security in Drupal:

- Publications:

  - Greg Knaddison, member of the Drupal Security Team, wrote the only book to provide a deep dive into security in Drupal: *Cracking Drupal: A Drop in the Bucket* (Wiley, 2009), `crackingdrupal.com`

  - *The Drupal Security Report* was written by Ben Jeavons and Greg Knaddison. This is a useful document for decision makers and people interested in understanding how Drupal has been handling security in the past. `drupalsecurityreport.org`

- Online resources:

  - Get familiar with Drupal's APIs at `api.drupal.org` where all Drupal functions and APIs are documented. Notes on security are included where relevant.

  - The *Develop for Drupal* handbook gives a higher perspective on how to leverage Drupal APIs at `drupal.org/documentation/develop`

  - The "Writing Secure Code" section of the *Develop for Drupal* handbook gives a series of examples with code snippets on how to use Drupal APIs in a secure manner at `drupal.org/writing-secure-code`

- Security blogs:

  - Heine Deelstra, Drupal Security Team lead, blogs about security in Drupal at `heine.familiedeelstra.com`

  - Greg Knaddison and Ben Jeavons write about security at `crackingdrupal.com/blog`

---

[6] Drupal, "common.inc," `http://api.drupal.org/api/function/l/7`, 2011.

[7] Wikipedia, "Cross-site request forgery," `http://en.wikipedia.org/wiki/Cross-site_request_forgery`, 2011

[8] Wikipedia, "SQL injection," `http://en.wikipedia.org/wiki/SQL_injection`, 2011

[9] Drupal, "Database API," `http://drupal.org/developing/api/database`, 2011.

- DrupalScout is building a Knowledge Base on security at
  `drupalscout.com/knowledge-base`

Dealing with Security Issues

The Drupal Security Team has a process for dealing with security issues found in the contributed projects hosted on `drupal.org`. As a developer, if you come across some piece of code that appears to contain a security vulnerability, you should know how to deal with such a situation.

You Found an Issue in Drupal core or a Contributed Project

The process is detailed in this section; note, however, that this process could change in the future, so check at `drupal.org/security-advisory-policy` for current information on the Drupal security policy.

First, make sure the code is hosted on `drupal.org`; the Drupal Security Team does not deal with code hosted elsewhere. Secondly, if the questionable code has not been released as part of a stable release (in other words, it's in a development snapshot, alpha, beta, or release candidate release), you are encouraged to discuss this issue publicly in the issue queue. If the code has been released as part of a stable release (e.g., 7.x-1.2), you should not discuss this vulnerability publicly, unless it requires one of these permissions to be exploited:

- Administer filters
- Administer users
- Administer permissions
- Administer content types
- Administer site configuration
- Administer views

Any user with any of the above permissions can already do a lot of damage to a site, so it is expected that only trusted users would be granted these permissions, and therefore it is fine to discuss these types of issues publicly. Please check `drupal.org/security-advisory-policy` for the current policy, which might change over time.

In any other case, don't discuss your findings publicly, but instead contact the Security Team by e-mail at `security@drupal.org` and explain in detail how to reproduce the issue and what version of Drupal core, modules, and themes you are using. The Security Team will investigate the issue and work with the project maintainer to create a fix, patch the code, create a release, and announce the release. You will be credited in any announcement made about this issue. At the time of this writing, issues should be reported to the Security Team by e-mail; however, this is likely to change in the future, so please check `drupal.org/node/101494` for current information on how to report an issue to the Security Team. Make sure to subscribe to the security mailing list to be notified of any change (see the beginning of the "Security Process" section).

Fixing a Security Issue in Your Project

If you find a vulnerability in one of your projects, contact the Security Team before doing anything about it. If the Security Team receives a report about a vulnerability in one of your projects, you will be contacted privately by e-mail. As a project maintainer, it is your duty to collaborate with the Security Team in order to keep the vulnerability secret until a fix is made available to the public. You will be invited to send a patch fixing the issue so that the Security Team can review it and possibly suggest a better way to solve the issue. When the patch is ready and has been approved by the Security Team, a date will be chosen for the patch to be committed and a security release to be published. You will be asked to help draft a Security Advisory (SA) for your project to be sent out on the day of the security release. Security releases usually happen on Wednesdays. You will be invited to commit the patch and push the fix to the drupal.org repository as soon as 24 hours before the agreed release date. Then you will be able to create a new release for all the branches that were affected by the vulnerability and tag it "Security update," as shown in Figure 6–8. Send the links of the releases to the Security Team so they can add them to the SA. The releases will remain unpublished until the Security Team publishes them and sends the SA at the same time.

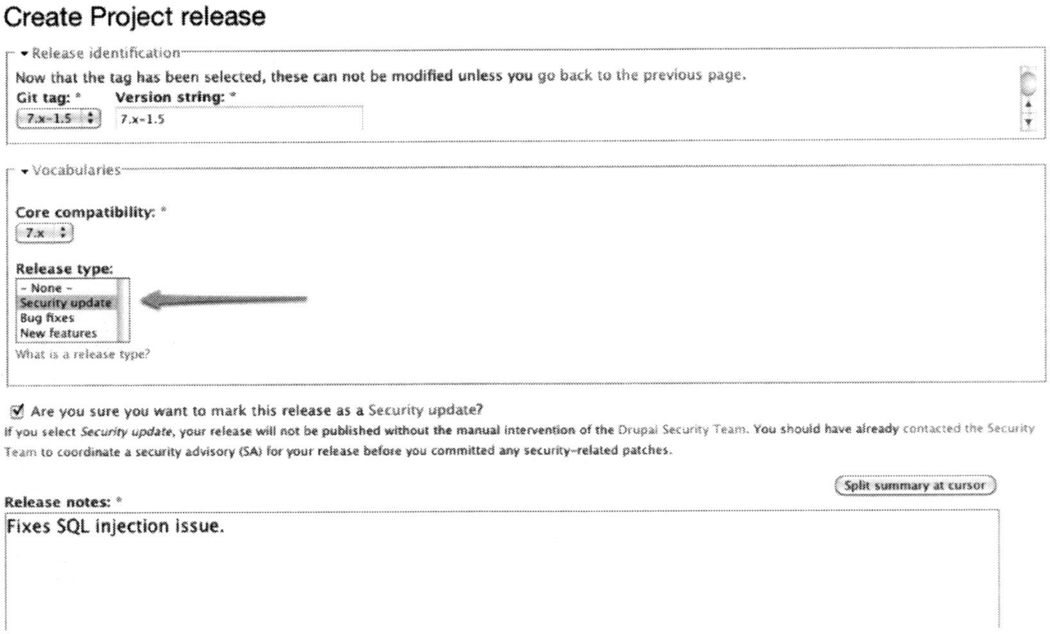

Figure 6–8. *The Create Project release form on drupal.org. Make sure to tag your release as "Security update" if it includes security fixes.You should already have contacted the Security Team at this point!*

Any issue reported publicly in the issue queue of your module can be fixed at your convenience as long as it is not present in a stable release. The new release can be marked as "Security update," as depicted on Figure 6–8, although you will need to contact the Security Team to get it published.

Summary

In this chapter you have learned the security processes to keep your Drupal site secure and how to leverage the infrastructure that the Drupal community has put in place to help site maintainers keep their code base secure. You've also learned that the APIs supplied by Drupal make it easy for module developers and themers to write secure code. Give it a try!

## CHAPTER 7

Updating Drupal

by Benjamin Melançon

"Another flaw in the human character is that everybody wants to build and nobody wants to do maintenance."

—Kurt Vonnegut, Jr.

Updating Drupal 7 means staying *within* Drupal 7. This is known as a minor version update. In Drupal core, the version numbers for a minor update such as the second and third updates to the Drupal 7 release look like 7.2 to 7.3. In contributed modules, version numbers for minor updates such as the eleventh and twelfth updates to the second version of a module for Drupal 7 look like 7.x-2.11 to 7.x-2.12. (Drupal version numbers do not have leading zeros, which can be confusing. Remember that the order is 7.1, 7.2, ... 7.8, 7.9, 7.10, 7.11.)

There is a very large difference between a minor version update and a major version upgrade. A major version upgrade such as Drupal 6 to Drupal 7 will require replacing all your modules with versions compatible with Drupal 7 core; your custom theme and custom code will need changes; and it will take a lot of work to get a complex site working well again. You don't have to worry about any of that in this chapter. When updating Drupal core from 7-point-something to 7-point-something-higher, nothing is supposed to break in the API. All the modules and the theme should continue to work, and nothing should need to be reconfigured. If you need to upgrade a Drupal 6 site to Drupal 7, Appendix A will get you started with that.

Why Update

Keeping Drupal core current, then, is easy. It's also very important. Primarily, it's critical for the security of your web site. Secondarily, bug fixes and other improvements will make it into the current release.

Drupal's security record, by the way, is excellent. As a rule, security vulnerabilities in Drupal are uncovered first by the security team (`drupal.org/security-team`) or other friendly Drupalistas—not fixed after they have been exploited by hostile parties. Once a security vulnerability has been identified and a release of Drupal made, however, it's easy for anyone with ill intentions to read the security advisory and take advantage of that vulnerability. This is why you must keep your site current.

It's worth noting that most of the security vulnerabilities fixed during the course of a Drupal release are unlikely to matter for a well-configured site; to exploit the vulnerability, you must give less-trusted users generous permissions. Chapter 6 covered Drupal's excellent security and other ways to make your web site secure.

■ **Tip** In addition to being easy and important, updating Drupal core is too rarely done. Show the world you know what you're doing and keep all your sites running on the latest security release of Drupal 7.

New versions of Drupal 7 core, the minor version updates, will be released for as long as the community supports Drupal 7 (which, officially, is until Drupal 9 comes out).

■ **Note** On `drupal.org`, only the current and previous releases are supported with bug fixes and security updates, but nothing stops someone in the community from offering more. Openflows Community Technology Lab has done just that: `http://openflows.com/drupal/security` has applicable security updates backported to older major versions of Drupal.

This chapter covers three approaches to updating core between minor version updates. First, you'll look at the manual update process described in Drupal core itself. Next, you'll look at the Drush command to update Drupal core. Last and perhaps least, you'll look at my preferred method of creating a `diff` via a shell script and applying it as a patch. This latter approach works best if you have a known modification to Drupal core that you wish to preserve (which does not necessarily mean you have hacked core; the `.htaccess` file, for instance, can legitimately be changed). The first approach is necessary if there are known or unknown modifications to core you need to be sure are removed and is, in general, the surest approach.

The following preparation steps apply no matter which approach you take to update Drupal core.

Preparation

Whenever you touch Drupal's code, there's the potential for something to go wrong. So even a minor-point–release update, as described here, should be:

- Tested offline and/or on a development server first.
- Scheduled to go live at a time when your site will be less heavily used.

■ **Tip** Take a look at your analytics to determine what time of day and time of week your site is least-visited. Get this insight with server-based statistic gathering and reporting such as AWStats (`awstats.sourceforge.net`) or use a service such as Google Analytics (which has a Drupal module for easier integration; see `drupal.org/project/google_analytics`).

Check the release announcements. If anything unusual is needed during the update process, it will be noted here. Are you updating through more than one minor release (for instance 7.0 to 7.3) at once?

Check *all* the release announcements. Go to drupal.org's Download & Extend ➤ Drupal core (drupal.org/project/drupal) and click on the "View all releases" link at the bottom (or go directly to drupal.org/node/3060/release).

■ **Tip** If an update is not a security release, you can safely choose not to update. The release notes and the available updates page at Administration ➤ Reports ➤ Available updates (admin/reports/updates) will tell you what is not a security update. This helps you avoid risking that changes not crucial to your site's security will affect the way your site operates. Drupal core is moving to a model where you can choose to apply only security releases. For contributed modules, skipping a non-security release will delay the need to update, but you'll have to do all updates when there is a security release.

Make sure everything in your version control is committed. If using Git, type git status while within a directory in your Drupal project. (And if you're working with others, make sure you git pull first.)

Back up your database immediately before the update, in addition to your regular nightly (or more frequent) backups. You can use a web graphical interface such as the one provided by phpMyAdmin or you can use Drush or the following command line:

```
mysqldump -u exampleuser -p examplepass example > example_backup.sql
```

■ **Note** Another option is the Backup and Migrate module at drupal.org/project/backup_migrate.

Manual Update

This approach follows the UPGRADE.txt recommendations included in every copy of Drupal core. It is, then, the officially recommended way of updating Drupal from one minor version to another. It's not the easiest way, and so for something that must be as regular and automatic as you can make it, not the best way. But it's important to know it as a failsafe way.

■ **Tip** The manual update process is not the most convenient, but it is the most robust. If you have a Drupal site and you don't know where it's been or the state of its code, this is the way to go.

All Drupalistas soon learn the rule **Don't hack core**. In general, you're not supposed to touch anything in your Drupal installation outside the **sites** directory. There are two files in Drupal core, however, that you won't be chastised for changing: **.htaccess** and **robots.txt**. You might not need to touch them, but modifying them is not considered hacking core. As these files live outside the sites folder (which you will preserve in its entirety, described shortly), they require special attention to preserve any changes you have made.

The final preparatory step for the manual update is to download the latest release of your version of Drupal via the following code (note that this code is for version 7.1; you will want the latest release):

```
cd ~/code
wget http://ftp.drupal.org/files/projects/drupal-7.1.tar.gz
tar -xzf drupal-7.1.tar.gz
```

■ **Hint** The latest release of Drupal is featured on the front page of Drupal.org at `drupal.org/home`.

Follow the Steps in UPGRADE.txt

These instructions follow the steps from UPGRADE.txt but I've changed them a little bit in certain cases, mostly because some of the work has been covered in the "Preparation" section.

1. Log in as a user with the permission "Administer software updates" (the first user created, also referred to as user 1, always works).

2. Go to Administration ➤ Configuration ➤ Development ➤ Maintenance mode (`admin/config/development/maintenance`). Checkmark the "Put site into maintenance mode" checkbox and press Save configuration at the bottom of the page. (You can put something personal and reassuring for your visitors as the "Maintenance mode message" since they will see that instead of your site.)

3. Copy all changed files out of your codebase. This should be the entire **sites** directory and possibly **.htaccess** and **robots.txt**. If you don't know if anything's changed in these files, copy them out; you can use the `diff` command to compare files later. Also, move out any other files you added or have changed outside of **sites**. I recommend copying everything. Then delete the entire codebase, and copy *only* the `sites` directory back in and optionally other changed files such as `.htaccess` and `robots.txt`.

    This is accomplished in the command line steps below by moving and then copying the desired files back in. In this example, the Drupal directory was **example/web**.

```
mv example/web examplewebtmp/
mkdir -p example/web
cp -pr examplewebtmp/sites/ example/web/
cp examplewebtmp/.htaccess example/web/
cp examplewebtmp/robots.txt example/web/
```

4. Copy the latest Drupal release into the codebase directory that is empty except for **sites** and other modified files. Don't overwrite anything in the **sites** directory.

    This command line step copies a new Drupal into its `install` directory around `sites` and other files you have put there (files are not overwritten):

```
cp -R drupal-7.1/* drupal-7.1/.htaccess example/web/
rm example/web/sites/default/default.settings.php
```

5. Re-apply any modifications to files such as .htaccess and robots.txt.

If the release notes indicate changes to settings.php, make these changes. If you've made changes to .htaccess and robots.txt, reapply them. If you're not sure what exactly has changed in any of these, use a comparison tool such as diff. Compare the new version of .htaccess to your old one that you moved back in; do the same for robots.txt. For settings.php, compare it with the new default.settings.php that's replaced your old default.settings.php.

You can use a graphical diff tool or these command lines to see changes between files:

```
diff -up example/websites/default/settings.php/
example/web/sites/default/default.settings.php

diff -up example/web/robots.txt drupal-7.1/robots.txt

diff -up example/web/.htaccess example/web/.htaccess
```

The first diff shows what has changed in the new recommendations for a settings.php file. The second and third diffs compare the new, core robots.txt and .htaccess files with your old, possibly modified versions. Evaluate what you see with + signs in front as things you may want to add or add back, and things with - signs in front as things you may want to remove— but most of these will be changes you yourself made.

▨ **Tip** If you don't know if core in the Drupal version you're dealing with has been hacked, and you know precisely what version of Drupal you are using, you can download a pure copy of it and diff between it and your copy to see what modifications, if any, have been made. See the "Diff Update" section for the commands.

---

6. Go to update.php, such as http://example.localhost/update.php on a local test site and http://example.com/update.php on a live site. Although this is not necessary if the point release (or releases) you are updating have not had any database changes, this information is not yet noted specially in the release notes. Go to update.php to check. Click continue; if it doesn't have to be run, it will tell you "No pending updates", as shown in Figure 7–1. If there are updates, run them.

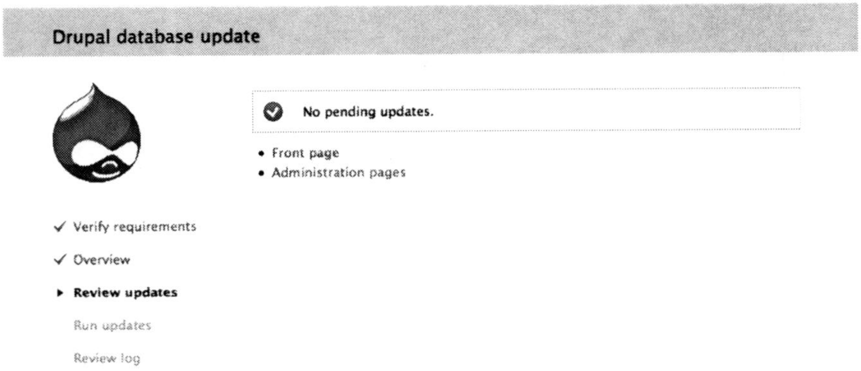

Drupal database update

✓ No pending updates.

- Front page
- Administration pages

✓ Verify requirements

✓ Overview

▶ **Review updates**

Run updates

Review log

Figure 7–1. No pending updates

7. Go to Administration ➤ Reports ➤ Status report (`admin/reports/status`) to see if Drupal has problems with anything. Visit all your key pages to test key functionality and also check Drupal's watchdog log (at `admin/reports/dblog` if using Database logging module or in your operating system's syslog if using the Syslog module).

8. This step (Step 8 from `UPGRADE.txt`) only applies if you couldn't log in and had to set `$update_free_access` to `TRUE` in `settings.php`; you probably won't have needed to do this.

9. Go back to Administration ➤ Configuration ➤ Development ➤ Maintenance mode (`admin/config/development/maintenance`). Uncheck "Put site into maintenance mode" and Save configuration.

Now Do It Live

If all goes well, commit your code changes, perform steps 1 and 2 on your production site (or better, first on a staging site), deploy the updated code to your live site, and repeat steps 6 through 10 on your live site. See Chapter 13 for deployment recommendations.

Drush Update

With Drush, the process is a lot easier. It first takes care of all contributed modules that need updating. The command for this is `drush pm-update`, or simply `drush up`.

Remember to always try this first on a copy of your site and database before trying it on a production site. Instead of the previous command, which combines code and database updates, you can use `drush upc` to update only code, which you can commit to your repository. With `drush updatedb` (for updating the database) tested successfully on a test site, you can deploy the code to a live site and immediately run `drush updated` there (or visit `update.php`).

Contributed module updates are discussed in a later section. To update only Drupal core with Drush, use the command `drush up drupal`.

As for most things Drush, see Chapter 26 for more complete coverage.

Diff Update

Now we come to the method that I personally use. It can be made a Drush script, I believe, but I haven't managed to do it yet, to my shame. So I leave it as an exercise for the reader!

Listing 7–1 is a script for downloading a fresh copy of the latest Drupal version *and* your current Drupal version, and applying the difference. This means that in many cases, none of your changes to Drupal will conflict with the changes that are simply re-applied over your existing code.

■ **Tip** You should still do a `diff` of your current site or use the module Hacked (`drupal.org/project/hacked`) to see what has changed on your site. Preserving hacks is not recommended without knowing exactly what they are and why they are necessary.

It should also be possible to generate this `diff` directly from `git.drupal.org`, which would be a more efficient and refined improvement than this script, but the same in effect. This improvement might be made to this script, which is another reason to download it from `dgd7.org/update`; don't try to type it in! The commands for using the script are following Listing 7–1.

Listing 7–1. Shell Script for Automating the Update of Drupal Core Using Old-to-New Version Difference

```
#!/bin/sh -e

if [ $# -lt 2 ]; then
    echo "Usage: $0 oldversion newversion (optional) directory (e.g. 5.5 5.6 dir)"
    exit 1
fi

# If you change TMP, you will have to change the -p3 option in the patch command!
TMP=/tmp
# Change the version below to what you have
VER_OLD=$1
VER_NEW=$2

if [ $# -gt 2 ]; then
  DRUPAL_DIR=$3
else
  DRUPAL_DIR=`pwd`
fi

# Change that to the directory where Drupal is installed
PATCH_FILE=$TMP/drupal-$VER_OLD-to-$VER_NEW.patch
cd $TMP

# Download your current version
wget http://ftp.drupal.org/files/projects/drupal-$VER_OLD.tar.gz

# Extract it
tar -xzf drupal-$VER_OLD.tar.gz
```

```
# Now, download the new version
wget http://ftp.drupal.org/files/projects/drupal-$VER_NEW.tar.gz
# And extract that too
tar -xzf drupal-$VER_NEW.tar.gz

# Now create the diff file
# echo "This command, or the next one, breaks the script so you'll just have to do the rest
yourself."
echo `diff -Naur $TMP/drupal-$VER_OLD $TMP/drupal-$VER_NEW > $PATCH_FILE`

# Now change to the directory where your Drupal installation is
cd $DRUPAL_DIR

# we'll want to see the output for this
set -vx

# Check that the patch would apply without errors
patch -p3 --dry-run < $PATCH_FILE

# turn off verbose output
set +vx
# turning it back off (naturally, on is a minus sign and off is a plus sign)

echo "If the above dry run patch applied without errors, you can press Y to apply the patch
for real."
echo "If there are errors, or you just aren't ready to apply the patch, press N to abort."
read YN
if ( test -z "$YN" )
then
  echo -e "Please enter either \"Y\" or \"N\" " ;
  eval "$0" "$@" ;
  exit ;
fi
# at this point 'YN' contains Y, y, N, or n
if ( test "$YN" = "N" -o "$YN" = "n" )
then
  exit ;
fi

set -vx
# Assuming there are no error from the previous step, you can
# now apply the patch for real

patch -p3 < $PATCH_FILE
```

To use the script, you need to provide the path to your Drupal site. I apologize for naming this script "upgrade," although it could possibly be used to start major version upgrades, too.

```
/path/to/version-upgrade-diff.sh 7.0 7.1
```

If the script is in your home directory scripts, and the site at hand is 'dgd7' in the code directory within your home directory, with the Drupal installation in web, this command will work when run from anywhere:

```
~/scripts/version-upgrade-diff.sh 7.0 7.1 ~/code/dgd7/web
```

Contributed Modules

It is also vital to keep your contributed modules current. The report page provided by update.module, Administration Reports ➤ Available updates (admin/reports/updates), will give you a list of ones that need updating. Modules are really updated not by the module, but by the project; some projects contain more than one module, and the update page indicates the modules contained in each project with the "Includes" line, as shown in Figure 7–2.

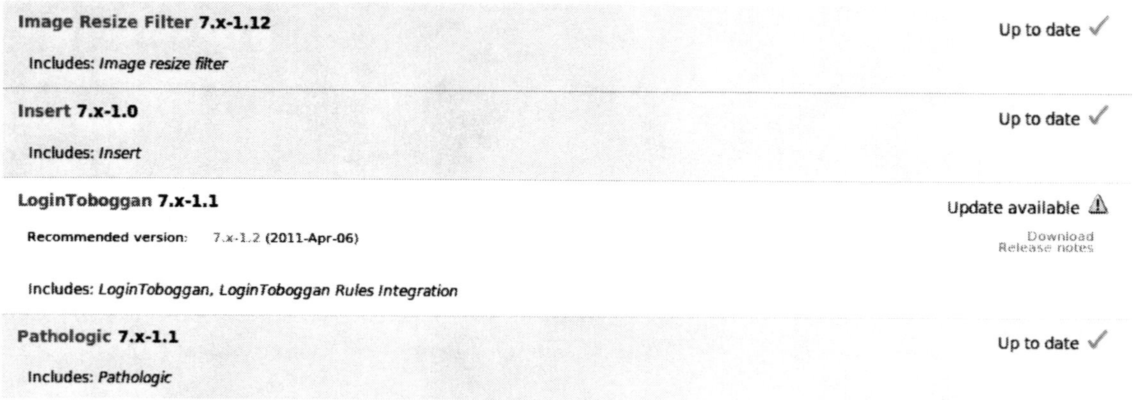

Image Resize Filter 7.x-1.12	Up to date ✓
Includes: *Image resize filter*	
Insert 7.x-1.0	Up to date ✓
Includes: *Insert*	
LoginToboggan 7.x-1.1	Update available ⚠
Recommended version: 7.x-1.2 (2011-Apr-06)	Download Release notes
Includes: *LoginToboggan, LoginToboggan Rules Integration*	
Pathologic 7.x-1.1	Up to date ✓
Includes: *Pathologic*	

Figure 7–2. Contributed modules shown in the available updates report, with links for download and release notes of modules with updates available

The manual way to update contributed modules is to delete each out-of-date module and untar a freshly downloaded latest stable release one in its place. Then go to update.php for your site, such as http://example.localhost/update.php for your test and http://example.com/update.php for your live site. There's really no reason to recommend the manual download approach over the automated options, which are described below.

No matter how you update, first test the results thoroughly on a *copy* of your production site. As with core, always perform contributed module updates first on a local or test copy of your live site. Much more than with core, you have to check carefully that contributed modules have not changed their behavior when you update them. See Chapter 13 on deployment or Chapter 26 on Drush for automated approaches to bringing copies of your live database onto a local or testing environment.

■ **Caution** A module with a major version upgrade means the module maintainer is telling you that there are major changes. There may not even be a clean upgrade path. If you need to go from 2.x to 3.x for a contributed module, for instance, read the release notes carefully and test thoroughly. Expect that you may need to adjust the configuration of the module. The release notes are linked directly from the module's page on drupal.org, right next to the download links for different versions of a module.

There are two easy, automated way to do the updates. (Neither of them, however, get you out of testing the update before applying it to your live site.)

Drupal's Automated Module Installer

To automatically update the modules that need updating, visit Administration ➤ Reports ➤ Available updates ➤ Update (`admin/reports/updates/update`) on your Drupal site. Checkmark the modules you want to update and press the "Download these updates" button at the bottom of the form, as shown in Figure 7–3.

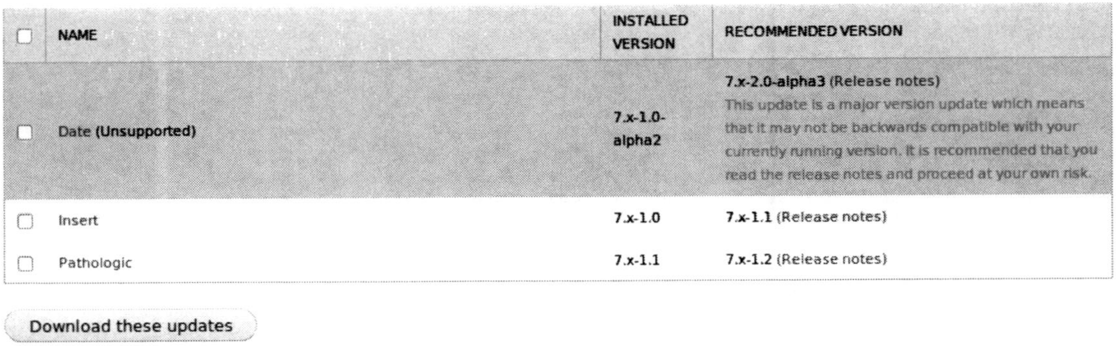

	NAME	INSTALLED VERSION	RECOMMENDED VERSION
☐	Date (Unsupported)	7.x-1.0-alpha2	**7.x-2.0-alpha3** (Release notes) This update is a major version update which means that it may not be backwards compatible with your currently running version. It is recommended that you read the release notes and proceed at your own risk.
☐	Insert	7.x-1.0	**7.x-1.1** (Release notes)
☐	Pathologic	7.x-1.1	**7.x-1.2** (Release notes)

Download these updates

Figure 7–3. *The automated update page with an example of a no-longer-supported branch of a module and two modules needing simple minor-point updates*

It's best to apply one or a limited number of related updates at a time, especially any with a major version upgrade warning, so that you can more easily identify the cause of any changes you notice in testing. After Drupal automatically places the code for you, don't forget to run the database updates (after you try, Drupal will tell you if none are necessary, as shown in Figure 7–1).

You can run Drupal's automated contributed module updater locally, and then commit the code to bring the changes to live. This allows you to continue to follow best practice of not changing code on the live server.

If Drupal's update manager module can't run the upgrade for you through the user interface (if it asks you for FTP information you are not sure you have), don't bother trying to make it work. That time would be much better invested making Drush work instead.

Updating Modules with Drush

The Drush commands for updating contributed modules are, as mentioned, exactly the same as for Drupal core. By default, Drush will try to do all at once: first all the contributed modules, and then Drupal core.

For installing Drush, see Chapter 2. For much more about Drush and the great things you can do with it, see Chapter 26.

At the time of this writing, there is a (long) issue (`drupal.org/node/1002658`) about making sure Drush checks for *all* available updates and somehow not take a minute or two looking them up (the behavior in the current patch). Drush will also sometimes claim that it failed in an update (because of an unavailable release or some other minor failure) and was unable to recover from its backups. In fact, Drush almost certainly succeeded in updating the code; you don't have to manually roll anything back and can instead run database updates, commit the code, and deploy and run database updates on stage and production sites. To avoid some of these issues, and as a matter of best practice for testing and identifying what caused (or solved) a problem, you can have Drush update one or a few projects at a time, such as updating only CTools and Views project code with `drush upc ctools views`.

To choose modules to update when using Drush, look at Administration ➤ Reports ➤ Available updates (`admin/reports/updates`) to decide what you want to update and hover over the download link to see what project name you should give Drush. (You can also run `drush up` to see what updates are available and cancel (n) before updating anything, so as to pick and choose one to run at a time.) From the previous example, the LoginToboggan module's download link is `ftp.drupal.org/files/projects/logintoboggan-7.x-1.2.tar.gz` which means the command you want to use to download it is

```
drush up logintoboggan
```

Not all projects have nearly identical human-facing and system-facing names. Image resize filter is `image_resize_filter` and Meta tags is `nodewords`. If there are several possible versions to update to (such as when there's a new major version upgrade available), you can include the version you want, also in the form seen in the download link, like so:

```
drush up logintoboggan-7.x-1.2
```

Summary

This chapter has served at least two purposes. It showed you several ways to keep your Drupal sites current, so just pick one and do it! It also showed that there are always multiple ways to do things within and around Drupal.

▓ **Tip** In addition to there being multiple ways of performing updates, there are (or will be) better ways than those discussed here. Check out `dgd7.org/update` for new information relevant to this chapter, and stay up on the latest ideas and practices for all things Drupal by getting involved in the community (see Chapter 9).

## CHAPTER 8

Extending Your Site

by Dan Hakimzadeh and Benjamin Melançon

"There is a great satisfaction in building good tools for other people to use."

—Freeman Dyson

Chapter 1 got you started with a Drupal site, Chapter 3 taught you the power of the Views module, and Chapter 4 gave you a sense of the variety of modules available for you to use. This chapter shows how far you can go building a site with fields and views, optional core modules, and chosen contributed modules—in short, configuring your site to within an inch of its life.

Showcasing Authors with Profile Pages

A multi-author book site cannot ignore its authors, so you might as well put them on the site. Authors who are also users of the site should be able to edit their own profiles, but it should *not* be assumed that authors will create and manage their own profile pages. You can give the Author role permission to create content of the type Profile and trust the authors not to create more than one profile piece for themselves.

■ **Tip** While building profiles on top of user accounts may seem to be the obvious step to take, it isn't always the best idea. Consider an About page featuring a board of directors; while all of them ought to be able to log in and edit their own profiles, how many actually will? Even for a Drupal-savvy crew like the authors of this book, not all can be expected to join a web site on demand. Besides, does creating user accounts with usernames, e-mails, and passwords really make sense when the immediate need is full names, a portrait photograph, and a short third-person biography? Profiles of the kind made possible by Profile2 module (`drupal.org/project/profile2`) make the most sense for people certain to be active users. When profiles or biographies are meant primarily as content, rather than a byproduct of a user account, consider the lighter weight option of a simple content type.

Let's get started:

1. As shown in Chapter 1, create a new content type by going to *Administration* ➤ *Structure* ➤ *Content types, + Add content type* (admin/structure/types/add).

2. Give it the name Author profile, and then click edit next to the automatically created machine name to bring it up in its own form field, enabling you to change author_profile to profile.

3. In the vertical tabs at the bottom of this form, under Submission form settings, change Title field label from Title to Name (see Figure 8–1).

Figure 8–1. *Submission form settings for the Author content type: Title field label changed to Name*

4. Next in the vertical tabs, in Publishing options checkmark *Create new revision* to add it to the default options.

5. In Display settings uncheck *Display author and date information* (see Figure 8–2).

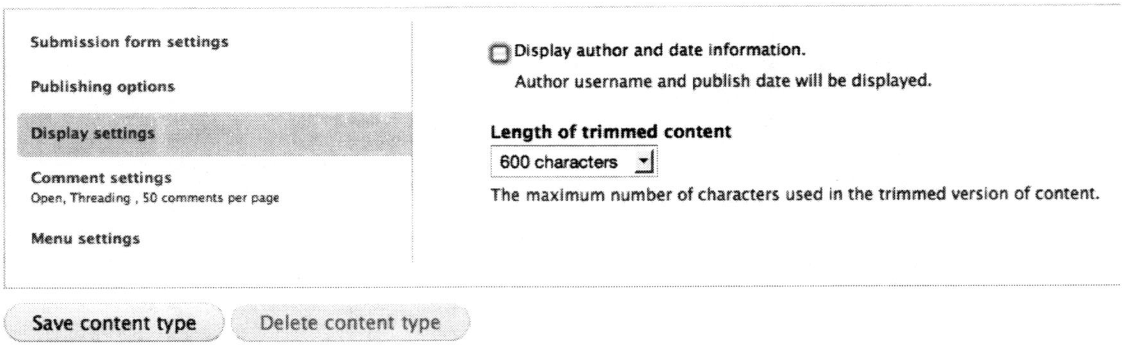

Figure 8–2. *Configuring a content type to not display posting (author and date) information*

6. Finally, change Comment settings to *Hidden* (don't show any comments) or *Closed* (don't allow any additional comments to be left). Both have the same effect if set before any comments are left.

The author profile content type should certainly have fields, so submit the form with Save and add fields. Now you are on the Manage fields tab of content type.

Giving Authors a Headshot Image

Good image handling capability is included in Drupal 7 core. Under Add new field specify:

- A label of **Headshot**
- A machine name of **headshot**
- A field type of **Image**

▓ **Tip** Avoid the temptation to reuse an existing image field for a use like this. Drupal 7 does heroic work at allowing most field settings to be specific to the content type or other bundle the field is attached to, but both the option for a default image and the number of images that can be uploaded are set globally per field, not per instance of a field on a content type or other bundle. Even if an existing field matches the global settings we need for a new field now, there is no good way to separate a shared field should a global setting need to change later. Unless you are certain their field-level settings will not diverge, *and* you know you need to use the same field from different sources in a listing, you should create a new field rather than reuse an existing field.

The default settings can remain the same on the instance (Author profile settings), though a subdirectory of "headshot" can keep the files directory more organized. Also, under Field settings, leave the Number of values set to 1. Providing a default image, which is optional, will help provide visual consistency until all authors provide headshots for their profiles.

Linking from Profiles to Web Sites

No web site is an island, and definitivedrupal.org should certainly link to the personal and professional sites of its authors (although sometimes the parable of the cobbler's children having no shoes applies to the web sites of Drupal developers). If we break the rules and judge a module by its name, Link module (`drupal.org/project/link`) is the front-runner. Indeed, Link has been the go-to module to provide a special field for URLs since the days of Drupal 4.7 and CCK, and it still is for Drupal 7 and Fields. In addition to the URL, Link module provides an option for a title (the text to be hyperlinked) and adding CSS classes and a link target, among other things. (You could use a text field to store links, but it wouldn't offer any of this.)

Before you can add Link fields to anything in Drupal, of course, you need to install the module. Chapter 4 covered installing modules; here we give the Drush instructions (see Chapters 2 and 26). Also shown are the commands for adding the module to version control using Git (see Chapter 2).

```
drush dl link
Project link (7.x-1.0-alpha2) downloaded to              [success]
/home/ben/code/dgd7/drupal/sites/all/modules/link.
git add sites/all/modules/link/
git commit -m "Link module for link fields."
drush en -y link
The following extensions will be enabled: link
Do you really want to continue? (y/n): y
link was enabled successfully. [ok]
```

▓ **Note** If enabling Link module through the user interface, a search for link on the Modules administration page (as with `control + f`) would find it grouped under the Fields package.

There is no configuration link on the Modules administration page for Link module because all its settings are per field. To begin doing anything, attach it to a content type. For this site, the content type that needs a Link field is Profiles, the content type for author bios. To add a link field:

1. Go to *Administration ➤ Structure ➤ Content types*.

2. Click on the Profile content type's Manage fields link (`admin/structure/types/manage/profile/fields`).

3. Go to the part of the form labeled Add new field.

4. Give it a label like **Web site** and the machine name **website** (which is automatically prefixed by field_) and the field type Link (see Figure 8–3).

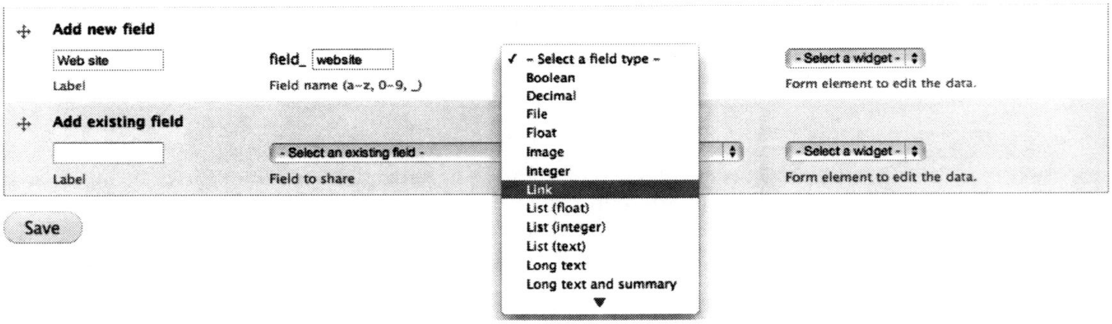

Figure 8–3. Adding a new field of type Link

5. Link module provides only one *widget* (a widget displays the field on the form for the person adding or editing), but the Field settings that you will come to next give all kinds of options that affect the widget, too. Click Save and you are there.

▓ **Tip** When adding a field, you can drag it to the position you want it to be in before submitting with Save. It's safe and it works! (This affects where it shows up on the node add/edit form; its display position can be arranged on the **Manage display** tab.)

---

6. On the Field settings page leave Optional URL unchecked–allowing that would be an unusual circumstance for a Link field–and leave the Link title as optional.

7. You may want to up the URL Display Cutoff to 120 characters because we do not want to cut off the display of an address unless it's going to impact page layout.

8. Leave Link Target set to the default, which is none, as forcing people's links to open in new windows is likely to confuse them, not help them get back to your site.

9. Finally, do not set the Rel Attribute. There are not many interesting things to do with rel on non-navigation links (see w3.org/TR/html401/types.html#type-links), unless you define your own. (Do not set "nofollow," as in the example; doing so is disrespectful to the people who use your site and against the nature of the Web.) An Additional CSS Class isn't likely to hurt anything, but on the other hand you can always come back and add it later if you want to theme web site links specially.

10. Now click **Save field settings**.

This takes you to a second settings page, divided into Profile settings (meaning settings that only apply to the Web site field when it is on the Profile content type) and Web site field settings (meaning settings that will affect the Web site field on anything you may attach it to). Pretty much all of these are duplicative of what you already filled out, but there is one important setting you have not seen before. Down the page a little, the first of the Web site field settings is Number of values (see Figure 8–4). By setting this, you can make your field able to be repeated and filled out with multiple values.

This means that rather than creating a Link field for company web site, another Link field for personal web site, another for secret project web site, and another for pet's web site–that is, trying to guess how many and what kind of web sites an author may be linking to–you can make one Web site field that can be repeated some number or an unlimited number of times.

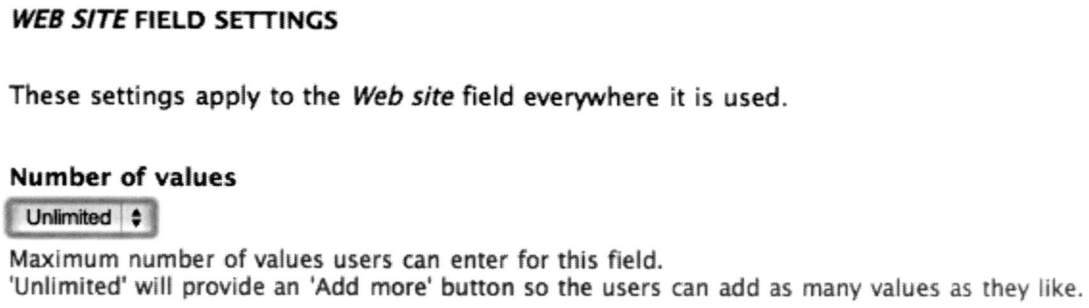

WEB SITE FIELD SETTINGS

These settings apply to the *Web site* field everywhere it is used.

Number of values

Unlimited ◆

Maximum number of values users can enter for this field.
'Unlimited' will provide an 'Add more' button so the users can add as many values as they like.

Figure 8–4. The Web site Link field configured to allow an unlimited number of values

Everything else you have already set. Save settings at the bottom of the form, and this field is ready for use. Drupal takes you back to the Manage fields tab of the Profile content type where you can edit or arrange the existing fields—or add more.

Authors' Other Homes on the Internet

As most of the authors are public figures in their own right (present authors excepted), the site should provide a standardized way of linking to their other most relevant pages (drupal.org user page, groups.drupal.org user page, and Twitter). These could have all been made Link fields, but with more work on the development side you can ensure consistent presentation by taking only IDs and wrapping a link around them yourself.

▓ **Note** Using the Link field to link to drupal.org and other specific web site accounts would be much easier, and perfectly acceptable. You won't get to the payoff for this until chapter 33 with some custom code.

Add two fields of type Integer (note: you have to add fields one at a time through Drupal's user interface, unless one of the fields you are adding already exists):

- *Drupal.org User ID*, which can take the machine name do_uid

- *Groups.Drupal.org User ID*, which can take the field name gdo_uid. (As always for fields created through the user interface, both machine names will be prefixed with "field_".)

You can immediately click past the Field settings page that comes next, as the integer fields have no settings to configure on this page.

▓ **Note** Perhaps empty configuration pages will be removed if this issue is resolved: `drupal.org/node/552604`.

Although it's best to store the data of user IDs as integers, they should each be displayed as links to user accounts on their respective web sites. Integer fields allow you to define prefixes and suffixes, which will be used on their input and edit forms and displayed with their values. This is a per-content-type settings, available on the second configuration screen after adding a field. (You can return to it at any time, as from *Administration ➤ Structure ➤ Content types ➤ Author profile ➤ Manage fields ➤ Groups.Drupal.org user ID*, `admin/structure/types/manage/profile/fields/field_gdo_uid`). However, these are meant for currency symbols or units of measurement. Attempting to provide the beginning of the HTML link code as prefix and the rest of the HTML link code as suffix does not work.

Sure enough, however, there's a module for this. Providing a special wrapper for fields could be done with Custom Formatters (`drupal.org/project/custom_formatters`)—define a custom formatter, make it available to integer or text fields as appropriate, and then define the HTML code to surround the data. Alternatively, you can write your own module to define a formatter, which could be cleaner (one or two formatters with options, rather than a formatter for every field) and more extensible (say with something crazy like looking up drupal.org account usernames). See Chapter 33 for more.

▓ **Tip** One of the great things about the field system is that we can collect data right away and finalize the display later.

Save it, and you are back at the Author profile content type's manage fields page, ready for the next field.

A Non-displaying Data Field: Approximate Pages

Create another integer field to hold the approximate number of pages each author contributed to the book. This will be used later for sorting the display of author names and profiles, described in the "Listing the Authors" section. Hiding it from display will then be covered, in the "Fine-Tuning Content Display" section, and you've already made integer fields, so there's not too much to cover here!

Connecting Author Profiles to Authors' User Accounts

We decided against making Author profiles tied to user accounts, but you can have the best of both worlds by allowing profiles to reference user accounts.

1. Node and user references are a powerful addition to Drupal's content type and Fields system that currently lives in the References project (drupal.org/project/references). We need to add it:

```
drush dl references
Project references (7.x-2.x-dev) downloaded to                    [success]
/home/ben/code/dgd7/drupal/sites/all/modules/references.

Project references contains 2 modules: node_reference, user_reference.

git add sites/all/modules/references
git commit -m "Added project references (node_reference, user_reference)."
```

2. Enable the User reference module (and you'll be needing Node reference later, so enable it at the same time).

3. Add new field with the Label **DefinitiveGuide.org account** and Field (machine) name field_**user**, and of course change the Type of data to store to User reference. As soon as you select this, the User reference field type provides three different widgets from which you can choose one for entering data: Select list, Check boxes/radio buttons, and Autocomplete text field (see Figure 8–5).

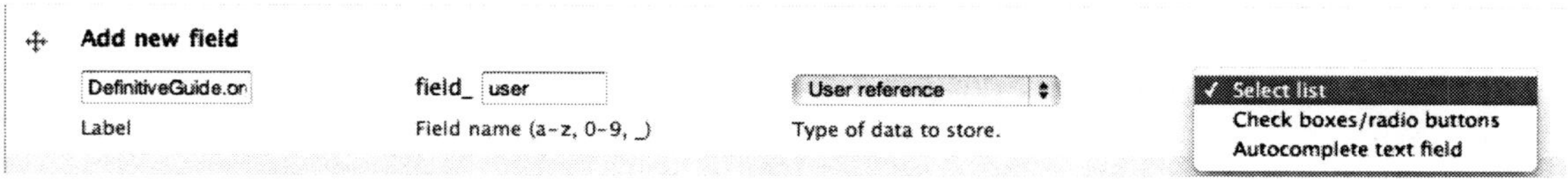

Figure 8–5. Adding a User reference field, with the three widget options shown

■ **Note** The Check boxes/radio buttons widget is radio buttons if the field is configured to allow a single value and checkboxes for a multiple value field. Likewise, the select list will be a select form rather than a drop-down if multiple values are allowed.

4. It would seem that since the site may have thousands of users to choose from, the only widget you can use is Autocomplete text field—since the other two both show all users, and choosing one out of a thousand is not a usable user interface. However, you'll find on the next screen that you can limit the users that can be referenced by role. Therefore, choose the Select list widget, as a compact way to show the site users available to be chosen.

5. You can come back to this page (the Author profile content type's Manage display tab) to change the widget at any time, so go ahead and Save.

6. You are brought to a configuration page that includes options for limiting referenceable users by role and status. Only users with the author role should be available, and there's generally not any harm in limiting to active users, so select that box (see Figure 8–6).

User roles that can be referenced

☐ authenticated user

☐ administrator

☑ author

☐ trusted

User status that can be referenced

☑ Active

☐ Blocked

(Save field settings)

Figure 8–6. Limiting the users available to be referenced by role and status

7. Click **Save field settings** and you get to move on to the next configuration screen.

8. Not much to do here: Don't make it a required field, don't set a default value, and leave the Number of values at 1. The point of this field is to associate an Author profile with that author's user account, if there is one. So click Save settings just to get off this page, and you are done!

Giving Authors Permission to Create Profiles

Permissions were introduced in Chapter 1, and you will be returning to that wall of checkboxes now and often as you build Drupal sites. The new content type you created, Author profiles, will be available to have its permissions set at *Administration* ➤ *People* ➤ *Permissions* (admin/people/permissions), under Node.

Checkmark the Author role for two permissions: Author profile: Create new content and Author profile: Edit own content.

▨ **Note** The Administrator role has not been given create, edit, and delete rights on this new content type, but it does not matter because the Administrator role already has the Node module permission "Bypass content access control."

▨ **Tip** Most sites should create a content editor or content administrator role that has both the Administer content and Access the content overview page permissions, probably the Administer comments and comment settings permission, and possibly the Bypass content access control permission. See the bonus chapter "Content Administrator Convenience" at `dgd7.org/content` for discussion about managing content and comments and creating views and other tools to make this more convenient.

You can create an author profile or two at *Add new content ➤ Create Author profile* (`node/add/profile`). You should test creating a profile as *a user account that only has the author role*—permissions are the most common way to look stupid by telling people to do something on your site and it does not work. Create a test account or use the Masquerade module (`drupal.org/project/masquerade`).

▨ **Tip** As an administrator, you can assign content to other users when you create it or at a later date. Under Authoring information, in the vertical tabs at the bottom of the node add/edit form, replace the user name in Authored by with the name of the user you want to be the owner (author) of that content. Type patiently—it will autocomplete.

You can also create users for willing authors at *Administration ➤ People, + Add user* (`admin/people/create`) and give them the author role right there. Finally, you can ask people to create their own accounts on the site, and add the author role to their user account after they register (see the online material for this chapter at `dgd7.org/moresite` for ways to set up notification of user registration).

Listing the Authors

The authors have the capability to have profiles now, but there's no way for visitors to find them. The book site should show off the authors a little. The profiles will be shown in three ways:

- A page, linked from the main menu, featuring a grid of author pictures and names, where each name and picture links to the full author profile, sorted at random.

- A page, available from the picture grid page, with small profile pictures and the first paragraph or two of short biographies, each linking to the full author profile, sorted by pages written.

- A block, in the footer of every page, with each author's name linked to his or her full author profile, sorted by pages written.

For all three of these purposes, the Views module is the natural choice.

■ **Note** For a short time before there was an official release of Views for Drupal 7, this site displayed author profiles using an excellent class provided by Drupal core, EntityFieldQuery. See dgd7.org/180 for how to make a page of author profiles without Views and only a few lines in a custom module.

Building the Authors Headshot View

The Views module can reach into the data stored when administrators or authors add author profiles and display just part of it to make the page of names and pictures that link to their author profile pages.

1. First off, go to *Structure* ➤ *Views* in the toolbar and click the Add new view link (admin/structure/views/add).

2. On this page go ahead and name your new view. In the View name field add **Author profiles** but change the automatically generated machine name to simply **profiles**.

■ **Note** Once the view machine name has been chosen, it cannot be changed.

---

3. Checkmark description to get the View description field and put a quick description such as **A view to show all the author profiles**.

4. The rest of this page helps you get your view built faster. Leave Show set to Content (meaning nodes) and change "of type" to Author profile.

5. Under Create a page, change the Page title that has been automatically filled in for you to Authors. That's the title that will be shown to visitors to this page. Set the last part of the path URL to authors. And change Display format to **Grid** of fields.

6. Now press the **Continue & edit** button. This brings you to the edit view page. Saying that a lot can be done here is an understatement. However, most of what you need to do has already been set up for you based on your settings on the previous page. All of that can be changed or tweaked. For instance, in the Grid settings change the Number of columns to 4.

■ **Tip** The theme developed for the site (see Chapters 15 and 16 and dgd7.org/theme for theming) is flexible width and includes an inline class in its stylesheet. Changing the Format to HTML List and using the class inline would give more perfect results. Drupal's separation of data and presentation lets you make this change later.

---

7. Head to the Fields section and again click the Add button to add some fields to your view. Here's where a lot of the magic happens. The Authors page requirements call for the authors profile image and name to be displayed in a grid with both the images and the author names linking to their corresponding authors profiles. So, go ahead and choose Content: Image (remember adding this to the author profile content type?) and Content: Title.

8. In the configuration for Content: Image, remove the Label text (uncheck "Create a label") and under Image style select thumbnail. Make sure "Link image to" is set to Content. In the Content: Title settings similarly remove the label text and make sure "Link this field to the original piece of content" is checkmarked.

9. Don't forget to save the view!

You just created a dynamic page on your site that queries the database and displays the image and title from profiles nodes (and only profile nodes), in a 4 column grid format. You can visit the page by going to the path you entered for it; in this case, `authors`.

Creating an Image Style

You could leave the view you just made just as is. But the drawback of this is that some authors may upload landscape style profile images and others may upload portrait. This means that the authors listing page could look like a jumbled mess of long and wide images. The default thumbnail image style that you selected for the image field display is only set to scale images down to a certain pixel width or height.

The capability of automatically resizing images is cool, but it's not good enough and Drupal is way cooler. What we want are profile images that are perfectly square, then our grid won't have so much white space or oddly shaped images. With Drupal's Image styles we can easily create an image style to do this for us using the Scale and Crop effect.

Can Drupal do even better? Of course. The Smart Crop module (`drupal.org/project/smartcrop`) provides alternatives to Image modules' cropping ability. Smart Crop tries to identify the center of action of a picture and make that the middle of its cropping. If you want to use it, download and enable Smart Crop.

▓ **Tip** Smart Crop tries harder than Drupal core's image crop, but it's not infallible. If you need images cropped to an exact size without cutting off anything important, try Imagefield crop (`drupal.org/project/imagefield_crop`), which has users crop their images when they upload them.

---

1. First, we have to edit an existing image style (by clicking on its name or the edit link) or create a new image style (by clicking the + *Add style*) link above the table (see Figure 8–7). Because thumbnail, medium, and large are always provided by the image module, every module that uses images can count on their existence. Any changes you make to one of these image styles will take effect everywhere they are used on your site, including as the default image styles used by modules you have not even thought of installing yet.

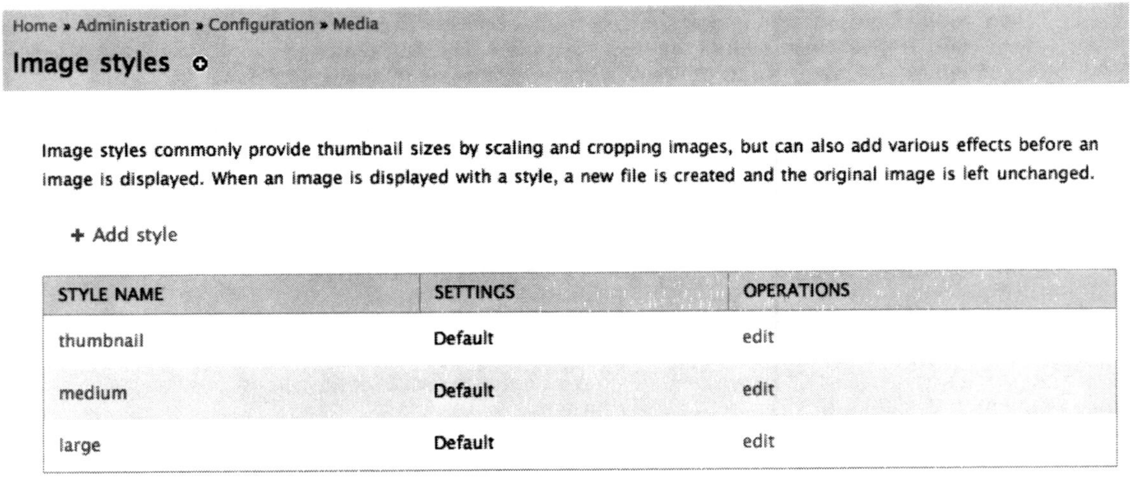

Home » Administration » Configuration » Media

Image styles ○

Image styles commonly provide thumbnail sizes by scaling and cropping images, but can also add various effects before an image is displayed. When an image is displayed with a style, a new file is created and the original image is left unchanged.

+ Add style

STYLE NAME	SETTINGS	OPERATIONS
thumbnail	Default	edit
medium	Default	edit
large	Default	edit

Figure 8–7. Image styles listing page. Clicking on the Style name or the edit link under Operations lets you edit.

■ **Note** You can edit a module-provided image style if you want to affect every module that might use that style. The first time you edit, when it still has its default settings, you will have to click Override defaults first.

---

2. The author views needs are pretty specific, so let's not override a default style. Instead, create a new style with the + *Add style* link. Give it a Style name such as **small_square**, and click Create new style.

■ **Tip** As image styles are about presentation, we recommend you name them based on their appearance, not their use.

---

3. You will be taken to the image style edit page where you can build your style by adding all kinds of different effects. In our case we want square images, so select and add the Scale and Smart Crop effect (see Figure 8–8). This takes you to another configuration page; set a width and height of 150px each and allow upscaling.

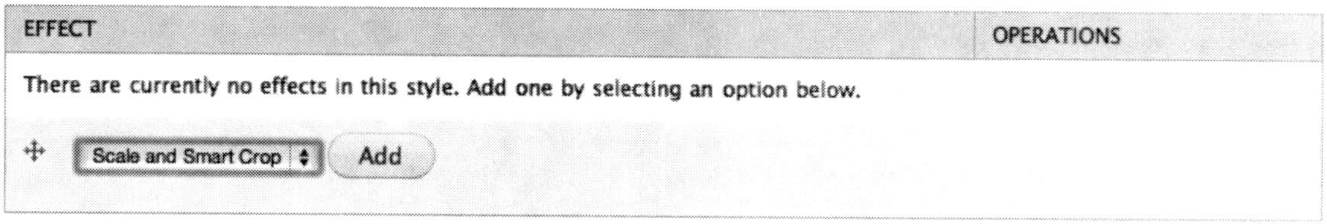

EFFECT	OPERATIONS

There are currently no effects in this style. Add one by selecting an option below.

⊹ [Scale and Smart Crop ⬍]   (Add)

Figure 8–8. Giving a new image style the effect Scale and Smart Crop

4. Submit this form by clicking the Add effect button. Now you are brought back to the image style edit page, which includes a preview of the example image with that style applied. If you see a beautiful hot air balloon scene, you have a special prize-winning copy of Drupal! Well, not really, but the example image was drawn special for Image module by its primary author, Nate Haug (quicksketch). Below the image preview, there is the effect you just added in the list of the effects used in this image style and an opportunity to add more.

■ **Caution** Although image styles allow you to change their name (which is effectively a machine name), views and other site elements using the image style don't get the memo. Therefore, it is strongly recommended you do not change your image style name, and if you do, remember to go through the site updating wherever it was used.

---

5. The last step is to go back into your authors view and set the image field to use your newly created image style instead of the default thumbnail one.

While you are back in your view and editing it again, this will be a good chance to also create a menu item for the biographies page so that your site's visitors can access it from a menu item and not just by entering the path.

Creating a Menu Link for a Page View

Start by editing the View page display you created.

1. Find Page settings and within it Menu: No menu. Click No menu to give it a menu link. (Views' new, more intuitive user interface did not get more intuitive here, sorry!) Be sure to select Main menu under the Menu option, as shown in Figure 8–9.

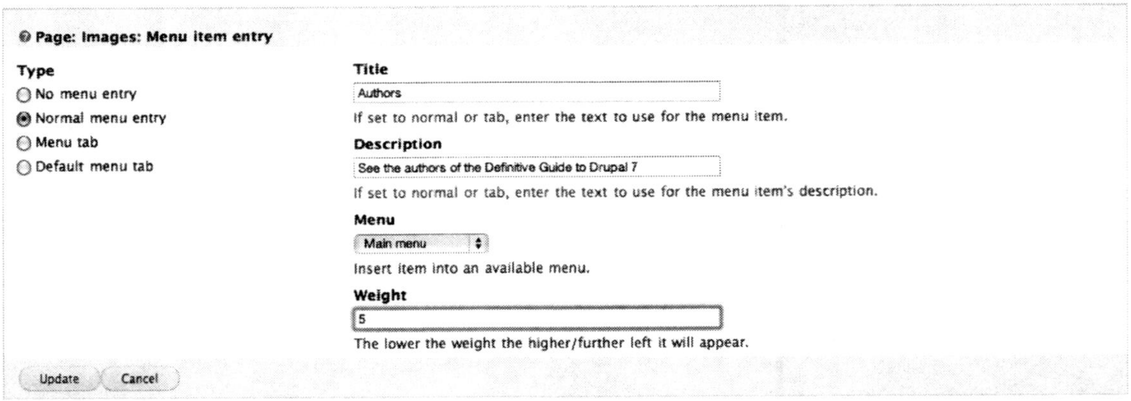

Figure 8–9. *Adding a menu link to a page view*

2. Click Apply and then Save. If the link is not where you want it in the menu, it's easiest to go to *Administration* ➤ *Structure* ➤ *Menu* (admin/structure/menu) and reorder the menu there.

■ **Note** You can also create menu links for View pages, as for all pages, through the Menu administration. Click Add link and give the path—the same way the Table of Contents menu link was created.

Building an Author Biographies View Page, Reachable As a Tab on the Authors View

The main way of showcasing the authors is the grid of images, but visitors should also be able to peruse the authors all at once in a listing that includes their short biographies. See Table 8–1 for the key elements for this display.

■ **Note** We won't be covering every aspect of this view. Refer to Chapter 3 for any additional Views reference you need.

CHAPTER 8 ▨ EXTENDING YOUR SITE

Table 8–1. The Key Elements of the View Page Display

Title	*(override)* Title: **Author biographies**
Advanced settings	Machine name: **biographies** Display name: Page: **Biographies**
Format	*(override)* Style: HTML List *(override)* Row style: Node (teaser)
Page settings	Path: **authors/biographies** Menu: **Tab: Biographies** (weight: 5)
Sort criteria	**Fields: field_pagecount** (desc)
Filters *(unchanged)*	*Node: Type = Profile* *Node: Published = Yes*

There is one more thing we have to do to make this menu tab show up on the existing author pictures view—we need to make that page a default tab (see Figure 8–10).

1. Go back to the profile view images display. In Page settings change the Path to authors/pictures, and in Menu select Default menu tab.

2. Keep the title Authors, and keep the same description.

3. Change the Weight to -5, as this is the weight for the default tab (rather than the link in the main menu), and it should always appear first.

4. Click Update. For the Parent menu item, you must choose Normal menu item (*not* Already exists).

5. Give this the title **Authors** and the same description, too. Put it in the Main menu (and expect to have to adjust its weight from Menu administration later).

▨ **Note** You cannot create these menus and tabs through the Menu administration user interface, only through Views (or your own code or something else that creates menu items, not merely menu links). To be perfectly clear: Even though you already have a menu link pointing to the path authors, you need to tell Views to create the menu entry for the parent of the default tab. When Views creates the menu entry for you, it is creating not simply a menu link but a menu item, which is substantial enough to peg tabs too. Also, the default tab must have a different path from its parent menu item. That is why the path "authors" was replaced with "authors/pictures" so that the parent menu item could have the "authors" path. See Chapter 29 to learn about the menu system.

Figure 8–10. *Two menu tabs, the Biographies and the default menu tab Authors, provided by your views*

■ **Tip** Even if two View displays are logically related, if structurally they are too different–different filters, fields, sorts, etc.–performance-wise it is best to make them as separate views. If a display will be overriding almost all defaults, it should be a separate display (unless it is an Attachment display, which needs to be in the same view as the displays it attaches to). The two displays in Figure 8–10 could justifiably have been split into separate views.

Fine-tuning Content Display

The ability to add fields to hold all different sorts of information is great, and the ability to flexibly change how this information is displayed is even better. The magic happens in the **Manage display** tab of every content type. With it, you have a great deal of control over the display of your content without the need to theme nor do any other coding.

Turn first to the Manage display page (see Figure 8–11) for the Author profile content type at *Administration ➤ Structure ➤ Content types ➤ Author profile ➤ Manage display* (admin/structure/types/manage/profile/display).

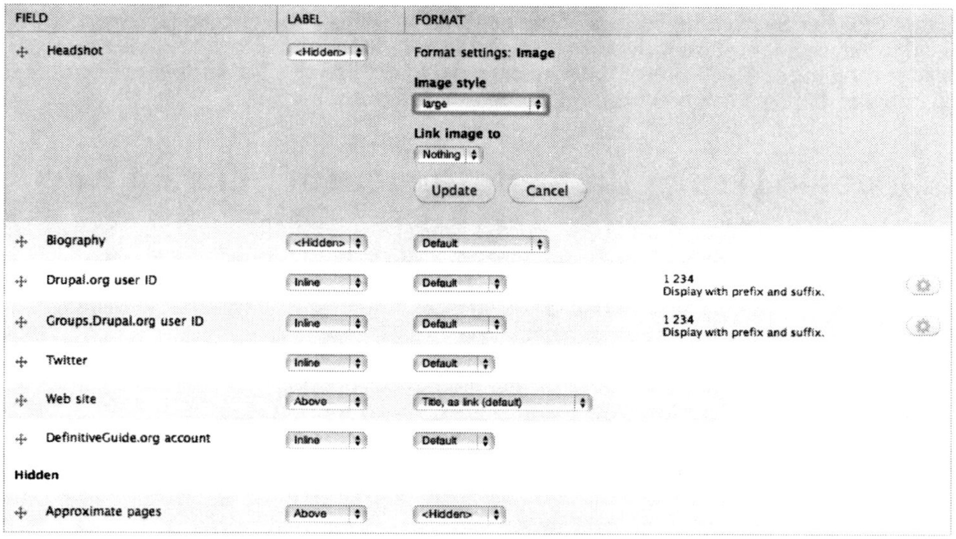

Figure 8–11. The Manage display page for the Author profile content type, Default view mode

---

■ **Note** This is a powerhouse of a page, and you have a version of it for every fieldable entity (nodes per content type such as here, comments per content type as seen in the tabs to the right, taxonomy terms per vocabulary, users, etc.).

Figure 8–11 shows an in-progress configuration of the default display of the Author profile content type (which you built earlier in this chapter). The Headshot image field has its label hidden and, more noticeably, has its format being set to display in the large image style. Those options were opened up by clicking the gear icon on the right of the Headshot table row. The main content Biography field also has its label hidden, and the various ID and account fields have their labels placed inline.

A field can be hidden from display by either selecting <Hidden> as its format or dragging it to the Hidden section at the bottom. This is the case with the Approximate pages field, which is only used for sorting the profile views, not for display. The order of fields can also be changed with drag-and-drop (or, optionally or without JavaScript, by weight textfields). In Figure 8–11, the DefinitiveGuide.org account should probably be placed above the multivalue web site field, so that it is with the other single-value, label-inline fields.

■ **Caution** Drupal warns you nice and clearly when you drag fields up and down that you need to submit your changes with the Save button at the bottom of the page. It does *not* alert you at all when you change label or format. Even when you use the gear to configure advanced display settings, you are not warned that these changes are not yet stored. (See issue at drupal.org/node/857312). In every case, none of your changes are saved until submitting by clicking Save at the bottom of the page.

Did you remember to click Save at the bottom of the page? Even though you clicked Update, Drupal isn't saving a blessed thing until you submit the form as a whole with the Save button. Now you know, though it might take getting burned a couple of times to get used to it: Field display settings are not saved until the full manage display form is submitted. So, Save this form.

Using View Modes to Display the Same Content in Different Ways

The previous changes were made to the Default view settings for the Author profile content type, as seen in the subtab selected beneath the Manage display tab. The other tab is Teaser, which is the other view mode automatically configured for node content.

When viewing the Default view settings, hidden in the collapsed fieldset labeled Custom display settings (toward the bottom of the page) are a set of checkboxes for view modes. For content (nodes) in a standard installation of Drupal core, these are Full content, Teaser, RSS, Search index, Search result, and Print. Two, notably, are provided by the Search module included in Drupal core.

By default, the teaser is the only specially configured view mode; everything else, including the full node view, falls back on the default configuration. Selecting an additional view mode will add it to the subtabs under the Manage display tab.

▓ **Tip** You can define additional view modes in a small custom module you write yourself (as will be done in chapter 33) or with Display Suite (`drupal.org/project/ds`). View modes (called build modes in CCK for Drupal 6) can be used to display referenced content when using the Node reference display formatter. View modes are also available when creating listings with the Views module (row style: node), which makes them a useful alternative to building field-based views that require a large number of fields. This is put to good use in the Anjali Forber-Pratt (Paralympic athlete and educator) case study (see `dgd7.org/anjali`).

Modifying Teaser Display and Setting Trim Length

The Teaser view mode is used in the view of author biographies, so you definitely want to pay attention to how it looks. The point of a teaser is to only show some of the content, so it's a good time to use the ability to hide fields from display.

1. Edit the teaser display (see Figure 8–12) at *Administration* ➤ *Structure* ➤ *Content types* ➤ *Profile* ➤ Manage display ➤ Teaser. (`admin/structure/types/manage/profile/display/teaser`).

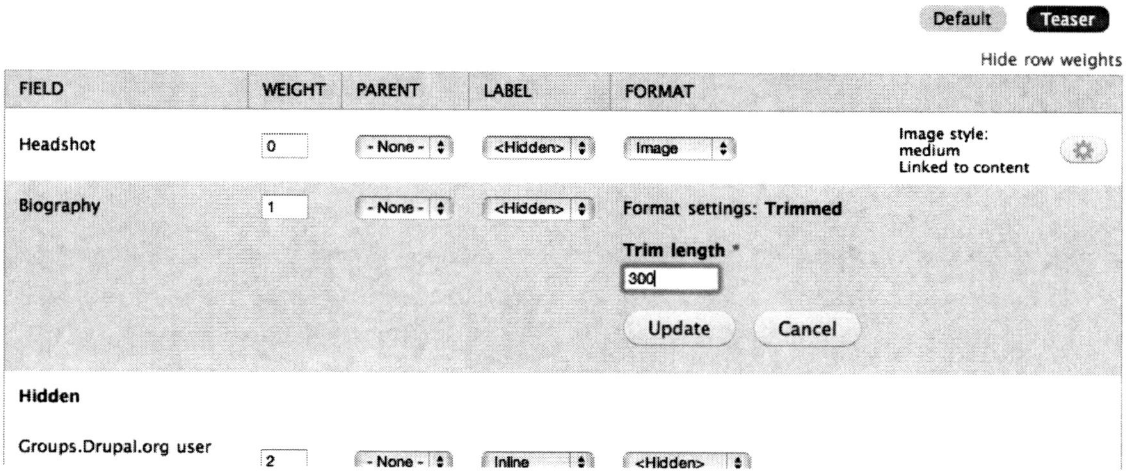

Figure 8-12. Setting the trim length for the Author profile Teaser view mode, with all other fields but headshot hidden. The Show row weights link has been clicked to show the way to move fields without drag and drop.

2. Change the Headshot Image style to *medium* and Link image to *content* (so that clicking on it will take people to the full author profile page).

3. The field you labeled Biography (machine name body) by default for the teaser has the format *Summary or trimmed* with its trim length set to 600 character. (Yes, that is characters, not words; Drupal gets points off its work for not showing units of measurement.) To change the default trim length, you need to click the gear icon at the left. To force the length to never be more than 300 characters, change the formatter to *Trimmed* and set the trim length.

▓ **Tip** The Summary or trimmed formatter will use an explicitly defined summary even if it is longer than its Trim length setting. The Trimmed formatter will always use the Trim length and ignore any summary. That means it takes the text it trims form the main content, not the summary. In Drupal 7, summaries are never considered a way of indicating the break point of the full content; if a summary is provided it is always separate and not considered part of the full content. Therefore, if you use textfields that allow summaries—as Drupal does by default for every content type, providing a body field of the type "Long text and summary"—you will likely need to educate users that the summary does *not* get shown when viewing the full content type.

---

4. Hide all the other fields, and you have nice tight teasers for the author biographies.

Making the Table of Contents with Book Module

Commonly, in the world of Drupal, modules already exist that will do what you want. That's the case with the next DefinitiveGuide.org web site requirements to take on: *The site should have a table of contents with optional chapter summaries that all authors can edit and rearrange.*

A table of contents made up of chapter titles and summaries is effectively an editable hierarchy of pages, which is precisely what the Book module provides: "A set of pages tied together in a hierarchical sequence," as its handbook page puts it (`drupal.org/handbook/modules/book`). You don't have to go far to find this module: it's in Drupal core. Go to *Administration* ➤ *Modules* (admin/modules) and you'll see the Book module says there that it "allows users to create and organize related content in an outline." Sounds good!

Although included with Drupal core, the Book module is left disabled by the standard installation profile. Enable it by checking the box to the left of the Book module name and submitting this change by clicking the Save configuration button at the bottom of the page.

■ **Note** The Book module's in-site documentation (admin/help/book) fails to say where the module is configured or mention that it creates a content type. Hunting around for what has changed when you enable a module is something you'll have do from time to time, but you can help make Drupal and its contributed modules better by improving documentation and by directly improving the user experience. Start by searching the appropriate issue queue and adding your observations or filing a new issue if no one has reported a problem. The issue to improve the Book module's help page is at drupal.org/node/1041498. (Changes to text may not be accepted except for Drupal 8, and even then, improvements will only happen if we step up and do them. See chapter 38 for more about contributing to the Drupal community.)

When enabled the first time, Book module runs an installation process that creates a new content type for you, *Book page*. The DefinitiveGuide.org web site plan does not call for using the Book module for any other purpose, so take over and edit its content type.

■ **Tip** If you want to add outlining ability to other content types, you can do so at any time at *Administration* ➤ *Content* ➤ *Books* ➤ *Settings* (admin/content/book/settings).

The book content type is edited like any other (and, new in Drupal 7, can be deleted; it is just like a content type you create yourself). Go to *Administer* ➤ *Structure* ➤ *Content Types* and click Book page's configuration link (admin/structure/types/manage/book), as shown in Figure 8–13.

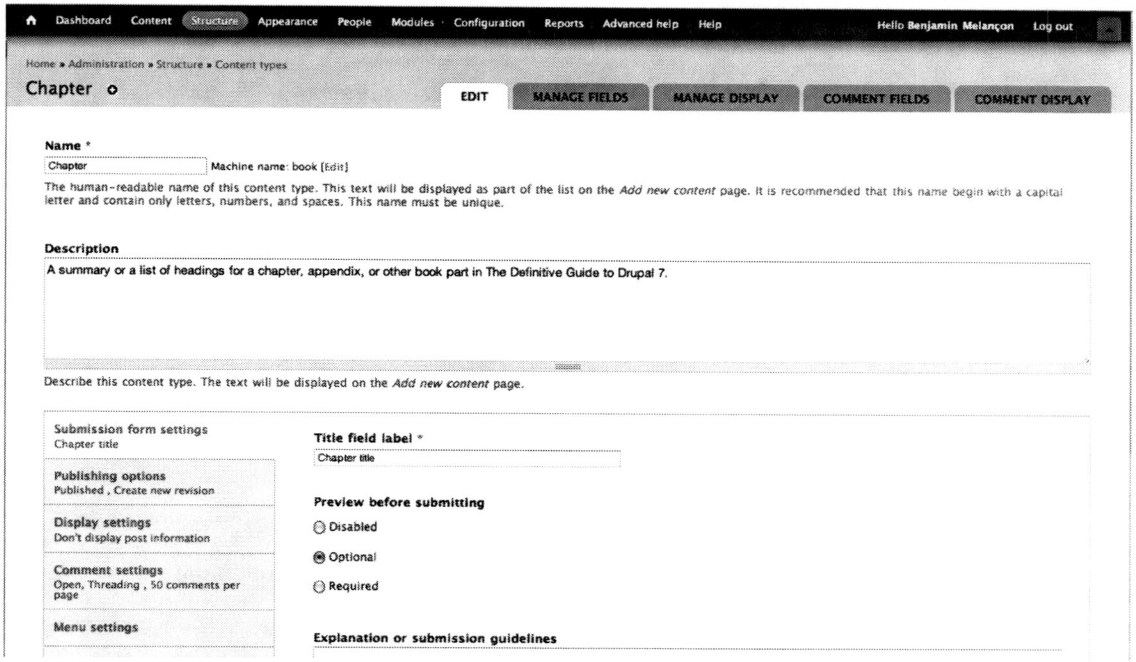

Figure 8–13. *The edit form for the book content type, modified to serve for Chapter content*

Change the name from Book page to **Chapter** (you can leave the machine name as book), and change the description to make sense for chapter summaries. You should also make some changes to the options stacked neatly into vertical tabs at the bottom of the content type edit form.

1. In Submission form settings, you can change the Title field label to **Chapter title**.

2. Next, in Publishing options, be sure Default options has both Published and Create new revision checked.

▓ **Tip** Turn on Create new revision for every content type. Be restrictive in which roles can delete content, and you can be generous in which roles can edit content with less fear of permanently losing anyone's work. We will set these permissions, among others, in the next section.

---

3. Then, in Display settings, uncheck the Display author and date information option. By default, a new node or post in Drupal includes the name of the user that posted it and the time it was first submitted. This should be removed on chapter summaries because it would be misleading to associate a chapter with the person who posted it, rather than the actual author or authors of that chapter (see Figure 8–14).

Submission form settings	☐ Display author and date information.
Chapter title	
	Author username and publish date will be displayed.
Publishing options	
Published , Create new revision	
Display settings	
Don't display post information	

Figure 8–14. Opting to not display author and date information ("submitted by" text) on content of a given type

4. Now save the content type. The content type originally provided by Book module is now configured to handle the chapter summaries for the DefinitiveDrupal.org web site.

Setting Permissions for Organizing and Writing Chapters

As mentioned in Chapter 1, it's best to set permissions soon after enabling a new module or defining a new content type. You've just enabled Book module and edited its content type, so it's definitely time to review permissions. These include the permissions provided specially by the Book module and content type permissions for the new content type (see Figure 8–15).

For the four permissions provided specifically by the Book module, Administrators can continue to have all powers, and people in the Author role should be able to *Administer book outlines* (to be able to arrange the table of contents) and *Add content and child pages to books* (to be able to add their chapters). There will be only one table of contents, so authors do not need the Create new books permission. Finally, the View printer-friendly books permission should be given to both anonymous and authenticated users, though you could reward the people who log in a little and only give the permission to the authenticated user role.

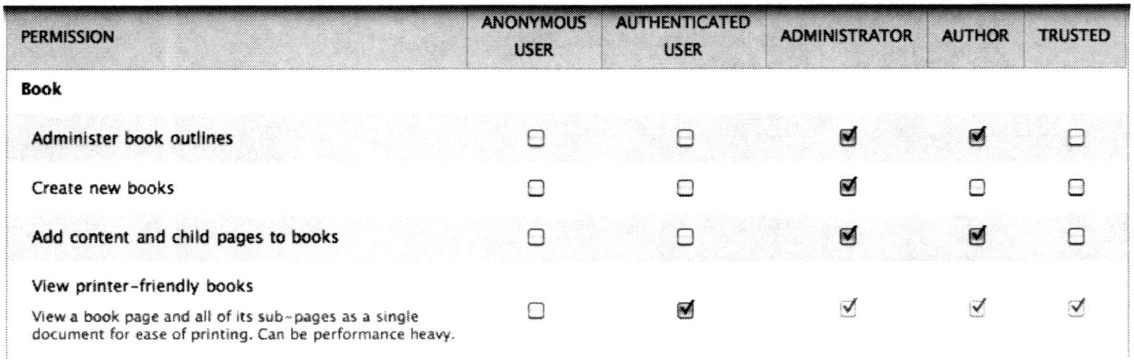

PERMISSION	ANONYMOUS USER	AUTHENTICATED USER	ADMINISTRATOR	AUTHOR	TRUSTED
Book					
Administer book outlines	☐	☐	☑	☑	☐
Create new books	☐	☐	☑	☐	☐
Add content and child pages to books	☐	☐	☑	☑	☐
View printer-friendly books View a book page and all of its sub-pages as a single document for ease of printing. Can be performance heavy.	☐	☑	☑	☑	☑

Figure 8–15. Permissions for Book module (admin/people/permissions#module-book)

You should also set the permissions for the Chapter content type you just modified while on the permissions page (see Figure 8–16). Again, let the Administrator role keep all permissions. Give the Author role all create and edit permissions but not delete permissions. With the Chapter content type having been set to keep revisions, authors can collaborate on each other's chapters but cannot permanently lose work.

PERMISSION	ANONYMOUS USER	AUTHENTICATED USER	ADMINISTRATOR	AUTHOR	TRUSTED
Chapter: Create new content	☐	☐	☑	☑	☐
Chapter: Edit own content	☐	☐	☑	☑	☐
Chapter: Edit any content	☐	☐	☑	☑	☐
Chapter: Delete own content	☐	☐	☑	☐	☐
Chapter: Delete any content	☐	☐	☑	☐	☐

Figure 8–16. *Permissions for Chapter (book) content type, found under the Node heading*

■ **Tip** Content types that you create and most content types provided by modules will be under the control of the Node module and so listed under Node on the permissions table, sorted by machine name (not the name shown).

Like most modules, once Book is enabled it adds new pages to your site's administration. In this case, the Book module adds a pages to the Content section. You should now see a Books tab at *Administration* ➤ *Content* (admin/content), as shown in Figure 8–17.

■ **Tip** The Configure link or the Help link added next to a module's listing on the Modules administration page can help you find your way to its settings page or pages.

Figure 8–17. *The Books content tab (admin/content/book) with its List and Settings subtabs*

On the administrative listing page for books, there is no link for creating new books. Instead, a book is made by creating an outline-enabled node. In the Settings subtab (admin/content/book/settings) next to the List subtab, you can assign which types of content can be added to book outlines, but because the Chapter content type was originally the Book content type provided by Book module, it is already selected.

Adding Metadata to the Chapter Content Type with Fields

In order to refer to chapters without numbers while the final order of the book is undetermined, they should have short internal names. (In the chapter drafts, these "machine names for chapters" are used instead of a number to refer from one chapter to another.) This information needs to be stored with the chapter summaries—clearly a case for adding a field to the Chapter content type.

1. From the content type listing page–*Administration* ➤ *Structure* ➤ *Content types*–you can click a manage fields link (`admin/structure/types/manage/book/fields`). (If you're already on a content type's edit page, you can get to the same place by the Manage Fields tab, which is up and to the left with the seven theme.)

2. While here, let's improve the label for the main text area (body) field. Edit the body field by clicking the edit link (`admin/structure/types/manage/book/fields/body`).

3. Change the Body label to **Chapter summary** and make sure Required field is not checked (keeping it optional to provide anything more than a title for a chapter) and click Save settings.

4. Now add a Chapter number field (see Figure 8–18). Making this field an Integer type feels like the right thing to do, but unfortunately chapters include appendices, which take letters, not numbers. Fall back on the Text field type.

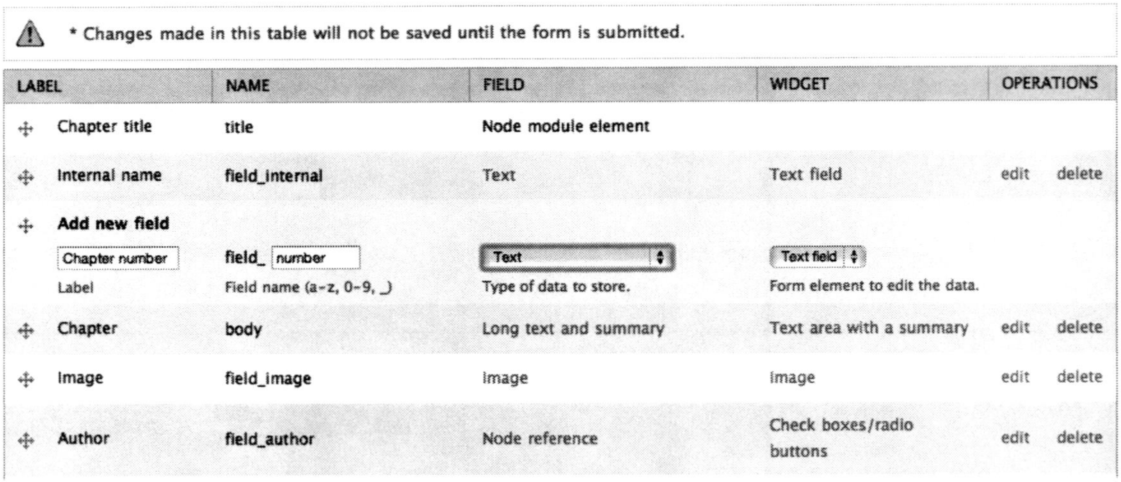

⚠ * Changes made in this table will not be saved until the form is submitted.

LABEL	NAME	FIELD	WIDGET	OPERATIONS	
✛ Chapter title	title	Node module element			
✛ Internal name	field_internal	Text	Text field	edit	delete
✛ **Add new field**					
Chapter number	field_ number	Text ⬍	Text field ⬍		
Label	Field name (a–z, 0–9, _)	Type of data to store.	Form element to edit the data.		
✛ Chapter	body	Long text and summary	Text area with a summary	edit	delete
✛ Image	field_image	Image	Image	edit	delete
✛ Author	field_author	Node reference	Check boxes/radio buttons	edit	delete

***Figure 8–18.** Adding the final field, the Chapter number text field, to the Chapter content type, in its desired position on the content editing form*

5. You can pretend you still have some control over the data type by limiting its maximum number of characters to only two, as shown in Figure 8–19.

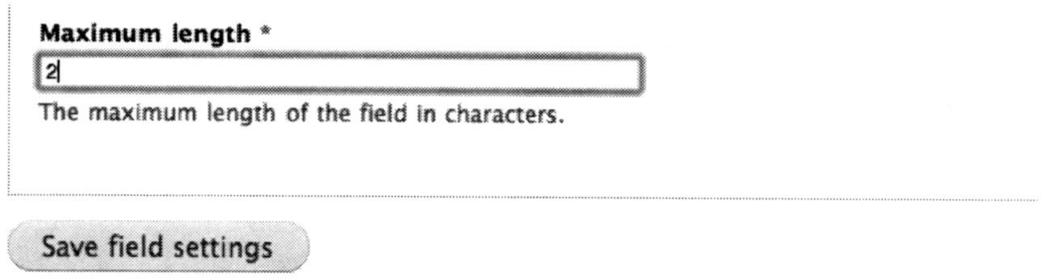

Maximum length *

`2`

The maximum length of the field in characters.

Save field settings

Figure 8–19. On the first field settings configuration page after adding a new text field, set its maximum length.

6. On the next configuration screen, the size of the field should not be greater than the maximum length, so cut that down to 2, too, as shown in Figure 8–20.

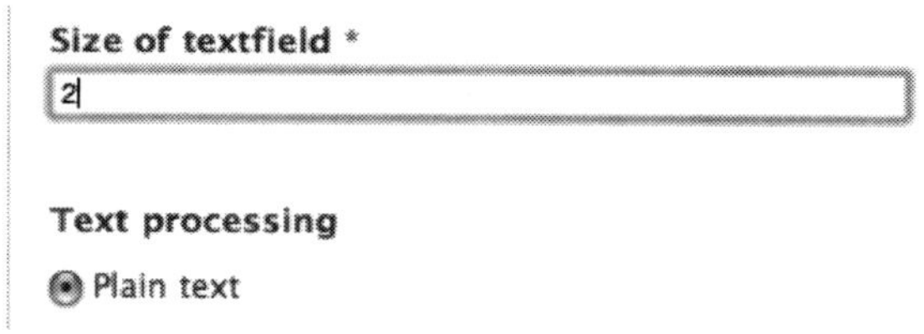

Size of textfield *

`2`

Text processing

◉ Plain text

Figure 8–20. Setting the size of the textfield in the Chapter settings for the Chapter number text field

7. Everything else can stay at its defaults, though adding help text for people who will be putting in values for the field is often a good idea: *The chapter number (integer) or an appendix letter.*

Setting How the Chapter Content Type Displays Its Fields

Immediately after setting up the fields for a content type (the Manage fields tab) is a good time to take a first pass at setting how they will look when displayed (the Display fields tab).

1. In this case, hide the labels of everything, move the chapter summary to the top image below the Chapter number, and set the image style to large, as shown in Figure 8–21.

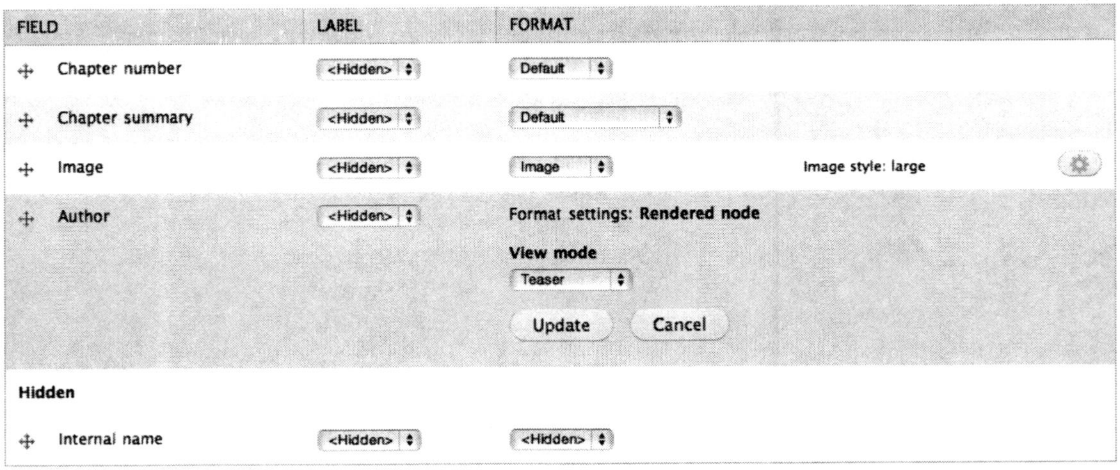

FIELD	LABEL	FORMAT		
⊹ Chapter number	\<Hidden\> ⬍	Default ⬍		
⊹ Chapter summary	\<Hidden\> ⬍	Default ⬍		
⊹ Image	\<Hidden\> ⬍	Image ⬍	Image style: large	⚙
⊹ Author	\<Hidden\> ⬍	Format settings: **Rendered node** **View mode** Teaser ⬍ Update Cancel		
Hidden				
⊹ Internal name	\<Hidden\> ⬍	\<Hidden\> ⬍		

Figure 8–21. Configuring the display of the fields of the Chapter summary content type for the default view mode (which includes full content view)–and setting the view mode for referenced Author content

---

▦ **Note** This section is called "Making the Table of Contents," but you'll note that what you really do is make a table of contents *possible*. If this causes a little cognitive dissonance, good—you are on the same wavelength as most people you will build web sites for. From the perspective of a Drupal site builder, a finished site is one that will accept particular content, put it in the right place, and generally do everything it needs to do. From the perspective of a site initiator, a finished site is one that has all the content written or added. In an ideal world the people who will be responsible for updating content will add the content in the first place, which achieves real content, testing, and training all at once. You need to be certain at this point that you won't lose their data; this is another benefit of capturing the development of site features in code (see Chapters 13 and 34 and Appendix A).

---

2. Always put in at least a couple of examples. Chapter 4 mentions the Devel module for generating content pre-filled with Lorem ipsum (fake filler text), random images, and meaningless taxonomy terms. For quickly pasting in filler text there is also a Firefox plug-in (sogame.cat/dummylipsum). Whenever possible, however, it is best to test your functionality and design with real examples.

3. For the table of contents, you need to start with making the "Chapter" that will be the top-level page and contain all the others. Go to *Add content* ➤ *Chapter* (node/add/book). The Chapter title in this one case is the book title, and the internal name can be dgd7. The summary is optional.

Note Book module would allow you to create the top level of the book as one content type and keep the children a different content type, but there was no compelling reason for the top level of the table of contents to have truly different functionality.

4. The action starts with a new vertical tab on the content adding form, Book outline. Change Book from <none> to <create a new book>, and Drupal updates the page in place to let you know "This will be the top-level page in this book." Don't worry about the confusing wording, you are indeed creating a new book outline (see Figure 8–22).

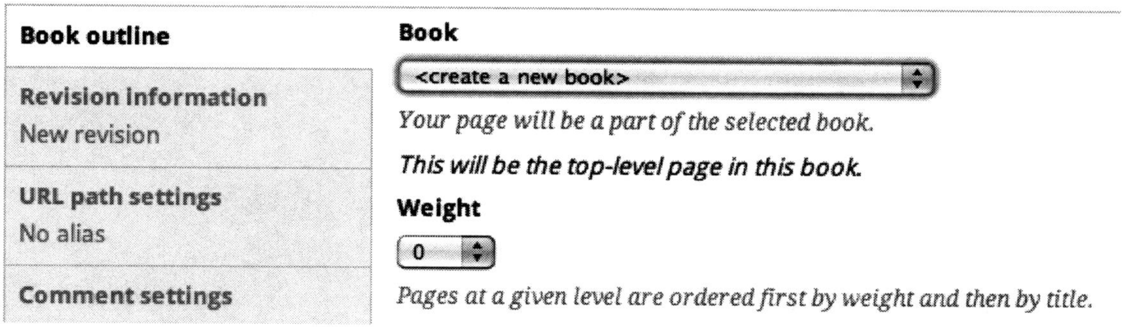

Book outline	Book
Revision Information New revision	<create a new book>
	Your page will be a part of the selected book.
	This will be the top-level page in this book.
URL path settings No alias	**Weight** 0
Comment settings	*Pages at a given level are ordered first by weight and then by title.*

Figure 8–22. Create the piece of content that will be the top level of a new book

Note When creating or editing outline-enabled content after a top-level page (and hence a book outline) already exist, you will be able to select that book here. You will then be given a further option to choose the parent item within the book for the new content you are creating.

5. After creating your first (or any) content that is part of a book outline, you will note that it displays a link for adding a child page. Use the Add child page link to add a section placeholder and a few chapter summaries to the outline (See Figure 8–23).

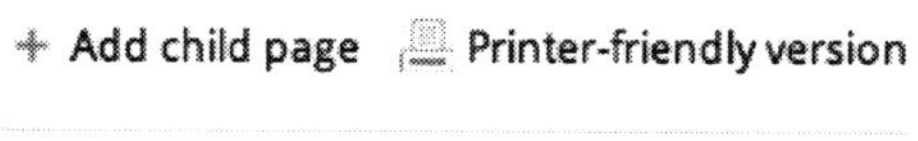

＋ Add child page ░ Printer-friendly version

Figure 8–23. The Add child page link (and Printer-friendly version link) provided by Book module

Using Menu Block to Display a Better Table of Contents

The outlining ability of Book module allows outline to go nine levels deep, but the book navigation only shows the first level. This means that if we divide the chapters into the Parts of the book, people visiting the site will only see the Parts listed below the top-level page and in the block provided by Book module. Surely Drupal can do better. And it can, with help from a contributed module you might not expect to be of help here: Menu Block.

Even though book outlines do not show up on the menu administration pages, Book module is secretly using Drupal's menu links under the hood. The fantastic Menu Block module takes advantage of this to let you create exactly the book navigation menu you want. Download and install the Menu Block module (project page `drupal.org/project/menu_block`).

When installing, Menu Block confirms its quality by going the extra mile and providing a message with a link to where and how to administer it (see Figure 8–24).

▓ **Tip** If you use Drush to install modules (`drush dl menu_block; drush en -y menu_block`), you still get a module-provided message (albeit not the link). See Chapters 2 and 26 for much more Drush!

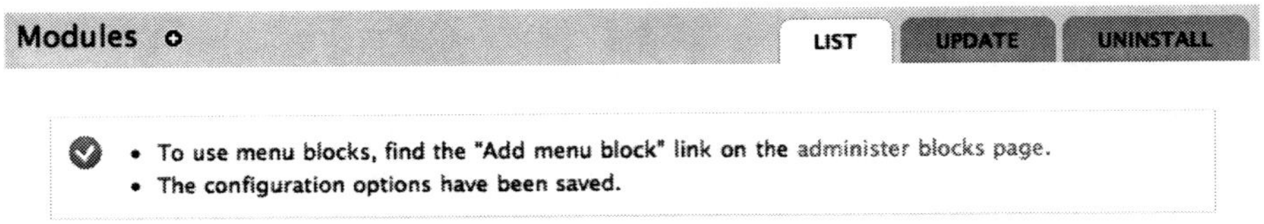

| Modules ○ | | LIST | UPDATE | UNINSTALL |

> ✓ • To use menu blocks, find the "Add menu block" link on the administer blocks page.
>   • The configuration options have been saved.

Figure 8–24. Helpful message and link from the Menu block module when it is installed

1. Couldn't be easier—follow the link to the usual Blocks administration page (admin/structure/block). There next to the + Add block link is a + Add menu block link (admin/structure/block/add-menu-block). Once on the Menu block form, immediately click over to the Advanced options tab—not to worry, it just shows (via JavaScript) a few otherwise hidden pieces of the form (see Figure 8–25).

2. Block title as link will make the block title link to the top-level book page, which happens to mimic the behavior of Drupal core's book block title when Show block only on book pages is checked. Might as well keep that behavior.

3. What gets interesting is that for the Menu you can select Definitive Guide to Drupal 7—which is a book outline. In a strange quirk, the Parent item allows something it calls `<root of Definitive Guide to Drupal 7>` but the real root, from the perspective of the Book module, is the top-level page, which is the next choice in the select drop-down: `Definitive Guide to Drupal 7`.

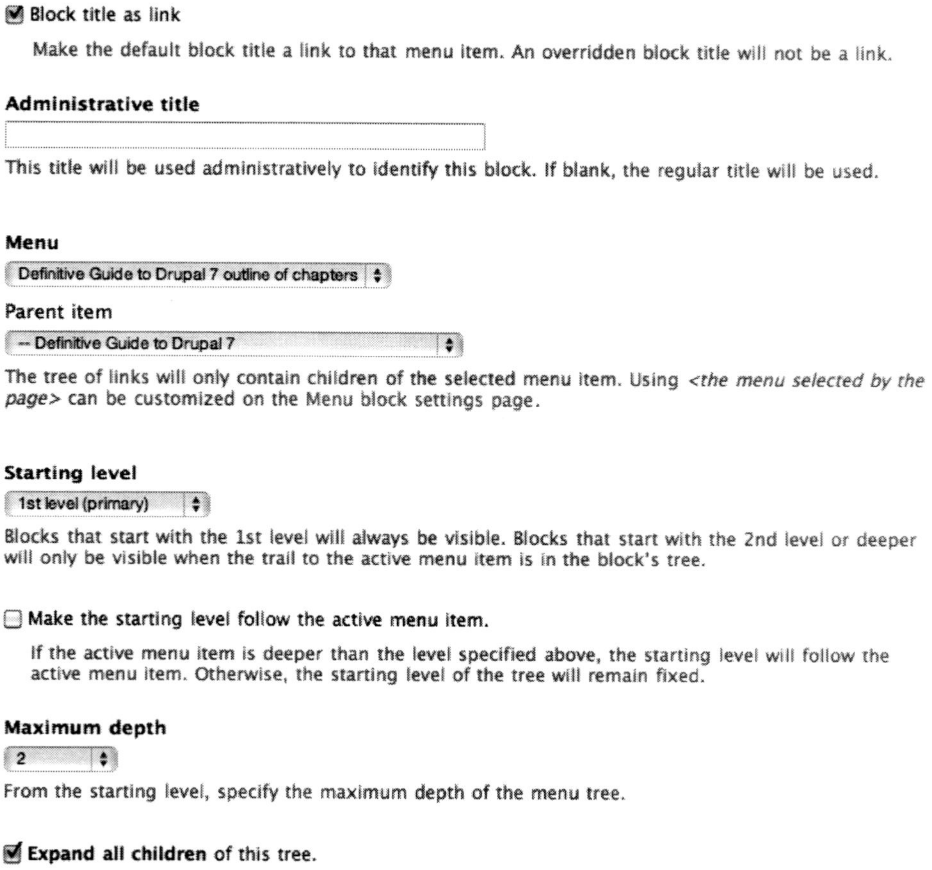

☑ **Block title as link**

Make the default block title a link to that menu item. An overridden block title will not be a link.

Administrative title

[   ]

This title will be used administratively to identify this block. If blank, the regular title will be used.

Menu

[Definitive Guide to Drupal 7 outline of chapters ▲▼]

Parent item

[-- Definitive Guide to Drupal 7   ▲▼]

The tree of links will only contain children of the selected menu item. Using *<the menu selected by the page>* can be customized on the Menu block settings page.

Starting level

[1st level (primary) ▲▼]

Blocks that start with the 1st level will always be visible. Blocks that start with the 2nd level or deeper will only be visible when the trail to the active menu item is in the block's tree.

☐ **Make the starting level follow the active menu item.**

If the active menu item is deeper than the level specified above, the starting level will follow the active menu item. Otherwise, the starting level of the tree will remain fixed.

Maximum depth

[2   ▲▼]

From the starting level, specify the maximum depth of the menu tree.

☑ **Expand all children** of this tree.

Figure 8–25. Key menu block settings for the table of contents (advanced options view required to set them all)

4. Below this, as a feature provided by the core Block module, you can immediately configure the region the new block should show in and its visibility settings. Put it in the left sidebar of all but the front page by setting the Region settings for your theme to Left sidebar and in Visibility settings set Pages to Show block on specific pages: All pages except those listed, and then listing in the box, <front>.

▪ **Tip** When selecting a region for a block through the main block listing administration page, the JavaScript-powered UI will whip it away and put it in that region. It may appear at the top of that region, but it will really place it at the bottom when you save (until this bug is fixed: drupal.org/node/1039666). Move it to the spot you want, or drag it down a slot and back up (you don't have to let go) to put it at the top for real.

■ **Tip** If using a theme that omits sidebars on the front page, or otherwise controls what blocks get seen on what pages, it is important to match those visibility options in the block configuration. Otherwise, Drupal is loading blocks only to throw them out, never to be displayed. The Omega theme (`drupal.org/project/omega`), which allows radical changes in presentation through the UI, recommends the Context module (`drupal.org/project/context`) to determine block visibility so as not to load blocks that are not displayed.

Adding the Table of Contents to the Main Menu

Site visitors need a way to see the table of contents, so link to it from the main menu.

1. Under *Administration* ➤ *Structure* ➤ *Menus*, click the Add link in the Main menu row (`admin/structure/menu/manage/main-menu/add`).

■ **Tip** While developing a site, you may want to add this Add menu link page to your Toolbar with the black plus sign.

2. Put in a title for the menu link and the path to the content you want to link to (in this case the root book page is node number 50).

   - Menu link title: Outline of Chapters

   - Path: node/50

   - Give it a little weight, a 3, just to see where it goes

3. The best you can do with weights on this page is guess, so don't worry much about it. After saving a new menu link, Drupal takes us to a page listing all the links in the menu, which you can reorder via drag and drop.

Linking Chapters to Their Authors

With both chapter summaries and author profiles represented on the site, we should make a connection between them. This could be done by editing the chapter summary text and inserting an HTML link to the main page holding the author profile. The Drupal way, as usual, is more complicated and more powerful.

What you're doing in the technical sense is referencing the Author profile content type from the Chapter summary content type. You will see later in this chapter one way to follow the connections in the other directions as well—viewing the author profile and seeing the chapters that author wrote. This is directly analogous to the user reference field added to the Author profile content type. This time, you'll configure fields on the Chapter summary content type (admin/structure/types/manage/book/fields) and add a node reference field limited to content of type Author profile. This same process is described in more detail in "Connecting Content Types with a Node Reference," the third part of the next section.

▓ **Tip** When the Relation project (`drupal.org/project/relation`) is mature (it is the more modestly named successor to the Awesome Relationships module), you will be able to use a field to reference any entity—for instance, if you had created the author profiles with the Profile2 module. Until then, the References project provides Node reference and User reference modules to connect anything that takes a field to nodes and to users.

Adding a Resource Content Type That References Chapters

For supplemental online material referenced from chapters in the book, we need to add another content type.

1. Give it a name, *Resource*. The machine name that Drupal gives it is just fine as it is, *resource*.

2. Give it a description, *A reference page or other resource for the Definitive Guide to Drupal 7. Connects to a book chapter.*

3. Set the default publishing options to published and create new revision. There's no reason to have any menus available in Menu settings, as resources will not be listed in any menu. Instead, we'll be making links to these resources from their respective chapters. Therefore, we uncheck the Main menu option.

4. Select to use the submit again button provided by the Add Another module (this module was ported from Drupal 6 to Drupal 7 in chapter 21).

5. Comments can stay enabled and other settings as default also.

▓ **Tip** You can administer most content type settings for all content types at once with the Content Type Overview module (`drupal.org/project/content_type_overview`) described in Chapter 4.

The normal textarea will work fine for people to write up the resource, but we still have some fields to add.

Reusing Chapter's Image Field

Like chapter summaries, resources can contain images and diagrams as well as written text.

■ **Note** When to reuse a field, and when to create a new one? The most important consideration is whether you will ever want to access data for that field type from two content types at once. If the data is dissimilar even though it uses the same field type–such as number of miles on a race course content type and number of gallons in a gas tank for a car content type, both stored as decimal–create a new field. However, content types that have the same relationship to a taxonomy vocabulary, for instance, should share the same field, as is done with Suggestions, Resources, and the original Articles all using the tag term reference field on the definitivedrupal.org site.

It's possible you'll want to create a view of all images attached to chapters or to resources and you do want image fields to act exactly the same on both content types. Therefore, reuse the chapter image field.

Allowing People to Attach Generic Files to Content

A basic purpose of the resource content type is to include anything associated with chapters that doesn't fit in the pages of the book—meaning it absolutely needs to allow authors to upload files. This is simply adding another field—of type File. Give it the label Attachments and the machine name file (or really, anything you like).

1. Two options unique to File fields (including Image fields, which extend the basic File type) are Allowed file extensions and File directory. We'll add sql to the allowed extensions, so database files ending in .sql can be attached, and make the directory used within the files directory resource (see Figure 8–26).

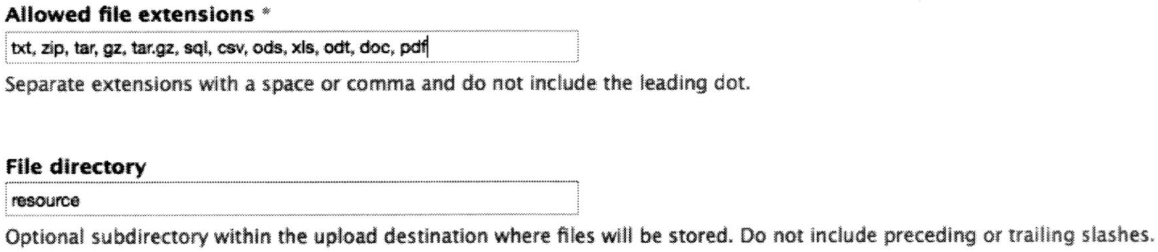

Allowed file extensions *

txt, zip, tar, gz, tar.gz, sql, csv, ods, xls, odt, doc, pdf

Separate extensions with a space or comma and do not include the leading dot.

File directory

resource

Optional subdirectory within the upload destination where files will be stored. Do not include preceding or trailing slashes.

Figure 8–26. File field settings specific to the a content type: Allowed file extensions and File directory

2. For the Attachments field everywhere settings, make the Number of values Unlimited. (Keep Enable Display field checked so that authors can choose to hide an attached file and link to it in the content, and for the preselected behavior keep Files displayed by default checked also.)

3. Next and finally, the resource content needs a way to reference the nodes it is attached to, the book chapter content type.

Connecting Content Types with a Node Reference

You've used the References modules, Node reference, and User reference, already in this chapter, so you know the drill.

1. On the Resource content type's Manage field's page (`admin/structure/types/manage/resource/fields`) add a new field of type Node reference, and on the next page you'll get to limit it to the chapter content type (see Figure 8–27).

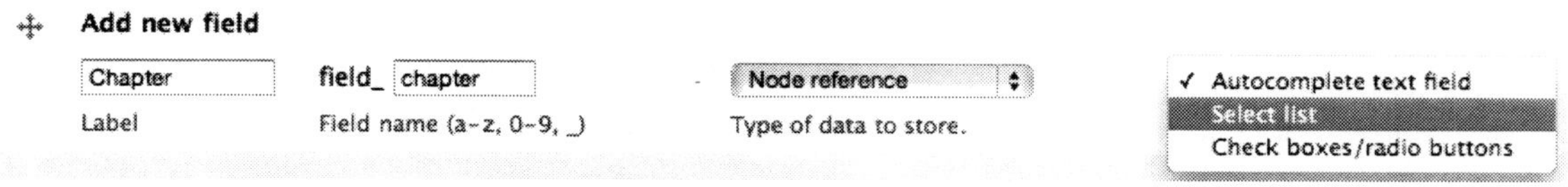

Add new field

Chapter	field_ chapter	Node reference ⬍	✓ Autocomplete text field
Label	Field name (a-z, 0-9, _)	Type of data to store.	Select list
			Check boxes/radio buttons

Figure 8–27. Add new field to the Resources content type that will reference Chapter summary content

2. Change the widget from the default Autocomplete text field to Select list, and Save the form.

3. For Content types that can be referenced, checkmark only Chapter summary and Save field settings.

4. Make it a Required field, leave the number of values at 1 and other settings as they are, and Save settings.

Managing Resource Content Type Display

Now that you've added all your fields, switch over to the Manage display tab (`admin/structure/types/manage/resource/display`) and do a quick tuning of the display of these fields. Do this for the Default view mode; resources are not expected to be seen as teasers so that and the other view modes can be ignored, at least for now. Hide the body label, change the file attachments display format to Table of Files, and make the chapter title inline (see Figure 8–28).

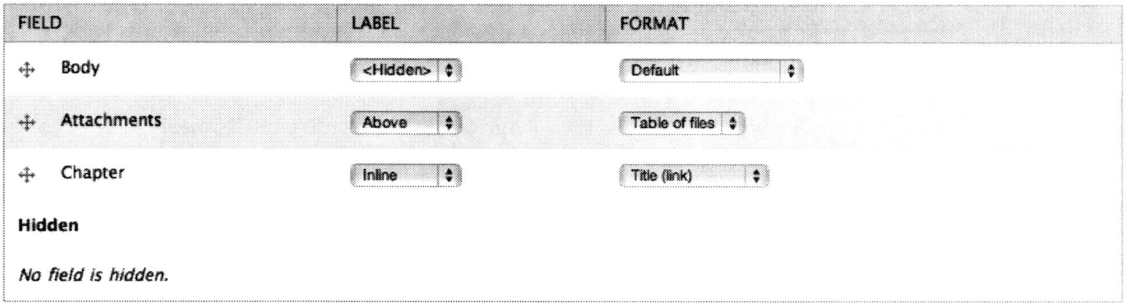

FIELD	LABEL	FORMAT
✛ Body	<Hidden> ⬍	Default ⬍
✛ Attachments	Above ⬍	Table of files ⬍
✛ Chapter	Inline ⬍	Title (link) ⬍

Hidden

No field is hidden.

Figure 8–28. Manage display form for the Resource content type, Default view mode

Showing Content That References the Post Being Viewed

You have made it so each Resource references the Chapter it belongs to, but how do you show these resources when someone views that chapter? Similarly, you have made it so the Chapter content type references the authors who wrote it. How, though, do people viewing an author profile get to see what chapters that author helped write?

At the time of this writing, the various modules that provided this capability in Drupal 6 have not been ported to Drupal 7, and the new Relation project (drupal.org/project/relation) is not ready. It should not be a huge surprise, though, that the powerhouse module you are already familiar with, Views, is up to the task. Let's do a view that shows related resources when viewing a chapter first.

1. Create a new view. You can name it Resources (machine name will be resources).

2. This will be an unusual view, compared to the listing page views built earlier in this chapter, but as usual, start with Filter. Uncheck Page, checkmark Block (the defaults here are fine), and Press **Continue & edit**.

■ **Tip** In the main Views edit page, these same filter criteria appear as Content: Published (yes) and Content: Type (=Resource), and here you could set more and more complex values.

---

3. Next, if only to make Views stop complaining about it, add a field, of group Content, Content: Title. Uncheck Create a label; people don't need to be told that it's a title. Leave Link this field to the original piece of content checked. Under Style settings, checkmark Wrap field in HTML and give it the HTML element H4. Press Apply.

Now, the most unique and important part of this view is the Contextual filters, found under the collapsed Advanced fieldset in the third column (in previous versions of Views, Contextual filters were called Arguments). This is how you can get one view to behave differently depending on its context—that is, depending on the arguments passed in. To show all the resources associated with a chapter, the view needs to know what chapter is being looked at and how all resources (potentially) relate to it. A more technical description: to show all the nodes of type Resource when viewing a node of type Chapter summary, the View needs to know the node ID of that chapter summary, and it needs to know which Resource nodes reference that node ID. Views contextual filters provides both these things.

1. Add a contextual filter from group fields, Fields: field_chapter (field_chapter) - nid. Views also provides here the information Appears in: node:resource. If you cannot find the field you are looking for by scanning the long list visually, nor by searching for the title with the **Search** box provided, a search in the modial dialog, as by typing control+f can allow you to search the "Appears in" text to bring you to the right field filter after a few tries. The addition of this field as an argument–really, an argument handler–takes care of the need to know which resources reference a chapter. Next, you need to hand in a chapter node.

2. A block view is considered as never receiving any argument. This means the setting that matters is When the filter value is NOT in the URL, which you need to set to Provide default value.

3. Once you've told the view that you'll provide the default value, you can proceed to set this default value to the Type Content ID from URL.

▦ **Note** Even if a node has a path alias (such as moresite for this chapter's page online), Views uses the internal path ('node/198' for this chapter's online summary), so it is always able to access the node ID (198) from the URL.

Save the view, and go to *Administration* ➤ *Structure* ➤ *Blocks* (admin/structure/block) to put the block just created by you and the Views module in the region in which you want it to display. The new block will be the name of the view followed by the machine name of the view followed by the human-readable name of the display (which is Block by default).

▦ **Tip** Views is so powerful it can be hard to figure out. It has good (and, with your help, continuously improving) documentation through the Advanced Help module (drupal.org/project/advanced_help), but clicking to configure and testing, clicking and testing, clicking and testing, and some more clicking and testing is inevitable at some point. Views is *also* wildly popular, which means at least two things. First, you can often find tutorials on Drupal.org and the blogs of Drupalistas for just what you need if you search for the right combination of words. Second, Views-related questions asked in IRC (that are not so obscure that no one has done anything like it before) have a pretty good likelihood of getting answered.

Giving Faces to the People Posting on Your Site

We love the people who leave suggestions and comments and would like to see their faces. Drupal has user pictures built in (and already enabled by the standard installation profile). A module created by Arnaud Ligny (Narno) and maintained by Dave Reid (davereid) uses the eponymous Gravatar service to use people's already associated avatars. (It allows the use of other services and will likely support libravatar.org out of the box.) Download and install this module, which you can read more about at drupal.org/project/gravatar.

1. Configure it at *Administration* ➤ *Configuration* ➤ *People* ➤ *Gravatar* (admin/config/people/gravatar). The module provides a large number of options for default images, including using a default you can upload yourself with the user module, and will preview the choices in real time as you select them (see Figure 8–29).

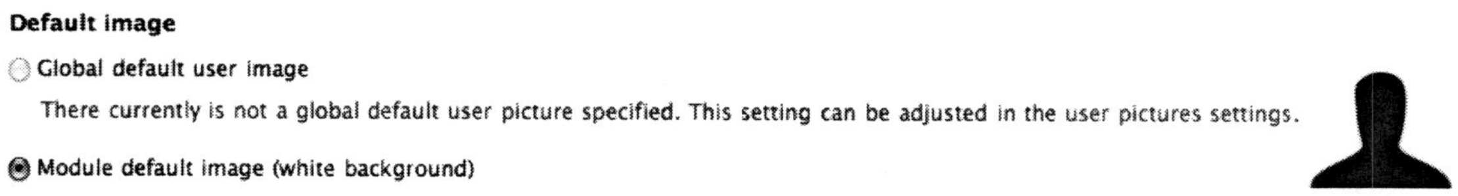

Default image

◯ Global default user image

    There currently is not a global default user picture specified. This setting can be adjusted in the user pictures settings.

◉ Module default image (white background)

Figure 8–29. The default image provided by the Gravatar module (which is in addition to ones provided by the Gravatar service)

2. Set the Gravatar size to be 100 pixels—the same as the thumbnail image style (see `admin/config/media/image-styles/edit/thumbnail`), which is the image style set for people's uploaded pictures (see `admin/config/people/accounts`).

3. For the book site, leave the Image maturity filter at G (you don't want everything listed as allowed in PG fit into a single image).

Now when people comment, whether registered with the site or not, if they are on Gravatar with the e-mail address they give, they'll get their picture with their comment.

Display Tricks: Tilting Images

The main use for Drupal 7 core's media styles is the different sizes you can assign, but there is a range of other effects you can apply to a given image style. The first step is finding where Drupal hides these image styles, which is *Administration* ➤ *Configuration* ➤ *Media* ➤ *Image styles* (`admin/config/media/image-styles`).

■ **Tip** You won't see anything happen when you apply rotate or desaturate effects to an image style if your site's Status report page (`admin/reports/status`) reports a problem with the GD library. You'll need to install it correctly; see `drupal.org/node/256876`. (Drupal core may be changed to allow these image effects using the alternative Imagemagick library, as discussed 27 comments into this issue: `drupal.org/node/758628`.)

Tilt thumbnails (and so user pictures) one degree up and to the left, just because you can (and to see if anyone notices).

If you do not want a tilt applied to every thumbnail to appear anywhere on your site—which includes, by default, the example shown after uploading an image—you will instead want to add a new style and configure user pictures to use it specially.

■ **Note** By the time you read this, the Gravatar module will very likely support image style transformations on gravatar images (see `drupal.org/node/334630`). For the moment, the tilt you see is done with CSS3 (see Chapter 15 and its online resources at `dgd7.org/86`). There's more than one way to munge an image!

Adding a Text Format That Allows Images

The Filtered HTML text format that exists allows users to post content that includes basic HTML—without allowing the inclusion of any scripts or code that could compromise the security of your web site. Unfortunately, malicious code can be placed in files included with the img tag, and so the ability for people to include images is left out. The Full HTML text format, for its part, allows images but is *far* less secure and should be restricted to administrators and other highly trusted users. (A user could easily add malicious or merely page-breaking code to your site unwittingly just by copying and pasting from something including script tags.) Conclusion: If you want to allow unknown users to include some HTML, and trusted users to include images, you need to create a new text format.

Text formats are collections of input filters. Input filters process people's text input—when the content is output. The Filtered HTML text format is different from the Full HTML text format (as provided by the Standard installation profile) because it includes a Limit allowed HTML tags filter. The tags to which content is limited is configurable per text format in Drupal 7.

The allowed HTML tags made available to content authors by default in the Limit allowed HTML tags input filter used in the Filtered HTML text format are a bit too limited. In addition to images, if you want to let people add headings or superscript text, you need to add the tags that make these possible: img, h1 or h2 through h6, and sup.

1. To create a new text format, go to *Administration* ➤ *Configuration* ➤ *Content authoring* ➤ *Text formats*, *+ Add text format* (admin/config/content/formats/add) and give it a Name like Filtered HTML Plus (the machine name will be filtered_html_plus).

2. Give it the Roles *administrator*, *author*, and *trusted* (provided you have created these last two).

3. Checkmark the same Enabled filters as Filtered HTML uses: Limit allowed HTML tags, Convert line breaks into HTML, Convert URLs into links, and Correct faulty and chopped off HTML. (Include Code filter if you installed that module when it was discussed in Chapter 4; be sure to set it to come after Limit allowed HTML tags in Filter processing order.)

▮ **Note** Through the miracle of JavaScript, any filter newly checkmarked enabled under Enabled filters will appear under Filter processing order for drag-and-drop sorting. (Without JavaScript or in a screen reader, all options are provided with weight select fields.)

---

4. The one change you want to make from the Filtered HTML text format is in the Filter settings. Here you will have a tab for Limit allowed HTML tags and will be able to edit the Allowed HTML tags. Here is an example of an expanded allowed tags list (see Figure 8–30):

`<a> <em> <strong> <cite> <blockquote> <code> <ul> <ol> <li> <dl> <dt> <dd> <img> <h2> <h3> <h4> <h5> <h6> <tt> <output> <q> <sub> <sup>`

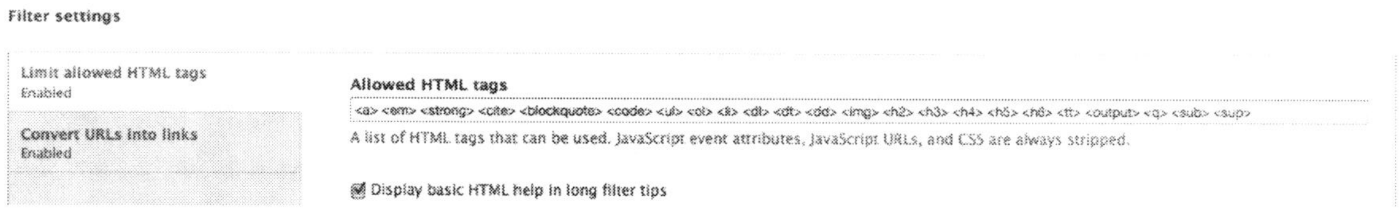

Figure 8–30. Allowed HTML tags configuration in the vertical tabs at the bottom of the text format form

5. Save it all with Save configuration at the bottom, and you have a new text format that allows images, available only to users to whom you have given a role indicating trust.

Bonus: Making It Easy to Insert Images into Posts

The authors will want to add pictures, screenshots, and diagrams to the draft chapters or bonus content hosted on the web site, and readers will undoubtedly want to leave comments with pictures of themselves with this book on Caribbean beaches and at the summit of Kilimanjaro. You can make this easy with two contributed modules for inserting and automatically resizing user-added images, cleverly named Insert (drupal.org/project/insert) and Image resize filter (drupal.org/project/image_resize_filter).

You know the drill with Drush by now:

```
drush dl insert image_resize_filter; drush en -y insert image_resize_filter
```

▓ **Tip** Many modules don't do anything until they are configured, and some do not have their own settings page but hide their configuration in some already-existing administration page. We always check the messages at the top of the page after installing modules, because some helpful modules provide notes and even links to their administration pages. (Drush reports back to you with the notes, but not links, when it installs modules.)

Image resize filter does an exemplary job of self-documenting and links to the text format administration page (admin/config/content/formats) following the note "The image resize filter has been installed. Before this does anything, the image resize filter needs to be added to one or more text formats." (Remember that you need to add <img> to the list of allowed HTML tags, as you just did previously, for Insert and Image Resize Filter to have the desired effect.)

Edit the Full HTML and your new Filtered HTML Plus text formats and under Enabled filters enable Image resize filter in each (don't forget to click Save configuration both times).

Now you need to configure the Insert module, which at the time of this writing did not provide any helpful notes on installation. Its settings are hidden in each Image field on every content type or other entity (including comments per content type, for which you may want to add an image field and use this setup).

Go to a content type and add a new image field or edit an existing image field. You can improve the image field for the Chapter summary (book) content type at *Administration* ➤ *Structure* ➤ *Content types* ➤ *Chapter summary* ➤ *Manage fields*, click the *edit* link in the Image row (admin/structure/types/manage/book/fields/field_image/edit). You shouldn't need to change any properties for this field, just make your way down to the Insert settings, which are collapsed and easy to miss.

▓ **Tip** Double-check that you have checkmarked Enable Alt field. This is a requirement for sites to meet basic accessibility standards: every information-carrying image should have alternate text conveying as best as possible the same information as the image. Read more about accessibility in Appendix E.

Expand the collapsed Insert fieldset and checkmark Enable insert button. Make the Maximum image insert width 600 pixels; this is very useful to make it easier for people to set the size of images they upload (and less likely for huge images on a page to ruin your site's design).

Now if users browse for an image for Chapter summary content and upload it right away, they will have an Insert button next to the images thumbnail. When they click the Insert button the HTML for displaying that image will be inserted into the text area. The magic of the Image resize filter module is it uses Drupal core's image handling to make a version of the image that is the size that the HTML img tag's height and width properties declare it to be. This correctly sized image is cached, giving much better performance than if a large uploaded image stays full size and is merely resized by the browser. If you have a WYSIWYG set up (see Chapter 4 and dgd7.org/modules) this often becomes dead simple for the user: resizing by dragging the images borders.

▪ **Tip** Insert module inserts the image with the full URL, so if you are doing any sort of content staging or simply working on the site at a temporary domain before taking it officially live, you will want to install the Pathologic module (drupal.org/project/pathologic) and enable its input filter Correct URLs with Pathologic (yes, yet another module that works its magic through the text formatting system) and configure it to convert your local, staging, or temporary domain to the live domain (for instance, tell it to consider http://dgd7.localhost/ as "local" to have it converted to http://definitivedrupal.org/ when on the live site). Pathologic can also ensure your in-site links and images work for people viewing your content with an RSS reader or on an aggregator like the Drupal Planet (drupal.org/planet).

Limiting Access to the Suggestion Status Field

You have hidden a field from site visitors, but how do you hide a field from people who are allowed to edit? That's what you need to do for the Suggestion content type's Status field—regular users should be able to submit suggestions, but only administrators should be able to set its status. Fortunately, there's a module for that: the Field Permissions module (drupal.org/project/field_permissions).

1. The Field Permissions module, once enabled, does not (at the time of this writing) provide a Configure link by its entry on the modules administration page. It does provide a Permissions link, but that is only for its own Administer Field Permissions permission, which Drupal has been kind enough to grant to the Administrator role already. There aren't any new field permissions on the permissions page, yet. The magic must start elsewhere... ah, there it is, in Structure: *Administration ➤ Structure ➤ Field permissions* (admin/structure/field_permissions).

2. The table on this page shows all the fields on your site and indicates for each whether any permissions handling is enabled for that field. Scroll down through the fields to the field_status row (they are sorted alphabetically by machine name) and click on Suggestion in the **Used in** column.

3. This takes you to the Suggestion content type's Field settings page for the Status field. This is the same page you reach when adding or editing a field; the Field Permissions module just gives you an easier way to get there than *Administration ➤ Structure ➤ Content types ➤ Suggestion ➤ Manage fields ➤ Status* (admin/structure/types/manage/suggestion/fields/field_status/field-settings).

4. Ignore the scary warning "There is data for this field in the database. The field settings can no longer be changed." Drupal core (at the time of this writing) doesn't understand that the Field permissions settings (unlike the locked Vocabulary setting, for instance) are perfectly acceptable to change at any time (see Figure 8–31).

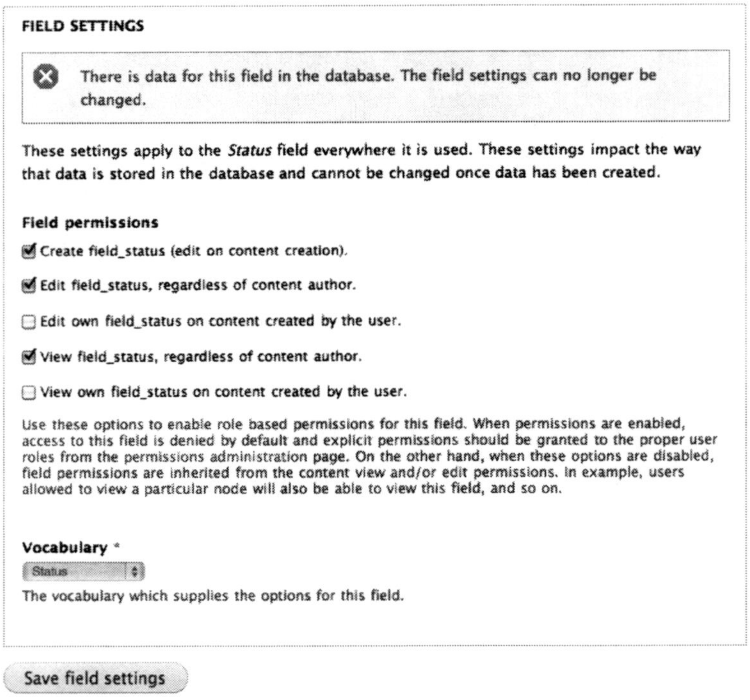

FIELD SETTINGS

❌ There is data for this field in the database. The field settings can no longer be changed.

These settings apply to the *Status* field everywhere it is used. These settings impact the way that data is stored in the database and cannot be changed once data has been created.

Field permissions

☑ Create field_status (edit on content creation).

☑ Edit field_status, regardless of content author.

☐ Edit own field_status on content created by the user.

☑ View field_status, regardless of content author.

☐ View own field_status on content created by the user.

Use these options to enable role based permissions for this field. When permissions are enabled, access to this field is denied by default and explicit permissions should be granted to the proper user roles from the permissions administration page. On the other hand, when these options are disabled, field permissions are inherited from the content view and/or edit permissions. In example, users allowed to view a particular node will also be able to view this field, and so on.

Vocabulary *

[Status   ◆]

The vocabulary which supplies the options for this field.

[Save field settings]

Figure 8–31. Field settings page with the new Field permissions options

---

■ **Note** The user interface for Field permissions may change to avoid such unhelpful warnings and other oddities, but the basic concepts are likely to remain the same: choose what fields you want to set permissions on, and then set their permissions via the usual Permissions pages. (One oddity that is unlikely to change, though, is that the Field permission settings are per field regardless of content type, yet can only be edited through a content type page. This approach is pretty baked into the Drupal 7 Field UI.)

5.   Checkmark three of these permissions: Create field_status (edit on content creation), Edit field_status, regardless of content author and View field_status, regardless of content author. This may seem backward, marking the very permissions we want to take away, but that is how Field permissions module works: once selected, each of these becomes a permission you can edit on the main Permissions page (see Figure 8–32).

■ **Note** Create field may seem to be a special case of edit field, but Field permissions module does not treat it that way—if you had not checkmarked it on the field settings page to make it available here on the permissions page, all roles would continue to be able to set status while creating Suggestion content.

---

6.   Do heed this warning from the Field permissions module: "When permissions are enabled, access to this field is denied by default and explicit permissions should be granted to the proper user roles from the permissions administration page." After you Save field settings, then, head over to *Administration ➤ People ➤ Permissions* (admin/people/permissions), and things are a little more interesting.

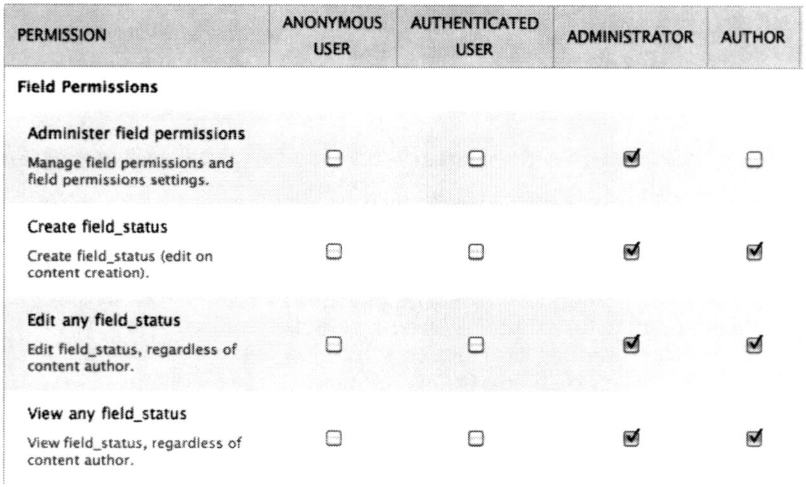

PERMISSION	ANONYMOUS USER	AUTHENTICATED USER	ADMINISTRATOR	AUTHOR
Field Permissions				
Administer field permissions				
Manage field permissions and field permissions settings.	☐	☐	☑	☐
Create field_status				
Create field_status (edit on content creation).	☐	☐	☑	☑
Edit any field_status				
Edit field_status, regardless of content author.	☐	☐	☑	☑
View any field_status				
View field_status, regardless of content author.	☐	☐	☑	☑

Figure 8–32. Field permission permissions. The first permission is about access to the module itself, but all additional permissions control access to fields and came into being when you selected them in field settings.

7.   For the three permissions you made available, give them to the administrator and author roles. With these settings, non-administrator, non-author users will not have any access to the Status field. Don't forget to Save permissions at the bottom of the form, and you are done limiting access to the status vocabulary on the Suggestion content type.

▓ **Note** If you only wanted to hide a field from non-privileged users on the node edit form, you could write a few lines of custom code implementing hook_form_alter() instead of using Field permissions module. You could of course write custom code to conditionally show a field based on users roles, but that's getting to be more trouble than it's worth. (In this case the site initiators can't decide whether visitors should see the Suggestion status or not, so making it controllable in the UI makes perfect sense.)

Autogenerating Human-readable URLs with Pathauto

Doing this is much slicker than that awkward headline. The first step, as always, is getting the required modules. Pathauto's project page (drupal.org/project/pathauto) requires Token module (drupal.org/project/token), which you have already installed if you set up a module that also requires it such as Comment Notify.

```
drush dl pathauto; drush en -y pathauto
Project pathauto (7.x-1.0-beta1) downloaded to                    [success]
/home/ben/code/dgd7/drupal/sites/all/modules/pathauto.
The following extensions will be enabled: pathauto
Do you really want to continue? (y/n): y
pathauto was enabled successfully. [ok]
```

▓ **Note** If Token module, which Pathauto requires, had not already been installed for the sake of another module, the first line would have had to be drush dl pathauto token; drush en -y pathauto.

Pathauto does not add a single link to the Configuration overview section of administration (nor to Structure or Content). If you are clever enough to look under *Administration* ➤ *Configuration* ➤ *Search and metadata* ➤ *URL aliases* you will find four new tabs provided by the Pathauto module. To get started go to the first one, Patterns (admin/config/search/path/patterns).

First, change the Default path pattern from containing the static text content. By default Pathauto prepopulates this fallback pattern as content/[node:title], but the word content is an uninformative space waster. Instead, use the content type machine name token, [node:content-type:machine-name], like this:

```
[node:content-type:machine-name]/[node:title]
```

▓ **Tip** You can insert tokens into the text field your cursor is in by clicking on the token's name.

The Basic page content type can have no prefix—just use the title token, [node:title]. This means, for example, that your About page path might be *about* rather than *page/about*. For everything else the recommended content type machine name and node title should work quite well.

▓ **Note** The Suggestion content type could do better than the generic suggestion replacement. It could use its value for the required suggestion type vocabulary–attached to the content as a single-value taxonomy term reference field–once Dave Reid's patches in `drupal.org/node/691078` are committed to Token module.

Summary

Congratulations! You've built a fairly complex site. By configuring Views and other selected contributed modules you were able to showcase the book's authors, present the table of contents, connect authors and resources to chapters, and allow visitors to participate. This is a taste of how far you can go in Drupal without writing any code. (You can go even farther by writing code, and after covering theming and module development in the next sections we will revisit this site in Chapter 33.)

Following publication of this book, the `DefinitiveDrupal.org` site will continue to have enhancements and new features built into it by adding contributed modules and configuring both core and contributed modules. To follow these developments as they are done, check in at `dgd7.org/moresite`.

PART III

■■■

Making Your Life Easier

Chapter 9 is perhaps the most important in the book: how to engage with the Drupal community.

Chapter 10 brings some more advice to bear on the critical and unavoidable practice of planning and managing projects.

Chapter 11 is about documenting your work for clients and colleagues, because it is only useful when understood by others.

Chapter 12 is all about getting your computer set up to help you in configuring or coding your projects.

Chapter 13 tackles the matter of getting your site online and then touches on how you can continue.

Chapter 14 carries a message of attaining joy from your coding or contributing by removing obstacles to unrestricted effort.

CHAPTER 9

■ ■ ■

Drupal Community: Getting Help and Getting Involved

by Ben Melançon and Susan Stewart

"Drupal: come for the software, stay for the community."

—Dries Buytaert, Drupal founder

You might be wondering how Drupal is made and where its thousands of contributed modules, themes, features, profiles, and other resources come from. The Drupal community is a somewhat nebulous concept from an outsider's perspective. Who are these people? What makes them part of the community? What's in it for me?

The Drupal community is anyone who has made Drupal better—through code, theming, translation, support, organizing, or other avenues. Becoming a community member is easy: hang around Drupal IRC, forums, or mailing lists and help people solve their Drupal problems. Hang around the issue queues on drupal.org and do bug triage, test patches, or contribute fixes. Create your own Drupal modules or themes and share them on drupal.org. Learn how to do something with Drupal, then write or improve the documentation on it.

There's a lot more to Drupal than the files delivered in one of its core downloads. Drupal 7 is great. Drupal 5 was great, too—back in 2007. Great software is constantly evolving to meet new demands. Powering Drupal's evolution is a living, breathing community that you can be part of.

There is no Central Authority assigning tasks in the Drupal ecosystem; thousands of individual Drupalistas find their own niches, all of which grow Drupal in some way. Documentation, support, issue queue triage, patch testing, bug fixing, bug reporting, test writing, and contrib module/theme maintenance are just a few of the many ways that Drupallers make Drupal better.

To the new Drupalista, or the Drupal user who is looking to contribute for the first time, this may seem like chaos. How could a bunch of strangers with different opinions, backgrounds, and motivations come together and build something as complex as a CMS—and succeed? There is order to the chaos, and this chapter intends to help you understand it and find your own niche in the Drupal ecosystem.

You'll find that during the support-giving, documenting, bug-fixing, code-writing, theming, patch-testing process you evolve from a mere consumer to a full-fledged community member. You will understand Drupal's development cycle better than a mere observer could. You'll know what to expect as Drupal's next version evolves because you are in the thick of getting it out. You'll become a more skilled, more aware, and more marketable Drupaller. You'll also be a more influential and efficient Drupaller; when you're the one reporting bugs and helping to fix them, you can draw attention to the ones that bug you the most. When you contribute code to the community, you get the eyes of other

Drupallers on it; those who want to use it will help improve it and you get more return for your time invested.

In short, the community member's Drupal-foo is always greater than the consumer's—not because you have to be awesome to be part of the community, but because being part of the community grows your awesome.

How to Get the Most from Your Participation

While there are many places to get your feet wet in the Drupal world, the fastest way to get into the thick of things is via our IRC (Internet Relay Chat) channels. The #drupal channel is something of a free-for-all while #drupal-contribute is dedicated to community activities—core development, contrib development, drupal.org infrastructure, and so on.

Perhaps the best way to get a feel for the drupal community is to idle in our IRC channels and watch the goings-on. Most of us multitask while chatting, or leave our clients logged on while we are gone, so no one minds folks who are in the channel but don't say anything, or who only chime in every now and again. It's a great place to ask questions and an invaluable resource when one begins to wander about the issue queues for the first time.

Where to Find the Community

There are literally hundreds of places to find the Drupal community. While some venues (such as the drupal.org web forums) are decidedly newbie-oriented, most cater to the entire breadth of Drupal experience. Because this book is written in English, we'll focus on English-language resources. Speakers of other languages can check drupal.org/language-specific-communities for resources in their preferred tongue. Chances are someone who speaks your language is already doing Drupal.

Reading, Listening, and Watching

There's a great deal going on in the Drupal community at any given moment. One great way to keep up on it all is through the blog posts, podcasts, and videos of your fellow Drupallers. Reading and listening aren't, strictly speaking, interacting with the Drupal community (unless you write or call back or post your own), but it's an easy way to keep up on things, learn new skills, and get into the community vibe.

Drupal Planet

The Drupal Planet aggregator (drupal.org/planet) collects Drupal-related blog posts from feeds submitted by community members to provide a central source for news and ideas from the wider Drupal community. Here you can read how-tos, announcements, wrap-ups of meetups and conferences, don't-do-what-I-did warnings, well thought-out questions, musings on Drupal's future, and reviews of Drupal distributions. In other words, you can read or watch whatever someone felt like posting that day.

Podcasts

Podcasts (lightly edited audio recordings of discussions made easily available online) have for several years been a popular, informal way for people interested in Drupal to keep up on goings-on in the community. Drupal podcasts (so far) are recorded, not done live, so you can't call in and ask questions. Nonetheless, and in part because you don't have to respond, they are a fantastic low-commitment way to get oriented and catch some of the excitement—and downright giddiness—people have about Drupal. Each episode also usually has a comment thread with links and follow-ups from the podcast.

- Lullabot (`lullabot.com/podcast`) is a high-profile Drupal consulting and training shop that has been doing podcasts since the beginning of 2006 without fail (if not quite on a regular schedule). These tend to be more than an hour long and cover a lot of ground with five or more Drupalistas participating. While at `lullabot.com/podcast`, be sure to check out Kent Bye's excellent Drupal Voices series in which he interviews a different person from the Drupal community each time; these podcasts are usually about five minutes long.

- DrupalEasy (`drupaleasy.com/podcast`) brings long-form but more focused interview-style discussions on topics relevant to the Drupal community.

- Acquia (`acquia.com/podcasts`), a company co-founded by the founder of Drupal, is focused on bringing Drupal to enterprise projects. It does short podcasts that usually feature a person currently making significant contributions to Drupal code.

- Geeks&God, a podcast helping Christian ministries use technology, has long discussion podcasts that include a Drupal spotlight. These podcasts may be of interest for their attention to applying Drupal solutions for specific communities: `geeksandgod.com/podcast`

Each of these sites are listed because they have a track record of releasing episodes up to the time of this writing. The authors will try to keep a current list of Drupal-related podcasts at `dgd7.org/podcasts`.

Drupal.org Forums

While most veteran developers don't frequent them, the forums at `drupal.org/forum` are extremely active and focus mostly on issues facing new users. The forums include places to post advertisements for paid gigs, places to get help with your Drupal questions, and more.

Groups.Drupal.org

`Groups.Drupal.org` (often abbreviated g.d.o) lets Drupalistas create groups around an interest or geographic area, so that it's easy to share news and information with others who want to hear it. So, if you are passionate about accessibility, live in the greater Indianapolis area, or want to use Drupal for your newspaper's web site, there is a Drupal group for you. If something else is your cup of Drupal tea, you can start your own group.

Mailing Lists

If you prefer to get the Drupal community delivered to your inbox, join one of Drupal's mailing lists. You can find a list of Drupal lists at `drupal.org/mailing-lists`. Lists are pretty straightforward: send an e-mail to the list address (be on-topic, please!) and it will go on to everyone subscribed to that list. You can read and reply to list messages just like any regular e-mail. Most people find it helpful to tell their mail client to sort e-mail list messages to specific folders to lessen inbox clutter.

Face to Face

Drupal has two large conferences per year, many well-attended but less formal and often free Drupal Camps, and innumerable meetups around the world. DrupalCons are always announced on the front page of drupal.org, among other places. The best place to find your local Drupal Camps and meetups is the groups.drupal.org group for your region.

DrupalCamps

Drupal Camps are perhaps the most newbie-accessible of in-person Drupal events. Camps are held in many locations throughout the world and are usually free or exceptionally low-cost to attend. Camps are generally put together by volunteers from the local Drupal group and you don't need to be a Drupal expert to help out at a camp. Help is always needed with setup and take-down, handing out lunch, recording sessions, or checking in the attendees.

Attending a Drupal Camp is a fantastic way to learn new things about Drupal on a budget; working a Drupal Camp gives you all that plus a chance to network with the local Drupal community and to become an active contributor yourself.

DrupalCons

DrupalCon is the Drupal community's twice-annual conference held in North America each spring and Europe each autumn. Thousands of Drupallers from scores of countries come together in one place, and the results are consistently astounding. DrupalCon has grown from about 300 attendees in 2007 (Sunnyvale, CA) to about 3,000 attendees in 2010 (San Francisco, CA), and even more attendees in 2011 (Chicago, IL). DrupalCon offers dozens of sessions on everything from community participation to the database abstraction layer, presented by people who create and maintain Drupal.

However, if you only attend formal sessions at DrupalCon, you are missing out. Smaller "BoF" (Birds of a Feather) gatherings provide opportunities for greater interaction while learning, and impromptu "hallway track" gatherings are just as valuable. Moreover, each night after hours, a ragtag bunch of Drupal hackers gather in the Chx Coder Lounge for all-night development. The coder lounge is a fantastic opportunity to get a little face time with some of our most prolific contributors and/or get help in making your own contributions come to life.

Drupal Meetups

If DrupalCon or DrupalCamp feels too big for your first foray into the face-to-face Drupal world, or if you need that Drupal fix more often than these events are held, the answer is your local Drupal meetup.

The most comprehensive list of Drupal happenings can be found on g.d.o at groups.drupal.org/events. This is a great way to find out where events are on a particular day, but unless you're prepared to perhaps fly thousands of miles to Mumbai for a Drupal meetup, looking up events by the day may not be the most practical way to go. Instead, take the time to join your local Drupal group(s).

■ **Tip** No authority bestows the right to call Drupal meetups. Anyone can do so. If you are in a place without a meetup group, even a neighborhood of a city, or a suburb, or just between regularly scheduled meetups, you can call one yourself. This is the other trick about meetups: you don't need to know any Drupal to call or help with them, let alone attend! It's better to do meetups with planning (line up at least one Drupal guru) and some promotion, but longtime Drupalista Cristefano set a responsiveness record by showing up at a Cambridge, Massachusetts, Drupal meetup called by this author with only a half-hour's notice. More on organizing and hosting meetups is in Chapter 38.

Knowing that it brings in people who may not have even seen g.d.o yet, some Drupalistas use their own funds to maintain Drupal groups on Meetup.com. In addition to true local Meetup.com groups, there is a Drupal Meetup group that tries to track Drupal events internationally (meetup.com/drupal-worldwide). However, anyone who posts a Drupal event on Meetup.com, Facebook, or any other service is encouraged to post to the appropriate groups.drupal.org group.

IRC

For the most immediate Drupal community involvement, head on over to IRC (Internet Relay Chat). You can find setup instructions and a full list of Drupal's IRC channels at drupal.org/irc. All the main channels are on irc.freenode.net: support questions are taken in #drupal-support, general discussion happens in #drupal, and anything involving community contributions can be discussed in #drupal-contribute. There are dozens more specific channels and language-based and regional channels as well.

IRC, like any other meeting place, has its own customs and courtesies. To help you jump in without feeling or looking like an outsider, here are some of the most important points to remember:

- Ask your question in the right channel. #drupal-contribute is not the place to ask for help with your site; #drupal-support is. See the list at drupal.org/irc for info on all of Drupal channels.

- Don't ask permission to ask a question; that's what we're here for. Don't ask who uses a module or if someone can help you with a problem. Do ask a specific question like "I have a view in a panel; how do I pass it an argument?" Assuring people that it's okay to ask or giving our resumes to every visitor is seen as a waste of time—and is disrespectful to the work our volunteers do.

- Ask your question to the entire channel. Only highlight someone (by saying their nickname in full) after they have begun to help you; this helps them easily follow the conversation.

- Do not pm (private message) any user without first asking and receiving permission in the channel. Support is kept in the channel so that everyone can participate and so that volunteers have one place to track all the people they are helping.

- Never paste large amounts (over a line or two) of code, log entries, or other text into an IRC channel. Instead, paste it into a pastebin (such as drupalbin.com) and provide the channel with a link to that paste.

- Do a quick Internet search before you ask a question. Chances are someone has already written documentation about your problem, and it will probably be more detailed than what you can get on IRC, or at least it will give you the information you need to ask a more informed question.

- Don't repeat your question, especially to multiple channels. If anyone who can help you is watching, they will help you. If not, you should consider posting your question on the forums or mailing list. Repetition harms our volunteers' workflow because it interrupts other conversations; in an empty channel, it alerts everyone to new conversation when there is none. (Trying again after half a day, or a different time of day, is reasonable, especially if you have refined your question and have an issue or forum post to which you hope to draw someone's informed attention.)

- Do be polite. Everyone on Drupal IRC is there because they enjoy the support side of the Drupal community. When people are rude and disrespectful, volunteers get frustrated and burn or leave. Keeping a pleasant atmosphere makes more people want to volunteer their time.

- Use correct English (or the appropriate language for non-English channels). Txtspk and 13375p34k (modern variants of the English language used for mobile and online communications) are obnoxious to some and completely incomprehensible to others. It only takes a few more keystrokes to use proper English and it makes your questions much more likely to be answered.

"How to Ask Smart Questions" (catb.org/~esr/faqs/smart-questions.html) and "The Anatomy and Habits of the Common Support Leech" (binaryredneck.net/support-leech) are must-reads for learning what to do and what not to do.

Newbies often find that IRC requires a bit more getting used to than the web forums. This is true, but the effort is certainly worth it. In return for taking the time to learn IRC customs, you get the chance to have your questions answered by any of the hundreds of experienced Drupalistas inhabiting these channels, including some of our most active contributors.

When you aren't asking a question, please idle (hang out) in the Drupal channels anyway. You may be able to help someone else with their question or even participate in a deep discussion about Drupal's future. You will certainly learn something new pretty regularly.

▨ **Tip** Have a thick skin. When the talented Amitai Burstein converted the popular Organic Groups project to take excellent advantage of Drupal 7's new capabilities (see Chapter 5), he also changed the name and asked the community for its input. A respected core contributor (and by many accounts a very nice person) advised against the name change in no uncertain terms. Amitai noted the harshness and received this reply: "Yes—I am being a bit harsh to try to make clear that I think it's really a bad idea." If every person with something to offer the community (or gain from the community) left and disengaged the first time someone was unreasonably (or reasonably) severe in critique, we wouldn't have anyone remaining here.

The Issue Queues

There are many great places to find the Drupal community, but at the center of it all are the Drupal issue queues. An issue queue is basically a collaborative to-do list where contributors come together to get things done. Drupal core and each contributed module and theme have their own issue queues on drupal.org.

Drupal core's issue queue can be found at drupal.org/project/issues/drupal, you can find a project's queue at drupal.org/project/issues/projectname where projectname is the name of a module or theme project or from the link on its project page on drupal.org.

Most of Drupal's major core code and community infrastructure decisions happen in the issue queues; the same goes for modules and themes. The issue queues are how Drupal gets better by thousands of incremental improvements. Someone posts a task, bug, or feature request. Others confirm, comment, etc. Someone posts a patch, others test it.

From your profile's edit page on Drupal.org, you can check Contributor Links under Block Configuration to give you a list of useful links for participating in Drupal development, including several ways to see different kinds of issues being worked on. Chapter 38 covers a little on how to use the issue queues, to review or submit patches, and Chapter 37, on maintaining a project with Git, covers how to submit your own project to drupal.org so that others can find it (and participate on its issue queue). Here are some tips worth knowing before you jump in:

- You do not have to be an expert to contribute in the issue queue. Issue triage (marking duplicates as such, asking for more info in vaguely-worded bug reports, and so on) is a huge help, as is testing the patches that others have written. These activities are also great ways to get to know other Drupal coders and become familiar with the code base. You can learn more about patch testing from Angela Byron's excellent blog post at webchick.net/6-pass-patch-reviews.

- Before filing a bug, search the bug tracker to see whether someone else has already filed it. Duplicates hamper progress because at best someone has to take the time to mark duplicates; at worst, no one notices the duplication until after energy has been expended on more than one copy of the same problem in parallel.

- When you write a bug report, be as specific as possible by including relevant information about both your Drupal install and the environment in which you are running it.

  - Describe the symptoms of the problem or bug (or missing feature) carefully and clearly.

  - Describe the environment in which it occurs (Drupal version, browser, server, operating system).

  - Describe the steps you took to try and pin down the problem yourself before asking the question.

  - Describe any possibly relevant recent changes in your server setup or web site configuration (even if it doesn't seem possibly connected).

  - Most importantly, provide everything others need to know in order to reproduce the problem.

- When you file a bug, follow up on it. Oftentimes, the people fixing issues need more information in order to reproduce the problem (and start fixing it).

Summary

The Drupal community includes site administrators, programmers, designers, and themers (or front-end developers), site owners, project managers, system administrators, community organizers, jacks of all trades, documentation volunteers, instructors, and even marketers spanning all six regularly inhabited continents. ("Noneck" Noel Hidalgo made a valiant attempt to bring Drupal representation to Antarctica as well, but he couldn't hitch a ride from the Southern tip of Chile.)

Most people fall into more than one role and often define new categories (like Noneck Noel, an "advocate for open communities, free culture, and transparent government"). The non-Drupal interests of those in the community are diverse and not cohesive, especially as many people discover Drupal when looking for an online platform for their own community of interest. (Indeed, Dries Buytaert initially created Drupal for people who wanted to talk to each other about new Internet technologies.) Although there is a strong sentiment that anything in a Drupal channel should be about Drupal, Drupal people's other interests and qualities are being increasingly accepted as part of their Drupal identities. The common thread in the Drupal community is doing things with Drupal—in particular, in the words of Drupal's founder: "innovating, collaborating, sharing, striving toward simplicity, and having fun."

What makes one a part of the Drupal community? It's not simply using Drupal. Even some site administrators and Drupal programmers may not play a significant part in the Drupal community, and of course site visitors and participants may never even know they are using a Drupal site.

The Drupal community is the people who participate in the Drupal community. This sounds tautological, yet it is the act of participation, of bringing something back, that builds the community. The something that we bring back does not have to be a contribution in the sense of something material; it can simply be our presence. Being part of the Drupal community might take the form of:

- Sharing a module or theme with the world on Drupal.org.

- Suggesting a line of code for someone else's module or theme.

- Providing a one-word correction to a comment that explains a line of code in Drupal.

- Calling a Drupal meetup in a local café or library–or simply showing up at one.

- Writing a blog post anywhere on the Internet about a Drupal problem solved or a cool thing done with Drupal.

- Giving a useful response to someone's question on any of a dozen means of communication.

- Discussing business practices and Drupal 8 settings API (Application Programming Interface) improvements while riding in the back of a pickup truck on a side trip to go skydiving during a Drupal conference.

- Demonstrating a site or asking a question (or responding to someone else's demonstration or question) in person at a Drupal event anywhere in the world.

Membership and status in the Drupal community is not based on anything like the academic concepts of merit or a professional certification. It's not what we know or what credentials we have that matters to other Drupalistas. What matters is what we do. Chapter 34 covers some of the many ways we can contribute back to Drupal (which includes much more than code).

Reading this book doesn't make us part of the Drupal community, either. Going and doing something with or for the Drupal community makes us part of the Drupal community. Seeking knowledge from others and sharing knowledge with others, building something and bringing something back, both makes the community and makes us a part of it. Welcome!

▒ **Tip** While most Drupal participation should revolve around the `*.drupal.org` family of sites, feel free to look for more help in getting involved with the Drupal community at this chapter's online home, `dgd7.org/participate`.

■ ■ ■

## CHAPTER 10

Planning and Managing a Drupal Project

by Amye Scavarda

Welcome! This chapter is about planning and managing Drupal web site projects. You've seen what Drupal has to offer, and you're ready to build yourself a web site.

Consider this chapter with a bit of measured enthusiasm: building web sites is harder than it looks, and I have lots of silly analogies for describing the difficulty. It's like trying to make a swing set out of an erector set, or like riding a rollercoaster without the rails. Get excited about the possibilities, but know that not everything will go smoothly. Building a web site in Drupal is also a creative process, because it takes thought, talent, and technical learning to meet the goals that you've set. The best advice for beginners is to remove any preconceptions about what's easy and what's hard. Just let yourself learn. Enjoy being a beginner.

This chapter is about laying out your goals, clearly defining what you need, setting yourself up to be able to tackle a large project in small chunks, and learning what you need to research to be able to finish. It's also about time management, a bit about project management methodologies to help keep everything running smoothly, and what a reasonable project plan looks like. I'll go through the various parts of Drupal that impact planning, what to be aware of, and what the biggest challenges are.

By the end of this chapter, you should be able to clearly define what it is you'd like to build and have a rough outline of what needs to be done where. You'll also understand the responsibilities of the project manager. Even better you'll have the ability to break those responsibilities down into manageable tasks and the tools to be able to complete those tasks.

The Role of Limitations

"It's not what you start in life, it's what you finish."

—Katharine Hepburn

Limitations are a necessary thing to be aware of when you're planning a project. Setting the expectation that you're awesome and that you'll have a fully built community site by this time tomorrow is great, but it's unreasonable. It's better to know your limitations, because you know what you can commit to in a reasonable amount of time—that's where the real awesome comes in.

Knowing how much time you have to devote to a project is the first step, so that when it looks like something really big is coming, you have clear boundaries around what effort you can put in and still stay sane. This is popularly referred to as "work-life balance," but it's really about being able to maintain the systems that maintain your own productivity. If you haven't set aside enough time to be able to keep up with your own e-mail, personal connections, and laundry, you won't have a life while you get this project done and it won't be fun for anyone.

It's possible to have a site up and running in about 60 minutes, but I usually schedule 4 hours of time for an initial site build. I want to make sure that I can get the development hosting environment right, get e-mail (Google Apps) and SMTP servers set up, the DNS servers pointing at the right place, the Drupal install done, modules installed, a theme applied, and some content up.[1] While these tasks can be broken up over several days with an hour or so here and there, I find that I lose track of what I need to do next. A fully functioning site with working e-mail and some placeholder pages gives me at least a place to start.

Putting Down Your Concept on Paper

Once you know how much time you can devote to building your site, think about what kind of web site you want to build.

Here's what I think of as the 1 to 10 scale of difficulty:

1. is "I have an idea for a web site, but I haven't totally decided on the concept". (Also known as "I'm going to install Drupal on my own computer and play with it.")[2]

2. is "I have an outline of what this web site is, and I might have an idea of what the title is. I have a domain name registered." (This is the bare site build that I'd budget 4 hours for.)

3. is "I already have a site that I built a long time ago in Dreamweaver/Publisher, but I can get the content out in straight text files. I don't want to improve it this week, but I'd like to migrate to a new site."

4. is "I built my site a long time ago, and it has a lot of content that I want to move, like a photo gallery or all of my blog posts going back to 2001."

5. is "I have a site that I need to migrate, and it had a custom design. I'd like to recreate that in this new system."

6. is "I have an idea for a new community site, I'm going to have some users, and I'll start with some content."

7. is "I want a new community site. I have lots of content that needs to be served dynamically, I'm going to have a lot of users, and I want them to be able to do six different things to communicate with each other. "

8. is "I have a community site already. I'd like to move over all of the content that I have now. I'd like to move over all of the users that I have now. Also, I want to add mapping, geolocation, feeds from different sites, and private messaging."

---

[1] More experienced developers may budget less time than that (maybe 2 hours). I don't do it often enough to trust that I won't forget a step when it's important, so I budget 4 hours to give myself the breathing room to move slowly.

[2] Note: You don't need to install Drupal on your own computer in order to be able to play with it (see Buzzr at http://buzzr.com or Drupal Gardens at http://drupal.gardens.com), but it's good practice.

9. is "I have three different sites that I want to move over to Drupal. They all need to work with the users I have now, but I don't want to change any of the passwords. Users are going to be able to interact with each other in 10 different ways. I have a lot of content now, but I don't want to move over all of it, so I need to decide what to move and what needs to be recreated in the new site. I'm also tired of my current design, so I want to do something new."

10. is the same as number 9, with the addition of "I need it to happen in three weeks. Or maybe yesterday. Can I build this today?"

These are just some rough sketches; there are thousands of different examples for each category. My hope is that you won't try to tackle anything above a 6 on your own. I deliberately left out "And I'd like to be able to sell things on my site," because adding a store generally pushes any of these projects up a notch in terms of complexity. So it's possible that this scale goes to up to an 11, but anything above a 5 will usually require more than one person's help, and anything above a 6 will require anywhere from 3 to 10 people's time and input.

If you have an idea of what you want to do, start taking notes about what category your idea might fit into. What's the purpose of your site? Who's going to use it? If you're having trouble narrowing it down, try thinking about what it isn't. This is your brainstorming space.

Before I get too deep into the brainstorming, take a look at Figure 10–1, which shows what the lifecycle of web site development looks like.

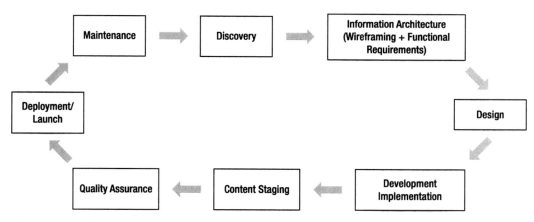

Figure 10–1. *Lifecycle of a project*

The difficulty scale takes this lifecycle into account. A site that's going through the first phases will be much less complex than a site that's moving through the fourth iteration. Sites that are more established are not starting from a bare idea anymore; they have established content, or established users, or they're moving from a system that isn't fitting all of their growth needs anymore. Consider that your project, too, may need to grow over time. Drupal is pretty good about accepting input from a wide variety of sources and outputting information in a wide variety of formats. It's flexible, but it's just a tool to put your requirements on paper. Let's walk through the project lifecycle using the stages in Figure 10–1.

1. Discovery

If you're just starting out, you're in the discovery phase: What do I want? What does it need to do? What does it look like? Who's participating in this project? Who are the decision makers?

Project plans come out of discovery; these plans inform the rest of the lifecycle. They're the guiding documents that help determine the scope and schedule of the project.

2. Information Architecture

Information architecture is about taking those brainstorms and putting them down concretely. Wireframing lets you build a prototype of what information the pages will contain. Think of it like the blueprints for a web site, just like an architect draws plans for a house. Figure 10–2 is an example of a video site wireframe created in GoMockingbird. (`http://gomockingbird.com`).

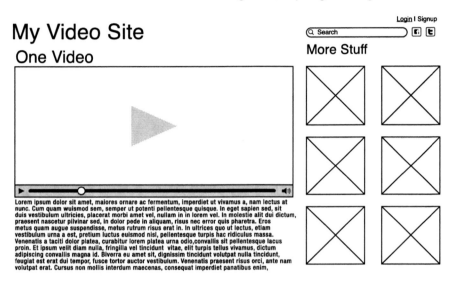

Figure 10–2. Example of a wireframe

This lays out information on the pages. There's a title for the whole site, which could also be an image. There are login and signup links, which means that there are users for the site. There's a search bar and links to Facebook and Twitter. There's a main content area where videos and text live. There's a sidebar for related content. This wireframe provides a visual reference that the designers can work with without having to recreate a web site from scratch.

Another part of the IA stage are functional requirements. Functional requirements are meant to capture all of the features that the site needs to have and what it needs to do. Functional requirements are not the "how" but rather the "what." If you're able to answer what needs to happen in plain English, that's the start of the functional requirements.

3. Design

Once you have the wireframe of where everything goes, the design stage puts clothes on it, adding a look and feel. Colors, fonts, how the site will look—it all happens here. After the design is complete, it will look like a web site, but it'll be just a Photoshop file. Warning: there's the expectation that anything that can be done in the Photoshop file can be exactly matched by the web site. Sometimes a Photoshop file goes beyond what's possible. Expecting an arrow to be exactly 3 pixels away from the link will lead to disappointment in the end. Changing the expectations to reflect that there will be an arrow next to a link is much easier to fulfill.

4. Development and Implementation

If the functional requirements are the "what", development and implementation (along with the timeline and project plan) are the "how." All of the things that you said you needed—this is where you decide how long it'll take and who's going to make it happen. This is where the wireframes get put into an actual working site, the design gets added, and the site starts to look like something that you'd see in your browser. But there's still something missing.

5. Content

The soul of a web site is content: stories and photos and videos. This is the stage of the project where you add the content. It's also leading into the quality assurance phase where you make sure that it works like you expected it to and it looks like you expected it to. If it doesn't, you either fix it or change your mind about what you need.

6. Deployment/Launch

Your site is completely done. It's ready to go live, but if you're doing it right, you have two separate environments: one for development that you can tinker with, and one for production that is the site the world sees in a browser. You'll need to migrate everything from the development site to the production site. This takes a bit of time and work.

You also need to check all of your work. Do the links work correctly? Did you remember to turn on the automatic path creator when you were adding content, so that /node/X isn't the URL? Did all of your images move over correctly? Did you lose the files directory in the migration? Is the theme working correctly for IE6/IE 7/IE8, Firefox, and Safari? Check your views to make sure that they're formatted correctly and display what you want. Did the favorite icon on the top of the URL bar in the browser get lost? This is also your chance to test multiple user roles. Can an anonymous user see things you didn't intend? Check and make sure. Keep a spreadsheet handy and note everything you need to change before you change the domain to point to your new site.

7. Maintenance

Your project will probably need updating as it goes along: modules get updated, Drupal core gets security updates, and new versions of Drupal come along. Eventually, you'll want to take advantage of new features or a new design, or you'll want to change the site entirely, and so the lifecycle will begin again.

Project Management Methodologies and Drupal

The lifecycle phases get documented into an overall project plan, and that project plan is also directed by methods to help you succeed. There are a few ways to think about this and some project management methodologies to touch on here. Drupal has adopted two basic methodologies: the more traditional "waterfall" style and the more iterative "agile" style.

Waterfall comes out of traditional project management. The planner assumes that there are a finite number of tasks, however large the list of tasks list may be, and that each of those tasks can be put in a sequence to bring the project to completion. Every task is estimated and known ahead of the start of the project. This style is usually used in large construction projects or projects that have a very concrete deliverable at the end. Waterfall also usually works off of an exact budget or an exact timeline. For example, when I'm planning an event, like a conference, I tend to use waterfall as a guiding principle to keep everything on track. I know that I can't adjust the timeline, so I do what I can do within the timeframe and make it work.

Agile is an iterative process for planning your projects. It assumes that you don't have as much knowledge about the finished deliverable. It's a collaborative process with all of the people who have a stake in the project. It emphasizes teamwork in planning, short bursts of development, and feedback at the end to adjust the project goals. I tend to use agile when I have an internal project that doesn't have billable hours attached to it or a project that doesn't have a very firm deadline. Agile works well to kick off a project that doesn't have enough information to let waterfall be effective; however, agile isn't helpful when trying to finish a project that has a set launch date, a concrete budget, and many required features.

Knowing both of these approaches is useful, because a Drupal project benefits from a combination of the two. In Table 10–1, I've broken out the tasks into tasks that benefit from a waterfall approach and tasks that benefit from an agile approach.

Table 10–1. Waterfall and Agile Breakdown by Drupal Project Stage

	Drupal Tasks That Use Waterfall	**Drupal Tasks That Use Agile**
Discovery	Documenting the project plan, timeline planning	Brainstorming
Information Architecture	Functional requirements	Wireframes
Design	(Very little about design work fits with waterfall)	Creating design layouts
Development	Only on a high level matching of functional requirements	Building out all of the features in a site, creating the site.
Content Staging	Deciding which content is added	Active work works best in sprints
Quality Assurance	Matching with functional requirements	Not as effective
Deployment/Launch	Checklists for launch	Not as effective
Maintenance	No methodology preference	No methodology preference

In general, if the project has a lot of uncertainties, agile will make for a better end product. You're better able to add more features later on in the process as you get more familiar with the project and its needs.

Waterfall will allow you to sketch everything out ahead of time, leaving very few uncertainties. You'll know when you're launching, what your minimum viable product is, and how much it'll cost. As you become more familiar with the project, you may not be able to take advantage of some brilliant thoughts without changing the scope of the project.

Site building and implementation is where "agile-fall" comes into play. Your team will probably work better in a focused agile environment to complete tasks, but your client may not be comfortable with watching agile happen. The project manager can lay out the lifecycle in a waterfall style (I'll be done with X by this time) but manage the team's work through agile user stories. It makes development and project management a lot less stressful if you don't have to explain how agile works at the same time as you're trying to discover what a client needs for a project.

Taking the Lifecycle into Account on Paper

You now have a good idea of what you're building and a rough idea of how to structure it. Now you need to answer these questions:

- Why you are building this?
- What it's going to do?
- When will each stage of the cycle be complete?
- When did they need to be completed?
- What needs to happen within each phase?
- Who's going to do this?

Understanding the complexity involved is helpful. This will all come together in the project plan.

What's a Project Plan?

A project plan is a document that speaks to the purpose and methods of a project. It defines what's at stake in the project, who the main stakeholders are, the scope of the timeline (as well as what that timeline is driven by), and the outcomes of the project. It also breaks down what happens in what order and who's both responsible and involved for each phase. It is a client-facing document because it's designed to create alignment between everyone involved. When a project plan is complete and clear, everyone knows why this project is being done, what sense of urgency is attached to it, and when the project is potentially launching. When it's done right, a project plan doesn't gloss over the hard parts: how difficult the project is, how fast it needs to be done, and who's actually committing to making it happen.

Purpose is a distinct part of the project plan, although it can be no more than a few sentences. With a startup, it can be: "This is the public face of our new start-up. We want to show off what we're working on and get our first sale." With a larger, more complex project that's migrating from an existing platform, the purpose can be: "We want to update our web properties to take advantage of a new level of customer engagement. We want to be able to have more satisfied customers and more sales." For a community site, "I want our users to find content that is relevant to their needs."

The purpose statement should be written in plain English: it articulates the goals of the project. Print it out. (Yes, a dead tree.) Keep it around for tricky meetings—those meetings where everyone comes to the table with something they're invested in seeing happen for the site, well after the scope has already been determined. This purpose statement can also be used to answer questions such as "Does X idea help fulfill our purpose? Is it worth changing the scope to incorporate this?" The purpose statement will help keep your project on track.

Example Project Plan for BeachHouse Non-Profit

Mission: BeachHouse is a nonprofit that wants to update their web properties to take advantage of online event management and donations.
Features:

- Static pages that are easily updated by non-technical staff

    - Images on pages

- Documents available for download

- Donations

- Events

- Email newsletter signup

- Photo gallery for past events

Timelines:

- Week 1: Kickoff, discovery, and planning, June 18 - 25

    - Kickoff meeting on Friday

    - Project plan and review on Monday

    - Layouts for home page, internal site pages

    - Thursday meeting: Theme discussion with site view, layout review

- Week 2: Initial site build, June 28 - July 3

    - Monday: choose theme

    - Site map for content

    - Feature review

    - Content strategy overview

    - Content types documentation

    - Roles documentation

- Week 3: Alpha site build, July 5 - 9

    - Monday: Themed site up and running

    - Wireframes for landing pages built

    - Content types built

    - Feature functionality built

    - Initial roles and permissions built

    - Thursday: review

- Week 4: QA, July 12 - 16

  - Monday: Review of site map

  - Content staged by development for landing pages

  - Content types, roles, and QA

  - Donations tested

  - Thursday: Review

- Week 5: Content Staging, July 19 - 23

  - Monday: Site review with available content

  - Content staging

  - Content checklists

  - Thursday: review

- Week 6: Beta Site, July 25 - 30

  - All content complete for launch

  - All QA completed

  - Site launch on Thursday, July 29

- Week 7: Post-Launch Support, August 1-7

  - Training screencasts reviewed with staff

  - Support time

  - Maintenance contract discussions

Estimating Completion Dates

Remember: Dates in Calendar Are Closer Than They May Appear. Be careful; allow yourself a reasonable amount of time according to what you've done before. In an ideal world, it might be possible to turn around a fully themed, content-complete site in less than two weeks. A site that will involve a lot of custom development or one that requires migrating from a legacy system will require more time.

To start with, go through the lifecycle on paper. How much is there to discover? Will you have to spend a week of active work reviewing the legacy site before you have a good idea what's there? Does the client want a very complex design? Plan for 30% more allotted time for a few revisions of design. Are the features they want something you'd heard about someone else doing? Have you installed those modules on another site? Your development estimates will be much lower if you don't have to build modules from scratch, but leave time for configuration. Estimating your time is a major part of succeeding at projects and keeping everyone satisfied with the pace of work.

What Happens If I Don't Do Anything?

Be willing to raise this question in the planning process. When the purpose is defined, it also raises other possibilities. If your community site doesn't have content that resonates with your users, what happens?

They might never come back and you could lose your advertising revenue and go out of business! It's possible, so you should be sure that you're doing the absolute best thing you can be doing for this project to support the business behind it. The answer may be that you shouldn't do this project until X is in place. If a project isn't set up to succeed, it won't, and there will be many awkward conversations. I guarantee it.

Risks

One of the biggest risks in a project is the integration/migration of the old system with current systems. This problem is usually compounded by the need to have the new site done yesterday in time for x event or y publishing event or z holiday. Whenever possible, those hard deadlines need to be known and factored into the plans. However, ours is not a perfect world: things happen and hard deadlines don't get met. For those deadlines, defining a minimum viable project is critical to maintaining the relationships.

When everyone knows what the minimum is, they know how bad it can be. It can also sometimes have the opposite effect, turning the project's deliverables into a "race to the bottom," cutting down on deliverables until the minimum amount of work is expected. It's the project manager's job to hold both ideals: the amazing web site project that was created in sales, and the bare bones version that will meet the client's needs, if not their expectations.

Minimum Viable Project/Product

This is the bare bones project that will meet the purpose of the project. This will probably not meet everyone's expectations for features or designs or both. For some projects, the MVP can be a domain name with a simple splash page featuring a logo and a color palette; it's a version of a "Coming Soon" page or the "Under Construction" icon.[3] Or it can be a newsletter signup or a contact form that gives the wider audience an opportunity to engage with the project, a series of static pages that speak to the project's mission. Think about the minimum that needs to be available at a given date when there's no engagement from the client, when the development team has been stalled by a tricky problem, or there's a change in the main stakeholders of the project. Laying this out in the project plan helps set the expectations of what's needed versus what's wanted; it's crucial to laying a foundation for expectations. Define this at the beginning, and then it's a question of being able to build up from it or scale down to it.

Keeping Track of Commitments

There's an estimated completion date, the milestones have been laid out, and there are clear deadlines. Something else is missing: the tracking/ticket system. This system needs to be something that will hold deadlines and help manage accountability for the entire team—including you, the project manager. It needs to track milestones and tasks against dates, and have a way to change the status of a task. It's also useful if it has a reminder system through e-mail or SMS.

Here are some personal favorites:

- Unfuddle
- Basecamp
- ManyMoon

---

[3] I rarely recommend the "Under Construction" icon. It looks like 1998 called and wants its Web back. But if you're into that sort of thing, great!

- 5pm

- LiquidPlanner

- Teambox

Note that none of these are Drupal-based task management systems. This list is about being able to manage large and small projects with ease. A system is for peace of mind, and the ability to manage more than one project at a time. When something is added to the ticket system, it's visible to the entire team that's working on it. Nothing is forgotten in an e-mail inbox somewhere, and there's a record of what's happening when.

So from this point on, everything is about putting this project plan into action. I'll let you in on a secret: you've already done a lot of the hard part. The build is not all smooth sailing, but you now have a road map.

You're now the project manager in charge. It's your main task to keep everything else organized, working on the right thing at the right time, and making sure that everything finishes when it's supposed to. You're also going to be the main person who communicates with the people who matter to the success of the project. This may be the people who are sponsoring this new web site within your organization, or the people who are paying you for it, or even Mom and Dad, if you're building Mom and Dad a blog. You're going to have to be able to ask questions without expecting the answers, and you're going to have to translate Drupal-speak into human language. On a good day, it's actually a lot of fun.

I'll lay out most of the events of a project manager having a good day, so that you'll be able to have more good days and less bad days.

Project Manager Tasks Beyond Development

The project manager's job doesn't end after the project plan. You're now in charge of producing the project through kickoff meetings, design meetings, check-ins, and milestone closing meetings. This is the "Day in the Life of a Project Manager."

Kickoff Meetings

These are the meetings when introductions happen, when all of the team gets to see each other for the first time. Finding out who's filling each role on the team is critical, and I find that face-to-face meetings have a much better outcome over the whole life of the project. This is a relationship-building time where everyone makes sure that they're talking about the same thing. Some terms might come up that people don't understand, so here's a quick glossary of some words I use when I talk about Drupal in a project kickoff meeting:

- *Wireframe*: The nonworking prototypes for what a site will look like. It's a skeleton.

- *Mockup*: Photoshop or other files that take the wireframe and add a look and feel to it. It looks like a full site, except that nothing works.

- *Layout*: How information (graphical or otherwise) is laid out on a page.

- *Concept design*: Another term for mockup.

- *Theme*: A set of files that change the look and feel of a web site. This is where design is involved.

- *Module*: Pieces of functionality that can be installed into Drupal. It's the system of interchangeable parts.

- *Features*: A set of files for Drupal that combine the functionality of a lot of different modules into one. It's sort of like interchangeable engines over interchangeable parts. However, the word "features" is also used to describe the simple functions of a site.

Design words for Drupal are more difficult because design is usually the only part of the site that most non-technical people can touch. You can see it, you can describe it, and it's something that you're comfortable looking at. Expect kickoff meetings to usually run about an hour or two. You'll be discussing the project plan, timelines, and resources for the project, and agreeing on any modifications.

The questions that everyone will want answered include the following:

- What are we building?

- Who will be working on it?

- Who's responsible for which part?

- What's the project cost?

- When will it be done by?

- Bonus question: What's driving this project?

Ideally, this will not be the first time that everyone in the project will have thought of these questions, but by the end, you should have the same answers.

Discovery Meetings

These are the brainstorming meetings. They're unstructured; there isn't a whole lot of deciding that goes on in these meetings, but they're integral to the success of the project. Documenting what comes out of these meetings is challenging, but it's invaluable to the designers as they put together concepts.

The following questions get answers in these meetings:

- What are some other sites you like?

- What features do they have?

- What do you not like?

- What message do you want to convey through design about your site?

- What are some examples of this that you've seen on the Web?

Know your own abilities here, so that you don't promise to implement the latest Facebook redesign for your first Drupal site. It's easy to get carried away with design, so be careful. Prioritize features over design if at all possible.

Information Architecture/Design Meetings

These meetings usually involve a deliverable of a wireframe or a concept design. They're meetings with the project manager, the information architecture expert, the designer, and the clients. It's a discussion about the features and what needs to be added, removed, or changed. It's also a conversation about the look and feel of a site: too light, too dark, wrong treatments, more rounded corners. These meetings are better if they're short (30 minutes) and frequent (twice a week) until the IA expert and designer have reached their final drafts.

The following questions get answers in these meetings:

- Is everything where it's supposed to be?

- What's missing?

- Out of these three designs, what elements do you like best?

- Is this the final design, or do we need another round of revisions? Based on the estimates, we're X dollars through the design phase. Adding another round of designs will increase the budget of the entire project by Y. Is this something that you want to do?

This is where budgets will start to get pinched. Watch carefully and be transparent about what resources are available.

Development Meetings

These meetings are usually internal between the project manager and the developers. They lay out what's been done, what's left to do, and what's blocking things. In agile, they're held daily and they're very short—no more than 20 minutes. These development meetings help coordinate the development team, make sure that everyone else knows that progress is being made, and can jointly solve problems. These meetings happen through the life of the project.

The following questions get answers in these meetings:

- What am I working on?

- What's next?

- What things will be/are a blocker?

Checkins

The project manager is the one that goes back and forth between the developer team and clients to make sure that questions are being answered. This requires translating between development and the client; the content will change depending on what phase of site building is occurring.

The following items are covered in these meetings:

- This is what we are working on.

- This is what's coming next

- What do we need your help on?

- How's your content coming?

Milestone Closing Meetings

As a phase of the cycle gets closed, the project manager, lead developer and client meet to make sure that everything that needed to get done during the phase has been completed and that the next phase can begin. If any changes need to be made, they should be small, or this will also turn into a change of scope conversation.

The following items are covered in these meetings:

- Here are all of the tickets we closed in this project.

- Here's where this is on the development site.

- Does this need to be added to the next phase, or is this complete?

- If we change this, it will add X amount of time to the project. Is this OK, or what else needs to be dropped to make this happen?

Launch Meetings

The final meetings before launching the site are when all of the developers, the project manager, and the client get together and discuss any final changes before the site goes live. If communication has been good all along, there will be no major surprises in this meeting. If something has gone awry, this meeting can bring up unpleasant surprises. As the project manager, you need to match any requests in this meeting with the functional requirements document. If it wasn't in the functional requirements document, it shouldn't be on the table for this particular meeting; it should be pushed out to a future phase of work.

The following items are covered in these meetings:

- Everything is done according to what we talked about before.

- What small changes need to be made?

- All of our content is here accurately.

- We've tested our work on the production site and we're ready to take this project live.

Post-Project Debriefs

Sweet! The site's live, everyone's happy, and now the team can sit down and talk about what went right, what didn't go so well, and what could be changed. This is usually an internal design/development/project management meeting because candid feedback is the main goal of this meeting.

Other Tasks for Project Managers

Outside of all of these meetings, a project manager has real tasks beyond tracking what's going on in a project. The project manager helps to create clarity around what is happening and why.

Creating User Stories

One of the best ways to know what the expectations are for your project is to break the scope down into a series of stories. What should a user be able to do? What kind of things should an administrative user be able to do? These are larger stories that tell concrete things, not a series of tasks. They will probably be written throughout the project, not just at the beginning. They're easy to take to the entire team as an explanation of what each element needs to do.

Here are some structures for the user stories:

- I want to [do something] with [x part of site] so that I can [reason]. Example: I want to be able to bookmark things within my profile so that I can find them again.

- As a [role], I want to [goal], so that I can [reason]. Example: As an administrator, I want to delete comments on a post so that I can moderate my site's user-created content.

A traditional agile workflow has these stories written on small cards: story, some concept, and confirmation that it works. These three things have to be present so that any single team member could complete this task without being dependent on another card being completed. It's a great ideal. More often, teams aren't big enough to need this sort of interchangeability, so these user stories serve as reminders for what complete features look like within a site.

Implementing Tasks and Task Workflow

Out of user stories, you'll need to create tasks. Tasks are small concrete things that need to be built/done/taken care of, and they integrate into a full workflow. Most ticket trackers can support this: a task can be in different workflow states.

A task will start out as "new" and will move to "assigned" after it's been assigned to a team member. That team member can "accept" that task if they feel like they have enough information to complete it. The task can also be "rejected" if the team member feels that it needs more clarification or shouldn't be done right now; the project manager and team member should discuss it with the whole development team or the client.

When a task has been completed, it will move to "resolved," and then it's the job of Quality Assurance (QA) to test it and confirm that it works as designed on a variety of platforms.

A task can be "closed" when there's no further action needed, or QA can "reopen" the task if there's something that needs to be changed. QA can report bugs back to the PM and development team.

It's helpful to have a separate bug tracker that isn't in the same space as a development workflow. The actual workflow is the same, but a different system allows for separation of development and fixing. Giving a client access to the bug tracking system (not the entire development ticket system) is helpful to move the project forward because it is easier to ask for and receive focused feedback.

Tasks are not always all in development. Design tasks can be to create Photoshop mockup for BeachHouse or create HTML/CSS layouts from approved mockups. Project management tasks can be to create project plan or populate discovery milestone with tasks. Tasks are assigned to milestones, with all of the estimated times for each task added together to create that milestones.

Tasks That Make up Milestones

When all of the tasks in a milestone are completed, the site can be reviewed by both the client and the project manager for approval. There's usually some time built into the project timeline to account for necessary review time before the meeting.

It's helpful for all sides to see what was accomplished, what's working, and what's left to do. These milestone sessions are also a good time to review the budgets. Ask the following questions:

- Based on the amount of work that's already done, how are our budgets looking?

- What's left to complete in the project?

- Do I have the budget for the next phase?

- If I don't have enough budget, what can be cut to make this work, or how do I get more budget?

Take the time to review and prioritize the next steps, and be honest about the project scope and the budget.

This can also be a time where things get added that weren't originally in the scope. It's the project manager's job to keep the original agreed-on scope in mind, manage the budgets to be able to meet the expectations, and get the project completed. Reviewing the scope before each milestone meeting is the best way to keep on track, but it's a struggle. The project manager has to set the tone; the best way to do this is to remain consistent throughout the entire project.

Bad Days

All of the above events and tasks happen as a normal part of a project manager's life. A bad day is when pieces of your project break, aren't meeting the expectations of a client, or are pushed aside entirely and forgotten.

You're the keeper of the relationships in all of these projects, and while it's your job to make sure that the project gets finished, sometimes that also means putting egos away and having the tough conversations.

Tough conversations include:

- "I need more communication."

- "I need more focused communication."

- "I've already talked about that, and we said we were done."

- "This is what it will take to change course."

- "We're out of budget."

- "I can't implement that design."

- "We're behind schedule."

Having the tough conversations is no fun, but not having them is worse in the long run. Don't let this happen to you! Take a deep breath. Be willing to have these conversations when necessary. Document what you needed to do, how you did it, and the outcome. Every conversation can be handled in a way that gives a good outcome for both parties. A good template is:

- What happened

- Taking responsibility

- Your team promises to do X by Y

- What happens next

Be willing to take a few hits for the team. Promises will get broken. Tests that should have happened won't happen. Designs that should have been delivered won't be. Content that should have been added won't be ready in time. E-mails will land more harshly than intended in stressful moments. It will feel awful.

If you can, let the rest of the team in on those calls/meetings. Let them watch how you handle the failures of your team without making it anyone's fault, how you take responsibility, how you manage the breakdown in communication, how you restore trust with the team, and how you help the project move forward.

In the end, the best projects are the ones that have the teams that understand each other the best. If you can communicate the goals of the project to different personalities, you'll have a much better time.

You'll also need to recognize various skill levels in every project, including your own. You're not only a project manager; you're a coordinator, leader, and mentor.

Have fun!

Further Resources

Managing Humans by Michael Lopp http://managinghumans.com

Making Things Happen by Scott Berkun www.scottberkun.com/books/making-things-happen/

Becoming Agile: In an Imperfect World by Greg Smith

More about Managing Budgets from a Drupal Project Manager - affinitybridge.com/blog/managing-budgets-and-billing-while-practicing-agile-development

---

▨ **Tip** Stop by dgd7.org/manage for more resources and recommendations on planning and running projects.

CHAPTER 11

■ ■ ■

Documenting for End Users and the Production Team

by Dani Nordin

Documentation is one of those things that many designers and developers hate doing, but it's important—not only for the happiness of clients and editors who have to take over a site but also for preventing the production team from making the same mistakes over and over again.

This chapter will give you an overview of creating effective documentation for Drupal project teams. Ideally, you'll be creating documentation for a specific site's eventual editors and administrators while also creating in-house documentation for the production team to help increase the efficiency of their workflow. I'll also discuss some ways that members of the Drupal community have found to create documentation for the benefit of their fellow Drupallers—and how you can do the same.

What Makes Good Documentation?

While there's no set formula for good documentation, there are a few things to bear in mind when creating your documents. Good documentation:

- Is easily editable and evolves with the site.

- Is consistently formatted so you don't have to reinvent the wheel every time you add to the documentation (includes visuals such as screenshots).

- Covers the most common things users need to worry about—preferably in the order that they need to worry about them.

- Discusses common errors users might run into and how to troubleshoot them.

- Is written in simple English.

That last point is the most important to bear in mind when creating documentation, whether it's for a client site, a Drupal module or theme, or your team's internal documentation. This is not to say that there's no place for code or technical requirements in documentation; rather, it's to say that it's important to assume that your end user is not the expert that you are but is willing to *gain* that expertise if you're willing to give it in a way that makes sense to them.

> ■ **Tip** A special supplement by Claudina Sarahe covers best practices for documenting for different audiences and tools for creating and maintaining documentation. Find it and more at this chapter's online home, `dgd7.org/document`.

Getting Clients into Content Entry Early

Since content curation, creation, and entry form such an important part of any Drupal site, it's important to get your client's intended content team to start entering content into the site as soon as possible. Doing this accomplishes several key goals:

- It gets the development team into the habit of rapidly iterating prototypes.

- It gets the client accustomed to interacting with the Drupal interface.

- It helps identify areas that need tweaking early in the process, which makes development easier.

- It gives the client a sense of the complete development process. Ideally, it moves them away from concerns about aesthetics (i.e., what things look like) and toward user experience and functional concerns—until it's truly time to talk about aesthetics.

This last point is the most important reason to get clients involved in the entry process early. It is easy for clients to get stuck on choices about fonts, colors, and images early in the site planning process. For the design process to work efficiently and produce effective results, that's a habit that both clients and designers need to break early and often.

The best way to get clients involved early in the content entry process is to set up a staging server (e.g., `staging.newsite.com`) on a password-protected URL as soon as you have a working prototype of the site. A staging server is a "work in progress" version of your web site; it allows both clients and the development team to see how a project is progressing and prevents the world from seeing the work as it's happening on the production (i.e., live) site. For more on this, check out Chapter 13.

If you set up a staging server, by the time the site goes live, your client's content team will (ideally) have enough experience with managing content in their Drupal site that it will become second nature. So why create documentation after the fact? The answer is simple: people change jobs. The person who's entering content into the site now isn't necessarily going to be the only person who enters content into this site until the end of time. Having good end user documentation, in the form of a PDF (or better yet, internal Wiki in a hidden area of the web site) that you deliver to the client, is an important way to create client good will. It also prevents anguished phone calls from the new client editor down the road.

Creating End-User Documentation Post-Launch

The best, and easiest, way to create effective documentation for clients is to do it during the site building process as soon as certain areas of the site have been approved. While every site is different, the key areas that should be covered include:

- Information on how to log into the site, including login URL, username, and password.

- A brief overview of the administration menu and any shortcuts that you've set up.

- How to add content and how to format each content type. While it can seem repetitive to include an entry in the documentation for each content type, getting into the habit can be extremely useful—especially for clients who aren't terribly tech-savvy.

- If applicable, information on how to create new users and how to assign them roles.

- A brief overview of the menu system and how to add/remove menu items.

- A brief overview of the taxonomy system and how to add/remove terms.

- A brief overview of the block system and how to add/remove blocks.

Note that the last three items are somewhat controversial. Many developers resist giving clients the level of control over their site's architecture and menu/block system that access to blocks, menus, etc. will offer—with good reason. However, experience shows that clients expect and often demand that level of control; after all, part of the reason they choose a content management system such as Drupal is that they want the ability to manage their content without having to call their web team.

For this reason, it is important during the development process to create ways for site editors to manage things like menu items and taxonomy without destroying the rest of the site. By using permissions, you can do the following:

- Allow site editors to create new taxonomy terms, but not new vocabularies.

- Allow site editors to create new menu items, remove, or move around menu items, but not create new menus.

- Allow site editors to create and place new blocks, but not change Views.

Another important thing to think about during the production of your site is how users will be entering content into the site. While WYSIWYG editors (such as the buttons you use in Microsoft Word to format copy) can be a controversial topic among Drupal site builders, it is safe to assume that almost any site that you build will eventually be managed by someone who isn't a site builder. Content editors for Drupal sites often include business owners, secretaries, interns, and volunteers. Some may be tech savvy, but it isn't fair to your clients (or your team, who will have to field support calls from confused site editors) to insist that clients learn HTML in order to enter content into a plain text editor. Clients expect some sort of WYSIWYG editor, and it's important as site builders that we give it to them. Fortunately, the WYSIWYG module (drupal.org/project/wysiwyg) supports multiple different libraries. For more information, check out Chapter 4.

The Anatomy of Good Client Documentation

Good documentation should be:

- Written in language that is easily understandable by people with a baseline of technical knowledge. Assume they don't know HTML.

- Easily updated by the development team as parts of the site change.

- Comprehensive; it covers everything that the client's management team is going to have to deal with when managing the site.

For these reasons, I use a simple word processing program such as Microsoft Word or OpenOffice to create site documentation. For the documentation team, it gives them the ability to create documentation quickly and to easily update it when the site changes. The files are delivered to the client as a PDF file, which helps ensure that things don't get deleted accidentally down the line.

The process of creating documentation is equally simple, but often requires a slight shift in thinking for someone who's used to being nose-deep in code. The basic process is to do everything that a site editor would have to do—from creating a new piece of content to changing a menu item to adding a taxonomy term—and document the process with screen shots.

For example, here's a bit of sample documentation from the site that we built in Chapters 1 and 8.

SITE DOCUMENTATION :: DGD7.ORG

This documentation will help you update content and work with the backend of your new Drupal site.

Logging into the Backend

On the left side of page, you'll see a "user login" box. Your username is editor, and your password it site_admin.

User login

Username*

Password*

- Create new account
- Request new password

Log in

Using the Admin Menu and Dashboard

The admin menu at the top gives you access to control the site's content. Clicking on the *Dashboard* link will show you a list of recent content, recent comments, and newly registered users.

About Content Types

The site's content is based on the following content types:
- **Chapter:** These are sample chapters of the book. They can only be posted by site authors and do not allow comments.
- **Suggestions:** These are suggestions, tips, and anecdotes for consideration in the next version of the book. These can be created by any registered user and must be approved by a moderator before they can be viewed on the site.

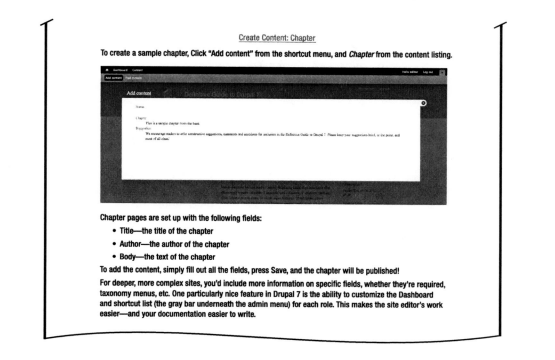

<u>Create Content: Chapter</u>

To create a sample chapter, Click "Add content" from the shortcut menu, and *Chapter* from the content listing.

Chapter pages are set up with the following fields:

- Title—the title of the chapter
- Author—the author of the chapter
- Body—the text of the chapter

To add the content, simply fill out all the fields, press Save, and the chapter will be published!

For deeper, more complex sites, you'd include more information on specific fields, whether they're required, taxonomy menus, etc. One particularly nice feature in Drupal 7 is the ability to customize the Dashboard and shortcut list (the gray bar underneath the admin menu) for each role. This makes the site editor's work easier—and your documentation easier to write.

Documenting for the Development Team

While client documentation is an essential piece of the Drupal development process, the importance of internal documentation for development teams can not be understated. As smart people, it's incredibly easy to keep things in our heads—which makes sense when we're the only ones touching things, but causes problems when other folks come into the picture, especially on larger projects.

Team documentation can take the form of almost anything from internal Wikis (which can be created using MediaWiki (`www.mediawiki.org/wiki/MediaWiki`) or built in Drupal!), to intranets (check out `openatrium.com` for a team intranet solution built in Drupal), to shared Evernote notebooks or Dropbox folders full of random code snippets. When creating your documentation, the most important part is to think of not only the team you currently have, but the team that you ultimately want to have. Teams grow; old members leave, new members come in. Having good internal documentation gets new team members up to speed quickly and helps avoid production bottlenecks.

The most important, and most difficult, factor in creating good internal documentation is creating a logical organization for it; having everything stored in a common location is important, as is adding comments or references for code snippets, blog entries, and other pieces of documentation you decide to save. Lastly, it's important to periodically look through documentation and weed out old or outdated information. Drupal evolves constantly, as does the team's development experience. The point of documentation isn't to cover everything you've ever done, but rather to compile a list of best practices that the team can share among themselves.

Good internal documentation should cover:

- Code snippets that the team uses over and over again, with a description of the use case.

- Idiosyncrasies with specific modules and what the team did to fix them (bonus points if you contribute the code as a patch to the module!).

- A site launch checklist, which covers commonly encountered issues (and how to recover from them) for launching sites.

- Site "recipes" (combinations of specific modules and configurations) for commonly built sites.

- Locations of commonly used files, modules, site configurations, and base themes (more on theming in Chapters 15 and 16).

- Coding and development standards shared by the team.

There are as many ways to organize documentation as there are ways to make macaroni and cheese. While the flavors may change depending on what you put in, the key ingredients are always the same: you can use any kind of cheese or shape of macaroni, but you still need cheese and macaroni.

Documenting for the Community

While contributing code is a great way to contribute to the Drupal community, contributing quality documentation is arguably even more important. Good documentation is essential not only for current Drupal site builders and designers in helping them work through sticky issues, but it helps new site builders ease into creating sites in Drupal, which makes the community stronger.

There are several ways that Drupallers can contribute documentation back to the community. One of the more popular ways is via webcasts; for example, the Lullabots (lullabot.com) have a number of paid and free webcasts that cover concepts related to working in Drupal. Bob Christenson's MustardSeed Media video podcast (mustardseedmedia.com/podcast) is a great way to get used to theming and working with display modules. The screencasts offered by Drupaltherapy (www.drupaltherapy.com/screencasts) focus on site building by using recipes of specific module combinations. Without people like these folks making the content that helps us learn how to use Drupal, many smart and talented designers and developers would not be part of the community.

So, if you are working in Drupal and you learn something new, blog about it or do a screen cast. If you find something that doesn't work with a module, contribute it to the issue queue on drupal.org or mention it on Twitter. And don't be surprised if you get an e-mail one day thanking you for your contribution.

The More You Know

Good documentation isn't about adding more work to an already busy schedule. It's about helping your clients, yourself, and the community enjoy the great sites you made with Drupal. It's about avoiding frantic midnight e-mails from clients who can't figure out how to add a page to the site. It's about saving the next Drupaller from the headaches you've been dealing with as you struggle to get a certain module or theme to work. It's about broadcasting a cool trick you learned in that one site that you wish you remembered now. Good documentation helps everyone. The sooner you start compiling it, the better.

■ **Tip** Documentation examples and lessons learned will be posted to dgd7.org/document as work continues on dgd7.org itself and on other model projects such as dgd7.org/anjali.

CHAPTER 12

■ ■ ■

Development Environment

by Kay VanValkenburgh

Pay special attention to this chapter. The topic may be as glamorous as visiting Home Depot on a first date, but this chapter will spare you reinventing the wheel. Whether you intend it or not, when you start a project of any sort, you set up a development environment: you choose tools and create spaces that define your processes and either limit or advance your efforts. So here's your chance to capitalize on the mistakes of others. In this chapter, I'll look at efficient, interrelated tools and appropriately defined spaces. I will focus on a handful of possible approaches, each of which takes minimal setup and maintenance. The result will be a development environment that positions your projects to run smoothly, that builds in flexibility for changes in size and complexity of projects and teams, and that lets you focus your energy on deliverables rather than on tinkering with an inadequate setup.

For people who have no experience with programming and want to get started with the bare necessities, go to the section called "The Most Basic Development Environment" for the bare-bones set of tools needed to complete essential tasks like uploading and installing a site. You can start there and return to other sections of the chapter to expand your development environment as your familiarity and needs grow. In short, here's what is covered in this chapter:

- Quickstart, a full-fledged, pre-configured development environment that is ready to use on startup. Download it, add credentials, add your project, and you're up and running with a powerful local setup. (For experienced developers as well as beginners who are on a developer career track.)

- Adding key tools to your existing development environment and the reasons for including these additions. (For experienced developers.)

- Signing up for and configuring a web hosting account and domain registration. (For beginners and non-programmers.)

- Installing and configuring basic graphical user interface (GUI) tools needed to create and maintain a simple Drupal site. (For beginners and non-programmers.)

■ **Note** The options for setting up your development environment are nearly limitless. This chapter describes two broad approaches: using a fully stocked Linux build in a virtual environment and using tools native to Windows or Mac. See dgd7.org/devenv for more approaches.

Starting with Quickstart

Quickstart (drupal.org/project/quickstart) is a virtual appliance for Mac and Windows machines that launches a preconfigured, LAMP-centric development environment in just a few steps. It eliminates hours of work, handing you a very well thought-out and thoroughly assembled environment that takes minutes to set up. Like Drubuntu (a Drush script that sets up a pre-configured development environment on Ubuntu; see Appendix G), Quickstart offers the considerable bonus of Drupal-specific documentation (drupal.org/node/788080), issue queue (drupal.org/project/issues/quickstart) and usergroup (groups.drupal.org/quickstart-drupal-development-environment)—in other words, all the benefits of a growing developer community that shares common tools in addition to codebase. Quickstart uses VirtualBox with Ubuntu, and is open source through and through.

As with most virtualization solutions, Quickstart can have performance challenges and requires significant resources. The Virtual Box application needs at least 1024MB RAM, and the Quickstart image will take 18GB of disk space as shipped, so check first whether you need to make room or install more RAM. Regarding performance, users on a variety of machines and host operating systems have complained of slowness. In a casual test, Quickstart ran flawlessly within Windows XP Pro on an older Intel Core Duo machine with only 2GB RAM. Yet a newer, more powerful machine had performance concerns (albeit mild ones): on a well-furnished MacBook Pro i7 (Snow Leopard, 8GB RAM, solid state drive), screen refresh was just jerky enough that the mouse was hard to use. Typical tasks like resizing a window required extra focus and patience. Brief experiments with upping base memory, video memory, and number of processors did not eliminate the jerkiness (see drupal.org/node/819720 for a few brief instructions on making Quickstart faster).

If you've not used a well-assembled development environment before, it's worth dealing with performance concerns to get familiar with this one. You can then choose what you find most valuable and take the time to install it on your preferred development OS. Here are the installation steps described on the drupal.org project page (drupal.org/project/quickstart). Note that installation requires importing an appliance rather than creating a new machine (when VirtualBox finishes installing, it will prompt you to create a new machine; you will need to cancel that operation and follow the directions here).

1. Download Quickstart 0.9.1 virtual machine with bittorrent. (Need a client? uTorrent (Win and Mac) from www.utorrent.com)

2. Install Virtualbox (version 4.0.4+).

3. Import Quickstart virtual machine.

   a. Start Virtualbox.

   b. File ➤ Import Appliance ➤ Choose file ➤ (select the downloaded ova file)

   c. Set RAM to 50% of your system RAM (min 1024MB, max 2048MB).

   d. Import ➤ (wait for import to finish).

4. Start the new machine from the list.

5. Username: Passwords

   a. Unix = quickstart:quickstart

   b. MySQL = root:quickstart

   c. Drupal = admin:admin

6. Update to latest official versions: drush, drush make, drush Quickstart, etc. To get the latest updates to drush commands:

    a.   cd ~/quickstart

    b.   git pull

    c.   bash -x update.sh

Once Quickstart is operational, open the readme file (shown in Figure 12–1) for links to documentation, tutorials, and a few of the browser-based developer tools. It's worth clicking through these links as well as looking closely at the Firefox toolbars that open above the page.

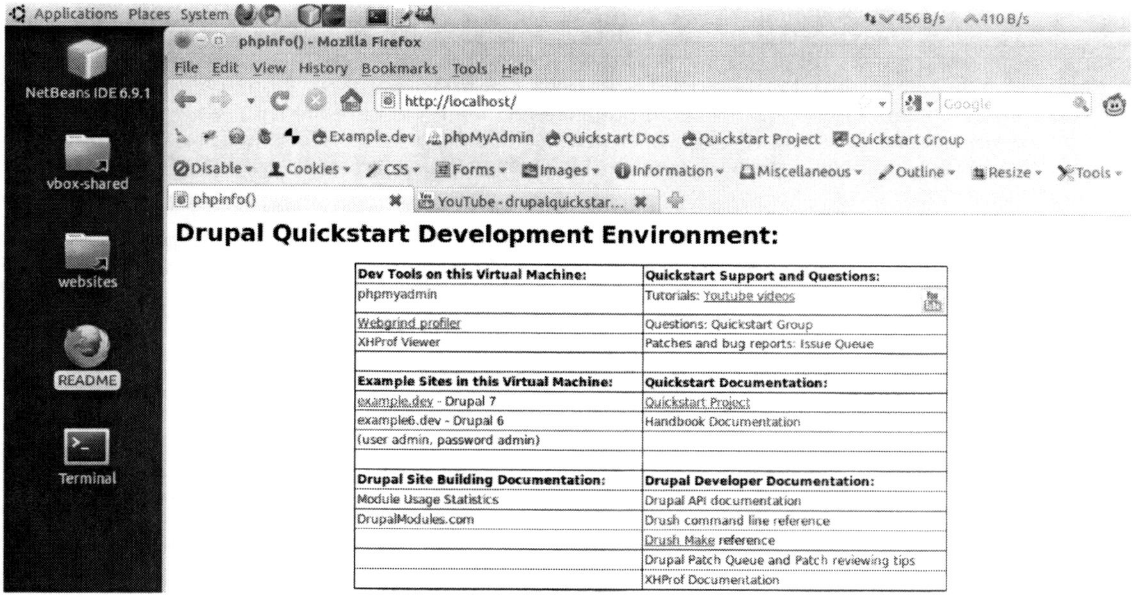

Figure 12–1. The readme file contains useful links to documentation, tutorials, and a few of the browser-based tools.

Virtualization has additional benefits. See the upcoming section on browser testing for a challenge particularly well addressed by virtual machines. If virtualization is not the direction you wish to take, though, continue to the next section of this chapter, which has instructions on installing several of the key components of a Drupal-friendly IDE on Windows and Mac operating systems.

Enhancing Your Existing Dev Environment

There's a developer tool for almost any task. The more often you perform a task, the more useful the "right" tool becomes and the more individualized your setup. This section will cover setting up some of the more common tools and look at the factors that might lead you to include them in your custom-assembled dev environment. I'll touch on the following major development needs:

- Hosting your site locally.

- Accessing the command line.

- Working with rendered HTML, CSS, and JavaScript.
- Testing for browser and device compatibility.
- Working with PHP files.

Hosting Your Site Locally

Hosting the site you are developing on your local machine is generally recognized both as a matter of convenience and as a best practice. With Git to facilitate the work of merging a team of developers' efforts, local development instances allow each team member to work with their own copies of files, database, and server software. This setup lets each team member experiment more freely and work out the kinks before uploading partially formed modifications that might interfere with other team members' work. As a bonus, local development travels with developers whether they are online or not, and network outages don't stop the entire team from working (both reasons for the lone developer also to adopt the practice).

Several reliable, comprehensive solutions for running the LAMP stack locally on Mac and Windows have been bundled into well-tested installation packages. The various systems each have somewhat different approaches and tools for the task; this book provides an appendix dedicated to each of the four common solutions.

- Appendix F covers local hosting on Windows with WAMP.
- Appendix G covers the setup of Drubuntu on Linux.
- Appendix H focuses on MAMP for the Mac.
- Appendix I focuses on Acquia Dev Desktop, which works on both Windows and Mac.

Another option on Windows is Microsoft WebMatrix (`microsoft.com/web/drupal`), which sets up Drupal to run locally on IIS.

Accessing the Command Line

From a distance, the command line strikes some developers as a relic of the dark ages, a pre-GUI tool probably used for torture. Despite its unfriendly appearance, the command line is an important, efficient, and powerful element of your development environment.

Mac and Linux ship with Terminal, the "go-to" command line interface. To open Terminal on the Mac, go to Applications ➤ Utilities ➤ Terminal; on Ubuntu go to Applications ➤ Accessories ➤ Terminal.

There are a few options for using Terminal with Windows. The two most common are hosting Linux via virtualization (e.g., Quickstart) or installing a Linux emulator. Cygwin (`cygwin.com/`) is widely used for the latter approach.

To install Cygwin, follow these steps:

1. Download the installer at `cygwin.com/setup.exe`.

2. Run `setup.exe`, accept the defaults, and follow the on-screen instructions until you reach the package selection screen

3. On the package selection screen, locate and enable the following choices (clicking once on a package selects the most recent version and clicking again selects a previous version, so resist the urge to double click):

a.   In Shells, "rxvt: VT102 terminal emulator for both X and Windows".

b.   In Net, "openssh: The OpenSSH server and client programs".

c.   In Archive, "unzip: Info-ZIP decompression utility".

d.   In Editors, "nano: A pico clone text editor with extensions" (you may also want to add vim).

e.   In Web, "wget: Utility to retrieve files from the WWW via HTTP and FTP".

▒ **Note** Terminal doesn't interpret spaces in file and directory names as Windows and Mac operating systems do. Use a backslash to escape spaces when you are entering paths, like so:

`$ cd Documents\ and\ Settings`

As an alternative to typing the full path of a file or directory, you can drag its icon onto a Terminal window.

When you have completed installing Cygwin, open Terminal by launching the Cygwin program. Type help to get a list of command-line functions. See other chapters in this book for instructions on using the command line.

Working with Rendered HTML, CSS, and JavaScript

The single most valuable tool for front-end developers is the Firebug plug-in (`http://getfirebug.com/`). At its most basic implementation, Firebug allows web developers to inspect and experimentally change setting in the CSS and HTML of a page while it runs in a web browser. Full functionality requires the popular open source Firefox web browser, though versions of the tool are available that provide partial functionality in other browsers. Some other browsers also implement their own tools that provide similar functionality, notably the Safari Developer Tools (to use these, turn on the Develop Menu in the menu Safari ➤ Preferences ➤ Advanced).

▒ **Note** Before you begin working with Firebug, ensure that CSS and JavaScript aggregation for your site is off at Administration ➤ Configuration ➤ Development ➤ Performance (`admin/config/development/performance`).

To enable Firebug, first add it to Firefox (browse with Firefox to getfirebug.com and click Install Firebug), then activate it by going to the menu Tools ➤ Firebug ➤ Open Firebug. By default, Firebug opens with an HTML view in the left pane and the styles associated with the highlighted element in the right pane. Styles are listed in order of precedence: styles at the top of the list supersede those listed lower down (note that this display order is the reverse of CSS stylesheets, well suited to the purpose of on-screen readability). Navigate the code either by expanding and selecting HTML elements or by enabling the inspector zoom tool (icon in upper left corner of the Firebug panel showing a mouse pointer and rectangle). To use the zoom tool, click the inspector zoom tool, then hover over the web page until the area you want to inspect is highlighted. Click the page and the HTML view will zoom to the nested HTML element associated with the highlighted area.

Once you are on the HTML element you wish to affect, you can change the values shown in the Style pane or in the HTML pane. Changes will immediately affect the loaded page accordingly. However, Firebug does not save these changes. The changes affect only the loaded instance of the page (that is to say, you leave the changed page in its existing window and open a new instance of the page in another window, you will see that the changes you made do not apply in the new window or tab).

To implement the changes you want to keep, open the related PHP or CSS documents in your text editor. As you develop the desired settings, modify the related PHP/CSS document accordingly. Remember only to modify your own custom theme or module files, not core or contributed code; see Chapters 15 and 16 on theming for the correct way to override rendered HTML, CSS, and JavaScript. Also keep in mind that best practice is to avoid making changes to the code of a live site; be sure to carry out your changes on a development server, then deploy to staging and production servers as appropriate.

Also check out the Drupal for Firebug module, which adds Drupal debugging and SQL query information to the Firebug window (see `drupal.org/project/drupalforfirebug`).

Browser and Device Compatibility Testing

As you fine-tune a site's theme, it is crucial to test the site thoroughly in each of the browsers and on each of the devices used by your target audience. As amazing as it may seem to the uninitiated, the display of a site can vary significantly between Internet Explorer and Firefox, the two most popular browsers available. It can also be disastrously different across IE versions themselves (IE6 has been very tenacious in certain markets, reportedly still with more than 15% of IE usage overall, even though IE9 is now available). Note, too, that some industries, and certainly academia, are more prone than others to continuing the use of old browsers rather than upgrading. As choices among web-enabled mobile devices grows, the challenge to test sites thoroughly becomes greater.

Limiting the breadth of the testing effort can be useful. Start by identifying which browsers and devices are most important. There are various sources of statistics on current browser market share; `en.wikipedia.org/wiki/Usage_share_of_web_browsers` references a good list of such sources. In the end, the best indicator of which browsers and devices you should test are statistics collected for the specific target audience of your project. If you are working with an existing site, you can typically get such data from the host's site statistics; you can also add the Browscap module to your Drupal install to capture browser version information (`drupal.org/project/browscap`). Keep in mind the rapid growth in mobile Internet use as you view historical data.

Even once you have identified a limited set of browsers and devices you need to account for, it can be a challenge to execute the tests. The most methodical approach to testing compatibility for desktop- and laptop-based browsers is to run (virtual) machines that host each combination of operating system and browser release of interest. For mobile devices, device manufacturers typically release emulators with their developer tools; visit their web sites for downloads and instructions.

Not everyone can justify the labor that goes into building and maintaining this array of test beds, and third party services can be engaged to handle testing. However, here are some potential shortcuts for desktop browser versions:

- Utilu IE Collection is a download of all the major releases of Microsoft Internet Explorer set up to run simultaneously on the same machine; find it at `utilu.com/IECollection`.

- Mozilla maintains a directory of Firefox releases at `releases.mozilla.org/pub/mozilla.org/firefox`.

- Multi-Safari offers individual downloads of Apple Safari, bundling the corresponding Web Kit framework of each version into the application (see description on the site; `michelf.com/multi-safari`); Apple also appears to leave the download pages in place for previous versions, findable via search engines.

- Opera maintains a number of downloadable releases at opera.com/docs/history.

- A resource for previous releases of Google Chrome has not yet surfaced.

When testing browsers, keep in mind that there may be different plug-ins installed on your target users' machines that can affect display and performance, not to mention the effect of screen resolutions and sizes, and the fact that visitors can resize windows (for the latter concern, be sure you resize the browser window on each test platform to ensure that any fluid or undefined widths behave as expected).

Working with PHP Files

Eclipse and Netbeans are two open source Integrated Development Environments (IDEs) well suited to the needs of Drupal development. They are quick to install and configure, and they provide a great way to navigate and modify your Drupal modules and themes. Get Eclipse PDT (PHP Development Tools) from eclipse.org/pdt; get Netbeans from netbeans.org. Here are the basic steps to get the Eclipse PDT package set up on your machine:

1. Start Eclipse. On the startup splash page, select Workbench.

2. Set preferences to recognize Drupal PHP content types at Window ➤ Preferences ➤ General ➤ Content Types; enter the following document types individually starting with the dot: .engine, .install, .inc, .module, .profile, .theme, .test)

3. Set text encoding and line delimiters at Window ➤ Preferences ➤ General ➤ Workspace; at the bottom of the window use Text file encoding ➤ Other ➤ UTF-8 and New text file line delimiter ➤ Other ➤ Unix

4. Set tabs to be converted to two spaces at Window ➤ Preferences ➤ General ➤ Editors; set Displayed tab width to two, and select Insert spaces for tabs.

The Most Basic Development Environment

This section is intended to help beginners and non-programmers put together a set of tools for occasional use.

Let's say you've never worked with Drupal, and you have no programming experience. You've heard the first step is to download a Drupal distribution (see Chapter 34), but for now you're still in the bookstore with this book in your hand. It's fallen open to this page. You want to know what tools are required when Drupal is in your plans: the essential set.

Here's the short list. Most computer owners today already have the majority of these things, but if you're new to web development, pay special attention to the last four on the list.

- A computer able to connect to the Internet.

- An Internet connection.

- A small amount of free disk space (you can do quite a lot with Drupal in 100MB, though you'll also need to account for file sizes of any media like video, audio, or large images).

- A web browser (the latest version of Firefox is strongly recommended).

- A code or text editor (important distinction: typical word processors are unsuitable for this work).

- A program for uncompressing gzip/zip files.

- To take your site online, you will also need:

    - A domain name (registered and managed either by your web site host or by a registrar).

    - A web server with database capabilities (typically a remote web server; Linux is the most common choice of operating system, Apache the most common web server, and MariaDB/MySQL the most common database; see `drupal.org/requirements` for system requirements).

    - A way to transfer files to and from a remote server (Drupal 7 provides a method for adding modules and themes through the administrative pages; it requires your server to have FTP properly configured, as most hosted servers do; you can also use software known as an FTP client).

The list of tools you need to get started is stunningly basic. Drupal and contributed modules provide the tools you will use most often, especially as you start out. All the other basic tools you need, and a good number of the advanced tools, are available as open source software (no matter what your operating system).

Each component in this section of the development environment chapter is relatively easy to set up and learn, so new users can focus their energy on climbing the Drupal learning curve. If you do the tasks repetitively, you will want to add some more complexity to your toolkit in exchange for greater efficiency.

You may also find you will try out a few FTP clients and text editors before identifying one you like. There are a lot of possibilities, especially with text editors, and many published discussions on the merits of certain solutions over others. For the sake of simplicity, I'll only look at a couple of good, all-purpose choices.

■ **Tip** Host your production web site with a professional host; hosting it yourself requires significant expertise and time. When choosing your host, be sure to refer to the recommendations at `drupal.org/requirements`.

Select Hosting Service

There are a lot of options when it comes to hosting configurations, and a large number of providers. See `drupal.org/hosting`; the providers listed are likely all to meet the minimum requirements to host Drupal. However, once those requirements are met, there are several important considerations and a few simple tasks you need to be able to complete. Here are some guidelines on choosing and setting up your host.

Choose a Host According to Performance and Service Needs

Right-sizing your hosting arrangement for the performance you will need is an important first step. Consider the expense and hassle that can go into changing hosts, or even changing server arrangements with the same host, choose a service that leaves room for increases in requirements. Here are some general categories of hosting with broad expectations of performance:

- Providers of Drupal as a Service (also known as Drupal SaaS) provide attractive combinations of price and performance; be sure to check that the specific functionality you need is part of their offering.

- If you are creating a basic Drupal site, can live with slower page loads, and expect light traffic (say not more than a few dozen simultaneous visitors), you can get by with one of the many readily available, inexpensive, shared hosting accounts.

- If you need fast page loads and capacity for higher traffic, the best balance of performance and budget is likely to be a virtual private server (VPS).

- If your site serves gigabytes of media to an international audience, you will likely need a content distribution network (CDN).

- If you anticipate severe traffic spikes, you will need an auto-scaling solution that is typical of cloud-based hosting.

Be sure that your host provides any services you are unable to provide. Some provide server space but leave the rest to you. You can get more details by comparing the services lists and reported up-time of various providers. (Review sites regarding hosts do not generally appear to be reliable). Key attributes include:

- A well-capitalized, well-run company.

- Adequately housed servers with complete, correctly configured software and equipment.

- 24×7 server software and equipment monitoring and issue resolution.

- Proactive performance of security and maintenance tasks.

- Adequate customer support.

- Acquisition of new infrastructure and expertise as appropriate.

In addition to hosting, you also need to register a domain and have it propagate to domain name servers. Not all hosts provide these services. If yours does not, you will need to sign up for an account with a registrar. Expect to pay around $10/year for this service (it is often included free with a hosting account). ICANN, the body responsible for coordinating internet addresses, also accredits registrars. They maintain a list of registrars at icann.org/en/registrars/accredited-list.html.

Once you have selected a host, the registration process is typically quick. Look for an e-mail once registration is complete. It will contain important information for the next steps. If you have a separate account with a registrar, the e-mail will also contain instructions on pointing your new URL to your hosting account (look for instructions regarding Domain Name Servers, also referred to as DNS).

FTP Client Setup

FTP clients let you transfer files between your local computer and a remote server. Start the setup of your FTP client after you receive a confirmation e-mail from your host provider. It will typically contain the URL, username, and password needed to access your online files.

A popular choice of standalone FTP utilities, Cyberduck is a powerful open source FTP client for both Mac and Windows (cyberduck.ch). A popular choice among Firefox add-ons is FireFTP (fireftp.mozdev.org). Setup of FTP connections is similar once these clients are installed, and both offer various ways to log in and transfer files.

The following sections show how to access your remote server.

1. Create a Bookmark with Your Server Access Settings

In Cyberduck: create a bookmark for your hosted account via the menu Bookmark ➤ New Bookmark.

In FireFTP: click Create an account in the upper left corner of the window, as shown in Figure 12–2.

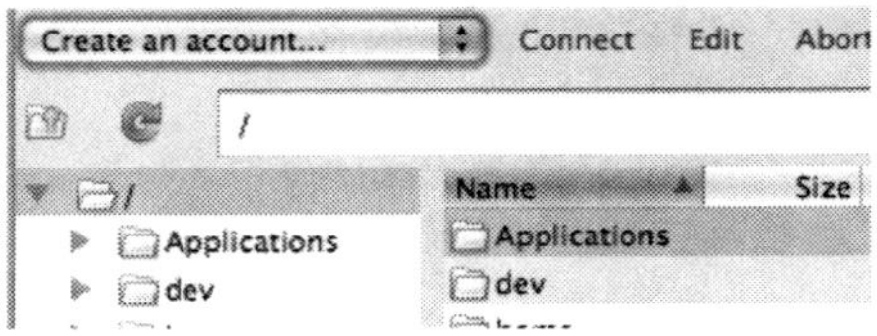

Figure 12–2. *In FireFTP, click Create an account to save your FTP login credentials.*

Always give the bookmark a clear nickname so you know at a glance where you are connected. Servers look identical when you are inside the file structures, so the nickname is often your surest landmark. The best nicknames contain the name of the project and indicate whether the server hosts a live, staged, or development version of your site.

2. Select a Security Protocol

In Cyberduck: select security protocols from the drop-down menu at the top of the New Bookmark window (see Figure 12–3).

In FireFTP: security settings are under the Connection tab of the bookmark window.

If your host offers SSH, you should be able to connect with SFTP using your SSH credentials. If it offers FTP-SSL, you should be able to connect with your FTP credentials. If it's not clear how to make a secure FTP connection, get in touch with their support.

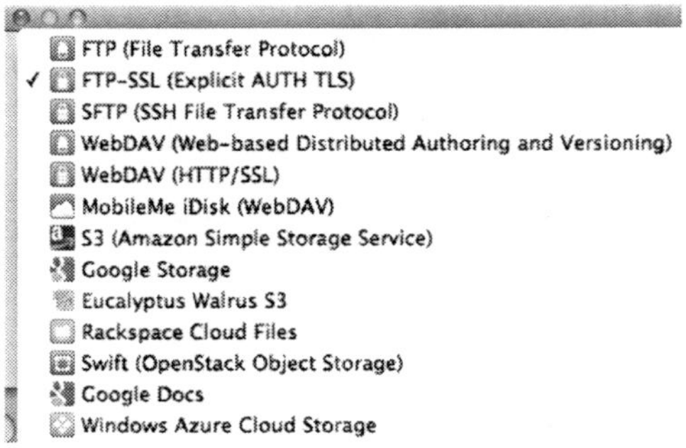

Figure 12–3. *Cyberduck connection types*

▩ **Tip** Most hosts provide a secure method of file transfer. Traditional FTP sends your password as plaintext, and broadly-available software makes it easy to record, especially on a shared network such as your favorite coffeehouse wireless hookup.

---

3. Enter Login Credentials Provided by Your Host

In the e-mail you receive from your host, you will find the server address, username, and password appropriate for the type of connection you have chosen. The various pieces of information may be named different ways. The server address may be called the host address or URL. For file transfer over SSH, the e-mail may use the acronym SCP. No matter the nomenclature, you should be able to recognize the pieces you need: a server address typically resembles a web URL; a username sometimes looks like an e-mail address; the password is typically a mix of letters, numbers, and symbols.

Fill in these pieces of information and be careful not to alter other settings in the window unless you have specific instructions to do so. Make sure the Anonymous Login box stays unchecked. Note that Cyberduck doesn't have a password field on this screen; once you click connect, it will ask for a password.

Save these settings. When you need to connect in the future, you will only need to click the bookmark.

4. Start a Connection and Upload Files

Click the bookmark. You should get a new screen showing a tree of files and directories. You will typically work within a directory labeled either public_HTML or www (sometimes both are listed and go to the same subdirectory).

You are now ready to upload your files. Both Cyberduck and FireFTP let you drag files from a local directory and drop them on the remote directory into which you want them loaded. See Chapter 1 for the steps to set Drupal in a directory on your server; the "Implementation" section provides the details.

If your connection fails, confirm that you have entered all credentials exactly as the host provided them. Small deviations can be hard to spot but almost always explain the problem (check that caps lock is off and that you are entering upper and lowercase letters as shown). The security protocol can be another source of trouble. To ensure you have the credentials entered correctly, you can also try with no security protocol. If you successfully connect with plain FTP but not with a secure protocol, contact your host about the correct settings.

5. Basic Text Editor Setup

Most every programmer has a favorite, no-frills text editor, even if they also have full-fledged Integrated Development Environments (IDEs) as well as high-end desktop publishing tools. A good, basic text editor is as handy as a Swiss Army knife.

The defacto standard for Windows machines is Notepad++ (`sourceforge.net/projects/notepad-plus`); Windows also ships with Notepad, which will suffice for small editing tasks in a pinch. If you use Notepad, be sure to save your documents with the UTF-8 encoding (see the drop-down menu in the Save dialog box).

For Mac, a very good choice is TextWrangler (free but not open source); the Mac also ships with TextEdit, which can be set to plaintext and is serviceable.

Linux users wanting a GUI-based text editor should try gEdit.

Don't attempt to use a word processor like Microsoft Word, WordPad, or OpenDoc. Servers and browsers can't easily digest the output of these programs. Sometimes you'll get instant feedback on their shortcomings (the page displays incorrectly or you get error messages). In the worst case you never see the problems on your own computer and only your site visitors experience the variety of issues that arise.

6. Configure Text Editor Preferences

Notepad++ and many other text editors typically need a few adjustments to the Preferences. TextWrangler and gEdit, on the other hand, ship with the default settings needed for web development. In Notepad++, go to Settings ➤ Preferences ➤ New Document/Default Directory. Set the New Document Format to Unix and set the Encoding to UTF-8.

One warning: TextWrangler, gEdit, and Notepad++ each inserts tab characters when you hit the tab key. Tab characters may produce unexpected results, often appearing as single spaces or collapsing with spaces around them. They do not typically cause fatal errors, but a better practice is to use two spaces to indent lines of code and to use CSS to indent lines of text.

7. Set Your FTP Client to Use Your Text Editor

At times, using your local text editor to modify a file that is on your remote development or staging servers can be the most efficient way to get things done (note that this practice is not recommended on production servers). FTP clients like Cyberduck and FireFTP let you associate file types (including images) with appropriate editing programs.

For Cyberduck: go to Edit ➤ Preferences, click the Editor tab, and select the program you want to use from the list. If the program isn't listed, click Add program.

For FireFTP: right-click any file in the FireFTP file view area, select Open With ➤ Add Programs. Under the Extensions window, click Add, and type an extension such as .txt. With the extension highlighted, click Add under the Programs window. Click Browse and locate your program. Type a name (e.g., Notepad++) and click Apply.

Uncompressing Archives

Most modern operating systems ship with a utility for uncompressing archives. If you've installed a command line interface on Windows (e.g., Cygwin, as described earlier in this chapter), one of the recommended packages is unzip. In Terminal, the command looks like $ unzip *filename*.

If you don't have a command line interface, the archive files you download from drupal.org will need to have a program associated with them (see Figure 12–4), and you may need to download one. (Double-click an archive to open it; if it doesn't open, you'll be invited to select a program to open it with). A popular open source utility for uncompressing common archive types is 7zip (sourceforge.net/projects/sevenzip/).

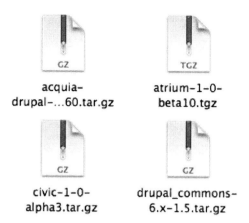

acquia-
drupal-...60.tar.gz

atrium-1-0-
beta10.tgz

civic-1-0-
alpha3.tar.gz

drupal_commons-
6.x-1.5.tar.gz

Figure 12–4. *When a program is properly associated with archives, the archives typically show a zipper icon.*

Server-Side Tasks and Tools

Once you have the aforementioned basic tools, your next tasks are to set up a database, upload files, and run the Drupal installer. The Introduction of this book and Chapter 1 describe these tasks in general terms. Since different hosts provide different tools and methods for completing these tasks, I'll cover a few common setups here in more detail. Some of the tools provided by hosts can actually introduce critical issues for Drupal, so we will look briefly at workarounds. If your host offers one-click installation, skip to the "Circumventing the One-Click Installers" section.

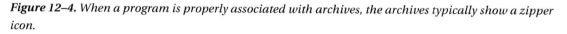

▤ **Tip** More details about creating a database can be found at `drupal.org/documentation/install/create-database`.

Database Setup with phpMyAdmin

Setting up a database can be quite simple. If your server includes direct access to the database creation features of phpMyAdmin, the broadly distributed open source database manager, the process requires these few steps:

1. Start phpMyAdmin, go to the Privileges tab, and click Add a New User.

2. Enter a username that relates to your project and phase (if you create several databases, a recognizable name will help you single it out if the need arises); note the name you use.

3. Select Local as the host and enter a password (or click Generate to have one created for you); note the password—you will be prompted for username and password when you run the Drupal installer.

4. In the box labeled Database for user, select Create database with same name and grant all privileges, then click Go at the bottom of the page.

5. In the left sidebar, click on the name of the database you created, then go to the Operations tab.

6. Set the collation to utf8_general_ci and click Go.

7. Upload your files and launch the Drupal installer as described in Chapter 1.

Database Setup with Wizards and Manual Tools

Hosts commonly provide a dedicated utility for database and user creation and disable the related tools in phpMyAdmin. In the best of situations, the host implements a manual form or a wizard that requests the same inputs described above.

Circumventing the One-Click Installers

The greatest pitfalls in setting up your Drupal site on a hosted server are likely to come in the guise of one-click installation utilities. You will typically be forced to use them if they are present. Unfortunately, they frequently introduce wholly avoidable issues that are relatively difficult to discover and fix. Fantastico and SimpleScripts are broadly used utilities of this sort. Each has its own problems. To add to the confusion, manual/wizard methods are frequently available alongside one-click installers. When both methods are available, the manual/wizard methods typically also result in installs that don't work. The best workaround appears to be to use the one-click utility. It will set up database, user, and the required non-Drupal files. You can then remove the Drupal files and tables created by the installer and proceed with a normal install.

Here are the steps for this workaround when you are forced to use a one-click install utility:

1. Follow the host's directions for installing Drupal; when it instructs you to create a new subdirectory for this version, give it an easily recognized name (e.g., fantastico-drupal7)

2. Once installation is complete, follow the 1-click installer's directions for launching the site; ensure the installation works as expected (you will see the front page as pictured in Chapter 1); if it doesn't, contact the host for support.

3. After confirming that the installation works, use your FTP client to place your own Drupal distribution in a different directory (e.g., public_HTML) as described in Chapter 1.

4. Navigate to the subdirectory created by the installation script (the one I suggested naming fantastico-drupal7 in step 1); inside the directory, navigate to sites/default/settings.php; open the file; and note the database name, username, password, host, and port, as shown in Figure 12–5.

```
 *   );
 * @endcode
 */
$databases = array (
  'default' =>
  array (
    'default' =>
    array (
      'driver' => 'mysql',
      'database' => 'databasename',
      'username' => 'username',
      'password' => 'password',
      'host' => 'localhost',
      'port' => '',
    ),
  ),
);
```

Figure 12–5. The settings.php file showing the connection information to note for use when running the Drupal installer

5. Next, launch phpMyAdmin and click the database name in the left sidebar that you noted from `settings.php`.

6. Scroll to the bottom of the list of database tables and click Check All; in the adjacent drop-down menu labeled With selected, choose Drop, then confirm your choice.

7. Click on the to the Operations tab, set the collation to utf8_general_ci, and click Go

8. Launch Drupal install as described in Chapter 1 of this book and enter the connection information recorded from `settings.php`.

Summary

In this chapter we have explored a few possible approaches to setting up your development environment. Most of the chapter focuses on two ways to build advanced suites of tools that offer significant gains in efficiency but also have a relatively steep learning curve. The last section of the chapter (Your Most Basic Development Environment) presents a vastly simplified setup suitable for occasional use, for casual beginners, and for non-programmers. We cover the basics of selecting, signing up for, and configuring a web hosting account and domain registration. Throughout, we touch on best practices and on workarounds for known issues related to development and shared web hosting. Further information on topics related to development environments can be found on the book's web site, `www.dgd7.com`.

■ ■ ■

## CHAPTER 13

Putting a Site Online and Deploying New Features

by Benjamin Melançon and Stefan Freudenberg

If only you can see it, your Drupal site isn't quite as useful as it could be. If something happens to it, and you can't restore it, that's really bad. If you need to take the site offline for a week to add a complex new feature, that's not great either. This chapter covers putting your site online, backing it up, and then treads lightly into Drupal's new frontier of deploying major features.

Putting Your Site Online

Your web site deserves to be on the Internet. This section covers the steps to put a site online (or "take it live") in general terms that apply no matter what software is available. We'll explain each step and we'll provide the command line steps that should work for any serious setup. If you deploy more than a couple times, you'll want to automate these steps. There is no Drupal community consensus yet on the best way to do this, but we'll include some tips and point to some resources for best-practice approaches.

Taking a site from your local computer or a development server to a live web server can be broken into five steps.

1. Export the database.

2. Transfer a copy of the site code, user files, and exported database to the server.

3. On the server, import the site's database.

4. Create or edit the site's **settings.php** on the server to use the database settings.

5. Direct traffic for your domain name(s) to the site's web root on the server.

These steps can be followed with different tools on any platform, such as graphical database and SFTP programs. Likewise, any build tool, such as rake or ant, can perform steps 2 through 4.

■ **Tip** When choosing a company to host your web site, look for one that will let you access your host server with SSH. See the online notes and resources for possible hosts at `dgd7.org/deploy`.

We'll look at the specific command line steps for Linux, Mac OS X, or Cygwin now. These steps should work even for environments you have not been able to set up. On the server side, the commands are based on a typical Debian or Ubuntu setup; if you're setting up your own server, see wiki.debian.org/LaMp.

When you're dealing with more than one site, you will certainly want to script the process. Deployment scripts are usually specific to your hosting and development workflow and needs. (For an example, the evolving practice of the Drupal collective I am part of is documented at data.agaric.com/deploying-the-agaric-way.) Aegir, which makes heavy use of Drush, is a Drupal deployment solution (using Drupal to help deploy Drupal) that has a significant, longstanding, and growing community. It is a free software hosting system for automating common tasks associated with deploying and managing web sites. For information and downloads, see aegirproject.org.

■ **Tip** See how Drush can enhance your deployment workflow in the "Using Remote Commands to Deploy Sites with Drush" section in Chapter 26.

---

1. Export the Database

Thus far, this book has had you work with your site installed locally on your computer. To take your configuration online with any content you've added, you will want to first export the database.

■ **Caution** This first step only applies the first time you take a site online. Exporting your development database and replacing an existing live database would, in most cases, be a mistake. If you aren't already backing up your live site (using tools mentioned in Chapter 2 or described later in this chapter), it would amount to a *colossal* mistake.

In the following commands, the key action is mysqldump. The other commands just refer to a place to put the database in the meantime.

The Drush command drush sql-dump can save you looking up the database connection information, when run from within the site root or with an alias.

```
# Change to your project's folder.
cd ~/code/dgd7
# If a database ("db") directory is not made already:
mkdir db
# Export the database, where dgd7 is the name of the database.
mysqldump -udgd7 -pdgd7 dgd7 > db/development.sql
```

The options used in the mysqldump command are the following:

- -u for database username, which can be followed immediately by the user (dgd7 here).

- -p for database password, which is followed immediately by the password (dgd7).

- The lone word (dgd7) is the database name itself. You can get these values from your local site's settings.php file.

■ **Note** Find out more about the `mysqldump` command by typing `man mysqldump` on the command line in UNIX-like environments (Linux, Mac OS X, Cygwin). The command `man` is short for manual, as in a user's manual; you can use it to get more information on almost any command.

---

2. Transfer to Server

This is the step you don't need to be reminded about: moving the site's code, any user files associated with it, and the exported database from your development environment to a server that is online. The remote file copy program secure copy (`scp`) will work.

```
scp -r ~/code/dgd7 username@host.example.com:/var/www/
```

■ **Tip** Don't forget to transfer the `.htaccess` file; as a "hidden" file beginning with a dot, it's easily missed.

Set Files Directories Permissions

After moving the codebase and user files, you need to make sure the user files directories are writeable. The `scp` command created the directory **dgd7** in **/var/www** while moving in your site code and dumped database, so after logging into your server, you can go to that directory to access them conveniently. (Note that it's assumed you are deploying to an Apache web server running as user www-data.)

```
ssh username@host.example.com
cd /var/www/dgd7
chown -R www-data:www-data web/sites/default/files
chown -R www-data:www-data private_files
```

The latter command only applies if you do a private files directory and should be done where you choose to create your private files directory (which should be outside of your web root).

3. Create a Database on the Server and Import Your Database

On your host server, log in to create a new database and load the transferred database dump into it.

■ **Note** It's quite possible your host will provide a control panel for creating database users and databases.

We name the database user and the database itself after the project name, which in this case is *dgd7*.

```
ssh username@host.example.com
mysqladmin -u root -p create dgd7
mysql -u root -p -e "GRANT ALL ON \`dgd7\`.* TO 'dgd7'@'localhost' IDENTIFIED BY↩
 'S3cUr3p4s5w0rD'"
```

You will be prompted for your MySQL root password after issuing each of the last two commands. It's better not to write this password inline, as that would put this important password in your server's shell command history. In this example, the third command gives the new database the password "S3cUr3p4s5w0rD", which you will then use to import the database, to use along with the database user and database name.

If you followed the steps in the "Set Files Directories Permissions" section, you are already logged into the host server and in the directory **/var/www/dgd7**, so the database directory used in the section before that, db, is right there.

```
mysql -h localhost -u dgd7 -pS3cUr3p4s5w0rD dgd7 < db/development.sql
```

The `mysql` command used to import the database has the same parameters as `mysqldump` when exporting the database, with one addition: `-h` for host, the server on which the database lives. Typically, the database will be on the same server as everything else, so you can use `localhost`. Note that the angle bracket is turned around—think of it as accepting the database file into the command.

4. Set the Database Settings in settings.php

Your Drupal site is almost ready to go live. The code is in place on your production server, the user files were transferred along with it, the databases are loaded, and now it needs to know about the database.

You can manually edit `settings.php` to use these values or you can use Drupal to set it up for you (if the file permissions in `settings.php` are set to allow it) by going to the site in your browser, for instance:

```
http://example.com/install.php
```

To edit the file manually, the following commands will open it in vim; go to the correct line (around line 181), and enter insert mode:

```
vi sites/default/settings.php
:181
i
```

Make the relevant section (the `$databases = array()` line) look something like this:

```
$databases['default']['default'] = array(
  'driver' => 'mysql',
  'database' => 'dgd7',
  'username' => 'dgd7',
  'password' => 'S3cUr3p4s5w0rD',
  'host' => 'localhost',
  'prefix' => '',
);
```

■ **Tip** Remember that the array you are defining is nested two deep (typically with the key 'default' for each)! It's not simply `$databases = array()` as Drupal starts you off; it is a twice-nested array and you might as well start off like `$databases['default']['default'] = array( ... );` The first default is for the default database rather than an additional one and the second default indicates that it is the main (master) database rather than a supporting (slave) database.

Every automation tool has to perform the steps described so far. We presume a functioning web serving environment, so this section on initial deployment is done with a final step: telling your web serving software the location of the document root of your web site. The preconditions we are not covering include a module capable of interpreting or running php (such as, for Apache, mod_fcgid or mod_php).

5. Point Incoming Traffic for Your Domain(s) to Your Site on the Server

This step is about pointing visitors looking for your domain to your site. This means configuring your web server software (most commonly Apache) to match the corresponding location and setup of Drupal from the previous steps. Before visitors can see your site at a public address (web domain), however, a few prerequisites need to be met.

- First, you need a domain name, which you can purchase through a domain name registrar (see icann.org/en/registrars/accredited-list.html for the full list of registrars).

- Second, you need the Domain Name System (DNS) settings for your domain name to point to nameservers you control. Your nameservers may be provided through your registrar, your host, or a dedicated DNS service.

- Finally, the nameservers need to be telling your domain to point to your server's Internet Protocol (IP) address.

■ **Note** After telling your domain to use new nameservers, it can take up to two days to resolve (start working). If you purchase hosting and domain names from the same company (not recommended), these steps may have already been done for you.

Once all that is established, you can configure the web server software to send incoming requests for your domain name to the folder that contains your site's web root. In this example, that folder is /var/www/dgd7/web. (Drupal's code was placed in the sub-directory web in the directory dgd7 in Chapter 1.)

■ **Note** As with most things you'll do in Drupal, there are multiple ways to serve a web site. Even if your host is using Apache, it may have a graphical user interface set up or command line tools to automate some or all of the upcoming tasks, so look for the easy solutions first!

Apache is the most-used web server; like Drupal, it's Free Software. A common way for Apache to direct visitors to your web site is with a virtual host configuration. These can be written as individual files, one for each web site, and added to /etc/apache2/sites-available (in a Debian installation). You can create a new file and begin editing it with the Vim editor (see Appendix I) with the command vi /etc/apache2/sites-available/dgd7 (where dgd7 can be any filename that lets you identify your site) and put something like the code in Listing 13–1 in it.

Listing 13–1. Example Apache Virtual Host Configuration File for definitivedrupal.org

```
<VirtualHost *:80>
    ServerAdmin webmaster@agaricdesign.com
    ServerName definitivedrupal.org
    ServerAlias www.definitivedrupal.org dgd7.org www.dgd7.org definitivedrupal.mayfirst.org
    DocumentRoot /var/www/dgd7/web
    <Directory />
        Options FollowSymlinks
        AllowOverride None
    </Directory>
    <Directory /var/www/dgd7/web>
        Options Indexes FollowSymLinks
        AllowOverride All
        Order allow,deny
        allow from all
    </Directory>
</VirtualHost>
```

A symlink to this file in Apache's sites-enabled directory can be created with the command sudo a2ensite dgd7 (where dgd7 is the name of the file you created in Apache's sites-available directory).

Apache must reload its virtualhost configuration files before they take effect. An error in one of these files can cause all web sites served by Apache to fail, so we highly recommend you test first (the first command here):

```
sudo /usr/sbin/apache2ctl -t
sudo /etc/init.d/apache2 reload
```

The second command reloads your configuration, and you should be able to see your web site at your domain name now! For more information about Apache virtual hosts, see apache.org/docs/current/vhosts.

Note the AllowOverride directive which permits Drupal's included .htaccess to give Apache instructions necessary for Drupal's proper operation.

■ **Note** You may have noticed that one of the domains listed as a server alias in the example Apache Vhost file was definitivedrupal.mayfirst.org, not one that acts as a public domain for the site. This allows you to test all the configuration done in this section *before* anyone can access your site through its usual domain name or names. This is especially useful when replacing an existing site. This particular domain and subdomain is set up by our host, May First People Link, for each project, but you could set up your own, even directing a subdomain such as livetest.definitivedrupal.org at your server for this purpose.

Your web site is online! Now (or earlier!) comes backups, and soon comes deploying updates and new features.

Before You Go Any Further, Back Up

"Another mortal mistake is not backing up your site."

—*Jeff Robbins(from a Lullabot podcast)*

Karen Stevenson immediately added that everyone has committed this sin, and most have horror stories. Permit us to help you avoid this fate. If you do nothing in this section, at least set up the Backup and Migrate module (`drupal.org/project/backup_migrate`) described in Chapter 2. Again, if you don't get going with a server-based backup solution such as the one described below, set up the Backup and Migrate module on every of your Drupal sites. Configure it to take daily backups, uploading them to a place on your server and/or sending them to your mailbox.

▨ **Tip** Do not skip this section. If you do not yet have automated backups, before you go any further, back up your work—and then set up your work environment and servers so that backups are automated.

If you are building anything you want to see again, you need to back it up. If you don't believe this, ask any developer who's had a server malfunction, user or developer error, or an attack on a site that wasn't backed up. Heck, ask anyone who has lost their computer or had a hard drive die.

Continually backing up your work is an essential practice for any web developer. As introduced in Chapter 2 and elaborated upon in Chapter 14, whether you are downloading modules to construct a site, authoring a theme, or coding a module, you can have peace of mind and comfortable creative flow by using version control.

Even more important than your code, however, are the words, the pictures, the stories and facts that people using your site have crafted and placed there. This content is a sacred trust; the worst thing you can do to your users is lose all their data. And that is, in fact, very bad. Don't do it.

Back up the database and the files. If you have configured a private file directory, don't forget to back the private files up as well, wherever you have placed them. Do whatever you need to do to make sure all data and files are regularly backed up, locally and to a separate computer. A server malfunction, user or developer error, or an attack on your site can mean that failure to back up comes at a very high price.

▨ **Note** A database backup that extends Drush is DGB, for Drush Git Backup. It provides Drush commands for backing up a Drupal database such that each table of the database is a separate file. This approach is more suitable for adding database exports to version control (the Git part), as you can see changes in a table with the `git diff` command (some tables are more useful to look at than others). It also improves on Drush's handling of cache_* tables, conveniently excluding data in these that doesn't need to be part of any backup. DGB is available on GitHub: `github.com/scor/dgb`.

See many more options for backing up a site at `drupal.org/node/22281`. Next, we present a proven approach with a handy tool, Backupninja.

BACKUPNINJA

Backupninja lets you drop simple config files in `/etc/backup.d` to coordinate system backups. It is a master of many arts, including incremental remote filesystem backup and MySQL backup. On systems using Debian's package management tools, you can install it by executing `apt-get install backupninja`.

■ **Note** For Linux without Debian's package manager, you can get backupninja through its project page, `https://labs.riseup.net/code/projects/show/backupninja`.

Running `man backupninja` gives some basic information; most notably, it mentions a small program called ninjahelper. It has a simple user interface offering the following two basic functions when you start it for the first time:

- new to create a new backup action
- quit to leave ninjahelper

A basic setup involving a dump of your database, system configuration, and remote storage involves creating three actions:

- sys
- mysql
- rdiff (make sure to include all the relevant directories mentioned earlier)

The last option requires a user account on a remote machine with ssh access. The really helpful ninjahelper creates and copies an ssh public key, installs required packages, and leaves you with a working backup configuration.

Testing Backups

Your site is not backed up if you can't restore it. Find out where your backups are (if you used the backupninja setup previously mentioned, it will all be specified in your `/etc/backup.d` directory).

Decide also what sort of restoration you need. If it's good enough that you can manually restore everything within a couple hours to a day if something catastrophic happens, you just need to know where everything is. If you need to have very rapid restoration no matter what happens, you will need to have a backup server ready to go and script your restoration.

■ **Tip** This is entirely unrelated to backups, but another scenario when a client or other site user will get upset about lost data is if they type a brilliant essay into the web site and something goes wrong (with the web site or their browser). Don't write anything of significance directly into a browser window, and tell others to avoid it. Edit your precious work in a text editor or word processor like MS Word or OpenOffice.org and copy and paste it into the form. Using a browser that tries hard to safeguard your data, such as Firefox or Chrome, can also make you much happier.

Your web sites aren't the only thing you should be backing up, of course. As mentioned in the next chapter, include your coding area in your personal computer's overall backup. If you aren't backing up your personal computer, now is the time to start. After all, it's not just treasured personal notes, irreplaceable photographs, and potential blackmail material anymore; we're talking truly precious lines of Drupal code.

Staging and Deployment

By staging and deployment, we mean the process of putting all the work going into a web site (the development and the content) somewhere they can be seen together (a staging site), and then taking this to a live web site where it can be seen in all its glory by everyone (deployment).

The trick is doing this when people are using the live web site every day and multiple people may be contributing to development.

■ **Note** Taking the security measures and bug fixes covered in Chapter 6 to a live site is a special case for deployment and by far the easiest case of what is described here; the most basic update code and running of update.php (after testing on stage) will work to deploy these sorts of updates. This process is described next.

There is no definitive way to stage Drupal. There are many ways. The best way depends on the specific needs of the web site project. In our experience, the most common needs involve adding features to an already operating web site. The recommended approach for deployment of new functionality is to make a distinction between content and configuration, and capture the configuration in code where it is version-controlled and easily moved from one environment (such as your local computer) to another (such as stage or live). This approach is commonly called "everything in code."

■ **Tip** No one in Drupal—not even Greg Dunlap, author of the Deploy module (drupal.org/project/deploy)—considers deployment a completely solved problem in Drupal 7. He and others do think we'll be able to solve it in Drupal 8. The Deploy module is not covered here; it is especially well suited when you need to push content as well as configuration from a staging site. In particular, the Deploy module is essential for a frequent content publisher staging and previewing lots of content on a staging site, then pushing it all forward to the live site.

Approach

The approach in this section assumes:

- Competent Drupal developers
- Straightforward publishing workflow (significantly, no need to stage content)

In this case, we recommend an "everything in code" approach to development by using the Features suite of modules to automate major parts of it, keeping the live database the final authority, and making all development impacts on the database testable and re-playable.

In this approach, the database of the live site remains canonical, correct, and never has to be merged. Database changes required for configuration can be replayed in a testable fashion on the staging site before being re-played on live.

If you have a Drupal site you've been working on for a while, you do *not* need to go back and move all existing configuration in the Drupal site into code. Development will always build on a copy of your working, live database. It does mean that new features must use code to make any changes to the database.

Drupal has some pitfalls when it comes to updates, like all applications that rely heavily on a database. That's an architectural decision that has its pros and cons. Applying "everything in code" to an application that follows at its core an "everything through the web" philosophy has its challenges, but the Drupal community is rising to meet them, as you'll see soon.

The Workflow

Given this approach, a model workflow would look like the following:

1. Make a copy of the live database and work with it locally.

2. Add functionality or change appearance through code (modules, themes, etc.). All changes made through pointing and clicking must be exported or otherwise reproduced in a form that is captured in code.

3. Test a fresh copy of the live database against your code from step 2 and run update.php if you have written code to change the database. You can do this on a staging server for other people to see and assess.

4. On the live site, apply the exact code updates you just tested in step 3 and immediately run any needed database update.

▓ **Tip** To always know what site you're looking at, you can use the Environment Indicator module (drupal.org/project/environment_indicator).

All content changes and additions, everything done by users, and the user accounts themselves flow from the live site. All code changes (including everything typically done by a site-building administrator exported to code) flow from the development site or sites. The database and user files meet the code on a quality assurance (QA), test, or stage site for, well, quality assurance and testing, before they meet again on the live site. Figure 13–1 diagrams the flows.

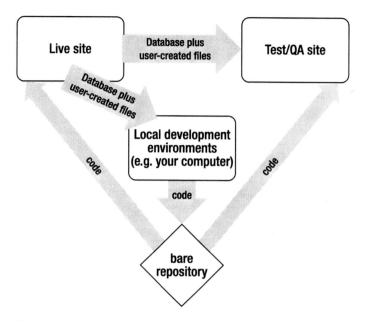

Figure 13–1. *Diagram of an "all configuration in code, all content changes on live" code and database/files flow*

A key thing about this setup is that the local development environments can be multiplied many times (one for every developer working on the site) and the code and data flow and the workflow remain the same. This is made possible by the *bare repository*, a common repository that you and other developers can push code changes to and pull code changes from. The staging and live sites should only pull changes. This is discussed in the "Bring Code Changes from Development to Stage, then Live" section later in this chapter.

Can you still make configuration changes on live? Of course. What we present here is a recommended ideal, not the laws of physics. A hybrid approach where content types and views are built in development and imported to live, but many other changes and tweaks are made directly on live, is quite common. Simply be aware that live configuration changes will burn you sooner or later: something will go wrong on live and you will not know how or why. The more people involved in a site, the more likely this will be. The less acceptable it is to roll back to the previous night's snapshot backup, the more serious this problem can be. Meanwhile, the more you put all your configuration changes into code, the faster you will get at it; likewise, the more everyone uses this approach, the better the community tools will be. Some of these tools are covered in the upcoming "How to put 'Everything in Code'" section.

Bringing Content from Production to Development (and Stage/QA)

The same commands from the "Putting Your Site Online" section can be used here. Dump and import the databases. Drush (`drupal.org/project/drush`) can do this even better; see Chapter 26. Don't forget to bring user files, which can be done with `rsync`.

Try to make this a one-command solution in your setup. To reduce unneeded strain on your live server, you may want to automate the nightly dump or simply get the copy from your most recent backup, rather than exporting the live database directly each time you sync production to development and stage. The important thing is to make it easy so that developers use it regularly. The database should always be considered to belong to live, and any changes you wish to keep must be captured in code.

▪ **Note** The Demonstration module (`drupal.org/project/demo`) can help your workflow of testing your code changes by re-loading a database.

Bring Code Changes from Development to Stage, then Live

Your code changes don't have to be major—you could simply updated core or contributed code (as from Chapter 7). It just has to be done on a development site first. So, download updates or make your code changes on your web site on your local development environment. Then commit these changes to your local repository, push changes to a shared repository, and pull the changes to a staging or QA site for testing. When everything checks out there, the code changes can go live.

A key part of this scenario is that all the environments talk to one repository. This repository can be hosted by a service such as `http://gitorious.org` or `http://github.com`, or you can create it yourself and place it on your own server.

SETTING UP YOUR OWN CENTRAL REPOSITORY

Git is a distributed version control system, which means it does not need a central repository— it carries its full version history with your project wherever you take it.

However, for the purpose of pushing code from one server to another and for working with a team, creating a central point of reference can be very valuable.

You can do this by making a bare clone of your project repository (which you set up in Chapter 2). Here, "bare" means the repository alone—those files in .git directory that mean nothing to a human, without the working copy around it.

From your local development environment, run a `git clone --bare` command and move the resulting folder (given the suffix .git, but a folder not a file) onto a server (this server has been set up to be accessible at the git.example.com address and to have a `/srv/git` directory).

```
git clone --bare ~/code/dgd7 dgd7.git
scp -r dgd7.git you@git.example.com:/srv/git/dgd7.git
```

Your new central repository is probably ready to go already, but from the server you can do a few extra things to make it work in every case.

```
ssh you@git.example.com
cd /srv/git/dgd7.git
git init --bare --shared
git update-server-info
```

To associate this new external repository with your original project on your local computer, do the following:

```
cd ~/code/dgd7
```

```
git remote add origin git
```

To access your project on another computer, including putting it on your staging or production server, do the following:

```
ssh you@test.example.com
cd /var/www
git clone you@git.example.com:/srv/git/dgd7.git dgd7
```

This gives you a repository with working copy in a **dgd7** folder. For more about putting a bare Git repository on your server, see Chapter 4.2 in the Pro Git book (`http://progit.org`).

With everything set up, the commands for adding and committing your changes to local version control and pushing to a shared repository are quite simple. Once you've done whatever you feel needs to be done to your code (much more on that in a following section) you can push it to your central repository, like so:

```
git add -A
git commit -m "Updated pathologic module to the latest security release."
git push
```

Note that `git add -A` captures every change you have made (added, edited, or removed files) and prepares them for committing. Use `git status` to see what you are proposing to commit (and `git reset` to undo an add before committing).

This pushes your code to the remote repository it's associated with. If it is associated with more than one repository, you may have to specify it in the push command (for instance, `git push origin master`).

Now the code is ready to be tested in a fresh environment. First, sync the database from the live site (manually, as in the "Putting Your Site Online" section, or using Drush), and likewise bring the user-created files from live by using the `rsync` command. Next, bring the code changes over to your test site (a clone and working copy of the repository). You can use something like the following commands:

```
ssh you@test.example.com
cd /var/www/dgd7
git pull
```

■ **Note** As with every step in this chapter, you can see an example of helper scripts in the (evolving) practice of one Drupal shop at `data.agaric.com/deploying-the-agaric-way`.

Don't forget to go to `update.php`, as in `http://test.example.com/update.php`, if your code changes include any database updates that need to be run. (Updated core and contributed code, even for security releases, can require updating something in the database, so if you aren't completely sure, go to `update.php` on your site to check.)

When everything has been checked out, you can make the code change on production (continuing to use source control as a deployment tool or using `rsync` for the go-live) and run `update.php`, exactly as you did on the test site.

How to Put "Everything In Code"

The approach outlined in this chapter is to export or otherwise capture in code all changes that you wish to make to a site. It's work—though the tools and techniques mentioned here make it less work—but the benefits are substantial.

- Code can be versioned and there are well-established procedures for resolving conflicts between different versions of the code using version control tools. You can see who did what change and when.

- The quality assurance (QA) environment enables you to test exactly what will happen when you take changes to production.

- Separated configuration and content means that your updates don't overwrite user activity on the live site.

In short, you want to capture in code every single *configuration* thing you possibly can. There's a movement in Drupal to make configuration exportable, and they have successfully implemented this idea for the most important elements of modern Drupal configuration: content (node) types, fields, and views. Arguably, most menus, blocks, and taxonomy can be considered configuration and thus given over to the control of code rather than the user interface on a live site. The Chaos Tools project (drupal.org/project/ctools) brought us the clearly defined concept of *exportables* and tools to help other modules export their configuration. Much of this has been further automated by the Features project, which is the most convenient way for most people to get configuration into code, and so is covered next.

Features

The Features project (drupal.org/project/features) is not the only approach to putting site configuration in code. Even within a single Drupal shop, some teams may only use update hooks (covered next), and some may use the Features module. However, there is pretty universal agreement that making Drupal configuration exportable is a key part of a robust deployment solution, and Features is helping drive the automation of this.

Variations of the word "feature" are used to mean different things in the Features world, and the distinctions are important. This book follows the official definitions:

- *Features*: The Drupal module that allows for the capture of configuration into code.

- *Feature*: A module that contains a collection of Drupal parts that do something specific.

- *feature*: Something you want your web site to do.

- *features*: A set of things you want your web site to do.

"Yes, I'm sorry. It seemed like a good idea at the time."

—Jeff Miccolis, *Development Seed,*
on the terminology used by Features

To use these forms in a sentence: A Feature module (which is created by the Features module) will typically have a tightly related set of features. See Figure 13–2 for a typical workflow of how a feature becomes a Feature module and can be deployed to another site.

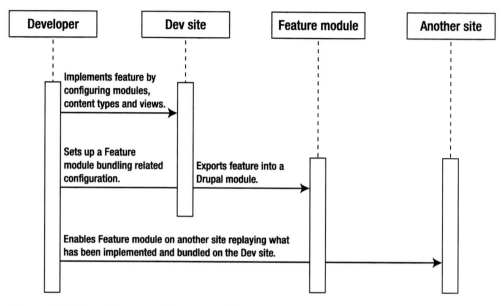

Figure 13–2. From feature to Feature module

Drupal developers working on a relatively simple site can choose to have just one Feature module for the whole site. The single sitewide update Feature evolves with the site. Separate custom Feature modules can be useful for multiple developers working on a complex site. The real ideal of Features, however, is a shareable Feature module that encapsulates useful functionality and configuration that can be deployed on multiple sites. See the Kit specification (`drupal.org/project/kit`) for best practices for making a shareable Feature.

■ **Tip** Major new developments related to a given piece of functionality should be done in a dedicated custom module or, better yet, a module you contribute on `drupal.org`. Use of Features for content types and views and other elements specific to your site does not prevent you from handling the export and storage of selected of these elements with individual modules, when their use can be generalized. These additional modules you make can also use and require the Features, or not. In either case, they would be required by the sitewide Feature module to keep everything tied together.

Features and Drupal 7 core do fairly well at exporting content types, fields, permissions, input filters, menu items, image styles, and taxonomy vocabularies. And if necessary, it's possible to hook up almost anything else to CTools' exportables framework yourself. In this way, you can make additional or custom modules' database-stored configuration exportable. (For contributed modules, check their issue queue first for other's progress!) Additional modules add to Features export and restore capabilities. In particular, the Strongarm module (`drupal.org/project/strongarm`), which also requires CTools, can be used by modules (including the Features module) to export and override settings stored in the much used and abused *variable* table.

What all this gives you is the ability to configure your Drupal site as always through the administrative UI (creating content types, views that use these content types, image styles that fields in these content types use in different views and view modes, etc.) and then, using Features UI or Drush, export it all to code and into a Feature module.

■ **Tip** The Features module allows you to automate and do through the graphical user interface what would be a lot of custom coding. You make your changes locally, and Features exports your changes into code in a special Feature module.

Telling a Feature to use what it has in code is called *reverting* a feature, which is confusing from the perspective of the workflow followed in this chapter because we're actually updating. Features calls this *reverting* because using a Feature module's saved configuration reverts to what is in code; it is only because you are not making any changes through the user interface on the live site that this always results in an update, and not what you would commonly think of as reverting.

Writing Update Hooks

This is the approach mentioned as an alternative to the Features approach, but really it's complementary. Export functionality is often still inconsistent and incomplete, but you can supplement exportables and Features-generated modules with your own custom code.

The essence of this approach is still the same: all changes are coded in a module. You write your own update code for every change you make. Each new change that affects the database goes in a `hook_update_N()` function, and the same change goes in `hook_install()` or `hook_schema()` to be kept in synch. See `api.drupal.org/hook_update_N` for the basics of update hooks.

■ **Tip** We highly recommend even if you are doing everything with features to also write an update hook to trigger the feature with `features_revert()`.

Try to use APIs, rather than direct database calls, whenever possible in your update hooks. (Note, though, that for creating content programmatically, API functions such as `node_save()` don't always pull in everything properly; faking out a form array and submitting with `drupal_form_submit()` may prove necessary.)

▨ **Note** Anything that can be done in your module by submitting a form should also be doable with a line of code. Indeed, the `submit` function that handles your form should always use an `API` function to save the change. Unfortunately, Drupal core itself is not there yet, so you will sometimes have to resort to faking out a form and using `drupal_form_submit()` rather than a proper API function. For instance, `node_save()` currently fails to accept free-tagging taxonomy terms except when called in the context of `drupal_form_submit()`.

Dependencies have to be really careful to do things in the right order. Keep in mind that update code runs for disabled modules, and in this case you must explicitly load any code you need for this module that is not in its `.install` file. First, check if a module is enabled with `if module_exists()`.

This chapter does not go into the details of using Feature modules nor writing update hooks. The latter is covered in the context of module development in Chapter 24. Look for updates and resources at `dgd7.org/deploy`; for examples using Features and update hooks to add features to a site, follow `dgd7.org/anjali`.

Creating, Editing, and Reviewing Content on Production

This chapter's approach entails that all content changes be made on a live site, with robust revision moderation as needed, using Drupal's capabilities as a CMS, and that you not try to deploy content changes from a staging site. (Instead of a place for content creation or configuration, the staging site in this workflow is the place where the live production site's database and the development sites' code are tested together.)

The approach discussed in this chapter takes staging content out of the equation. Do it on live. Use the staging site for confirming that bringing the literally codified development changes to a copy of the live database works as expected, then bring the code changes live and enable the feature/run `update.php`.

For "staging" content on live (creating or editing and reviewing before anything is made public), there are several options for main content that extend Drupal's content management capabilities. For instance, the Revision moderation module (`drupal.org/project/revision_moderation`) allows content to be edited without the edits going public until after they have been reviewed. (At the time of this writing, it was in the process of being ported to Drupal 7.)

Another module to protect live content from breaking is the Path redirect (`drupal.org/project/path_redirect`) module. Path redirect ensures that even if Pathauto module changes the path of a piece of content because, for instance, the title changed, the old path redirects to the new URL.

If your publishing needs mandate that content be staged on a separate site, we refer you again to the Deploy module (`drupal.org/project/deploy`). However it happens, if significant content is already or does get generated on a development or staging site, Deploy or possibly Feeds (`drupal.org/project/feeds`) or Migrate (`drupal.org/project/migrate`) may be called for.

Node export (`drupal.org/project/node_export`) could also work, and it can create code that can be run in update hooks by `update.php` to import the exported content. If doing this, the Pathologic module (`drupal.org/project/pathologic`) can be used to fix absolute paths in content.

Pages or Content Sections That Require Functionality

Pages and sections with a great deal of functionality can be created via `hook_menu()` and callback functions instead of as nodes. See `api.drupal.org/hook_menu` and Chapter 29.

■ **Tip** If the PHP Filter module is enabled, try to disable it. PHP Filter module should not be used to provide functionality on node (content) pages. Avoiding that is a good idea from both code quality and deployment perspectives. For placing functionality, rather than content, on a page or part of a page, use Drupal's `hook_menu()`, `hook_block()`, or `hook_page_build()`.

You can make content to go with your functionality—you can have code create content—but this is problematic where content has to relate to each other (e.g., primary key issues). This is a priority for Drupal 8, and a lot of thought is being put into Universally Unique Identifiers (UUIDs).

Development Workflow Recap

There are many possible development workflows. It's important that you safeguard production data and incorporate testing, and that everyone you are working with understands and follows the same approach. A basic development workflow is to pull content and user data from a live site (if any), add features and fix bugs locally, push the changed code to a staging site for people to test it, and only after testing, push it to the live site.

- New functionality is added to an existing or new module. Database-related aspects of this functionality are exported using Features (and committed to a module) or more manually encoded into a module.

- Other developers can pull from the developers repository (or from a central repository), run `update.php` in a browser on the development environment, and have a working version of the site.

- Fresh imports of the production database are taken regularly in the development process, but particular attention is paid to taking a fresh copy and doing quality assurance on stage with code updated and `update.php` run, but with no manual configuration changes, before updating the code and running `update.php` on live.

- If necessary, create shared development environments for collaboration on database configuration (before these changes are exported to code) but keep stage for quality assurance.

■ **Tip** Set up testing for your development (in part, an automated deploy to staging) with Jenkins Continuous Integration tool (`jenkins-ci.org`). See `groups.drupal.org/node/47686` for a Drupal-oriented setup. (Note that Jenkins was called Hudson until 2011; it is the same software but was renamed to preserve its independence as a Free Software project.)

Summary

This is just one approach to deployment. The concept of "everything in code" is most comfortable to people who like making modules, but the Features project makes it a reasonable approach for people who prefer the site builder role.

■ **Note** See reader comments and updated links to resources at `dgd7.org/deploy`. To see the principles of code-driven deployment put into practice, follow the Anjali project at `dgd7.org/anjali`.

We encourage you to consider deployment from the needs of your site and your team's workflow. You may find that a variation of the approach outlined here works best, or you may find a completely different alternative to be preferable. This is an area of a lot of movement and potential in Drupal, and the more people who get involved, the better it can be. See the Packaging & Deployment group at `groups.drupal.org/build-systems-change-management` to follow some of the conversations about developing better deployment tools and techniques in Drupal 7 and beyond.

CHAPTER 14

■ ■ ■

Developing from a Human Mindset

by Károly Négyesi

This book seeks to give you the tools to understand Drupal, to use it to do great things, and to contribute back to the Drupal community. This chapter will help in making your work not just highly productive but a source of joy.

Use Revision Control

To put it simply, revision control stores a copy of your files whenever you instruct it to do so, thereby allowing for later restoration. Of course, it stores the files more efficiently by storing only changes. It offers many other features, but for the purpose of this section, only the "restore later" feature is important.

The code repositories on Drupal.org have migrated to a modern revision control system, Git (`http://git-scm.com`), and I recommend using it. Keeping track of your work with Git is as simple as running the following code snippet once:

```
git init .
git add .
git commit -m 'Initial commit.'
```

Also, every time you save, run a `git commit -a -m "something"`. The "something" is a message; it doesn't matter what it says, so don't fret. You can also enter the date by using a system command to enter it for you (`git commit -a -m "'date'"`) or by defining a keyboard shortcut. The important thing is that you make it effortless to keep every revision of your work. (The importance of being effortless will be clear later.)

In a better world, the OS would do this for you; more often than not, it doesn't. When you reach a milestone, write a meaningful commit message in case you want to share the work with someone else. But the commit-by-the-minute routine is not about sharing; it's about making sure you can get back to any previous state. Study `git bisect` on how to find the revision where the error occurred. For more information on Git, see Chapter 2.

Backup

You should use mysqldump (`dev.mysql.com/doc/refman/5.5/en/mysqldump.html`) or the Backup and Migrate project (`drupal.org/project/backup_migrate`) to provide SQL dumps. SQL dumps are text files, so you can commit them into Git, too. Indeed, it doesn't matter what kind of text file you work on—throw them into version control!

Your web site probably has files, so don't forget to back up those as well. Windows and Mac OS X have GUI tools (Windows Backup and Time Machine) to achieve this; Linux has some command line tools (tar and rsync) to help. I recommend both the free and commercial offerings from r1soft (r1soft.com).

Experiment Freely

If you learn nothing else from this book, learn this: experiment freely. It's a very important component of being a successful web developer. Don't be afraid—you can't break it. That's why I use revision control constantly and why I back up regularly. Never work on a production server; setting up a development environment is very important and not difficult (and it is the focus of Chapter 12).

I often see people on IRC or other forums asking "What would happen if...?" Well, here's news for you: nothing serious! At worst, you get an error message. If you get one, remove the pieces that are too specific (like the local path to Drupal) and throw the error message into Google to find out why it occurred. Experiment freely not just by trying various strategies to a given problem but also with web searches.

A web search takes a fraction of a second and you just can't do too many of them. Search on something, take a look at the findings, rephrase your search based on them, and sooner or later you'll find what you were searching for. It's an iterative process and the only way to master it is to experiment a lot.

This is true not just for searches but for everything. The phrase "lifelong learning" means continuous learning. And if what you learn isn't useful right now, it might be useful later. My motto is "a day when I learned nothing is a day wasted."

On the other hand, don't learn rote facts! Google simply knows more rote facts than we could ever, ever learn but continues learning them at speeds far exceeding any human. Learn patterns instead; learn the vocabulary that's useful for searches. In this age of the ubiquitous web search, the very meaning of "knowledge" changes. If you know how to wield the search engine weapon well, you can just carry the skeleton of the necessary knowledge in your head; the meat can be filled with a quick search.

Experimenting freely is a step toward flow. Flow is a curious state where the mind, according to Mihaly Csikszentmihalyi, is "completely involved in an activity for its own sake. The ego falls away. Time flies. Every action, movement, and thought follows inevitably from the previous one, like playing jazz. Your whole being is involved, and you're using your skills to the utmost." Reaching flow is joyous and leads to outstanding performance. Some expressions for this mental state include "in the moment," "in the zone," "in the groove," and "keeping your head in the game."

We are not saying you always should be in a state of flow, nor is it advisable to always strive for flow (that probably would make it impossible to reach it). Rather, just organize things in a way so that flow can happen. Alas, there is no simple recipe, but the following things definitely help:

Have clear goals. This can easily be achieved if you're working on a well-defined project. (This is another reason why a good specification is vital to success!) If the specification has problems, break it down to tasks that are themselves clear.

Concentrate. I recommend listening to music to help you concentrate. It can put you in the mood, and it can mask other distracting noises.

Enjoy direct and immediate feedback. This is the reason why flow is easier to achieve for a web programmer: direct and immediate feedback is a given in our profession. Save the code, press refresh in the web browser, and ta-da! *Immediate* is important here; waiting for the code to compile or a test to finish does not fit this pattern.

Make the activity neither too easy nor too difficult. This is a tricky one to achieve in a work setting. Consider yourself lucky when it happens.

A sense of personal control over the situation or activity. Remember what I said about breaking down the problem into tasks? Doing so gives you a feeling of control. Working on a non-fixed schedule helps, too.

The activity is intrinsically rewarding, so there is an effortlessness of action. Have you ever felt elated because your code worked?

Contribute

Contributing to open source projects might not present you with a paycheck biweekly, but it will benefit you in other ways. First, if you want money, there is a community involved, so your professional network grows, which leads to more job opportunities. This is especially true with Drupal where the demand for quality workers far exceeds supply (for now, but it's so uneven that it is expected to continue for quite some time).

Second, peer reviews provide you with a chance to learn. This is one of the reasons why open source is such a great opportunity—we learn together.

Third, we humans are social animals. Belonging to a community and receiving the praise of our peers is important to everyone.

Fourth, review the flow list above! When working on your own issue, you have clear goals, so choose one that is doable (but only just). Of course, you have total personal control over the whole situation.

Finally, although there is no paycheck to receive, it's intrinsically rewarding.

So, how can you contribute? Contribution takes many forms (marketing, event organization, etc.), but the two I would like to highlight are documentation and code.

Documentation is best written by those who have just reached the point where they feel they understand their topic. Once you are intimately familiar with something, it takes an unusual talent to be able to reflect on what was hard to understand in the beginning. So while you struggle to understand something, write notes on the problems you find. At the end, write down the answers you learned and you have a handbook page. It might not be smooth. It might be in slightly broken English. Don't worry. It's way easier to clean up a handbook page than to write one.

Code contributions most often happen in the form of writing patches or reviewing them. Both are very important. You can go to any project page, click the "open issues" link, and then either fix an outstanding bug or review a patch. There are excellent handbook pages that help with this process at `drupal.org/patch`, `drupal.org/patch/apply`, and `drupal.org/handbook/git`.

Once again, don't try to come up with the perfect solution. Do something that works and then work with the community. Note that many patch reviews are terse and not too flattering; remember that the negative criticism is about your code, not you! We love everyone who contributes. Spending time with their contribution is appreciation in itself, as time is the scarcest commodity in an open source community.

You can make a valuable contribution to the issue queue even if you don't code. You can open a bug report and check whether it contains enough information to be reproduced. If not, mark it as "needs more information." If it does, try reproducing it. If it's not reproducible any more, close it as "fixed." We need a lot of people doing this so those who are more familiar with Drupal—like you after reading this book, putting it into practice, and spending time—can concentrate on fixing the real problems.

For more on this and many other ways to contribute to Drupal, see Chapter 38.

▨ **Tip** For more discussion about developing from a human mindset, visit `dgd7.org/think`.

PART IV

■ ■ ■

Front-End Development

Chapters 15 and 16 take you on a thorough tour of using Drupal's theming system to transform how your site looks in ways that are both powerful and maintainable.

Chapter 17 introduces another key part of front-end development, enhancing site visitor experience with JavaScript, and in particular the powerful and relatively easy-to-use, even fun, jQuery library.

See also Appendix D, which covers designing for Drupal.

■ ■ ■

## CHAPTER 15

Theming

by Jacine Luisi

Drupal's theme layer, and the themes that use it, are responsible for the look and feel of a Drupal web site. Good themes consist of all the same elements that you would find on any reputable web site, including standards-compliant XHTML markup, CSS, and JavaScript. How it all comes together is what is so special and what makes Drupal themes so flexible and powerful.

Drupal themes can be as simple or as complex as you need them to be. Themes have the final say and ultimate control over almost every aspect of each page. Like Drupal itself, themes are flexible and powerful. Admittedly, taking full advantage of Drupal's theme layer means overcoming a rather steep learning curve, and without a general understanding of what's going on under the hood, it is easy to make mistakes early on.

In this chapter, you will learn about the basic aspects of Drupal's theme layer. You'll learn how to go about making customizations and changes in a sustainable way and best practices for common tasks. You will be well on your way to creating flexible and sustainable custom Drupal themes in no time! The next chapter will build on this one and will cover the more advanced intricacies of Drupal themes.

Some of the examples you'll find throughout this chapter and the next can be found in the DGD7 theme. It's available at `https://github.com/jacine/dgd7` for download if you'd like to follow along.

The Core Themes Directory

When starting out, one of the first things people do is navigate to the core `/themes` directory and take a look at the files in the themes to get an idea of the general structure and contents. Unfortunately, many people make the mistake of starting out by directly customizing core themes. Do not make this mistake! They usually run into roadblocks and frustration shortly thereafter. Drupal has a large and diverse user base, and the main goal of a core Drupal theme is to cater to the masses.

Aesthetics aside, core themes have many requirements and different use cases to satisfy. A few themes support the Color module in order to make it easy for site administrators to change color schemes in the user interface. This is not a bad thing; however, it can easily become confusing and frustrating when trying to customize colorized themes because CSS is generated programmatically and stored outside of the theme directory. Core themes must also function if used as an administration theme and they must support bidirectional text; in general, they can't stray far from Drupal's default regions and settings.

It's not easy to please everyone, and Drupal core themes have the tough job of trying to do just that. As a result, core themes are nowhere near as flexible or as cutting edge as they could be. Most of the time, your goal and approach will be very different when creating custom themes. You'll be able to focus on coding your own front-end or back-end focused design, customize the markup, decide which CSS files to use (if any), and other exciting decisions.

Core Themes

Drupal core contains four themes. They are introduced in the following sections.

Bartik

Bartik is a new and welcome addition to Drupal 7. Drupal enables Bartik as the default user-facing theme upon installation. It is a clean and simple theme that supports the color module and makes excellent use of regions (see Figure 15–1). In addition to the default regions Drupal recommends, the Bartik theme has seven custom regions for laying out blocks in the footer and sub-footer.

***Figure 15–1.** Bartik is a clean and simple theme.*

Garland

Garland originally made its debut as a core theme in Drupal 5. It is a more complex theme with excellent color module support (see Figure 15–2). It contains fifteen color schemes and provides an option to toggle between a fixed or fluid layout.

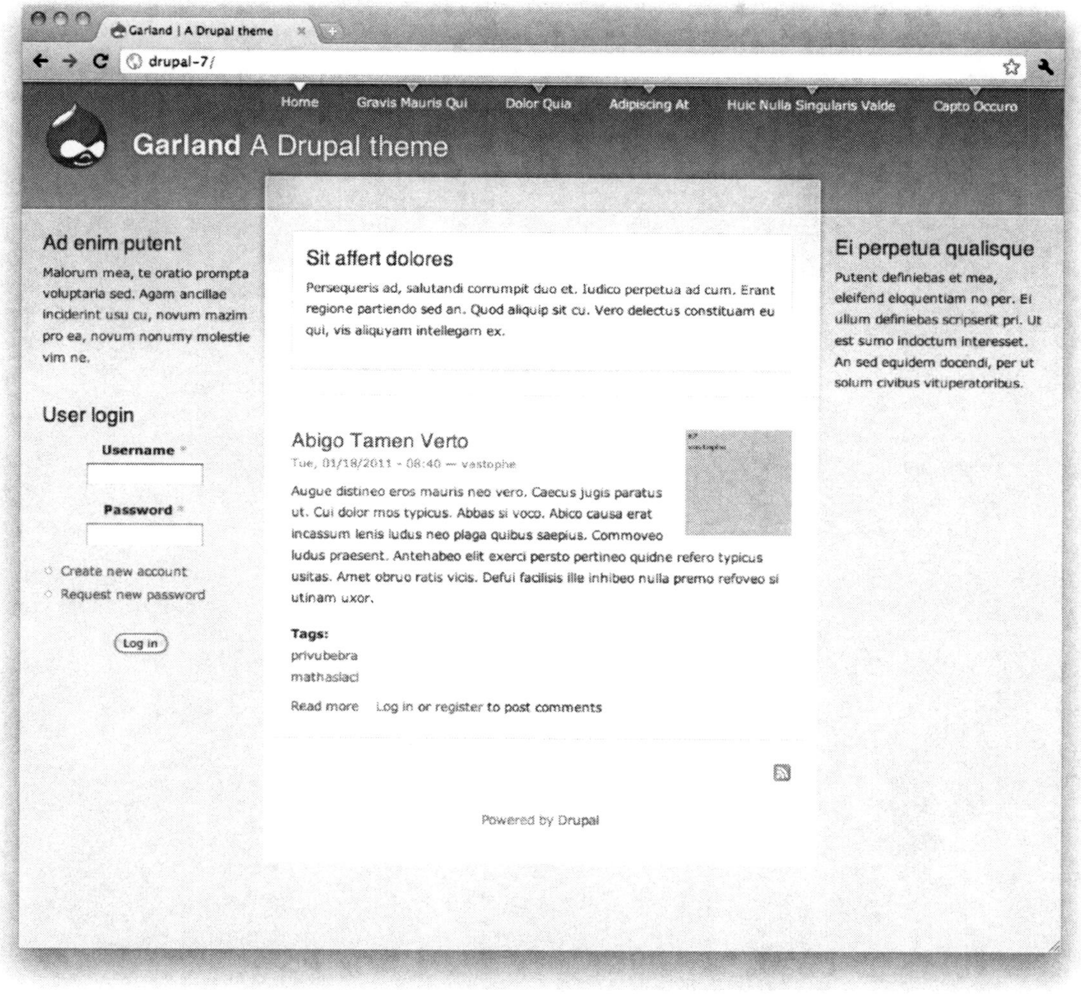

Figure 15–2. Garland is a more complex theme with excellent color module support.

Seven

Also new to Drupal 7, Seven is Drupal's default administrative theme. Born out of the Drupal 7 User Experience project (http://d7ux.org), Seven drove many of Drupal's user interface improvements. It contains very few regions, as its focus is on performing administrative tasks (see Figure 15–3).

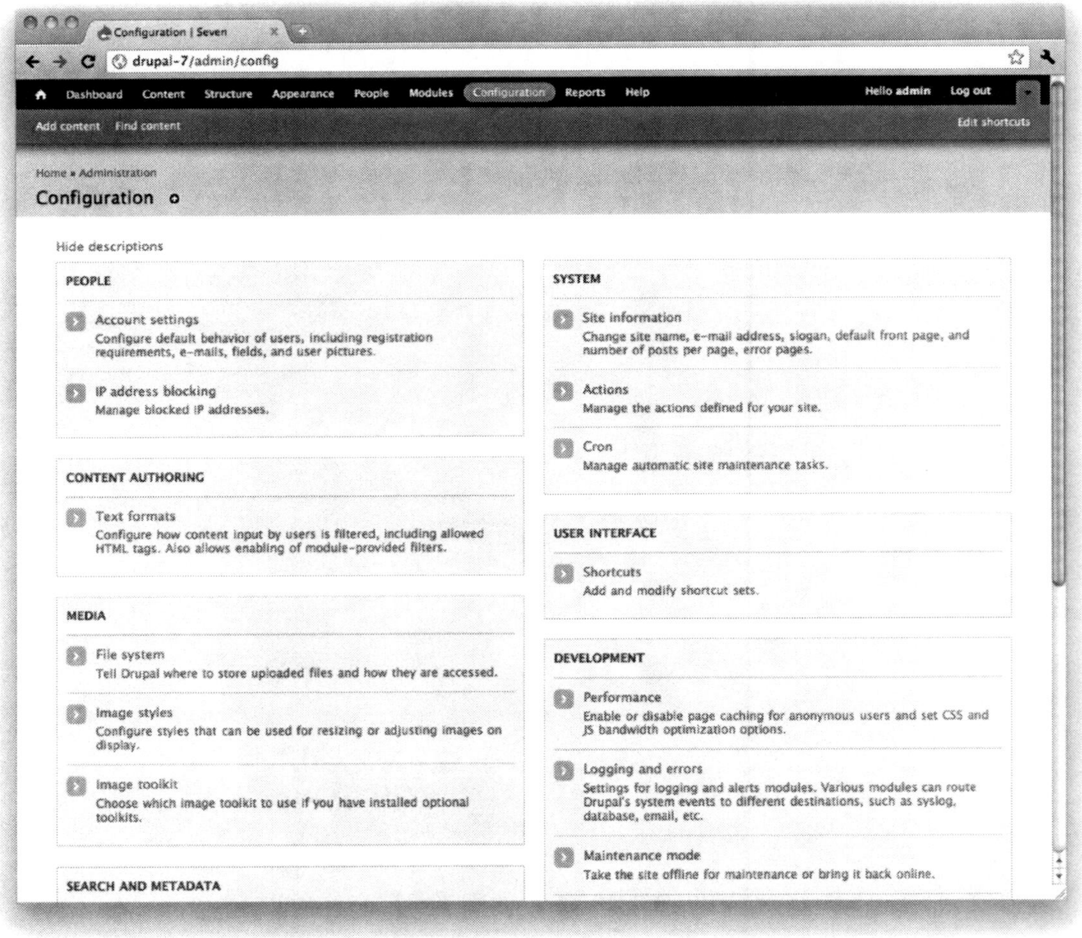

Figure 15–3. Seven is Drupal's default administrative theme.

Stark

Stark is a unique and literally minimal Drupal theme (see Figure 15–4). Its main purpose is to expose Drupal's default HTML markup and CSS. It does not provide any template files and barely provides any CSS at all, other than basic layout styles that place the default sidebar regions. Don't let its simplicity fool you; it is actually quite useful. Stark is the perfect theme for developers to code against when writing CSS for their modules. It can also assist theme developers when trying to troubleshoot issues where they're not positive if the problem is with their theme or another module.

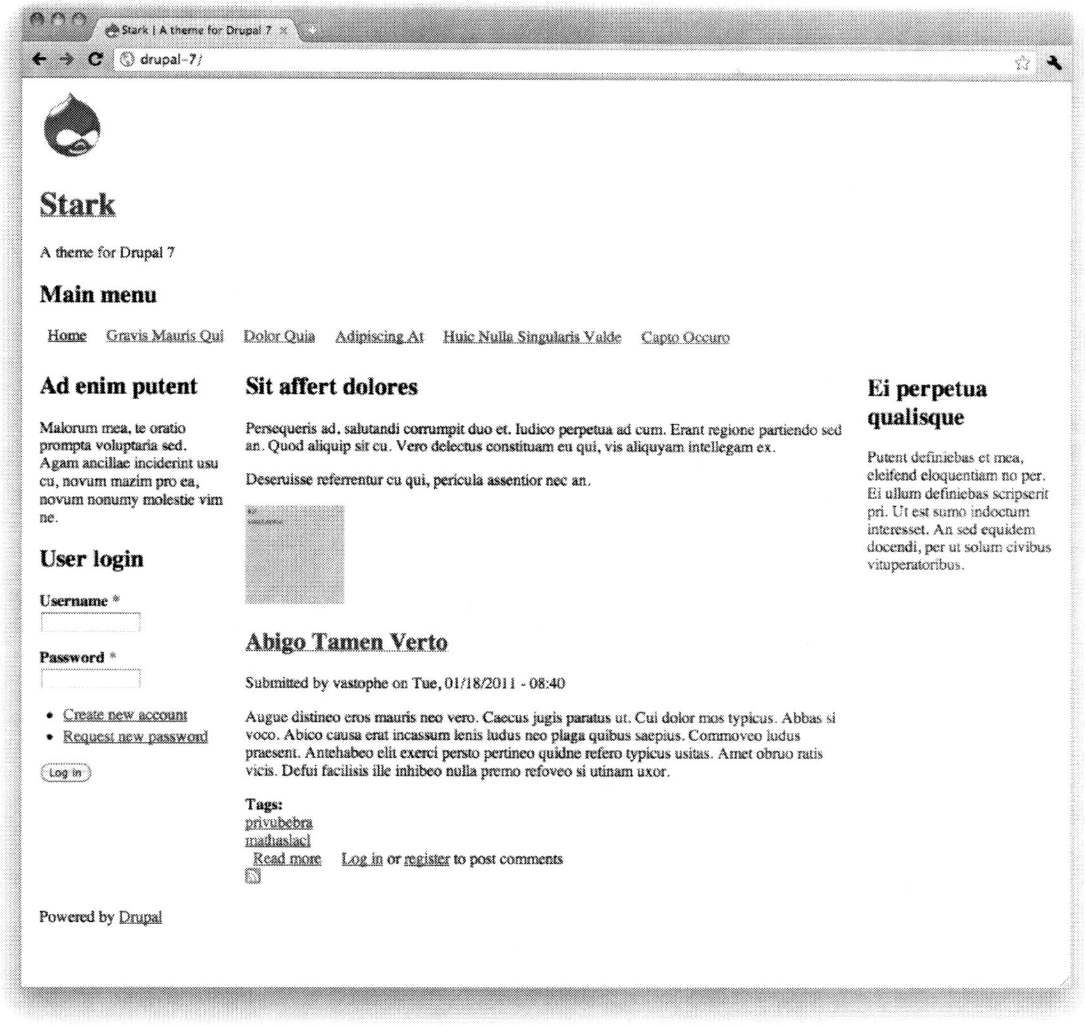

Figure 15–4. Stark is a unique and literally minimal Drupal theme.

Theme Engines

Drupal's theme directory also has an engines directory that contains a theme engine called PHPTemplate. Theme engines provide an easy way to separate themable output into template files as opposed to plain old PHP. The main benefit of using the PHPTemplate engine is that separating logic from presentation is simplified. Those who are unfamiliar with PHP can accomplish a great deal because they are able to work in template files that mainly contain markup and print variables.

While other theme engines such as Smarty, XTemplate, and PHPTal may be used, PHPTemplate is Drupal's default theme engine and is by far the most popular theme engine used by Drupal themes (and many popular contributed modules), so we will cover it in this chapter. It is also possible to write pure PHP Drupal themes. See the Chameleon theme for an example of a pure PHP theme at `http://drupal.org/project/chameleon`. For a full listing of available theme engines, visit `http://drupal.org/project/theme+engines`.

Theme Administration

Theme configuration tasks are located in the Appearance section of Drupal's administration. This is where you can control things like which themes you want to enable or disable, which settings you want to apply, which color scheme you want to use (if your theme supports the color module), and more.

Enabling and Setting a Default Theme

In a fresh installation of Drupal 7, the default theme (Bartik) appears at the top of the Appearance page, followed by other enabled and disabled themes (see Figure 15–5). What is a default theme? Simply enabling a theme is not enough with Drupal. Setting a theme as the default is what makes it the front-end theme (the theme your site visitors will see).

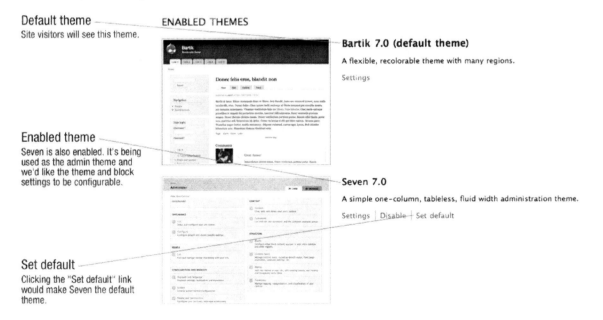

Figure 15–5. The Appearance page in a default installation showing enabled themes

Enabling a theme without setting it as the default is useful when you want your site to utilize multiple themes at once. This setting is typically more useful when used in conjunction with contributed modules. An example of this is the SwitchTheme (`http://drupal.org/project/switchtheme`) module, which allows users to change the site theme by selecting the name of a theme from a list that is populated with all enabled themes.

Administration Theme

In Drupal 7, the Seven theme is the default administration theme. The administrative theme is used when performing all administrative tasks, most of which happen under the `/admin` path. You can also choose to allow the administrative theme to be used when editing site content. Although some themes support Drupal's administrative interface better than others, any Drupal theme can be used as an administration theme if desired.

The administration theme's configuration settings are located below the theme listings on the `admin/appearance` page. To use the same theme in both the front and back end of your Drupal site, simply choose Default theme as the Administration theme.

Global Theme Settings

Drupal comes with some theme settings that can be configured in the administrative interface. This is where most of the site identity assets are defined, as well as a couple of other miscellaneous settings. A Global Settings page located at `admin/appearance/settings` contains these settings. When global settings are saved, the settings apply to all themes. Each theme also has its own Settings page accessible via a Settings link located next to each enabled theme on the `admin/appearance` page. When theme settings are applied on an individual theme's Settings page, they override the global settings. The following sections will detail what each of these are and where you'll encounter them in your themes.

Quite a few of these settings determine whether or not variables are populated and therefore printed in template files. The settings pictured in Figure 15–6 represent the defaults provided by Drupal. These can be overridden by themes by defining features in the theme's `.info` file, which is discussed further in the "Defining Theme Metadata" section. When specifying features in `.info` files, you'll need to make sure you include all the features you want to support, as having just one will override all of the defaults provided by Drupal. The following is a quick reference of these settings as they'd be entered in a `.info` file:

```
features[] = logo
features[] = name
features[] = slogan
features[] = favicon
features[] = main_menu
features[] = secondary_menu
features[] = node_user_picture
features[] = comment_user_picture
features[] = comment_user_verification
```

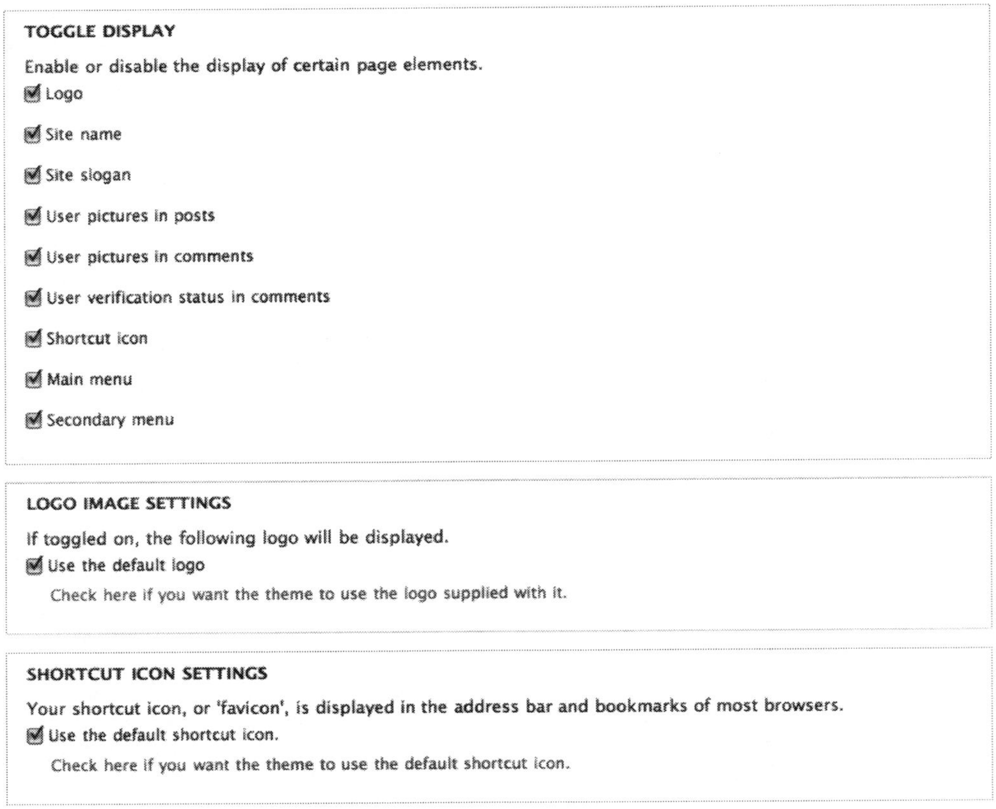

TOGGLE DISPLAY

Enable or disable the display of certain page elements.

☑ Logo

☑ Site name

☑ Site slogan

☑ User pictures in posts

☑ User pictures in comments

☑ User verification status in comments

☑ Shortcut icon

☑ Main menu

☑ Secondary menu

LOGO IMAGE SETTINGS

If toggled on, the following logo will be displayed.

☑ Use the default logo

    Check here if you want the theme to use the logo supplied with it.

SHORTCUT ICON SETTINGS

Your shortcut icon, or 'favicon', is displayed in the address bar and bookmarks of most browsers.

☑ Use the default shortcut icon.

    Check here if you want the theme to use the default shortcut icon.

Figure 15–6. The Global Settings page

Logo

By default, Drupal will look for a file named logo.png in the root of the theme directory. There is also an option to specify a path to a different file to use for the logo, as well as the ability to upload a logo to use. When the Logo checkbox is checked, a variable called $logo is populated with the path to the logo, which will be available in page.tpl.php. If unchecked, the logo will not print.

Name and Slogan

The site name is defined during the installation process. Both the site name and slogan can be changed on the admin/config/system/site-information page. On the theme's Settings page, you can toggle their visibility. Both are available in page.tpl.php as $site_name and $site_slogan.

Shortcut Icon

The shortcut icon, also known as the favicon, is the small Drupal icon that appears in the address bar, bookmarks, and tabs of most browsers. Like the logo, the shortcut icon's visibility can be toggled and a custom file can be used. The default file is `misc/favicon.ico`.

User Pictures in Posts and Comments

These settings control whether or not the variables `$user_picture` in `node.tpl.php` and `$picture` in `comment.tpl.php` are populated, and therefore whether or not the pictures are displayed when viewing nodes and comments.

User Verification Status in Comments

This option will display "(Not verified)" next to the user name for users that do not have a verified account. This text is defined in `template_preprocess_username()` and printed in `theme_username()` as `$variables['extra']`. See the "Preprocess and Process Functions" and "Theme Functions" sections to learn how to change this.

Main and Secondary Menus

When the checkboxes for the Main and Secondary menus are checked, `$main_menu` and `$secondary_menu` variables are populated in `page.tpl.php` with arrays containing the menu links for each menu. On the Menu Settings page, located at `admin/structure/menu/settings`, you can choose which menu is used for each. By default, the Main menu, which can be managed at `admin/structure/menu/manage/main-menu,` is used as the source that populates `$main_menu`. The default menu for the source of the Secondary menu is the User menu, which can be managed at `admin/structure/menu/manage/user-menu`.

These are simple one-level menus output using the `theme_links()` function (which will be covered later in this chapter) in `page.tpl.php`. This makes them hard to use when styling complex navigation designs. Because complex navigation is often required, many theme developers create regions for navigation and use blocks to output their menus instead of using these menus. We highly recommend the Menu Block module (`http://drupal.org/project/menu_block`), which allows you to do pretty much anything you'll ever need to do with menus very easily.

Custom Theme Settings

Custom theme settings are similar to the global theme settings and can be provided by themes and modules. An example of custom theme settings can be found in the Garland theme in the `garland.info` file. It creates a setting called garland_width that can be set to fixed or fluid. The Shortcut module also provides a setting to display the "Add or remove shortcut link" used in the Seven theme to provide the icon you see in the Overlay next to the title. To learn how to create custom theme settings for your theme, visit `http://drupal.org/node/177868`.

Installing a New Theme

Drupal scans its theme directories for available themes, so it's important that you place your themes in the right place for Drupal to recognize them. You might also be tempted to add themes to Drupal's `/themes` directory, but technically this is considered "hacking core" and should be avoided. After downloading and unpacking your theme, choose one of the following directories in which to place the theme. Using one of these directories will help ensure that any updates you make to Drupal itself will not result in accidentally overwriting your theme.

- sites/all/themes: Use this directory when you want the theme to be available to all sites in your Drupal installation.

- sites/sitename/themes: Use this directory when you only want the theme available to a specific site in your multisite Drupal installation.

You may also use the theme installer to download and install contributed themes by clicking the Install new theme link at the top of the Appearance page. This will bring you to a form where you can enter the link to the project download's tarball location and click Install. The theme installer will automatically download your theme and place it in the sites/all/themes directory. Once completed, you can enable the theme as usual on the admin/admin/appearance page.

Defining Theme Metadata (.info Files)

.info files (pronounced "dot info files") contain important metadata about your theme, such as the name of the theme, which version of Drupal it supports, as well as things like the stylesheets and regions the theme will contain. Writing a .info file is usually the first step you take when creating a Drupal theme.

The first part of the file name is the machine-readable name of the theme, which Drupal uses to store information about your theme in the database. Dashes and other special characters are not allowed. While underscores are allowed, it is considered a best practice to avoid using them when naming your .info file. Use themename.info instead of theme_name.info. This name will also be used to prefix function names when implementing theme function overrides. When overriding theme_menu_link(), for example, a function named themename_menu_link() is considered easier to read than theme_name_menu_link() when trying to determine the override being performed.

■ **Caution** Your theme (machine) name must be unique. Do NOT to give your theme the same name as any existing modules as it will likely cause namespace issues and make it difficult to track down PHP errors.

Each theme requires some basic properties to be set in the theme's .info file. The name, core, and engine properties are the bare minimum requirements for all Drupal themes. The following sections contain a brief description of each available property followed by an example of the syntax.

■ **Tip** To add comments to your .info file, add a semicolon to the beginning of each line, like so:

```
; This is a comment. Comments are good. Make frequent use of them.
```

Required Properties

Core: Drupal will only allow your theme to be enabled if the core setting is set to support the current major version of Drupal. Major versions are simply 6.x, 7.x or 8.x, and so on.

```
core = 7.x
```

Name: The human-readable name of your theme. It doesn't need to match or resemble the machine-readable name, so feel free to be creative here.

```
name = Theme Name
```

Additional Properties

Base theme: Drupal allows themes to establish a relationship with each other. Creating a subtheme allows you to inherit the functionality and assets of the base theme (more on this in the next chapter). When creating a subtheme, you'll need to specify the base theme. It's important that the machine name of the base theme is used here.

```
base theme = themename
```

Description: The basic features or purpose of the theme should be described here. The description will appear in the admin/appearance page and may contain HTML.

```
description = The description of my theme
```

Engine: Specifies the theme engine. PHPTemplate is the default and most common, so unless you want to change this, it doesn't have to be manually set. Other options include smarty and theme for a pure PHP theme (see Chameleon at http://drupal.org/project/chameleon for an example).

```
engine = phptemplate
```

Features: Setting features are a way of overriding Drupal's default global theme settings. The following is a list of the default theme settings provided by Drupal. These settings can be toggled on an off in the administrative interface on the Settings page of each theme. Specifying even one will disable Drupal's defaults and use yours.

```
features[] = logo
features[] = favicon
features[] = name
features[] = slogan
features[] = node_user_picture
features[] = comment_user_picture
features[] = comment_user_verification
features[] = main_menu
features[] = secondary_menu
```

PHP: Drupal 7 supports PHP version 5.2.5, and by default, so does your theme. This is something you will probably never need, but in case your theme has code that only works with a certain version PHP, you may specify it here.

```
php = 5.3
```

Regions: Regions are sections of your page layout where content (blocks) are placed. Each entry is prefixed with `regions` and contains the system name of the region in brackets with the human readable name as the value. For example, `regions[system_name]` = `Human readable name`. The default regions are as follows:

```
regions[page_top] = Page Top
regions[header] = Header
regions[highlighted] = Highlighted
regions[help] = Help
regions[content] = Content
regions[sidebar_first] = Sidebar First
regions[sidebar_second] = Sidebar Second
regions[footer] = Footer
regions[page_bottom] = Page Bottom
```

Settings: The setting property is reserved for custom setting implementations in themes. The Garland theme provides a theme setting for the type of layout (fixed or fluid), which the site administrator can choose. While we won't be covering custom theme settings, we highly recommend checking out the Omega (`http://drupal.org/project/omega`) and Fusion (`http://drupal.org/project/fusion`) themes to get an idea of how theme settings can be used. For more information, visit `http://drupal.org/node/177868`.

```
settings[garland_width] = fluid
```

Screenshot: Drupal will automatically look for a file named `screenshot.png` in the root of your theme directory, so this line is only required if you want to use an alternative path or file name for your theme's screenshot. The recommended dimensions for the screenshot image are 294 x 219 pixels.

```
screenshot = screenshot.png
```

Stylesheets: There are quite a few options for adding CSS files in Drupal 7. You'll want to add stylesheets via the theme's `.info` for CSS files you want to load on every page. I'll cover this in much more detail in the Managing CSS Files section in the next chapter.

```
stylesheets[screen][] = path/to/screen-stylesheet.css
stylesheets[print][] = path/to/print-stylesheet.css
```

Scripts: JavaScript files can be defined in `.info` files using the `scripts` property. Like stylesheets, you'll only want to load JavaScript files here that need to be loaded on each page.

```
scripts[] = path/to/script.js
```

version: Specifying the version is discouraged for both contributed themes and modules. This is because `drupal.org` has a packaging script that takes care of adding the version when releases are created. However, you may use this for custom themes, if desired.

```
version = 7.x-1.1
```

Now let's see the basics in action by taking a look your DGD7 theme's `.info` file, as shown in Listing 15–1.

Listing 15–1. The Top Portion of the DGD7 Theme's `.info` *File*

```
name = DGD7 Theme
description = A theme written for The Definitive Guide to Drupal 7 book website.
core = 7.x
```

With the exception of the core property, all of the above can be seen in the user interface on the admin/appearance page, as shown in Figure 15–7. This is all you'll need to get started with your theme.

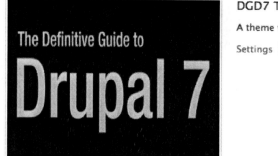

DGD7 Theme

A theme written for The Definitive Guide to Drupal 7 book website.

Settings | Disable | Set default

Figure 15–7. DGD7 theme as shown on the theme listing page admin/appearance.

CREATE YOUR FIRST THEME!

Taking into account what you have learned so far, create a custom theme.

1. Start by creating a new folder in `sites/all/themes` called dgd7.

2. Inside the dgd7 folder, create a new file named `dgd7.info` and add the following code inside it:

```
name = DGD7 Theme
description = A theme written for The Definitive Guide to Drupal 7 book website.
core = 7.x
```

3. Grab the `screenshot.png` file from the chapter source code and copy it into the dgd7 directory. This is an optional step. If the screenshot is not defined, you will see the text "No screenshot" instead.

4. Now visit `admin/appearance` and reload the page. You should now see the theme under Disabled Themes. Click the "Enable and set default" link to begin using this theme on your site.

■ **Tip** You will need to clear your site caches in order for changes in `.info` files to take effect! To clear the site caches, visit the Performance page at `admin/config/development/performance`.

Working with Regions

Most of the content found on Drupal pages is output inside a region. Typical regions include the header, footer, sidebars, and content (see Figure 15–8); these regions often play a large part in defining the high-level structure of your HTML markup. An option appears in the blocks interface at `admin/structure/block` for each region, allowing site administrators to control and position the blocks inside them.

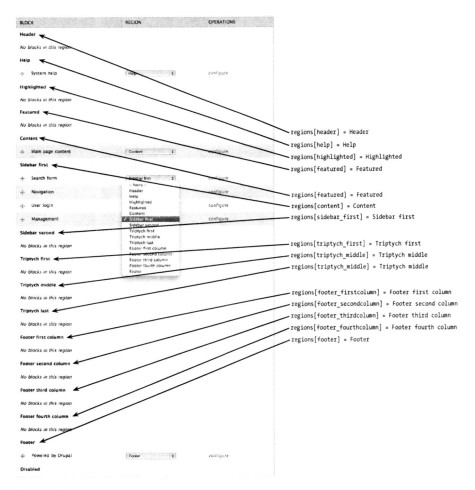

Figure 15–8. The Bartik theme's regions and block placement options on the Blocks administration page

Themes have full control over defining and determining the placement of printing and styling regions. An example of what this looks like in the Bartik theme is shown in Figure 15–9.

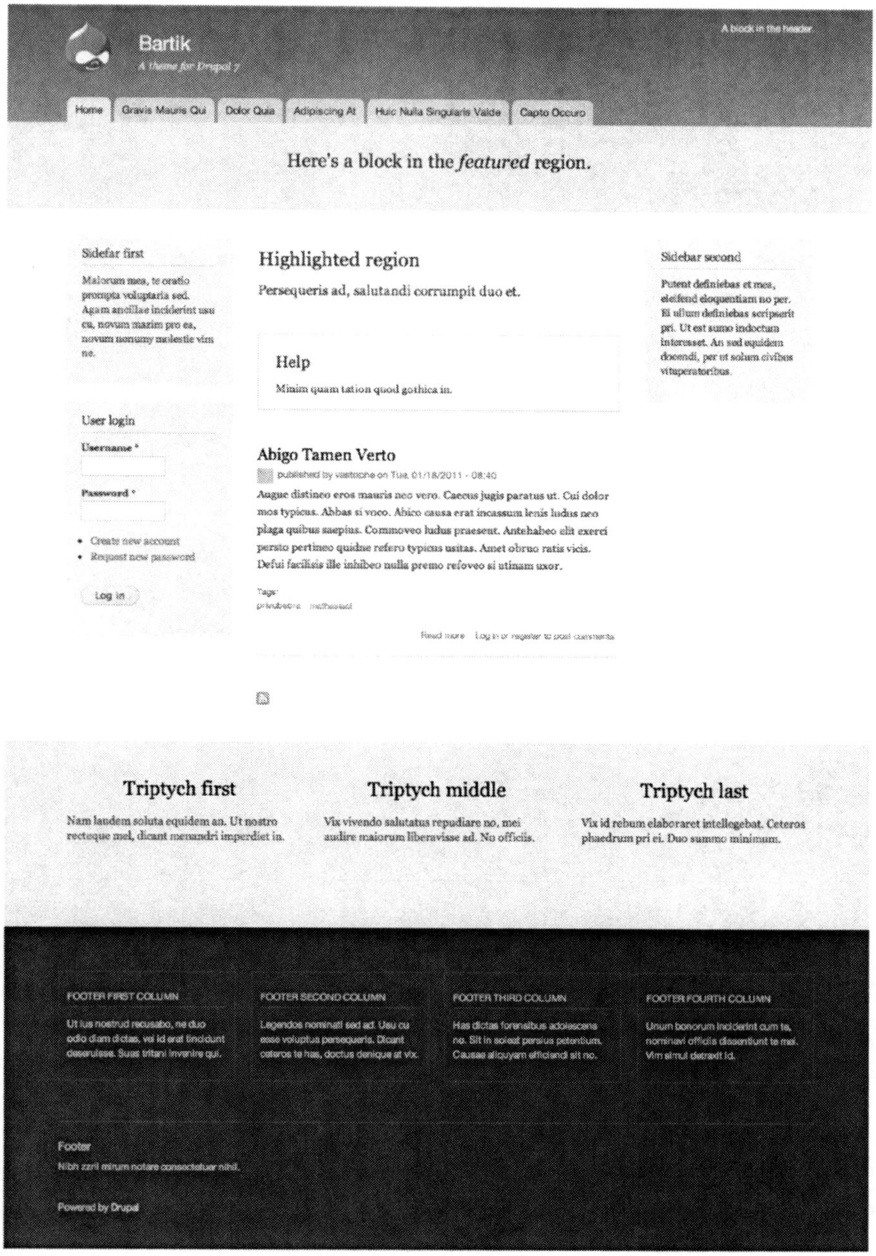

Figure 15–9. Bartik regions filled with custom blocks

In addition, themes may also use regions for less obvious purposes in combination with JavaScript or jQuery. Common use cases for regions include containing modal or hidden content to enhance the user interface or embedding blocks into node content.

Default Regions

Drupal core defines nine regions for themes to utilize programmatically by default. The code in Listing 15–2 duplicates the default core regions in .info file format. Like most theme layer implementations, the reason themes define regions is because they want to modify or add to the defaults. Until a theme defines its own regions, Drupal will use the defaults. This means that if the default regions are sufficient for your design, you will not need to define regions in your theme's .info file.

Listing 15–2. Drupal's Nine Predefined Theme Regions in Chronological Order

```
regions[page_top] = Page Top
regions[header] = Header
regions[highlighted] = Highlighted
regions[help] = Help
regions[content] = Content
regions[sidebar_first] = Sidebar First
regions[sidebar_second] = Sidebar Second
regions[footer] = Footer
regions[page_bottom] = Page Bottom
```

However, including this code in your theme's .info file to begin with is a good practice. Once you define a single region in your theme, it will override core defaults, so having the full list of defaults and commenting out regions that you have disabled (instead of deleting or omitting them entirely) is a good way to keep track of what you're doing with them. You will need some of these regions, namely the page_top, content, and page_bottom regions. These are required and must be printed in every Drupal theme to maintain a properly functioning site. An example of how one might organize regions in an .info file, taking defaults into account, is shown in Listing 15–3.

Listing 15–3. An Example of Region Implementation in a Theme's .info File

```
; CORE REGIONS - DISABLED
;regions[highlighted] = Highlighted
;regions[help] = Help
;regions[header] = Header
;regions[footer] = Footer

; CORE REGIONS - REQUIRED
regions[page_top] = Page Top
regions[content] = Content
regions[page_bottom] = Page Bottom

; CORE REGIONS
regions[sidebar_first] = Sidebar First
regions[sidebar_second] = Sidebar Second

; CUSTOM REGIONS
regions[my_custom_region] = My Custom Region
```

As shown in Figure 15–10, the intended display of Drupal's default regions is a standard three-column layout. The gray regions are required and the rest are optional. Header, `sidebar_first`, `sidebar_second`, and `footer` are layout regions. The `page_top` and `page_bottom` are special regions; they are discussed in the "Hidden Regions" section of this chapter.

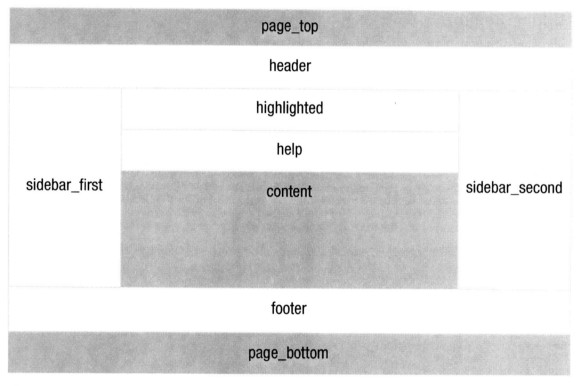

Figure 15–10. *Drupal's default layout for regions*

The `highlighted` region replaces the old Site Mission, which used to be a static variable containing the site's mission statement or a brief summary text that was output manually in `page.tpl.php`. The prior implementation was not ideal for a few reasons, but mainly because its display was limited to the front page. It was decided that using a custom block to display this information was a better option, so the highlighted region was created.

The Help region also used to be a `page.tpl.php` variable that printed error and status messages. The status messages are now displayed in a block called System help and the Help region was created to contain it. However, the System help block may easily be placed inside the Content region, weighted above the Main content block for the same effect.

The Content region is new to Drupal 7. It was introduced to contain the Main page content block, which is somewhat special because it can be moved from region to region but can't be disabled. Since the Block module is optional and the contents of the Main page content block are critical to operate a Drupal site, the contents of this block will always display via the $page['content'] variable in page.tpl.php.

As a result, some of the Block module's functionality doesn't work as you might expect. If you place the Main page content block in the disabled area or set block visibility settings to exclude it from a page, the Block module's UI will lead you to believe that it has been disabled. However, the content will still appear. You'll also notice changes in the markup, which may lead to undesired results, such as un-styled content, depending on how your CSS is written.

Hidden Regions

Notably missing from the options on the Blocks administration page in Figure 15–8 are the page_top and page_bottom regions. Both are hidden regions, which Drupal intentionally excludes from the user interface so that site administrators can't interact with or control their content. The main purpose of hidden regions is to act as a placeholder where modules or themes can dynamically add markup to in a structured way. Themes may declare hidden regions within .info files by using the following syntax, with each region on a separate a line:

```
regions_hidden[] = the_region_name
```

Both the page_top and page_bottom regions are printed in html.tpl.php (see Listing 15–4) and should not be removed or rearranged. The page_top region, for example, is utilized by the Toolbar module to add the markup needed for the administrative toolbar shown at the top of each page when a user is logged in as a site administrator. The page_bottom region exists for modules to add any final closing markup, which specifically needs to be at the very bottom of the page. An example of this is the Google Analytics module, which adds markup to load JavaScript files that track the site visitor activity and needs to be loaded last. The page_bottom region replaces the $closure variable that was used in prior versions of Drupal.

Listing 15–4. The Contents of html.tpl.php, Highlighting the Placement of the page_top and page_bottom

Regions

```
<!DOCTYPE html PUBLIC "-//W3C//DTD XHTML+RDFa 1.0//EN"
  "http://www.w3.org/MarkUp/DTD/xhtml-rdfa-1.dtd">
<html xmlns="http://www.w3.org/1999/xhtml" xml:lang="<?php print $language->language; ?>"
version="XHTML+RDFa 1.0" dir="<?php print $language->dir; ?>"<?php print $rdf_namespaces; ?>>
<head profile="<?php print $grddl_profile; ?>">
  <?php print $head; ?>
  <title><?php print $head_title; ?></title>
  <?php print $styles; ?>
  <?php print $scripts; ?>
</head>
<body class="<?php print $classes; ?>" <?php print $attributes;?>>
  <div id="skip-link">
    <a href="#main-content" class="element-invisible element-focusable"><?php print t('Skip to
main content'); ?></a>
  </div>
  <?php print $page_top; ?>
  <?php print $page; ?>
  <?php print $page_bottom; ?>
</body>
</html>
```

■ **Tip** Drupal uses hook_system_info_alter() to declare the page_top and page_bottom hidden regions. For more information, see http://api.drupal.org/api/function/system_system_info_alter/7.

Module-Specific Regions

The Dashboard module's Dashboard Main and Dashboard Sidebar regions are an example of regions created by a module. These regions are nontraditional in the sense that they can't be administered via the Blocks administration page, and the theme does not control defining or printing them. The Dashboard module defines them programmatically using hook_system_info_alter() and takes care of displaying them on the administrative Dashboard located at /admin. The Dashboard module allows you to drag and drop available blocks to those regions to create a dashboard for site administrators (see Figure 15–11).

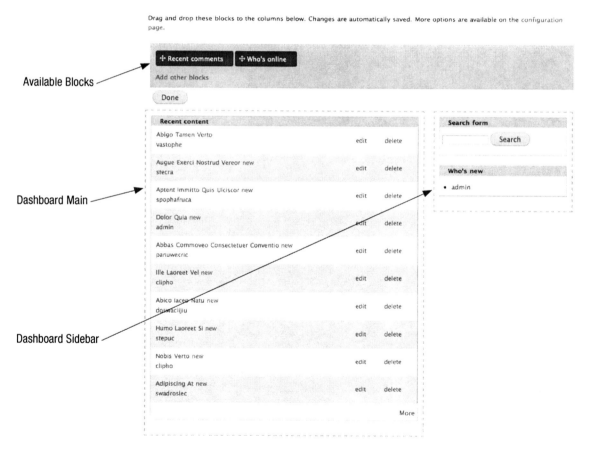

Figure 15–11. Administrative Dashboard in edit mode

Regions and Your Theme

Getting started with your theme regions requires taking a good look at design requirements as well as planning for the unexpected. There are many things to consider, including how site administrators will need to work with blocks and regions, what types of content you have, and how regions play a part in your general layout strategy. As discussed earlier, the default regions are a great starting point. We recommend that you begin defining the defaults in your theme's `.info` file and tweaking from there, as shown in Listing 15–5.

Listing 15–5. Drupal's Default Regions

```
regions[page_top] = Page Top
regions[header] = Header
regions[highlight] = Highlight
regions[help] = Help
regions[content] = Content
regions[sidebar_first] = Sidebar First
regions[sidebar_second] = Sidebar Second
regions[footer] = Footer
regions[page_bottom] = Page Bottom
```

■ **Tip** In addition to defining regions in your theme's `.info` file, you'll need to print it in the appropriate template file. The page_top and page_bottom regions print in the `html.tpl.php` template and the rest print in `page.tpl.php`. Printing regions and template files are discussed in more detail later in the chapter.

Using Regions vs. Hard-coding Variables in Template Files

When deciding whether or not to use regions in your theme, it's useful to consider the content that will be included in each section, how likely the position of the content is to change, and who needs to be able to change it. Blocks are flexible by nature and were designed to allow site administrators to easily move them around. This can cause problems if blocks are expected to be in a certain region and then moved or reordered.

When working on a site alone, or when only a few trusted individuals have control over the configuration of blocks, this is probably not something you need worry about. Alternatively, in cases where less trusted individuals have access and can potentially cause problems, taking extra measures to identify potential problem areas and doing what you can to prevent them is well worth it. For example, headers and footers are especially prone to this sort of problem. They usually have a tightly defined design and CSS to match. When blocks are moved around inside these regions, especially highly styled content such as the main menu navigation, things can go wrong quickly in the wrong hands. Sometimes defining an additional region, even if its purpose is to hold only one block, is a safer option compared with placing the block in the header region with other blocks. This will help ensure it is always printed in the right location and reduce the chance of user error. If site administrators do not need control over positioning, it may be best to print using a hardcoded variable in `page.tpl.php`, where it can't be affected by actions taken in the blocks interface.

As a general rule, consider using a region when content needs to be moved between regions or rearranged in the Blocks interface. When content doesn't need to be controlled via the Blocks interface, and it is risky for it to be there, consider hardcoding it in template files so it can't be affected by actions taken in the Blocks interface.

■ **Tip** The main menu (`$main_menu`) and secondary menu (`$secondary_menu`), which are located in `page.tpl.php`, are examples of hardcoded variables.

Layout Strategies

The core defaults for sidebars (Sidebar First and Sidebar Second) were designed to handle multiple sidebar combinations with the help of body classes. Drupal is extremely flexible, and pages can be changed on a whim. Whether this will actually look good or not depends on how flexible and well coded the theme is. Since Drupal only prints regions that contain content, having a well planned and flexible layout is very important.

For example, let's say you have a two-column layout theme where the first column contains the main content and the Sidebar First region contains a single block. If you were to set the visibility of that block to only show on the home page, the entire Sidebar First region would only print on the home page and the inside pages would print just the main column. If your layout CSS only accounts for having both of those columns on each page, instead of including CSS for both a single column and the two-column, your layout will break. While regions are fairly easy to add or modify at any given time, oversimplifying the layout in the beginning of a project may come back to bite you in the form of extra CSS work. However many sidebars your theme will have, it's generally best to account for all possible sidebar combinations (one, two, or three columns) to avoid running into problems down the line. A great way to do this easily and sustainably is to use an established base theme.

There are also certain types of content that often work better in separate regions. For example, custom blocks containing advertisements and blocks that have significantly different design requirements are often easier to work with and write CSS for when they are abstracted. Figure 15–12 shows what adding a region for an ad banner and main navigation might look like.

It is also important to consider how the pages will be built and who will be working with them. If your site is going to be using regions and blocks to implement more complicated designs and you want to make it easy for site administrators to use, it may make sense to predefine multiple regions to lay out smaller sections of your pages. A good example of this is the Bartik theme, which contains seven additional regions to organize blocks in the footer, as shown in Figure 15–13. The same look could be achieved by defining two regions (Footer First and Footer Second) instead and style them using CSS to float the blocks in each to the left, but Bartik's implementation, shown in Listing 15–6 and illustrated in Figure 15–13, is arguably easier to understand for those who are not interested in the inner-workings of the code and just want to use the theme.

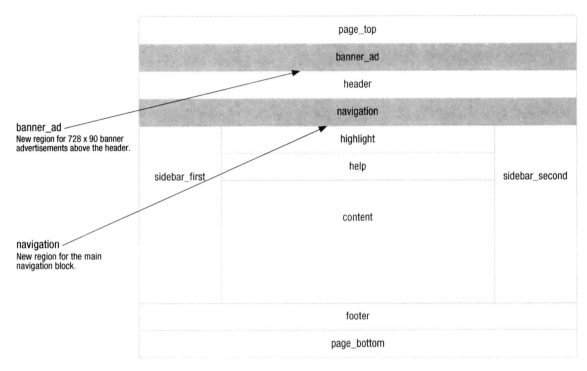

Figure 15–12. Example of custom advertisement banner and navigation regions

Listing 15–6. Excerpt from Bartik Theme's .info File Where Its Seven Custom Regions Are Defined

```
regions[triptych_first] = Triptych first
regions[triptych_middle] = Triptych middle
regions[triptych_last] = Triptych last
regions[footer_firstcolumn] = Footer first column
regions[footer_secondcolumn] = Footer second column
regions[footer_thirdcolumn] = Footer third column
regions[footer_fourthcolumn] = Footer fourth column
```

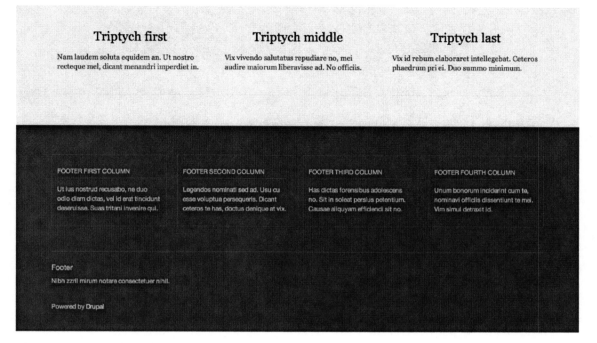

Figure 15–13. Populated footer regions in the Bartik theme

CREATING NEW REGIONS

The creation of a new region is a two-step process. Using the example in Figure 15–12, here's the process of creating the new Banner Ad and Navigation regions.

1. Define the regions in the `dgd7.info` file. Begin by adding the code for your new regions to the defaults you started with in Listing 15–3, plus the definition of the banner_ad and navigation regions to your `dgd7.info` file.

```
; DEFAULT REGIONS
regions[page_top] = Page Top
regions[header] = Header
regions[highlight] = Highlight
regions[help] = Help
regions[content] = Content
regions[sidebar_first] = Sidebar First
regions[sidebar_second] = Sidebar Second
regions[footer] = Footer
regions[page_bottom] = Page Bottom

; CUSTOM REGIONS
regions[banner_ad] = Banner Ad
regions[navigation] = Navigation
```

2. Print the regions in the `page.tpl.php` template file. Once you clear your site caches, you'll be able to see and populate the new regions on the Blocks administration page at `admin/structure/block`. In order to get them to display on the page, you'll need to override the `page.tpl.php` file in your theme and print the new regions.

Navigate to the `modules/system` directory, copy the `page.tpl.php` file and paste it into the `sites/all/themes/dgd7` directory you created earlier.

Open the `page.tpl.php` file in the theme and scroll down to the `<div id="page-wrapper">` and paste the code to print the region below it, and above the `<div id="header">`.

```
<div id="page-wrapper"><div id="page">
  <?php print render($page['banner_ad']); ?>
  <div id="header"><div class="section clearfix">
```

Remove the default markup for the `$main_menu` and replace it with the region code for your new navigation region.

Remove this code:

```
<?php if ($main_menu || $secondary_menu): ?>
      <div id="navigation"><div class="section">
        <?php print theme('links__system_main_menu', array('links' => $main_menu,
'attributes' => array('id' => 'main-menu', 'class' => array('links', 'inline',
'clearfix')), 'heading' => t('Main menu'))); ?>
        <?php print theme('links__system_secondary_menu', array('links' =>
$secondary_menu, 'attributes' => array('id' => 'secondary-menu', 'class' =>
array('links', 'inline', 'clearfix')), 'heading' => t('Secondary menu'))); ?>
      </div></div> <!-- /.section, /#navigation -->
    <?php endif; ?>
```

Replace with this code:

```
<?php print render($page['navigation']); ?>
```

3. Technically you're finished, but let's add some content to illustrate what you've done.

Add a new custom block for the Banner Ad code. Title the block "Banner Ad" and add the following code to fake the appearance of an ad banner in the Block body (be sure to select the Full HTML text format). Then, select the Banner Ad region for the region settings and save it.

```
<img style="width: 728px; height: 90px; border: solid 1px #000;" alt="728 x 90 Banner
Ad" src="image.png" />
```

Go back to the `admin/structure/block` page. Find the Main Menu block and place it inside the Navigation region and click Save blocks.

You've just added and populated two new custom regions!

Template Files

Drupal core, its modules, and contributed modules provide much of their output in the form of template files. Template files consist of HTML markup and PHP variables. This makes it fairly easy for those with little or no PHP experience to make changes to HTML code.

A simple example of a template file is `user-picture.tpl.php` (see Listing 15–7). This template is located in the `modules/user` directory and its purpose is solely to print a site user's picture as either an image or an image with a link (depending on whether or not the user viewing the photo has access to view user profiles). It wraps the picture in a `<div class="user-picture">`. This template file will be used anywhere the user_picture theme hook is called, such as the user profile page and author information for nodes and comment (where enabled).

Listing 15–7. Contents of user-picture.tpl.php File

```php
<?php
// $Id: user-picture.tpl.php,v 1.5 2009/08/06 05:05:59 webchick Exp $

/**
 * @file
 * Default theme implementation to present a picture configured for the
 * user's account.
 *
 * Available variables:
 * - $user_picture: Image set by the user or the site's default. Will be linked
 *   depending on the viewer's permission to view the users profile page.
 * - $account: Array of account information. Potentially unsafe. Be sure to
 *   check_plain() before use.
 *
 * @see template_preprocess_user_picture()
 */
?>
<?php if ($user_picture): ?>
  <div class="user-picture">
    <?php print $user_picture; ?>
  </div>
<?php endif; ?>
```

A typical page on a Drupal site is essentially a big tree of nested template files and theme functions. As Figure 15–14 illustrates, this tree begins with larger templates such as `html.tpl.php` and `page.tpl.php` files and goes all the way down `field.tpl.php`, which is used to print fields.

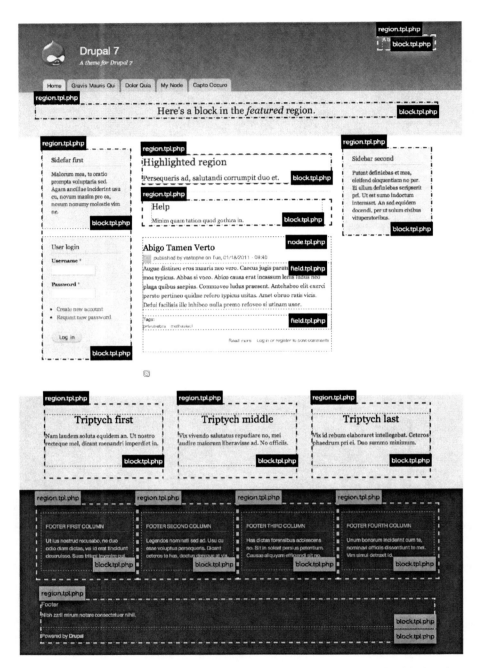

Figure 15–14. *An example home page using the Bartik theme, which highlights the use of major template files and many custom regions*

Common Core Templates

Drupal core contains over forty template files, but there are six major template files (described in Table 15–1) that are tasked with making up the majority of each page. These major template files are the ones you'll be working with most when writing Drupal themes and they will allow you do most of the heavy lifting in your theme.

Table 15–1. *Common Core Template Files*

Name	Origin	Purpose
html.tpl.php	modules/system	Prints the structure of the HTML document, including the contents of <head> tags, e.g. $scripts, and $styles, as well as opening and closing <body> tags with $page_top, $page and $page_bottom regions printed inside. Unless you need to change the DOCTYPE, there's probably no reason to override this file.
page.tpl.php	modules/system	Prints the page level regions and other hard-coded variables such as $logo, $site_name, $tabs, $main_menu, etc. Full control of the site layout is possible by manipulating this file, and most themes provide their own version of it.
region.tpl.php	modules/system	Prints the HTML markup for regions.
block.tpl.php	modules/block	Prints the HTML markup for blocks.
node.tpl.php	modules/node	Prints the HTML markup for nodes.
comment.tpl.php	modules/comment	Prints the HTML markup for comments.
field.tpl.php *	modules/field/theme	Prints the HTML markup for fields. There are many different types of fields, and since this file needs to cover every case, its implementation is very general. If having semantic markup is important to you, you'll probably end up with a few versions of this template.

* field.tpl.php is used only when overridden by a theme. The one in modules/field/theme is only provided as a base for your work.

Overriding Template Files

The template files provided by Drupal core and contributed modules represent the default markup implementation chosen by the original author or team, but every last one of these template files—and the markup and variables printed inside of them—is customizable. When developing a theme, if you decide the default implementation is not going to suit your needs, you can simply choose to override it. Drupal's theme layer is designed to be extremely flexible and easy to manipulate in this way.

The beauty of theming Drupal sites is that you can easily make changes without having to modify templates where they originate. The process of overriding template files is extremely simple:

1. Find the original template file by browsing through code or checking http://api.drupal.org

2. Copy and paste it into your theme directory.

3. Clear the site cache and reload!

After following these three steps, Drupal will begin using the theme's version of the file, and you are free to make whatever changes you wish. It's that simple.

▪ **Tip** A quick way to ensure that Drupal is using the template file you've just overridden in your theme is to add text to the top of the template file, like "Hello World." If your text appears when you reload, you'll know you're working with the correct file.

Global Template Variables

Template files usually contain a few more variables than they actually print. In some cases there are many more. This is a great thing for theme developers because it opens up many possibilities for manipulating the display of markup without the need for much PHP knowledge. Table 1-2 describes some of the helpful variables available in all templates (with the exception of the attribute variables; these are covered section the "HTML Attributes" section). Identifying available variables is covered in detail in the next chapter.

Table 15–2. Variables Available in All Templates

Variable	Description
$is_admin	Helper variable that equals TRUE if the currently logged in user is an administrator, and FALSE otherwise.
$logged_in	Helper variable that equals TRUE if the current user is logged in, and FALSE otherwise. The $user->uid is used to determine this information, as anonymous users always have a user ID of 0.
$is_front	Helper variable that uses the drupal_is_front_page() function to determine if the current page is the front page of the site. Equals TRUE on the front page (unless the database is offline), and FALSE otherwise.
$directory	The directory in which the template being used is located.

Variable	Description
$user	An object that contains account information of the currently logged in user. It may be accessed by adding the line global $user; to the template you are working in. Never print any properties of it directly because it contains raw user data and thus it is insecure. Instead, use theme('username'); for example, theme('username', array('account' => $user)).
$language	An object that contains information about the language currently being used on the site, such as $language->dir, which contains the text direction, and $language->language which would contain en for English. It may be accessed by adding the line global $language; to the template you are working in.
$theme_hook_suggestions	An array containing other possible theme hooks, which can be used as variants for naming template files and theme functions or to determine context. See the "Theme Hook Suggestions" section.
$title_prefix and $title_suffix	Render arrays containing elements, such as contextual links, to be printed before and after the title in templates or at the top and bottom of template files where a title does not exist.

HTML Attributes

In Drupal 7, we began storing attributes in arrays. Part of the reason this was done is the RDF module. The RDF module utilizes these variables to tack on its data during the preprocess phase. Another reason was to allow theme developers more control over the classes printing out in their template files in preprocess functions.

Each of these variables, described in Table 15–3, has an array and string version. The array version, which contains the suffix _array in the variable name, is populated during various preprocess functions, such as template_preprocess() and template_preprocess_node() or template_preprocess_block(). Then, during the template_process() phase, new variables containing a flattened or string version of these arrays is created for use in templates. This process is illustrated in Figure 15–15. See the "Preprocess and Process Functions" section of this chapter for more details.

Table 15–3. Pluggable HTML Attributes

Variable	Description
$attributes	Contains HTML attributes provided by modules (mainly RDF), except for the class attribute, which is handled separately (see below). $attributes, available as $attributes_array in preprocess, is usually reserved for the top-level HTML wrapper element, such as <body> or outermost <div> in other template files.
$classes	Contains HTML classes for templates. Usually reserved for the top-level HTML wrapper element, such as <body> or outermost <div> in other template files.
$title_attributes	Contains classes for the top-level heading, such as a node or block title, of the template file, which is usually an <h2> for node teaser or block content.
$content_attributes	Contains classes for the content wrapper <div>, or post body of templates. An example of how these variables are used can be found in the node.tpl.php file.

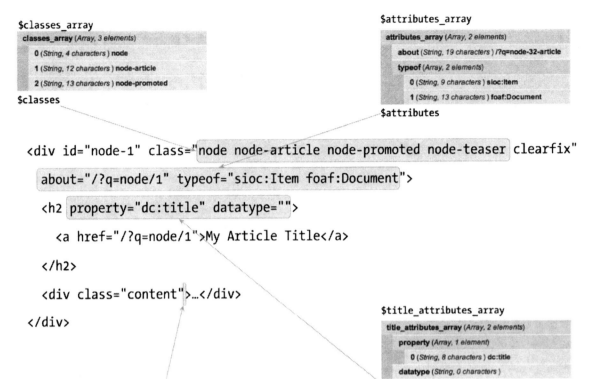

Figure 15–15. Excerpt from node.tpl.php, which highlights how the pluggable HTML attributes are used

---

■ **Tip** If you don't see these attributes in your source code, be sure to enable the RDF module.

All of the common core templates provide detailed documentation of the available variables. A quick look at the default block.tpl.php template file, located in the modules/block directory reveals that most of the contents of the file is actually documentation for the available variables. As shown in Listing 15–8, you can get a good idea of what you have to work with by just looking at the documentation and code.

Listing 15–8. Source Code for Default modules/block/block.tpl.php, Including Variable Documentation

```php
<?php
/**
 * @file
 * Default theme implementation to display a block.
```

```
 *
 * Available variables:
 * - $block->subject: Block title.
 * - $content: Block content.
 * - $block->module: Module that generated the block.
 * - $block->delta: An ID for the block, unique within each module.
 * - $block->region: The block region embedding the current block.
 * - $classes: String of classes that can be used to style contextually through
 *   CSS. It can be manipulated through the variable $classes_array from
 *   preprocess functions. The default values can be one or more of the following:
 *   - block: The current template type, i.e., "theming hook".
 *   - block-[module]: The module generating the block. For example, the user module
 *     is responsible for handling the default user navigation block. In that case
 *     the class would be "block-user".
 * - $title_prefix (array): An array containing additional output populated by
 *   modules, intended to be displayed in front of the main title tag that
 *   appears in the template.
 * - $title_suffix (array): An array containing additional output populated by
 *   modules, intended to be displayed after the main title tag that appears in
 *   the template.
 *
 * Helper variables:
 * - $classes_array: Array of html class attribute values. It is flattened
 *   into a string within the variable $classes.
 * - $block_zebra: Outputs 'odd' and 'even' dependent on each block region.
 * - $zebra: Same output as $block_zebra but independent of any block region.
 * - $block_id: Counter dependent on each block region.
 * - $id: Same output as $block_id but independent of any block region.
 * - $is_front: Flags true when presented in the front page.
 * - $logged_in: Flags true when the current user is a logged-in member.
 * - $is_admin: Flags true when the current user is an administrator.
 * - $block_html_id: A valid HTML ID and guaranteed unique.
 *
 * @see template_preprocess()
 * @see template_preprocess_block()
 * @see template_process()
 */
?>
<div id="<?php print $block_html_id; ?>" class="<?php print $classes; ?>"<?php print
$attributes; ?>>
  <?php print render($title_prefix); ?>
<?php if ($block->subject): ?>
  <h2<?php print $title_attributes; ?>><?php print $block->subject ?></h2>
<?php endif;?>
  <?php print render($title_suffix); ?>
  <div class="content"<?php print $content_attributes; ?>>
    <?php print $content ?>
  </div>
</div>
```

At the top of the file there is a @file block, which briefly describes the purpose of the file. Underneath, there is a long list of variables, some of which are printed in the template file and some that are not. There are also @see references to applicable preprocess and process functions, which are discussed in more detail in the next chapter.

To get an up-close idea of what this template file produces, take a look at a block produced by the Bartik theme. Bartik does not include a `block.tpl.php` file; it uses Drupal's default, which is provided by the Block module. Create a custom block with the title "My Custom Block" and some dummy text as the body, and place it in the Sidebar First region of the Bartik theme.

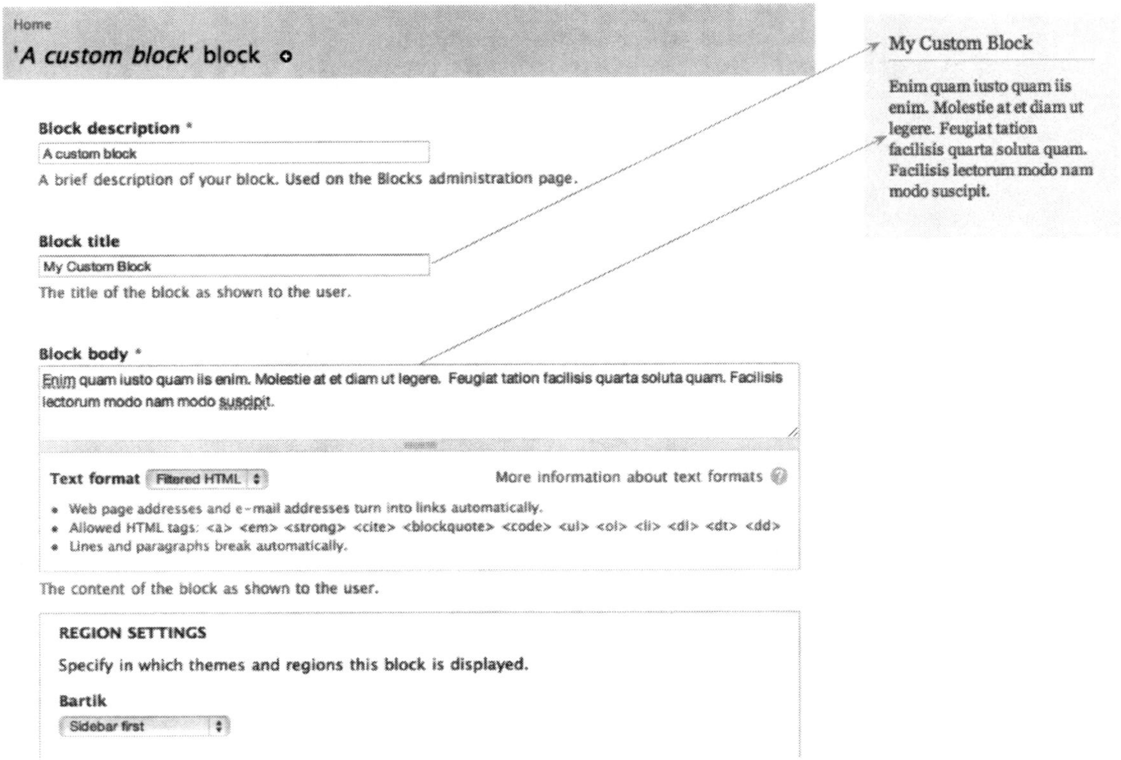

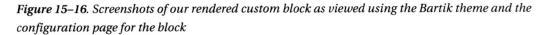

Figure 15–16. *Screenshots of our rendered custom block as viewed using the Bartik theme and the configuration page for the block*

Your custom block, shown in Figure 15–16 along with the `block.tpl.php` template file in Listing 15–9, produces the output displayed in Listing 15–9 for anonymous users. The block title is printed by `<?php print $block->subject ?>` and the body is printed by `<?php print $content ?>`. Drupal will only populate variables and display content that the user viewing it has access to.

Listing 15–9. *HTML Output of a Custom Block Titled "My Custom Block" When Logged Out*

```
<div id="block-block-1" class="block block-block">
  <h2>My Custom Block</h2>
  <div class="content">
    <p>Enim quam iusto quam iis enim. Molestie at et diam ut legere. Feugiat tation facilisis
quarta soluta quam. Facilisis lectorum modo nam modo suscipit.</p>
  </div>
</div>
```

Listing 15–10 shows the HTML for the same block as it is displayed to users logged in as administrators. You'll notice that the code is different. Administrators have access to contextual administrative links, added by the Contextual Links module. These links are printed via the `<?php print render($title_prefix); ?>` line. The Contextual Links module also adds a class to the wrapper `<div>` identifying it as a contextual-links-region. This behavior is not specific to the Block module or the `block.tpl.php` template file. The `$title_prefix` and `$title_suffix` variables were created to allow modules to inject content before and after titles in template files, which the Contextual links module takes advantage of.

Listing 15–10. HTML Output of a Custom Block Titled "My Custom Block" When Logged In as an Administrator, Highlighting the Output of $title_suffix

```
<div id="block-block-1" class="block block-block contextual-links-region">
  <h2>My Custom Block</h2>
  <div class="contextual-links-wrapper contextual-links-processed">
    <a class="contextual-links-trigger" href="#">Configure</a>
    <ul class="contextual-links">
      <li class="block-configure first last"><a
href="/admin/structure/block/manage/block/1/configure?destination=node">Configure
block</a></li>
    </ul>
  </div>
  <div class="content">
    <p>Enim quam iusto quam iis enim. Molestie at et diam ut legere. Feugiat tation facilisis
quarta soluta quam. Facilisis lectorum modo nam modo suscipit.</p>
  </div>
</div>
```

Theme Functions

The purpose of a theme function is the same as a template file in that its goal is to provide HTML markup in a way that makes it customizable by themes (and modules, too). There are many, many theme functions in Drupal core, from form elements to menu items to full administration page implementations. For a full list of theme functions available in Drupal 7, visit `http://api.drupal.org/api/group/themeable/7`.

How Theme Functions Are Created

Drupal core and modules usually define theme functions, but they can be defined by themes as well. `hook_theme()` implementations are where all the juicy information about most generic theme functions resides, including what parameters these functions accept. Theme hooks are covered in detail in the "Theme Hook Suggestions" section later in this chapter, but Listing 15–11 shows what a simple `hook_theme()` implementation looks like.

Listing 15–11. Example hook_theme() Implementation

```
<?php
/**
* Implements hook_theme().
*/
```

```
function mymodule_theme() {
  return array(
    'my_theme_hook' => array(
      'variables' => array('parameter' => NULL),
    ),
  );
}
?>
```

Implementations of hook_theme() let Drupal know about theme hooks. Once Drupal is aware, it will search for a theme function called theme_my_theme_hook() in this case, which might look like the code in Listing 15–12.

Listing 15–12. Example Theme Function Implementation

```php
<?php
function theme_my_theme_hook($variables) {
  $parameter = $variables['parameter'];
  if (!empty($parameter)) {
    return '<div class="my-theme-hook">' . $parameter . '</div>';
  }
}
?>
```

Calling Theme Functions

Throughout this chapter we refer to theme functions as theme_this() and theme_that(). That's what the functions are named and usually referred to as. However, you should never call a theme function directly. Doing so will reverse the wonderful functionality that comes along with Drupal's theme layer, such as overrides, suggestions, etc. Always use the theme() function to generate theme output. It takes care of routing the request to the appropriate theme function. For more information on how this works, see http://api.drupal.org/api/function/theme/7.

Using theme_image(), Listings 15–13 and 15–14 illustrate the right and wrong way to call theme functions, respectively.

Listing 15–13. The Correct Way to Call a Theme Function.

```php
<?php print theme('image', array('path' => 'path/to/image.png', 'alt' => 'Image description')); ?>
```

Listing 15–14. The Wrong Way to Call a Theme Function

```php
<?php print theme_image(array('path' => 'path/to/image.png', 'alt' => 'Image description'));
?>
```

Overriding Theme Functions

Overriding theme functions is very similar to overriding template files. The main difference is that you are working with functions, and your overridden theme functions all reside in template.php. The steps involved in overriding a theme function are as follows:

1. Find the original theme function by browsing through Drupal's source code or checking http://api.drupal.org.

2. Copy and paste it into your `template.php` file.

3. Change the beginning of the function name from `theme_` to `yourthemename_`.

4. Save `template.php`, clear the site cache, and reload!

■ **Caution** If creating `template.php` from scratch, remember to include `<?php` at the top of the file. Also note that a closing tag should not be added at the bottom of the file. Omitting the closing PHP tag prevents unwanted whitespace, which can cause "Cannot modify header information" or "Headers already sent" errors. For more information, visit `http://drupal.org/node/1424`.

LET'S OVERRIDE A THEME FUNCTION

Here is a theme function called `theme_more_link()`. It is used to print a link to additional content in blocks. To find the code for the theme function, take a look at `http://api.drupal.org/api/function/theme_more_link/7`.

1. Copy and paste the original theme function code into `template.php`.

```php
<?php
/**
 * Returns HTML for a "more" link, like those used in blocks.
 *
 * @param $variables
 *   An associative array containing:
 *   - url: The url of the main page.
 *   - title: A descriptive verb for the link, like 'Read more'.
 */
function theme_more_link($variables) {
  return '<div class="more-link">' . l(t('More'), $variables['url'], array('attributes'
=> array('title' => $variables['title']))) . '</div>';
}
?>
```

2. Change the beginning of the function name to your theme's name, save it, and clear the site cache.

```php
<?php
/**
 * Returns HTML for a "more" link, like those used in blocks.
 *
 * @param $variables
 *   An associative array containing:
 *   - url: The url of the main page.
 *   - title: A descriptive verb for the link, like 'Read more'.
 */
function dgd7_more_link($variables) {
```

```php
    return '<div class="more-link">' . l(t('More'), $variables['url'], array('attributes'
=> array('title' => $variables['title']))) . '</div>';
}
?>
```

3. Drupal will now use your version of the theme function, so make changes!

```php
<?php
/**
* Overrides theme_more_link().
*   - Changed the text from "More" to "Show me More"
*   - Changed the class from "more-link" to "more"
*/
function dgd7_more_link($variables) {
  return '<div class="more">' . l(t('Show me MORE!'), $variables['url'],
array('attributes' => array('title' => $variables['title']))) . '</div>';
}
?>
```

■ **Tip** In Step 3, you'll notice that the comment block has been changed to indicate what function was overridden and the changes that were made. Documenting your code is always a good idea, and explicitly listing the reasons why you've overridden a theme function can be a big time saver in the future. Theme functions change, and some aren't as small as a few lines. When upgrading major versions of Drupal, such as Drupal 7 to Drupal 8, such comments will make your life a lot easier.

Theme Hooks and Theme Hook Suggestions

Theme functions and templates are defined by theme hooks. By making use of theme hook suggestions, you have a lot more flexibility to override theme functions or templates in certain situations. This section covers both ways to greatly increase the power and maneuverability of your custom theme.

What Is a Theme Hook?

In Drupal, theme hooks refer to template files and functions that have been specifically registered via hook_theme(). This may sound scary or over-technical to non-PHP developers, but honestly it's not. You've already learned about template files and theme functions, so technically you already have a pretty good grasp on theme hooks.

Whether a template file or function is implemented in core is decided on a case-by-case basis, and the criteria for making this decision is usually a balance between how likely it is to be reused by other modules, how often it is expected to change, and whether or not it makes sense for performance reasons. Template files are slightly slower than theme functions so they are not always desirable. Smaller bits of markup for things like form input elements are more efficiently implemented as theme functions, whereas larger chunks like nodes and blocks are better as a template file.

- Both theme functions and template files exist as a way for Drupal and its modules to create output consisting of markup and variables in a way that you, the themer, can override and make it your own. They are both entirely YOUR domain, and you get the last word as to how they should look.

- Both share the same exact theme hook. For example, a template file called node.tpl.php and a function called theme_node() share the same node theme hook. The difference is in the implementation, as both cannot be used at the same time.

- Both can take advantage of preprocess functions, which allow you to intercept and alter variables before rendering. Using the node hook as an example, this would look like template_preprocess_node(); in your theme it would be yourtheme_preprocess_node().

Theme Hook Suggestions

The default implementation of template files and theme functions offer a very generic set of markup that is sufficient, but not ideal in all cases. When doing a standard override, such as copying block.tpl.php into a theme, the changes made will apply site-wide whenever a block is rendered. At times this the desired result, but you'll often want to make changes to a specific block, a set of blocks provided by a specific module, or even a group of blocks in a specific region.

Theme hook suggestions allow you to implement targeted overrides in your theme for both template files and theme functions with naming patterns. The options and naming patterns vary depending on what type of object you are working with. During the preprocess stage, before each template is rendered, a variable called $theme_hook_suggestions is created and populated with alternative hook suggestions.

Suggestions and Template Files

All of the common template files listed in Table 15–1 can be overridden to allow for more targeted customization by simply changing the name of the template file. When working with blocks, for example, Drupal suggests the options in Listing 15–15 during template_preprocess_block().

Listing 15–15. *Excerpt from template_preprocess_block() where template suggestions for block template files are defined*

```php
<?php
  $variables['theme_hook_suggestions'][] = 'block__' . $variables['block']->region;
  $variables['theme_hook_suggestions'][] = 'block__' . $variables['block']->module;
  $variables['theme_hook_suggestions'][] = 'block__' . $variables['block']->module . '__' .
$variables['block']->delta;
?>
```

Drupal automatically converts the underscores to dashes and searches for these templates in your theme when determining which one to use. This code translates to the suggestions shown in Table 15–4.

Table 15–4. Template Suggestions for Blocks

Suggestion	Template File Equivalent	Description
block	block.tpl.php	Default block implementation.
block__REGION	block--REGION.tpl.php	REGION is replaced with the theme region name, and the template targets blocks in that region.
block__MODULE	block--MODULE.tpl.php	MODULE is replaced with the name of the module that created the block. For example, a template file that targets custom blocks would be block--block.tpl.php and a block created by the menu module would be targeted by using block--menu.tpl.php.
block__MODULE__DELTA	block--MODULE--DELTA.tpl.php	The DELTA value, which used to be a number in previous versions, is the system name of the block as defined by the module. For example, to target the System module's Navigation block, you would use block--system--navigation.tpl.php. In this example, "system" is the module and "navigation" is the delta.

Page-Level Suggestions

Because of their special nature as the highest-level template files in Drupal, both html.tpl.php and page.tpl.php are given special attention when it comes to generating their suggestions. A function called theme_get_suggestions() is used to automatically generate suggestions using arguments based on the context of the current page. This means that if you wanted to, you could literally have a different version of these template files for every page on your site. Of course, this is something you should never even think about doing, but in certain cases, like a very different home page or landing page, having a different page.tpl.php makes perfect sense.

As mentioned, the theme hook suggestions for these files are generated with the help of arguments. Arguments in Drupal are the elements or pieces of system path of a page. For example, when viewing the URL http://yoursite.com/node/1, the first argument is "node" and the second argument is "1." Understanding arguments in Drupal is one of the key things that will help you understand Drupal. They are extremely useful in determining context and can allow you to perform more advanced manipulations in your theme.

Figure 15–17 illustrates how you can use theme hook suggestions and arguments to make separate page.tpl.php and html.tpl.php templates for just about any page on your site.

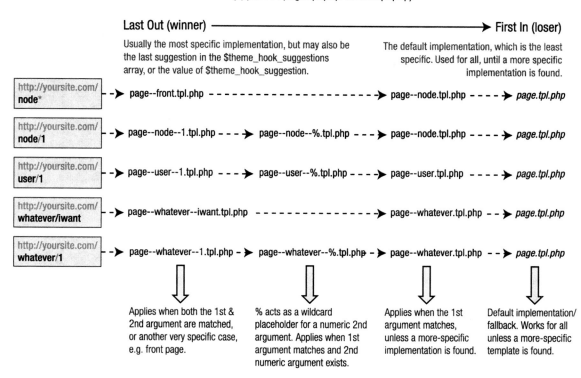

Figure 15–17. Suggestions for page.tpl.php on different types of pages

* Drupal's front page is set to "node" by default under Admin ➤ Configuration ➤ Site Information. This page is not a typical node. It is a custom page provided by the node module's node_page_default() function. It lists posts that have been marked as "Promote to front page." The "front" suggestion is specific to the front page (or home page), regardless of what type of page it is. Should you change your front page to a different path, additional suggestions will become available to you.

■ **Caution** Figure 15–17 lists examples of named paths that you'll likely encounter when using contributed modules such as views and panels. These become system paths and can be used as template suggestions. However, attempting to create a template file using a path that was created using a custom alias (or the Pathauto module) such as about/team for a node/1 will not work. The same applies to taxonomy, terms, and user profiles. The real system path is always required when working with templates.

Some observations of $theme_hook_suggestions include:

- Underscores are used instead of dashes.

- File extensions are not present because these hooks can be implemented as theme functions or template files. At this stage in the process, it doesn't matter whether a template or a theme function will be used. When it's time to render the content, theme() will determine which should be used and make the necessary adjustments.

- Each suggestion begins with a hook__ (double-underscore) prefix. In the example shown in Listing 15–15, that hook is block. This allows Drupal to fall back on the generic theme hook, which in this case is block, and use block.tpl.php when a more specific template, like block--module.tpl.php, doesn't exist.

The order in which these suggestions appear in the $theme_hook_suggestions variable determines which hook/template file will be used in FILO (first in, last out) order. When it comes time to render the template, the last suggestion will be used, with one exception. A variable called $theme_hook_suggestion (note that it is singular, not plural) is also available. If it's set by a module or theme, it will take precedence over anything defined in $theme_hook_suggestions.

■ **Tip** Use the dpm() function (provided with the Devel module) inside the generic template file you are working with to find out what options are available. `<?php dpm($theme_hook_suggestions); ?>` will show the options that are available for the page you are working on.

Suggestions and Theme Functions

As explained in the "Suggestions and Template Files" section, alternate $theme_hook_suggestions are usually defined in the preprocess function for that hook. This works well because template files usually serve a specific purpose, like printing a specific entity such as a node or block. Theme functions, however, are much more diverse and end up being used within many different types of output, such as form elements, fields, and render elements. Module developers may also use theme functions to create one-off, custom content. This makes the prospect of implementing a theme function override of a widely used function such as theme_links() much less attractive, as it could potentially break styling in unexpected places all over your site.

Luckily, theme hook suggestions also exist for many theme functions, and Drupal core has implemented suggestions for some of the popular theme functions, like theme_links(). Using theme hook suggestions with theme functions simply means that you can choose to override a theme function in a specific context as opposed to overriding the base theme function, which would have a site-wide effect.

As mentioned, theme_links() is a good example of where to use theme hook suggestions when overriding theme functions. This theme function is used in many, many places, such as the main navigation, node, comment, and contextual links. Note that to implement the functions named in the "Theme function equivalent" column in Table 15–5, you need to replace THEME with the name of your theme in template.php.

Table 15–5. Some Example Template Suggestions for theme_links()

Suggestion	Theme Function Equivalent	Description
links	THEME_links()	Default implementation, which is used for all implementations unless a more specific implementation like those below is specified.
links__node	THEME_links__node()	Targeted implementation of theme_links() that only applies to links lists inside of nodes.
links__comment	THEME_links__comment()	Targeted implementation of theme_links() that only applies to links lists inside of comments.
links__contextual	THEME_links__contextual()	Targeted implementation of theme_links() that only applies to links generated for contextual links.
links__contextual__node	THEME_links__contextual__node()	Targeted implementation of theme_links() that only applies to contextual links inside of nodes.

You'll notice in Drupal's default page.tpl.php file, located in the modules/system directory, that both the main and secondary menus are printed using suggestions. You might also notice that theme functions called theme_links__system_main_menu() and theme_links__system_secondary_menu() do not exist, and that's okay. In this case, the base hook, or the fallback, theme_links() will be used unless a more targeted theme function is created (see Listing 15–16).

Listing 15–16. Excerpt from modules/system/page.tpl.php

```php
<?php if ($main_menu || $secondary_menu): ?>
  <div id="navigation"><div class="section">
    <?php print theme('links__system_main_menu', array('links' => $main_menu, 'attributes'
=> array('id' => 'main-menu', 'class' => array('links', 'inline', 'clearfix')), 'heading' =>
t('Main menu'))); ?>
    <?php print theme('links__system_secondary_menu', array('links' => $secondary_menu,
'attributes' => array('id' => 'secondary-menu', 'class' => array('links', 'inline',
'clearfix')), 'heading' => t('Secondary menu'))); ?>
  </div></div> <!-- /.section, /#navigation -->
<?php endif; ?>
```

In this situation, the theme hook suggestions are hardcoded into the function arguments. When theme() processes this, it will check to see if an implementation of theme_links__system_main_menu() exists first. If the function is found, it will be used to render the content. If not, the original (or fallback) theme_links() will be used instead. theme() handles this automatically and can determine the base hook from the use of the double underscore that appears directly after it.

■ **Caution** It's important to note that theme hook suggestions are NOT the same as theme hooks. Given what you've learned about theme hook suggestions, it's natural to think that preprocess and process functions can be written for the specific suggestion. Theme hooks, which are the default implementation and suggestion, are specifically registered in an implementation of hook_theme(). This means that you may create a preprocess function called THEME_preprocess_page() but you may not use THEME_preprocess_page__front().

Summary

This chapter has covered the basics of Drupal themes, including how to:

- Define .info files and work with regions.
- Override and create targeted template files and theme functions.
- Make sense out of theme hooks and suggestions.

Armed with this knowledge, it's time to move onto some more advanced theme topics in the next chapter.

■■■

## CHAPTER 16

Advanced Theming

by Jacine Luisi

One of the best things about Drupal's theme layer is the sheer amount of flexibility it provides. In the previous chapter you learned the basics of creating a theme: working with .info files, template files, and theme functions. When implementing more custom themes, sometimes these tools alone are not enough and you need to dig deeper. This is the point where the line between front-end developer and back-end developer gets a little blurry, but stay with us.

By the time you finish reading this chapter you'll know how to work with variables in preprocess functions, customize forms, and use the new render API. I'll also cover the ins and outs of working with CSS files and the basics of subtheming, and leave you with basics rules for creating sustainable Drupal themes. You'll be transformed into a theming ninja in no time.

Finding Available Variables in the Theme Layer

When working in the theme layer, you'll find that the variables are different depending on the type of entity with which you are working. You'll also find that the various templates and theme functions don't use or document all of the variables that are available, so one of the things you'll often need to do is print the contents of arrays to the screen.

There are various ways to print arrays using PHP. One of the most common ways is to use the print_r() function. There's also var_dump(), get_defined_vars() and Drupal's own debug(). These functions are great for small arrays, but Drupal's arrays are known for being tremendous, thus using these functions while coding the front end of a site is annoying, to say the least. Luckily, thanks to the Devel module (http://drupal.org/project/devel) and the Krumo library, printing compact and easily readable arrays is a piece of cake. Upon installing the Devel module, you'll have access to functions like dpm() and kpr() among others.

When working with templates and preprocess functions, you'll usually print $variables using dsm() or dsm(). As an example, try adding <?php dpm($variables); ?> to the top of your node.tpl.php file.

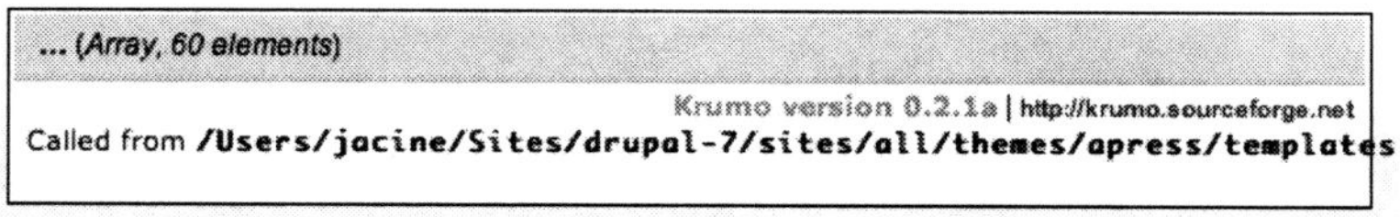

... (Array, 60 elements)

Krumo version 0.2.1a | http://krumo.sourceforge.net
Called from **/Users/jacine/Sites/drupal-7/sites/all/themes/apress/templates**

Figure 16–1. The result of printing `<?php dpm($variables); ?>` *in* node.tpl.php

In Figure 16–1, you see the result of printing the contents of the $variables array using the dpm() function. What's nice about using dpm() is that the array is neatly printed using the $messages variable in `page.tpl.php`, which is where system status messages are located. As shown in Figure 16–2, you can click the heading and expand the contents of each part one by one.

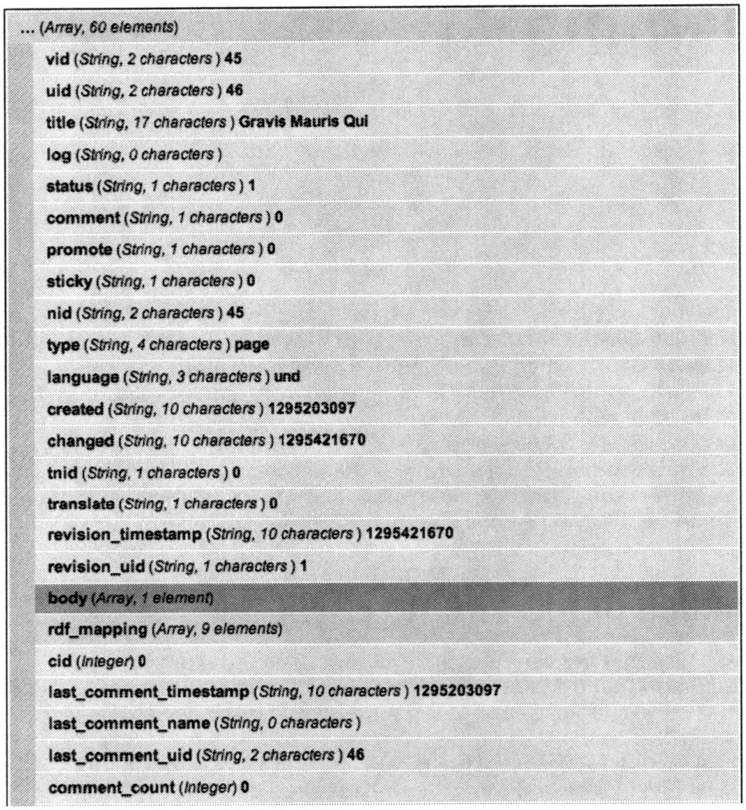

Figure 16–2. An expanded array printed using the dpm() function

When working inside template files, these variables are made available as top-level variables. This is done as a convenience for theme developers. For example, instead of printing $variables['status'], just print $status in templates. When working inside functions, such as theme functions or preprocess functions, use $variables['status'].

Using the Theme Developer Module

Of course, when you're first starting out with Drupal, you'll need to get an idea of where the code is located and what you need to override in the first place. The Theme Developer module (http://drupal.org/project/devel_themer) is the perfect tool to help you figure this out. Once enabled, a checkbox will appear in the bottom right corner of the page. When clicked, a semi-transparent, resizable, and draggable window appears in the top right corner of the page. You can then move it around and click on any element of the page and the window will populate with all the information you need to know—and more (see Figure 16-3).

For example, when clicking a node, the following information is made available in the window:

- The parent functions and templates that affect the element
- The template or theme hook suggestions (candidates)
- The preprocess and process functions being used
- A printout of the variables available

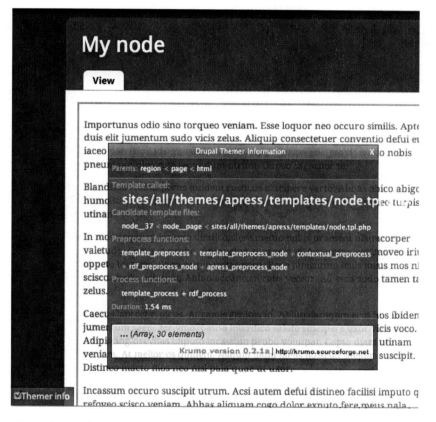

Figure 16–3. *The Theme Developer window shows theme-related information about the element that was clicked (a node in this case).*

Preprocess and Process Functions

Preprocess functions are a theme developer's best friend. There are so many use cases where preprocess functions can make your life easier, your code more efficient, and your template files clean and crisp. If you haven't used them before, either because you think you don't need them or are afraid of delving too deep into PHP, you are truly missing out. We hope to change that.

By now you are familiar with the general purpose of template files, which is mainly to provide markup and print variables. But what if you'd like to change those variables or add your own? Your first inclination might be to create a template file and do everything there, but that is often the wrong way to go.

Preprocess functions were designed for this exact purpose. When implementing a preprocess or process function you are basically telling Drupal, "Hey, wait! I have some changes to make to this data before you send it off for rendering." It's sort of like an editor getting a final review of an article before it's allowed to be published. By definition, "preprocess" is a phase of processing that happens before templates are rendered. "Process" functions, which are new in Drupal 7, serve the same purpose, with the only difference being that they run later (after preprocess) in the processing cycle.

A good example of how Drupal uses preprocess and process functions is the $classes_array and $classes variables. In template_preprocess() in Listing 16–1, which is the default implementation of preprocess by Drupal and the first preprocess function called, the $classes_array variable is initialized; see http://api.drupal.org/api/function/template_preprocess/7.

Listing 16–1. Excerpt from template_preprocess() Where $classes_array Is Defined

```php
<?php
function template_preprocess(&$variables, $hook) {
  // Initialize html class attribute for the current hook.
  $variables['classes_array'] = array(drupal_html_class($hook));
}
?>
```

This first step provides a class indicating the hook that's being used. For example, if this preprocess function is being called for a node, this code will add the class node to this array. After this function runs, all modules and themes also have a chance to run it themselves and add or change any of the variables. Next up is the Node module, which implements template_preprocess_node(); see http://api.drupal.org/api/function/template_preprocess_node/7. As you can see in Listing 16–2, quite a few classes are added to this array.

Listing 16–2. Excerpt from template_preprocess_node() Where Additional Classes Are Added to the

$classes_array Variable

```php
<?php
function template_preprocess_node(&$variables) {
  // Gather node classes.
  $variables['classes_array'][] = drupal_html_class('node-' . $node->type);
  if ($variables['promote']) {
    $variables['classes_array'][] = 'node-promoted';
  }
  if ($variables['sticky']) {
    $variables['classes_array'][] = 'node-sticky';
  }
  if (!$variables['status']) {
    $variables['classes_array'][] = 'node-unpublished';
  }
  if ($variables['teaser']) {
    $variables['classes_array'][] = 'node-teaser';
  }
  if (isset($variables['preview'])) {
    $variables['classes_array'][] = 'node-preview';
  }
}
?>
```

Once again, after `template_preprocess_node()` runs, all modules and themes have a chance to implement their own version, making any changes or additions they want. Once all the preprocess functions have completed, the process functions have their chance. In Drupal core, there are only two process implementations for nodes: `template_process()`, the default implementation, and `rdf_process()`, an implementation by the RDF module.

In `template_process()`, after all the modules and themes have had a chance to modify it, a new variable called `$classes` is created. It contains a string version all of the classes provided in `$classes_array`. The `$classes` variable is printed in the class attribute of the wrapper `<div>` in the `node.tpl.php` template file. This is shown in Listing 16–3.

Listing 16–3. Excerpt from template_process() Where $classes Is Created from the $classes_array Variable

```php
<?php
function template_process(&$variables, $hook) {
  // Flatten out classes.
  $variables['classes'] = implode(' ', $variables['classes_array']);
}
?>
```

Listings 16–1 through 16–3 illustrate some of the flexibility and power that Drupal provides with preprocess and process functions as well as the order in which these functions occur. The most important thing to understand is that in the theme layer, you've got the last call on all of these variables. You can easily add, modify, and remove any variables you please by simply implementing preprocess and process functions in your theme; this will be covered in more detail in the following pages.

The big advantage of using preprocess functions is that they allow you to keep most of the logic outside of your template files. This allows for cleaner and easier to understand template files plus more efficient themes that are easier to maintain, manage, and extend over time. There are many changes you can make, such as affecting classes and modifying existing variables, that don't require any changes to template files at all—just a few simple lines of code.

Implementing Preprocess and Process Hooks

Preprocess functions are implemented by creating a function that is named in a certain way. Listing 16–4 shows an example of this naming convention.

Listing 16–4. Naming Convention for Preprocess and Process Hooks

```php
<?php
/**
 * Implements template_preprocess_THEMEHOOK().
 */
function HOOK_preprocess_THEMEHOOK(&$variables) {
  // Changes go here.
}

/**
 * Implements template_process_THEMEHOOK().
 */
function HOOK_process_THEMEHOOK(&$variables) {
  // Changes go here.
}
```

There are four points to consider in naming these functions:

1. The hook of a default implementation, usually created by a module, is "template." In all other implementations, the hook is replaced by the system name of the module or theme implementing it.

2. Which stage of the process do you want to affect? There are two options: the preprocess, which runs first, or process, which runs after all of the preprocess functions have been executed.

3. The theme hook matches the theme hook as defined in hook_theme(), which is ultimately output using either a theme function or a template file.

4. The &$variables parameter contains data needed by the theme function or template file rendering it. Since preprocess functions run before templates are rendered, you can make all sorts of changes and additions to its contents.

■ **Caution** By default, only theme hooks that have been explicitly defined in hook_theme() are able to use preprocess hooks. For example, hook_preprocess_node() is perfectly fine, but hook_preprocess_node__article() will not work. This is because node__article is a theme hook suggestion, which is a variation of a theme hook but is not actually a real theme hook.

Default Implementations

Listing 16–5 illustrates what a preprocess implementation for a default theme hook looks like, using template_preprocess_node(), which creates variables for the node.tpl.php template file as an example. This function resides in node.module along with a hook_theme() implementation, node_theme(), where it defines "node" as a theme hook.

Listing 16–5. Naming Convention for Default Implementations of Preprocess and Process Hooks

```php
<?php
function template_preprocess_node(&$variables) {
    // Changes go here.
    // See http://api.drupal.org/api/function/template_preprocess_node/7 for contents.
}

function template_process_node(&$variables) {
    // Changes go here.
    // See http://api.drupal.org/api/function/template_process_node/7 for contents.
}
```

■ **Tip** Browsing http://api.drupal.org and looking through the default implementations is a great way to learn how the variables were created.

Theme and Module Implementations

Both modules and themes are able to use preprocess functions in the same way, and a given theme hook can have many preprocess implementations, originating from both modules and themes. This introduces the opportunity for conflicts to occur, so keeping that in mind and knowing the order in which these functions run is important. Preprocess implementations from modules run first, and implementations by themes run last. When dealing with base and subthemes, the base theme will run first and the subtheme will run last. A good way to remember this is that the active theme always wins.

Preprocess functions implemented by Drupal core and modules reside in various files, such as `modulename.module` or `theme.inc`, and many others, while preprocess functions implemented by themes always reside in `template.php`.

As an example, implement a preprocess function for a theme called "dgd7" for the node theme hook. As shown in Listing 16–6, you simply place a function in `template.php` beginning with the theme name (the implementing hook), followed by `_preprocess_` and the theme hook, which in this case is "node." Finally, you pass in the `&$variables` parameter by reference (the & before the $ indicates a variable being passed by reference).

Listing 16–6. Implementation of template_preprocess_node() in a Theme

```php
<?php
/**
 * Implements template_process_node().
 */
function dgd7_preprocess_node(&$variables) {
  // Changes go here.
}
```

The code in Listing 16–6 is all that's needed, along with a quick cache clear, for Drupal to pick up your preprocess function and run it before rendering a node. Now the fun can begin!

Finding the Contents of $variables

The contents of the `$variables` array are different for each theme hook; even the contents of the same theme hook vary based on other factors, such as the view mode or user role.

The first thing to do after creating the function is to print the array and find out what's inside for you to work with. As explained in the "Finding Available Variables in the Theme Layer" section, using the `dpm()` function is a great way to do this, as shown in Listing 16–7.

Listing 16–7. Printing Variables to the Screen for Debugging Purposes

```php
<?php
/**
 * Implements template_preprocess_node().
 */
function dgd7_preprocess_node(&$variables) {
  dpm($variables);
}
```

■ **Caution** Debugging functions should only be used temporarily during development.

Preprocess Functions in Action

There are so many things you can change using preprocess functions that we can't possibly get into all of them. Now that you've got your preprocess function all set up and are aware of how to view existing variables, you are equipped with enough knowledge to start making some changes. Let's just jump right in and get started with a few practical examples of how to use preprocess functions.

Add Classes to Template Wrappers

In the DGD7 theme at http://definitivedrupal.org, the header, sidebar, and footer areas are black and the content area is white. In order to style the contents of each of those sections more easily, you can add a couple of helper classes to the region wrapper. To do this, you'll need to implement a preprocess function for the region theme hook in your template.php file; see Listing 16–8.

Listing 16–8. Adding Classes to Region Wrapper <div> Using the $classes_array Variable in

template_preprocess_region()

```php
<?php
/**
 * Implements template_preprocess_region().
 */
function dgd7_preprocess_region(&$variables) {
  $region = $variables['region'];
  // Sidebars and content area need a good class to style against. You should
  // not be using id's like #main or #main-wrapper to style contents.
  if (in_array($region, array('sidebar_first', 'sidebar_second', 'content'))) {
    $variables['classes_array'][] = 'main';
  }
  // Add a "clearfix" class to certain regions to clear floated elements inside them.
  if (in_array($region, array('footer', 'help', 'highlight'))) {
    $variables['classes_array'][] = 'clearfix';
  }
  // Add an "outer" class to the darker regions.
  if (in_array($region, array('header', 'footer', 'sidebar_first', 'sidebar_second'))) {
    $variables['classes_array'][] = 'outer';
  }
}
```

$variables['classes_array'] turns into $class in the process phase, and the class(es) added during preprocess are automatically modified as a result. So, just like that you've added a class to a region wrapper <div>.

The alternative in template files is lengthier. Adding logic to each affected template file would be required, which means you'd need to override the file, even if you didn't need to change the markup. If you have multiple template files for regions, the change would have to be made manually across all of them, which is clearly less efficient as you can see in Listing 16–9.

Listing 16–9. Adding Classes in Preprocess Functions Can Dramatically Increase the Efficiency of Your CSS

Code.

```css
/* Using classes and ID's provided by default. */
#header fieldset,
#footer fieldset,
```

```
.sidebar fieldset {
  border-color: #333
}

/* Using the class added in Listing 16-8, which is more efficient. */
.outer fieldset {
  border-color: #333;
}
```

■ **Tip** This example changes classes for the region template, but this technique can be applied to any of the major templates, including `html.tpl.php`, `block.tpl.php`, `node.tpl.php` and `comment.tpl.php` in their respective preprocess functions.

Making Changes to Nodes

Listing 16–10 demonstrates making three changes:

1. Drupal's page title prints in `page.tpl.php`. When a node title prints inside of the `node.tpl.php` file, it's usually because it's being viewed in teaser mode, and therefore, the node title is marked up with an `<h2>` by default. Usually, the content inside the node body also contains one or more `<h2>` tags. Adding a class to single out the node title can make styling easier. Listing 16–10 utilizes the `$title_attributes_array` to add a `node-title` class to help make styling easier.

2. When viewing a node that has a comment form directly under the node links, it doesn't make much sense to have an "Add new comment" link as well. In Listing 16–10, the comment links are hidden when the comment form is below it by using the `hide()` function, which will be covered in more detail later in this chapter.

3. Designs often call for differences when viewing the teaser of a node versus the full page. Listing 16–10 demonstrates using `$variables['teaser']` to suppress the `$submitted` information and truncate the node title to 70 characters when viewing in teaser mode.

Listing 16–10. Demonstrates Making Changes to the Display of Node Content During Preprocess

```php
<?php
/**
 * Implements template_preprocess_node().
 */
function dgd7_preprocess_node(&$variables) {
  // Give the <h2> containing the teaser node title a better class.
  $variables['title_attributes_array']['class'][] = 'node-title';

// Remove the "Add new comment" link when the form is below it.
  if (!empty($variables['content']['comments']['comment_form'])) {
    hide($variables['content']['links']['comment']);
  }
```

```
    // Make some changes when in teaser mode.
  if ($variables['teaser']) {
    // Don't display author or date information.
    $variables['display_submitted'] = FALSE;
    // Trim the node title and append an ellipsis.
    $variables['title'] = truncate_utf8($variables['title'], 70, TRUE, TRUE);
  }
}
```

Add a Change Picture Link Underneath the User Photo

As you've probably noticed by now, there are many variables available to you within the $variables array. These variables can be used to create new variables very easily. You know the path to edit a user profile is user/UID/edit, so you can use the information inside of $variables to determine whether or not the user viewing the page is the account holder. Once you've determined this, you can easily create a variable containing a link for the user to edit the photo everywhere it appears on the site by implementing template_preprocess_user_picture(), as shown in Listing 16–11. Once you do this, you'll be able to print it in the corresponding template, user-picture.tpl.php, as shown in Listing 16–12.

Listing 16–11. Creating a Custom Variable for the user-picture.tpl.php by Implementing

template_preprocess_user_picture().

```php
<?php
/**
 * Implements template_preprocess_user_picture().
 * - Add "change picture" link to be placed underneath the user image.
 */
function dgd7_preprocess_user_picture(&$vars) {
  // Create a variable with an empty string to prevent PHP notices when
  // attempting to print the variable
  $vars['edit_picture'] = '';
  // The account object contains the information of the user whose photo is
  // being processed. Compare that to the user id of the user object which
  // represents the currently logged in user.
  if ($vars['account']->uid == $vars['user']->uid) {
    // Create a variable containing a link to the user profile, with a class
    // "change-user-picture" to style against with CSS.
    $vars['edit_picture'] = l('Change picture', 'user/' . $vars['account']->uid . '/edit',
array(
      'fragment' => 'edit-picture',
      'attributes' => array('class' => array('change-user-picture')),
    )
  );
  }
}
```

Listing 16–12. Printing Your Custom Variable Into the user-picture.tpl.php File, Which You've Copied Into Your Theme to Override

```php
<?php if ($user_picture): ?>
  <div class="user-picture">
    <?php print $user_picture; ?>

    <?php print $edit_picture; ?>

  </div>
<?php endif; ?>
```

Using the Render API

What Is a Render Array?

Many of the variables in template files are straightforward, but you'll notice that some of the variables are printed along with a function called render(). Render arrays are structured arrays that contain nested data and other information needed by Drupal to turn them into HTML using Drupal's Render API. Variables that are render arrays are generally easy to spot in template files because they are printed using a function called render().

In page.tpl.php, you'll notice that all of the regions are printed using the render() function. Each region is an element (another array) nested inside the $page array. The code in Listing 16–13 is all that's needed to render each region. Each render() call returns fully formatted HTML for all the contents of the render array.

Listing 16–13. Printing Regions in page.tpl.php Using the render() Function

```php
<?php print render($page['sidebar_first']); ?>
```

In prior versions of Drupal, you would just include <?php print $sidebar_first; ?>, which contained a fully formatted HTML string ready for printing. This worked, of course, but it wasn't very flexible. Let's face it; there are only so many things you can do with a big glob of HTML markup at that stage.

In Drupal 7, these variables are sent to templates as nicely structured arrays. Instead of a glob of HTML markup, you get an array containing all sorts of information about the content inside it, down to attributes of specific links deep inside of it. This makes it incredibly easy to target specific content of the arrays and make any sort of changes you want to it at the last possible minute before it's rendered in the first place.

To find out what's inside this array, use the dpm() function provided with the Devel module to print it inside of page.tpl.php: <?php dpm($page['sidebar_first']); ?>. As you can see in Figure 16–4, there are two top-level render elements inside this array, the Search form block and the Navigation block, which are currently printing in the first sidebar.

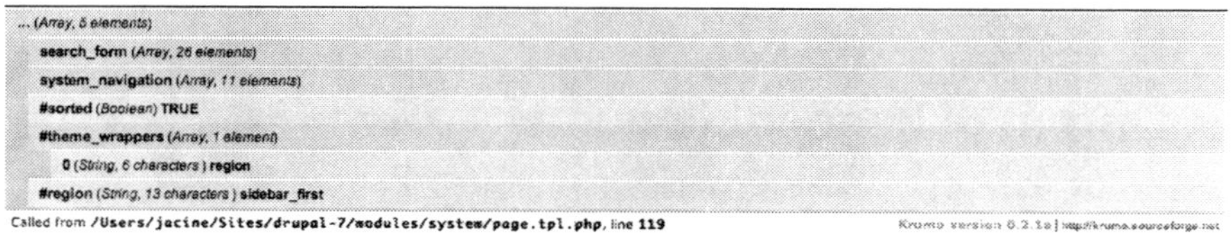

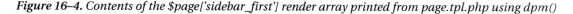

Figure 16–4. Contents of the $page['sidebar_first'] render array printed from page.tpl.php using dpm()

Identifying Render Elements

An easy way to identify arrays as render elements is the presence of properties. Render elements are always arrays, and they always contain properties that always begin with a hash tag. In Figure 16–4, you can immediately tell that $page['sidebar_first'] is a render element because it contains a few properties: #sorted, #theme_wrappers, and #region. These properties are used by drupal_render()which is called when using drupal_render() to determine how to render the output. For details about drupal_render() see http://api.drupal.org/api/function/render/7.

As themers, you won't be getting deep into the more developer-centric properties, but there are a few that will be helpful for you to make sense of out what these arrays mean. These are described in Table 16–1.

Table 16–1. Helpful Render Element Properties

Property	Description
#theme	Specifies the theme hook, which can be either a function or a template to use when rendering the element.
#theme_wrappers	An array containing theme hook(s) to be used to wrap the rendered children of the element. For example, when theming a block, the #theme property would be block and the #theme_wrappers property would contain region. This ensures that after the block(s) are rendered, the children would be run through the region template as well.
#type	The type of element that will be rendered. The default properties for element types are defined in hook_element_info() implementations.
#prefix & #suffix	A string containing markup to be placed before (prefix) or after (suffix) the rendered element.
#weight	A number that is used to sort the elements to determine the order in which they will print.
#sorted	A Boolean (TRUE or FALSE) that indicates whether or not the children have been sorted. For example, this is used in conjunction with the #weight property to sort the blocks in a region. When reordering blocks in a theme via hook_page_alter(), you'll need to specify #sorted => FALSE in addition to the #weight to trigger a new sort when you need to move a block to any other position than below the already sorted elements.
#attached	The #attached property is used to specify corresponding CSS, JavaScript, or libraries to load when the element is rendered.

See the documentation at http://api.drupal.org/api/function/drupal_render/7 for more information.

Manipulating the Output of Render Elements

As mentioned, having a structured array to work with is far more flexible than a bunch of HTML. This allows you to make only the changes you want to make with ease, whether big or small, without having to re-write code from scratch.

The prospect of using render arrays to generate markup and using alter hooks in general are completely new concepts to Drupal theme developers. It's very different than what you are used to, in a good way, but it takes some getting used to. In a lot of ways it's easier than creating templates and theme functions for one-off implementations. The biggest issues front-end developers face when using the Render API are:

1. Thinking about generating markup differently.

2. Figuring out how to modify the content of a render array.

3. Getting comfortable with implementing alter hooks.

Unlike theme hooks, render arrays are modified using alter hooks, not preprocess functions and templates. This can be confusing at first because render arrays are similar to theme hooks in that their purpose is to ultimately generate HTML markup, and they use templates and theme functions to do so. With render arrays, the #theme property, which allows you to define which theme function or template should be used to render the element, is just one of many properties used and can be changed at any time. In general, you'll use templates and theme functions to modify the markup itself, and you'll use alter hooks to modify contents, structure, or placement of the elements before it's rendered.

The following sections contain a few examples of things you can do with render arrays.

Generate New Content on the Fly

Generating new content is as simple as adding a new element to the page array. Listing 16–14 shows the addition of a new element called "new_stuff" to the pre-existing Highlighted region by implementing hook_page_alter() in a theme's template.php.

Listing 16–14. Adding a New Element to the Highlighted Region

```php
<?php
/**
 * Implements hook_page_alter().
 */
function mytheme_page_alter(&$page) {
  $page['highlighted']['new_stuff'] = array(
    '#type' => 'container',
    '#attributes' => array('class' => 'my-container'),
  );
  $page['highlighted']['new_stuff']['heading'] = array(
    '#type' => 'html_tag',
    '#tag' => 'h2',
    '#value' => t('Heading'),
    '#attributes' => array('id' => 'my-heading'),
  );
  $page['highlighted']['new_stuff']['list'] = array(
    '#theme' => 'item_list',
    '#items' => array(
      'First item',
      'Second item',
      'Third item',
    ),
  );
}
```

The first thing you did was name your new element "new_stuff," gave it a #type of container, and defined a class attribute of my-container. Note that container is an element, defined in system_element_info(), which uses the theme_container() theme function as a theme wrapper by default. This means the children of your element (heading and list) will be run through theme_container(). The resulting markup is shown in Listing 16–15.

Listing 16–15. The Output Generated for $page['highlighted']['new_stuff'] by theme_container()

```
<div class="my-container">
  ...
</div>
```

Then you added a subelement called "heading" and specified the #type element property as html_tag. This will cause the element to use theme_html_tag() when rendering. You also specified #tag, #value, and #attributes properties. These are parameters of the theme_html_tag() function as you can see at http://api.drupal.org/api/function/theme_html_tag/7. The resulting markup is shown in Listing 16–16.

Listing 16–16. The Output Generated for $page['highlighted']['new_stuff']['heading'] by theme_html_tag()

```
<h2 id="my-heading">Heading</h2>
```

Finally, you added a subelement called "list." Here you specified item_list as the #theme property and included an array containing your #items, which is a required parameter for theme_item_list(). The resulting markup is shown in Listing 16–17.

Listing 16–17. The Output Generated for $page['highlighted']['new_stuff']['list'] by theme_item_list()

```
<div class="item-list">
  <ul>
    <li class="first">First item</li>
    <li>Second item</li>
    <li class="last">Third item</li>
  </ul>
</div>
```

When the Highlighted region is rendered, the code in Listing 16–14 produces the final result shown in Listing 16–18.

Listing 16–18. The Final Rendered Result of Listing 16–14

```
<div class="my-container">
  <h2 id="my-heading">Heading</h2>
  <div class="item-list">
    <ul>
      <li class="first">First item</li>
      <li>Second item</li>
      <li class="last">Third item</li>
    </ul>
  </div>
</div>
```

■ **Caution** The previous examples are meant to illustrate how the Render API works to generate content. However, it's worth noting that it should not be abused to output every piece of HTML on a page as separate elements because there can be serious performance implications. Using the `markup` `#type` is preferred for small bits of markup, such as headings, instead of `html_tag`, as it requires the `theme_html_tag()` theme function to determine the output.

Move Content from One Region to Another

Inside a hook_page_alter() implementation, you can move the content of regions around at will. Listing 16–19 contains a few simple lines of code that move the contents of the entire first sidebar to the second sidebar, which results in the layout changing from a left sidebar layout to a right sidebar layout on full node pages. In Listing 16–19, you've also moved the breadcrumbs to the bottom of the footer region.

Listing 16–19. Relocating the sidebar_first Region to sidebar_second and Adding Breadcrumbs to a New Element in the Footer Region

```php
<?php
/**
 * Implements hook_page_alter().
 */
function dgd7_page_alter(&$page) {
  // Check that you are viewing a full page node.
  if (node_is_page(menu_get_object())) {
    // Assign the contents of sidebar_first to sidebar_second.
    $page['sidebar_second'] = $page['sidebar_first'];
    // Unset sidebar_first.
    unset($page['sidebar_first']);
  }

  // Add the breadcrumbs to the bottom of the footer region.
$page['footer']['breadcrumbs'] = array(
    '#type' => 'container',
    '#attributes' => array('class' => array('breadcrumb-wrapper', 'clearfix')),
    '#weight' => 10,
  );
  $page['footer']['breadcrumbs']['breadcrumb'] = array(
    '#theme' => 'breadcrumb',
    '#breadcrumb' => drupal_get_breadcrumb(),
  );
  // Trigger the contents of the region to be re-sorted.
  $page['footer']['#sorted'] = FALSE;
}
```

Altering Content Inside a Render Array

Altering the contents of a render array to change bits and pieces of the actual content is where you get into a very gray area. It could be argued that a change like this belongs inside a module. When making changes like this, it's important to ask yourself whether or not the changes you are making should still apply when the theme you are developing is not active. Listing 16–20 changes the View and Edit tabs to read Profile and Edit profile on user profile pages.

Listing 16–20. Implements hook_menu_local_tasks_alter() to Change Tab Names on User Profile Pages

```php
<?php
/**
 * Implements hook_menu_local_tasks_alter().
 */
function dgd7_menu_local_tasks_alter(&$data, $router_item, $root_path) {
  if ($root_path == 'user/%') {
    // Change the first tab title from 'View' to 'Profile'.
    if ($data['tabs'][0]['output'][0]['#link']['title'] == t('View')) {
      $data['tabs'][0]['output'][0]['#link']['title'] = t('Profile');
    }
    // Change the second tab title from 'Edit' to 'Edit profile'.
    if ($data['tabs'][0]['output'][1]['#link']['title'] == t('Edit')) {
      $data['tabs'][0]['output'][1]['#link']['title'] = t('Edit profile');
    }
  }
}
```

Notable Render Arrays in Core Templates

There are quite a few render array variables scattered across core templates that are worth noting. hook_page_alter() contains the entire page so it can always be used to alter anything. However, finding that particular anything is not always trivial as other modules can move stuff around, so using more specific alters is advised. Table 16–2 is a quick reference of notable render arrays. This is by no means a full list, but it covers quite a bit and should give you an idea of how to begin figuring out where to look to edit these things.

Table 16–2. Notable Render Arrays in Core Templates

Variable	Found in	Alter Hook	Description
$page	page.tpl.php	hook_page_alter()	Contains the entire page from regions down to fields and comments.
$content	node.tpl.php, comment.tpl.php, taxonomy-term.tpl.php	hook_node_view_alter(), hook_comment_view_alter(), hook_taxonomy_term_view_alter()	Contains the contents of each entity. For more details see http://api.drupal.org/hook_entity_view_alter.
$tabs	page.tpl.php	hook_menu_local_tasks_alter()	Contains primary and secondary tabs, themable via theme_menu_local_tasks() and theme_menu_local_task().

Variable	Found in	Alter Hook	Description
`$action_links`	`page.tpl.php`	`hook_menu_local_tasks_alter()`	Contains action links, themable via `theme_menu_local_actions()`.
`$item`	`field.tpl.php`	`hook_field_display_alter()` and `hook_field_display_ENTITY_TYPE_alter()`	Contains display settings for fields, which can adjust label settings or control the formatter used to display the contents of `field.tpl.php`.

Introducing render(), hide(), and show()

One of the best new theming features of Drupal 7 is the ability to selectively render bits of content in templates. As detailed in the previous sections, the content of some variables (render arrays) is sent to templates as structured arrays instead of chunks of HTML. This is really awesome news for the theme layer.

To understand just how awesome this is, you need to look into the past. In prior versions of Drupal, theming complex nodes with fields wasn't the easiest task. Fields were lumped into the $content variable, and while they could be printed and manipulated individually, there were issues. You had to be very careful to properly sanitize variables, and once you decided to break up the content variable, you needed to rebuild it entirely. This was not future-proof, as the addition of new fields would often require going back to the template file and printing the new field.

In Drupal 7, those problems have been solved quite gracefully. You now have the ability to very easily render individual pieces of content, such as fields, with three new functions called render(), hide(), and show(). They can be used inside theme functions and templates files as well as preprocess and process functions. All three of these functions take a single argument, which is the element (or child) you wish to target.

- *hide():* Hides a render element or part of a render element by tricking drupal_render() into thinking it has already been printed. Example usage:

  ```php
  <?php hide($element['something']); ?>
  ```

- *show():* Does the opposite of hide(). It can be useful to revert a previously applied hide() status. Example usage:

  ```php
  <?php show($element['something']); ?>
  ```

- *render():* Converts a render array to HTML markup. It returns HTML, so it should be used along with print in templates. Example usage:

  ```php
  <?php print render($element); ?>
  ```

To illustrate these functions in action, look at node.tpl.php (see Listing 16–21).

Listing 16–21. Excerpt from the Default node.tpl.php Template

```php
<div id="node-<?php print $node->nid; ?>" class="<?php print $classes; ?> clearfix"<?php print
$attributes; ?>>
  <?php print $user_picture; ?>
  <?php print render($title_prefix); ?>
  <?php if (!$page): ?>
    <h2<?php print $title_attributes; ?>><a href="<?php print $node_url; ?>"><?php print
$title; ?></a></h2>
  <?php endif; ?>
  <?php print render($title_suffix); ?>
  <?php if ($display_submitted): ?>
    <div class="submitted">
      <?php print $submitted; ?>
    </div>
  <?php endif; ?>
  <div class="content"<?php print $content_attributes; ?>>
    <?php
      // Hide the comments and links now. so they can be rendered later.
      hide($content['comments']);
      hide($content['links']);
      print render($content);
    ?>
  </div>
  <?php print render($content['links']); ?>
  <?php print render($content['comments']); ?>
</div>
```

As you can see in Listing 16–21, this template is already making use of both render() and hide()
functions out of the box. There are three render arrays in this node template: $title_prefix,
$title_suffix, and $content. Inside the <div class="content"> wrapper, both $content['links'] and
$content['comments'] are hidden using hide(), and then $content is rendered directly underneath.

The reason that the comments and links are hidden is to break them out of the $content variable
and allow them to be placed outside of the <div class="content"> wrapper. Both of the items are then
rendered afterward using render() individually.

Of course, the fun doesn't have to stop at top-level variables. These functions work as deep into the
array as you can go. As long as you pass in a proper render element (see the "Render API" section), you'll
be able to manipulate it with these functions.

As an example, say you wanted to hide the "Add new comment" link when viewing a node that has a
comment form on the page you're viewing. You can simply check to see if the form exists in your array,
and then hide that specific link group (comment). The code in Listing 16–22 demonstrates how to do
this.

Listing 16–22. Hiding the "Add new comment" Link when the Comment Form Is Present

```php
<?php
// Hide the "Add new comment" link when the comment form is present.
if (!empty($vars['content']['comments']['comment_form'])) {
  hide($vars['content']['links']['comment']);
}
// Print the rendered links afterward.
print render($content['links']);
```

Because the show() function resets the print status but does not print anything, it can be helpful to revert a previously applied hide(). In most cases, you'll likely just use render() because it will allow you to print the element as many times as you need, as shown in Listing 16–23.

Listing 16–23. Hiding the "Add new comment" Link when the Comment Form Is Present, but Showing It Again if Some Other Condition Is Met

```php
<?php
// Hide the "Add new comment" link when the comment form is present.
if (!empty($content['comments']['comment_form'])) {
  hide($content['links']['comment']);
  if ($some_exception) {
    show($content['links']['comment']);
  }
}
// Print the rendered links afterward.
print render($content['links']);
```

■ **Tip** For complex templates, this code begins to get very messy in templates files. In those situations, it's best to do these operations in preprocess or process functions in order to keep your templates clean and more manageable.

Theming Forms

Theming forms is a little different than working with the usual template file or theme function. Form markup is generated using Drupal's Form API. This makes it really easy for modules to build forms and guarantees consistency among generated elements. While the process of theming forms is quite different from what most front-end developers are used to, we think you'll begin to appreciate the consistency and flexibility of theming Drupal's forms.

One thing Drupal is famous for is the ability to accomplish a single task in many different ways. Although none of Drupal's forms ship with template files, they can easily be made to use them. Forms can also use preprocess functions, process functions, and alter hooks. So, how do you know when to use one over the other? This section will explain how forms are generated and will present a couple of examples using each method.

How Form Markup Is Generated

Forms are generated by modules. The simple function shown in Listing 16–24 is all that is required to generate form markup. It looks really easy, doesn't it? It is. Of course, there is more to the process to make it functional, such as validating the form and saving the submitted values, but the rest is not your concern in the theme layer. What's important to you is the structure of a form and how it's transformed from the $form array to actual markup.

Listing 16–24. A Simple Unsubscribe Form

```php
<?php
function exampleform_unsubscribe(&$form, $form_state) {
  $form['email'] = array(
    '#type' => 'textfield',
    '#title' => t('E-mail address'),
    '#required' => TRUE,
  );
  $form['submit'] = array(
    '#type' => 'submit',
    '#value' => t('Remove me!'),
  );
  return $form;
}
```

In Listing 16–24, you define a very simple form with two elements: a textfield for the e-mail address and a Submit button. When rendered, the result looks like those in Figure 16–5. The resulting markup is shown in Listing 16–25.

E-mail address *

Remove me!

Figure 16–5. Rendered form based on the code from Listing 16–24

Listing 16–25. The Markup Generated by Drupal for the exampleform_unsubscribe() form in Listing 16–24

```html
<form action="/example/unsubscribe" method="post" id="exampleform-unsubscribe" accept-
charset="UTF-8">
  <div>
    <div class="form-item form-type-textfield form-item-email">
      <label for="edit-email">E-mail address
        <span class="form-required" title="This field is required.">*</span>
      </label>
      <input type="text" id="edit-email" name="email" value="" size="60" maxlength="128"
class="form-text required" />
    </div>
    <input type="submit" id="edit-submit" name="op" value="Remove me!" class="form-submit" />
    <input type="hidden" name="form_build_id" value="form-jKkl1KLWJLnvOhM4DSVd8-
4OboTgBQAzWWhUn44c15Q" />
    <input type="hidden" name="form_token" value="LBO7DqsDXK9idWdOHLxUen7jKxm52JqTyHiR7-pNumA"
/>
    <input type="hidden" name="form_id" value="exampleform_unsubscribe" />
  </div>
</form>
```

Form API Elements and Default Properties

In the exampleform_unsubscribe() form, you've defined two form elements: the e-mail address and the submit element. The e-mail element's #type property is textfield, which provides a single line text input. The submit element's #type is submit, which is the Form API equivalent of <input type="submit" />.

If you look closely at the generated markup in Listing 16–25, you'll see that you only set two properties in each element, but your markup ended up with some additional attributes. This is because Drupal assigns a default set of properties to each element. In this case, you are using form, textfield, and submit elements, which are defined in system_element_info(), as shown in Listing 16–26. When the form is processed, Drupal merges the properties defined in the form with the default properties.

Listing 16–26. Default Element Properties As Defined in system_element_info() for Textfield and Submit Elements

```php
<?php
$types['form'] = array(
  '#method' => 'post',
  '#action' => request_uri(),
  '#theme_wrappers' => array('form'),
);
$types['textfield'] = array(
  '#input' => TRUE,
  '#size' => 60,
  '#maxlength' => 128,
  '#autocomplete_path' => FALSE,
  '#process' => array('ajax_process_form'),
  '#theme' => 'textfield',
  '#theme_wrappers' => array('form_element'),
);
$types['submit'] = array(
  '#input' => TRUE,
  '#name' => 'op',
  '#button_type' => 'submit',
  '#executes_submit_callback' => TRUE,
  '#limit_validation_errors' => FALSE,
  '#process' => array('ajax_process_form'),
  '#theme_wrappers' => array('button'),
);
```

▓ **Tip** This form only touches on a few of form elements, but Drupal has many of them. For a full list of elements available through the Form API and their default properties, see

http://api.drupal.org/api/file/developer/topics/forms_api_reference.html/7.

Rendering of Form Elements

The element properties contain critical information required to render them. Of these properties, two are very important in the theme layer: #theme and #theme_wrappers. When it's time to render the form, these properties tell Drupal which theme functions to use. There's also the option to use the #pre_render property to define a function(s) that should run prior to rendering.

- #theme: Specifies the theme function to use when rendering the element.

- #theme_wrappers: Specifies a theme function or functions that should be used to wrap the rendered children of the element.

To illustrate this process, let's use the $form['email'] field from the previous form to walk through the process:

1. theme('textfield', array('element' => $form['email'])) is called. This results in the following markup:

```
<input type="text" id="edit-email" name="email" value="" size="60" maxlength="128"
class="form-text required" />
```

2. theme('form_element', array('element' => $form['email'])) is called. This results in the following markup:

```
<div class="form-item form-type-textfield form-item-email">
  <label for="edit-email">E-mail address
    <span class="form-required" title="This field is required.">*</span>
  </label>
  <input type="text" id="edit-email" name="email" value="" size="60" maxlength="128"
class="form-text required" />
  <!-- RESULT OF THE RENDERED TEXTFIELD -->
</div>
```

3. Finally, after all of the form elements are rendered, the form itself is run through theme_form(), which is specified as the #theme_wrappers in the form element. The theme_form() function takes care of generating the rest of the form markup, including the hidden elements form_build_id, form_token, and form_id.

■ **Caution** As mentioned previously, you never use theme_ to call a theme function directly, and similarly theme functions are entered in #theme and #theme_wrappers without the prefix theme_.

First Steps for Theming Forms

Find the Form ID

Before you can do anything, you'll need to find the ID of the form you're working with. It appears in the following two places in the markup of every form:

1. There's a hidden field near the bottom of the form named form_id that contains what you're looking for.

```
<input type="hidden" name="form_id" value="exampleform_unsubscribe" />
```

2. Although it's not copy/paste ready because it contains dashes instead of underscores to separate words, the `<form>`'s ID attribute also contains the form ID.

    ```
    <form id="exampleform-unsubscribe">
    ```

Each Form ID has a corresponding function, which follows Drupal module naming conventions. In this example, exampleform is the module name and unsubscribe is what the form is named by the module.

Sometimes it helps to look at the original form and code comments when theming. You'll often find the original function that generates the form in the `.module` file of the module that created the form. If you find that the form doesn't exist in the `.module` file, it's definitely inside the module somewhere, but you may have to look around. Sometimes developers use `.inc` files for organization and code efficiency purposes.

Implement hook_theme()

In order to be able to use template files, preprocess, or process functions with forms, the first thing you'll need to do is register the form ID as a theme hook. This is necessary so that Drupal knows about the theme hook. Drupal core does this for some forms in core, mostly for administrative forms that use tables, but chances are you'll need to do this manually.

In your theme's `template.php` file, you'll create an implementation of hook_theme(), with your theme's name in place of the hook prefix. As an example, you'll theme the contact form located at `/contact` when the Contact module is enabled, whose form ID is `contact_site_form`. Inside you'll specify the form ID as the key and the render element as form, as shown in Listing 16–27. The render element key is required for theme hooks that use the render API to generate markup, such as forms. Its value indicates the name of the variable that holds renderable element, which in this case is form.

Listing 16–27. A hook_theme() Implementation that Defines the contact_site_form() Theme Hook As Render Element "form"

```php
<?php
/**
* Implements hook_theme().
*/
function THEMENAME_theme() {
  return array(
    // Defines the form ID as a theme hook.
    'contact_site_form' => array(
      // Specifies 'form' as a render element.
      'render element' => 'form',
    ),
  );
}
```

After doing this and clearing the cache, you'll be able to create a theme function and use preprocess and process functions for this form, which you'll get into later in the chapter.

Tip When registering theme hooks, if you are unsure what to enter, look at some of the default implementations. In this case, you are dealing with a form, so a quick look at `http://api.drupal.org/api /function/drupal_common_theme/7` reveals the defaults for the original form theme hook, which are exactly what you need here.

Theming Forms with Theme Functions

The decision of whether to use a theme function or a template file is a personal/team preference. If you're comfortable using PHP, you might be inclined to use theme functions. If not, you'll probably prefer a template file, which is explained in the next section.

As discussed above, you'll need a hook_theme() implementation, without a template or path index, as shown in Listing 16–28. After doing this, `hook_contact_site_form()` is an official theme hook that can be overridden like any other theme function. Even though a theme_contact_site_form() function doesn't exist, you still name it as you would any other theme function override: THEMENAME_contact_site_form().

Listing 16–28. *The Basic Required Code for Theming a Form with a Theme Function*

```php
<?php
/**
 * Implements hook_theme().
 */
function dgd7_theme() {
  return array(
    'contact_site_form' => array(
      'render element' => 'form',
    ),
  );
}

/**
 * Implements theme_forms_contact_site_form().
 */
function dgd7_contact_site_form($variables) {
  // Renders all elements of a form.
  return drupal_render_children($variables['form']);
}
```

Using drupal_render_children() Is a Must!

drupal_render_children() takes care of rendering all of the children of the form. This function alone will result in the exact same code Drupal would have provided without your theme function, which makes the function in Listing 16–28 pretty useless by itself, but it's worth stressing that it's VERY important to always use drupal_render_children($variables['form']) at the bottom of your function.

Even if you call render() on every element you have added to the form, Drupal will have added some important hidden elements identifying the form and those need to be rendered, too. So calling drupal_render_children($form) at the end of the theme function is mandatory. This won't re-print $form['foo'] because drupal_render() knows it has printed already. As an added bonus, it will take care of any additional elements added by other modules.

Manipulating Form Elements in Theme Functions

Now that you've gotten that out of the way, let's make some changes to the markup. Just like any theme function, the code this function returns will be inserted directly into the page markup. Since forms are render elements you need to render them. The code in Listing 16–29, does the following:

1. Changes the labels of the name and mail elements.

2. Renders the name and mail elements individually.

3. Arranges the markup and individually rendered elements in a variable called $output.

4. Includes drupal_render_children($form) in the $output at the bottom of the theme function.

5. Finally, it returns the $output.

Listing 16–29. Implements theme_contact_site_form()

```php
<?php
/**
 * Implements theme_contact_site_form().
 */
function dgd7_contact_site_form($variables) {

  // Hide the subject field. It's not required.
  hide($variables['form']['subject']);

  // Change the labels of the "name" and "mail" textfields.
  $variables['form']['name']['#title'] = t('Name');
  $variables['form']['mail']['#title'] = t('E-mail');

  // Create output any way you want.
  $output = '<div class="something">';
  $output .= '<p class="note">'. t("We'd love hear from you. Expect to hear back from us in 1-2 business days.") .'</p>';
  $output .= render($variables['form']['name']);
  $output .= render($variables['form']['mail']);
  $output .= '</div>';

  // Be sure to include a rendered version of the remaining form items.
  $output .= drupal_render_children($variables['form']);

  // Return the output.
  return $output;
}
```

Forms and their contents are render elements, so you can use hide(), show(), and render() functions to manipulate the elements of the form. When using hide() or making changes to the form array inside the theme function, you'll need to make sure you do so before attempting to render. There are a lot of other things that can be done here. We can't possibly cover all of them, but here are a few quick examples of what can be done:

- Adjust the #weight property of an element to change the order in which they print. The following code would cause the message element to print at the top of the form:

```
$variables['form']['message']['#weight'] = -10;
$variables['form']['message']['#sorted'] = FALSE;
```

- Add a description underneath an element by setting the element #description property, like so:

```
$variables['form']['mail']['#description'] = t("We won't share your e-mail
with anyone.");
```

- Set the default value of form element, such as checking the "Send yourself a copy" checkbox, by default setting the #checked property to TRUE, like so:

```
$variables['form']['copy']['#checked'] = TRUE;
```

- Unset the #theme_wrappers property to remove the label and wrapper <div> and re-create the markup exactly the way you want it, like so:

```
unset($variables['form']['mail']['#theme_wrappers']);
```

- More advanced changes include making the form display in a table by using the theme_table() function.

- ... and so on!

■ **Tip** Using theme functions over templates is slightly faster performance-wise, but the difference is very minimal. Performance isn't something you should worry about when deciding whether to use a template file over a theme function.

Theming Forms with Template Files

Creating template files for forms is surprisingly easy given what you've already learned. As mentioned in the "First Steps for Theming Forms" section, you'll need to open template.php and implement a hook_theme() function. Instead of just defining the render element, you'll need to add two more things, as shown in Listing 16–30:

1. A path key (optional) that contains the path to where the template file is located in your theme.

2. A template key that contains the name of the template file, without the .tpl.php suffix.

▨ **Caution** Template files defined this way are not auto-discovered. If the path is omitted, Drupal will only look for your template file in the root of the theme. Specifying the path of the template directory is only required if your file exists in a subdirectory of your theme.

Listing 16–30. hook_theme() Implementation for Using Templates with Forms

```php
<?php
/**
 * Implements hook_theme().
 */
function mytheme_theme() {
  return array(
    'contact_site_form' => array(
      'render element' => 'form',
      'path' => drupal_get_path('theme', 'mytheme') . '/templates',
      'template' => 'contact-site-form',
    ),
  );
}
```

After creating the hook_theme() function shown in Listing 16–30, you'll need to create the template file. In this case, it's located in the templates directory within your theme:

sites/all/themes/mytheme/templates/contact-site-form.tpl.php.

Once that's complete, simply clear the cache and Drupal will begin using your template file.

If there's nothing in your file to begin with, you'll get a blank page where the form used to be. The first thing you should do is add this line back to the template file: <?php print drupal_render_children($form); ?>. This will get the entire form back, and even though you may not want to keep everything in the form, you need to print the contents of this at the bottom of the form to ensure everything works properly as we detailed in the "Using drupal_render_children() is a Must!" section.

Manipulating Form Elements in Template Files

For the sake of covering this topic in detail, let's use the example from the "Manipulating Form Elements in Theme Functions" section. The code in Listing 16–31 represents the result of completing the following tasks:

1. Changing the labels for the name and mail elements.

2. Rendering the name and mail elements individually.

3. Arranging your markup and individually rendered elements as you want them.

4. Finally, printing drupal_render_children($form) at the bottom of the template.

Listing 16–31. contact-site-form.tpl.php Implementation of the Contact Form

```php
<?php // Change the labels of the "name" and "mail" textfields.
$form['name']['#title'] = t('Name');
$form['mail']['#title'] = t('E-mail');
```

```
?>
```

```php
<?php // Render the "name" and "mail" elements individually and add markup. ?>
<div class="name-and-email">
  <p><?php print t("We'd love hear from you. Expect to hear back from us in 1-2 business
days.") ?></p>
  <?php print render($form['name']); ?>
  <?php print render($form['mail']); ?>
</div>

<?php // Be sure to render the remaining form items. ?>
<?php print drupal_render_children($form); ?>
```

While there are slight differences, it's mostly the same (with less PHP). All of the possibilities that apply in theme functions apply just as well in template files. The variables themselves are slightly different. In theme functions and preprocess functions, the name element would be located in $variables['form']['name']. In template files, that same variable would be $form['name']. This is done specifically to make Drupal's monster arrays easier on template authors.

■ **Caution** Be sure not to hide or omit required form elements. In Drupal, presentation is totally separate from form processing. Drupal will expect those elements and prevent the form from being submitted if they are not filled in. These types of changes should be done in a hook_form_alter() implementation, using the #access property. See the "Modifying Forms Using Alter Hooks" section and Chapter 22 for more information.

Keep Your Template Cleaner with Preprocess Functions

In our example of theming a form with a template file, the template is quite messy. The definition of a clean template file is one that contains hardly any logic and that simply prints variables and maybe an occasional IF statement. If you are dissatisfied with the appearance of the template file, this is a perfect opportunity to use preprocess functions. To make this really clean, you'd do the following in a preprocess function:

■ Perform all modifications to the form array.

Create any new variables.

Render each field individually and provide easy variables for templates.

Of course, this is not something you'd want to do on every form on your site. However, it's very useful and convenient for highly styled user-facing forms that you want to take extra care to get right, such as the login, registration, and contact forms. The process of doing this is very easy, as demonstrated in Listing 16–32 with the contact form.

Listing 16–32. Using a Preprocess Function to Do the Heavy Lifting for the Template

```php
<?php
/**
 * Implements hook_preprocess_contact_site_form().
 */
function mytheme_preprocess_contact_site_form(&$variables) {
```

```
  // Shorten the form variable name for easier access.
  $form = $variables['form'];

  // Change labels for the 'mail' and 'name' elements.
  $form['name']['#title'] = t('Name');
  $form['mail']['#title'] = t('E-mail');

  // Create a new variable for your note.
  $variables['note'] = t("We'd love hear from you. Expect to hear back from us in 1-2 business
days.");

  // Create variables for individual elements.
  $variables['name'] = render($form['name']);
  $variables['email'] = render($form['mail']);
  $variables['subject'] = render($form['subject']);
  $variables['message'] = render($form['message']);
  $variables['copy'] = render($form['copy']);

  // Be sure to print the remaining rendered form items.
  $variables['children'] = drupal_render_children($form);
}
```

Because you've done all the work in the preprocess function, the template file in Listing 16–33 is crispy clean. Adding markup and classes and moving elements around is a piece of cake, and it's very easy to see what this template file does at first glance.

Listing 16–33. A Preprocess Function Can Provide a Clean, Minimal Template for the Contact Form.

```
<p class="note"><?php print $note; ?></p>
<p><span class="form-required">*</span> <?php print t("Denotes required fields."); ?></p>
<ol>
  <li><?php print $name; ?></li>
  <li><?php print $email; ?></li>
  <li><?php print $subject; ?></li>
  <li><?php print $message; ?></li>
  <li><?php print $copy; ?></li>
</ol>
<?php print $children; ?>
```

Modifying Forms Using Alter Hooks

The ability of themes to use alter hooks is new in Drupal 7. Templates are great for situations where you want to have a lot of control over the markup itself, but there are quite a few situations where simply using hook_form_alter() can make things a lot easier, especially if you are comfortable with Drupal's form markup either by default, or in combination with changes you can make site-wide via theme functions. Using an alter hook is perfect for quick changes like:

- Simple changes to form labels, descriptions, and other properties.

- Changing the order in which the form elements print using the #weight property.

- Wrapping a few elements in a <div> or <fieldset>.

- Hiding or removing form elements that are not required.

- Adding some markup to a form.

It's also arguably easier because there are fewer steps involved in the process. You don't need to implement hook_theme(). You also get full control over the elements. There are certain limitations to the changes you can make within theme functions, as it's already too late in the process.

Technically, there are two hooks you can use.

■ hook_form_alter(): Runs for all forms.

hook_form_FORM_ID_alter(): Runs for a specific form ID.

There are reasons for using hook_form_alter() over hook_form_FORM_ID_alter() all the time, but those reasons mainly apply to the tasks a module developer needs to perform. Unless you are specifically targeting more than one form to do the same thing, as shown in Listing 16–34, it's probably best to use hook_form_FORM_ID_alter(), as shown in Listing 16–35.

Listing 16–34. Implementation of hook_form_alter() to Target all or Multiple Forms

```php
<?php
/**
 * Implements hook_form_alter().
 */
function mytheme_form_alter(&$form, &$form_state, $form_id) {
  // Changes made in here affect ALL forms.
  if (!empty($form['title']) && $form['title']['#type'] == 'textfield') {
    $form['title']['#size'] = 40;
  }
}
```

Listing 16–35. Implementation of hook_form_FORM_ID_alter() to Target a Specific Form

```php
<?php
/**
 * Implements hook_form_FORM_ID_alter().
 */
function mytheme_form_contact_site_form_alter(&$form, &$form_state) {
  // Add a #markup element containing your note and make it display at the top.
  $form['note']['#markup'] = t("We'd love hear from you. Expect to hear back from us in 1-2
business days.");
  $form['note']['#weight'] = -1;

  // Change labels for the 'mail' and 'name' elements.
  $form['name']['#title'] = t('Name');
  $form['mail']['#title'] = t('E-mail');

  // Hide the subject field and give it a standard subject for value.
  $form['subject']['#type'] = 'hidden';
  $form['subject']['#value'] = t('Contact Form Submission');

}
```

Managing CSS Files

Every good Drupal theme needs a stylesheet or two, or ten! You might be caught off guard by the sheer number of CSS files that Drupal loads, before you even start on your theme. Being the modular framework that it is, Drupal uses that same approach for CSS stylesheets and JavaScript files. CSS and JavaScript files are provided separately by module—and sometimes a few per module. This is done on purpose for the following reasons:

- It's easier to read and understand the purpose of the code and what module it belongs to.

- It allows Drupal to load only the code needed on a given page.

- It's easier for Drupal to maintain these files and their contents.

That said, in Drupal's theme layer you have full control over all stylesheets and scripts. You can do whatever you want with them, literally. If you decide you don't want to load any stylesheets from modules, you can remove them all. If you aren't happy with a few files, you can override them individually by removing them or override them and change the contents within the theme. You can even change the order in which the files load if you want to. This section will show you how to do all of that.

Aggregation and Compression

As mentioned, Drupal has many stylesheets. Of course, you want to keep the number of files at a minimum on your live sites for performance reasons, so Drupal has a way of handling this. During development, it's normal to deal with anywhere from 10-40 CSS files, and even more if you are working on sites in languages that display text in right-to-left order. In the Performance section at `admin/config/development/performance` there are options to aggregate and compress CSS and JavaScript files. When turned on, Drupal will minify and combine the files into as few automatically generated files as possible. This also effectively works around the Internet Explorer 31 stylesheet limit bug. Drupal aggregates files in two ways: it creates a per-site aggregation file from files that would be loaded on every page, and it creates a per-page aggregation files for the remaining files that are conditionally loaded depending on the page. For CSS files, it further aggregates by media type. To remain correct, if the contents of CSS and JavaScript files are changed, when the site cache is cleared Drupal will regenerate the aggregated versions of the files and give them a different name. Enabling aggregation and compression for CSS files on all live sites is highly recommended, as it will speed up page loads quite a bit. This process is very effective and allows themers and developers to continue developing sites in a modular manner, without having to worry about the number of CSS files.

■ **Caution** Do NOT use the `@import` directive to load CSS files manually within Drupal. Doing so will cause performance and possible aggregation issues when combined with `<link>`'ed stylesheets and will cause the files to be excluded from override features.

Patterns and Naming Conventions

In your theme, you are free to name your CSS files whatever you want. Many themes tend to create a directory called "css" in which they place a few stylesheets. It's very common to create a `layout.css` for page layout styles and `style.css` for the rest. Some themes, like Zen, take it much further with almost 30 stylesheets. How you decide to organize your CSS is completely up to you. There are no restrictions on how many stylesheets a theme can have. Most front-end developers have their own way of working, and Drupal is happy to oblige.

Core and Module CSS Files

Most modules that provide CSS will typically include a file in the root of the module directory called `module-name.css`. Some of the modules have a few CSS files, and the better modules create a separate file for any CSS used to style the administrative user interface. Modules are not restricted to any number or specific organization of CSS files, but developers are generally urged to be conservative and style elements as little as possible.

It's also worth mentioning that Drupal's System module, located in `modules/system`, contains quite a few CSS files that seem to all be dumped there because there is no better place to put them. Table 16–3 is a quick description of each, so you have an idea of what their purpose is and can decide whether or not to keep them in your theme.

Table 16–3. System Module's CSS files, Excluding RTL Versions

CSS File	Purpose	Loads...
system.base.css	Contains CSS that is heavily relied upon by JavaScript for certain functionality, including collapsible fieldsets, autocomplete fields, resizable textareas, and progress bars.	Every page.
system.theme.css	Contains general styles for many generic HTML and Drupal elements.	Every page.
system.menus.css	Contains default styling for menu tree lists, tabs, and node links.	Every page.
system.messages.css	Contains default styling for error, warning, and status messages.	Every page.
system.admin.css	Contains styles needed on administrative pages throughout Drupal.	Admin pages.
system.maintenance.css	Contains styles for installation, maintenance, and update tasks.	Maintenance pages.

Bi-Directional Text Support

One of the things Drupal is known for is its superb language support. This includes bi-directional text support. While most languages display text from left-to-right (LTR) on screen, certain languages, such as Arabic and Hebrew, display text from right-to-left (RTL) on screen. Browsers handle much of the styling differences needed by reading the dir attribute defined in the <html> tag and using User Agent CSS files, but many times CSS floats, text alignment, and padding need to be accounted for in CSS, especially when you are running a site with multiple languages.

Drupal handles RTL stylesheets in an automated way based on CSS file naming conventions. If you have a stylesheet named style.css, which contains the CSS for the LTR version of the site, you can simply create another file called style-rtl.css to contain the necessary tweaks to fix the display for the RTL version. Drupal will automatically load it when needed, directly after the original file so that the same selectors can be used and RTL styles will override the LTR styles, taking advantage of the natural CSS cascade. When writing CSS for a site that will support both LTR and RTL displays, it is customary to write the CSS for the LTR version first, while keeping track of what will need to change (per property) with a comment. This is one of the coding standards Drupal has adopted for core and contributed CSS files. Listing 16–36 shows an example.

Listing 16–36. Example CSS Denoting a LTR Property and the RTL Version

```
// In style.css:
// .my-selector floats content to the left, which is LTR-specific, so an inline comment is
added to note this.
.my-selector {
  border: solid 1px #ccc;
  float: left; /* LTR */
}

// In style-rtl.css:
// The RTL version of .my-selector needs to be overriden and floated right instead of left.
.my-selector {
  float: right;
}
```

Adding, Removing, and Replacing CSS Files

There are three ways to manipulate CSS files within Drupal themes. This section will explain what the implementation options are, the reasons for each method, and when it's advantageous to use certain methods over others.

Quick and Dirty Stylesheets via .info Files

Adding stylesheets via your theme's .info file is the easiest way to add a CSS file to your theme; see Listing 16–37 and Listing 16–38. However, there are a few drawbacks to doing this in certain situations.

1. Any stylesheet you define in the .info file will load on every page.

2. You don't have the full use of the features available in drupal_add_css(). For example, you can't add conditional stylesheets for Internet Explorer or change the weight of a module's CSS file in your .info file.

Listing 16–37. .info Syntax for Adding Stylesheets

```
stylesheets[CSS media type][] = path/to/file.css
```

Listing 16–38. Typical .info Stylesheet Definition Example

```
stylesheets[all][] = css/layout.css
stylesheets[all][] = css/style.css
stylesheets[print][] = css/print.css
```

■ **Caution** Stylesheets may also be removed via .info files by creating an entry for a file as if you were overriding it, but then not actually including the file in the theme directory. However, there is a bug that allows these stylesheets to return when AJAX rendering occurs. To be safe it's best to remove stylesheets in hook_css_alter(); this is explained later in this section.

Conditionally Loading Stylesheets with drupal_add_css()

drupal_add_css() is the main function used by modules and themes to add CSS files via PHP code. Some themes use it in their template.php file, typically within preprocess functions. One of the advantages of using drupal_add_css() in the theme layer as opposed to defining CSS files in a .info file is that files can be conditionally loaded based on certain criteria or context. For example, you may want to create a special CSS file that only loads on your site's home page. In your theme's template.php, you could do this within template_preprocess_html(), as shown in Listing 16–39.

Listing 16–39. Adding a Stylesheet that Loads Only on the Home Page

```php
<?php
function mytheme_preprocess_html(&$variables) {
  // Add a stylesheet that prints only on the homepage.
  if ($variables['is_front']) {
    drupal_add_css(path_to_theme() . '/css/homepage.css', array('weight' => CSS_THEME));
  }
}
```

There are many different options for adding CSS to your pages in Drupal using drupal_add_css(), some of which include:

- Specifying the type as "inline" to print a block of CSS code within <head>, as opposed to adding a CSS file.

- Specifying the group of a file to determine where the file should appear using constants such as CSS_SYSTEM (top), CSS_DEFAULT (middle), and CSS_THEME (bottom).

- Specifying the weight of a file to control the order in which it loads within its group.

- Adding conditional stylesheets to serve different files to different browsers.

- Adding externally hosted CSS files.

- Forcing a CSS file to be excluded from the aggregation and compression process.

Adding Conditional Stylesheets for Internet Explorer

According to Wikipedia at the time of this writing, about 43 percent of users are visiting web pages using Internet Explorer. This statistic varies from source to source, but for many of you, supporting older versions of Internet Explorer is a fact of life. Using conditional stylesheets is considered a best practice when the need arises to write CSS that targets Internet Explorer.

One of the great new features in Drupal 7 is that conditional stylesheets can be added using `drupal_add_css()`. In fact, all three of Drupal's core themes do this in `template_preprocess_html()`. The reason this is done in `template.php` is that `.info` files only have very basic support for `drupal_add_css()`. Listing 16–40 and Listing 16–41 demonstrate how this works using code from the Seven theme as an example.

Listing 16–40. *Excerpt from the Seven Theme, Using drupal_add_css() to Add Conditional Stylesheets for IE in template_preprocess_html()*

```php
<?php
function seven_preprocess_html(&$vars) {
// Add conditional CSS for IE8 and below.
  drupal_add_css(path_to_theme() . '/ie.css', array('group' => CSS_THEME, 'browsers' =>
array('IE' => 'lte IE 8', '!IE' => FALSE), 'preprocess' => FALSE));
  // Add conditional CSS for IE6.
  drupal_add_css(path_to_theme() . '/ie6.css', array('group' => CSS_THEME, 'browsers' =>
array('IE' => 'lt IE 7', '!IE' => FALSE), 'preprocess' => FALSE));
}
```

Listing 16–41. *The Source Code that Results from Adding IE Conditional Stylesheets*

```
<!--[if lte IE 8]>
<link type="text/css" rel="stylesheet" href="http://drupal-7/themes/seven/ie.css?l40z2j"
media="all" />
<![endif]-->

<!--[if lt IE 7]>
<link type="text/css" rel="stylesheet" href="http://drupal-7/themes/seven/ie6.css?l40z2j"
media="all" />
<![endif]-->
```

The code in Listing 16–40 and Listing 16–41 gives you two conditional stylesheets that will load for Internet Explorer only. The first stylesheet will load for Internet Explorer 8 and under, and the second stylesheet will load for versions of Internet Explorer prior to IE7.

Completely Control Stylesheets Using hook_css_alter()

Drupal core and modules add CSS files individually via the `drupal_add_css()` function. During `template_process_html()`, a variable called `$styles` is created; it contains the fully formatted HTML output for all the stylesheets that are specified for each page. This variable is eventually printed inside the `<head>` tags in the `html.tpl.php` template file, as shown in Listing 16–42.

Listing 16–42. *$styles Variable Is Created in template_process_html() for Use in html.tpl.php*

```php
<?php
/**
* Implements template_process_hmtl().
```

```
*/
function template_process_html(&$variables) {
  ...
  $variables['styles'] = drupal_get_css();
  ...
}
```

During the call to drupal_get_css(), Drupal gathers up all the CSS files previously added, and then provides an opportunity for any modules or themes to make changes by calling drupal_alter('css', $css). At this time, Drupal looks for functions in modules and themes that fit the naming pattern hook_css_alter(), where the word "hook" in the function name is replaced by the module or theme name implementing it. This function allows for the most granular control over all aspects of your CSS files.

An example of why a module might want to implement hook_css_alter() can be found in the Locale module. The Locale module checks to see if the language direction is right-to-left, and if so, finds the related RTL versions of the CSS files and adds them to the page.

In themes, the main reasons to implement hook_css_alter() is to remove or override CSS files provided by modules. An example of this can be found at the bottom of Seven theme's template.php file (see Listing 16–43). Seven chooses to override the stylesheet vertical-tabs.css file provided by core with its own version.

Listing 16–43. The Seven Theme's hook_css_alter() Implementation

```php
<?php
/**
 * Implements hook_css_alter().
 */
function seven_css_alter(&$css) {
  // Use Seven's vertical tabs style instead of the default one.
  if (isset($css['misc/vertical-tabs.css'])) {
    $css['misc/vertical-tabs.css']['data'] = drupal_get_path('theme', 'seven') . '/vertical-tabs.css';
  }
  // Use Seven's jQuery UI theme style instead of the default one.
  if (isset($css['misc/ui/jquery.ui.theme.css'])) {
    $css['misc/ui/jquery.ui.theme.css']['data'] = drupal_get_path('theme', 'seven') . '/jquery.ui.theme.css';
  }
}
```

■ **Caution** Overriding a module's CSS files in .info files (creating an entry with the same CSS file name) will work, but not always in an efficient way. Stylesheets that are defined in .info files will load on every page. Whether or not they are actually needed is never taken into account. This is not the case when using hook_css_alter() as you are given the opportunity to make sure the file is set to load before attempting to replace it.

MANAGING STYLESHEETS IN YOUR THEME

In this section, you've learned quite a few ways to manipulate CSS files in Drupal's theme layer. Now you'll go through the steps again with practical examples.

Exercise A: Define stylesheets for all pages in the .info file

1. Begin by creating a new directory in your theme called css in `sites/all/themes/mytheme`. This step is optional but helpful for theme file organization.

2. Create two files inside the css directory called `style.css` and `print.css`.

3. Open the `sites/all/themes/mytheme/mytheme.info` and add the following two lines to define the stylesheets so Drupal knows to load them:

```
stylesheets[all][] = css/style.css
stylesheets[print][] = css/print.css
```

4. Clear the site cache at `admin/config/development/performance`. Once you return to the front end of your site, you'll see that both files have been added.

Exercise B: Add a conditional stylesheet for IE using drupal_add_css()

1. Create a file inside the css directory called `ie.css`.

2. Create a file in the root of the theme directory called `template.php` if you haven't already done so, and make sure to include `<?php` at the top of the file.

3. Use the following code to implement `template_preprocess_html()` and load the IE stylesheet using `drupal_add_css()`:

```php
<?php
/**
 * Implements of template_preprocess_html().
 */
function mytheme_preprocess_html(&$vars) {
  // Add conditional stylesheet that targets Internet Explorer 8 and below.
  drupal_add_css(path_to_theme() . '/css/ie.css', array('weight' => CSS_THEME,
'browsers' => array('IE' => 'lte IE 8', '!IE' => FALSE), 'preprocess' => FALSE));
}
```

Exercise C: Add a custom stylesheet for the homepage using drupal_add_css()

You'll use the `$is_front` variable, which already exists, to detect if the home page is being displayed and then add the `homepage.css` stylesheet. Add this code directly above the conditional stylesheet code you added in Exercise B.

```php
<?php
// Add a stylesheet that prints only on the homepage.
if ($variables['is_front']) {
  drupal_add_css(path_to_theme() . '/css/homepage.css', array('weight' => CSS_THEME));
}
```

Exercise D: Override and remove module CSS files using hook_css_alter()

To implement `hook_css_alter()`, you'll need to create a function called `mytheme_css_alter()` in your `template.php` file. The `$css` parameter, which is passed by reference, contains all the stylesheets in array format, and you can do what you please with it. The following code shows how to remove the `node.css` file if it's set to load.

```php
<?php
function mythemename_css_alter(&$css) {
  // Remove the node.css file.
  if (isset($css['modules/node.css'])) {
    unset($css['modules/node.css']);
  }
}
```

Working with Base and Subthemes

Chances are you have a certain way you do things. You may tend to structure your markup similarly in all your themes. You might frequently override certain theme functions, or have special way you like to style forms, or maybe you tend to use a certain grid framework for your layout. These are all great reasons to take advantage of Drupal's base and subtheming functionality.

Subthemes share a special relationship with their base (parent) theme(s). They inherit template files and assets from their parent themes. This makes them a great tool to help streamline your theming workflow and essentially create your own "frameworks" or "resets" for theming Drupal sites. Of course, you can also use an existing base theme. Drupal offers quite a few base themes, which we'll tell you more about later in this section.

Creating a Subtheme

Both base and subthemes are regular Drupal themes as far as characteristics go, and any theme can be a base theme. The process of creating a subtheme is very straightforward.

1. Start by creating the shell of a new theme. Create a directory for it, and create the `.info` file containing at least the `name` and `core` properties.

2. In the `.info` file, add the "base theme" property containing the name of the theme you want to use as a base, like so:

    `base theme = basethemename`

3. If the base theme has regions and/or features defined in the `.info` file, you'll need to copy those to the subtheme as well.

For basic Drupal themes, these three steps are all you'll need to do to create your subtheme. Once you've done this, you'll be able to enable the theme on the `admin/appearance` page. It's also worth noting that the base theme you are using does not need to be enabled in the UI to function properly.

■ **Caution** Most of the popular contributed base themes require a little more to set up. Themes like Zen, Omega, and Fusion come with a starterkit or starter directory, which you can copy and use to start your subtheme. Make sure you refer to each theme's README.txt file for full instructions on how to begin using it, as each is different.

Inheritance and How It Works

You already know that Drupal provides a lot of markup in its modules, and that this markup comes in the form of templates, theme functions, or the Render API. In Drupal themes you have the opportunity to override and take over this behavior. So, technically, you are inheriting it in the first place. Using subthemes allows you to add one more step to the process. When using a parent theme, all of the assets—including template files, CSS files, JavaScript files, theme functions, and pretty much everything in template.php—are inherited.

CSS, JavaScript, template files, and theme functions defined in a base theme will automatically be available for the subtheme. The subtheme doesn't have to do anything for this to happen. It just works. Preprocess and process functions will run for both the base and the subtheme, so they can be used in both themes simultaneously without issue. Of course, the subtheme can override anything the base theme has done.

Some things don't work this well. Regions are not inherited, and neither are features or theme settings. In order for these to work properly, you'll have to copy the information from the base theme into the subtheme's .info file. Table 16–4 shows which assets are automatically inherited and which ones are not.

Table 16–4. Inheritance of Assets from Base Theme to Subthemes

Asset	Automatically Inherited?
CSS files	Yes
JavaScript files	Yes
Template files	Yes
Theme Screenshot	Yes
Regions	No
Theme Settings	No

Finding a Good Base Theme

Thousands of contributed themes are available at http://drupal.org/project/Themes. Unfortunately, Drupal themes have a reputation for being ugly. While there is some truth to that, there are many gems out there; you just need to know what to look for. Themes on drupal.org are sorted by popularity, based on project usage stats, so it is easy to see which themes are the most popular. However, popularity is not always the best measure. There are a few things you should understand when evaluating a contributed Drupal theme.

- *Type:* All of the themes on drupal.org are lumped together into one, uncategorized list. As you can see on http://drupal.org/project/themes, a large portion of the themes on the first page are base themes. While any theme can technically be used as a base theme, it's important to read the project information so you know what to expect. Maintainers will be a lot less inclined to help you with a problem if you're not using the theme how they intended.

- *Maintenance and development status:* Each project has a Maintenance and a Development status which can be viewed on the project page. These will give you a good idea of how the module is supported. If the project has an "Actively maintained" maintenance status and an "Under active development" development status, chances are that the module developer intends to fix bugs and will entertain feature requests made in the issue queue.

- *Usage statistics:* On each project page, the Project Information section contains the number of reported installations and a link called "View usage statistics" that shows a long term graph and table of this data and how it has changed over time. Usage statistics can be a good indication of whether or not a theme has been well tested. If many people are using it or it shows steady growth, chances are that it's a better theme.

- *Issue queue:* Most projects contain issues queues where users can report bugs and request features. Reading through the issue queue is a good way to gauge the community participation in a project. It is also a great way to learn what bugs the theme may have and how quickly the community and maintainer(s) respond to such issues.

Popular Base Themes

There are many great base themes available from seasoned theme developers on drupal.org. A comprehensive list of available base or "starter" themes is available at http://drupal.org/node/323993. Some of the most popular base themes available for Drupal 7 include:

Zen: http://drupal.org/project/zen

Fusion: http://drupal.org/project/fusion

AdaptiveTheme: http://drupal.org/project/adaptivetheme

Genesis: http://drupal.org/project/genesis

Basic: http://drupal.org/project/basic

Blueprint: http://drupal.org/project/blueprint

NineSixty: http://drupal.org/project/ninesixty

Omega: http://drupal.org/project/omega

Mothership: http://drupal.org/project/mothership

Tips for Creating Your Own Base Themes

- *Don't do too much:* It's important not to make too many assumptions in your base themes. Ask yourself if what you are doing will fit in well on any project you work on. If the answer is no or maybe, it's likely not a feature you should include in your base theme.

- *Look at contributed themes:* Looking at what other contributed themes have done is one of the best ways to learn. Chances are you'll find some things you like and some things you don't from each of them. Don't be afraid to mix and match.

- *Provide styles for layout and others structural elements:* Take care of things that you consistently do on each project. For example, normalize font sizes, provide CSS resets, and make sure that the general padding and margins are set so blocks and nodes are not on top of each other.

- *Use multiple CSS files:* Aggregation and compression will take care of combining these files automatically, so don't be afraid of using a few CSS files. This will allow you to easily choose between what you want and don't want in your subthemes.

Sustainability and Best Practices

Drupal contains many, many template files. For a front-end developer, these are one of your greatest tools in taking over a Drupal theme and turning it into exactly what you need it to be. However, with power comes responsibility. Because working with template files is so easy, it's also an area where you can get in trouble quickly.

Most front-end developers experience some frustration working with Drupal's markup. Because it's relatively easy to go in and make changes, doing exactly that is often a first reflex. Resist it. While you'll definitely feel the power and control you have over things, changing too many template files is often the wrong approach. Just because you can change things doesn't always mean you should.

Start With a Good Base

A great way to ensure minimal template overrides is to define your markup in such a way that it is flexible enough to work in most cases. Think of the major template files like node.tpl.php, views-view.tpl.php and block.tpl.php, for example, as having two purposes. The first is to provide a container and the second is to provide the actual content, which can include any number of different elements inside it. Drupal does this reasonably well to begin with, but there is always room for improvement, and your needs may vary from site to site depending on the design.

As an example, look at the contents of the block.tpl.php file, shown in Listing 16–44, which is provided by Drupal's Block module and can be found in modules/block/block.tpl.php. Most blocks, even those produced by other modules, will use this template file to output their contents. There could be a menu inside the block, a few paragraphs in a custom block, a snippet of JavaScript that will load an advertisement, a poll, a user listing, and so many other possibilities.

Listing 16–44. Default block.tpl.php Implementation

```
<div id="<?php print $block_html_id; ?>" class="<?php print $classes; ?>"<?php print
$attributes; ?>>
  <?php print render($title_prefix); ?>
  <?php if ($block->subject): ?>
```

```
    <h2<?php print $title_attributes; ?>><?php print $block->subject ?></h2>
  <?php endif;?>
  <?php print render($title_suffix); ?>
  <div class="content"<?php print $content_attributes; ?>>
    <?php print $content; ?>
  </div>
</div>
```

▪ **Tip** The Bartik theme uses Drupal's default `block.tpl.php` template file. This is easy to determine because the Bartik theme does not include a `block.tpl.php` file in its directory.

Using a simple custom block as an example, the template code in Listing 16–44 translates to the output in Listing 16–45.

Listing 16–45. Block Output Using the Default block.tpl.php Implementation

```
<div id="block-block-1" class="block block-block first last odd">
  <h2>Block title</h2>
  <div class="content">
    <p>Block content.</p>
  </div>
</div>
```

The resulting code is pretty minimal. In most cases, when creating custom themes, you will not want these to look the same, so you will use CSS to style them differently. It may not be immediately apparent, but there are some potential problem areas to take note of with the default `block.tpl.php` implementation. Certain design aspects need more flexible markup. Some examples of this include:

- *Grids:* You may choose to lay out your blocks within regions using a CSS grid framework. This will prevent you from adding left and right padding directly to the `.block` class.

- *Background images:* Your design might require adding multiple background images to achieve a design for the block that is content agnostic. Sounds easy enough, right? The top and tiling background image can be declared in `.block`, but where can the bottom background image be defined? As soon as you add padding to the `.block` class itself, you lose the ability to place the second background image on the existing `.content` class.

The previous examples are a small taste of what you might encounter while coding a Drupal theme. You may be tempted to take the minimalist markup approach and deal with problems as they arise, and this is where we would stop you! As mentioned, these main template files are responsible for containing many types of content. You don't want to create a new template file for every different kind just to modify structural aspects. It's much more sustainable, not to mention easier to code, to create solid and flexible defaults and deal with exceptions as they arise.

This can be achieved fairly easily by separating structure from content. As shown in Listing 16–46, by simply adding `<div class="inner">` to surround the contents, you can solve many potential problems before they arise. In the example of grids, padding can be applied to the `<div class="inner">`. As for background images, the top background image can be applied to `.block`, and the bottom can be applied to `.block .inner` or vice versa.

Listing 16–46. Modified block.tpl.php Containing a More Flexible Container Structure

```
<div id="<?php print $block_html_id; ?>" class="<?php print $classes; ?>"<?php print
$attributes; ?>>
  <div class="inner">
    <?php print render($title_prefix); ?>
    <?php if ($block->subject): ?>
      <h2<?php print $title_attributes; ?>><?php print $block->subject ?></h2>
    <?php endif;?>
    <?php print render($title_suffix); ?>
    <div class="content"<?php print $content_attributes; ?>>
      <?php print $content; ?>
    </div>
  </div>
</div>
```

Override Template Files with Purpose

While core template files are less likely to change during the course of a major release cycle, there are usually massive changes to template files for each major Drupal release, and contributed modules are a constantly moving target. Template files can change at any time, and sometimes drastically. There are many potential reasons for these changes. A module developer may decide to take a different approach, there might be new features or security updates, or there may be no good reason at all. The point is that once you override a template file by adding it to your theme, you are responsible for maintaining it. This can easily get out of hand if you have too many template files.

Another thing to remember is that Drupal is a framework. The whole idea of using Drupal is to take advantage of its modularity. Having too many template files in your theme can essentially remove that modularity; once that happens, your theme can become more of a hassle to maintain than all of Drupal and whatever custom modules you have combined. The key to avoiding this problem is to use overrides sparingly and take advantage of the many tools that Drupal provides.

Just adding the <div class="inner"> as you did in Listing 16–46 can go a long way in saving you the need to create additional template files. The following tips will help you stay out of trouble when working with templates in Drupal themes:

- *Structure for the majority.* Explore options for handling one-offs separately by using preprocess functions where possible.

- *Take advantage of theme hook suggestions.* When the differences between the markup warrant it, use node--article.tpl.php to style article nodes and use theme_links__node() to target only node links.

- *Take advantage of CSS classes as arrays.* If all you need is a class, don't create a new template file. For example, block titles are output in a simple <h2> tag by default. When applying even minimal CSS to .block h2, you run the risk of affecting <h2> tags that may end up inside <div class="content">. Add a class to the title to style against, so you can prevent these issues.

Leverage Default CSS Classes

Don't just rip out or change CSS classes without good reason for doing so. Think about it. While many front-end developers and web designers gasp at the sight of all the CSS classes that Drupal makes available, there really is a purpose to the madness. These classes (especially body classes) not only provide helpful information that guides you through figuring out what is generating the markup and what characteristics the contents of a given <div> might have, but they are designed to give you the opportunity to do a large portion of your theme development within the CSS.

Keep in mind, especially when using contributed modules, that you will need to update and likely upgrade your site at some point in the future, and that you can't control the changes that may be made to templates and often to the classes applied inside them. It's also important to note that modules may rely on classes and certain CSS files, such as system.base.css to be loaded in order to function properly. Of course, you can try to manage these things, but we can report from experience that this can easily turn into a frustrating waste of time. We're not saying there's not room for improvement or that you shouldn't code your site the way you want to. We simply want to make you aware of some of the risks involved when stripping markup down to barebones.

Do My Changes Belong in a Module?

With each new release of Drupal, the theme layer becomes more and more powerful. With the advent of Render API and the ability to use alter hooks in themes, Drupal 7 is packed with more power than ever. As powerful as Drupal themes can be, there are still many things that just do not belong in the theme layer. As you are plugging away coding your awesome Drupal theme, constantly ask yourself these questions:

- Does what you are trying to accomplish require an SQL query? These should never be in a theme. Period.

- Does your task seem particularly difficult to accomplish? Are you completely rebuilding data?

- Are your changes really theme-specific? For example, if you are changing form labels and descriptions, shouldn't these be available if you were to disable your theme?

If the answer to any of these questions is yes, then your changes belong in a module.

Summary

Throughout this chapter we've covered more of the many different methods you can use to bend Drupal themes to your will. We've covered almost everything you'll need to know to create truly awesome and sustainable themes, including how to:

- Find the variables that are available to you in the theme layer.

- Understand and use preprocess and process functions.

- Use and alter contents of render arrays.

- Theme forms with templates, theme functions, and alter hooks.

- Manage CSS and JavaScript files in your theme.

- Work with base and subthemes.

It's easy to become overwhelmed with Drupal's theme layer in the beginning. Just remember that your themes can be as simple or as complex as you need them or want to be. We hope that you'll take this knowledge and use it to create awesome Drupal themes, and contribute them back to the community.

CHAPTER 17

■ ■ ■

jQuery

by Jake Strawn with input from Dmitri Gaskin

jQuery has become an essential part of Drupal since Drupal 5. Many of the interfaces in the administrative area use jQuery to enhance the user experience, and Drupal 7 is no exception, continuing to improve the ability for developers and themers to implement advanced JavaScript functionality.

Drupal 7 currently ships with jQuery 1.4.4 and now also ships with jQuery UI 1.8 (jqueryui.com) in core which enables advanced User Interface elements/widgets and effects.

Implementing jQuery and JavaScript

This first section will be dealing with the basics of getting your own custom JavaScript/jQuery functionality added to your Drupal 7 project.

I will be going over the basics of including new JavaScript files in your theme or module, adding entire JavaScript libraries, overriding JavaScript and/or jQuery that has already been included, using Drupal Behaviors, and finally, ensuring that your jQuery/JavaScript degrades nicely for those users that are unable to or choose not to view JavaScript functionality.

Including JavaScript

It is possible for theme and module developers to add JavaScript and jQuery functionality in a variety of ways depending on the needs of the code being implemented. This first section will deal with adding basic JavaScript to your site and will cover the various methods and use cases. In some instances, you may want your JavaScript coded added to every page on the site; in other circumstances, it may only be necessary to include it on a single page if certain requirements are met.

Adding JavaScript in Your .info Files

Themes and modules have the ability to include JavaScript files very easily in the .info file, as demonstrated in Listings 17–1 and 17–2. In the same manner that stylesheets can be added using stylesheets[all] = file.css, JavaScript files may be added by simply using scripts[] = file.js.

Listing 17–1. Adding JavaScript in a Theme's .info File

```
name   = Gamma
description = Omega Sub-Theme starter kit
screenshot = screenshot.png
core = 7.x
```

```
base theme = omega

stylesheets[all][] = css/text.css
stylesheets[all][] = css/regions.css
stylesheets[all][] = css/gamma.css
stylesheets[all][] = css/dark.css
```

scripts[] = js/gamma.js

Any scripts that are included in this manner are automatically loaded on every page where the theme that implemented the JavaScript is being used. So, if you use this method, your JavaScript would not apply to the administrative section of your site when using Seven as the administrative theme.

The location of gamma.js in Listing 17–1 is relative to the root path of the theme or module. So since the .info file for this theme is likely in /sites/all/themes/gamma/gamma.info, the JavaScript you are attempting to load here would be located in /sites/all/themes/gamma/js/gamma.js.

Listing 17–2. Adding JavaScript in a Module's .info File

```
name = DGD7 Test Module
description = An example module
core = 7.x

files[] = dgd7_test.module
```

scripts[] = dgd7_test.js

Adding JavaScript in your module's .info file will ensure the file is included on every page load.

drupal_add_js()

Themes may also add JavaScript files in template.php using drupal_add_js(). This is the preferred method if you only wanted your JavaScript to be included under certain conditions and not on every page. Modules also use drupal_add_js() to include any JavaScript files related to the functionality or presentation of the output it produces.

The following examples of drupal_add_js() can be placed either in your theme OR module, but keep in mind that any calls to drupal_add_js() declared in your theme will only be present on pages where your theme is being used. If you need a JavaScript file included on every page site-wide, including administrative pages (possibly to manipulate a node form), you will want to include the JavaScript in a module using drupal_add_js() or by adding it to the .info file for the module (as described previously) so that it will appear on any page, regardless of the theme being used to render the page. The full documentation for this function can be found at http://api.drupal.org/drupal_add_js.

So, to add a JavaScript file from the local filesystem, use the following code:

```
drupal_add_js('misc/machine-name.js');
drupal_add_js(drupal_get_path('module', 'example') . '/example.js');
drupal_add_js(drupal_get_path('theme, 'omega') . '/js/example.js');
```

With just a single parameter, Drupal assumes the JavaScript you are including is a type of 'file'. In the first line, using the relative path to the file misc/machine-name.js is fine, since machine-name.js, a JavaScript include that handles creating system names (replacing spaces with dashes or underscores, making all text lowercase, etc.) for generic text input, is included in Drupal core and is unlikely to move. However, if you are including a JavaScript file that is located in a module or theme directory, the best practice is to use drupal_get_path() to properly find the location of the module or theme, then append the location in the directory the JavaScript file would be stored. Using drupal_get_path() is quite important since if you were using the file example.js in your module called example, the path could be any number of locations including:

- sites/all/modules/example/example.js

- sites/default/modules/example/example.js

- sites/example.com/modules/contrib/example/example.js

With all these potential locations where a valid module could be stored, calling drupal_add_js(drupal_get_path('module', 'example') . '/example.js'); will ensure that the example.js file is loaded, no matter where the module is stored.

In previous versions of Drupal, it was not possible to add a JavaScript include from a remote server using drupal_add_js(), but this is now possible in Drupal 7. This is a great way to add JavaScript code from other locations—a very common need if you are running many sites that need the same JS functionality across your network of sites. Previously, this had to be done creatively with symlinks on the server to appropriately map a relative path to the location or by managing multiple copies of the same JavaScript includes. The following code shows how easy it is to now add a remote JavaScript file:

```
drupal_add_js('http://example.com/example.js', 'external');
```

It is also possible to quickly add a line or two of JavaScript inline (instead of creating an entirely new .js file) and implement the code by adding it directly to the page. The following code shows how you can quickly add an alert to the page using the inline property in drupal_add_js():

```
drupal_add_js('jQuery(document).ready(function () { alert("Drupal Love!"); });', 'inline');
```

```
drupal_add_js('jQuery(document).ready(function () { alert("Drupal Love!"); });',
  array('type' => 'inline', 'scope' => 'footer', 'weight' => 5),
);
```

This method should only be used for JavaScript that can't be executed from a file. When adding inline code, make sure that you are not relying on $() being the jQuery function. Proper namespacing for jQuery will make sure that another JavaScript library doesn't conflict with jQuery when using the $(). In order to ensure your JavaScript/jQuery snippet works as you expect when using inline JavaScript, wrap your code in (function ($) { $('div').addClass('page-div')})(jQuery);.

Note also that this method, rather than just passing 'inline' as the second parameter, uses the array of options to further manipulate how the JavaScript will be added to the page. Using the 'scope' => 'footer' setting, you are telling Drupal to render the JavaScript at the end of the page in the $page_bottom region, making it appear just before </body>. In addition, you are telling Drupal that you would like this JavaScript include to be weighted a little heavier than normal, ensuring that if other items are declared in the scope of 'footer', this will be rendered after any items with a weight less than 5.

Weight and Group in drupal_add_js()

A couple of the fantastic new features available to drupal_add_js() in Drupal 7 are the weight and group options inside of $options. In the past, adding JavaScript using this function happened in the order in which it was called during the page building process.

The weight and group options allow you to reorder JavaScript inclusions any way you like; so if late in the page build process certain conditions have been set, you can make a new file included using drupal_add_js() appear early (or even first) in the source order. Following up on that idea, you can add an included file early but ensure that it is the absolute last item to be included in the source code by making the weight a higher number.

The ordering of JavaScript in Drupal page rendering adheres to the following rules:

- First by **scope**, with 'header' first, 'footer' last, and any other scopes provided by a custom theme coming in between, as determined by the theme.

- Then by **group**.

- Then by the 'every_page' flag, with TRUE coming before FALSE.

- Then by **weight**.

- Then by the **order** in which the JavaScript was added. For example, all else being the same, JavaScript added by a call to drupal_add_js() that happened later in the page request gets added to the page after one for which drupal_add_js() happened earlier in the page request.

Examples of Weight in drupal_add_js()

With weights, Drupal can place JavaScript includes in a logical order. Just as when the jQuery library (jquery.js) is added in early so that other files may rely on it being available, you can also add weights to your own JavaScript since you may also have code that needs to be included early in the page so other includes or inline JavaScript can build off of that.

The following code declares no weight; items are sorted by scope, group, every_page flag, and then the order in which they are called:

```
drupal_add_js('misc/machine-name.js');
```

In the following code, the weight being set to -10 will place the file higher up in the default scope of header and the group it is associated with:

```
drupal_add_js('misc/machine-name.js',
  array('type' => 'file', 'weight' => -10),
);
```

In the following code, the scope of 'footer' will ensure this file is included before the </body> tag at the end of the document:

```
drupal_add_js('misc/machine-name.js',
  array('type' => 'file', 'scope' => 'footer', 'weight' => 5),
);
```

Examples of Group in drupal_add_js()

In addition to simply adding weights to JavaScript, you can also now declare them into default groups (see Listing 17–3). JS_LIBRARY includes core Drupal includes like drupal.js, jquery.js, and other high level JavaScript files. JS_DEFAULT is by default where JavaScript included in modules is grouped. JS_THEME is by default where includes from the theme layer will be included.

It is good to have the ability to regroup your JavaScript files; under certain circumstances, you may need a JavaScript file included via your theme to be included at a very high level with the other JS_LIBRARY functionality.

Listing 17–3. *The Default Groups: JS_LIBRARY, JS_DEFAULT (module JS), and JS_THEME (theme JS)*

```
drupal_add_js('misc/machine-name.js',
  array('type' => 'file', 'scope' => 'header', 'weight' => -15, 'group' => JS_LIBRARY),
);
drupal_add_js('misc/machine-name.js',
```

```
  array('type' => 'file', 'scope' => 'header', 'weight' => -15, 'group' => JS_DEFAULT),
);
drupal_add_js('misc/machine-name.js',
  array('type' => 'file', 'scope' => 'header', 'weight' => -15, 'group' => JS_THEME),
);
```

Groups are declared in the order you see them in Listing 17–3.

- JS_LIBRARY includes, like the core jQuery library, need to be declared first in order for other files and libraries to use them.

- JS_DEFAULT is the default value when using drupal_add_js() in the module layer.

- JS_THEME is the default when using drupal_add_js() in the theme layer (template.php).

Using drupal_add_js(), many other options are available to you for advanced placement, grouping, ordering, and caching/aggregation options. You can find further details on the API page for drupal_add_js() at http://api.drupal.org/drupal_add_js.

JavaScript Libraries

With a revival of usage since the days where it was shunned as "that thing that needs to be turned off in Internet Explorer," JavaScript and its many powerful libraries are now common on a huge percentage of the sites you rely on every day. Facebook, Twitter, NY Times, and even the Drupal.org site all rely heavily on JavaScript libraries to provide you with enhanced functionality and a cleaner interface.

jQuery is a cross-browser JavaScript library, and there are literally thousands upon thousands of libraries out there. Not all are as complex as jQuery, but the one thing they have in common is they work towards providing a certain level of functionality or interactivity with your web page.

jQuery is a library that is already included by default in Drupal and is always available for use. This section will discuss how you can add other JavaScript libraries into your site and/or module.

▓ **Note** Drupal 7 features more flexible jQuery and JavaScript.

---

hook_library()

When adding or defining a custom JavaScript library in your site, the first Drupal function you will come to learn and love is hook_library(). Adding a library can be simply implementing your own custom code as a library or including a library already available from the web. hook_library() registers JavaScript/CSS libraries associated with your module. This hook is always located in your custom .module file or an appropriate include file for your module.

To really get an understanding of the basics, you can look at the documentation at http://api.drupal.org/hook_library.

The definition of each library contains the following items:

- **Title:** The human readable name of the library

- **Web site:** The URL of the library's web site

- **Version:** A string specifying the version of the library

- **Js:** An array of JavaScript elements

  - Path to JavaScript file => array()

- **CSS:** An array of CSS elements

  - Path to CSS file => array()

  - Type = file/external/etc.

  - Media = screen/print/all

  - See drupal_add_css() for type and media options

- **Dependencies:** An array of libraries on which this library depends

  - Uses the formatting of drupal_add_library(), which will be defined in the next section on including a defined JavaScript library

Listing 17–4 demonstrates the basic elements available to hook_library(), and you will see how quickly you can add a robust library to your module to implement anything from simple functionality to a full blown interface overhaul, depending on the code your library is including and how it's implemented.

Listing 17–4. The Basic Elements Available to hook_library()

```
function hook_library() {
  // Library One.
  $libraries['library-1'] = array(
  'title' => 'Library One',
  'website' => 'http://example.com/library-1',
  'version' => '1.2',
  'js' => array(
    drupal_get_path('module', 'my_module') . '/library-1.js' => array(),
  ),
  'css' => array(
    drupal_get_path('module', 'my_module') . '/library-2.css' => array(
      'type' => 'file',
      'media' => 'screen',
    ),
  ),
);
    return $libraries;
}
```

Listing 17–5 defines your library as two JavaScript files (js-file-one.js and js-file-two.js) and a single CSS file (css-file-one.css), and it declares that your library will not function without the default jQuery UI core and autocomplete libraries that are provided by the system module.

Listing 17–5. Defining Your Library

```
function mymodule_library() {
  $libraries['my-first-library'] = array(
```

```
      'title' => 'My First JavaScript Library',
      'website' => 'http://himerus.com',
      'version' => '1.0.1',
      'js' => array(
        drupal_get_path('module', 'mymodule') . '/js-file-one.js' => array(),
        drupal_get_path('module', 'mymodule') . '/js-file-two.js' => array(),
      ),
      'css' => array(
        drupal_get_path('module', 'mymodule') . '/css-file-one.css' => array(
          'type' => 'file',
          'media' => 'all',
        ),
      ),
      'dependencies' => array(
        array('system', 'ui'), // require the core ui library
                array('system', ' ui.autocomplete'), // require autocomplete library
      ),
  );
    return $libraries;
}
```

You can see that actually implementing a new library is quite easy using hook_library(). The actual labor of this process is getting your JavaScript code built (assuming it is custom). The actual definition and inclusion of the library is very simple.

drupal_add_library()

Now that you have defined your custom library, you can quickly add it to your site in a variety of ways. I will outline a few examples here, but there are literally dozens of ways you can include your library and call it in specific locations.

In the past, including the necessary JavaScript and CSS to provide certain functionality required many calls to drupal_add_js() and drupal_add_css(). Now, using the previous examples in hook_library(), you are able to quickly load all the JavaScript, CSS, and other libraries it may depend on by using a single call to drupal_add_library(), as shown in Listing 17–6.

Listing 17–6. Comparison of Including Libraries in Drupal 6 and Drupal 7

Drupal 6

```
// add required dependencies
drupal_add_js('misc/autocomplete.js');
// add relevant JS files
drupal_add_js(drupal_get_path('module', 'mymodule') . '/file1.js');
drupal_add_js(drupal_get_path('module', 'mymodule') . '/file2.js');
// add relevant CSS files
drupal_add_css(drupal_get_path('module', 'mymodule') . '/file1.css');
drupal_add_css(drupal_get_path('module', 'mymodule') . '/file2.css');
```

Drupal 7

```
// add my library and all its dependencies
drupal_add_library('mymodule', 'mylibrary', TRUE);
```

The drupal_add_library() function takes three arguments: module name ($module), name of library ($name), and a Boolean flag ($every_page) to define if it is to be included on every page. If the flag is set to FALSE, the JavaScript and CSS with the library can't be aggregated, which is how Drupal combines multiple cacheable JS/CSS files into single files to present on page load, so when possible, it's best to set this to TRUE. The primary time when the $every_page flag would be set to FALSE will be for a module or implementation where the JavaScript library is only needed on a single form or on a single page.

The difference in required work between Drupal 6 and Drupal 7 is dramatic, as you can see in Listing 17–7. Instead of declaring a long list of files to include your appropriate JavaScript/CSS and required dependencies, you can now define your requirements in hook_library() to tell Drupal that you have X number of JavaScript files, Y number of CSS files, and Z number of dependencies that Drupal should include before adding your files. drupal_add_library() does have a return value of TRUE or FALSE. It will return TRUE should the function have returned appropriately with all files and dependencies included properly, or FALSE if one of the items failed to be found or load.

Overriding JavaScript

You have learned how to implement JavaScript via standard calls to drupal_add_js(), how to add an entire library at one time using drupal_add_library(), and how to implement your own libraries using hook_library(), but the fun isn't over yet. You now have the ability, as seen elsewhere in the Drupal APIs, to alter some of those elements before they are output to the page. This allows you to manipulate the JavaScript files being included or to completely change the definition of a library on the fly through your own module.

hook_js_alter()

In previous versions of Drupal, modifying the script output to the page was quite cumbersome and lacked some level of elegance. The jQuery Update module used a method to scan $variables['scripts'] in hook_preprocess_page() to look for items to replace, assign the new replacements, then unset the originals. It worked, but it was a rather messy solution to a problem that could be handled better.

In Drupal 7, you now have the highly useful hook_js_alter() function. This will be easy to understand for those familiar with hook_form_alter(), hook_menu_alter(), etc. The hook_js_alter() function is available in both the theme and module layer, so you can include your mymodule_js_alter() function in your .module file or mytheme_js_alter() in your template.php file for your theme. When using hook_js_alter(), the function you will create starts off as follows:

```
function mymodule_js_alter(&$JavaScript) {
  $search = drupal_get_path('module', 'some_module') . '/some-file.js';
  if(array_key_exists($search)) {
    // reset the weight for this item, making it appear higher in the source
    $JavaScript[$search]['weight'] = -100;
  }
}
```

Changing the weight of a JavaScript include that was already included is as simple as shown. Taking this into account, you can easily replace all of the settings for a JavaScript file and even replace the file itself. You can also reset any of the attributes you learned about in this chapter regarding drupal_add_js(). This comes in handy when, for example, you would like to replace a version of jQuery core that was included to a newer version that is not packaged with Drupal core. You can simply use hook_js_alter() in your module or theme and replace the default jquery.js file with one of your choosing.

The following code example shows altering the weight of the toolbar.js file, which is provided by the toolbar module in Drupal 7. If some other JavaScript was conflicting and this needed to be added earlier in the page source, it can be accomplished this easily. Note that this applies to ANY JavaScript included in Drupal.

```
function mymodule_js_alter(&$JavaScript) {
  $search = drupal_get_path('module', 'toolbar') . '/toolbar.js';
  if(array_key_exists($search)) {
    $JavaScript[$search]['weight'] = -100;
  }
}
```

hook_library_alter()

Now that you've seen how you can alter individual JavaScript files, this section shows how you can manipulate an entire JavaScript library defined by hook_library() by using hook_library_alter().

The API documentation (http://api.drupal.org/hook_library_alter) offers a great example of usage. The code in Listing 17–7 replaces the JavaScript file defined by hook_library() if its version number is less than 2.

Listing 17–7. Replacing the JavaScript File Defined by hook_library()

```
function hook_library_alter(&$libraries, $module) {
  // Update Farbtastic to version 2.0.
  if ($module == 'system' && isset($libraries['farbtastic'])) {
    // Verify existing version is older than the one we are updating to.
    if (version_compare($libraries['farbtastic']['version'], '2.0', '<')) {
      // Update the existing Farbtastic to version 2.0.
      $libraries['farbtastic']['version'] = '2.0';
      $libraries['farbtastic']['js'] = array(
        drupal_get_path('module', 'farbtastic_update') . '/farbtastic-2.0.js' => array(),
      );
    }
  }
}
```

Listing 17–7 demonstrates the two parameters for hook_library_alter(), which are $libraries, an array of included libraries keyed with the system name of the library as declared in hook_library(), and $module, the name of the module implementing the library. Usage of this hook should come with caution or at the very least a stern warning from your mother. If you were to update the version of a library such as jQuery or Farbtastic (in Listing 17–7), it could be possible that another module that relies on that same library could be dependent on a specific version, so your updating it could adversely affect the functionality of other items in your site.

That being said, there are a lot of possibilities, even many that the core contributors who implemented the addition of hook_library(), hook_library_alter(), and hook_js_alter() couldn't possibly have thought of at the time of implementation into Drupal 7 core. Regardless, this new flexibility in Drupal gives module developers and themers a much more robust method to add and manipulate JavaScript/jQuery functionality into projects.

Drupal Behaviors

Drupal Behaviors provide some great benefits that make enhancing your modules with JavaScript and jQuery much simpler. Drupal.behaviors is a property of the Drupal object, as you can see:

```
var Drupal = Drupal || { 'settings': {}, 'behaviors': {}, 'locale': {} };
```

In Drupal 7, JavaScript behaviors are now objects with two methods: attach and detach. Drupal.detachBehaviors() was introduced to allow AJAX elements to remove attached elements before a page element is processed or removed.

Attaching Behaviors

Rather than attaching behaviors using the traditional $(document).ready(); method to ensure your code is fired after the DOM has loaded all objects, you will define your jQuery code the Drupal way using behaviors, which lets your code properly interact with the page on initial load. It also deals with the situation when AJAX or another method has added objects to the DOM at a later time, attaching your behaviors to new objects in the DOM simply by calling Drupal.attachBehaviors(). Defined in drupal.js, any property added to the Drupal.behaviors object will be called automatically when Drupal.attachBehaviors is called, as shown here:

```
Drupal.attachBehaviors = function (context, settings) {
  context = context || document;
  settings = settings || Drupal.settings;
  // Execute all of them.
  $.each(Drupal.behaviors, function () {
    if ($.isFunction(this.attach)) {
      this.attach(context, settings);
    }
  });
};
```

The next method works as expected when the page loads, adding a new CSS class (custom-css-class) to any H3 element on the page using $(document).ready(). This is fine in most cases, but this will only affect H3 elements that were loaded into the DOM when the page was first loaded and when Drupal.attachBehaviors was called.

```
$(document).ready(function(){
  // act on all h3 elements and give them a custom class
  $('h3').addClass('custom-css-class');
});
```

The following code demonstrates the proper usage in Drupal 7, using Drupal.behaviors attach method to define your custom code. Now, any time new elements are added to the DOM and Drupal.attachBehaviors() is fired, your code will apply to the new elements.

```
Drupal.behaviors.myModuleHeaders = {
  attach: function(context, settings) {
    // act on all h3 elements and give them a custom class
    $('h3').addClass('custom-css-class');
  }
};
```

Detaching Behaviors

New to Drupal 7 is the `Drupal.detachBehaviors` method. In previous versions, there was no way to remove a behavior that was attached using `Drupal.attachBehaviors`. This can be useful when your JavaScript code is attaching itself to elements that don't persist on a page until another page load. An example of this would be a WYSIWYG editor loaded in a modal window that allows editing or saving new content; upon submission, the modal window closes, leaving extra behaviors in the DOM that are no longer relevant.

It is optional to supply a detach method inside your module's behavior. As of yet, there aren't many examples of the detach method, with the exception of usages in `modules/file/file.js`. Line 49 of `file.js` demonstrates attaching and detaching behaviors to links that are added to uploaded files:

```
/**
 * Attach behaviors to links within managed file elements.
 */
Drupal.behaviors.filePreviewLinks = {
  attach: function (context) {
    $('div.form-managed-file .file a, .file-widget .file a',
context).bind('click',Drupal.file.openInNewWindow);
  },
  detach: function (context){
    $('div.form-managed-file .file a, .file-widget .file a', context).unbind('click',
Drupal.file.openInNewWindow);
  }
};
```

Degrading JavaScript/jQuery Nicely

An issue with using JavaScript/jQuery functionality in your web applications is when a user, for various reasons (preference, disability, etc.) has JavaScript disabled in their browser. The days when users were told it was good to turn off JavaScript in their browsers for security are long past. In fact, most of the sites we visit on a daily basis rely heavily on the use of JavaScript, jQuery, and similar libraries. So the issue is not those who actually choose to turn those features off, but instead the users who do not have the option to view them in the first place.

The more common reason today for users to have JavaScript disabled would be blind or sight impaired users that rely on screen readers to access Internet content. Site visitors using screen reader technology should have the same ability to interact with the site as a user that is not visually impaired. For many of us, testing this type of accessibility can be tough, but there are continual pushes in Drupal to ensure everything (core and contributed code) is as accessible as possible; thanks to many visually impaired contributors in Drupal, the community as a whole has become much more aware of and considerate to these issues.

It is critical when designing your user interfaces and interactions that the functionality works without JavaScript enabled, and that when JavaScript IS enabled, your functionality is simply enhanced by it.

Drupal core is very accessible without JavaScript enabled, and for those of us with JavaScript capabilities, greatly improved. A good example of this in Drupal core can be seen in the weights property, which allows you to drag and drop to reorder menu items (see Figure 17–1). This same method is applied throughout usages of weights in Drupal including taxonomy term weights, block positions inside of a region, field ordering on content types, and many more areas.

As a simple rule, the best practice when ensuring your JavaScript degrades nicely and will function for those users without JavaScript capabilities is to build your JavaScript enhancements only after the application works as expected without JavaScript (see Figure 17–2).

Menu link		Enabled	Operations		⊡
✛ Home		☑	edit	delete	
✛ AJAX Examples		☑	edit	reset	
✛ Simplest AJAX Example		☑	edit		
✛ Generate checkboxes		☑	edit		
✛ Generate textfields		☑	edit		

Figure 17–1. Menu links with JavaScript enabled, using tabledrag for reordering of menu items

Menu link	Enabled	Weight	Operations	
Home	☑	-50 ⬍	edit	delete
AJAX Examples	☑	-49 ⬍	edit	reset
Simplest AJAX Example	☑	0 ⬍	edit	
Generate checkboxes	☑	1 ⬍	edit	
Generate textfields	☑	2 ⬍	edit	

Figure 17–2. Menu links with JavaScript disabled, using standard select menu option for reordering of menu items

jQuery UI

jQuery UI (http://jqueryui.com) provides abstractions for low-level interaction and animation; high-level, themeable widgets; and advanced effects. These are built on top of the jQuery JavaScript library that you can use to build highly interactive web applications.

jQuery UI in Drupal Core

In Drupal 5 and Drupal 6, in order to easily include jQuery UI interactions, you needed the help of the jQuery UI module for Drupal (http://drupal.org/project/jquery_ui). In Drupal 7, jQuery UI 1.7 is included in core, making advanced, enhanced interfaces readily accessible to module and theme developers without the need of an additional module or manually implementing the jQuery UI code in your site/project.

In order to start implementing jQuery UI functionality, refer to the drupal_add_library() function discussed earlier in this chapter. You are able to quickly include the relevant pieces of jQuery UI needed to start building out your enhancements.

jQuery UI Elements in Drupal Core

The examples in this section are taken directly from the documentation available at www.jqueryui.com, adding just the relevant PHP code to implement in Drupal 7 and the appropriate JavaScript to declare your functionality via Drupal.Behaviors. Further examples and usage can be found in the jQuery UI documentation.

accordion

Let's start with accordion. The following is the PHP to include the accordion library:

```
drupal_add_library('system', 'ui.accordion');
```

The following is the JavaScript for creating your Drupal.behavior to implement the accordion:

```
Drupal.behaviors.myModuleAccordions = {
  attach: function(context, settings) {
    // add accordions to all h3 elements wrapped in a div with a class of accordion
    $('.accordion').accordion();
  }
};
```

And finally, the following is an HTML example for accordion (which is shown in Figure 17–3):

```
<div class="accordion">
  <h3><a href="#">Header 1</a></h3>
  <div><p>Lorem Ipsum dolor sit amet. Lorem Ipsum dolor sit amet</p></div>
  <h3><a href="#">Header 2</a></h3>
  <div><p>Lorem Ipsum dolor sit amet. Lorem Ipsum dolor sit amet</p></div>
  <h3><a href="#">Header 3</a></h3>
  <div><p>Lorem Ipsum dolor sit amet. Lorem Ipsum dolor sit amet</p></div>
</div>
```

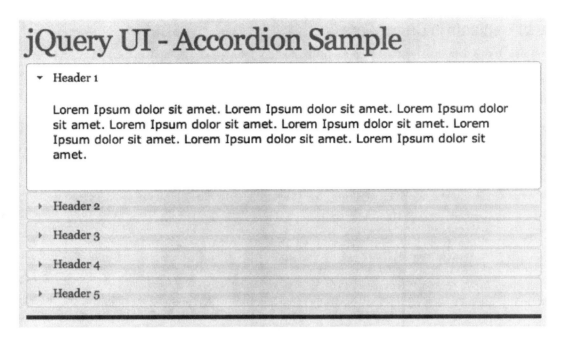

Figure 17–3. *Accordion in action*

datepicker

Now let's look at datepicker. The following is the PHP for including the datepicker library:

```
drupal_add_library('system', 'ui.datepicker');
```

The following is the JavaScript for creating your `Drupal.behavior` to implement the datepicker:

```
Drupal.behaviors.myModuleDatepicker = {
  attach: function(context, settings) {
    // add the jQuery UI datepicker to all inputs with a class of datepicker
    $('.datepicker').datepicker();
  }
};
```

The following code is an HTML example for datepicker. You can see the results in Figure 17–4.

```
<p><label for="custom-datepicker">Date:</label> <input id="custom-datepicker"
class="datepicker" type="text"></p>
```

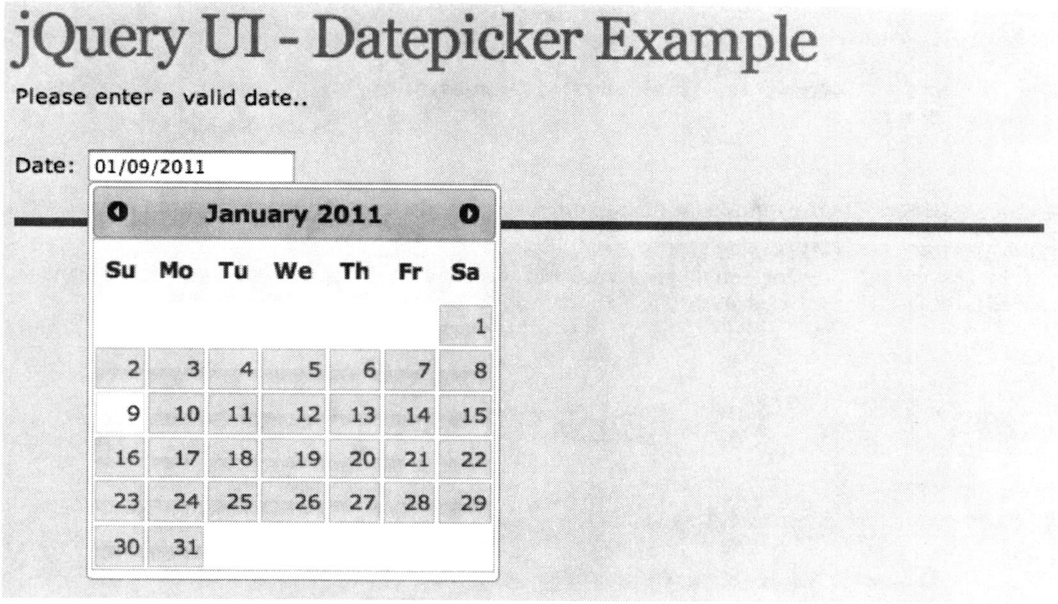
jQuery UI - Datepicker Example
Please enter a valid date..
Date: 01/09/2011
January 2011
Su Mo Tu We Th Fr Sa

Figure 17–4. Datepicker in action

dialog

Next up is dialog. The following is the PHP for including the dialog library:

```
drupal_add_library('system', 'ui.dialog);
```

The following is the JavaScript for creating your `Drupal.behavior` to implement the dialog:

```
Drupal.behaviors.myModuleDialog = {
  attach: function(context, settings) {
    // add the jQuery UI dialog to all elements with id of dialog
    $('.dialog').dialog();
  }
};
```

The following is an HTML example for dialog, the results of which are shown in Figure 17–5:

```
<div class="dialog" title="Basic dialog">
  <p>This is the default dialog which is useful for displaying information. The dialog window
can be moved, resized and closed with the 'x' icon.</p>
</div>
```

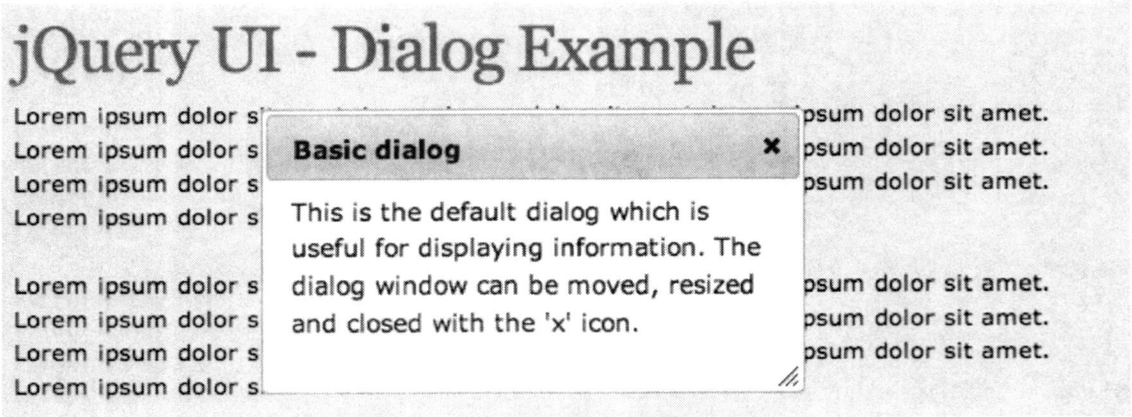

Figure 17–5. Dialog in action

draggable

The next example is a draggable, which you can drag around the screen. This is the PHP to include the draggable library:

```
drupal_add_library('system', 'ui.dialog');
```

This is the JavaScript for creating your Drupal.behavior for the draggable element:

```
Drupal.behaviors.myModuleDraggable = {
  attach: function(context, settings) {
    // make all elements with a class of draggable, well… draggable…
    $('.draggable').draggable();
  }
};
```

And this is an HTML example for draggable; you can see the results in Figure 17–6:

```
<div class="draggable ui-widget-content">
  <p>Drag me around</p>
</div>
```

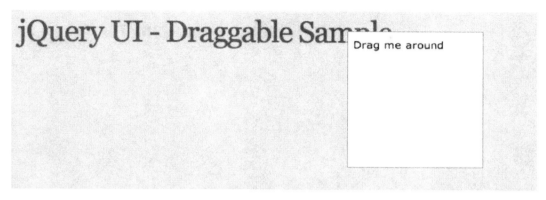

Figure 17–6. *Draggable elements in action*

droppable

What's a draggable without a droppable? The following is the PHP for including the droppable library:

```
drupal_add_library('system', 'ui.dialog');
```

The following is the JavaScript for creating your `Drupal.behavior` for the droppable element:

```
Drupal.behaviors.myModuleDroppable = {
  attach: function(context, settings) {
    // make all elements with an id of droppable, well… droppable…
    $( ".droppable" ).droppable({
      drop: function( event, ui ) {
        $( this )
          .addClass( "ui-state-highlight" )
          .find( "p" )
          .html( "Dropped!" );
      }
    });
  }
};
```

The following code is an HTML example for droppable. Figures 17–7 and 17–8 show the before and after of the droppable action.

```
<div class="draggable ui-widget-content">
  <p>Drag me to my target</p>
</div>
<div class="droppable ui-widget-header">
  <p>Drop here</p>
</div>
```

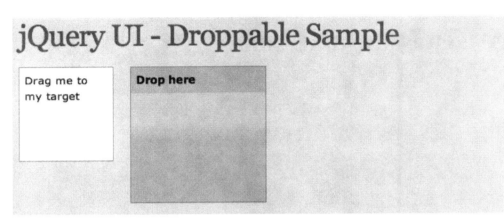

Figure 17–7. The droppable zone before dropping a draggable element inside

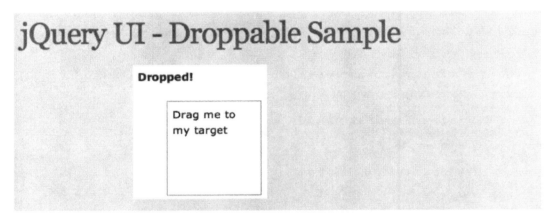

Figure 17–8. The droppable zone after dropping a draggable element inside

progressbar

There is usually a time in any web app when you need to indicate progress, so let's see how. Here's the PHP to include the progressbar library:

```
drupal_add_library('system', 'ui.progressbar');
```

Here's the JavaScript to create your Drupal.behavior for the progressbar:

```
function dgd7progressbarUpdate(){
    var progress;
    progress = $("#progressbar").progressbar("value");
    if (progress < 100) {
      $(".progressbar").progressbar("value", progress + 5);
      setTimeout(dgd7progressbarUpdate, 500);
    }
  }
```

```
Drupal.behaviors.dgd7progressbar = {
    attach: function(context, settings) {
      $(".progressbar").progressbar({ value: 1 });
      setTimeout(dgd7progressbarUpdate, 500);
    }
};
```

And here's an HTML example for droppable, with the results in Figure 17–9:

```
<div class="progressbar"></div>
```

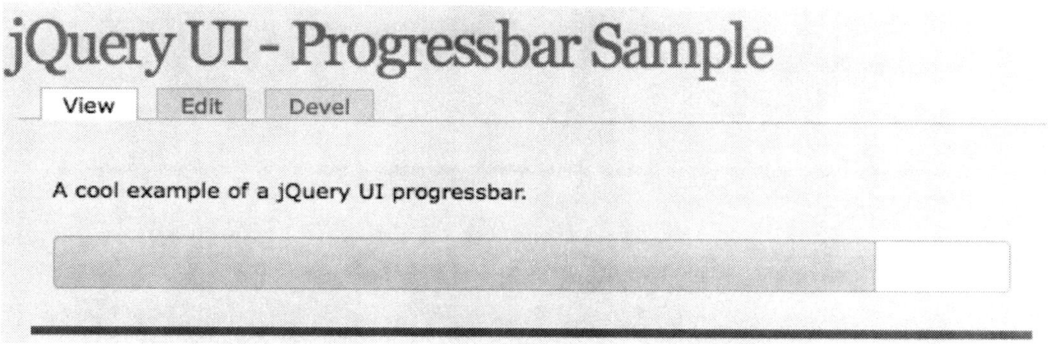

jQuery UI - Progressbar Sample

| View | Edit | Devel |

A cool example of a jQuery UI progressbar.

Figure 17–9. Progressbar in action

resizeable

The next example shows how to place a resizable element on the screen. Here's the PHP to include the resizable library:

```
drupal_add_library('system', 'ui.resizable);
```

Here's the JavaScript for creating your Drupal.behavior for the resizable element:

```
Drupal.behaviors.dgd7resizable = {
    attach: function(context, settings) {
      $('.resizable').resizable();
    }
};
```

And here's an HTML example for resizable element, the results of which can be seen in Figure 17–10:

```
<div class="resizable ui-widget-content">
  <h3 class="ui-widget-header">Resizable</h3>
</div>
```

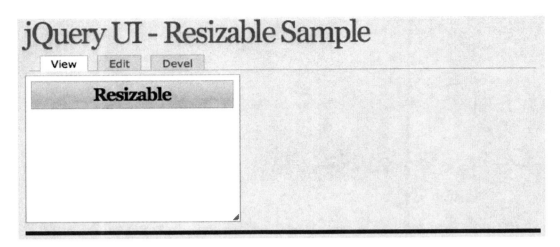

Figure 17–10. The resizable element

selectable

Web apps often need to gather user input, so you can use the selectable element instead of the usual list. Here's the PHP to include the selectable library:

```
drupal_add_library('system', 'ui.selectable');
```

Here's the JavaScript for creating your Drupal.behavior for the selectable element:

```
Drupal.behaviors.dgd7selectable = {
    attach: function(context, settings) {
      $('.selectable').selectable();
    }
  };
```

And here's an HTML example for selectable element, the results of which can be seen in Figure 17–11:

```
<ol class="selectable">
  <li class="ui-widget-content">Item 1</li>
  <li class="ui-widget-content">Item 2</li>
  <li class="ui-widget-content">Item 3</li>
  <li class="ui-widget-content">Item 4</li>
  <li class="ui-widget-content">Item 5</li>
  <li class="ui-widget-content">Item 6</li>
  <li class="ui-widget-content">Item 7</li>
</ol>
```

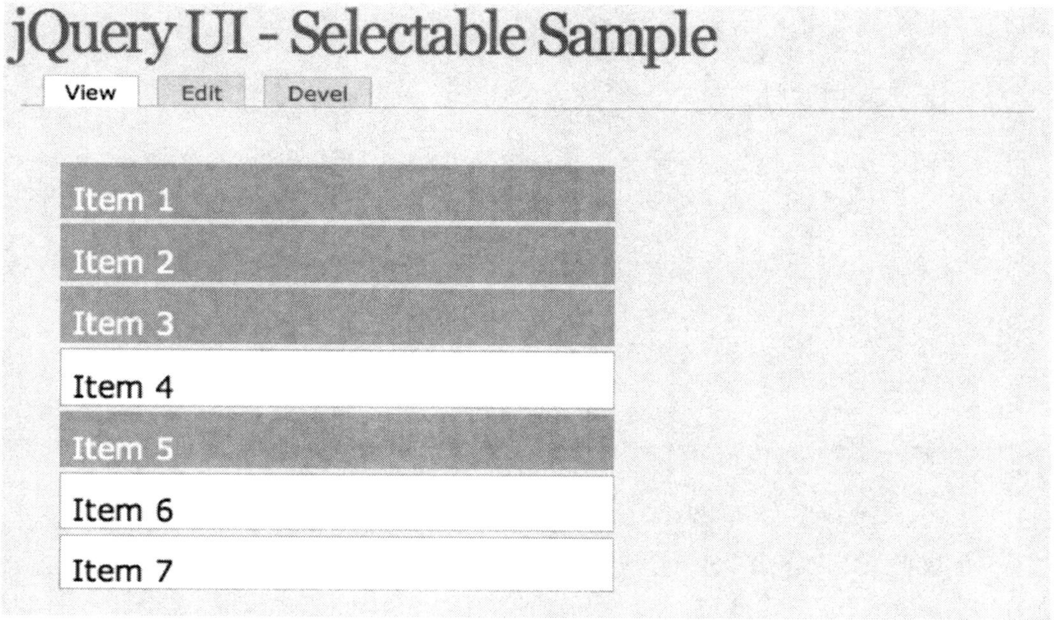

jQuery UI – Selectable Sample

| View | Edit | Devel |

Item 1

Item 2

Item 3

Item 4

Item 5

Item 6

Item 7

Figure 17–11. The selectable element

slider

The slider element adds a slider to the page so you can gather fine-grained values. This is the PHP to include the slider library:

```
drupal_add_library('system', 'ui.slider);
```

This is the JavaScript for creating your Drupal.behavior for the slider:

```
Drupal.behaviors.dgd7slider = {
    attach: function(context, settings) {
      $('.slider).slider();
    }
};
```

And this is an HTML example for sortable element; you can see the results in Figure 17–12:

```
<div class="slider"></div>
```

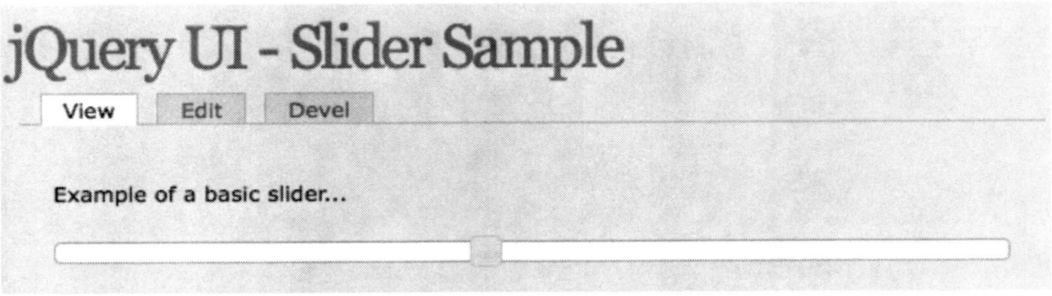

jQuery UI - Slider Sample

| View | Edit | Devel |

Example of a basic slider...

Figure 17–12. The slider element

sortable

When displaying lots of data to the user, it's sensible to allow them to sort it. Use this PHP to include the sortable library:

```
drupal_add_library('system', 'ui.sortable);
```

This JavaScript will create your `Drupal.behavior` for the sortable element:

```
Drupal.behaviors.dgd7sortable = {
    attach: function(context, settings) {
      $('.sortable').sortable();
    }
  };
```

And this is an HTML example for sortable element, the results of which can be seen in Figure 17–13:

```
<ol class="sortable">
  <li class="ui-state-default"><span class="ui-icon ui-icon-arrowthick-2-n-s"></span>Item
1</li>
  <li class="ui-state-default"><span class="ui-icon ui-icon-arrowthick-2-n-s"></span>Item
2</li>
  <li class="ui-state-default"><span class="ui-icon ui-icon-arrowthick-2-n-s"></span>Item
3</li>
  <li class="ui-state-default"><span class="ui-icon ui-icon-arrowthick-2-n-s"></span>Item
4</li>
  <li class="ui-state-default"><span class="ui-icon ui-icon-arrowthick-2-n-s"></span>Item
5</li>
  <li class="ui-state-default"><span class="ui-icon ui-icon-arrowthick-2-n-s"></span>Item
6</li>
  <li class="ui-state-default"><span class="ui-icon ui-icon-arrowthick-2-n-s"></span>Item
7</li>
</ol>
```

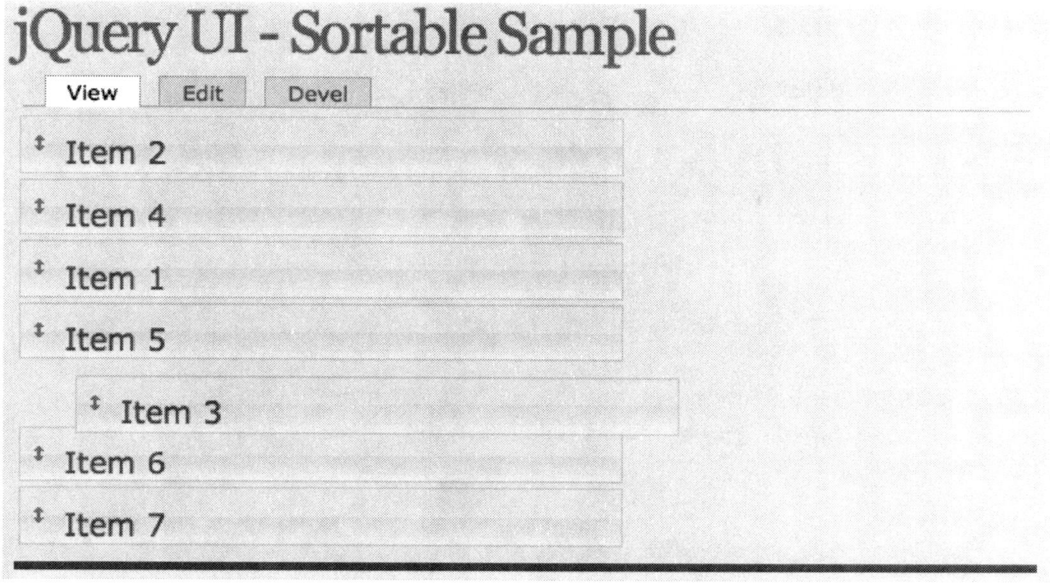

jQuery UI - Sortable Sample

| View | Edit | Devel |

‡ Item 2

‡ Item 4

‡ Item 1

‡ Item 5

‡ Item 3

‡ Item 6

‡ Item 7

Figure 17–13. The sortable element

tabs

A cool way of implementing menus is to use tabs. The following is the PHP to include the tabs library:

```
drupal_add_library('system', 'ui.tabs);
```

The following is the JavaScript for creating your Drupal.behavior for the tabs:

```
Drupal.behaviors.dgd7tabs = {
    attach: function(context, settings) {
      $('.tabs').tabs();
    }
};
```

The following is an HTML example for tabs; you can see the results in Figure 17–14:

```
<div class="tabs">
  <ol>
    <li><a href="#tabs-1">Nunc tincidunt</a></li>
    <li><a href="#tabs-2">Proin dolor</a></li>
    <li><a href="#tabs-3">Aenean lacinia</a></li>
  </ol>
  <div id="tabs-1">
    <p>Lorem Ipsum Dolor Sit Amet…</p>
  </div>
  <div id="tabs-2">
    <p>Lorem Ipsum Dolor Sit Amet…</p>
  </div>
  <div id="tabs-3">
```

```
    <p>Lorem Ipsum Dolor Sit Amet…</p>
  </div>
</div>
```

jQuery UI - Tabs Sample

| View | Edit | Devel |

Nunc tincidunt | Proin dolor | Aenean lacinia

Lorem Ipsum Dolor Sit Amet... Lorem Ipsum Dolor Sit Amet... Lorem
Ipsum Dolor Sit Amet... Lorem Ipsum Dolor Sit Amet... Lorem Ipsum
Dolor Sit Amet...

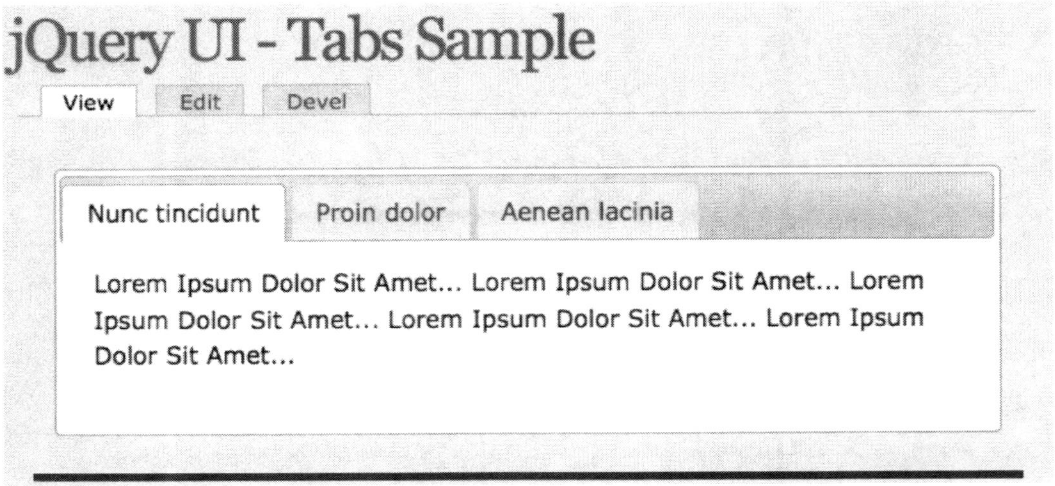

Figure 17–14. Tabs in action

jQuery UI Effects in Drupal core

In addition to the many widgets already described, there are several effects that can be used for animations and enhancements by simply including the appropriate library and then calling the appropriate effect in your jQuery animations. Try the following for yourself:

- blind

    ```
    drupal_add_library('system', 'effects.blind');
    ```

- bounce

    ```
    drupal_add_library('system', 'effects.bounce');
    ```

- clip

    ```
    drupal_add_library('system', 'effects.clip');
    ```

- drop

    ```
    drupal_add_library('system', 'effects.drop');
    ```

- explode

    ```
    drupal_add_library('system', 'effects.explode');
    ```

- fade

    ```
    drupal_add_library('system', 'effects.fade');
    ```

- fold

  ```
  drupal_add_library('system', 'effects.fold');
  ```

- highlight

  ```
  drupal_add_library('system', 'effects.highlight');
  ```

- pulsate

  ```
  drupal_add_library('system', 'effects.pulsate');
  ```

- scale

  ```
  drupal_add_library('system', 'effects.scale');
  ```

- shake

  ```
  drupal_add_library('system', 'effects.shake');
  ```

- slide

  ```
  drupal_add_library('system', 'effects.slide');
  ```

- transfer

  ```
  drupal_add_library('system', 'effects.transfer');
  ```

Further jQuery Resources

When it comes to JavaScript and jQuery, there are countless resources available on the Internet and many resources available via drupal.org that will help answer your questions on implementing specific functionality. When searching for information on an issue or question you're having, you may be surprised at how many times it has been answered for you on drupal.org.

- Drupal 7 JavaScript API Documentation: http://drupal.org/node/751744

- Documentation for jQuery JavaScript Library: http://docs.jQuery.com

- Resources for jQuery UI: http://jqueryui.com

Summary

Many popular web sites, including Facebook and Twitter, rely heavily on JavaScript interactions to enhance the usability of their web sites. Drupal 7 and the JavaScript framework have more than enough flexibility and power to accomplish anything you can imagine or have seen on any other site!

As demonstrated throughout this chapter, the JavaScript framework in Drupal 7 has added a wealth of functionality; it's modified many of the ways our applications utilize the power of JavaScript and the jQuery library. The basic examples in this chapter should get you well on your way to providing powerful JavaScript enhancements to your already powerful Drupal 7 site.

■ **Tip** For more resources and recommendations on JQuery and AJAX in Drupal 7, including the #attached render property and the #ajax form properties, check out this chapter's online home at dgd7.org/jquery.

## PART V

Back-End Development

Chapters 18, 19, and 20 form one unit, originally written as one chapter, covering everything you need to know to get started writing your own modules.

Chapter 21 covers porting a Drupal 6 module to Drupal 7, which can be a great way to learn module development.

Chapter 22 provides another good onramp to writing modules—"glue code," or site-specific modules, to make the final tweaks you cannot quite achieve with configuration. This chapter can be read without reading any of the previous chapters first.

Chapter 23 covers writing tests for your module, an essential part of reliable and sustainable code.

Chapter 24 introduces the concept of an API module and goes into some of the strategy of writing these building blocks of Drupal functionality.

■ ■ ■

## CHAPTER 18

Introduction to Module Development

by Benjamin Melançon

By now, you know that Drupal is a powerful and modular system. Indeed, much of Drupal's power is in its modules, dynamos of drop-in functionality that build on Drupal's base system and on one another to do wonderful things.

How do you tap into this power to add your own original features? You can write a module. All you need to do is make two files. The first file tells Drupal about the module; it's not code. The second file can have as little as three lines of code in it. In the first section of this chapter, you'll create the contents of both these files, thereby making a working module. Making a module is something that *anyone can do*. There are many (mostly simple) rules to follow and tons of tools to use—and lots of exploration to do. Every person developing a module is still learning.

This chapter is an introduction to module building, and Chapters 19 and 20 will build on it. This chapter provides the following:

- The basics of a module and how Drupal uses hooks in nearly everything it does to allow modules to extend and modify Drupal.

- An overview of technical skills required to develop a module, including PHP basics and Drupal coding standards.

A Very Simple Module

In this section, you'll take a quick spin through a small module, and then you'll come back and revisit the route in detail. When feature-complete at the end of Chapter 19, this module will help site builders and module developers investigate sites; ideally, they'll see the skeletal structure of a site, so the module is called X-ray. This module will print the form ID at the top of each form on a site.

Two Files in a Folder

The simplest module is composed of two files together in a folder: one to identify the module, and the other containing the code (the instructions for what the module should do). The information file is named for the module followed by .info (pronounced "dot info") while the file with the code is the module name followed by .module (pronounced "dot module"). Your module can have any human-readable name, but the name needed at the start is its *machine name*: a lowercase version of the name without spaces or special characters. You will use this name consistently for the folder and file names and the functions within the code. So in this case, the machine name of X-ray module will be xray, so xray.info and xray.module files, defined in Listings 18–1 and 18–2, should go in a folder called xray. You will cover this and the code in detail later.

Listing 18–1. The xray.info File

```
name = X-ray
description = Shows internal structures and connections of the web site.
core = 7.x
```

*Listing 18–2. The xray.module File, Including Comments (Text between /** and */)*

```php
<?php
/**
 * @file
 * Helps site builders and module developers investigate a site.
 */

/**
 * Implements hook_form_alter() to show each form's identifier.
 */
function xray_form_alter(&$form, &$form_state, $form_id) {
  $form['xray_display_form_id'] = array(
    '#type' => 'item',
    '#title' => t('Form ID'),
    '#markup' => $form_id,
    '#weight' => -100,
  );
}
```

Now you know you can make a module! The whole thing fits on a half page and you will know what the code means by the end of this section. To use the module, do the same thing you would do with a module someone else wrote: put it within a directory where Drupal looks for modules and enable it. Within your development site, put the xray folder in a modules folder such as sites/all/modules/custom (creating the "custom" directory if necessary). Then, use your browser to view your development site and enable the X-ray module on the Administration ➤ Modules (admin/modules) page. (Sure, you could enable it with Drush, but the first time you enable a module you've made, it feels good to see it on the Modules page and do it manually.) X-ray works as soon as you turn it on. You'll see the changes right on the modules page: X-ray alters forms on the site, making them print their internal form ID; the Modules administration page is one big form provided, you now know, by the system_modules() function (see Figure 18–1).

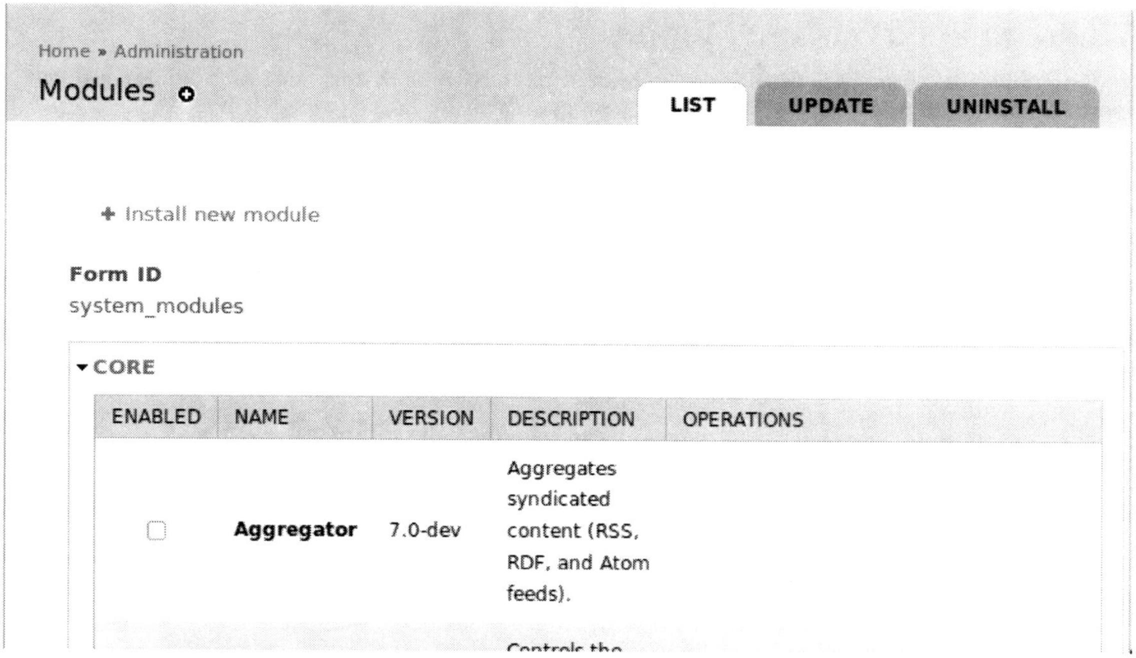

Figure 18–1. The internal form ID system_modules *(the name of the function producing the form) printed at the top of the modules administration form*

It's not the most exciting module, granted, but a fully-functional module all the same, affecting your site with only a few lines of code. The mythology of module development as the exclusive domain of Drupal ninjas has been definitively smashed. You can proceed with confidence. You will gain the knowledge needed to put extra power under the hood of your Drupal site with modules you make yourself.

■ **Note** Don't get caught up in trying to do something unique or awesome or even particularly useful with your first module. A module created as a learning exercise doesn't have to something never done before; all it needs to be is new to you. See Chapter 20 to make modules that are both simple and useful.

Still, that was a *bit* exciting. A very little code and you're adding something to every form on your site! How does it work? Let's do a slow-motion replay, with a play-by-play analysis and lots of color commentary for background information.

Where to Put a Custom Module

Your module is self-contained in its folder and can be put anywhere Drupal looks for modules, just like modules you get from `drupal.org`. But, where *should* you put it?

You know you want it somewhere within the sites folder because *every* customization you make to a Drupal distribution belongs in sites. This chapter follows the practice of putting custom modules in `sites/all/modules/custom`, which will need to be created the first time you put a module there.

▓ **Note** When making your own distributions, as in Chapter 34, you can bundle modules with your installation profile. Modules included with the example_profile would end up placed in `profiles/example_profile/modules`.

Every module downloaded from `drupal.org` can go in the `sites/all/modules/contrib` directory (as shown in Chapter 4 for placing manually downloaded or drushed modules; once you create a `sites/all/modules/contrib` directory, Drush will automatically put modules it downloads from `drupal.org` there).

As an alternative to putting custom modules in `sites/all/modules/custom`, many developers adopt a convention of placing custom modules in `sites/default/modules` and contributed modules directly in `sites/all/modules`). This works well as long as you aren't using Drupal's multisite capability. (*Multisite* means using a single installation of Drupal to serve multiple sites by putting additional folders in `sites`. Often, multiple *installations* of Drupal will serve you as well or better than multiple sites on one installation. However, some methods for deploying many Drupal sites, such as Aegir (`aegirproject.org`) do make heavy use of multisite. See `INSTALL.txt` in the web root of any copy of Drupal for instructions on setting up your own multisite.)

Table 18–1 lists recommended directories for custom modules.

▓ **Note** In the directories in which Drupal looks for modules, it does a serious job looking: it will keep burrowing down through all nested subdirectories and find any modules that are there. Therefore, because Drupal looks for modules in `sites/all/modules`, it will also find John Albin Wilkin's Bad Judgment module if you put it in `sites/all/modules/contrib/experiments/set_a/johnalbin/amusements/bad_judgment`. But that doesn't mean you should put it, or any other module, there. (Module projects that contain multiple modules necessarily make use of this feature to have Drupal find additional modules in their project folder, and some will put sub-modules nested a layer or two deeper, such as in a modules sub-directory, an approach used by core's Field module.)

Table 18–1. Recommended Locations for Custom Modules

Directory	Use case
`sites/all/modules/custom/`	For a single site or to be available for all sites in a multisite installation.
`sites/example.com/modules/custom/`	To be available for only one site, example.com, in a multisite installation.
`sites/default/modules/`	Acceptable shortcut location for custom modules when using a single-site installation.

You will be developing the X-ray module within a local development site that is a single-site install, so any of these will work. (Such a local site is also called a sandbox site, meaning it's a playground and is not used for production.)

■ **Tip** To develop your module, you should have a working Drupal site on your computer. If you don't have this yet, see Chapter 12 on setting up your development environment and Appendix F (Windows), G (Linux), H (Mac), or I (for the cross-platform Drupal stack installer from Acquia) for serving web pages locally. Alternatively, some developers do all their work SSHing or FTPing into a remote development server.

USING THE COMMAND LINE

You can use your computer's graphical user interface (GUI), or you can use the command line. In the time it takes to create a modules folder, and then create an xray folder inside it, and then open a text editor to create the `xray.info` file, you might have written that whole file already using commands. (The `mkdir` command for making directories and the `cd` command for changing directories are shown below, and the `vi` command for using a common text editor is the subject of the online appendix at `dgd7.org/vi`.)

The ability to use the command line is a particularly handy skill to have as you learn web development because it allows you to navigate, view, and edit files on servers, which are typically Linux and set up without an available GUI. (Don't use the ability to edit files on a server to touch the code on a live site, though!)

I wanted to say "Do not fear the command line," but there is no undo on the command line, so in some ways it is to be feared—but then, that's why we use source control. Bottom line: using the command line opens up a range of useful, powerful, and convenient tools in your work as a web developer. The command line is available to you through Terminal on Linux and Terminal.app on Mac OS X.

While you can create folders with a graphical file management tool (such as the Mac OS X Finder or the Microsoft Windows Explorer), this chapter shows how to do this with the command line (see Listing 18–3). It will help make you a better and faster developer, and it probably builds character, too.

Listing 18–3. Commands to Create the xray Folder, Its Parent Folder Called modules, and Change

Directory to It

```
mkdir -p sites/default/modules/xray
cd sites/default/modules/xray
```

Create a Repository for Your Module

This step has nothing to do with making your module work and everything to do with your workflow when making your module. Chapter 2 introduced version control with Git and Chapter 14 expounded on its benefits for achieving a state of flow as a developer: you want to feel free to try anything and always know you can get back to a working state. You want to develop your module while using source control and to commit your changes constantly.

From the root of the module you are developing (in this case, in the folder xray; on my computer, this directory is at `~/code/dgd7/web/sites/all/modules/custom/xray`), initialize a Git repository. Then make your first commit, which can be as soon as you've created your first file, like so:

```
it init
```

▪ **Note** You can create a repository in your module's directory even if it is already in a web site project that is version controlled. This will let you separate your module from your site for sharing the module with the world.

After initializing the repository, add and commit the changes you've made in your module directory. These are steps you will do again and again and again at each juncture or pause or breath you take while coding your module, ensuring that you can get back to any step of the journey should you need to.

```
git add .
git commit -m "Basic xray.info and .module files."
```

In Chapter 14, Károly Négyesi, one of the most prolific contributors to Drupal core, said not to worry about what the commit message says. The most important thing is to make recording all your changes effortless and natural. (I commit frequently but don't yet follow this practice myself. You can see every commit made in the development of X-ray module at `drupal.org/node/953650/commits`.)

Another great benefit of version control is that you can now easily share your work with the world. See Chapter 37 for how to link your module with a sandbox project on `drupal.org` so that anyone can try out your work. Chapter 37 also has much, much more on using Git to track changes, share code, and collaborate with other developers.

The .info File

This file only tells Drupal about your module, but there's still a lot to look at there. A `.info` file tells Drupal "Hey, this is something you can play with." Drupal reads only the `.info` and ignores the rest of the module until the module is enabled. The information Drupal displays on the Modules administration page (admin/modules) therefore comes entirely from the .info file for modules that are not enabled. (Once a given module is enabled, Help, Permissions, and Configure links, which are dependent on the module's code to work, may appear).

Basic .info Directives

The contents of the .info file are simple and formulaic. I will cover many common directives in the next few pages, but all directives can be found at drupal.org/node/542202. The following is the minimum contents of a .info file as self-describing examples, as would be found in machine_name.info:

```
name = Human-readable name of our module
description = Describes what our module does in a sentence or two.
core = 7.x
```

There can be additional values, but these are the essentials. The syntax is a simple *label equals value* pairing. It's always the label (or name) and the value, separated by a space, an equals sign, and another space. For instance, in the last directive (or property) above, core is the label and 7.x is the value.

■ **Note** As of Drupal 7, there's no need to show Id. The old version control system used by drupal.org, CVS, required that every file hosted on cvs.drupal.org have an Id comment at the top which it replaced with the time when it was committed and the name of who committed it. This is unnecessary now with Git and git.drupal.org, but Git still knows who committed what and when.

The human-readable name is required for the module to be selected (and thus enabled) on the Module administration page. There is no machine name directive; this is read from the .info file name. Though not technically required, including a description is minimum module developer courtesy. The core directive must be set to 7.x or Drupal 7 will refuse to work with the module. (Drupal doesn't currently allow modules to require a certain minor "point release" version of Drupal, but you can work around this by declaring a certain version of core's system module as a dependency of your module. The dependencies directive is covered next.)

dependencies[ ]

One of the most common optional directives is the dependencies[] directive, which lists the system names of any modules required by your module to work. If you decided to make the previous example dependent on the Views module, you would add the line dependencies[] = views to the .info file.

You should only list immediate dependencies. For instance, Views depends on CTools, but you should only list CTools in your module if your module directly uses CTools. This helps you avoid listing false (outdated) dependencies. By the same token, if you change your module so it is no longer dependent on another, remove that from the dependencies so that site builders aren't forced to install the extra module.

What's with the brackets? When a directive can have multiple values, the name has array notation, [], appended to it so that the directive can be repeated as many times as necessary. Thus, a module that depends on both the core Help module and the contributed Views module would repeat the dependencies[] directive twice, as shown in Listing 18–4.

■ **Note** As of Drupal 7, each dependency must be listed on a separate line, repeating dependencies[] = system_name for the system name of each module on which your module relies.

Listing 18–4. A .info File of a Module Requiring Two Other Modules

```
; Require the core Help module and the contrib Views module to be enabled.
dependencies[] = help
dependencies[] = views
```

The first line in Listing 18–4 is a comment. In .info files, comments are indicated by a semicolon (;) at the very beginning of a line. So any line beginning with a semicolon in a .info file will be ignored by Drupal. Comments aren't usually necessary in module .info files because .info files are so simple and self-explanatory. The next two lines in Listing 18–4 are the two dependencies, the machine names of the Help and Views modules. (Remember that the machine name can vary greatly from the human-readable name. The machine name for Views Bulk Operations module, for instance, is vbo.)

Version-Specific Dependencies

Dependencies can specify particular versions of modules, such as >=3.x for any major version 3 or above. For contributed modules, this is the second part of a module's version string, after the Drupal version, so dependencies[] = views (>=3.x) will allow Views 7.x-3.0 (and the 4.x series, when that exists) but not Views 7.x-2.9. Note that the parentheses are required even for the most simple version string. The following is an example of a complex version-aware dependency specification, courtesy Károly Négyesi (chx):

```
dependencies[] = foo (>=2.x, <4.17, !=3.7).
```

It means that you need foo module's major version to be at least 2 and any version up to (but not including) 4.17, aside from 3.7 which was horribly buggy.

As mentioned, you can use this form of the dependencies[] directive to require certain versions of Drupal core. If a bug in Drupal 7.0 that prevents your module from working properly is fixed in Drupal 7.1, you can require that system module (a core module which is required to always be enabled) be version 7.1 or above, like so:

```
dependencies[] = system (>=7.1)
```

configure

The configure directive, optional but highly recommended, lets you provide the path to your module's configuration page. Drupal uses this path to provide a link on the Modules administration page when the module is enabled. The following is an example of a configure directive from the core search module:

```
configure = admin/config/search/settings
```

(The X-ray .info file does not have a configure line at this point, but you will add one when you create a configuration page to link to later.)

■ **Note** As of Drupal 7, the `configure` directive greatly improves the experience of site builders by providing a link to a module's configuration page from its listing on the modules page. (I really like the configure link.)

package

Another optional directive is `package`, which is used to group modules on the Modules administration page (admin/modules). If you don't know what to put as your module's package, you are encouraged to skip it entirely. Leaving package out will group your module in the "Other" category. If your module belongs with a group of modules, you can place it with them by using the same package.

■ **Note** The best approach to grouping modules with the package directive is not a settled matter in Drupal. Keep an eye on the handbook page (`drupal.org/node/542202#package`) for updates to policy and the other eye on the package wiki page (`groups.drupal.org/node/97054`) for the choices module maintainers are making. As noted, when in doubt, leave it out.

You'll put your X-ray module in the Development package, which is the suggested location for development-related modules. You can create and edit your module's .info file using any code- or plain-text editor; do **not** use a rich text editor or word processor. (See `dgd7.org/vi` for a little information on how to use the Vim editor, which is present in most webserving environments.) Create or edit the .info file for your X-ray module to include the package directive set to "Development", as shown in Listing 18–5. (Note that this directive, unlike dependencies[] but like name and description, uses proper capitalization.)

Listing 18–5. The xray.info File with Added Package Information

```
name = X-ray
description = Shows internal structures and connections of the web site.
package = Development
core = 7.x
```

There you have it—a .info file that tells Drupal your module's name, its description, what package it belongs to for grouping on the Administration ➤ Modules page, and the version of core with which it works. Your module is all set to rock Drupal's world; the only thing it's lacking is... code.

■ **Hint** If you're not near this book or another reference when you need to write a .info file for a new module, you can look at a core module's .info file or another contributed module's .info file (and ignore everything below the "Information added by `drupal.org` packaging script" line), or you can find the handbook page on Drupal 7 .info files at `drupal.org/node/542202`.

The .module File

The second file, a .module ("dot module") file, is what tells your module to do something. Its importance doesn't dictate length; it can be even shorter than the .info! (Admittedly, it is usually much longer.)

The .module file must have the same machine name as the .info file, which for both should be the same name as the folder they are in. (Modules do not have to be named the same as the folder they are in, but it is common courtesy to do so for the sake of site builders and other module developers. Even for projects that include multiple modules, each module ought to receive its own folder, and the machine name of all modules in a multi-module project should begin with the project name.)

For the X-ray module, the project name, folder name, and machine name are all xray, and so the main module file name will be xray.module. Open your .module file, as you do every PHP code file, with the full <?php tag that identifies the file as containing PHP code to process, like so:

```
<?php
```

I emphasize this because numerous code samples in this book will *not* include this line, but all code is presumed to go in a file that starts with the <?php line. No PHP code will work without an opening line.

Next, for the .module and every code file, add a comment explaining the purpose of the entire file. It uses docblock comments, one of the two PHP comment styles approved by Drupal coding standards. Comments are so important that they are described in their own section of this chapter.

Code Comments

The one-line style of comment that begins with // is for use inside functions, such as the function xray_form_alter(). Everything following the two slashes to the end of the line is ignored, so inline comments that span multiple lines need to have each line begin with //. The X-ray module does not have an example of inline comments inside functions yet, but you will see and write plenty very soon.

The first lines of the .module file are comments of a different kind, called *docblock* for *doc*umentation *block*. Let's break them down. The first is the @file notation that describes the purpose of the file as a whole (see Listing 18–6). For a .module file, it will often be similar to the module description from the .info file.

Listing 18–6. Code Comments in Docblock Format at the Beginning of a File and Before a Function

```
/**
 * @file
 * Helps site builders and module developers investigate a site.
 */

/**
 * Implements hook_form_alter() to show each form's identifier.
 */
function xray_form_alter(&$form, &$form_state, $form_id) {
  // This is an inline comment telling you the code has been removed.
}
```

PHP's /* */ C-style commenting goes from the beginning /* to the ending */, commenting out everything in between, and can span multiple lines. In Drupal, it is only used *outside* of functions and usually to introduce functions. In Listing 18–6, this block style of comment introduces the file with the aid of the @file identifier. Note that Drupal coding standards require more than simply opening and closing comment tags: the start of the comment has an extra asterisk (/**); each line of the comment is prefaced by an indent of one space, an asterisk, and another space (*); the closing is indented one space (*/).

The same docblock notation is used to introduce the one function you have in your module so far. This comment must be immediately above the function, with no blank lines between them. Its first sentence must fit on a single line, including the period it must end with, and additional lines of description or explanation must be separated by an empty comment line. In this case, as a simple hook implementation, a single-line sentence of documentation can be the only line. The comment informs anyone reading the code that the function `xray_form_alter()` implements `hook_form_alter()`.

Wait, "implements `hook_form_alter()`"? What is that even supposed to mean?

Hooks

Hooks are the magic portals that let any module, including your module, appear in another part of Drupal and do something. When Drupal takes an action it considers important (loading content, saving a user account, displaying a comment, etc.), it takes a moment to invite any installed module to observe or intervene. Every hook is an opportunity for your module to take action in response to something Drupal is doing—and there are 251 hooks in Drupal core, according to the list at `api.drupal.org/hooks`.

The "hook" in a hook name is a placeholder for the short name of the implementing module. It signifies the naming convention that allows functions to behave in this special way. When a typical hook is invoked, Drupal looks through all enabled modules for functions that start with the module name and end with the hook name, not including the word "hook." Thus, to implement a hook, take the "hook" part off the front of the hook name and replace it with your module's short (machine) name. This is why `hook_form_alter()` is implemented in the X-ray module by the function `xray_form_alter()`.

■ **Tip** If you see a function `hook_anything_whatsoever()`, it's a demonstration of how to use that hook (and as such should live in an `.api.php` file such as `modules/system/system.api.php`). Your module's functions will not start with the word "hook." A function that implements a hook *will* say which hook it is implementing in its documentation block comment, but the function name itself will use the module's short name in place of the word "hook."

In computer science terms, Drupal's hooks fit the event-driven design pattern in the Inversion of Control family of design patterns. Every use of `module_invoke_all()` (or a variant method of invoking hooks) is an event that other parts of Drupal, including contributed modules, can respond to (or not respond to; that's also perfectly fine). For example, when comment module shows a comment, it runs this code

```
module_invoke_all('comment_view', $comment, $view_mode, $langcode);
```

to give any module a chance to act on the comment by implementing `hook_comment_view()`. The comment object is passed to implementing functions by reference so that changes can be made on it directly. The view mode and language code are provided as context that can be taken into account when reacting to the comment being viewed. The hook function signature describes what is passed to a hook, and every function signature can be seen on `api.drupal.org`. For instance, `hook_comment_view()`'s definition can be found at `api.drupal.org/hook_comment_view`. Each hook's API documentation will also explain if and what a hook implementation should return.

Larry Garfield (crell) writes that in a procedural system, which PHP applications historically are, this hook method is a very good way to keep code loosely coupled, meaning that your code doesn't have to know squat about how the code you're talking to works, as long as you know what the other code wants. For more about approaches to programming and how some of them relate to Drupal, you can read crell's blog at garfieldtech.com/blog/language-tradeoffs. For what this means for your module, read the sidebar on how Drupal displays help text on a page.

■ **Tip** The best way to learn how to use hooks is to download several contributed Drupal modules and find where the hooks are really used, says Drupal developer and educator Chacha Sikes. Then you can compare the hooks in use to the hook definitions on `api.drupal.org` to see how the module developer figured out how to implement the hook.

All hooks defined in Drupal core can be looked up at `api.drupal.org`. Many that are defined in contributed modules can be looked up at `drupalcontrib.org`. All this documentation is being generated by comments in Drupal's code, so you can put in some work yourself to install the (currently Drupal 6) API module (`drupal.org/project/api`) or simply look at the code of the module you are interested in. If a module defines hooks, it should have a .api.php module with examples of how to use them.

HOW DRUPAL USES HOOKS TO DISPLAY HELP TEXT ON A PAGE

The X-ray module will make heavy use of `hook_help()` to show text in the help region on pages it investigates. Placing the following code in the `xray.module` file is sufficient to add text to the help block when visiting the page Administration ➤ Structure (`admin/structure`):

```php
<?php
// [Existing code not shown due to space considerations]...
/**
 * Implements hook_help().
 */
function xray_help($path, $arg) {
  if ($path == 'admin/structure') {
    return t('This site has stuff!');
  }
}
```

Displaying the text "This site has stuff!" at the top of the Structure administration page seems like a simple task—all right, it *is* a simple task—yet the complexity of how that text gets there is the secret source of Drupal's power. You don't need to know how hooks work to use them, but understanding how Drupal works never hurts (much). Let's take a short tour of how Drupal puts help text on a page.

Drupal Turning Paths into Pages: hook_menu()

Drupal is going about its business, which usually means displaying a web page. You've clicked on the Structure link in the toolbar (`admin/structure`). Your browser tells Drupal that's where you want to go. Every path ultimately matches up to a menu item with a page callback function that has chief responsibility for displaying the page at that path. These menu items are provided by implementations of `hook_menu()` and stored in the menu_router table. (The menu system is covered in greater detail in Chapter 29.)

Menu items can include information to calculate whether the user requesting the page has access or not, and if there is any file that should be included before calling the page callback function. Having taken care of the main content (typically a renderable array or chunk of HTML that, in this case, is a list of the administrative links within the Structure section), Drupal looks to load up all the other regions of the page, too. It gets the regions available from the theme in use at the time, and it gets the blocks assigned to each region of that theme from the block system. All that information is provided by Drupal calling hooks. Other parts of Drupal's core code or contributed or custom code you've added answer the calls with functions that implement those hooks.

And you still have another major hook to go before you reach your little help hook.

Drupal Showing a Block: hook_block_view()

When the system_help block (which by default assigns itself to the help region) is reached, Drupal calls a specific implementation of hook_block_view(). That is, rather than following the common pattern of invoking a hook in all modules that implement it, Drupal here follows an alternate pattern of invoking the hook as implemented in only one specific module. Drupal constructs a function name from the name of the module providing the block (system)and the hook's name(block_view). The naming convention of calling a function based on the combination of a module's name and the hook name is the same one used when invoking a hook in multiple modules. It allows you to say that the function system_block_view() *implements* hook_block_view(). (Some distinguish this from true hooks by calling them callbacks; see drupal.org/node/1114032 to see if this gets done in Drupal 8.)

When invoking system module's implementation of hook_block_view() for the system_help block, Drupal passes in the text "help" as a parameter. Inside the function system_block_view() is a switch statement that decides what code gets run. When the parameter given is "help," the switch statement (and subsequently the function) gives back information for the system_help block. It sets the title of the block to nothing and sets the body of the block to the value returned by the function menu_get_active_help().

Drupal Gathering Help for a Page: hook_help()

It is now that Drupal finally invokes the hook which your module implements, hook_help(). Inside the function menu_get_active_help(), Drupal gets the internal router path of the page that is currently being visited. Then it says, pretty much literally, "for each module that implements the hook "help," give me what you've got for this path." It takes what it receives, if anything, from all the implementations of hook_help() and combines them into a single string. It returns that output to be used as the body of the system_help block. Your module is named xray, the hook is named help. Therefore, you named your function xray_help() and stated in its code comment that it implements hook_help(). As noted, the entire hook system is based on this naming convention of module name plus hook name; if a function exists with that name, Drupal considers the hook to be implemented and calls that function when invoking the hook.

■ **Note** The "for each module that implements hook x" step is the same thing that happens whenever Drupal calls `module_invoke_all('x')`, where 'x' is the hook name without the preceding "hook." Whether or not the function `module_invoke_all()` is used, something very similar occurs each time a hook is invoked.

The `hook_help()` function signature lets you know that your function will receive a parameter (you can think of a *parameter* or *argument* as a piece of information) represented by `$path` and that your function needs to return some text. The function signature for `hook_help()` is defined at `api.drupal.org/hook_help` and also in Drupal core's code at `modules/help/help.api.php`.

■ **Tip** You can look up any hook the same way you look up any function—by searching for it on Drupal's API site at `api.drupal.org`. You can get to a function or hook, for instance `hook_menu`, by typing it into the search address directly (`api.drupal.org/api/search/7/hook_menu`) or, even more concisely when searching within the current version of Drupal, by simply adding the function name or hook name onto the API site's address: `api.drupal.org/hook_menu`. Be sure you are looking at the function or hook documentation for your version of Drupal; `api.drupal.org` provides tabs for Drupal 5, Drupal 6, and Drupal 7.

The function `menu_get_active_help()`, when called for the Structure administration page by the sequence of events I just went over, hands the parameter `$path` with the value `admin/structure` to each function that implements `hook_help()`. Block module's `block_help()` function checks and tells Drupal it has nothing for it at that path. Node module's `node_help()` also checks and reports nothing. Taxonomy module's `taxonomy_help()` function and all the other modules that implement `hook_help()` check to see if they have anything to say for the path `admin/structure`, and they all say no. (This doesn't have to be the case; they could all return text for a path and Drupal would combine the help text and display it on the page, but this is why `admin/structure` had no help on it before— all of this happens whether your module is enabled or not.) Finally, `menu_get_active_help()` asks X-ray module's `xray_help()` if it has anything for the path `admin/structure`.

```
function xray_help($path, $arg) {
  if ($path == 'admin/structure') {
    return t('This site has stuff!');
  }
}
```

Inside `xray_help()`, it takes the `$path` parameter and checks if it is equal to the text "admin/structure". Upon realizing that it is, your function exclaims OMG! and immediately returns the text "This site has stuff!" to `menu_get_active_help()`, which in turn passes the same text back up the stack to `system_block_view()`, which returns the same text, now combined with the empty title it set earlier, back to the Block module, which you last saw a half-dozen paragraphs ago, but fortunately Drupal works a lot faster than this story.

■ **Tip** See the hook_help() function signature in Chapter 20 for details about the $path parameter and the as-yet unmentioned $arg parameter.

It worked to good dramatic effect, but X-ray module was only last to be asked about the path because it came last alphabetically. If you had a Zebra module with the function zebra_help(), or a module that has been intentionally set to a heavier weight, either of those would be called after your module. All implementations of hook_help() get called. The order doesn't make much difference, unless you care about whether your help text is before or after another module also providing help text on the same page. Also note that your xray_help() function gets called by this chain of events on *every* page, but on all those other pages it compares $path to "admin/structure", realizes they are not equal and that it has nothing to say, and returns nothing.

Drupal Allowing Blocks to be Modified: hook_block_view_alter() and hook_block_BLOCK_ID_view_alter()

Block module, immediately after it receives its response from system_block_view(), builds the block. Then it fires off yet another hook using drupal_alter() to allow any module to implement hook_block_view_alter() and change the title or the body of the block, based on the block machine name (system_help in this case). Actually, Drupal gives you two alter hooks at this point; the second one is the precisely named hook_block_view_system_help_alter() for any module that wants to pinpoint the system_help block for changes. You don't implement either hook, and no other module does either, but the point is you could; it's one more way Drupal builds in flexibility and extensibility.

■ **Note** Don't use alter hooks unless absolutely necessary. You could have given X-ray module a function named xray_block_view_system_help_alter() and tacked your text onto the help block's content by altering that specific block. This would have required you to figure out the path you are on yourself, but more importantly it's the wrong way to do it because it's farther outside the system Drupal has set up for help text. You should always do things at the first opportunity Drupal gives you to do them. Doing things later means missing out on tools Drupal provides for you and takes away opportunities for other modules to react to and act on what you're doing in your module.

Hooks Open Drupal to Change and Extension

You really get a sense of how Drupal thinks from the story of how Drupal uses hooks when it displays help text on a page. Drupal doesn't hardcode a set of regions for its pages; it gets that from a theme. It lets any module provide a block that can be put in any of those regions. And in its own code, when it provides the help block, it lets any module stick help messages in there. Then, for good measure, it lets any other module take a crack at modifying this block. (The page rendering layer gives still another chance to alter parts of the page before it is output.) In general, there's a hook for everything Drupal does, which is why, no matter what you need to do, there's a module for that—or soon will be!

■ **Note** The previous story was told by a debugging tool. Chapter 12 and `dgd7.org/ide` talk about the tools you need to read your own "Page request in the life of Drupal" adventure stories whenever you want.

Technical Skills

Even if you're familiar with PHP and Drupal's coding standards, it may be worth your while to skim this section. There's usually something you can pick up. In fact, I learned new things writing this section.

PHP Basics

Some would tell you that you should know PHP and SQL before embarking on a journey into Drupal's innards. To them, you can say you're sure the authors will remind you what those acronyms mean in a minute, and you'll be good to go. PHP is the programming language in which Drupal is written. (Its acronym doesn't stand for much of anything anymore; officially it is a recursive acronym for PHP: Hypertext Preprocessor.) PHP will run, and is likely to be found, nearly anywhere you can run a web server. SQL (Structured Query Language) is for communicating with relational databases, which is where Drupal stores its configuration and content by default.

Studying PHP and SQL is a good idea, certainly, but it is possible to get started with Drupal development and learn as you go. As this is one book, and not a multi-volume series, it takes the learn-it-all-through-Drupal approach. I will go over some PHP basics here; SQL will be touched on in the section on Drupal's database layer in Chapter 19.

Programming, with PHP or anything else, is just logic—almost literally—which makes it easy in some ways and hard in others. You can learn the fundamentals of any programming language by learning its syntax and applying a little logic. On the other hand, people get PhDs in logic, and that's without the quirks of different programming languages. But don't worry; you will jump in and learn the basics of PHP and apply it in practice within the structure of Drupal programming.

The best learning advice is to look at a lot of Drupal code. Whenever you see something and you don't understand what it's doing, look up the operator or function on `php.net` or, for Drupal-specific functions, on `api.drupal.org`. (If you see a function in Drupal core, and it's not on one of those sites, it's on the other.)

■ **Tip** The official PHP web site—`php.net`—is an excellent resource with good documentation for every function and many comments by people who have been there and done that before you. Furthermore, it's easy to find function definitions by typing the function name directly after the site URL. To get the definition for the function `substr()`, you would enter into your browser `php.net/substr` or, if you didn't remember the function name exactly, you would give your best guess. Picking one of `php.net`'s suggestions, and always checking out the See also section underneath most function definitions, is usually a faster way to find the function you need than searching the web as a whole. If I have a guess, I make `php.net` my first stop.

Terminology

There are some words in code that initially seem like they are just there to confuse things; however, after using them for a while you won't know how to speak without them.

- A *string* is literally a string of characters. It could be a word, a phrase, or a random group of characters. The closest non-jargon term is probably "chunk of text." It could be a single character or there could be no text in a string at all, which is called an *empty string*.

- An integer is a whole number (no decimal places), positive or negative, or, as the PHP manual puts it, "a number of the set $\mathbb{Z} = \{..., -2, -1, 0, 1, 2, ...\}$." (php.net/integer)

- An *array* can hold any assortment of other variable types (strings, integers, objects) or it can hold more arrays! The latter happens disturbingly often in Drupal and is called *nested arrays*. An associative array has keys, which are integers or strings pointing to values, which, as mentioned, can be anything.

- An *object* is sometimes used in Drupal similarly to arrays to hold a collection of related data (such as the $user object or $node object). Objects can do much more, such as inheriting information and functionality from a parent object and defining their own methods, which are functions specific to objects of that type.

- A *variable* is a labeled holder for some value that can be changed. Variables in PHP have to start with a dollar sign, such as $name_of_variable. A variable can be a string, number, array, object, or another variable type such as non-integer numbers, called *floats*.

- A *function* is a set of code that can be called by name. It can receive variables (as parameters, covered next) and can return a value. You can define your own functions and each has a local scope for variables used within it, such that the function code is discrete from other code. All code written for a module should be within functions you define. Both xray_form_alter() and xray_help(), already seen, are functions.

- *Parameters* (also called *arguments*) allow the code calling a function to send information to that function. The parameter or parameters a function expects constitute that function's signature.

Although PHP only mildly complains if it comes across an empty variable that it has not been told about before, you should always *initialize* your variables. This means to define them before, or in the act of, your first use of them. Functions allow default parameters to be defined, which can have the effect of ensuring the initialization of those variables. For instance, a function with the name of example_takes_arguments and defined as function example_takes_arguments($text = 'Hi.') { ... } will have the variable $text available inside it (the code that would replace the ... here), set to the value 'Hi.'

Operators and Conditional Statements

An operator is something that receives one or more values and returns a value. A value is also called an expression, which makes the point that any combination of things that returns a value is, indeed, a value.

Assignment Operators

The most common operator is the assignment operator (the equals sign), which is used to assign any variable a value or the result of an expression.

```
$num = 5;
$an_array = array(
  'a_number' => $num,
  'a_letter' => 'k',
);
$another_array = array(
  'a_letter' => "If merged this will overwrite k with a sentence. Oops.",
);
$function_result = array_merge($an_array, $another_array);
```

These silly examples all have the assignment operator, "=", in common, and indeed you will use it constantly to set the value of variables. Note that at the end, the variable $function_result has the value

```
array('a_number' => 5, 'a_letter' => If merged this will overwrite k with a sentence. Oops.",
```

String Operators

String operators include the concatenation operator, which per Drupal coding standards is always separated on both sides by a space, like so:

```
$end = " completion of string";
$msg = "Start of string" . $end;
```

The concatenating assignment operator can take everything in the string already and add onto the end of it.

```
$msg .= "!!!";
```

The resulting string $msg is

```
Start of string completion of string!!!
```

Arithmetic Operators

From simple addition to getting the remainder in division, the operators work the same as the symbols on your calculator.

- 5 + 2 returns 7

- 5 - 2 returns 3

- 5 * 2 returns 10

- 5 / 2 returns 2.5

- 5 % 2 returns 1

Comparison Operators

Comparison operators compare two values. For instance:

- 5 == 2 returns FALSE (is equal to; don't forget both of the equals signs, or it becomes the assignment operator and so is always true when comparing a variable to a value or another variable) and "apple" == "apple" returns TRUE.

- 5 != 2 returns TRUE (is not equal to).

- 5 < 2 returns FALSE (is less than).

- 5 > 2 returns TRUE (is greater than).

- 5 <= 2 returns FALSE (is less than or equal to), and 3 <= 3 returns TRUE.

- 5 >= 2 returns TRUE (is greater than or equal to), and 3 >= 3 returns TRUE.

There are two more comparison operators that are quite important. These are the *identity comparisons* that check if two values are of the same type before trying to compare them. This means, for instance, that FALSE will not equal an empty array, and strings are not converted to integers for comparison (which is a nice bonus because that conversion can lead to unexpected results). They also are faster than the equality comparisons. Examples include:

1 === TRUE returns FALSE, and 1 === 1 returns TRUE.

'' !== array() returns TRUE.

Ternary Operator

The *ternary operator* is an occasionally allowed exception to Drupal's bias toward more spread out, easily understood code. The ternary operator is compact and confusing.

$resulting_value = ($condition) ? "If TRUE value" : "If FALSE value";

Let's start in the parenthesis (which aren't required, but are best practice). The expression in this first location is evaluated. It can be a simple variable or it can be a complex set of logic. Usually it will be a variable or a straightforward comparison such as ($maybe_seven == 7). If the evaluation is TRUE, then the value immediately following the question mark is returned. If the first expression evaluates to false, the value after the colon is returned. (Technically these latter two values could be expressions and so are called the second and third expressions.) For more information, see Comparison Operators page at php.net/ternary.

■ **Note** You will frequently come across situations where you want to set a variable equal to a value *if* that value is non-empty or non-zero, such as $result = ($value) ? $value : "default". In these situations, the ternary operator seems less than compact because you are repeating the variable for the test and for the assignment. All you can do is wait for Drupal 8: Drupal 7 requires a minimum PHP version of 5.2, and it is not until PHP 5.3 that you can leave out the middle part of the ternary operator. In PHP 5.3, the expression $value ?: "default" returns $value if $value evaluates to anything other than FALSE, and "default" otherwise. (If you have a more compelling reason to require PHP 5.3 and above, you can declare it the minimum version your module or theme will support by adding the line `php = 5.3` in your `.info` file.)

Logical Operators

The more common comparison operators you will see in Drupal are the following:

- `$a && $b` which returns TRUE if both $a **and** $b are TRUE.

- `$a || $b` returns TRUE if either $a **or** $b is TRUE.

- `!$a` returns TRUE if $a is **not** TRUE.

The words "and" and "or" can also be used and act as lower-precedence (evaluated later) versions of `&&` and `||`, respectively. (There is one more logical operator, `xor`, that works such that the expression `$a xor $b` returns true if only *one* of $a and $b is true.)

You can find more kinds of operators (along with more detail on the ones covered) at `php.net/operator`.

Control Structures

PHP uses control structures to decide what code gets run, or *executed*. Often this decision is made with the help of conditional statements like equals (`$a == $b`), identical (`$a === $b`), is less than (`$a < $b`), is greater than or equal to (`$a >= $b`), etc., that were discussed in the previous section on comparison operators.

The if, elseif, and else Statements

An `if` statement can stand alone, it can be followed by an `else` statement that is executed instead if the conditional for the `if` statement evaluates to FALSE, or it can come in a chain of `if` statements using the `elseif` syntax. This can also end in an `else` statement, which gets used if none of the above evaluated to true. See Listing 18–7 for examples.

Listing 18–7. Chained if/else Statements

```
if ($advice == 'good') {
  $do = 'Follow it.';
}
elseif ($advice == 'bad') {
  $do = 'Don\'t follow it.';
}
else {
  $do = 'Who knows?  If all else fails, do as you please.';
}
```

■ **Caution** Note the apostrophe in the string *Don't follow it.* It is *escaped* with a backslash (\) because in plain text the apostrophe is the same character as a single quotation mark, which is the character used to indicate the start and end of the string. If you had used double quotation marks to bound your string, you wouldn't have needed to escape the single quotation mark—but you would have needed to use the backslash to escape any double quotation marks in the string.

These if() statements used comparison operators. An if() statement can also do an implied comparison when given just one expression to evaluate; if the expression has any non-zero, non-empty value the statement will evaluate to TRUE, so there's no need for an "== TRUE". Use simply

```
if ($condition) {
  // Take example action when condition is true.
  take_example_action();
}
```

A single exclamation point before an expression reverses its true/false evaluation, so for instance:

```
if (!$condition} {
  // Take example action when condition is false.
  take_example_action();
}
```

The switch and case Statements

Another control structure, the switch statement, using any number of case statements inside it, doesn't do anything a chain of if, elseif, elseif, elseif… statements couldn't do, but it is considered a cleaner and more readable way to compare one value to multiple options.

You used to have a single case, handled by the statement if ($path == 'admin/structure')… Now, you're comparing the path variable to more possibilities (five in the Listing 18–8), so you have replaced the if statement with the switch/case syntax. (You've also offloaded the messages to helper functions. You'll look at what you're doing in them later.)

Listing 18–8. A Switch Statement Used in One Version of xray_help()

```
switch ($path) {
    case 'admin/content':
      return _xray_help_admin_content();
    case 'admin/structure':
      return _xray_help_admin_structure();
    case 'admin/appearance':
      return _xray_help_admin_appearance();
    case 'admin/people':
      return _xray_help_admin_people();
    case 'admin/modules':
      return _xray_help_admin_modules();
  }
```

The switch statement does the equivalent of a (`$path == 'admin/content'`) comparison for the first case statement, and if it evaluates to true, it executes the code beneath the `case 'admin/content':` line, and so on for each case statement. Note that when executing the code beneath a case statement, a `break;` statement is usually used to leave the switch after a case matches, but a `return;` statement ends the entire function and so makes anything else unnecessary. For more, see `php.net/switch`.

Loops

The other control structures you will see most commonly in Drupal are loops. A `while ($expression) {` `... }` statement continues to run the code inside its brackets so long as `$expression` evaluates to TRUE; the value of variables in the expression must of course be changed by this code within the statement so that the loop will stop eventually. See `php.net/while` for more on while. A `for ($i = 0; $i < 5; $i++) {` `... }` statement will execute the code within its brackets five times in this example, for the values of `$i` from zero to four; see `php.net/for` for more information. Finally, the special `foreach ($array as $key` `=> $value) { ... }` will iterate over all the items in an array, providing the repeated code within the brackets with the key and value for each item. Listing the key is optional.

```
foreach ($lumps as $lump) {
  $variables['extra'] .= krumo_ob($lump);
}
```

Drupal Coding Standards

Why, one might ask, is how the code *looks* as important as how it *works*? PHP ignores extra white space, so you could write your entire module on one line if you wanted, and it would work. The code would also be unreadable. Sure, that's an extreme case—a straw man argument. But in Drupal, the standards are a lot higher than being able to read something yourself. Your code must be as clear as possible to other Drupalistas; following coding standards is very important for collaboration. And if beauty and logic are not enough to convince you to keep your code up to scratch, you'll be called out, repeatedly, when you violate the standards. This is the character-building chapter, and good coding habits are best formed early, so do the right thing.

Some Important Standards, Explained

Keeping code readable and maintainable is easier when you know what you need to do and why you should do it. The following commandments are among the most important when writing modules. More rules and explanation can be found at `drupal.org/coding-standards`.

Use <?php Opening Tag

Always use full `<?php` tags, not any of its abbreviations. Aside from being uncouth to the eye, anything other than `<?php` is not guaranteed to work in all configurations of PHP.

Don't End Files with the Closing PHP Tag

In most files, you don't use a closing PHP tag at all. Every module file (`.module`), include file (`.inc`), install file (`.install`), `settings.php` file, and `template.php` file (in themes) should have `<?php` *immediately* at the top and not have any closing PHP tag.

Leaving closing PHP tags off prevents a common problem caused by white space after a closing tag. It can be seen in the form of an error such as *"Warning: Cannot modify header information - headers already sent by (output started at /var/www/example/drupal/sites/default/oops/oops.module.php:37) in /var/www/example/drupal/includes/bootstrap.inc on line 568"*. Any white space after a closing PHP tag is sent to the browser and can interfere with when output is supposed to start.

Of course, there's an exception to this rule: template files (.tpl.php), which are already supposed to be sending output. Generally, a template file starts with HTML, dips into PHP, returns to HTML and goes back and forth between them, usually ending with HTML again. Therefore, closing PHP tags are not only allowed but necessary. The closing PHP tag is simply ?> and should only be used in templates.

Precede Internal Functions with an Underscore

Functions with names that start with an underscore, such as _function_name(), are meant for a module's internal use. They should not be called by other modules.

The underscore naming convention for private functions has two major benefits. First, it lets everyone know the function is for internal use and that if they use it, they are doing it wrong, because you reserve the right to remove or modify the function on a whim. You can also change non-underscored public API functions, but you should strive never to do this unless you are also releasing a new major branch of your module (for instance, changing the release number from 1.x to 2.x). Second, preceding internal functions with an underscore helps prevent you from accidentally implementing a Drupal hook (there are, remember, more than 250 hooks in core alone).

■ **Caution** You still need to precede internal function names with your module's name as well as the underscore, in the form _modulename_function(), or you risk having a function with the same name as someone else's function. Two functions with the same name is a namespace collision that causes PHP to have a fatal error, which is nearly as bad as it sounds.

Indent Two Spaces

You should indent functions, control structures like loops and if statements, array definitions, and pretty much anything that looks indentable; and do so with two spaces, not a tab. (You can configure some IDEs and code editing tools to use two spaces whenever you hit the tab key; see Chapter 12 and dgd7.org/ide.)

Everything within a function, for instance, starts on a new line and is indented two spaces; everything within an if statement within that function is indented two more spaces, for a total of four.

All Control Statements, Including else, Start a New Line

The else clause in an if statements goes on a new line, starting fresh, following the closing bracket:

```
if ($following_coding_standards) {
  drupal_set_message("Good job!");
}
else {
  drupal_set_message("Follow this example!");
}
```

Use a Space Between Control Statements and Their Opening Parenthesis

To make these control statements more distinguishable from functions, separate their condition (in parenthesis) from the control statement name with a space; this can be seen in the if statement line in the previous example. As with functions, the opening curly brace is also separated with a space. That accounts for both spaces in the "if ($following_coding_standards) {" line. The same goes for foreach statements, while loops, etc.

Use Spaces Between Parameters

Put spaces between parameters in function definitions and function calls, like so:

```
function space_standard($parameter, $another_parameter, $last_parameter) {
  _space_standard($parameter, $another_parameter, $last_parameter);
}
```

Use Spaces on Either Side of All Binary Operators, Concatenators, and the Like

A binary operator is simply something that acts, or *operates*, on *two* values at once, to return a new value. This includes comparison operators such as == or >=, arithmetic operators such as + or /, string operators such as . or .=, logical operators such as && or ||, and assignment operators such as = or += (the latter is a combined arithmetic and assignment operator, as .= is a combined string and assignment operator). The general rule is whenever something is between two values, give it a single space on each side.

    The following code is thick with operators. The point is that every single one of them is politely buffered by a single space on each side.

```
if ($budget < $money || ($is_broke && !$has_credit)) {
  $message = 'Your remaining $' . $money - $budget . ' is not enough.';
}
```

AN ASIDE ON WHAT THE CODE IS SAYING

It may or may not help to know what the previous code example is saying, but here it is, with *values* in italics and **operators** in bold: If *budget* is **less than** *money* **or** the person both *is broke* **and** *does not have credit*, then set the *message* **to equal** a phrase made up of a *text string* ('Your remaining $') **concatenated with** the result of *money* **minus** *budget*, further **concatenated with** a final *text string* (' is not enough.').

A few code tricks are worth noting in this example. First, negation is signified by the exclamation point. In the code example, it changes the meaning of $has_credit to its opposite: if $has_credit is true, the expression !$has_credit evaluates to false. Second, the dollar symbol is everywhere a mark of a variable, except in one place—inside the single quotation marks the dollar symbol does not designate a variable and is simply a character in the string. Finally, the two ampersands—&&—join $is_broke and !$has_credit together, so *both* must evaluate to true for the combined expression to be true. On the other hand, the or symbol—||—signifies that if either expression to its left or right evaluates to true, then the whole expression is true.

Automating Adherence

Thanks to the fantastic work of Stella Power (stella), Doug Green (douggreen), and Jim Berry (solotandem), the art of conforming to coding standards can be automated. You'll get to see this in practice when you polish your module for contributing in Chapter 20.

Stella's Coder Review module (part of the Coder project at `drupal.org/project/coder`) will review source code files for code that does not satisfy Drupal coding standards, flagging each violation as having minor, normal, or critical severity. The use of this module is explained in Chapter 20, before you share your module with the world.

Solotandem's Grammar Parser library (`drupal.org/project/grammar_parser`) will go a step farther and put in an effort to rewrite a module file to conform to coding standards. This author, for the moment, eschews the Grammar Parser approach in favor of the "eat your veggies" philosophy and corrects coding standards lapses by hand (after Coder Review automatically points them out), but it's only a matter of time before the sheer awesomeness of the Grammar Parser contribution overwhelms all objections.

■ **Tip** JavaScript also has coding standards. See `drupal.org/node/172169` and Chapter 17.

Development Tip #1: When Something Isn't Working, Clear Caches

For the sake of performance, Drupal has dozens of places where information is cached, or stored in an easily accessible way, rather than read and interpreted from the database and code every time it's needed. Therefore, when developing, if you don't see the changes you made in your code, it's not necessarily a problem with your code; it may be that Drupal's caches and registries are out of date.

You can manually clear caches and rebuild the theme and menu registries at Administration ➤ Configuration ➤ Development ➤ Performance (`admin/config/development/performance`) by clicking the Clear all caches button. You may want to link to this page using the Shortcuts module, or use a module such as Admin menu that enables you to clear all caches with a single click on a link.

You can also clear caches by placing the function `drupal_flush_all_caches();` in a part of your code that is run (that is, not where it is cached); a can't-miss spot is `index.php` between `drupal_bootstrap()` and `menu_execute_active_handler()` but remember to remove it later.

As usual, the most convenient way to clear all caches including the theme registry is with Drush: `drush cc all` (you can alias this in your shell to be even shorter, see `dgd7.org/162`).

However you clear caches, learn to like the method(s) you use, because you'll be doing it a lot.

■ **Tip** See Chapter 27 for a way to disable caching entirely while developing. However, Drupal also has registries, including for `hook_menu()` and `hook_theme()`, that are rebuilt using the clear all caches methods mentioned previously.

Development Tip #2: When Anything's Missing, Check Permissions

You add a new page, block, or feature of any kind; you reload the page, clear the cache (see above), shift-reload the page to make sure it's not the browser cache, and still nothing. It's time to check access control and permissions. In code, when a page or tab isn't working, you should check if there is an access argument or access callback defined for the related menu item. When it comes to configuration, you want to be sure you've granted proper access to the user you are testing between the Permissions page (admin/people/permissions) and the roles assignment on the given user's edit page (user/[uid]/edit), where [uid] is the user's numeric ID.

■ **Tip** If something works when you're logged in as the superuser or an administrator but not when you're logged out or logged in with a lesser role, the problem is pretty certainly in your permissions configuration.

Development Tip #3: Set Your Site to Show All Errors

When developing a module, you want every bit of feedback as quickly as possible from the system. Adding the code in Listing 18–9 into your local settings.php should ensure that all notices and errors are immediately printed to the screen. (In Drupal 6 it's a little more work; see randyfay.com/node/76.)

Listing 18–9. Lines to Add to settings.php to Show All Notices and Errors

```
error_reporting(-1);
$conf['error_level'] = 2;
ini_set('display_errors', TRUE);
ini_set('display_startup_errors', TRUE);
```

The first line sets PHP to report every conceivable notice and error (the -1 is an undocumented shortcut). The second line tells Drupal to show all these notices and errors as messages on your screen (2 equals the constant ERROR_REPORTING_DISPLAY_ALL, but that constant is not defined yet when settings.php is loaded). The last two lines help ensure that the infamous "White Screen of Death" (WSOD) from PHP errors becomes instead a screen with the error printed on it.

Summary

This chapter introduces you to module building, and provides you with the basics of a module and how Drupal uses hooks in nearly everything it does to allow modules to extend and modify Drupal. It also includes an overview of technical skills required to develop a module, including PHP basics and Drupal coding standards, and it offers helpful development tips.

You're now ready to take on a full module, which is where Chapter 19 comes in.

■ **Tip** More tips and discussion online at dgd7.org/intromodule.

CHAPTER 19

■■■

Using Drupal's APIs in a Module

by Benjamin Melançon

The nature of the game in making modules for Drupal is using the tools Drupal provides you. API stands for Application Programming Interface and is a fancy way of saying that code has clearly defined ways of talking to other code. This chapter is devoted to introducing APIs, the hooks and functions Drupal provides to you, in the context of building the X-ray module introduced in Chapter 18. As each feature of the module requires using another tool from the extensive selection in Drupal's API toolbox, I will introduce it and use it.

At the time of this writing, Drupal core provides **251** hooks. This chapter covers some of the most-used ones. Hooks, though the stars of the show, are but one part of the ensemble you have to work with. You have a fantastic supporting cast in the form of Drupal's excellent utility functions. These functions, too, are a part of Drupal's APIs.

The module made in this chapter is loosely based on a suggestion posted to the Contributed Module Ideas group (`groups.drupal.org/contributed-module-ideas`) by Zoë Neill-St. Clair. She proposed a module to give a technical summary of a Drupal site, with relationships between content types and explanations of what in Drupal produces each page. You don't know how to do this yet, but you know it can be done; everything else is filling in details.

In this chapter, you will see instructions and examples for using the hooks and functions provided by Drupal. These are covered in the course of building a complete module and include the following:

- Altering forms.

- Localization (providing a translatable user interface).

- Making modules themeable and styling your module.

- Creating pages with hook_menu().

- Using and defining permissions.

- Retrieving and storing data using the database abstraction layer.

Altering Forms

Changing anything about forms calls for my all-time favorite hook: hook_form_alter(). Whether you want to modify a form element, change the order of form elements, remove something entirely, or add something new, this is the hook for you. It comes in two varieties: the original, general hook_form_alter() that runs for every form Drupal outputs, and any number of hooks in the pattern hook_form_FORM_ID_alter(), which are specific to particular forms.

As always, you can find documentation for any function or hook on api.drupal.org, so for this hook, type api.drupal.org/hook_form_alter. The first parameter your implementation of hook_form_alter() will receive is the nested array that represents the form. The reason this hook is so powerful is because Drupal holds all the information about the form in this array when it renders and processes the form, so any change you make affects the form cleanly and more than cosmetically.

Form elements are exhaustively documented at api.drupal.org/api/drupal/developer--topics--forms_api_reference.html/7. (For convenience, I'll link to this and related documentation from dgd7.org/forms.) Fortunately, to begin altering forms, you don't need to know about every possible form element—you can simply look at the elements present in the form you choose to alter.

That's another nice thing about hook_form_alter(), everything you learn while messing with other forms is applicable when you build your own forms. Whether creating a new form or adding to an existing one, the form element definition looks exactly the same.

As a refresher, the X-ray module you started in Chapter 18 prints the form identifier for each form on the site. Instead of just showing the code this time, I'll explain what code to write. Add the code in Listing 19–1 to the xray.module file (if you have already defined xray_form_alter(), only add the debug line within it—PHP can't have two functions with the same name).

Listing 19–1. Implementation of hook_form_alter() by the X-ray Module, Containing Only Debug Statements

```
/**
 * Implements hook_form_alter().
 */
function xray_form_alter(&$form, &$form_state, $form_id) {
  debug($form, $form_id, TRUE);
}
```

▓ **Tip** After creating any modulename_form_alter() or modulename_form_FORM_ID_alter() function for the first time, *clear your caches.* You can do this, for instance, with the Drupal shell command drush cc all. (For more on the marvelously powerful and convenient Drush, see Chapter 26.)

The debug() function takes any variable, including an object or an array (such as your form) and prints it to the screen. If you don't see any debug output, it could be that something is interfering (as can be the case when Devel module's backtrace logging option is selected) rather than because your code is not running (such as due to the module not being enabled, the hook name being incorrectly formed, or caches not having been cleared yet). You can put an exit('Show me a sign'); line in your code (with the status text of your choice) as a quick way to establish whether it's being run at all.

▓ **Tip** Drupal 7 introduces a debug() function, which is a great convenience when developing (or, naturally, debugging). To use it, you can put any variable or output-generating function as the first parameter, optionally followed by a label to help you keep track of multiple uses of debug(). For instance, debug($user, 'User object'); prints the contents of the $user variable, which in most places in Drupal is an object representing the currently logged-in user.

Visiting any page with a form (which is every public page if the Search module and block are enabled) will result in a message for each form printing the array of all form elements (which are more arrays), both visible and hidden. The only part of the form that looks likely to always be of interest, however, is the Form ID which is printed as the label for the form array in Listing 19–1.

For your informative addition to forms, you don't want to use a form element of a type that can be submitted. The usual display-only #type is 'markup' (and because 'markup' is the fallback if #type is not defined, it does not have to be stated explicitly).

■ **Tip** New in 7, the output of a default #type 'markup' form element must be given in a #markup property, like so: `$form['just_for_show'] = array('#markup' => t('Form, not function.'));`

However, Drupal provides another form element type, 'item', that is also for static markup but includes the trappings of a real form element, such as #title and #description properties. This information-only form item is what you'll use to print out the form ID at the top of every form (see Listing 19–2).

Listing 19–2. Implementing hook_form_alter() to Add a Markup-Only Item to Every Form

```
/**
 * Implements hook_form_alter().
 */
function xray_form_alter(&$form, &$form_state, $form_id) {
  $form['xray_display_form_id'] = array(
    '#type' => 'item',
    '#title' => t('Form ID'),
    '#markup' => $form_id,
    '#theme_wrappers' => array('container__xray__form'),
    '#attributes' => array('class' => array('xray')),
    '#weight' => -100,
  );
}
```

■ **Note** Using #prefix and #suffix for markup can be a quick shortcut while developing; indeed, this form element was originally built not with #theme_wrappers and #attributes but simply with '#prefix' => '<div class="xray">' and '#suffix' => '</div>', but that's not what should be used in a finished module. (You can see the correction made in the X-ray module's repository at drupalcode.org/project/xray.git/commit/839927e.) See Chapter 33 for the journey of discovery, but the properties to use instead, as used in this example, are '#theme_wrappers' => array('container__xray__form') and '#attributes' => array('class' => array('xray')). These have identical HTML output to the manual prefix and suffix but eliminate the risk of unmatched markup (such as missing the closing </div>). More importantly, they allow themers to change the markup without trying to re-alter the form. The double underscores in front of "xray" and "form" in the theme wrapper `container__xray__form` mean that they are optional for theme functions overriding your container markup. If a theme function with the name `THEME_container__xray__form()` or `THEME_container__xray()` exists (where THEME is the name of one's theme), it will be used; if not, then `THEME_container()` will be used. If no theme function overrides it, see `api.drupal.org/theme_container` for the function that will theme the wrapper to this form element. Making your module themeable is covered later in this chapter.

The #markup property will print its value directly into HTML, so you need to make sure the argument passed to your function is HTML safe. Most of the time $form_id is a PHP identifier that can only contain numbers, letters, and the underscore, so it's considered safe in any HTML context; in the very rare other cases, it's the module author's responsibility not to allow unfiltered user input to become a $form_id. Drupal core itself prints $form_id in the form HTML as a hidden variable.

The large negative weight (-100) ensures that in almost any conceivable form, this added form element will be printed at the top.

▓ **Note** The Form API is a very important API in Drupal. Where one might expect a special API for modules to talk to each other for a particular reason, Drupal sometimes relies on its robust Form API to bring in new functionality. Node module enhances Block module with block visibility based on content type by implementing a form alter hook. In `node.module` the function `node_form_block_admin_configure_alter()` is an implementation of `hook_form_FORM_ID_alter()`, where `block_admin_configure` is the form ID in that pattern of the form that is altered. Similarly, Open ID module alters the login form with `openid_form_user_login_alter()` or `openid_form_user_login_block_alter()` (for the main `user_login` form or the `user_login_block` form, respectively).

Localization with t() and format_plural()

There is one function in the `form_alter()` implementation that is easy to overlook as it is only one character long: `t()`. The *t* stands for *translate* and the `t()` function is Drupal's most-used function. It is part of the localization system that makes it possible to translate Drupal's user interface—the parts of Drupal generated by code, as opposed to content written by users. This translatable user interface should include all text you put in any modules you make. For the most part, this means that it should all be wrapped in the `t()` function.

■ **Note** The tools for translating content (words written by the site's users) are frequently called *internationalization* and are not part of Drupal core. The gray area of administrator-defined words in Drupal (such as site name and slogan; welcome messages; and structure like menus, some taxonomy, and content type names) also falls under the rubric of internationalization and is where translation gets most difficult, er, fun. These forms of translation are usually not your concern when writing modules, rather, only localization is. In Drupal discussions and even module names, localization is frequently abbreviated as *l10n* and internationalization as *i18n*. (The abbreviations come from each word's first and last letter and the number of letters in between.) A current list of resources for both tasks is at `dgd7.org/translate`.

The point may seem obvious, but only text that you write can be translated in advance to be available to people who download your module (if you or others take the time to do the translation). Text that is modified by users or administrators and output by your module—anything that can't be known ahead of time—should not be wrapped in a translation function. Moreover, don't try to translate variables. From the X-ray module, the subheading on the reports page `t('Content summary')` is a classic example. Strings for translation are always written in English; if you can provide immediate translation for your module into another language, that's fantastic! The text in your code, however, must be in English so that all localizations can start from the same base.

This is straightforward. It gets more interesting with the ability to take placeholders for the parts of strings that should not be translated. The `t()` function has built-in security for showing such (potentially) user-submitted data when you use its placeholder array. You'll see this used in examples throughout this chapter—placeholders prefaced with @ to sanitize the variable, % to sanitize and emphasize, and ! to insert without any safety checks or changes (by the way, only use ! placeholders when you know the source is safe (never from a user) or already escaped). These placeholders are well documented at `api.drupal.org/t`. The following code shows the use of the % emphasis placeholder: %func is replaced with a sanitized value of the %func key from the array (the $page_callback variable concatenated with a pair of parenthesis) and wrapped in <em> tags:

```
$output = t('the function %func', array('%func' => $page_callback . '()'));
```

When you need text that changes based on the quantity of items being discussed (singular or multiple), Drupal has a function for you, `format_plural()`. Note that the `t()` function is used inside it (see Listing 19–3).

Listing 19–3. Using the format_plural() Function

```
$output .= format_plural(
  xray_stats_content_type_total(),
  'The site has one content type.',
  'The site has @count content types.'
);
```

The first parameter that the `format_plural()` function takes is a number. This should always be an integer (one that will vary, of course, because if you already knew if it were a single or a multiple value, you could just write your text string accordingly). In this case, that number is being supplied by your function `xray_stats_content_type_total()`. The second parameter is the string to use if the number given as the first parameter is just one; the third parameter is what string to use if it is two or more (or zero). The @count placeholder (which is the number provided by the first parameter) is always available to both strings, but you can provide more placeholders and values (just like for the t() function) in an array in the fourth parameter.

Finding a Drupal Function That Does What You Need

Finding a function that does what you need can be a three-step process of identifying a page that does something similar to what you want to do or displays information you are also interested in, looking up what function produces that page, and looking within that function to see what functions it calls.

The example below is not the cleanest (this book uses real examples, not contrived ones, precisely to show how applying methods like these really work) but don't be put off by the pages spent tracking a function down. The basic steps really are as easy as 1, 2, 3!

1. Identify a page that produces output like what you want to see.

2. Look up the page callback function for that page's menu item.

3. See what functions are used (or database queries made) in the page callback function.

■ **Tip** An analogous process can be followed to see how Drupal produces a given block; see dgd7.org/233.

You're looking to display a summary of theme information. As before, you can look directly in the database to find your information (themes, along with modules, are in the system table). Whenever possible, however, you want to use functions Drupal already provides rather than creating duplicates, even if you are just pulling data. You should put in due diligence trying to find a function that does what you need before writing your own database queries.

Finding code that uses the database table that holds information you care about can be a good way to find such a function. Even already knowing that themes are in the system table, searching the code for the word system isn't going to help you much. The system.module file alone is nearly 4,000 lines of code. Something more precise is needed to find the function related listing theme information.

This is why you look for a page in Drupal that is doing something similar to what you want to do. Especially in Drupal core, often this will be an administrative page. A look through Drupal's administration section for a listing of themes brings a swift victory: Administration ➤ Appearance (admin/appearance) appears to show all the themes!

With a debugger (see dgd7.org/ide), you can try to watch all the functions called as this page loads. Without using a debugger, this can sometimes be done even faster and is usually a two-step process. First, you find the menu item that loads the page. Second, you see what functions the menu item call. You can find the menu item by searching Drupal's code for the path of the page.

You know the enabled and available themes are shown to you when you visit the Appearance administration page (admin/appearance). Paths are provided by implementations of hook_menu(), hook implementations generally live in .module files, and you know this page is provided by Drupal core, so you can restrict your search to the top-level modules folder, like so:

```
grep -nHR --include=*.module 'admin/appearance' modules
```

A search using the powerful command line text search utility grep returns a number of matching lines, but this is the hit that's interesting to you:

```
modules/system/system.module:590:   $items['admin/appearance'] = array(
```

Now you've reached the second step: follow the code to this function. You're told what file the function is in (`modules/system/system.module`) and the line number the function appears on (590). The "`$items`" is an indicator that this is part of a menu definition (`hook_menu()` implementations are supposed to return an array of menu items). The search output has told you where to look, so you open `system.module` to see for yourselves (see Listing 19–4).

Listing 19–4. The admin/appearance Path Definition at Line 590 in system.module

```
// Appearance.
$items['admin/appearance'] = array(
  'title' => 'Appearance',
  'description' => 'Select and configure your themes',
  'page callback' => 'system_themes_page',
  'access arguments' => array('administer themes'),
  'position' => 'left',
  'weight' => -6,
  'file' => 'system.admin.inc',
);
```

Menu items are fantastic because they tell you exactly what makes a page and where it's done. The page callback is the function that makes the page and the file, if specified, is the file where the page callback function lives. In this case, it's `system.admin.inc`. If no file is specified, the page callback function is in the same `.module` file as the implementation of `hook_menu()`.

Therefore, go to `system.admin.inc` and look for the `system_themes_page()` function. And there it is. Early in this function, it calls `system_rebuild_theme_data()` to get the list of themes.

But wait. This should work... but based on the function name alone, it seems a bit much. Rebuild theme data? You just want to know what the themes are! You can look a little deeper in the function to assess if it is one you want to use.

Inside the function `system_rebuild_theme_data()`, it calls the internal function `_system_rebuild_theme_data()` (note the preceding underscore that indicates it's not meant as a public function for any module to use). You can look this function up in your code, but you can also look it up on Drupal's API site at `api.drupal.org/api/function/_system_rebuild_theme_data/7`. Doing the latter lets you know it is called by exactly two functions. One, of course, is `system_rebuild_theme_data()`, which is how you found it. The other is `list_themes()`, which is functionally equivalent to `system_rebuild_theme_data()` but has a more comforting name. (There is an issue filed to reduce this code duplication in Drupal 8 at `drupal.org/node/941980`.)

■ **Note** The `list_themes()` function also has static caching; if it happens to be called twice on a page load, the second call will hardly take any resources. Most statically cached functions can be easily spotted by a line at the top of the function similar to this one in `list_themes()`:

```
$list = &drupal_static(__FUNCTION__, array());
```

Investigating What the Function Gives You

So, you have a function list_themes() that... lists themes. X-ray needs to give a summary of how many themes are present on a site, what themes are enabled, and anything else that might be useful to a site administrator.

Watching the Appearance administration page load in a debugger would let you look into the variable returned by _system_rebuild_theme_data(), which, as noted, is the source for everything given out by list_themes(). Or you can make a test PHP file that bootstraps Drupal and prints the output of list_themes(). Or, since you already have a module you're working on, you can stick a debug() call into our code. Let's do that last one; see Listing 19–5.

Listing 19–5. Printing the Data from list_themes() *with* debug() *within an X-ray Module Stub Function*

```
/**
 * Implements hook_help().
 */
function xray_help($path, $arg) {
  switch ($path) {
// ...
    case 'admin/appearance':
      return _xray_help_admin_appearance();
// ...
  }
}

/**
 * Help text for the admin/appearance page.
 */
function _xray_help_admin_appearance() {
  debug(list_themes());
}
```

The important addition is in bold—**debug(list_themes());**. The rest is an excerpt from our old friend hook_help() calling a function when someone visits the Appearance administration page (the admin/appearance path). That function, _xray_help_admin_appearance(), is just a stub, now, with nothing in it but your debug code.

The information about themes is lengthy, so please look at your own output or refer to dgd7.org/145 for the full result. Getting accustomed to huge nested arrays is something you have to do when developing with Drupal (see Listing 19–6).

Listing 19–6. Information for the Bartik Theme Excerpted from the Output of the Function list_themes()

```
Debug:

array (
  'bartik' =>
  stdClass::__set_state(array(
     'filename' => 'themes/bartik/bartik.info',
     'name' => 'bartik',
     'type' => 'theme',
     'owner' => 'themes/engines/phptemplate/phptemplate.engine',
     'status' => '1',
     'bootstrap' => '0',
     'schema_version' => '-1',
```

```
'weight' => '0',
'info' =>
array (
  'name' => 'Bartik',
  'description' => 'A flexible, recolorable theme with many regions.',
  'package' => 'Core',
  'version' => '7.0-dev',
  'core' => '7.x',
  'engine' => 'phptemplate',
  'stylesheets' =>
  array (
    'all' =>
    array (
      'css/layout.css' => 'themes/bartik/css/layout.css',
      'css/style.css' => 'themes/bartik/css/style.css',
      'css/colors.css' => 'themes/bartik/css/colors.css',
    ),
    'print' =>
    array (
      'css/print.css' => 'themes/bartik/css/print.css',
    ),
  ),
  'regions' =>
  array (
    'header' => 'Header',
    'help' => 'Help',
    'page_top' => 'Page top',
    'page_bottom' => 'Page bottom',
    'highlighted' => 'Highlighted',
    'featured' => 'Featured',
    'content' => 'Content',
    'sidebar_first' => 'Sidebar first',
    'sidebar_second' => 'Sidebar second',
    'triptych_first' => 'Triptych first',
    'triptych_middle' => 'Triptych middle',
    'triptych_last' => 'Triptych last',
    'footer_firstcolumn' => 'Footer first column',
    'footer_secondcolumn' => 'Footer second column',
    'footer_thirdcolumn' => 'Footer third column',
    'footer_fourthcolumn' => 'Footer fourth column',
    'footer' => 'Footer',
    'dashboard_main' => 'Dashboard main',
    'dashboard_sidebar' => 'Dashboard sidebar',
  ),
  'settings' =>
  array (
    'shortcut_module_link' => '0',
  ),
  'features' =>
  array (
    0 => 'logo',
    1 => 'favicon',
    2 => 'name',
    3 => 'slogan',
```

```
      4 => 'node_user_picture',
      5 => 'comment_user_picture',
      6 => 'comment_user_verification',
      7 => 'main_menu',
      8 => 'secondary_menu',
    ),
    'screenshot' => 'themes/bartik/screenshot.png',
    'php' => '5.2.5',
    'scripts' =>
    array (
    ),
    'overlay_regions' =>
    array (
      0 => 'dashboard_main',
      1 => 'dashboard_sidebar',
    ),
    'regions_hidden' =>
    array (
      0 => 'page_top',
      1 => 'page_bottom',
    ),
    'overlay_supplemental_regions' =>
    array (
      0 => 'page_top',
    ),
  ),
    'stylesheets' =>
  array (
    'all' =>
    array (
      'css/layout.css' => 'themes/bartik/css/layout.css',
      'css/style.css' => 'themes/bartik/css/style.css',
      'css/colors.css' => 'themes/bartik/css/colors.css',
    ),
    'print' =>
    array (
      'css/print.css' => 'themes/bartik/css/print.css',
    ),
  ),
    'engine' => 'phptemplate',
  )),
// ...
)
```

in xray_help_admin_appearance() (line 109 of
/home/ben/code/dgd7/web/sites/default/modules/xray/xray.module).

The Garland, Seven, Stark, and Test themes, and the Update test base theme have all been removed from this output. The test themes you've probably never heard of; they have an extra attribute in this array: hidden, which is set to TRUE. You will want to account for this and not list them with the regular themes (see Listing 19–7).

Listing 19–7. Initial Code to Count and Display the Number of Hidden Themes

```
/**
 * Fetch information about themes.
 */
function xray_stats_enabled_themes() {
  $themes = list_themes();
  // Initialize variables for the data you will collect.
  $num_hidden = 0; // Number of hidden themes.
  // Iterate through each theme, gathering data that you care about.
  foreach ($themes as $themename => $theme) {
    // Count each hidden theme.
    if (isset($theme->info['hidden']) && $theme->info['hidden']) {
      $num_hidden++;
    }
  }
  return compact('num_hidden');
}

/**
 * Help text for the admin/appearance page.
 */
function _xray_help_admin_appearance() {
  $output = '';
  $data = xray_stats_enabled_themes();
  $output .= format_plural(
    $data['num_hidden'],
    'There is one hidden theme.',
    'There are @count hidden themes.'
  );
  return theme('xray_help', array('text' => $output));
}
```

The $num_hidden variable is originally set to zero. A foreach function goes through the array of themes, and inside an if statement you add one to the $num_hidden variable each time you are dealing with a hidden theme. $num_hidden++ is a shortcut way of writing $num_hidden = $num_hidden + 1;. The if statement identifies what is a hidden theme by checking if the 'hidden' item in the theme info array exists *and* has a value equivalent to TRUE. That first isset() function is needed or else PHP will complain about you asking it to look for a non-existent piece of information; non-hidden themes don't necessarily have the 'hidden' item in their info array at all. If it's not there, the if statement exits immediately and moves on to the next code. (In this case, that is the continuation of the foreach loop and when that's done, the return of the information you are gathering.) If the 'hidden' item *is* there, the isset() function returns TRUE and so the if statement continues on to the second expression (after the &&) and reads the value of $theme->info['hidden']. If this also evaluates to TRUE (which the number 1 will), the code inside the if statement is run.

■ **Tip** Two expressions that are joined with && both have to be evaluated if the first expression returns TRUE but can stop immediately if the first expression returns FALSE (because no matter what the second expression is, the combination is FALSE and && is asking "are this expression AND that expression both TRUE?"). It's the opposite for two expressions joined with ||. Here, if the first expression is TRUE, the next need not be evaluated; if the first expression is FALSE, the next expression needs to be evaluated because the entire condition will be TRUE if either the first OR the second is TRUE.

The compact() function creates an array out of the named variables (if they are present), and this is the value you return. Here it is only 'num_hidden' (which uses the $num_hidden variable) but it could be a list of several variable names, as you will see in the next code listing.

You only want a count of the hidden themes, but you'll show administrators more information about the other themes. To do that, you need to continue to look at the information in the theme objects. Looking at the printout of data for Bartik in Listing 19–7, one clearly important attribute is status. That's whether the theme is enabled (1) or not (0). Most of the rest of the interesting information is nested a layer deeper in an info array. The regions, features, and stylesheets are all things you can easily count, at least. They are in arrays, which means you can use the count() function, as shown in Listing 19–8. (See php.net/count for a definition of that function.)

Listing 19–8. Extracting and Summarizing Information from an Array of Data about Themes

```
/**
 * Fetch information about themes.
 */
function xray_stats_enabled_themes() {
  $themes = list_themes();
  $num_themes = count($themes);
  // Initialize variables for the data you will collect.
  $num_hidden = 0; // Number of hidden themes.
  $num_enabled = 0;
  $summaries = array();
  // Iterate through each theme, gathering data that you care about.
  foreach ($themes as $themename => $theme) {
    // Do not gather statistics for hidden themes, but keep a count of them.
    if (isset($theme->info['hidden']) && $theme->info['hidden']) {
      $num_hidden++;
    }
    else {  // This is a visible theme.
      if ($theme->status) {
        $num_enabled++;
        // This is an enabled theme, provide more stats.
        $summaries[$theme->info['name']] = array(
          'regions' => count($theme->info['regions']),
          'overlay_regions' => count($theme->info['overlay_regions']),
          'regions_hidden' => count($theme->info['regions_hidden']),
          'features' => count($theme->info['features']),
          'kindsofstylesheets' => count($theme->info['stylesheets']),
```

```
        'allstylesheets' => isset($theme->info['stylesheets']['all']) ? count($theme-
>info['stylesheets']['all']) : 0,
        );
      }
    }
  }
  return compact('num_themes', 'num_hidden', 'num_enabled', 'summaries');
}
```

Everything used in this much larger function has just been discussed; it's taking place in the same foreach loop, using the ++ shortcut (note that the variable is defined first), and count() to return the number of elements in an array. The ternary operator and isset() are thrown in at the end to only count the 'all' sub-array of the 'stylesheets' if the 'all' sub-array is present, and return zero otherwise. See dgd7.org/262 for the code used to display all of this theme information!

■ **Tip** One of the great benefits of working in an open source free software community is that you can expect others to see and comment on your code and suggest improvements. You don't have to wait for that to happen by chance, however. If something seems a little off, ask about it in IRC. If you've done enough investigating to have found one or more possible answers but you are unsure about the best answer, no one in a development discussion channel or forum will mind you asking a question such as, "I'm trying to show a list of themes, what is the simplest way to do it? I have so far only found system_rebuild_theme_data()." Whether you get an answer or not depends on if anyone knows the answer, of course, but an interesting question can inspire people to look into the answer even when they don't know! If your question can be answered with yes or no (such as "Is there a better way to do X?"), it's a sign that you could phrase it better. Try "I'm trying to do X and have tried Y and Z. What is the best way to do it?"

Creating a Page with hook_menu()

Defining a whole page is one of the ways you get to feel the power of making your own modules. You can put the page at any path you want and make anything display there, yet still have all the surrounding design, blocks, login functionality, and everything else that Drupal provides.

■ **Tip** Check out the Examples project's (drupal.org/project/examples) menu_example module and api.drupal.org/hook_menu for just-the-facts implementations of hook_menu(), and see Chapter 29 for more about the menu (router) system's role in Drupal.

Sure, you could make a node and use Path module to place it at almost any path you want. User-editable nodes are a bad fit for module-provided information, though. And how does Drupal know how to understand the underlying node/1883 path to show you the node with ID 1883 when you go there? That's right: hook menu. If you want your own, better system for handling pieces of data, you could define the path megabetternodes/ that takes arguments in the form of *letters* instead of numbers, like megabetternode/rg. That is a terrible idea; the node system is excellent and easily extended with the Node API hooks (api.drupal.org/api/group/node_api_hooks/7), fields, and many great things it would be foolish to try to reproduce. The fact remains, however, that all Drupal's major subsystems with dedicated paths for displaying entities (think node/, user/, taxonomy/term/) are brought to you by hook_menu(), and it gives you access to the same power.

Let's start with a more modest goal. The X-ray module needs a page of its own. This page will display all the information that you've been displaying on certain administration pages with hook_help() and more.

Choosing a Path for an Administration Page

What path shall you give this page? In a system as extendable and popular as Drupal, you always have to try to avoid namespace conflicts—two pages can't have the same path. Therefore, it's a best practice to incorporate your module name into paths created by your module, because every project hosted on drupal.org has a unique system name.

■ **Note** The convention of using the module system name in paths provided by the module is followed in Drupal core by Node and Contact modules, among others. This is the case both for their user-facing paths (such as node/99 or contact) and also in their administration paths (such as admin/content/node and admin/structure/contact). (User module has user-facing paths like user/3/edit and user/register, but as of Drupal 7 its administrative pages are at admin/people and admin/config/people. Moral of this story: On occasion, core can do things you should not do yourself.)

As currently conceived, X-ray module is meant for administrators. Therefore, it should be displayed in the administration section of the site, which is every single page that falls under admin/ in the path. But you're not done yet—a path like admin/xray is completely possible with the power of hook_menu() but terribly presumptuous. That's like saying your module is as important as the entire configuration section (admin/config) or the modules listing (admin/modules)! You must look a little more carefully and play well with others.

Every module in Drupal core fits its administration pages under the following categories, the top level of administration menu items: Dashboard, Content, Structure, Appearance, People, Modules, Configuration, Reports, and Help. Really, the best choice for most module administration pages is between the Structure and Configuration sections, and in most cases somewhere under Configuration. X-ray is a little different, however. It is providing information about the site, and so naturally fits under the Reports menu. This would give your page the path admin/reports/xray.

Defining a Page with a Normal Menu Item

Now you know where you want to put your page; all you have to do is put it there. At the root of every page displayed in Drupal (for nodes, administration pages, or anything else) is hook_menu().

> ▓ **Note** Drupal's Menu system isn't accurately named because it does so much more than menus. In addition to making possible every page in Drupal, whether they have a link in any menu or not, hook_menu() is ultimately responsible for every path, whether it returns a page or not. Some paths used in AJAX requests just return a little bit of data.

As with every Drupal hook or Drupal function, you can get great documentation on hook_menu() by adding it in after the address of Drupal's API site. Case in point: api.drupal.org/hook_menu, which redirects to api.drupal.org/api/function/hook_menu/7.

You can also look for an example of hook_menu() in most any module's .module file, including for the core modules mentioned in the note with regard to their administrative paths, Node module and Contact module.

Let's look at the file node.module, which is located within a download of Drupal's code in the modules/node folder. Implementations of hook_menu() must return an array containing one or more menu items. The menu items themselves are also arrays. Drupal likes arrays. (And arrays of arrays of arrays of arrays of arrays. If you are not writing an array about every 5-10 lines, you are probably doing something wrong.) I'll discuss their structure after Listing 19–9.

Listing 19–9. Excerpt from Node Module's Implementation of hook_menu()

```
/**
 * Implements hook_menu().
 */
function node_menu() {
  $items['admin/content'] = array(
    'title' => 'Content',
    'description' => 'Find and manage content.',
    'page callback' => 'drupal_get_form',
    'page arguments' => array('node_admin_content'),
    'access arguments' => array('access content overview'),
    'weight' => -10,
    'file' => 'node.admin.inc',
  );
// ...
  return $items;
}
```

> ▓ **Caution** Looking at examples from core and other Drupal code is a great way to learn, but you can never expect any given section of code you look at to match up one-to-one with your needs.

The array of menu items is keyed by the all-important path; the path for the menu item in the code excerpt above is admin/content.

The first element in the menu item array is the title. (PHP and Drupal don't care what order the elements of a keyed array are in, but the Drupal developers are noting something about the importance of the title by putting it first.) If present, the description element is frequently listed second. For pages, meaning menu items such as the above with the default type of MENU_NORMAL_ITEM, the description is used for the title text (the hover-over tool tip) on menu links to the page. It is also shown on administrative listings. You won't see the text "Find and manage content." at the path admin or hovering over the Content link in the Toolbar on your standard Drupal install, however, because Comment module changes the description for admin/content to "Administer content and comments." in its implementation of hook_menu_alter().

■ **Note** As of 7, the title and description of menu items are by default passed through the t() function, so you don't wrap them in the t() function yourself, as you do for all other user-facing text in your modules. It is possible to have the title handled by a different function or no function by setting the title callback to another function or FALSE. In that case, you should handle running text you provide through a translation function yourself. The description is always passed through t().

Not even the title is a required element for a menu item, but clearly certain elements must be present for the menu item to do anything useful; the required elements depend on a menu item's purpose. The most important element when showing a page is the page callback. Drupal calls the function named as the page callback when the menu item's path is visited. The page callback function must provide the main content of the page.

■ **Tip** Node module is showing you a neat trick with the file attribute. Putting 'file' => filename.extension in a menu item tells Drupal to include the named file. This allows the function in the page callback to be in that other file, outside the .module file. This can help you organize the code for a complex module in a sensible way by grouping functions related to one page's functionality together in one file. It also can boost Drupal's performance (on sites without an opcode cache such as APC) by excluding unneeded code from being loaded and parsed. That is why Drupal frequently puts code related to administration in separate files, as it is doing here with the admin/content path and the node.admin.inc file. Unlike code related to showing nodes (content), taxonomy terms, or blocks, the code for administering nodes only needs to be loaded when a user with sufficient privileges goes to this page.

The code excerpt in Listing 19–9 was the first menu item defined at the top of Node module's long and complex implementation of hook_menu(), and it is a pretty good model for what you want to do. It defines an entire administrative section, which you do not want to do, but you can move it down a level just by adding to the path; instead of admin/content, you're going to have admin/reports/xray, as discussed earlier.

Defining a Tab with a Local Task Menu Item

You could stop there, but the Node module is doing something pretty cool with a second menu item. It is defined in only five lines, as shown in Listing 19–10.

Listing 19–10. Excerpt from Node Module's Implementation of hook_menu(), Second Menu Item Defined

```
$items['admin/content/node'] = array(
    'title' => 'Content',
    'type' => MENU_DEFAULT_LOCAL_TASK,
    'weight' => -10,
);
```

This second menu item provides a tab that is selected by default. That is how the type `MENU_DEFAULT_LOCAL_TASK` is interpreted. The first menu item did not specify a type attribute, which means it defaults to `MENU_NORMAL_ITEM`, a page, so that the page defined by the first menu item can be extended with multiple tabs (see Figure 19–1).

Figure 19–1. The Content local task (tab) is provided by Node module's admin/content/node menu item.

Local tasks work such that you see them as a tab on the page you extend. Because it is the default local task, the page is identical whether you go to admin/content or admin/content/node.

You'll use this to make your page not just a page but also the Overview tab for X-ray reports. This way you can easily add new, more in-depth report pages as additional tabs.

▓ **Note** Drupal does not display any description for local tasks, which Drupal themes as tabs—not even as link title tool-tip text. This may change in Drupal 8 (drupal.org/node/948416), but for Drupal 7 avoid confusion by leaving off the description element for menu items of type MENU_LOCAL_TASK or MENU_DEFAULT_LOCAL_TASK.

Declaring Menu Items for X-ray Module

After much ado, Listing 19–11 shows a menu declaration of your own.

Listing 19–11. X-ray Module's Implementation of hook_menu()

```
/**
 * Implements hook_menu().
 */
function xray_menu() {
  $items['admin/reports/xray'] = array(
    'title' => 'X-ray technical site overview',
    'description' => 'See the internal structure of this site.',
    'page callback' => 'xray_overview_page',
```

```
    'access callback' => TRUE,
  );
  $items['admin/reports/xray/overview'] = array(
    'title' => 'Overview',
    'description' => "Technical overview of the site's internals.",
    'type' => MENU_DEFAULT_LOCAL_TASK,
    'weight' => -10,
  );
  return $items;
}
```

■ **Gotcha** For your menu item—and page—to appear, the menu_router table must be cleared. **Saving the modules page (without enabling or disabling any modules) no longer does this, as it did in Drupal 6.** You can instead put the menu_rebuild() function directly into your code— outside of the hook_menu() implementation, which is only called when menus are rebuilt! (See data.agaric.com/node/3376 for the code that skips over flushing all caches if nothing changes on the modules page.) The reliable drush cc all (or the more precise drush cc menu) also work to rebuild menus.

I still haven't explained everything going on in the menu declaration. A very important part of every new path is access control. In other words, can a user view the page (or access another callback)? The access callback is typically a function that returns TRUE if access is allowed and FALSE if access should be denied. (By default, it is the user_access() function, and so Drupal can simply take a permission name in the access arguments to evaluate if a given user's role has access to the menu item.) By setting the value of access callback to TRUE, you short-circuit any of this and make the page always viewable by anyone. This is not recommended but it will hold you over until you choose or define a permission.

■ **Caution** Menu items deny access by default. If you provide no value for either the access callback or access arguments attributes, use of your menu item (including trying to visit a page it defines) will be denied to everyone—even user 1, which typically bypasses access checks.

As a menu item that defines an administration page, X-ray module's admin/reports/xray should limit access to authorized users. To set this access, you can create a new permission with hook_permission() or re-use an existing permission.

Using Existing Permissions in Your Module

The Permissions administration page (admin/people/permissions) is one of the more intimidating configuration pages in Drupal—or in any content management system. Drupal's fine-grained permission system is a great strength, but it means a large grid of checkboxes to be able to configure all the permissions for each role. For a new site based on Drupal core's default installation profile, this is just three roles (listed across the top) and about 60 permissions (listed down the side), as shown in Figure 19–2.

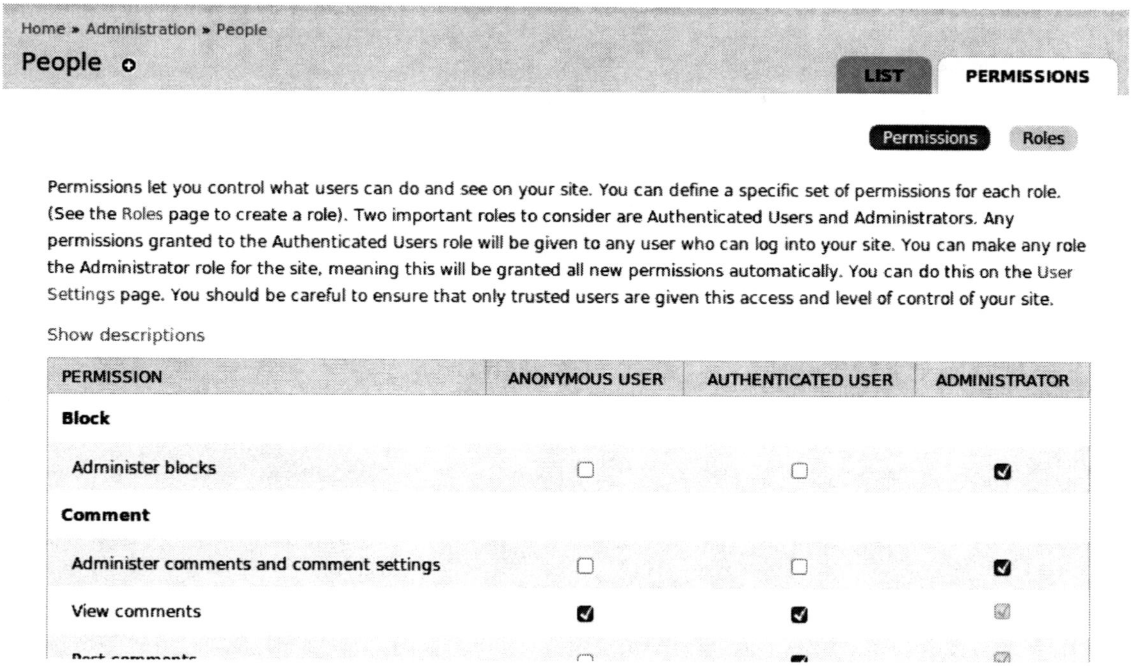

Figure 19–2. The top of the Permissions configuration page of a fresh Drupal core default installation profile

As the number of roles on a site increases, and as functionality increases along with the number of permissions, this page becomes more visually overwhelming. Every new content type adds separate create, edit, and delete permissions, and then there's extra edit and delete permissions per content type for the author of the piece of content in question.

The normal rule in Drupal is *when in doubt, make it configurable or extendable.* In other words, don't try to guess the use cases someone else will need; instead, try to make anything possible. If there's an option, provide it. When it comes to administrative options and especially permissions, however, I prefer to avoid contributing to the wall of checkboxes unless a clear use case is present. People who need a specific permission can file an issue asking for it; a site developer who needs finer-grained permissions for an unusual use case can create her own and make a page require it by modifying the existing menu item with hook_menu_alter().

■ **Note** When you do want to create your own permission or permissions, hook_permission() is a very straightforward hook, as seen in the example from system.module, documented at api.drupal.org/hook_permission.

So you want to re-use an existing permission rather than create your own. There's a catch, however. The permissions you can see at Administration ➤ People's Permissions tab (`admin/people/permissions`) are not named exactly the same as their system or internal name, which your module must use. For one thing, all the internal names are (almost always) lower-case only, but the words can change, too. This is not something you want to guess at; access will be denied because no user can have a permission that doesn't exist (except user 1, which ignores user access checks).

■ **Note** As of 7, permissions have human-readable names and descriptions. This is great for humans, but you developers, trying to write code that speaks to machines, get left out in the cold a little bit.

There will undoubtedly be a module for matching up Permission's public human-readable names with internal system names—you'll incorporate the functionality into X-ray, in fact—but as developers, you should know how to get this information without a helper module, even if you always use the convenience.

Finding Permissions' System Names in the Database

Longtime Drupal developer Moshe Weitzman celebrates exploring the database as a way of understanding Drupal (in general and in the case of a particular site). To list all the internal names of permissions you can start by looking at your Drupal site's database. Looking at all the tables in it (via the command line as in Listing 19–12 or with a more graphical application such as phpMyAdmin), you can see that table role_permission is the only table with a name that mentions permissions. You can then look inside the role_permission table to see the permissions it holds.

Listing 19–12. SQL Commands for Listing Drupal's Database Tables and the System Names of Permissions

```
mysql
mysql> SHOW DATABASES;
mysql> USE d7scratch;
mysql> SHOW TABLES;
mysql> SELECT * FROM role_permission WHERE rid=3;
```

■ **Tip** The command line steps in Listing 19–12 use all UPPERCASE letters for SQL commands to help distinguish the commands from information like database, table, and field names; however, you don't need to type SQL commands in all caps, and it's much easier to not mess with hitting the Shift or CapsLk key.

As you will see, there are a lot of permissions even for an untouched Standard install of Drupal. The rid (Role **ID**) of 3 is Drupal's administrative role which is given all permissions by default (see Listing 19–13). Selecting only for this role allows you to see all the permissions present in the fresh installation, without duplication. The purpose of the role_permission table is to track which roles have which permissions. This is why permission machine names can appear more than once (or for permissions never granted to a role, not at all).

*Listing 19–13. Output of the SELECT * FROM `role_permission` WHERE `rid=3` Query on a Fresh Standard Installation of Drupal*

```
+-----+------------------------------------+------------+
| rid | permission                         | module     |
+-----+------------------------------------+------------+
|   3 | access administration pages        | system     |
|   3 | access comments                    | comment    |
|   3 | access content                     | node       |
|   3 | access content overview            | node       |
|   3 | access contextual links            | contextual |
|   3 | access dashboard                   | dashboard  |
|   3 | access overlay                     | overlay    |
|   3 | access site in maintenance mode    | system     |
|   3 | access site reports                | system     |
|   3 | access toolbar                     | toolbar    |
|   3 | access user profiles               | user       |
|   3 | administer actions                 | system     |
|   3 | administer blocks                  | block      |
|   3 | administer comments                | comment    |
|   3 | administer content types           | node       |
|   3 | administer filters                 | filter     |
|   3 | administer image styles            | image      |
|   3 | administer menu                    | menu       |
|   3 | administer modules                 | system     |
|   3 | administer nodes                   | node       |
|   3 | administer permissions             | user       |
|   3 | administer search                  | search     |
|   3 | administer shortcuts               | shortcut   |
|   3 | administer site configuration      | system     |
|   3 | administer software updates        | system     |
|   3 | administer taxonomy                | taxonomy   |
|   3 | administer themes                  | system     |
|   3 | administer url aliases             | path       |
|   3 | administer users                   | user       |
|   3 | block IP addresses                 | system     |
|   3 | bypass node access                 | node       |
|   3 | cancel account                     | user       |
|   3 | change own username                | user       |
|   3 | create article content             | node       |
|   3 | create page content                | node       |
|   3 | create url aliases                 | path       |
|   3 | customize shortcut links           | shortcut   |
|   3 | delete any article content         | node       |
|   3 | delete any page content            | node       |
|   3 | delete own article content         | node       |
|   3 | delete own page content            | node       |
|   3 | delete revisions                   | node       |
|   3 | delete terms in 1                  | taxonomy   |
|   3 | edit any article content           | node       |
|   3 | edit any page content              | node       |
|   3 | edit own article content           | node       |
|   3 | edit own comments                  | comment    |
```

```
|      3 | edit own page content           | node       |
|      3 | edit terms in 1                 | taxonomy   |
|      3 | post comments                   | comment    |
|      3 | revert revisions                | node       |
|      3 | search content                  | search     |
|      3 | select account cancellation method | user    |
|      3 | skip comment approval           | comment    |
|      3 | switch shortcut sets            | shortcut   |
|      3 | use advanced search             | search     |
|      3 | use text format filtered_html   | filter     |
|      3 | use text format full_html       | filter     |
|      3 | view own unpublished content    | node       |
|      3 | view revisions                  | node       |
|      3 | view the administration theme   | system     |
+------+----------------------------------+-----------+
61 rows in set (0.00 sec)
```

There, toward the top of the list and provided by the required core System module, is a nice permission for X-ray's overview page: "access site reports." It's the same permission used by the other pages available at Administration ➤ Reports (admin/reports). You can use it for X-ray's page too.

■ **Tip** Drupal stores all kinds of interesting and important information in its database. It's worth putting in some time to look around in there.

Finding Permissions' System Names in Code

An alternative way to find the machine name is to search for it in Drupal core. As mentioned, a permission only exists in the database if there is at least one role that has been given it. Once you've seen "view site reports" on the Permissions administration page (admin/people/permissions), you can search for it in the code of Drupal's core modules. Listing 19–14 shows a grep command that can be run from terminal; your operating system's file browser or IDE can also search for a text string in your Drupal code. If run from the root of a Drupal install, this grep command searches only .module files within the modules folder for the text "view site reports."

Listing 19–14. Command Line Step (in Bold) to Search for "View site reports" Text in Drupal's core

```
grep -nHR --include=*.module 'View site reports' modules
modules/system/system.module:233:      'title' => t('View site reports'),
```

As the grep command (or other search) tells you, the one place your text appears is line 233 of system.module, which is shown in Listing 19–15.

Listing 19–15. Excerpt from System module's Implementation of hook_permission()

```
/**
 * Implements hook_permission().
 */
function system_permission() {
  return array(
// ...
```

```
  'access site reports' => array(
    'title' => t('View site reports'),
  ),
// ...
  );
}
```

■ **Tip** This is also, of course, how to define your own permission. Chapter 24 describes it in more depth, but it's as simple as the code in Listing 19–15: the array returned by an implementation of hook_permission().

Every implementation of hook_permission() needs to return an array of permission arrays keyed by the internal system name (and including, at minimum, a title element with the human-facing name). The key for the permission with the title "view site reports" in the array returned by system_permission() is "access site reports" so that is what you use as the access argument in your menu item, as shown in Listing 19–16.

Listing 19–16. Menu Item Using the "access site reports" Permission for Access Control

```
$items['admin/reports/xray'] = array(
  'title' => 'X-ray technical site overview',
  'description' => 'See the internal structure of this site.',
  'page callback' => 'xray_overview_page',
  'access arguments' => array('access site reports'),
);
```

The default local task will inherit this access control (but other tasks, or tabs, will not).

A Second Local Task to Complement the Default Local Task

As mentioned, when you created the first local task, a default local task, no tabs appear from these local tasks until there are at least two defined and accessible to the user, as shown in Listing 19–17.

Listing 19–17. Menu Item Defining a Local Task (Displayed as a Tab) for the X-ray Permission Names Page

```
function xray_menu() {
  $items = array();
// ...
  $items['admin/reports/xray/permissions'] = array(
    'title' => 'Permissions',
    'page callback' => 'xray_permission_names_page',
    'type' => MENU_LOCAL_TASK,
    'weight' => 10,
    'access arguments' => array('access site reports'),
  );
// ...
  return $items;
}
```

You gave it a weight of ten so it will appear after the Overview tab which was given a weight of negative ten. Lower (lighter) and negative values are said to float to the top (for elements displayed vertically) and front (for elements displayed horizontally). In left-to-right languages, this means the local tasks with the lightest (most negative or lowest) weights are displayed as tabs to the left of heavier-weighted tabs, as you can see in Figure 19–3.

Xray technical site overview ⚙   **OVERVIEW** **PERMISSIONS**

Figure 19–3. When at least two local tasks are defined, the tabs are shown.

■ **Gotcha** While the default tab (MENU_DEFAULT_LOCAL_TASK) inherits its access control from the parent menu declaration, other tabs (MENU_LOCAL_TASK) do not. You must declare access arguments and/or an access callback in your menu item declaration.

Now let's make the function for the page callback you defined, xray_permission_names_page(), and make this page give you permission names, both human-readable and machine!

Call All Implementations of a Hook

You know from your investigation into finding permissions' machine names that the information you need is in modules' implementations of hook_permissions(). How do you get this information for yourself? There's a function for that: module_invoke_all() is used for invoking all implementations of a given hook. From a module, all implementations of hook_permission() in Drupal can be invoked, and their data gathered, with the following single line:

```
$permissions = module_invoke_all('permission');
```

The $permissions variable is now an array keyed by permission machine name, but the values are another array that includes the permission description and other information you don't need. It can be cycled through quickly and the extra data dropped, like so:

```
// Extract just the permission title from each permission array.
foreach ($permissions as $machine_name => $permission) {
  $names[$machine_name] = $permission['title'];
}
```

Now let's put these names in alphabetical order by title before handing them off to a theme function. PHP.net has excellent built-in search, so you can just go to php.net/sort to see what it gives you. It takes you directly to PHP's sort() function, but reading the notes for that function indicates it's not good enough. It assigns new keys to the array, and you are using a keyed array: the system names are the keys, pointing to the human-readable title. Throwing out the machine name key would defeat your purpose of showing what the machine or system permission names match the titles. So, you'll use asort(), like so:

```
// Put permission names in alphabetical order by title.
asort($names);
```

■ **Tip** Always read the Notes and See Also sections of PHP manual pages. The related functions listed in these sections, in particular, can teach a great deal about PHP and picking the function you really want, and not your first guess.

The next step, handing the sorted $names array to a theme function for formatting as a table, will require a little research.

Format Data for Display as a Table

You'd like to show your permission machine names and permission titles in a nice grid as an HTML table. This is such a common need that surely Drupal has helper functions, an API, for printing tables. Let's find a place in core that does this. As this is a user interface element, instead of looking at code, you can start by browsing the user interface.

Clickety, clickety... aha! The Permissions page itself, at admin/people/permissions, is a table (a complicated table that is also a form with lots of checkboxes, but a table). Searching the code for 'admin/people/permissions' to find what creates this page and table turns up these two functions in modules/user/user.admin.inc: user_admin_permissions() and theme_user_admin_permissions(). You can also see the full functions online at api.drupal.org/user_admin_permissions and api.drupal.org/theme_user_admin_permissions.

While stealing code, you can steal your doxygen documentation block from User module. The function theme_user_admin_permissions() has the in-code documentation shown in Listing 19–18.

Listing 19–18. Doxygen Documentation Block for theme_user_admin_permissions()

```
/**
 * Returns HTML for the administer permissions page.
 *
 * @param $variables
 *   An associative array containing:
 *   - form: A render element representing the form.
 *
 * @ingroup themeable
 */
```

As with all theme functions, it takes one parameter, $variables. Sometimes $variables contains a single render element—in this case, 'form'—but it is still provided in an associative array, as noted in this docblock.

Documenting Themeable Code with @ingroup themeable

Furthermore, User module put its theme_user_admin_permissions() function in a theme-related group with the line @ingroup themeable in the introducing docblock. Using the @ingroup instruction is a way to make your code self-documenting.

This theme function is quite complex, as it is dicing and splicing a large form. You don't need any of that and can skip down to the end to see how the table is generated. That's the following line:

```
$output .= theme('table', array('header' => $header, 'rows' => $rows, 'attributes' =>
array('id' => 'permissions')));
```

The $rows variable needs to be an array of rows, and each row is itself an array of cells. Each cell, in turn, can be just a string, or it too can be an array, that separates data (the contents of each cell) from HTML attributes to apply to the table cell. See more at api.drupal.org/theme_table.

Listing 19–19 is X-ray module's version of a simple themed table, built from the data returned by invoking all occurrences of *hook_permission()*.

Listing 19–19. *Theme Table for Permission Names (for Machines and for Humans)*

```
/**
 * Display the X-ray permission names page.
 */
function xray_permission_names_page() {
  $names = xray_permission_names();
  return theme('xray_permission_names', array('names' => $names));
}

/**
 * Collect permission names.
 */
function xray_permission_names() {
  $names = array();
  $permissions = module_invoke_all('permission');
  // Extract just the permission title from each permission array.
  foreach ($permissions as $machine_name => $permission) {
    $names[$machine_name] = $permission['title'];
  }
  // Put permission names in alphabetical order by title.
  asort($names);
  return $names;
}

/**
 * Returns HTML of permission machine and display names in a table.
 *
 * @param $variables
 *   An associative array containing:
 *   - names: Array of human-readable names keyed by machine names.
 *
 * @ingroup themeable
 */
function theme_xray_permission_names($variables) {
  $names = $variables['names'];
  $output = '';
  $header = array(t('Permission title'), t('Permission machine name'));
  $rows = array();
  foreach ($names as $machine_name => $title) {
    $rows[] = array($title, $machine_name);
  }
  $output .= theme('table', array('header' => $header, 'rows' => $rows, 'attributes' =>
array('id' => 'xray-permission-names')));
  return $output;
```

```
}
```

The final theme function receives an array of permission names with the machine names as the key and the version of the name intended for people to look at as the value, which was created by the xray_permission_names() function defined immediately above it.

Neither theme function theme_xray_permission_names() nor any function to override it will receive anything or be called at all if you don't register it with the Drupal theme system. This is covered next.

Making Modules Themeable

Modules and themes go together perfectly, as made famous in the Drupal power ballad, "I can be your module, you can be my theme" (drupal.org/project/powerballad; listen at your own risk). A well-made module allows all elements of its presentation to be overridden by the theme of the site on which it is used. This is done by using the theme() function whenever you want to send output to the screen or by providing a renderable array to parts of Drupal that will accept one, which includes all page and block output. (In the case of providing a renderable array, Drupal calls theme() for you, making use of #theme and #theme_wrapper properties.) For complex output, several theme functions may feed into another theme function.

For its theme functions to be recognized, your module must implement hook_theme(), which returns an array of theme hooks or callbacks and associated information; most of the time, you just need to give the name that you will put 'theme_' in front of and a theme will put its THEMENAME_ in front. So from the code in Listing 19–19, it's just 'xray_permission_names' and you tell it whether it gets a single render element or an array of variables (which you can name and provide defaults for). Listing 19–20 shows an implementation of hook_theme() for X-ray module, defining the xray_permission_names theme hook with a single variable and so called 'render element.'

Listing 19–20. Defining the xray_permission_names Theme Hook with a Single Variable and 'render element'

```
/**
 * Implements hook_theme().
 */
function xray_theme() {
  return array(
    'xray_permission_names' => array(
      'render element' => 'names',
    ),
  );
}
```

Although 'xray_permission_names' is stated here to take a single renderable array, when passed to a theming function such as theme_xray_permission_names(), it's nested within another array and so can be treated exactly as the $variables array for passing multiple variables to a theming function, which you'll see later.

▓ **Tip** Whenever you make changes to your implementation of hook_theme(), you need to rebuild the theme registry for those changes to take effect, including when you first define the hook, if your module was already enabled. You can do this in code by placing the function drupal_flush_all_caches(); in a part of your code that is run; remember to remove it later. You can manually clear caches and the theme registry at Administration ➤ Configuration ➤ Development ➤ Performance (admin/config/development/performance) by clicking the Clear all caches button. And as usual, the most convenient way is with Drush via the command drush cc all.

Resources for Theming in Modules

Reading Chapter 15, on making themes, will certainly help you understand theming for modules. See more on producing quality, overridable output from your module code on drupal.org.

- Read more about hook_theme() at the Drupal API site at api.drupal.org/hook_theme.

- See every theme_ function in Drupal core—every function a themer can override to change the way Drupal's output looks—at api.drupal.org/api/group/themeable/7.

- Read "Using the Theme Layer (Drupal 7.x)" in the Module Developer's Guide at drupal.org/node/933976.

- See the Drupal Markup Style Guide at groups.drupal.org/node/6355 for a working proposal on the kind of HTML modules should produce.

▓ **Note** Drupal.org manual pages are entirely written and maintained by volunteers. You may find one talking about how to do something in Drupal 6 but not find a handbook page explaining the Drupal 7 equivalent. As you figure something out, you can edit or create the appropriate handbook page.

A More Drupal 7 Approach: Leveraging the Power of Render Arrays

As noted, the permission names table example was taken from Drupal 7 core, but nevertheless there is a more Drupal 7 way to do it! (User module, from which you took the example, could use some love and attention.) Renderable arrays are now accepted and preferred as the result from a page callback function. In essence, Drupal gathers all the information to display a page as a giant structured array and knows what theming function needs to be run on each part of that array, but doesn't run anything until it has everything together. This lets anyone come and easily move pieces of the page around (and is described in Appendix C). You call to your own theme function in the xray_permission_names_page() callback and your subsequent call to the table theming function short-circuited that page, altering ability a bit. Adopting the renderable array approach also makes it sensible to refactor your code to not need a custom theming function at all, as shown in Listing 19–21.

Listing 19–21. Refactoring the X-ray Permission Names Page Callback to Take Advantage of Drupal 7's Render System

```
/**
 * Display permission machine and display names in a table.
 *
 * @return
 *   An array as expected by drupal_render().
 */
function xray_permission_names_page() {
  $build = array();
  // Gather data, an array of human-readable names keyed by machine names.
  $names = xray_permission_names();
  // Format the data as a table.
  $header = array(t('Permission title'), t('Permission machine name'));
  $rows = array();
  foreach ($names as $machine_name => $title) {
    $rows[] = array($title, $machine_name);
  }
  $build['names_table'] = array(
    '#theme' => 'table__xray__permission_names',
    '#header' => $header,
    '#rows' => $rows,
    '#attributes' => array('id' => 'xray-permission-names')
  );
  return $build;
}
```

You're using the same data gathering function and setting up the data in the same way, and you're using the same theme_table() function you identified before, but you're telling Drupal to call that function by identifying it in the #theme property in the sub-array you are returning. What before was the array of variables handed to the theme table call becomes additional properties (#rows, #header, #attributes) that Drupal will hand to table theming function for you.

Did you just undo the work you did? Well, yes. Letting go of old code is how code gets better. But everything you learned about theming still applies and will be used again shortly!

You added one innovation here: the extension of the name of the table theming hook from 'table' to 'table__xray__permission_names'. Each double underscore means that everything after the double underscore is optional, so core's theme_table() function still handles theming for you, but you've now enabled themers who want to tweak your table to override theme_table() in this instance only (or for all X-ray tables, stopping at the first set of underscores) rather than the unworkable proposition of changing the theming of all tables in Drupal. This could also have been done for the table function when calling via theme().

Removing your custom function from the mix means that if themers wanted to add text, for example, instead of overriding your theme function, they would be better off adding it to the renderable page array with hook_page_alter(). See Appendix C for more about renderable arrays and the flexibility they provide in altering pages after the fact.

Calling a Drupal Function Directly

Hooks are not the only way to interact with Drupal's code; it has many useful functions you will want to call directly. The example in Listing 19–22 is a pretty internal-focused function used in this case (because the goal of X-ray module is to show Drupal's internal functioning), but it demonstrates the principle of getting data from a Drupal function and using parts of it.

Listing 19–22. Displaying Router Information with menu_get_item() Information

```
/**
 * Provide the page callback function (and other router item information).
 */
function xray_show_page_callback() {
  // Do not hand in the path; menu_get_item() finds dynamic paths on its own
  // but fails if handed help's $path variable which is node/% for node/1.
  $router_item = menu_get_item();
  // menu_get_item() can return null when called via drush command line.
  if ($router_item) {
    return theme('xray_show_page_callback', $router_item);
  }
}

/**
 * Theme the page callback and optionally other elements of a router item.
 */
function theme_xray_show_page_callback($variables) {
  extract($variables, EXTR_SKIP);
  $output = '';
  $output .= '<p class="xray-help xray-page-callback">';
  $output .= t('This page is brought to you by ');
  if ($page_arguments) {
    foreach ($page_arguments as $key => $value) {
      $page_arguments[$key] = drupal_placeholder($value);
    }
    $output .= format_plural(count($page_arguments),
      'the argument !arg handed to ',
      'the arguments !arg handed to ',
      array('!arg' => xray_oxford_comma_list($page_arguments))
    );
  }
  $output .= t('the function %func',
            array('%func' => $page_callback . '()'));
  if ($include_file) {
    $output .= t(' and the included file %file',
            array('%file' => $include_file));
  }
  $output .= '.</p>';
  return $output;
}
```

The first function assigned the return value of menu_get_item() to a variable, $router_item, and handed it to a theme function. The default implementation for this theme function is the second function in Listing 19–22. It checks the information available and adds it to an output variable, which it returns at the end. Note that it uses another function created for X-ray module, xray_oxford_comma_list(), which is defined later in this chapter.

▓ **Tip** Theme functions are always handed arrays, even for a sole render element. A quick way to deal with the array, as demonstrated in theme_xray_show_page_callback() in Listing 19–22, is to make the first line of theming function extract($variables, EXTR_SKIP);. This converts a single element in $variables into a variable of the name provided for 'render element' and multiple $variables into the names provided for 'variables' in the implementation of hook_theme(). The EXTR_SKIP parameter is a security precaution preventing any existing variable from being overwritten.

Remember that this theme_xray_show_page_callback() function (and any function that would override it), which you are counting on to display the information you gathered, will not be found by the Drupal theme system unless you register it with Drupal in hook_theme(); see Listing 19–23.

Listing 19–23. Addition to hook_theme() Defining the xray_show_page_callback Theme Function with Three Variables

```
/**
 * Implements hook_theme().
 */
function xray_theme() {
  return array(
// [existing code not shown to save space]
    'xray_show_page_callback' => array(
      'variables' => array(
        'page_callback' => NULL,
        'include_file' => NULL,
        'page_arguments' => NULL,
      ),
    ),
  );
}
```

Don't forget to clear caches!

Any variable passed to a theming function in the $variables array will be available to the theming function, but only the ones defined in hook_theme() (in this case, these are page_callback, include_file, and page_arguments) can be absolutely counted on to be initialized—to exist and have the values set, all NULL in this case, but any defaults can be given. (In this unusual case of providing an entire function's result to the theme, instead of defining the three variables you plan to use, as in Listing 19–23, you could have run menu_get_item() in the theme hook just for the purpose of defining every key it returns as NULL or an empty string.)

One final thing necessary to start seeing this work is to use hook_help() to print it; this can be seen at dgd7.org/259.

Styling Your Module: Adding a CSS File

The first duty of a module, regarding how it looks, is to be modifiable by themes. That doesn't mean it can't provide its own default appearance. And far be it for Drupal to cramp your style! Modules can have their own cascading style sheets (CSS) added to every page by listing them in their .info file, just like themes can. The CSS file uses the classes or IDs you gave to the module's HTML output to style it.

Add stylesheets with the stylesheets[TYPE][] directive, where TYPE is the type of media (print, screen, etc.) that the stylesheet should be used for. The second set of brackets is because there can be multiple stylesheets for a given medium. If you want your stylesheet to be used no matter what medium the site is viewed through, use 'all' for the type, as shown in Listing 19–24.

Listing 19–24. The .info File with Stylesheets Directive

```
name = X-ray technical site map
description = Shows internal structures and connections of the web site.
package = Development
core = 7.x
stylesheets[all][] = xray.css
```

■ **Note** Stylesheet files are listed in the .info file with the stylesheets directive, *not* the files directive.

Listing 19–25. A CSS file for the X-ray Module Boringly (but Properly) Called xray.css

```
p.xray-help,
div.xray {
  display: block;
  color: white;
  padding: 5px;
  background-color: black;
  border: 4px solid white;
  -webkit-border-radius: 8px;
  -moz-border-radius: 8px;
  border-radius: 8px;
}
```

In Listing 19–25, the line added to xray.info tells Drupal to add this CSS (the contents of the specified file, xray.css) on every page. The files xray.info and xray.css are both at the same level in the xray directory, or else xray.info would have had to provide the path to xray.css. The style defined in Listing 19–25 gives the help messages and form-identifying divs a stylish, slimming black background and rounded borders. This works because you wrapped your output in classes when printing via hook_help() and hook_form_alter().

■ **Caution** Always namespace your module's CSS files; that is, use your module's name as the name of your CSS file or as the first part of the name of your CSS files. This is because Drupal lets themes automatically override CSS files simply by having them named the same, and you do not want a theme accidentally overriding your stylesheet.

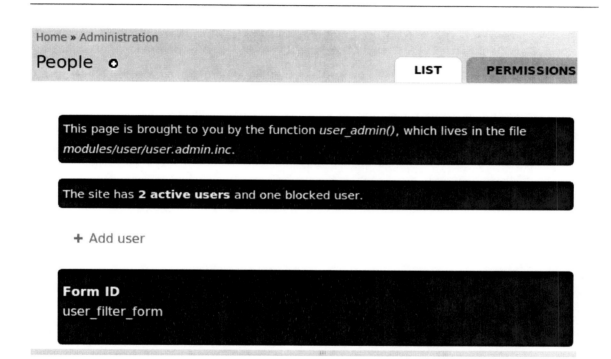

Figure 19–4. X-ray module's display (including two help-area messages and the form ID printed in the form)

Listing 19–26. Additions to the xray.css File

```
/* Make non-help xray font size consistent with help text size. */
div.xray {
  font-size: 0.923em;
}

/* Remove extra form item padding in X-ray output (for form ID). */
div.xray .form-item {
  margin: 0;
  padding: 0;
}
```

Once you have entries in your CSS file that apply to the HTML you need to affect (and have cleared Drupal's CSS aggregation and your browser's cache) you can use an HTML/CSS inspection tool such as Firefox's Firebug to tweak properties until you have the visual effect you want. Listing 19–26 shows additions to the xray.css file. Your module's style should be tested in at least the core themes of Stark, Bartik, and Garland. If your module will output anything that will be seen in the administration section, such parts should also be tested in core's Seven theme.

Database API

Drupal 7 introduced a robust database layer built on PHP Data Objects (PDO), a lightweight, consistent interface for accessing databases. Dubbed DBTNG (Database The Next Generation) by its lead developer, Larry Garfield (crell), the Drupal 7 Database API provides object-oriented tools for adding, changing, and reading SQL data.

The vendor-agnostic abstraction layer for accessing multiple kinds of database servers is designed to preserve the syntax and power of SQL when possible but more importantly, it:

- Allows developers to use complex functionality, such as transactions, that may not be supported natively by all database engines.

- Provides a structure for the dynamic construction of queries.

- Enforces security checks and other good practices.

- Provides modules with a clean interface for intercepting and modifying a site's queries.

The most obvious benefit is that your Drupal application can run with any database (or more than one database) that has a driver written to work with the Drupal 7 Database API. All queries properly written to take advantage of the database layer will not care what database your site is using. Drupal core, out of the box, works with MariaDB/MySQL, PostgreSQL, and SQLite. Database back ends already exist for MSSQL (drupal.org/project/sqlsrv) and Oracle (drupal.org/project/oracle). (The so-called NoSQL MongoDB database used to help scale Drupal in Chapter 27 makes use of pluggable storage for Field API and does *not* use the database abstraction layer, which is designed for SQL databases.)

■ **Note** As of 7, Drupal provides transaction support. This means that if you are making changes to the database and it's critical to your application that these changes be all or nothing—the classic example is debiting one account to credit another account—then you need to wrap your interaction with the database in a transaction. This is done by declaring a transaction variable with the function described here, api.drupal.org/db_transaction. The transaction continues until that variable is destroyed (which includes at the close of the function in which it is defined).

One additional large benefit, derived from the unified structure for dynamic queries (including all insert, update, and delete queries), is that the intelligent database layer helps your site scale. Multiple insert operations will be performed in one query for databases that support this (a much faster approach allowed by the very common MariaDB/MySQL database, among others), and fall back to repeating a series of single queries for databases that do not support it.

All in all, DBTNG is one of the key developer-experience initiatives of the Drupal 7 release cycle. Next, I will cover how to use it. You can also refer to the excellent documentation at drupal.org/developing/api/database and api.drupal.org/api/group/database, along with the DBTNG Example module in drupal.org/project/examples.

Fetching Data with a Select Query

Pulling data out of the database is the most common database-related task you'll see in Drupal core, contributed modules, and your own modules.

For the summary X-ray provides at the top of the Structure administration page, it would be nice to show how many content types the site has. This means counting the number of content types, of course. You can get the number of content types by looking in the node_type table. Use a command line database client or an application such as phpMyAdmin to browse your site's database tables and the columns and content within them.

Out of the box, Drupal stores its data in relational databases (that's what MariaDB/MySQL, Postgres, and SQLite are). The data can be accessed, manipulated, and saved by using the standardized structured query language SQL. As noted, all dynamic queries (which include manipulating and saving) should use the Database API query builder, but non-dynamic, or *static*, queries can and should use SQL directly. (There are lapses in standardization, and working around these is one of the purposes of the Database API, but this is not a concern in most cases of selecting data.)

You're encouraged to use straight SQL for data access queries (when possible; more on that in a moment). This means using the db_query() function for SQL queries starting with SELECT, as shown in Listing 19–27.

Listing 19–27. Basic SQL Query to Count Content Types from the node_type Table

```
db_query("SELECT COUNT(*) FROM {node_type}")->fetchField();
```

The SQL is within the quotation marks. Frequently, such SQL will take the form of "SELECT column_a, column_b FROM table_y". In this example, instead of selecting data with a column name, it selects a count of all rows from the table node_type. When a method for fetching a single field, ->fetchField(), is added to it, db_query() returns a number directly. That number is 2 for the two content types (Article and Basic page) in a fresh Standard installation of Drupal.

The db_query() function passes whatever you give it to the database almost exactly; it does prefixing and expands array-placeholders, but that's it. This is the simplest and fastest way for Drupal to get data that can be fetched with a single standard SQL query.

■ **Tip** You can't attach methods to db_query() *except* for the fetch*() methods.

To be complete, this query should not return anything for disabled content types. That means adding a WHERE clause.

■ **Tip** Use phpMyAdmin or the command line `mysql` to test queries. You'll need to use actual table names (without brackets) and values (not placeholders). You will also have to do escaping yourself (quotes around strings but not numbers); with `db_query()` and `db_select()` queries properly written using placeholders, Drupal does this for you. The advantage is that you can test the query instantly, and tools like phpMyAdmin can help you construct the query.

The code in Listing 19–28 is an example of a raw SQL query that could be run in the command line or with an application such as phpMyAdmin.

Listing 19–28. Raw SQL to Return the Number of Available Content Types from the Node Type Table

```
SELECT COUNT(*) FROM node_type WHERE disabled = 0;
```

■ **Gotcha** If you aren't familiar with SQL, here's your first gotcha—the equality comparison is a single equals sign, not two. In SQL, you should use `<>` for the "does not equal" comparison, which will also work in PHP.

To use this query in Drupal, you use the `db_query()` function and make several modifications to the SQL. Listing 19–29 is the same query as Listing 19–27 but in the style that Drupal needs as the content of a `db_query();` in other words, it has brackets around the table name and values passed in via placeholders.

Listing 19–29. Recommended Basic-SQL Query to Count Content Types from the node_type table

```
db_query("SELECT COUNT(*) FROM {node_type} WHERE disabled = :status", array(':status' => 0))->fetchField();
```

You have replaced node_type with {node_type} so that your module will work on sites that use database table prefixes. The second, bigger change is using a placeholder. Instead of `disabled = 0`, you have `disabled = :status`. In this case, it's replacing a hardcoded zero, and isn't strictly necessary. When it's a variable that may come from a user, it is absolutely necessary. You should never see something like `disabled = $status`; it should always be `disabled = :status` with the `array(':status' => $status)` in the select queries second parameter. Note that you can have as many placeholders in this array as you want.

Using the placeholder array is a best practice and is absolutely required for potentially user-sourced variables, so it should always be used for all variables. Placeholders also take care of quoting string values for you (and handing in numeric values without quotation marks).

Drupal's more complex database function `db_select()` can also be used to make unchanging (static) queries that fetch data, although this use is not recommended. If you already know even a little SQL, the simple `db_query()` approach will be easiest for you. If you are not familiar with SQL, learning both normal SQL and Drupal's object-oriented syntax for databases can be a lot at once. The same simple select query written using the `db_select()` function can look the one in Listing 19–30, which counts the number of content types on a site, needlessly using the full Database API (for example only).

Listing 19–30. A Simple Select Query

```
db_select('node_type')
  ->fields('node_type')
  ->condition('disabled', 0)
  ->countQuery()
  ->execute()
  ->fetchField();
```

This query selects the table `node_type`, adds all fields for the `node_type` table just so the query runs, adds a condition that is equivalent to a "`WHERE disabled = 0`" clause, adds the `countQuery()` method, executes (runs) the query, and fetches the single field. The `countQuery()` method makes this query return a count of the rows in the result set rather than the content of any of the fields. For more counter-examples of `db_select()` versions of static queries, see `dgd7.org/235`.

▨ **Note** Best practices for realizing the virtues of avoiding duplicate code and writing maintainable code dictate that you investigate other ways to get this information from Drupal's APIs, rather than writing your own query. And Drupal has APIs coming out of its ears. A new API in Drupal 7 that is eminently relevant to getting information about content types (and, as you shall see, other central components of Drupal) is the Entity API. This is covered in the upcoming section "Drupal Entities: Common Structure Behind Site Components" (after a whole lot more on the Database API).

Before moving on to dynamic queries that require `db_select()`, let's look at a few more examples of static queries that put their SQL in the `db_query()` function.

Fetching Data with a Static Query with a Join on Two tables

Another piece of information the X-ray module can provide is the number of blocks enabled for each theme. There are several queries in `modules/block.module` that get information from the block table, but they don't fetch precisely this information, and in any case they aren't in stand-alone API functions that you could use. You therefore have every justification in writing your own query. You can wrap it in a function for easy re-use later, as shown in Listing 19–31.

Listing 19–31. Static Query to Count the Number of Blocks Enabled for Each Theme

```
/**
 * Fetch the number of blocks enabled per theme.
 */
function xray_stats_blocks_enabled_by_theme() {
  return db_query("SELECT theme, COUNT(*) as num FROM {block} WHERE status = 1 GROUP BY
theme")->fetchAllKeyed();
}
```

The ->fetchAllKeyed() method provided by Drupal's Database API for db_query() objects takes any two-column result set (here, the theme and the count of blocks) and makes an array in which the values from the first column are the keys to the values from the second column.

Listing 19–32. The Array Returned by db_query("SELECT theme, COUNT(*) as num FROM {block} WHERE status = 1 GROUP BY theme")->fetchAllKeyed();

```
array (
  'bartik' => '10',
  'garland' => '7',
  'seven' => '9',
  'stark' => '7',
)
```

■ **Caution** The ->fetchAllKeyed() method returns *only* the first two columns of a result set and silently ignores the rest.

There are still two things wrong in Listing 19–32. First, this section is titled "Static Query with a Join" and this query doesn't have a join yet. Second, this query is returning the number of enabled blocks for every theme, when restricting the report to enabled themes would make more sense. Let's revise the query to solve both those problems, as shown in Listing 19–33.

Listing 19–33. Static Query Involving a Join from the Block Table to the System Table to Restrict Data Reported to Enabled Themes

```
/**
 * Fetch the number of blocks enabled per enabled theme.
 */
function xray_stats_blocks_enabled_by_theme() {
  return db_query("SELECT b.theme, COUNT(*) as num FROM {block} b INNER JOIN {system} s ON
b.theme = s.name WHERE s.status = 1 AND b.status = 1 GROUP BY b.theme")->fetchAllKeyed();
}
```

The first necessary new part of this query is that the reference to the {block} table is followed by a letter b (which could be most any characters or word) that acts as its *table alias*. The next major addition is the join statement, which is what makes the table alias necessary; it's now possible to have two columns with the same name from different tables. That b is then used in front of the where condition status = 1, such that it becomes b.status = 1. This is necessary for database engines to differentiate between block status and theme status because the table you are joining to the block table, system, also has a status column.

The system table, for its part, is also given an alias, s, as can be seen in the join statement, which immediately follows and becomes part of the from statement, such that together it reads FROM {block} b INNER JOIN {system} s ON b.theme = s.name.

An inner join means that there has to be a match in each table for a row to exist in the result set, and the "ON" part of the statement declares the columns to match the tables on; in this case, it's the block (b) table's column theme (which contains theme system names) with the system (s) table's column name (which contains project names including themes). Table aliases are used consistently throughout to prevent any ambiguity, although in this case there is no theme column in the system table, and no name column in the block table, so the table alias 'b' for the block table could be left off when referring to the theme column and the alias 's' left off when referring to the name column, but once you start making joins, it's important to be explicit.

A Non-Database Interlude: Displaying the Same Data in Two Locations

Before moving on to dynamic, structured queries, let's take a moment away from the database to close the loop and show X-ray's information to site builders. First, Listing 19–34 shows a function for providing a full summary of the Structure page which calls the function you just defined, xray_stats_blocks_enabled_by_theme(), and a couple others defined elsewhere.

Listing 19–34. Displaying Summary Data on the Structure Page

```
/**
 * Summary data for Structure section (admin/structure).
 */
function xray_structure_summary() {
  $data = array();
  $data['blocks_enabled_by_theme'] = xray_stats_blocks_enabled_by_theme();
  $data['block_total'] = xray_stats_block_total();
  $data['content_type_total'] = xray_stats_content_type_total();
  // @TODO menu, taxonomy
  return $data;
}

/**
 * Implements hook_theme().
 */
function xray_theme() {
  return array(
// [existing code not shown for space reasons] ...
    'xray_structure_summary' => array(
      'variables' => array(
        'data' => array(),
        'attributes' => array('class' => 'xray-help'),
      ),
    ),
  );
}
```

```
/**
 * Implements hook_help().
 */
function xray_help($path, $arg) {
  $help = '';
// [existing code not shown for space reasons] ...
  switch ($path) {
    // Summaries for main administrative sections.
// [existing code not shown for space reasons] ...
    case 'admin/structure':
      $variables = array('data' => xray_structure_summary());
      return $help . theme('xray_structure_summary', $variables);
// [existing code not shown for space reasons] ...
    default:
      return $help;
  }
}

/**
 * Returns HTML text summary of Structure section (admin/structure) data.
 *
 * @param $attributes
 *   (optional) An associative array of HTML tag attributes, suitable for
 *   flattening by drupal_attributes().
 * @param $variables
 *   An associative array containing:
 *   - data: result of xray_structure_summary().
 *
 * @ingroup themeable
 */
function theme_xray_structure_summary($variables) {
  // Make direct variables of xray_structure_summary()'s data elements.
  extract($variables['data'], EXTR_SKIP);
  $attributes = drupal_attributes($variables['attributes']);

  $output = '';
  $output .= "<p $attributes>";
  $output .= t('This site has @total blocks available. Of these,',
             array('@total' => $block_total));
  $output .= ' ',
  $list = array();
  foreach ($blocks_enabled_by_theme as $theme => $num) {
    $item = '';
    $item .= format_plural($num, '1 is enabled', '@count are enabled');
    $item .= ' ' . t('on %theme', array('%theme' => $theme));
    if ($theme == variable_get('default_theme', 'bartik')) {
      $item .= t(', the default theme');
    }
    elseif ($theme == variable_get('admin_theme', 'seven')) {
      $item .= t(', the admin theme');
    }
    $list[] = $item;
```

```
  }
  $output .= xray_oxford_comma_list($list, array('comma' => '; '));
  $output .= '. ';
  $output .= format_plural($content_type_total,
    'The site has one content type.',
    'The site has @count content types.'
  );
  return $output;
}
```

The `xray_oxford_comma_list()` function is defined in Chapter 20 in the section titled "Writing a Utility Function when Drupal's APIs Miss Your Need." For now all that matters is that it turns the array of items provided to it into a text string output.

Listing 19–35. Reusing the Summary on the X-ray Reports Overview Page

```
/**
 * Overview page with summaries of site internal data.
 */
function xray_overview_page() {
  $build = array();
  $build['intro'] = array(
    '#markup' => '<p>' . t("Technical overview of the site's internals.  These summaries also
appear / can be configured to appear on main administration section.") . '</p>',
  );
  // Repeat each summary from the top of each administrative section.
// [existing code not shown for space reasons] ...

  $build['structure_title'] = array(
    '#theme' => 'html_tag',
    '#tag' => 'h3',
    '#attributes' => array('class' => 'xray-section-title'),
    '#value' => t('Structure summary'),
  );
  $data = xray_structure_summary();
  $build['structure_summary'] = array(
    '#theme' => 'xray_structure_summary',
    '#data' => $data,
    '#attributes' => array('class' => 'xray-report'),
  );

  return $build;
}
```

The overview page is built as a renderable array. Unlike the somewhat antiquated Help system, where you must call `theme()` yourself to process your array of variables to an HTML string, in the page callback function `xray_overview_page()` you can build and return an entire renderable array and Drupal will know what to do with it. A site builder could alter this page array by changing the #theme function or even adding to the #data array, but it's unlikely anyone would need to get this fancy. Most themers' needs will be met with CSS, and so you also hand in a different class (in the #attributes array) to make it very straightforward to style it differently with CSS should you or anyone else choose to do so.

There are two more functions providing data for the information you just themed and presented about the site's Structure administration section. This data is also provided by SQL queries.

Using variable_get() and Another Static Select Counting and Grouping Query

The other inputs for presenting structure-related information also came from static (db_query()-style) SQL queries. The one that fetched content type statistics was the function xray_stats_content_type_total() returning the query you showed in Listing 19–26 for selecting the count of non-disabled content types.

The other piece of data used was the total number of blocks available, which can be calculated from the block table, filtered by theme as the block table has a row for every block for each theme.

Listing 19–36. *Query to Return the Total Number of Blocks Available to a Site*

```
/**
 * Fetch the total number of blocks available on the Drupal site.
 */
function xray_stats_block_total() {
  // Get count of total blocks.  All blocks are repeated in the block table
  // for each theme, so you filter for one theme (it could be any theme).
  return db_query("SELECT COUNT(*) FROM {block} WHERE theme = :theme", array(':theme' =>
variable_get('theme_default', 'bartik')))->fetchField();
}
```

Listing 19–36 uses Drupal's variable_get() function. The variable_get() function is funny because it must always provide its own default value as the second parameter (here, 'bartik'). This should be the same value a corresponding variable_set() function uses. This is because the variable_set() function may not have ever been run, if for instance no one has saved the settings page on which it is used. In this case, the configuration value does not exist in the {variable} table (which is loaded into the $conf array on every page load), and the variable_get() will return nothing.

Analogous queries and theming functions are used in the module to get information about other sections of the site; see the code or dgd7.org/252.

■ **Tip** Drupal doesn't have the most consistent naming scheme for its tables. Usually this is due to the need to avoid words that are reserved for special use by various databases. Hence, although the rule is that tables take the singular form of what they hold (*comment*, *block*, *variable*), the table of user records is called *users* because the term *user* is reserved in MySQL.

Dynamic Queries

As mentioned, it's best to use the simple SQL queries when possible, and you have begun to demonstrate the query builder alternative, but you have not defined what "when possible" means. The Database API's functions and methods (for all the goodness of DBTNG described in the opening section) must be used for all dynamic queries, which includes using db_select() instead of db_query() for dynamic select queries. A dynamic query is:

- *All* INSERT, UPDATE, or DELETE queries (for which the Database API provides db_insert(), db_update(), and db_delete() respectively).

- SELECT queries that Drupal may need to modify, such as to provide access control.

- SELECT queries that you want to change based on user input (meaning the structure of the query changes, as db_query can handle what is passed in).

- SELECT queries that make use of functionality that is not implemented consistently across different database engines. For instance, if you use db_select() with LIKE (or NOT LIKE) as the third parameter of a ->condition() method, you can be sure the comparison will be done in a case insensitive manner.

▓ **Note** The need to provide access control includes every time you query the node table, so you must use the db_select() query builder and include the method ->addTag('node_access') before the ->execute() method. Leaving off this tag constitutes a security hole in that site visitors may see content they are not authorized to see, such as unpublished nodes. Don't tell anyone you read it here, but if you are new to SQL and learning it along with the Database API, there's nothing horribly wrong with sometimes using the heavier Database API functions even when you don't need them, if you're simply more comfortable with them. However, the db_query() SQL approach has several additional qualities that argue for its use whenever possible: you learn the underlying queries (which is valuable for using the query builder approach also); you will be able to test a query more rapidly than with the db_select() query builder (such as directly on the database without Drupal at all), and finally, you may need to do complex queries that the query builder can't do.

You've been looking at the database a lot in this chapter. In an ideal Drupal world, your module would not be looking at the database tables of another module; instead there'd be an API to get whatever information it needs. Practically, it would be an exercise of premature optimization for a module developer to try to make a function for anything that another module might want from its data. The database layer, as mentioned, is very robust in Drupal 7 and lets the storage of data be handled by any database that provides integration with Drupal's database layer, without your code having to care what database gets used. When your module needs to store data, however, it is undoubtedly your job to use the database layer!

You've seen one contrived example of a query-builder; now let's look at some real ones. But first, if your module is going to be manipulating its *own* data with SQL, it needs to make a database table.

The .install File

In case you couldn't guess, creating a database table involves another hook: hook_schema().

Every hook you have looked at so far has been implemented in the .module file, but there are four main types of hooks that go in a different file: the .install file. These hooks are hook_install(), hook_schema(), hook_uninstall(), and hook_update_N(). When your module has its own database table, you need a .install file that implements hook_schema(). There are other reasons to have a .install file, too. Your hook_install() can insert data into that database table (or another module's) and it can be used to add a nice message with drupal_set_message() to help people know what to do when your module is enabled. One or more implementations of hook_update_N(), such as example_update_7000 and example_update_7001(), are needed if the schema of your database tables have changed. While you should always ensure hook_schema() has the most current schema, if you've released versions of your module and then changed the schema, you need hook_update_N() to catch people up who installed your module with the old schema.

Other .install module hooks (or really, all of these are callbacks as they are called for the one module being installed only) include hook_requirements(), to have any requirement you can code checked before your module is installed, and hook_update_dependencies(), to make sure hook_update_N() functions that rely on another module's hook_update_N() function don't run before it. See dgd7.org/253 for conveniently clickable links to api.drupal.org for these functions and for more information on all .install callbacks.

■ **Note** As of 7, if all your module needs to do is define a database table, you can skip implementing hook_install() and hook_uninstall(). If Drupal sees a hook_schema() implementation in your .install, it figures out that you want the tables defined in it created on install and removed on uninstall. Note that if your module puts any configuration settings in the variable table, you'll still have to use hook_uninstall() to clean that up yourself with variable_del() or your own SQL call via db_delete().

Figuring Out Your Data Model

Before creating your database tables, and ideally before coding related parts, you need to decide what data model will serve your purposes.

The X-ray module needs a database table to store a record of hook invocations that are made on a site, so that it doesn't have to start fresh at each cache refresh, and so that it can combine hook information from multiple sources in one, sortable table. The information you'd like to store is:

- The name of the hook invoked.

- The time you first recorded the hook being invoked.

- The time you last recorded the hook being invoked.

- The list of modules that implement this hook, if any.

The code that gather shook information, the invocation of the hook module_implements_alter(), only runs when the hook implementation cache is cleared, so recording the total number of times you recorded the hook being invoked doesn't seem likely to mean anything definite. You'll put a count in there anyway to see if any patterns arise.

■ **Note** When Drupal stores additional data that may have varying structures or amounts and that it will not want to sort, Drupal often chooses to stuff it all into a single column as a serialized array.

Because a database can't sort on a list of information such as you will be storing in the modules column, you can add another piece of information you'd like to store separately: the number of implementing modules. (You could also store the implementing modules in a separate database table with two columns, hook and module, where the two together provide a unique combination—but a separate table for this violates the common-sense rule of starting simple and adding what you need when and *if* you need it. Initially, X-ray even skipped its own table at all, pulling information for what hooks were invoked from Drupal's cache_bootstrap table; see dgd7.org/255.)

Creating a Database Table

Drupal core's .install files and their hook_schema() implementations are a great place to look for how to define various data types. For the hook name, you'll need a basic text string: varchar. For timestamps, numbers are used: int. A database field type for a moderately-sized serialized array was harder to find, but system_schema() had it for the {system} table's info array, so you'll copy and modify its definition, where the type is blob. For a count, you want an integer again (int). The primary key is the hook (each hook should appear only once in the table), and you're going to be certain to add an index for each additional column (field) that you wish to sort by. Note that the primary key is automatically indexed.

That's been enough ado. Now let's define a database table. Create the .install file, if you don't have one yet, and implement hook_schema(). Listing 19–37 shows the schema definition for X-ray module for a table to hold hook invocation and implementation information, with four columns (or fields).

▓ **Note** While every module with its own database tables should define them in its .install file, when data storage is handled on your module's behalf, such as is the case with the Field API, you don't define the table yourself.

Listing 19–37. This Entirety of the xray.install File

```php
<?php
/**
 * @file
 * Install, update and uninstall functions for the X-ray module.
 */

/**
 * Implements hook_schema().
 */
function xray_schema() {
  $schema['xray_hook'] = array(
    'description' => 'A record of hook invocations (using module_invoke_all).',
    'fields' => array(
      'hook' => array(
        'description' => 'The primary identifier for a node.',
        'type' => 'varchar',
        'length' => 255,
        'not null' => TRUE,
        'default' => '',
      ),
      'first' => array(
        'description' => 'Timestamp of when the hook was first recorded.',
        'type' => 'int',
        'unsigned' => TRUE,
        'not null' => TRUE,
        'default' => 0,
      ),
      'last' => array(
        'description' => 'Timestamp of when the hook was last recorded.',
```

```
        'type' => 'int',
        'unsigned' => TRUE,
        'not null' => TRUE,
        'default' => 0,
      ),
      'count' => array(
        'description' => 'Total count of times the hook is recorded as invoked.  Note that
this is only recorded after a cache clear.',
        'type' => 'int',
        'unsigned' => TRUE,
        'not null' => TRUE,
        'default' => 0,
      ),
      'modules' => array(
        'description' => 'A serialized array of module machine names for the modules which
implement this hook.',
        'type' => 'blob',
        'not null' => TRUE,
      ),
      'modules_count' => array(
        'description' => 'Count of the number of implementing modules.',
        'type' => 'int',
        'unsigned' => TRUE,
        'not null' => TRUE,
        'default' => 0,
      ),
    ),
    'indexes' => array(
      'xray_hook_first' => array('first'),
      'xray_hook_last'  => array('last'),
      'xray_hook_count' => array('count'),
    ),
    'primary key' => array('hook'),
  );
  return $schema;
}
```

While you no longer have to tell Drupal to create a database table on install or destroy it on uninstall, if you have an existing, released module, you *do* have to tell it to create the table in an update hook. Moreover, you need to copy the schema into that update hook because it needs to be the baseline against which any other updates are run. Imagine you add a database table in version 1.2 of your module, add a column to it in version 1.3, and change the unique indexes in version 1.4. Someone who downloads 1.4 should have a version of hook_schema() that includes all of that. However, your true fan (the person you really care about) who had version 1.1 of your module and upgraded to 1.2 needs an update hook that creates the database table. When updating to version 1.3, the same fan will need an update hook that adds a column. And so again when updating to version 1.4. (In fact, X-ray had a beta release before this table was added, and so needs the install-a-whole-table update hook. Details on this and the more common uses of hook_update_N() at dgd7.org/261.)

Inserting and Updating Data

You have a database; now it's time to populate it. Frequently you will be either inserting new rows of data or updating existing rows of data in about the same place in the code. As noted later, db_merge() is often the best function to use for that. That isn't always the case, though, and isn't so here: you need both db_insert() and db_update() when adding or updating hook information to the {xray_hook} table defined in the previous section.

The reason you can't use db_merge() is that you want to set the "first time" if you are inserting, but leave it alone if you are updating. You also want to increment the count value. Therefore, you need to check if the hook has been saved already and fetch the value from the count column. This should be done with straight SQL and can be done in one statement. Listing 19–38 shows the use of the db_insert() and db_update() Database API functions. Because there are a few bumps in the road on the way to the two DBTNG functions you care most about, that portion of the code is in bold.

Listing 19–38. Use of the db_insert() and db_update() Database API Functions /**

```
 * Implements hook_module_implements_alter().
 */
function xray_module_implements_alter(&$implementations, $hook) {
  // Because hook_module_implements_alter() is invoked for X-ray before the
  // xray_hook table is created, check if the table exists and bail on this
  // function if it does not.  Because this hook can be called many times on
  // page loads after a cache clear, statically cache this check.
  static $table = NULL;
  if ($table === FALSE || !($table = db_table_exists('xray_hook'))) {
    return;
  }

  $is_existing = (bool) $count = db_query('SELECT count FROM {xray_hook} WHERE hook = :hook',
array(':hook' => $hook))->fetchField();
  // Increase the count of times this invocation has been checked by one.
  // $count++ does not work if $count is FALSE.
  if ($is_existing) {
    $count++;
  }
  else {
    $count = 1;
  }

  // You don't want first and last timestamp potentially varying by a second
  // in cases where they should be the same.
  $timestamp = time();

  $fields = array(
    'last' => (int) $timestamp,
    'count' => (int) $count,
    'modules' => serialize($implementations),
    'modules_count' => (int) count($implementations),
  );

  if ($is_existing) {
```

```
    // Update the hook.
    db_update('xray_hook')
      ->fields($fields)
      ->condition('hook', $hook)
      ->execute();
  }
  else {
    // The hook has not been recorded yet, insert it into the database.
    $fields['hook'] = (string) $hook;
    $fields['first'] = (int) $timestamp;
    db_insert('xray_hook')
      ->fields($fields)
      ->execute();
  }
}
```

■ **Tip** If you didn't need to check if the first time existed (and provide it or not accordingly), you could use the wonderfully convenient db_merge() function that automatically does the equivalent of a db_update() if the primary key already exists and the equivalent of a db_insert() if it does not. See api.drupal.org/db_merge and drupal.org/node/310085.

I ran into a bunch of errors when doing this code originally. Many debug() statements were deployed in figuring out the places I went wrong; see dgd7.org/256 to commiserate with me about (or laugh at) my problems.

Displaying Data in a Sortable Table

You know the drill by now. Find something you like in core. The Recent log messages page of the Database logging module looks like a good choice. Three of the columns are sortable and there are no administrative checkboxes bringing the complications of a form into it. The section "Finding a Drupal function that Does What You Need" will take you to where this table is created—or X-ray will tell you: "This page is brought to you by the function dblog_overview() and the included file modules/dblog/dblog.admin.inc." Off you go.

■ **Tip** The dblog_overview() function and its helper functions in modules/dblog/dblog.admin.inc also have an example of using a filter query and filter form that allow users to filter a table.

Nearly every part of the table in Figure 19–5 is a simpler version of the log messages table used as ¹le code. It uses the renderable array structure to pass several parameters (as properties of the a table theming function ('#theme' => 'table'). The first function that chooses to implement 'table' (and you've fancied it up even more with the double underscore magic, using '#theme' => 'table__xray__hooks' to allow a theming function to take over for 'table__xray' or 'table__xray__hooks') will get to make the HTML table. In this case (and in practically all cases), no modules or themes choose to take on the task of theming a table and Drupal core's theme_table() has the job. You've already looked at theme_table() and as before you can look up what it expects at api.drupal.org/theme_table. Even better, you have the dblog.admin.inc example.

The code in Listing 19–39 introduces a legitimate use of the db_query() function (in bold, since this section is purportedly about the Database API). With the method ->extend('TableSort') added to the query, and fields using the same table nickname ('h') in the query as they do in the table's headers, the theme_table() function fairly magically knows what query to manipulate to sort the table in different ways.

The use of array_keys() on the array of implementing modules (which is unserialized from the database) warrants a moment of explanation. This goes back to the way Drupal handed the implementations to xray_module_implements_alter(), which is where you saved this information to the database. The implementing modules were listed with the key as the module name and the value as only FALSE. If a module's name is present as a key, that means the module implemented the hook; the value is not used. Drupal does this because searching on the key is faster than searching on the value. (Elsewhere in Drupal identical keys and values are sometimes used for this same reason.) As you did not change this before saving it to the database, you need to use array_keys() to make an array out of the keys (and drop the values) before handing it to any listing function.

Let's go to the code! The first segment is adding this menu callback so the page is shown. You'll have to clear caches to see the new Hooks tab added to the Administration ➤ Reports ➤ X-ray section.

Listing 19–39. The Callback Showing the Information from the {xray_hook} Database Table as a Sortable HTML Table

```
/**
 * Implements hook_menu().
 */
function xray_menu() {
// [existing code not shown due to space considerations] ...
  $items['admin/reports/xray/hooks'] = array(
    'title' => 'Hooks',
    'page callback' => 'xray_hook_implementations_page',
    'type' => MENU_LOCAL_TASK,
    'weight' => 20,
    'access arguments' => array('access site reports'),
  );
  return $items;
}

/**
 * Table of available hooks and the modules implementing them, if any.
 */
function xray_hook_implementations_page() {
  $build = array();

  $header = array(
    array('data' => t('Hook'), 'field' => 'h.hook'),
    array('data' => t('Implementing modules'), 'field' => 'h.modules_count'),
    array('data' => t('First recorded'), 'field' => 'h.first'),
    array('data' => t('Last recorded'), 'field' => 'h.last'),
  );
```

```
    $rows = array();

    $query = db_select('xray_hook', 'h')->extend('TableSort');
    $query->fields('h', array('hook', 'modules', 'modules_count', 'first', 'last'));
    $result = $query
      ->orderByHeader($header)
      ->execute();

    foreach ($result as $invocation) {
      // Prepare the implementing modules text.
      if (empty($invocation->modules)) {
        $modules_text = t('<em>None</em>');
      }
      else {
        $modules = array_keys(unserialize($invocation->modules));
        $modules_text = xray_oxford_comma_list($modules);
      }
      $rows[] = array(
        // Cells.  Must be in the correct order to match $headers!
        $invocation->hook,
        $modules_text,
        format_date($invocation->first, 'short'),
        format_date($invocation->last, 'short'),
      );
    }

    $build['hook_table'] = array(
      '#theme' => 'table__xray__hooks',
      '#header' => $header,
      '#rows' => $rows,
      '#attributes' => array('id' => 'xray-hook-implementations'),
      '#empty' => t('No hooks recorded yet (this is unlikely).'),
    );

    // Return the renderable array that you've built for the page.
    return $build;
}
```

A little more on the code in a moment, but first... it works!

There's one cool thing a little bit hidden here that's not from the Recent log messages table. The Hooks HTML table is showing data that comes from one column in the database table, but sorting that HTML column based on the data from a different database table. This is what allows the modules listing, which is coming from an unsortable blob in the database (literally), to be sorted by the number of modules.

HOOK ▲	IMPLEMENTING MODULES	FIRST RECORDED	LAST RECORDED
action_info	comment, node, system, and user	2011-04-03 08:21	2011-04-03 08:21
action_info_alter		2011-04-03 08:21	2011-04-03 08:21
admin_paths	block, book, node, openid, shortcut, system, taxonomy, and user	2011-04-03 07:12	2011-04-03 08:21
admin_paths_alter		2011-04-03 07:12	2011-04-03 08:21
advanced_help_topic_info_alter		2011-04-03 07:12	2011-04-03 07:12
block_info	block, book, comment, menu, menu_block, node, search, shortcut, system, user, and views	2011-04-03 08:21	2011-04-03 08:21
block_info_alter	dashboard	2011-04-03 08:21	2011-04-03 08:21

Figure 19–5. Success! You now have a beautiful and sortable table of every hook Drupal has called via
`module_implements()`.

▓ **Tip** If you are wondering if something can be done, just try it. No one knows everything up front, and coding in a development environment with version control means you can always recover from a failure.

Inconveniently, the first time you click on *Implementing modules*, it sorts by the number of modules ascending, which means it starts with those hooks with no modules implementing them, which is less interesting than the most-used hooks. There's an issue for allowing a descending sort to be the initial one when clicking a table header: see `drupal.org/node/109493`. How did I find that issue? I found it while searching for "drupal table sort different column," which did not come up with an answer. How did I actually discover you could use a different field than is shown to sort a column? I just tried it. This is perhaps the most important way of learning and succeeding, as advocated in Chapter 14. If you're wondering about it, give it a try. It won't hurt, and you may make a cool discovery.

▓ **Note** An initial iteration of this table used Drupal core's `item_list()` function—`theme('item_list', array('items' => $modules));`—to format the list of implementing modules, but the rows for the most-used hooks became unreadably high. The `xray_oxford_comma_list()` defined in the next chapter came to the rescue. Another common trick is to use CSS to make HTML lists display inline.

One final thing: while the guess about sorting the implementing modules column using the `modules_number` field from the database succeeded pretty much right away, twenty other things went wrong the first time coding this section. The database errors took the longest, but even printing out the list of implementing modules first silently failed because I left out the 'modules' field from the query (doh!), then failed very loudly because I had a typo in "$invocaton", and then failed moderately loudly because I forgot to unserialize that column's data. Three different causes of one problem! (This is disturbingly common in programming.) Authors of other books and other chapters are probably less error-prone, but trust me, no one gets everything right the first time, and you shouldn't even try. (But don't leave out a field you want to display. Or leave serialized data serialized. Or make typos. Skip my stupid mistakes and reach for intelligent, ambitious mistakes. And when things don't work, fix the errors. And enjoy it all the more when it finally works out!)

Drupal Entities: Common Structure Behind Site Components

Drupal 7 introduced the concept of *entities* to standardize its treatment of essential data objects. Users, nodes, comments, taxonomy vocabularies, taxonomy terms, and files—these are all entities in Drupal 7 core. Contributed modules can register additional entity types by implementing `hook_entity_info()`; this is covered in Chapter 24.

Nodes, the main content object on Drupal sites, are the prototypical entity; the creation of the entities concept in Drupal 7 had a lot to do with making the other objects act more like nodes. In particular, the introduction of Fields in Drupal core made it seem necessary to give non-node objects something analogous to content types (also called node types). In Drupal 6, the Content Construction Kit project (drupal.org/project/cck) and related modules made it possible to add fields (text fields, number fields, e-mail address fields, file fields, image fields, etc.) to content types. Every content type represented a set of fields. In Drupal 7, any entity can have fields (if its entity type definition declares it a "fieldable entity") but it was also desired for one entity type to have entities with different sets of fields. The word *bundle* was forcibly conscripted into service in Drupal to describe this generic sense of "thing with fields," the analog of content type for non-node entities.

■ **Note** Entities introduce the concept of *bundle* and content types are examples of *bundles*. In other words, a content type is a bundle—the most common bundle you are likely to deal with in Drupal 7.

You can get information about every bundle on a Drupal site with a function named `field_info_bundles()`. While figuring out what to display and how to display it on the Structures administration page, you can print the output of this and other functions or variables with the `debug()` function. (You can also, of course, use a debugger; see dgd7.org/ide.) In a bootstrapped `test.php` file (dgd7.org/testphp) or a function that is called such as a callback in `hook_help()` or a page callback, place the code `debug(field_info_bundles())`;

The output is a wealth of information about your site's entities. It would take 11 pages if placed in this book, so please look at your own output (or refer to dgd7.org/151) for the full result. This is an excessively large array, but huge nested arrays are expected when developing with Drupal.

From this entity and bundle information, output by the function `field_info_bundles()`, you learn there are six types of entities on your site already in a typical install. These entities are *comment*, *node*, *file*, *taxonomy_term*, *taxonomy_vocabulary*, and *user*. Each entity type is further divided into at least one bundle. The *file* entity type, for instance, defines only the *file* bundle, while the *comment* entity type has bundles for every content type to which comments attach.

▓ **Gotcha** The node type is not stored in the comment table. It's only available in the comment entity, and so through a function such as `field_info_bundles()`. Don't expect all bundle information to be easily found in the database!

You can use `field_info_bundles()` to provide a listing of all entities and bundles with X-ray. See `dgd7.org/254` for turning the debug statement into a nicely formatted informative table—but you can get all the information you need from the debug output, of course.

Summary

This chapter introduces you to APIs and teaches you how to write a whole module. You saw instructions and examples for using the hooks and functions provided by Drupal, which include altering forms, localization, making modules themable, creating pages with hook_menu(), and using and defining permissions. These were covered in the course of building a complete module. As each feature of the module requires using another tool from the extensive selection in Drupal's API toolbox, I introduced the tools and showed you how to use them.

Now you know what it takes to write a whole module, but there is still more to the module story, which is finished off in Chapter 20 where you will learn to create a configuration page and settings form and refine your module into a drupal.org-worthy module, including fixing errors and reviewing for coding standards.

▓ **Tip** Also check out `dgd7.org/intromodule` for discussion about confusing parts of this chapter and the continued development of X-ray module.

■ ■ ■

Refining Your Module

by Benjamin Melançon

Chapters 18 and 19 have shown you how to write your module, but there's more to a module than just the code you've written. In this chapter you'll see how to:

- Create a configuration page and settings form.

- Refine your module into a `drupal.org`-worthy module, including fixing errors and reviewing for coding standards.

Creating a Configuration Page for Your Module

X-ray module could get away with setting sensible defaults and having no configuration page. The design philosophy of Don't Make Me Think (in general, but in particular the now-classic book of that name by Steve Krug) argues for removing non-essential options. Whenever possible, replace choices to be made by the user with sensible defaults. Almost as good as or better than leaving out configuration options, perhaps, is a configuration page most administrators using your module will never have to visit.

X-ray module will allow administrators to turn off the display of administrative section summaries, page callbacks, and form IDs. These will all be on by default so that the module just works out of the box.

Where to Put a Configuration Page

There is an entire section of Drupal's administration called Configuration, so there's not too much question of where to put a configuration page. It's not that simple, of course. The Configuration section in Drupal 7 is divided into many subsections, including (in core Drupal) People, Content authoring, Media, Search and metadata, Regional and language, System, User interface, Development, and Web services. As X-ray is clearly a development aid, its configuration should go under Development (`admin/config/development`), but you'll need to decide for each module you create (that has a configuration section) what category it belongs in, based on core modules and on any related, respected contrib modules. Personally, I dislike the fragmentation of a module's administration pages into wholly separate sections, as it doubles the number of places administrators must look for things. This separation, however, is the way of Drupal 7; indeed, it is the way of the future as well. A module providing reports for administrators, as X-ray does, should put them in the Reports section of Administration; if that module provides any configuration options they go in Configuration. This does make sense in the long run, as it makes modules work in a way consistent with Drupal core, but for the site builder who just enabled a module and is trying to figure out how to use it, the separation adds to the difficulty of navigating an already overwhelming interface. You will use hook_help() again in the

"Using hook_help() as Drupal intended" section to make a helpful link from X-ray's reports page to its configuration and vice versa.

Defining a Menu Item for a Settings Form

Configuration forms are such a common need, in Drupal core as well as for contributed modules, that Drupal provides a number of helpful functions and shortcuts (see Listing 20–1).

Listing 20–1. A Menu Item for the X-ray Settings Page

```
/**
 * Implements hook_menu().
 */
function xray_menu() {
  $items = array();
  // ...
  // Administration page.
  $items['admin/config/development/xray'] = array(
    'title' => 'X-ray configuration',
    'description' => 'Configure which elements of internal site structure will be shown.',
    'page callback' => 'drupal_get_form',
    'page arguments' => array('xray_admin_settings'),
    'file' => 'xray.admin.inc',
    'access arguments' => array('administer site configuration'),
    'weight' => 0,
  );
  return $items;
}
```

The most interesting parts of this menu item declaration, compared to what you have looked at before, are the 'page callback', 'page arguments', and 'file' instructions. The 'page callback', rather than being a custom function as in other examples, is a Drupal core function for getting forms. This function, drupal_get_form(), needs to be given an identifier for a form, which is usually the name of a function that returns a form structure as an array of arrays, but it can also be an identifier registered with hook_forms() that returns the real function. This form ID is passed in here as the only item in an array given to 'page arguments'. Finally, the 'file' is specified because the argument 'xray_admin_settings' that you are passing drupal_get_form() means that the function xray_admin_settings() will be called—and that function, as I will cover below, is defined in a separate file.

■ **Tip** For pages that are solely forms, as many administration pages are, Drupal frequently makes use of a code-saving trick. Instead of a custom function, the menu item's page callback is 'drupal_get_form' and via page arguments, it is passed a form identifier. This saves creating a function just to handle the page callback to display the form.

You'll borrow the code for this menu definition, as you will for the settings form it calls, from Drupal core. User module provides a good example. This code is directly modeled on the definition of the Account settings administration page by user_menu() in user.module. X-ray itself will tell you, regarding admin/config/people/accounts, that "This page is brought to you by the argument user_admin_settings handed to the function drupal_get_form(), with the help of the file modules/user/user.admin.inc."

Creating a Separate File for Administration Code

Dividing your code into files provides two advantages. First, it helps you organize your code into manageable segments. Second, it allows Drupal to avoid loading the code into memory when it's not going to be used. (This is the point of the file instruction in the admin/config/development/xray menu item definition. The file xray.admin.inc is only included when this path is visited.)

Your page callback is the function drupal_get_form(), which is loaded in Drupal bootstrap. The form identifier it is handled is the name of a function returning a form array. The file xray.admin.inc and this xray_admin_settings() function are modeled on user.admin.inc and user_admin_settings().

Note Not everything in a core file will match your needs, of course. User module's implementation of hook_menu() defines the path admin/config/people and with the callback system_admin_config_page(). Most modules you create will not need to do this because their configuration pages will go in a subsection of Configuration that already exists. X-ray module, for its part, is in the Development subsection (admin/config/development).

Building a Settings Form

With an assist from a specialized function of Drupal's Form API, your settings form can be lean indeed. The system_settings_form() function used right before returning the $form array takes the fieldset and three checkbox options you provide and takes care of adding the submit button as well as doing all the submit handling for anything with a form key that matches the variable name! Note how 'xray_display_section_summaries' is both the identifier in the form array and the default value in the variable_get() function. Drupal will use variable_set() to save the value chosen when someone submits the form; you don't have to handle any of it! Listing 20–2 is an administration file that holds the form definition for X-ray's settings form, which is only loaded when admin/config/development/xray is visited, with the form building function for administration settings.

Listing 20–2. An Administration File That Holds the Form Definition for X-ray's Settings Form

```php
<?php
/**
 * @file
 * X-ray module settings UI.
 */

/**
 * Form builder; Configure which X-ray information is shown.
 *
 * This form provides feeds the menu callback for the X-ray settings page.
 *
 * @ingroup forms
 * @see system_settings_form()
```

```
  */
function xray_admin_settings() {
  $form = array();
  // X-ray output visibility settings.
  $form['display'] = array(
    '#type' => 'fieldset',
    '#title' => t('Display options'),
  );
  $form['display']['xray_display_section_summaries'] = array(
    '#type' => 'checkbox',
    '#title' => t('Show summaries on administration sections.'),
    '#default_value' => variable_get('xray_display_section_summaries', 1),
    '#description' => t('If unchecked, the summaries will still be visible on the ↵
<a href="@xray-overview">X-ray reports</a> page.',
      array('@xray-overview' => url('admin/reports/xray'))
    ),
  );
  $form['display']['xray_display_callback_function'] = array(
    '#type' => 'checkbox',
    '#title' => t('Show the page callback function on all pages.'),
    '#default_value' => variable_get('xray_display_callback_function', 1),
  );
  $form['display']['xray_display_form_id'] = array(
    '#type' => 'checkbox',
    '#title' => t('Show form ID in forms.'),
    '#default_value' => variable_get('xray_display_form_id', 1),
  );
  return system_settings_form($form);
}
```

As you can see in Figure 20–1, you are now producing a form on the administration page you defined.

Figure 20–1. Administration page with three checkboxes on by default

---

LETTING DRUPAL STORE CONFIGURATION SETTINGS VS. CREATING A DATABASE TABLE

There are two ways to store configuration settings in Drupal: letting Drupal do it, and doing it yourself. Drupal makes it easy for you to store configuration in the global configuration variable (the $conf array, from which individual settings can be retrieved with variable_get()). By default, system_settings_form() wraps a naked form array in a submission handler that automatically saves all form elements with variable_set() into the variable table. This is loaded into the global $conf variable for every page load.

For once, I don't think it is necessarily best practice to follow the path of least resistance in Drupal. The configuration information available on every page load should not be bloated with settings that are only needed in specific situations. Module authors should go through a little extra effort to store separately any large amount of data that isn't required in Drupal's global context.

■ **Tip** There is an initiative for Drupal 8 to make Drupal's settings saving more intelligent and pluggable; see dgd7.org/config for links, including anything that is backported to Drupal 7.

If X-ray module were to have settings that were used only when visiting the X-ray reports page, it would make sense to save them in your own database table. The settings you have, however, affect many or every page view and so should go in the variable table that is loaded into the $conf array.

Defining New Permissions

You still have a very big step to take: making your code honor your new settings. Before doing so, however, let's take another look at X-ray's permissions, or lack thereof. If you're going to allow administrators to turn off certain types of messages, you can accept that some people will want to hide X-ray's messages from whole classes of users. (Such people will not be you or me, as we will be following the deployment practices in Chapter 13 and will never have X-ray enabled on a live site, but there's an outside chance people who have not read this book will use X-ray.)

This calls for a "View X-ray messages" permission. A look at admin/people/permissions shows that there is no appropriately fine-grained permission for X-ray module administration. "Administer site configuration" is a permission likely to be handed out to most administrators of any kind, while the ability to toggle X-ray settings on and off only makes sense to users with at least some developmental bent. You could try to save a permission by intuiting that someone with "Administer site configuration" and "View X-ray output" should be able to configure displays, but Drupal frowns on such trickery that will be opaque to administrators. So two new, straightforward permissions it is: "Administer X-ray" and "View X-ray output". These are shown in Listing 20–3.

Listing 20–3. X-ray Module with an Implementation of hook_permission() with Two New Permissions Defined

```
/**
 * Implements hook_permission().
 */
function xray_permission() {
  return array(
    'view xray messages' => array(
      'title' => t('View X-ray messages'),
      'description' => t('Allows users to see X-ray output.'),
    ),
    'administer xray' => array(
      'title' => t('Administer X-ray'),
      'description' => t('Allows administrators to configure which X-ray messages are↵
  shown.'),
    ),
  );
}
```

You will have to clear caches before these permissions show up on the admin/people/permissions page.

■ **Caution** Remember when using single quotation marks to delineate strings, as above, that using an apostrophe in the string will break everything. Use double quotation marks for those strings or escape the apostrophe with a \.

Back in your most recent additions to xray_menu(), you need to replace 'administer site configuration' with 'administer xray' to have your new, finer-grained permission have any effect. And for the "View X-ray messages" permission to mean anything, you need to check for it in the code at the same time as you check the display-or-not configuration of different types of X-ray messages.

Conditionally Taking Action Based on Configuration or User Access

In Drupal code you will frequently want to take some action only in the case of certain configuration settings or depending on the user's permissions—or, in the case of X-ray, check both at once.

Conditionally taking an action on a configuration setting is usually as simple as checking the result of a variable_get(). An if statement loads a configuration variable with variable_get() and proceeds if that setting is TRUE; for more complex settings, it can compare several possible values from the setting to the condition you care about. The simple case can look like the following:

```
if (variable_get('xray_show_formid')) { ... }
```

Conditionally, taking an action on a permission a user may or may not have calls for the user_access() function. It takes a string with the machine name of a permission. It, too, can go in an if statement that wraps around the code you only want run if the user has permission to access it (based on the permissions given to roles and the roles granted to users). Alternatively, within a function, the if statement can reverse the check and return immediately, meaning all the remaining code is skipped; see Listing 20–4.

Listing 20–4. Using a Permission Check to Bail on an Entire Function if the User Doesn't Have the
Required Access

```
function example_something($account = NULL) {
  if (!user_access('do something complex', $account)) {
    return;
  }
  // lots of complex code here that never gets looked at if the user
  // does not have the permission 'do something complex'.
}
```

It's a best practice to separate a function from reliance on any global variables, such as the user account of the currently logged-in user. With proper separation, the function can be reused for different purposes. The user_access() function performs the check for the current user when the $account parameter is not present, which would tie the function to checking the access of the presently logged-in user only. It's best if user access checks are done outside of the function that does the work or, at the least, able to accept a user account that can be set to something other than the currently logged-in user. That is the approach taken in Listing 20–4. When $account is NULL, which is the default there, user_access() checks access for the currently logged-in user, but the example_something() function has the potential to do the check for any user account handed in.

The code in Listing 20–5 is not in a potentially reusable function but in a hook implementation, where you *can* expect the global environment variables, such as the currently logged in user, to be the only ones that matter. It contains the addition of a configuration check (should you be showing the form ID at all?) and a user access check (does this person have the permission to view X-ray messages granted to a role they are in?) added to xray_form_alter().

Listing 20–5. xray_form_alter() with Configuration Check and User Access Check Addedfunction

```
xray_form_alter(&$form, &$form_state, $form_id) {
  if (variable_get('xray_show_formid', TRUE) && user_access('view xray messages')) {
    $form['xray_display_form_id'] = array(
      '#type' => 'item',
      '#theme_wrappers' => array('container__xray__form'),
      '#attributes' => array('class' => array('xray')),
      '#title' => t('Form ID'),
      '#markup' => $form_id,
      '#weight' => -100,
    );
  }
}
```

Only the code in bold is new: the opening of the if statement and its closing with a }. The code in between has been indented to meet coding standards for clarity. If both the xray_show_formid setting is TRUE and user_access returns TRUE, the xray_display_form_id item will be added to the form array.

■ **Caution** Don't forget the default value of `variable_get()`! Drupal won't throw an error, but leaving it blank is the equivalent of claiming the default is FALSE, which is the opposite of what you mean in this case. Every use of `variable_get()` should have two parameters: the variable's name and its default value.

Writing a Utility Function when Drupal APIs Miss Your Need

After several dozen pages on Drupal's APIs, you can be forgiven for thinking that all your coding needs can be met by `drupal.org` and `PHP.net`. And in a way, that's true; the code you write is of course for Drupal and the language it is written in is PHP. But every function in Drupal was created to fill a need, and you can write your own.

■ **Note** JavaScript, the client-side scripting language that enhances Drupal's front end, is the exception to the all-PHP rule. Even for this, Drupal supplies some PHP API functions for working with JavaScript. And in JavaScript, Drupal provides functions for translation and other Drupal-specific capabilities. Not to mention that Drupal includes the JQuery library to provide many, many utility functions that make JavaScript much easier to work with, especially for cross-browser support.

Listing Data as Human-Readable, Properly-Punctuated Text

The X-ray module so far has been more than liberal in sprinkling `t()`s everywhere, and it probably sets a record for the number of times `format_plural()` has been used in a module. Both provide good handling of including variables. Nonetheless, in turning data into natural text, X-ray module had a recurring need not met in Drupal core: taking an array of items and making it into a sentence-ready list with commas and a conjunction.

The function I found after searching for "comma separated list PHP" and similar search terms could have been in any PHP project—a snippet put up by anyone. Yet it was shared by a Drupalista because the community rocks. Building on that snippet is the utility function shown in Listing 20–6.

Listing 20–6. The Oxford Comma Function

```
/**
 * Make an array of items into a proper, punctuated, and sentence-ready list.
 *
 * Based on www.drupaler.co.uk/blog/oxford-comma/503
 * Grammatically fun helper to make a list of things in a sentence, i.e.
 * turn an array into a string 'a, b, and c'.
 *
 * @param $list
 *   An array of words or items to join.
 * @param $settings
 *   An array of optional settings to use in making the Oxford comma list:
 *   - type
```

```
 *      The text to use between the last two items. Defaults to 'and'. Pass in
 *      'or' and 'and' without translation; translate any other join.
 *   - comma
 *      The join for the list. Defaults to a comma followed by a space.
 *      To make an Oxford comma list with semicolons, use '; '.
 *   - oxford
 *      Change this from default 'TRUE' and you are a philistine.
 */
function xray_oxford_comma_list($list, $settings = array()) {
  // Set default settings.
  $comma = ', ';
  $type = 'and';
  $oxford = TRUE;
  // Overwrite default settings with any passed-in settings that apply.
  extract($settings, EXTR_IF_EXISTS);
  // Translate 'and' and 'or'.
  if ($type == 'and') {
    $type = t('and', array(), array('context' => 'Final join'));
  }
  elseif ($type == 'or') {
    $type = t('or', array(), array('context' => 'Final join'));
  }
  //
  if ($oxford && count($list) > 2) {
    $final_join = $comma . $type . ' ';
  }
  else {
    $final_join = ' ' . $type . ' ';
  }
  // Take the last two elements off of the $list array.
  $final = array_splice($list, -2, 2);
  // Combine the final two removed elements around the final join string.
  $final_string = implode($final_join, $final);
  // Add the combined elements (now a single element) back onto the list array.
  array_push($list, $final_string);
  // Return the list as a text string joined together with commas (or other).
  return implode($comma, $list);
}
```

This function was fun to write, not least because most of the work had already been done. It introduces the concept of *context* for translation functions, making clear with a third parameter given to the t() function that this use of 'and' and 'or' are for final joins and not whatever inappropriate use someone else might come up with for them.

Another new thing is the use of extract() with a new constant to tell it to *extract if exists*. (Rule of thumb: never use a bare extract; always add a second argument.) See dgd7.org/245 for an older, more verbose version of the default settings code that was made leaner and cleaner with this use of extract().

As you do more with Drupal and PHP, you will get a consistently better sense of what is possible (most everything), and, knowing something is possible, also know that you can find a way to get there. Actually, there will be multiple ways to get there. One beautiful thing about writing code that encapsulates its functionality in functions and methods is that readability or performance improvements can be made in one piece of code without always having to pay attention to all the rest of the code. The xray_oxford_comma_list() function went through several overhauls for adding capability and then purely for code elegance—and will undoubtedly go through more.

Making Mistakes and Embracing Error Messages

Following the advice to write what you know, I've decided to do a whole section on messing up. There's no such thing as bug-free code, especially not on the first writing. Knowing what to do when your code breaks something is the route to victory.

Searching for Answers

Web search is your friend, as always, when it comes to error messages. Be sure to remove any parts of the message that are unique to your environment, such as web site URLs or Drupal directory paths.

■ **Tip** Quote enough of the error message to return precise results, but cut out any parts that are specific to your site or system (such as site name or the system path to your home folder). Effective searching for solutions to errors you encounter will involve trial and error even after you get good at the initial search. It's usually worth trying `drupal.org`'s search and the general Internet.

See what other occurrences of the error have been posted and read other people's comments. With luck, and perhaps some perseverance, you'll find someone who has a solution. Searching for answers works most of the time, but it's also good to know how to recognize and solve certain types of errors like those listed below.

Syntactic Fatal Errors

Fatal errors mean we are alive. They mean our code is having an effect. And they are usually easy to fix by adding, removing, or moving a semicolon, parenthesis, or curly bracket. As PHP isn't a compiled language, it's almost as fast to fail trying to run the code for real (loading a web page from a local server) as it is for code syntax checking in an editor to give you a heads up. However, any good PHP IDE provides syntax checking.

■ **Tip** Enable syntax checking with the Vim editor; see `dgd7.org/vi`.

Drupal lines should end with a semicolon in most cases (when the line represents a statement); when it's part of a multi-line array definition, each item is separated with a comma. Mistakes like these will mostly be easy to fix, with PHP telling you which line the error is on. The hardest syntax error to fix is a mismatch in opening and closing curly braces. A missed closing curly brace (also called bracket) can produce an error pointing to the end of the file as the problem, when of course the actual cause can be much further up the file.

Runtime Fatal Errors

As mentioned, syntactic fatal errors manifest at runtime since PHP is not compiled, but because it's easy to catch them before running the code in the context of the whole application (just loading the code triggers the error), they are treated separately here. What I will call runtime fatal errors can occur only when taking an action (including visiting a page) that uses your code:

```
Fatal error: Cannot use object of type stdClass as array in↩
 /home/ben/code/dgd7/web/sites/default/modules/xray/xray.module on line 186
```

If your development environment is properly set up, this error will be printed to your screen. Even on a production site, this will be written to the error log on the server, which is helpful because all that you see may be the less-than-informative White Screen of Death (WSOD). (Even better, a properly set up development environment will provide a call stack of all the functions called. The next section shows how to enable a stack trace with the Devel module. Also, see Chapter 30 for a walk through a stack of function calls, similar to what you did at the beginning of this chapter.)

PHP is being very helpful and telling you precisely where and what the problem is. It's on line 186 and you are trying to use an object as an array. The code in Listing 20–7 shows the error-triggering code and the corrected code.

Listing 20–7. *The Line That Breaks Everything and the Corrected Code*

```php
<?php
// Line 186 looks like this:
    if (isset($theme['info']['hidden']) && $theme['info']['hidden'] == TRUE) {
// ...
}

// But it needs to look like this:
    if (isset($theme->info['hidden']) && $theme->info['hidden'] == TRUE) {
// ...
}
?>
```

The point is not that code that looks like the former is always wrong (if $theme were an array, it would be correct); the point is that when you have an error stating "Cannot use object of type stdClass as array", it means that you are dealing with an object and should be using object notation, the arrow (->).

Tracking Down the Cause of Errors and Warnings

If a new error pops up on your site while you're coding your module, odds are it's something you did. However, the error message may point to some core file that you have never touched. In this case, it is almost certain that the error has its origin somewhere else, whether caused by code you wrote or something you installed or configured. The process of figuring out where an error or bug came from and fixing it is called *debugging*. Figure 20–2 shows one such error that came up while coding the X-ray module.

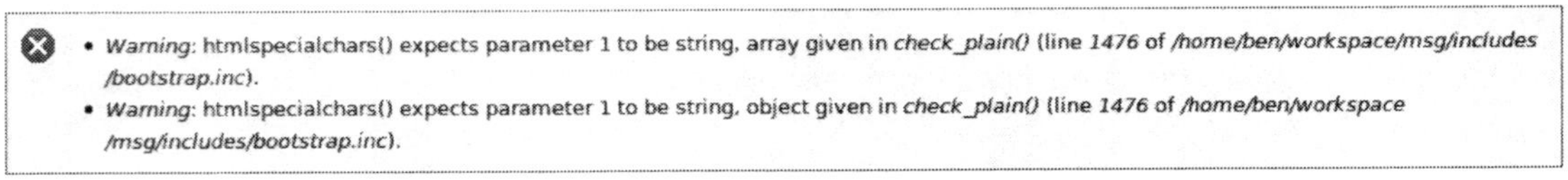

- • *Warning*: htmlspecialchars() expects parameter 1 to be string, array given in *check_plain()* (line 1476 of /home/ben/workspace/msg/includes /bootstrap.inc).
- • *Warning*: htmlspecialchars() expects parameter 1 to be string, object given in *check_plain()* (line 1476 of /home/ben/workspace /msg/includes/bootstrap.inc).

Figure 20–2. "Warning: htmlspecialchars() expects parameter 1 to be string" error message

Warning, array given, warning, object given, on line 1,476 of `bootstrap.inc`? What are you to do with that? You've never even looked at `bootstrap.inc`! You could take a look now to see how the function `htmlspecialchars()` is used in the Drupal function `check_plain()`, and then you could search through all the code of Drupal for the 157 functions that call `check_plain()`. Yes, 157; see `api.drupal.org/check_plain` for the list. It would be overkill to point out that one of the functions that calls `check_plain()` is the `t()` translation function, which, at 1,246 calls in core alone, is the most-used function in Drupal. So you could look through everywhere that `t()` is used, and everywhere else that `check_plain()` is used, and the functions that are calling them, and so on up the tree to try to find the one that's making `htmlspecialchars()` angry at you...

Or you could let a tool take care of this in an instant. There are standalone debugging tools and Integrated Development Environments (IDEs), which are discussed at `dgd7.org/ides`, but, as this is Drupal, there's also a module for that. The Devel module includes the option to print a backtrace from a PHP warning or error back up the chain of functions, formatted for readability with Krumo. Let's take a look at how it works.

Using Devel Module Trace an Error Back Up the Stack

Devel module contains tools for Drupal development and deserves to always be on hand. Let's install Devel module with Krumo and watch it transform the error message.

1. Download Devel module from `drupal.org/project/devel` or with Drush: `drush dl devel` (and give thanks to Moshe Weitzman, creator of both Devel and Drush).

2. Enable the module at `admin/modules` or with Drush: `drush -y en devel`.

3. Go to `admin/config/development/devel` (you can get there via the Configure link on `admin/modules`).

4. Scroll down the page to find Error handler, change it from Standard drupal to Backtrace, and then submit the form with Save configuration.

5. Navigate to a page that causes the error message and enjoy.

Now, back to your `htmlspecialchars()` warnings (see Figure 20–3).

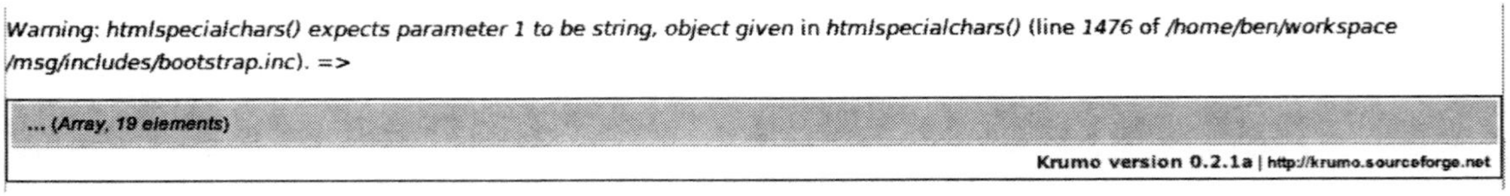

Warning: htmlspecialchars() expects parameter 1 to be string, object given in htmlspecialchars() (line 1476 of /home/ben/workspace /msg/includes/bootstrap.inc). =>

... (Array, 19 elements)

Krumo version 0.2.1a | http://krumo.sourceforge.net

Figure 20–3. "Warning: htmlspecialchars() expects parameter 1 to be string" error message with Devel and Krumo

All right, that's not helping much yet. Click the "... *(Array, 19 elements)*" text (where 19 will be the number of elements in your backtrace array) to expand the Krumo-formatted array); see Figure 20–4.

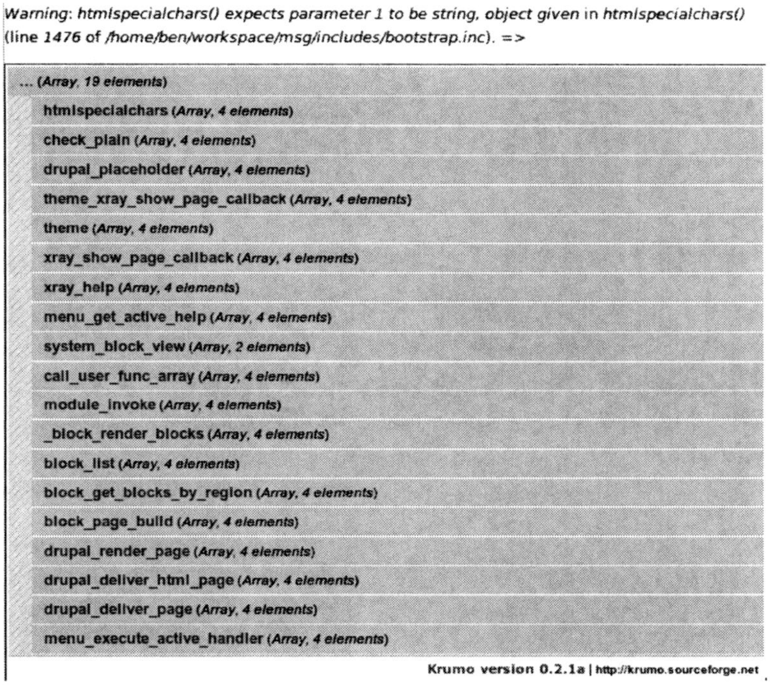

Warning: htmlspecialchars() expects parameter 1 to be string, object given in htmlspecialchars() (line 1476 of /home/ben/workspace/msg/includes/bootstrap.inc). =>

```
... (Array, 19 elements)
    htmlspecialchars (Array, 4 elements)
    check_plain (Array, 4 elements)
    drupal_placeholder (Array, 4 elements)
    theme_xray_show_page_callback (Array, 4 elements)
    theme (Array, 4 elements)
    xray_show_page_callback (Array, 4 elements)
    xray_help (Array, 4 elements)
    menu_get_active_help (Array, 4 elements)
    system_block_view (Array, 2 elements)
    call_user_func_array (Array, 4 elements)
    module_invoke (Array, 4 elements)
    _block_render_blocks (Array, 4 elements)
    block_list (Array, 4 elements)
    block_get_blocks_by_region (Array, 4 elements)
    block_page_build (Array, 4 elements)
    drupal_render_page (Array, 4 elements)
    drupal_deliver_html_page (Array, 4 elements)
    drupal_deliver_page (Array, 4 elements)
    menu_execute_active_handler (Array, 4 elements)
```

Krumo version 0.2.1a | http://krumo.sourceforge.net

Figure 20–4. Krumo-formatted backtrace array for "Warning: htmlspecialchars() expects parameter 1 to be string" error

Now you're in business. You can see every function involved from htmlspecialchars(), the function that is complaining, up through the function that calls it and the function that calls that function and the function that calls *that* function all the way to menu_execute_active_handler(), the function in index.php that starts off Drupal most of the time (see Chapter 30 to view Drupal through the eyes of this function). In that long list are several functions from X-ray module, which are far more likely culprits than a core function spontaneously generating an error.

You can click on theme_xray_show_callback in the function stack and drill down to the arguments given to it. As the error message indicated, the page_arguments array has an object in it and this is the fault of xray_show_page_callback().

■ **Tip** If you don't have Devel module or anything else handy, you can put a debug(debug_backtrace()); call where Drupal reports the error, but the output won't be nearly as easy to read as Krumo makes it.

To prevent the error, you will have to check each page argument and make sure it is not an object or array when you hand it to `drupal_placeholder()`. This level of complication in a theme function (or template) is a clear indicator it should have a preprocess function cleaning up the variables before it.

Making a Preprocess Function

When making a preprocess function for a theming function or template file, you can (as is so often the case) turn to Drupal core for examples. Node module yields `template_preprocess_node()` as a possible model (after a search for 'preprocess', for instance, with the command line search `grep -nHR 'preprocess' modules/node`).

■ **Note** As of 7, theme functions can have preprocess functions just like templates. It's still considered more friendly to themers to be able to copy and modify template files rather than override theme functions in `template.php`. Theme functions have better performance than templates, however, and are preferred for small things or things where re-theming is unlikely. See `drupal.org/node/933976` in the module developer's guide for more on using the theme layer in your module.

Preprocess functions defined in a module begin their names with `template_` (themes use the theme name here); next is `preprocess_`; and finally the name of the theme function or underscore. There's no need to add anything to your implementation of `hook_theme()`; Drupal is already looking for preprocess functions. Preprocess functions look and act the same whether for a template file or a theme function. A key point is that the `$variables` array is passed in by reference, so any changes or additions to this array need to be to the referenced copy. See Listing 20–8 for an example.

Listing 20–8. A Preprocess Function to Prepare Variables for theme_xray_show_page_callback()

```
/**
 * Process variables for show page callback theme function.
 */
function template_preprocess_xray_show_page_callback(&$variables) {
  if ($variables['page_arguments']) {

    foreach ($variables['page_arguments'] as $key => $value) {
      // Arrays and objects can't be easily printed in a message, so instead
      // identify what they are.
      if (is_array($value)) {
        $value = t('array') . ' ' . $key;
      }
      elseif (is_object($value)) {
        $value = t('object') . ' ' . $key;
      }
      // Sanitize for security and add emphasis to each argument.
      $variables['page_arguments'][$key] = drupal_placeholder($value);
    }
  }
}
```

```
/**
 * Theme the page callback and optionally other elements of a router item.
 *
 * @param $variables
 *   An associative array, as generated by menu_get_item(), containing:
 *   - page_callback: The function called to display a web page.
 *   - page_arguments: (optional) An array of arguments passed to the page
 *     callback function.
 *   - include_file: (optional) A file included before the page callback is
 *     called; this allows the page callback etc. to be in a separate file.
 *
 * @see template_preprocess_xray_show_page_callback()
 *
 * @ingroup themeable
 */
function theme_xray_show_page_callback($variables) {
  extract($variables, EXTR_SKIP);

  $output = '';
  $output .= '<p class="xray-help xray-page-callback">';
  $output .= t('This page is brought to you by ');
  if ($page_arguments) {
    $output .= format_plural(count($page_arguments),
      'the argument !arg handed to ',
      'the arguments !arg handed to ',
      array('!arg' => xray_oxford_comma_list($page_arguments))
    );
  }
  $output .= t('the function %func',
              array('%func' => $page_callback . '()'));
  if ($include_file) {
    $output .= t(' and the included file %file',
                array('%file' => $include_file));
  }
  $output .= '.</p>';
  return $output;
}
```

Arguably this data cleanup should be done even before the preprocess function. There's no way of requesting review quite like publishing your code in a book, so tune into this chapter's online companion at dgd7.org/61 for what will undoubtedly be more critiques and improvements of this code.

■ **Note** The code in Listing 20–8 has been enhanced (and made more complicated) by offering Krumo output. See dgd7.org/259 for the improved and expanded version, which includes a helper function for dealing with arrays and objects.

Final Considerations

You've seen a dozen APIs and looked at a lot of code and written your own code, but did you make a module? Pretty much, yes! Not every line of the X-ray module has been shown (in particular, the repetitive parts), but you can find it, along with all the code from this book, at dgd7.org/code.

This module lends itself to extension, but you didn't provide an API for other modules to extend it; instead, patches (additions or modifications to code that can be easily applied by a project maintainer) are very welcome! Now let's cover some final considerations, including coder module review and peer review.

The biggest final consideration, of course, is if you met the minimum requirement for what you were trying to do. Everything else is secondary—but still important.

- Try to ensure there's nothing hardcoded that people will want to change.

- Look very carefully for security vulnerabilities. Using Coder review module (covered next) will help catch many, but it can't catch everything. Is user access checked before anyone is able to see or change anything administrative? Is anything a user might enter *ever* output again without being escaped? The need to escape potentially dangerous markup includes user-submitted data being shown after it has been saved in the database; the protections the Database API provides against SQL injection attacks have nothing to do with the protection against HTML and JavaScript injection attacks that sanitization functions such as t(), check_plain() (which t() uses), and filter_xss() provide. See Chapter 6 for an overview of security considerations.

- Go over your code to ensure that it follows coding standards; see drupal.org/coding-standards. The Coder review module can help with this; see the next section.

■ **Note** Most of your code has gone into the .module file, but where in the file should you put, say, your next hook implementation? There's no official coding standard or widely agreed-upon best practice. Use something that helps you find your code (a good code editor will let you jump easily to specific functions) and don't spend too much time thinking about it. I keep all hook implementations together at the top of the .module file and favor importance, with a fallback on alphabetical order when indecisiveness strikes. Another approach is to put them in order of execution (see Chapter 30 for that order). I group the rest of the code by functionality, which is more art than science.

Coder Module Review

It's never too early to run an automated review of your module's code with Coder review module, in the Coder project found at drupal.org/project/coder. But it should definitely be run as the last thing you do before a release, too.

Download and enable the Coder review module (drush dl coder; drush -y en coder_review). Then go to Administration ➤ Configuration ➤ Development ➤ Coder (admin/config/development/coder) and leave everything at their defaults, which means the enabled reviews will be Drupal Coding Standards, Drupal Commenting Standards, Drupal SQL Standards, Drupal Security Checks, and

Internationalization. You can select "minor" so that coder will show every error or perceived problem it comes across. Under "Select specific modules," find the one you are working on among the module machine names, listed alphabetically.

Running this for X-ray resulted in this message: "Coder found 1 projects, 3 files, 1 critical warnings, 12 normal warnings, 9 minor warnings, 0 warnings were flagged to be ignored". Fortunately the critical warning was a false positive where the parser had not yet been updated to the new Database API way of doing queries.

The other errors, however, brought to light a coding mistake that wasn't documented anywhere really except by Coder review module: text in `t()` functions should not begin or end with a space. The logic is that translators are not likely to understand or notice the space, but in trying to build sentences that depended on whether, say, any page arguments existed at all, I repeatedly violated this rule. (This has been fixed in the code in the module and the code shown in the book.)

The moral of the story is always do a final pass with the automated code review before expecting people to look at and use your code. And having people look at your code can be a great way to learn, just as you learn from looking at other people's code.

Peer Review

"Contributing to Drupal is like pair programming with the entire community."

—Mark Ferree (`twitter.com/mrf`)

Contributing to an open source project means potentially thousands of reviewers will help make your code better. When you contribute to Drupal core, your work will be reviewed as a matter of course. When you publish your first project to its own project page on `drupal.org` (see Chapter 37), it will get a code review, too. The rest of the time, you have to ask specifically.

For a long time Drupal didn't have a recommended process for soliciting a review of your work. The best contributors ask; even when contributing a patch to core, top contributors find others to review their code, often swapping reviews, to keep things moving along. IRC, as is frequently the case, is usually the most effective place to ask. You might also find some interest on `groups.drupal.org` if the module relates to an existing group.

There is now a process for soliciting code reviews, centered around the Peer Review group on at `groups.drupal.org/peer-review`. This initiative aims to match people who want reviews for their projects with people willing to do the review. Remember that *giving* as well as receiving reviews is an excellent way to learn and to build relationships in the community. To request a code review, follow these steps:

- Before seeking a review, you'll need to get your code on `drupal.org`. See Chapter 37 for instructions on starting to use a Git sandbox project.

- Create a new issue for your own project that you want reviewed—the issue should be dedicated to the overall project review, rather than the tag being added to an existing issue. The category for the issue should be "task" and the status, naturally, is "needs review." (This is a bit of an abuse of the "needs review" status, as usually it means there is a patch that needs review, but here you are using it to apply to your whole project.) In the description, state what you are most looking for from a review and make clear your commitment to make improvements when they are recommended.

- Before submitting the issue, add the peer-review tag (with a dash between peer and review). All issues requesting peer review use this tag. You can optionally focus the kind of review you are looking by adding tags such as code-review, ux-review, accessibility-review, etc. See groups.drupal.org/peer-review/requests for the current list of tags.

- Any person who volunteers to review will post responses in that issue. The reviewer can change the status from "needs review" to "needs work" if he or she found issues (which should be described in a comment or created as separate issue reports on your project). Normally the "Assigned" attribute is for the person working on the code, but as you posted the issue and it's understood you will be working on the code, this should be used by a person reviewing to claim the primary reviewer role.

- After you've fixed any problems found, set the status back to "needs review." With luck, the reviewer will come back and mark it "Reviewed and Tested by the Community (RTBC)" if he or she has approved your work!

- Feel free to add "Reviewed by [username (linked to user account)] on [date (linked to the issue)]" to the description on your project page!

Just as for core contributors, it helps a great deal to get a timely review if you solicit one; offer to swap a review in exchange. Hanging out in IRC (see Chapter 9) is usually how such casual requests are made. Drupal meetups can also be a place to swap code reviews!

▨ **Note** It's very important that you follow the best practices described in this book and stick to coding standards (at drupal.org/coding-standards) before asking someone to invest their time in making your code better.

The best reviewers are people motivated to use your module because they need it. You don't necessarily have to solicit this review— bug reports, feature ideas, and support requests will be filed in your issue queue. If you have an opportunity to watch someone try to use your module, that can provide invaluable feedback. Many usability problems people run into don't get self-reported. The best way to get a usability review is to watch people try to use something and solicit their feedback immediately. It doesn't have to be done in a lab for you to learn a lot. If you can't find willing victims/participants in person to test your module, ask people you know are interested in using your module to try it out and report any bugs or confusion they encounter.

Using hook_help() as Drupal Intended

The most common usage of hook_help() is the one you haven't used it for yet. But first, I promised a full look at the hook's definition.

The hook_help() Function Signature

Every hook has a function signature: the parameters passed in to implementations of the hook and the nature of the value the invocation expects returned (if any). What you start with and what type of data you end with are defined; in the middle you can do whatever you want. That is the nature of APIs.

■ **Note** Implementations of hook_help() are expected to return an HTML string, most likely because it was overlooked during Drupal 7's conversion to renderable arrays. See Appendix C for more about the render system that applies everywhere else in Drupal!

The Parameters $path and $arg

What you receive to start with are called *parameters* or *arguments* to a function. The $path variable passed in to functions that implement hook_help() is the router path, which is Drupal's idealized understanding of what path it is on, based on the paths defined by implementations of hook_menu(). This just means that on code-defined pages such as admin/structure, the router path is also admin/structure, while on pages that might be created by the user, such as node/1, the router path is node/%. Therefore, to put a message on only a certain node (or user, or taxonomy term), you could still implement hook_help(), but you will have to use the $arg parameter to see the actual path you are on.

One way to see what these paths are for any page, as it isn't always intuitive, is to implement hook_help() and have it print the path and arg variables on every page. In a module called test (thrown in here just so you remember you can make modules that aren't named X-ray), this function would do that; Listing 20–9 shows the contents of test.module that, with a basic test.info file and when enabled, would print the path and arguments as interpreted by help on every page.

Listing 20–9. Contents of test.module

```php
<?php
function test_help($path, $arg) {
  return $path . '<pre>' . var_export($arg, TRUE) . '</pre>';
}
```

The same effect could be achieved by adding the return line to xray.module's xray_help() function.

■ **Tip** You can also use the debug() function almost anywhere in Drupal to print any variable to the screen, like so: debug($path, 'path'); debug($arg, 'arg'); The second parameter, a label, is optional. (For variables that are large arrays or objects, a third parameter TRUE may be necessary to avoid errors.)

Using this, you can visit node/add/article and see that the content type machine name (article) is present in the router path, node/add/article. This is true even if it is a content type you modify or create yourself, because the paths for add node pages for all content types are defined dynamically in node_menu(). The paths for edit forms for whole content types, however, like the edit form for nodes, make use of a wildcard placeholder in the router path. When you go to admin/structure/types/manage/article to edit the Article content type, for instance, the $path parameter for this path looks like the following: admin/structure/types/manage/% (*article* has been replaced by a percentage symbol, %, which signifies the wildcard placeholder). To see what content type you are editing, you need to look at the $arg parameter, which is an array that includes each part of the real path ('admin', 'structure', 'types', 'manage', and 'article').

On-site Documentation for a Module

Your use of hook_help() for the X-ray module (to add summaries and pieces of information to various places throughout the site) has been unusual. The usual use is for documenting how a site administrator should use the module itself. This may be as help messages on configuration pages for the module, which works the same as your path-based usage, but the most common use of hook_help() is, ironically, a special case as far as the code is concerned. When an implementation of hook_help() returns text for the path admin/help plus a hash sign (#) followed by a module name (in your case, admin/help#xray), Drupal creates a help page for the module at admin slash help slash module name (admin/help/xray for your module) and links to this dedicated help page from admin/help.

Let's close out this chapter by adding a proper, ordinary help page for X-ray module; note the path it returns on (see Listing 20–10).

Listing 20–10. Classic Help Page for the X-ray Module

```
/**
 * Implements hook_help().
 */
function xray_help($path, $arg) {
  $help = '';
  // Display in a help message the function that provides the current page.
  $help .= xray_show_page_callback();
  switch ($path) {
    // Summaries for main administrative sections.
    case 'admin/content':
      $variables = array('data' => xray_content_summary());
      return $help . theme('xray_content_summary', $variables);
    case 'admin/structure':
      $variables = array('data' => xray_structure_summary());
      return $help . theme('xray_structure_summary', $variables);
    case 'admin/appearance':
      $variables = array('data' => xray_appearance_summary());
      return $help . theme('xray_appearance_summary', $variables);
    case 'admin/people':
      $variables = array('data' => xray_people_summary());
      return $help . theme('xray_people_summary', $variables);
    case 'admin/modules':
      $variables = array('data' => xray_modules_summary());
      return $help . theme('xray_modules_summary', $variables);
    // The main help page for the module itself.
    case 'admin/help#xray':
      // This is shown as a regular page; do not include the
      // xray_show_page_callback $help or it is shown twice.
      return _xray_help_page();
    default:
      return $help;
  }
}

/**
 * Help page for the X-ray module.
 */
function _xray_help_page() {
```

```
  $output = '';
  $output .= '<h3>' . t('About') . '</h3>';
  $output .= '<p>' . t('X-ray module provides a look at the skeletal structure of your site↵
from several perspectives intended to benefit developers and site builders.') . '</p>';
  $output .= '<p>' . t('It adds an accounting summary of relevant objects to the help above↵
the main administrative sections (blocks, content types, menus on <a href="@structure">↵
Structure</a>; themes on <a href="@appearance">Appearance</a>; etc).', array('@structure' =>↵
url('admin/structure'), '@appearance' => url('admin/appearance'))) . '</p>';
  $output .= '<h3>' . t('Uses') . '</h3>';
  $output .= '<dl>';
  $output .= '<dt>' . t('Page callback and arguments') . '</dt>';
  $output .= '<dd>' . t('X-ray exposes the function that is primarily responsible for↵
providing a given page in a help message at the top of that page.  It precedes the name of↵
the function with the arguments handed it, if any.  It also provides the name of the file↵
where this function lives if available (the file is only available if the callback does not↵
live in a .module).  Note that just because arguments are handed in to a function does not↵
mean they are used.') . '</dd>';
  $output .= '</dl>';
  return $output;
}
```

The many other functions for displaying summary data about the site on various administration overview pages, such as People and Modules, are very similar to those shown for the Structure page in this chapter and can be found at dgd7.org/252. It's worth noting again that in addition to a data-gathering function and a theme function, X-ray's summary data require implementations of hook_theme(), hook_menu() (plus a page callback function), and hook_help(). Like every module hosted on drupal.org, you can look at X-ray's code to see how these messages and any new features are implemented.

Summary

By now, you may have figured out that if I can do this, you can do this. After reading Chapters 18, 19, and 20, I hope that you feel ready to take on the rewarding work of building your own modules to add power to your web projects and to contribute to Drupal.

▨ **Tip** Discuss Chapters 18, 19, and 20, continuing work on X-ray module, and module development generally at dgd7.org/intromodule.

## CHAPTER 21

Porting Modules to Drupal 7

by Robin Monks and Benjamin Melançon

Drupal, like many open source projects, relies on volunteer contributors to keep its ecosystem of development active and current. This is one of the key strengths of open source software; the downside is that people who used to volunteer time to Drupal often drop out when other commitments take over.

As a result, you'll occasionally discover a module that's exactly what you need, but the module developer hasn't upgraded it to Drupal 7 yet. In this chapter, I will upgrade a simple Drupal 6 module to Drupal 7. I'll examine the different processes to perform module upgrades, and I'll show you some of the common changes necessary to *port* a module from Drupal 6 to 7.

The Add another module is designed to save time when adding lots of items of the same content type to a site by presenting an "add another" message after submitting a node. This useful module could make your site more usable for contributors. Unfortunately, it's only available as a Drupal 6 version; there's no Drupal 7 version yet. Happily, with some simple effort, you can fix this!

Note that even if you don't know of a module that you personally need ported to Drupal 7, you can look for one for which other people have requested a port. Porting a module provides a triple benefit:

The community gets the functionality it wants.

Porting is easier than making your own module from scratch.

You get to expand your Drupal knowledge in two powerful ways—from examining the code you are upgrading, and from noting the changes Drupal made between versions 6 and 7.

You don't need to understand every aspect of the project you are upgrading (nor every change in Drupal) to upgrade the project to Drupal 7 successfully. You will, however, learn a great deal from the process. You may not immediately understand every nuance of how the code works, but in looking at another developer's code and understanding it enough to make changes to the parts where APIs have changed, you can't help but learn.

Deciding to Upgrade a Module

Whenever you have a need for a feature for your Drupal site, it's important to search the existing Drupal community to see if someone else has had the same itch. If so, that someone has probably already scratched their itch—most likely with a contribution to the Drupal community in the form of a module.

With very few exceptions, it's better to take someone else's similar or out-of-date module (or even code snippet, in some cases) and form it to match your own needs than it is to begin development from scratch.

Fortunately, upgrading a module from Drupal 6 to Drupal 7 can be an easy way to gain the functionality you need for your project and, as previously mentioned, a fun way to learn more about Drupal and contribute back to the community.

Before you begin the fun part of actually working on the upgrade, you need to make a few beginning steps to make sure you're not duplicating effort. You also need to let others know that work is happening to upgrade the module.

Throughout this chapter, you'll be working with the Add another module as your example. It's publically available at `drupal.org/project/addanother`; I ported it from Drupal 6 to Drupal 7 using the methods described here.

■ **Tip** As soon as you determine that a module ought to be upgraded—or that any feature, bug fix, or other change should be made to any Drupal project—you should investigate whether anyone else has posted the same idea to the project's issue queue. If not, go ahead and post it yourself.

Posting the Issue

When working with code in a community setting, you first need to announce your intentions with the code to everyone who might care. While shouting from the rooftop can be a fun first crack at this, it's best to climb down and go to the project's issue queue.

A project's issue queue is always linked to from the project's page on `http://drupal.org`, as shown in Figure 21–1.

You can also get to a project's issue queue directly at `drupal.org/project/issues/`*projectname*. For the Add another module's issue queue, go to `drupal.org/project/issues/addanother?status=All` to see what issues people have submitted. The optional "?status=All" query shows all issues; the issue page filters out closed ones by default. Issues are shown with the most recently updated ones first; you are able to filter by status (if the issue has work being done on it or a patch that needs review), version (such as all 6.x or all 7.x issues), and priority (relative importance of the issue), among other criteria.

■ **Tip** To filter without searching, leave the **Search for** text field blank and use the drop-downs you need to filter the list of issues:

Status filters by the current stage of the issue (e.g., active, fixed)

Priority filters by the urgency of the issue (e.g., major, minor)

Category filters by the type of issue (e.g., bug report, support request)

Version filters by the version of Drupal and the module version

Component filters by the component of the project (e.g., code, documentation). You still press **Search**, but without text in the search field, the filters are applied against all issues.

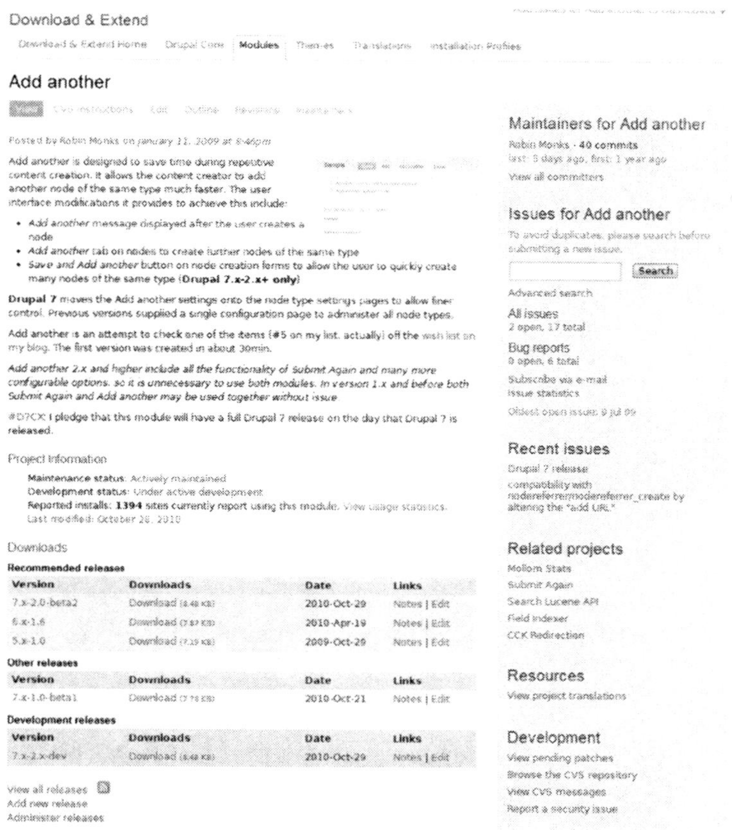

Figure 21–1. *The block issues for Add another include a summary of open versus total numbers of issues and bug reports.*

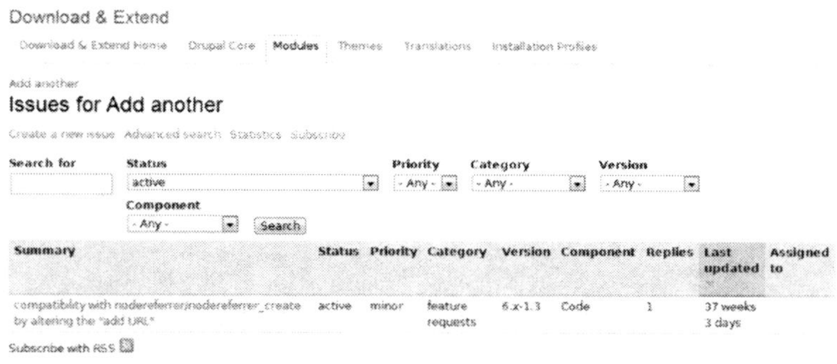

Figure 21–2. *Excerpt from the issues listing for the Add another module*

Look at all of the information in Figure 21–2; you can see each issue's title (ideally a short and accurate **Summary**); to whom the issue is **Assigned to**, if anyone; and the information you can use to filter the listing. Issues are color-coded based on their current **Status** (which is also written out in the second column). You can sort by any of the bold-print headers of this table. **Last updated** is, as mentioned, the default sort (click it to reverse it and view the oldest issues first).

If all issues or all open issues take up more than a page, reading the issue titles will be tedious, so use the **Search for** box to find an issue similar to your own. In the Add another issue queue, you can search for "Drupal 7", "port" and "7.x version" and you'll find that they come up empty or not related to upgrading.

From the listing of all issues, follow the Create a new issue link (which, in the case of the Add another module, takes you to `drupal.org/node/add/project-issue/addanother`).

In the issue creation form, **Version** is a required field; since no 7.x version exists yet, use the latest 6.x version. The project's maintainer (or *a* maintainer; a project can have more than one) will have to create a 7.x branch for this issue to be resolved. The issue can be properly assigned the 7.x version tag at that time. **Component**, another required field, is *code* (most functionality-related issues will be), and **Category** can be *task* (more typically, you will be filing *feature requests* or *bug reports* when recommending changes to a module's code). **Priority**, **Assigned**, and **Status** can be left to their defaults.

You can get really creative with the title: *7.x port*. Most issues will take more than a line to describe, but in the case of an upgrade, one sentence suffices: "This simple and useful module needs a Drupal 7 port."

Why Not Custom Code?

If a module does not exist for your version of Drupal, does not exist at all, or does not do precisely what you need, a custom, site-specific module is always a possibility. (For a site with highly customized functionality, this is often necessary. See Chapter 22 for more about writing modules like this, which are frequently called *glue code*.) In general, it's easier to write code that works just for your site but not in other situations. If you know exactly what you need, you don't need to make configuration through a user interface possible. Even in the case of upgrading an existing module, grabbing and modifying the essential lines of code might be easier than porting the whole module.

Nevertheless, from a purely selfish perspective, there are two strong reasons to upgrade (or make or extend) a proper, publicly released module with a user interface. First, you (and the people you work with) can make changes without modifying code. For instance, if a new content type is added that should also have the Submit and make another option, this can be done with a simple checkbox through the administrative UI. Second, by sharing your code with the community as a `drupal.org`-hosted module, you get the benefit of other people's eyes on the functionality and code; someone else may catch bugs or security holes before they bite you. Someone may even add features or upgrade the module to Drupal 8 when the time comes! It does happen, just as you are upgrading the Drupal 6 version of the Add another module to Drupal 7.

Undertaking the Upgrade

If you put Add another into a modules directory of a Drupal 7 site, you would see it listed on the modules page with its Drupal 6 version number (6.x-1.6) and description ("Presents users with an option to create another node of the same type after a node is added"). After that, though, Drupal adds the note "This version is not compatible with Drupal 7.x and should be replaced." You can't even try to enable it, as shown in Figure 21–3.

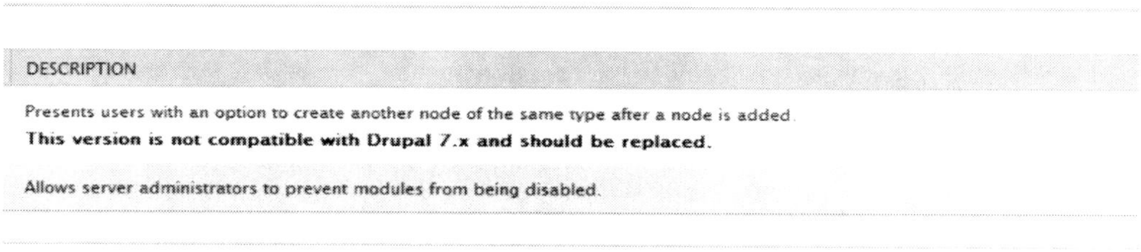

DESCRIPTION

Presents users with an option to create another node of the same type after a node is added.
This version is not compatible with Drupal 7.x and should be replaced.

Allows server administrators to prevent modules from being disabled.

Figure 21–3. Drupal will display an error if a module was written for an earlier version.

▓ **Tip** As soon as you start work, you can assign the issue you created to yourself. You should only do this when you actively start work; set it back to *unassigned* if you have to step away for more than a day. The issue queues have lots of issues assigned to people with no work done for months or years.

That would have been fun if it had worked, but we will have to put some effort into making the Add another module work in Drupal 7. For the simplest modules, changing only the core version specified in the .info file might work, but blind attempts are not actually the best way to get a module working.

Keeping Track of What You Need to Know

As changes are made to Drupal to create the next major version, a comprehensive list of API changes is recorded. These changes can be found on drupal.org in the handbook under *Developing for Drupal ➤ Module Developer's Guide ➤ Updating Your Modules*. The Drupal 6 to Drupal 7 changes are in a page called "Converting 6.x modules to 7.x" at drupal.org/update/modules/6/7.

Documenting the changes between major versions of Drupal and keeping this list up-to-date is a fantastic effort by the Drupal community. As worthy of honor as this effort is, do you really want to review the 200+ items on this list? For a learning exercise, this is an excellent and recommended use of a long afternoon … but for each module you upgrade?

A few stalwarts have taken the effort to improve the Drupal developer experience (sometimes abbreviated *DX*) even further.

Automating (Part of) the Module Upgrade

Jim Berry, with help from Jon Duell and others, has graced us all with the Coder Upgrade module. You can get it as part of the Coder project package at drupal.org/project/coder.

Coder Upgrade requires the Grammar Parser module to go through code and make changes and suggestions, so you must download drupal.org/project/grammar_parser also. See the "Command Line Steps" section in this chapter for the fastest way to do all of this.

▓ **Tip** You can also use these tools as an online service at upgrade.boombatower.com.

As with all development work, you do this on your computer or test server, not on the live site on a public server. You don't even need to be working on a copy of your site (although you will be doing so in this example); a new Drupal 7 installation will suffice for upgrading a module. Because you are using a development sandbox, you should put Coder and Grammar Parser in sites/all/modules even though they are developer modules that you don't intend to become part of the site project.

On your local install of Drupal, visit *Administer* ➤ *Modules* (admin/modules). There you should enable Coder, Coder Upgrade, and Grammar Parser (which Coder Upgrade requires).

Now you need to get the module you're going to upgrade. Go to the module project page and look for the latest version code. Typically this is in a *-dev* branch called HEAD; you want to use this most recent, in-development version of the code when upgrading a project or adding a feature to a project. For the Add another module, visit its project page at http://drupal.org/project/addanother and you will find that the latest version available is a full official release. A look at the repository (available for you to browse via a link on the project page) shows that no work has been committed since then. Therefore, download the latest version, 6.x-1.4, to begin the port. Unzip and untar the module's compressed tarball and put the resulting folder and files in the staging area that Coder Upgrade asks you to use; this is within your Drupal site's files directory (typically sites/default/files) in a coder_upgrade subdirectory and an 'old' directory within that (coder_upgrade/old). In other words, it's sites/default/files/coder_upgrade/old. Note that you can create parent directories as needed.

Command Line Steps

From the web root of a Drupal installation, which is drupal7 in this example, enter the following:

```
drush dl coder grammar_parser
drush en coder coder_upgrade grammar_parser
mkdir -p sites/default/files/coder_upgrade/old
cd ../
drush dl addanother --default-major=6 --select --
    destination=drupal7/sites/default/files/coder_upgrade/old
```

■ **Note** The -p flag for mkdir stands for --parents; it automatically creates, in this case, the coder_upgrade directory while creating the old directory.

In the steps above, we have to step back from the Drupal 7 site to get Drush to download a Drupal 6 module, which is what the cd (change directory) line does for us.

■ **Tip** The --select option for drush will show all currently available versions of a module and allow you to select the one you want.

For installing modules and fetching the module you are upgrading, using the command line as above is highly recommended. The remaining upgrade steps, however, are performed through Coder Upgrade's user interface.

■ **Tip** Many modules have excellent help built in, see `admin/help`. You can read Coder Upgrade module's particularly extensive in-module documentation on your own site at `admin/help/coder_upgrade`.

To begin the automatic upgrade, go to *Administer* ➤ *Configuration* ➤ *Development* ➤ *Coder* ➤ *Upgrade* (`admin/config/development/coder/upgrade`), click on the *Directories* vertical tab, and find the module you want to upgrade. The modules are listed by system name and Add another's system name is addanother. Coder Upgrade also gives the path—`coder_upgrade/old/addanother`—so you can be sure you have the module you just downloaded. Checkmark it, and click on the Convert files button at the bottom, as shown in Figure 21–4.

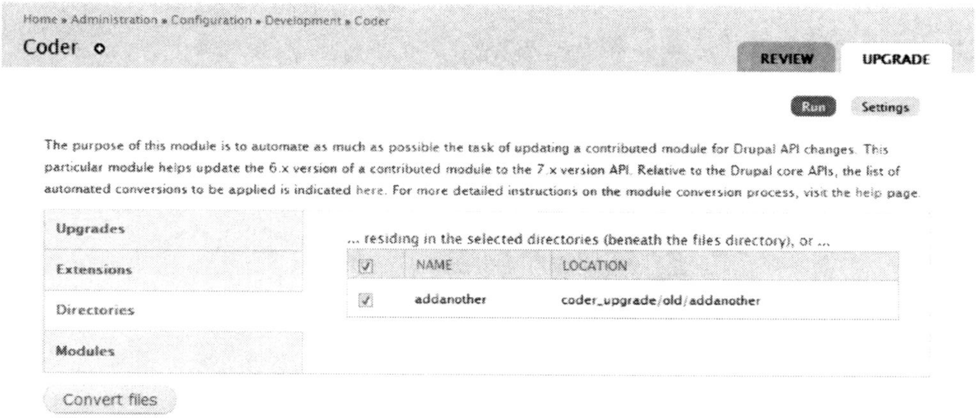

Figure 21–4. Coder provides an admin interface to simplify module upgrades.

You will receive these exciting system messages:

- Module conversion code was run
- Click to view the conversion log file
- Patch files may be viewed by clicking on Name links in the Directories and Modules tabs below

You can click the conversion log file link, but there isn't much there of interest: just a list of the hooks the upgrade looked for. Looking at the patch file is much more interesting. The patch file shows you everything that was changed in the module by Coder Upgrade.

As a rule, an automatically upgraded module is only partially upgraded, but it's worth testing out.

You can move the upgraded module from where Coder Upgrade placed it in `sites/default/files/coder_upgrade/new` to your `sites/all/modules` or `sites/default/modules` directory, or you can upgrade the 6.x version of your module in place with the patch Coder Upgrade provides. You can choose the latter to avoid dealing with permissions.

Command Line Steps

```
mv sites/default/files/coder_upgrade/old/addanother sites/default/modules/
patch -p0 < sites/default/files/coder_upgrade/patches/addanother.patch
```

▪ **Tip** Drupal has good documentation on how to apply patches at `drupal.org/patch/apply`. I consider this link the quickest and easiest-to-find refresher for which direction the angle bracket goes when using the `patch` command. (Another option: remember that the patch command "eats" the patch. Thus, the last line of the previous code could be read as "patch -p0 < aiee-the-alligator-is-going-to-get-me.patch.")

If nothing else, the key change the automatic upgrade must do is changing the core directive in the module's .info file to 7.x. This line may appear twice because `drupal.org` adds a datestamp and some other automatic information to downloaded modules, as noted in the comment (note that comments in .info files start with a semicolon (;) character at the beginning of each comment line). These lines added by the packaging script can be safely deleted, even if `coder_upgrade` tried to update the core line. Also, at the time of this writing the supported release of Coder Upgrade is incorrectly adding files[] directive lines for `.install` and `.module` files; this has been corrected in the development version of Coder Upgrade, but if you see these created, a relic of an earlier phase of Drupal 7's development, you can delete them.

```
name = Add another
description = "Presents users with an option to create another node of the same type after a
node is added."
core = 7.x

; Information added by drupal.org packaging script on 2010-04-19
version = "6.x-1.6"
core = 7.x
project = "addanother"
datestamp = "1271637006"
```

▪ **Note** If you had checked out the module directly from `drupal.org`'s version control, you wouldn't get this information added by the packaging script; Drupal only modifies .info files that are packaged into downloadable versions.

Now you should enable the module and check for additional configuration options added by the module (again on your development site, not a production site of any kind). Most modules add something to the administrative user menus: new settings under *Configuration*, a new node type under *Create content*, or a new menu link or tab somewhere in the administrative UI. You won't see anything for this module, though. It should have added an "Add another" link under *Configuration*, but nothing is there.

That automatic port would have been really great if it had worked.

However, even if the automatic upgrade had fully worked, you would still want to review the code. Time to look into the module!

Identifying What's Wrong

Having something specific that isn't working is a pretty good place to be when programming. It means you have a very clearly defined task in front of you. In fact, test-driven development (see Chapter 23) takes the approach of writing an automated test of what ought to happen, knowing that the test will fail. Programmers then make the test pass and can refactor (improve) the code, secure in the knowledge that they'll know right away if they break any part of it. In this case, it would mean testing for the presence of the Add another menu item under *Configuration*.

Regardless of whether you use test-driven development or not, you need to look inside the module to fix the code.

The module is right where you left it, in `sites/default/modules`. Open up the file addanother.module in the addanother directory.

Command Line Steps

From the web root, enter the following:

```
cd sites/default/modules/addanother/
vi addanother.module
```

Now you are in the module. Where do you start looking?

Whenever you need to make a menu item in Drupal, you'll need to deal with hook_menu in some form. In Drupal 7, the manner in which you specify paths for configuration pages changed slightly. With Drupal 6, you could specify a menu path to be `admin/settings/YourModuleName`; Coder Upgrade will actually reformat that as `admin/config/YourModuleName`. Sadly, this isn't up to Drupal 7 standards for displaying items from the Configuration page, as you need to pass another element in the path to show the group of configuration pages where yours belongs, the most basic of these being **system**. This would make your link `admin/config/system/YourModuleName`. Let's look at this change in practice.

Coder Module Output

```
/**
 * Implements hook_menu().
 */
function addanother_menu() {
  $items = array();
  $items['admin/config/addanother'] = array(
    'title' => 'Add another',
…
}
```

Corrected Code

```
/**
 * Implements hook_menu().
 */
function addanother_menu() {
  $items = array();
```

```
$items['admin/config/system/addanother'] = array(
  'title' => 'Add another',
...
}
```

Whenever you make changes to the menu system in Drupal, you need to clear the menu cache for the changes to appear. There are two ways to accomplish this. The first is to go to *Configuration*, then *Performance* under *Development* and then click the Clear all caches button. The second method is to use Drush to clear the caches; you can do the directly from the command line with the following command:

```
drush cc
```

However you choose to clear your page cache, the Add another menu item should now appear on your site's Configuration page. You can now access the Add another page and enable Add another for the Article content type that comes with Drupal by default. You can also enable all three of the display settings for the purposes of testing the rest of the module's features: Display the Add another message after node creation, Display the Add another tab on supported node types, and Also display the Add another tab on supported node edit pages (as shown in Figure 21–5).

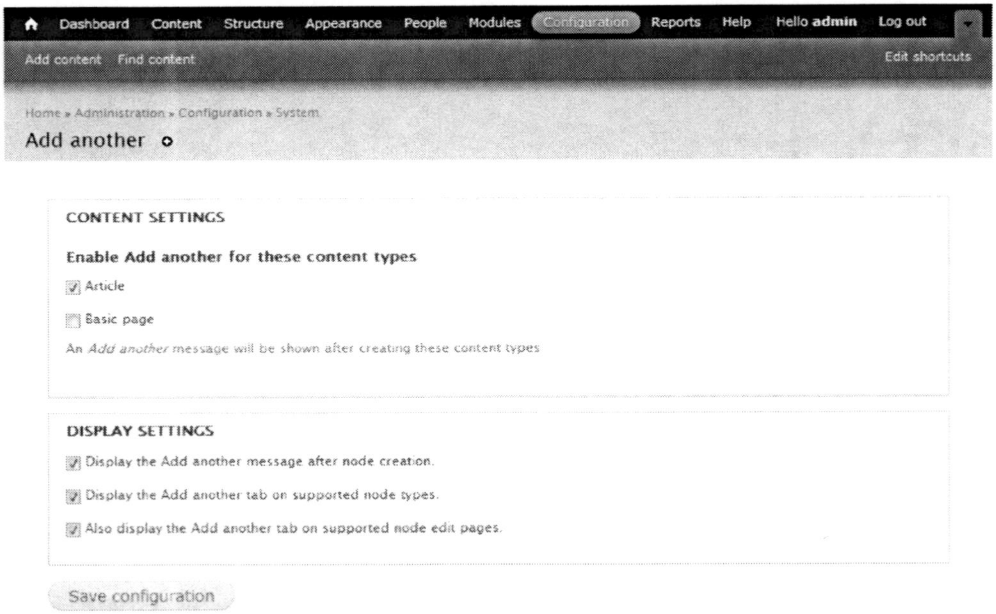

Figure 21–5. The Add another configuration page is edging closer to the functionality you want.

OK, so, you're getting much closer to the functionality you want. However, if you try to create an Article node type, you'll see a couple errors appear instead of your desired message:

```
Notice: Undefined index: access in _menu_translate() (line 776 of
C:\xampp\htdocs\d7\includes\menu.inc).
Notice: Undefined index: access in menu_local_tasks() (line 1890 of
C:\xampp\htdocs\d7\includes\menu.inc).
```

This is due to yet another change in Drupal 7 that Coder doesn't catch automatically. Since Add another's Drupal 6 version contained a function called addanother_access, Coder assumes it was a node access function and renames it to addanother_node_access for Drupal 7. This is incorrect; you'll need to rename the function back. So this code

```
/**
 * Check if we should display the Add another verbiage on a node.
 */
function addanother_node_access($nid) {
...
}
```

becomes

```
/**
 * Check if we should display the Add another verbiage on a node.
 */
function addanother_access($nid) {
...
}
```

Now if you create an article, you're definitely getting somewhere! You can see the Add another tab working properly, but the Add another message still isn't displaying. This is due to a change in processing order in Drupal 7 that you can actually take advantage of by moving your drupal_set_message call into the addanother_node_insert function. You can also perform some clean-up at the same time by removing legacy code to deal with the now-depreciated Submit Again module. The changes are as follows:

Original

```
/**
 * Implements hook_node_insert().
 */
function addanother_node_insert($node) {
  if ($node->op == t('Save and create another')) {
    // This prevents Add another's message from clashing with Submit Again.
    return;
  }
  $allowed_nodetypes = variable_get('addanother_nodetypes', array());
  if (user_access('use add another') && isset($allowed_nodetypes[$node->type]) &&
$allowed_nodetypes[$node->type]) {
    global $_addanother_message;
    $_addanother_message = t('Add another <a href="@typeurl">%type</a>.', array(
        '@typeurl' => url('node/add/' . str_replace('_', '-', $node->type)),
        '%type' => node_type_get_name($node)
        ));
  }
}

/**
 * Implements hook_nodeapi().
 */
function addanother_nodeapi_OLD(&$node, $op, $a3 = NULL, $a4 = NULL) { }
```

```
/**
 * Implements hook_form_alter().
 */
function addanother_form_alter(&$form, &$form_state, $form_id) {
  if (isset($form['#node']) && $form['#node']->type . '_node_form' == $form_id
      && variable_get('addanother_message', TRUE)) {
    $form['buttons']['submit']['#submit'][] = '_addanother_message';
  }
}

/**
 * Display the Add another message if set by addanother_nodeapi().
 */
function _addanother_message($form, &$form_state) {
  global $_addanother_message;
  if (isset($_addanother_message)) {
    drupal_set_message($_addanother_message, 'status', FALSE);
  }
}
```

Updated

```
/**
 * Implement hook_node_insert().
 */
function addanother_node_insert($node) {
  $allowed_nodetypes = variable_get('addanother_nodetypes', array());
  if (user_access('use add another') && isset($allowed_nodetypes[$node->type]) &&
$allowed_nodetypes[$node->type]) {
    $_addanother_message = t('Add another <a href="@typeurl">%type</a>.', array(
      '@typeurl' => url('node/add/' . str_replace('_', '-', $node->type)),
      '%type' => node_type_get_name($node)
      ));
    drupal_set_message($_addanother_message, 'status', FALSE);
  }
}
```

As you can see, you've been able to remove the empty hook_nodeapi function as well as remove the no longer needed _addanother_message function and the hook_form_alter that calls it. This is a wonderful example of how some of the changes introduced in Drupal 7 can make the module writing process easier.

■ **New in 7** Drupal coding standards call for functions that are implementations of hooks to be identified with the comment Implements hook_somethingorother(). (See drupal.org/coding-standards and in particular the "Module Documentation Guidelines" page at drupal.org/node/161085.) Beginning function descriptors with present-tense third-person (he/she/it) verbs such as "implements" is new to Drupal 7.

After saving the module and creating another article, as shown in Figure 21–6, savor the smell of sweet success!

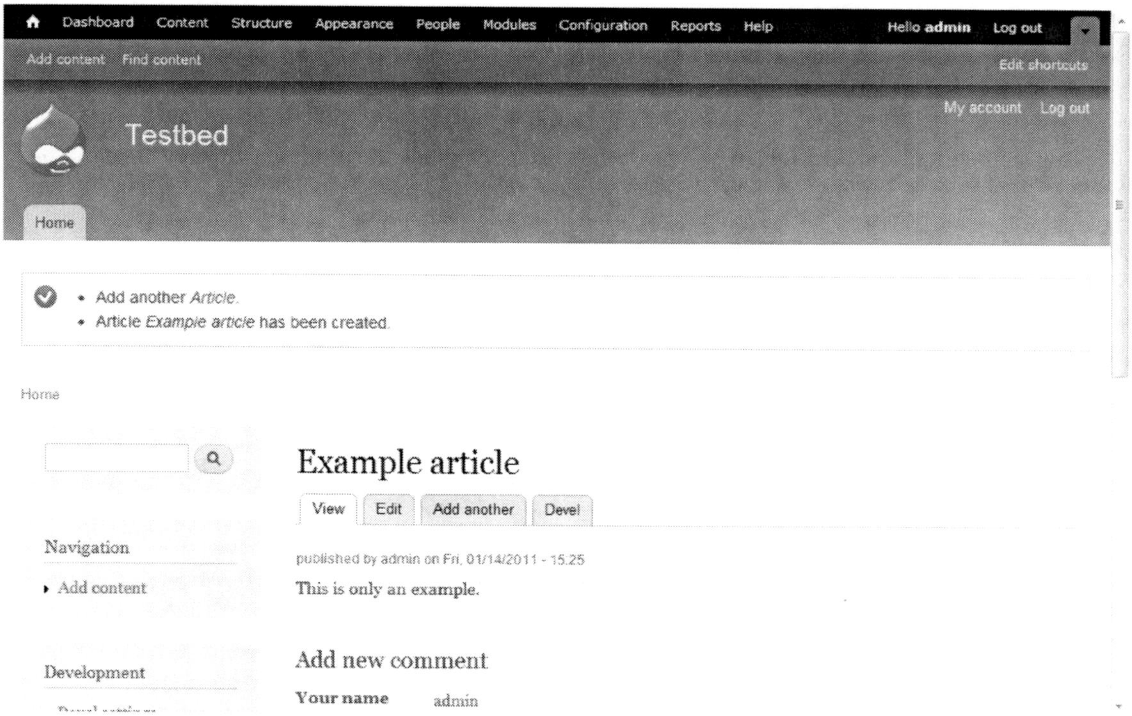

Figure 21–6. Add another message is finally working!

Finding Models to Follow

Looking at the Drupal core code is one of the best ways to learn to write Drupal code well. Although parts of core are not (ironically) up to the latest and greatest as far as doing things "the Drupal way," core code usually has the most eyes on it and the most work put into it. You can feel certain that the code works well.

■ **Tip** Another great place to look for model code is the suite of modules in the Examples project at `drupal.org/projects/examples`.

In the case of this module, you would have been able to compare the menu hooks with another module in core that produces system menus such as comment.module. You can also look at similar contrib modules on drupal.org that perform functions similar to your own to use as models.

■ **Note** Core and contributed modules also frequently have code in include files alongside the module or in subdirectories. In the case of Comment module (aside from several theme template files, CSS files, a JavaScript file, and the .install and .info files), it contains comment.admin.inc, comment.pages.inc, and comment.tokens.inc.

This chapter focused on doing just what was needed to upgrade the module, but you can learn more about Drupal from any module you upgrade or work on simply by exploring its code.

Contributing the Upgrade to Drupal.org

You're not done until you contribute a patch.

Open source free software is fantastic. You're building on someone else's work (and looking at the core software's code for guidance). Now you get to share the work you've done with the community, and you'll have the benefit of at least one or two people reviewing and testing it. After your work is incorporated into the module on drupal.org, you will be able to use any fixes or improvements others make, rather than having a version separate from what other Drupalistas use and contribute to.

Okay, you know all that. How exactly do you contribute your changes? The traditional Drupal way (which is common to many software projects) is for all code changes to come in the form of a patch file. Instructions for making a patch are on the "Creating Patches" page at drupal.org/patch/create (and in the "Contributing Code" section of "Getting Involved" in the handbook).

In most parts of this book, command line text is presented as an option—the recommended option, but an option. For creating patches, it's the only option described, although there are various GUI programs such as http://winmerge.org that you can try. To create a patch without using a version control system, you need a copy of your code. Any UNIX-like system (Linux, Mac OS X, or Cygwin on Windows) will provide you with the diff command to create a simple file showing the differences between your version and the original.

Use of this command is simple. It takes some flags to create patches in the style the Drupal community expects: **u** and **p** for unified context (the three lines of non-changed code before and after every change) plus the function that the code is within, and **r** to recurse through directories (to be able to patch more than one file). Then it takes two arguments, or operands: the original code (file or directory) and your modified code (an equivalent file or directory). Finally, you can point the output of the command to a file with the > (right angle bracket) character and a filename. Filenames for patches posted on drupal.org should include the relevant project name, a very brief description of changes (usually taken from the issue title), the node ID of the issue, and the comment number to which the patch will be attached.

That's a lot to process, but note how it all fits together in a one line command. First, you must start in the module's directory, because project patches should be able to be applied from within the project root. For the Add another project, it should apply from within the Add another folder. (Likewise, all Drupal core patches should apply from the drupal root.)

Go back to drupal.org/project/issues/addanother and find the issue, *7.x port*. You can get the issue's node ID from its URL, http://drupal.org/node/554504, and look at what the number the next comment will be (simply add one to the last comment number on the issue). Now you're ready to make the patch, the culmination of all your work, like so:

```
cd sites/default/modules/addanother
diff -urp ../../files/coder_upgrade/old/addanother/ . > addanother-7.x-port-554504-5.patch
```

You can test that the patch applies to the Add another module (you should always check for the latest version) by using the `patch` command. Copy the patch over to a fresh directory, get a fresh copy of the Drupal 6 version of Add another, and try out the patch, like so:

```
wget http://ftp.drupal.org/files/projects/addanother-6.x-1.4.tar.gz
tar -xzf addanother-6.x-1.4.tar.gz
cd addanother
patch -p0 < ../addanother-7.x-port-554504-5.patch
```

As long as no errors appear, the patch applied correctly. Now you simply need to post a comment to the issue and attach the .patch file. Don't ever expect everything to work the first time, especially for everyone who then tries to apply your patch. Once in the issue queue, people will try to help.

You'll have the opportunity to tweak or further modify the module as other people check and review you code, but for the most part, you're done. Congratulations on your first Drupal module upgrade!

■ **Tip** Check in at `dgd7.org/upmodule` for more tips on porting different kinds of modules and for current patching best practices with Drupal.org's still-new move to Git version control.

## CHAPTER 22

Writing Project-Specific Code

by Florian Lorétan

One of the great strengths of Drupal is the wide selection of available modules, providing everything from the integration of external media to complex access restrictions, with many modules expanding standard functionality to fit specific use cases.

Combining existing modules can cover most of your needs, but every project is different and has unique details that are not covered by any module. This where *glue code* comes in—project-specific code that fills the gap between the functionality provided by existing modules and the exact requirements of your project. Glue code allows you to bring projects to 100% completion with full customer satisfaction.

Note Many modules provide configuration options to let users adapt the functionality to their needs. Make sure to look at these options before you start writing your own custom code.

The following are terms you need to know:

- *Core module*: a module that is included in the standard download of Drupal. These modules are maintained by the same people who maintain the core system.

- *Contributed (contrib) module*: a module made available for download on drupal.org. Some of these modules are widely used, while others are only used by very specific people.

- *Custom module*: a module written by you while working on a project. It only contains project-specific functionality such as customizations of core and contrib modules.

Custom Modules

Like any functionality in Drupal, glue code resides in modules. There is no technical difference between a custom glue code module and a contributed module from drupal.org, but it is important to separate your code from code maintained by other people. This separation makes it possible to apply updates to contributed modules and benefit from security updates and improved functionality without losing your customizations.

The biggest mistake made by developers new to Drupal is making changes directly to existing modules or even to core Drupal files. I must admit to having done so in the early days of my Drupal career, and it cost me a lot more time than I would have spent reading this book, had it existed at the time.

The right way to write glue code is to create a custom module, clearly separated from contributed modules. Each type of module has a different standard location, making it easy to tell them apart. Directories are indicated relative to the main Drupal directory, where the index.php file resides.

- Core modules are stored in the modules directory. You shouldn't ever modify the content of this directory.

- Contributed modules are stored in the sites/all/modules/contrib directory. The content of this directory should only be modified when you are updating modules.

- Custom modules are stored in the sites/all/modules/custom directory. These are the modules that you are writing, and you are free to modify them as needed.

In addition to storing custom modules in sites/all/modules/custom, you also want to follow the following conventions:

- To avoid potential conflicts with existing names, the names of custom modules should be prefixed with the project name, e.g., myproject_comment.module.

- For small projects, everything can be in one module. If you need more than one module, make sure that the dependencies between your own modules are clear.

- If a custom module extends the functionality provided by another module, make sure to include that module in the dependencies listed in the .info file.

For example, a module customizing the comment form for a project called "MyProject" would have the following structure:

sites/all/modules/custom/myproject_comment/myproject_comment.info

```
name = "MyProject Comment Customizations"
description = "Customize the comment form for MyProject."
core = 7.x
package = "MyWebSite"

; Add any modules that we rely on.
dependencies[] = comment
```

sites/all/modules/custom/myproject_comment/myproject_comment.module
```
<?php
```

For now, myproject_comment.module can be left empty. You can enable the module from the module administration page, but it doesn't do anything yet.

▨ **Note** Many of the examples given in this chapter could be solved using existing contributed modules; such solutions are referenced in the text. These modules generally take a similar approach to the presented custom code. The decision whether an existing module is more appropriate than a custom module is dependent on the project and is left to the reader.

Hooks

As mentioned earlier, glue code modules do not provide functionality on their own, but they expand the functionality provided by existing modules. In Drupal, the standard mechanism to let modules interact with each other is the *hook system*.

The hook system is a very flexible way to let one module give other modules the possibility to react to certain events. For example, the comment module defines a hook called hook_comment_presave(), which is executed before a comment is saved. Any module interested in modifying a comment before it is saved can define a function named by replacing "hook" with the name of the module. In your example, you have a "myproject_comment" module implementing hook_comment_presave, which results in the following function:

```
function myproject_comment_comment_presave($comment) {
  // Do something here.


}
```

The hook system makes it possible to have many modules building on top of each other at the same time. The flexibility it provides has been one of the success factors of Drupal as a development platform, but that flexibility also means that developers who are new to Drupal sometimes have a difficult time following the execution of the code. A standardized method for adding custom functionality to the existing module is very helpful to keep a good overview of the various interactions happening between modules.

The Method

Now that you have a place to put your code, let's see what you can put in there. However, before I get into the details of the various APIs and how to use them, let's have a look at the general method for achieving what you want using custom code. No matter if you are an experienced "Drupal Ninja" or if you are writing your first module, writing custom code is always a discovery process consisting of the following questions:

What is it that I need to modify and why am I doing it?

Where can I hook into?

What is already there?

How can I modify existing functionality for my own needs?

What is it that I need to modify and why am I doing it?

I am not going to spend much time discussing the reasons for wanting a specific functionality, but "Why am I doing this?" is always an important question to ask before starting to write code.

Custom code, by nature, modifies the standard behavior of existing functionality. Before you start coding, make sure that the changes you want to bring into the system are meaningful. The standard functionality is often the standard for a reason, and it's important to consider the implications that your changes will have.

Where can I hook into?

Drupal has a very flexible architecture that makes interaction between different modules very easy, but it also means that there are many different ways to achieve similar results. The main concept used for module interaction is the *hook*. When a module provides certain functionality, a hook is a way to let other modules know about it and react accordingly. This makes it possible to have modules that build on top of others. In fact, you can look at Drupal as a sort of layered architecture, with the core systems at the very bottom, some basic modules building on top of that, and more modules extending that basic functionality.

Each of these modules building on top of each other is using the hooks of the modules below it. Your custom module will come on top of existing modules, but knowing the best way to hook into them is important to build solid functionality. This question pretty much comes down to what hook you want to implement.

There is no absolute rule, but a good starting point is to find out what kind of element or main component you will be dealing with. In most cases, it will be a node, a form, or a menu router item. A search on api.drupal.org should help you find the relevant hooks, but Table 22–1 shows some of the basic ones.

Table 22–1. Basic Hooks

Component type	Alterable with
Form	hook_form_alter(&$form, &$form_state, $form_id)
Node	hook_node_presave(), hook_node_insert(), etc.
Menu router item	hook_menu_alter(&$items)

What is already there?

Once you have a place to hook into existing functionality, you need to know what's there to play with. This is the point where some debugging tools, such as the debug() function, come in handy. Custom modules work mostly with structures defined by other modules and being able to visualize those structures is critical to interacting with them.

▪ **Tip** The Devel module provides a set of tools that makes it easy to investigate the different structures involved in a Drupal site. This module does not provide any functionality to end users and should be disabled on production environments, but I absolutely recommend using it during the development of any project.

How can I modify existing functionality for my own needs?

This is the last step of the process, but it's the one where you actually get things done. You know what you want, where you can hook into, and what data is available; now you just need to write the code that does it. If you ever find yourself at this point not knowing how to continue, going back to the previous steps should help.

An Example: Changing the Label of a Submit Button

Here's a simple example to illustrate this method:

1. **What is it that I need to modify and why am I doing it?**

   You have a form provided by a contributed module, but the client for whom you are building the web site wants to replace the standard submit button that says "Save" with one that says "Store this information".

2. **Where can I hook into?**

   There are a few places where you could hook into to perform the change, but since what you want to modify is a form element, you are going to implement hook_form_alter(), which takes three arguments: $form, $form_state, and $form_id:

```
function mymodule_form_alter(&$form, &$form_state, $form_id) {

}
```

3. **What is already there?**

   Use the Devel module and its helper function dpm() to figure out the content of the parameters, like so:

```
function mymodule_form_alter(&$form, &$form_state, $form_id) {
  dpm($form);
  dpm($form_state);
  dpm($form_id);
}
```

It turns out that $form is a Form API structured array in which you can identify the submit button that you want to modify (see Figure 22–1). The $form_state has additional information about the state of the form, such as the submitted values. The $form_id parameter is there to identify this specific form; you can use it to make sure that you don't affect other forms.

Note that hook_form_alter() has another variant, which is specific to a certain form, takes the form hook_form_FORM_ID_alter(), and doesn't take the $form_id parameter. This variant has the advantage of only affecting a specific form, thus slightly improving performance and reducing the likelihood of unwanted side-effects.

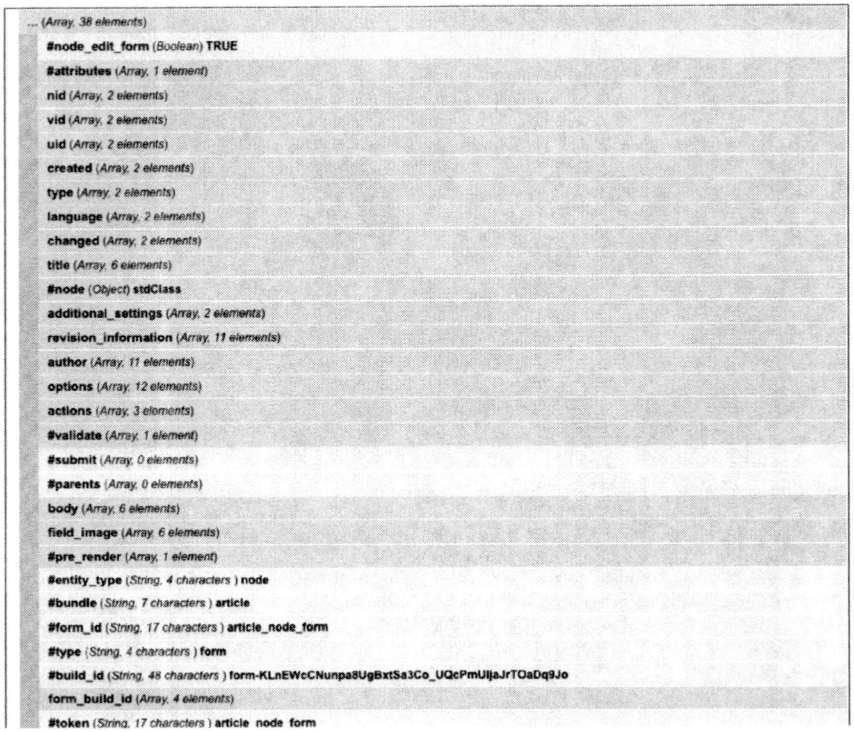

Figure 22–1. The output of dpm()

4. **How can I modify existing functionality for my own needs?**

Now that you have targeted the key elements that you are going to use, you can write the code. We know the ID of the form, so we can also use the hook_form_FORM_ID_alter() variant to only affect this specific form. Supposing that the ID of the form in question is article_node_form, our hook implementation would look like this

```
function mymodule_form_ article_node_form alter(&$form, &$form_state, $form_id) {
  // Replace the #value attribute of the submit button.
  $form['submit']['#value'] = t('Store this information');
}
```

Specific Use Cases

The possibilities provided by the different hooks in Drupal are endless. Documentation about how to use each of them is available at api.drupal.org, so listing them all here wouldn't make much sense. Instead, I am going to show examples of common tasks and how to solve them.

Hiding Elements from the User Interface

When I talk about customizing the functionality provided by an existing module, I am not necessarily going to expand it. In fact, one of the most common tasks of glue code is to hide elements from the user interface. The purpose can be either to streamline the user experience by removing superfluous elements, or it can be functional—to purposefully limit the options given to the end user in order to match your needs.

When you need to hide elements from the user, the first idea that comes to mind is simply to completely remove the element. While this can work most of the time, there are cases where such an approach will have negative side effects. Other modules might be counting on those elements to be there, so rather than removing them, the best solution is to deny access to them, like so:

```
/**
 * Implements hook_form_alter().
 * Remove the comment settings from the article form.
 */
function mymodule_form_alter(&$form, &$form_state, $form_id) {
  $form['comment_settings']['#access'] = FALSE;
}
```

This code illustrates how to use hook_form_alter() to set the #access attribute of a form element to FALSE, which has the effect of hiding it from all users. The form element is not visible but is still present in the form structure and will be processed correctly. In this case, you hide the comment settings from the article creation form, but articles created with this form will still have the default comment settings applied to them.

The next example uses the same principle with menu elements. Access callbacks are usually functions that define whether or not a user has access to a page, but by setting the access callback to TRUE or FALSE you can allow or deny access unconditionally to all users.

```
/**
 * Implements hook_menu_alter().
 *
 * Make the http://example.com/node page unreachable.
 */
function mymodule_menu_alter(&$items) {
  $items['node']['access callback'] = FALSE;
}
```

This second example uses the same principle with menu elements. Access callbacks are usually functions that define whether or not a user has access to a page, but by setting the access callback to TRUE or FALSE we can allow or deny access unconditionally to all users.

Sometimes instead of removing an element, you only want to change the way it looks or behaves. This can generally be done by changing its type. Basic form elements can easily be converted from one type to another. The next example turns a text field into a select field to let the user choose from predefined options instead of entering arbitrary input. Note that form elements can only be converted into elements types with compatible values. The value of a text field is a string, whereas the value of a group of checkboxes is an array; turning a text field into a group of checkboxes will have unpredictable results.

```
/**
 * Implements hook_form_FORM_NAME_alter().
 *
 * Instead of using a text field for filtering a view by type, you limit the options↵
 * using a select element.
 */
```

```
function mymodule_form_views_exposed_form_alter(&$form, &$form_state) {
  // Change the type of the filter field to a select element.
  $form['title']['#type'] = "select";

  // Set the options to only search for Drupal or Open Source.
  $form['title']['#options'] = array(
    '' => t('List everything'),
    'Drupal' => t('List only articles whose title includes "Drupal"'),
    'Open Source' => t('List only articles whose title includes "Open Source"'),
  );
}
```

This last example is a very common one. Tabs such as those found on node pages or on the user registration form are often undesired, although the pages they link to still need to be available. This effect can be easily obtained by changing the type of the corresponding menu definition from MENU_LOCAL_TASK to MENU_CALLBACK, like so:

```
/**
 * Implements hook_menu_alter().
 *
 * Hide the tab to edit an article, you are going to create a link at the end of the↵
 content instead.
 */
function mymodule_menu_alter(&$items) {
  // The default type is MENU_LOCAL_TASK, which displays a tab.
  $items['node/%node/edit']['type'] = MENU_CALLBACK;
}

/**
 * Implements hook_node_view().
 *
 * Add our own link.
 */

function mymodule_node_view($node, $view_mode) {
  $node->content['links']['mymodule_link'] = l(t('Edit'), 'node/' . $node->nid .
'/edit');
}
```

Execution Order of Hooks

Knowing the order in which hook implementations are executed is very important when adding glue code. It often happens that the module that you want to extend uses the same hook as your custom module, in which case you generally want your module's implementation to be executed explicitly before or after the original module.

By default, the order in which hooks are executed is determined by the corresponding module's weight, which is stored in the system table and can be set using hook_install(). (For an example, look at the Devel module's implementation of hook_install() in devel.install.) Modules having the same weight are sorted alphabetically based on the path, which means that core modules stored in the modules directory have their hooks executed before those of contrib modules, which are stored in sites/all/modules.

However, sometimes you need to control just one hook, not all of them. This can be done using hook_module_implements_alter(&$implementations, $hook). Suppose that you want to do some form alterations after all other modules have done theirs. This could be done with the following code:

```
/**
 * Implements hook_module_implements_alter().
 */
function mymodule_module_implements_alter(&$implementations, $hook) {
  if ($hook == 'form_alter') {
    $my_hook_implementation = $implementations['mymodule'];
    unset ($implementations['mymodule']);
    $implementations['mymodule'] = $my_hook_implementation;
  }
}
```

Working with Fields

One of the most important new features of Drupal 7 is the inclusion of the Fields API into Drupal core.

While the Field API was inspired by the widely used CCK module, some substantial changes occurred that made the Field API even more central to the functionality of a web site. Whereas fields used to be limited to nodes, they can now be attached to any entity. This means that users, comments, taxonomy terms, and any other defined entity can now have additional attributes. As a consequence, you are going to encounter structures from the Fields API very often when writing glue code for Drupal 7.

The standard structure of a field is the following:

```
$entity->field_name[language_code][delta]['attribute_name']
```

By looking at the field structure of an article defined in a standard installation with the Devel module, you will notice the following:

- The field name often starts with the field_ prefix, but this is not always the case. The body of an article is a field, for example, but its field name is simply 'body'. Fields created through the user interface will always have the field_ prefix.

- When the locale module is not enabled, the language code is always 'und', which is the value of the constant LANGUAGE_NONE. However, when the locale module is enabled, the language code corresponds to the language of the article in some cases, but some fields such as the field_tags are still language-independent. The field_language() function helps us determine the language code for a field, but we can also use the field_get_items() function, which handles the whole logic for us.

```
/**
 * Implements hook_node_presave().
 */
function mymodule_node_presave($node) {
  // Use field_language() for a specific field.
  $body_language_code = field_language('node', $node, 'body', $node->language);
  $body_value = $node->body[$body_language_code][0]['value'];

  // Alternatively, get the items directly.
  $body = field_get_items('node', $node, 'body');
  $body_value = $body[0]['value'];
}
```

Note that when dealing with the form elements related to a field's widget, the language code is accessible in the #language form API attribute and should be retrieved that way.

```
/**
 * Implements hook_form_alter().
 */
function mymodule_article_node_form_alter(&$form, &$form_state) {
  // Right:  $body_language_code = $form['body']['#language'];
  // Wrong:  $body_language_code = field_language('node', $node['#node'], 'body');
}
```

- The delta is a numeric index used with multiple-valued fields to identify the each of the different values. However, the delta is part of the structure of any attached field to maintain consistency. For single-valued fields, the delta is always 0.

```
// You can iterate through the multiple values of a field.
foreach (field_get_items('node', $node, 'field_tags') as $delta => $item) {
  // Do something with each value.
}
```

- Each field type can have many different attributes. Many field types, such as text and numbers, have one main attribute called 'value', but this is not always the case. Taxonomy term reference fields only have one ' tid' attribute with the identifier of a referenced taxonomy term. Image fields have much more information about the referenced file. When in doubt about what data is available, make use of the Devel module to check. If the data you need is not available, you can generally load it based on the existing attributes.

▊ **Note** The Field API provides many more possibilities that can be very practical for custom modules. Writing custom widgets or custom formatters can be a very elegant way to take advantage of existing field structures while keeping your code generic and clean. More information about the Field API can be found at api.drupal.org/api/drupal/modules--field--field.module/group/field/7.

Adding Dynamic Front-End Interaction

The Web 2.0 movement has popularized the use of JavaScript and Ajax for user interface improvements to the point where they have become an integral part of the expected user experience. Fortunately, Drupal 7 includes many tools that greatly facilitate the creation of dynamic user interfaces. For more details about how to use these various APIs, have a look at Chapter 17.

jQuery UI

The jQuery UI library is a set of user interface tools built on top of jQuery, which is included in Drupal 7. It provides helper functions to facilitate the creation of behaviors such as resizable, draggable, or selectable components. It also provides JavaScript tabs, accordions, sliders, and other common user interface components.

Listing 22–1 is an example of using jQuery UI to turn the sidebar blocks into an accordion using hook_page_alter().

Listing 22–1. Using jQuery UI

```
/**
 * Implements hook_page_alter().
 *
 * Turn the sidebar blocks into a an accordion.
 */
function mymodule_page_alter(&$page) {
  if (isset($page['sidebar_first'])) {
    // Adapt the HTML structure of the sidebar using a custom theme function.
    $page['sidebar_first']['#theme'] = 'mymodule_sidebar_accordion';

    // Add the accordion library from jQueryUI.
    $page['sidebar_first']['#attached']['library'] = array(
      array('system', 'ui.accordion'),
    );

    // Add the code to transform the sidebar into an accordion.
    $page['sidebar_first']['#attached']['js'][] = array(
      'data' => '(function($) {
                  Drupal.behaviors.sidebarAccordion = {
                    attach: function(context, settings) {
                      $("#sidebar-first").accordion();
                    }
                  };
                })(jQuery);',
      'type' => 'inline',
    );
  }
}
```

#ajax and #states

Interactivity is very often related to forms. The #ajax and #states attributes are recent additions to the Form API that greatly simplify the creation of Ajaxified components and the definition of dependencies between form elements. Such tasks once required custom jQuery code but can now be handled directly from PHP by altering form arrays inside an implementation of hook_form_alter(). See the Form API reference at api.drupal.org/api/drupal/developer--topics--forms_api_reference.html/7 for documentation and examples on how to use these attributes.

Making Code Reusable

Even though the glue code that you put into custom modules is mostly project-specific, it would be nice to be able to reuse the same functionality on a different project without having to start from scratch or spending hours adapting your custom code to the new project. The following sections contain guidelines that will help you keep your code generic and reusable.

Make Functionality Configurable

When you want to act on a specific component, the easiest way to specify it is to hardcode the component's name into your module. The drawback is that from this point, your module will depend on a component with a specific name. Instead of hardcoding the component's name, you can make your functionality configurable.

For example, you want a small module that notifies users about potentially outdated content because your information is extremely time-sensitive. The hardcoded version would look like this:

```
/**
 * Implements hook_node_view().
 */
function mymodule_node_view($node, $view_mode, $langcode) {
  $display_outdated = $node->type == 'article';
  $age = time() - $node->created
  $is_outdated =  $age > 60*60*24*7;

  if ($display_outdated && $is_outdated) {
    drupal_set_message(t('This article was posted over 1 week ago and might be outdated.'));
  }
}
```

If you use this code on a different project that needs the same functionality—but for a content type called "story" and with a threshold of one month instead of one week—you would need to change the code in four places. This creates a high risk of forgetting something and ending up with broken code. A better solution would be to make the code configurable, like so:

```
/**
 * Implements hook_node_view().
 */
function mymodule_node_view($node, $view_mode, $langcode) {
  $delay = variable_get('mymodule_outdated_delay_' . $node->type, 0);
  $age = time() - $node->created
  $is_outdated = $age > $delay;
  if ($delay && $is_outdated) {
    $type = node_type_load($node->type);
    drupal_set_message(t('This @type was posted over @delay ago and might be↵
outdated.', array('@type' =>  $type->name, '@delay' => format_interval($age, 1));
  }
}
```

This code is not dependent on the existence of a specific content type anymore. Instead, it defines variables that can be set for any content type. To make this configuration available to the end user, you can simply extend the node type configuration form, as shown in Listing 22–2.

Listing 22–2. Extending the Node Type Configuration Form

```
/**
 * Implements hook_form_FORM_NAME_alter().
 */
function mymodule_form_node_type_form_alter(&$form, &$form_state) {
$form['mymodule_outdated_delay'] = array(
    '#title' => t('After how long do you want to warn users.'),
    '#type' => 'select',
    '#default_value' =>  variable_get('mymodule_outdated_delay_' . $form['#node_type'],↵
```

```
  60*60*24*7),
    '#options' => array(
      0 => t('Do not warn about outdated content'),
      60*60 => t('1 hour'),
      60*60*24 => t('1 day'),
      60*60*24*7 => t('1 week'),
    ),
  );
}
```

This code will let the user configure functionality along with other node settings. These settings are stored as variables that you can access from other parts of your code as you did in your implementation of hook_node_view(). Now that the configuration is independent from the functionality, you can reuse the same code on a different project with similar functionality but a different configuration.

Tie Components Together

Glue code is, in most cases, dependent on other structures such as content types, views, and other configuration components. In Listing 22–2, you made the code generic in order to be able to attach functionality to any content type, but there are cases where you need a specific structure to be present.

For example, a custom blog module would not make much sense without a content type for blog articles and a view to list the blog posts. Rather than leaving it up to the person installing the module to create those components, you can have your custom module define them itself. You could use hook_node_info() to define a new node type and hook_views_default_view() to define a view for the blog listing.

However, defining these structures by hand can be tedious and updating such structures is difficult. The Features module can greatly help with the task of exporting configuration components to code, but it adds an additional dependency to your module. Chapter 34 contains more details about how to use features.

Document Your Code

You've probably already heard this many times, so I won't spend too long on this point, but just because you are writing project-specific code does not mean that you shouldn't document your code. As a PHP developer on a Drupal project, custom code is where you will spend most of your time, so a lack of documentation can do a lot of damage and definitely reduces code reusability.

Follow Drupal's Coding Standards

Like many projects, Drupal has coding standards that guarantee a clean and consistent coding style. Although you are free to do whatever you want when writing your own code, using the same coding style as other Drupal module developers will make it easier to keep all your projects consistent and will improve the readability.

More information about the official Drupal coding standards is available at drupal.org/coding-standards.

Release Your Work

No matter what kind of custom functionality you need, it is likely that there are other people who have similar needs. If you have been good at keeping your code clean and generic, it's an excellent idea to release your code on drupal.org. (This doesn't have to be as a full, supported project, either— many people will be able to benefit from you sharing custom code as sandbox projects.)

All Drupal modules are released under the GPL 2 license. If you are being paid for your development work (whether you an employee or a contractor), check with your contact person to make sure they have no problem with making the code you wrote for them public.

In addition to garnering good karma for contributing to an open source project, there are many other reasons why releasing code publicly can be beneficial to everyone involved. Having more people use your module means that there will be more eyes on the code, and it is likely that your users will contribute bug reports and new features.

Patching Existing Modules

Modifying the code of existing modules is generally considered to be a bad practice. However, it makes sense when you're working on improving the module itself—as long as the improvements are contributed back to the maintainer so that they can be included in future releases. Note that such changes should always be done on a development environment (not on a live server) and that you should use a version control system to make sure that you can revert your changes if necessary.

In most cases, you will be fixing a bug or adding a new feature to the original module. Although the details might be different, here are the basic steps to follow:

- Look at the module's issue queue to see if anybody else has reported something similar and eventually solved it.

- If a bug hasn't been reported yet, write an issue describing the problem and how to reproduce it.

- If a new feature hasn't been requested yet, write an issue describing the new feature and why it's needed.

- If there are any suggested solutions, try them and report if they worked or not.

- If there are no suggested solutions and or the suggested solutions don't work, try to resolve the problem yourself.

- Make sure to post an update of what you found. Even an unsuccessful attempt can result in useful information.

- Once you have a solution that works, you can keep it in your code base. Make sure to have a reference to the issue and a copy of the patch saved in case it needs to be reapplied at a later date.

Releasing a New Module

Finally, there are cases where the new functionality you created does not belong to an existing module but deserves a module of its own. The steps to get a module maintainer account on drupal.org are beyond the scope of this chapter, but you can find more information about it at drupal.org/node/7765 (and see Chapter 37 on maintaining a project on drupal.org using Git).

Before you release your code, please make sure to check the following points:

- The code is clean, well documented, and follows Drupal's coding standards.

- The functionality provided can be useful to other people.

- There is no existing module that serves the same purpose. If there is, try to work with that module's maintainer. Duplicated modules cause confusion for end users.

- The code has no security holes that you are aware of.

Summary

With each new release, Drupal's APIs have made it possible to do more without having to hack existing modules. As of Drupal 7, hacking modules should never be necessary. Using the APIs correctly to write your own glue code can not only save you from causing yourself problems, but it will also make you a better Drupal developer.

Keeping your code clean makes it easier to take advantage of the development community surrounding Drupal, and contributing bug fixes and new features as you encounter them is probably the easiest way to bring your own contribution and becoming an active member of the community yourself.

■ **Tip** Stick around `dgd7.org/glue` for the links from this chapter, more resources, and reader tips.

■ ■ ■

## CHAPTER 23

Introduction to Functional Testing with Simpletest

by Albert Albala

The release of Drupal 7 marks a turning point, specifically with regards to automated testing, as it allows core and contributed module developers to validate that their code works as intended. Because content management systems were originally designed for simpler web sites, the relative complexity of automated testing has traditionally made it a low priority. However, in recent releases, and especially with version 7, Drupal has become much more than a simple content management system. It is a *platform*, a complex application making use of modern concepts such as exception handling, object-oriented programming, and, yes, automated testing.

Two types of automated tests are now supported by Drupal:

- *Unit tests* validate units of code (especially functions). For example, a unit test could feed the value 9 to a `square_root()` function and confirm that it returns 3.

- *Functional tests* validate that particular use cases involving a real user produce a desired outcome. An actual example found in Drupal's core node module test (`modules/node/node.test`) validates that a user with the "create page content" permission can go to Add content ➤ Basic page and successfully create a page.

This chapter will focus exclusively on functional tests, which are by far the most widely-used in Drupal and the most adapted to the way Drupal is written. The Drupal community has modeled its Simpletest testing framework on the PHP library of the same name, although that library is not required by Simpletest in Drupal (for Drupal 6, see drupal.org/simpletest). In fact, Simpletest is now so tightly integrated into the Drupal core development workflow that all new core code is practically required to be validated by a functional test.

This chapter will show you how to leverage Simpletest for functional testing in your own modules and patches (see Chapter 18 for more on developing modules). Think of functional testing as *validating that a module actually interacts as intended with a real user*. For example, let's say you wanted to develop a simple module to display the text "Over 25 active users!" if more than 25 users have posted at least one node in the last month.

Without automated functional testing, you would write the module and then test it by creating 25 users and a post for each. Only then could you be sure that the text "Over 25 active users!" actually appears when it should. Simpletest allows you to define these steps in a functional test so they can be repeatedly simulated any number of times, automatically, within a brand new temporary Drupal site one you can't manipulate directly, but only through the code in your testing file (as you'll see later on).

In fact, you'll create this exact module and functional test later in this chapter. But first, let's start with a quick overview of some key Simpletest concepts. Then you'll learn how to set up a Simpletest working environment in Drupal 7. (Don't worry; it's really not that complicated.)

Advantages (and Caveats) of Using Simpletest

Your first question is probably about whether incorporating Simpletest into your workflow adds to development time. If you consider development time over the life of your project (and you should!), in most cases you'll find that using Simpletest actually saves you time. Yes, you'll spend a lot more time defining your tests at the very beginning of a project. The real payoff comes later on in the lifecycle of your project. Here's how:

- *Automated testing allows you to validate that your code is actually doing what it should* by running particular use cases in a brand new, temporary Drupal installation. This allows you to catch problems early (hopefully before the users of your site) and do away with assumptions about your code.

- *Tests are a vital part of a module's documentation.* As you look at the sample test later in this chapter or the tests included with Drupal core (see modules/node/node.test), you'll find that tests *tell a story* about what the module actually does—from a user's perspective. This will save future programmers (including you) valuable time figuring out what a module was meant to do in the first place.

- *Automated testing helps avoid regressions.* Once some functionality is validated by a test, it will be more difficult to break later on. If a bug fix you're implementing introduces a *regression* (breaks functionality that worked fine before), the problem will be brought to your attention as soon as you run your tests on the new code. You'll spend less time fixing mistakes and maintaining your code.

Keep in mind, though, that tests, just like any other code, are prone to bugs and need to be maintained. Beware of logical errors in the tests you write, especially tests that succeed when they should fail.

When to Use Simpletest

Using Simpletest is time consuming at first. Although in a perfect world all code would be validated by a functional test, you'll find Simpletest yields its highest dividends in the following scenarios:

- On widely-used modules, where bugs are more likely to appear.

- On modules you expect will be under active development for a long time.

- On modules that are mission-critical to your web site.

- On modules that require several steps to test a desired use case.

For the most effective tests, don't limit yourself to normal workflows. Make sure you also test what happens when a user tries something that should not be permitted (for example, a test could validate that an anonymous user can't create content). Don't forget: your tests are only as good as you make them.

What Is Test-Driven Development (TDD)?

Test-driven development takes automated testing to its logical next step. On a TDD project,

- The current version of your module should not contain any failing tests (and thus should not contain any half-baked functionality).

- Tests should be defined in parallel with (or even *before*) your code. This allows you to focus on the task of satisfying your tests as you code.

- In a pure TDD model, the current version of your module should not even contain any features that are not validated by tests.

The more you apply these concepts to your code, the harder it will be for bugs to creep in. the following is the basic TDD workflow for a given task:

- Add a test that fails, proving that your bug exists or your feature is not implemented.

- Modify the module (including its test) until the test passes.

- Once your test passes and you have validated that your modifications work, you're done.

Of course, satisfying your tests does not guarantee that your code is any good! Both your tests and your module code should still be written conscientiously.

How Simpletest Works

In Drupal, any module that defines the user interface can (and should!) define one or more functional tests. You can then run these on any Drupal site with Simpletest enabled (see the "Setup and Running a Test" section). But in most cases, tests will be run only on your development site; once your modules are stable, they will run on production sites and the tests will be ignored.

Where are these tests defined? Drupal modules are folders with at a minimum two files: `mymodule.info` and `mymodule.module`. (For more about developing modules, see Chapter 18.) Tests are defined in another file, `mymodule.test`. For example, your test file could be at `sites/all/modules/mymodule/mymodule.test`.

■ **Note** In Drupal 7, files containing classes must be explicitly referenced in the `.info` file. So in addition to creating a `.test` file, you'll add the line: `files[] = mymodule.test` to your `.info` file.

You'll take a closer look at the specifics later in the "Anatomy of a .test File" section; you'll also find all the code from this chapter at dgd7.org/167 and on the book's page at www.apress.com. Basically, each test defines something specific that a module should do *on a brand new Drupal installation, not on your current site*. If a test depends on some content or users being present, these should be created within the test itself (you'll see how this is done later in this chapter).

Once a test exists, you will be able to run it through the Simpletest module (see the "Setting up and Running a Test" section). Running even a basic test can take several minutes (you might even think your site is frozen; it's not). This is because Simpletest creates a brand new temporary Drupal site for each test, then deletes it when the test is done.

■ **Note** It is important to understand that each test, as it is run, completely ignores whatever is in your site's current database or what's in other tests. This is to avoid tests becoming "contaminated" by outside data. Although work is being done to enable running tests on a clone of your site instead of a brand new installation (see `drupal.org/node/666956` and `drupal.org/project/simpletest_clone`), such functionality is not currently ready for prime time.

For each test, Simpletest creates a new site by installing all database tables; and at the end of each test, these tables are discarded. The database used by Simpletest is the same one used by your development Drupal site (on which you enabled the Simpletest module), with the same username and password; to avoid naming conflicts, each temporary table is created with a random unique prefix.

■ **Note** I don't recommend using table prefixes when you install your development site (the one on which you enable Simpletest), but if you must, keep them short. Simpletest will add its own prefix to your prefix before each temporary table name, which will result in errors if the table names become too long. The maximum length of table names varies between systems, but I've had problems using prefixes of over six characters. Avoid prefixes altogether if you can.

Setting up and Running a Test

Before Drupal 7, one had to download and install the Simpletest module, then patch core before performing tests. With Drupal 7, Simpletest is now a bona fide member of Drupal core, so all you have to do is enable it on any Drupal 7 web site and you're ready to start testing. There's no fiddling with the server.

Because you will be testing *modules* and not your *web site*, and because running tests is processor-intensive, you should not run tests on your production web site. It is best to set up a dedicated Drupal site (on your laptop, for example) specifically for developing and testing. This is where you'll develop your modules, enable Simpletest, and run your tests. The temporary Drupal sites used for testing will be created on the same database as this development site. Do not enable Simpletest on your production site.

■ **Note** Although the Simpletest module's machine name is `simpletest`, its human-readable name is Testing. So if you enable the module through the web interface at `admin/modules` (see Figure 23–1), look for Testing, not Simpletest. If you're enabling the module through Drush (see Chapter 26) on the command line, use `drush en simpletest`.

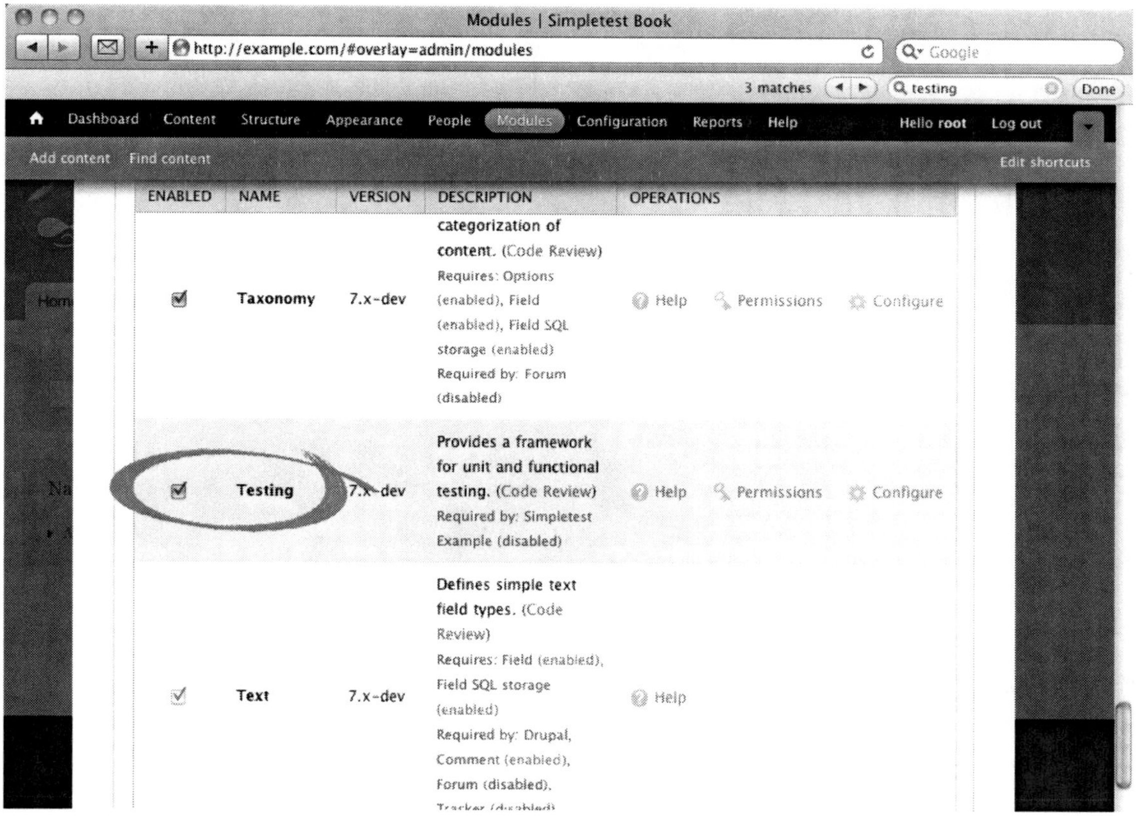

Figure 23–1. Enabling the Testing module

Let's start by running a test that ships with Drupal core: the functional test included with the core blog module. Install a new Drupal 7 site, enable the Testing module, then go to Configuration ➤ Development ➤ Testing. Here, you'll see all modules (even if they're not active) that have associated automated tests (see Figure 23–1). Click the blog checkbox, and then the Run tests button.

Running the blog test takes a few minutes (your site is not frozen; be patient) because it's installing a brand new Drupal web site in a virtual browser, creating some users and content, and making sure everything works as expected. This is all done in the background while you're staring at a progress bar.

If you expand the results section on the resulting page, you'll see about 250 tests in green and a number of *verbose messages*. Clicking on any of the verbose messages shows you a snapshot of how the temporary test site looks at a particular stage of a test. This is not a screenshot but the actual HTML code of a given page exactly as the testing robot sees it at a given time. This is an invaluable tool when you have failing tests in your modules—you get to see exactly what went wrong and when.

■ **Note** On the Simpletest settings page at Configuration ➤ Development ➤ Testing ➤ Settings (`admin/config/development/testing/settings`) the "Provide verbose information when running tests" option should be on by default in Drupal 7. If you are developing a test and running it repeatedly—and expecting differences in your HTML snapshots—your browser might display a cached version due to the way these verbose snapshots are stored. Just refresh your browser if you are seeing an out-of-date snapshot.

Anatomy of a .test File

Examining existing .test files (such as `modules/node/node.test`) can quickly become overwhelming—they use functions and an object-oriented structure that might not be familiar to some Drupal developers and can seem very complex. To get a feel for the structure of a .test file, Listing 23–1 provides its most basic skeleton. Testing code goes into a special file with the .test extension that is placed in your module's directory, next to the .module and .info files. Then you add a line referencing your .test file in your .info file (see the "How Simpletest Works" section earlier in the chapter).

Listing 23–1. Structure of a .test File

```php
<?php
/**
 * @file
 * Describe your file here.
 */

/**
 * The following class is a test case. Test cases have a name and
 * description and are what appears in the Simpletest user interface. They
 * may include any number of tests that all share the same setup.
 * When you run a test case through Simpletest, each test inside the test
 * case will run by creating a new temporary Drupal site, running the
 * common setup code, running the test itself, then destroying the
 * temporary Drupal site. There can be more than one test case class
 * in a .test file.
 */

class MyModuleTestCase extends DrupalWebTestCase {

  /**
   * Info for this test case.
   */
  public static function getInfo() {
```

```
    return array(
      'name' => 'One-line description of your test case',
      'description' => t('Longer description of your test case.'),
      'group' => 'mymodule',
    );
  }


  /*
    Common setup for all tests within a test case.
  */
  public function setUp() {
    // set up a new site with default core modules, mymodule, and
    // dependencies.
    parent::setUp('mymodule');
    // create a new user with some permissions you need; then log in.
    $admin = $this->drupalCreateUser(array('permission one', 'permission two'));
    $this->drupalLogin($admin);
  }


  /*
    Tests—recognizable as such because the function name starts with 'test'.
    For every test, Simpletest will create a completely new Drupal
    installation, run the common setUp() function, and go through this code.
  */
  public function testMainTest() {
    // your testing code goes here. Note that at this point
    // setUp() has already been run so if, in the setUp() function,
    // you have logged in as a specific user, you are still logged in.
  }
}
```

If you are familiar with object-oriented programming, you'll notice that you just defined a new class that contains information about your test case. A test file can contain any number of test case classes, and each test case class can contain any number of tests. Each test function in a test case *must begin with the lowercase "test"*. This is what makes Simpletest recognize it as an actual test.

For example, if your test file contains three test cases with three test functions each, nine new temporary Drupal sites will be created and then destroyed. If you're running several test cases on several modules, you'll have time to go for a jog before the results come in.

Writing Your First Test

Running an existing test is all fine and good, but the real fun begins with writing and running your own tests.

You'll first write a module that displays "Over 25 active users!" in a custom block. Then you'll write a test to make sure it works. The block should render only if there are over 25 users who have authored at least one node in the previous month.

Call your module *mymodule* if you want this code to work as is. (See Chapter 18 on writing custom modules.) First, in your Drupal 7 site, create the directory mymodule in sites/all/modules. Place the code in Listing 23–2 in a new file at sites/all/modules/mymodule/mymodule.module (note that you can find this code on the companion web site at dgd7.org/167 and on the book's page at www.apress.com).

Listing 23–2. mymodule.module

```php
<?php
/**
 * @file
 * This file defines a block which displays t('Over 25 active users!')
 * if more than 25 users have created a post in the last 30 days.
 */

/**
 * Implements hook_block_info().
 */
function mymodule_block_info() {
  $blocks[0]['info'] = t('Number of users');
  return $blocks;
}

/**
 * Implements hook_block_view().
 */
function mymodule_block_view($delta = '') {
  if ($delta == 0 && mymodule_active_users() >= 25) {
    $block['subject'] = t('Number of users');
    $block['content'] = t('Over 25 active users!');
    return $block;
  }
}

/**
 * mymodule_active_users().
 * Returns the number of active users, defined as being users who posted a
 * node in the last 30 days.
 * @return
 *    number of active users (see above).
 */
function mymodule_active_users() {

  return db_query('SELECT COUNT(DISTINCT uid) FROM {node} WHERE
  :time - created < :threshold', array(
    ':time' => REQUEST_TIME,
    ':threshold' => variable_get('mymodule_threshold', 60*60*24*30),
  ))
  ->fetchField();}
```

Basically, you are defining a block that displays "Over 25 active users!" only if the function mymodule_active_users() returns 25 or more. The mymodule_active_users() function counts how many users exist as authors of nodes created less than a month ago.

To test this module without Simpletest, one would have to create 25 users and a post for each, which is quite unwieldy. This is also the perfect opportunity to write a functional test! Create the test file at sites/all/modules/mymodule/mymodule.test and populate it with the code in Listing 23–3, which is your test.

Listing 23–3. mymodule.test

```php
<?php
```

```
/**
 * @file
 * This file contains tests of the functionality of mymodule,
 * a test module designed to demo Simpletest.
 */

/**
 * This class corresponds to a family of tests (called a test case).
 * Complex modules will have several of these. Inside the same
 * test case, all tests will have the same setup.
 */

class MyModuleTestCase extends DrupalWebTestCase {

  /**
   * Info for this test case.
   */
  public static function getInfo() {
    return array(
      'name' => 'mymodule functionality',
      'description' => t('Test the functionality of mymodule'),
      'group' => 'mymodule',
    );
  }

  /*
    Common setup for all tests within a test case.
  */
  public function setUp() {
    // set up a new site with default core modules, mymodule, and
    // dependencies.
    parent::setUp('mymodule');
    // create a new user with some permissions you need; then log in.
    $admin = $this->drupalCreateUser(array('administer blocks', 'create blog
      content', 'administer nodes'));
    $this->drupalLogin($admin);

    // go the block management page and set the region of your block
    // to sidebar_first, making sure it will be visible to Simpletest when
    // it is run. Because this involves filling in a form, drupalPost()
    // is used. See the "Simpletests and Forms" section in Chapter 23 of
    // the Definite Guide to Drupal 7 (dgd7.org)
    $this->drupalPost('admin/structure/block', array('blocks[mymodule_0]
      [region]' => 'sidebar_first'), t('Save blocks'));
  }

  /*
    Test—recognizable as such because it starts with 'test'. For every
    test, Simpletest will create a completely new Drupal installation, run the
    common setUp() function, and go through this code.
  */
  public function testMainTest() {
    // note that at this point, the setUp() function has already executed.
```

```
$this->assertNoText(t('Over 25 active users!'), t('Make sure the block is
  not yet visible, because no content has been created yet.'));

// create 25 users, and for each user create a blog post.
for ($i = 0; $i < 25; $i++) {
  // each user has the permission to create a blog post.
  $user = $this->drupalCreateUser(array('create blog content'));

  // note that we are still logged in as the main (admin) user (see
  // the setUp() section). We'll visit the blog creation page and set a
  // random title, and make sure the author name is set to the name of
  // the user we just created, then click Save.
  $this->drupalPost('node/add/blog', array('title' =>
    $this->randomName(32), 'name' => $user->name), t('Save'));
}

$this->assertText(t('Over 25 active users!'), t('Make sure the block
  is now visible, because we just created 25 users and a blog post for
  each.'));
  }
}
```

Finally, create the file sites/all/modules/mymodule/mymodule.info, as shown in Listing 23–4.

Listing 23–4. mymodule.info

```
name = My Module
description = Displays t('over 25 active users') if 25 users or more have posted at least one
node in the last month. This module was created to demo simpletest as part of the book
definitivedrupal.org.
dependencies[] = blog
files[] = mymodule.test


core = 7.x
```

Running Your First Test

Congratulations, you just built your first test! Go ahead and run it. On your Drupal 7 site, enable Simpletest. You will see your module's test case (if you don't, clear your caches) in the list of tests at Configuration ➤ Development ➤ Testing (see Figure 23–2), and you can run your test!

▓ **Note** If Simpletest is already enabled and you're adding new tests, you might not see them in this list. In such cases, you might have to clear your caches by visiting System ➤ Performance and clicking Clear all caches.

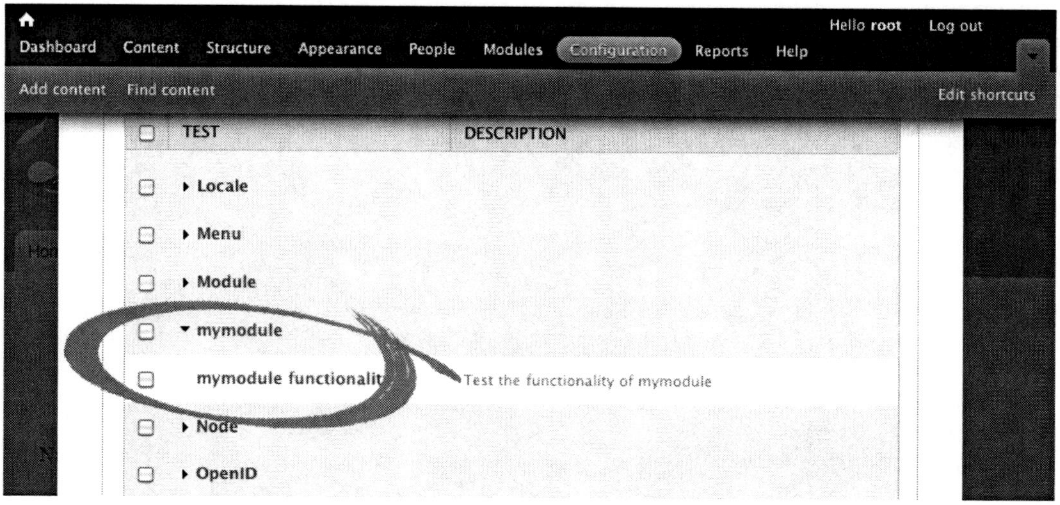

Figure 23–2. *List of available tests at* Configuration ➤ Development ➤ Testing

On the test result page (see Figure 23–3), you will be able to click through the verbose messages that show you snapshot after snapshot stored by Simpletest as it created 25 users, a blog post for each, and confirmed (asserted) that the text "Over 25 active users!" actually appeared on the temporary Drupal site as a result.

There's a lot going on here. If you go back to the code in Listing 23–3, you'll notice that your test contains a number of assertions such as assertText(), which makes sure some text appears on the current page (see "The Simpletest API and Further Reading" section) and actions such as drupalPost(), which fills forms (see the "Simpletest and Forms" section), but not 189 of them! So why are there 189 checks here? For each function call you write, Simpletest runs a number of behind-the-scenes steps and checks; each is documented on the test result page.

Now, to get a more realistic feel for Simpletest, try generating an error: replace all instances of 25 for 50 in your .module file (but not your .test file) and run your test again. Notice how the results page now lets you pinpoint the failure.

■ **Exercise** Astute readers will have noticed that there is a small anomaly in the "Over 25 active users!" module: the block displays even if there are exactly 25 users. To fix this, change your test to assert that the text does not appear if there are 25 users, but does appear if there are 26. Then, fix the module code itself until your new test passes. This is test-driven development in action!

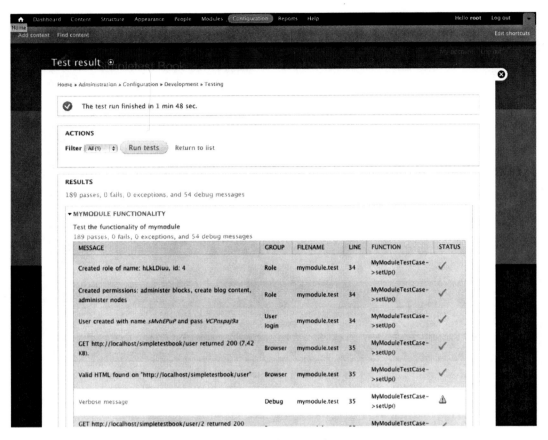

Figure 23–3. The verbose messages on the test result page of a test

Simpletests and Forms

The test in Listing 23–3 needed to fill in quite a few forms in order to validate the functionality of the module. For example, if you want Simpletest to "see" a block's contents, you need to assign your block to a region in your test or setUp() function or it won't be visible to Simpletest when the test is run.

Assigning a block to a region in Simpletest involves mimicking what a human user would do. Remember, Simpletest knows nothing of your current site's configuration. Go to the block configuration page and fill in a form. Filling in forms in Simpletest is done with the drupalPost() function. In Listing 23–3, you saw the following line:

```
$this->drupalPost('admin/structure/block', array('blocks[mymodule_0]
    [region]' => 'sidebar_first'), t('Save blocks'));
```

This line simulates finding the block configuration page and setting the region of your module to the left sidebar, then submitting the form. Here's how you would decide what to write in this function:

1. You first need to navigate to the form you want to include in your test. In this case, it's http://example.com/#overlay=admin/structure/block (replace example.com with your actual domain name). Take note of the Drupal path in this URL; in this case, it is admin/structure/block.

2. On the form, for each form field you want to modify, use a tool such as Firebug for Firefox to identify within the page's HTML source code the value of the name attribute of the form input element. In the case of your module, the HTML you're looking for is <select name="blocks[mymodule_0][region]" ...>, so the name of this field is blocks[mymodule_0][region], as shown in Figure 23–4.

3. Then you need to find the desired value for that form element; in this case, it is sidebar_first (again, see Figure 23–4).

4. Finally, you need to embed the name of the submit button into Drupal's t() function; in this case, it is t('Save blocks'), as shown in Figure 23–4.

Figure 23–4. Determining the name of a form field

With this information, you can build a function call that tells Simpletest to go to the block page and move your block to the sidebar_first region, like so:

```
$this->drupalPost('admin/structure/block', array('blocks[mymodule_0]
    [region]' => 'sidebar_first'), t('Save blocks'));
```

Similarly, to create a node within your test, you'll mimic filling a node creation form. Here is another line from Listing 23–3:

```
$this->drupalPost('node/add/blog', array('title' =>
    $this->randomName(32), 'name' => $user->name), t('Save'));
```

It visits the blog node creation page, inserts a random name as the title, sets the name of the author to the specified user name, and then clicks Save. To better understand this line, on your Drupal site, make sure the blog module is enabled, go to Add content ➤ Blog entry (node/add/blog), then use Firebug for Firefox to examine the form to see which fields are being manipulated by this code ('title' and 'name').

The Simpletest API and Further Reading

To get the most of Simpletest, it is useful (although not necessary) to brush up on your object-oriented PHP skills. You'll also need to get familiar with Simpletest's API, the functions you can use within your tests. You can see a few of Simpletest's functions in Listing 23–3; feel free to use any code in this chapter as a basis for your own projects.

Some oft-used functions are listed below. Because you are writing your tests in a class, don't forget to add $this-> before each call (as in Listing 23–3).

- drupalGet('*path*') points Simpletest to the path provided.

- drupalPost('*path*', array('*input1*' => '*value1*', '*input2*' => '*value2*', t('*Button Name*')) points Simpletest to the path provided, fills in the form with the provided values, then clicks on a given button (see the "Simpletests and Forms" section).

- assertText('*text*') makes sure some text is present on the current page.

- assertNoText('*text*') makes sure some text is *not* present on the current page.

- assertRaw('*html*') makes sure some HTML is present in the source code of the current page.

- assertNoRaw('*html*') makes sure some HTML is *not* present in the source code of the current page.

- $user = drupalCreateUser(array('*permission 1*', '*permission 2*')) creates a user object with the given permissions.

- drupalLogin($user) logs in with a user object created with drupalCreateUser().

- randomName() generates a random string, which is useful for creating temporary nodes and users.

- verbose($text) displays some text in your test output. Helpful for debugging your test.

Some more Simpletest resources:

- The complete list of Simpletest functions can be found by heading to `api.drupal.org/DrupalWebTestCase.`

- Look at existing tests for Drupal core modules to see how tests are written. In Drupal 7, most core modules contain test files, for example `modules/contact/contact.test` or `modules/node/node.test.`

- Look at `modules/simpletest/drupal_web_test_case.php` for the source code of all Simpletest functions.

- Look through the handbook on Simpletest at `drupal.org/simpletest.`

- Install and examine `drupal.org/project/examples`, a module containing further commented sample code.

Submitting a Patch to Drupal.org

Every so often (sometimes several times a day!) you'll come across a bug in Drupal core or in a contributed module, or you may think of a useful new feature you'd like to see. Because Drupal is open source software, you can (and should) contribute your thoughts to `drupal.org` via an issue (see Chapter 38) where you can describe the problem and, if you have the technical skills, submit a patch.

A patch is a great place to use Simpletest. Because your patch changes the way a module works, an automated test goes a long way in showcasing what your code actually does. As stated in the introduction to this chapter, if you're patching core, including a functional test is all but a requirement.

Rather than simply fixing the bug or adding the feature and submitting a patch to `drupal.org`, why not integrate test-driven development into your workflow? Here's how:

1. First, add a `.test` file to the module you are patching if one does not exist.

2. Add a failing test.

3. Modify the code (and the test) until the test passes.

4. Create your patch.

5. Submit it to the project's issue queue at `drupal.org.`

Summary

By now you should have all the tools to go out and add tests to your modules and patches. Start using tests on hard-to-test use cases in mission-critical and widely-used modules. Some key points to remember:

- By design, **Drupal uses functional testing more than unit testing**. This is due to the way Drupal is written, primarily as a content management system geared toward the end user experience.

- Functional testing **tests the user interface and the interaction of your site with a fictional human user**.

- Tests are meant to **validate a module, not a site**. Everything on your site (and in other tests) is ignored while running each test, thus isolating tests from outside contamination. Need users, nodes, or anything else to make your test run? You must define them within the test itself.

- Each functional test you write, enclosed in a `test...()` function, will create a **brand new, isolated, temporary, fully-functional Drupal site** in which to run; this temporary site will be destroyed as soon as the test is over. You'll never have direct access to these temporary sites; all manipulation needs to be done by code in your test file.

- Make sure "Provide verbose information when running tests" is checked on Simpletest's settings page (`admin/config/development/testing/settings`) to allow you to pinpoint where things are going wrong (they will!).

- Automated testing is now **tightly integrated into the workflow of Drupal core development** and currently being deployed for contributed modules.

■ **Tip** Check in at `dgd7.org/test` for more notes and resources.

■ ■ ■

## CHAPTER 24

Writing a Major Module

by Benjamin Melançon

"You need me and I need you / Without each other there ain't nothing people can do."

—Aretha Franklin (Think)

The dictionary definition of "module" is "one of multiple distinct but interrelated parts that can be used to construct a more complex structure." That describes how complex web sites are built with Drupal: module by module. (And you didn't think anything in Drupal was sensibly named.)

A module, by definition, never exists on its own but rather in relation to other modules with which it forms a working whole. Drupal's modularity makes it possible for separately written and maintained projects to extend what Drupal can do.

■ **Note** The fact that modules never exist on their own has legal implications by the interpretation given by legal advisors to the Drupal Associations. Drupal is Free Software licensed under the GNU General Public License (GPL). Because a Drupal module is by definition a derivative work, any module we make and distribute must be available for anyone else to see, copy, and modify (that is, modify their own copy!). Modules built for ourselves or a single client are not considered distributed, but it is worth noting that the ethos of sharing and collaboration—with its range of practical benefits—is backed by a legal framework.

In the terms used in this chapter, a basic module is a module that extends Drupal and a major module is additionally meant to be extended itself. A major module is modular (ready to be modified or extended), a mirroring of Drupal's modularity. By this definition, LoginToboggan (drupal.org/project/logintoboggan) is a basic module, as it changes the way Drupal works, and Advanced help (drupal.org/project/advanced_help) is a major module, as it exists for other modules to plug in to. The more common term for this latter type of module is API module, but that term is reserved in this chapter for a pure API module.

A major module has an API for other modules to use. API, recall, stands for Application Programming Interface. It is how code talks to code (when being proper and going through official channels). The hook invocations and implementations (such as the ones described in Chapter 19), plus the utility functions available to our module, are Drupal's API.

The module we will begin to build in this chapter will enable other modules to extend it just as it extends Drupal 7. Called Form messages, its goal is to do immediate inline validation of form elements. (Originally named AJAX form messages, this module was re-named as during development it became clear that only doing AJAX calls was not the best approach.) It will modify forms to have inline notices and errors as provided by an API and accompanying UI. Other modules will be able to use the Form messages API to provide error messages and inline validation routines. This module, therefore, will have APIs coming and going: making use of Drupal's APIs to build on Drupal (like every module must) and defining its own API so other modules can build on it. We won't complete the module or even get close in this chapter (though the work and documentation will continue at `dgd7.org/strategy`). Instead, the groundwork will be laid for a major module.

This chapter has two main goals:

- To present a module development strategy (along with a bunch of tips) that will help set you up for building any kind of API-providing module.

- To cover some concepts core to much of Drupal 7 development: entities and fields.

How Not to Build a Module

This section is not a worst-case scenario module-making disaster story (although negative examples are quite fun and informative—for a classic satire of four Drupal versions old and still applicable, see Nick Lewis' Road to Drupal Hell, `drupal.org/node/77487`). No, the premise of this section is simpler than that: the best module is one you do not have to build.

When setting out to build a module, you will want to do the due diligence of searching for a module to meet your need. You will want to be certain you are not duplicating someone else's work. If after searching `drupal.org` and the World Wide Web you haven't found an existing module doing what you want to do, go to `groups.drupal.org` (often abbreviated g.d.o by Drupalistas) and join the Contributed Module Ideas group, `groups.drupal.org/contributed-module-ideas`. Here you can post a discussion (at `groups.drupal.org/node/add/story?gids[]=5445`—entirely beside the point, but you can see from this URL that the machine name for a g.d.o discussion is story and the node ID of the contributed module ideas group is 5,445. Remember to keep checking back at your post if you don't have notifications set up! Ask IRC, including in `#drupal-contribute`, which modules exist in the problem space you are addressing.

■ **Tip** If you find a similar project already developed or in progress, join forces with other developers whenever possible. Module duplication not only wastes your time as a developer, but it makes it harder for users and contributors to choose what to use or where to put their effort. See `drupal.org/node/23789` for more information.

For the Form Messages module, a search for *Drupal AJAX form messages, drupal AJAX form validation*, and *drupal inline form validation*, among other variations, did not come up with a comparable module or effort. I posted the module's goals in the Contributed Module Ideas group and cross-posted it to the Form API and Usability groups (see this post at `groups.drupal.org/node/113564`).

Nothing came of asking the final attempt, `#drupal-contribute`: "What work (if any) has been done in Drupal toward giving immediate, inline feedback when filling out forms? (Ideally including for field combinations on node forms.)" You can craft a better question than that, assuredly, but remember the rule of thumb that any question that can be answered with yes or no is not the best one you can ask. (See Chapter 9 for more IRC tips and etiquette.) Any question asked on IRC is a shot in the dark—even if someone knows the answer, they have to be online, see it, and be in a mental state of coherence sufficient to craft an answer. A question about a topic big enough to be a major module, yet that no one is working on already, is even more of a long shot. But that doesn't mean it's not worthwhile.

The mere act of asking—the work of posing the question even if no one joins you in bouncing ideas around—helps you better understand what you are trying to do. You may even be able to begin to answer your own question. I was reminded while asking my questions that there is one place in Drupal core that provides instant feedback when you fill out a form: the password strength indicator. A core model to follow is a very good thing.

Later, as you build your module, report your progress to people who expressed interest (or anyone who might be interested). Your project page and issue queue are good public places to state plans, track progress toward implementing targeted capabilities, and collaborate with others. On the latter point, never count on people participating until long after you've built something useful. See Chapter 37 for how to set up sandbox projects on `drupal.org`.

Know the Tools Drupal Gives You

On any project, you will get off to a better start (and, subsequently, a better finish) with a thorough knowledge of the tools you have to work with. Some commonly used APIs in Drupal were introduced in Chapter 21. There are many more.

> *"You can blow a very long weekend trying to walk through [Drupal] with a—what's the opposite of a bird's-eye view?—worm's-eye view."*

> —Jeff Eaton

A piece of this worm's-eye view is given in Chapter 34. You can continue the exploration by setting up a debugger and watching Drupal step through its code as it does different things.

Knowing what Drupal provides can help in recognizing if you're trying to make Drupal do something it's not actually good at. That's step one to any project: evaluating potential tools. Just as there are many ways to do something with Drupal, there are many ways to do something without Drupal. If it has anything to do with content, users, permissions, showing things on a web site, and much more, of course, you probably do want Drupal.

Drupal at its literal core is a collection of APIs. Drupal architect Jeff Eaton highlights not Drupal's hook-providing modules but first and foremost all the useful things that live in the `includes` directory. Drupal's `include` files define functions to help with:

- Menus (routing)
- Database abstraction
- Session handling
- Caching
- File storage and stream wrappers
- Locale and language
- Theming (Rendering)
- Forms and form processing
- Date handling

- Image manipulation
- Paging and table sorting
- Batch processing
- Tokens
- E-mail
- Entities
- Module system
- XMLRPC
- AJAX
- Unicode and other common utilities
- Updates
- … and more

Nobody automatically remembers all these helper libraries (includes/graph.inc provides a function to do a depth-first search on a directed acyclic graph, by the way), let alone knows how to use them all, but they are our baseline, always-present toolbox before we even begin to enable or download modules. Drupal's core modules, of course, provide additional critical functionality, such as user handling and input filtering. Contributed modules can provide their own utility functions and APIs, and some modules are meant *only* to provide tools for other modules. CTools and VotingAPI are pure API modules.

Should Your Module Provide an API?

In general, any module you make should provide an API for modules that might want to work with your module or build on it. Also, in general, an API is hard to do well; it will usually need to be revised or expanded as other modules try to use it.

If your module is simple and uses enough of Drupal's APIs, it doesn't need to create its own API. If your module creates its own user interface for settings, though, it should always at the least have an accompanying API for those settings.

Keep API and UI Separate

Anything that can be done in a module by submitting a form (the user interface) should also be doable with a line of code. Indeed, the submit function that handles a form should always use an API function to save the changes.

If you make a database query directly in a submit function, you are doing it wrong. You should never see db_insert(), db_update(), or db_delete(), nor db_ anything, nor drupal_write_record() in a form submission function. This would mean that saving, changing, or deleting the information affected by the form can only be done through the user interface—or by recreating these functions or faking a form submission. This makes it harder and uglier for other modules to work with the services and information your module provides. (Having any database changes in form validation is even worse.) Instead, the form submitting function should be handing data from the form over to an API function that is cleanly abstracted from form submission. (Unfortunately, Drupal core is not yet a consistent model in this regard.)

The ultimate expression of keeping API and UI separate is having the user interface in a separate module in your project, which can be turned off. Drupal core's Fields module is complemented by a Fields UI module, which can be diabled. Views module likewise has a Views UI module, which you can disable.

Use APIs to Hide Complexity

The benefit for another module to build on yours is that the author of that module does not have to think about all the things that your module is doing. This is especially true of modules whose entire point is to provide for common functionality, an API module. Jeff Eaton told the story of the VotingAPI module (drupal.org/project/votingapi) at DrupalCon DC. He was working on one of his first larger sites and needed voting functionality. He found a number of cool voting modules, but none of them worked with each other. "So I took the one with the nicest flash widget and shamelessly ripped out its guts," he said.

Thus was born VotingAPI, with two functions for getting and setting votes. And after asking other people maintaining voting modules, "Can you make my module a dependency for no good reason?" he had one person take him up on it. Immediately, he had to add three more functions to meet the more refined needs of that module.

"We always get it wrong the first time," Eaton said. And the second. And the third. The rule of thumb is that APIs need to be tested with at least three implementations—cases in which they are used to do something specific—before you can expect them to be of general utility.

By the time your API can handle three different use cases, it's likely hiding an awful lot of complexity.

■ **Tip** Mercenary module development—developing a module for hire—can be a lot of fun, especially with a good client, because the requirements are figured out and laid out for you. Even with the best requirements, a module, like a web site, will evolve as it is built and tested against real needs. When trying to develop a module that will be useful for many people, consider your client's specification as only *one* of the use cases—and don't expect all of your development hours to be paid. Making a generally useful module is always more work than a one-off, but you, your client, and the community can benefit in the long run.

Making Your Module Modular

Providing an API for its core functionality is the most important way to make your module extendable by other modules, but not the only way.

There are many ways to make the Form Messages module modular, as there will be in any major module. The common thread for almost all ways is separating functionality into encapsulated pieces so that your module is working with its own APIs internally. When parts of your code go through channels to talk to other parts of your code, these same channels are available to the code in other modules.

Unleashing the Power of Hooking Into Your Module

Just as your module will use the hooks Drupal provides to change its behavior (such as hook_menu() to show a page or do something at a URL), and may very well use hooks that other contributed modules provide (such as hook_views_default() to provide a default view), your module can make hooks available for other modules to implement.

The main API for Form Messages will be offering the ability of modules to define messages. This will probably take the form of defining to allow modules to provide default messages in the same way hook_default_views() allows modules to provide default views. This fundamental hook for Form Messages will be covered in this chapter's online companion, dgd7.org/strategy. It's important to note that when defining hooks, you should document an example implementation of each hook in a modulename.api.php file that you include with your module.

There are lighter-weight ways to allow modules to hook into yours than defining your own complete hook. Whenever your module gathers an array of data, it can give other modules a chance to manipulate that data. The easiest way to do this is the delightful drupal_alter() function. Frequently, a module first defines its own hook to let other modules give it information. Then it uses drupal_alter() to create an alter hook that comes along and lets modules modify this *after all the data has been gathered*.

■ **Note** A one-line patch adding a drupal_alter() statement to an existing module is frequently the easiest way to get functionality you seek into someone else's module. Adding a big feature that meets others' needs and the module maintainers' approval may be impossible, but convincing a maintainer to commit a change enabling you to build on features from your own module should be much more achievable.

There are, of course, persuasive solidly selfish reasons for opening up our modules to the meddling of the masses. Well-placed hook invocations allow other people to do the hard work for us. The more our module is built this way, the more we can say, as Jeff Eaton did (pausing to straighten his imaginary tie), "Solving that isn't my problem; I just maintain the API."

When building a pure API module, this focus on maintaining the API and making it possible to address many use cases—but not solving them in your module—is particularly important. Jeff Eaton ended his API module presentation urging us to "stay focused—do one thing really well. Drupal is moving toward things that work together; the key is making them work together really well." This is the famous Unix philosophy. Doug McIlroy, the inventor of Unix pipes and one of the founders of this Unix tradition, summarized it this way: "Write programs that do one thing and do it well. Write programs to work together."

■ **Tip** As early in the process as possible, start talking with other people who are doing work in the area in which you are working.

Progressive Enhancement: Making Use of Other Modules If They Are Enabled

If the point of your module is to extend another module or you are calling one of its functions, you have to list it as a dependency. Most of the time, though, your module can be enhanced by another module or your module can enhance another module by providing more choices or power. If your module stores data in any way, for instance, you probably want to expose that data to Views. (In many cases, you can get this for free by using Drupal's Field API.)

Wherever possible, make these module dependencies optional. You don't want to force people to use half a dozen modules in addition to yours. Instead, check if the specific function you want to use exists, and degrade gracefully if it doesn't. In this context, degrading gracefully can mean your module loses some extra functionality but does not break, and it continues to provide its base features. Your goal should be to build your module to have conditional enhancements rather than dependencies.

Many excellent modules are designed to pick up on what other modules offer. This is better thought of as *progressive enhancement* than *graceful degradation* because there is no workaround for missing functionality, simply the addition of functionality when modules making it possible are enabled.

For example, Drupal's core Menu module integrates with the Block module but doesn't require it. In the implementation of hook_help(), which takes the path of the current page as an argument (variable piece of information) to act on, there is this code:

```
if ($path == 'admin/structure/menu' && module_exists('block')) {
  return '<p>' . t('Each menu has a corresponding block that is managed on the <a
href="@blocks">Blocks administration page</a>.', array('@blocks' =>
url('admin/structure/block'))) . '</p>';
}
```

The exciting bit is module_exists('block'). As long as Block module is enabled, Menu module offers each of its menus as blocks. As long as Help module is enabled, you are told about this at the top of the menu administration page. Both uses of other modules are examples of progressive enhancement.

▓ **Note** Why would anyone not have Help module enabled? Why would anyone not have Block module enabled? It is not the job of a module author to judge the choices of a site builder. The Block module, for its part, is in fact not (yet) as powerful and flexible as some Drupal sites demand it to be. Some developers use Panels module instead (which includes code to call blocks itself). Others use Context module. Both Panels and Context modules exemplify the modularity of Drupal—to allow replacements of core functionality—and remind us to never make our module require another module if it doesn't absolutely have to.

The use of Drupal's hook system is the easiest way for one module to react to something another module is doing.

You can provide default views and expose your data to Views. You can provide tokens for use in PathAuto and dynamic text areas, and you can provide Drush commands. You can provide basic Drupal core help by implementing hook_help(), another hook provided by a module that no module *has* to implement. And you can provide pages of Advanced Help documentation by invoking that module's hooks; they will only be used when Advanced Help is enabled.

Getting Started with a Test Environment

Starting a major module warrants setting up a fresh test environment for it. Grab a copy of Drupal, name the installation after the project you are working on, and install it from the command line. See Chapters 2 and 26 for more on Drush, which is what makes this easy. Here are the command-line steps to create a test site using drush site-install (si), naming the site after the module we are developing.

▨ **Note** A word on naming—one of the first things you have to do when starting to write a module. Module names, as far as your directory and code, must be only lowercase letters, numbers, and underscores, and must start with a letter. It is recommended that the name be descriptive rather than short, and that if a noun it take the singular form (so as to be compatible with recommended naming practices for classes and database tables). I have violated both recommendations in naming the module formmsgs, to my public disgrace. I don't apologize for avoiding underscores in module names, though; this is based on my paranoia about namespace conflicts (naming the module `form_messages` and implementing `hook_help()` would mean that a module named form implementing a potential `hook_messages_help()` would have a fatal error due to duplicate function names).

```
cd ~/workspace
cd formmsgs
drush dl drupal --drupal-project-rename=formmsgs
drush si --db-url=mysql://root:rootpass@localhost/formmsgs
```

By default, `drush site-install` will use the standard installation profile and give the superuser (user ID 1) the username admin and password admin.

▨ **Tip** You can automate these steps even more. For an example of automating the creation of the test site and its installation of Drupal, see `dgd7.org/sh`.

Next, make a directory for the new module; within `sites/default` is fine for a test site. (If the modules directory doesn't already exist in `sites/default`, the `-p` flag tells `mkdir` to make it before making the formmsgs directory.) Also, immediately start a Git repository for the module like so:

```
mkdir -p sites/default/modules/formmsgs
cd sites/default/modules/formmsgs
git init
```

As you add and edit files, have Git keep track of all of your changes by using the command `git add .` (used to add both new and changed files, the period signifies adding everything available) and `git commit`.

Stealing Some Code to Start

I start my .info file by stealing the one from the Unique fields module because I expect to be working closely with this module (or at the very least learning a lot from it), so I can study and borrow at the same time.

```
drush dl unique_field
cp ../../../all/modules/unique_field/unique_field.info formmsgs.info
gvim formmsgs.info
```

Modify the contents. Info files are simple, and there won't be much duplicated. But it's nice to start from a template and, if that is also a module you're interested in, that's great. Copying an entire .module file is not such a good idea, but looking at an example and even copying out parts can work nicely.

```
name = AJAX form messages
description = "[formmsgs] Provides immediate, in-form validation."
core = 7.x
```

■ **Note** Including the module machine names in the description is a convention (favored by me, if no one else) that helps people searching for the module on their module administration page to find it.

Sharing Your Code in a Sandbox on Drupal.org

All I have is a .info file, but it is great to get in the habit of committing and sharing early and often (see Listing 24–1). The commands for sharing a project are discussed in Chapter 38 and are given to you after you create a project via drupal.org/node/add/project-project.

Listing 24–1. Start Sharing Your Code on Drupal.org

```
git add .
git commit -m "Initial commit for AJAX form messages module; the .info file."
git remote add origin mlncn@git.drupal.org:sandbox/mlncn/910490.git
git push origin master
git checkout -b 7.x-1.x
git push origin 7.x-1.x
```

The steps in Listing 24–1, tailored to your project, are on your project's Git instructions tab. This is drupal.org/node/910490/git-instructions for Form Messages, and the instructions for your full or sandbox project can be found at the same path (with the node ID of your project substituted in for 910490).

■ **Tip** Sharing, fortunately, works both ways. For best practices in code, look to core and widely worked on and used modules such as Views, Token, Administration Menu, Date, Webform, Devel, Voting API, and others (including those covered in this book such as Commerce in Chapter 25 and Apache Solr in Chapter 31). Know, however, that you may have to go your own path and revise significantly as you learn more. On that note, also sign up for updates to the code and approaches taken by the Form Messages module at dgd7.org/strategy.

Planning Your Approach

I keep saying I'm going to provide an API, but what does that mean? It means a lot more—and in some cases, it means something different—than simply having the user interface in a different module. One way to look at being an API means your module doesn't do anything. It just is. The API for Form Messages would handle interaction with the form, based solely on what it is told to do by other modules.

This means I must distill what's needed to show a message as its essential parts. You can't assume that your module has any way to know on its own when or how it's supposed to do something.

Here are some of the questions Form Messages module must ask, then, of modules that would work with it. Posing this question for your own module will tell you what data the API module must store and process, and how it interacts with these other modules—in short, just what kind of API it needs.

- What on the form triggers evaluation for a message?

- What determines if the message will be shown and what information does it need?

- What does the message say?

- Does the trigger also run when the form is submitted (normal validation) or only for inline AJAX validation?

Outlining what your application must know is critical to defining what API functions it will need (and the data it must store, discussed in the section "Defining Your Data Model"). However, answering questions like these also helps you figure out what your application must do, and it can definitely be worth making something work before planning out every detail of the API.

Outlining an API

AJAX Form Messages, at its heart, wants to say: "I'm on a form. What do you want me to do when stuff happens to each element?"

The centerpiece of the API must be a hook or other way for modules (including users through a UI module) to register all the information about a message. (For performance reasons, this should probably not be done when loading the form.) I'll get into the details of what information must be registered, expanding on the questions introduced in the "Defining Your Data Model" section.

Once storing and getting this information is taken care of, and a way for modules to alter this information has been created, the fundamental API is complete. Another module could even access the information and replace AJAX Form Messages' implementation of interacting with the form.

Other aspects of the API could include a way for modules to affect the output defaults (such as where messages are placed), but most other potential API functions will be ancillary to what information can be defined about messages and making this information alterable.

Diving Into Doing

If you feel your questions are getting into the realm of the theoretical, it's time to dive into writing some code that produces some result *even if you already know you'll want to introduce an API for that*. Abstracting out an API can be premature. As noted, however, *first* asking the kinds of questions the API needs to answer does help you write better code right away, even if you skip implementing some of the API in your first iteration.

In the case of AJAX Form Messages, you're going to want to aggregate and store all the information it needs in a central place, rather than poll all modules each time a form is displayed. But dealing with that is getting in the way of figuring out how the triggers and messages themselves will work. And the questions and answers brought to light by focusing on the API have given rise to lots of ideas and directions to try out.

For instance, what must trigger the error or other message is a function akin to a validation function. Ideally, you'll be able to reuse validation functions to evaluate if an error message should be shown. However, validation functions frequently take an entire form, and I'm talking about AJAX requests that can happen multiple times a form, and that needs to be fast. Efficiency is important. What information has to be sent to the evaluation function?

The whole form is definitely easiest, but maybe it can be made to either expect a form (which could include only the parts you care about, but still be processed by any normal, non-over-zealous validate function) or a single specific element. Upon investigation, it's clear the date validation function date_validate()—see api.drupal.org/date_validate—is one that (despite its parameter name "$form") clearly expects a form element, not an entire form.

▓ **Note** By choosing to use FormAPI, we've already made sure we won't be only limited to node (content) forms, at least not at the fundamental API level.

Investigating Form Elements

AJAX Form Messages is going to be listening in on form elements as people type and then sending messages back to form elements. It will provide a structure for storing a function that is used to check what people type and decide what message to send back. This means it needs a reliable way to identify these elements within and across forms—so you're going to have to take a close look at the structure of forms and the form elements with which they are built. This approach has already been used in Chapter 19, implementing the form alter hook in order to see the structure of site forms.

```
/**
 * Implements hook_form_alter().
 */
function formmsgs_form_alter(&$form, &$form_state, $form_id) {
  debug($form, $form_id, TRUE);
}
```

Giving the form ID as the second parameter for debug() is a neat trick to show exactly what form you are dealing with. The third parameter TRUE is a good habit to get into so that debug() uses a less pretty but more robust (less likely to die) function to print the output.

▓ **Gotcha** If you have a debug() statement that isn't printing anything at all, check your logging and errors settings at Administration ➤ Configuration ➤ Development ➤ Logging and errors (admin/config/development/logging). Always show messages like this by adding $conf['error_level'] = 2; to your local settings.php file. Show every error by adding four lines to settings.php as described earlier in this book and at dgd7.org/err.

Listing 24–2. Excerpt from Printing the Form Variable on the node/add/article Page

```
'title' =>
array (
  '#type' => 'textfield',
  '#title' => 'Title',
  '#required' => true,
  '#default_value' => NULL,
```

```
    '#maxlength' => 255,
    '#weight' => -5,
),
```

All form elements are defined by an array. The title element in Listing 24–2 was an immediate child of the $form array, but it could also have been nested within a group. Its name, 'title', is the key to the array shown. Its location (nesting) and name ('title'), together, are unique on this form but could be used for an entirely different element on another form. Therefore, you have an imprecise instrument with which to target form elements.

Form element location is a bit messy. (Even the phrase "form element location" is awkward.) You have to decide to either try to find form items even if they've been moved inside a fieldset grouping or if you require implementations of form message hooks to say exactly where a form item is in the form array. The more helpful way to find the form element wherever it has moved is done by form_set_error() (api.drupal.org/form_set_error) as used by form_error() (api.drupal.org/form_error) is slower. To simplify things to start, at least, you'll require the full location.

But you're getting ahead of yourself a little bit. Before you figure out how to store the identity of a form element, you should make sure you can do what you need to with a test-case form element.

■ **Note** Investigating the JavaScript that powers the password strength check on user edit pages, you'll discover that it does not use AJAX at all but does the entire password strength check directly in JavaScript. This indicates another possible flexibility for your API: instead of handling the JavaScript yourself, you could allow modules to define custom JavaScript. They might, therefore, not provide a function to call via AJAX at all. (I found the user password JavaScript by looking at the form structure by implementing hook_form_alter() and, seeing that the 'pass' form element was defined as #type 'password_confirm', searching for 'password_confirm'. The password_confirm form type is expanded with the function form_process_password_confirm() in includes/form.inc, which adds the classes 'password-field' and 'password-confirm' to the first and second password fields, respectively. Searching for either class brought me to the JavaScript file modules/user/user.js. There are probably more direct ways to find things, but never hesitate to explore!

Proving a Concept

Time to prove you can take a form element and, when a user types something in it, display a message based on a function in Drupal. But let's raise the difficulty just a little bit; let's experiment with running a validation function.

The way Drupal can assign validation functions to particular form elements is described in the Form API documentation at api.drupal.org/api/drupal/developer--topics--forms_api_reference.html/7#element_validate (that monstrous URL is linked from dgd7.org/strategy). This would be a perfect anchor for adding AJAX callbacks to an element via a general hook_form_alter() implementation.

Searching Drupal core's modules for 'element_validate' (as with grep -nHR 'element_validate' modules/ on the command line from the Drupal web root) brings an example worth trying. On line 77 of modules/image/image.admin.inc the element_validate property is set to use the function image_style_name_validate().

Visiting the administration page for adding image styles (admin/config/media/image-styles/add) with the debug($form, $form_id); in your implementation of hook_form_alter(), you can see the structure of this element, this candidate for inline validation.

```
'name' =>
array (
  '#type' => 'textfield',
  '#size' => '64',
  '#title' => 'Style name',
  '#default_value' => '',
  '#description' => 'The name is used in URLs for generated images. Use only lowercase
alphanumeric characters, underscores (_), and hyphens (-).',
  '#element_validate' =>
  array (
    0 => 'image_style_name_validate',
  ),
  '#required' => true,
),
```

You can't write a module called AJAX Form Messages without a fair amount of asynchronous JavaScript, but this chapter is just covering the basics. See Chapter 17 on JQuery for more about JavaScript, and the online follow-up to this chapter at dgd7.org/strategy for what will surely be a steep learning curve for me.

■ **Tip** If for your module you write a set of JavaScript and/or CSS files that could be considered a package, provide it as a library to other modules by implementing hook_library(), and include it in your own pages by using either #attached['library'] or drupal_add_library(). See api.drupal.org/hook_library and drupal.org/node/756722 for more.

Borrowing directly from the excellent AJAX module in the Examples for Developers project (drupal.org/project/examples), you can use hook_form_alter() to add an AJAX callback to the 'name' form element. None of the examples in Drupal's Form API documentation for AJAX seem to refer to text entry in a form text field as a triggering event, but it does link to api.jquery.com/category/events where there are several options, including keyup().

```
/**
 * Implements hook_form_alter().
 */
function formmsgs_form_alter(&$form, &$form_state, $form_id) {
  if ($form_id == 'image_style_add_form') {
    $form['name']['#ajax'] = array(
      'callback' => 'formmsgs_image_style_name',
      'event' => 'keyup',
      'wrapper' => 'formmsgs-image-style-name',
    );
    $form['name']['#suffix'] = '<div id="formmsgs-image-style-name">Default message.</div>';
  }
}
```

Remember, this is all proof of concept and hardcoded to a specific form and element, quite unlike the API we plan to build. It allows you to test that your AJAX callback is in fact called, without having to worry that the failure might be somewhere else.

```
/**
 * Test callback.
 */
function formmsgs_image_style_name() {
  return 'Change-o presto.';
}
```

That works! The "Default message." text under the form is changed to "Change-o presto." when you started to type anything in the name form field.

■ **Gotcha** When returning a straight string and using the default 'replace' method, the entire placeholder element you are matching with the 'wrapper' directive is replaced. This includes, for instance, the div with the ID you matched. This means that unless your return text includes the wrapper element and ID again, the AJAX will not be able to find that it to replace or change anything again. The AJAX commands used next are modeled from the Examples project (drupal.org/project/examples) and documented at api.drupal.org/api/group/ajax_commands/7 allow much more.

Independently, you can check what information you have to work with. Here is the same callback function, but this time with both the variables that are passed to it, the form array and the form state array:

```
function formmsgs_image_style_name($form, $form_state) {
  die(var_export($form,TRUE));
}
```

From this, you get to see the variables that are passed to your callback via AJAX. See dgd7.org/273 for the full output; the most important thing in there is that we have the current value—what you just typed—of the name element.

```
function formmsgs_image_style_name($form, $form_state) {
  image_style_name_validate($form['name']);
  $message = form_get_error($form['name']);
  if (!$message) {
    $message = "Default message.";
  }
  $commands = array();
  $commands[] = ajax_command_html('#formmsgs-image-style-name', $message);
  return array('#type' => 'ajax', '#commands' => $commands);
}
```

This replaces the text "Default message" with the text "Please only use lowercase alphanumeric characters, underscores (_), and hyphens (-) for style names," as shown in Figure 24–1.

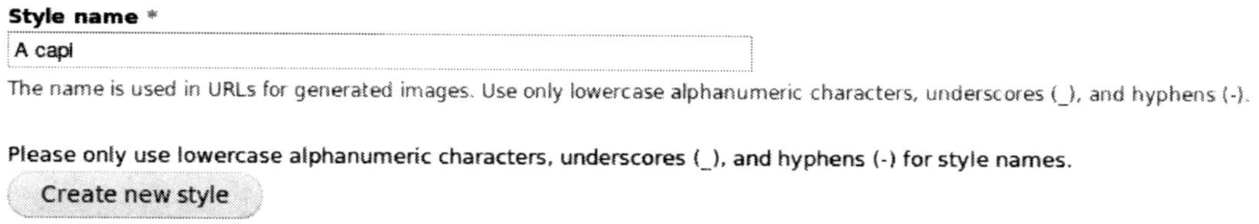

Style name *

A capl

The name is used in URLs for generated images. Use only lowercase alphanumeric characters, underscores (_), and hyphens (-).

Please only use lowercase alphanumeric characters, underscores (_), and hyphens (-) for style names.

Create new style

Figure 24–1. The validation error message for image style names shown immediately on the form via AJAX.

This looks impressive and fairly clean—run the validation function, fetch the error, and return it using the AJAX html command—but in fact it barely works. It has done its work, however, as a proof of concept inline validation function using a normal validation function. The Please only use lowercase alphanumeric... message, or nothing, is correctly returned each time. Unfortunately, it causes the text area to lose focus when a user is typing. Also, it passes the whole form and form_state variables, not restricting itself to the needed parts, which is too much overhead for per-keystroke validation. Indeed, it's becoming evident that in-line validation for allowed characters like this (as opposed to preventing duplicate names, which would require checking the database) should be done with JQuery alone and no AJAX calls to Drupal.

Remember, this is a proof of concept. Aside from letters lost in the lag while typing, an unwanted progress throbber, and other problems stemming from Drupal's convenient #ajax property (you can take more control using the #path property instead of the #callback property), you're doing unholy things with Drupal's existing validation functions and form_get_error() that may not prove durable. But the concept is proven! You can continue establishing an API while working out performance and implementation details.

Defining Your Data Model

For Form messages to do inline validation, it needs to get the messages it should show, when it should show them, and a whole lot more information. This is part of the API and should be thought of as such, but you're also thinking of it as the data you want to store. Regular form validation is done without a data model per se, but if you are going to be allowing people to both use a UI to define messages and modules, you need a data model where both meet.

This is where you get into a lot of detail about exactly what information AJAX Form Messages needs to know, thinking through what it needs in full detail. Each message can apply to multiple forms— think node forms with the same field, or the search block form and the main search form. It seems legitimate for now for each form message to have a primary perspective from a single form element, even if there are multiple fields relevant to the validation.

Thinking through issue after issue like this, you'll come up with an initial list of data to store. Each message and evaluation rules combination needs to provide the following:

- A form ID or multiple form IDs or a pattern for matching form IDs.

- Optional further conditional logic on whether to apply the evaluation and message. (This will frequently be needed, as the form ID is not enough; all content types use the same node form, for instance.)

- The trigger/receptor form element. This is the place the user is typing or clicking that triggers the message, and also the place that receives the message— where the message should be shown. Perhaps the trigger/receptor can also be multivalue, such as two phone number fields that should receive identical validation and messages.

- Optional form elements of interest. This can allow the inline validation to take into account the value entered into other form fields, such as requiring a selection in one vocabulary to have a unique combination with a selection in another vocabulary.

- One evaluation function to run. It receives at least one value: the value in the triggering receptor, and an array of the values in other form elements, if any are specified. A third parameter is also optional, a context array, such as to hold the user ID. If context is provided, it would be an array of callback functions, which are used to create an array of keyed values.

- A static message to show when the evaluation function returns a hit (anything other than strictly equal to false, "=== FALSE").

- A message callback function—an optional replacement to using the message set in the field above, so you can do whatever message you want, but the AJAX Form Messages API doesn't have to care. This callback function would receive the result of the evaluation function and whatever data the evaluation function was given.

- Is this a warning that allows the form to submit, or an error that will be added to the form's validation routine? (Or an error that is already applied to the form validation routine, which is a much better way of doing things than counting on a module named "Form Messages" to do your form validation for you.)

- An optional message to show at the default state.

- An optional message to provide for a successful selection or entry.

And Form Messages module will take care of the rest. Well, once it is coded.

The message will always be shown at the form element that triggers the error. Unless touchpad forms of entry allow some unholy three-finger action, there is only one form element that is truly in play at any time: the one value is being entered or selected in. Call it a rationalization to keep the code simpler, but the user interface should only be showing changes where you are entering text or selecting something, not elsewhere on the form.

How to Store the Data and How to Edit It in the UI

"In theory, theory and practice are the same. In practice, they are not."

—Yogi Berra

Storing the data and editing it in the UI should be separate questions. They really should. Define the data model. Define its storage. Make things work without a user interface. Build a user interface on top of that.

But the practical matter of re-using the tools Drupal provides changes the approach. It can make sense to think of a complex configuration object, like the one outlined in the previous section, as an entity with fields. This is controversial in Drupal. I personally really like the idea of finally having an administrative interface that tracks who did what, when— and this would be easily possible with revisions on a form message entity.

When it comes to having a user interface that works flawlessly with the same information captured in code, you're asking for the configuration to be exportable, which, if using an entity, means making an entity exportable, CTools style. On the one hand, this is big and scary. On the other hand, it's a natural progression of where Drupal is that some other crazy person must be working on doing the same thing. It's not easy to find, but the indefatigable Wolfgang Ziegler (fago) has documented using his Entity API module to create exportable entities for the very purpose of using them to store configuration. This documentation is at drupal.org/node/1021526. (Unfortunately, that approach to exporting entities is separate from the CTools approach, and the two have not yet developed an integrated method.)

Again, using entities to store configuration is controversial. The upcoming section also serves as an introduction to entities no matter what you use them for! Note that the export I am talking about is not to export entity type definitions (which are in code anyway), but rather to export the content held in entities' fields. This is why this approach is controversial; many feel that data in fields should always be data and never configuration. Is there anything you can do to use a code-based definition of a form message before creating an exportable entity? Maybe, but it seems it would involve coding a storage mechanism when Drupal can provide one.

Ideally, it would be a JSON export because JSON allows safe copy-pasting to import. Allowing people to paste in PHP can't be made safe, and CTools is planning to switch to JSON. Based on playing around with Profile2 and Message modules, which use Entity API, it does indeed export to JSON.

Also ideally, that export would live only in code if the UI were never needed. On this point, unfortunately, Entity API always automatically imports to the database, rather than reading from code at runtime. But on balance, exportable entities using the Entity API module fits your preferences quite well.

Plus, you'll get to use entityFieldQuery(), which all the first-adopter Drupal 7 devs are raging about. EntityFieldQuery (api.drupal.org/EntityFieldQuery) or Views is what to use for displaying entities— avoid creating your own query and display system. See dgd7.org/entities to find examples.

▪ **Tip** Make your module exportable. Closely related to good APIs is making your module's configuration **exportable**. There are two major approaches to aiding the export of configuration in Drupal at the moment: for entities, Entity API, and for anything that you can put in a database table, CTools. The first rule of exportability is not relying on numeric keys, which both these solutions address. CTools is more common and better tested, and it is documented by example in modules such as Views and Panels.

Providing a New Entity Type

With all the caveats that exportable entities are not universally endorsed by Drupal developers, let's go ahead and make one, because it seems to fit our use case well.

While entities are new to Drupal 7, creating them is hardly uncharted territory. The entire node system is now based on entities, as are comments, terms, vocabularies, files, and users. Contributed modules can and do define their own entity types, and so can your module.

When to Create an Entity Type

The most common reason for creating an entity type is to have your own fieldable entities. Always seek to extend existing entities with fields before creating new entities. However, don't use nodes for anything that isn't content—that's the most common time to create your own entities. Commerce module (see Chapter 25) uses entities for products, among other things, because products have distinct needs from content. In the case of products, they in particular have a need for many subtypes that would be, at best, an abuse of content types.

How to Create an Entity Type

Entity types are declared by implementations of hook_entity_info(). See, as usual, the excellent Examples project at drupal.org/project/examples; api.drupal.org/hook_entity_info; and, for an updated list of tutorials and examples online, dgd7.org/entities.

AJAX Form Messages chose to use entities for storing configuration (have I mentioned that is controversial?) in part for the export capability of Entity API (drupal.org/project/entity), a contributed module that adds a lot of capabilities to core entities. This means your entity definition will differ slightly from an implementation based only on core, especially when you take advantage of the capabilities Entity API offers. You can follow the contributed Entity API's online documentation for making an exportable entity at drupal.org/node/1021526.

The first step to using Entity API, as for relying on any module, is to declare it as a dependency—it's easy to forget to do this later, and your users will not thank you when your module breaks their site when they try to enable it.

```
name = AJAX form messages API
description = "[formmsgs] Provides immediate, in-form notice of validation requirements."
package = AJAX Form Messages
core = 7.x
dependencies[] = entity
```

There are a few other things to note in this .info file. Because the main module is meant to be an API module and have a UI and several optional supporting modules packaged with it (and possibly more contributed separately), you include API in the name and give it a package directive, which will have all modules given the package "AJAX Form Messages" grouped together on the modules administration page (admin/modules).

When defining an entity, the next step can take place in your .install file. Every entity requires a database table to hold basic information about it. This includes a serial integer ID column (or field, as they are called in the schema definition in Listing 24–3) required for any entity and machine-readable name column, which is critical for the entity being exportable.

Listing 24–3. Implementation of hook_schema() in Form Messages Module's formmsgs.install File

```
<?php

/**
 * @file
 * DB schema, install, and uninstall functions for AJAX Form Messages.
 *
 * The entity base table is defined here.
 */

/**
 * Implements hook_schema().
```

```
*/
function formmsgs_schema() {
  $schema = array();
  $schema['formmsgs'] = array(
    'description' => 'Stores information about all formmsgs entities.',
    'fields' => array(
      'fmid' => array(
        'type' => 'serial',
        'not null' => TRUE,
        'description' => 'Primary Key: Unique form message ID.',
      ),
      'name' => array(
        'description' => 'The machine-readable name of the form message.',
        'type' => 'varchar',
        'length' => 32,
        'not null' => TRUE,
      ),
      'label' => array(
        'description' => 'The human-readable name of this form message.',
        'type' => 'varchar',
        'length' => 128,
        'not null' => TRUE,
        'default' => '',
      ),
      'status' => array(
        'description' => 'Boolean indicating whether the form message is active.',
        'type' => 'int',
        'size' => 'tiny',
        'not null' => TRUE,
        'default' => 1,
      ),
    ) + entity_exportable_schema_fields(),
    'primary key' => array('fmid'),
    'unique keys' => array(
      'name' => array('name'),
    ),
  );
  return $schema;
}
```

One neat trick to note is + entity_exportable_schema_fields(), which uses a handy function provided by the Entity API module to add a couple more columns to the entity's table. These columns (or fields) are for the exportable status and the name of the providing module, and Entity API needs them for its export capability but saves you the trouble of defining them yourself.

The next step for making a new kind of entity is to implement hook_entity_info() in your module. This is pretty formulaic. A key element is identifyng the base table defined in the implementation of hook_schema() (which we just did in the .install file). A good model for any content-like entity is node_entity_info() in modules/node/node.module, so borrow a little from that and from Entity API's documentation at drupal.org/node/878804. Parts unique to Entity API are the controller class, discussed later, and the ability to set an 'exportable' property to TRUE. See Listing 24–4.

Listing 24–4. Definition of a New Form Message Entity in formmsgs.module

```php
<?php

/**
 * @file
 * Provides immediate, in-form validation requirements.
 */

/**
 * Implements hook_entity_info().
 */
function formmsgs_entity_info() {
  $return = array(
    'formmsgs' => array(
      'label' => t('Form message'),
      'controller class' => 'EntityAPIController',
      'entity class' => 'Formmsgs',
      'base table' => 'formmsgs',
      'fieldable' => TRUE,
      'exportable' => TRUE,
      'entity keys' => array(
        'id' => 'fmid',
        'name' => 'name',
        'label' => 'label',
      ),
      'access callback' => 'formmsgs_entity_access',
      'module' => 'formmsgs',
      'admin ui' => array(
        'path' => 'admin/structure/formmsgs',
        'file' => 'formmsgs.admin.inc',
      ),
      'bundle keys' => array(
        'bundle' => 'name',
      ),
      'bundles' => array(
        'formmsgs' => array(
          'label' => t('Message'),
        ),
      ),
      'view modes' => array(
        'full' => array(
          'label' => t('On form'),
          'custom settings' => FALSE,
        ),
      ),
    ),
  );
  return $return;
}
```

The 'controller class' is EntityAPIController, which is what makes your entity take advantage of Entity API's capabilities. Defining an 'entity class' requires it. In the previous code, the entity class is Formmsgs. This class has to be defined and will be in the next section.

As you want to be able to use Field API to gather and store data for form messages, you set 'fieldable' to TRUE. This is core entity functionality, as opposed to the 'exportable' property that came from Entity API.

The 'base table' needs to be the name of a table defined in hook_schema(). While the entity type property 'label' is simply 'Form message' (what to call this type of entity), within the 'entity keys' property, 'label' is the column in your base table that holds labels for individual Form messages (also called label). The ID (fmid) and the name (name) columns are likewise matched here in the 'entity keys' property.

The entity key 'name' is another feature provided by Entity API; it will allow form messages to be exported with a machine name. Importing and exporting does not work well across deployments or separate sites when trying to use a sequential numeric ID.

All bundle-related properties could be left off because the formmsgs entity will have only one bundle, which in the absence of being told otherwise, Drupal automatically names after itself. The chance to define a single bundle and its label is available and, as with all the code here, follows examples in core, contributed modules, and drupal.org documentation. The links in this chapter (and more) can also be found at dgd7.org/entities.

▒ **Note** When creating an entity type without the aid of Entity API, you will likely want to define your own controller class, such as FormmsgsController and extend a Drupal-provided class such as DrupalDefaultEntityController. In it could go a create method and extensions to inherited methods. Classes that aren't used all the time (such as classes used when creating an entity) should live in an outside file identified in .info with the files[] directive. This helps performance on sites not using an opcode cache. In this example, Entity API module is taking care of that for us. Drupal will only load its includes/entity.controller.inc file when it needs to use the EntityAPIController class. EntityAPIController extends DrupalDefaultEntityController and does a whole lot, but should you need more, you can make your own class that extends EntityAPIController.

Setting the property 'entity class' to Formmsgs means you must define this class. If it were more than these few lines it would make sense to put it in an include file referenced from formmsgs.info with the files[] directive.

```
/**
 * The class used for form message entities.
 */
class Formmsgs extends Entity {

  public $label;
  public $status;

  public function __construct($values = array()) {
    parent::__construct($values, 'formmsgs');
  }
}
```

This is a very lightweight extension of Entity API's Entity class; chiefly, it calls the constructor function from the Entity class. It also declares the label and status variables, making them available without errors, even as empty variables when a form message is created.

Defining an Entity Access Callback Function

Entity API requires an access callback function. In the 'access callback' property for the previous implementation of hook_entity_info(), you named the function formmsgs_entity_access(). When listing the names of callback functions, the parenthesis () are left off. This access callback function is adapted from entity_metadata_comment_access() in entity/modules/callbacks.inc.

```
/**
 * Access callback for Entity API-provided formmsgs administration section.
 *
 * @TODO Patch Entity API to accept hook_menu style 'access arguments' to
 * make this function unnecessary for the straight user_access() case.
 */
function formmsgs_entity_access($op, $entity = NULL, $account = NULL) {
  return user_access('administer formmsgs');
}
```

Entity API requires an access callback in return for it providing an entity management and editing user interface. As noted in the @TODO, it seems when all you want to do is determine access based on a simple user permission, you should be able to provide the permission string as an argument and not create your own access callback to wrap user_access(). Either way, for the access callback to work and have permissions specific to the entity, you need to define a permission or two for the new entity.

Defining a Permission

Chapter 21 advised to avoid defining a new permission if not necessary, but you should define a new permission if your module makes something new possible that site administrators should be able to allow or deny depending on users' roles. Listing 24–5 shows permissions being defined.

Listing 24–5. Excerpt from System Module's Implementation of hook_permission()

```
/**
 * Implements hook_permission().
 */
function system_permission() {
  return array(
    'administer modules' => array(
      'title' => t('Administer modules'),
    ),
    'administer site configuration' => array(
      'title' => t('Administer site configuration'),
      'restrict access' => TRUE,
    ),
// ...
  );
}
```

The 'restrict access' => TRUE directive instructs Drupal to print a notice under the permission name (after the description, if any) on the Permissions administration page: *Warning: Give to trusted roles only; this permission has security implications.* It has no other purpose; it is a convenience for module builders that provides a consistent way to alert administrators to permissions that should not be tossed around freely.

If you want to give a more precise warning to an administrator about giving a permission, you can put the message directly in the description. The core Filter module does this for the Filtered and Full HTML formats (and any format that is not configured to be the fallback format). Filter module is also dynamically generating a permission for each text format, which is cool, but the custom warning in the description is the present topic and is emphasized in bold here:

```
// Generate permissions for each text format. Warn the administrator that any
// of them are potentially unsafe.
foreach (filter_formats() as $format) {
  $permission = filter_permission_name($format);
  if (!empty($permission)) {
    // Only link to the text format configuration page if the user who is
    // viewing this will have access to that page.
    $format_name_replacement = user_access('administer filters') ? l($format->name,
'admin/config/content/formats/' . $format->format) : drupal_placeholder($format->name);
    $perms[$permission] = array(
      'title' => t("Use the !text_format text format", array('!text_format' =>
$format_name_replacement,)),
      'description' => drupal_placeholder(t('Warning: This permission may have security
implications depending on how the text format is configured.')),
    );
  }
}
return $perms;
```

▪ **Note** One more thing from the excerpt from Filter module's implementation of hook_permission() that's too cool not to remark upon: The title of each text format links to the configuration page *if* the administering user has access to configure text formats. It is using a permissions, check with the user_access() function to enhance the usability of its permission definitions!

Form messages' implementation of hook_permissions() is not nearly as exciting. It does have a bypass permission, modeled on Unique Field module.

```
/**
 * Implements hook_permission().
 */
function formmsgs_permission() {
  return array(
    'administer formmsgs' => array(
      'title' => t('Administer AJAX form messages'),
      'description' => t('Allows administrators to configure errors and warning messages.'),
    ),
    'bypass formmsgs' => array(
      'title' => t('Bypass form message errors'),
      'description' => t('Allows users to ignore errors set through form messages.'),
```

```
      ),
    );
}
```

Giving Your Entities an Administrative Interface

Entity API puts a fair amount of work into providing an administrative UI for managing entities based on it, but there's still some routine setup you have to do yourself. Previously, in Listing 24–4, the definition of the Form messages entity via hook_entity_info(), you defined an administrative user interface path and a separate admin file with the lines:

```
      'admin ui' => array(
'path' => 'admin/structure/formmsgs',
'file' => 'formmsgs.admin.inc',
),
```

You make good on this promise with a couple functions in a formmsgs.admin.inc file (see Listing 24–6). Entity API picks up the main administrative form automatically when the function has the name of the entity followed by '_form'. (If you had a module that both defined an Entity API enhanced entity with the same name as the module and an old-style, module-owned node type, this callback would conflict with the node form callback— but that's unlikely.)

Listing 24–6. An Administration UI for Form Messages Entities as Defined in formmsgs.admin.inc

```php
<?php
/**
 * @file
 * Forms and functions only needed on administration pages.
 */

/**
 * Generates the form message entity add/edit form.
 *
 * This form is automatically picked up by the administrative UI provided by
 * Entity API module.
 */
function formmsgs_form($form, &$form_state, $formmsg, $op = 'edit') {

  if ($op == 'clone') {
    $formmsg->label .= ' (cloned)';
    $formmsg->name .= '_clone';
  }

  $form['label'] = array(
    '#title' => t('Label'),
    '#type' => 'textfield',
    '#default_value' => $formmsg->label,
  );
  // Machine-readable form message name.
  $form['name'] = array(
    '#type' => 'machine_name',
    '#default_value' => isset($formmsg->name) ? $formmsg->name : '',
    '#disabled' => ($op === 'edit') ? TRUE : FALSE,
```

```
    '#machine_name' => array(
      'exists' => 'formmsgs_load_by_name',
      'source' => array('label'),
    ),
    '#description' => t('A unique machine-readable name for this form message. It can only
contain lowercase letters, numbers, and underscores.'),
  );
  $form['status'] = array(
    '#type' => 'checkbox',
    '#title' => t('Active'),
    '#default_value' => $formmsg->status,
  );

  field_attach_form('formmsgs', $formmsg, $form, $form_state);

  $form['actions'] = array('#type' => 'actions');
  $form['actions']['submit'] = array(
    '#type' => 'submit',
    '#value' => t('Save form message'),
    '#weight' => 50,
  );
  return $form;
}

/**
 * Form API submit callback for the formmsgs entity add/edit form.
 */
function formmsgs_form_submit(&$form, &$form_state) {
  $formmsg = entity_ui_form_submit_build_entity($form, $form_state);
  // Save and go back.
  $formmsg->save();
  $form_state['redirect'] = 'admin/structure/formmsgs';
}
```

There is a very key line in formmsgs_form() that you are not using yet: the field_attach_form()
function. It will allow fields defined for the Form message entity to be filled out along with the label and
machine name. You will programmatically define fields in the next section.

The next function, formmsgs_form_submit(), is a simple implementation of a submit function for the
form. With a helper function from Entity API, calling the ->save() method on the form message object is
all you need.

The form, though, even with Entity API's help, is not enough for you to be able to list and edit Form
messages in the administrative UI yet. You need to define a few loading functions that Entity API draws
on first. The code in Listing 24–7 goes in formmsgs.module because it has more general utility, but its
immediate need is to support the administrative operations.

These load functions are modeled on Profile2 module (also by fago, the creator of Entity API). The
odd one out, formmsgs_load_by_name(), is modeled on profile2_get_types(). It fills a special need of the
Entity API provided administrative UI.

The other two functions are directly analogous to node_load() and node_load_multiple(). You will
see that, like the node loading functions, formmsgs_load() works by calling formmsgs_load_multiple().
This respects Garfield Law: *One is a special case of many.* For Larry Garfield (crell)'s current eight
aphorisms of API design, see my notes on his presentation (data.agaric.com/aphorisms-api-design) or
the DrupalCon Chicago recording the notes are based on (or catch him revisiting this topic at a future
DrupalCon or Drupal camp).

Listing 24–7. *Entity Load Functions Required for Entity API's Administrative UI to Work as Defined in* ***formmsgs.module***

```
/**
 * Fetches an array of all form messages, keyed by the formmsg machine name.
 *
 * Also used to check if machine name is used for an existing form message.
 *
 * @param $name
 *   If set, the form message with the given name is returned.
 * @return $formmsgs
 *   An array of form messages or, if $name is set, a single one.
 */
function formmsgs_load_by_name($name = NULL) {
  $formmsgs = entity_load('formmsgs', isset($name) ? array($name) : FALSE);
  return isset($name) ? reset($formmsgs) : $formmsgs;
}

/**
 * Fetch a form message object.
 *
 * @param $fmid
 *   Integer specifying the form message id.
 * @param $reset
 *   A boolean indicating that the internal cache should be reset.
 * @return
 *   A fully-loaded $formmsg object or FALSE if it cannot be loaded.
 *
 * @see formmsgs_load_multiple()
 */
function formmsgs_load($fmid, $reset = FALSE) {
  $formmsg = formmsgs_load_multiple(array($fmid), array(), $reset);
  return reset($formmsg);
}

/**
 * Load multiple profiles based on certain conditions.
 *
 * @param $fmids
 *   An array of form message IDs.
 * @param $conditions
 *   An array of conditions to match against the {formmsgs} table.
 * @param $reset
 *   A boolean indicating that the internal cache should be reset.
 * @return
 *   An array of form message objects, indexed by fmid.
 *
 * @see entity_load()
 * @see formmsgs_load()
 */
function formmsgs_load_multiple($fmids = array(), $conditions = array(), $reset = FALSE) {
  return entity_load('formmsgs', $fmids, $conditions, $reset);
}
```

All of these load functions ultimately rely on Drupal core's `entity_load()` function (see api.drupal.org/entity_load), for which EntityAPIController provides its own implementation.

You can now create, list, edit, and delete Form message entities, but each one is only a label, a machine name, and a status. To get the full power and flexibility you were seeking when going the entity route, your module needs to define Drupal 7 fields.

Programmatically Creating and Attaching Fields

Fields can be created and attached to entity bundles (such as content types) through the User Interface. This is indeed a key reason and purpose for fields, but they can also be defined in code. In the unusual case of using fields to store configuration information (a use case which is controversial, it should be noted again), AJAX Form Messages doesn't even *want* the fields configurable in the user interface. To provide users of Form messages with all the fields to match the data model brainstormed earlier, you most certainly need to create and attach the fields in code.

Finding a Model

Several places in core programmatically attach fields to content types, which is analogous to attaching fields to your own entity and bundle. Node module has a function that encapsulates adding the body field to content types, `node_add_body_field()`, which you can see in `modules/node/node.module` or at api.drupal.org/node_add_body_field. The Standard installation profile also attaches a Taxonomy field, which can be seen around line 283 in `profiles/standard/standard.profile`.

For the message, you want a text field. To see precisely what text fields are available for you to use, look directly at Drupal core's Text module, a submodule of the Field module found at `modules/field/modules/text.module`.

```
function text_field_info() {
  return array(
    'text' => array(
      'label' => t('Text'),
      'description' => t('This field stores varchar text in the database.'),
      'settings' => array('max_length' => 255),
      'instance_settings' => array('text_processing' => 0),
      'default_widget' => 'text_textfield',
      'default_formatter' => 'text_default',
    ),
    'text_long' => array(
      'label' => t('Long text'),
      'description' => t('This field stores long text in the database.'),
      'instance_settings' => array('text_processing' => 0),
      'default_widget' => 'text_textarea',
      'default_formatter' => 'text_default',
    ),
// ...
  );
}
```

The maximum length (`max_length`) of the text field may appear to be 255 characters, so it would behoove you to choose the `text_long` format. However, that 255 characters is a setting; it can be set to something different, and much higher, when the field is created. (The longest safe value is about 50,000 bytes, see drupal.org/node/1052248.)

Putting this together, to add a field you return to your .install file. It is a two-step process of defining (creating the field) and attaching to an entity (creating an instance of the field), and both steps can go together in an implementation of hook_install().

```
/**
 * Implements hook_install().
 */
function formmsgs_install() {
  // Define a field.
  $field = array(
    'field_name' => 'field_message',
    'type' => 'text_long',
    'entity_types' => array('formmsgs'),
    'translatable' => TRUE,
  );
  $field = field_create_field($field);

  // Attach a field.
  $instance = array(
    'field_name' => 'field_message',
    'entity_type' => 'formmsgs',
    'label' => t('Message'),
    'bundle' => 'formmsgs',
    'description' => t('Message to show on error.'),
    'widget' => array(
      'type' => 'text_textarea',
      'weight' => -5,
    ),
  );
  field_create_instance($instance);
}
```

The process of defining a field is a simple matter of creating an array of information about the field and calling field_create_field() on that array. Attaching a field works analogously. It does not need to be handed the field you created; instead it uses the same field name as the field you just created and also provides the name of the entity type you are attaching to. It then optionally takes instance-level settings. The real trick is looking through core and contrib .install files for examples of different fields. You can also, if necessary, define your own field types. The creation of custom field types for AJAX Form Messages will be documented at dgd7.org/strategy.

▨ **Note** Remember that once you have released a beta version of your module (at which point users expect to be able to upgrade safely), you need to define and attach any new fields in implementations of hook_update_N() in addition to hook_install().

Define Done

"Walking on water and developing software from a specification are easy if both are frozen."

—Edward V. Berard

This section on defining "done" should have come at the beginning, of course. (There's a reason I didn't write Chapter 10 on project planning and management.) But don't let that scare you off some good advice: clearly define goals first.

Almost any project can be almost infinitely extended; the more you work on it, the more cool things you will think about doing. Defining early the minimum criteria needed to ship helps maintain focus. Use your own issue queue to post feature requests, but don't let them get in the way of getting to done. Ship it to meet a first use case, and try to budget time to revisit it later.

▨ **Tip** What you do not want to cut corners on is leaving yourself the flexibility to do things differently later. You want to encapsulate functionality and define boundaries and interfaces between parts of your code whenever a decision about how best to do something is best left until later. This also means abiding by your own API and not special-casing the needs of your code; your module should not privilege itself over others. Code as if you will not be able to edit your own code. If you need more flexibility, make that flexibility available to other modules also.

Of course, in open source, anyone can then decide it is not done enough and put some work in themselves. One of the great strengths of the Drupal community is the frequency with which new people coming to a project have made significant contributions, including by taking over maintainership for established modules.

For this module, in its purpose as a case study, done is defined as *this book needs to be published*. Follow the continuing adventure of the Form message module at dgd7.org/strategy and drupal.org/project/formmsgs.

PART VI

■■■

Advanced Site-Building Topics

Chapter 25 covers building an online store and brings you inside the decisionmaking of the ground-up rearchitecture of Ubercart–the number one e-commerce suite for Drupal 6–for Drupal 7 as Drupal Commerce. This chapter is valuable to any person building a commerce site, but it also invites you into the Commerce developer community.

Chapter 26 provides insight into advanced Drush usage to revolutionize your site developing experience as much as using Drush, Drupal's command-line shell, did when you started using it in the first place. It includes examples to get you started writing your own Drush scripts and commands.

Chapter 27 goes over the concepts and practice of using Drupal's pluggable caching and storage mechanisms to scale to millions of site users—not simply visitors, which is relatively simple to scale, but people interacting heavily with your site. See also Appendix B.

Chapter 28 gives the theory and practice of bringing the power of the Semantic Web to Drupal, and vice versa—making data on your web site linked to precise meanings that computers can understand and connect to data elsewhere on the Internet. (SEO hint: Computers include search engines.)

Chapter 29 tours the Drupal's routing system, providing critical background for module developers and site builders alike.

Chapter 30 takes you on a tour of what goes on inside Drupal during a page request, a perfect follow-up to Chapter 29 and a great approach to truly understanding Drupal.

Chapter 31 explains using and extending the Solr module for much more powerful search capabilities. In this latter capacity it provides an example of integrating Drupal with a web service and making use of object-oriented code.

Chapter 32 gives an in-depth look at user experience improvements in Drupal 7 and the decisions behind them and how you can use new best practices and consistent interface design decisions in your own development.

Chapter 33 takes on advanced configuration and lots of glue code–indeed, whatever it takes–for completing the DefinitiveDrupal.org site built out in Chapters 1 and 8.

Chapter 34 covers some popular Drupal distributions–packaged collections of Drupal and modules to serve specific purposes, which are spreading Drupal like never before–and shows you how to make your own distributions with Drupal's installation profile capability.

■ ■ ■

## CHAPTER 25

Drupal Commerce

by Ryan Szrama

E-commerce with Drupal is more powerful than ever before thanks to the development of Drupal Commerce for Drupal 7. The Drupal Commerce project is comprised of a core set of Commerce modules and an implementation strategy that leverages the many new Drupal 7 features and API improvements. This chapter begins with a broad overview of Drupal Commerce, highlighting its key features before moving on to a closer examination of the core systems, their implementation, and how they should be used together. It also includes words of wisdom for site builders and developers seeking to implement Drupal Commerce on their own sites. The chapter ends with a discussion of the project's development history, design philosophy, and utilization of key Drupal 7 features.

Drupal Commerce Overview

In many ways Drupal is the ideal platform for e-commerce web sites. Its core modules and systems define APIs for deeply integrating contributed modules into the behavior of the site and for communicating with external web services. It includes a plethora of features for content management and community building, enabling you to build a community around your products and services or promote your brand through your customers' existing social network relationships.

All of the major e-commerce modules dating back to Drupal 4.5 have built on Drupal's base feature set as a foundation for e-commerce instead of integrating with external applications, and Drupal Commerce is no exception. As Drupal has matured, this base of core features and major contributed systems like Views has also grown, giving modules building on them even greater flexibility and power. For this reason, Drupal Commerce was started from scratch with a fresh architecture designed around the latest features in Drupal 7 and greatest developments among Drupal's contributed modules such as Rules and Views.

The end result is an e-commerce solution that can be built from the ground up to address your business needs, no matter how great or small. Drupal Commerce sites benefit from Drupal's security, its ability to scale, and the interoperability of its vast selection of contributed modules. With the content management and social commerce tools baked into the core itself, Drupal is a very robust platform for today's online businesses without requiring integration with external e-commerce applications.

Key Features

The scope of the core feature set is intentionally limited, as the goal of Drupal Commerce has been to provide the building blocks of e-commerce as tools for site builders and developers to create customized e-commerce solutions. However, the Commerce module still encompasses the basic set of features expected of an e-commerce application. These features are mostly enabled by the user interface (UI) modules of some of the core module pairs, such as Product and Product UI, and by strictly UI modules that focus on the customer experience, like Cart and Checkout.

A basic summary of the core features includes:

- Products with any number configurable product image and data fields.

- Dynamic product pricing allowing for UI-based discounts and tax-inclusive price display.

- Flexible product display based on Drupal 7's Fields system, enforcing a separation of the product definition from the point of display.

- "Smart" Add to Cart form that displays differently based on the number and types of products represented on it

- Shopping cart system that includes a cart block and cart update form, with carts implemented as special case order objects.

- Orders consisting of line item and customer profile references and other metadata.

- Line items of various types used for describing items on an order like products, taxes, shipping fees, etc.

- Customer profiles of various user configurable types allowing the collection of data necessary to fulfill or complete an order.

- Flexible checkout form builder with a drag-and-drop user interface supporting single and multi-page checkout.

- Payment system integrating onsite and offsite payment solutions into the normal checkout workflow and allowing for tracking and manual entry by administrators.

- Complete order, customer profile, and payment transaction logging.

- Support for multicurrency and multilingual stores.

Digging Into Drupal Commerce

You can find out more about the origins, philosophy, and core Drupal innovations behind Drupal Commerce later in this chapter and through the project's homepage at `drupalcommerce.org`. Digging into the Commerce modules themselves first will provide you with the appropriate context for the more advanced topics. Accordingly, this section covers downloading and installing the Commerce modules with a thorough examination of the various entities and fields that make up the project's core systems organized as a walkthrough of a simple store configuration.

The project's source code is hosted in two locations: a development Git repository on GitHub that is mirrored to a repository on `drupal.org`. To get started quickly, you can simply download the latest release from the project page at `drupal.org/project/commerce` and extract it to your site's modules directory. If you plan on contributing code back to the project or want to develop against the freshest code, you can clone the Git repository and pull from the most active development repositories by following the instructions in the *Code Workflow* handbook available at `drupalcommerce.org/development/workflow`.

■ **Tip** Ryan Szrama, the Drupal Commerce project lead, maintains the most active development repository where most of the code that gets committed to the main project repository originates. To find his and other developers' active repositories, you can refer to the developer documentation at
drupalcommerce.org/development/workflow/repositories.

Before you can enable the Commerce modules, you also need to download and extract the latest Drupal 7 version of the following dependencies to your site's modules directory:

- Address Field (drupal.org/project/addressfield)

- Chaos tools suite (drupal.org/project/ctools)

- Entity API (drupal.org/project/entity)

- Rules (drupal.org/project/rules)

- Views (drupal.org/project/views)

With these modules in place, you are ready to start enabling the modules that you will use to build your store. If you are starting from a Standard installation of Drupal 7, you should already have the optional core Drupal modules that the Commerce modules depend upon enabled: Contextual links and Field UI. If these are not enabled, you should enable them when you enable the following dependency modules from the projects you have downloaded:

- Address Field

- Entity CRUD API

- Entity Tokens

- Rules

- Rules UI

- Views

- Views UI

- Modules in the Chaos tools suite listed as dependencies of the Views module

■ **Tip** While not a dependency, the Administration Menu module is highly recommended for navigating the Commerce UI in conjunction with the core Overlay module. You can download the latest Drupal 7 version from its project page at drupal.org/project/admin_menu.

You are now prepared to enable the Commerce modules. While the Commerce fieldset on the module installation page lists modules in alphabetical order, they are listed here in order of dependency:

- *Commerce/Commerce UI* defines features and API functions common to the Commerce modules, like currency handling and Field API helper functions.

- *Price* defines a dynamic Price field with multiple display formatters

- *Product/Product UI* defines the product entity and user interface for creating and managing product types and products.

- *Physical Product* defines fields for offering physical products for sale.

- *Line Item/Line Item UI* defines the line item entity, API for modules to define line item types, and the line item reference field used to add line items to orders.

- *Product Reference* defines the product reference field used to display products on other entities and a product line item type.

- *Product Pricing/Product Pricing UI* enables Rules based product sell price calculation for dynamic product pricing.

- *Tax/Tax UI* defines tax types with an API and user interface for defining tax rates and managing tax inclusive price displays.

- *Customer/Customer UI* defines the customer profile entity, user interface for creating and managing customer profile types and profiles, and a customer profile reference field used to add customer information to orders.

- *Order/Order UI* defines the order entity and user interface for creating and managing the default order type and orders.

- *Payment/Payment UI* defines the payment transaction entity and user interface for accepting and managing payments via the checkout form and administration form.

- *Checkout* defines a flexible checkout form with a drag-and-drop checkout form builder supporting single and multi-page checkout.

- *Cart* defines the special shopping cart order status and user interface components like the cart block, update form, and checkout integration.

Upon installation, some of these modules will perform automatic field creation to configure some entities for use. For example, when Product Reference is enabled, the Line Item module defines a new line item type with a default price field based on Product Reference's implementation of hook_commerce_line_item_info(). The rest of this section examines the systems and features defined by each module, highlighting aspects requiring further configuration. These configuration tasks include:

- Enabling supported currencies and setting the default store currency.

- Creating product types and adding products.

- Creating a product display node type.

- Enabling payment methods.

- Customizing the checkout form.

- Reviewing the default Rules.

■ **Tip** Due to the number of modules involved in running Drupal Commerce, you can use the Commerce Kickstart installation profile that automatically installs the necessary modules during the normal Drupal installation. To locate and download installation profiles and find resources for creating your own, refer to the documentation at `drupalcommerce.org/development/installation-profiles`.

Commerce

The Commerce module defines a variety of API functions used by the other modules to simplify commonly used features of Views and the Forms API. While this library of functions and general store settings will surely grow as Drupal Commerce matures, the main feature it is responsible for at present is currency definition and formatting. Every possible currency is defined in the Commerce module according to ISO 4217, while the module allows the name and formatting data to be altered via `hook_commerce_currency_info_alter()`.

The Commerce UI module defines a top level Management menu item called Store under which all the other UI modules place their menu items and a Configuration beneath Store to hold Commerce module settings forms. It also adds a Currency settings item in the Configuration menu, as shown in Figure 25–1. Before adding products to your site, you should select the default currency for the store and enable any other currencies that you intend to use in product pricing. Default price fields added by Commerce modules to bundles of entities like products and line items use the default store currency on currency selection widgets, because the default values for these "locked" fields cannot otherwise be adjusted via the Field UI.

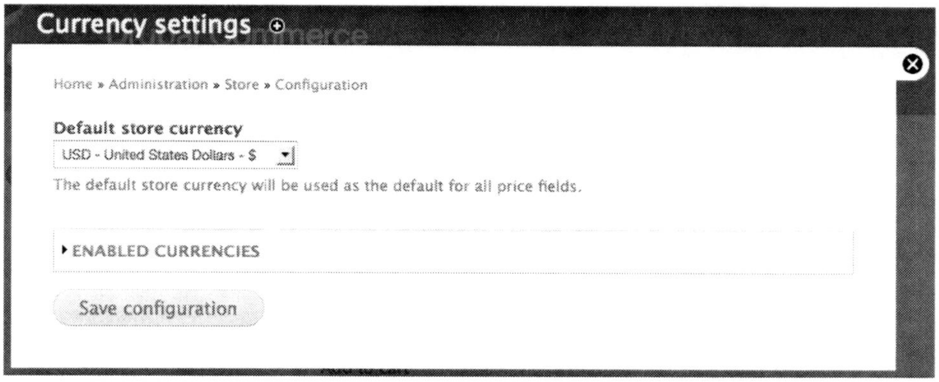

Figure 25–1. The currency settings form lets you specify a default store currency and enable any other currencies.

Price

The Price module primarily defines the price field that can be attached to entities allowing the entry of currency specific pricing. The price field stores an amount and an ISO 4217 currency code for every price value, and it comes with two display formatters that display price values as raw numbers or as numbers formatted for the specified currency. Entering prices is possible via one of two default widgets shown in

Figure 25–2, a Price textfield widget that allows price entry for a specific currency and a Price with currency widget that lets you choose a currency from the list of enabled currencies on data entry.

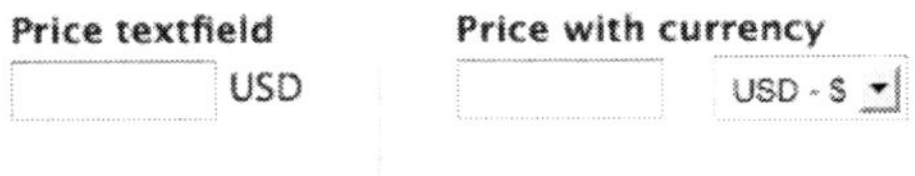

Price textfield

    [   ] USD

Price with currency

    [   ] USD - $ ▾

Figure 25–2. The Price module defines these two standard widgets used for entering price values.

While the Price module does not create any price fields on its own, it does provide an API function called `commerce_price_create_instance()` that other modules in Drupal Commerce use to add required, locked price fields to their entity bundles. The Product module uses this function to add default price fields to product types to ensure every product you create has a price value, like so:

```
/**
 * Ensures a base price field is present on a product type bundle.
 */
function commerce_product_configure_product_type($type) {
  commerce_price_create_instance('purchase_price', 'commerce_product', $type, t('Price'));
}
```

If multiple calls to `commerce_price_create_instance()` use the same first argument representing the field's name, the same field will be used for each instance. In the case of products, this allows Views and other functions to assume they can find price data in the same field across every product type. Without this ability, it would be nearly impossible to build reliable product catalogs and multipurpose Add to Cart forms.

Additionally, price fields created with this function are "locked," meaning instances of these fields cannot be deleted or altered via the Field UI. For this reason, they all default to the Price with currency widget for data entry, as it uses the default store currency and alters its form elements based on the number of available currencies. While the widget will also accommodate currencies that are disabled after prices have already been entered using those currencies, you should consider it a best practice to plan for and enable the currencies your site will use prior to entering your product data.

Dynamic Pricing

Price fields have the ability to enable other modules to dynamically alter a price's amount and currency on display. Altering prices for various types of discounts and adjusting price displays for things like tax-inclusive pricing and multicurrency support is a major consideration of many e-commerce web sites. The Price module accommodates these needs via integration with Rules in the Product Pricing module, allowing you to configure price adjustments via the Rules UI.

Altering prices based on the point of display or some set of discount parameters on its own is not a difficult task, but because using Rules for dynamic pricing requires Drupal to load and execute code, this data is not readily available in the database for the purpose of sorting or filtering query results. In other words, a View that orders products from lowest to highest price would have incorrect ordering if the most expensive product is discounted when the page is generated to be the cheapest in the list. To avoid this problem, the Price module has the ability to pre-calculate and cache prices derived from independent Rules that use a consistent set of parameters to produce predictable and reproducible price alterations.

Product

After your initial store and currency configuration, your next step will be to implement your site's product strategy. You should have a clear understanding of what types of products you will be selling and how your customers will be paying for them as you begin to interact with the product system. The Product module uses Drupal 7's entity system to define a new fieldable product entity that can have any number of bundles referred to as product types. The entity also defines several view modes that allow you to control how the fields on each product type are displayed in various locations.

Any module can define new entities in the same manner using hook_entity_info(). As you contribute modules to Drupal 7 or write your own modules to extend Drupal Commerce, you should consider using the entity system any time your code depends on a displayable data object with bundles that should be configurable via a user interface. See the development discussions later in this chapter for a code example discussing the definition of an entity type.

Creating a Product Type

In addition to defining product types in code, you can use the default interface provided by the Product UI module to add and configure product types. This interface is located under the Products menu item in the Store menu. The main Products page is a view listing all products on the site in a table with a Product Types tab that lists all currently available product types with some administrative links for managing the types and their fields (see Figure 25–3).

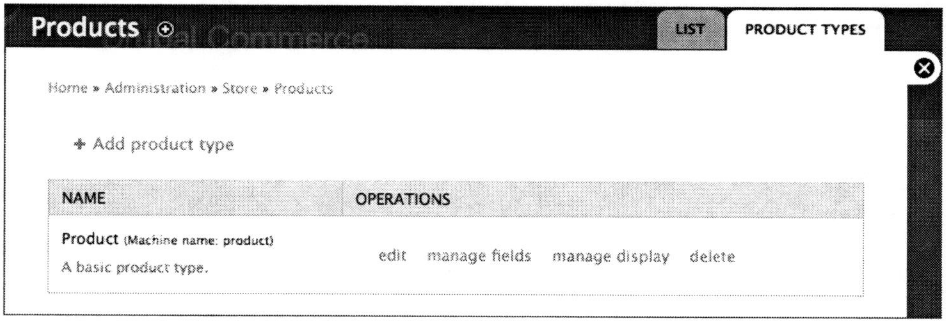

Figure 25–3. The Product Types tab allows you to add and configure product types on your site.

While the Product UI module creates a basic product type on install, most sites will need to define additional product types or at least customize the basic product type. You should add a separate product type for each group of products you sell that share a common set of attributes or features, like the size of a shirt or type of cover on a book. These attributes are represented as fields on the various product types and are added via the manage fields link for the product type. As discussed later in the Cart section, the Add to Cart form adjusts its display to allow product selection based on any required, single-value fields with a definite set of options that each of the products on the form contain.

Follow these instructions to build a t-shirt product type that might be used in an apparel store:

1. Click the Add product type link pictured above and enter *t-shirt* as the product type name. Notice that a valid "machine name" is automatically created for the product type that will be used throughout the code to refer to this type.

2. Submit the form using the Save and add fields button to create the new product type and redirect to its Manage Fields tab.

3. Drag the Add new field row in the field table to a position between the Title and Price rows. Enter *Size* in the new field's label textfield and *size* in its name textfield. Select List (text) as the type of data to store, leave the widget at Select list, and click the Save button to create the new field and redirect to its settings form.

4. Leave the Allowed values for the field settings blank, as these allowed values apply to any instance of your Size field and cannot be updated later if you decide you need additional options. Submit the form using the Save field settings button.

5. You are now viewing a form with settings specific to the Size field on the t-shirt product type and other general field settings. In the t-shirt settings fieldset, check the Required box beneath the Label textfield to require every t-shirt product to have a size value. In the Size field settings fieldset, ensure the Number of values is set to 1 and enter a few size options in the Allowed values textarea one per line.

6. Submit the form using the Save settings button to be returned to the Manage Fields tab, which should now resemble Figure 25–4. You can add any additional fields you need using the same process, including fields of other types like images.

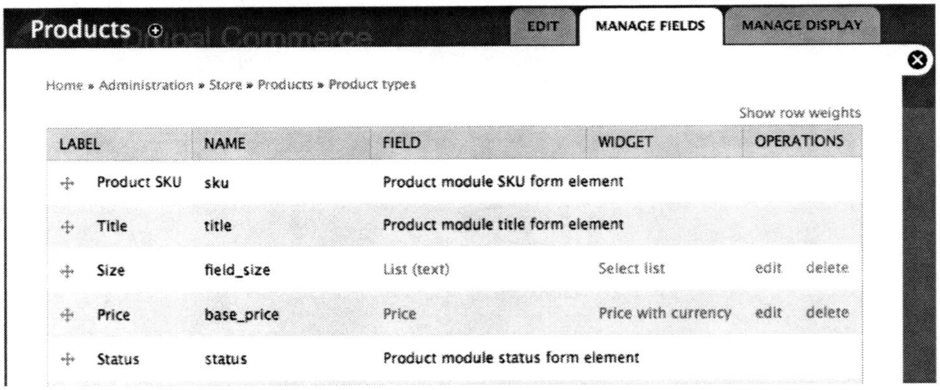

Figure 25–4. The Manage Fields tab of a product type shows the default fields added by modules and any additional fields you add via the Field UI.

Adding Products

Once you have configured the product type, you are ready to start adding products to the site. Returning to the *Store ➤ Products* page, you can use the Add a product link to choose the product type and start creating products. When you list products of types that have single-value fields like the t-shirt product type, you must add a separate product for each variation you intend to sell.

The keen observer will realize how many products this will result in for stores that have product types with multiple attribute fields and many options. In Drupal Commerce you can end up creating several to dozens of products that differ from one another in only one field value. This is due in large part to the project's prioritization of normalizing the product data model and is an extension of its emphasis on separating the API from the UI as discussed later.

Drupal Commerce began with discussions on how to better define products in response to the poor developer experience in the Ubercart Product API, resulting from the inconsistency of attribute data, unreliability of SKU adjustments, and opacity of critical data stored as serialized arrays. The main corrective measure architected into the Commerce product system was to enforce a full definition of every possible variation of a product, including a unique product ID and SKU. This approach combined with the storage of attribute data in fields makes the product data much easier to work with and simplifies the product creation API.

■ **Note** SKU stands for Stock Keeping Unit and refers to the merchant-defined unique identifier of each variation of a product or billable entity. SKUs often contain meaningful abbreviated product information but can just as well be simple numeric values, especially for stores that don't depend on the data or are in markets where other methods of tracking sold items are dominant.

This move to focus on the API and data model at the expense of a simpler core UI was intentional. A critical part of the product strategy involves introducing usability layers on top of the product system to simplify repetitive tasks. One of Drupal's Google Summer of Code 2010 projects focused on this problem, resulting in Commerce Bulk Product Creation available from drupal.org/project/commerce_bpc. If you need to create multiple variations of the same product at once, this module allows you to create them through a form that lets you choose the attribute field options to create products for and specify a token-based pattern to use for their SKUs.

At this point, you still don't have any way to display the products you are creating to your customers for purchase. The product definition exists solely on the back end and will be displayed on the front end through a product display node type utilizing a product reference field, as discussed in the Product Reference section. As mentioned, this separation of a product's definition from its point of display is an extension of Drupal Commerce's emphasis on separating APIs from the default UI. This separation allows the same product to be referenced in multiple places, like on language specific nodes or across multiple domains, without requiring manual data synchronization to ensure that product SKUs, prices, and other information is uniform across all displays. While it may take more work to set up an initial product display, the greater flexibility is well worth the cost.

Finally, using Drupal's entity system to define products enables modules to use special fields to add functionality to different product types. The Physical Product module does just that, defining fields that you can use to describe a product's dimensions, weight, and packaging information. This data is then available on the checkout form where it can be aggregated and used to calculate shipping costs and collect additional information from the user necessary to fulfill orders of physical products.

Line Item

Drupal Commerce line items are used to represent anything on an order that contributes to calculating the order's total or fulfilling the order. The line item entity defined by the module is fieldable and can be configured in any number of module-defined bundles called line item types. Changes to line items are tracked via line item revisions, much like nodes. Every line item contains the following default properties and fields in addition to line item type-specific fields added by the module defining the type:

- Label
- Title

- Display options

- Quantity

- Unit price

- Total price

Any module needing to represent other information on the order, like a discount from a coupon code, can define a new line item type in the same manner using `hook_commerce_line_item_info()`. An example implementation may be seen in the Product Reference module, which defines the product line item type and uses a default product reference field to relate the line item to the actual product in your database. For current documentation of the line item type data structure, refer to the Line Item page of the "Info hooks" section in the *Drupal Commerce Specification* handbook at `www.drupalcommerce.org/specification`.

■ **Tip** Bookmark the Specification handbook (`drupalcommerce.org/specification`) and refer to it often for the most current system overviews, hook explanations, and API utilization strategies.

The line item reference field defined by the Line Item module can relate any number of line items to another entity using their `line_item_id` values. The field itself doesn't store any data other than IDs, but it comes with a very robust Line item manager widget that lets you add, edit, and delete line items via a dynamic form powered by the new `#ajax` support in the Forms API (see Figure 25–5). Modules like Cart that want to add line items to orders via the API are responsible for both creating the line items and associating them to the orders by adjusting the values of the order's line item reference field. Refer to `commerce_cart_product_add()` in `commerce_cart.module` for an example implementation of this process.

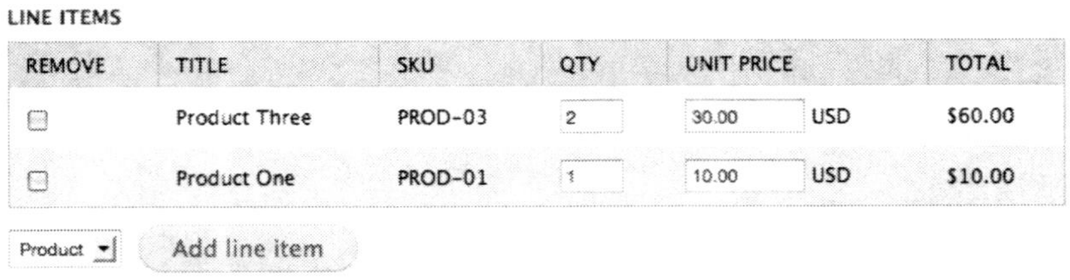

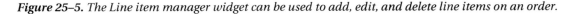

LINE ITEMS

REMOVE	TITLE	SKU	QTY	UNIT PRICE		TOTAL
☐	Product Three	PROD-03	2	30.00	USD	$60.00
☐	Product One	PROD-01	1	10.00	USD	$10.00

| Product ▾ | Add line item |

Figure 25–5. The Line item manager widget can be used to add, edit, and delete line items on an order.

Line items can be displayed using Views via a line item relationship or argument, as in the shopping cart block and Line item View display formatter, and by using the API to build a content array based on the line item type's field display configuration. You can access a list of line item types and manage their field display settings through the Line items item in the Store ➤ Configuration menu. Note that line item types can't be added or edited via the user interface because they depend on module-specific code to operate effectively. If you must alter another module's line item types, you can do so using `hook_commerce_line_item_info_alter()`.

In addition to Product Reference and Cart, Tax is the other core module that heavily interacts with the line item system. The Tax module allows modules to define tax rates via `hook_commerce_tax_info()` that may apply to line items on an order. Storing tax collected in line items allows you to easily create tax reports using Views and access tax rate information via a field referencing the particular rate used to calculate the line item's price.

Product Reference

The Product Reference module defines both a product reference field and the product line item type, which uses the field to reference product data from the line item. The product reference field is the primary tool you will use to build product displays and Add to Cart forms. When the field is placed on a node type, Product Reference pulls the referenced product's fields into the node for display, using both the product and node types' field display settings to format and order the product's fields along with the node's fields. Product reference fields may reference single or multiple products, and using the Add to Cart form display formatter provided by the Cart module may be displayed as Add to Cart forms in the node display. The field also integrates with Views to provide a relationship from the display node to the referenced product's data for use in product catalog Views and other types of displays.

As you can see, this field is quite versatile and is a key part of Drupal Commerce's product strategy. By pulling product fields into node displays, image and price information can be defined and maintained on the single product entity and then referenced from any number of places throughout the site. Any updates to the product will automatically appear wherever it is displayed using a product reference relationship.

Building a Product Display Node Type

Follow these instructions to build a basic Product display node type for your site:

1. Browse to Structure ➤ Content types in the Administration menu and click the Add content type link. Enter Product display as the content type name and adjust the settings in the vertical tabs to your liking.

2. Submit the form using the Save and add fields button to create the new content type and redirect to its Manage Fields tab.

3. In the Add new field row in the field table, enter *Product* as the new field's label and *product* in its name textfield. Select Product reference, leave the widget at Autocomplete text field, and click the Save button to create the new field and redirect to its settings form.

4. Leave the "Product types that can be referenced" checkboxes unchecked, allowing the field to reference products of any type. Submit the form using the Save field settings button.

5. You are now viewing a form with settings specific to the Product field on the Product display content type and other general field settings. In the Product display settings fieldset, check the Required box beneath the Label textfield to require every Product display node to reference a product. In the Product field settings fieldset, leave the Number of values set to 1 and submit the form using the Save settings button to be returned to the Manage Fields tab.

6. Click the Manage Display tab to see how the content type fields (Body and Product) and referenced product fields (Product: Size and Product: Price) will be ordered and displayed. Only T-shirt products will have the size field, and you don't need to display the field itself via the product display node. You will also want the node's product field to be displayed as an Add to Cart form, requiring you to select that display formatter in the field's Format select box. Update your default field display settings to resemble Figure 25–6 and repeat the process for any other display modes.

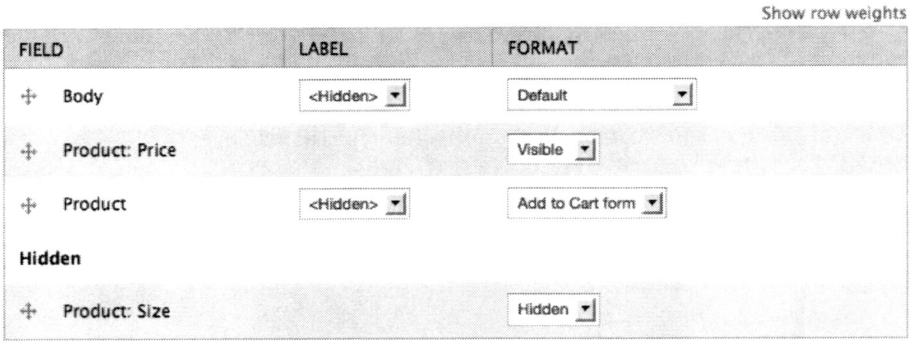

Show row weights

FIELD	LABEL	FORMAT
⊹ Body	<Hidden> ▾	Default ▾
⊹ Product: Price		Visible ▾
⊹ Product	<Hidden> ▾	Add to Cart form ▾
Hidden		
⊹ Product: Size		Hidden ▾

Figure 25–6. The pictured field display configuration hides unnecessary fields and orders the price field from the referenced product to be displayed right above the product reference field rendered as an Add to Cart form.

7. Finally, you should review the display settings for the product fields that will be displayed in the node context. These settings are configured via the manage display forms for each product types listed at Administration ➤ Store ➤ Products ➤ Product types. Product fields can be displayed differently on each node view mode, so you may need to configure the field display settings for multiple product view modes.

Following those steps will give you a node type you can now use to list products for sale on your site. The Autocomplete text field widget adds a text field to the Node Edit form where you can enter products by SKU to reference from the node, and it autocompletes on the product SKU or Title during data entry. Nodes of this type will display a simple Add to Cart form that adds the referenced product to the customer's shopping cart.

While this simple product display is good for selling a single product at a time, it will not be sufficient for selling sets of products from the same node. For example, you might want to create four t-shirt products that all have the same style or design but are different sizes. Drupal Commerce's product data model demands each size to be listed as a separate product, but the customer only needs to see a single product display where he or she can choose the appropriate size. To accomplish this, you use a content type with a product reference field whose Number of values setting is greater than one or set to unlimited. The autocomplete text field will function just the same but support a comma separate list of SKUs, and the Add to Cart form will automatically adjust to allow the customer to choose the proper product he or she wants to add to the cart.

The inclusion of product fields on display nodes is a critical feature for this whole system, but it is not without its difficulties. For single value product reference fields, it is easy enough to pull the referenced product's fields into the node for display, and it is clear to see that any display data for the product is best stored in fields on the product type. The most common example would be to add an image field to the product type and upload your images to the products themselves so they can be displayed easily on product display nodes or on other custom displays and Views. However, for multiple value product reference fields, it is more difficult to know which product's fields should be displayed by default and whether or not some data should be stored on the products despite the potential for duplication, like the case of images for t-shirts listed only as separate products to accommodate various size options. As Drupal Commerce matures, your approach is likely to change, but at this point the best strategy is to keep as much raw data about your products, including any related images, stored in fields on the products themselves.

Customer

The Customer module defines a customer profile entity and the related customer profile reference field that works much like the line item reference field to associate customer profile data with orders. The customer profile entity supports any number of module-defined fieldable bundles known as customer profile types. Changes to customer profiles are logged via revisions, and special attention is given to ensure that customer profiles are duplicated instead of merely updated to preserve customer data for profiles referenced by previous orders. Each customer profile type can have its own set of fields to collect data pertinent to the profile type, allowing you to collect different information for billing and shipping profiles if necessary. Customer profile types like the default Billing information type use the postal address field defined by the Address Field module to collect name and address information in conformance with international standards.

Customer profiles are intended to serve as the primary method for collecting the information you need from customers in order to fulfill your orders. This information is maintained separate from the normal user account system to provide several key points of flexibility. First, this model lets users maintain multiple profiles of each type, much like the address book functionality common to most major e-commerce web sites. Second, allowing repeat customers to refer to previously used profiles, creating new profiles only when some information has changed, reduces data duplication. Third, stores that allow group purchasing can grant multiple users access to the same customer profile information, entrusting the ability to create new profiles to the managers of each group. Fourth, customer profile data can be collected and stored in relation to an order for anonymous users such that a store does not need to create user accounts at all if it does not desire. This level of anonymous checkout would not be possible if customer data were tied directly to user accounts.

Customer profile types are defined via modules via hook_commerce_customer_profile_info(). As with line item types, modules can perform configuration steps on these profile types when they are first enabled to ensure the presence of default fields. The Customer module provides checkout form integration for each customer profile type to give customers a place to supply their information, and it adds customer profile reference fields to the order object to give administrators a place to add and edit the profiles. Unlike the line item manager widget, the customer profile manager widget only supports referencing a single profile at a time. Finally, the module adds a Customer profiles item to the Store menu that allows you to create, view, update, and delete customer profiles with a separate tab allowing you to view a list of all the customer profile types and manage their fields. Any fields you add to the profile type will appear on the checkout and order edit forms and in customer profile displays.

Order

The order system consists of the order entity, order state, and status information plus an API designed to assist you in working with order data and updating orders. The order entity defines a single fieldable bundle that supports revisions for any change in the order's data. Tracking changes to orders through their entire workflow is very important from both a marketing and security perspective, allowing administrators to track a customer's interactions with the site leading up to checkout and to track the updates other administrators make to the order afterward. Therefore, special attention is paid to ensure orders and the line items and customer profiles associated with them are also revised as necessary.

In addition to the line item and customer profile data mentioned previously, orders contain metadata that tracks the order's status, creation and update timestamps, and owner information. The order status is its current step in the life-cycle of the order that provides administrators with information on what has occurred to the order and what the next step in processing the order will be. Order statuses range from shopping-cart-related and checkout-related statuses to various post-checkout statuses ending in a completed status. They are organized into containers called order states that represent the larger phases an order goes through. The owner information includes both the ID of the user who created the order, whether it was through a shopping cart or administrative form, and a contact e-mail address that defaults to the user's e-mail if he or she is logged but may be different or supplied by anonymous users on the checkout form.

The default user interface for order administration is a View listing all orders with an order creation link at the Orders item in the Store menu and a settings area in the Store ➤ Configuration menu that includes field management tabs. The default order View shows the most recent orders first and displays the order number, which can be any alphanumeric value even though it defaults to the order ID, along with other metadata including the order's total and current status.

While the default order View is fairly basic, it is here that the decision to standardize Drupal Commerce's default UI on Views really pays off. Many stores require tailor-made order administration interfaces that accommodate their unique order workflows and fulfillment needs. Site builders can use the familiar Views interface and theme system to customize the existing interface, add additional sorting and filtering options, and extend it with a variety of contributed Views modules like Views Bulk Operations for batch updating.

Payment

The Payment module defines a payment transaction entity that logs payment attempts for any module-defined payment method, relating these transactions to orders through the checkout process or an order's payment form. Payment methods are defined by contributed modules for each possible method of payment provided by any given payment service. As mentioned, no real payment methods are included in the core project to allow payment service integration code to mature independent of the core development cycle. The Payment module does offer reusable code for common types of payment methods that you should reuse in your integration modules, such as a standardized credit card data entry form.

Payment transactions are created any time a payment is attempted, logging the time and details of the attempt, the data returned by the payment service, and the result or current status of the payment. The payment transaction entity defines bundles for each of the enabled payment methods, but it does not allow fields to be attached to these bundles. Updates to a payment transaction are logged via revisions, with the exception of payload data received from the payment service. This data is maintained in a serialized array with a new value for each message pertaining to the transaction, and it is only visible to payment administrators for debugging purposes.

As payment transactions are created for orders, they are visible in a payment tab on the orders' Payment tab pages. This tab contains a View listing all transactions for the order sorted chronologically with a footer containing the remaining balance to be paid and a form to enter payments manually. During development and testing, you may take advantage of the Payment Method Example module to test the receipt and logging of payments, resulting in fully paid orders as shown in Figure 25–7.

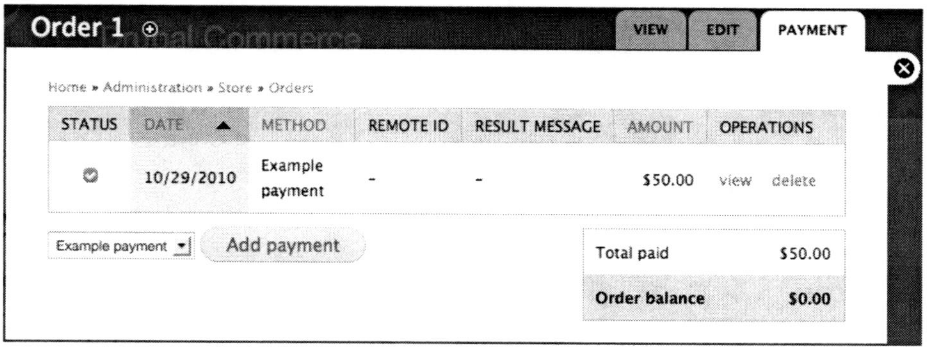

Figure 25–7. Payments are listed in chronological order on the Payment tab, where you will also find links to perform any necessary operations on the payments and a form to manually add new payments to the order.

Enabling Payment Methods

The Payment Method Example module is also useful as a model for developing your own payment method modules. Defining new payment methods is not a terribly complicated process, involving the implementation of hook_commerce_payment_info() and the definition of callbacks governing the collection and communication of information from the customer to the payment service. There are additional accommodations for payment methods that require redirection to a third party web site for the submission of payment details, ensuring these payment methods fit properly into the normal checkout workflow. As with the line item type documentation, refer to the Payment page of the "Info hooks" section in the *Drupal Commerce Specification* handbook for up to date information on integrating with the payment system properly.

The Payment module defines two checkout panes that handle payment from customers on the checkout form. The basic Payment pane displays any available payment methods to the customer for selection on the Review checkout page and will automatically update itself to include any additional form elements needed to collect process payments of the selected method. If an off-site payment method is selected, the customer will be redirected from the Payment checkout page via the Off-site payment redirect checkout pane that also handles customers returned from the off-site payment service. This page is skipped for payment methods that can be processed directly from your web site.

The list of available payment methods is determined via integration with the Rules module. Each payment method will receive a default rule configuration that you must enable for the payment method to appear on the checkout form. Each payment method will also likely have additional settings that must be configured in the form of the action on the rule configuration that enables it. Additionally, if necessary, you can add any conditions in the rule configuration that must be met for the customer to pay using this method.

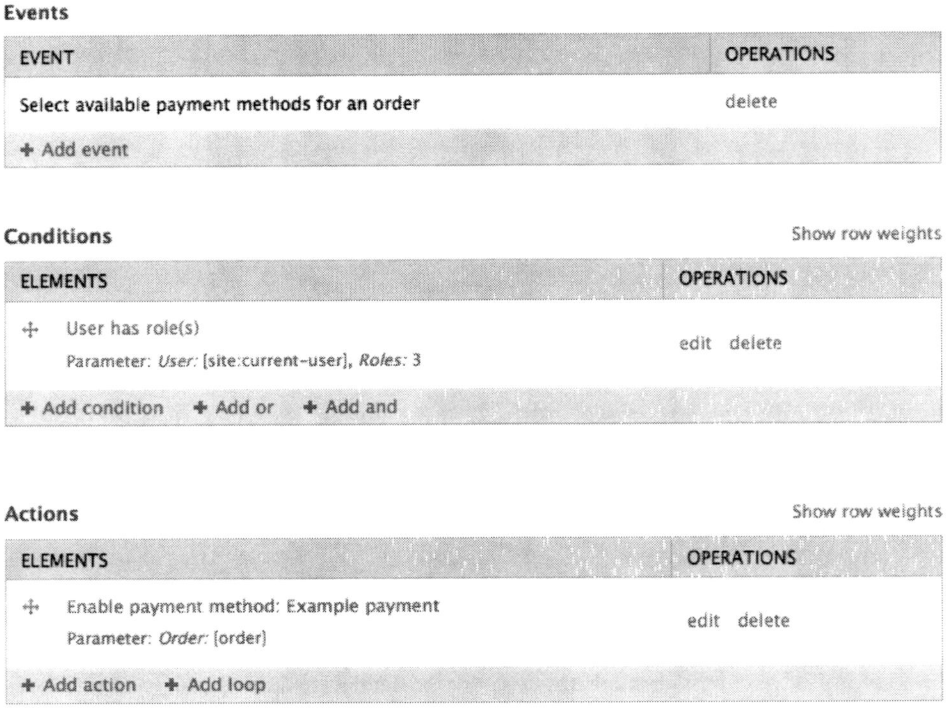

Events

EVENT	OPERATIONS
Select available payment methods for an order	delete
✚ Add event	

Conditions   Show row weights

ELEMENTS	OPERATIONS
✤ User has role(s) Parameter: *User:* [site:current-user], *Roles:* 3	edit delete
✚ Add condition ✚ Add or ✚ Add and	

Actions   Show row weights

ELEMENTS	OPERATIONS
✤ Enable payment method: Example payment Parameter: *Order:* [order]	edit delete
✚ Add action ✚ Add loop	

***Figure 25–8.** Payment methods are enabled by rule configurations like the one pictured here for the Example payment method.*

Follow these instructions to enable the Example payment method for use by users with the Administrator user role, resulting in the rule configuration pictured in Figure 25–8:

1. Browse to the Payment settings page in the Store ➤ Configuration menu.

2. Click the Enable operation link for the Example payment rule configuration in the Disabled payment rules table and confirm the action on the following form.

3. Click the Edit operation link for the rule configuration to view an overview form listing the event that executes this rule, "Select available payment methods for an order," the conditions that will be checked on execution, and the actions to perform upon successful evaluation. The only action will be the "Enable payment method: Example payment" action. View its configuration form via the Edit operation link to see where you would normally enter payment method settings.

4. Return to the overview form for the rule configuration and click the Add condition link in the footer of the Conditions table. Select the "User has role(s)" condition and submit the form via the Continue button.

5. You now need to tell Rules what user it should check for which role. In the User fieldset, select or specify site:current-user in the Data selector text field. This Token tells Rules to evaluate this condition using the currently logged in user. In the Roles fieldset, specify Administrator as the Value and submit the form via the Save button.

6. Your overview form should now resemble Figure 25–8 and will result in users with the Administrator role having access to the Example payment method on the checkout form.

You will need to repeat this process for any other payment methods you want to enable on your checkout form. The administrative payment form does not depend on Rules, however, displaying any available payment method that can be processed by an administrator. Redirected payment methods will typically not work, as they are often dependent on checkout-specific information or a customer's username and password.

■ **Tip** Most major payment services will have modules integrating them into Drupal Commerce, so search the e-commerce modules on `drupal.org` before developing your own integration.

Checkout

The checkout system consists of a pluggable checkout form and an administrative checkout form builder that lets you order and configure the components of the checkout form using a drag-and-drop interface. The checkout form is comprised of checkout pages containing a set of module-defined checkout panes, which are fieldsets used to display order details and collect customer and payment information.

While the form defaults to using a two-step process with review and payment on a standalone page, it can be configured with a few clicks of the mouse to use a single-step configuration that processes the order upon form submission and redirects to the completion page immediately upon success. Whether or not such a configuration works for your store will depend on the payment methods you are using and any business rules your store has that might require additional checkout steps.

■ **Tip** The two-step process is the default so customers can review the full details of their orders prior to submitting payment information. For security reasons, some payments must be processed immediately upon form submission, meaning payment should occur at the final step before checkout completion. Understand the limitations of your payment methods before making the decision to implement to a single-step checkout form.

The purpose of the checkout form is to collect any information needed for the order to be properly fulfilled, including processing payments as discussed in the "Payment" section. As an order progresses through the checkout form, its status is adjusted to reflect the page it is currently on, allowing you to retain information on where an order was when abandoned during checkout. The data on the order may be critical for recovering those sales and streamlining the checkout process to improve your conversion rate.

The default checkout pages defined by the Checkout and Payment modules include:

- *Checkout* displays the cart contents and collects customer profile information.

- *Review order* displays a summary of data entered and collects payment details.

- *Payment* is the point of redirection for off-site payment methods; skipped if not needed.

- *Checkout complete* is the final landing page showing an order summary, pertinent order links, and order fulfillment information.

The checkout panes appearing on each page are fully customizable, with any page without panes getting skipped in the checkout workflow. You can expose additional checkout pages and panes to the checkout form builder pictured in Figure 25–9 using the hooks described on the Checkout page of the "Info hooks" section in the *Drupal Commerce Specification* handbook referred to earlier.

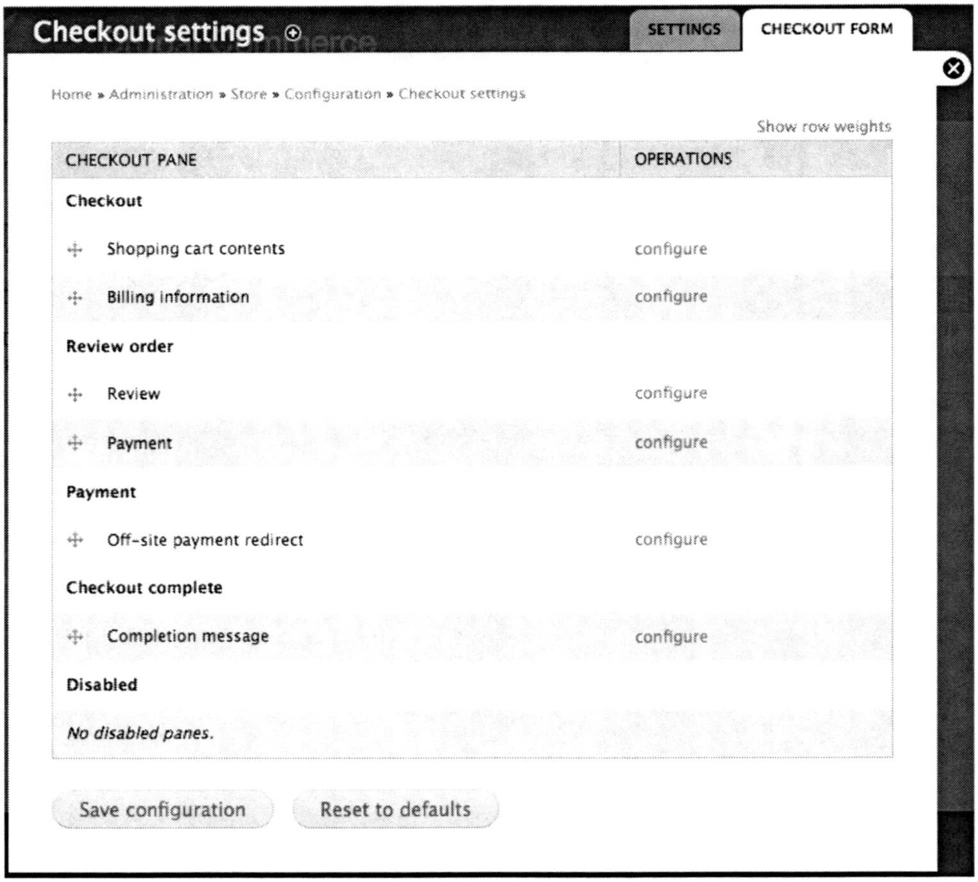

Figure 25–9. The checkout form can be easily reconfigured using the drag-and-drop checkout form builder.

The Checkout module actually does not have a dependency on the Cart module, meaning you can enable the checkout form but devise some other method to create orders based on customer action or give customers checkout links to Administrator-created orders. The basic checkout URL is actually defined by the Cart module as a router to an order specific checkout URL – checkout/#. The checkout form does not use Drupal's multi-step form capabilities to progress through the form on a single URL, so the current checkout page will actually be reflected in the URL as the customer progresses through the form.

You are mostly left to your own devices to configure Drupal to provide an optimal checkout experience. There are many web sites and articles discussing best practices for e-commerce web sites with an eye toward increasing conversions, and the flexibility of Drupal will serve you well to optimize your checkout pages. At the very least, you should disable unnecessary blocks and menus on the checkout pages and use theming to highlight the buttons your customers should use to access the checkout form and progress through it.

Cart

The Cart module enables a fairly standard shopping cart system, allowing customers to add products to shopping cart orders that can then be purchased via the checkout form. As soon as an item is added to a customer's cart, a new order is created that will exist until it is completed via checkout. There is a default Shopping cart order state and status, but additional statuses can also tell the Cart module they are shopping cart statuses, as with the statuses representing the default Checkout and Review steps in the checkout form. This allows customers to update the contents of the shopping cart until they actually submit payment.

The shopping cart is represented by a Drupal block shown in Figure 25–10 that consists of a View listing the line items on the cart order with a footer summarizing the items on the order and linking to the cart page and checkout form. The block is quite dynamic and can be easily customized via the Views user interface and themed to match your site. The cart page provides a form also built through Views that lets users update the contents of the shopping cart and proceed to checkout.

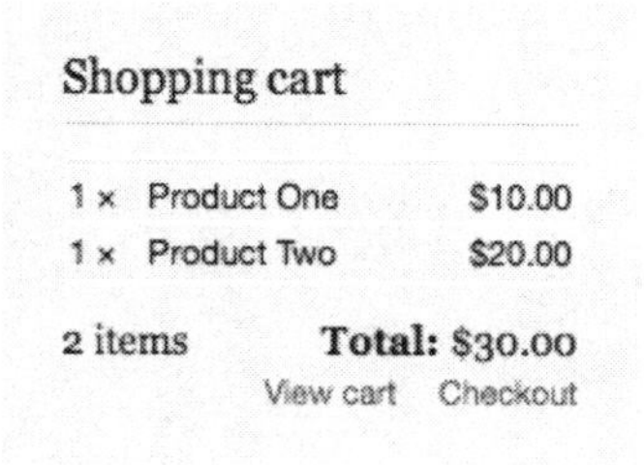

Shopping cart		
1 ×	Product One	$10.00
1 ×	Product Two	$20.00
2 items	**Total:** $30.00	
	View cart Checkout	

Figure 25–10. *The default shopping cart block is entirely configurable via the Views user interface.*

The Cart API includes functions for loading and updating shopping cart orders along with a versatile Add to Cart form function. The Add to Cart form display formatter for Product reference fields passes the referenced product IDs to this form, which examines the values passed in to determine how to display the form. Single product forms simply display an Add to Cart button for the product signified in a hidden form value while multiple product forms will vary in appearance; they might either appear as a single select list, radio buttons group, or check boxes group allowing the customer to select products to add based on the products' titles or as a set of dynamically generated widgets representing the common attribute fields on the referenced products. As the customer updates the product or attributes selected, the form uses the #ajax property of the Forms API to update elements on the page accordingly prior to adding the product to the cart.

Summarizing the Main Components

Much more can be written about how the various systems are architected, but this quick examination of the core modules should give you a functional understanding of how the major pieces of Drupal Commerce work together. The key thing you should take away is that even though the core modules do not provide you with a complete e-commerce application out of the box, the necessary systems are in place to be extended by other modules and fleshed out in the site-building process to provide the e-commerce experience your site requires.

Tables 25–1, 25–2, and 25–3 summarize the main Commerce components, specifically all the entities and fields mentioned in the previous module discussions.

Table 25–1. *Core Drupal Commerce Entities*

Name	Base Table	ID	Bundles	Revisions
Customer profile	commerce_customer_profile	profile_id	Yes; module-defined customer profile types	Yes
Line item	commerce_line_item	line_item_id	Yes; module-defined line item types	Yes
Order	commerce_order	order_id	API level support for multiple, UI for one	Yes
Payment transaction	commerce_payment_transaction	transaction_id	Yes; one per payment method	Yes
Product	commerce_product	product_id	Yes; module- and UI-defined product types	No

Table 25–2. *Core Drupal Commerce Fields*

Name	Widget(s)	Display formatter(s)
Customer profile reference	Customer profile manager	Customer profile display
Line item reference	Line item manager	Line item View
Price	Price text field	
Price with currency	Raw amount	
Formatted amount		

Name	Widget(s)	Display formatter(s)
Product reference	Autocomplete text field	
Select list		
Check boxes/radio buttons	Add to Cart form	
SKU		
Title		

Table 25–3. Default Order States and Statuses

Order state	Order status(es)
Canceled	Canceled
Shopping cart	Shopping cart
Checkout	Checkout: Checkout (functions as cart)
Checkout: Review (functions as cart)	
Checkout: Payment	
Checkout: Complete	
Pending	Pending (allows completion page access)
Processing (allows completion page access)	
Completed	Completed (allows completion page access)

Implementing Drupal Commerce

Having read through the discussion introducing the various systems, entities, and fields, you should be able to see the power and flexibility this approach to designing an e-commerce system provides. However, as you also likely surmised, the loosely coupled components that make up Drupal Commerce will require an extra dose of intentionality and expertise on your part to ensure they are successfully configured.

The old adage proves true: with great power comes great responsibility. It is now up to you to ensure that you are using the tools as intended while providing an e-commerce experience customized to your site's needs and client's expectations. Setting up Drupal Commerce sites will require extra planning effort in advance, so this final section of the chapter provides a few tips to help you get started and to mitigate some of the repetitive tasks you will encounter developing multiple sites.

Because e-commerce is just one part of your Drupal site, you should ensure that you are following Drupal site-building best practices. Plan your content types, Views, roles, and permissions in advance to ensure the foundation of the web site is strong and secure. Configuring the Commerce components is then just an extension of your normal process, requiring you to plan product types in addition to content types and add roles specifically for store administration.

Additionally, you should take extra precaution to ensure your Drupal site is secure. Plan on regular maintenance to keep Drupal and your contributed modules current; fully test your payment system and checkout workflow to ensure payment data is not exposed and orders are not fulfilled before payment Is complete. When dealing with on-site credit card payments, ensure your checkout configuration allows the payment method module to process payment when the checkout page containing the payment checkout pane is submitted. You should also take advantage of other contributed modules to beef up your security, like using Secure Pages to add SSL protection to your site.

Finally, it has been the project's goal from the beginning to enable site builders and developers to create reusable Drupal Commerce distributions and Features modules targeting specific e-commerce use cases. The amount of work involved in setting up a Drupal Commerce installation is not something you will want to repeat afresh with each new site, and it requires a level of proficiency with Drupal that will be beyond the grasp of most new users. As targeted distributions of Drupal are becoming more popular, aided by the automatic installation profile packaging features of `drupal.org` itself, the vision for Drupal Commerce is to see many of these geared toward e-commerce sites such as:

- Clothing and apparel stores with ready-made product types and displays.

- Premium content and membership sites selling user roles, node access, and other types of permissions with flat fees and recurring payments.

- Outreach and donation collection sites for non-profit organizations.

- Community-based event registration and support sites.

With this strategy and vision in mind, the Commerce components were also designed to be usable by Features and other modules enabling exportable site configurations. Additionally, the use of Views for the default user interfaces and Rules for order workflow automation allows you to export your setup along with your Commerce configuration. The standardization on entities and fields for all the Commerce objects provides a consistent data model for importing and exporting your e-commerce data. Using all these pieces to develop reusable sites and custom distributions requires intentional planning on your part, but the payoff in your own site building workflow and in community usage is well worth the effort.

Development History

Parts of Drupal Commerce are best understood in light of its development out of the Drupal based e-commerce projects that have gone before it. The Drupal Commerce feature set and usability goals have their roots in Ubercart, and its development philosophy was influenced by both the community experience of developing for Ubercart and the radical changes enacted in the latest version of the e-Commerce module. However, the code and user interface for the Commerce modules look and act almost nothing like the former projects, as the new modules were written specifically for Drupal 7 in conformity with a strict set of development standards outlined later in this chapter.

The principle goals of Commerce in its original departure from Ubercart included desires to:

- Establish a better-documented, easier-to-use API for contributed module developers.

- Separate plug-in modules from the core systems to allow each group of modules to mature independently of the concerns of the other.

- Establish a data object model based on Drupal 7's Entity and Field systems, depending on the UI to reduce any repetitive data entry that might ensue.

- Provide full test coverage for the core modules using Drupal's Testing framework.

- Take advantage of installation profiles and modules like Features to provide default configurations instead of focusing on a complete user experience in the modules alone.

- Provide a migration path from Ubercart to Drupal Commerce. Without a one-to-one feature correlation, a direct module update from one to the other is impossible.

Development has been accomplished in rounds since the project's inception, with systems being proposed and discussed in the project forums, IRC, and physical code sprints before being developed. To learn more about the project's history and stay on top of development proposals and roadmaps, refer to the forums and documentation at drupalcommerce.org.

Design Philosophy

When you first look at the list of Commerce modules, two things are likely to stand out that require a bit of explanation. The first is the raw number of modules available, including the separation of some modules into pairs of API and UI modules. While some users are turned off by the amount of setup required to install and configure the various modules, this division was made intentionally so the same set of modules can be adapted to a wider variety of e-commerce web sites. As your experience grows, you can enable only the modules you need for a particular site, while installation profiles and other modules can provide default configurations for common use cases.

For example, by separating the default UI from the modules that actually define the data objects and core APIs, site builders are freed to provide full drop-in replacements for parts of the UI that do not suit their sites. Additionally, by separating some systems into their component parts, like keeping Cart and Checkout separated, the same core set of Commerce modules may be used for traditional shopping-cart–based stores, sites with no checkout process that use shopping carts to deliver quotes, and invoicing sites where administrators create orders and send customers checkout links to provide payment.

■ **Note** This practice should be familiar to most users of Drupal 6, as Views and Rules have separated their default user interfaces to separate modules since then. Drupal 7 continues this practice with its division of the Field system into the Field and Field UI modules.

The second thing that stands out is the lack of modules adding common e-commerce features like product promotion tools, discounts and coupons, and integration with third party payment and fulfillment services. In the earliest planning stages of Drupal Commerce, the project's goal was to include in the core project only the systems and data objects without which it would not be a coherent project and which are necessary to build and support all necessary non-core features. This does not mean features not included in the core modules are not essential or deserving of special attention and maintenance. This is instead an architectural decision designed to improve the development process overall by freeing the core systems to iterate to new versions without first requiring every plug-in module to be updated.

A great example is the presence of the Payment module in the core project without any modules that actually integrate with the major payment services. It might be inconvenient to include modules integrating with the common payment services in the core project, but decoupling the development of the integration modules from the core project allows the various projects to mature and incorporate new features on their own timelines. The core Payment module can be improved and released without first requiring a collection of payment modules to be tested and updated on the new system, while at the same time the integration modules are free to respond to API and feature changes at the integrated service without having to wait on a new release of Drupal Commerce.

A final major point of the project's design philosophy is a dependence on installation profiles and modules like Features to simplify the process of starting a new Drupal Commerce site for a variety of targeted use cases. The core modules do not make any assumptions about the use case or business needs of sites that will implement them. Instead they focus on being flexible and extensible, supporting exportable configurations, and developing forms to be embedded anywhere instead of limiting them to the default UI implementation. The goal for the project is to see distributions provide an out of the box experience for niche markets, like apparel stores, event registration sites, and non-profit organization donation sites.

Development Standards

In addition to adopting a design philosophy that focuses on modularity and reproducible configurations, Drupal Commerce has adopted and enforced a strict set of development standards to ease development and maintenance. The main objective was to provide a well-documented, consistent API for developers to integrate with in their contributed modules and installation profiles. No patches are accepted that do not conform to the development standards listed at `drupalcommerce.org/development/standards`.

While the standards do occasionally change in response to core Drupal updates and issues that require the adoption of new standards, the current list of standards addresses the following topics:

- Code syntax and documentation based on Drupal's own coding standards.

- Module file and directory structures.

- Module .info file package naming.

- Function and hook naming to avoid common PHP inconsistencies and provide pattern-based namespacing for hooks.

- Proper utilization of Drupal's Testing framework.

- Using core and contributed module APIs.

- Embracing fine-grained permissions and extensible access control.

- Localization and user interface string storage.

- Template files and theme functions.

- Appropriately separating core APIs from the default UI.

- Performance considerations covering database and memory usage.

- Normalized data storage via entity and field data tables.

Building on Drupal 7

The Commerce modules were written to take advantage of many improvements in Drupal 7, most notably its fieldable entity system. They also owe much of their flexibility to Views, the query builder providing displays including the shopping cart and product lists, and Rules, the contributed system for performing conditional actions in response to events like checkout completion and order updates. The rest of this book was written to cover the many improvements in Drupal 7, but a few are highlighted here as holding special significance for Drupal Commerce.

Core Entities and Fields

The hallmark new feature of Drupal 7 is its system of fieldable entities. No longer must everything be a node to benefit from modules like Drupal 6's Content Construction Kit, resulting in a rethinking of major systems like user groups and e-commerce. Contributed modules can standardize on the entity system to define new data objects that can be bundled with any number of module-defined or user-configurable fields.

The Product Entity

Drupal Commerce has fully embraced the new system, defining all of its custom data objects as fieldable entities with varying use of bundles and revisioning based on the entity type. For example, whereas previous e-commerce projects for Drupal relied on the node system to implement products, Drupal Commerce defines a specific product entity. This entity has multiple bundles, each constituting a different product type that may contain fields to describe the product and choose from among a group of products on an Add to Cart form.

To define the product entity, the Product module uses the code in Listing 25–1.

Listing 25–1. Defining the Product Entity

```
/**
 * Implements hook_entity_info().
 */
function commerce_product_entity_info() {
  $return = array(
    'commerce_product' => array(
      'label' => t('Product'),
      'controller class' => 'CommerceProductEntityController',
      'base table' => 'commerce_product',
      'fieldable' => TRUE,
      'entity keys' => array(
        'id' => 'product_id',
        'bundle' => 'type',
      ),
      'bundle keys' => array(
        'bundle' => 'type',
      ),
      'bundles' => array(),
      'load hook' => 'commerce_product_load',
      'view modes' => array(
        …
      ),
```

```
    …
  );

  foreach (commerce_product_type_get_name() as $type => $name) {
    $return['commerce_product']['bundles'][$type] = array(
      'label' => $name,
    );
  }

  return $return;
}
```

Notice that the structure of the entity array includes keys related to product storage in the database and the controller class, CommerceProductEntityController, used to perform CRUD operations on products via save, load, and delete functions. Any of these values may be altered using hook_entity_info_alter() to change the nature of product data storage, though you should be cautious when making such a decision as you may interrupt the ability of other modules like Views to take advantage of the data.

The omitted portions of the previous code snippet handle the definition of the various display modes available for products and the definition of various callbacks that Rules uses to work with the product entity. The foreach loop populates the product entity's bundles array with data from commerce_product_type_get_name(), an API function that invokes hook_commerce_product_info() to gather information from enabled modules on available product types.

The Order Entity

Again, the order object is defined as an entity, allowing administrators to easily add fields to the default order bundle based on the site's business needs. These orders then take advantage of entity revisioning to track all the changes made to the data on an order.

When an entity is not defined to support multiple bundles, it defaults to a single bundle with the same machine name as the entity itself. In the case of orders, a single bundle is explicitly defined, making this unnecessary, a shown in Listing 25–2.

Listing 25–2. Explicitly Defining a Single Bundle

```
/**
 * Implements hook_entity_info().
 */
function commerce_order_entity_info() {
  $return = array(
    'commerce_order' => array(
      'label' => t('Order'),
      'controller class' => 'CommerceOrderEntityController',
      'base table' => 'commerce_order',
      'revision table' => 'commerce_order_revision',
      'fieldable' => TRUE,
      'entity keys' => array(
        'id' => 'order_id',
        'bundle' => 'type',
        'revision' => 'revision_id',
      ),
      'bundle keys' => array(
        'bundle' => 'type',
```

```
    ),
    'bundles' => array(
      'commerce_order' => array(
        'label' => t('Order'),
      ),
    ),
    'load hook' => 'commerce_order_load',
    'view modes' => array(
      …
    ),
    …
  ),
);

  return $return;
}
```

Notice that the bundles array contains only a single bundle. Should you need to enable multiple order bundles for some reason, you would have to alter this array with hook_entity_info_alter(). The initial version of the Order module defaults to a single bundle with database and API level support for multiple bundles.

If you encounter a situation where you need to define your own revisable entity, you can use the order entity as a model. Notice that you must specify both the revision table and the revision key that links an order to its currently revision. Your controller class must add its own support for saving revisions, but you can depend on Drupal's default entity controller to properly load revision information into the object. In your controller class's save method, the revision should be saved prior to using the Field Attach API to add or update field data to the object to ensure it gets saved with the proper revision.

A full list of entities and their properties is included later in the chapter. You may also want to bookmark drupalcommerce.org/specification/entities as a reference during your development.

Various Commerce modules also take advantage of the field API to link data objects together, add data to entities that would benefit from user configurable display options, and embed Add to Cart forms on any entity in the site. These fields operate in much the same way that CCK fields did in Drupal 6 and will be listed below alongside the core entities. You may also want to bookmark drupalcommerce.org/specification/fields as a reference during your site building.

Forms API Improvements

There are a couple of improvements to the Forms API, both of which are covered in this section.

Dynamic Forms via the #ajax Property

One of the most visible new features of the Forms API that the Commerce modules leverage is the new #ajax property for form elements. With the #ajax property, it is possible without writing a single line of JavaScript to create forms whose elements automatically validate and update on changes and other user interactions.

In the Commerce modules, this functionality is utilized in a few places. On the order edit form, the line items table uses the #ajax property to allow you to add and update line items without a page refresh. The Customer module integrates with the Address Field module that uses it to provide name and address elements that automatically update to reflect the format and vocabulary of the selected country.

The following code shows just how easy it is to implement a dynamic form using #ajax. It is taken from the Payment module form element that updates the checkout form when a customer selects a payment method option. The full implementation is found in commerce_payment.checkout_pane.inc.

```
// Add a radio select widget to specify the payment method.
$pane_form['payment_method'] = array(
  '#type' => 'radios',
  '#options' => $options,
  '#ajax' => array(
    'callback' => 'commerce_payment_pane_checkout_form_details_refresh',
    'wrapper' => 'payment-details',
  ),
);
```

The `callback` function the element specifies simply has to return the portion of the form array that should be rendered into the area of the DOM targeted by the wrapper value which corresponds to an HTML ID. Forms using this functionality are tested without JavaScript enabled to ensure graceful degradation, relying on the ability of form submit handlers to request the form be rebuilt based on the button used to submit the form.

Automatic File Inclusion

Another innovation in the Forms API that the Commerce modules rely on heavily is the ability to specify in a form array the files Drupal should include when rebuilding the form. This allows modules to put forms in include files that can be automatically loaded when the form is processed on submission instead of depending solely on active menu item file handlers. All of the Commerce entity forms use this feature so they can be instantiated at URLs specific to the default UI module or by other contributed modules wherever necessary. The code to allow this is quite simple, as shown in this example from `commerce_product.forms.inc`:

```
function commerce_product_product_form($form, &$form_state, $product) {
  // Ensure this include file is loaded when the form is rebuilt from the cache.
  $form_state['build_info']['files']['form'] = drupal_get_path('module', 'commerce_product')
    . '/includes/commerce_product.forms.inc';
  …
}
```

Both of these new features in the Drupal 7 Forms API are very important for Drupal Commerce. The first enables the project to have dynamic forms that greatly improve the user experience for customers and administrators. For example, the checkout form can be configured to operate on a single page that will gracefully degrade for users on devices that do not support JavaScript. Second, the ability to define forms by Commerce modules that can be embedded anywhere perfectly supports the project's philosophy of a strict separation of the API from the UI.

Contributed Module Dependencies

As part of the strategy to start Drupal Commerce from scratch on Drupal 7, the project determined to make the best possible use of other major contributed modules to avoid duplicating code and effort. This involved introducing dependencies on the ubiquitous Views module, the Rules module, and their dependencies.

Views 3 powers almost the entire default user interface provided by the various Commerce UI modules. This means every listing page, the shopping cart block, and some table displays embedded on other forms are configurable via the Views UI. The Commerce modules rely heavily on Views 3's new pluggable area handler feature to create more powerful displays entirely through Views, like the shopping cart block and Payment tab on orders. Both of these displays use custom area handlers in their footers to add links and forms onto Views.

The dependency on Rules is just as important. The Entity API module, itself a Rules 2 dependency, makes it easy to expose custom entity and field data to Rules. The Commerce modules integrate with Rules to allow administrators to configure dynamic pricing, parts of the checkout form, and the order workflow via a single user interface. This latest version of Rules also makes it easy to embed parts of the UI at various locations, so the Commerce modules can place filtered configuration lists at appropriate places in the default UI.

Address Field, a dependency of the Customer module, is also maintained as a separate contributed module. This project defines a field that lets users enter name and address information via a dynamic set of form elements that update based on the country selected. It was started with the goal of implementing a subset of the xNAL standard for names and postal addresses and remains separate to allow it to mature independently of the core Commerce modules and to enable other projects and sites to use it.

Summary

The Drupal Commerce project is still maturing, and innovations in the core code and contributed module ecosystem are likely to change rapidly in ensuing releases. Be sure to follow along at the project's home page (`drupalcommerce.org`) and in the issue tracker (`drupal.org/project/issues/commerce`) to see how the systems outlined here mature and to find places where you can contribute documentation, testing, code, and more. You can also generally find assistance in the #drupalcommerce IRC channel on `irc.freenode.net` when dealing with issues or guidance when developing contributed modules that extend the functionality of Drupal Commerce.

CHAPTER 26

■■■

Drush

by Greg Anderson

Drush is the Drupal shell—a program that allows you to examine and modify your Drupal site by entering instructions from the command line. It's also a toolbox full of useful utilities and a scripting environment to help you quickly divide, conquer, and control your Drupal sites.

Drupal itself provides a sophisticated graphical interface that exposes a wide array of configuration options through the web browser. Being able to visually navigate through these settings is very useful, especially when first learning the features available in core, or some new modules that you just installed. However, once you are familiar with an operation, and you need to be able to do it over and over again, shell scripting provides a degree of reproducibility and efficiency that cannot be matched by GUI work. The more that you do with Drupal (and in particular, the more sites you build with Drupal), the more compelled you will be to script common operations so that you will have more time for more important things.

Many people do, in fact, utilize shell scripts to speed up their Drupal site configuration, management, and development; a quick Google search will show that some of them use Drush and some of them don't. Using Drush has a lot of very serious advantages over rolling your own scripts, one of the biggest being that Drush brings the power of the Drupal community to the shell. There are currently six Drush maintainers, and many contributors from the larger community have also collaborated to provide patches and features that make Drush both comprehensive and reliable. It is very likely that Drush already does many of the things that you would like it to—and more—already written and tested. Going beyond that, Drush also provides a sophisticated framework for bootstrapping the Drupal environment, which allows scripts to be written in PHP and utilize Drupal APIs directly. Drush has its own set of APIs and functions that provide abstractions for the different databases and different versions of Drupal, which means that your scripts are more likely to continue to work as the Drupal environment evolves.

Drush is also highly configurable; it allows you to provide named aliases for all of your Drupal sites, and you can control how Drush will interact with each site in very flexible ways. If these configuration files are shared among members of a development team, for example, by checking them in to a version-control system, then every team member's interaction with the sites they are working on can be standardized. In this way, Drush can help define and disseminate a team's development process.

In this chapter, I will go beyond the basics and give you a walk-through on how to get the most out of Drush. If you have been following along with the examples in this book, then you've probably already installed and used Drush at least a few times, but if you have not, visit the Drush project page at `http://drupal.org/project/drush`, download the latest stable release, and consult the `README.txt` file to get it installed and running. After that, you will be ready to go on my guided tour through Drush's capabilities. I will show you how to:

- Get up and running quickly with Drush by setting up some basic configuration options and defining an alias or two for the Drupal sites you're working on.

- Speed up your Drupal site maintenance at the command line with Drush shell enhancements.

- Apply code updates to Drupal core and your installed modules.

- Install Drush extensions to add even more power to Drush.

- Go more in-depth with Drush configuration to further streamline your environment.

- Deploy a site with Drush, and then safely copy back user-contributed content from the live site for further testing and development offline.

- Write shell scripts with Drush.

- Extend Drush by writing your own Drush commands.

Becoming proficient in all of these different aspects of Drush will turbo-charge the maintenance of your Drupal sites. Let's get started.

Getting Started with Drush

Drush works on Drupal version 5 through 7, and on MySQL, Postgres, and SQLite databases. It can work on multiple Drupal sites on the same system, or on Drupal sites on remote servers. It supports both the Drupal multisite configuration, where multiple sites share a common set of Drupal core files, and single-site configurations, where each site contains its own copy of Drupal core. Additionally, Drush can be extended with new commands that are packaged either with a Drupal module or theme, or bundled separately. In order to support all of these different configurations in all of the different ways that they may appear on a system, Drush provides a wide array of settings and configuration options to make things easier for you.

■ **Tip** If you would like to make a temporary Drupal site to test Drush commands on, you can quickly do so using the Drush site-install command. Just enter the following lines:

```
$ mkdir dgd7
$ cd dgd7
$ drush dl drupal --drupal-project-rename=web -y
Project drupal (7.0) downloaded to dgd7/web.
Project drupal contains:
 - 3 profiles: minimal, standard, testing
 - 4 themes: seven, bartik, garland, stark
 - 47 modules: node, trigger, system, statistics, simpletest, php, poll, contextual, shortcut,
field_ui, tracker, contact, path, profile, help, overlay, aggregator, toolbar, image, update,
locale, translation, menu, blog, file, comment, dashboard, syslog, user, book, filter, dblog,
taxonomy, search, block, rdf, forum, color, number, options, text, list, field_sql_storage,
field, openid, drupal_system_listing_incompatible_test, drupal_system_listing_compatible_test
$ cd web
$ cp sites/default/default.settings.php sites/default/settings.php
$ chmod -R o+w sites/default
```

```
$ drush site-install --db-url= pgsql://www-data:yoursqlpw@localhost/dgd7db --account-
name=admin --account-pass=secretsecret -y
```

To view your temporary Drupal site in a web browser, you would also need to make a virtual host configuration file for it; however, it's not necessary to do that just to run Drush commands on it.

Drupal Site Selection in Drush Commands

The first step in learning how to effectively configure Drush is to understand how Drush selects the Drupal site to operate on when you run a command. The drush status command provides a summary of Drush's current environment. If you run it after Drush has just been installed, you will see output that looks something like that in Listing 26–1.

Listing 26–1. Using core-status Command to Check Your Drush Environment

```
$ drush core-status
 PHP configuration        :  /etc/php5/cli/php.ini
 Drush version            :  4.1
 Drush configuration      :
 Drush alias files        :
```

This shows you that you have installed Drush version 4.1, and have not yet provided any Drush configuration files. The path to php.ini is also displayed as a convenience. You now know that Drush is installed and working, but you have no information about your Drupal site. Drush needs to be provided with the location of your site before it can do anything with it. There are a number of different ways that this can be done. Perhaps the most straightforward way is to change the current working directory to the sites folder for the Drupal site you are working on. This is the folder that contains the settings.php file (see Listing 26–2).

Listing 26–2. Running core-status from the Sites Directory at dgd7.org

```
$ cd dgd7/web/sites/default/
$ drush core-status
 Drupal version           :  7.0
 Site URI                 :  http://default
 Database driver          :  pgsql
 Database hostname        :  localhost
 Database username        :  www-data
 Database name            :  dgd7devdb
 Database                 :  Connected
 Drupal bootstrap         :  Successful
 Drupal user              :  Anonymous
 Default theme            :  bartik
 Administration theme     :  seven
 PHP configuration        :  /etc/php5/cli/php.ini
 Drush version            :  4.1
 Drush configuration      :
 Drush alias files        :
 Drupal root              :  /srv/www/dgd7/web
 Site path                :  sites/default
 File directory path      :  sites/default/files
```

Now the output of the status command shows additional information about your site. If you were to run other Drush commands from this directory, they would operate on the site indicated by drush status.

■ **Note** Every time Drush runs a command, it runs through a process called *bootstrapping* where the Drupal environment is initialized. I will examine the bootstrapping process later in this chapter, but for now it is sufficient to understand that drush status displays information that Drush gathers during the bootstrap, so it is therefore a good way to diagnose your Drush configuration and insure that everything is working correctly.

From here, it is possible to get Drush to operate on the site you just selected. For example, as Listing 26–3 shows, you could clear the Drupal caches with the cache-clear command.

Listing 26–3. Using the cache-clear Command on the Selected Drupal Site

```
$ drush cache-clear
Enter a number to choose which cache to clear.
[0] : Cancel
[1] : all
[2] : theme
[3] : menu
[4] : css+js
1
'all' cache was cleared
```

When you have Drush at your fingertips, it's no longer necessary to navigate through the web admin interface if you make a configuration change that requires a cache flush; you can fire it off quickly from the command line. drush cache-clear all works just like the previous example but does not display the interactive menu.

Drush can do much more than clear the Drupal cache, though; it comes with over fifty commands that covers such diverse topics as examining your Drupal configuration, copying files, manipulating the database, running cron, rebuilding the search cache, installing Drupal, updating Drupal modules and core files, running unit tests, adding and editing fields and users, and more. Drush can even be used to update itself! A complete list of commands is always available via the drush help command, which is shown in Figure 26–1. You will see that many of the commands have shortened forms, called *command aliases*; these appear in parenthesis after the command name in the help page. For clarity, the long form of Drush command names will always be used; however, you will probably find yourself quickly learning and using the shorter aliases as you become more comfortable with Drush.

Core drush commands

cache-clear (cc)	Clear a specific cache, or all drupal caches.
core-cli (cli)	Enter a new shell optimized for drush use.
core-cron (cron)	Run all cron hooks in all active modules for specified site.
core-rsync (rsync)	Rsync the Drupal tree to/from another server using ssh.
core-status (status,st)	Provides a birds-eye view of the current Drupal installation, if any.
core-topic (topic)	Read detailed documentation on a given topic.
drupal-directory (dd)	Return path to a given module/theme directory.
help	Print this help message. See `drush help help` for more options.
image-flush	Flush all derived images for a given style.
php-eval (eval, ev)	Evaluate arbitrary php code after bootstrapping Drupal (if available).
php-script (scr)	Run php script(s).
search-index	Index the remaining search items without wiping the index.
search-reindex	Force the search index to be rebuilt.
search-status	Show how many items remain to be indexed out of the total.
self-update (selfupdate)	Update drush to the latest version, if available.
site-alias (sa)	Print site alias records for all known site aliases and local sites.
site-install (si)	Install Drupal along with modules/themes/configuration using the specified install profile.
site-upgrade (sup)	Run a major version upgrade for Drupal (e.g. Drupal 6 to Drupal 7).
test-clean	Clean temporary tables and files.
test-run	Run tests. Note that you must use the --uri option.
updatedb (updb)	Apply any database updates required (as with running update.php).
variable-delete (vdel)	Delete a variable.
variable-get (vget)	Get a list of some or all site variables and values.
variable-set (vset)	Set a variable.
version	Show drush version.
watchdog-delete (wd-del, wd-delete)	Delete watchdog messages.
watchdog-list (wd-list)	Show available message types and severity levels. A prompt will ask for a choice to show watchdog messages.
watchdog-show (wd-show, ws)	Show watchdog messages.

Field commands

field-clone	Clone a field and all its instances.
field-create	Create fields and instances. Returns urls for field editing.
field-delete	Delete a field and its instances.
field-info	View information about fields, field_types, and widgets.
field-update	Return URL for field editing web page.

Project manager commands

pm-disable (dis)	Disable one or more extensions (modules or themes).
pm-download (dl)	Download projects from drupal.org or other sources.
pm-enable (en)	Enable one or more extensions (modules or themes).
pm-info (pmi)	Show detailed info for one or more extensions (modules or themes).
pm-list (pml)	Show a list of available extensions (modules and themes).
pm-refresh (rf)	Refresh update status information.
pm-releasenotes (rln)	Print release notes for given projects.
pm-releases (rl)	Print release information for given projects.
pm-uninstall	Uninstall one or more modules.
pm-update (up)	Update Drupal core and contrib projects and apply any pending database updates (same as pm-updatecode + updatedb).
pm-updatecode (upc)	Update Drupal core and contrib projects to latest recommended releases.

SQL commands

sql-cli (sqlc)	Open a SQL command-line interface using Drupal's credentials.
sql-connect	A string for connecting to the DB.
sql-drop	Drop all tables in a given database.
sql-dump	Exports the Drupal DB as SQL using mysqldump or equivalent.
sql-query (sqlq)	Execute a query against the site database.
sql-sync	Copy and import source database to target database. Transfers via rsync.

User commands

user-add-role (urol)	Add a role to the specified user accounts.
user-block (ublk)	Block the specified user(s).
user-cancel (ucan)	Cancel a user account with the specified name.
user-create (ucrt)	Create a user account with the specified name.
user-information (uinf)	Print information about the specified user(s).
user-login (uli)	Display a one time login link for the given user account (defaults to uid 1).
user-password (upwd)	(Re)Set the password for the user account with the specified name.
user-remove-role (urrol)	Remove a role from the specified user accounts.
user-unblock (uublk)	Unblock the specified user(s).

Figure 26–1. Drush command summary

Using the available Drush commands as building blocks, it is easy to create simple aliases and shell scripts to do common operations. In a scripting environment, though, it is desirable to be able to select the target Drupal site without changing the current working directory. Happily, Drush provides other ways for specifying the site. One way is to use the `--root` and `--uri` options to provide the location of the Drupal root, and the URI of the Drupal site in the `sites` folder that you wish to target, like so:

```
$ drush --root=/srv/www/dgd7.org/web --uri=dgd7.org core-status "Site URI"
  Site URI : dgd7.org
```

The URI used on the command line should be the same as when the site is being accessed from a web browser. It is also possible to use the name of the folder that contains the `settings.php` file for the URI (e.g. `--uri=default`). This works, and is, in fact, equivalent to Listing 26–2 in terms of the site URI that Drush will use when calling in to Drupal; you can confirm this by comparing the output of the "Site URI" line in Listing 26–2 with this output. Having a correct site URI is not always required, but some modules might need it if, for example, they are generating absolute URLs or making HTTP requests back to the same host; it's therefore advisable to set a correct URI whenever possible.

It's also possible to combine the information from the `--root` and `--uri` options into a single command line argument to Drush. In this form, the Drupal root and the site URI are concatenated together, separated by the '#' character, as shown:

```
$ drush /srv/www/dgd7.org/web#dgd7.org core-status "Site URI"
  Site URI : dgd7.org
```

This is a little more compact than the previous option, but it is still a bit lengthy to type. In the next section, I will discuss different ways to keep things brief by customizing the Drush configuration files to match your installation. There are two kinds of configuration files for Drush: Drush resource files (`drushrc.php`) that contain configuration options, and alias files (`aliases.drushrc.php`) that contain information about the various local and remote Drupal sites that you are working on. I will discuss both of these in the sections that follow.

Drush Alias Files (aliases.drushrc.php)

You can greatly increase the convenience of working with multiple Drupal sites by defining shorthand names for each site using Drush aliases. Aliases are not defined in `drushrc.php`; rather, they are stored in a separate file, named `aliases.drushrc.php`, that may be stored in the same locations as the standard `drushrc.php` configuration files. As you will see later, Drush also allows more flexibility in how aliases may be grouped and organized; you can place aliases that you share with team members in one alias file, and keep your personal and temporary aliases elsewhere. For now, you will consider only `aliases.drushrc.php`. There is an example alias file in the examples directory; let's start by copying it to your Drush configuration folder, like so:

```
$ cp examples/example.aliases.drushrc.php $HOME/.drush/aliases.drushrc.php
```

If you open up `example.aliases.drushrc.php` and take a look inside, you will see that it begins with the following introduction:

```
Aliases are commonly used to define short names for local or remote Drupal installations;
however, an alias is really nothing more than a collection of options. A canonical alias named
"dev" that points to a local Drupal site named "dev.mydrupalsite.com" looks like this:
  $aliases['dev'] = array(
    'root' => '/path/to/drupal',
    'uri' => 'dev.mydrupalsite.com',
  );
```

If you copy this definition into your aliases.drushrc.php file, and change the root item to point to the Drupal root and the uri item to your site's uri, then you will be able to use shorthand notation to select your development site. Rather than using --root and --uri, you can use your new alias, as shown in Listing 26–4.

Listing 26–4. Using a Site Alias to Specify a Site

```
$ drush @dev core-status
Drupal version            :  7.0
Site URI                  :  http://dgd7.org
Database driver           :  pgsql
Database hostname         :  localhost
Database username         :  www-data
Database name             :  dgd7devdb
Database                  :  Connected
Drupal bootstrap          :  Successful
Drupal user               :  Anonymous
Default theme             :  bartik
Administration theme      :  seven
PHP configuration         :  /etc/php5/cli/php.ini
Drush version             :  4.1
Drush configuration       :  /home/user/.drush/drushrc.php
Drush alias files         :  /home/user/.drush/aliases.drushrc.php
Drupal root               :  /srv/www/dgd7/install/dgd7/web
Site path                 :  sites/default
File directory path       :  sites/default/files
```

▨ **Note** The alias, @dev, comes *before* the command name. This differentiates it from the arguments to the command.

Once you have defined aliases for each of the Drupal sites that you're working on, you can more easily manipulate them individually merely by employing the appropriate symbolic name in front of the Drupal command. In the next section, you'll see how you can make site selection even easier with the Drush interactive shell.

Using the Drush Shell

Drush isn't called the Drupal Shell for nothing; it even comes with its own interactive shell, which can be entered via the command drush core-cli. The Drush interactive shell is actually just a *bash subprocess*; that just means that Drush runs another copy of bash whenever core-cli is used. When the core-cli command is entered, Drush will dynamically generate a bash configuration file that is optimized for use with Drush. Then, the bash shell is executed again, this time with Drush's custom configuration. To return to your regular shell, just type exit or CONTROL-D. The Drush shell is designed to reduce the amount of typing that you need to do when using Drush. One important way that it does this is by creating bash aliases for every Drush command, so it is not necessary to type drush before the command name. Combine this with a few custom commands exclusively optimized for this shell with the power of bash, and what you get is a very powerful environment for Drupal site maintenance from the shell. Let's examine some of the things that this shell can do.

For starters, when you enter core-cli, Drush will remember which site you selected and apply every subsequent command to that site. Consider the example in Table 26–1 of adding some modules to a couple of Drupal sites; in the left column are the commands you need to type when using core-cli with Drush's command aliases, and on the right are the equivalent command in longhand form, as entered from the bash shell.

Table 26–1. Adding a Few Modules to Some Drupal Sites

Drush core-cli	Bash

$ drush @site1 core-cli
@site1> dl og
@site1> en og
@site1> cd @site2
@site2> dl devel coder
@site2> en devel coder
@site2> cd %devel
@site2> use
$
	$ drush @site1 pm-download og
	$ drush @site1 pm-enable og
	$ cd \`drush drupal-directory @site2\`
	$ drush @site2 pm-download devel coder
	$ drush @site2 pm-enable devel coder
	$ cd \`drush drupal-directory @site2:%devel\`

The shorthand command aliases shown on the left are available when using Drush from an ordinary bash shell, but the convenience of cd and use really makes the Drush shell shine. The cd command will behave just like the built-in cd when moving between directories; use cd with a Drupal site alias, and you will select that site and change the working directory to the site's Drupal root. There are also a number of path aliases that Drush recognizes; if you use %modulename as the argument to cd, then you will change directories to the location where the module with the specified name has been installed. The Drush use command is similar to the cd command, but for two differences. First, it does not change your working directory; it only selects a new site to serve as the target for future Drush commands. Second, it also works on remote site aliases; if you select a remote site with use @remotealias, then every subsequent Drush command will operate on that remote site via ssh. This requires that a public/private ssh key pair be set up between the sites, as discussed in the upcoming section on deploying remote sites with Drush.

If you use core-cli frequently, you might want to convert your login shell into a Drush shell. To do this, run drush core-cli --pipe; this will dump the bash configuration file that Drush generates, and exit. If this configuration file is placed where bash reads configuration files from, then this will have the effect of permanently applying the capabilities of the core-cli command to the bash shell that you use every day. The location and names of the files that bash reads can vary from platform to platform; .bashrc and .profile in your $HOME directory are two locations that are commonly supported. If you are using a Debian-based Linux distribution such as Ubuntu, the file .bash_aliases (also in your $HOME directory) starts off empty, but will be read if it exists. This makes it a particularly good place to put your Drush configuration.

```
$ drush core-cli --pipe > $HOME/.bash_aliases
$ source $HOME/.bash_aliases
```

■ **Tip** The source command will read a bash configuration file and execute all of the configuration directives found inside, exactly the way it happens when you log in to your account. When reading bash scripts, you will find that the source command is used frequently, although it is often used in its shorthand form, "." (a single dot).

After you do this, your shell will not immediately appear to behave any differently than it did before; Drush tries to "stay out of the way" until it is needed. However, the power of Drush is now always at your fingertips. Type the command help. You will see the output of the drush help command rather than the usual bash help! You can still access bash help by typing builtin help. Next, try typing status. This time, you will see an error message; the regular Linux status command takes precedence over the Drush command in this case. If you enter use @alias, then Drush will change your prompt to @alias>, signaling that any subsequent Drush command will target the site indicated by that alias. Now if you enter the status command, you will see the output from Drush status. To go back to your regular bash prompt, enter use without an argument; you will see your prompt return to normal.

This facility, where Drush will select the Drush command when appropriate or call through to the standard command as needed, is called *contextual commands*. This is a very powerful capability; it allows Drush commands to be available in just a few keystrokes—without changing the default behavior of the shell that you are accustomed to. I have all of my bash shells configured like this; it really speeds things up.

Applying Code Updates with Drush

One of the good things about Drupal is that there are frequent bugfix and security releases that help to keep your site stable and secure. One of the bad things about frequent releases is that it can make maintenance a real time sink. Even with the advances in the update_status module, it still takes a lot of clicks in the online GUI to find the modules to be upgraded, optionally review their release notes, and apply the change. Drush makes it much easier. Before you get started, though, it is important to remember that code updates should always be made on a *copy* of your production site, and not on the live site itself. Upgrades take some time to process and test, and it's not desirable to leave the production site offline the whole time this process is going on. The most important reason for using a scratch site, though, is that upgrades do not always go as planned; sometimes, you might apply an upgrade to a module you are using, only to discover that some new bug or incompatibility has crept in. Sometimes, you simply might not like the way some new features work. If you always test your upgrades on a development site first, if anything does go wrong, it's very easy to just throw away the upgrade-in-progress and start over. I will cover how to copy sites in a later section; if you do not yet have a development copy of your site, you can always create an empty test site to use as you follow along.

Let's run through the steps of applying code updates to a development site. First of all, if you are to try out the update process on a scratch site that you just installed, it is important that you have something to update. Use the --select flag of pm-download and pick an old release of the logintoboggan module; you add in the --all flag so that Drush will not filter out "uninteresting" releases (see Listing 26–5).

Listing 26–5. Picking an Old Release of a Module to Install

```
$ drush @dev pm-download logintoboggan --select --all
Choose one of the available releases:
 [0]  :  Cancel
 [1]  :  7.x-1.x-dev     -  2011-Jan-06  -  Development
 [2]  :  7.x-1.0         -  2011-Jan-06  -  Supported, Recommended
 [3]  :  7.x-1.0-alpha3  -  2010-Aug-10  -
 [4]  :  7.x-1.0-alpha2  -  2009-Oct-25  -
 [5]  :  7.x-1.0-alpha1  -  2009-Oct-21  -
4
Project logintoboggan (7.x-1.0-alpha2) downloaded to
/srv/www/dgd7/web/sites/all/modules/logintoboggan.
$ drush @dev pm-enable logintoboggan
The following extensions will be enabled: logintoboggan
Do you really want to continue? (y/n): y
logintoboggan was enabled successfully.
```

Choose the "alpha2" release; now you know that if you run pm-updatecode, there will be something to update (see Listing 26–6).

Listing 26–6. Running pm-updatecode to Update the Modules on a Drupal Site

```
$ drush @dev pm-updatecode
Refreshing update status information ...
Done.
Update information last refreshed: Sat, 01/15/2011 - 19:57

Update status information on all installed and enabled Drupal projects:
Name            Installed version  Proposed version  Status
Drupal core     7.0                7.0               Up to date
LoginToboggan   7.x-1.0-alpha2     7.x-1.0           Update available


Code updates will be made to the following projects: LoginToboggan [logintoboggan-7.x-1.0]

Note: A backup of your project will be stored to backups directory if it is not managed by a
supported version control system.
Note: If you have made any modifications to any file that belongs to one of these projects,
you will have to migrate those modifications after updating.
Do you really want to continue with the update process? (y/n): y
Project logintoboggan was updated successfully. Installed version is now 7.x-1.0.
Backups were saved into the directory                          [ok]
/home/user/drush-backups/20110101170457/modules/logintoboggan.
'all' cache was cleared                                        [success]
You have pending database updates. Please run `drush updatedb` or  [warning]
visit update.php in your browser.
```

Note that pm-updatecode proposes that the 1.0-alpha2 release be updated to the 1.0 release, even though there is a newer development release available. It does so because the 1.0 release is marked as the recommended release. In general, pm-updatecode will always update to the recommended release; the only exceptions to this is if you explicitly give pm-updatecode the version of the project you would like to update to, or if the recommended release is older than the release that you currently have installed. If you would like to update from a stable release of a module to the development release, you can download it again using drush pm-download modulename --dev.

Returning to Listing 26–6, if you add the --notes option when running pm-updatecode, Drush will show you the release notes for any module that has an available update. You can also show the release notes directly, without running pm-updatecode, if desired, via the pm-releasenotes command, as shown in Listing 26–7.

Listing 26–7. Showing the Release Notes for a Drupal Module

```
$ drush @dev pm-releasenotes logintoboggan
--------------------------------------------------------------------------------
> RELEASE NOTES FOR 'LOGINTOBOGGAN' PROJECT, VERSION 7.x-1.0-alpha2:
> Last updated: December 24, 2010 - 23:18 .
> Installed
--------------------------------------------------------------------------------

Changes since DRUPAL-7--1-0-ALPHA1:
* arguments -> variables per change to hook_theme.
```

The actual output from the pm-releasenotes command will contain all of the release notes from the installed version through the recommended version, inclusive; Listing 26–7 shows truncated output from the point in time when logintoboggan-7.x-1.0-alpha2 was installed.

If you do not want to spend time upgrading and testing a site unless there are security updates, then the --security-only flag can be used. The code in Listing 26–8 will filter out the bugfix/feature releases and show only those projects that have security updates.

Listing 26–8. Running pm-updatecode to Update the Modules on a Drupal Site

```
$ drush @dev pm-updatecode --security-only
Refreshing update status information ...
Done.
Update information last refreshed: Sat, 01/15/2011 - 19:57

Update status information on all installed and enabled Drupal projects:
 Name            Installed version  Proposed version  Status
 Drupal core     7.0                7.0               Up to date
 LoginToboggan   7.x-1.0-alpha2     7.x-1.0           Update available

No security updates available.
```

In Listing 26–8, none of the releases of logintoboggan after 7.x-1.0-alpha2 through the current recommended release were marked as security updates, so Drush reports that there is nothing to update in this instance.

After you update your code, you must update the database (update.php). You can do this with Drush as well, as shown in Listing 26–9.

Listing 26–9. Running updatedb from Drush

```
$ drush @dev updatedb
The following updates are pending:

logintoboggan module :
  7000 -    Remove hardcoded numeric deltas from blocks.

Do you wish to run all pending updates? (y/n): y
Finished performing updates.
```

Since this is such a common operation, Drush provides a single command, pm-update, that will call pm-updatecode followed by updatedb.

Just as Drush makes it easy to update code, it also makes it easy to *not* update code. There are a number of reasons why you might not want to update some module on your site; a module will change in a way that you don't like, for example. You can prevent Drush from updating the module by using the --lock option shown in Listing 26–10.

Listing 26–10. Locking a Module via Drush

```
$ drush @dev pm-updatecode --lock=logintoboggan
Refreshing update status information ...
Done.
Locking logintoboggan
Update information last refreshed: Sat, 01/15/2011 - 19:57

Update status information on all installed and enabled Drupal projects:
 Name            Installed version  Proposed version  Status
```

```
Drupal core     7.0              7.0              Up to date
LoginToboggan   7.x-1.0-alpha2   7.x-1.0          Locked via drush. (Update available)
```

No code updates available.

The lock is persistent; you will not be able to update the locked module unless you unlock it with --unlock=module_name or --unlock=all.

RAM and CPU time on a live site are valuable. Why use the CPU that is handling your user requests to check for code updates? You can turn off update status on your live site and test for code updates via Drush. If your dev site has a copy of the code that is deployed on the live site, then use the following code:

```
$ drush @dev pm-updatecode --pipe
logintoboggan 7.x-1.0-alpha2 7.x-1.0 Update-available
```

The --pipe option is supported in many Drush commands. It causes Drush to convert the output from its usual human-readable form into something that is designed to be processed by a script. With pm-updatecode, it also causes Drush to print only the current status of the installed code. If there are no updates available, there will be no output. Call the previous command in cron, and if there are updates available, it would be pretty easy to have your script copy the site and perform an update on it—and maybe even run some unit tests. Scripting provides a lot of options; automating frequent tasks will quickly pay off.

■ **Note** The module update_advanced also allows you to select modules that you do not want to have updated. If you do this, Drush will also support this setting. Update_advanced is not yet available for Drupal 7, but it probably will be shortly.

Installing Drush Extensions

In addition to all of the commands I have already discussed, Drush also allows for extensions that define new commands for you to use. Some examples of projects that provide additional Drush commands include drush_extras, drush_make, drubuntu, and devel. It is also possible for regular Drupal modules to provide Drush commands; devel and features are two examples of modules that do. The capability for any Drupal module to also add Drush command files is a very powerful facility, because it allows module developers to provide command line interfaces to the functionality provided by the module. A large number of Drupal modules take advantage of this capability; there is a link to a list of modules that provide Drush integration on the Drush project page (http://drupal.org/project/drush).

Drush extensions by convention must place the Drush commands that they define in PHP source files called Drush command files. The file name of a Drush command file always ends in ".drush.inc". Drush will search for these files during the bootstrap process, and any command file that is found will be added to an internal list that is used to find and dispatch commands. Drush will look for command files in the following locations:

- The folder named commands inside of Drush's installation location (/path/to/drush/commands)

- Folders listed in the include option, which can be set either on the command line (--include=/path/to/my/drush/commands) or in a drushrc.php file ($options['include'] = /path/to/my/drush/commands).

- The system-wide Drush commands folder, e.g. `/usr/share/drush/commands`

- The .drush folder in the user's $HOME folder.

- All enabled modules in the current Drupal installation

The Drush `pm-download` command is smart enough to put Drush extensions into a location where they can be easily found for future use. For example, were you to `pm-download drush_extras`, Drush would place it in `$HOME/.drush/drush_extras`. This location is only suitable for projects that consist only of Drush commands. For projects that contain both Drupal modules and Drush command files, such as the devel module, it is necessary that Drush place these inside a Drupal site, usually in `sites/all/modules`. This must be done because the module can't work outside of a Drupal site, and the project can't be split up and installed in different locations. This limitation is important to understand, because it means that Drush commands that are bundled with modules will not be visible unless that module is enabled, and the site that it is installed in has been selected (bootstrapped) when Drush was executed. Listing 26–11 shows how to install the devel module on your @dev site to see it in action.

Listing 26–11. Downloading and Showing Help for the devel Module

```
$ drush @dev pm-download devel
Project devel (7.x-1.0) downloaded to /srv/www/dgd7/web/sites/all/modules/devel.
Project devel contains 4 modules: devel_generate, performance, devel_node_access, devel.
$ drush @dev pm-enable devel
The following extensions will be enabled: devel
Do you really want to continue? (y/n): y
devel was enabled successfully.
FirePHP has been checked out via svn to /srv/www/dgd7/web/sites/all/modules/devel/FirePHPCore.
$ drush @dev help --filter=devel
All commands in devel: (devel)
 devel-download          Downloads the FirePHP library from http://firephp.org/.
 devel-reinstall         Disable, Uninstall, and Install a list of projects.
 (dre)
 devel-token (token)     List available tokens
 fn-hook (fnh, hook)     List implementations of a given hook and explore source of
                         specified one.
 fn-view (fnv)           Show the source of specified function or method.
```

In Listing 26–11, you run `drush @dev help` to tell Drush to include command files from the @dev Drupal site in the help text. The `--filter=devel` flag instructs Drush to only show those commands that come from the command file named devel. If you left off the `--filter` flag, then the output of Drush help would be much longer; if you left off the @dev alias, though, the devel Drush commands would not appear anywhere in the output.

You may also notice that the devel module automatically downloads its dependency, FirePHP, when it is enabled. This is a bit of Drush magic that is easy to replicate; I explain how in the section on altering Drush command behavior.

Going In-Depth with Drush Configuration Options and Aliases

Now that you've seen a little of what Drush can do, let's return to the topic of configuration files. You have already seen how to configure site aliases in an `aliases.drushrc.php` file, but I skipped over the more basic Drush configuration file, `drushrc.php`. Drush will search for configuration files in multiple locations, the primary places being `$HOME/.drush/drushrc.php` for per-user configuration. Other options will be discussed shortly, but first, let's take a look at some simple configuration options. Inside the drush folder, there is a directory called examples that includes a number of sample files to help us get started on various activities. One of these is example.drushrc.php. Let's start out by copying this file to $HOME/.drush/drushrc.php, like so:

```
$ mkdir $HOME/.drush
$ cp examples/example.drushrc.php $HOME/.drush/drushrc.php
```

All of the configuration options in the default file are commented out at first, so you will need to edit your new configuration file before it will do anything for you. Here's how to specify your default site:

```
// Specify a particular multisite.
# $options['uri'] = 'http://d7dg.org';
// Specify your Drupal core base directory (useful if you use symlinks).
# $options['root'] = '/srv/www/d7dg.org/drupal';
```

Now, if you execute the drush core-status command, you will see that your sample site was selected, even without specifying --root or --uri on the command line. Note also that specifying these options in your configuration file will take precedence over the Drush feature that selects a particular Drupal site based on the current working directory. If there are multiple Drupal sites on the local machine, it is usually preferable to *not* specify the root and URI in your configuration file so that you can continue to use cd to select your Drupal site. This configuration option is a big time-saver on systems with more than a single Drupal instance on them, however.

Drush Contexts

Specifying options in a configuration file rather than on the command line is even more flexible than it first appears. As previously mentioned, Drush will search for configuration files in multiple locations, some of which may be loaded conditionally depending on the context that Drush is invoked. Each configuration file is loaded into a separate *context*; the Drush contexts are labeled by type and ordered by priority. Configuration options that are loaded into a higher-priority context will mask options of the same name that were loaded into a lower-priority context. Some of the more important contexts are as follows:

- **CLI**: The command line options that the user entered are loaded into the cli context.

- **Specific**: Command-specific options become active when the specified command is executed.

- **Site**: Holds options from a drushrc.php file loaded from the Drupal site directory (the directory where settings.php is found).

- **Drupal**: Holds options from a drush.php file loaded from the Drupal root directory (the directory where Drupal's index.php is found).

- **Alias**: Options that are defined in a site alias are copied into the alias context when the alias is referenced.

- **Home**: Holds options from a drush.php file loaded from the users $HOME/.drush directory

By defining options in these different contexts, it is possible to change Drush's behavior on a per-site or per-alias or per-command basis. The priority of the context are as shown previously, with the options context being one of the highest priority in the list; this insures that any option the user explicitly enters on the command line will override options in configuration files. Similarly, options defined in an alias will override options in a global configuration file, and options that are specific to a Drupal site will take precedence over alias options.

Command-Specific Options

In addition to the global options previously shown, Drush also allows command-specific options to be defined in a configuration file. Command-specific options give you a great deal of control over the way Drush behaves. For example, both the pm-download and pm-updatecode commands will show release notes if the --notes option is specified. If you would like pm-updatecode to always display release notes, but leave the behavior of pm-download unchanged, you can define a command-specific option for pm-updatecode like this:

```
$command_specific['pm-updatecode'] = array('notes' => TRUE);
```

It is also possible to put command-specific options into an alias record (see Listing 26–12). The syntax should not be surprising in the least.

Listing 26–12. *Command-Specific Option in an Alias Record*

```
$aliases['dev'] = array(
  'root' => '/srv/www/dgd7.org',
  'uri' => 'http://dev.dgd7.org',
  'command-specific' => array(
    'status' => array('show-passwords' => TRUE),
  ),
);
```

In Listing 26–12, the option --show-passwords will be set any time the command drush @dev core-status is executed. This might be useful if you wanted to be able to easily see your temporary passwords in the status display for your scratch sites, but do not want to display passwords for production systems.

Site Lists

In addition to simple single-site aliases, Drush also supports alias lists that represent a number of sites. There are two ways to create such a list. The first is to define the list explicitly, and name every alias that should appear in the list, like so:

```
$aliases['all-scratch'] = array(
  'site-list' => array('@dev', '@stage'),
);
```

When you have a site list like this, you may use it to execute Drush commands on multiple Drupal sites sequentially, like so:

```
$ drush @all-scratch core-status "Drupal Version"
You are about to execute 'core-status Drupal Version' on all of the following targets:
  @dev
  @stage
Continue? (y/n): y
@dev   >> Drupal version : 7.0-dev

@stage >> Drupal version : 7.0
```

The other way to make a site list is implicitly through a group alias file. A group alias file is just like a regular alias file, except that its filename begins with the name of the group. For example, to create a group of aliases to represent the live site, the staging site, and the development site for dgd7.org, you could create a file named `dgd7.aliases.drushrc.php` and populate it with aliases to your three sites. It might look something like the code in Listing 26–13.

Listing 26–13. *A Group Alias File dgd7.aliases.drushrc.php*

```php
$aliases['dev'] = array(
  'root' => '/srv/www/dgd7.org',
  'uri' => 'http://dev.dgd7.org',
);
$aliases['stage'] = array(
  'root' => '/srv/www/stage.dgd7.org,
  'uri' => 'http://stage.dgd7.org',
);
$aliases['live'] = array(
  'remote-host' => 'host.isp.com',
  'remote-user' => 'wwwadmin',
  'root' => '/srv/www/dgd7.org',
  'uri' => 'http://dgd7.org',
);
```

Drush will do a couple of special things for every group alias file that it encounters. First, it will make additional names for each of the defined aliases with the group name prepended, so the @dev alias could also be addressed as `@dgd7.dev`. (If multiple alias group files define aliases named @dev, then the simplified name will become ambiguous, and the longer name with the group name must be used.) Second, an implicit site list is named after the alias group; in Listing 26–13, that would be equivalent to the following alias definition:

```php
$aliases['dgd7'] = array(
  'site-list' => array('@dgd7.dev', '@dgd7.stage', '@dgd7.live'),
);
```

The definition for your @dgd7.live site in Listing 26–13 includes items called `remote-host` and `remote-user`. When these keys are set in an alias record, it indicates that the Drupal site in question resides on a remote machine. If you use one of these aliases as the target to a Drush command, you will find that Drush allows for the remote execution of commands using remote site aliases. In order for that to work, however, you must first do some preliminary configuration. This process is discussed in the next section.

Using Remote Commands to Deploy Sites with Drush

When you have an alias like @live that describes a Drupal site that resides on a remote server, it is possible to run remote commands on that site as easily as running a local command. Drush makes this possible by using ssh to invoke a remote instance of Drush. In this section, I will show how this facility can greatly ease the work involved in managing multiple Drupal sites running on multiple remote servers—or perhaps just make a single local copy of your only Drupal site for development and testing purposes.

Setting Up an SSH Key Pair

In order for remote Drush command execution to work, you first need to set up an ssh key pair allowing the local machine to connect to the remote machine. This isn't too hard to do if you know how, and it's even easier to do if you use Drush to do it. There is a command called pushkey that is available in the drush_extras module that will do all of the work for you. To use drush_extras, you must first download it. Drush_extras is not a Drupal module; it contains only Drush commands. When you download a project like this, Drush will automatically place it in a location where its commands can be found by Drush. Therefore, pushkey is available for use as soon as drush_extras is downloaded (see Listing 26–14).

Listing 26–14. Downloading drush_extras and Using pushkey to Set Up a Public/Private Key Pair

```
$ drush pm-download drush_extras
Project drush_extras (7.x-4.0) downloaded to                    [success]
/home/user/.drush/drush_extras.
$ drush pushkey @live
Enter passphrase (empty for no passphrase):
Enter same passphrase again:
Generating public/private rsa key pair.
Your identification has been saved in /home/user/.ssh/id_rsa.
Your public key has been saved in /home/user/.ssh/id_rsa.pub.
The key fingerprint is:
d1:72:ed:7c:05:c4:cb:75:75:dc:3b:c4:ba:95:0d:1e user@localhost
The key's randomart image is:
+--[ RSA 2048]----+
|           o+.=|
|        . . E+*|
|       o o .oo=*|
|        + o .+*.|
|       S   o + .|
|           o    |
|                |
|                |
|                |
+-----------------+
wwwadmin@host.isp.com's password:
$ drush @live core-status
 Drupal version             : 7.0
 Site URI                   : http://live.dgd7.org
 Database driver            : pgsql
 Database hostname          : localhost
 Database username          : www-data
 Database name              : dgd7livedb
 Database                   : Connected
 Drupal bootstrap           : Successful
 Drupal user                : Anonymous
 Default theme              : bartik
 Administration theme       : seven
 PHP configuration          : /etc/php5/cli/php.ini
 Drush version              : 4.0-dev
 Drush configuration        : /home/user/.drush/drushrc.php
 Drush alias files          : /home/user/.drush/live.aliases.drushrc.php
                              /home/user/.drush/dev.aliases.drushrc.php
```

```
Drupal root            :  /srv/www/dgd7-live/web
Site path              :  sites/default
File directory path    :  sites/default/files
```

In order for the core-status command to work, you must have Drush installed on the remote machine. Once Drush is installed remotely, you can quickly and easily run remote commands to affect your Drupal sites on other machines without having to explicitly log in. Drush will do an implicit remote login via ssh for every command; if your public key is password-protected (as is advisable), you may need to enter your password for the first command and after periods of inactivity, but beyond that, remote administration of multiple sites running on different servers is much more convenient using remote aliases. If there is some reason why you cannot install Drush on your remote servers, it is still possible to use the drush core-rsync and drush sql-sync commands described later without a remote copy of Drush. If you need to do that, skip ahead to the end of this section; for now, though, I will presume that you have Drush installed on both machines, and the remote core-status command shown in Listing 26–14 is working.

Making a Local Copy of a Remote Drupal Site

Once you have remote execution set up, the Drush core-rsync and sql-sync commands can be used to quickly copy a Drupal site from one location to another. The basic operation is the same regardless of whether one site is remote or both are local. If you would like to do a dry run once to see what Drush parameters Drush will pass to core-rsync for any particular set of sites, then you may run the command with the --simulate option first, as shown in Listing 26–15.

Listing 26–15. Copying all Drupal Files from a Remote Server to the Local System with drush rsync

```
$ drush core-rsync @live @dev --include-conf --simulate
Calling system(rsync -e 'ssh ' -az --exclude=".bzr" --exclude=".bzrignore" --
exclude=".bzrtags" --exclude=".svn" wwwadmin@host.isp.com:/srv/www/dgd7-live/web/
/srv/www/dgd7/web/);
$ drush core-rsync @live @dev --include-conf
You will destroy data from /srv/www/dgd7/web/ and replace with data from
wwwadmin@host.isp.com:/srv/www/dgd7-live/web/
Do you really want to continue? (y/n): y
```

The option --include-conf tells Drush to also copy the settings.php file. Settings files often have some variable sections between the live and dev sites, so Drush skips it by default when copying sites. Use --include-conf the first time you copy a site over, but leave it off thereafter, and Drush will not overwrite your settings.php file. Speaking of which, if you need to change your database settings for your development site, now is a good time to open up the copy of settings.php you just made and adjust it to suit. If both sites are running on the same machine, then you will, at a minimum, need to change the database name; when the Drupal sites are running on different machines, though, it is possible that they may be able to use the same settings.php file without any changes.

Once the files have been copied over, you can pull the database across. Note that you don't need to create the database in advance; you can tell Drush to do that for you (see Listing 26–16).

Listing 26–16. Copying the Drupal Database from a Remote Server with drush sql-sync

```
$ drush sql-sync @live @dev --create-db
WARNING:  Using temporary files to store and transfer sql-dump.  It is recommended that you
specify --source-dump and --target-dump options on the command line, or set '%dump' or '%dump-
dir' in the path-aliases section of your site alias records. This facilitates fast file
transfer via rsync.
```

You will destroy data from dgd7devdb and replace with data from host.isp.com/dgd7livedb.

You might want to make a backup first, using the sql-dump command.

Do you really want to continue? (y/n): **y**
DROP DATABASE
CREATE DATABASE

If the sql-sync command results in an error, "Access denied for user 'www-data'@'localhost'", then you can specify the username and password of a more privileged user with --db-su and --db-su-pw.

That's pretty much it; if you have configured your web server to serve content at the dev site, then you'll be able to pull it up in your web browser and view your local copy. There may be some need to fix up file permissions; for example, the files folder must be writable by the web server. You can enhance your experience by setting some options, though. For example, Drupal caches a lot of information in a site's SQL database. You can save time by excluding these tables from the sync operation, like so:

```
$ drush sql-sync @live @dev --structure-tables-key=common
```

The structure tables list is defined in your drushrc.php file. Here is the list of tables that appears in example.drushrc.php:

```
$options['structure-tables'] = array(
 'common' => array('cache', 'cache_filter', 'cache_menu', 'cache_page', 'history', 'sessions',
'watchdog'),
);
```

You may need to add some more tables to this list. A good place to start would be to consider the list of tables that contain "cache" in their name via drush sql-query 'show tables;' | grep cache. Remove from this list tables such as imagecache_action and so on, and add the remainder to your structure tables list.

After you do an sql-sync with skipped tables, you will need to clear the cache on the target site to make sure that things work right. drush cache-clear all will do the trick.

Drush will also help you fix up your sql database when syncing a site. The --sanitize option selects this operation (see Listing 26–17).

Listing 26–17. Sanitizing a Database Sync to a Scratch Site for Testing

```
$ drush sql-sync @dev @test --sanitize
```

You will destroy data from testdb and replace with data from devdb.

The following post-sync operations will be done on the destination:

  * Reset passwords and email addresses in user table

You might want to make a backup first, using the sql-dump command.

Do you really want to continue? (y/n):

It is possible to extend Drush with your own sanitization operations; you can find an example of how to do this in the file docs/drush.api.php. The default operations will replace all of the user passwords with a default password (like "password"). This makes it easy to log in as any user for testing and also means that sanitized copies of the database can't be used to perform dictionary attacks to get actual user passwords. The other thing the default sanitization operation does is set every user's e-mail address to a specified test address. This is useful both for privacy and for testing. For example, you can test e-mail notification code on a sanitized copy of your database without actually sending test e-mails to all of your users.

■ **Note** Drush makes it very easy to make copies of your site; however, if you have a lot of sites, you might want to look into Aegir, which includes the provision and hostmaster projects. To get started with Aegir, visit the Aegir community site at `http://community.aegirproject.org/`, where you will find instructions on how to install it either with the provided installation script or by using Drush.

Managing Dump Files

By default, `sql-sync` will dump the source SQL database into a temporary file that is deleted after being imported into the destination database. This is fine for syncing sites that are hosted on the same machine, but for syncing sites across the network, there are often benefits to using persistent dump files. Drush does an `sql-sync` in three steps. First, the source SQL database is exported from the source machine via `mysqldump` or `pg_dump`, as applicable. Next, the database dump is copied to the target machine using core-rsync. In the final stage, the target dump file is imported into the target SQL database. If your sql database is fairly large, and the changes are comparatively small, then the core-rsync operation that Drush uses to transfer the dump file will complete a lot faster if the target file is similar in content to the source. Drush has a number of facilities for managing dump files so that you can benefit from this intrinsic characteristic of core -rsync.

The simplest way to utilize dump files is to set `$options['dump-dir']` in your Drush configuration file. With this setting, Drush will generate the name of the dump file automatically, and store it in the directory specified by this option. While this is simple to set up, it is not very flexible, as the same location will be used for both the source and destination database dumps. This has the obvious implication that the same filesystem directory structure must exist on both machine; if this is not the case, then the dump file must be individually specified on a site-by-site basis.

There are two ways to specify the location of the dump files that allows individual control over where each dump file is stored. The most straightforward way is to use the `--source-dump` and `--target-dump` command line options. These should be set to the full path to the exact file that the database should be stored in. This is perfectly functional, but might be a little tedious to type out every time you need to synchronize your databases. To ease this burden, Drush also allows you to record your dump file paths in the site alias record for your source and target sites. This is done by setting a value in the `path-aliases` section of the alias record, like so:

```
$aliases['dev'] = array(
  'root' => '/srv/www/dgd7.org',
  'uri' => 'http://dev.dgd7.org',
  'path-aliases' => array(
    '%dump' => '/path/to/dumpfile.sql',
);
```

When this configuration is used, the `--source-dump` option will be set to the value of the `%dump` item when the alias is the source argument of the sync, and it will set the `--target-dump` option when it is used as the target argument.

When using dump files, it is also important to be aware of Drush's automatic caching behavior. The `sql-sync` command has a `--cache` option that specifies the maximum time, in hours, that a cached persistent dump file will stick around. If not specified, the cache setting defaults to twenty-four hours; if you try to sql-sync using the same database more frequently than this, then you will end up re-using the last dump file instead of getting a fresh dump. To override this behavior, set $options['cache'] = 0; in your configuration file to disable caching. You should in particular be careful to disable the cache whenever you change the settings for the structure-tables or skip-tables options, or you may be surprised by the results.

Using sql-sync Without Installing Drush on the Remote System

The previous code snippet shows that with just a couple of simple site aliases and a properly-configured ssh public / private key pair, Drush can easily copy databases from one system to another. Doing this manually takes quite a few steps, and requires knowledge of the database parameters for both the source and the target system. Using Drush saves you the trouble of having to look up these settings every time you need to migrate a database. All of this convenience is wonderful, but you might be left wondering just how it is that Drush knows what the database settings are for the remote machine.

You may recall that in the previous section, I mentioned that it is necessary to install Drush on the remote machine before running the sql-sync example. This is required because Drush will use the remote copy of Drush via an ssh call to request the database settings for the remote system if it cannot determine that they should be using information available locally. Drush uses the sql-conf command to look up the information. It is possible to watch Drush do this if you run the sql-sync command with the --debug flag, like so:

```
$ drush sql-sync @live @dev --debug
[ some debug information removed for brevity ]
Running: ssh -o PasswordAuthentication=no 'wwwadmin'@'remoteserver.com'        [command]
'drush  --all --uri='\''http://dev.dgd7.org'\'' --root='\''/srv/www/drupal'\''
sql-conf --backend' [0.05 sec, 3.7 MB]
```

From this, you can see that Drush is using ssh to call the Drush command sql-conf with the --all flag. Sql-conf is a hidden command that does not show up in drush help; however, you can still run this same command ourselves and see its output directly (see Listing 26–18).

Listing 26–18. Using sql-conf to Inspect Remote Database Credentials

```
$ drush @live sql-conf --all --show-passwords
Array
(
    [default] => Array
        (
            [default] => Array
                (
                    [driver] => pgsql
                    [username] => www-data
                    [password] => secretsecret
                    [port] =>
                    [host] => localhost
                    [database] => dgd7db
                )

        )

)
```

The --all flag instructs Drush to include information on all available databases rather than just the active database. --show-passwords overrides Drush's default privacy modes, which attempts to avoid printing sensitive information in the console output. The sql-conf command shows only information on the database connection; a similar command, site-alias, will show information about a site in the same format that is used in a Drush aliases.drushrc.php file (see Listing 26–19).

Listing 26–19. Using site-alias to Show a Site Alias with a Database Record for a Remote Drupal Site

```
$ drush site-alias @live --with-db --show-passwords
$aliases['live'] = array (
  'remote-host' => 'host.isp.com',
  'remote-user' => 'wwwadmin',
  'uri' => 'http://live.dgd7.org',
  'root' => '/srv/www/dgd7',
  'databases' =>
  array (
    'default' =>
    array (
      'default' =>
      array (
        'driver' => 'pgsql',
        'username' => 'www-data',
        'password' => 'secretsecret',
        'port' => '',
        'host' => 'localhost',
        'database' => 'dgd7db',
      ),
    ),
  ),
);
```

The output of this command is suitable to use directly in your `aliases.drushrc.php` files; just copy it into place. Once you do that, the `sql-sync` command will no longer need to make an extra remote call to fetch the database information. The disadvantage to storing the database information in the alias record, though, is that there is some potential that the information could become stale if the database information in the settings.php of the remote Drupal site is changed. Whether you prefer to use manually-cached database settings, or dynamically fetch them on every call to `sql-sync` is largely a matter of preference and requirements. Drush gives you the flexibility to choose the method that works best for you.

Using the Drush Site Context to Control sql-sync Options

You now know enough to construct a more advanced example. Imagine that you have a certain set of configuration options that you always want to apply to `sql-sync`. For example, perhaps you wish to insure that you never overwrite the users or user_roles tables when using `sql-sync` with your live site. As you have seen, it is possible to remove tables from an `sql-sync` operation via command-line options, and you also know that you can define command-specific options in a configuration file or an alias. Beyond this, Drush will also allow alias files to define command-specific options for `sql-sync` and `core-rsync` that are only applied when the alias is used as the source of an operation, and other options can be applied when the alias is used as the destination site (see Listing 26–20).

Listing 26–20. Specifying SQL Tables to Skip when an Alias Is the Target of an sql-sync Command

```
$aliases['live'] = array(
  'remote-host' => 'host.isp.com',
  'remote-user' => 'wwwadmin',
```

```
  'root' => '/srv/www/dgd7.org',
  'uri' => 'http://dgd7.org',
  'target-command-specific' = array(
    'sql-sync' => array('structure-tables' => 'users,user_roles'),
  ),
);
```

If this alias definition is used, then the command drush sql-sync @dev @live will include the option --target-structure-tables='users,user_roles', but no such option will be set when the sites are reversed (i.e. drush sql-sync @live @dev). If this alias record is shared by different users, then it would be more convenient to avoid overwriting the users and user_roles table when writing to the site @live, but a full copy of all tables would still be done when syncing from @live.

In the previous section, I showed that Drush will fetch the database records for the source and destination sites of an sql-sync command. It turns out that Drush will also pick up special configuration options for the sites at the same time. In order for this trick to work, two preconditions must be met. First, the alias record must *not* define the database record for the site. If the database record is defined, then Drush will not make a remote (or local) call to fetch it, and therefore there will be no opportunity to fetch configuration options either. The other requirement is that the configuration options to be shared must be defined in the site context for the alias record. As was previously explained, the site context is loaded from a drushrc.php file located in the same folder as the settings.php file for a Drupal site. Therefore, the same effect from Listing 26–20 can be achieved by defining the options in the sites folder of the @live site, like so:

```
$options['target-command-specific']['sql-sync'] => array('structure-tables' =>
'users,user_roles');
```

The effect here is the same; the users and user_roles tables will be skipped when @live is the target, but not when it is the source of a sql-sync operation. The difference is that these options do not need to be stored in the alias file; when they are defined in the site context, any change made to that one drushrc.php file will affect any target that selects that Drupal site.

■ **Caution** Do not confuse the purpose of pre-defined configuration options. Command-line options specified by the user will always take precedence over options defined in any configuration file or alias record. Default options, therefore, are nothing more than a convenience. They cannot be counted on to protect your data from careless mistakes.

Scripting with Drush

If you are at all familiar with Linux and the bash shell (or similar variants), you have probably encountered the venerable shell script. Listings 26–21 and 26–22 show other ways to write Hello World.

Listing 26–21. "Hello World" Script in bash

helloworld.sh:
```
#!/bin/bash
echo "Hello world!  This machine's name is:" `uname -n`
```

Listing 26–22. Running helloworld.sh

```
$ chmod +x helloworld.sh
$ helloworld.sh
Hello world!  This machine's name is: genkan
```

Well, it turns out that you can do the very same thing with Drush; see Listings 26–23 and 26–24.

Listing 26–23. "Hello World" Script in Drush

```
helloworld.drush:
#!/usr/bin/env drush
drush_print(dt("Hello world!  This site's name is: @name", array("@name" =>
variable_get('site_name', 'unknown'))));
```

Listing 26–24. Running helloworld.drush

```
$ chmod +x helloworld.drush
$ cd /srv/www/dgd7.org
$ /path/to/drush/examples/helloworld.drush
Hello world!  This site's name is: The Definitive Guide To Drupal 7
```

■ **Note** If it bothers you to see a php script without the "<?php" start-marker, you may include it, but it is not necessary. Neither is it necessary to make your Drush shell scripts end in .drush, nor do your bash scripts need to end in .sh, for that matter. Scripts may be named anything and located anywhere, provided that they are in your PATH. It is usually considered best practice to *not* put the filename extension on your scripts; that way, if you ever re-implement a command in another language, the name of the command does not need to change.

In the Drush examples folder, there is an example script called drush/examples/helloworld.script; it is more comprehensive than the helloworld.drush example shown in Listing 26–23.

When you run your Drush shell script, Drush will first bootstrap your site before running your code. This means that Drupal APIs such as variable_get are available, and they will operate on your site's database. It really is that easy—you just call the function and leave it up to Drush to prepare the Drupal site and insure that the code has been included. This makes Drush shell scripts a very quick and convenient way to save little snippets of PHP code that you may need to occasionally run on your sites. One way to get started with Drush scripts is to write scripts that run sequences of Drush commands. Of course, you can do this with a bash script, but Drush lets you do the same thing in PHP.

Processing Script Command Line Arguments and Options

Drush makes it easy to get the command line arguments and options that were passed to your script. As mentioned, there is a more comprehensive hello world example in drush/examples/helloworld.script; it includes such useful tidbits as how to iterate over the script command line arguments, like so:

```
while ($arg = drush_shift()) {
  drush_print(' ' . $arg);
}
```

```
// Fetch the value of the --target option; return "@self" if --target was unspecified
$target_value = drush_get_option('target', '@self');
```

Running External Commands

There are quite a few convenience functions that help you run shell and Drush commands from within your Drush scripts. The sections below describe some of the more important commands available for use; the http://api.drush.ws site contains a comprehensive API reference that contains even more information.

drush_shell_exec and drush_op_system

The commands drush_shell_exec and drush_op_system allow you to easily call a shell command from your Drush script. Of these two functions, drush_op_system is the easier one to call, but it is also much more limited; it always discards the output of the shell command and expects the caller to correctly escape any arguments passed to the command. If you need to record the output of the shell command, use drush_shell_exec instead. It will escape parameters for you, and returns the shell output. The following is an example call to drush_shell_exec:

```
drush_shell_exec("tar -tf %s", $tarpath);
$output = drush_shell_exec_output();
$project_dir = rtrim($output[0], DIRECTORY_SEPARATOR);
```

Be careful when switching between these two functions; drush_op_system returns 0 on success, whereas drush_shell_exec returns TRUE on success.

drush_invoke

The function drush_invoke will call a Drush command using the current bootstrapped state and the current command line options. Here's a simple script that will clear all of the Drupal caches and enable the devel and hacked modules. You might want to run this after sequence after syncing your live site to your dev site.

```
#!/bin/env drush
drush_invoke('cache-clear', 'all');
drush_invoke('pm-enable', 'devel', 'hacked');
```

drush_dispatch

The function drush_dispatch is very similar to drush_invoke, but it executes a command based upon a full command record. This is occasionally useful if you wish to participate in the command dispatching process for some reason; for example, the Drush command core-topic looks up the list of commands that are topic commands, allows the user to select one, and then executes it via drush_dispatch.

```
$commands = drush_get_commands();
$command_name = function_to_select_one_command($commands);
return drush_dispatch($commands[$command_name]);
```

drush_invoke_process and drush_invoke_sitealias

The functions drush_invoke_process and drush_invoke_sitealias are both very similar to drush_invoke; the main difference is that the process and sitealias APIs execute the desired commands in a new process with a new environment. In the case of drush_invoke_sitealias, a site alias record is also provided to target a different Drupal site; the target may be either local or remote. The most convenient way to get a site alias record is to look one up from the available Drush alias files using the function drush_sitealias_get_record.

```
// Run the core-status command on the site named @dev, and pass it "Drupal version"
// as its argument.  This is the same as: drush @dev core-status "Drupal version"
$site_record = drush_sitealias_get_record('@dev');
$result_record = drush_invoke_sitealias($site_record, 'core-status', "Drupal version");
drush_print($result_record['output']);
```

When drush_invoke_sitealias is called, it runs a new Drush command in a new process, bootstrapping the specified Drupal site and executing the specified command. This process works equally well regardless of whether the site alias represents a local or remote Drupal site. The command results appear in the output item of the returned object; this is explained in more detail later in the chapter.

drush_invoke_process_args and drush_invoke_sitealias_args

To pass command options on to the invoked commands, use one of the variant APIs, drush_invoke_process_args or drush_invoke_sitealias_args. These functions work just like their non-arg counterparts, except for the fact that the former allows the command line arguments and command line options to be passed in using array variables.

```
// Call sql-conf with --all to determine the configuration settings for
// all databases associated with the provided alias record.
$result_record = drush_invoke_sitealias_args($alias_record, "sql-conf", array(), array('all'
=> TRUE));
$database_records = $result_record['object'];
```

This example is the technique that sql-sync uses to look up the database configuration when the alias record does not include them inline. It passes no arguments, and the only option passed is --all to instruct sql-conf to return all databases, not just the primary one. If you would like to invoke another command on either the bootstrapped site (drush_invoke_process_args) or on some other site (drush_invoke_sitealias_args) using the same options the user passed in to the current command, you can use the function drush_redispatch_get_options, which will look them up for you.

Processing Invoke Process Results

As shown in the previous section, the functions drush_invoke_process, drush_invoke_sitealias, and the _args variants of these functions return an associative array that contains the results of the executed command. You may have noticed that one example took the results from output, and the other looked at a different item called object. These fields and the other contents of the invoke process results are explained here:

- **output:** This item contains the textual output of the command that was executed. This is the text that you would see if you ran the same Drush command from the shell.

- **object**: The object item is not provided for every Drush command. When it is available, it will contain the PHP object representation of the result of the command. This will usually be an associative array; for example, the `sql-conf` command returns an array that contains the database configuration information.

- **self**: The self object contains the alias record that was used to select the bootstrapped site when the command was executed. All of the options from the site context are merged into this record before it is returned; this is how the `sql-sync` command obtains the shared options from the site context of remote (or local) sites.

- **error_status**: This item returns the error status for the command. Zero means "no error."

- **log**: The log item contains an array of log messages from the command execution ordered chronologically. Each log entry is an associative array. A log entry contains following items:

  - **type**: The type of log entry, such as "notice" or "warning."

  - **message**: The log message.

  - **timestamp**: The time that the message was logged.

  - **memory**: Available memory at the time that the message was logged.

  - **error**: The error code associated with the log message (only for log entries whose type is "error").

More information about the meaning of type and error appears in the section on logging and error reporting.

- **error_log**: The error_log item contains another representation of entries from the log. Only log entries whose error item is set will appear in the error log. The error log is an associative array whose key is the error code, and whose value is an array of messages—one message for every log entry with the same error code.

- **context**: The context item contains a representation of all option values that affected the operation of the command, including both the command line options, options set in a drushrc.php configuration files, and options set from the alias record used with the command. This item is initialized with the result of the function `drush_get_merged_options`, which simply merges together all options from all Drush contexts.

Output and Logging

When writing scripts or commands for Drush, it is important to follow the established conventions for output and logging. Using the provided functions described in this section will insure that your Drush scripts will return the correct result code and that output will be available for inspection by other scripts as well as to the end user. Drush commands can be executed remotely and non-interactively; a well-behaved Drush command can be used as a building block by a larger script that will then be able to separate out the output from the error log and respond as warranted by the situation. This makes it easier to integrate Drush commands into other scripts that may wish to parse and act on the command's output. Conversely, ignoring the available Drush utility routines will make it harder for others to re-use your scripts.

Use drush_print and dt for Simple Output

Drush provides functions drush_print, drush_print_r, and dt that should be used in place of print, print_r, and t, respectively. Drush provides automatic character encoding conversion in the drush_print function, which is important for correct interoperability with systems that can't process UTF-8 output directly. See the output_charset option in examples/examples.drushrc.php for information on how to configure this feature.

Similarly, the dt function should be used to wrap all output before it is sent to drush_print or other output functions. This serves the same purpose as the Drupal function t: it allows user-visible text to be identified for translation. A Drush script can't simply use the existing Drupal t function, because t is only available when a Drupal site has been bootstrapped. Sometimes Drush will produce output before Drupal has been bootsrapped, and some Drush commands do not bootstrap a Drupal site at all. The pattern for the dt function is the same as for t, and should be familiar to you.

```
drush_print(dt("The command !command said !exclamation", array('!command' => $command,
'!exclamation' => $exclamation)));
```

Before using drush_print, you should first consider whether it might be more appropriate to use one of the available Drush logging functions, as is explained in the following sections.

Use drush_print_pipe to Output Data for Use by Shell Scripts

Drush provides a facility that allows scripts to produce an alternate representation of their output for easier processing by scripts. For example, the command pm-list will by default display information about the available Drush extensions in a human-readable table. When called with the --pipe flag, pm-list will instead output just the name of the extensions and nothing else.

To achieve this result, a Drush script need only call drush_print_pipe with the output to include in the alternate representation. There is no need to check for pipe mode; the pipe output is only displayed when requested. The ordinary output of the script is also suppressed, so a script may simply produce both kinds of output and leave it up to Drush to determine what to do with it.

Formatting Tabular Results with drush_print_table

The function drush_print_table will take a representation of tabular information with text in every cell and format it so that the column widths of the output are balanced and the text in each cell is wrapped to fit within the established boundaries. It is actually a wrapper around the Pear Consol Table library by Richard Heyes and Jan Schneider; it is available in source form from its primary source, http://pear.php.net/package/Console_Table. The Console Table code is not actually distributed with Drush; rather, Drush will download and install it if possible the first time Drush runs.

To use this function, simply build an array of table rows, each of which is itself an array of table cells. Each cell should contain a string (see Listing 26–25).

Listing 26–25. *Building an Array of Arrays for drush_print_table*

```
$header = array(dt('Id'), dt('Date'), dt('Severity'), dt('Type'), dt('Message'));
while ($result = drush_db_fetch_object($rsc)) {
  $row = core_watchdog_format_result($result);
  $table[] = array($row->wid, $row->date, $row->severity, $row->type, $row->message);
}
if ($tail) {
  $table = array_reverse($table);
}
array_unshift($table, $header);
drush_print_table($table, TRUE);
```

The code in Listing 26–25 is a simplified version of the Drush command `watchdog-show` that prints out entries from the Drupal watchdog table to the console. This command has a tail mode that continuously prints the results from the log as they are added; when doing this, the results are reversed so that the newer entries are on the bottom. The header is added on at the end; the parameter TRUE indicates that the first row of the table contains the header. For example, let's watch the `watchdog-show` command in action. If the output of watchdog-show is

```
$ drush watchdog-show
Id  Date           Severity  Type    Message
61  15/Jan 09:01  notice    user    Session opened for admin.
60  15/Jan 08:47  notice    cron    Cron run completed.
```

then the watchdog-show function will build an array of arrays that looks like

```
array(
  array ( 'Id', 'Date', 'Severity', 'Type', 'Message',   ),
  array ( '61', '15/Jan 09:01', 'notice', 'user', 'Session opened for admin.', ),
  array ( '60', '15/Jan 08:47', 'notice', 'cron', 'Cron run completed.',   ),
);
```

If you do not need to manipulate the contents of the table before display, then it is, of course, possible to just put the header row directly into the table and append the data after it. There is also a third optional parameter to `drush_print_table`, not shown here, that allows you to specify the exact width to use for some or all of the columns. If you want to build a simple table with a column of labels and a column of values, just like `drush core-status` does, then you can use the convenience function `drush_key_value_to_array_table` to do the conversion, like so:

```
$status_table['Drush version'] = DRUSH_VERSION;
$status_table['Drush configuration'] = implode(' ', $configuration_list);
drush_print_table(drush_key_value_to_array_table($status_table));
```

The actual implementation of drush `core-status` is slightly different (and more extensive) than this, of course, but this is the general idea. As you can see, these functions will allow you to very quickly write code that produces formatted tabular output.

Rendering HTML Output for Textual Display with drush_html_to_text

Drupal contains a function `drupal_html_to_text` that is very useful in a command line scripts. As previously mentioned, though, Drush commands are not always running in an environment that has a bootstrapped Drupal site available; therefore, Drush provides the `drush_html_to_text` function that serves as a simpler replacement for this function.

This function is not intended to be a replacement for a textual web browser, but it is often useful for displaying information on HTML pages that are known to have a simple enough structure to be compatible and appropriate for textual output. For example, the Drush command `pm-releasenotes` uses `drush_html_to_text` to convert the requested release notes HTML page into a format that can be displayed in the terminal. If you need to parse HTML in a Drush command that always bootstraps a Drupal site, though, you might as well use the `drupal_html_to_text` function and utilize its enhanced capacity to convert HTML into plain text.

Prompting the User

Drush also has helper functions to process user input in different ways. Using the provided wrappers where possible will help keep the behavior of scripts consistent. The three functions available are as follows:

- **drush_confirm** will prompt the user for a yes/no response.

- **drush_prompt** will prompt the user to enter a string. The caller can also provide a default value that the user can select by typing ENTER without providing any input.

- **drush_choice** will present the user with a number of options that can be selected by numeric label. The available selections are passed to drush_choice in an associative array, where the keys are the identifiers that are returned if the user selects that item, and the values are the human-readable strings that are displayed to the user. The display of drush_choice is formatted via drush_print_table; if the caller provides a data table where the values are arrays of strings, then these arrays will be included in each row array, so the values of the array will be formatted into aligned columns. Drush uses this facility internally in the pm-download command when the --select option is used, so the version numbers and release dates of the available releases are aligned.

Here is an example of drush_choice use from the Drush pm-download command. The associative array $releases is pre-populated with items keyed by version; each release item contains a date string and a release_status array. Drush loops over this structure and builds an associative array of options that it passes to drush_choice.

```
foreach($releases as $version => $release) {
  $options[$version] = array($version, '-', gmdate('Y-M-d', $release['date']), '-', implode(',
', $release['release_status']));
}
$choice = drush_choice($options, dt('Choose one of the available releases:'));
```

This will display each line from drush_choice in columns, with the version in the first column, the date of the release in the second column, and the release status values, which include terms such as "Supported" and "Recommended," in the last. You will also notice two extra columns containing only "-" characters are also included to provide some separation between the columns. You have already seen what the output from this function looks like; it was shown in Listing 26–5 in the section "Applying Code Updates with Drush."

The user can instruct Drush to autoconfirm all prompts with either an affirmative or negative response by using the --yes and --no options, respectively. When Drush runs another chained command either on the local machine or on a remote machine, it automatically sets the --yes option to prevent the command running in the background from getting hung up on user input. When in autoconfirm mode, drush_prompt will also always return the default value without waiting for the user.

If a user cancels out of a command, either by responding "no" to drush_confirm, or selecting the first option from drush_choice, which is always "cancel," the best thing to do is to exit the current function via return drush_user_abort();. This will insure that Drush will exit from the function cleanly. See the section on Drush Command Hooks for more information.

Logging and Error Reporting

Drush has specific rules on how errors should be reported and how log functions should be used. Understanding when to use drush_print, and when to instead to use drush_log or drush_set_error is key to producing scripts that are convenient and behave appropriately when used in different contexts. This section describes what you need to know to do this correctly.

Use drush_log to Display Significant Events

It is better to use `drush_log` in place of `drush_print` when the message indicates that something noteworthy has happened during execution, or, alternatively, when auxiliary information is being provided. Drush provides two additional levels of output control, `--verbose` and `--debug`. Some log messages are only displayed in these modes, whereas others are by default always displayed. However, Drush also provides facilities for other scripts to call Drush commands and retrieve the results, and `drush_log` is useful in these contexts as it provides the type of message as well as the message text to the caller, which can be helpful to the caller in determining how to format and display the results. The default `drush_log` output will also format the results, putting the message type description on the right-hand side of the first line of the message, appropriately colored to match the status level of the message. This makes it really easy to notice errors that may slip into the output of your command as they will be rendered in red text so as to stand out from the rest of the information displayed. Finally, Drush will also send the output of all log messages to the standard error stream rather than to standard out, which helps give the caller control over separation of log and ordinary output. As you can see, there are many reasons why the Drush logging functions increase the user's control over and comprehension of output messages. Moreover, a call to `drush_log` looks very much like a call to `drush_print`:

```
drush_log(dt('!extension was enabled successfully.', array('!extension' => $extension->name)),
'ok');
```

The different log levels supported are as follows:

- **'ok'** or **'success'**: These log levels indicate that some operation completed successfully. Drush is a little bit inconsistent in its use of 'ok' vs. 'success', but a good guideline to use would be to use 'ok' when a sub-operation works and execution is (or may be) continuing, and to use 'success' for the final message once a command or script has concluded execution satisfactorily. One example of an 'ok' log message is in the `pm-enable` function, shown previously, where `drush_log` 'ok' is used to inform the user that one of the modules specified is already enabled.

- **'warning'**: This log level indicates that a situation that the user must be aware of has come up, but execution of the current script or command can still continue. For example, the command pm-updatecode will use `drush_log` 'warning' to notify the user that one of the modules that was updated required database updates and updatedb must be run at some point.

- **'notice'**: The notice log level informs the user of progress or situations that might be interesting, but that do not warrant any specific action or response. Notices are not displayed unless the `--verbose` flag was specified. One example of a Drush command that uses a notice is `pm-releasenotes`, which notifies the user after the HTTP request to fetch the release notes text completes.

- **'debug'**: These debug log level includes additional information that the user might need if investigating the root cause of some failure. These messages are not displayed unless the `--debug` option was specified. One example of a debug log message can be found in the `php-script` command, which displays the list of filesystem paths it uses when searching for the script to run.

- **'error'**: An error log is used to indicate that some condition prevented the command from doing what it was intended to do. Usually, this log level should not be used as it is better to instead call the `drush_set_error` function, which is described below. Drush uses `drush_log` 'error' internally to report that a Drush command or script returned an error condition and can't continue.

Using the drush_log function can make your scripts much more transparent and friendly to the user, but take care to not log gratuitously. If a log message of any type does not provide any additional information to the user, leave it out. Sometimes just the progress information that a log message provides is enough to make it useful; it often comes down to a judgment call as there is not always one right answer to fit all situations. The best way to fine-tune logging is to analyze the output of your script at different log levels and under differing conditions (e.g. success and failure), and adjust the log messages to optimize the amount of useful information that is displayed, so that the user can determine what happened, and what else might need to be done without needing to page through a lot of text that is not relevant to the situation.

Use drush_set_error to When Unrecoverable Errors Occur

The function drush_set_error should be called whenever something completely unrecoverable happens. It is a convention that any time a Drush command calls drush_set_error, it should also return FALSE as its function result. To make this easier, Drush has also established the convention that the return result of drush_set_error is always FALSE, so a function can be concisely aborted, as shown:

```
return drush_set_error('DRUSH_CRON_FAILED', dt('Cron run failed.'));
```

The first parameter to drush_set_error is a string constant that another script may test for when examining the cause for a particular failure condition. To see a list of all of the defined Drush error codes, run the command drush topic docs-errorcodes. This will display a list of error codes with their corresponding error message; the list is sorted by error code. The second parameter, the error message, is optional. If missing, Drush will attempt to look up the error message by concatenating "error:" with the Drush error code (e.g. "error:DRUSH_CRON_FAILED"). The Drush command help hook is used to do the lookup; this hook is described later.

Writing Drush Extensions

Drush shell scripts are a fine way to get started, and they are a particularly appropriate way to build tools that are tailored expressly for use on one particular Drupal site. If you want to write a general-purpose tool that is intended to work on any Drupal site, it's preferable to write a Drush command. The good news is that all of the techniques described in the previous section are also usable and relevant to Drush commands, so if you develop a useful Drush script that you would like to make more general and turn into a Drush command, it's possible to do so simply by naming the file appropriately and implementing the required Drush command hook files. This section will explain how to do all of that.

Drush includes a sample command file, drush/examples/sandwich.drush.inc that shows how commands are defined. The key difference between Drush commands and Drush scripts is that Drush commands contain a command hook that returns an array of items that describe the command, including its arguments, options, and help text. Additionally, Drush commands are managed by Drush; they are stored in a PHP file called a Drush command file, and they must appear somewhere that Drush will search for them.

Drush command files must be named following a particular pattern. The filename begins with the name of the command file, and ends with .drush.inc. The name of the command file is extremely important, as it is used to compose the function names that Drush will call at various points to give the command file an opportunity to define commands and other Drush hooks. In this way, Drush is very similar to Drupal. This section will describe the different responsibilities of a Drush command file that you will need in order to create your own Drush commands.

The Drush Command Hook

The primary entry point for a Drush command file is hook_drush_command. So, if the command file's name is sandwich, then it must have a function called sandwich_drush_command that declares all of the commands it provides. The drush_command hook is very similar to the menu hook in Drupal; it is expected to return an associative array of items that describe its commands. The drush_command hook for the example sandwich command file is in Listing 26–26; it defines a single command called "make-me-a-sandwich".

Listing 26–26. Implementation of hook_drush_command for the Sandwich Command File

```
/**
 * Implementation of hook_drush_command().
 *
 * In this hook, you specify which commands your
 * drush module makes available, what it does, and
 * description.
 *
 * Notice how this structure closely resembles how
 * you define menu hooks.
 *
 * @See drush_parse_command() for a list of recognized keys.
 *
 * @return
 *   An associative array describing your command(s).
 */
function sandwich_drush_command() {
  $items = array();

  $items['make-me-a-sandwich'] = array(
    'description' => "Makes a delicious sandwich.",
    'arguments' => array(
      'filling' => 'The type of the sandwich (turkey, cheese, etc.)',
    ),
    'options' => array(
      '--spreads' => 'Comma delimited list of spreads (e.g. mayonnaise, mustard)',
    ),
    'examples' => array(
      'drush mmas turkey --spreads=ketchup,mustard' => 'Make a terrible-tasting sandwich that
is lacking in pickles.',
    ),
    'aliases' => array('mmas'),
    'bootstrap' => DRUSH_BOOTSTRAP_DRUSH, // No bootstrap at all.
  );
  return $items;
}
```

The items description, arguments, options, and examples are used only to display the help text for the command and have no affect on actual operation. However, it is important to always include these items so that new users can discover how to use your command. Also, it is possible that a future version of Drush may parse the options item and reject command line options that are not defined in the command or global options list, so be sure to be complete in your command definitions. Commands that take no arguments or options may omit these items from their definition, though.

The aliases item provides alternate, shorter forms for the command name. The example command in Listing 26–26 can be executed either via drush make-me-a-sandwich, or via drush mmas. Multiple aliases can be included by placing multiple items in the array.

The bootstrap item regulates how this Drush command will interact with the specified Drupal site, if one is available. DRUSH_BOOTSTRAP_DRUSH means that Drush should initialize itself and go no further. In this mode, the Drush command can't call any code from Drupal, because the Drupal site will not be bootstrapped, and no Drupal code will be loaded. Conversely, DRUSH_BOOTSTRAP_DRUPAL_LOGIN means that Drush should fully bootstrap the selected Drupal site and log in the default user. DRUSH_BOOTSTRAP_DRUPAL_LOGIN is the default bootstrap level for commands that do not explicitly specify a desired bootstrap level. There are other bootstrap options as well; for example, it is possible to bootstrap to the Drupal root but not select any specific site. Any of these bootstrap levels that attempt to initialize Drupal will abort with an error if the initialization fails. The special exception is DRUSH_BOOTSTRAP_MAX, which will attempt to bootstrap the current site to the farthest level possible, but will stop bootstrapping and continue execution of the Drush command if any problem is encountered. This allows Drush commands to run quickly without a Drupal site or provide additional information or functionality when a Drupal site is present. For example, the pm-releases command will tell you which version of a module is installed if a Drupal site is selected, or it will show the available releases without this information if not.

There are other items in a command record besides the ones shown here; they are explained later. Additionally, the command drush docs-commands contains a table that lists all of the available items with a summary of its function.

Providing the Command Implementation Function

By default, Drush will compose the name of the function to call from its command name and the name of the command file. The default command implementation is composed by concatenating drush, the name of the command file, and the full name of the command. Each item is separated by an underscore ("_"); any dashes in the command name are also replaced with underscores. Since it is common for Drush commands to be prefixed with the name of the command file that they appear in, the default implementation name is simplified by replacing adjacent occurrences of the command file name with a single instance. For example, the Drush command record for the command sql-sync is defined in the command file named sql (the full filename is sql.drush.inc). The default implementation function name is composed by concatenating "drush", "sql", and "sql-sync" to form drush_sql_sql_sync, which is then simplified to drush_sql_sync. Drush will call the specified function, converting all command line arguments into function parameters. Ergo, the function that implements sql-sync will look something like this:

```
Functoin drush_sql_sync($source = NULL, $destination = NULL) {
  $source_settings = drush_sitealias_get_record($source);
  $destination_settings = drush_sitealias_get_record($destination);
  // Implementation of sql-sync continues…
}
```

As you can see, when it comes right down to it, Drush commands are just regular PHP functions. This makes it pretty easy to convert a Drush script into a Drush command; just wrap a function definition around the code and define the Drush command hook. Drush provides a lot more control than this, but that's the basics of it. I'll continue to explore more of the capabilities of Drush commands in the remainder of this section.

Return an Array to Pass Structured Data to Other Drush Scripts

In some instances, a Drush command or script may use a complex data structure such as an associative array to render its output. These data structures are not always easy to represent in a form that would be useful to output with drush_print_pipe, or, even if they were, it would take a lot of effort for a PHP script that is calling a Drush command to parse the textual output and reconstruct the original data structure. Drush makes it easy to pass these structures unaltered to the caller. If the primary hook function for a command returns a result, then the object returned will be placed in the 'object' item of the result structure returned by drush_backend_invoke. Drush makes use of this facility internally in a couple of places; for example, the Drush function sql-conf returns the associative array with the database connection information; as previously mentioned, the sql-sync command uses this mechanism to fetch the database information for remote Drupal sites.

Manually Specify the Command Function with a Callback Item

It is also possible to provide a callback item in the command structure; the callback will be used in place of the default implementation if it appears. It is recommended that you use the default implementation function name whenever possible, and only provide your own callback function name when the command can be implemented by an existing function. For example, the various Drush topic functions are for the most part implemented by using drush_print_file to display an existing file to the user. The command record for the topic command docs-readme can be found in Listing 26–27.

Listing 26–27. Using a Callback Item to Implement a Drush Command with an Existing Function

```
$items['docs-readme'] = array(
  'description' => dt('README.txt'),
  'hidden' => TRUE,
  'topic' => TRUE,
  'bootstrap' => DRUSH_BOOTSTRAP_DRUSH,
  'callback' => 'drush_print_file',
  'callback arguments' => array(DRUSH_BASE_PATH . '/README.txt'),
);
```

The items hidden and topic are particular to Drush topic commands. Hidden means that the command will not show up in the Drush help listing, although it is available for execution, either via the command line, or programmatically via drush_dispatch. The topic item will cause the command to show up in the topic list when the user runs the drush topic command.

The item callback was previously mentioned; it instructs Drush to call the function drush_print_file instead of the function name that would normally be used, which is to say drush_docs_readme. The item callback arguments will be added onto the front of whichever arguments the user specified on the command line. Since the function drush_print_file takes but a single argument, this means that the command docs-readme will always result in a call to drush_print_file (DRUSH_BASE_PATH . '/README.txt'), which will display the README.txt file.

Placing the Command Implementation in a Separate File

If the implementation for a Drush command is particularly large, it can be placed in a separate file. Before drush_invoke calls a command hook, it will first check to see if there is a separate .inc file for the command. The filename is composed by splitting the command name on the dashes in the name, reversing them, and adding ".inc" onto the end. For example, the command sql-sync is implemented in a file named sync.sql.inc.

The Drush Help Hook

The Drush help hook is optional and does not need to be implemented. It is a place where longer command descriptions may be placed, if desired. If the shorter description in the description item of the command record is adequate, though, then there is no need to provide the longer form. When implemented, the Drush help hook looks the code in Listing 26–28.

Listing 26–28. The Drush Help Hook

```
function sandwich_drush_help($section) {
  switch ($section) {
    case 'drush:make-me-a-sandwich':
      return dt("This command will make you a delicious sandwich, just how you like it.");
    case 'meta:sandwich:title':
      return dt("Sandwich commands");
    case 'meta:sandwich:summary':
      return dt("Automates your sandwich-making business workflows.");  }
}
```

In addition to providing longer command descriptions, the help hook can also specify metadata values that are used to format the output of Drush help. The available metadata items are meta:COMMANDFILE:title and meta:COMMANDFILE:summary. These items are used to describe all of the commands defined in the command file as a group. One place where you will see them is when you run drush help --filter, which allows the user to display the help for just one section of commands (see Listing 26–29).

Listing 26–29. Show Help Just for the Sandwich Command File

```
$ drush help --filter --include=examples
Select a help category:
 [0]  :  Cancel
 [1]  :  Core drush commands
 [2]  :  Field commands: Manipulate Drupal 7+ fields.
 [3]  :  Project manager commands: Download, enable, examine, and update your modules and
themes.
 [4]  :  SQL commands: Examine and modify your Drupal database.
 [5]  :  Sandwich commands: Automates your sandwich-making business workflows.
 [6]  :  User commands: Add, modify, and delete users.
5
Sandwich commands: (sandwich)
 make-me-a-sandwich  Makes a delicious sandwich.
 (mmas)
$ drush help make-me-a-sandwich --include=examples
This command will make you a delicious sandwich, just how you like it.

Examples:
 drush mmas turkey                  Make a terrible-tasting sandwich that is lacking in pickles.
 --spreads=ketchup,mustard

Arguments:
 filling                            The type of the sandwich (turkey, cheese, etc.)

Options:
 --spreads                          Comma-delimited list of spreads (e.g. mayonnaise, mustard)

Aliases: mmas
```

The Drush help hook also has a secondary purpose that was mentioned previously. The function drush_set_error will use the Drush help hook to look up error messages if a message string was not provided as the second argument of the call. These help messages begin with "error:" rather than "drush:" but otherwise they work the same.

Altering Drush Command Behavior

When Drush executes a command, it actually goes through a series of stages before its main implementation function is executed and continues with one more stage after the command is finished. If there is an error anywhere along the way, Drush also provides a rollback hook which some commands use to put things back the way they were if something goes wrong. Table 26–2 summarizes how the hooks work.

Table 26–2. Descriptions of Rollback Hooks

Hook Name	Function Name	Description
Init	drush_HOOK_init	The init function is called before any other stage begins. The init stage is allowed to load additional command files, if desired, usually via a call to drush_bootstrap_max. The utility for doing this is discussed in the section on altering other commands.
Validate	drush_COMMANDFILE_HOOK_validate	The validate function is called to confirm that a command can run. It may do initialization, but should not alter the state of any persistent object.
Pre-command	drush_COMMANDFILE_pre_HOOK	Called before the main command hook.
Command	drush_COMMANDFILE_HOOK	The main command hook that should provide the main implementation for the command.
Post-command	drush_COMMANDFILE_post_HOOK	Called after the main command hook.
Rollback	[*]_rollback	If any function in the Drush command dispatch sequence calls drush_set_error, then any command that had previously completed without causing an error may participate in the rollback stage. A rollback function is created by adding "_rollback" to the end of the function that it reverts. For example, if the function drush_pm_updatecode fails, then the function drush_pm_updatecode_rollback will be called.

In all cases, the string HOOK in the function name is replaced by the name of the command being executed, and COMMANDFILE is replaced by the name of the command file where the command hook is defined; this is exactly as explained previously. Note, however, that it is not only the command file that defines a command that participates in the command dispatch process; *every* command file is given the opportunity to hook in to any command that the user runs. For example, the devel module has a Drush command file called devel.drush.inc. The devel command file patches into the Drush pm-enable command with the following hook:

```
function drush_devel_post_pm_enable() {
  $modules = func_get_args();
  if (in_array('devel', $modules)) {
    drush_devel_download();
  }
}
```

This code is called every time the Drush pm-enable command finishes execution without calling drush_set_error. The devel module then checks to see if it was one of the modules that was just enabled; if it is, then it calls drush_devel_download, which downloads the external libraries that the devel module needs to run. This is a useful pattern to follow for other modules that have external dependencies. If the external code is needed in order to successfully enable the module, then you might try patching in to the pre_pm_enable hook.

As you can see, Drush commands are easy to patch into, and there are a number of situations where doing so is useful. Sometimes, though, the hook function name composition algorithm may seem a little mysterious. To view a complete list of all of the hook function names, run the command that you want to hook into with the --debug --show-invoke options. This will cause Drush to print out a list of all of the function names that could participate in the command dispatch process. Functions that have already been defined are marked with a "[*]". This mechanism is a good way to get a quick list of function names available for your command file; just combine it with grep. For example, if you would like to create a command file named mycommand, and you would like to hook the Drush status command, do the following:

```
$ touch $HOME/.drush/mycommand.drush.inc
$ drush status --debug --show-invoke 2>&1 | grep --color=auto mycommand
drush_mycommand_core_status_validate
drush_mycommand_pre_core_status
drush_mycommand_core_status
drush_mycommand_post_core_status
```

The modifier "2>&1" may not be familiar to you. The "2>" tells the shell to redirect the standard error output from the command, and "&1" means that it should be redirected to the standard output. By default, Drush sends all notices, including the --show-invoke output, to standard error; you need to redirect it to standard out in order to filter it with grep. --color=auto tells grep to highlight matches in red, so they stand out; this is the default setting on many Linux distributions. From this output, you can see the names of the functions you would need to implement in order to hook into the validate, pre, post, or main hook for the status command.

In addition to the command hooks described previously, there are other hooks that Drush defines that any Drush command file can hook into. Drush uses the functions drush_command_invoke_all and drush_command_invoke_all_ref to enable this capability; both of these functions behave the same way, save for the fact that the later passes its first argument by reference, allowing the hook function to modify it as desired. As you might imagine, the later is more useful and more often will be the variant used to define a hook. For example, the Drush function drush_print_help, which displays the help text for a single Drush command, invokes the drush_help_alter hook as follows

```
drush_command_invoke_all_ref('drush_help_alter', $command);
```

This gives all Drush command files the opportunity to change the $command record to add additional text, options, or examples. In this way, command files that change the behavior of a Drush command with a pre or post hook can also alter the help text for that command to document the adjustment. Drush also uses the help alter hook for its own purposes; topic_drush_help_alter will modify commands that declare that they have topics, and copy the topic description into the command help so that this information does not have to be duplicated in every command that cross-references to one or more topics. The implementation of topic_drush_help_alter is shown in Listing 26–30.

Listing 26–30. topic_drush_help_alter

```
function topic_drush_help_alter($command) {
  $implemented = drush_get_commands();
  foreach ($command['topics'] as $topic_name) {
    // We have a related topic. Inject into the $command so the topic displays.
    $command['sections']['topic_section'] = dt('Topics');
    $command['topic_section'][$topic_name] = dt($implemented[$topic_name]['description']);
  }
}
```

Your Drush commandfiles can use similar techniques to hook into this and other Drush APIs. To see the complete list of available hooks, view the Drush API documentation using the command drush topic docs-api.

Summary

In this chapter, you used Drush to streamline and automate many common Drupal site maintenance task, including downloading and enabling modules, applying code updates, copying sites between remote systems, checking site status, and clearing the Drupal caches. You also breezed through Drush scripting and Drush command creation, and examined some of the more useful Drush APIs and utility functions to help you get a quick start on writing your own code tailored specifically to your sites needs.

There many more Drush commands and options than the ones covered here; fortunately, there is plenty of excellent documentation on Drush, and most of the functions of Drush are very easy to use. The following sources of information are very helpful places to find out more about Drush:

- The README.txt file in the drush folder covers basic installation and configuration.

- The command drush help will list all of the available Drush commands.

- The command drush topic will show documentation on different Drush-related topics.

- The Drush home page, http://drush.ws, contains all of the information on Drush-related topics, plus the Drush FAQ, the API reference, and a list of important Drush resources.

- The Drush issue queue, http://drupal.org/project/issues/drush, contains the most current information on the current Drush release in process.

With this knowledge, you will find yourself spending less time stepping through GUI administrative pages and more time just getting things done. Once you start using Drush regularly, you'll wonder how you ever got along without it. The power of Drush is now in your hands; go forth and script.

## CHAPTER 27

Scaling Drupal

by Károly Négyesi

To define scaling, let's look at a little café. When it opens up, because it's little, the owner does everything: she takes the order, prepares the drink, and takes the payment in exchange for the coffee. Some time passes and the café becomes popular so the owner hires a barista and a waiter. Now the waiter takes the order and gets the money. The barista gets a slip with the order, prepares the drink, and gives it to the customer. What you should notice here is that when one person did everything, the exchange of the money and the drink happened at the same time. But now the customer hands over the money first and only *eventually* gets a drink. Is there a risk involved with handing over money before getting the coffee? If a fire broke out suddenly, the customer would have paid his money but received nothing in exchange. However, no one is really bothered by this possibility; they would rather take this extremely small risk in order to get their coffee a lot faster. By separating the "taking of money" and the "serving coffee" actions, the shop can serve a lot more customers a lot faster. It can hire any number of baristas and any number of cashiers to better accommodate the traffic. This is scaling: to accommodate the traffic in such a way that more customers do not slow down the process.

But note that adding baristas does not make the time between paying and receiving any shorter. The shop owner makes sure there is always a free barista, but you still need to wait for him to prepare your drink. If, however, the shop employs crafty red robots that make coffee much faster, this will help shrink this waiting time. This is performance: the time that a web application takes between receiving a request and finishing serving it.

Performance is important because people tend to abandon slow web sites; scaling enables a web site to perform when there is a lot of traffic but scaling in itself won't make a web site fast. It is performance that makes it fast. However, if you have enough visitors, even the fastest web site will end up having to make some visitors wait before it begins serving their requests.

Now that I have defined scaling and performance, I'll spend the next part of the chapter telling you why you should care about them. Then I'll discuss some of the available scaling options for Drupal 7. That discussion will focus mainly on databases, because databases are integral to scaling Drupal. Drupal isn't always as scalable as one wants it to be, but the changes I'll discuss can make Drupal scale much more effectively.

Do You Need to Care About Scaling?

When you start out building a web site, handling more traffic is not usually your focus. Getting any traffic at all is usually what concerns most people. After all, only people with big, successful web sites need to worry about traffic. No web site started with millions of users. However, in time, you might just achieve that number or more. If you are aggressively marketing your site, that's all the more reason to plan for growth. Even if you just get a fixed percentage of all Internet traffic, you might be in for a surprise; new devices, even new *kinds* of devices, allow more and more people to spend more and more time browsing. What are you going to do when success strikes? Will your site be able to adapt?

If your site is not able to adapt to an increase in visitors, you are in for a lot of suffering: what should be success is instead frustrated users, both the new arrivals and the long-time fans, waiting for pages to load and perhaps receiving no response from the site at all. To make this worse, very often the web site is coded in such a way that adding additional hardware doesn't help much; in that case, the site needs to be rebuilt, often from the ground up. This can't happen overnight, of course, and it typically happens at a time when the business is busy with other things: growing. Simply put, more traffic very likely means more potential business, so at the same time the company is trying to cope with the necessary growth to deal with new demand, it suddenly needs to deal with a significant refactoring of the web site. While that happens, the web site might crash daily. The company or organization struggles to keep the lights on, in effect, instead of realizing the success that seems to be tantalizingly close. This is a scenario to avoid.

But there is another pitfall: becoming obsessed with scalability in the beginning of the life cycle of the site to the point where this takes away precious resources from developing functionality. Drupal's modularity has always provided a solution to these issues, and Drupal 7 rises to new heights in this regard.

Cache

Caching means to temporarily store some processed data. It can be structured data or a string of HTML-formatted text. While serving cached data is faster than retrieving and processing it from multiple database tables, the data is not really editable, so processing it into another format is not possible. Because of this, the raw data needs to stay in the database. So now you have more than one copy of the data, and the original data and the cache can become out of sync. In this case, the cache data is "stale." Sometimes that's fine; if you produce a few articles a day, it probably doesn't matter if fresh content is not visible to anonymous users for a few minutes after the original publication date. This is another important lesson in scalability: the practical trumps the theoretical. Scalability is always a matter of making compromises; it's just a question of which compromises are acceptable for a given web site.

▪ **Tip** Take careful note of that phrase "for a given web site." There is no silver bullet, no single solution to all scaling challenges. Scalability is always web-site–specific, although some practices apply to many similar sites.

Drupal can utilize caching to store the whole page, the HTML as it is, for anonymous visitors. Enabling this is very simple at `admin/config/development/performance` and it works even on the simplest shared hosting. Note that it only works for anonymous users but more often than not, a significant portion of the traffic is anonymous. By default, submitting new content deletes this cache, but a minimum lifetime can be set up. As mentioned, it's very site-specific.

▪ **Tip** Another option that works with shared hosts and is even faster than the built-in page caching is the Boost module (`drupal.org/project/boost`). This module can serve pages to your anonymous visitors, completely bypassing PHP.

Let's look at how developers can utilize caching to store the results of a slow query. Suppose you have a very slow function called `very_slow_find()`. This is how to utilize caching:

```
$cache = cache_get('very_slow');
if ($cache) {
  $very_slow_result = $cache->data;
}
else {
  // Run the very slow query.
  $very_slow_result = very_slow_find();
  cache_set('very_slow', $very_slow_result);
}
```

First you try to retrieve the cache. If yes, the stored data is used; if there is a cache miss, you run your query and store its results. This way the very slow query rarely needs to happen, but see the previous caveats about stale caching. In this example, very_slow is the cache ID (cid) or cache key and $very_slow_result is the data you store.

Cache is used very widely and it's stored in various bins. While it's certainly possible to store everything in one big pile, there are two advantages of separating them into what Drupal calls bins: the contents of a bin can be trashed separately from the other bins as necessary to avoid stale data, and different storage mechanisms can be set per bin to store data. (I will describe some examples of available storage mechanisms later in the chapter). While using cache_get and cache_set and the other functions that the Drupal caching API provides, you don't need to worry about which storage mechanism is in place. That's why pluggable subsystems are so useful: you can pick a different storage mechanism and you don't need to change any code.

Drupal, by default, uses the database to store cached data—not because it's the best way, but because Drupal knows it's there. Fortunately, there are alternatives. First, you'll see an example that has more to do with helping development and shows how to configure pluggable subsystems; then you'll see some performance and scalability solutions.

Disabling Caching During Development

For development purposes, I recommend the simplest cache implementation: nothing. There is a cache implementation that is the equivalent of a black hole: cache writes and clears don't do anything, reads always fail. Drupal uses this fake cache during installation because there is no information yet available about where it could store its data. This fake cache is quite useful while developing, too. One caveat is that multistep (and consequently AJAX) forms require a working cache, and so will not work when all caches are black-holed in this way. To short-circuit Drupal's caching using its own fake cache, add the three lines below to settings.php, which will be in the /sites folder for your site; typically it will be (relative to the root directory of your Drupal install) at /sites/default/settings.php.

```
$conf['cache_backends'][] = 'includes/cache-install.inc';
$conf['cache_class_cache_form'] = 'DrupalDatabaseCache';
$conf['cache_default_class'] = 'DrupalFakeCache';
```

By doing this, complex data structures like the theme registry will be rebuilt on every page load (adding classes and menu items still require an explicit cache flush on the admin/config/development/performance page). This slows down the site significantly but simplifies the life of the developer because changes to code are reflected immediately in Drupal's behavior.

The $conf array in settings.php is the central place to specify Drupal configuration. While some configuration options have a UI and store their state in the database, there are too many options to provide a UI for each, and most of these UI-less options are not necessary for the typical user. Another reason to use $conf instead of a UI is that some configuration is necessary before the database is available. Cache is an example of both: it's not something a user needs to set from the UI—most will never need to—and it can be used before the database is loaded. Most people are fine with the default cache implementation but also the cache can be used before the database is available. However, because the database is not available yet, settings for the cache is a bit more complicated than usual; you need to specify the file (in $conf['cache_backends']) not just a class to be used (as in $conf['cache_default_class']). For other settings, most of the time just specifying the class is enough because Drupal can read the location of the file containing the class from the database.

memcached

The solutions from now on will not work on shared hosts. You need to be able to control your environment to be able to perform and scale well.

memcached is a separate program that stores cached data in memory and allows access to it across the network. Being a separate program isn't so unusual; the database Drupal uses (like MySQL) is also such an application. The distinguishing feature of memcached is that it stores data solely in memory, which makes it very, very fast. Using this program instead of a database for caching can help Drupal performance quite a lot. And not just Drupal—this solution is very mature and used practically on every large web site.

Note that memcached is not just a performance solution but also one that scales very well and very easily: you just need to start as many instances of it on as many servers as necessary and configure Drupal to use them. There is nothing to set up in memcached because the separate memcached instances don't need to know about each other. It's Drupal that talks to every one of them. This is very different from, say, MySQL, where master-slave configuration needs to be configured explicitly.

There are three parts to the memcached puzzle: the application itself, a PHP extension, and a Drupal module. memcached is available at memcached.org. The installation and configuration are detailed on the web site. As mentioned, you need to add a PHP extension to allow PHP to communicate with memcached. There are two, confusingly named "memcache" and "memcached." Even experts have different opinions on which one is better. I cautiously recommend the newer "memcached" one. PHP extensions can be installed with

```
pecl install memcached
```

You can install them in operating system-specific ways, too, such as the following on Debian or Ubuntu:

```
apt-get install php5-memcached
```

Third and finally, you make Drupal use memcached by installing the Memcache module, drupal.org/project/memcache. The project page has extensive documentation that I won't repeat here.

Varnish

Another important part of the scalability toolset is Varnish. Varnish is an external program for storing and serving full pages. Normal page caching requires a request to reach your web server, which in turn bootstraps Drupal, loads the page, and then Drupal sends the request. Boost module provides a faster solution because now the request only needs to reach your web server but Drupal is not started. Varnish is even faster because it handles the request itself. It's a really, really fast, and massively scalable solution to serve anonymous pages. Its motto is "Varnish makes web sites fly" and it lives up to that. The application is at www.varnish-cache.org/ and the Drupal integration lives at drupal.org/project/varnish.

On Databases

So far you've seen how some pluggable subsystems are configured and you've briefly reviewed various solutions to serve anonymous pages quickly. By only employing the solutions listed so far, you can make your site perform well (thanks to memcached) and scale well for anonymous visitors (thanks to Varnish). However, social web sites are all the rage today and they require serving logged in users. It gets harder; while memcached does buy you some performance, there are many problems to overcome. You need to step back and get an overview of how web sites operate, store, and retrieve data; the problems encountered; and a fairly new solution that solves many somewhat unrelated problems.

On a high level, most web sites do the same basic actions: collect data (either a user/administrator entering it via a form in the browser or aggregating it from another web site), store that in a database, and later show the data to users. The operations to show and modify data are commonly referred to as Create, Read, Update, and Delete (CRUD for short). A typical web site would use some sort of SQL database to execute these operations on.

As you will soon see, SQL and especially the currently widespread SQL implementations (including MySQL/MariaDB/Drizzle, PostgreSQL, Oracle, and Microsoft's SQL Server) are not always the best fit for many problems that a web site faces. But if SQL isn't optimal, why is it so widespread? Similarly, if it is widespread and working, is going another route really a good idea? In short, people have always used these SQL databases, so what's the fuss?

Good questions. Let's look at just how long that "always" is. Most databases that are in use today have their roots in the late seventies. True, a given database program such as MySQL or PostgreSQL might have no code remains from say, UNIREG (the ancestor of MySQL) and Postgres or even INGRES (the ancestors of PostgreSQL). Like the folklore of the axe used by Abraham Lincoln, proudly kept as a piece of history by a family that honored it with use, the handle was replaced five times and the head three times over the centuries. The mindset when SQL databases were designed and the resulting limitations, alas, do not go away as easily as the code is replaced. Abraham Lincoln's axe is still an axe.

In the years since these databases were constructed, factors like CPU speed, available memory, and available disk space have grown a millionfold. Note that disk speed did not keep up. And although the tasks have grown as well, few tasks have grown a millionfold. And finally, operating systems have grown more sophisticated.

All this means that some new, previously unthinkable design decisions are necessary and now make a lot of sense. Because disk space is abundant and disk speed is now the throttling factor, you can focus on making databases faster rather than smaller. Sacrificing disk space to benefit performance looks like a terrific investment when there is such an abundance of cheap storage. One can presume the whole database fits in memory; if not, the operating system will handle the problem. These design decisions affect more than databases: Varnish, for example, employs these modern programming paradigms and that's one of the reasons it's so fast.

MEMORIES OF MEMORY

The first personal computer hard drive, the Shugart Technologies ST-506 in 1980, had a 5MB capacity, was as big as a DVD drive today, and cost $1,500. Thus, 1GB cost $300,000 in 1980 dollars; in current dollars, that would be fairly close a million. Today the fastest hard disk can store 300GB, costs less than $300 (thus a gigabyte is less than a dollar), and is as small as the hard drive in a typical laptop. Slower hard disks are available up to 3000GB (3TB) and the lowest per gigabyte cost for a hard disk at this moment is around 0.04 cent with some 2TB disks available for $80.

However, not everything changed so much: the ST-506 had a seek time of 170ms and the ST-412 in 1981 had a seek time of 85ms, but today the average disk has a 8-10ms seek time and the absolute fastest disk has a 3ms seek time—not even a hundredfold growth. (The seek time is the time it takes the drive to get to where the data is stored.) Once there, the ST-506 would read about half a megabyte per second whereas a typical disk today might be able to read a bit more than 100 megabytes per second—a mere 200 times speedup.

Flash memory drives help this situation somewhat by eliminating the seek time and about doubling the raw reading speed. There's still a long road ahead for these new devices: their reliability can't match a hard disk yet and they are about a hundred times slower than main memory still.

In 1980, 64 kilobytes of memory was the max for a personal computer and cost about $400, making the per-megabyte cost $6,200 (in 1980 dollars). Today, 64 gigabytes (one million times as many) of server memory costs less than $2000, making the per-megabyte cost about 3 cents. That's about half a million times cheaper.

The fastest 1980 microprocessors ran 1-2 million instructions per second (Intel iAPX 432, Motorola 68000). Today, the speed record is above a teraflops (IBM POWER7)—a million times that. Commodity processors were introduced at $200-350 and they still are in that range.

Aside from design decisions made before disk space and memory became cheap and plentiful, the fundamentals of SQL also mandate a critical look. SQL is based on tables that have columns. For example, you might have a profile table that contains a column for first name and a column for last name. This means that every single profile will have a first name and a last name—exactly one of each. Even staying within the Western culture, it's easy to find examples where such a rigid structure crumples. For example, what happens when Hillary Diane Rodham Clinton wants to register? Or people who take their online nickname as a legal name and consequently have only one name? For better storage you would also need a profile names table that has a profile ID and a name column, making it possible to store as many names as you want. You will see shortly the drawback of this approach. In Drupal 7, you can easily make a "name" multiple-value text field, but despite Drupal hiding the ugliness from us, it doesn't mean it's not there.

While names are known to be problematic like that, it's not too hard to find a problem with almost every kind of data. For example, if you are describing cars, then you have a table called car and a column called horsepower that stores a number, a column called transmission steps that again stores a number, and a column called color that stores a string. After all, a car has an engine with a fixed horsepower, right? (Well, not exactly; there are cars with both a gas and an electric motor, which of course have different horsepower ratings and remember, you can only enter a single number.) As for transmission steps, continuously variable transmission can't be stored as nicely as a number. As for color, the list is endless: there are widely successful two-colored small cars as well as thermochromic paints that make your car a chameleon. This problem could be resolved by storing more complex data structures than a single string or number.

The point of all this is that you can't store all the data in a single table with SQL. Why is this such a big deal? Let's look at how the database finds data to answer this question.

Indexes

How do you find a recipe in a cookbook? You look in the index, of course. While alphabetic ordering of the recipes help, will you remember the name of the excellent salad with chorizo and avocado? Even if you do, cookbooks are often ordered by some other topic like seasons or occasion, so even the exact recipe name won't be of much help. So let's build an index on ingredients that contains the page numbers where the ingredient appears, like so:

```
avocado
 40, 60, 233
chorizo
 50, 60, 155
```

This is somewhat helpful but to find anything you would need to go over every recipe listed because there is absolute no information of what's on those pages. Let's create an alphabetical index per ingredient and then per name, like so:

```
avocado
 Guacamole
   40
 Tortilla Soup
   233
 Warm Chorizo Salad Cesar style
   60
chorizo
 Black Bean Chorizo Burritos
   50
 Scrambled Eggs Mexican style
   155
 Warm Chorizo Salad Cesar style
   60
```

While this index is useful, it is only useful if you are searching for ingredients or ingredients and names. It is also useful if you want to list recipes containing an ingredient, ordered by recipe name. However, if you want to search for a name, it becomes completely useless. For example, if you want to find the Scrambled Eggs Mexican style, you need to go over to the avocado recipes first, then the bacon recipes, then the chorizo—not much better than just paging through the whole book itself.

Remember that you started browsing your cookbook looking for a recipe containing both avocado and chorizo. How would you create an index that makes this search simple and fast? If you start your index with recipe names, then you need to go through every single recipe to find them, so that's not a good idea. If you do something like your first index, you can easily find all the recipes containing avocado and also all the recipes containing chorizo. Say you had 1000 avocado and 1000 chorizo recipes but only one that has both. You would need to compare 2000 numbers to find the single one. To make this operation fast you actually need an index like the following:

```
avocado
 bacon
   30, 37, 48
 chorizo
   60
bacon
 avocado
   30, 37, 48
 chorizo
   70
```

That's plain horrible. It's not just that the storage requirements would be quite high but more importantly, in real life where data changes, maintaining something like this would become untenable very quickly. Say the average recipe had a mere eight ingredients; you can make 8*7 = 56 pairs so every change would require updating 56 index entries! (Even if you don't store both avocado-bacon and bacon-avocado, merely halving this does not solve anything and in fact raises several problems when querying, as an ingredient-name index could not be used backwards.) This is the very same way SQL stores and indexes data and this is the very problem with scaling with SQL: you can't use indexes on most queries spanning multiple tables—and you are forced to use multiple tables due to the rigidity of SQL. Let's see a Drupal example!

In Drupal, nodes have comments on them. Nodes are stored in one table (Node) and because there can be multiple comments on a single node, comments are stored in a separate table (Comment). If you want to show the ten 'page' nodes most recently commented on then you are facing a similar problem: you can have a list of comments ordered by creation date and the nodes belonging to them if you have an index on creation date, and you can have a list of 'page' nodes if you have an index on node type, but if, say, the last 200,000 comments are all on 'story' nodes and you have 50,000 pages, then you can either go over 200,000 comments first to find that none of them are pages or you need to go over all 50,000 pages to find the latest comment on each. That's certainly not fast.

This example can easily be fixed by storing the node type in the comment table because node type does not change. But if you wanted to do something with the node change information and comment together then you would be forced to store node change information in the comment table and a node edit would trigger an update of hundreds of lines in the comment table. Such a practice is called denormalization and it is used widely. However, it should raise red flags: what sort of system are you working with that can only be made to perform by throwing out its very fundamental theory (normalization)? I will show one very good solution to this problem later but let's continue with listing the problems with SQL.

NULL in SQL

NULL is a wonderful construct that defies conventional logic; its usage is contradictory and it's not even consistent across databases. NULL is used to signal that some data is missing or invalid and is never equal to anything else but then again it's neither less or greater than either. Whatever you do with it, the operation will result in a NULL. You need a special IS NULL operator to detect NULLs, like so:

```
mysql> SELECT 0 > NULL, 0 = NULL, 0 < NULL, 0 IS NULL, NULL IS NULL;
+----------+----------+----------+-----------+--------------+
| 0 > NULL | 0 = NULL | 0 < NULL | 0 IS NULL | NULL IS NULL |
+----------+----------+----------+-----------+--------------+
|     NULL |     NULL |     NULL |         0 |            1 |
+----------+----------+----------+-----------+--------------+
```

This is called a three-valued logic. Instead of a statement being true or false, it can be NULL. This leads to many weird problems with NULL columns. Drupal (not by any conscious decision, mind you) doesn't have many NULL columns which just by sheer luck avoids most of this madness. Alas, this is not consistent and sometimes you are forced to enter the NULL pit.

There is even more to NULL than just the common-sense–defying three-valued logic, such as:

```
CREATE TABLE test1 (a int, b int);
CREATE TABLE test2 (a int, b int);
INSERT INTO test1 (a, b) VALUES (1, 0);
INSERT INTO test2 (a, b) VALUES (NULL, 1);
SELECT test1.a test1_a, test1.b test1_b, test2.a test2_a, test2.b test2_b
FROM test1
LEFT JOIN test2 ON test1.a=test2.a
WHERE test2.a IS NULL;
```

```
+---------+---------+---------+---------+
| test1_a | test1_b | test2_a | test2_b |
+---------+---------+---------+---------+
|       1 |       0 |   NULL  |   NULL  |
+---------+---------+---------+---------+
```

There is, of course, no such (NULL, NULL) row in test2. But, LEFT JOIN uses this to display the result for so called anti-joins. These are used to SELECT rows from the first table where no matches are found in the second table.

Now, if 1 = NULL is true, it would have found the single row you inserted into test2. It didn't do that. 1 = NULL, remember, is neither true nor false; it's just NULL. But just from looking at the results this is absolutely not evident; after all, the results contain a test2_a being NULL and didn't the JOIN prescribe test1.a=test2.a? Yes, it did but in this particular case the JOIN part does not need to be true. The result has missing data that is indicated by a NULL and it has nothing to do with the JOIN. If you find this confusing, it is. Not only do you need to live with a three-valued logic but you need to make exemptions for LEFT JOINs.

There's one more database architecture detail to cover before I can show what the answers to these problems. The current SQL implementations are focused on transactions (the term comes from financial transactions but it can mean any unit of work the database executes). You will quickly see that the effects of this focus fly against the expectations of the user of web sites— as the expectations of a user of a web site are different from the expectations of a user of a bank.

A CAP Between ACID and BASE

The typical example of a transaction is sending money to someone else. This is a very complex process, but at the end of the day you expect that your balance is decreased by the amount you sent and the receiver's balance is increased by that amount (minus fees). You also expect that once the bank has said "you sent money," it is actually sent, no matter how long the actual sending takes (it's completely ridiculous how long a so long called SWIFT transfer can take). Another expectation is that if the money disappears from your account, it will appear in the account of the other party, no matter what happens to the computer system of the bank. You certainly don't expect your money to disappear without a trace if a computer crashes. A set of properties on the database is necessary to make transactions work according to these expectations—these are commonly abbreviated as ACID:

- *Atomic*: Either the complete transaction succeeds or none of it.

- *Consistency*: The database is in a consistent state between transactions. For example, if a record refers to another record and such a reference is invalid by the end of a transaction, then the whole transaction must be rolled back.

- *Isolation*: Transactions do not see data changed by other transactions before those are finished.

- *Durability*: Once the database system notified the user about the success of a transaction the data is never lost.

On the other hand, most web applications want a whole different set of properties, aptly named BASE:

- *Basically Available:* Users have the silly expectation that when they point the browser to a web page, some kind of information appears. You expect this to happen even if some parts of the system you are reaching are down. This is not as trivial as it sounds; there are many systems where if one server goes down, the whole system goes down.

- *Scalable:* Adding more servers makes it possible to serve more clients. Adding more servers instead of trying to create a single huge monster server is much more future-proof and usually cheaper, too. Once again, this is a user expectation: information not just appears but it appears fast. (Note that this user expectation also requires performance not just scalability.)

- *Eventually Consistent:* It's enough if data eventually becomes available in all the places to which it is copied (you can have many copies, as described in the previous bullet point). The expectation is that the information appearing fast is somewhat current. When you post an ad to Craigslist, it does not immediately appear in lists and searches, which is not really a problem. It would be a problem if it took days for an ad to appear; no-one would use the site.

On this last point, if you have a consistent system as described in the ACID property list, it is also "eventually consistent" because it follows a stronger requirement: data immediately become available for all copies. (I'll get back to this one in detail just a little bit later.)

It would be awesome if there were a database system that could be both ACID and BASE, but alas that's not actually possible. Remember that BASE was basically about having a system consisting of a big number of servers. If you mandate that all writes are strongly consistent, then every write needs to go out to every server and you need to wait until all of them finish and communicate back this fact. Now, if you have servers scattered in datacenters around the globe, then network problems can be expected. Let's say a transatlantic link goes down—this is called a network *partition*. If you want consistency, then the system must go down together with the transatlantic link—even if all other servers are still up—because writes in Europe can't get to USA and vice versa so the parts will have inconsistent data. You need to give up something: either the Availability from BASE (system goes down to achieve consistency) or Consistency from ACID (you stay up but the system is inconsistent). In other words, out of Consistency, Availability, and Partition Tolerance (CAP), you can pick two but not three. So far, I have only defined consistency for databases, so it's time to be more generic about it: at any point in time it doesn't matter which server responds to a request, all of them will provide the same answer. Availability, as described above, means that even when some servers go down, the whole system doesn't. Finally, partition tolerance means that some communication between two servers can be lost and yet the system will work. Note how "soft" these two criteria are, and yet they pose a hard problem when you want them together with consistency.

I have just shown that the three parts of CAP don't work together and I can show that any two can live together easily. If you made sure parts of the network never fail, then providing Consistency and Availability is not a problem. However unlikely this sounds, Google's BigTable, used by more than 60 Google projects, is actually such a system. If you throw out Availability then the other two requirements are easily met: just don't switch on the servers, the data will stay consistent even if parts of the network fail. Finally, if you don't care about Consistency then you can simply not replicate writes from one server to the next—this system will certainly not care about network partitions (because it doesn't use the network at all) and if you reach a working server, it will answer something. While the latter two examples are extreme and don't describe a useful system, the point is, once again, that while Consistency, Availability, and Partition Tolerance can't all live together, any two of them can.

Once again, remember the tale of the coffee shop: in order to be able to employ more baristas (to scale) you need to accept that for a short time the customer is without money and without coffee (eventually and not immediately consistent). And people accept that even with a web application. If your comment takes a short time (even a few minutes) to appear to everyone in the world, that's fine. Of course, you expect it to appear to the poster of the comment immediately or at least as soon as the data is sent to the server and a reply has arrived. But for others, it takes some time to load a web page over the Internet anyway and so whether the server shows that new comment to those who have started loading the page just before or just after the Send button has been pressed matters little. It's more important that the web page is always responsive (available) no matter how many are browsing at the same time (scalability).

So while the SQL databases are mainly ACID compliant, databases that are BASE-focused fit a lot better with web applications. On top of that, the following databases take the vastly changed hardware and operating system possibilities into account to become an even better fit for these purposes. One of the first databases built along these principles is CouchDB which was first released in 2005. Cassandra was released to the public in 2008, and MongoDB was first released in 2009.

It was also in 2009 that these new, non-relational database systems got the somewhat catchy "NoSQL" moniker. This is, of course, just a buzzword, as it would be possible to drive a non-ACID compliant database with SQL (in fact MySQL was using SQL for more than a decade without being ACID compliant) but the feature set of these database is so different from what SQL is geared to work with that it would be pointless to try. For example, none of these databases offer the ability to JOIN tables.

As MongoDB is the best fit for many Drupal tasks, I will discuss it now in detail.

MongoDB

Getting started with MongoDB is super easy: just point a browser to `try.mongodb.org`. It provides a tutorial and lets you play with the database without downloading anything. If you want to use it on your own computer, you can download from `mongodb.org/downloads` and get up and running in no time; there is no complicated configuration file to write. The Drupal integration project is at `drupal.org/project/mongodb`.

MongoDB fits Drupal 7 surprisingly well despite the fact that much of Drupal 7 development predated MongoDB. It's a database designed for the Web so it's no wonder it matches so well the world's best software for making web sites—Drupal.

Basically, MongoDB stores JSON encoded documents (the actual difference is minor). A document is the rough equivalent of an SQL record. Any number of documents constitutes a collection, which is the rough equivalent of an SQL table. Finally, databases contain collections, much like MySQL databases contain tables.

While a MySQL table can only have fixed records, a single MongoDB collection can store any kind of documents, like so:

```
{ title: 'first document', length: 255 },
{ name: 'John Doe', weight: 20 }
```

And so on. Anything goes. There is no CREATE TABLE command because one document can wildly differ from the next.

Remember the problems with storing names in SQL? Not a problem here!

```
db.people.insert({ name: ['Juan', 'Carlos', 'Alfonso', 'Víctor', 'María', 'de', 'Borbón',
'y', 'Borbón-Dos', 'Sicilias'], title: 'King of Spain'})
```

If you wanted to get a list of the documents of people named Carlos, you could run `db.people.find({name: 'Carlos'})`. It will find the king of Spain, regardless of where Carlos is in the list of names.

Also, properties can be a lot more than just numbers or strings.

```
db.test.insert({
  'title': 'This is an example',
  'body': 'This can be a very long string. The whole document is limited to a number of
megabytes.',
  'votes': 56,.
```

```
'options':
  {
    'sticky': true,
    'promoted': false,
  },
'comments': [
  {
    'title': 'first comment',
    'author': 'joe',
    'published': true,

  },
  {
    'title': 'first comment',
    'author': 'harry',
    'homepage': 'http://example.com',
    'published': false,
  }
]
});
```

So a document has properties (title, body, etc. in the previous example) and the properties can have all sorts of values, such as strings (title), numbers (votes), Booleans (options.sticky), arrays (comments) and more objects (also called sub-documents, an example is options). There is no limitation of how complex the document can be. There is, however, a limit on document size (it was 4MB for quite some time; it's currently 16MB but plans call for 32MB); for most web pages this limit doesn't pose a real problem. Sticking with this example, just how many comments will any post have? There's space for several thousands. If that's not enough, the actual body (which is never queried) can be stored separately.

So compared to an SQL table, the major advantages are no need to specify schema ahead of the time, no fixed schema actually, and the values can be complex structures.

Here are a few more interesting find commands against the document shown previously:

```
db.test.find({title: /^This/});
db.test.find({'options.sticky': true});
db.test.find({comments.author': 'joe'});
```

As you can see the, the find command uses the same JSON documents as insert. The first find command shown uses a regular expression to find posts where the title starts with "This". The second shows how easy it is to search inside objects. The third shows that arrays of objects are equally easy. It's also possible to make all three of these queries indexed.

If you look at a Drupal 7 entity with fields, it's actually an object containing arrays. You can store and index those as a whole into MongoDB. And that's what matters most: in SQL, while you could store entities that have the same structure (for example, nodes of the same type) in a single table, if you need to query across these (for example, to show all the recent content favorited by a user, regardless whether they are articles or photos), then you can't index that query. Remember, to make such a query fast, you need to denormalize; in other words, keep copies of the data you need to query together in a single table. This is hard to maintain and slow to upgrade because every piece of data has so many copies. In MongoDB, you can easily do this cross-content–type query because all nodes can sit in a single table and you can just create an index on 'favorite' and 'created' and you're all set.

In summary, SQL is not able to store complex structures. While MongoDB is not the only solution to this problem, it is much simpler to implement and maintain than SQL's approach of using multiple tables and denormalization. This problem existed in Drupal 6 with CCK but became central in Drupal 7 with entities and field API.

To use MongoDB as the default field storage engine, add

```
$conf['field_storage_default'] = 'mongodb_field_storage';
```

to settings.php (in sites/default or the relevant sites directory). If you are creating fields from code, then setting the 'storage' key of the field array also works. The UI doesn't offer this choice so if you are solely using the UI, you can't pick the storage per field.

There is even more to MongoDB than being a very nice field storage engine, although that's probably the best thing about it. But it solves other problems, too. Once again, it's not the only solution but it's a very nice one.

First, let's look at some more features relating to writes. Let's increment the votes in our test document, like so:

```
o = db.test.findOne({nid: 12345678});
o.votes++;
db.test.save(o);
```

While this code works, it's ugly and prone to a race condition. Race conditions are the bane of developers as they are extremely hard to reproduce but can produce mysterious failures. Let's look at an example. Here is what can happen in the listed order when two users try to vote:

User A runs o = db.test.findOne({nid: 12345678}); -- votes are at 56.

User A runs o.votes++

User B runs o = db.test.findOne({nid: 12345678}); -- votes are at 56.

User A runs db.test.save(o); setting votes to 57.

User B runs o.votes++

User B runs db.test.save(o); setting votes to 57.

In MongoDB, you can do instead:

```
db.test.update({nid: 12345678}, {$inc : { votes : 1 }});
```

- User A runs this command, votes are incremented by 1 to 57
- User B runs this command, votes are incremented by 1 to 58

This is an atomic operation. There is no possibility for errors caused by a race condition. Note that update also operates with JSON documents; there are special update operators like $inc shown but it's still the same syntax.

You can also specify a multiple document update

```
db.test.update({nid: {'$in': [123, 456]}, {$inc : { votes : 1 }}, {multiple:1});
```

and while single documents will be incremented atomically (without a race condition0, a multiple update is not atomic. When I listed transaction properties previously, I mentioned that in the context of a transaction, atomicity means that either all documents update or none. This is not the case here, as there are no transactions in MongoDB: it's possible that the update of one document fails but has no consequence on the other documents, which update successfully. MongoDB also lacks another capability for transactions, namely isolation: while one document already is updated for every client, the others can still have their old values.

Atomic per-document increments make MongoDB ideal to store various statistics. For example, you might want to store and display the number of times a node is viewed. First, add a numeric field to the node called 'views.' Next, you will see a little script that takes a node ID as an argument and increments the value of the views field by one. Note that it emits the same headers Drupal does to stop browsers and proxies from caching it and finally, prints a 1x1 transparent GIF.

```php
<?php
if (!empty($_GET['nid']) && $_GET['nid'] == (int) $_GET['nid']) {
 define('DRUPAL_ROOT', getcwd());
 require_once DRUPAL_ROOT . '/includes/bootstrap.inc';
 drupal_bootstrap(DRUPAL_BOOTSTRAP_CONFIGURATION);

 require_once DRUPAL_ROOT . '/sites/all/modules/mongodb/mongodb.module';
 $find = array('_id' => (int) $_GET['nid']);
 $update = array('$inc' => array('views.value' => 1));
 mongodb_collection('fields_current', 'node')->update($find, $update);
}

header('Content-type: image/gif');
header('Content-length: 43');
header("Last-Modified: " . gmdate("D, d M Y H:i:s") . " GMT");
header("Expires: Sun, 19 Nov 1978 05:00:00 GMT");
header("Cache-Control: must-revalidate");
printf('%c%c%c%c%c%c%c%c%c%c%c%c%c%c%c%c%c%c%c%c%c%c%c%c%c%c%c%c%c%c%c%c%c%c%c%c%c%c%c%c%c%c%c
', 71, 73, 70, 56, 57, 97, 1, 0, 1, 0, 128, 0, 0, 0, 0, 0, 0, 0, 0, 33, 249, 4, 1, 0, 0, 0, 0,
44, 0, 0, 0, 0, 1, 0, 1, 0, 0, 2, 2, 68, 1, 0, 59);
```

Now all you need to do is to save this as stats.php in your Drupal root, add an <img src="<?php print base_path() . 'stats.php?nid=' . $node->nid; ?>"/> in your node.tpl.php. By counting node views this way, even if the page is served from cache or Varnish, the view will be counted.

Is this going to kill the site's performance? That depends. It does cause a PHP hit every time someone loads a page, which may or may not be acceptable. For most sites, it's OK. If the site works with that, MongoDB won't cause a problem. Given that MongoDB works with the database in memory and occasionally writes back to the disk, writes are a lot faster as they need to happen only into memory. Also, it works hard to update values in place so that indexes don't need to be updated needlessly.

New in 2011 is the ability to not lose any writes even when using a single server. One of the biggest complaints about MongoDB was that because it was only writing back occasionally, data might get lost if the server crashed. Previously this was mitigated by making the application wait for the write to be replicated to another server, hoping that two servers won't crash at the same time. But now, if mongod is started with the –dur option, writes don't get lost.

Watchdog, Session, and Queue

Drupal has other areas that write a lot: watchdog and session. The session subsystem keeps the user logged in; therefore it needs to write on every single page load. The fast writes of MongoDB make this a non-issue. Once you have mongod running and the Drupal module installed, just add

```php
$conf['session_inc'] = DRUPAL_ROOT
. '/sites/all/modules/mongodb/mongodb_session/mongodb_session.inc';
```

to settings.php (in sites/default or the relevant sites directory) and MongoDB takes over the sessions, speeding up the site again.

Watchdog is problematic because if for some reason there are a lot of error messages (like a massive worm outbreak that tries to retrieve nonexistent URLs), a SQL table might grow into such sizes that the only viable option is to trash it completely (TRUNCATE). Deleting older rows might not be able to catch with the torrent of writes, plus writes are a bit slow. The traditional solution is to use syslog, which is just a text file so it's not the simplest to query it. With MongoDB, you can specify that a collection should only keep the last N documents and then automatically start over, overriding the oldest messages, so there never will be more than the specified number of messages, making it easy and convenient to query. Also, the Drupal implementation of watchdog puts different messages into different collections so there won't be more than the specified number of messages recorded for each message. For example, "comment created" messages won't be crowded out by php error messages. To use this facility, enable mongodb_watchdog and disable dblog modules.

Finally, Drupal 7 has a message queue, which can also be implemented with MongoDB. There are many queues but if you have already deployed MongoDB for field storage, watchdog, and session, then just the write speed of MongoDB is handy enough here to use it instead of SQL. Just add

```
$conf['queue_default_class'] = 'MongoDBQueue';
```

to settings.php and you're done. You have seen how to utilize MongoDB as a field storage engine, to store session data, to log watchdog messages, and as a queue mechanism. It's also possible to use it as a cache but for that purpose memcache is simply better (because of the trivial scalability of it).

Null Values in MongoDB

So far you have seen how MongoDB solves some of the SQL problems. Let's see if it ameliorates SQL's previously-discussed weirdness with NULLs (and while you do that, you'll learn more about MongoDB and see more examples on MongoDB queries).

The way MongoDB handles NULL is a little bit saner than SQL but it surely has its own NULL quirks. The following find is completely valid and shows that NULL values need no special operator:

```
db.test.find({something:null}) ;
```

This will find the documents where something has a NULL value. Very easy. NULL is a type in itself and comparing different types are always false because MongoDB is strictly typed and never casts values for you. So comparing a number to NULL is always false but the same is true to comparing a number to a string. This is not really a problem—just something you need to be aware of. An example will be shown soon. At least MongoDB does not employ three-valued logic; comparisons can only be true or false, never NULL.

However, there is a caveat to NULLs: nonexistent values are treated as NULLs.

```
> db.test.drop()
> db.test.insert({a:1});
> db.test.insert({something:null});
> db.test.insert({something:1});
> db.test.find({something:null});
{ "a" : 1 }
{ "something" : null }#
```

To actually find what you wanted, do this:

```
> db.test.find({something:{$in: [null], $exists:true}});
{ "something" : null }
```

The new operators are $in and $exists. And here is the example for comparing NULL to 1:

```
> db.test.find({something: {$gte: null }});
{ "a" : 1 }
{ "something" : null }
```

Once again, the first document doesn't contain a something property so when comparing, it matches. The second document contains a something: NULL pair and the operation is "greater than equal" ($gte) so it matches again. You have a document where something is 1 but that won't match—NULL is not zero.

Summary

As you've seen, thinking about scaling in the early stages of a site is not always a high priority. However, it always pays to think about it early before your headaches really start. This chapter went over why you *should* care about scaling early and what techniques are available in Drupal 7 to sort out scaling.

The main focus was on databases, because they are absolutely integral to scaling in Drupal. Caching and the like are of course useful, too, so you looked into that as well. All in all, this chapter's changes will take your Drupal site some way towards scaling effectively.

■ **Tip** Stay up to speed with occasional updates, discussion, and resources at **dgd7.org/scale**.

CHAPTER 28

■■■

Spice Your Content Up
With Tasty Semantics

by Stéphane Corlosquet

It used to be that search engines had to guess which parts of a page to show to make your site look relevant and attractive in their search results. Now Drupal gives you the tools to clearly express what meaning your content carries, thus helping other applications on the Web to truly understand your site and reuse your content in potentially useful and attractive ways (see Figure 28–1).

Salad - **Thai** Green **Mango Salad** Recipe

☆☆☆☆☆ 7 reviews - 20 mins
You asked for a one-page printable version of my step-by-step Green **Mango Salad** recipe, so here it is! This salad will blow you away with its ...
thaifood.about.com/od/thaisnacks/r/greenmangosalad.htm - Cached - Similar

Figure 28–1. Drupal offers the tools to clearly express your content.

Thanks to the semantic markup used on this recipe page, it shows up in a Google search for Thai mango salad with a picture and the rating users on the site gave it. When your web site's pages provide information in ways that machines can understand, Google can give selected pieces of information (such as the picture and the rating) a privileged place in its presentation of the search engine results page (SERP).

With Drupal 7, you can easily add semantic markup to your pages. The ways to do this through your site's user interface will be covered in the RDF UI section. The challenge and promise of the growing Semantic Web are much greater, however, and Drupal 7 is set to play an important role helping you both navigate and build this information-rich future.

Information Overload

The Web contains more than 20 billion publicly available pages, to which one can add 900 billion *deep pages*[1] (password-protected pages or dynamic pages generated after a search). If you combine all the personal computers, data servers, and other devices connected to the Web, the online storage capacity is

---

[1] LLRX, "Deep Web Research 2007," www.llrx.com/features/deepweb2007.htm, 2006.

estimated to be above 600 exabytes (that's 600 billion gigabytes). Together with the fact that memory is cheap and an ever growing number of users are joining the Web, the amount of information we, as humans, process on a daily basis is skyrocketing. It's crucial to understand that without the help of the machines, we won't be able to digest this information overload.

But aren't we already using machines today to surf the Web? Yes, we are, but we're not using them to the best of their ability; you still need a human reader in order to understand the structure and content of most web pages. Search engines like Google, Yahoo!, and Bing are constantly harvesting pages on the Web and mirroring them into their server farms in order to achieve very fast search results for end users. But there's something broken here. All the search engines have access to are HTML pages or plain text in PDF files. RSS feeds provide more structured information in the form of XML, but it is limited to title, date, and content; it can't express the type of item (news, blog post, user profile, item for sale, event), nor can it express the amount of reviews, the image, or the price.

It is fairly trivial for the human brain to identify the various bits of information on a page and guess what type of information it is reading: text, date, or image. The same goes for the relationship between the elements of the page and what they refer to. (Is this the name of the author who wrote the page or the topic of the page?) These exercises are much more challenging for machines as they lack the ability to infer this sort of knowledge from contextual clues that we, as humans, use throughout our day-to-day lives.

In other words, a machine visiting a web site will mostly see plain text that links to other pages or images. Experts have to run many complex algorithms to attempt to reverse engineer the process used to put the page together. A very simple, resource-intensive example is to find dates in a page using regular expressions by searching for slash-separated digits. With a date like 08/07/10, how could a machine guess whether the date is July 8th or August 7th when even an English reader and an American reader would read this date differently? Machines need a clear, non-ambiguous way to interpret this information.

The same thing goes for words. What would a machine infer when coming across the word "apple?" Many terms in the English language have several meanings and nuances. The Semantic Web is a set of tools and standards designed to tackle these issues by adding a layer of semantics on top of the Web that we know today. It's important to understand that the Semantic Web is not trying to replace the existing Web, but rather enhance its content with clues for machines to understand context, as if a Web chef was adding spices to blend content in order to make it more tasty and meaningful for machines.

The Semantic Web has had increasing real world impact over the years and was recently adopted by the big players on the Web. Among all the Semantic Web standards, RDFa (RDF in attributes) is the one that has seen the largest adoption. In 2008, Yahoo! Search Monkey initiated the trend by supporting RDFa-enabled pages. Google followed with its Rich Snippets a year later. In April 2010, Facebook announced they were using RDFa as part of the Open Graph protocol, which has since been deployed on millions of web pages. You have probably come across RDFa-enhanced web sites without even knowing it: the White House, O'Reilly, Best Buy, The New York Times. And you can also add most Drupal 7 sites to that list.

THE RESOURCE DESCRIPTION FRAMEWORK

The Resource Description Framework (RDF) is a set of W3C specifications for modeling information. In RDF, each piece of information or statement contains a subject, verb, and object, much like basic sentences in natural language. When combined together, these statements can model knowledge about many things. Let's take the example of a recipe for an apple pie. It takes 30 minutes to prepare and has 25 reviews. In RDF, each statement follows the same structure of subject-verb-object, so here's how the previous sentence would be expressed:

```
[recipe] - [name] - "Apple pie"
[recipe] - [preparation_time] - "30 min"
[recipe] - [number_reviews] - "25"
```

This subject-verb-object pattern used to assert basic elements of information is sometimes called a *triple* in RDF jargon. The verb is often referred to as a *predicate* or a *property*. To ensure interoperability on the Web, it is crucial to reuse the same verbs so that when someone else reads this recipe, they understand what the number 25 represents. In natural language this is achieved by agreeing on a common meaning for the words we use. For machines, and in RDF, this is done via the use of URIs. Linked Data[2] best practices encourage the use of HTTP URIs because they provide a means for machine and humans alike to look up the meaning of a verb. If you are unsure about what a verb means, you can just paste it in your browser to find out more about it. This process, known as "following your nose," can also be used by machines to discover the meaning behind a URI. It's similar to looking up a word in a dictionary.

These dictionaries in RDF are called *ontologies*, *vocabularies*, or *schemas*. They contain a set of definitions for the URIs specific to a given topic. One popular example is the Friend of a Friend (FOAF)[3] vocabulary that includes terms to describe people and their friends. This enables exciting possibilities for machines to learn and infer new knowledge, such as if two verbs from different vocabularies are in fact synonyms, or if a particular verb brings a set of extra statements. For instance, using foaf:img in an RDF statement implies that the subject is a person and that the object is an image.

Note the shorthand notation of foaf:img to refer to the img verb of the FOAF vocabulary. This notation is the *CURIE syntax*[4] (for Compact URI) and is useful to avoid using full URIs, which tend to be verbose and error-prone. CURIEs are always used within a context where the prefix used before the semi-colon is bound to the namespace of the vocabularies. In the case of foaf:img, the foaf prefix is bound to the FOAF namespace `http://xmlns.com/foaf/0.1/` as defined in the FOAF vocabulary specification. The full URI for foaf:img (the one that refers to the img term) is the concatenation of the namespace and the term: `http://xmlns.com/foaf/0.1/img`.

Let's look at another example where RDF can be useful: web page metadata. The following describes the title, creation date and one of the topics of a webpage:

```
<http://example.org/home.html>    dc:title      "Joe's homepage"
<http://example.org/home.html>    dc:created    "Dec 1, 2005"
<http://example.org/home.html>    dc:subject    "London"
```

Note the new prefix here: dc, which in the context of the example refers to Dublin Core, a vocabulary used to describe physical resources (e.g. books) as well as digital items like video, text files, or web documents. The dc prefix is generally bound to the namespace `http://purl.org/dc/terms/`.

The object of the last statement is a string. Another feature of RDF is that it allows the object to be a URI, so the last statement could be

```
<http://example.org/home.html>    dc:subject    <http://dbpedia.org/resource/↵
London,_Ontario>
```

The advantage of using a URI instead of a string is to avoid any ambiguity that a plain text string would have. Secondly, the URI can also provide the coordinate of the city and country where it's located, some pictures, various statistics, and much more information than what a string alone can express.

---

[2] W3C, "Linked Data," `www.w3.org/DesignIssues/LinkedData`, 2006.

[3] XMLNS, "FOAF Vocabulary Specification 0.98", `http://xmlns.com/foaf/spec/`, 2010

[4] W3C, "CURIE Syntax 1.0: A syntax for expressing Compact URIs," `www.w3.org/TR/curie/`, 2010.

Note that knowledge representation in RDF is very generic and not bound to any particular syntax. This means you can embed RDF in a variety of languages such as HTML, JSON, XML, RSS, and Atom.

Continuing with the analogy of natural language, the same information can be expressed in many different ways: ideas and concepts can be expressed as words (in English, French, etc.) or diagrams (whiteboard style or the ancient hieroglyphs). Similarly, a photo can be saved as a jpg file, a png file, or printed on a piece of paper; all these mediums carry essentially the same information contained in the photo. Typically, you would choose the medium or language that works best for you and the recipient with whom you want to communicate: if you're chatting with your Spanish friend, you might speak Spanish, or if both parties are comfortable with English, you might choose English. Similarly, RDF offers various formats to express or *serialize* the same information. In the context of web pages, RDFa (RDF in attributes) is the most appropriate syntax because it offers to embed RDF directly in HTML via the addition of a thin layer of attributes.

How Did We Get There?

Any source of data tends to be made available on the Internet so that it can be shared, reused in accordance with the license of the site, and mashed up with other data. Content management systems like Drupal help people to produce content online. Whether it's via self-hosted web sites, software as a service (SaaS), or free platforms (such as Facebook, Twitter, MySpace, or Gmail), ordinary users of the Web have many ways to produce content online.

From the 140 character update on Twitter to the four paragraph blog post to the one hundred page PDF documentation, all these pieces of information land on the Web in one form or another. Some are public; others are behind firewalls or password-protected. Much of this content ends up being visible as HTML, although other formats exist, like text files, PDF documents, and images. Some of this data results directly from the content the user has put on the Web (content, ideas, thoughts) but there is also a lot of metadata surrounding this user input, like the date it was entered, the number of page visits, or the number of comments the page has received.

Navigating the Web and contributing to it has become very easy with the wide adoption of the browsers like Mozilla Firefox and Google Chrome; these browsers are now available on a variety of platforms such as desktop computers, laptops, tablets, and mobile devices. E-mail clients are another means to publish content on the Web; mailing lists are a good example.

Decentralized Dataspaces

When Sir Tim Berners-Lee created the World Wide Web in 1990, he envisioned a globally distributed information space in which everyone was free to say anything about anything without having to deal with heavy bureaucratic procedures, corporate policies, or any form of centralized control authority. Most importantly, this information space was to remain free and open for every single person: you may have to pay your local Internet Service Provider (ISP) for the service to get access to this information space, but once you're connected to it, you're free to do what you want. Each user can own her dataspace and can claim what she thinks is true, share her ideas with the rest of the world, and link to other people's dataspaces in agreement or disagreement.

Web applications such as Drupal empower Internet users to build their own dataspace, create content, and link it to other dataspaces. The collection of all these dataspaces is what is commonly called the Web, built on top of the Internet infrastructure that has been developing since the 1960s.

Linking Data at the Global Web Scale

Before you dive into the details of Drupal and RDF, it's important to understand another aspect of the Semantic Web and how it allows you to address information beyond the boundaries of your web site. Most applications store their data using the concept of foreign keys, which allows them to address each data item in their database and find the data relating to each data item easily across tables. This works well on a closed system where it is easy to enforce constraints on these foreign keys, such as making each identifier unique. This does not work on a global scale because each site on the Web does not rely on a centralized authority for assigning identifiers.

While my user ID on my personal site is 1, it does not mean I have the same user ID on all sites on the Web. On `drupal.org`, my user ID is 52142 and on `groups.drupal.org` it's 3258. Likewise, my username on `identi.ca` is "scor" but on twitter this username was already taken so I had to choose the username "scorlosquet" instead. The bottom line is that talking about plain IDs or usernames does not mean anything in a totally distributed system such as the World Wide Web and is ambiguous at best!

To work around this, RDF uses URIs (Uniform Resource Identifiers) as a means to name and address resources on the Internet. URIs look much like URLs, starting with http:// or https://. So instead of referring to a user as an integer, RDF will use strings of the form "`http://drupal.org/user/52142`". With that, we can claim things like `http://drupal.org/user/52142` and `http://groups.drupal.org/user/3258` are two user profile pages of the same person. With URIs, each web site can own its dedicated namespace and create as many resources as needed without having to consult with anyone else. Drupal typically will assign an ID to each user and build their URI as http://sitename/user/{userid}; ditto for nodes, taxonomy terms, etc. This path can be customized using URL aliases; Drupal will ensure that each URL alias points to a unique resource on your site and thus avoid any ambiguity.

Now that you've seen the importance of URIs, you can move along and see in what context they are useful. You've learned that a username is meaningless on the Web without some kind of namespace, such as the web site to which it belongs. Beyond this use case, think of the problem of ambiguity when talking about concepts, such as tagging a blog post with "apple." You're back to using a string for identifying a potentially ambiguous concept, and like the username case, this is something RDF can help you with. You could host your concepts yourself on your namespace, but for common concepts like "name" or all the countries in the world, it makes more sense to use a somewhat agreed upon centralized repository.

Wikipedia[5] contains a huge amount of information about objects, concepts, famous people, cities, countries, organizations, etc. Each entry has a URI on Wikipedia that displays some information about the topic at hand. Talking about "apple" can mean either the fruit or the company. If you were instead using URIs, you could easily get rid of any ambiguity; `http://en.wikipedia.org/wiki/Apple` is about the fruit and `http://en.wikipedia.org/wiki/Apple_Inc` describes the company. Making this distinction might not be necessary for humans who understand from the context which meaning was intended, but it's crucial for machines. The more sites that use the same identifiers, the easier it is for machines to make cross references to infer whether a set of posts is talking about the same topic or not.

---

[5] Wikipedia (`http://en.wikipedia.org/`) is an online multilingual encyclopedia composed of more than 17 millions articles. Dbpedia (`http://dbpedia.org/`) is a separate project aiming at extracting structured information from Wikipedia and making it available online as RDF. With DBpedia it becomes possible to run complex queries against Wikipedia content and to reuse this data more easily within RDF applications.

Do You See What I Mean?

Drupal offers a user-friendly interface to produce HTML. When submitting data, Drupal will typically store it in the database and then process it to build the HTML output. Drupal knows exactly from which tables and columns the data should be pulled; when building the page, it knows what corresponds to the title of the page, the date it was created, and its main content. It knows the current version of the node and can pull it from the right database record. However, once it has put together the page as HTML, all this structure is lost; the actual data is laid out on the page properly and formatted for the human eye, but the semantics have been lost.

The first versions of HTML were not designed to make this structure explicit to machines, but imagine if HTML tags offered a way to specify what type of data the tag contains and how it related to other pieces of information on the page or on other pages of the Web? This is what a recent World Wide Web consortium working group addressed in the "RDFa in XHTML" W3C Recommendation,[6] released in October 2008.

RDFa, or How HTML Can Be Augmented with Semantics

From a web developer perspective, RDFa is no more than a few XHTML attributes that can be added to web pages in order to explicitly state the semantics of the data contained in the HTML tags (see Figure 28–2). The RDFa markup does not change the way the page is rendered in a web browser; it looks just the same to the user. However, the difference is visible to any RDFa-capable software reading the page because it can understand the semantic markup.

Web browsers can then enhance the user experience depending on the type of data the page contains: some browser extensions can, for example, provide additional functionalities based on the RDFa markup contained in the page. Search engines typically also make great use of this data, as it allows them to better understand the information at hand and display it accordingly in search results; it's easy to extract the title, the date, and an image for the page, which can drastically improve the visibility in search results and aid the search engine optimization (SEO) of a given site. The price, ratings, and the number of reviews are also relevant elements that can drive more traffic to an e-commerce site. Yahoo! has reported up to 15 percent increase in click-through rate due to RDFa (www.slideshare.net/NickCox/ses-chicago-2009-searchmonkey).

---

[6] W3C, "RDFa in XHTML: Syntax and Processing," www.w3.org/TR/rdfa-syntax/, 2008.

Figure 28–2. *By adding a few simple XHTML attributes to existing HTML tags, RDFa enriches the content of a webpage with machine-readable hints.*

The RDFa processing model relies on a DOM traversal technique where each DOM element is visited, starting from the document object and making its way to each child element in a recursive manner. RDFa is best explained with some basic examples. Remember that RDFa is all about adding attributes to existing XHTML markup. First of all, some adjustments need to be made to the top of the XHTML template so that they are compliant with the RDFa specification.

```
<!DOCTYPE html PUBLIC "-//W3C//DTD XHTML+RDFa 1.0//EN"
  "http://www.w3.org/MarkUp/DTD/xhtml-rdfa-1.dtd">
<html xmlns="http://www.w3.org/1999/xhtml" xml:lang="en" version="XHTML+RDFa 1.0" dir="ltr">
<head profile="http://www.w3.org/1999/xhtml/vocab">
```

Secondly, let's set some prefixes so you can use the CURIE syntax discussed in the section on RDF. This is done in the HTML tag using the syntax xmlns:prefix="http://somenamespace.org/". For FOAF, it would be

```
xmlns:foaf=http://xmlns.com/foaf/0.1/
```

Drupal 7 takes care of all of the above and includes a set of commonly used namespaces. Modules can declare additional prefixes and namespaces.

You are now all set to start using RDFa markup in your HTML document. To denote the attributes in HTML, we'll prefix them with an at sign (@). The RDFa attributes are @about, @content, @datatype, @href, @property, @rel, @rev, @resource, @src, and @typeof. Each RDFa attribute will have an effect on how RDF statements are built from the structure and the content of the HTML document. You might recognize some of these attributes (rel, href, or src), and you will soon see what role they play in RDFa and how RDFa can reuse existing attribute values.

The attributes @property, @rel, and @rev specify the verb of an RDF statement. To understand how they work, it's best to look at the following examples:

```
<h1 property="dc:title">Joe's homepage</h1>
<div rel="sioc:has_creator"><a href="/user/9">John Smith</a></div>
```

dc:title and sioc:has_creator are two different RDF verbs that specify the title and the author of a page. In the first example, the @property forces the object of the RDF statement to be a string. In the second example, the @rel is used instead of @property in order to force the object of the statement to be a URI pointing to the author page; in other words, it's a resource as opposed to a simple string. Doing so allows the markup to include much more information about the author than if it was just a string. The author resource can include not only his name, but his bio and links to his other articles, allowing for content discovery.

An exhaustive description of RDFa is beyond the scope of this chapter, so please consult the RDFa primer at www.w3.org/TR/xhtml-rdfa-primer/ for a more detailed understanding of how RDFa markup is processed. See also these excellent articles on RDFa published in the *A List Apart Magazine*:

www.alistapart.com/articles/introduction-to-rdfa/
www.alistapart.com/articles/introduction-to-rdfa-ii/

RDFa, Microformats and Microdata

RDFa is not the only syntax for adding semantics to HTML. Microformats (microformats.org) were the first syntax to see a wide adoption by the web developer community. However, Microformats were never standardized and due to its design, the development of its vocabularies (hCard, vCard, etc.) was centralized and limited to one organization. RDFa, on the other hand, can be freely extended due to the nature of RDF: external vocabularies can be combined and custom domain-specific vocabularies can be built when needed. RDFa also benefits from all the work that has been put into the Semantic Web stack in the last decade. Many tools are available for parsing, storing, and querying RDF data. Most notably SPARQL en.wikipedia.org/wiki/SPARQL, the RDF querying language similar to SQL for relational databases, allows running queries over data federated from any RDF source.

RDFa has been a W3C standard since 2008 and has been adopted by many prominent companies on the Web such as Google, Facebook, BBC, and Best Buy. Recent research from Yahoo! shows that RDFa saw an explosive growth in 2010 and is the fastest growing data markup format (http://tripletalk.wordpress.com/2011/01/25/rdfa-deployment-across-the-web). Microdata (www.whatwg.org/specs/web-apps/current-work/multipage/links.html#microdata) is a new syntax part of the HTML5 specification, which is still under development at the time of this writing. Microdata shares more in common with RDFa than microformats, such as the use of URIs to allow for extensibility. Microdata and HTML5 were still too new during the development phase of Drupal 7, and the more established RDFa standard was more promising and a better fit to Drupal's native XHTML output. While version 1.0 of RDFa is only valid with XHTML markup, the upcoming RDFa 1.1 will allow RDFa in both XHTML5 and HTML5. See the HTML+RDFa 1.1 draft document at http://dev.w3.org/html5/rdfa/. RDFa 1.1 also includes feedback from the microformats and the microdata communities, allowing for a simpler syntax and more use cases. Given that RDFa 1.1 is backward compatible with Drupal 7 RDFa 1.0 markup, expect to see RDFa-enabled HTML5 pages soon on Drupal 7. Join the conversation on HTML5 in Drupal at http://groups.drupal.org/html5.

Drupal 7 and the Semantic Web

You might have already noticed an **rdf** folder while browsing Drupal 7's modules directory or seen it on the Modules page in the administration interface. If you have installed the standard profile, this module will be already enabled (see Figure 28–3).

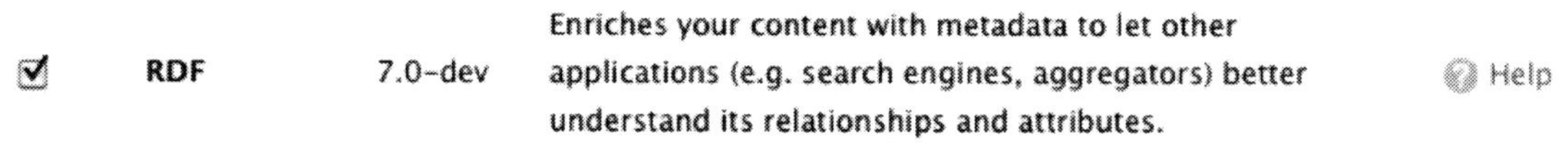

☑ **RDF** 7.0-dev Enriches your content with metadata to let other applications (e.g. search engines, aggregators) better understand its relationships and attributes. ⚲ Help

Figure 28–3. *Make sure the RDF module is enabled by visiting the Modules page in the administration section of your site.*

All the work of the RDF module happens behind the scene. In fact, it does not include any user interface and only provides an API for other modules to use (much like the Field module). Many modules in core leverage the RDF module, including Node, Comment, User, Taxonomy, Forum, Blog, and Tracker.

The RDF module does essentially two things: it describes the data structure of a Drupal site in terms of RDF mappings (which relates a Drupal field to one or more RDF terms) and then takes these mappings and inserts them into the HTML output in the form of RDFa attributes. The RDF module takes advantage of the new concepts of entities, bundles, and fields introduced in Drupal 7. Let's have a closer look at the lifecycle of these RDF mappings.

Starting at the higher level, entity types such as node have a set of attributes like title or date that can be mapped to an RDF property. Whenever this value is output in HTML, this RDF property can be added to the HTML, so that agents looking at this HTML from an outside point of view can still understand a piece of data's origin and significance. A very simple example of a node whose title is "My trip to Belgium" would then be output to HTML as

```
<h2 property="dc:title">My trip to Belgium</h2>
```

Note the extra property attribute that is added to the wrapping h2 tag, indicating clearly the title of the node. Aside from the attributes of an entity type, a special kind of mapping exists for the actual type of an entity. This might sound redundant from a Drupal standpoint, but remember that the RDF mappings are there to help external applications that do not know anything about the internal structure of your web site.

The entity type is yet another element of information that gets lost and does not appear clearly in the HTML, but the RDF module offers a chance to solve this with the rdftype key of the RDF mapping structure (see Listing 28–1). This RDF-type mapping will appear accordingly in the page in the form of RDFa.

Listing 28–1. *RDF Mapping Structure for the User Entity Type as Defined in user.module*

```
/**
 * Implements hook_rdf_mapping().
 */
function user_rdf_mapping() {
  return array(
    array(
      'type' => 'user',
      'bundle' => RDF_DEFAULT_BUNDLE,
      'mapping' => array(
        'rdftype' => array('sioc:UserAccount'),
```

```
    'name' => array(
      'predicates' => array('foaf:name'),
    ),
    'homepage' => array(
      'predicates' => array('foaf:page'),
      'type' => 'rel',
    ),
  ),
  ),
);
}
```

The second level of the RDF mapping lifecycle happens with the content types and other bundles (see Chapter 18). Entity types never get instantiated as such; they first go through a level of specialization to become bundles, where they can get other optional features such as revisions, comments, taxonomy, and most importantly, fields. An entity type with a small set of attributes can suddenly be extended with a customizable set of fields depending on the needs of the site administrator. Fields can be attached to bundles via the Field user interface that is part of Drupal 7 core.

The same can be done programmatically, such as in the Drupal 7 standard profile. Nodes are the ideal use case for understanding the concept of a bundle: when installing Drupal 7 with the standard profile, you will find two predefined content types: Article and Basic Page, which are simply two bundles of the node entity type. While these two content types share some attributes such as title and date, they have a different set of fields. For example, Basic Page has a title and a body, while Article comes with some additional fields: tags and image. Each bundle will inherit the RDF mapping structure of its parent entity type.

This is very convenient in the case of nodes where some attributes are common to all bundles and are unlikely to change (such as the title and date). Similarly to the way the RDF mappings are defined for each entity, they can be defined for each bundle when necessary. Most of the time, because each bundle inherits the entity type RDF mapping structure, it is only necessary to specify the RDF mappings for the fields specific to a bundle, as shown in Listing 28–2. Note how only the RDF mappings for the specific fields need to be specified.

Listing 28–2. RDF Mapping Structure for the Article Bundle as Specified in the Standard Installation Profile

```
array(
  'type' => 'node',
  'bundle' => 'article',
  'mapping' => array(
    'field_image' => array(
      'predicates' => array('og:image', 'rdfs:seeAlso'),
      'type' => 'rel',
    ),
    'field_tags' => array(
      'predicates' => array('dc:subject'),
      'type' => 'rel',
    ),
  ),
),
```

Note that the RDF mapping structure for the bundle and entity type are similar, the only difference being that an RDF mapping structure affecting an entity type must specify RDF_DEFAULT_BUNDLE as the value for the bundle key. By contrast, an RDF mapping structure for a bundle should explicitly state what bundle the mapping is for.

Understanding the Structure of RDF Mappings

An RDF mapping is a nested associative array defining a relation between Drupal's internal attributes and meaningful RDF predicates, which are designed to be understood by and interoperate with external applications. A mapping structure contains three required keys. The type and bundle keys refer respectively to the entity type and the bundle to which the RDF mappings pertain. The third key, mapping, lists the Drupal attributes that should be mapped to RDF.

Besides the special rdftype key that was described earlier, the other keys refer to either Drupal custom attributes (title, date, author) or to fields defined by the core Field module. Each item contains an array listing the RDF predicates of this attribute in the predicates key. This is sufficient when dealing with a string value (such as the title of a node or the name of a user in Listing 28–1). But when dealing with attributes that refer to some other resource with a URI (link, image, or another entity), the developer should specify a type for a mapping element. This type indicates the direction of the relation between the two resources with regards to the RDF predicate used.

In most cases, type => rel is what's required; the rel relationship indicates that the parent HTML element is the subject. For instance,

```
<div>Lora is interested in <a rel="foaf:interest" href="http://drupal.org">Drupal</a></div>
```

states that the user Lora is interested in Drupal.

The rev value can be used when a reverse relation is needed, like so:

```
<div about="http://drupal.org">Drupal is interesting to <a rev="foaf:interest"
 href="user/5">Lora</a></div>
```

This nuance in direction is inherited from the RDF model, which is based on directed graphs. It is generally easier to use the rel type; few developers will need to use the reverse type. Thus, the rel type for any non-string linkage is all you need to bear in mind.

Going back to Listing 28–2, the Drupal 7 standard installation profile maps the field_image of the article bundle to the og:image RDF predicate. In other words, it links each article node to its image via the og:image directed relation. This relation is automatically reflected in the form of RDFa inside the HTML output of the page, clearly helping any application such as a search engine understand what image is associated with an article. The same thing goes for the field_tags field mapping element, which makes an explicit semantic relation between an article and the subjects it covers via the dc:subject predicate. Once these relations have been established in the RDF mapping structure, the RDF module will take care of adding them where they need to be in the HTML markup; the developer does not need to worry about placing the RDFa elements.

Working with RDF Mapping Structures

Drupal developers have basically two options for working with RDF mappings. Module developers who create their own entity types and bundles are encouraged to use hook_rdf_mapping() in order to associate RDF predicates with their attributes. Drupal core modules should be used for reference (namely Node, User, Comment, and Taxonomy).

Secondly, in keeping with Drupal's traditions of extensibility and flexibility, the RDF module also provides API functions to alter the RDF mappings defined by the modules. This is what the standard installation profile uses in order to add RDF mappings to the image and tag fields upon installation, right after creating these fields and attaching them to the article bundle via the Field API. All RDF mappings defined with these CRUD functions are stored in the database. The CRUD functions rdf_mapping_load(), rdf_mapping_save(), and rdf_mapping_delete() can be used to specify the RDF mappings of new bundles and fields, as well as alter existing RDF mappings that have been saved to the database on module installation and are not alterable without the CRUD API. Listing 28–3 is an example of altering some of the mappings of the article content type. Note that only the RDF mappings of the fields to change need to be specified.

Listing 28–3. *PHP Code Example to Alter Some RDF Mappings*

```
$article_rdf_mappings = array(
  'type' => 'node',
  'bundle' => 'article',
  'mapping' => array(
    'field_image' => array(
      'predicates' => array('og:image', 'rdfs:seeAlso'),
      'type' => 'rel',
    ),
    'field_tags' => array(
      'predicates' => array('dc:subject'),
      'type' => 'rel',
    ),
  ),
);
rdf_mapping_save($article_rdf_mappings);
```

RDF Vocabularies in Drupal 7

As you saw earlier, many schemas already exist on the Web, and some of them are quite well understood by applications like search engines. The major vocabularies that Drupal 7 uses are as follows:

- *Dublin Core* caters to online media such as generic documents, news articles, or date of publications. See the Dublin Core specification at `http://dublincore.org/documents/dcmi-terms/`.

- *Friend of a Friend (FOAF)* describes the relationships between people, as well as their name, address, picture, location, and their social web attributes like e-mail, home page, OpenID, or interests. FOAF also contains some broader terms to define documents, organizations, groups and their members, and projects. See the FOAF specification at `http://xmlns.com/foaf/spec/`.

- *Semantically-Interlinked Online Communities (SIOC)* is used to model the connections between the content created online and the users who create this content. It can describe several channels of discussion such as forums, blogs, polls, and news in general. See the SIOC specification at `http://rdfs.org/sioc/spec/`.

- *Simple Knowledge Organization System (SKOS)* tailors the representation and sharing of knowledge organization systems like thesauri, taxonomies, subject heading systems, and classification schemes. It is a good match to Drupal taxonomies for both controlled vocabularies and free tags. See the SKOS specification at `www.w3.org/TR/skos-reference/`.

Figure 28–4 depicts how these vocabularies are used natively in Drupal 7.

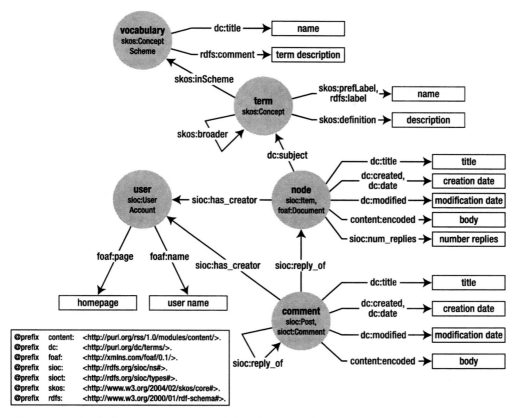

Figure 28–4. Default RDF mappings as defined in Drupal 7

Modules can add new namespaces and their associated prefix by implementing
hook_rdf_namespaces(). The snippet in Listing 28-4 adds the WGS84 Geo Positioning namespace to
Drupal, which will be serialized along with the other namespaces defined by the other modules in the
HTMl output. The prefix "geo" can then be used when defining the RDF mappings using the WGS84 Geo
Positioning vocabulary.

Listing 28–4. RDF Mapping Structure for the User Entity Type as Defined in user.module

```
function mymodule_rdf_namespaces() {
  return array(
    'geo'  => 'http://www.w3.org/2003/01/geo/wgs84_pos#',
  );
}
```

Using RDF Beyond Drupal Core with the Contributed Modules

The previous sections only addressed what Drupal 7 core APIs enable, but there are more functionalities that the contributed modules space offers. The following are a few contributed projects that extend Drupal 7's RDF capabilities. These projects are evolving fast, so please check their description on their project page to get up to date information on what they do.

The RDF Extensions project downloadable at `http://drupal.org/project/rdfx` offers a set of useful modules to directly interact with the Drupal 7 core RDF module. Site administrators who prefer a user interface to writing code will use the RDF UI module to alter the RDF mappings, as illustrated on Figure 28–5. This package also offers more RDF serialization formats such as RDF/XML, N-Triples, and Turtle.

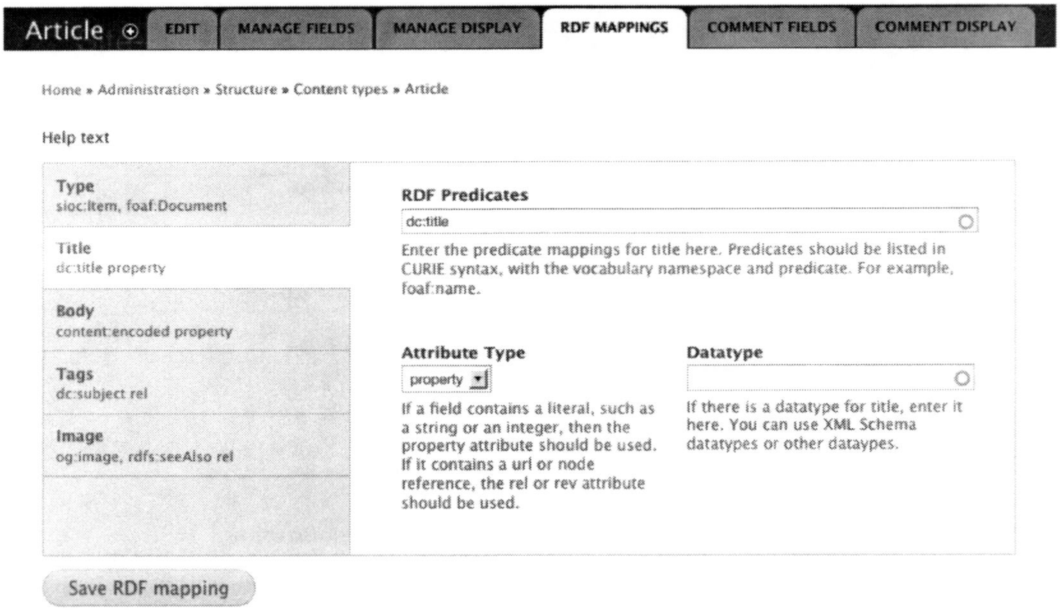

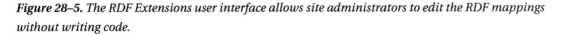

Figure 28–5. The RDF Extensions user interface allows site administrators to edit the RDF mappings without writing code.

The SPARQL project can turn your Drupal site into a SPARQL endpoint by indexing all its RDF data. Site administrators can also register external endpoints that other modules can use to get their data from. The SPARQL package also exposes an API for other modules to run SPARQL queries on the fly without having to worry about setting up a SPARQL endpoint locally. Download SPARQL at http://drupal.org/project/sparql.

SPARQL Views is a query plug-in for Views 3 allowing you to bring data from SPARQL endpoints into Views. Download SPARQL Views at `http://drupal.org/project/sparql_views`.

The Examples project includes a module showing some examples of RDF mappings. Download Examples at `http://drupal.org/project/examples`.

Summary

In this chapter, you learned about the Resource Description Framework, an abstract data model used to describe information and make statements about Web resources in the form of subject-verb-object expressions. You've also seen how RDF can be embedded directly into XHTML and HTML5 in order to annotate the bits of information it contains, making it easier for machines to understand the content at hand, which in turn helps Internet users to find the information they need.

You've seen how Drupal 7 makes use of RDF in its internal data modeling via the RDF mappings and how this structured information is surfaced during the rendering of HTML. Many of the RDF mappings are set by default for generic content types; for example, blogs and articles include the author, the tags, and the comments. More complex or domain-specific sites can make use of Drupal's RDF mapping API to add new vocabularies and choose the appropriate mappings for their data.

■ **Tip** Semantic web technology is hot. Set your machine to read `dgd7.org/semantic` for the Drupal community's take on new developments.

## CHAPTER 29

The Menu System and the Path Into Drupal

by Robert Douglass

A versatile and easily understood architecture sets the stage for wide community involvement, as exemplified by Drupal's menu system—responsible for associating paths on a Drupal site with just what the site returns to the visitor.

Open by design, Drupal's simple and extensible architecture on the inside equates to high levels of participation on the community side.

This chapter looks at one of the features that leads to Drupal's openness and flexibility. It is a dispatcher that takes the incoming Drupal path and maps it to a callback function. Along the way it resolves any access considerations and loads the data objects that are needed. Drupal calls this the menu system since the paths can also be used to build the visible navigation structures (i.e., menus) of the web site.[1]

Every web application solves the problems of dispatching URLs and resolving access in one way or another, so the mere existence of the menu system is not groundbreaking. What makes the menu system beautiful is its low barrier to entry and its power to reach into every corner of the code base to modify, extend, or replace what is already there.

Drupal's Menu System by Example

A typical first task for a developer starting out with Drupal would be to integrate some existing code and have its output displayed within the context of a Drupal site. The requirements of this task include that the Drupal application gets fully loaded (including user authentication and making the database connection), that the page containing the output has its own Drupal path, and that this page be available in the visible navigation of the Drupal site.

Listing 29–1 shows the code needed to display an outrageous message within the context of a XHTML page. It lives within a hypothetical module called the outrageous module, and it fills the three requirements.

---

[1] The current menu system, first added in Drupal 6, was conceived of and implemented by Károly Négyesi with help from Peter Wolanin. Numerous others have contributed along the way.

Listing 29–1. An Outrageous Message

```php
<?php

function outrageous_menu() {
  $items['outrageous'] = array(
    'title' => 'Outrageous message',
    'access callback' => TRUE,
    'page callback' => 'outrageous_message',
  );

  return $items;
}

function outrageous_message() {
  // Create an outrageous message. Based on a quote by Gill Davies.
  // t() is a wrapper that allows text to be localized.
  $message = t('A teddy bear is a cuddle with four paws on the end.');

  // Get a formatted date.
  $time = date('M d, Y');

  $page = array(
    '#markup' => "$time: $message",
  );

  return $page;
}
```

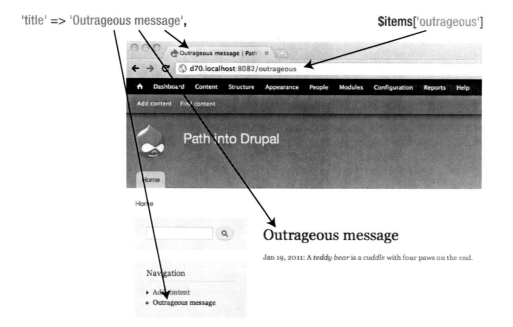

Figure 29–1. *The code from Listing 29–1 defined a path, "outrageous," which displays an outrageous message within a fully bootstrapped Drupal application. A link in the main navigational menu was created to access the "outrageous" page.*

In Listing 29–1 the first function, outrageous_menu(), defines the path to the page, the title of the page, the access conditions, and the callback function that will generate the content of the page. This is all in the form of a simple PHP array. The second function, outrageous_message(), generates the output that is displayed in the content area as shown in Figure 29–1.

This code would live in a module that is a file named outrageous.module. The outrageous_menu() function is an implementation of a core Drupal hook called hook_menu().[2] The naming convention states that if your module's name is outrageous and the hook is generically called hook_menu, the function outrageous_menu() is the name of the function that will get called. Implementations of hook_menu() will get called whenever Drupal builds the menu router table in the database that is used when dispatching Drupal paths to callback functions. The pattern of calling functions based on the naming convention "module name" plus "hook name" is used extensively throughout Drupal.

---

[2] For more information on Drupal's hooks, see api.drupal.org/api/group/hooks. For more information on hook_menu in particular, see api.drupal.org/api/function/hook_menu/6.

DRUPAL'S HOOKS

Listing 29–1 introduces the concept of a hook. Hooks are the very basis of how Drupal operates, and the menu hook is but one of many hooks available to developers writing Drupal modules.

In essence, a hook is a contract between Drupal and its modules that certain functions will be called with specific arguments at certain points in the page execution. The name of these functions follows a naming convention that uses the module name and the hook name to dynamically come up with the name of a PHP function to call. The module in Listing 29–1 is defined in the file `outrageous.module`, thus Drupal knows its module name to be `outrageous`. When page execution comes to a point where a hook needs to be invoked, Drupal takes `outrageous`, along with all of the other modules that are enabled, and for each one calls `outrageous_hookname()`. Thus when it comes time to compile the menu router table, Drupal invokes `hook_menu`, and `outrageous_menu()` is one of the functions that will be called.

This whole mechanism is facilitated by PHP's awareness of the functions it has available at runtime. The PHP function `function_exists($function_name)` makes it possible for Drupal to check in the middle of a page execution whether a certain function exists before actually trying to call it.

All incoming Drupal requests are directed at a single point of entry, which is the index.php file that lives in the base Drupal directory. This isn't apparent in the example or on many Drupal sites, however, because behind the scene the web server is always rewriting the incoming URLs to point to index.php. Thus a URL of `http://example.com` will get rewritten to `http://example.com/index.php`. The rest of the URL is what is referred to as the Drupal path. It gets rewritten, too, so that `http://example.com/outrageous` will be represented internally as `http://example.com/index.php?q=outrageous`. Drupal refers to the q parameter as the path, and the path in this case is `outrageous`.

Given the code in Listing 29–1, a URL of `http://example.com/outrageous` will map to an internal path of `outrageous`, and this will match the menu item defined in the `outrageous_menu()` function based on the key of the array, `$items['outrageous']`. Once the dispatcher has matched the incoming path to the appropriate entry in the menu's router table, a callback function will be sought. In this case it is defined in the `$items` array with the key `'page callback'`, and the `outrageous_message()` function will be called.

The `$items` array also defines a title that will be displayed on the page. Here the title is a hardcoded string, but a later example shows how this can be dynamically generated via a callback.

Access to this menu router item is set with the `'access callback'` key. The value of this key can either be a Boolean (TRUE in this case means that everybody has access) or the name of a callback function, which must return a Boolean value.

You can see in Figure 29–1 that a visible navigation item appears in the navigation menu on the site. Although not covered here, this and the other navigation items can be configured, renamed, hidden, or moved around using Drupal's administrative interface. The site administrator, not the coder, has final say in the matter.

Here are all the steps, from URL to Drupal page, laid out in order:

1. `http://example.com/outrageous` gets rewritten to
   `http://example.com/index.php?q=outrageous`.

2. The q parameter, `outrageous`, gets recognized as the Drupal path.

3. Based on the path, the menu router item originally defined by
   `$items['outrageous']` from the example code, now loaded from the database
   at runtime, is chosen to handle this page callback.

4. An access check is done based on the `'access callback'` item of the menu
   router. The value is `TRUE`, so access is allowed.

5. The page title is set based on the `'title'` item of the menu router. The title is
   now "Outrageous message."

6. The function named in the page callback parameter, `outrageous_message`, is
   invoked. This defines what appears in the content area of this particular page.

7. Drupal builds the rest of the page using the presentation layer and the
   application's configurations. This is where the logo, the navigation menu, and
   the shaded regions seen in Figure 29–1 come from.

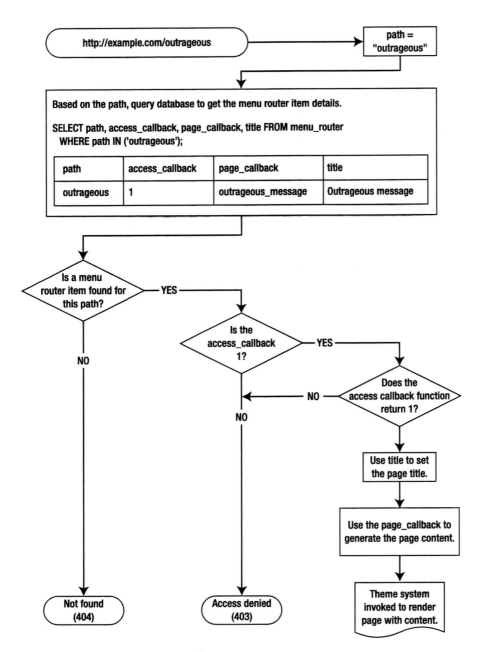

Figure 29-2. Handling a request from URL to page output

A web developer who is new to Drupal will usually grasp the essence of this example right away and experience satisfaction that he can freely write code that gets included and executed within Drupal at the right time. All that is needed is a simple PHP array and some code to generate the output. The first barrier to entry has been overcome and Drupal has been extended.

MENU ROUTER ITEMS

One of the tables in the Drupal database is the `menu_router` table. In Listing 29–1 you saw how menu router items consist of paths and the metadata that describes the paths' behavior. All of the menu router item definitions from all of the installed and enabled modules get stored in the `menu_router` database table.

The Never-ending Path

In Listing 29–1, the Drupal path was outrageous. A practical feature of the menu system is that this path is open ended. The same callback definition will also match and handle the path `outrageous/dog/friend`. The path gets broken into segments based on the slash, and each segment beyond `outrageous` will be available to the callback function as arguments. In Listing 29–2, the callback function has been rewritten to accept and use two arguments. If there are no arguments, it works the way it did in Figure 29–1.

Listing 29–2. The Outrageous Message with Two Arguments from the Drupal Path:

http://localhost/outrageous/dog/friend

```
/**
 * Now with arguments that default to the original version of the message.
 */
function outrageous_message($animal = 'teddy bear', $noun = 'cuddle') {
  // Create an outrageous message template. Based on a quote by Gill Davies.
  $message = 'A %animal is a %noun with four paws on the end.';

  // Replace the %animal and %noun placeholders with the $animal and $noun
  // arguments.
  // The t() wrapper not only allows localization, it performs the
  // placeholder replacement.
  // t() also guarantees that $animal and $noun are plain text, thus
  // protecting against XSS attacks.
  $message = t($message, array('%animal' => $animal, '%noun' => $noun));

  // Get a formatted date.
  $time = date('M d, Y');

  $page = array(
    '#markup' => "$time: $message",
  );

  return $page;
}
```

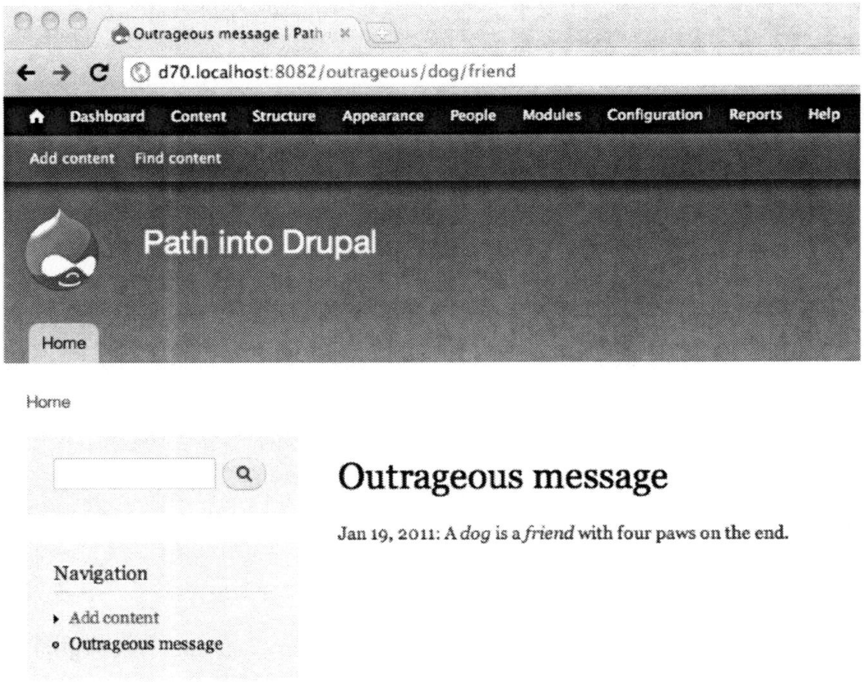

Figure 29–3. The message is composed from the path segments in the Drupal path.

Structure of a Path

Being able to accept arbitrary arguments into the callback function is fine for some cases, but usually a more nuanced and exact approach is needed. A typical pattern in Drupal is to refer to data objects (called entities in Drupal-speak) using their primary key identifiers. The main object type for content in Drupal is called a node, which is just a generic term for content such as an article, blog post, image, or calendar event. Nodes have integer primary key identifiers. The paths in Table 29–1 all do various things with the node number 42.

Table 29–1. Various Node Paths and Their Actions

Path	Action
node/42	Load and display node #42
node/42/edit	Load and display the editing form for node #42
node/42/revisions	Show the revision history for node #42

A pattern is emerging:

```
node + id + action
```

In each of the cases just shown the second segment of the path signifies the primary key id and the third segment specifies the action (with an implicit "view" action on node/42). One might be tempted to handle this pattern in a single callback function as shown in Listing 29–3.

Listing 29–3. *Not Recommended: How Not to Handle the Node Paths*

```
/**
 * $arg1 corresponds to the integer id.
 * $arg2 corresponds to the action.
 */
function node_callback($arg1, $arg2) {
  // If $arg1 is an integer, use it to load the node.
  if (is_numeric($arg1)) {
    $node = node_load($arg1);
  }

  // If we have a node, go about our business.
  if ($node) {
    if ($arg2 == 'edit') ...

    if ($arg2 == 'revisions') ...
  }
}
```

This approach has a lot of drawbacks:

- It is hard to extend. What if you later want to write a module that handles node/42/send? If all node/integer/action type paths are handled by one function you'd either have to hack that function or replace it altogether.

- All of the if {...} statements clutter up the code.

- The whole picture gets more difficult when you consider this path, which Drupal also handles: node/add

This path displays a page with links to add new content. Now the second segment isn't an integer at all, so clearly we need a way to differentiate between all of the different possibilities in paths.

The menu system handles this wide range of dynamic paths quite elegantly. The use of a wildcard notation simplifies not only the handling of dynamic paths but also the task of loading common objects. Consider the hook_menu implementation in Listing 29–4.

Listing 29–4. *Recommended: How Drupal Handles the Node Paths*

```
/**
 * Implementation of hook_menu().
 */
function node_menu() {
  $items['node/add'] = array(
    'title' => 'Add content',
    'page callback' => 'node_add_page',
    'access callback' => '_node_add_access',
  );
```

```
$items['node/%node'] = array(
  'title callback' => 'node_page_title',
  'title arguments' => array(1),
  'page callback' => 'node_page_view',
  'page arguments' => array(1),
  'access callback' => 'node_access',
  'access arguments' => array('view', 1),
);

$items['node/%node/edit'] = array(
  'title' => 'Edit',
  'page callback' => 'node_page_edit',
  'page arguments' => array(1),
);

  return $items;
}
```

This is a slightly simplified version of the actual Drupal implementation for handling the node paths discussed previously. The original code can be found in Drupal's node.module, and by the naming convention, the node_menu()[3] function gets called whenever Drupal needs to build the menu router table.

Callback Functions

There are several things to observe here. The first item maps to the path 'node/add', and it uses the node_add_page() callback to generate a page that displays links to add various content to the system. To access this page at all, however, the user has to have the right access permissions. Whether the user has the right access permissions is decided by the function _node_add_access(), as specified by the 'access callback' key. In Listing 29–1 this bit was 'access callback' => TRUE, which is simply shorthand for saying that everyone has access. Now, in Listing 29–4 there is an example of access control being handed off to a dedicated callback function.

■ **New in 7** Drupal 7 has some new elements to modify the behavior of your menu items. The "delivery callback" can be defined to let a custom function handle rendering; you will usually be fine with the default, drupal_deliver_html_page. When replacing a default function with your own, you need to ensure that the replacement handles all the cases that the original function takes care of. The delivery callback function handles the cases of access denied, not found, site offline, and rendering the content. Another new element, context, can allow a menu item to be used as a contextual link (see Chapter 24 for an example). The rarely used "theme callback" and "theme arguments" elements allow you to provide a function to specify a different theme to be used when that menu item's page loads. Read the API introduction for a complete list with brief explanations.[4]

---

[3] Drupal's node_menu() function: api.drupal.org/api/drupal/modules--node--node.module/function/node_menu/7

[4] api.drupal.org/api/drupal/modules--system--system.api.php/function/hook_menu/7

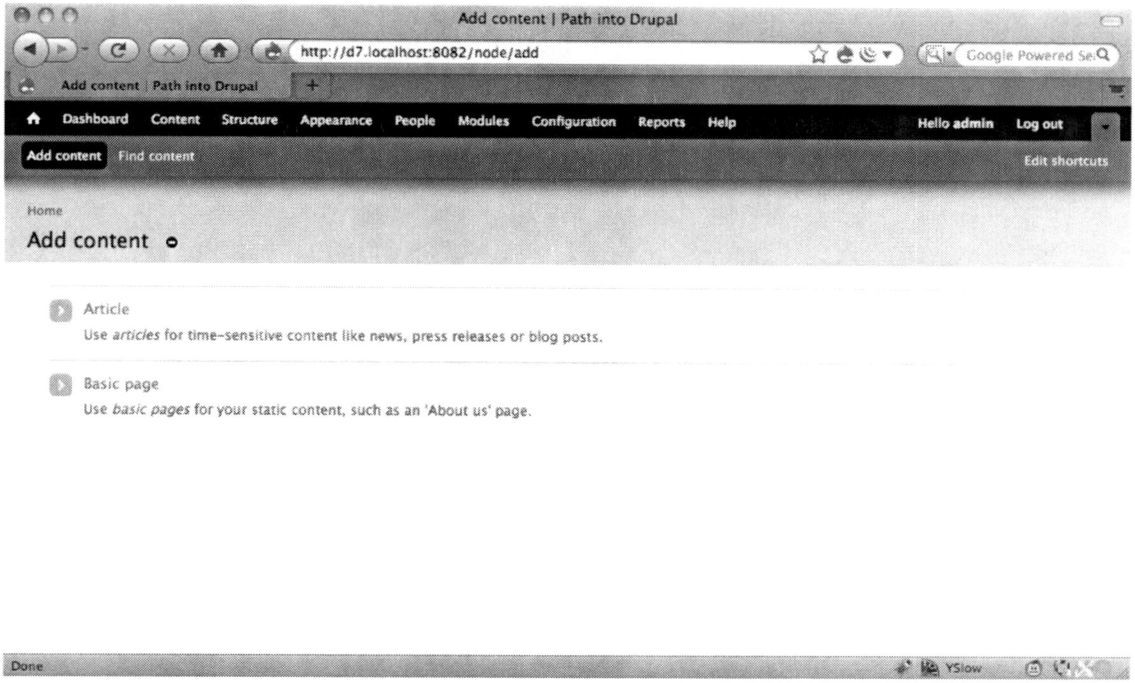

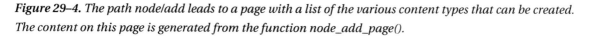

Figure 29–4. *The path node/add leads to a page with a list of the various content types that can be created. The content on this page is generated from the function node_add_page().*

The menu router item 'node/%node' has a wildcard segment in it, %node, which will match anything found in that segment. This item will match paths node/42, node/foo, and so forth. Although it would normally match node/add as well, it won't in this example because there is a menu router item that defines node/add exactly, and the exact match takes precedence over wildcard matches.

Loader Functions

Whenever the menu system matches an incoming Drupal path to a wildcard segment with a notation like %node, it attempts to call a special loader function to automatically load an object for later use by any callback functions. The specific loader function is determined by a naming convention; when the percent sign is followed by a string (e.g., %foo), the system will look for a loader function, foo_load(). The loader function for %node is node_load(). Thus the path node/42 will invoke the function node_load(42), sending in the matched integer as an argument. The result is a fully loaded and built $node object with the primary id of 42. This object, in turn, becomes available for use as an argument to the various callback functions. In Listing 29–4 it is being passed on to the page callback that is responsible for generating the content output for this request. In Listing 29–5, look at the page callback keys for the 'node/%node' item.

Listing 29–5. Detail of the node/%node Menu Router Item

```
$items['node/%node'] = array(
...
  'page callback' => 'node_page_view',
  'page arguments' => array(1),
...
);
```

These keys tell the menu system to use node_page_view() as the main page callback and to pass in a single argument. The argument is addressed with the 'page arguments' key, and the array contains the segment from the path that should be used as the argument. This is array(1) in the example, so path segment 1 should be used. Path segment numbering starts with zero, so array(1) refers to the %node part of the path. As was just shown, this is a fully loaded and built $node object, and it is this object that will be passed into the callback function. The code that executes for path node/42 is functionally equivalent to this snippet:

```
// Invoke the _load function for node with the argument 42.
$node = node_load(42);
// Invoke the page callback function with the built $node object.
return node_page_view($node);
```

Let's look again at the full definition for the 'node/%node' menu router, which is shown in Listing 29–6.

Listing 29–6. node/%node Menu Router Item

```
$items['node/%node'] = array(
  'title callback' => 'node_page_title',
  'title arguments' => array(1),
  'page callback' => 'node_page_view',
  'page arguments' => array(1),
  'access callback' => 'node_access',
  'access arguments' => array('view', 1),
);
```

In Listing 29–1 our menu router item had a key, 'title', in which the title was set directly. The 'node/%node' menu router item has 'title callback' and 'title arguments' keys instead. These allow for the title of the page to be dynamically set. The callback function responsible for setting the title is node_page_title(), and it receives the same loaded $node object as node_page_view(), as specified by 'title arguments' => array(1). In this way the title of this page can be formed using dynamic information from the $node object.

In the same fashion, this menu router item's access callback function takes some parameters, one of which is the dynamically loaded $node object. Based on the 'access callback' and 'access arguments' keys, code similar to the following snippet will be executed to determine whether the user issuing the request can access the 'node/4711' path:

```
// Segment 1 gets passed into the loader function for %node.
$node = node_load(4711);
// The loaded $node object gets passed to the access callback function.
return node_access('view', $node);
```

The 'node/%node' menu router item is a great example of how much functionality can be wired together with a relatively simple array of metadata to specify callback functions and their parameters.

The menu system handles the loading of data objects and the invocation of callbacks to set the page title, checks if the current user is allowed to access this path, and generates the page content.

The developer uses the menu router item definitions to describe to the system what is supposed to happen, but how it all actually ends up happening is handled behind the scenes. The advantage of doing things this way—using data arrays to describe desired behavior—as opposed to simply writing the few lines of code to load and display the node directly, will be seen later when hook_menu_alter is discussed. The ability for developers to rewire menu router items, even those described in Drupal's core, is fundamental to allowing contributed modules the chance to change anything and everything, if desired. Remember, "Do it in contrib" has to be a viable option, even for the most far-fetched ideas that come along.

Fitness

What happens when a path comes in that can be matched by more than one menu router item? How is the one true item chosen? Which item is the most fit to handle any given request? Consider the path node/12345/edit. This path can be matched by both of the following menu router items from Listing 29–4:

```
$items['node/%node']
$items['node/%node/edit']
```

The node/%node item is considered to be an ancestor of node/%node/edit because they have all but the last segment, edit, in common. When searching for a menu router item to handle a path, Drupal starts by calculating all of the possible ancestors of the path. Here is the complete theoretical ancestry of node/12345/edit:

```
node/12345/edit
node/12345/%
node/%/edit
node/%/%
node/12345
node/%
Node
```

Wildcard segments are simplified and represented by the % placeholder. There is not any guarantee that any of these menu router items are actually defined, but by generating the list of ancestors Drupal at least knows which router items to look for. This translates roughly into SQL like this:

```
SELECT * FROM menu_router
  WHERE path IN
  ('node/12345/edit',
  'node/12345/%',
  'node/%/edit',
  'node/12345',
 'node/%',
 'node')
```

This will find all of the possible menu router items that can handle a request, but which one is the best one to handle node/12345/edit? Here is where the concept of fitness comes in. Any menu router item path is broken down by segment and converted into a series of 1s or 0s. Discreet segments (such as node or edit) become 1s and wildcards become 0s. The resultant string of 1s and 0s is then interpreted as a binary integer to calculate that menu router item's fitness. Applying these rules to the ancestors of path node/12345/edit produces the list in Table 29–2.

Table 29–2. Drupal Path Ancestry and Fitness. From `drupal.org/node/109134`

Path	Fitness Base 10	Fitness Binary
node/12345/edit	7	111
node/12345/%	6	110
node/%/edit	5	101
node/%/%	4	100
node/12345	3	11
node/%	2	10
Node	1	1

The base ten fitness value is always saved along with any path in the menu router database table. Fitness is used for ordering the paths as shown in the following SQL query. Out of any set of menu router items, the one with the highest fitness will be used to handle a given request. The actual SQL generated by node/12345/edit thus becomes:

```
SELECT * FROM menu_router
  WHERE path IN
    ('node/12345/edit',
     'node/12345/%',
     'node/%/edit',
     'node/12345',
     'node/%',
     'node')
  ORDER BY fit DESC
  LIMIT 0, 1
```

Exactly one item from the ancestry of the actual path will be selected—the one with the highest fitness. If querying the menu_router table produces no results, a 404 Not Found page is generated. Understanding how fitness is calculated is usually not necessary for Drupal module developers, but it is one of the aspects of the menu system that makes it a beautiful architecture.

Hopefully this exercise of deconstructing Drupal's menu router paths has illustrated some of the tools available to developers for *extending* a Drupal application. The ability to define new paths, wire them to callbacks, preload objects, and manage access, all within the Drupal application, gives one enough power to add virtually any new feature. In the next section, I'll show you how existing features can be *modified* using hook_menu_alter.

Modifying Existing Router Items

The examples so far have been focused on extending Drupal. What does one do to modify or replace existing functionality? How does a developer alter core Drupal behavior without resorting to changing the core Drupal code itself? Drupal lays bare its entire menu router to any module to be able to change.

The mechanism for doing this is called hook_menu_alter. Modules may implement their own hook_menu_alter function and simply change any of the defined menu router items.

Let's go back to the first example in this chapter, the outrageous message. If someone comes up with a custom implementation for developing outrageous messages, but doesn't want to or isn't able to convince the maintainer of the outrageous module that the new implementation is better, he can implement their own module that alters the way outrageous messages get created (see Listing 29–7).

Listing 29–7. Review of the Outrageous Module

```php
<?php

function outrageous_menu() {
  $items['outrageous'] = array(
    'title' => 'Outrageous message',
    'access callback' => TRUE,
    'page callback' => 'outrageous_message',
  );

  return $items;
}

function outrageous_message() {
  // Create an outrageous message. Based on a quote by Gill Davies.
  // t() is a wrapper that allows text to be localized.
  $message = t('A teddy bear is a cuddle with four paws on the end.');

  // Get a formatted date.
  $time = date('M d, Y');

  $page = array(
    '#markup' => "$time: $message",
  );

  return $page;
}
```

The moreoutrageous_menu_alter() function in Listing 29–8 implements hook_menu_alter by following the naming convention of modulename + hook name, and it receives the entire menu router item table in the form of an $items array.

Listing 29–8. The Moreoutrageous Module

```php
<?php
function moreoutrageous_menu_alter(&$items) {
  // Change the callback function for the path 'outrageous'.
  $items['outrageous']['page callback'] = 'moreoutrageous_message';
}

function moreoutrageous_message() {
  // Juicy (mis)quote by Károly Négyesi.
  $message = t('I am a machine for turning orange juice into Drupal patches.');

  // Get a formatted date.
  $time = date('M d, Y');
```

```
$page = array(
  '#markup' => "$time: $message",
);

return $page;
}
```

The $items array is the sum total of all menu router items returned by all of the hook_menu implementations from all enabled modules. Since the array is passed in by reference any alterations made to it will persist beyond the scope of the function. The code changes the 'page callback' value that was designated in the outrageous_menu() function in the outrageous module and specifies that it should instead be handled by the moreoutrageous_message() function in the moreoutrageous module.

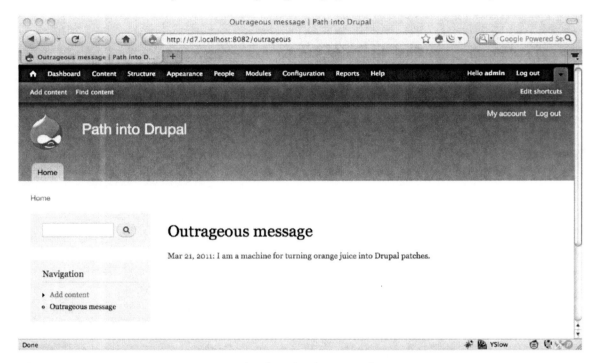

Figure 29–5. *A more outrageous message, thanks to hook_menu_alter*

Building the menu router table is a relatively expensive operation. First hook_menu is invoked, which results in all modules being checked for implementing functions. Once the menu router items from all of the modules are collected and concatenated into a large array, hook_menu_alter is invoked, affording each module the chance to alter that array. Fortunately this is not done on every page request. The menu router table is rebuilt whenever something about the fundamental state of the Drupal application changes. Examples include installing new modules, defining new content types, or creating new views of content. Once the final array of all menu router items is built it is persisted in the menu_router database table. Subsequent page requests are able to query this table to find callbacks and router items until the next occasion that necessitates a total rebuild occurs.

Summary

The menu system is a tool that offers a great deal of control and opportunity. It is easy to grasp and developers with a wide range of skills and abilities are able to use it effectively. It isn't the only tool available for extending or altering Drupal. Other tools exist if your goal is to alter a form or extend the definition or behavior of nodes or content types. Used together, these tools allow for the enhancement and alteration of Drupal's core functionality and behavior while avoiding the need to hack the core code. By embracing this need for an architecture that is open and accessible, Drupal supports a very significant amount of community participation, has become the choice of platforms for hundreds of thousands of people and organizations, and has enabled thousands of developers to become open source contributors.

■ ■ ■

## CHAPTER 30

Under the Hood: Inside Drupal When It Displays a Page

by Stefan Freudenberg

The moment a web browser requests a page, Drupal begins running a complex series of steps that result in a fully rendered page being returned to the browser. With every page request, Drupal has to do those same calculations, so understanding them is key to making the best development decisions for your modules or sites.

In this chapter you will learn what happens when a Drupal URL is requested, for instance, http://definitivedrupal.org/node/84. Chapter 29 covered how the URL is sorted out by the web server to become index.php?q=node/84. In this chapter, I'll start with what happens when the web server hands the path node/84 to Drupal's index.php.

The web server's PHP interpreter parses index.php and executes the code. Drupal's developers have organized the process of creating a Drupal page into two sequences: bootstrap and execution of the page callback associated with the current path. This division allows the use of a working Drupal environment for applications other than generating web pages. A good example is Drupal's own cronjob which executes hook_cron() after bootstrapping and performing some basic checks.

```
/**
 * Root directory of Drupal installation.
 */
define('DRUPAL_ROOT', getcwd());


require_once DRUPAL_ROOT . '/includes/bootstrap.inc';
drupal_bootstrap(DRUPAL_BOOTSTRAP_FULL);
menu_execute_active_handler();
```

Bootstrap always runs the same for a full page load. The execution of the page callback depends on the path handed in, node/84 in this example.

Bootstrap

The task of the bootstrap is to set the stage for business logic and theming to take place by including all necessary libraries, preparing a database connection, and reading the configuration. It is accomplished in separate phases, and each phase must be executed only once and in a particular order. This is enforced by the drupal_bootstrap() function and by having a constant integer assigned to the phases that represent their processing order (see Table 30–1). `drupal_bootstrap()` is called with the bootstrap phase that should be reached as a parameter.

Table 30–1. Drupal Bootstrap Phases

#	Phase	Purpose
0	DRUPAL_BOOTSTRAP_CONFIGURATION	Initialize configuration
1	DRUPAL_BOOTSTRAP_PAGE_CACHE	Try to serve a cached page
2	DRUPAL_BOOTSTRAP_DATABASE	Initialize database layer
3	DRUPAL_BOOTSTRAP_VARIABLES	Initialize the variable system
4	DRUPAL_BOOTSTRAP_SESSION	Initialize session handling
5	DRUPAL_BOOTSTRAP_PAGE_HEADER	Set up the page header
6	DRUPAL_BOOTSTRAP_LANGUAGE	Find out the language of the page
7	DRUPAL_BOOTSTRAP_FULL	Load modules and initialize theme

First Bootstrap Phase: Initialize Configuration

In phase one, `settings.php` is read from the sites/default folder and the most important global variables are set, either directly from `settings.php` like `$databases` or by computing their value based on the server environment. Here are three you will need in your daily site developer's life:

- `$base_url`: The base URL all your Drupal pages share. Each path is appended to it. It must be a valid URL without a trailing slash. This only needs to be set if Drupal does not determine it correctly.

```
$base_url = 'http://www.example.com/drupal'; // NO trailing slash![1]
```

- `$base_path`: The base URL's path component (either '/' or anything following the domain part) with a trailing slash appended. It is derived from `$base_url` and can be handy on its own.

```
$base_path = '/drupal/';
```

- `$base_root`: Contains the protocol and domain parts of the URL. It is either the base URL or derived from it by removing the base path if there is any.

```
$base_root = 'http://www.example.com';
```

---

[1] Jeff Eaton tried to get in a patch documenting this requirement in a more dramatic way. See `drupal.org/files/issues/settings.php_1.patch`

Second Bootstrap Phase: Try to Serve a Cached Page

During the second bootstrap phase Drupal tries to deliver the whole page from its cache in case page caching is enabled in the Performance section of the configuration interface and the visitor is not logged in. If a cached version of the page can be found and is not expired, it is sent between invoking hook_boot() and hook_exit().

If the cache back end requires a database connection (determined by $conf['page_cache_without_database'] in settings.php), the third and fourth bootstrap phases are executed before fetching the cached page.

Debugging page caching is eased by an additional HTTP header the Drupal developers have introduced for this purpose: if the page is actually served from cache, the X-Drupal-Cache HTTP header is set to HIT (see Figure 30–1); otherwise, its value is set to MISS (see Figure 30–2).

Figure 30–1. The X-Drupal-Cache HTTP header is set to HIT. You need the Firebug plug-in to view HTTP headers in Firefox.

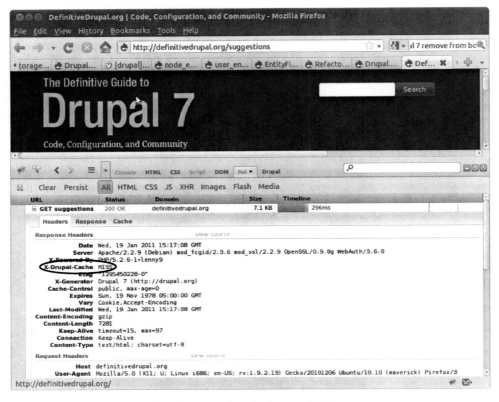

Figure 30–2. The X-Drupal-Cache HTTP header is set to MISS.

■ **Tip** The cache back end is pluggable. By default, Drupal uses database tables for caching pages, blocks, etc. Alternative back ends can be registered in settings.php by adding a filename to $conf['cache_backends']. The file must include a class implementing DrupalCacheInterface. Drupal ships with a database cache implementation and a mock implementation that is needed during installation. A popular alternative cache implementation is provided by the memcache module (drupal.org/project/memcache) that uses memcached as a back end (see Chapter 27 for details). To support page caching by a reverse proxy caching agent such as Varnish (www.varnish-cache.org/), replacing Drupal's built-in page cache for anonymous visitors, hook_boot() and hook_exit() must be deliberately disabled. This is necessary to ensure consistent behavior for requests hitting the origin server and for requests hitting the cache-serving intermediary server. Add the following lines to your settings.php[2]:

---

[2] See http://drupal.org/node/797346

```
$conf['page_cache_invoke_hooks'] = FALSE;
if (!class_exists('DrupalFakeCache')) {

 $conf['cache_backends'][] = 'includes/cache-install.inc';
}
// Rely on the external cache for page caching.
$conf['cache_class_cache_page'] = 'DrupalFakeCache';
```

Third Bootstrap Phase: Initialize the Database Layer

The database abstraction layer is set up in this phase. Because there's no need to open a connection yet, only the base classes and utility functions (db_query, et al) are included. In addition, callbacks for autoloading classes and interfaces are registered with the Standard PHP Library (SPL) autoload stack[3]. The files containing classes and interfaces are declared by modules' .info files or live in the main include folder, and Drupal maintains a registry to track them. The first time a class or interface is needed during execution, the callbacks use this registry to include the necessary file.

■ **Note** The database abstraction layer in Drupal 7 has undergone one of the most drastic changes from Drupal 6. Instead of the functions we used to love (and hate)—such as db_query()–there's now a modern database layer based on PHP 5's PDO: query builders, a fluent interface, result sets providing iterator interfaces, named placeholders, and consistent transaction and master/slave replication support. (If you liked db_query(), there's good news: it's still there as a wrapper for non-dynamic queries.)

Fourth Bootstrap Phase: Initialize the Variable System

In the fourth bootstrap phase, Drupal fetches all values from the variable database table (which includes both configuration settings and persistent variables) and merges them with those defined in settings.php in the global variable $conf. Values set in the file via $conf['variable_name'] take precedence over those stored in the database; in other words, you can prevent variables from being overridden through the UI by defining them in the settings.php file.

The $conf variable takes the form of a giant associative array. Its values can be obtained by calling variable_get('key_name', 'a default value'). Variables can be persisted by calling variable_set('key_name', 'value') in your code.

In addition to the variables, all modules required during bootstrap are loaded, implementing hooks called during bootstrap, hook_boot(), hook_exit(), hook_language_init(), and hook_watchdog(). The pluggable locking system is also included. Pluggable means you can provide an alternative

---

[3] http://php.net/manual/en/function.spl-autoload-register.php

implementation and make Drupal use it by defining `$conf['lock_inc'] = 'path/to/your/lock.inc'`. You have already encountered this pattern earlier in this chapter.

■ **Tip** Drupal's excellent in-code documentation explains how locking works: "Drupal implements a cooperative, advisory lock system. Any long-running operation that could potentially be attempted in parallel by multiple requests should try to acquire a lock before proceeding. By obtaining a lock, one request notifies any other requests that a specific operation is in progress that must not be executed in parallel."

An example of this can be seen in the variable initialization code. Fetching all data from the variable table has proven to be a performance issue, so in Drupal 7, the result of this query will be cached. A problem arises when more than one process attempts to populate the variables cache when it is not yet primed. This is solved by means of the locking system. Before variables data is fetched from the database, a lock must be acquired. If another process already has the same lock, code execution pauses for a second; afterwards, another attempt is made to get the variables data. This happens as long as the lock is not released by the process that has originally acquired the lock. As such, it is guaranteed that only the first process claiming the lock fetches the variables from the database and stores them in cache for subsequent requests. See more at `http://api.Drupal.org/api/Drupal/includes--lock.inc/group/lock/7`

Fifth Bootstrap Phase: Initialize Session Handling

Things covered so far: database, settings, variables, some common Drupal functions and constants, global variables, and bootstrap modules.

In this phase, Drupal registers its session handler and a session is associated for already authenticated users. Usually, anonymous users won't get a session at all unless something needs to be stored in `$_SESSION`; for this case, a session ID is pregenerated. This allows HTTP proxy caching for anonymous visitors. If Drupal can't detect a logged in user, a dummy user object is created during this phase that represents the anonymous visitor with a user ID 0 in Drupal's database.

If you need fancier session handling than Drupal's own database solution, you can include an alternative by pointing `$['conf']['session_inc']` in `settings.php` to a file containing the functions that need to be implemented. Sites with many authenticated visitors can benefit from a more efficient session storage. The Mongodb module explained in Chapter 27 provides such an alternative.

Sixth Bootstrap Phase: Set up the Page Header

After all that nice setup, the first output is generated to be sent to the site's visitor: the HTTP headers. The default headers Drupal sends to the client only affect caching. To be precise: No byte is sent on its way to the visitor because Drupal operates in output buffering mode. In other words, nothing leaves the server until the buffer is flushed, which happens at the final stage of the cycle. Wait! Something happens before: `hook_boot()` is invoked, giving modules a first opportunity to intervene in the page creation cycle. Note that this hook must be disabled to support external caching mechanisms (see the Tip in phase 3).

Seventh Bootstrap Phase: Find out the Language of the Page

The next-to-last step in the bootstrap process deals with language selection for the current visitor if the site is multilingual. Once the language is determined, implementations of hook_language_init() can react, for instance by setting language dependent variables.

Language Negotiation Algorithms

Negotiation algorithms that determine which language to use can be provided by hook_language_negotiation_info() and existing ones can be modified by hook_language_negotiation_info_alter(). The providers will have a chance to determine a language in the order they are set by the site admin at the language configuration page (admin/config/regional/language/configure). Each defined negotiation algorithm must provide a callback to determine the language. Language selection stops as soon as a provider returns a valid language.

Here is an example of a language provider:

```
$providers[LOCALE_LANGUAGE_NEGOTIATION_URL] = array(
  'types' => array(LANGUAGE_TYPE_CONTENT, LANGUAGE_TYPE_INTERFACE, LANGUAGE_TYPE_URL),
  'callbacks' => array(
    'language' => 'locale_language_from_url',
    'switcher' => 'locale_language_switcher_url',
    'url_rewrite' => 'locale_language_url_rewrite_url',
  ),
  'file' => $file,
  'weight' => -8,
  'name' => t('URL'),
  'description' => t('Determine the language from the URL (Path prefix or domain).'),
  'config' => 'admin/config/regional/language/configure/url',
);
```

Final Bootstrap Phase: Load Modules and Initialize Theme

Finally drupal_bootstrap_full() is executed. All files containing the Drupal utility functions are included. Enabled modules are loaded (in other words, the .module files are included). Modules get a chance to register stream wrappers[4] by means of hook_stream_wrappers() and modify existing ones with hook_stream_wrapper_alter(). (By now you know that all hooks registering things also have an alter hook). The path in $_GET['q'] is normalized and the theme is initialized.

■ **Note** You can replace all or some of the original functions of Drupal's menu system and path handling functions by providing an alternative menu.inc or path.inc in settings.php. You might want to do this to improve the performance of your Drupal site...if you have lots of guts and nerves of steel. Be careful; you might accidentally change core Drupal behavior.

---

[4] http://api.drupal.org/api/drupal/modules--system--system.api.php/function/hook_url_inbound_alter/7

Path normalization is the task of drupal_get_normal_path(). It checks if the path stored in $_GET['q'] is a path alias or a custom URL that needs to be mapped onto an internal Drupal entity URL (node/84, user/123). If ordinary stored aliases are not enough for you, implementations of hook_url_inbound_alter() can add some magic. This hook is called after aliases from the URL alias table have been mapped to system paths. See the API documentation for a usage example.

Initializing the theme layer involves looking up the active theme, which can either be the theme set as the default theme in the UI, a user's personally preferred theme, one returned by an implementation of hook_custom_theme(), or a theme explicitly set for the active path via the menu system. All CSS and JavaScript declared in the theme's .info file is added to the page and the theme's hook_init() implementation is called if it exists.

At the very end of this phase when Drupal is fully set up, hook_init() is invoked. On using hook_init(), the API documentation states: "It is typically used to set up global parameters that are needed later in the request." Drupal core's Locale module implements hook_init() to initialize date formats based on the user's current language.

▓ **Note** In Drupal 6, hook_init() was commonly used for adding CSS or JavaScript files intended for every page load. While you can still do it in this fashion, these assets can now also be listed in the module's .info file, like scripts[] = example.js or stylesheets[all][] = example.css. The system module's implementation of hook_init(), system_init(), then takes care of adding those files.

Execution of the Page Callback

After completing the bootstrap phase, Drupal is ready to build, render, and deliver content. Because every request is routed to index.php by the rewrite rules in .htaccess, Drupal needs an internal mechanism to dispatch a given request URL to something that handles the request. In Drupal, that something is the active menu item's page callback. A menu item is a collection of information about how to respond to a client's request to a given path. You learned how the menu system works in Chapter 29. The most important part is the page callback—a function returning a renderable data structure. Rendering is explained in Appendix C.

Drupal has a few cases to consider:

- The site is in offline mode.

- No menu item for the requested path is found in the menu_router table.

- The visitor does not have permission to view the resource associated with the menu item.

- Everything works as expected and the page callback is executed.

The result of this algorithm is either an integer equaling the corresponding HTTP status code or a render array in the format expected by drupal_render(). It is handed over to drupal_deliver_page(), which lets the delivery callback produce the output. By default, this is drupal_deliver_html_page(). It makes use of drupal_render() to merge the render array returned by the page callback with likewise structured region data and turn the whole page into HTML. Figure 30–3 illustrates the whole page load cycle indicating when Drupal's hooks get called.

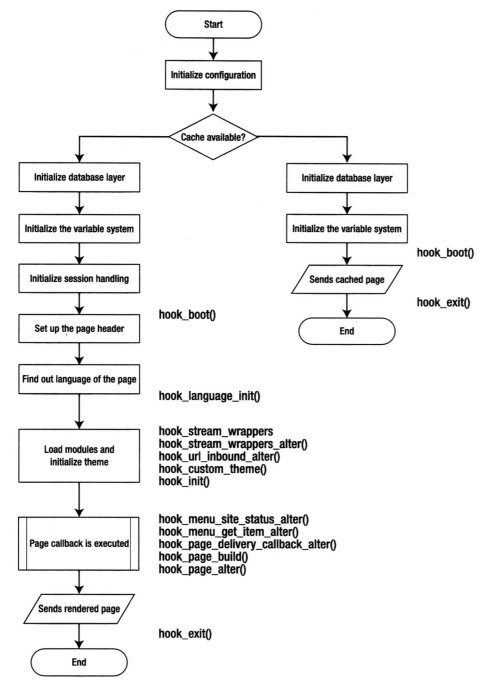

Figure 30–3. Page load cycle detailing the bootstrap

A Typical Example

Let's come back to the example URL from the beginning of this chapter: node/84. Drupal's menu system takes care of loading the node identified by the node ID 84 by calling node_load(84). Under the hood, DrupalDefaultEntityController and its subclass NodeController take care of fetching the matching record from the database and invoking hook_load(), hook_entity_load(), and hook_node_load(), thereby giving modules opportunities to manipulate the node object or trigger other actions. Associated fields are loaded via field_attach_load(). Modules implementing hook_field_storage_pre_load() or hook_field_attach_load() have the opportunity to add and alter field data on the fly for each field. Node 84 is a node of type book, provided by the book core module. Figure 30–4 shows a debugger's view of the node object after loading is completed. Properties and fields added by various modules are indicated.

In the following example code you see book_node_load(), the book module's implementation of hook_node_load(). Like all its implementations, it takes two arguments, an array of nodes, and an array of their types. If the node loaded is part of a book, additional data is attached to the node to extend its behavior: the node becomes aware of being part of a book. Types are ignored here but might be important for other modules. For you as a developer, it's important to understand that the complex loading process actually takes a lot of the burden away from you. You only need to implement the appropriate hooks.

```
/**
 * Implements hook_node_load().
 */
function book_node_load($nodes, $types) {
  $result = db_query("SELECT * FROM {book} b INNER JOIN {menu_links} ml ON \
b.mlid = ml.mlid WHERE b.nid IN (:nids)", array(':nids' => \          array_keys($nodes)),
array('fetch' => PDO::FETCH_ASSOC));
  foreach ($result as $record) {
    $nodes[$record['nid']]->book = $record;
    $nodes[$record['nid']]->book['href'] = $record['link_path'];
    $nodes[$record['nid']]->book['title'] = $record['link_title'];
    $nodes[$record['nid']]->book['options'] = unserialize($record['options']);
  }
}
```

After loading the node object, it is passed to the page callback for the given path, node_page_view(). It sets the node's title as the page title and adds a canonical and a short link[5] to the HTML head elements (not rendered yet) and the HTTP headers. Building the render array is the responsibility of node_show(), which delegates it to node_view_multiple(). In this function, each node's render array is built by node_view(). Fields are prepared for rendering and modules get an opportunity to act on the content to be displayed via hook_entity_prepare_view(). That hook is especially important; developers implementing a new entity should make sure it is invoked in an ENTITY_build_content() or ENTITY_view_multiple() function by calling entity_prepare_view(), like node_view_multiple() does. Read the API documentation of entity_prepare_view()[6] for further details.

---

[5] Canonical links are very useful to avoid being punished by search engines for advertising more than one URL for the same content. A very common case is the short URL, which is quite popular with SMS services.

[6] api.drupal.org/api/drupal/includes--common.inc/function/entity_prepare_view/7

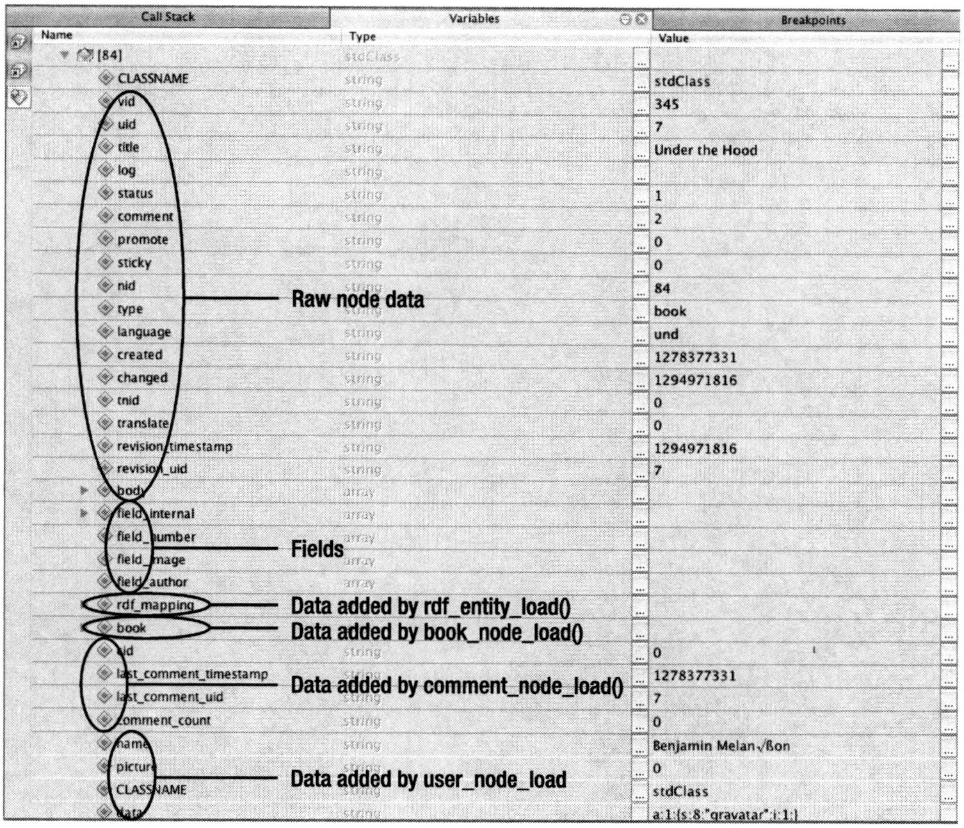

Figure 30–4. *Netbeans debugger view of a completely loaded node object*

Each individual node (there's only one for this page) is rendered by node_view(), delegating the bulk of the work to node_build_content(). Fields and links are turned into render arrays and modules are given the possibility to further add to the render array by means of hook_entity_view() and hook_node_view(). The book module implements the latter using it to add the book navigation element, as shown in Figure 30–5. How it looks on the finished page is shown in Figure 30–6. Before leaving the page callback context, hook_entity_view_alter() and hook_node_view_alter() are invoked as a last chance to modify what other modules have done before.

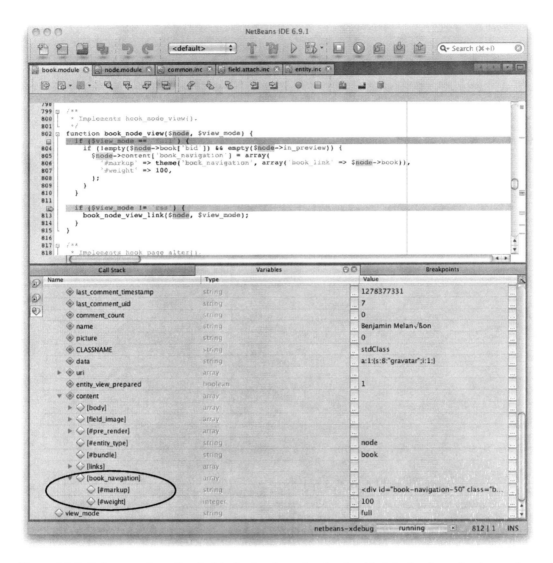

Figure 30–5. *Debugger view of node 84 after book_node_view() added the book navigation to the render array*

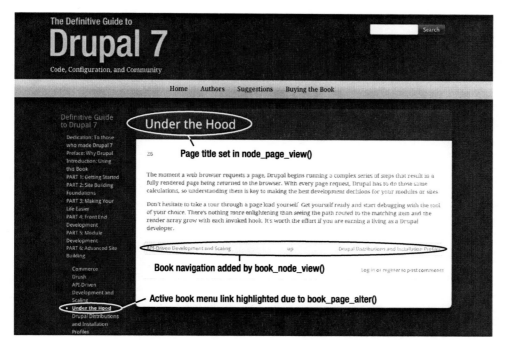

***Figure 30–6.** The final outcome*

When the render array is finally returned by the page callback, it is passed to drupal_deliver_page(), which leaves rendering to the delivery callback drupal_deliver_html_page(). It makes sure other modules have a last chance to alter the outcome by invoking hook_page_build() and hook_page_alter() before drupal_render() traverses the render array to generate the markup. hook_page_build() is used by the block module to add content to the regions defined in the theme. book_page_alter() takes advantage of the powerful new hook_page_alter() to add the book menu to the active menus.

```
/**
 * Implements hook_page_alter().
 *
 * Add the book menu to the list of menus used to build the active trail when
 * viewing a book page.
 */
function book_page_alter(&$page) {
  if (($node = menu_get_object()) && !empty($node->book['bid'])) {
    $active_menus = menu_get_active_menu_names();
    $active_menus[] = $node->book['menu_name'];
    menu_set_active_menu_names($active_menus);
  }
}
```

To conclude this example of a typical page load cycle, the details of rendering can be found in Appendix C. Once the markup is ready, the page in all its beauty is sent to the browser of the visitor. Figure 30–7 illustrates the most important hooks covered in the second part of this chapter.

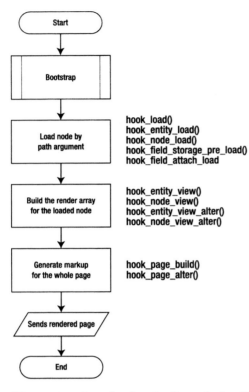

Figure 30–7. *Page load cycle of a node detailing the execution of the page callback*

After digging through a full load cycle of a Drupal page, it's a good idea to review it from a bird's eye perspective. The bootstrap has set the stage for modules to deliver content to the visitor. It's the same procedure for all the pages of your website. A number of hooks are invoked at the various phases, presenting opportunities to influence your site's behavior at a global level. When contributing to Drupal modules or creating your own, think carefully about when a certain piece of code needs to be executed and pick the most fitting hook. It doesn't make sense to figure out the language selection at a later stage of the page load; everything that's needed for the task is available during the bootstrap and all pages can benefit from a resolution at that point.

Summary

Drupal 7 has introduced several new concepts, most prominent among them entities and fields. Numerous hooks are at your disposal to affect the behavior and presentation of your content. These hooks make it easy to create big effects with lean code and little effort. Examine some of the core modules to see how they leverage the entity and field API.

Don't hesitate to take a tour through a page load yourself. Start debugging with the tool of your choice—there's nothing more enlightening than seeing the path routed to the matching item and the render array grow with each invoked hook. It's worth the effort if you are earning a living as a Drupal developer. A summary of tools for looking under Drupal's hood—including your suggestions—will be kept up-to-date at dgd7.org/inside.

## CHAPTER 31

Search and Apache Solr Integration

by Peter Wolanin

This chapter will discuss the Apache Solr Search Integration module in terms of how it implements the Drupal core Search module hooks, as an example of how to make a custom search, and in terms of its functionality. This chapter also highlights some of the additional hooks that allow the module's behavior to be customized and extended. This module can be seen as an example of integrating Drupal with a web service, and it makes use of some object-oriented code.

The Search module in Drupal core provides a framework and API for modules to provide search functionality. The Search module itself does very little except provide a search form and some administrative configuration options. In order to have the search form show up, one or more modules must implement the Search module hooks. Within Drupal core, both the Node module and User module implement the search hooks.

The Node module provides the ability to do keyword searches of content. Since it is part of Drupal core, it uses the SQL database as the storage and searching mechanism. While the Node module's search implementation provides very good keyword matching, its use of the database can cause significant performance issues for larger sites. In addition, while it can handle some filtering (for example, by user or taxonomy term via the advanced search form), this is rather limited.

The Apache Solr Search Integration module (found at `drupal.org/project/apachesolr`) provides an alternative and replacement for the Node module's search for indexing and searching content. A wider range of content indexing and filtering functionality is available, and Solr server can be accessed from many Drupal sites. A number of the enhancements and changes to the Search module API in Drupal 7 were driven by the limitations encountered when creating Apache Solr Search Integration with the Drupal 6 Search module. There are several key features that distinguish it from the Node module search:

- Faceted search using Facet API module.

- Multiple user-selectable sorts for results.

- Highly customizable boosting that allows you to tune the relevancy score for search results to control what is listed first.

- Fast searches for large amounts of content (e.g., > 10,000 nodes).

- The potential to do multi-site searches or federated searches, such as showing user and content searches in the same result set.

■ **Note** The term "facet" refers to an attribute of the documents in the search results (or the whole search index), such as a taxonomy term. "Faceted search" refers to an interface for filtering search results based on facets, which is a technique for helping the user find the desired result and avoid dead-end searches.

Apache Solr is its own open-source project. Actually, it's a part of the Lucene Java project: Lucene is the actual search library that Solr is built upon. Apache Solr provides the HTTP interface and hence can be integrated with Drupal (or almost any other application) while residing on the same server or a totally separate server. The fact that Solr can be run on a separate server is one reason for its popularity in the Drupal community: it allows a site administrator to reduce the load on the database server and get fast search results even for sites with hundreds of thousands of nodes. Solr also has built-in support for master-slave replication, so it can easily provide high availability for search requests; it can also scale horizontally in the event that search traffic exceeds the capacity of one server. The Drupal module is primarily intended to work with the stable Solr 1.4.x release series, though most or all functionality should work with the forthcoming Solr releases.

If you want to run Solr, you have the following options:

- Run it yourself. Generally this option is suited for those with at least one dedicated server or VPS. It requires, at the least, the ability to deploy Solr in a Java servlet container (like Jetty or Tomcat) and control access to it via firewall rules, HTTP authentication, or other authentication.

- Pay for a hosted Solr index. Acquia provides a Solr index for every customer with a Drupal support subscription. Other companies provide more generic services.

- Pool resources via a non-profit or cooperative such as May First People Link.

The Apache Solr project comes with a simple-to-run Jetty deployment that almost anyone interested in trying the module can get running in a few minutes on a local machine. The steps are outlined in the README.txt that comes with the Apache Solr Search Integration module. However, this simple kind of deployment does not include any authentication mechanism, so access to Solr needs to be protected by a firewall, at minimum, when used for a production site on a public server.

Search Module Administrative Options

The administrative interface for the Search module provides some key configuration options in Drupal 7 that were not available in Drupal 6. Both the Search module and Apache Solr Search Integration settings are found in the Search and metadata section at the admin/config path, as shown in Figure 31–1.

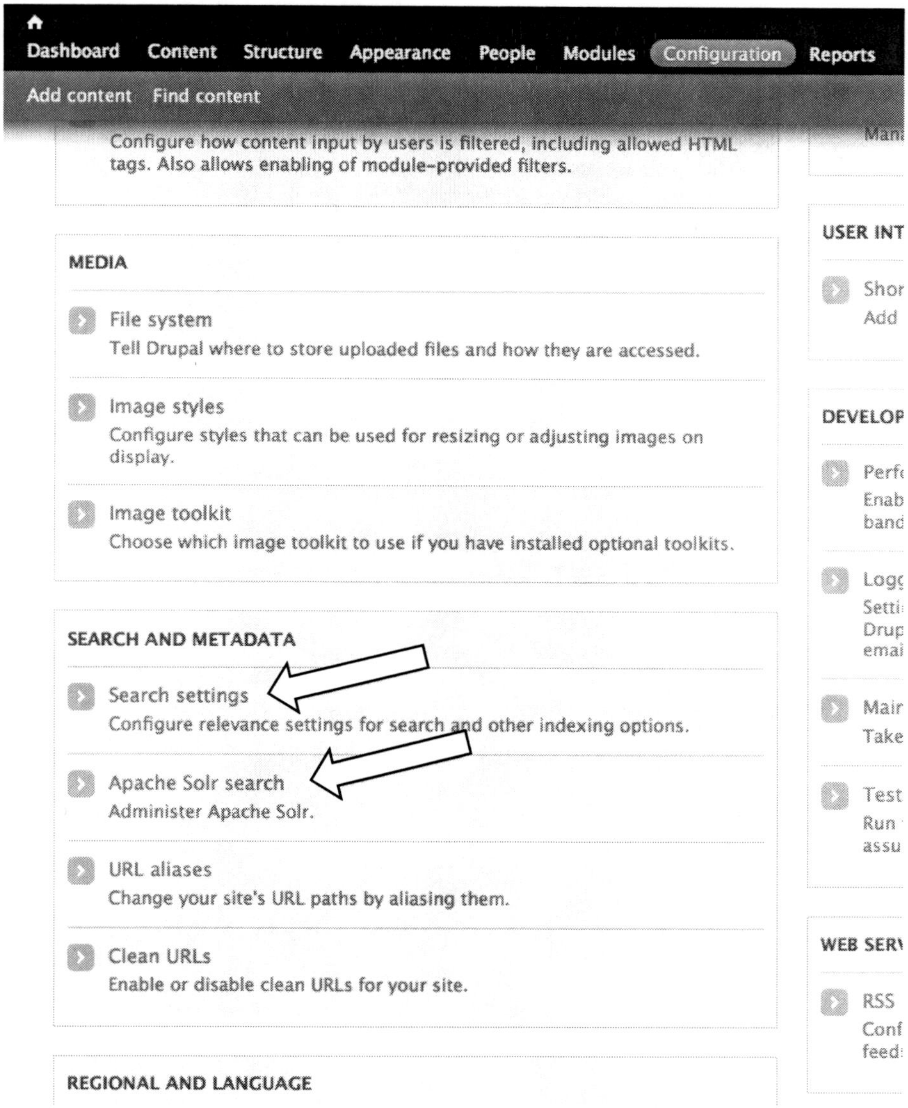

Figure 31–1. *The Search settings in the Admin Configuration screen*

Of particular note for the Search module, shown in Figure 31–2, the form at `admin/config/search/settings` allows you to selectively enable any or all of the modules that implement the search hooks. You can also choose any one of them to be the default search (the search that is run from the search block form and the default tab). If you want to use Apache Solr Search Integration as the main search, you should make it the default and likely disable the Node module search.

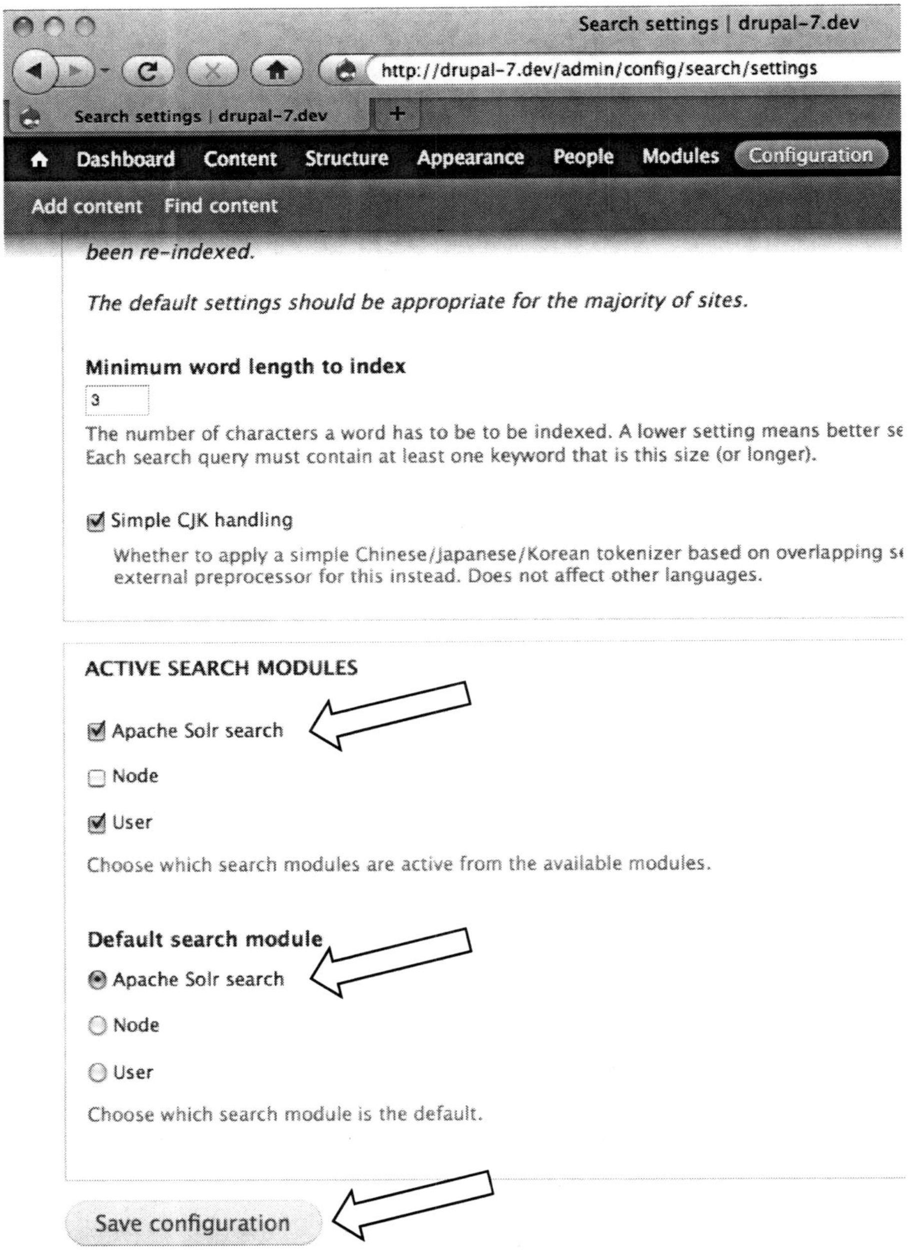

Figure 31–2. Search module configuration options

Search Results and Facet Blocks

Further configuration will be discussed later in the chapter, but what you get when appropriate filters are enabled and blocks are configured is a default search that allows you to see the current keywords and filters so that you can narrow your search or make it broader by removing one of the current filters. The enabled filters that are relevant for the current search results will show up in a facet block. Each link in this block will apply one additional filter to narrow the result set. The default settings show the facets with a checkbox (this is added via JavaScript). Once a facet filter is applied to the search results, you can also check the Retain current filters checkbox, which essentially gives you the option to search again with different keywords and the current filters (see Figure 31–3).

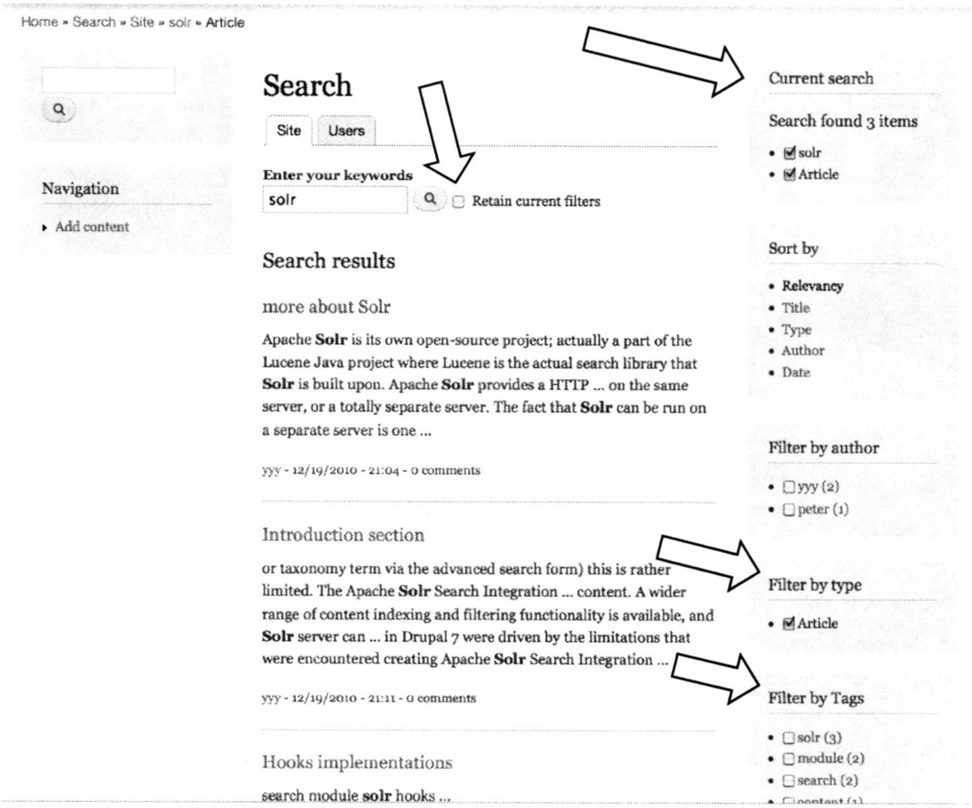

Figure 31–3. Search results with current search block, facet blocks, and the checkbox to retain filters when using new keywords

Search Module API

The Search module in Drupal core provides a framework that other modules can use. In particular, they can take advantage of the search interface and standard result formatting from the Search module.

Much more detail on these hooks can be found in the search.api.php file that comes with the Drupal 7 Search module; the same documentation can be accessed online at api.drupal.org. This section will focus on the hooks implemented by the Apache Solr Search Integration module, which are basically the minimal set of hooks any module would need to implement to create a custom search implementation.

Hooks Implementations Required to Create a Search

The following hooks are essential to define a new search that shows up as a search tab. It's a conscious limitation that a single module can only define one search—this helps keep the API simpler.

```
hook_search_info()
hook_search_execute()
```

With just these two hooks, your new search functionality can appear. hook_search_info() lets the Search module know about your search implementation, what title to give the search tab, what path you want to use to run searches, and (optionally) the name of a callback function that adds other conditions like filters to the search in addition to keywords. The other essential hook, hook_search_execute(), is called when a user visits the search path and finds either keywords or conditions present. Note that while the search form submits via a POST request, the search module actually takes all the search parameters from the URL. So you can, for example, bookmark and search and visit the URL to run it again to find new results. The return value from hook_search_execute() is an array of results, each of which is an array with certain key/value pairs expected by the theme function.

■ **Note** The fact that all the search parameters are passed in via the URL with a GET request has benefits beyond allowing you to bookmark searches. For example, since Drupal uses the page URL as a cache key, you can benefit from Drupal page caching for search pages for any commonly run searches on your site, such as providing users with links to particular search URLs.

Additional Search Module Hooks

The following hooks are optional but they allow your module more control over the search process and the indexing process (if using the search module's indexing facilities), or they allow you to add to the Search module administrative interface:

```
hook_search_access()
hook_search_reset()
hook_search_status()
hook_search_admin()
hook_search_page()
hook_search_preprocess()
hook_update_index()
```

If you implement hook_search_page(), you can take total control over the processing and display of search results, in which case the return format from hook_search_execute() can be altered for your convenience rather than conforming to the format expected by the Search module. The implementation shown in Listing 31–1 mirrors closely what's in the core search module but adds an additional possible output to browse all facets' blocks.

The apachesolr_search Integration module implements five of these hooks plus the callback that is optionally specified in hook_search_info(). This last callback is important because it allows the code to pull additional filter parameters out of the query string and to use these to run a search even when there are no keywords. It was added to the core Search module based on this need for Apache Solr Search Integration. You'll notice also that the info returned for hook_search_info() is actually the content of a variable, though this variable is not (currently) exposed for configuration in the user interface. This will allow developers to change the name and path for the search tab without needing to use hook_menu_alter().

Listing 31–1. Basic Search Module with Additional Possible Output

```
/**
 * Implementation of hook_search_info()
 */
function apachesolr_search_search_info() {
  return variable_get('apachesolr_search_search_info', array(
    'title' => 'Site',
    'path' => 'site',
    'conditions_callback' => 'apachesolr_search_conditions',
  ));
}

/**
 * Implementation of hook_search_execute()
 */
function apachesolr_search_search_execute($keys = NULL, $conditions = NULL) {
  $filters = isset($conditions['filters']) ? $conditions['filters'] : '';
  $solrsort = isset($_GET['solrsort']) ? $_GET['solrsort'] : '';

  try {
    return apachesolr_search_run($keys, $filters, $solrsort, 'search/' . arg(1),
pager_find_page());
  }
  catch (Exception $e) {
    watchdog('Apache Solr', nl2br(check_plain($e->getMessage())), NULL, WATCHDOG_ERROR);
    apachesolr_failure(t('Solr search'), $keys);
  }
}

/**
 * Implementation of a search_view() conditions callback
 */
function apachesolr_search_conditions() {
  $conditions = array();

  if (isset($_GET['filters']) && trim($_GET['filters'])) {
    $conditions['filters'] = trim($_GET['filters']);
  }
  if (variable_get('apachesolr_search_browse', 'browse') == 'results') {
```

```
      // Set a condition so the search is triggered.
      $conditions['apachesolr_search_browse'] = 'results';
   }
   return $conditions;
}

/**
 * Implementation of hook_search_reset()
 */
function apachesolr_search_search_reset(){
   apachesolr_clear_last_index('apachesolr_search');
}

/**
 * Implementation of hook_search_status().
 */
function apachesolr_search_search_status(){
   return apachesolr_index_status('apachesolr_search');
}

/**
 * Implements hook_search_page()
 */
function apachesolr_search_search_page($results) {
   if (!empty($results['apachesolr_search_browse'])) {
      // Show facet browsing blocks.
      $output = apachesolr_search_page_browse($results['apachesolr_search_browse']);
   }
   elseif ($results) {
      $output = array(
         '#theme' => 'search_results',
         '#results' => $results,
         '#module' => 'apachesolr_search',
      );
   }
   else {
      // Give the user some custom help text
      $output = array('#markup' => theme('apachesolr_search_noresults'));
   }
   return $output;
}
```

Obviously the code here mostly wraps calls to other internal module functions; the status and reset hooks are implemented simply to allow status and reset operations to work with the Search module administrative page as well as within the Apache Solr Search Integration administrative pages. Note that hook_search_page() is implemented so that it can provide either facet block browsing or customized help text when there are no search results. The code to format normal search results is the same as the default implementation in Search module.

Apache Solr Search Configuration

The administrative interface for the Apache Solr Search Integration provides a number of configuration options that will meet the needs for most initial customization. In particular, by configuring the boost setting and doing some basic tests of end user satisfaction with the ordering of results, you can help make the search results become more relevant.

Enabled Filters

In order to let end users navigate via a particular facet, you need to follow a two step process. First, you have to enable the filter via the Apache Solr Search Integration settings, and then you need to enable the corresponding block via the normal Block module interface. The act of enabling a filter means that extra processing is performed by the Solr server and additional data is returned. Thus, you should only enable those filters where you will use the block or will use the data for some other purpose. For example, in order to make a facet block available for the Tags field, the last filter needs to be enabled (see Figure 31–4) and then the block is configured.

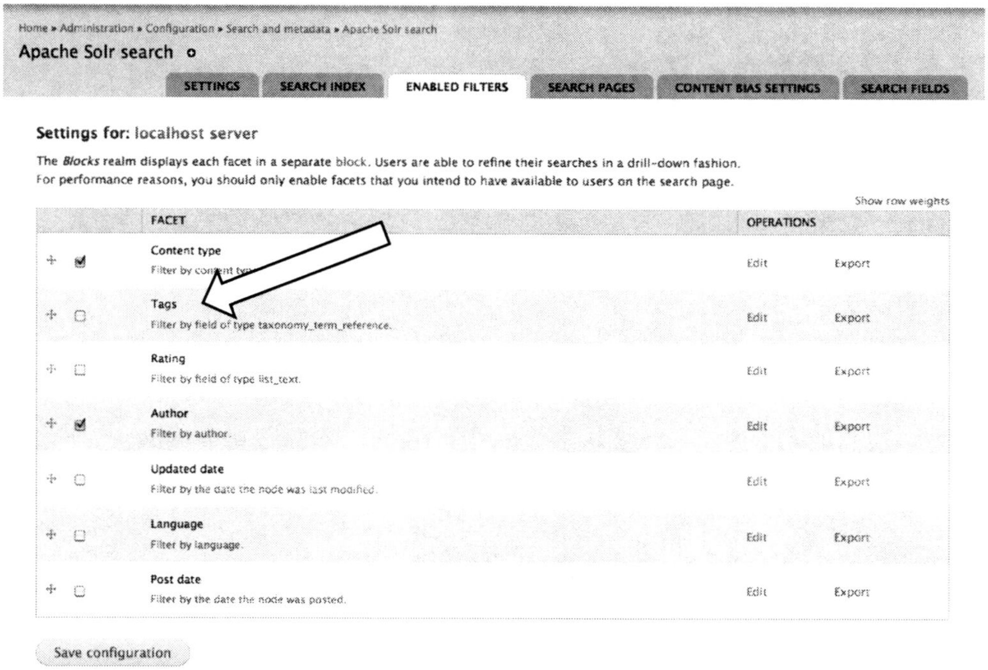

Figure 31–4. Enabling a filter makes an additional facet available in the search results.

Type Biasing and Exclusion

A common need for sites is that content of a certain type should receive a boost in search results or a certain content type should not be added to the search index at all. For example, you may wish to steer users toward blog posts. Alternately, you may want them to first find documentation represented by book nodes. Initially, all content types are treated equally. By setting a value to something other than "Ignore" you indicate that a certain node type within your site content has greater importance and should receive a higher score in search results. In contrast, there may be some content that should not be indexed at all. This may be true for nodes of a type that is automatically generated or represents data rather than actual site content.

The administrative interface lets you configure boosting and exclusion per content type (see Figure 31–5). The module will attempt to immediately delete from the search index all relevant nodes if you add a type to the excluded list, so do not make this change casually.

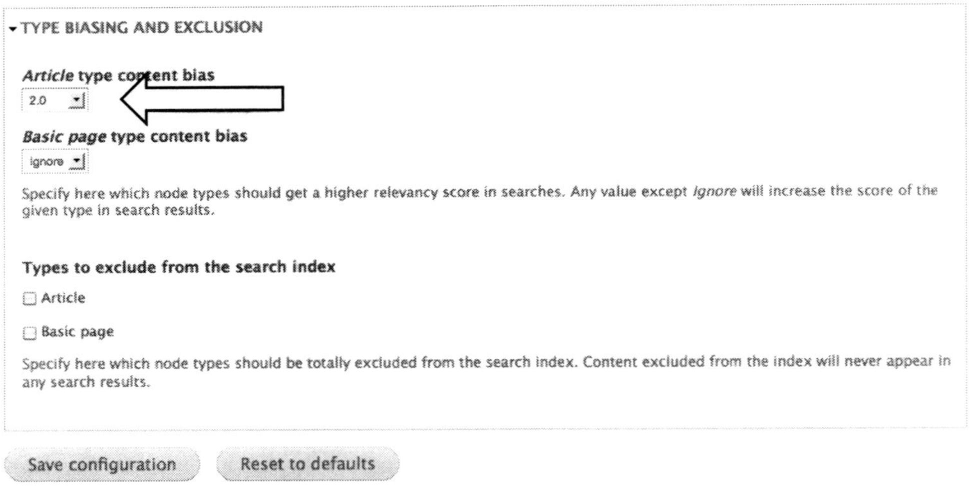

Figure 31–5. Setting the search result bias and exclusion settings for specific content types

Apache Solr Search Customization

The Apache Solr Search Integration module is only a starting point if you want an interface that is fully optimized for your Drupal site. In addition, the filtering and sorting capabilities of Solr make it attractive to use as a data source for certain kinds of listing pages such as ecommerce sites, library sites, or on drupal.org itself for the page that lists all modules. There are a wide number of hooks documented in apachesolr.api.php, but only a few of them are necessary for most typical customizations.

Hooks for Getting Data into Solr

When indexing a node, Apache Solr Search Integration will add certain fields to the document by default. If you want to do custom filtering, boosting, etc., you will want to add additional fields to the document in the index. To do so, you can implement hook_apachesolr_update_index($document, $entity, $namespace). This hook is used to add more data to a document before it's sent to Solr; it can also be used to alter or replace data added to the document by Apache Solr or another module. It works like an alter hook, although there's no need to pass the variable by reference because the document is an object. When adding data to the Solr index, it's helpful to look at the schema.xml file to see the names of types of the dynamic fields. You can control how the data is indexed simply by naming a property on the document with the right prefix. For example, you could add a single-value like so:

```
function MYMODULE_apachesolr_update_index($document, $node, $namespace){
  if ($node->type == 'site_product' && $document->entity_type == 'node') {
    // Add an additional custom node field to the index.
    $document->fs_price = $node->price;
  }
}
```

There are several ways to get searchable data into the index. The simplest way is to simply add more content to the node to be rendered at index time. Another approach is to implement hook_node_view($node, $view_mode, $langcode), and look for a $view_mode of 'search_index'. Yet another option is to add content via hook_node_update_index($node). Any content returned from that hook is appended to the content sent to the search index. However, in the latter two cases, this content will simply be found as part of a keyword search and can't be used to create facets or sorts.

A big feature of the Drupal 7 core release is the Fields API. The Apache Solr Search Integration module has built-in support for indexing the fields on nodes or (potentially) other entity types, based on either the field type or even on a per-field basis. This feature was created based on the support for Content Construction Kit (CCK) fields in the 6.x-2.x version of the module; for 7.x, it has been extended to include handling the taxonomy term reference fields. By default, only taxonomy and all the list-type fields (e.g. list_text) will be indexed as separate fields in the Solr document. If you need to add to or change this indexing, you can implement hook_apachesolr_field_mappings_alter(&$mappings). See apachesolr.api.php for more details.

A last thing to consider is actually keeping data out of the search index. Previously, you saw the administrative interface for excluding all nodes of a certain type, but you might need to exclude content on a more selective basis. In that case, you can implement hook_apachesolr_node_exclude($node, $namespace). If any module returns TRUE, the node is not sent to the index.

Hooks for Altering Queries and Results

The first and most common reason to alter the query sent to Solr is to retrieve an additional field from the document in the search result. This is the complement to adding an extra field to the document via hook_apachesolr_update_index($document, $node, $namespace). Usually when you modify a query, you don't want the modification to be visible to the end user in the facet links, etc. In this case, you should use hook_apachesolr_modify_query($query, $caller) and append your field name to the 'fl' parameter sent to Solr, like so:

```
function MYMODULE_apachesolr_query_alter($query){
  // Also return any price data from the index in the results.
  $query->addParam('fl', 'fs_price');
}
```

hook_apachesolr_modify_query() can also be used to add filters to a search that are not visible to the end user. This is important, for example, in the implementation of the Apache Solr node access module. This module adds filters to search queries based on the node access system using node_access_grants(). It also uses hook_apachesolr_update_index() as described previously to index as additional fields the node access information with each Solr document derived from a node.

A very similar hook is hook_apachesolr_ query_prepare ($query). Any changes made using this hook may end up being visible to the user on the search results page, so its use is much more limited than hook_apachesolr_query_alter().

There are also several hooks (and theme hooks) that can be used to modify or enrich the search results before they are displayed to the user. The most common one is hook_apachesolr_search_result_alter($doc, $extra), which allows each document in the result set to be individually altered.

Integrating with the Apache Solr Server

To understand a little bit about how and why the Search module hook implementations in Apache Solr Search Integration are written as they are, it's useful to have a broad conceptual understanding of how the Apache Solr server works. Drupal interacts with Solr via an HTTP request, which for Drupal means using the drupal_http_request function (though it could also be done other ways in PHP including via the curl functions or file_get_contents(), depending on the PHP install). Solr has a RESTful API interface, but, at least in version 1.4.x, it doesn't support the full range of HTTP methods as verbs so it's not a *true* REST interface for this reason. Instead, different URL paths are used (and can be configured per search index); POST requests are used for data changing operations and GET requests are used for querying.

A PHP library was adapted to provide some of the low-level logic of getting data into and out of Solr. That library can be found at code.google.com/p/solr-php-client. The Apache Solr Search Integration module provides a class adapted from the main library class, which alters its behavior. The most important alteration is to use Drupal_http_request() instead of file_get_contents() so that all Drupal sites can work with the module. This is class DrupalApacheSolrService, which extends Apache_Solr_Service. The document class is used from the library with minimal modification.

Managing Data in the Solr Index

Data is added to the Solr index as XML documents sent via POST request to the /update path on the Solr server. Solr stores data as documents, and each document must have a unique string ID value. Solr does not have any native concept of relationships between document nor any ability to JOIN documents together. In this sense, it's like document-based NoSQL databases, such as MongoDB, so you have to store together all attributes of the node or other entity that you wish to be able to search on or retrieve in the search result. Documents are deleted with a POST request of an XML document that either specifies the document ID or by a query that deletes all matched documents.

Searching and Analysis

Normal searches are run based just on the URL path and query string. Depending on your configuration, different paths may be used for different searches, such as a keyword search versus a "more like this" search. If something is not working as expected, having Solr running locally is very helpful since you can type your query directly into the URL or use other features of the Solr administrative interface. In particular, the analysis feature is useful to help understand how indexed content or search keywords are transformed by the analyzers and filters configured in the Solr schema.xml. If running Solr locally using the example Jetty deployment, you'll be able to get to the interface at http://localhost:8983/solr/admin/. Figure 31–6 shows the admin interface: in parentheses at the top is the name of the schema in use, then the link to the analysis interface and the text box where you can initiate a search.

Solr Admin (drupal-7.1.0)
10.19.128.78:8983
cwd=/Users/pwolanin/apache-solr-1.4.1/example SolrHome=solr/

Solr	[SCHEMA] [CONFIG] [ANALYSIS] [SCHEMA BROWSER]
	[STATISTICS] [INFO] [DISTRIBUTION] [PING] [LOGGING]
App server:	[JAVA PROPERTIES] [THREAD DUMP]

Make a Query	[FULL INTERFACE]
Query String:	solr
	Search

Assistance	[DOCUMENTATION] [ISSUE TRACKER] [SEND EMAIL]
	[SOLR QUERY SYNTAX]
	Current Time: Sun Jan 02 14:21:58 EST 2011
	Server Start At: Sun Jan 02 14:21:34 EST 2011

Figure 31–6. The Apache Solr admin page, including the link to the analysis interface

Summary

By using Apache Solr Search Integration, you can enhance the quality of the search results and the search interface on your site, which will help keep users on your site and help them find what they are looking for.

The Drupal 7 version of Apache Solr Search Integration will be enhanced as indexing for additional entities like users and files is available and as the Drupal 7 version of Views is released.

■ **Tip** Find updates at dgd7.org/solr.

■ ■ ■

## CHAPTER 32

User Experience

by Bojhan Somers and Roy Scholten

Learning how Drupal works takes a lot of time—and that's just core. As modules get added, the complexity grows. As a Drupal developer, you don't want this complexity to get in the way of users and site administrators getting the full benefit of your work. This creates some challenges in terms of design. How does this module fit together with all the other modules? How do we design Drupal administration to fit endless possibilities?

This is when the practice of design—and most importantly, interaction design, which focuses on the behavior of the user—comes in. For example, the single biggest change in Drupal 7's design was the introduction of the admin theme named Seven.

Not having a default admin theme caused confusion from the very first second people started using Drupal 6 because it doesn't map to how they think a CMS would work. It confused people that the administrative interface was visually within their site, instead of there being a separate admin interface.

Modularity

The ability to plug in functionality without hacking the application is at the core of Drupal. However, once you start to use the modules in combination with each other, workflow issues begin to occur. Can you imagine needing to use several plug-ins within Firefox or the iPhone to achieve one goal?

Human API

We like to think that humans are reasonable, rational beings that take conscious action based on careful thinking. The truth is that many, if not most, of our decisions are made unconsciously, driven by emotion and automatic triggers coming from parts of the brain we don't have conscious access to.

This subconscious part of the brain is a pretty darn fast and smart processor of inputs—as it should be—because our five senses capture about 11 million pieces of information every second. Only 40 of those are processed consciously. Good thing we have the unconscious to handle all the others or we'd be overloaded in seconds.

Memory

Have you ever walked into a room and can't remember what you were going to do there? You've just run into the restrictions of your short term memory and also experienced your ability to get distracted easily. In the interface world, we have to account for this, as users are easily disrupted from their task flow by many events throughout the day, such as a colleague walking in or e-mail popping up.

Short term memory, which goes from a couple seconds to about 30 seconds, has limited storage. George A. Miller, a psychology professor, wrote in a famous paper "The Magical Number Seven, Plus or Minus Two" (1956) that a person can remember about 7 (±2) items. As research progressed on this topic, it was discovered that humans are likely to remember even less (about 4 (±1) items), and that we tend to remember information in chunks, such as telephone numbers. This is why in game shows it is easier for participants to remember a larger group of similar or related names than a small number of unrelated ones.

As we design interfaces, we need to take into account how users are easily disrupted in the task flow and that they struggle to remember larger bits of information from one screen to the next, especially if it contains unfamiliar information. Repeating important collections of information in logical chunks across screens will help users work through the task at hand.

Long Term Memory

Do you remember studying for an upcoming school test? You may have tried all the tricks from spaced repetition (gradually increasing the interval between repetitions of learned material) to the advice of your mom that you need sleep to process and properly organize those memories. When users approach interfaces, a lot of long-term memory kicks in by recognizing familiar elements—how these work, what the next step would be, etc.

Semantic memory is about the memory of concepts and meanings. It's not the story of when you first learned how to use the checkbox form element, but rather a specific piece of knowledge on how it works and how it is distinctive from other form elements.

Procedural memory is our memory of the steps involved in the execution of tasks. This allows us to tie our shoe and allows seasoned Drupalistas to set up a module without much thinking. It's often when we break with these learned processes that user confusion occurs.

By creating a deeper understanding of the users' long-term memory (the concepts, previous experience, and existing processes), we can provide a better interface. We can match their expectations of how things work and possibly even exceed their expectations by guiding them towards more possibilities.

How Drupal modules work is part of an eco-system from the Web to content management systems to Drupal specifically. All these systems introduce concepts and processes that are leveraged by the user when using your module. By adhering to standards, you are more likely to avoid obvious mismatches with concepts and processes. However, as Drupal modules get more and more complex, it's likely you will have to do additional research to understand how users perceive the concepts involved in your module and which existing knowledge can be applied to make it easier.

Mental Model

Before users get to Drupal, they already have a mental model of how it might work, not just from previous experience with content management systems but from computer experience in general. When thinking about mental models, we differentiate between the way the system works (system model) and the way users think about achieving their goals with the system (interaction model).

The interface of a system tries to close the gap between these two models and is called the representational model—the way we as developers or designers choose to display functionality. A poor understanding of the interaction model that a user has before actually using the functionality often leads developers and designers to model the interface after the system model instead. This usually results in hard-to-use interfaces. For example, Drupal 7 has the Fields UI; its interface is modeled after the system requiring the user to shift his focus from the interaction model of creating forms and boxes of content to making a database column.

Taking a step back and thinking about how the user thinks about achieving their goals with your module (before they ever see it) is key to creating a usable interface. It's also a step that is often forgotten in the process of building an interface.

Figure 32–1 shows a simplified version of the user's interaction model against that of the system model. What do I want a list of? Where do I want to show it? How do I want to present it, using which format for each item?

Views "sitemap"

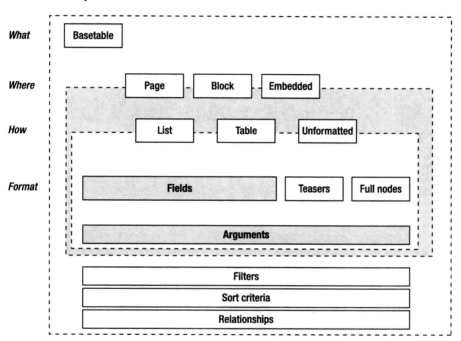

Figure 32–1. A concept model of the Views module

Perception

Understanding why humans see certain things as foreground and others as background is fundamental to designing a good interface. As our surroundings give stimuli to our sense organs, we start talking about perception—the interpretation of these stimuli.

> *"Perception is not determined simply by stimulus patterns; rather it is a dynamic searching for the best interpretation of the available data."*

> —Richard L. Gregory

Top-down perception explains the perception processing as something that is built constructively from our knowledge, expectations, and thoughts. Bottom-up perception processing is described as primarily driven by physical elements.

A famous video from one of the usability tests on Drupal 6 showed a participant struggling to find the "Create content" link that was placed in the left menu and always visible. Still, it took the user over 5 minutes to find it on the screen, after going through various places in the administration screen. It was a clear example of how expectations and prior knowledge drove where the user looked and that Drupal failed to prominently display the most important link in a Content Management System.

When designing, we have to remember how to work with what is perceived outside of the center of the gaze—what is referred to as the peripheral vision. As people move through a page, they identify many objects in their peripheral vision. Designing with this principle in mind means visually grouping related elements and demoting the visual importance of less critical functionality.

Perception is one of the oldest fields in psychology and has a lot of theories and applicable understanding to designing your modules interface. We will cover only two: that of Gestalt (the form and harmony between elements on your page) and some general color usage tips. When we think of form and color, the following qualities drive the meaning:

- Form
  - Line orientation
  - Line length
  - Line width
  - Size
  - Spatial grouping
- Color
  - Hue
  - Chromaticity
  - Saturation
  - Luminance

A lot of what goes into understanding perception is about designing for grouping information more logically to manage the complexity of your interface. For modules like Views and Rules, these challenges are immense and have a deep impact on the usefulness, efficiency, effectiveness, learn ability, and overall satisfaction of the module.

Gestalt Psychology

When looking at the interface, we do not consider the different stimuli of different pieces on the page as individual elements, but rather we see it as a larger whole. Gestalt psychology focuses on understanding how humans perceive certain elements as foreground and others as background, how we differentiate between forms, and how we find similarity between forms.

Research by Kurt Koffka, Wolfgang Köhler, and Max Werheimer from 1920-1940 introduced this idea of considering the perception of object or environment as a whole form where one would have foreground parts and background parts. Gestalt perception is introduced as the law of prägnanz, where the following laws are part of and applicable to the Drupal context:

- Law of similarity

- Law of proximity

We will briefly cover each law and its application in Drupal. These laws often help in exploring and evaluating your module forms.

Law of Similarity

We group together items that have similar characteristics, such as color, shape, orientation, size, space, etc. When we see the elements shown in Figure 32–2, such as a row of circles in a field of blocks, we perceive this as a row or line rather than separate circles.

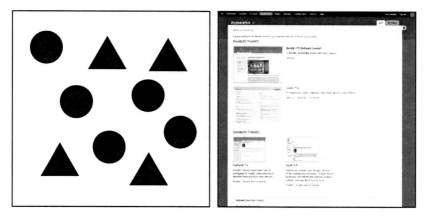

Figure 32–2. *Bigger screenshots for active themes, smaller thumbnails for inactive ones*

This pattern is often applied in Drupal to differentiate items among many others, as shown in the right of Figure 32–2 where size is used to group similar items. It's a pattern also used for grandeur in architecture—and in the retail store by repeating similar parts to look grand.

Law of Proximity

As shown in Figure 32–3, a common pattern is to put visual elements close to each other. Psychologically, when we see two people standing close to each other, we assume they know each other. This pattern is used all over the Internet. A notable example is Flickr, which uses this pattern for almost everything on the page and only occasionally uses lines for closure. Drupal also uses it, as shown in Figure 32–3.

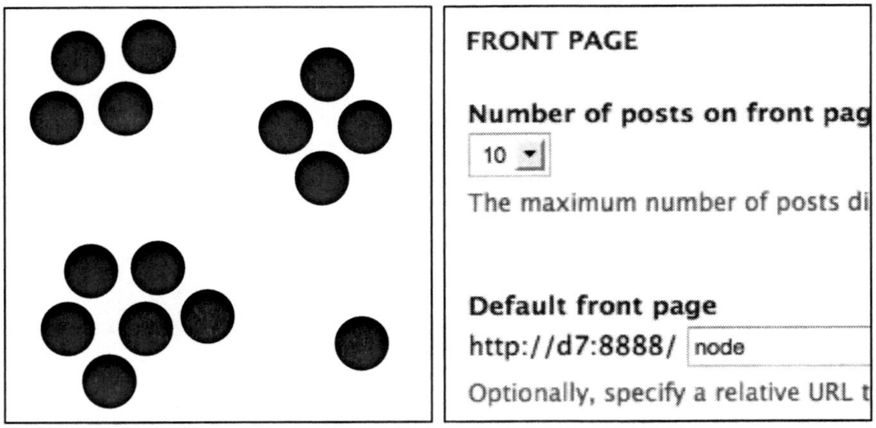

Figure 32–3. White space is used to define the relationships between form labels and form elements.

We apply this principle all over Drupal to layout all kinds of listing pages but also on the detailed level, using white space to define relationships between the elements of a form. The key to applying this principle is to look at the page as a whole and group page elements in a way that helps guide the eye.

This very basic law is often misapplied by using either too much or too little white space. A trick for applying this pattern correctly is taking a step back. By blurring the page a bit, can you still see the groups on your page? If not, you might have to make the groups more explicit or reduce the number of groups.

Color

Beyond making things look beautiful, color is used to give structure, attention, and meaning to elements on the page. The "Perception" section covered a few cases where color could be used to enhance the composition of elements on the page and help convey meaning. Describing color itself is both technical and confusing as we put different meanings to words like "dimmed" or "bright," especially in a black-and-white book like this. In technical terms, color is described by its hue, chromaticity, saturation, and luminance.

- **Hue** is when we try to identify the primary color. Red, green, blue, and yellow are referred to as the unique hues.

- **Chromaticity** is the purity of a color—the absence of other colors. For example, a shiny dark blue would have a high chroma where as purple would have a medium chroma.

- **Saturation** is how a color changes as it gets darker or lighter; more importantly, it's about the intensity of a given color—how one color can appear pale while another looks strong.

- **Luminance** is a measure for the brightness of a color.

Drupal's administrative interface (Seven) uses color sparingly. This is primarily a branding and usability decision. We tried to add as little visual distractions to the actual form interactions on the page as possible. Another consideration is accessibility, because a good part of our society has a form of color vision deficiency. Seven makes use of the neutral colors described in Table 32–1.

Table 32–1. *Seven's Colors*

Seven's Colors	Usage
#a6a7a2 (light gray)	Tabs, selected table column header
#e1e2dc (light gray)	Table header backgrounds
#0074bd (blue)	All links
#008800 (green)	Success messages, enabled modules
#b14400 (orange)	Warnings
#8c2e0b (dark red)	Errors
#b4d7f0 (light blue)	Demonstrate blocks back background

As shown in Table 32–1, there is a whole range of colors you can use out of the box, and the large majority of modules will be fine leveraging any one of these. For modules that need to step beyond these supplied colors, there are several principles that apply.

Color Harmony

In Drupal we use light gray because it doesn't draw attention, unlike shades of blue, red, and green. When you choose color, there are many different types of color combinations to be made from analogous color (combinations of colors that are close to each other on the color wheel) to complementary colors (combinations of colors that are on opposing ends of the color wheel) to different types of hues and chromaticity of colors.

It's important to understand what type of meaning and attention you want to draw to the element you are coloring. Nonetheless, try to limit the usage of new colors because it's likely that colors will conflict, harmony will collapse, and the eye will be left wondering what the colors are trying to communicate.

Color theory is an extensive field and we have only skimmed the basics here. For more information, we suggest these books: *The Art of Color: The Subjective Experience and Objective Rationale of Color* by Johannes Itten (John Wiley & Sons, 1997) and *Color: A Natural History of the Palette)* by Victoria Finlay (Random House Trade Paperbacks, 2003). But most importantly it's a field of experimentation—finding harmony and meaning through carefully chosen colors.

Practice

"In theory, theory and practice are the same. In practice, they're not."

—Yogi Berra

So with all this theory, how do you bring the principles into practice? It's all about having a process that considers design as an activity during the creation of your module, rather than something done at the last moment.

This is an important aspect of building a good UI: the willingness to take the necessary steps by doing sketches, wireframes, and mockups, and then running them by a few users. The process described in this section is applicable to most digital projects, but we specifically target it on Drupal.

We believe strongly that the role that design takes in the current module design process has to change if we want to make a more compelling Drupal where the user experience of its contributed modules fits in seamlessly in with Drupal core and each other.

The Process

Most Drupal modules serve a very specific need which is often only a part of the larger goals in building the web site. The act of designing focuses on two major parts: understanding what people want to accomplish with your module, and how they can do this the best through your UI.

The design process is about a very simple idea: in order to get to good design, you need to explore possibilities and iterate on these with feedback from users. It's important to realize that your module is often part of a larger workflow; therefore, not breaking with existing interaction patterns and not breaking that flow is key.

We will describe the following process:

- **Concept:** Define what you are making.

- **Design:** Sketch your module's screens and relations.

- **Build:** Build your user interface, checking against core interaction patterns.

- **Optimize:** Test with users and optimize on findings.

- **Release:** Prepare your project files for sharing on drupal.org.

This process can be applied fully or partially, depending on what stage in the cycle you are; nonetheless, each step will be revisited from time to time as you are making iterations. As we walk through the process, it will become clear which activities you can use to step out of the role of programmer and into that of the designer; it should also create an understanding why design based on just the implementation model tends to not account for user needs.

The design activity is about seeing the larger picture for where and how your part fits in. How is your module used with other modules? To what task flow are you adding a feature? At what point in this flow might people want to use it? How do you do it in a way that blends in and enhances the user experience?

In the practice section, you will apply this process to the administrative interface of the Rules module. The interface for this module had grown organically over the years but for Drupal 7 got a bigger overhaul to better fit the needs of the people using it in their sites. As is the case with many others of the more technical modules, its domain can be incredibly complex. Thus, the user interface has to account for large amounts of data and configuration to actually become useful and enable users to get their things done—not an easy task.

The Challenges

Designing a good UX is hard. Once you've got your version 1.0 out of the door, your module enters a new phase: it will actually get used by others. It may take some time, but eventually issues will pop up in your issue queue. Gasp! Bugs are found. Or worse: feature requests!

Designing a piece of a modular, extensible, and flexible framework like Drupal is a tough job. Let's look at some of the main challenges you may encounter when designing your application within the Drupal ecosystem.

Keep the Focus on the Essentials (Say No!)

As your module progresses, it's likely that new features will be added. Over time, the original simplicity and focus of the module might get lost. This is a threat to any software project, but especially in modules where there is little feedback on the actual use of functionality—its common module functionality is really only used by the module maintainer himself.

As we have experienced in Drupal core, the issue queue is not the best place for receiving feedback on your UI. The people in this queue are often far more experienced Drupal users (expert users, in fact) and take the time to actually write up an issue. These users often do not reflect common user needs or problems with the UI, so just keep this in the back of your mind as you approach these issues.

For example, if we went solely by the feedback we received in the issues queue, Drupal 7's biggest problem would have been the permission page and the second biggest problem the module page. However, from testing, we saw that most of the problems were in finding how to create content and where to actually find functionality. Therefore, Drupal 7 added an add content link in the administration section, reorganized this section, and introduced contextual links for editing and configuring; while the modules and permissions pages await Drupal 8 for their overhaul.

Be bold and say no to a feature request if it diverges from your original vision for your module. Some modules do this by providing additional modules for specific feature requests or by providing the option in the code but not the UI. Keeping the focus means you are able to deliver the core value of the module easily and your interface will stay clean of distracting settings.

How to Make Informed Design Decisions

It's rare that an issue starts with "While observing and talking to a user…" because it's not exciting information to share. Fundamentally, however, this is what informs your decision best: how it affects users. How do you know who your target audience is and what intermediate users want to achieve? How do you build a solid understanding of your users so you can make informed design decisions?

The quickest and best way to do this is by talking to them and observing them as they use your module. This might seem like a big step, but often you can find people in your close surroundings who can give you this kind of feedback.

Throughout the Drupal 7 design process, we often spoke with users in the issue queue, visitors of local camps and technology conferences, and those who update their local scouting web site. From all these stories, we were able to make more informed design decisions on how it affects the user, the code, and the work they do together.

Design with Limited Resources

It's common in software development environments for the amount of developers to far outnumber that of designers; in open source projects, this is even more drastic. However, for your design to work, you often need feedback from designers to make sure that visual affordances such as alignment, color usage, and the relationships between elements on the page are in balance.

Concept: What Exactly Are You Building?

This is primarily about taking a step back and looking at the larger picture. To help you set the scope of the project and map the different audiences that will be using it, the two primary questions are:

- What are you building?

- Who will use it (excluding yourself)?

Both questions can be defined quickly and expanded on when needed. Actually, documenting both answers sets a good stage for discussing further development and helps communication towards the community. So what goes into answering the question: "What are you building?"

This answer is not primarily expressed in the functions and features of the tool but on a somewhat more abstract level concerning the user goals this module wants to support. The opportunity here is to tie the technological abilities of your module to real user needs.

The question of "Who will use it" is primarily about understanding who your users are in a way that goes beyond putting them into beginner, intermediate, and advanced groups. Research the different needs people have and consider how your module will be used in the larger workflow.

Let's take a look at these two questions for the example project, the Rules module (`drupal.org/project/rules`). The Rules module lets site administrators define conditionally executed actions that can be triggered by events that occur in the site or application. You could create a rule to send the site manager an e-mail when new people register on the site. E-commerce sites have many uses for rules, too: calculating shipping costs or applying promo-codes for lower prices, for example.

Let's try to answer these two questions that help define the concept for this tool.

Rules: What Are You Building?

Rules wants to provide users with a complete set of tools for defining the business logic in a Drupal application. The intended scope is large: Rules aims to be the primary, extensible platform for defining and handling events on your site.

The concept model in Figure 32–4 explains the general problem that Rules wants to tackle.

RULES CONCEPT MODEL

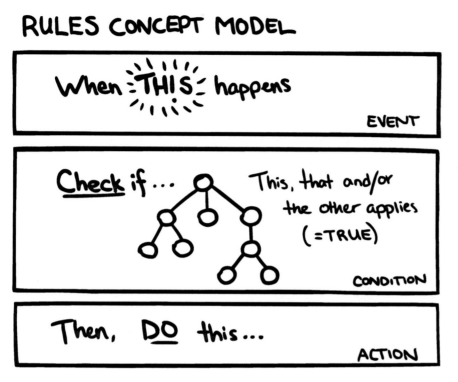

Figure 32–4. *The concept model of Rules*

Rules: Who Will Use It?

The main audience for the Rules module can be grouped into three roles or people: developers, site builders, and business developers.

They all share the main reason to use for Rules: to define the business logic of the site or application. Developers use the Rules API to customize system workflows. Site builders use the Rules interface to define how different interactions on the site make other things happen. Business-minded people have order processing and marketing campaigns to implement and improve.

Design

Now, how do you translate these ideas about your project and its audience to actual screens for your software? You explore multiple ideas with sketches, refine the best options in wireframes, and create a mockup of the one selected solution.

Don't fear the bad ideas. Explore freely.

Getting Ideas: Sketching

"The best way towards a good idea is to have many ideas" is how the saying goes. Getting towards a good design is very much about exploring multiple ideas first.

It's an almost universal problem in software design that very little time and energy are spent on exploring multiple possible solutions. Often it is simply the first, and therefore un-optimized, design that is chosen.

On the abstract level, the practice of design consists of switching back and forth between two opposing mental states: divergent thinking and convergent thinking, as shown in Figure 32–5. With divergent thinking, you look for multiple ideas and opportunities. Convergent thinking is about evaluating those ideas and making choices on which to throw away and which to elaborate on.

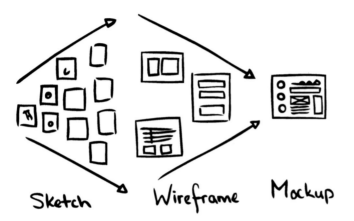

Figure 32–5. *Showing the design deliverables in the process from divergent thinking to convergent thinking*

Sketching can be done in any kind of medium: pen and paper, wireframe software, graphic software, and even code. When exploring designs, you can grab a pencil and make a quick drawing of how things could look. It's all about the activity of putting technical boundaries aside for a bit and just brainstorm about how it might work in a perfect world. Explore, explore, and explore some more. Get those (crappy) ideas out of your system, make a quick note of them, and move on to the next idea.

In the book *Sketching User Experiences: Getting the Design Right and the Right Design* by Bill Buxton (Morgan Kaufmann, 2007), sketches are defined by the following attributes:

- **Quick**: It doesn't take much time to make one.

- **Timely**: It can be provided when needed.

- **Inexpensive**: Costs should not restrict possibilities to explore.

- **Disposable**: The investment is in the concept, not in the execution.

- **Plentiful**: Sketches work best in series or collections.

- **Clear vocabulary**: There's a specific style to them that identifies them as sketches.

- **Distinct gesture**: It's not tight and precise, but open and fluid.

- **Minimal detail**: It includes only what is needed to communicate the concept.

- **Appropriate degree of refinement**: The level of precision matches level of refinement of the actual project itself.

- **Suggest and explore rather than confirm**: Don't dictate solutions, but suggest ways towards answers.

- **Ambiguity**: Leave room for multiple interpretations.

You might have noticed that nowhere in this list does it say that you have to be able to draw well. It's not about that. Nor is it about having to use pen and paper. Sketches can be done in code as well. Just focus on generating multiple ideas. Work only as long as needed to get the gist of the idea across. Take a screenshot or document it in another way, and move on to the next idea. We're using pen and paper in our examples here because that's what we're comfortable with. Pick the tool that you are comfortable with and that lets you work quickly.

The feedback loop starts here. Show it to others with the intention of getting more ideas first, not necessarily for separating the good from the bad ones. If you get suggestions for other ideas, sketch those out quickly.

If you choose to narrow down your selection yourself, make sure you review your ideas with relatively fresh eyes. Put some time between sketching and selecting. Look at them upside down and from a distance.

Sketching the Rules User Interface

Let's look at an example from the Rules module. If you explore the Rules interface, you'll see many of the basic core UI ingredients like tabs, tables, and fieldsets at work. But what stands out even more is that there are a few deliberate deviations from core patterns. There are a couple of pages that present multiple tables on one page. There's the Rules listing page that groups active and inactive rules each in their own table. And there's the Rules edit page, where there are no less than three tables shown below each other. Let's retroactively explore some ideas for both of these cases and find out why those design decisions were taken.

The Rules Listing Page

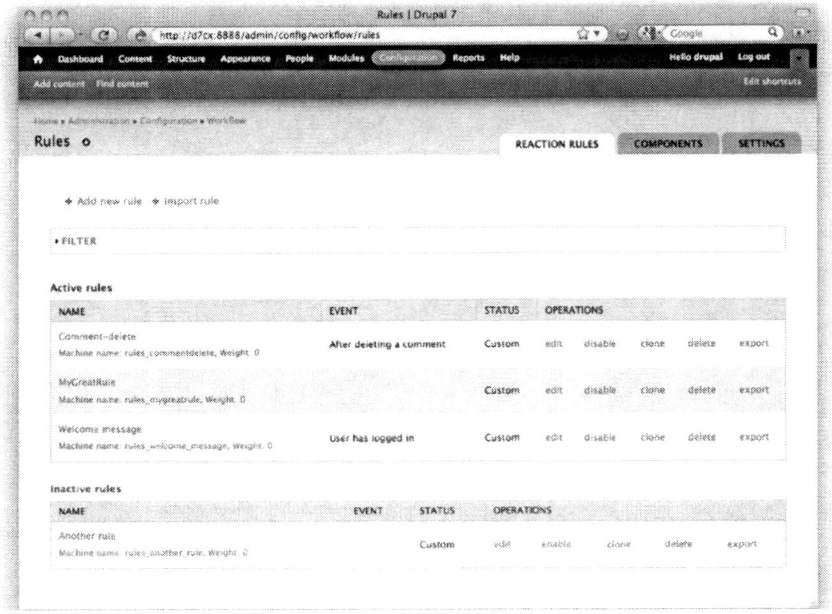

Figure 32–6. A screenshot of the Rules listing page. Note how active and inactive rules are each presented in their own table

As you can see in Figure 32–6, all rules in the system are grouped into two tables: one table with all active rules and another table with inactive rules underneath it. Is this the best way to separate the two? Let's see if we can come up with some ideas for doing this differently, shown in Figures 32–7a through 32–7g.

ACTIVE & INACTIVE RULES

① "2 TABLES"

Figure 32-7a. The current situation: a table for active rules and another for inactive ones

ACTIVE & INACTIVE RULES

② "DRAG & DROP"
2 sections in 1 table, like in Fields UI

Figure 32-7b. One table with an inactive part at the bottom. You make rules active or inactive by dragging-and-dropping them to the desired section of the table. This is a variation on a pattern used in the Fields UI where this interaction is used to show or hide individual fields on an entity.

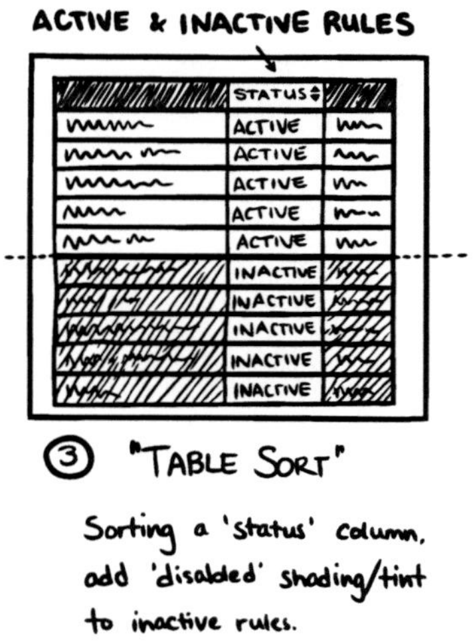

ACTIVE & INACTIVE RULES

③ "TABLE SORT"
Sorting a 'status' column, add 'disabled' shading/tint to inactive rules.

Figure 32-7c. What if all rules were in a single table that can be filtered to show only active or inactive rules?

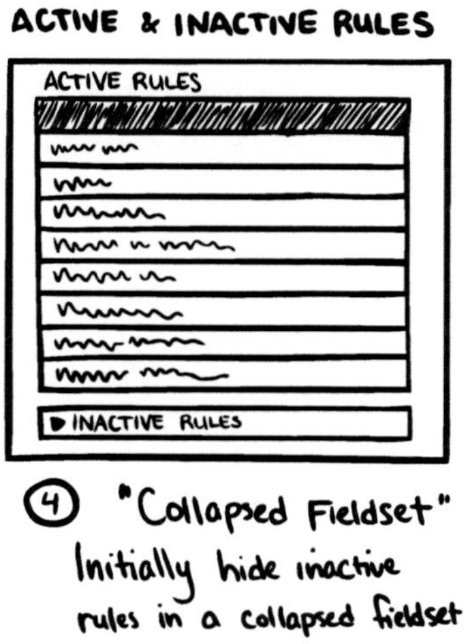

ACTIVE & INACTIVE RULES

④ "Collapsed Fieldset"
Initially hide inactive rules in a collapsed fieldset

Figure 32-7d. What if all inactive rules are put into a collapsible fieldset below the active ones?

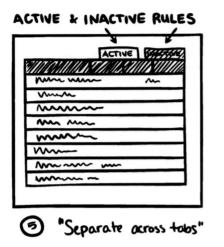

⑤ "Separate across tabs"

Figure 32–7e. Would spreading them out across separate tabs be a workable solution?

⑥ "Don't group, just use different visual styles"

Figure 32–7f. Do you even have to group rules bases on active or inactive? Can the inactive ones just be styled differently (greyed out)?

⑦ "Filter select list"

Figure 32–7g. What if all rules were in a single table that can be filtered to show only active or inactive rules?

As you can see, a few ideas can easily be discarded (32–7e and 32–7f), but the filter (32–7g) and fieldset ideas (32–7d) seem promising. The filter could work because there's already a fieldset with filter options present. Further explorations would investigate if that could be designed to accommodate this active/inactive filter.

The other option with all inactive rules (in a table) inside a collapsible fieldset seems nice, too, because it makes them less prominent in the interface. You can safely assume that when people are on this page, they come much more often to work on an active rule. Having the inactive rules take up less screen space would support that. The two groupings are clearly different from each other, which makes it easier to tell them apart.

Get feedback on page concept from real people. Ask them how it aligns with their mental model, show sketches, ask what they see.

For really complex problems, you might need ten or more idea-sketches to get the feeling that you have sufficiently explored the problem space. For less complex scenarios, three sketches can easily be enough. But even then, you'll have material to choose from, which still puts you ahead because now you can make an informed decision on which route you are going to take and explore further.

How? you ask.

Wireframes

Wireframes can serve many purposes: prioritizing content, initial design briefings, validating requirements, evaluating copy writing in context, or as paper prototypes that can be usability tested. This versatility brings the risk of trying to communicate too much to multiple audiences. When making a wireframe, know its purpose and stick to it. Keeping that focus will make it most effective.

Wireframes can be made with many tools: pen and paper, dedicated diagramming software, drawing software, and even office productivity tools have some basic capability for drawing labelled boxes onto the screen. As with sketches, the medium isn't important. A digitally created wireframe might be easier to share online since you'll need to scan or photograph pen-and-paper drawings first.

Say you want to wireframe a Drupal admin screen. From your sketches you have picked two or three ideas that seemed to point towards a solution. You narrowed down your options. Now it's time to look at those ideas and explore each in more detail.

It's entirely possible that by now it is already perfectly clear what you need to do because your project scope is small.

- Wireframing is about collecting and arranging the bits and pieces needed, where the bits are form elements and the pieces are interaction patterns (more on these later).

- Use the Seven theme. It imposes interesting restrictions like a one-column layout and provides a beautiful baseline that can be extended. The visual language is one of restraint. That leaves a lot of room to experiment. And you definitely should. There are many complex interfaces in contrib for which core does not have a ready answer. But to make the Drupal admin UI shine is to make it disappear. You should also honour that restraint and be picky about what is added to the visual language.

Get Feedback on Your Wireframes

As pointed out earlier, it's important to know the purpose of your wireframe and stick to it. This is especially important when asking other people for feedback who don't have the background information (meaning your process up till now). Present the wireframe in a way that best serves its purpose. Whatever the tool you use, make sure to include the following elements for an effective visualisation:

1. **Title and a description.** Yes, that's obvious but also easily forgotten. Without knowing what they're looking at, it will be hard for people to give meaningful feedback. It's best to add the title to the graphic itself. Doing it this way ensures that the wireframe is not dependant on surrounding text for this basic clarification.

2. **Main page areas.** For a web page, outline the header, footer, content area, and sidebar(s). For a Drupal admin screen, put in a box for the toolbar and shortcuts. Add one underneath for the breadcrumbs, page title, and tabs. It's unlikely that your module changes things in these areas but put them in to provide context.

3. **Highlight and annotate** the specifics that are part of your design. Put a number close to the part you want to highlight. Repeat that number in a column next to the wireframe and write a short description of what's going on in that particular spot.

Once again, it's time to get some input from others on your designs.

Reality Check

Stress-test your design with the four basic screen states: normal, empty, flooded, and error. All of these screen states will eventually happen and you should design each of them.

Normal

Figure 32–8. *Normal state*

Figure 32–8 shows a manageable list of content, a handful of tags, menus with a moderate amount of links. This is probably the state your wireframe already depicts. Everything is about average—no extreme cases.

Empty

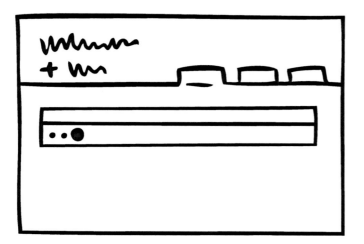

Figure 32–9. *Empty state*

If your module generates listings of objects, you'll want to use a table for that list. But what if no items are available yet? On the one hand, this case is very much an exception. On the other hand, most listings start out empty. So while this state (Figure 32–9) doesn't happen often, you can be sure it does happen at the very important first-time use scenario. Drupal 7 introduces a standard empty pattern for tables that you'll want to implement as well.

Flooded

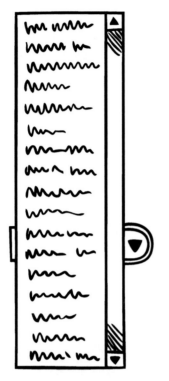

Figure 32–10. Flooded selectlist state

"I have so many active modules that the Site Configuration drop-down menu extends beyond the height of my screen." What happens when you have 68,000 content items? Or 1429 taxonomy terms, 5 million comments, or a content type with 63 fields? If this is a likely scenario for your module (such as in Figure 32–10), what kind of tools will the user interface expose to help people manage that amount of data? Search, sorts, filters?

Error

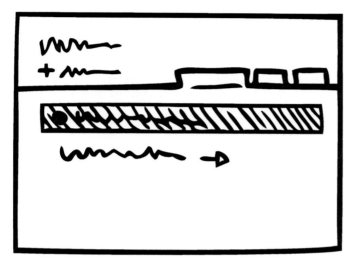

Figure 32–11. *Error state*

Figure 32–11 is the screen you don't want to show. And of course the best error message is no error message at all. Still, you will want to handle this situation constructively. Drupal provides basic patterns for how and where system status messages are shown. What wording will you use for your error message and how do you guide people towards fixing the problem?

This review will help you find parts of the UI that you might not have thought about yet. Rework your wireframe where needed. Sketch multiple options if necessary; take care to not simply bolt on some fixes.

Mockups for Detailed Design

While wireframing or reviewing your design, you might have run into a few specific parts of the interface that are particularly tricky. Maybe you noticed people had a hard time finding a particular bit of info or functionality when you were testing.

Then it's time to take the fidelity of your designs one last level further and create some mockups. You've sketched ideas to come up with general ideas. Then you made wireframes to work through individual screens. When you find that a particular element in a screen needs even more detailed design exploration, that's when you want to create mockups. Mockups look exactly like the interface. You can make them with Photoshop or other image editing software. If you already have functional code, then tweaking the design with the Firebug plug-in or directly in the module code itself is perfectly fine as well and probably even more efficient.

Create mockups to sweat the details and get the design exactly right. It's possible that using default patterns and styling gets the interface working at about 80 percent. It's very much worth it to dive deeper and get that last 20 percent in order.

Build: Build an Alpha and Verify with Users

You've defined the scope and intended audience for your project. You have explored different options for the layout of your screens and chosen a direction. It's time to start actually building your project.

Make it your goal to get a working prototype as quickly as possible, meaning to focus on building only the main functionality you want to achieve. If your project consists of multiple screens, then get the main flow through those screens/states up and running. Work on the big picture; filling in the details comes later.

Why such a strong focus on a working prototype? Because a working proof of concept can be tested by others. All the nice little extras you might want to add are useless if people cannot achieve the main goal your project wants to support. Verify it with *other people*. Simply because you already know too much about how things (should) work, you are *not* the best person to verify if the functionality matches user goals. Because you know, it has become impossible for you to imagine how things are perceived when you *don't* know. It's called the Curse of Knowledge and it's a barrier towards simplicity. You might feel that you are dumbing things down and over-simplifying. Seeing other people use your application will, in most cases, correct that and tell you that you need to clarify.

So, get the essentials up and running and observe other people using it. There is more about getting the best results from simple usability testing a bit later in this chapter.

But let's say you are at a stage where most things seem to be working as planned. People successfully use the interface to get things done. Then it is time to do a check you *can* do yourself, and that is verifying if your interface elements follow core conventions, which can be found at `drupal.org/ui-standards`.

It's important to realize that when you are building a module, your UI will be seen in context of core and multiple other contributed modules. That's why the consistency mantra is so important: you will almost never know the exact context in which your UI will show up. The best strategy then is to not try to be different but to do your very best to blend in.

Optimize: Observations and New Versions

Once your module is built and designed, you should have a good idea what the user wants and whether your module achieves this. The final stage is to optimize your module for reality. As your module goes into alpha, it's likely you will get feedback from users.

This alpha stage is also the best moment to do a more thorough usability test. The primary goal of any usability test is to inform design decisions.

- Does the module serve its purpose? Is it useful?

- Does it help people achieve their larger goals?

- Is it effective, efficient, and perhaps even a pleasure to use?

This chapter will go into some of the basics of running a qualitative usability test, which is quick to run and applicable to module development. We follow a fairly basic process for running a usability test:

- Development of test plan.

- Recruitment of participants.

- Set up of module, recording, and logging.

- Running the usability test.

- Analysis of results.

- Reporting of issues.

- Develop a test plan.

The test plan is your blueprint for the usability test, making sure that you prepare your test sufficiently and can run each individual session consistently. But it also serves as the tool to convince others that you didn't just run it by users but performed a well thought-out plan.

Test Plan Outline

- Why are you testing?
- What kind of user are you testing?
- How are you testing?
- Method
- Scenario
- Task
- Environment
- Analysis method
- Reporting method

This is a very basic test plan, which leaves out a lot of detail work you would otherwise do for a large site. The idea here is that you can repeat this test plan more often, and others can help by performing it on participants around. So let's use this test plan outline to set up a usability test of Rules.

Why Are You Testing the Rules Module?

You are testing to find out whether users can set up a rule using the Rules 2 interface. Specifically, you want to know:

- How closely does the module workflow match the user's expectations?
- Are the basic Event, Condition, and Action relationships clear?
- How confident are users that their rule will be triggered?

You are also testing to provide material to the community that will help people make better design decisions for the user interface of this module in the future.

What Kind of User Are You Testing?

In the concept phase, you identified three audiences for this module. Now you have to make the evaluation of which users and how many you should test in this phase.

- **Developer**: The developer can provide valuable insights to whether the flow they see in the interface matches their expectations, especially since they are looking at this from an implementation model.
- **Site builder**: Can the site builder set up a rule and is he confident enough that this rule will be executed successfully? What are the triggers that help the user understand the required steps in the interface?

- **Business developer (sales, content strategist, shop owner):** Is the rules interface leading enough to understand which steps they need to take? How does it match their mental model?

Both Site builder and Developer audiences should be easy to recruit from the people around you, but the last group will be considerably harder, given that they are also a small portion of your target audience. For the test, refer to the spread shown in Table 32–2.

Table 32–2. The Test Spread

Participant Type	Number of Participants
Developer	2
Site builder	2
Business developer	1
Total Number of Participants	**5**

Let's avoid recruiting participants who are familiar with the Rules 2 UI or Rules 2 implementation. These participants will be recruited through the Drupal.org forums, IRC, and from the people around you.

How Are You Testing?

This usability test will be an explorative one, where each user is asked to create two rules using the Rules 2 UI. The test will be recorded and shared with the community.

Method

You will do five individual sessions that will last for about 20 minutes each. During this session, the participant will be asked to perform two tasks. Ideally, the scenario and tasks for each session will be adapted to the context of the participant.

The test moderator will introduce the tasks and ask questions whenever appropriate as well as take notes and assure the video is running.

Scenario

You are building a web shop for a small store that sells shoes online, and you are using Rules to send notifications to shop management when you are running over 20 orders of a specific shoe (to check the store's stock) and to have a scheduled discount on shoes during the summer sale.

Tasks

1. Send a promotion e-mail to a user when that user hasn't visited the web site for more than three months.

2.   Offer a 20 percent discount on all shoes from June 1 till August 31.

Environment

You need to have a web shop with at least a Carlos shoe. This web shop system needs to leverage Rules; this can be set up using an e-commerce system like Drupal Commerce or Ubercart, or Drupal core using a price field on a shoe content type.

Since you will be recording each session, you will require a video recording tool. If you are testing remotely, you need a screen sharing tool as well (`remoteusability.com/tools/` for remote testing tools).

Choosing an Analysis Method

For this test, let's use a qualitative usability test that is explorative on the actual UI. This method was chosen because of Rules 2 release cycle and ability to change significant parts.

Having an idea of how you will perform analysis helps you determine exactly what data you want to collect. A typical way of analyzing results is writing down each problem you find during the test from going through your notes and video to answer the research questions formulated in the "Why are you testing?" section.

Reporting test results is all about sharing your information so that others can act upon it, too. It can not only help make your module more usable, but also those modules in the same domain and even Drupal core; for example, your findings can help Drupal core optimize its actions module because in some parts they are similar.

Recruitment of Participants

In the test plan you identified which participants you wish to recruit; now you need to actually find these participants. In order to verify whether they meet the requirements you set, you have to do a quick interview or questionnaire.

Where Do You Find Participants?

Finding participants requires a bit of creativity. Since this is open source, it's likely you are on a shoestring budget for everything so using a recruitment form or offering compensation is probably a bit too much to ask. Here are some places we have looked for finding participants.

- **Forums and IRC**: If you are trying to recruit developers, it is relatively easy to find them on IRC and in the Forums. For recruiting participants from the Forums, it's important to inform them that you want them to be "fresh" to avoid that they will try out the module before you do a test with them.

- **Module Page Signup**: If you want to recruit people who are about to use your module, or already are using your module, include a link to sign up for testing on your module's page. This is an effective way to recruit participants. The signup form could include a few questions and ask for some indicators when they are available. Make it as easy as possible to select the right participants for you and the participants themselves.

- **Drupalcamps, User Groups and Contribution Sprints**: There are many local events that give you the possibility to do quick 15-20 minute usability tests. We have tested at Drupalcamps before; with some coordination with the organizers, it's usually possible to do tests before the camp starts, during lunch breaks, or possibly during sessions. It all depends on the willingness of the participant to miss other sessions. A request for test participants can be done up front, on the website/blogpost about the event, or during the event (for example, in the opening presentation).

- **Colleagues, friends, and family:** You might be working at a web development company, have friends that build web sites, or have a really excited cousin that is into building web sites. It's likely that they meet the requirements you set for the usability test, so recruiting them should be possible. A risk here is that the relationship you have to the person influences the test (not feeling free to criticize) so keep this in mind.

Schedule Participants

Scheduling participants is relatively easy. We often schedule sessions in the evening or during lunch. Keep them in close contact and confirm once or possibly even twice before the session to assure it's in their agenda. Always try to schedule participants, even when people come from IRC. This way you can assure they have dedicated a block of time for just your test, rather than something adhoc where they can be disturbed by work or other stuff.

Inform Them of Privacy Considerations

It is important to inform the participant on what test involvement means in terms of information that will be released. If you are recording and sharing this with the community, you have to get permission from the participant. Be clear on how the data of the test will be used, including any material, and that this will be anonymized.

If you share any information with the community, make sure that there are no names on recordings or in notes. An easy way to make sure this happens is to use participant numbers rather than names during the test and analysis.

For sharing video, you also have to make sure it's clear that videos can be shared—without showing their face or anything—purely for sharing insights.

Setup of Module, Recording, and Logging

Running a smooth usability test means taking away any worries about the technical environment and recording. The following are a few tips for the setup process:

- Have backup installs ready.

- Run a dry test (test it yourself).

- Evaluate whether the timing set for tasks is realistic.

- Is all the information you give correct?

- Test the microphone and video quality.

- Disable core update notifications.

Running the Usability Test

Now, onto actually running a usability test! Much of this is common sense. It's primarily the techniques you use to get the most out of your participants in terms of insights that are important. For a traditional test we use the following setup:

- Introduction (Purpose, setup, duration)
- Expectations (What the user should do, such as speak loudly)
- Comfort (You are not being tested, ask any questions, you can skip stuff if needed)
- Introduce scenario
- Introduce task
- "Thinking aloud" technique
- Post-test questions
- Closing (evaluation)

It's very difficult to understand what people are thinking and which small considerations they make each second as they browse through the interface. You are testing because you want to rise above your own assumptions. Interpreting silence from participants brings you back to assuming. Use the "thinking aloud" technique, in which you ask the participant to say what they think as they use the interface. It is extremely effective in learning about all of the small problems they run into and how decisions affect their ability to use the interface; it gives valuable hints towards their mental model. It also keeps participants in the flow of talking about what they are doing. The participant has to be open to this technique; to some it will feel unnatural or they will forget to do it because they are moving through the interface fast. It's okay to ask the participant during the session to keep thinking aloud.

Questioning the Participant

The participant will do a lot of things where you want to more deeply understand the thinking behind them. Feel free to ask the participants how they feel about it, what is expected, or their thoughts about what happened.

By asking questions, as if you where the student trying to learn from the participant, the participant should feel more at ease.

Don't Turn the Participant Into the Designer

You are looking for problems. Don't ask for solutions. It's okay if the participant suggests solutions. Dig a bit deeper if they do, but don't suggest improvements yourself ("Do you think it would work better if that button would be below instead of to the right of the object?") or ask which color might communicate a message better.

These suggestions can often cloud your judgment in later processes when you are looking for recommendations.

Wait an Extra 20 Seconds Before Offering Assistance

It's quite often that the participant will run into problems that are either hard to solve or are still undoable in the prototype. It's human nature to want to be friendly and help. But it's best to wait a bit. It's through the struggle of a participant you get a deeper understanding.

So whenever the participant feels lost and truly can't complete the task, give it a bit more time and see if you can ask questions regarding the mental model and how, for example, the error messages give information.

We Are Testing the Software, Not You

This is a sentence that makes the participant more at ease. During a test you want to make sure the participant doesn't shy from giving a critique and even being very negative when necessary.

Analysis of Results

Now that you have collected all this data, you can start doing analysis. For qualitative tests, this is a fairly chaotic process of looking through your notes and writing down the trends you see on each task and the larger trends you see in the interface.

It's key in analysis to create direct connections between the trends you see and the material. This helps you verify your understanding and makes it easier to describe the trend in reporting.

A common method for analysis is building an affinity diagram (KJ Analysis), which is often done by doing the following:

- Writing down individual issues on a Post-it.

- Counting how often it was found.

- Grouping similar issues.

- Removing duplicate issues.

- Grouping issues on trends.

While doing this, it's often easy to spot the trends. Some issues might occur often or one issue is leading in a lot of other issues.

During this rather chaotic process it's important to keep in mind that you are mapping the problems; you are not yet finding solutions. As a developer, it's easy to jump into the activity of coming up with solution, but that's not the activity here—and it will cloud your ability to do a thorough analysis.

Reporting of Issues

How do you want to report your findings with the community? It's not always easy to communicate usability test results. We have applied the following method in previous tests:

- Single report page (important findings, list of problems)

- Project issues (describing a specific problem)

- Video

The most important part here is that you are always reporting the problem, not the possible solution. This is to create greater separation between the two mental activities and to avoid communicating the solution as something that will definitely be usable.

The single report page is an overall view of what was learned, but it's also a centralized place from which you can go to the individual issues and the videos. There are many ways to communicate specific problems; for example, in a Drupal 6 core test, we described the problem shown in Table 32–3.

Table 32–3. Drupal 6 Core Test Problem

Object	Observation	Importance
Administrative overlay	Users were confused that the administrative interface was overlaying the web site. Their mental model of CMS software is an administrative interface and a separate interface to view the site.	Major

Using a simple table, we could communicate about 30 identified problems, which were turned into issues.

Essentially, reporting is all about isolating problems into workable chunks that you and contributors on your module can work on. Since a usability test is likely to expose a large number of issues, the activity of reporting helps you finalize which major issues you want to work on, what strategy you want to adopt, and how you hope to potentially attract other developers to work on the low-hanging fruit.

Feedback from Issue Queues

When your module is in beta or even alpha, it's likely others are already trying it out and giving feedback through the issue queue. This feedback is vital for improving your module and often allows for a more direct conversation than through other methods such as testing. Additionally, this feedback will be continuous in any phase your module is in.

However, it's always important to remember these reports come from the very small percentile that has the skills and desire to actually let you know about it by posting an issue in the first place. Although this is an important audience, it's likely that this audience is more advanced and doesn't necessary reflect the issues the majority of your users face.

Understanding when certain feedback is describing an obscure edge case or when it's actually dealing with a common case is helpful. There is danger in jumping in to changing the UI; quite often these edge cases introduce edge case interface elements, which can potentially make it confusing for the common case.

Release: Project Page and Documentation

When you have released your module, there is one step that remains: creating a useful project page and documentation for your audiences. With the many modules out there now, finding the right module is a difficult task—even more so for those who don't understand all the points involved in evaluating a module. Usability starts by helping your potential users find and evaluate your module.

What Does Your Module Do?

The primary question people ask is "What does your module do?" Let's look at how Rules describes itself.

- *The Rules modules allows site administrators to define conditionally executed actions based on occurring events (known as reactive or ECA rules). It's a replacement with more features for the trigger module in core and the successor of the Drupal 5 Workflow-ng module.*
- *Example use cases*
- *Build flexible content publishing workflows changes*
- *Send customized mails to notify your users about important updates*
- *Create custom redirections, system messages, breadcrumbs, and many more*

It's a fairly compact description that entails what it does (touching upon some specifics known to experienced Drupal users) and gives examples. It's most likely the examples are most interesting aspect as they give people an idea what they can do with the module.

Having a clear description at the top of your project description explaining what your module does is obvious but an often missed step.

Another example is Pathauto.

> The Pathauto module automatically generates path aliases for various kinds of content (nodes, categories, users) without requiring the user to manually specify the path alias. This allows you to get aliases like /category/my-node-title.html instead of /node/123. The aliases are based upon a "pattern" system which the administrator can control.

Again, compact and clearly showing what you can do using an example. So what can you do to improve page sections like these? Let's take the last example of Pathauto. A user scanning over this whole page might miss the most important information: the example that clearly shows what it does. Rewriting this piece could look like the following:

> The Pathauto module automatically generates path aliases for various kinds of content (nodes, categories, users) without requiring the user to manually specify the path alias.
>
> Example:
>
> Turn www.example.com/node/123 into www.example.com/category/my-page-title.html
>
> The aliases are based upon a "pattern" system which the administrator can control.

Ideally your project page is as short as possible, sending people to additional handbooks when you want to explain specific errors or frequently asked questions.

A common structure for project pages is the following:

- Overview
- Features
- Requirements
- Known problems

- Tutorials
- Pledges
- Credits
- Recommended modules

For a more in depth description on how to make a usable project page, please see an article by Lisa Rex at growingventuresolutions.com/blog/module-owners-how-make-your-module-description-useful.

Copywriting

The quickest and most effective way towards a more usable interface is through good copywriting. In most cases, the text is the interface. In Drupal 6, we saw the impact of badly written descriptions; they were often superfluous and not targeted at the task at hand. It was a serious issue that could be found in a majority of Drupal interfaces, so in Drupal 7 almost all descriptions and labels got a major overhaul, optimizing them for the task at hand and knowledge of the user.

An example of this was found during a usability test of Drupal 6. A smart and web-savvy participant was tasked with categorizing some of her content. She actually quickly found the taxonomy page but then wasn't sure if she was in the right place. She started reading the very long help text at the top of the page. This text confused her so much, she left the page.
At least three things stand out here.

- The help text somehow didn't provide enough clues for the participant to inform her she was at the right place.

- Even a multi-paragraph help text gets ignored at first.

- The more help text, the further the actionable part of the page is pushed into peripheral vision.

The reason that many descriptions in Drupal are wrong is because they are trying to provide too much information—from the concept, the place where it will be used, to the interactions on the page. With all that information, often the most important part—the concept—gets lost. For example, look at the Taxonomy page description in Drupal 6.

"The taxonomy module allows you to categorize your content using both tags and administrator defined terms. It is a flexible tool for classifying content with many advanced features. To begin, create a 'Vocabulary' to hold one set of terms or tags. You can create one free-tagging vocabulary for everything, or separate controlled vocabularies to define the various properties of your content, for example 'Countries' or 'Colors'.

Use the list below to configure and review the vocabularies defined on your site, or to list and manage the terms (tags) they contain. A vocabulary may (optionally) be tied to specific content types as shown in the Type column and, if so, will be displayed when creating or editing posts of that type. Multiple vocabularies tied to the same content type will be displayed in the order shown below. To change the order of a vocabulary, grab a drag-and-drop handle under the Name column and drag it to a new location in the list. (Grab a handle by clicking and holding the mouse while hovering over a handle icon.) Remember that your changes will not be saved until you click the Save button at the bottom of the page."

The top paragraph explains the concept and the second paragraph explains what this page is about, what vocabularies can be tied to it, and how to use the interactions on this page. As we went through the process of changing this description, we established the following principles:

- We need to explain the concept of terms and vocabularies; this concept is often unknown to the user who thinks in terms of categorizing content.

- We should avoid explaining how to use the interactions on this page and what effect it will have in other places; this should be obvious from the interactions themselves.

- We should bring forward familiar concepts in terms of categorizing content.

With all that in mind, we rewrote the description to the following:

"Taxonomy is for categorizing content. Terms are grouped into vocabularies. For example, a vocabulary called "Fruit" would contain the terms "Apple" and "Banana."

As you can see, this is far more to the point. It starts by validating that Taxonomy is indeed about categorizing your content and goes on with one example that clearly explains how a vocabulary is used to contain terms.

The next step is validation with users. Does the new description cause confusion or does it help users? We did a number of usability tests of which this page was a step. The large majority of users that did read this text understood what taxonomy is about and how vocabulary and terms are related.

Causes of Unhelpful Copy

Taking a step back, what causes all this unhelpful copy in Drupal and its contributed modules?

- **Not focused on the task at hand**: Users are relentlessly task-focused. In order to achieve their goal, they know the page is only a step; thus reading descriptions will only be done if really necessary.

- **The wrong attitude towards the user**: We rarely see the kind of writing that sounds relaxed and confident in the user. Instead a lot of text is trying to lecture and assumes the user doesn't care. You can see this in the amount of places where we say "please note," "warning," etc. Lecturing users is never a good thing.

- **Developer documentation bubbling up into the UI**: Often descriptions are trying to explain technical concepts from the usage of the word "node" in the interface to explaining the effects of certain performance options.

- **Explaining a broken UI**: We often see descriptions that are trying to make up for a hard-to-use interface. When you find yourself having to write a description explaining parts of the page, you're creating an interaction that doesn't work.

- **Not understanding where your users are**: Your interface is rarely the first one they see in Drupal, so consider where they are coming from and where they want to go. This will set boundaries to what you need to explain.

- **No clarity in choice of words**: The copy in your interface should be as clean as possible. It should be active and stripped of any unnecessary words or long words that could be short. Using "now" over "currently" and other quick wins will help bring clarity to your writing.

Users often blame themselves when they missed the meaning of a description; they go back read it again or just go on and ignore it. As an interface developer, you are stepping into the shoes of a writer, composing sentences with great clarity and meaning. Revise your writing until it's totally clear what you are trying to say.

Just like good design, good writing is no accident. It often comes from a thorough process of rewriting.

Principles

The principles outlined below are the ones we use for Drupal 7 core. Obviously, more principles apply to writing like good spelling, grammar, and tone of voice.

- **Use active voice**: Active voice is about the subject doing an action; passive voice is about having done it. For example, the user creates content (active), the content was created by the user (passive). This principle applies to most text in Drupal where we try to direct towards a certain action.

- **Focus on the task at hand**: The description or label should only be about the task at hand, not about any preceding or follow-up tasks.

- **Clarity over precision**: It's in the programmer's nature to be as precise as possible; in copywriting, this usually means long, dense, and very complex sentences. Always consider clarity over precision. It's likely your precision will not be understood by the user and your most important point is overlooked. It is often better to refer to documentation when you are getting to the point where you need to explain how it affects different use cases.

  You will encounter this problem more often in modules that are more technical, such as Drupal 7's field interface, which is basically an interface for setting up database tables; the copywriting is precise enough for those who are familiar with database concepts to use it effectively. However, this means anyone who is not completely familiar with database concepts will not get the information they need in an easy-to-digest manner.

- **Cut 50 percent; cut another 50 percent**: As you're writing, especially when you're incorporating other people's feedback, it's easy to grow your text into a long paragraph. A trick applied by many writers is constantly cutting big parts of the text; this forces you to let go of those carefully crafted sentences when they don't convey the meaning. It's about constantly reevaluating whether each word in your text has a function. You'll be surprised how much you can improve your interface only by going through and cutting text. The earlier mentioned Taxonomy page has seen many revisions; during the Drupal 7 lifecycle, it changed several times from a lot to too little (not conveying the meaning) to just right. It's likely you will have to rewrite a sentence three, four, maybe even ten times before you get it right; getting it right will save many module users many hours of time.

- **Only add descriptions when needed**: This might sound obvious, but in Drupal 6 we had a really tough time removing all the places where the description was either repeating the label above or adding little to no additional meaning.

Whenever you can add two or three extra words in the label to make the description superfluous, it's best to do so. We definitely recommend that module maintainers avoid having any descriptions in their forms; it's a good practice because it means your labels are descriptive enough.

- **Be consistent with core terminology**: There are many existing text patterns applied all over Drupal 7 from the way we label our menu items, buttons, and links to proper usage of plural and singular. When writing interface text, compare your work with similar interfaces in Drupal core. This helps you maintain consistency in both terminology and tone-of-voice.

In Drupal core we also have a number of words we avoid using, which are displayed in Table 32–4.

Table 32–4. *Words We Avoid Using in Drupal Core*

Don't use	Use	Why
Drupal	Site	This complicates distributions.
Please	-	It sounds pushy; it's often possible to leave this word out.
We	The user, the admin, name the person	"We" is often not descriptive as to which user it applies, so specifically name whom this is affecting.
Node	Content, piece of content	"Node" is an unknown concept to users.
Post	Piece of content	"Post" can be used as verb; "post" can be confused with other concepts.
Input format	Text format	The word "text" is a better trigger to the user's mental model.
Plug-in, Extension	Module	These words can have other meanings.

We hope you feel prepared to design for the user experience and help make Drupal great!

■ **Tip** Visit dgd7.org/ux for links to resources mentioned in this chapter (and more) and to track continuing developments in Drupal UX.

■ ■ ■

## CHAPTER 33

Completing a Site: The Other 90%

by Benjamin Melançon

> *Hofstadter's Law: "It always takes longer than you expect, even when you take into account Hofstadter's Law."*

You've built out content types and views and blocks and menus (and if you haven't, get back to Chapter 1). You've done some more of this and a bunch of other configuration, too (see Chapter 8). You've made a custom theme (see Chapters 15 and 16). The site is indisputably 90% built. It's just that the final 10% can easily take as much time as you've already put in. Getting a site to done usually means a lot of messing and obsessing until everything works and looks just right.

If the site is high visibility and has to look great and work easily, keep going until, as the song goes, "you've" done did everything that needs done."

This chapter will touch on advanced configuration, but mostly you will use glue code to polish off DefinitiveDrupal.org with custom rims and modded cupholders. (Glue code is theming functions or modules written to meet site-specific needs; see Part V, Back-End Development, particularly Chapter 22 for full coverage of this approach.) You'll even see a spin-off module built for the site but made general enough to contribute to drupal.org.

This chapter does *not* cover theming. For this essential part of completing a site, see Chapters 15 and 16 and also the DefinitiveDrupal.org theme itself. Jacine Luisi is contributing the theme to the community as its own project, and the as-is production version is also in the site's source code. See dgd7.org/theme and dgd7.org/code.

■ **Note** The online resources and discussion related to this chapter are at dgd7.org/other90.

Creating a View Mode

View modes, called build modes in Drupal 6, were mentioned in Chapter 8, and they have not become any less fantastic for changing the display of content or other site entities depending on context. On DefinitiveDrupal.org, author profiles use the Full Content view mode (which inherits the Default view mode's display settings) for the standalone pages and the Teaser view mode for one of the author list views. When author profiles are shown on chapter content, however, it would be best to have another, still-smaller display of author profile content.

This is when you turn to the magic of view modes. The code in Listing 33–1 goes in a module file called dgd7glue.module; it is adapted from a presentation Benjamin Doherty made at DrupalCamp Florida and published afterward to his GitHub account at github.com/bangpound/fldrupalcamp-demo. The first function defines a view mode; it's not intuitive that this would require implementing *hook_entity_info_alter()*, but it's not difficult once you know how.

Listing 33–1. Defining a New Build Mode, Compact, for Nodes

```php
<?php
/**
 * Implements hook_entity_info_alter().
 *
 * Reveals new view mode for node entities. If you don't see your view mode
 * in the Field UI's "manage display" screen, you may need to clear cache
 * or rebuild menus more than once until you do.
 */
function dgd7glue_entity_info_alter(&$entity_info) {
  $entity_info['node']['view modes']['compact'] = array(
    'label' => t('Compact'),
    'custom settings' => FALSE,
  );
}

/**
 * Implements hook_preprocess_node().
 *
 * Adds classes and theme hook suggestions specifically for view modes.
 */
function dgd7glue_preprocess_node(&$vars) {
  $view_mode = $vars['view_mode'];
  $vars['classes_array'][] = 'node-' . $view_mode;
  $type = $vars['type'];
  $vars['theme_hook_suggestions'][] = 'node__' . $type . '__' . $view_mode;
}
```

This second function, an implementation of *hook_preprocess_node()*, is not necessary to have and use view modes, but it is a tremendous theming aid. For example, the addition to 'classes_array' allows CSS to target content displayed with the Compact view mode by looking for the class node-compact. The addition to the 'theme_hook_suggestions' array allows a themer to copy node.tpl.php to node--profile--compact.tpl.php or node--article--teaser.tpl.php, for example, and make modifications that only affect profile content shown in Compact mode or article content in Teaser mode. Using the theme hook suggestion to create a custom template for a view mode is covered later.

■ **Note** As *hook_preprocess_node()* can also be implemented by themes in template.php, this ability to use theme hook suggestions for view modes may already have been added there.

When writing or modifying a preprocess function (as in so many places in Drupal), you can use a debugger or use debug functions to print output to your screen. The set of variables available to *hook_preprocess_node()* tends to be too large for debug() to handle gracefully, so installing Devel module and using a Krumo-enhanced debug output function, such as kpr(), is recommended.

A kpr($vars); in an implementation of *hook_preprocess_node()* will run for every node you display, so looking at a list of nodes while your variable printing code is in your module is not recommended. Also remember that you need Devel module present and enabled to use kpr(). There is a *lot* you can do with preprocess functions. Anything you change or add in a preprocess function, as a rule, becomes available for use in the corresponding theme function or template. Something added to the variables array in *hook_preprocess_node()*, such as $vars['current_time'] = date('Y M d H:m:s', time());, will be available in node.tpl.php (and all its variations including node--article.tpl.php and the now-available node--article--teaser.tpl.php) as $current_time, to be used with print $current_time; or for render array variables print render($complex);. You will see more usage of preprocess functions later in this chapter.

■ **Note** The code in Listing 33–1 needs to go in a file called **dgd7glue.module** which should go in a folder called **dgd7glue** which could be put in your site at **sites/all/modules/custom/**. Then your custom module needs a .info file also, **dgd7glue.info** (see Listing 33–2), which goes in the **dgd7glue** folder with **dgd7glue.module**. (Making modules is covered exhaustively in Chapters 18 to 20 and for the same purpose as here, making a site-specific module, in Chapter 22.)

Listing 33–2. dgd7glue.info

```
name = DGD7 Glue Code
description = [dgd7glue] Site-specific custom code for DefinitiveDrupal.org.
package = Custom
version = 7.x-1.0
core = 7.x
```

■ **Note** The version directive is only included because this site-specific code will not be hosted on drupal.org; for contributed code, the d.o packaging script adds that line itself.

Now—after enabling the DGD7glue module or, if it is already enabled, clearing caches, very likely more than once—you can visit the manage display tab of a content type, such as Administration ➤ Structure ➤ Content types ➤ Author profile ➤ Manage display (admin/structure/types/manage/profile/display) and see that in the collapsed formset **Custom display settings**, there is a new view mode: Compact (see Figure 33–1).

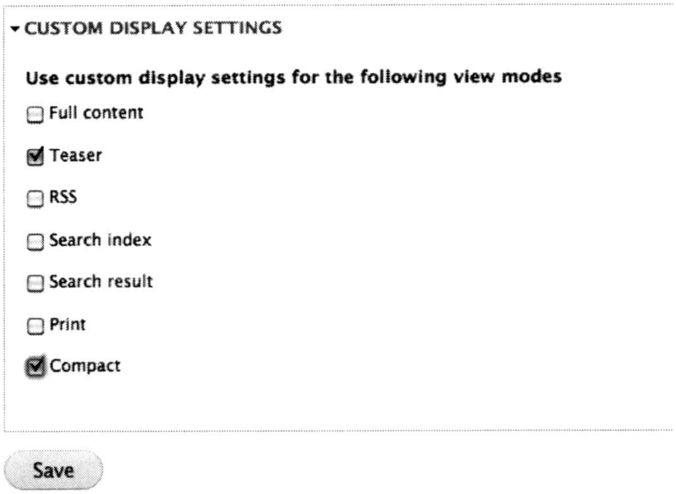

Figure 33–1. *Checkbox to enable custom display settings for view modes, now with the option for Compact*

▓ **Tip** If you want custom settings for your new view mode to be enabled automatically for all content types (the way Teaser is), you can change the custom settings line to `'custom settings' => TRUE`, for your `$entity_info['node']['view modes']['`*viewmodename*`']` array in the *hook_entity_info_alter()* implementation. It may start out with no fields displayed using this approach.

Figure 33–2. *New view mode, Compact, visible at the Manage display tab*

Go to the Compact sub-tab, shown in Figure 33–2, and configure the fields that should show when using the Compact view mode. You can make it show the author's picture, as a thumbnail linked to its content; the drupal.org User ID, as the account link; and the biography text, trimmed to just 300 characters. Hide all the other fields.

Next, go to the Chapter content type and manage the display of its fields. You can give it custom settings for the Compact display mode too, but the present goal is to tell its node reference Author field to use the Compact view mode for displaying author profiles. For the Author field, the Format options will probably be a drop-down containing Title (link), Title (no link), Rendered node, and <Hidden>. Choose Rendered node, and then click the gear icon to the right of the drop-down to configure settings for the Author field rendered node. This is where you can select Compact as the View mode (see Figure 33–3).

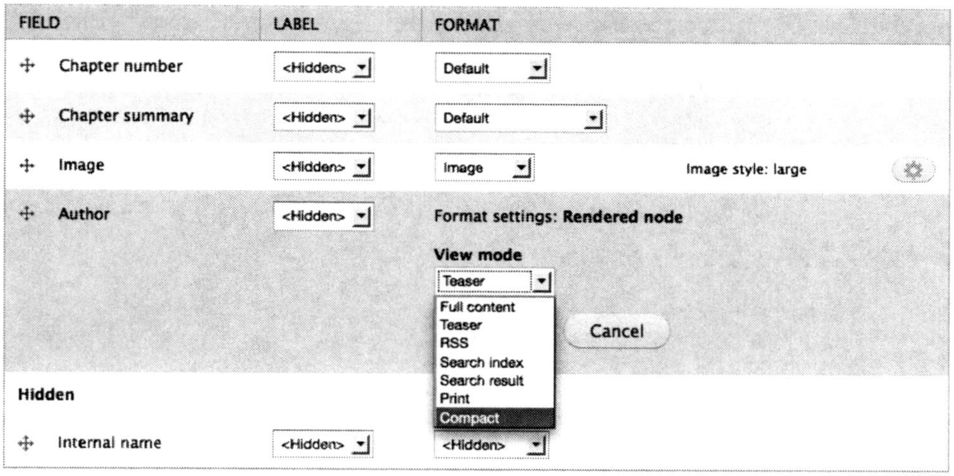

Figure 33–3. Using the Author profile in the Compact view mode when it is displayed on Chapter content. This is set via Chapter content type's Manage display page for its Default view mode.

The next section describes how to theme your view mode.

Creating a Custom Theming Template

The process of creating a custom template file for a theme hook suggestion you define yourself is exactly the same as when creating a custom template file for a template suggestion provided by core. Many suggestions, such as those based on content type, are built in. To use your own template files for all author profiles, you would create a `node--profile.tpl.php` file in your theme (where *profile* is the machine name for the Author profile content type). Below, you're going to do the same for the theme hook suggestion you created that is aware of both content type and view mode.

1. Make sure you have a `node.tpl.php` file in your custom theme's folder (or within a `templates` subdirectory in your theme's folder). Drupal won't recognize your variation of a template unless you have a version of the base template in your theme.

2. Copy this `node.tpl.php` file to match the pattern of the template suggestion you want to use a custom template for. In the case of the theme hook suggestion defined previously, that pattern is `node__content_type__view_mode`. Underscores are replaced with dashes in template files, so it would look like `node--content-type--view-mode.tpl.php`. For the Author profile with the Compact view mode, this is `node--profile--compact.tpl.php`.

3. Modify this file to match your theming needs.

■ **Note** In Drupal 7, you need two dashes (or underscores for functions) separating each part of a suggestion. In Drupal 6, you only needed one— as you might guess from the node--*content-type--view-mode*.tpl.php example. Having two dashes prevents confusion when working with a content type that has an underscore in its machine name.

Listing 33–3 is a look at the modified node template file (you can view the original in your source code, the node.tpl.php that you copy, and at api.drupal.org/api/modules--node--node.tpl.php). The file is node--profile--compact.tpl.php as noted previously. In your theme, it goes in the templates folder. The first three lines are how to learn about the variables available; they should be deleted before use on a live site.

■ **Caution** The code in Listing 33–3 uses a function provided by the Devel module— you'll need to download and enable it if you haven't already, or substitute a core Drupal function such as debug() or a PHP function such as print_r(). Devel's dpm() and core's debug() both send their output to Drupal's messages area; Devel's kpr() and PHP's print_r() both print out right where they are (by default), which works in template files and preprocess functions.

Listing 33–3. Custom Node Template for Author Profiles Shown with the Compact View Mode

```php
<?php
  kpr($content);
?>
<div id="node-<?php print $node->nid; ?>" class="<?php print $classes; ?> clearfix"<?php↩
  print $attributes; ?>>
  <?php print render($content['field_image']); ?>
  <div class="author-info">
    <h3<?php print $title_attributes; ?>><a href="<?php print $node_url; ?>"><?php↩
print $title; ?></a></h3>

    <?php
      // We hide the comments and links.  Shouldn't be any.
      hide($content['comments']);
      hide($content['links']);
      print render($content);
    ?>
  </div>
</div>
```

This template removes and rearranges some markup and adds a div, but the most significant thing it is doing is using the line print render($content['field_image']); to print out the author picture before the node title (the author's name). Note that when the rest of the content is printed with render(), the image is not re-printed. This is all explained in Chapters 15 and 16.

The HTML produced by the template in Listing 33–3 works with the accompanying CSS shown in Listing 33–4, developed mostly by experimenting in Firebug (see getfirebug.com).

Listing 33–4. *Addition to style.css in the Theme's Directory Making Use of the New View Mode and the Custom Template to Theme the Compact Author Profiles*

```
/**
 * Compact author profiles.
 */
.node-compact .field {
  padding: 0;
}

.node-compact .field-name-field-image {
  position: absolute;
}

.node-compact .author-info {
  margin-left: 130px;
}
```

The absolute positioning works because the .node div is already defined as position: relative. Altogether this makes the page look pretty good, as you can see in Figure 33–4.

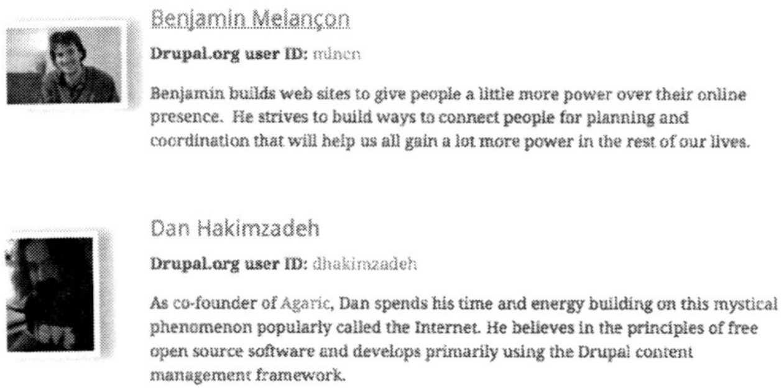

Benjamin Melançon

Drupal.org user ID: mlncn

Benjamin builds web sites to give people a little more power over their online presence. He strives to build ways to connect people for planning and coordination that will help us all gain a lot more power in the rest of our lives.

Dan Hakimzadeh

Drupal.org user ID: dhakimzadeh

As co-founder of Agaric, Dan spends his time and energy building on this mystical phenomenon popularly called the Internet. He believes in the principles of free open source software and develops primarily using the Drupal content management framework.

Figure 33–4. *Two author profiles, as attached to a chapter, with the compact view mode and CSS styling*

■ **Tip** Making a template file should never be your first choice; they are hardest to maintain as things change. Other approaches, such as styling with CSS, configuring through the Drupal user interface, and manipulating variables in preprocess functions can often give you all the flexibility you need.

Remember you may be able to get pretty far with CSS (especially with the view mode added to the node body classes), and then even farther with preprocess functions, and not need to create a node template, which can be a lot of work to maintain when changes to a content type are made. As noted in Chapters 15 and 16, while you can implement theme_node__suggestion() or node--suggestion.tpl.php, there is **no** "hook_preprocess_node__suggestion" equivalent to these. Instead, you can use the many variables available in a *hook_preprocess_node()* implementation to check the value of one or two variables, such as the content type (in $vars['type']) or the view mode (in $vars['view_mode']), to decide if you want to mess with any of the other variables. (Note that $vars can be $variables or whatever you put in the parenthesis when implementing hook_preprocess_node(), and note further that this all applies the same to hook_preprocess_page(), hook_preprocess_comment(), etc. These hooks can be used in either a module or a theme and are covered in Chapters 15 and 16.)

■ **Note** The template in Listing 33–3 looks clean, and it worked for your purposes, but when Drupal prints it out, there's a div each for field, field-items, and field-item. This is great for consistency: the same CSS will apply if it is a single-value field or one with fifty items. If it offends your sensibilities or gets in the way of your design, you can change the output that surrounds fields. In an approach directly analogous to providing theme hook suggestions in hook_preprocess_node(), you can provide theme hook suggestions for fields by implementing hook_preprocess_field(). See dgd7.org/222.

Modifying the Chapter Number Field's Display

As noted, you can also use preprocess functions to modify fields before they are output. The Chapter number/Appendix letter field was set up to take only two characters. Drupal does not currently allow a textfield to be re-sized (though a module can override this, perhaps even safely; see dgd7.org/226), so you have to provide a code solution where it might have been better to let people type out "Chapter 1" and so forth. The good news, of course, is that an elegant code solution is possible.

As usual, you can begin your investigation by looking up relevant API functions (such as template_preprocess_field()) and, most usefully, printing out the variables available to your hook_preprocess_HOOK() implementation, in this case dgd7glue_preprocess_field(), while continuing to use the same custom module.

■ **Note** The various preprocess hooks are considered special cases of hook_process_HOOK() (see api.drupal.org/hook_process_HOOK) and do not have API documentation of their own at this time.

You can also implement preprocess hooks in your theme's **template.php**; prefix it with your theme's name instead of your module's name (see Listing 33–5).

Listing 33–5. Using Krumo to Display All Data Available to the hook_preprocess_field() Implementation

```
function dgd7glue_preprocess_field(&$vars) {
  kpr($vars);
}
```

■ **Tip** Functions for debugging that use Drupal's message system, including debug() and Devel module's dpm(), can be inconsistent in their functioning from within preprocess functions. It is late enough in the page building, rendering, and theming cycle that printing output directly from these functions does work, so print_r() for small arrays and krumo() (with Devel module enabled) for larger arrays and objects works well. The function kpr() shown in Listing 33–5 will use krumo for arrays and will print scalar variables.

With krumo—via Devel module's kpr()—you can see that the variables available for a given field in a highly readable structure. It starts out with all sub-arrays and sub-objects collapsed; you click to open the ones you are interested in. In Figure 33–5, the *element* variable is expanded; you can see it provides very useful information such as the field name in #field_name, the view mode in #view_mode, and the content type in #bundle. The *element* variable is meant for the Render API layer (see Appendix C) and is just information at the theming layer where preprocess acts, but it is very useful information.

The rest of the variables are the ones you can change in the preprocess function; in particular *items*, shown fully expanded, is where you can change the value output by the field, which is currently 29. The several-deep array nesting for *items* translates to $vars['items'][0]['#markup'] in code.

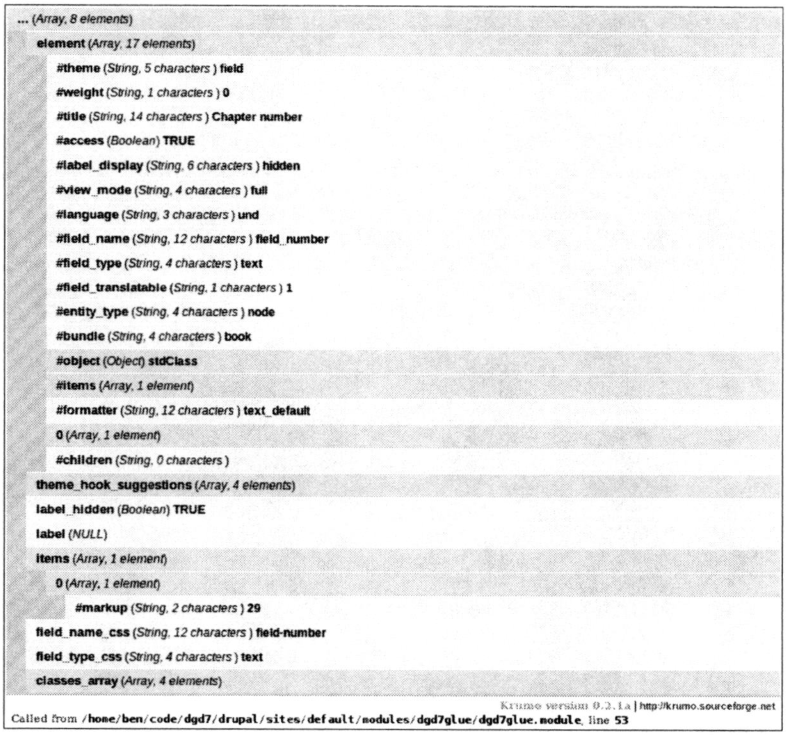

Figure 33–5. Krumo output, the result of calling kpr($vars); for an implementation of hook_preprocess_field() when viewing a page with a node that includes the 'number' field.

I'll mention this again, because it will save you a lot of time wondering why your changes are not taking effect. Information you can read to decide when and how to take action is in the *element* variable; the data you can change to affect the display of the field is in the *items* and other variables.

■ **Gotcha** None of the values in the element array have any effect. Only `$vars['items'][0]['#markup']` changes what the field outputs for its value (for the first value for the field; the second value would be in the 1 position instead of 0). I don't know how you would know this without having read it here. A couple hours of wondering why manipulating such things as `$vars['element']['#items'][0]['safe_value']` had no effect was my approach. See `dgd7.org/225` for some excerpts from that fun journey.

Putting this information together, you can write code for the preprocess function that checks if it is the field and content type (bundle) you care about, prints Chapter for numbers, Appendix for letters, and further checks the view mode to print shorter text for the Compact view mode.

The end result of the code in Listing 33–6 is to print **Chapter 33** instead of **33** when viewing the node for this chapter (at `dgd7.org/other90`), Appendix C instead of C (for `dgd7.org/render`), and Ch 33 and App C for these when shown on a compact list such as `dgd7.org/chapters`.

Listing 33–6. Implementation of hook_preprocess_field() that Converts the Number or Letter to the Text Chapter [number] or Appendix [letter], Respectively, Using a Short Form for the Compact View Mode

```
/**
 * Implements hook_preprocess_field().
 */
function dgd7glue_preprocess_field(&$vars) {
  if ($vars['element']['#field_name'] == 'field_number'
      && $vars['element']['#bundle'] == 'book') {
    $v = $vars['items'][0]['#markup'];
    if (is_numeric($v)) {
      if ($vars['element']['#view_mode'] == 'compact') {
        $v = t('Ch !n', array('!n' => $v),
          array('context' => 'Abbreviation for Chapter'));
      }
      else {
        $v = t('Chapter !n', array('!n' => $v));
      }
    }
    else {
      // It's not a number, so it is an Appendix.
      if ($vars['element']['#view_mode'] == 'compact') {
        $v = t('App !n', array('!n' => $v),
          array('context' => 'Abbreviation for Appendix'));
      }
      else {
        $v = t('Appendix !n', array('!n' => $v));
      }
    }
    $vars['items'][0]['#markup'] = $v;
  }
}
```

As a coder, you have full control of field output with preprocess functions. It's also possible to give site administrators ways to change field display by coding field formatters, covered next.

Linking to Drupal.org and Twitter Accounts with Field Formatters

As constructed in Chapter 8, Author profiles include fields for very specific connections to other web sites: a drupal.org ID, a groups.drupal.org ID, and a Twitter username. The two IDs were made integer fields and the username was made a plain text field. The task of turning this data into human-readable (and clickable) links was punted to here. Fortunately, making field formatters is fun.

You've seen formatters in action, for instance, when choosing whether a text field should be displayed as Default, Plain text, and Trimmed. To make your own formatters, you can get started by looking at Drupal's own code directly or finding an answer on api.drupal.org. Taking the latter route this time, going to api.drupal.org and clicking Topics takes you to api.drupal.org/api/drupal/groups/7 which is a long list of things that have been grouped together—two pages worth—but Field API is on the first page. In fact, Field API in some form is listed eight times (see Figure 33–6).

Field API	Attach custom data fields to Drupal entities.
Field API bulk data deletion	Clean up after Field API bulk deletion operations.
Field Attach API	Operate on Field API data attached to Drupal entities.
Field CRUD API	Create, update, and delete Field API fields, bundles, and instances.
Field Info API	Obtain information about Field API configuration.
Field Language API	Handling of multilingual fields.
Field Storage API	Implement a storage engine for Field API data.
Field Types API	Define field types, widget types, display formatter types, storage types.

Figure 33–6. *Field API topics listed on api.drupal.org*

The first listing, "Field API", links to all the other Field API topics (after providing a lot of background information on fields). But it's the last listing, Field Types API, that's exactly what you're looking for: "Define field types, widget types, *display formatter types*, storage types" (emphasis added). Click through to api.drupal.org/api/group/field_types (that's the shortest URL that works; you'll be taken to the long version) and at the bottom of a list of hooks, two are specially documented:

> *The Field Types API also defines two kinds of pluggable handlers: widgets and formatters, which specify how the field appears in edit forms [widgets] and in displayed entities [formatters]. Widgets and formatters can be implemented by a field-type module for its own field types, or by a third-party module to extend the behavior of existing field types.*

You can extend the behavior of existing field types with a module. The referenced hook is hook_field_formatter_info(), defined at api.drupal.org/hook_field_formatter_info, and it has example code! You can change the module name part of the function name, and a few other details, and add it to the glue module (see Listing 33–7).

Listing 33–7. Basic Implementation of hook_field_formatter_info() for dgd7glue.module

```
/**
 * Implements hook_field_formatter_info().
 */
function dgd7glue_field_formatter_info() {
  return array(
    'dgd7glue_number_account_link' => array(
      'label' => t('Account link'),
      'field types' => array('number_integer'),
    ),
    'dgd7glue_text_account_link' => array(
      'label' => t('Account link'),
      'field types' => array('text'),
    ),
  );
}
```

Clear caches and visit an administration page for fields display that includes text or integer fields, such as the Manage Display page for the Author profile content type at Administration ➤ Structure ➤ Content types ➤ Author profile ➤ Manage display (admin/structure/types/manage/profile/display) and you will see that you have an **Account link** option for the formatter of text and integer fields. It won't do anything, but it shows up! See Figure 33–7.

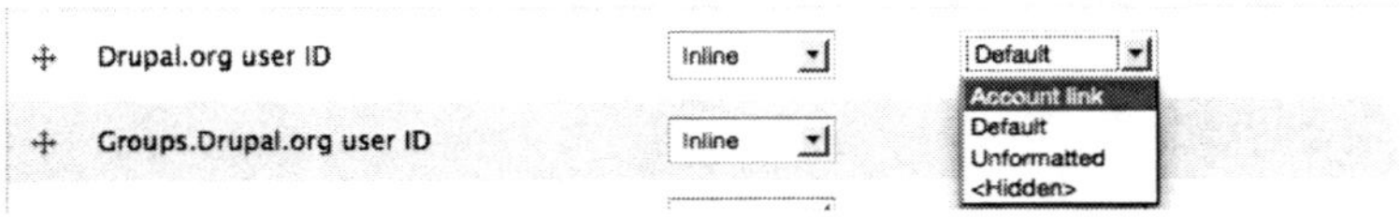

Figure 33–7. Account link formatter option for an integer field

If the two formatters you are defining need to be configurable, they will need some settings. You can get an example of formatter settings from both the text and integer fields provided by Drupal core. The integer field type is defined in the number module, which is inside the field module; the Number module's main file is located at modules/field/modules/number/number.module. The text module is also inside the field module. Both define much more than formatters, but you are only interested in the various formatter functions: hook_field_formatter_*() implementations– info, settings_form, settings_summary, and view.

▓ **Note** You could add settings to the existing text and integer field formatters with hook_field_formatter_info_alter(), but adding a link around the field data will require its own formatter view, and so needs a new formatter.

To add settings forms and settings summaries to the field display form, you need to first add settings defaults to your implementation of hook_field_formatter_info(); see Listing 33–8.

Listing 33–8. Adding Settings Defaults for the Custom Account Link Formatters for Integer and Text Fields

```
/**
 * Implements hook_field_formatter_info().
 */
function dgd7glue_field_formatter_info() {
  return array(
    'dgd7glue_number_account_link' => array(
      'label' => t('Account link'),
      'field types' => array('number_integer'),
      'settings' => array('web_site' => 'drupal_org'),
    ),
    'dgd7glue_text_account_link' => array(
      'label' => t('Account link'),
      'field types' => array('text'),
      'settings' => array('web_site' => 'twitter_com'),
    ),
  );
}
```

This provides defaults but administrators don't yet have a way to change these defaults. You need a settings form with a select list—a form element with pre-defined options. The Number module's field formatter settings form hook implementation has a select list element from which you can borrow (api.drupal.org/number_field_formatter_settings_form). The options in this select list will be drupal.org and groups.drupal.org in the case of the number account field and twitter.com and identi.ca in the case of the text account field. The code in Listing 33–9 borrows from the number form structure and select list and adds an if statement to provide different options depending on if it is the formatter for number fields or the formatter for text fields. The select options themselves are moved to helper functions.

Listing 33–9. Settings Form for the Account Link Formatters for Text and Integer Fields

```
/**
 * Implements hook_field_formatter_settings_form().
 */
function dgd7glue_field_formatter_settings_form($field, $instance, $view_mode, $form,↵
&$form_state) {
  $element = array();

  $display = $instance['display'][$view_mode];
  $settings = $display['settings'];

  if ($display['type'] == 'dgd7glue_number_account_link') {
    $options = _dgd7glue_number_account_link_options();
  }
  else {
    // Field type is dgd7glue_text_account_link.
    $options = _dgd7glue_text_account_link_options();
  }

  $element['web_site'] = array(
    '#title' => t('Web site or service'),
    '#type' => 'select',
    '#options' => $options,
```

```
        '#default_value' => $settings['web_site'],
        '#required' => TRUE,
    );

    return $element;
}

/**
 * Provides Account link formatter options for integer fields.
 */
function _dgd7glue_number_account_link_options() {
  return array(
      'drupal_org' => t('Drupal.org'),
      'groups_drupal_org' => t('Groups.Drupal.org'),
  );
}

/**
 * Provides Account link formatter options for text fields.
 */
function _dgd7glue_text_account_link_options() {
  return array(
      'twitter_com' => t('Twitter.com'),
      'identi_ca' => t('Identi.ca'),
  );
}
```

Drupal's Field API requires you to provide a summary of the settings selected. Rather than again drawing from the number field for an example, the need to state which option has been selected maps closely to the simpler one-line summary of text.module (api.drupal.org/text_field_formatter_settings_summary); see Listing 33–10.

Listing 33–10. A Summary of the Settings Selected

```
/**
 * Implements hook_field_formatter_settings_summary().
 */
function dgd7glue_field_formatter_settings_summary($field, $instance, $view_mode) {
  $summary = '';

  $display = $instance['display'][$view_mode];
  $settings = $display['settings'];

  if ($display['type'] == 'dgd7glue_number_account_link') {
    $options = _dgd7glue_number_account_link_options();
  }
  else {
    // Field type is dgd7glue_text_account_link.
    $options = _dgd7glue_text_account_link_options();
  }

  $summary .= t('Web site') . ': ' . $options[$settings['web_site']];

  return $summary;
}
```

Test that this worked by going back to the Author profile manage fields display page, selecting Account link for the Drupal ID field and see that the options drupal.org and Groups.Drupal.org appear.

■ **Caution** The settings form link (gear icon) will not be displayed if the settings summary hook is not also defined.

A first draft of Listings 33–9 and 33–10 did not have helper functions for the formatter options. Realizing that both dgd7glue_field_formatter_settings_form() and dgd7glue_field_formatter_settings_summary() should have the display-friendly version of the option (for instance 'Drupal.org' for 'drupal_org'), they were refactored to put the options in their own functions. This way, the settings form function and the settings summary function can both call them. (Repeating information in two places in the code would have been a bad thing; when something needs to be changed, you or the next developer would be likely to miss one of the places.) In retrospect, it might be even cleaner to have one options-gathering helper function (instead of two) and do an if or switch statement on the field formatter type within it. However, the point of custom code is to do something effective and specific on your web site in a maintainable way, not to be endlessly refactored for elegance.

The next step is to implement hook_field_formatter_view(). While developing, you will likely want to look in a debugger or throw a debug($items) into dgd7glue_field_formatter_view() to see exactly what it gets for items, as shown in Listing 33–11.

Listing 33–11. Implementation of hook_field_formatter_view() to Investigate What It Is Handed

```
/**
 * Implements hook_field_formatter_view().
 */
function dgd7glue_field_formatter_view($entity_type, $entity, $field, $instance, $langcode, ↩
$items, $display) {
  foreach ($items as $delta => $item) {
    debug($item);
  }
}
```

Viewing an author profile page that has values for a drupal.org ID and a Twitter account now result in messages printed to the screen, for the former, a numeric field:

```
array (
  'value' => '64383',
)
```

and for the latter, a text field item

```
array (
  'value' => 'mlncn',
  'format' => NULL,
  'safe_value' => 'mlncn',
)
```

Knowing the structure of the items handed in to dgd7_field_formatter_view() and knowing the structure of the display settings form you just defined, you can write a function that combines the two.

■ **Note** If you need to examine the structure of the variable $display you can look at in a debugger (see dgd7.org/ide) or output with debug() as done with $item above.

The function in Listing 33–12 has a switch statement to assign the base URL according to the web site setting (such as http://drupal.org/ for a drupal.org-designated field) and another switch statement to set the key for accessing the field's value correctly. As seen above, 'value' is the only property available for the integer field. This is because a validated integer field is inherently safe. Drupal provides the 'safe_value' property for the text field because a sanitized version is needed for you to print it safely. A user-input string could contain malicious JavaScript code.

Listing 33–12. Implementation of hook_field_formatter_view() to Show Account IDs as Links

```
/**
 * Implements hook_field_formatter_view().
 */
function dgd7glue_field_formatter_view($entity_type, $entity, $field, $instance, $langcode,↵
$items, $display) {
  $element = array();

  // Allow a definition of a function to get the account link title.
  $title_callback = NULL;
  $item_key = 'safe_value';

  // Ordinarily, view formatters switch on the display type, but for the
  // account link formatters dgd7glue defines, the web site is what matters.
  switch ($display['settings']['web_site']) {
    case 'drupal_org':
      $href = 'http://drupal.org/user/';
      $title_callback = 'dgd7glue_drupal_page_title';
      break;
    case 'groups_drupal_org':
      $href = 'http://groups.drupal.org/user/';
      $title_callback = 'dgd7glue_drupal_page_title';
      break;
    case 'twitter_com':
      $href = 'http://twitter.com/';
      break;
    case 'identi_ca':
      $href = 'http://identi.ca/';
      break;
  }

  switch ($display['type']) {
    case 'dgd7glue_number_account_link':
      $item_key = 'value';
      break;
    default:
      $item_key = 'safe_value';
  }
```

```
  foreach ($items as $delta => $item) {
    if ($title_callback) {
      $title = $title_callback($item[$item_key], $href);
    }
    else {
      $title = $item[$item_key];
    }
    $href = $href .= $item[$item_key];
    $element[$delta] = array(
        '#type' => 'link',
        '#title' => $title,
        '#href' => $href,
    );
  }

  return $element;
}

/**
 * Get the title of a page on a Drupal site.
 *
 * Callback for account link titles in dgd7glue_field_formatter_view().
 */
function dgd7glue_drupal_page_title($account_id, $href) {
  return $account_id;
}
```

The first switch statement, above, provides the base for the URL depending on which web site is set in the field's display settings, and optionally a title callback to generate the text part of the link. That last function, dgd7glue_drupal_page_title(), provides that callback. As shown, however, it's only a placeholder: it doesn't do what you really want it to do. In the next section, you'll change it to fetch the author's username from drupal.org and groups.drupal.org profile pages.

The main function ends with a foreach() statement (which would handle the case if the field were to allow multiple values) that builds the element to return as a renderable array. By setting the '#type' to 'link', Drupal knows to create a link. (As described in Appendix C, returning a render array instead of an HTML string gives other Drupal modules and the theme a chance to make changes, such as adding a class or a target attribute.)

Fetching the Username

The dgd7glue_drupal_page_title() function used previously needs to do what it says and fetch users' names from their profile pages on drupal.org and groups.drupal.org.

Even for the craziest ideas, someone may have blazed the trail for you in Drupal. In this case, that someone is Kevin Hemenway, better known as Morbus Iff. His Bot module powers Druplicon in #drupal and other IRC channels (see Chapter 9). It can be configured to magically fetch the title of a node when given the URL on a Drupal, such as http://example.com/node/523. (For issues on drupal.org, it can also get the project, status, and other information. But the interesting thing for your present use case is that it somehow grabs the title of sites with which it has no special integration.)

Knowing this, why not drush dl bot, even though you don't plan to use it—just look at it (see Listing 33–13).

Listing 33–13. Excerpt from bot_project.module

```
/**
 * Listen for URLs or a numerical ID and respond with information about it.
 *
 * @param $data
 *   The regular $data object prepared by the IRC library.
 * @param $from_query
 *   Boolean; whether this was a queried request.
 */
function bot_project_irc_msg_channel($data, $from_query = FALSE) {
// [Code not of interest for present purposes not shown...]
      $result = drupal_http_request($url);
      if ($result->code != 200) { continue; }

      // we'll always display a title, so grab that first for db storage.
      preg_match('/<title>(.*?) \|.*?<\/title>/', $result->data, $title_match);
      $title = $title_match[1] ? $title_match[1] : '<' . t('unable to determine title') . '>';
// ...
```

The code is littered with caveats from Morbus, the module's author, about how it's not the best way to do it—but it works. You can adopt it directly, as shown in Listing 33–14.

Listing 33–14. Function to Scrape User Names from Drupal.org User Page Titles (or Any Drupal.org Page Title)

```
/**
 * Get the title of a page on a Drupal site.
 *
 * Callback for account link titles in dgd7glue_field_formatter_view().
 */
function dgd7glue_drupal_page_title($account_id, $href) {
  $result = drupal_http_request($url);
  // Use $account_id as title if cannot get one.
  if ($result->code != 200) {
    return $account_id;
  }
  // Extract the first part of the title from the page's HTML source.
  preg_match('/<title>(.*?) \|.*?<\/title>/', $result->data, $title_match);
  $title = $title_match[1] ? $title_match[1] : $account_id;
  return $title;
}
```

This code works and is pretty awesome, replacing a number with a name. There's still a problem with it, though: it causes drupal.org to be contacted twice every time someone views an author's profile, downloading an entire profile web page each from drupal.org or groups.drupal.org. One way or another, the name needs to be cached locally instead.

■ **Tip** Before you implement caching, make sure you need it. You can test if the code you are planning to cache is called with a debugger, a query logger (as provided by Devel module, drupal.org/project/devel), or by including a watchdog() logging command (api.drupal.org/watchdog), which you could use temporarily even on a live site. See Appendix B for ways to find performance problems on your site that need optimization.

Caching Simple Data Using Drupal's Default Cache Table

To be nice to drupal.org, to say nothing of your own site's performance, don't grab an entire page each time you want to look up a username.

Doing this work at the formatter level means it is too late for Field API's built-in caching. Defining a new cache_* table or adding a row or rows to the generic cache table are both possibilities. To implement some basic caching, you can look in the cache table and work your way backwards. Searching for keys from the cache table in the site code quickly shows that cache_set() and cache_get() are the functions Drupal uses to put and take data from cache. Searching for 'cache_set' or 'cache_get' (as with grep -nHR 'cache_get' modules from the root of Drupal's code) finds plenty of examples.

■ **Note** Drupal's caching functions take care of static caching for you, which is nice. It's probably not necessary in this case, but static caching means that when the data is fetched from the cache with a database query, it doesn't repeat this query during a page request. (See api.drupal.org/_cache_get_object which is called by cache_get().)

Taking as an example the caching for language metadata in **locale.module**, you can incorporate caching into the page title fetching function. The caching-related additions are shown in Listing 33–15 in bold.

Listing 33–15. Caching Added to the Function for Fetching Page Titles from Standard Drupal Sites

```
/**
 * Get the title of a page on a Drupal site.
 *
 * Callback for account link titles in dgd7glue_field_formatter_view().
 */
function dgd7glue_drupal_page_title($account_id, $href) {
  $url = $href . $account_id;
  if ($cache = cache_get('dgd7glue:' . $url, 'cache')) {
    $title = $cache->data;
  }
  else {
    $result = drupal_http_request($url);
    // Use $account_id as title if cannot get one, but do not cache it.
    if ($result->code != 200) {
```

```
      return $account_id;
    }
    // Extract the first part of the title from the page's HTML source.
    preg_match('/<title>(.*?) \|.*?<\/title>/', $result->data, $title_match);
    $title = $title_match[1] ? $title_match[1] : $account_id;
    cache_set('dgd7glue:' . $url, $title);
  }
  return $title;
}
```

The request to load a page is now made only once, and is thereafter retrieved from the cache until caches are cleared—which can be weeks on a production site (not in development).

Streamlining an Awkward Form Element with CSS

The *Suggestion* content type has the *Book element* vocabulary attached to it. This vocabulary has a dozen terms, of which only one can be selected, presented as radio buttons listed vertically by default. This significantly increases the amount of scrolling a person needs to do when posting a suggestion.

To fix this, there is (of course) a module for that, one with a most impressive name: Multi-column checkboxes radios (drupal.org/project/multicolumncheckboxesradios). However, at the time of writing, it was still buggy for Drupal 7. Also, the Book element vocabulary doesn't have so many terms that it needs columns; it would look fine horizontal instead of vertically, and you can do that with CSS.

■ **Note** Drupal 7 improves the classes added to divs surrounding form items. In Drupal 6, it was hardcoded to 'form-item'. Now the form element name and the type of form element are added as form-item-*name* and form-item-*type*. You can see how Drupal does this (and also see the theme function you would override to change it) at api.drupal.org/theme_form_element.

Unfortunately, you can't easily add custom classes to forms that you define or alter. However, between classes based on the type and the name, you can generally target form items with CSS or JavaScript as you need to. In general, you will be able to style your form without adding another div or other wrapping element and without overriding the theme_form_element() function; see Listing 33–16.

Listing 33–16. CSS Added to the Theme to Make the Book Element Vocabulary's Radio Buttons Span Side-to-Side

```
/* Make the Book element radio buttons flow horizontally. */
.form-item-field-element-und {
  display: inline-block;
  padding-right: 7px;
}
```

Contextual "Add New" Links for Content Types

When a user is looking at the list of suggestions or an individual suggestion, she should also be invited to submit her own, if she has permission to create a new suggestion.

Drupal 7 provides for a similar action primarily found on Administration pages, for example the + *Add content* link above the content listing (`admin/content`).

■ **Note** Action links are a new interaction pattern for Drupal 7 (see Chapter 32). They are Drupal's way of saying things like "If you're on the content overview page, there's a good chance you want to add new content." While other local tasks in Drupal take you to settings or listing pages, action links perform actions, usually adding something. Rather than being rendered as tabs like other tasks are by default, they are rendered as links directly below the help region through an `$action_links` variable in the page template.

Personally, these action links (such as the + *Add content type* at the top of `admin/structure/content-types`) might as well be invisible to me—whether it's the slight indent or, more likely, being used to Drupal 6 which only ever had help text in that area, this new Drupal 7 convention hasn't become natural to me yet. However, the benefits of adopting a standard (which probably will be natural to native Drupal 7 users in any case) trumps personal taste. The fundamental concept of treating a certain type of links a certain way is sound.

■ **Note** The first approach described next turns out not to be the best way to add existing pages as action links, so if you're looking for a straight answer, you can skip down to the second solution. I'm showing this one here because it's a viable solution (and the proper way to add new pages as action links) and, more importantly, demonstrates the process of investigation.

Finding and Following a Model

As discussed in Chapter 18, it's always good to look to Drupal core for examples, but a contrib implementation of a core convention is a good place to look, too—especially when the contributed modules is Views. On the Administer ➤ Structure ➤ Views page (`admin/structure/views`), atop the listing of existing views, is the signature plus sign with text + *Add new view*. You can search for the text in the Views code to learn how it gets there; see Listing 33–17.

Listing 33–17. Using Grep to Search for "Add new view" within the Views Project, with Result Shown

```
cd ~/workspace/dgd7
grep -nHR "Add new view" sites/all/modules/views/
sites/all/modules/views/views_ui.module:38:    'title' => 'Add new view',
```

The search output in Listing 33–18 tells you that in the Views UI module, on line 38, the text you searched for ("Add new view") is present. Go there and you can see that it is within an implementation of hook_menu(); see Listing 33–18.

Listing 33–18. Code that Defines the "Add New View" Link in views_ui.module

```
$items['admin/structure/views/add'] = $base + array(
  'title' => 'Add new view',
  'page callback' => 'views_ui_add_page',
  'type' => MENU_LOCAL_ACTION,
);
```

This is quite instructive. The menu item definition indicates that the page it is appearing on is at the path admin/structure/views, as you know it is. Its **title** is the text you see, "Add new view". The special part seems to be the menu item **type** of MENU_LOCAL_ACTION.

Do a quick search of Drupal code for MENU_LOCAL_ACTION and you can find other examples; see Listing 33–19.

Listing 33–19. Menu Item Defined in node.module Gives Link on admin/structure/types

```
$items['admin/structure/types/add'] = array(
  'title' => 'Add content type',
  'page callback' => 'drupal_get_form',
  'page arguments' => array('node_type_form'),
  'access arguments' => array('administer content types'),
  'type' => MENU_LOCAL_ACTION,
  'file' => 'content_types.inc',
);
```

That's not the link that needs to be added to the top of the listing of suggestions, though. The link you want to include as an action link is 'node/add/suggestion'. Searching for node/add in node.module (skipping past the menu item that defines the listing page of *all* content types that users can create) brings you to a set of menu items defined in a foreach loop—one menu item for each content type; see Listing 33–20.

Listing 33–20. Code in node.module's Implementation of hook_menu() that Creates a

node/add/CONTENT_TYPE Page for Each Content Type

```
foreach (node_type_get_types() as $type) {
  $type_url_str = str_replace('_', '-', $type->type);
  $items['node/add/' . $type_url_str] = array(
    'title' => $type->name,
    'title callback' => 'check_plain',
    'page callback' => 'node_add',
    'page arguments' => array($type->type),
    'access callback' => 'node_access',
    'access arguments' => array('create', $type->type),
    'description' => $type->description,
    'file' => 'node.pages.inc',
  );
```

Is there any way to make this show up outside its location? It might seem there is no easy way, but actually you can create a second menu item at a different path that calls the same page callback and page arguments as the node add form you want. (As you'll see later, this is not the best approach here.) In this case, that's the suggestions path defined by your view and the suggestion content type.

The most important thing to note is the page callback, which is the node_add() function, and the page arguments, which is just one argument, the node type machine name.

■ **Tip** The X-ray module created in Chapters 18 through 20 and available at drupal.org/project/xray provides the page callback and page arguments passed to it for every page you visit, and could give this information for node/add/suggestion without the need to look at *hook_menu()* implementations directly.

Enough looking at existing code. Time to write some code! The code in Listing 33–21 is a menu item definition that combines the definition of a node/add menu item with the MENU_LOCAL_ACTION type.

Listing 33–21. Defining a Local Action Menu Item in Your Custom Code

```
/**
 * Implements hook_menu().
 */
function dgd7glue_menu() {
  $items = array();
  $items['suggestions/add'] = array(
    'title' => "Add a suggestion",
    'page callback' => 'node_add',
    'page arguments' => array('suggestion'),
    'access callback' => 'node_access',
    'access arguments' => array('create', 'suggestion'),
    'file' => 'node.pages.inc',
    'file path' => drupal_get_path('module', 'node'),
    'type' => MENU_LOCAL_ACTION,
  );
  return $items;
}
```

■ **Gotcha** Menu item definitions do *not* use underscores in their keys ('page arguments', 'page callback', and 'access callback', etc.).

Clear caches (and make sure the module is enabled) and presto! It's there, your own action link.

PROBLEMS BETWEEN KEYBOARD AND CHAIR (PEBKAC)

When your author first did this, the action link did not show up. I cleared caches, added it below an `admin/` path (rather than the Views-created path `suggestions`), and of course cleared caches again, and it still did not show. I looked in the menu table, and the entry was there. It wasn't until I decided to directly manipulate the example I was following (the Add content type link) that I noticed that I had left off the most critical part of the example: `'type' => MENU_LOCAL_ACTION`!

Let it be said again, if I can make modules, you can make modules.

Another mistake made I made was attempting to put the full path to the node module in `'file'`. That did not work, and my mistake was quickly corrected by a visit to `http://api.drupal.org/hook_menu`. The path to the module that contains code I am borrowing must be listed separately in the `'file path'` directive. (The path to the node module was obtained from the `drupal_get_path()` function, which your author found by searching for 'path' on `api.drupal.org`.)

Some things are just difficult, and a typo can take serious time to debug. Often, when things are difficult, it's a sign that Drupal may provide a better way. This is true this case, so read on.

Noticing and Adopting a Better Way

This method of defining a new menu item for the action link works, but is there a better way? Repeating the use of the page callback function in a new menu item means that the page to add a suggestion now exists at *two* paths on the site: node/add/suggestion, as expected, and the new suggestions/add. This will confuse Shortcut module (allowing the same page to be added to the shortcut bar twice) and also might confuse people using the site, reducing their feelings of comfort and understanding.

While looking at node.module's implementation of *hook_menu()*, you might have noticed that the + *Add content* action link at the top of admin/content is not defined as a MENU_LOCAL_ACTION. Searching all the files of node.module for "Add content" only brings up the node/add page itself. How does it get added to admin/content? Searching for admin/content brings the answer almost immediately: the function node_menu_local_tasks_alter(). Check it out in node.module or at api.drupal.org/node_menu_local_tasks_alter because you can take and modify the code very directly and make it your own, as done in Listing 33–22.

Listing 33–22. Adding an Action Link by Implementing hook_menu_local_tasks_alter()

```
/**
 * Implements hook_menu_local_tasks_alter().
 */
function dgd7glue_menu_local_tasks_alter(&$data, $router_item, $root_path) {
  // Add action link to 'node/add/suggestion' on 'suggestions' page.
  if ($root_path == 'suggestions') {
    $item = menu_get_item('node/add/suggestion');
    if ($item['access']) {
      $data['actions']['output'][] = array(
        '#theme' => 'menu_local_action',
        '#link' => $item,
      );
    }
```

```
    }
}
```

Excellent! This replaces the menu item defined previously with a much more elegant solution (thank Drupal that "there's a hook for that"). Now you have added a custom action link to an existing page the correct way. It's easy when you know how. But if there's any moral to be learned from your author's stumbling around, it's that not knowing but trying anyway is one way to end up knowing how.

Views-created listings featuring one or two content types are very common in Drupal. It is a great boost to usability to place atop them links for creating the same content. Now you know how to do that with a snippet of a dozen lines.

Making a Custom Text Filter

Drupal's text format filters are a fairly simple and powerful way to change how your content is displayed. (Previous versions of Drupal called these *input filters*, which was misleading because Drupal, ever-respectful of user-submitted data, filters content on *output*.) In this section, you will once again see how easy, non-scary, and useful making a module can be, even for someone as prone to false starts as your author in this chapter.

The Definitive Guide to Drupal 7, as well as other Apress books, emphasize tips, notes, and other types of commentary by setting it apart—between two lines and in a different font.

▨ **Tip** At the start of any project, you won't know exactly how to do it, but knowing it can be done somehow is the crucial first step in figuring it out and doing it.

For the DefinitiveDrupal.org web site, you can produce a similar effect using HTML and CSS. The HTML with a div and spans for the CSS to change might look like this:

```
<div class="featured-element tip"><span class="featured-element-type">↵
<span class="leading-square">T</span>ip</span> Hand-entering HTML code that involves↵
 divs or spans and classes or IDs is a strong sign we're doing it wrong.</div>
```

However, you don't want the authors to have to type in HTML code each time they want a highlighted tip. Apart from the tedium, it would increase the chances of making a minor mistake that makes display inconsistent. Instead of typing the previous HTML, let's let the authors use pseudo-markup that can be replaced with the previous HTML, such as:

```
[tip] Hand-entering HTML code that involves divs or spans and classes or IDs is a strong  sign
we're doing it wrong.[/tip]
```

That is much harder to mess up. You know what you want to do. You have the simplified markup you want to use, and the HTML you want to produce from it. Now where do you start?

Looking for a Module that Does What You Need

The best module is one you don't have to write yourself. Look around for a module that does that has to do with creating HTML tags from other markup. Searching online for such keywords as "drupal text format transform tags," "drupal replace markup," "drupal input filter tags," "drupal 7 text filters exportable" and searching `drupal.org` modules specifically for similar keywords (minus the "Drupal") did turn up some prior art.

■ **Tip** When searching Drupal.org for a module, apply the module filter. The URL might look like:

`drupal.org/search/apachesolr_multisitesearch/replace%20tags?filters=ss_meta_type%3Amodule`

Similar to what `DefinitiveDrupal.org` needs, Markdown Filter (`drupal.org/project/markdown`), and Textile (`drupal.org/project/textile`) modules (in the sense that they process text) are the BBCode (`drupal.org/project/bbcode`). These, however, are for known markup systems, not for meeting custom needs. They and others, like the Typogrify module (`drupal.org/project/typogrify`), can serve as examples for how to create filters.

Another module turned up in search: SimpleHTMLDOM (`drupal.org/project/simplehtmldom`), a wrapper for the namesake library available from `simplehtmldom.sourceforge.net`, could be useful as a tool, but your need to manipulate text is not that complex.

There *is* a Drupal 6 version of a module doing tag replacing, including some that looks like it does the before and after tags that you need: Rep[lacement] tags (`drupal.org/project/reptag`). However, it doesn't use filters and the text format system, instead relying on NodeAPI. Furthermore, the Drupal 6 version never hit a stable release. This should ease your conscience a bit about making a duplicate module, rather than porting and extending.

It's also very possible that these markup replacement needs could be done or should be done with configuration or as a sort of submodule of Flexifilter module (`drupal.org/project/flexifilter`), which is intended to make creating custom filters easier. A project in the same vein, Custom filter (`drupal.org/project/customfilter`) has been around even longer and is more actively maintained. Neither had D7 branches as of this writing, nor felt compelling enough to adopt the approach of porting and then building a submodule.

Given a short timeline, specific goals, and coding abilities, this is a justifiable time to make your own module. (It may not be the smartest or best decision, but it is not, on the face of it, a terrible idea.)

Choosing an Approach

Deciding to make a module is, of course, only the first step. How to make it is also pretty important.

Having learned about hooks and nodes in the part of the book on module development, you might be tempted to intercept nodes when they are saved using `hook_node_insert()` or `hook_node_update()` and make your changes there. You should resist this temptation. One of Drupal's distinguishing characteristics is that it does not lay a finger on content. What you see before you save is exactly what you see when you edit it again. This means your data is never corrupted. Accepting that as the Very Good Thing it is, you may then think you should replace the placeholder markup with your cool styling using a manipulation in `hook_node_view()`. But that means Drupal might have to do that work of processing the text every time it displayed a node. Before building a mechanism for manipulating the existing text and adding a new caching layer, it's time to take a step back and look outside the node system. (Or, if really stumped, ask on IRC, as discussed in Chapter 9.)

Note For the full cornucopia of node-related hooks in Drupal 7, see `api.drupal.org/node.api.php` or open `modules/node/node.api.php` in any copy of Drupal 7.

Changing the way user-inputted text looks is a common problem in Drupal. In fact, this is a problem that has long been solved by Drupal core itself. A method of managing modifications to content when it is displayed has lived in its own module, Filter module, since Drupal 5.

In Drupal 7, Filter module shows up in the administration interface at Administration ➤ Configuration ➤ Content Authoring ➤ Text formats (`admin/config/content/formats`). Looking at this core module from the code side (in the directory `modules/filter`) shows ten files (`filter.admin.inc`, `filter.css`, `filter.js`, `filter.test`, `filter.admin.js`, `filter.info`, `filter.module`, `filter.api.php`, `filter.install`, and `filter.pages.inc`), which seems a little intimidating. Let's take a look at it, but it would be nice to find a module that implemented just the provision of a filter, not the entire text format system.

Finding an Example (Hint: the Examples Project)

Where can you find a good example?

A project initiated by Randy Fay (rfay) while Drupal 7 was still in development provides the excellent (and now obvious) answer: the Examples suite of modules. You can download it just like any other project at `drupal.org/project/examples`. Sure enough, it has a `filter_example` module demonstrating how to define an input filter.

Tip Whenever you need to implement a core API (a hook defined by Drupal core) look for examples in the Examples project (`drupal.org/project/examples`).

Giving a Module an Interim Name

Now that you know your approach and have an example to follow, it's time to start coding. Which leads to question zero: what to name the module? (You could start adding functions to your glue code module, but when starting major new functionality, it's cleaner to start in a separate module—especially when there's a chance of contributing the code to the Drupal community.) If inspiration for the name does not strike right away, to avoid expending energy coming up with the perfect name before the module even exists, you can use a temporary name.

There are a few guidelines in choosing an interim name, however. If you named the module "tip" and later decided to contribute it to `drupal.org`, you would want to rename it so as not to claim the common word "tip" when that is not a particularly apt description of what the module does. The problem is that running a find-and-replace on those common three letters would not be pretty.

Even for a module you plan to contribute, for its temporary name, follow the same practice as for custom modules and namespace it with the name of your site project. Your project name plus any distinctive word you choose should make it easy to fix all function names with find-and-replace.

> ■ **Tip** This module will use an underscore in its provisional name, but certain aspects (such as where CSS classes and IDs, which historically use dashes instead of underscores) would be easier with both the provisional and the ultimately chosen name avoiding any underscore.

So let's have at it! Make a directory named whatever you choose to name the module (in this case dgd7_tip) and start making the necessary module files, also named after the module, starting with dgd7_tip.info (see Listings 33–23 and 33–24).

Listing 33–23. Command-Line Steps to Create the Module Directory and a .info File with Vim

```
cd sites/all/modules/custom
mkdir dgd7_tip
cd dgd7_tip/
vi dgd7_tip.info
```

Listing 33–24. Initial Working Content for dgd7_tip.info

```
name = Tip formatter
description = [dgd7_tip] Text format filter for tips, notes, hints and other emphasized⏎
 paragraphs of text.
core = 7.x
```

> ■ **Note** This author considers it a basic matter of usability for administrators and developers to be able to see module's system (or machine) names on the admin/modules page and will continue to put the system name in the description until this basic functionality is accepted into core. This style is not accepted practice so only follow it if you also feel strongly.

Now create a .module file and give it its first hook, an implementation of hook_filter_info() (see api.drupal.org/hook_filter_info) adapted from the Filter example module, as shown in Listing 33–25.

Listing 33–25. Initial Contents of dgd7_tip.module

```
/**
 * Implements hook_filter_info().
 */
function dgd7_tip_filter_info() {
  $filters = array();
  $filters['dgd7_tip'] = array(
    'title' => t('Tip formatter'),
    'description' => t('Allows simple notation to indicate paragraphs of text to be⏎
emphasized as tips, notes, hints, or other specially featured interjections.'),
    'process callback' => '_dgd7_tip_process',
    'tips callback' => '_dgd7_tip_tips',
  );
```

```
  return $filters;
}

/**
 * Implements filter process callback.
 */
function _dgd7_tip_process($text, $filter) {
  return $text;
}

/**
 * Implements filter tips callback.
 */
function _dgd7_tip_tips($filter, $format, $long = FALSE) {
  $tips = '';
  return $tips;
}
```

There! That looks neat and tidy. Your module won't even have any undefined function errors if you enable it—though the filter callback functions are mere stub functions so they won't do anything, either. (The 'prepare callback' in the *hook_filter_info()* definition and in filter_example.module proved unnecessary for a simple filter; it is useful for complex filtering that requires making changes to content before other filters do their work. Your author initially made a stub function for it but removed it from the example. Warning: An empty prepare or process callback, or one that for whatever reason does not return a value, will result in empty content anywhere that input format is applied!)

■ **Note** This module only provides one filter, but it could provide more by repeating the $filters['dgd7_tip'] array with different key and values. If you do intend to provide more than one input filter, the key should not be your module name, 'dgd7_tip', but rather the module name *plus* something descriptive of that particular filter. The same convention applies for callback names. This module is not intended to provide other input filters, so the precaution of explicit function names is premature. (The process and tips callbacks are internal functions, meant only for use in your module, as indicated by the underscore in front of them. For any API function—a function that may be called by other modules—you may want to take the precaution of choosing future-proof names.)

Start a Repository for Your Module

Because this module may be destined for an independent existence from the rest of the web site project, you can initiate a separate version control repository for it. With Git (see Chapter 2 and Chapter 37 for more information and resources), this is a few words typed on the command line, as shown in Listing 33–26. Do this from within the dgd7_tip directory you made.

Listing 33–26. Command-Line Steps for Starting a Repository and Making the Initial Commit of the Provisionally-Named dgd7_tip Module

```
git init
git add .
git commit -m ".info and .module file with stub filter API functions."
```

You can now commit constantly (as advocated in Chapter 14) without commit messages or with them when you have something particular to note. The git add commands and commit messages will not be marked with the code in this chapter, but you can be sure that after every significant change and many insignificant ones, there was a commit.

▓ **Note** The module created in this section is linked from the online chapter notes at dgd7.org/other90, and you can see every commit made to it.

Making the Tags and Replacement Markup Form

For a completely custom module, you could skip the settings form and just hardcode the processing you want to apply to content. No need to make a user interface for administrators to use, no need to make an API for modules to use. Because there is no Drupal 7 solution for the wrapping tag replacement called for by DefinitiveDrupal.org's needs, and because you may want administrators to be able to make changes to the filter without requiring modifying a module, you can try to make a module with both a UI and an API.

Normally you would start with the API. In this case, Drupal provides an API for filter settings forms but not for filter settings data, so you can implement the form first and work backwards to understand what Drupal is doing with the data.

Each tag and replacement markup set needs to contain three pieces of data: the tag being replaced, the markup that will replace the opening version of this tag, and the markup that will replace the closing version of the tag. By adopting the HTML convention of closing tags including a slash, you can ask for only the closing tag and derive the opening tag by removing the slash. So for instance, the form could accept {{/pony}} as the tag and in the content {{pony}} would be replaced with the opening markup entered into the form and {{/pony}} would be replaced with the closing markup.

Defining a Settings Callback

For your filter to save settings, the first thing you need to do is add another callback to the filter definition in your implementation of *hook_filter_info()*. A settings callback allows you to define form elements that accept values from administrators. Drupal will then have those values available in the process callback (and the prepare callback, if defined).

You need to add a line giving your filter a settings callback function. Add the following to the $filters['dgd7_tip'] array you created in dgd7_tip_filter_info(). I'll show this filter-defining function again after a bit more work.

```
'settings callback' => '_dgd7_tip_settings',
```

Then, of course, you need to define the _dgd7_tip_settings() function. This function should return form elements that Drupal will stick into the filter-specific options on the text format edit pages. There is an example, naturally, in filter_example.module, and you will define a filter settings callback to suit your needs later.

Building a Form that Accepts Multiple Elements

Each tag and replacement markup set needs its own place on the form, which means the form needs to take a variable number of these sets of form elements.

Know When to Fold 'Em

The slickest way to add additional sets of form elements as they are needed is with AJAX, which can pull HTML into your page on demand. Drupal's fields provide an example of this.

■ **Note** For readers who can't tell from the section title alone: you won't get any development done in this section.

Unfortunately, the "Add another item" link that is used by unlimited value fields is specific to the Field module. The code for the AJAX callback `field_add_more_js()` and related functionality in `modules/field/field.form.inc` may be instructive, but there's nothing in Drupal 7's FormsAPI to automate it for you.

So what do you do at this point in building a module? Punt. Make it as simple as possible. It's not worth getting bogged down in complex user interface enhancements at this point. (In fact, it's best to make your module with no user interface at all in the first pass. That rule is only broken here because the usual method of saving filter information is unfortunately not API-friendly; a text format is saved as a whole.)

■ **Note** As of 7, every instance of a filter has its own settings. That is, every filter on each text format is configured independently: If you change the settings of the image resize filter on the Filtered HTML text format, the settings for image resize filter on the Full HTML text format won't change. This greatly increases flexibility, but makes it a little more work to keep settings of shared filters consistent.

Making a Filter Settings Form that Always Accepts Two Additional Rows

The settings form will instead adopt a much simpler pattern: when first presented and whenever it's saved, it will always provide at least two sets of blank form elements.

All form elements returned by the settings callback function are saved with the filter object and available at `$filter->settings`. The filter object, including its settings array, is available in all the filter callbacks (process, prepare, tips, and settings itself). You can put any settings you want in this array in their own nested array, such as `$filter->settings['rm']` for the replacement markup information you need to store now. (Your author considered saving each tag and replacement markup pair directly to the settings array, but that way lies madness when it comes to generating the form.) The form elements for gathering the replacement markup information from administrators should also nest inside an 'rm' array.

Given that you need a set of form elements for each saved value, and then two more blank ones, this is a natural time for a foreach loop. However, it's not possible to add two blank tag arrays to the replacement markup settings array because each has an empty string ('') as its key and so are combined into one. Rather than repeating the code to create the form elements in two separate loops, you can factor out the creation of the form elements into its own function so you can call it as many times as you want without code duplication. The three things each set of form elements need are the (closing) tag, the opening markup that will replace its opening variation, and the closing markup (see Listing 33–27).

Listing 33–27. Defining a Set of Form Elements for the Tag and Replacement Markup in a Function that Can Be Called Repeatedly

```
/**
 * Add a set of form fields for adding a new tag and replacement markup pair.
 */
function _dgd7_tip_add_rm_formset(&$settings, $i, $tag = '', $replace =↵
array('before' => '', 'after' => '')) {
  $settings['rm'][$i]['tag'] = array(
    '#type' => 'textfield',
    '#title' => t('Tag'),
    '#maxlength' => 64,
    '#default_value' => $tag,
  );
  $settings['rm'][$i]['before'] = array(
    '#type' => 'textfield',
    '#title' => t('Before'),
    '#maxlength' => 1024,
    '#default_value' => $replace['before'],
  );
  $settings['rm'][$i]['after'] = array(
    '#type' => 'textfield',
    '#title' => t('After'),
    '#maxlength' => 1024,
    '#default_value' => $replace['after'],
  );
}
```

This function is doing a couple interesting things. Mostly, it's plainly defining three form elements of type textfield. It also accepts an iterator ($i) so that it can add itself to the $settings['rm'] array as many times as needed with a different integer each time. The $settings array itself is passed in by reference (as indicated by the ampersand in front of it in the function definition) so the function doesn't need to return any value; it's making changes to the $settings variable directly. Finally, it takes default values for the tag and the replacement markup, and the function definition itself sets these to empty if none are provided to make adding blank form fields easier. That is what the $tag = '', $replace = array('before' => '', 'after' => '') part of the _dgd7_tip_add_rm_formset() function definition line does.

Listing 33–28 shows the function that provides a form with rows of elements (to edit each tag and replacement markup set that is saved) and two rows of blank form elements to allow administrators to add additional tag and replacement markup sets

Listing 33–28. Settings Callback Function

```
/**
 * Settings callback for tag filter.
 */
function _dgd7_tip_settings($form, $form_state, $filter, $format, $defaults) {
  // Declare the array that will hold our settings form elements.
  $settings = array();

  // Get the default settings.
  $filter->settings += $defaults;
  // "rm" is short for replacement markup.
  $rm = $filter->settings['rm'];
```

```
  $i = 0;
  foreach ($rm as $tag => $replace) {
    _dgd7_tip_add_rm_formset($settings, $i, $tag, $replace);
    // Increment our number of filters by one.
    $i++;
  }
  // Always add two empty sets of form fields to be filled in.
  $total = $i+2;
  for ($i; $i < $total; $i++) {
    _dgd7_tip_add_rm_formset($settings, $i);
  }
  return $settings;
}
```

The _dgd7_tip_add_rm_formset() function is called in two different loops. One iterates through any existing or default tag and replacement markup sets (I'll get to the concept of default settings in a little bit) and the second adds two more blank sets of fields to however many are already there. The $i variable keeps count so each set of fields has its own unique key. However, this integer key only makes sense when gathering the data with the form; it would be nice to get rid of it when saving the data.

Manipulating Values Before Saving with a Validate Function

Indeed, the code in Listing 33–28 doesn't quite work: the form will be saving data by its $i iteration integer, which is necessary for allowing multiple sets to be saved at once, but this arbitrary value means nothing when it comes time to get the data. The attempt at retrieving assumes that $rm array will have the tag as the key, not a number.

The following two things let you work around this in the context of filter settings on the text format form (see Listing 33–29):

- A validation function can be added to any form element by setting the #element_validate property.

- Validation functions can do more than validate. They can change the data that will be saved with form_set_value().

Listing 33–29. Additions to the Settings Callback Function to Set a Validation Function to the Element Containing the Tag and Replacement Markup Sets of Form Elements

```
function _dgd7_tip_settings($form, $form_state, $filter, $format, $defaults) {
  // Declare the array that will hold your settings form elements.
  $settings = array();
  $settings['rm'] = array(
    '#element_validate' => array('dgd7_tip_rm_form_keys_validate'),
  );
  // [Other previously shown code not shown to save space...]
  return $settings;
}
```

After a good bit of experimentation, it seems the test array structure in Listing 33–30 saves into settings in a way that comes back out fine.

Listing 33–30. Experimental Function to Discover Data Structure that Drupal's Filter API Saves the Right Way

```
function dgd7_tip_rm_form_keys_validate($element, &$form_state) {
  $rm = array();
  $rm['{/testtag}'] = array(
      'before' => 'value for before markup',
      'after' => 'value for after markup',
  );
  form_set_value($element, $rm, $form_state);
}
```

The process for experimenting was saving the form and seeing if these hardcoded values showed up as expected (with {/testtag} as the tag and value for before markup and value for after markup in the replacement markup fields). One would never use a validation function to hardcode values, but it provided a convenient way to test the structure to use for saving the data. All the other parts of the form can be dispensed with, apparently, so you shall do so (see Listing 33–31).

Listing 33–31. Validation Function that Reorganizes Data to Save with Tag as the Key, Dropping the Integer Series Key

```
/**
 * Rearrange form elements to be keyed by tag before filter_format_save() runs.
 */
function dgd7_tip_rm_form_keys_validate($element, &$form_state) {
  $rm = array();
  // Create a tag-keyed version of each element.
  foreach ($element as $i => $value) {
    // Skip non-value form elements (the ones we care about have numbers).
    if (!is_numeric($i))  continue;
    $key = $value['tag']['#value'];
    // Do not save empty keys.
    if (!$key) continue;
    $rm[$key] = array(
      'before' => $value['before']['#value'],
      'after' => $value['after']['#value'],
    );
  }

  form_set_value($element, $rm, $form_state);
}
```

That may not win any prizes for elegance, but it gives sane data storage which helps an upcoming task, a task more tied to the immediate use case for this module, which is providing defaults in code. But first, let's look at a more normal use of validation.

Validating the Filter Settings

For the tag replacement to work, the module needs to make sure that the tag provided is a closing tag, with a / (forward slash) included. Surprisingly, there is no built-in validation of text filter settings, which means no obvious model to follow.

You could implement hook_form_alter() and add a form-wide validation function, just as you could if you were defining the whole form yourself. The easier, gentler approach is to use the #element_validate form property on a specific form element.

■ **Tip** Read more about the element_validate form property at api.drupal.org/forms_api_reference.html#element_validate. As always, you can also look for examples in core, as with the command-line on Unix-like systems: grep -nHR 'element_validate' modules/

As with most hooks and functions, the most important thing about functions for validating elements is their function signature: $element, &$form_state, $whole_form. The ampersand, again, indicates that even though $form_state is an array, it is passed to your validating function by reference, and changes made within the function apply to the original.

The precise information you need to validate the tag to replace is verifying the existence of a slash. Searching the web for "*php count number characters in a string*" (and some clicking around) brought the author to php.net/substr_count (see Listing 33–32). (If you think you can guess the function name or even get close, going directly to php.net/bestguess is the fastest way to find a function, as it will automatically provide a range of possible matches.)

Listing 33–32. Validate the Tag to Be a Closing Tag That can Be Interpreted

```
/**
 * Validate each tag to include one and only one slash.
 */
function dgd7_tip_rm_form_tag_validate($element, &$form_state, $whole_form) {
  if (strlen($element['#value']) && substr_count($element['#value'], '/') !== 1) {
    // We describe where the error is because after submission it is likely
    // to be in a non-visible vertical tab.
    form_error($element, t('In the Replacement markup Filter settings, each tag must be in↵
the form of a closing tag with exactly one slash ("/").  The opening tag is calculated by↵
removing the slash.'));
  }
}
```

Your data-munging validation function already throws out replacement markup form data with nothing in the tag textfield, so this validation function first checks if there's anything in the form element with strlen($element['#value']). If not, it does nothing (doesn't throw an error). The second half of the if statement uses the substr_count() function; if there's not exactly one slash, then it throws the error.

Providing Instructions on the Filter Setting Form

This module should provide instruction on filling in the fields for the tag and the before and after markup. The usual Drupal way of providing a #description in your form element array is not a good fit because you want to describe all fields together (not one field or even field set at a time) and you want it before the form elements it describes (not after as #description does by default). You only want some text that's above the form.

The Image Resize Filter module (drupal.org/project/image_resize_filter), which the site is already using, happens to have this same sort of disembodied help text. So it is conveniently available to

steal how its author, Nathan Haug (quicksketch), did it. Taking a look in image_resize_filter.module;
you can see he pasted it right into a theme function, theme_image_resize_filter_form().

Well, you can build on that idea and make it a little more elegant—still using a form theme function,
but using it to rearrange a description that is properly defined in the form array. Step 1 is to implement
hook_theme() so you can define a theme function. Step 2 is to add two properties to a form element
containing the form elements you want to describe: description text and an instruction to use the theme
function. Step 3 is to define that theme function and have it print the description before the rest of the
form. Listing 33–33 shows this theme function; note that most of the settings callback function
_dgd7_tips_settings() is not shown.

*Listing 33–33. Implementing a Theme Function to Put a Description at the Top of a Form Element Instead
of the Bottom*

```
/**
 * Implements hook_theme().
 */
function dgd7_tip_theme() {
  return array(
    'dgd7_tip_settings' => array(
      'render element' => 'form',
    ),
  );
}

function _dgd7_tip_settings($form, $form_state, $filter, $format, $defaults) {
// ...
  $settings['rm'] = array(
    '#description' => t('To set tags and replacement markup, enter only the closing tag↵
(such as &lt;/tip&gt;); the opening tag will be calculated automatically by removing the↵
slash (&lt;tip&gt; in this example). Then enter the before and after markup which will↵
replace the opening and closing tag, respectively.'),
    '#theme' => 'dgd7_tip_settings',
    '#element_validate' => array('dgd7_tip_rm_form_keys_validate'),
  );
// ...
}

/**
 * Theme callback to print description with settings form.
 */
function theme_dgd7_tip_settings($vars) {
  $form = $vars['form'];
  return '<p>' . render($form['#description']) . '</p>'
       . drupal_render_children($form);
}
```

See Chapter 9 for more about defining and using theme functions. And as described in Chapters 14
and 15, Appendix C, and elsewhere in the book, using render() to show an element will mean that
element is not shown again (unless you render just it or expose it again with show()). When displaying
the rest of the form, the function drupal_render_children() is needed instead of render() to avoid an
infinite loop.

Making Your Own Hook

Now for the fun part. When developing Drupal, you implement other modules' hooks all the time. It's something of a rare treat to create your own hook! It's your module's chance to give back, and ask if any other modules want to join its party. The occasion is adding the tag and replacement markup sets when the filter is newly added to a format.

Creating a hook is a little metaphysical: if a hook is defined and nobody implements it, does it exist? (You can implement the hook yourself later if that question keeps you up at night.) Hooks come into being by the act of offering other code the opportunity to heed their call. The most common way of putting out this call, and so creating a Drupal hook, is to use the function module_invoke_all(), as shown in Listing 33–34.

Listing 33–34. Invoking a Hook to Give Other Modules a Chance to Provide Default Settings for a Filter

```
/**
 * Implements hook_filter_info().
 */
function dgd7_tip_filter_info() {
  $filters['dgd7_tip'] = array(
    'title' => t('Replacement markup'),
    'description' => t('Allows simple notation to indicate paragraphs of text to be wrapped↵
in custom markup, for instance to emphasize tips, notes, or other featured interjections.'),
    'process callback' => '_dgd7_tip_process',
    // Allow other modules to declare default tags and replacement markup.
    'default settings' => array(
      'rm' => module_invoke_all('dgd7_tip_defaults'),
    ),
    'settings callback' => '_dgd7_tip_settings',
    'tips callback' => '_dgd7_tip_tips',
  );
  return $filters;
}
```

The module_invoke_all() function is built to take data from multiple sources and put it together. It uses the PHP function array_merge_recursive() to do this, so anything that has a new key gets added to the array it returns and anything that has the an identical key overwrites the previously existing data. For the replacement markup, if there happen to be two modules implementing this hook and providing markup for the same short tag, the last-called module will win. This is common to the way hooks work and not something you need to worry about.

Ordinarily you would pass some contextual information along when invoking your hook, even if you can't think of a reason to use it. In this case, there isn't any meaningful context that can be passed, but be attentive to your issue queue if maintaining a public module: always figure on someone else doing something stranger with your API than you could ever imagine.

Note that this solution combines code-provided defaults and administrator-set overridden or new settings, but it doesn't do so as flexibly as a true exportable configurations such as made possible with CTools. Implementing that, should this module gain respectable usage, is left as a later exercise for the author—or you.

Filtering the Content

Weren't you doing all this for a reason? Oh yes! To take the content people input and format it differently when it's displayed. To convert tags into their replacement markup, you need to implement your filter's process callback, as shown in Listing 33–35.

Listing 33–35. Process Callback for the Replacement Markup Text Filter

```
/**
 * Process callback for tag filter.
 */
function _dgd7_tip_process($text, $filter) {
  if (!isset($filter->settings['rm']) || !is_array($filter->settings['rm'])) {
    return $text;
  }
  foreach ($filter->settings['rm'] as $ctag => $replace) {
    dgd7_tip_replace_tags($text, $ctag, $replace['before'], $replace['after']);
  }
  return $text;
}
```

The first part of this function checks that there is any replacement markup to apply at all; if not, it bails early, returning the text unaltered. (Perhaps it should not be possible for there to be unset settings, but it doesn't cost much to be a little forgiving here).

■ **Caution** Remember, if the process callback doesn't return any value, the text, far from displaying unchanged, will be gone entirely.

The Regular Expression

Looking at a regular expression—and looking at the code surrounding this regular expression—can be an experience of seeming to face the incomprehensible. Maybe a lot of other code you've looked at has already felt this way to you. It's not the ideal approach—to use something without understanding it—but you can't become an expert in everything right away. To succeed in practice as a developer, you will have to push the boundaries of your knowledge. With use comes familiarity. With familiarity may come understanding, and if not, the recognition that something you are using more than once is something you should put further effort into researching and understanding. This section takes the use-first approach, but first give yourself the ability to experiment freely.

MAKE YOUR OWN TEST.PHP FILE

Make your own test script to rapidly test code within a Drupal environment. Make a file called test.php or anything you like and keep that in the same folder as index.php. Use the first three code lines of index.php, and you have a fully bootstrapped Drupal that you can use to test all sorts of code much more quickly than setting up a page through the menu system.

Here is an example that prints out all the configuration information available to Drupal:

```
<?php
define('DRUPAL_ROOT', getcwd());
require_once DRUPAL_ROOT . '/includes/bootstrap.inc';
drupal_bootstrap(DRUPAL_BOOTSTRAP_FULL);
```

```
drupal_test();
function drupal_test() {
  global $conf;
  print '<pre>';
  var_export($conf);
  print '</pre>';
}
```

■ **Note** The contents of the global $conf variable are available to you throughout Drupal with the variable_get() function (api.drupal.org/api/function/variable_get/7).

You can test out any function here (not hook implementations, however) without needing to create and enable a module.

This section was adapted from a presentation by Chad Phillips (hunmonk) who in turn credited Karoly Negyesi (chx). It's sharing skills the open source way, and now I pass them on to you. A few more tips:

- As soon as you get in trouble, start looking at your variables.

- Use exit($var); to end code execution at the part you care about (and optionally dump a variable available at the time).

- Find an example in core. Search an install of Drupal core or ask for an example of how core does X in channel #drupal (or #drupal-contribute if you are contributing back the module you are working on).

- Clear your cache.

- Document your work. Otherwise, when you come back in a week or a year, you won't have any idea what you thought you were doing.

Testing the Regular Expression

Using a test PHP file, you can try the basics of a regular expression. (This file, using PHP functions and not Drupal ones, would not even need to bootstrap Drupal.) Because the intended use of the module is replacing pairs of opening and closing tags, you want a regular expression that matches both at once, not one alone. This makes it all a bit trickier; see Listing 33–36.

■ **Tip** See dgd7.org/regex for links to regular expression resources.

Listing 33–36. A Test Regular Expression

```php
<?php
$text = "This is text surrounding a note.

[note] This is a note. [/note].

More text.

[note]This is another note,
a multi-line note.[/note]";
$otag = "[note]";
$ctag = "[/note]";
$before = "BEFORE";
$after = "AFTER";

$text = preg_replace('@' . preg_quote($otag) . '(.+?)' . preg_quote($ctag) . '@s',
  "$before $1 $after",
  $text);

print $text;
```

The resulting output is:

```
This is text surrounding a note. BEFORE This is a note. AFTER. More text. BEFORE This is
another note, a multi-line note. AFTER
```

The regular expression syntax used inside the `preg_replace()` function is successfully matching the text *between* [note] and [/note]. The `preg_replace()` function provides the value of this inner portion of the match, the part within parenthesis, in the variable $1, which is available to the second parameter, the replacement text. (The third parameter is the original text.)

The first line builds the regular expression string; that is all it is, a string, and each dot connects one part of the string to the next. Things go crazily to hell if you don't use `preg_quote()` on the strings you want to match because they are likely to contain characters that have special meanings to the regular expression. (The author found this function courtesy of searches for "*regular expression do not interpret string*" and "*php escape regex special characters.*")

The @ symbol in this string delineates where the regular expression begins and ends. This can be any character, but it can't, of course, be one that is appearing in that regular expression otherwise. Often a / is used for this but the closing tag will always have a slash, so in testing @ was used. The chosen delimiter can be escaped specifically, however, so a more robust approach for the function you are building could check for the presence of delineator characters in the opening and closing tags. In fact, because you have already validated the closing tag to contain exactly one slash, you can escape that slash and be certain that there will be no conflicts between the characters in the tag strings that get searched for and the delineators of the expression. That will be the approach you will take next.

Finally, the s modifier that follows the delineator of the end of the regular expression allows the wildcard to match a newline character, so that a line break can be within a note, as in the test. Listing 33–37 puts this together in a function or two for the module.

Listing 33–37. Function for Replacing Opening and Closing Tags with Defined Markup

```
/**
 * Replace with tags with markup given a closing tag (containing a /).
 *
 * @param $text
 *   String to be modified to use markup in place of tags, passed by reference.
 * @param $ctag
 *   A closing tag, identical to the opening tag except it includes a /.
 * @param $before
 *   Markup to replace the opening tag.
 * @param $after
 *   Markup to replace the closing tag.
 * @return NULL
 */
function dgd7_tip_replace_tags(&$text, $ctag, $before = '', $after = '') {
  $otag = preg_quote(dgd7_tip_otag($ctag));
  $ctag = str_replace('/', '\/', preg_quote($ctag));
  $text = preg_replace(
    '/' . $otag . '(.+?)' . $ctag . '/s',
    "$before$1$after",
    $text
  );
}

/**
 * Take a closing tag and strip the slash to present the opening tag.
 */
function dgd7_tip_otag($ctag) {
  return str_replace('/', '', $ctag);
}
```

The creation of the opening tag by removing the slash from the closing tag is in a separate function, though it could easily fit in the one line in the replace tags function and could just as well have gone there; it simply felt like something likely to be used again. The work of quoting special characters in the search strings ($otag and $ctag) is handled along with this manipulation before putting them in the preg_replace() function, which makes that look a little cleaner. Note that replacing the slash with an escaped slash (/ with \/) in the closing tag is done *after* special characters are escaped. Finally, "$before$1$after" looks messy and mashed together, but PHP treats each variable separately and strings them together without spaces, which is perfect for creating the replacement text.

To test, you'll have to configure a text format (under admin/config/content/formats), enable Replacement markup filter for it, and put in a few test tags and markup.

The order of input filters is very important for achieving expected results, whether it's a filter you've created or one from modules contributed by others. The Replacement markup filter has to follow the "Limit allowed HTML tags" filter (if present); otherwise the latter may strip out tags added by the former. Then you can go to any node, edit it using a text format that has Replacement markup filter configured, and stick in the opening and closing tag pair to see how the replacement turns out.

You will run into errors when developing your own code. I did, frequently. Putting every error encountered during development would make this description impossible to follow, but expect to have to fix errors. An error printed to the screen is nice; it usually tells you exactly where something is wrong. An error where nothing happens can take longer to track down, but pulling out parts of code into a test.php file to try independently can help. Finally, it's worth noting that the author did this without any deep understanding of the filter form saving system nor the `preg_replace()` function when he started—or necessarily when he finished. But it worked.

Renaming Your Module

You've put a lot of work into this module. You should share it, but "dgd7_tip" is not a good name at all.

After an embarrassing amount of time spent considering possible names Tagfilter? It sort of indicates that it is a filter module. Tagreplace? Reptags? Replacemarkup? Repmark? Remark! It's tempting to take the 'remark' project namespace, but let's leave it for something awesome having to do with the English word remark, rather than "replacing markup." This module will be named Remarkup.

Some IDEs provide tools for replacing text in multiple files, and some provide tools for renaming files, but you can handle this with the command line, too.

With a little help from searches that lead to the Drupal handbook page "sed - replace text in single or multiple files" (`data.agaric.com/raw/sed-replace-text-multiple-files`) and the post "Easily renaming multiple files" on the shockingly non-Drupal site Debian Administration (`debian-administration.org/articles/150`), you can rename your module with four lines typed into your terminal, as shown in Listing 33–38. The last two commands are for moving outside the module folder and renaming the folder. The commands start from the directory that holds your module.

Listing 33–38. *Command-Line Steps to Replace All Occurrences of a String in Multiple Files and Rename the Files*

```
cd sites/all/modules/custom
sed -i 's/dgd7_tip/remarkup/g' *
rename 's/dgd7_tip/remarkup/' *
cd ../
mv dgd7_tip remarkup
```

This changes every function name and your API hook name, which incorporates your module name, per best practice to avoid namespace conflicts. Your module name is guaranteed to be unique (if the same as your project hosted on `drupal.org`), so prefacing your hook name with your module name helps ensure that no one else is using the hook for some other purpose. This means that once you are hosted on `drupal.org`, renaming a module is something you do not want to do.

■ **Note** In a sign of the strength of the Drupal community, the first hit for this author's search for "replace text in multiple files" on Google (not logged in, so theoretically not customized search results) was `drupal.org`. When he started out, many times a post on a Mambo (now Joomla) forum would come up for general web-related tasks; now it is increasingly Drupal sites.

Conditionally Including a Stylesheet for an Administration Page

The Settings page needs some cleanup. A function for adding CSS to a page (as opposed to all pages, which can be done via a module or theme's `.info` file) is `drupal_add_css()`. Yet, there is an even better, more Drupal 7 way to conditionally include CSS when it relates to any element that is rendered, which includes forms. That way is the `#attached` property.

▓ **Note** There is no hard line between what you should just know and what is just as well looked up when you need it. Clearly, the more you do, the more you just know. This author needs pretty much everything noted and looked up each time, but most people doing Drupal show a higher capacity to learn.

The drupal_add_css() function (which is used internally for the #attached property) should be used only when there is no renderable array with which to use the #attached property. Implementation of hook_help() is an example of a place where you can't use #attached. There are numerous examples of both methods in Drupal core. You can see examples of the function at api.drupal.org/drupal_add_css because the api.drupal.org site links to usages of functions. Skip some examples from themes using it and take a look at how block module uses it: api.drupal.org/block_admin_display_form. This is almost exactly as you would want to use it, in the function for displaying an administrative form! Right at the top of the form is

```
drupal_add_css(drupal_get_path('module', 'block') . '/block.css');
```

But Block module should use the #attached property on the form returned rather than calling drupal_add_css() directly. I filed an issue for core (drupal.org/node/1122584); Listing 33–39 shows how to do it right.

Listing 33–39. Using #attached Property to Include a CSS File when Pages with a Renderable Element Are Viewed

```
/**
 * Settings callback for tag filter.
 */:
function _remarkup_settings($form, $form_state, $filter, $format, $defaults) {
  // Declare the array that will hold our settings form elements.
  $settings = array();
  // [Additional already-seen code not shown...]
  $settings['rm'] = array(
    // [Additional already-seen code not shown...]
    // Add CSS to make _remarkup_add_rm_formset() form elements look good.
    '#attached' => array(
      'css' => array(drupal_get_path('module', 'remarkup') . '/remarkup.css'),
    ),
  );
  // [Additional already-seen code not shown...]
}
```

The CSS file attached in this way does not have to be large, as you can see by Listing 33–40.

Listing 33–40. remarkup.css Styles the Settings Form for Remarkup Text Filter

```
.remarkup-formset .form-item {
  display: inline-block;
  padding: 0;
  margin-bottom: 5px;
}

.remarkup-formset {
  margin-bottom: 10px;
```

This CSS file is attached when someone views the text format settings page, even though you did not define that page yourself. There is one important thing still missing, though: the HTML container with classes for this CSS to apply to!

Adding a Container Form Element with a Specified Class

Originally the div and class for the CSS to act on was added with a #prefix property on the tag with a line like:

```
$settings['rm'][$i]['tag'] = array(
  '#prefix' => '<div class="remarkup-formset">',
  '#type' => 'textfield',
```

It then had a corresponding #suffix on the final markup form element. This worked, but it feels ugly. A little investigation into the Drupal API's page on form generation (api.drupal.org/api/group/form_api) uncovered, in a long line of *theme_* functions meant for forms, theme_container() (api.drupal.org/theme_container). It could be set directly with the #theme_wrappers property on a form element that holds the three textfield form elements, as shown here:

```
$settings['rm'][$i] = array(
  '#theme_wrappers' => array('container'),
  '#attributes' => array('class' => array('remarkup-formset')),
);
```

But investigating how to use the container theme wrapper found a particularly relevant example: the form element type container. You can use the container form element for slightly cleaner code and the identical effect as the above. Listing 33–41 shows it all together in the function defining the set of form fields for the tag and replacement markup in a function that can be called repeatedly, now wrapped in a containing div and with sizes set for presentation. Note that this is the same function that was called _dgd7_tip_add_rm_formset() previously.

Listing 33–41. Defining a Set of Form Elements for the Tag and Replacement Markup, Now Wrapped in a Containing Div and with Sizes Set for Presentation

```
/**
 * Add a set of form fields for adding a new tag and replacement markup pair.
 */
function _remarkup_add_rm_formset(&$settings, $i, $tag = '', $replace = array('before' => '',
'after' => '')) {
  $settings['rm'][$i] = array(
    '#type' => 'container',
    '#attributes' => array('class' => array('remarkup-formset')),
  );
  $settings['rm'][$i]['tag'] = array(
    '#type' => 'textfield',
    '#title' => t('Tag'),
    '#maxlength' => 64,
    '#size' => 10,
    '#default_value' => $tag,
    '#element_validate' => array('remarkup_rm_form_tag_validate'),
  );
  $settings['rm'][$i]['before'] = array(
    '#type' => 'textfield',
    '#title' => t('Before'),
```

```
    '#maxlength' => 1024,
    '#size' => 45,
    '#default_value' => $replace['before'],
  );
  $settings['rm'][$i]['after'] = array(
    '#type' => 'textfield',
    '#title' => t('After'),
    '#maxlength' => 1024,
    '#size' => 45,
    '#default_value' => $replace['after'],
  );
}
```

With the CSS file, its attachment, and the additions to the function that add sets of form elements, the settings for Remarkup looks pretty good. Figure 33–8 shows it with one set of tag plus markup pair filled in and one set blank.

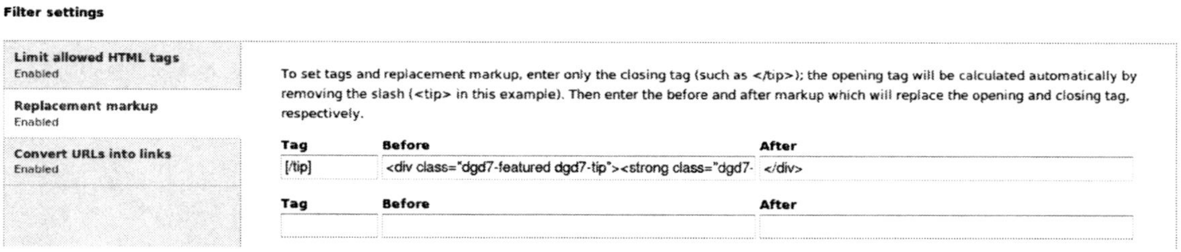

Figure 33–8. *Settings form with three form elements in a row per set using CSS and wrapped HTML elements*

Sharing Your Module on Drupal.org

Like sharing on `Gitorious.org` or `GitHub.com`, `drupal.org` lets every user create sandboxes that require no more of an application process than accepting the guidelines. In the case of `drupal.org`, this primarily means agreeing to post only GPL code. (If you don't yet have the ability to create full name-spaced projects on `drupal.org`, posting code to your sandbox is still the first step. And if you have been granted permission to promote a sandbox to a full project, a sandbox project is still the best place to start sharing your work early— it even comes with an issue queue. There's still nothing like putting the code on `drupal.org` as a properly released project, though, to get the attention of users and reviewers alike.)

After accepting the Drupal Git policies and adding your public key to your `drupal.org` account, you can create a sandbox project and push the repository for your module there (see Listings 33–42 and 33–43).

▨ **Tip** The public key for a user on a UNIX-like computer or virtual machine can usually be found in a file located in the user's .ssh folder in a file named id_rsa.pub (less ~/.ssh/id_rsa.pub) or by creating a public-private key pair if necessary (ssh-keygen). See drupal.org/node/1027094.

Listing 33–42. Command-Line Steps for Sharing Code to git.drupal.org as a Full Project

```
git checkout master
git remote add origin mlncn@git.drupal.org:project/remarkup.git
git push origin master
git branch 7.x-1.x
git push origin master:7.x-1.x
git checkout 7.x-1.x
```

Listing 33–43. Sharing New Modifications with add, commit, and push

```
git add .
git commit -m "Include form CSS with #attached instead of drupal_add_css()."
git push
```

See Chapter 37 for more about sharing your projects on drupal.org, including using Git sandboxes.

Coda on a Contributed Module

You made plenty of compromises in making this module, but you got some essential things correct:

- It has an API.

- It has a UI.

By going beyond your immediate needs—and by providing an API that allows your module to be extended without patching it—you make it much more likely that people will use your module and a little more likely someone else will pick up where you left off.

Even if you skip building a UI for site administrators and an API for module builders, it would be a good idea to share your module: git.drupal.org sandboxes are provided for you to share code that you do not necessarily intend to support.

■ **Note** The source code of the module developed in this section is available at drupal.org/project/remarkup.

Making a Site-Specific Module that Uses Your API

Wait, didn't you have some goal of your own, quite apart from making a module that other people might find useful?

It's time to write site-specific code that makes use of the module you made. The cool thing, with all the work you've already done, is that your glue code module can be quite small, as shown in Listing 33–44.

Listing 33–44. An Inefficient, Error-Prone Approach to Defining a Custom Implementation of the Remarkup Hook

```
/**
 * Implements hook_remarkup_defaults().
 */
function dgd7_remarkup_defaults() {
  return array(
```

```
  '[/tip]' => array(
    'before' => '<div class="dgd7-featured dgd7-tip"><span class="featured-name"><span↵
class="leading-square">T</span>ip</span>',
    'after' => '</div>',
  ),
  '[/reality]' => array(
    'before' => '<div class="dgd7-featured dgd7-tip"><strong class="dgd7-name">↵
Reality</strong>',
    'after' => '</div>',
  ),
);
}
```

But this can introduce inconsistencies due to the duplicate HTML code. Even when doing the very simple, supply-data step, you can still automate stuff, as shown in Listing 33–45.

Listing 33–45. Implementation of the Hook to Provide Default Remarkup that Abstracts Out the Repetitive Code

```
/**
 * Implements hook_remarkup_defaults().
 */
function dgd7glue_remarkup_defaults() {
  $rm = array();
  // Define the simple tips-style replacements, machine and human-readable.
  $tips = array(
    'tip' => t('Tip'),
    'note' => t('Note'),
    'hint' => t('Hint'),
    'reality' => t('Reality'),
    'caution' => t('Caution'),
    'gotcha' => t('Gotcha'),
    'new' => t('New in 7'),
  );
  foreach ($tips as $type => $name) {
    $rm['[/' . $type . ']'] = array(
      'before' => '<div class="dgd7-featured dgd7-' . $type . '">↵
<strong class="dgd7-name">' . $name . '</strong>',
      'after' => '</div>',
    );
  }
  return $rm;
}
```

That, if not easier, ensures consistency in the HTML code used for the tips, notes, hints, etc.

■ **Gotcha** Don't forget the return statement; unless implementing a hook that receives its data by reference, it's rather important. The hook system is generally robust and is not going to complain about getting no response. So when your hook implementation seems to have no effect, the first place to look is at the bottom for a `return` `$data` statement!

You can now provide CSS in your module for this default-provided markup. Put the CSS in a file, such as **dgd7.css**, saved in the dgd7glue module directory. I won't take up space with the CSS here; it's in the project code available at `dgd7.org/other90` and you can also see it, as on any web site, by viewing the CSS through your browser's view source option or with a tool such as Firebug.

Don't forget to keep your custom module's .info file current, as shown in Listing 33–46.

Listing 33–46. Adding a Dependency and Styles File to dgd7glue.info

```
name = DGD7 Glue Code
description = [dgd7glue] Site-specific custom code for DefinitiveDrupal.org.
package = Custom
version = 7.x-1.0
core = 7.x
dependencies[] = remarkup
styles[] = dgd7.css
```

The Payoff

Enable both modules. Now you have to edit the text formats you want to use, such as Filtered HTML at `admin/config/content/formats/filtered_html` and Full HTML at `admin/config/content/formats/full_html`.

■ **Gotcha** New tags and markup pairs provided by implementations of the replacement markup defaults hook will not have any effect until you edit a text format so that your default settings are imported, and save it.

The way Remarkup currently implements its defaults hook, it is true defaults—the moment you save a text format form, the values you provided are saved to the database. New default tags you add will be noticed, but updates to defaults that already have been saved once will not be seen. CTools-style exportables could be implemented to make in-code updates easy, but that's not an issue to cover in this chapter. Indeed, if it's something you want, you can file an issue in the Remarkup queue (`drupal.org/project/issues/remarkup`) and perhaps provide a patch! (A patch, as described in Chapter 38 and elsewhere, is a contribution of code in the form of an easily-applied file of changes from the existing code.)

Adding Custom Markup for Output

With the framework in place, you can add new tag and replacement markup definitions as you need them, as shown in Listing 33–47.

Listing 33–47. *Additional Remarkup Definitions for Text Files, PHP Code, and Command-Line Steps*

```
function dgd7glue_remarkup_defaults() {
  $rm = array();
// Removed code, see above for context.
  // A few rules are unique.
  $rm['[/file-txt]'] = array(
      'before' => '<code>',
      'after' => '</code>',
  );
  // Requires codefilter module, with its filter set to run after remarkup.
  $rm['[/file-php]'] = array(
      'before' => '<?php',
      'after' => '?>',
  );
  $rm['[/cli]'] = array(
    'before' => '<h4>Command-line steps</h4>
    <tt>',
    'after' => '</tt>',
  );
  return $rm;
}
```

Making Next and Previous Links That Mimic Book Navigation

When viewing any individual posts that can be seen as part of a series (blog posts, news articles, featured profiles), it's good usability and just plain nice to give readers a way to get to the next one or the previous one directly, without having to go back to a listing page. For reading through all the suggestions submitted to the dgd7.org site one-by-one to review them, next and previous link buttons were all but an absolute requirement.

This could be done in a theme, but being able to move to the next item is a matter of functionality more than presentation, which calls for a module. Also, in a module it's possible to make a more re-usable solution.

A search for *"Drupal 7 next previous links"* and related keywords turned up several projects, all in Drupal 6. Your author hadn't used custom_pagers in Drupal 6 and could not grok exactly what it was doing from its in-progress Drupal 7 port (on GitHub at the time of writing). It allowed PHP and Views in the administration of pagers, yet seemed to be calling SQL from a custom table to run the query—that is, storing SQL in SQL. It definitely seemed a heavy solution to port for the simple use case of being able to see the previous and next suggestions. Writing custom code seemed a reasonable choice.

Pulling the Information

You can look at api.drupal.org/node.api.php and decide *hook_node_view()* is how you want to add previous and next links to chosen nodes. The next step is to know how to get the links. Putting Devel module's dpm() function in an implementation of *hook_node_view()*—for the site-specific module used throughout this chapter, that function name would be dgd7glue_node_view()—will show you the data you have available. Consulting the database layer handbook gives static queries, with methods such as ->fetchAssoc() for returning results as an array, in examples on drupal.org/node/310072.

■ **Note** If not using Devel's dpm(), be aware that because Drupal is a bit silly, calling debug($node) in an implementation of *hook_node_view()* does not work. In multiple places, such as where it loads taxonomy term entities, Drupalrecursion blows up the var_export() function used by debug() by default. You can instead call debug() with its optional third parameter (the second parameter is the label) set to TRUE, which makes it use the harder-to-kill print_r() function, for instance debug($node, 'Node when viewed', TRUE);.

Based on the information gathered, you can create a quick proof of concept. Note that while the code in Listing 33–48 tests two different things, it tests them independently. It does not try to query the database and use the result to add text to the node, because if that didn't work, you wouldn't know immediately where the problem lies. Doing both at once can wait until you are certain that both work separately. For now, use a debug function to show the result of the query and add straight markup.

Listing 33–48. Proof-of-Concept Code (with LIMIT Function that Is Not Cross-Database Compatible) for Querying the Database and Adding Text to Display on a Node

```
/**
 * Implements hook_node_view().
 */
function dgd7glue_node_view($node, $view_mode, $langcode) {
  // Print prev/next links on Suggestion node pages.
  if ($node->type == 'suggestion' && $view_mode == 'full') {
    $markup = 'i can print something';
    $next = db_query('SELECT title, nid FROM {node} WHERE nid > :nid AND status =↵
1 LIMIT 1', array(':nid' => $node->nid))->fetchAssoc();
    debug($next, 'next'); // the query works
    $node->content['dgd7glue_prevnext'] = array(
      '#markup' => $markup,
      '#weight' => 100,
    );
  }
}
```

The code in Listing 33–48 prints out a node ID and title from the query and the static text assigned to #markup. It shows you that the query runs and that you can add things to the display of the node. It still needs to be updated to run a query that filters to show only suggestions, and the output needs to be based on this result, but the concept is proven.

While making it work correctly, the query should also be made cross-browser compatible. You may vaguely remember that LIMIT is not a part of SQL that works in a standard way across all types of databases, and that Drupal provides some assistance for getting around this. A grep for 'LIMIT' in Drupal core's modules directory shows that it is not used in an SQL query except for one commented out query in a testing file. Conclusion: Using LIMIT in SQL is not best practice. A grep for 'limit' (in lower case) to see where the code comments or anything are just talking about limits brings up a lot of results including this query in modules/user/user.install, shown in Listing 33–49.

Listing 33–49. Query in user.install Containing the Text Limit

```
$result = db_query_range('SELECT f.*, u.uid as user_uid FROM {users} u INNER JOIN↵
{file_managed} f ON u.picture = f.fid WHERE u.picture <> 0 AND u.uid > :uid ORDER BY↵
u.uid', 0, $limit, array(':uid' => $sandbox['last_uid_processed']))->fetchAllAssoc('fid',↵
PDO::FETCH_ASSOC);
```

That gives you the function you want, db_query_range(), and pretty much shows you how to use it, too. You can look up more information about it at api.drupal.org/db_query_range. It also uses the ->fetchAllAsoc() method to return all the rows of the result at once as a nested associative array.

Moving from the proof of concept to working custom code takes a number of significant but not overwhelming changes. This code is still not generalized, but it is not meant to be a contributed module this time; it is site-specific code. The dgd7glue_nextprev_suggestion() function, defined second in the code in Listing 33–50, runs the query and returns an array with the node ID and the title. To this array, in the next line, is added a 'text' key with 'Next >' or '< Prev' values.

Listing 33–50. Create and Display Previous and Next Links on Suggestion Node Pages

```
/**
 * Implements hook_node_view().
 */
function dgd7glue_node_view($node, $view_mode, $langcode) {
  // Print prev/next links on Suggestion node pages.
  if ($node->type == 'suggestion' && $view_mode == 'full') {
    $markup = '';
    $next = dgd7glue_nextprev_suggestion($node->nid);
    $next['text'] = t('Next >');
    $prev = dgd7glue_nextprev_suggestion($node->nid, TRUE);
    $prev['text'] = t('< Prev');
    $markup .= '<div class="nextprev">';
    $markup .= dgd7glue_format_link($prev);
    $markup .= ' | ';
    $markup .= dgd7glue_format_link($next);
    $markup .= '</div>';
    $node->content['dgd7glue_prevnext'] = array(
      '#markup' => $markup,
      '#weight' => 100,
    );
  }
}

/**
 * Get the next or previous suggestion node nid and title.
 */
function dgd7glue_nextprev_suggestion($nid, $previous = FALSE) {
  // Set the ORDER BY direction and the comparison operator ($co).
  if ($previous) {
    $direction = 'DESC';
    $co = '<';
  }
  else {
    $direction = 'ASC';
    $co = '>';
  }
```

```
    return db_query_range("SELECT title, nid FROM {node} WHERE nid $co :nid AND type =↵
:type AND status = :status ORDER BY nid $direction", 0, 1, array(':nid' => $nid, ':type' =>↵
'suggestion', 'status' => 1))->fetchAssoc();
}

/**
 * Format a next/prev link.
 */
function dgd7glue_format_link($link) {
  return l($link['text'], 'node/' . $link['nid'], array('attributes' => array('title' =>↵
$link['title'])));
}
```

The method used to get an array from the query is ->fetchAssoc() as the query will always return only one record: there is no need to fetch all at once (nor iterate). A drush cc all on the live site or a visit to admin/config/development/performance for the Clear all caches button is necessary to make the prev/next links show up after adding your code to dgd7glue.module. Drupal is pretty aggressive with caching!

This works for most suggestion posts, but it doesn't account for the very first and last nodes in the series. Let's see what the array returned by the query looks like empty. (Again, the query is wrapped in the dgd7glue_nextprev_suggestion() function, but inside there it is the db_query_range() function with a ->fetchAssoc() method returning directly.) Immediately below it, you can add a debug($prev); statement.

If you go to node 90, the first suggestion that was made (pulled in from the live database, or you could make your own example), is at http://dgd7.localhost/node/90.

Viewing this page, the output in the message area is:

```
Debug:
false
```

That makes your test very easy. If any value is returned, print the link. If not, do not. This may be best fixed in the display, and it's time to take a second look at the theming. It is currently simple, but not consistent with anything else on the site.

Reusing Book Module Templates to Display Non-Book Navigation

The site is already using the Book module for the outline of chapters, so it would be good to borrow that navigation.

■ **Caution** This is one of those ideas that might sound like a good idea but isn't— yet it can still prove workable.

Take a look inside modules/book. There is a template file called book-navigation.tpl.php. (There is no double-hyphen because this is not a suggestion for the book content type but its own template for navigation that is incorporated into the display of outline-enabled nodes.) The line in book.module that uses the book navigation template book-navigation.tpl.php is in an implementation of hook_node_view(), book_node_view(), shown in Listing 33–51

Listing 33–51. Calling the book-navigation.tpl.php file and Handing It the $node->book Array

```
$node->content['book_navigation'] = array(
  '#markup' => theme('book_navigation', array('book_link' => $node->book)),
  '#weight' => 100,
);
```

The key line is the #markup line. You aren't going to have $node->book for a non-book page, but you can make something that works the same. You can see in **book-navigation.tpl.php** what variables you'll have to provide to match the $node->book array.

▧ **Note** In the interest of ending this chapter, I won't show the many wrong and otherwise incorrect paths that eventually led to the solution shown. To see some of them, visit dgd7.org/230.

The function template_preprocess_book_navigation() (see api.drupal.org/template_preprocess_book_navigation) is what prepares the variables for the book-navigation.tpl.php template, and it is what you will have to replace. It is possible to implement hook_theme_registry_alter() to tell Drupal to make such a substitution. The result is the ability to take the basic next and previous data and hand it the Book module's theme templates padded out with all the variables necessary to display; see Listing 33–52.

Listing 33–52. The Revised hook_node_view Implementation, Registry Alter, and the

template_preprocess_book_navigation.tpl.php It Lets You Replace

```
/**
 * Implements hook_node_view().
 */
function dgd7glue_node_view($node, $view_mode, $langcode) {
  // Print prev/next links on Suggestion node pages.
  if ($node->type == 'suggestion' && $view_mode == 'full') {
    $next = dgd7glue_nextprev_suggestion($node->nid);
    $prev = dgd7glue_nextprev_suggestion($node->nid, TRUE);
    // Make a fake book link array.
    $link = array();
    $link['dgd7glue'] = TRUE;
    $link['prev'] = $prev;
    $link['next'] = $next;
    $node->content['dgd7glue_prevnext'] = array(
      '#markup' => theme('book_navigation', array('book_link' => $link)),
      '#weight' => 100,
    );
  }
}

/**
 * Implements hook_theme_registry_alter().
 */
function dgd7glue_theme_registry_alter(&$theme_registry) {
  // Replace the default preprocess function with our own.
```

```
    foreach ($theme_registry['book_navigation']['preprocess functions'] as $key => $value) {
      if ($value == 'template_preprocess_book_navigation') {
        $theme_registry['book_navigation']['preprocess functions'][$key] =⤸
'dgd7glue_template_preprocess_book_navigation';
        // Once it's found it we're done.
        break;
      }
    }
  }

/**
 * Replaces template_preprocess_book_navigation() when using tpl for non-books.

 */
function dgd7glue_template_preprocess_book_navigation(&$variables) {
  if (!isset($variables['book_link']['dgd7glue'])) {
    // This is a normal book, just use the usual function.
    template_preprocess_book_navigation($variables);
    return;
  }
  // Use our fake book_link variable to provide all the same variables.
  $link = $variables['book_link'];
  $variables['book_id'] = 'dgd7glue-nextprev';
  $variables['book_title'] = t('Suggestions');
  $variables['book_url'] = url('suggestions');
  $variables['current_depth'] = 0;
  $variables['tree'] = '';
  $variables['has_links'] = TRUE;
  $variables['prev_url'] = NULL;
  $variables['next_url'] = NULL;
  if ($link['prev']) {
    $prev_href = url('node/' . $link['prev']['nid']);
    drupal_add_html_head_link(array('rel' => 'prev', 'href' => $prev_href));
    $variables['prev_url'] = $prev_href;
    $variables['prev_title'] = check_plain($link['prev']['title']);
  }

  $parent_href = $variables['book_url'];
  drupal_add_html_head_link(array('rel' => 'up', 'href' => $parent_href));
  $variables['parent_url'] = $parent_href;
  $variables['parent_title'] = $variables['book_title'];

  if ($link['next']) {
    $next_href = url('node/' . $link['next']['nid']);
    drupal_add_html_head_link(array('rel' => 'next', 'href' => $next_href));
    $variables['next_url'] = $next_href;
    $variables['next_title'] = check_plain($link['next']['title']);
  }
}
```

The dgd7glue_nextprev_suggestion() function is the same as it was when presented previously—most everything else is new or changed!

▓ **Note** Relying on functions provided by Book module means you should include Book module as a requirement to your .info file, with the line

dependencies[] = book

added to your **dgd7glue.info** file.

Configuration Clean-Up

Although you are not using a view to get next and previous links, you need to make a view to show the suggestions (built off-camera). To this view, you add a sort by node ID criteria. Its configuration page looks like that in Figure 33–9.

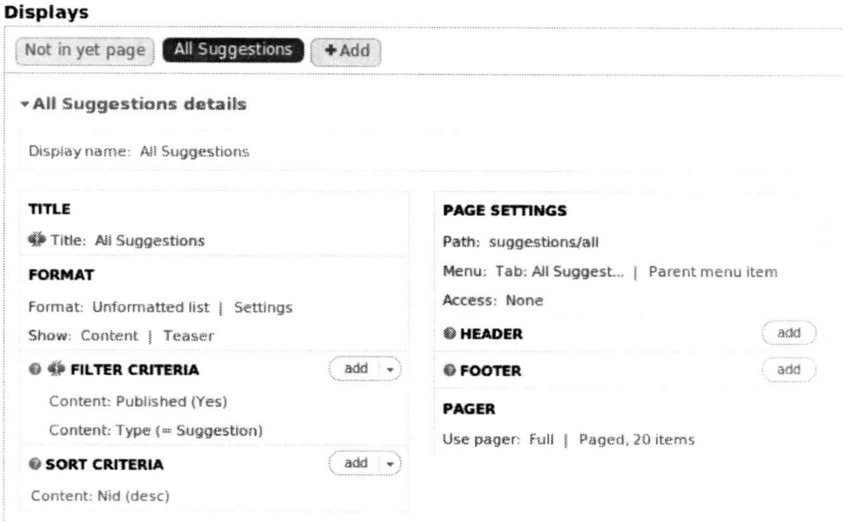

Figure 33–9. Suggestion view with sort by Node ID, descending

Creating a View to Make User Pages Have Hackable URLs

In the interest of hackable URLs (the ability to navigate a site by taking off everything after a / in the URL), you can use Pathauto module (`drupal.org/project/pathauto`) to give all user paths a sensible prefix and then provide a view of all users at that prefix. Pathauto settings, recall, are hidden under Administration ➤ Configuration ➤ Search and metadata ➤ URL aliases on a tab called **Patterns** (`admin/config/search/path/patterns`). The pattern for paths to user account pages is well down the page.

In the spirit of extreme optimism, figure that anyone who registers on the site is reading the book so make the prefix for user paths *readers*, followed by a slash separator and the token for the user's name: `readers/[user:name]`. Thus, a user account with the name Dries Buytaert would have the path readers/dries-buytaert. To have this work retroactively for users who are already on the site, go to the **Bulk update** tab of the path configuration (admin/config/search/path/update_bulk), checkmark **User paths**, and Update.

That path alias does nothing to make the path readers exist. If you go to readers, you will get *Page not found*. To improve user experience and assuage your own sense of feng shui as a web developer, you will need to put something sensible at this path, such as a list of all users.

Create a new view at admin/structure/views/add and, for a change, tell the wizard to **Show** Users.

▧ **Tip** Before creating a user (or any) view, check to see if Views has provided a default view to do generally or precisely what you want. There is no default User-based view, but there are views to take over Drupal core functionality such as a Comment-based view and a Node-based view that takes taxonomy term IDs.

Give your Page display a Path of readers and a Display format of perhaps HTML List (this or Unformatted will need to be themed; Grid may look good without theming). Give it a big number such as 50 for Items per page. After you Continue and Edit, you can leave the filter set to User: Active Yes and add Fields for User: Picture in addition to User: Name. Uncheck the Create a label option so it won't display labels.

Whether or not you want to make a menu item for the view of users or not, if someone hacks the URL of a user from readers/john-smith to readers, just as if they hack the URL of a suggestion path aliased at suggestions/installing-drubuntu to suggestions, they will come to a sensible list and not page not found. It's a small detail to make it seem right to call the site complete.

In Conclusion

Calling this chapter "Completing a Site" was a little misleading. As long as you have a Drupal site, you will not be done. Drupal sites are about living communities, breathing with the information that content administrators and users contribute. They will surely want new features sooner or later. If truly no one is using your site, if visitors are only viewing it, export it to static HTML. See Chapter 7 for the bare minimum to keep contributed code up to date, see Chapter 13 for deploying new features, and subscribe to dgd7.org/signup to learn how any new features are added to the DefinitiveDrupal.org web site!

▧ **Tip** Discussion and updates pertaining directly to this chapter will be at dgd7.org/other90.

■■■

## CHAPTER 34

Drupal Distributions and Installation Profiles

by Florian Lorétan

Installation profiles are lists of Drupal modules and themes coupled with automatic configuration to allow you to quickly and easily create a full-featured site or development testbed. They are packaged within distributions, which guide you through the installation and provide the site code. For example, the default Drupal distribution ships with two profiles, standard and minimal. Standard enables a set of modules and configuration that will be useful for most sites; it also includes some placeholder content and examples that can be helpful for a new user exploring Drupal's capabilities. Minimal installs just the barest set of modules and configuration needed for Drupal to run; it's recommended for someone who knows just what modules the new site will need.

Profiles are also great learning resources. If you want to build a site but aren't sure how to proceed, a profile can lay much of the groundwork for you, thus allowing you to focus on your new features. Profiles also use a wide range of modules and configuration options; if you find a profile that provides a function you like, it's a good idea to study how it implements that function. You can discover more profiles at `http://drupal.org/project/installation+profiles` or from their individual providers' web sites.

Site Templates

When you need to create many very similar sites, say for business or academic departments, profiles can provide standard features and themes to each so that new sites can be launched with very little effort.

Drupal Gardens (`http://drupalgardens.com`) is a hosted service for quickly building and styling web sites and microsites. It has both free and paid subscriptions, a powerful Theme Builder, and an increasing number of features.

You have the option of exporting your Drupal Gardens site as a fully-packaged and configured Drupal installation. The service also lets you clone a site, copying over theme, configuration, and selected content. This allows you to rapidly prototype or template many kinds of sites. You can also investigate how to accomplish things on your own site by building a Gardens site to do what you want, exporting it, and studying the configuration.

For example, Drupal Gardens provides a template that allows you to set up a blog with a few clicks. If you're familiar with how the core Drupal blog module works, you may notice some different behavior navigating a Drupal Gardens blog. For instance, the links at the bottom of each blog node may link back to a site-wide blog instead of the individual author's blog, which is nice for a blog with only one author. How is this accomplished?

Under the Configuration menu, there is a Blog settings option that controls this at /admin/config/content/blog. To see how Gardens manages these changes, export the site from /admin/config/system/site-export, get a site archive, and inspect the code.

A good way to find how something works is to search the code base for a text string you've seen associated with it in the UI. The help text or labels on forms often work well, as does the menu path of a configuration screen. One caveat to this method is that strings in code may be using placeholders, so if you're searching for text that looks dynamic—say, something that contains a user name—it's best to search for the surrounding text or something on the same page that looks static.

In this case, to search for the menu path, run this code from within the docroot directory of the export:

```
> grep -ri 'admin/config/content/blog' *
```

It should return one result:

sites\all\modules\flexible_blogs\flexible_blogs.module.

So that's the module that causes these changes, but how does it work? This module provides good examples of several hooks, and the different link behaviors are handled in an implementation of hook_node_view_alter(). As you work on creating your own sites and profiles, inspecting how others have accomplished goals similar to yours is often useful as a starting point. Perhaps you will find the code you need has already been written.

Full-Featured Services

A profile can allow you to easily offer a service that would normally take a long time to install and configure. The Drune music player (discussed later in this chapter) is an example of a service provided by a distribution.

Drupal Commons (acquia.com/products-services/drupal-commons) is social business software powered by a Drupal distribution. It is designed to allow companies and organizations to quickly create targeted social networks or communication platforms. Drupal Commons was created by Acquia specifically to compete with commercial closed source social business providers as an open source alternative.

Some features of Drupal Commons you can use and study are the personalized dashboard provided by the Homebox module and the real-time member activity stream provided by the Heartbeat module. Commons also provides integration between the User Relationships and Rules modules, which is a nice example of how to use both of those modules' APIs. Drupal Commons, like Open Atrium, uses Organic Groups and Features; comparing their configurations can give you ideas of different ways to manage and configure these modules within your own sites or profiles.

Development Profiles

If you're developing your own modules or features, you can create a profile that will allow you to easily create a suitable test site in moments. Include scripts to download the required contributed modules and external libraries, and set up some sensible default fields and configuration.

The Media module (drupal.org/project/media) provides tools for inserting images into a rich text or WYSIWYG editor, mass-uploading files, pulling in external video, and many other media management tasks. The developer profile for Media (http://drupal.org/project/media_dev) sets up a Drupal installation for a developer interested in contributing to the Media project. Since Media is a complex and abstract project, this distribution creates some sample images and audio files, which gives other developers concrete examples to work with.

The Feeds module (drupal.org/project/feeds) lets you import or aggregate data into your site. It also has a developer profile (drupal.org/project/feeds_test) focused on tests. With this, contributors to the project can easily run their changes through the Simpletest testing suite, which is covered in more detail in Chapter 23.

If you have a module or other project you'd like to ask the community for help with, consider creating a development install profile. The easier you can make it for people to contribute, the more contributions you'll see. Plus, if you ever want to try out a branch of your project, or need to work on a computer other than your own, you'll be able to set up a proper environment easily. An example development profile is discussed later in this chapter.

An Example Distribution: Drune

Rather than using generic examples, you are going to have one example distribution which will guide you through the different sections of this chapter: Drune. Drune is a web-based music player built on top of Drupal that lets users listen to their music from their browser (see Figure 34–1). More information about Drune can be found at drune.org.

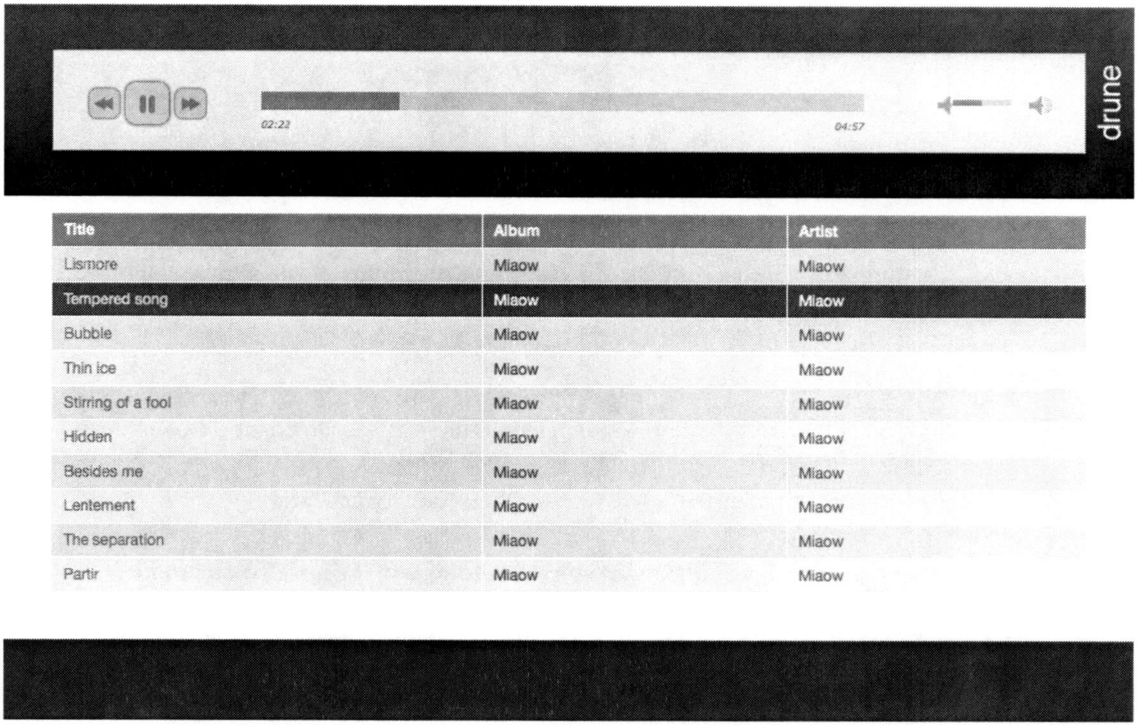

Figure 34–1. The Drune web-based music player

Creating Installation Profiles

The very first page a user sees when installing Drupal 7 is the choice between a standard and a minimal installation (see Figure 34–2). As mentioned previously, the standard installation creates a web site with a common configuration so that users can get started quickly. The minimal installation contains the minimum necessary setup and is meant for advanced users who know exactly what they want. These two options are the installation profiles that are included in Drupal core.

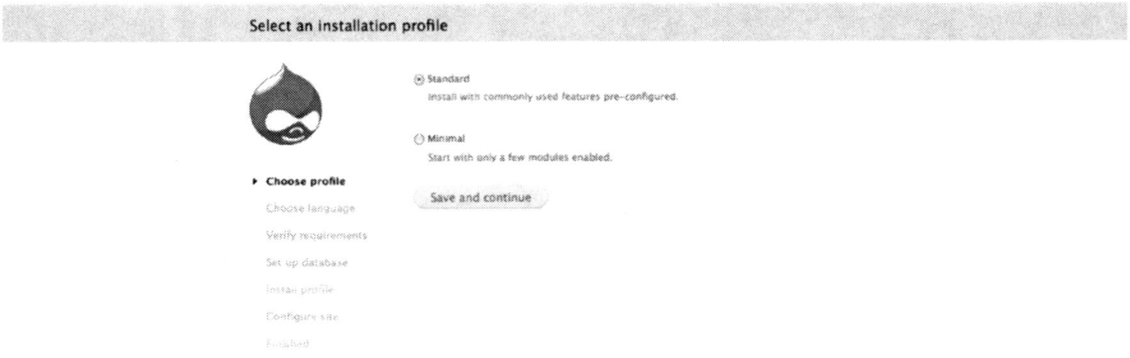

Figure 34–2. *The installation profile selection form*

In addition to the built-in installation profiles, you can create your own. This installation profile will be responsible for setting up the initial configuration for your distribution. It will also be responsible for guiding the user through the installation procedure and gathering input from the user as needed.

Structure of an Installation Profile

An installation profile has a structure similar to that of a module. You need to create a new folder inside of the profiles folder that contains at least the following two files:

- profilename.info contains metadata such as name, description, and dependencies.

- profilename.profile is a PHP file that contains the code of the installation profile itself.

Note that "profilename" is replaced with the name of the installation profile. In your case, you'll have two files called drune.info and drune.profile.

▨ **Tip** Developing an installation profile is an iterative process, so you will need to run the installation procedure multiple times until you get everything absolutely right. In order to save time when re-running the installer, use the drush site-install command; it lets you run the whole procedure from the command line.

---

drune.info

The `profilename.info` file contains essential metadata about our installation profile. Your **drune.info** file has the following content:

```
core = 7.x
name = Drune
description = A web-based music player built on top of Drupal.
files[] = drune.profile
dependencies[] = dblog
dependencies[] = features
dependencies[] = drune_track
dependencies[] = drune_player
```

The `core` attribute on the first line indicates the version of Drupal core with which your installation profile will be compatible (Drupal 7). The `name` and `description` attributes define the text to be displayed to the user on the installer profile selection form. The `files` attribute defines the list of PHP files to be included. The dependencies attribute defines the modules that need to be available in order for the installation to begin. Without these modules, an error message will be displayed to the user. They will be enabled automatically at the beginning of the installation procedure, right after the required system modules have been enabled.

The `drune_track` and `drune_player` are features, which are a specific kind of module. I will cover these later in this chapter.

drune.profile

The `profilename.profile` file is a PHP file. This file can contain hooks just like modules, but they will only be active during the installation procedure.

The installation procedure consists of a sequence of steps. The basic steps, such as the check for a `settings.php` file or the activation of module dependencies, are defined by Drupal itself. Installation profiles can add their own steps by implementing `hook_install_tasks()`. Listing 34–1 contains your implementation for Drune.

Listing 34–1. Your Implementation for Drune

```php
/**
 * Implements hook_install_tasks().
 */
function drune_install_tasks() {
  $tasks = array(
    // Display a welcome text.
    'drune_welcome' => array(
      'display_name' => st('Welcome'),
      'type' => 'normal',
    ),
    // Set up the basic configuration.
    'drune_setup' => array(
    ),
    // Let users enter information about the location of their music library.
    'drune_config_form' => array(
      'display_name' => st('Drune Configuration'),
      'type' => 'form',
    ),
```

```
    // Import files from their music library.
    'drune_import' => array(
      'display_name' => st('Import audio files'),
      'type' => 'batch',
    ),
  );

  return $tasks;
}
```

Your implementation of hook_install_tasks() returns a structured array defining four tasks: display a welcome text, set up the basic configuration, prompt the user for information, and use that information to import content. The key of each task is the name of a function callback. The kind of return value expected from the callback is defined by the type attribute of the task. Let's take a look at each of the callbacks.

```
function drune_welcome() {
  drupal_set_message(st('Welcome to Drune'));

  return st('We are going to walk you through the remaining steps required to set up Drune on
your server.');
}
```

This task has a type of normal, which is the default. Text returned by the callback is simply displayed on the page.

■ **Note** During the installation process, the standard Drupal configuration is not fully in place. This means that some subsystems like translation are not available. For that reason, you need to use the st() function instead of the standard t() function when outputting localized strings.

```
function drune_setup() {
  variable_set('site_frontpage', 'library');
}
```

The second task is also of type normal, but it doesn't have a return value. The code is executed and the installer automatically continues to the next task. Note that such a step could be replaced by implementing hook_install() in a profilename.install file.

Form Tasks

Form tasks let you gather input from the user. In your case, you ask the user to enter the location on the server where audio files are stored so that they can be imported (see Listing 34–2).

Listing 34–2. Importing Audio Files Form Task

```
function drune_config_form($form_state) {
  drupal_set_title(st('Drune configuration'));
  $form = array();
```

```
  $form['drune_import_source_dir'] = array(
    '#type' => 'textfield',
    '#title' => st('Where are your files located?'),
    '#description' => st('Enter the absolute path to the directory where your music files are
currently stored.'),
    '#default_value' => variable_get('drune_import_source_dir', NULL),
  );

  $form[] = array(
    '#type' => 'submit',
    '#value' => st('Save and continue'),
  );

  return $form;
}

function drune_config_form_validate($form, &$form_state) {
  $source_dir = $form_state['values']['drune_import_source_dir'];
  if (!empty($source_dir) != '' && !is_dir($source_dir)) {
    $error_text = st('%dir is not a directory.', array('%dir' =>
$form_state['values']['drune_import_source_dir']));
    form_set_error('drune_import_source_dir', $error_text);
  }
}

function drune_config_form_submit($form, &$form_state) {
  if ($form_state['values']['drune_import_audio_files']) {
    variable_set('drune_import_source_dir', $form_state['values']['drune_import_source_dir']);
  }
}
```

Tasks of type form need to return a Form API structured array. The usual rules for validation and submission handler names apply. Once the form has been submitted successfully, the installer continues onto the next task.

Batch Tasks

Some tasks in the installation procedure can take a long time, potentially more than the timeout defined in the PHP configuration. For these cases, you can use a task of type batch and return a structured array from your callback using the format used by batch_set().

In your case, you gather all the mp3 files located inside the directory specified by the user and use a batch process to create a node for each file. Note that you are creating nodes of type track, a content type defined by the drune_track feature that has been marked as a dependency (see Listing 34–3).

Listing 34–3. Batch Task

```
function drune_import() {
  $batch = array(
    'title' => st('Importing audio files'),
    'error_message' => st('The audio file import has encountered an error.'),
    'finished' => '_drune_import_finished',
  );
  $files = file_scan_directory(variable_get('drune_import_source_dir', NULL), "/.*\.mp3/");
```

```
  foreach ($files as $file) {
    $batch['operations'][] = array('_drune_import', array($file));
  }

  return $batch;
}

function _drune_import($file, &$context) {
  global $user;

  $node = (object) array(
    'uid' => $user->uid,
    'type' => 'track',
    'title' => $file->filename,
  );
  $file = file_copy($file, 'public://music/' . $file->filename);
  $node->field_audio_file[LANGUAGE_NONE][] = (array)$file + array('display' => TRUE);
  node_save($node);
  $context['message'] = st('Importing: @filename', array('@filename' => $file->filename));
}

function _drune_import_finished($success, $results, $operations) {
  drupal_set_message(st('Audio file import completed'));
}
```

Dealing with Configuration: Features

While installation profiles give you a good starting point to let users get started with a predefined configuration, they don't really cover everything you need. Some of the issues are:

- The configuration is set using direct calls to API functions. This method works for simple configurations where you only need a few variables but it is not appropriate for creating the node types, views, permissions, and other components needed by a full-blown distribution.

- The installation profile only controls the original setup of a project. There is no update mechanism that would allow maintenance updates.

- The original configuration is stored in the database along with the eventual modifications done by users after the installation. It is then impossible to separate the standard configuration from the modifications.

All solutions to these issues involve exporting the configuration away from the database and into files that can be released with the installation profile. The Features module has become the standard way of doing this by providing a unified mechanism to export different kinds of configuration components. All functionalities related to the Features are available from the administrative interface and from the command-line using Drush commands. More details about using Drush can be found in Chapter 26.

Many modules use a standard mechanism for letting other modules define default structures. The most common example of this is probably the Views module, which lets other modules create default views. Such default structures are originally defined in a module's code using a specific hook, but the user is then free to override that structure with a new version which is then stored in the database.

Structures that behave in such a way are called *exportables*. The Features module works as a wrapper for exportables and makes it easy to turn a set of structures into a custom module defining these structures.

There are other kinds of structures that do not have an API that lets modules define default structures. Field configurations, block placement, and user permissions fall into this category and are generally referred to as *faux-exportables*. Fortunately, the Features module provides a mechanism to deal with those almost in the same way as you deal with exportables.

For your Drune example, you are going to create a feature defining the track content type and all the associated fields that store the audio file, artist, album, cover thumbnail, etc.

Once these components have been created and the Features module has been activated, you can go to `admin/structure/features/create` to create a new feature (see Figure 34–3). The version and URL of update XML fields can be left blank for now.

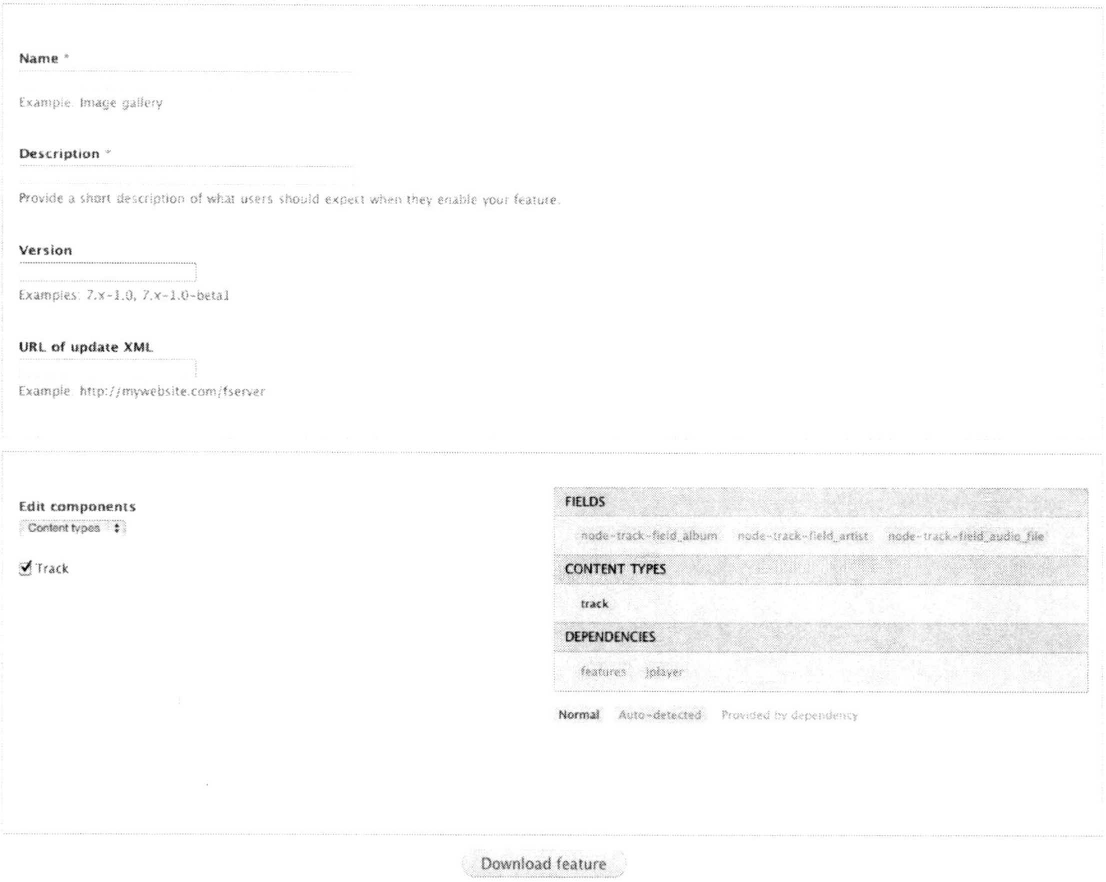

Figure 34–3. The user interface for creating new features

811

■ **Note** There are no strict rules on how to separate components into different features, but grouping them into logical entities will make your work much easier in the long term.

The features interface creates an archive containing a custom module that you can simply copy to your modules directory, but it's worth taking a quick look at the content of the generated code shown in Listing 34–4.

Listing 34–4. drune_track.info

```
core = "7.x"
dependencies[] = "features"
dependencies[] = "file"
dependencies[] = "jplayer"
dependencies[] = "text"
description = "Provide a track content type with the associated structure and functionality. "
features[field][] = "node-track-field_album"
features[field][] = "node-track-field_artist"
features[field][] = "node-track-field_audio_file"
features[node][] = "track"
features[user_permission][] = "create track content"
features[user_permission][] = "delete any track content"
features[user_permission][] = "delete own track content"
features[user_permission][] = "edit any track content"
features[user_permission][] = "edit own track content"
name = "Drune Track"
package = "Features"
```

Besides the fact that attributes are sorted alphabetically, notice the presence of the features attribute. Components are grouped by component type and each has a unique identifier.

drune_track.*.inc

The Features module generates different include files containing the actual definition of the components listed in the drune_track.info file. Components are grouped by type; for example, all default views would be in a .default_views.inc file and all field definitions would be in a .features.content.inc file (the presence of "features" in the filename indicates components that are not exportable and whose export to code is managed by the Features module).

drune_track.module

The .module file generated by the Features module contains a single line of code that takes care of including the various include files that define the individual components (see Listing 34–5). However, you are free to add any code in here that would be allowed in a module. This can typically be used to add glue code (see Chapter 22 related to the components defined in the feature).

Listing 34–5. Drune_track.module

```php
<?php

include_once('drune_track.features.inc');
```

Overrides

Once a feature is activated, it's still possible to change the configuration provided by the feature. The Features module automatically detects when the configuration of a feature has been modified and displays its status as "overridden" in the features administrative interface. A detailed list of which component types are overridden is also available.

When a feature is overridden, it's possible to go back to the configuration stored in the code by reverting the feature. This can be done in the features administrative interface by selecting the individual components to revert, but it can also be done from the command-line using the drush features-revert command.

Updates

One of the advantages of using the Features module is that it doesn't only provide a mechanism to export configuration to code, it also makes it possible to update that configuration over time. As a developer, you simply need to override the feature to match the desired state, and then update the feature. This can be done either by re-exporting the feature from the user interface and replacing the old version of the feature with the new one, or simply by using the drush features-update command to update the feature from the command-line.

When the Features module recognizes that the code has a new version of the configuration, it will either load it directly or indicate its status as "Needs review," in which case reverting the feature is necessary.

Table 34–1. A Comparison of the Behavior of Exportables and Faux-Exportables in Different Situations

	Exportable	**Faux-Exportables**
Example components	Views, image presets	Content types, permissions, fields
Default status	Configuration only in code	Configuration in database matches the configuration in code
Overridden	Configuration both in the database and in the code. The version from the database takes precedence over the one in the code.	Configuration in database is different from configuration in the code
New changes are in the code	The new version is loaded automatically, but clearing the Drupal cache is necessary in most cases.	Reverting the feature is necessary in order to synchronize the database with the code.

■ **Note** Besides making it easier to build distributions, the Features module also solves many issues related to deployment and team collaboration. Many developers use it as a standard tool in all of their Drupal projects.

Exceptions

Unfortunately, not everything in a Drupal project's configuration can be exported with features. The features API makes it easy to add support for the configuration of additional modules, but even then not everything can be exported.

The problem comes mainly from the use of sequential numbers as the primary identifier for components. Because these sequential numbers are automatically generated from the database by picking the next available integer, you have no guarantee that identifiers are consistent across different environments. Some faux-exportables, like menu links, circumvent this problem by using a different identifier (the menu link path) instead of the internal numeric identifier.

In order to support the creation of configuration that isn't managed by features in an installation profile, you need to write your own code to manage it. For example, you can use this method to create default nodes or user accounts. The code can be located in one of the following places:

- hook_install() in the installation profile .install file, if the configuration is related to the whole installation profile.

- An installation task in the installation profile. This is particularly useful if the configuration is based on information entered by the user in a previous task.

- hook_install() in a custom module's .install file, if the configuration is related to that specific module.

- hook_update_N() in a custom module's .install file, if the configuration is related to that specific module and should also affect existing instances that need to be updated.

Choosing the right location depends on the context to which your configuration is related, but the same syntax can be used in all locations. Listing 34–6 contains an example creating an about page and a default non-admin user for your Drune installation profile in drune.install.

Listing 34–6. Creating an About Page

```
/**
 * Implements hook_install().
 */
function drune_install() {
  // Create the about page.
  $node = new StdClass;
  $node->type = 'page';
  $node->title = t('About');

  // … Set additional node attributes

  node_save($node);

  // Create a default non-admin user.
  $default_user = new StdClass;
```

```
  $default_user->name = 'drune';
  $default_user->pass = 'drune';
  user_save($default_user);
}
```

See Chapter 22 for more details about writing custom code.

Using Installation Profiles and Features as a Development Tool

The combination of installation profiles with the Features module allows you to define the whole configuration of a project and to go from a codebase without any database to a functional Drupal site in just one step. This functionality is great for creating distributions, but it can also be incredibly powerful in the development of any Drupal project.

Imagine, for example, the development of a complex web site. Each functional section is exported to a feature that contains the required components and the related custom code. The installation profile can be a simple listing of module dependencies (including features) and an empty profilename.profile PHP file. The content of the **profilename.info** file would look like that in Listing 34–7.

Listing 34–7. Contents of profilename.info

```
name = "Complex Web site"
description = "Custom installation profile for Complex Web site."
core = 7.x

; List of our exported features.
dependencies[] = complex_web site_registration
dependencies[] = complex_web site_forums
dependencies[] = complex_web site_forums

; List of additional modules which are not required by any feature
dependencies[] = dblog
dependencies[] = toolbar

; Development modules, these will be deactivated on the live site.
dependencies[] = devel
dependencies[] = simpletest
dependencies[] = views_ui

files[] = profilename.profile
```

As mentioned, the profilename.profile file can be left as an empty PHP file. Using this installation profile would enable all the features with their dependencies, as well as any other specified modules. The result is a new instance of the project with all the configuration in place, ready for people to add content.

Content can be created programmatically by adding a task in the profilename.profile file, but this approach is only practical when the content can be imported in bulk from an external source. Creating editorial content programmatically can be tedious, so this method does not apply well for projects based mostly around editorial content.

Packaging Your Code

You now have all the required components for someone to recreate your installation profile: an installer profile, a list of dependencies, a few custom modules and features, eventually a theme, and some additional external libraries. The problem is that a user would need to get code from many different sources. Sometimes you also need a very specific revision of a module that can only be obtained directly from the version control system. What you need is a way to formally define how to build the code required to run your distribution.

Makefiles are a well-known tool in software development, generally used in combination with the make command to automate the compilation of executable files. While building a Drupal project is very different from compiling a C++ application, some of the same general concepts still apply. The Drupal equivalent of the **make** command is drush make, an extension to drush that turns a makefile into a Drupal project ready to be installed.

Drush Makefiles

The makefile syntax used by drush make is similar to the syntax of *.info files that you have already encountered multiple times. Listing 34–8 shows what this would look like for your Drune distribution.

Listing 34–8. profilename.make for the Drune Distribution

```
; Specify the drush make API version
api = 2

; Specify the compatible core Drupal version.
core = 7.x

; List of packages to be downloaded from Drupal.org.
projects[] = ctools
projects[] = features
projects[] = views

; Modules can be downloaded directly from version control.
projects[jplayer][type] = module
projects[jplayer][download][type] = "git"
projects[jplayer][download][url] = "git://git.drupal.org/project/jplayer"
projects[jplayer][download][tag] = "6.x-1.0-beta2"

; Patches can also be applied automatically. In this case the port of the jPlayer module to
Drupal 7.
projects[jplayer][patch][] = "http://drupal.org/files/issues/jplayer_d7_1.patch"

; Also specify external libraries.
libraries[jplayer][download][type] = "get"
libraries[jplayer][download][url] =
"http://www.happyworm.com/jquery/jplayer/latest/jQuery.jPlayer.1.2.0.zip"
```

This file is called profilename.make and is located directly in the root of the installation profile (in your case, it would be profile/drune/drune.make).

Note that this makefile does not include Drupal core in the list of projects. Because it is located inside the profile folder, it's expected to be taking place inside of an existing Drupal project. You can create a simple makefile that would get Drupal core and your installation profile, and drush make will parse the makefiles recursively, like so:

```
api = 2
core = 7.x
projects[] = drupal
projects[] = drune
```

Hosting on drupal.org

Installation profiles hosted on drupal.org can also make use of a special makefile named drupal-org.make. This file is automatically parsed by the drupal.org packaging script and will create an archive containing the Drupal project and your installation profile ready to be installed by users.
Due to the hosting policy of drupal.org, the inclusion of external libraries is not allowed. The drush verify-makefile command can be used to check that all the requirements for hosting on drupal.org are met. If a makefile does not meet the requirements, it can be converted into a compliant makefile using the drush convert-makefile command.

Packaging

Even if your installation profile is hosted on drupal.org, you probably want to give users of your distribution the possibility to download an archive containing everything needed for the installation right from your web site. Among the many options provided by drush make, the --tar option does exactly that, like so:

```
drush make --tar drune.make
```

For a complete documentation of all the possibilities offered by drush make, have a look at the README.txt file included inside the drush make download.

The Future of Distributions

Distributions are vitally important to the future of Drupal. They make it competitive against single-task, difficult-to-extend systems. Drupal Commons, for example, was developed to compete with other closed-source social business services. By lowering the barrier to site creation and creating unique feature sets, distributions also bring Drupal into niche markets.

Since providers of distributions depend on Drupal to offer their products, it's in their interest to contribute to the Drupal project. And since Drupal is strengthened by having distributions, this feedback cycle creates a better product for everyone.

If you worked with profiles in Drupal 6, you'll be happy to hear they've received significant attention in Drupal 7 as part of the effort to recognize this future. They are built essentially like a module with .info and .install files; no more need to learn an additional (somewhat esoteric) API. If you can write a module, you can write an install profile. In addition, they've received much more prominent treatment on drupal.org and are now placed on par with modules and themes. Making distributions even easier to create and maintain will be the next challenge the community faces.

The Drune music player used as an example in this chapter was thrown into existence when the author's desktop music player stopped interacting with his music library due to a change in the proprietary protocol being used. The examples in this chapter are somewhat simplified versions of the actual code. The current development status of the project is available at drune.org.

Summary

In this chapter, you have learned that profiles and distributions allow you to create a pre-configured site quickly and easily. Distributions and profiles are an important part of the Drupal ecosystem, and you should consider creating a profile to support development of your Drupal project. Writing your own profile is similar to writing your own module, and you can learn a lot by inspecting how existing profiles are built and using them as a template. You can quickly and easily pull together the resources your profile needs from multiple locations by using drush makefiles. You can also package logically-grouped parts of your site configuration together as exportable, reusable features. Most things features can't export can be stored in code in `hook_install()` and `hook_update_N()`.

■ ■ ■

## PART VII

Drupal Community

Chapter 35 gives the story of Drupal's beginnings as an open source project and some key events to its development into the thriving community it is today.

Chapter 36 tackles what it takes to make a living with Drupal, including taking a hard look at problems with Drupal software—and suggests ways you can mutually sustain your success and Drupal's success.

Chapter 37 goes over maintaining a project shared with the world on Drupal.org and making use of the Git revision control system.

Chapter 38 caps off the book with a discussion of effective ways to contribute back to Drupal to make the software you work with, and the community you work in, better. And, perhaps, help make the world better.

CHAPTER 35

■■■

Drupal's Story: A Chain of Many Unexpected Events

by Kasey Qynn Dolin

"For me the history of Drupal is a chain of interesting surprises."

—Dries Buytaert, Drupal Founder and Project Lead

I considered titling this chapter "History," but decided that that would be misleading. Even though the Drupal project is only ten years old at the time of this printing, a complete history of Drupal would fill hundreds of pages and document the experiences of literally hundreds of thousands of people.

And in the interest of full disclosure, if you are looking for an exhaustive biography of key contributors, you will have better luck checking out their profile pages. While many key contributors are fascinating, intelligent characters whose decisions, actions, and beliefs undoubtedly left their mark on the community that so many people worldwide have come to know and love, this history is not a story about the People-with-a-capital-P who shaped Drupal.

It is instead a story about the events that shaped Drupal, and how the community as a whole responded to those events. Speaking of the community...

As an outside observer, I have come to feel that the truly amazing thing about Drupal is its appeal to a bizarrely wide range of users. Drupal users run the gamut from hobby hackers to entrepreneurs, radical grassroots organizers to national governments, FOSS evangelists to corporate strategists—and the community includes a multitude of entities and individuals who combine traits from all of the above.

It is completely just to say that the quality and flexibility of Drupal's code explains its wide appeal, and that it should come as no surprise that an elegant, adaptable, and useful technology will have an impressive range of applications...

...but it is equally just to point out that Drupal is a collaboratively-produced enterprise. Members of every group described above from every inhabited continent must communicate, work together, and rely on one another in order to get the most of what they want from the software—and in so doing, push the project forward as a whole. What has made this implementation of open source values on a huge scale possible? What is it about the Drupal project that inspires this type of devotion, which has in turn resulted in its phenomenal success?

The answer: the aforementioned chain of many unexpected events,[1] and the community's response. This chapter will provide snapshots of a few events that shaped how and why the community survived and grew, and in so doing, will hopefully capture a little of the flavor that defines Drupal (though I will leave it up to the reader to define for themselves exactly what that flavor is). After a brief reccounting of Drupal's origins, the first section describes events that resulted in Drupal attracting the critical mass of developers it needed to thrive. The next two sections outline the events that determined the shape of Drupal's infrastructure, and how that infrastructure balances the open source values that give Drupal its strength with the ability to support a wide range of commercially-viable applications.

The Original Accident

The experiment that we now know as the Drupal project began in 1998, when Dries Buytaert, a Belgian undergraduate student seeking his Licentiate in Computer Science at the University of Antwerp, began construction on a local area network to connect his dorm-mates (and avoid the high cost of Internet access at the university). The message boards that Dries created allowed his fellow computer science students to discuss the latest in internet technology and to just plain keep in touch.

The latter is important because it was this sense of community that inspired Dries, upon his graduation and move from the dorms, to keep the discussions going by moving the internal web site to the Internet. On April 28, 2000, drop.org was born.

■ **Note** Just in case there are any readers out there who have somehow managed to escape familiarity with the origins of Drupal's name, here's the condensed version: *In the beginning, there was a typo. And Dries looked upon his typo, and he saw that it was good...so he went with it.* When registering his new site's domain, Dries meant to type an abbreviation of the Dutch word *dorpje* (meaning village), but misspelled it as the English word *drop*. Later, when naming the software, he back-translated *drop* into Dutch *(druppel)*, which he then spelled phonetically (in English) as *drupal*.

In a move that would define the character of the Drupal community forever after, Dries, rather than trying to implement the deluge of suggestions, complaints, and advice himself, chose to make the software available to anyone, for free, under the GNU General Public License. This meant that anyone who was willing to put their time and effort into trying out their ideas was able to experiment with the code that would become Drupal at will—providing they agreed to make the results of their experiments just as freely available to others. On January 15, 2001, the Free and Open Source Software (FOSS) movement gained a new member with the official release of Drupal 1.0.

While it was originally intended that the content of the discussions on drop.org be about Internet technologies in general, the commentary quickly began to trend toward the very specific—as in, the software powering drop.org web site itself.

Shortly after Drupal 2.0 was released on March 15, 2001, Dries decided to provide a place for all of the specifically Drupal-related activity that had been overwhelming the drop.org site, and so drupal.org was born.

---

[1] Dries Buytaert uses the phrase "a chain of many unexpected events" to describe Drupal in an interview with Noel Hidalgo, 26 July 2007, "episode 13–dries on drupal," http://luckofseven.com/vlog/episode13.

Drupal Gains a Foothold

Drupal continued to evolve in relative obscurity until early 2002, when Dries initiated a relationship with Jeremy Andrews, owner and operator of kerneltrap.org. A news site reporting on issues relating to Linux Kernel and the FOSS world at large, kerneltrap.org would periodically go down under an onslaught of traffic due to a mention on the popular technology-related news site slashdot.org/. Dries contacted Jeremy and suggested Drupal as an alternative to PHP-Nuke, and Jeremy, after converting kerneltrap.org to Drupal 3.0.2 on February 14, 2002, developed the throttle module (which was eventually included in Drupal 4.1 core).

While the throttle module "is little more than a Band-Aid, attempting to work around a problem rather than solving it,"[2] and was removed from Drupal 7 core, the impact of that early relationship was significant. Jeremy would go on to be an active member of the Drupal community for many years, with over 4400 commits to his credit. But more relevant to the purposes of this chapter, he reported on his early conversion to and work with Drupal on kerneltrap.org itself. The publicity generated by this most sincere form of endorsement has been identified by Dries as something that "opened the eyes of many other people in the technical world"[3] to Drupal's unique capabilities.

If the 2002 mention on kerneltrap.org represents Drupal's "coming out" to the world of techies, July of 2003 represents the beginning of Drupal's "coming out" to the world at large. While the Drupal community was hacking its way through versions 4.2, 4.3, and 4.4, a group of politically active young people were using the still relatively obscure content management system in an attempt to get a relatively obscure candidate elected president of the United States.

While candidate Howard Dean did not get elected, he did make it on to the national scene in a big way—thanks in part to the organizing capacity of the Drupal software and the dedication of the activist/developers who constructed the web sites that drove the campaign. While the organizers used Drupal software to create DeanSpace, a site used to connect and organize Dean volunteers around the United States and therefore expand exponentially the number of people the campaign reached, the campaign's expansion caused the Drupal software to undergo its own exponential growth.

As more and more Drupal-run Dean sites popped up, the number of developers constructing modules to meet the needs of these sites grew as well. David Cohn, in writing about this period of Drupal's history, uses the figure of a 300% increase in created content on drupal.org. This reciprocal push of development continued even after Dean's campaign collapsed; in fact, the end of the campaign ushered in a period of rapid expansion of Drupal into a variety of grassroots and not-for-profit applications, much of it driven by former Dean-volunteer Drupal developer talent. On July 23, 2004, it was officially announced that the DeanSpace was dead, and CivicSpace, "the first company with full time employees that was developing and distributing Drupal technology"[4] had begun. Advomatic, Chapter Three, and Echo Ditto are examples of other Drupal-based companies founded by Dean volunteers that continue to contribute significantly to the Drupal community.

---

[2] Tag1 Consulting, Inc., "Section 3: The Throttle Module," http://books.tag1consulting.com/scalability/drupal/performance/throttle

[3] Dries Buytaert, 26 July 2007, interview with Noel Hidalgo, "episode 13 – dries on drupal," http://luckofseven.com/vlog/episode13.

[4] DigiDave, Drupal Nation: Software to Power the Left, http://blog.digidave.org/2008/12/drupal-nation-software-to-power-the-left

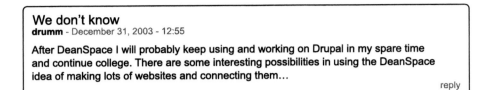

We don't know
drumm - December 31, 2003 - 12:55

After DeanSpace I will probably keep using and working on Drupal in my spare time and continue college. There are some interesting possibilities in using the DeanSpace idea of making lots of websites and connecting them...

reply

Figure 35–1. 2004 New Year's Eve prediction by Neil Drumm, future co-founder of CivicSpace and Drupal core developer

Oh, That's How You Say Your Name!

Seven months after all of this very visible and large-scale activity was taking place on the North American continent, on the other side of the Atlantic Drupal was experiencing the advent of a tradition that has become definitive to the character of the culture itself, as ultimately significant as the events of 2004 (though on a far more intimate scale).

■ **Tip** It involved lots of beer and power strips.

On February 26, 2005, a major milestone occurred: what is widely recognized as the first Drupal Conference (though technically, the first stand-alone DrupalCon would not occur for another seven months). FOSDEM, or the Free and Open Source Developers' European Meeting, is a conference that is still being held annually in Brussels, Belgium, "organized by volunteers to promote the widespread use of Free and Open Source software" and to "provide developers with a place to meet."[5] FOSDEM 2005 was attended by between 3,000 and 3,500 people from all over the world. In addition to scheduled speakers and short project presentations in the form of lightning talks, FOSDEM 2005 hosted eighteen developers' rooms, including Drupal's.[6]

DrupalCons, however, are not the tradition to which the hint above refers. The really significant event occurred during the two days prior to FOSDEM.

On February 24 and 25, 2005, four months after the release of Drupal 4.5, Drupalistas gathered in Antwerp, Belgium for the first official Drupal developer sprint. Twenty-six Drupal developers from eleven countries met up to work collaboratively (and face to face) on issues that sprint organizers had identified as needing concentrated attention prior to the meet-up. Roughly 80% of these developers traveled from outside of Western Europe for the event, with twelve of the twenty-six coming from different continents entirely.

The tradition of flying out in order to meet up was born.

---

[5] FOSDEM, About page, www.fosdem.org/2010/about/fosdem

[6] FOSDEM, Archive of 2005, http://archive.fosdem.org/2005/

The Extended Weekend from Hell

Drupal 4.6 was released April 15, 2005. By any measure or definition, the Drupal community was continuing its trend of rapid expansion: by July 2005, there were 26,772 users and 455 service providers registered to drupal.org. In practical terms, this meant that a massive number of people were affected by the events of July 7-11, 2005—what Steven Wittens dubbed "the Extended Weekend from Hell."[8] On July 10, users attempting to log on to drupal.org were greeted with the following message: "http://drupal.org temporarily offline. We can't get the server back online without help from our hosting company, and after 48 hours they still have not responded to our support requests."[9]

Steven provided a (less terse/stressed/desperate sounding) blow-by-blow description of events in his July 12 News and Announcements drupal.org post on the subject: "Thursday evening, this server was hacked. One of the other sites on our server provided the hole through which the hackers entered; it appears someone wanted to turn us into a warez FTP, but completely messed it up instead. We discovered the intrusion quickly and were able to regain control of the server soon afterward. However, the entire incident occurred only a few hours before a scheduled power outage at our current ISP; problems with remote administration and the lack of install media meant we were unable to fix the server remotely. Over the weekend we called to try and rectify the situation, but due to miscommunication with our ISP we had to wait until Monday morning before we could reinstall the OS and get the server purring again."[10]

While the server crash may have hit drupal users like a slap to the face, the community was by no means unaware that problems with infrastructure could prove to be an issue, as illustrated in Figure 35–2.

> **Please give the Donate button better exposure!**
> **adrianrf** - June 29, 2005 - 13:59
>
> This project clearly needs to raise enough cash - now, and on an ongoing basis - to prevent space and bandwidth limitations undercutting everyone's hard work, by damaging confidence in the professionalism of that project through lapses in how its own brand-marquee site operates. Let's:
> 1. Quickly pick a significant number as a short-term funding target.
> 2. Until that amount is raised:
>   a. Move the Donate block to the top of a column.
>   b. Make its appearance non-discretionary (not selectable per site visitor).
>   c. Make it appear on every page.
> 3. Ideally, have that block display a) the goal amount and b) the amount raised to date, or the delta remaining.
>
> reply

Figure 35–2. The Drupal community was aware that problems with infrastructure could be an issue.

Dries had already prepared for publication prior to the server crash a message that Charlie Lowe posted to the main page of drupal.org on July 10, addressing the need to get a new server. At the time of the crash, drupal.org was running on a Pentium Xeon 3Ghz server with 1GB of RAM that it shared with approximately 20 other sites; Drupal veteran Kjartan Mannes (http://drupal.org/user/2) both maintained the server and footed the bill.

---

[7] Groups.Drupal, Growth Charts, http://groups.drupal.org/node/1980

[8] Drupal, "Restoring Drupal.org and Murphy's Law," http://drupal.org/node/26545

[9] Internet Archive WayBack Machine, http://web.archive.org/web/web.php, http://www.drupal.org/

[10] Drupal, "Restoring Drupal.org and Murphy's Law," http://drupal.org/node/26545

In the month of June alone, according to Dries' post "Help Drupal.org Buy a Dedicated Server," drupal.org generated 100GB of traffic, serving over 3 million pages; in his words, "our current server doesn't cut it anymore." The message to the Drupal community begins "Quite a few people have pointed out that drupal.org has been slow lately. We know it's been slow, and have been working on optimizing drupal.org...The fact remains that as the result of Drupal's growing popularity, the server is saturated pretty much all day. This explains drupal.org's poor performance."[11]

The post goes on to outline a plan for moving drupal.org to a new server hosted by Oregon State University's Open Source Lab (OSUOSL, OSL). The Open Source Lab was officially created in January of 2004 with the stated mission of "help[ing to] accelerate the adoption of open source software across the globe and aid[ing] the community that develops and uses it."[12] These fairy godmothers of FOSS had come to the aid of Drupal veteran Jeremy Andrews two months prior to the drupal.org server meltdown; when Jeremy found himself looking for a new host for http://kerneltrap.org, OSL was the first organization that he contacted.

As Associate Director of OSL, Scott Kveton explained to Jeremy, "*The goal of the Open Source Lab is to bring FOSS communities together and so by doing promote cross-pollination of ideas and people to help create an atmosphere of innovation around open source.*" Particularly well-positioned to meet this goal, by mid-2005 OSL was already hosting projects such as Arklinux, Debian GNU/Linux, Freenode.net, Gentoo Linux, the Mozilla Foundation, the PowerPC Kernel Archives, and SPI.

OSL gathered this impressive list of participants mostly by keeping their ears to the FOSS grapevine and offering their assistance when and where it was needed; as Scott explained to Jeremy, the OSL team would hear that "*such-and-such project had a machine that died and needs help or so-and-so is reaching the limits of their existing infrastructure and needs help.*"

This pretty neatly describes where Drupal was in June of 2005. Drupal also passed the selection criteria that the OSL staff used to evaluate prospective hostees: it was community-focused; it had "committed, energetic, and most importantly, realistic leadership;" its community would interact well with those of the projects already hosted at OSL; it would use the services provided by OSL to help its community grow; and the OSL's resources and services would enable the community to focus on rapid innovation (rather than simply keeping the lights on).

> *Let's face it, open source is gaining traction everywhere. With its success comes additional drains on already strapped resources. We want to be an option for these open source projects that don't want to be indentured servants of the big companies that want to provide help. We're not anti-company or anti-people-making-money-from-open-source; we just know that projects want to ensure the future of their communities and so are very careful about who they partner with. We know this will take time and as with everything in open source; it's all about the relationships we develop.*
>
> —Scott Kveton, 2005[13]

Only a few weeks prior to Drupal's server meltdown, the conditions of the deal had already been worked out: OSL would provide free hosting—rack space, bandwidth, power, domain name service,

---

[11] Internet Archive WayBack Machine, http://web.archive.org/web/web.php, www.drupal.org/

[12] KernelTrap, "KernelTrap: New Home At The Open Source Lab," http://kerneltrap.org/node/5083

[13] KernelTrap, "KernelTrap: New Home At The Open Source Lab," http://kerneltrap.org/node/5083

database, back-ups, and mail relay. All the Drupal community would have to do was provide the hardware.[14] The price tag on the desired equipment was US$3,000.

The call for donations was posted on the temporary main page of drupal.org (the only one accessible at the time) on July 10, 2005. Shortly after that, a piece explaining Drupal's plight was posted to slashdot.org/.[15] Sixteen hours after the initial drupal.org posting, the US$3,000 target had been reached and exceeded. By July 12, the Drupal community had donated more than US$10,000 and Drupal organizers had more than enough money to meet their needs, literally. Without a foundation or any other formal not-for-profit status, Drupal's bounty was potentially taxable—and sitting in the PayPal account of a private individual. This situation emphasized another long-recognized but long-postponed need of the community, and the formation of an Association became an acknowledged priority.

The generosity that the FOSS community exhibited toward Drupal during the Extended Weekend from Hell did not end with the contributions of OSL and private donors. Tim Bray, who Dries describes as "Sun Microsystems employee, W3C member, co-inventor of XML, and Drupal fan"[16] came across the slashdot.org/ piece describing Drupal's situation (which had been posted at 3:39 p.m. on Sunday, July 10). Sympathetic, Tim passed the story up the chain of command at Sun, along with the request that something be done to help.[17] It was still Sunday when Dries received the e-mail from Hal Stern, Software CTO of Sun, informing him that Drupal was the proud new owner of a free Sun Fire V20z server. Paperwork was signed on Monday, and by Tuesday, the server arrived at its new home at OSL.[18]

> *Amusing side note: Dries Buytaert of Drupal wrote wondering "under what terms we'd get such machinery from Sun" and Hal wrote back saying a mention on the site would be nice, "and no offense, but the legal cost of any more 'terms' than above exceeds our cost of the hardware."*
>
> —Tim Brays[19]

By July 19, all of the donations had been transferred to OSL (and out of Dries' PayPal account), and implementation of the infrastructure proposal developed by the team at OSL and FireBright (CEO Jonathan Lambert) could begin with the purchase of three Dell PowerEdge 1850 1Us. By August 25, the team including Kjartan Mannes, Corey Shields (OSL Infrastructure Manager, a.k.a. cshields), Mike Marineau (System Administrator at OSL), Matt Rae (Community Systems Administrator and drupal.org infrastructure manager at OSU, aka raema) had successfully moved the drupal.org database to the new server[20], which made many people very happy.

---

[14] Internet Archive WayBack Machine, web.archive.org/web/web.php, www.drupal.org

[15] Slashdot, "Drupal Needs a New Home," developers.slashdot.org/article.pl?sid=05/07/10/1924256&tid=169&tid=8

[16] Drupal, "The future Drupal server infrastructure," drupal.org/node/26707

[17] Tim Bray, "Iron for Drupal," www.tbray.org/ongoing/When/200x/2005/07/14/Drupal-Server

[18] Drupal, "The future Drupal server infrastructure," drupal.org/node/26707

[19] Tim Bray, "Iron for Drupal," www.tbray.org/ongoing/When/200x/2005/07/14/Drupal-Server

[20] Various. kveton.com/blog/2005/08/26/drupalorg-before-and-after/, drupal.org/node/29670

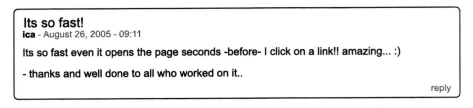

Its so fast!
ica - August 26, 2005 - 09:11

Its so fast even it opens the page seconds -before- I click on a link!! amazing... :)

- thanks and well done to all who worked on it..

reply

Figure 35–3. Drupal.org user expresses joy about new server speed

If You Have a Problem, Please Search Before Posting a Question

By 2006, Drupal was positioned to step into the role of major player in the world of Free and Open Source Software and the world of web site development at large. But physical infrastructure of the sort provided by OSL is not the only type of infrastructure necessary to make sure that an entity like Drupal is scalable enough to survive into adulthood, so to speak; the infrastructure of the community itself is just as crucial.

The next section will outline the formation of an important piece of that community infrastructure: the Drupal Association. The process was long, and plenty of other exciting activity was taking place in the Drupal community while the research and debate on what form the Association should take continued; however, a detailed look at how the Association came to be is informative on many levels. Not only does the framework established within the statutes and internal regulations of the Association charter define how Drupal is allowed to grow (and who is allowed to influence that growth), but peeking at the process that the community used to craft it can be revealing.

Just as the Drupal community had been discussing the need for new infrastructure months before the server crash made obtaining it an inescapable and immediate priority, discussion concerning the formation of some sort of not-for-profit entity capable of handling Drupal's financial affairs had been bouncing around for a while.

More predictions
Kjartan - January 4, 2004 - 12:06

...Kjartan will cave and set up some method for people to donate to the Drupal project. This will end up in $200,000 donated, making for one kick ass party. The leftover change will cover a new server to power http://drupal.org and hosting.http://drupal.org. ...

Disclaimer: These predictions may or may not be serious, figuring out which are intended as serious is left to the reader.

reply

Figure 35–4. (Facetious?) New Year's Eve prediction for 2004, posted by then maintainer of drupal.org's server, Kjartan Mannes

Speaking seriously, it was well understood that any structure that was established would have far-reaching consequences (economic, legal, and cultural) for the Drupal community and potentially for the software itself. As Steven Peck explained to an individual concerned by Drupal's lack of an intensive fundraising initiative in a June 29, 2005 `drupal.org` forum reply, "Discussions are occurring. Stuff just takes time to do right."[21]

Days after the server crash, Dries' July 14, 2005 `drupal.org` announcement of the plan to disburse the entirety of the fundraising windfall to OSL galvanized another round of public debate on the foundation issue. Folks expressing their concerns that none of the US$10,000 had been used to set up some sort of a foundation were assured (with varying degrees of politeness) that:

1.   Money had indeed been located for the purpose of creating some sort of not-for-profit-entity, in the form of promised matching funds (to be delivered when needed).

2.   It was a deemed wise to hand all of the server donations over to a third party (which incidentally did, unlike Dries, hold not-for-profit status) that would spend the money on servers and hosting because that was what donors expected their money to be spent on, and issues of fiscal responsibility can become hazy when solicited donations are sitting in a private individual's account, no matter how trustworthy and dedicated that private individual may be.

3.   Members of the Drupal community with very personal stakes in the matter had already been working on this complex issue, doing careful and extensive research, and would continue to work on it until a satisfactory solution could be reached.

In other words, funds were not the main issue. The undisclosed amounts promised by Advomatic, CivicSpaceLabs, Google, and Packt Publishing would be sufficient to cover costs; the main issue was the scope of the task. To proceed, the Drupal community had to come to some sort of internal consensus as to what it needed and wanted—and perhaps more importantly, did not need or want—from a foundation. As Chris Messina (factoryjoe) pointed out in his July 14, 2005 `drupal.org` comment "Regarding the Drupal Foundation," in addition to "scoping out various legal service providers," another priority was "looking into the vast open source community for ideas, opinions, and other helpful insights into how to do this right—there's no sense in reinventing the wheel if we don't have to!"[22]

DrupalCon Portland 2005 (a free conference from August 1-5 held alongside the O'Reilly Open Source Convention in Portland, Oregon) provided the venue for a roundtable discussion about needs, wants, and concerns regarding a Drupal Foundation. OSCON itself provided a venue for picking the brains of those involved in the formation of other FOSS Foundations. Boris Mann's `drupal.org` News and Announcements post "DrupalCon Portland 2005: Drupal Foundation meeting" summarizes the takeaways from the meeting as follows:

"Some examples of needs include:

•   Ability to accept and give out funds

•   Hold assets (e.g., servers and other hardware)

•   Bookkeeping to track funds and how they are spent

A selection of the group's thoughts on goals for the Drupal foundation:

•   Attract more users and developers

•   Provide server infrastructure for related projects

---

[21] Drupal, Comments on "Why does drupal.org choke so much?", `drupal.org/node/25982#comment-45105`

[22] Drupal, Comments on "Why does drupal.org choke so much?", `drupal.org/node/25982#comment-45105`

- Manage Intellectual Property (trademarks, copyrights, licensing, etc.)
- Fund developer meet-ups"[23]

Later in the post, Boris mentions that Dries identified an additional goal—the creation of a funded position to lift the substantial burden of maintaining the drupal.org web site off the shoulders of the volunteers (Dries, Steven Wittens, etc.) who spent approximately eight hours a week on such housekeeping tasks. Incidentally, the same post also details the input from a community member who felt that the formation of a foundation was not a necessary step:

"Kieran...had a more pragmatic view. The Drupal community has figured out how to get money, we've got a great ecosystem that can come up with solutions on the fly. With free hosting from OSL and a great set of server infrastructure, we're fine as we are now. [24]

- Boris Mann

■ **Note** Boris is referring to Kieran Lal, a.k.a. Amazon (drupal.org/user/18703), the then Development Manager for CivicSpace who would go on to serve on the Drupal Association's Board of Directors every year from its inception to the current day, first as Fundraiser and then as Director of Business Development.

Now we skip ahead almost a full year to June 25-30, 2006. While it may seem like a long time to let an issue sit, keep in mind that Drupal does not and has never stood still; the same people who were discussing options for a foundation also had day jobs to work, code to write, bugs to fix, and Cons to organize and attend (and, in Dries' case at least, a fiancée to marry)[25].

About a month and a half after the official release of Drupal 4.7, Dries announced on his blog buytaert.net his intent to continue his research into questions of community infrastructure by picking the brains of "some of the smartest people in the FOSS and Internet community." The itinerary for Dries' "Drupal road trip to San Francisco" included personal meetings with Tim O'Reilly (Founder and CEO of O'Reilly & Associates), Chris DiBona (Open Source Programs Manager at Google), Mitch Kapor (Co-Founder of Lotus-1-2-3, Founder of the Open Source Applications Foundation, Co-Founder of the Electronic Frontier Foundation, and Chair of the Mozilla Foundation), Jeffrey Veen (Co-Founder of Adaptive Path, Project Lead of Measure Map, and User Experience Leader at Google), Chanel Wheeler a.k.a. chanel (drupal.org/user/4733, Software Applications Developer at Yahoo!), Bradley Greenwood (Lead Software Engineer/Open Source Software Evangelist at Yahoo!), Janice Fraser (CEO of Adaptive Path), Guido van Rossum (Founder of the Python project and Google employee), Larry M. Augustin (Founder and CEO of VA Linux), Anders Tjernlund (Vice President of Support Services at SpikeSource), and Brian Behlendorf (Co-Founder of the Apache Foundation)[26].

---

[23] Drupal, "DrupalCon Portland 2005: Drupal Foundation meeting," drupal.org/node/28338

[24] Drupal, "DrupalCon Portland 2005: Drupal Foundation meeting," drupal.org/node/28338

[25] Drupal, "Dries and Karlijn married," drupal.org/node/55814

[26] Various. http://buytaert.net/drupal-road-trip-san-francisco, www.adaptivepath.com/about, www.linkedin.com/in/jeffreyveen/, www.linkedin.com/in/chanelwheeler, younoodle.com/people/bradley_greenwood

These discussions provided the starting point for months of intensive research by Dries Buytaert, Dries Knapen, and Steven Wittens. None of these individuals had any previous expertise in the field of international tax law, but (in classic open source fashion) they spent hours soliciting input from those who did. By September 2006, they had produced a draft of the statutes and by-laws of what would become the Drupal Association.

But wait, aren't we talking about a foundation? What's this association?

As a result of their research, one of the decisions that Dries Buytaert, Dries Knapen, and Steven Wittens made was to incorporate the Association in Belgium, rather than in the United States. Belgian law differentiates between an Association and a Foundation, and according to the Drupal Association FAQ, the most significant differences between the two are:

- An Association is incorporated by several individuals, who agreed upon the goals of the Association after voting and discussion, whereas a Foundation can be incorporated by one person (or a small number of people)

- When incorporated, the founders must bring in initial assets (funds) in a Foundation. This is not the case for an Association

- An Association has members. A Foundation can't have members, only a Board of Directors...In other words, an Association allows for a far more democratic operating mode than a Foundation....[and] therefore reflects the way a real (or online) community of people works to a much higher extent than a Foundation.[27]

After some review and revisions of the draft by members of a mailing list created for this purpose, Dries used the venue of DrupalCon Brussels 2006 to publicly announce what had been accomplished.[28] Attendees of the session provided feedback, and the Association mailing list grew. In November, Dries Buytaert, Dries Knapen, and Steven Wittens selected the first round of Permanent Members from the individuals who had submitted their candidacies through this mailing list, which was the first step in establishing the membership of the Association.[29] On December 7, 2006, The Drupal Association's statutes were legally recognized by the Belgian courts,[30] and on February 26, 2007, the formal announcement of the Association was posted on drupal.org and association.drupal.org.[31]

So what did those statutes contain? After years of discussion, months of research, weeks of intensive work, and a constant flow of input from the community, what did three tech-geeks with little to no experience writing legal documents manage to come up with?

In short, they managed to come up with a structure that ensured that control of Drupal would always be in the hands of those who work to create it, and that those same individuals would not have their time and energies diverted from improving the project to carrying the burden of administrative duties.

As the Association is very careful to make clear, **"The Drupal Association has no say in either the planning or development of the Drupal open source project itself.** The Drupal Association could, however, do any of the following:

---

[27] Drupal, FAQ, association.drupal.org/about/faq

[28] Google video, DrupalCon, 2006. video.google.com/videoplay?docid=7038940559530825104

[29] Drupal, FAQ, association.drupal.org/about/faq

[30] Drupal, "Announcing: The Drupal Association," association.drupal.org/node/71

[31] Drupal, various announcements, drupal.org/node/122835, association.drupal.org/node/71, association.drupal.org/node/87

- Accept donations and grants.

- Organize and/or sponsor Drupal events, and represent the Drupal project at events.

- Engage in partnerships with other organizations.

- Acquire and manage infrastructure in support of the Drupal project.

- Support development by awarding grants or paying wages.

- Write and publish press releases and promotional materials."[32]

The body of members who vote on these issues (Permanent Members, who together make up the General Assembly) are differentiated from the body of members who pay dues in support of the Association (Admitted Members), ensuring that an inability to afford membership dues does not make one ineligible to take part in the decision-making process.

The statutes and bylaws also clearly define and restrict the role that corporations, companies, and other "legal persons" are allowed to play in the Association. While corporations and companies may purchase memberships and so become Admitted Members, they are explicitly barred from having voting rights in the Association's decision-making body, the General Assembly. If, however, they have the recommendation of a member of the General Assembly, a corporation or other legal person can become an Advisory Member. While Advisory Members aren't allowed to vote, they are allowed to attend meetings of the General Assembly and...well...advise.[33]

This setup allows business entities in the community to stay informed of the issues being discussed by the Association, and for the voting members of General Assembly to receive informed input from those business entities, without the possibility of a commercial interest controlling the award of Association contracts, grants, or wages. Additionally, the Board of Directors is given the right to deny admission to any entity applying for Admitted Membership "if in the judgment of the Board of Directors there is evidence that the actions, ideas/views/beliefs, and/or motivation of the new member applicant are adverse to the Association's interests,"[34] and at any time, "an Admitted Member can have his/her membership terminated by simple resolution of the Board of Directors."[35]

For Permanent Members, the process of admission (and termination) is more democratically arranged. To become a Permanent Member, an individual must be recommended by someone who is already a Permanent Member. Once the individual has their recommendation, they then send an application to the President of the Board. The General Assembly votes on whether or not to admit the applicant; if two-thirds of the Assembly agree, the individual is accepted as a Permanent Member. As the name suggests, there are no terms for Permanent Members ("Permanent membership has an unlimited duration.") but Permanent membership can be revoked by a two-thirds majority vote of the General Assembly.[36]

---

[32] Drupal, About page, association.drupal.org/about/introduction

[33] Drupal Association Statutes, 1.3.1 Article 10, association.drupal.org/system/files/statutes-en.pdf

[34] Drupal Association Internal regulations 1.2.3 Article 4, association.drupal.org/system/files/internal-regulations-en.pdf

[35] Drupal Association Statutes 1.2.4 Article 8, Section 3, association.drupal.org/system/files/statutes-en.pdf

[36] Drupal Association Statutes 1.2.3, Article 7, Section 3 & Section 2 association.drupal.org/system/files/statutes-en.pdf

> ### 1.2.3. Article 4: Admission and Duties
>
> Following are the factors that come into play when establishing the conditions for admission of members.
> - Permanent Members shall be judged on the contributions they make to the Drupal project and on their role within the Drupal community. A Permanent Member shall serve as an Ambassador of the Drupal community and shall make decisions in the sole interest of the Association and thus with the best interests of the community in mind.

Figure 35–5. Drupal Association Internal Regulations ➤ Membership ➤ Admission and Duties

The General Assembly also votes (by open ballot) on which of their number gets elected to the Board of Directors. Any Permanent Member seeking a position on the Board must submit an application to the President listing their motivations and proposed contributions. If the candidate receives approval in a two-thirds majority vote of the General Assembly, they are then officially a Director, though it is the rest of the Board—not the General Assembly—that votes to determine which Director fills which office. In other words, the Assembly cannot vote a President into office, but only someone that the Assembly has approved has a chance of becoming President of the Association.[37]

The Story Continues

As stated at the beginning, the history of Drupal is much more than covered here. Among other things it includes the commercial growth of Drupal, the evolution of Drupal as enterprise-level software, and the development of Drupal 7 implicit in this book. Drupal is an absurdly chaotic system that produces bizarrely functional results...just like nature. Yet it is not completely random; the events recounted in this chapter suggest that key actions affecting Drupal's ecosystem have helped the success the Drupal community has enjoyed. Moreover, it is evident that this growing software project remains open to having the course and breadth of its history altered—perhaps by another typo or server crash, perhaps by you.

Note Discussion, updates, and related material for this chapter can be found at dgd7.org/history.

---

[37] Drupal Association Statutes 1.4.2 Article 18 & 1.4.3 Article 19, association.drupal.org/system/files/statutes-en.pdf

CHAPTER 36

■ ■ ■

Now You're in Business: Making a Living with Drupal

by Allie Micka

You're ready to strike out on your own and become the next Drupal rockstar! There's plenty of work out there for experienced Drupal developers, and this book has armed you with the technical foundation you need to get started. To make a living, you just need to find people who are willing to pay you to do some work. Then you do that work and you get paid. It really is that simple!

Yet many new Drupal developers find themselves struggling with miscalculations and feel unprepared when things get complicated. For the first few projects, many Drupal developers feel that they are barely earning enough to hang on, while their clients or managers are increasingly disappointed that the promise of a Drupal web site just isn't panning out.

We want to prevent this, which means we want to plan carefully, involve everyone who should be part of the process, and work together to make each project the next Drupal success story. As you work with Drupal's strengths and leverage the community, you might even find yourself working as a contributing member of Drupal itself.

Building a Drupal Site: New Rules for New Technologies

Drupal introduces a lot of functionality right out of the box and allows an experienced administrator to accomplish a lot with minimal effort. This power and flexibility are often misinterpreted as "Drupal will do everything I need without any effort at all." Perhaps it sounds silly to put it that way, but we're all capable of falling into the trap of assuming too much. And when inflated expectations collide with a developer's inexperience, the results can be disastrous.

By contrast, a successful Drupal project is a collaboration between clients and developers that lets everyone focus on their strengths. By recognizing this collaboration and planning to work together on common goals, an experienced Drupal developer really *can* do a lot with a little and build a solution that works well for many years to come.

"I Hate Drupal:" Things That Can Go Wrong

It takes a lot of character to figure out what you need to learn and apply yourself to figuring it out. My day job involves helping developers and site owners become self-sufficient Drupal users. Many of our clients are just getting started and want to start on the right foot, while others are ramping up their skills for challenging new tasks. Unfortunately, we also encounter many Drupalers who open the conversation with, "I hate Drupal."

We hear this sentiment from both developers and site owners who feel they have a Drupal mess on their hands. It's an over-budget, overdue, overwrought enigma that just doesn't do what it's told. There are common themes to this disappointment, such as:

- Drupal is complicated

- A Drupal site is expensive to upgrade and maintain

- I can't find out where to get support

- Drupal developers are expensive

- My developer vanished!

The frustrating situations that developers and clients encounter stem from applying old assumptions to a new technology. They find themselves working against Drupal rather than leveraging its strengths. Sometimes it's just too much and an under-experienced developer, confronted with a client whose expectations are set high, switches into an avoidance mode and bugs out.

Let's try and avoid that!

Understanding Drupal

It's easier to harness Drupal's power when you approach a Drupal project with a clear understanding of what it provides out of the box and what's required to build upon it. The first step to sidestepping a problem project is developing this understanding so that you can see the warning signs when a client is making some dangerous assumptions.

Drupal and "Done"

If you were to build a fence around your yard, your first step would include taking measurements and selecting the material. You can figure out how long the installation will take based on the first few sections or, better yet, a professional fence installer can provide a more accurate estimate based on how long it takes take to dig the required number of posts and complete the project. The more experience your professional has, the more deftly they can avoid obstacles such as rocky patches of ground or gas lines. The end result will probably match what you pictured in your head before you began.

Historically, software and web development could be predicted by similar mechanisms. Starting with an empty field, a list of requirements presents a series of sections to complete. You select your materials—or programming language—and begin the process of writing function after function, file after file, and page after page until the functionality matches the requirements. It's certainly predictable to work this way, but it can also be much more costly and repetitive, and the end product will not change as new technologies become available.

Over the years, developers have created programming libraries, methodologies, and frameworks that aim to reduce repetition. Drupal can be considered a framework, and one of its goals is to reduce coding repetition to zero. Extend the fencing analogy to a Drupal project, and it might look like something out of a futuristic show like the Jetsons (let's pretend they had yards to fence in!). With the push of a button, a magical robotic fence unfolds before your very eyes, and in just a few seconds you're done! Or are you?

What Does "Done" Mean?

Drupal lets you point-and-click your way to new functionality. And because so many people use and support Drupal, there's a good chance that it's community-tested and will work well for your needs.

However, the functionality that exists may not match the specific image that a client pictures in his head. For example, when the client says, "I would like a forum on my web site," he has a picture in his head of a forum he has used on a forum-centric web site. He is imagining e-mail notifications, quality ratings on each comment, and little animated smiley faces that automatically appear when you type ":)".

His developer hears, "I would like a forum on my web site," and she remembers that Drupal includes a forum module right in its core distribution. Since there's no need to research or download any modules, she estimates that adding a forum to the web site will take just one hour. But the client is deeply disappointed when he sees the result of this effort. "Where are my smilies?" he cries!

While it's still possible to deliver something that matches the client's expectations, it will take *much* longer than the budgeted hour and will require many more modules, configuration changes, or custom theming. Someone must pay for this time. Perhaps the developer will end up working for minimum wage on a fixed bid, or maybe the client will cover the changes and his budget expectations are shattered. The process of making things right is founded on disillusionment, and everyone begins thinking that Drupal isn't all that it's cracked up to be.

What Does "Done" Look Like?

Imagine what might happen if you carried a photograph of your favorite dish into a well-regarded restaurant, insisting that the chef prepare something that looks exactly like the picture. By rejecting the chef's culinary expertise you're adding unnecessary complexity and you'll probably end up with an inferior meal. This is what happens when design expectations are set by a graphic artist or business analyst who is not experienced with Drupal. The client may fall in love with mockups that present a specific aspect of a design, layout, or workflow that is different from what Drupal provides out of the box. The result of this is can be a costly customization project.

Does this mean that Drupal is generic, boring, or inflexible? Not at all! It's always possible to season to taste by re-theming or restructuring the out-of-the-box functionality to meet your goals. However, you can sink a lot of time and money into chasing a specific mental picture when your goals might be addressed just as well—if not better—by leveraging what's already available and then building on top of it.

Drupal will never be as predictable as building something from scratch, but that's a good thing. You can leverage the experience and track record of thousands of people who are working on goals that are in common with yours, and you can profit from ideas you would never have thought of on your own.

Content Needs Managing

It was easy to draw a line between "webmaster" and "client" when a web site could be approached as a compartmentalized work effort. We could collect the content in various documents and files, put it up on the site, design some appealing graphics, and get the go-ahead from the client when it's ready to launch. A client's role was relegated to providing documents and confirming that they look right.

Drupal's biggest strength is that it allows the client to become a contributing editor, content manager, or even a site administrator, limited only by his time and inclination to become acquainted with the details. With these new job titles come new skills and responsibilities that kick in well before the site goes live. If these roles are important after launch, then the people filling these roles are important during the development cycle. That's a pretty big change from the old way of doing things.

Control over a site is a good thing, because it means current content and the autonomy to make changes without hiring a developer. And while Drupal gets easier and easier with each new release, you can't expect to have total control without learning at least a little bit. Unfortunately, developers often forget to acknowledge the learning curve of their clients. They don't always account for the time it takes to develop a foundation of knowledge and don't include the post-launch support necessary to keep things running smoothly. This can leave a client feeling left in the dark, resenting Drupal rather than embracing their newfound powers.

"Now I'm Hiring Rock Stars?"

We often hear that Drupal takes a "building block" approach to site building. An experienced Drupal developer can point and click her way to victory, developing complex business applications without opening a text editor. This has obvious benefits: nearly anyone can advance to this skill level, including people who have an intimate understanding of a particular field or business process.

The big secret is knowing where to point and what to click on. Which modules should be downloaded? When *should* you open a text editor? You can't just turn on a module that works as advertised; you're often tasked with weaving together a whole bundle of modules just to perform one simple task. This idea is foreign and intimidating to new users, including new developers who make a lot of rookie mistakes and create some expensive Drupal messes.

Experienced Drupalers can get expensive, but that's usually because they're offsetting a lot of time spent sharing best practices and improving Drupal itself. I have seen countless projects where a single well-trained Drupal developer was able to develop an application in a matter of weeks, replacing an existing solution that cost millions of dollars to build.

This applies to small and large projects alike. Consulting with a trusty Drupal guide, if only for a few hours, can prevent a lot of drama while helping you see possibilities you couldn't have imagined. Fortunately, it's getting easier to prosper from sage advice. With more books, more training materials, and a variety of "prepackaged knowledge" in the form of distributions, it's even easier to find your way.

Drupal Does Things You Don't Care About

When you're under deadline it's incredibly easy to lose sight of the fact that in most cases, you're going to be responsible for the care and feeding of the project for a long time. After adding up the perceptions that Drupal is difficult to grok, expensive to customize, and requires special training to operate, many developers and site managers run for their do-it-yourself frameworks and custom solutions.

With that in mind, the fact that the Drupal community is working to add more bizarre-sounding technologies to the mix, perhaps it sounds like more of a liability than a boon. But all technologies were bizarre-sounding before they became important. By the time RSS became an important means of sharing content, Drupal sites had been providing RSS feeds for years. And with well-structured content and nice-looking URLs, Drupal was SEO before SEO was cool. Clear separation between form and content has made it easy and affordable for many Drupal sites to work on phone technologies. When the next important web technology comes to the forefront, do you want to be using it or playing catch-up?

Building on Drupal

Most Drupal mishaps are based on the fact that some of Drupal's biggest strengths are actually weaknesses. As developers, we're responsible for the attitude that our clients develop, so it's important to nurture a positive and forward-thinking attitude. Throughout each project, it helps to set expectations correctly by focusing on the short-term goals, long-term results, and accounting for the needs of everyone involved along the way.

Start with Goals

The biggest mistake any developer or client can make is in making assumptions about what's possible without enough advance planning or research. Behind every "Drupal mess" is a project where the costs, features, and timeline was established without a clear recognition of the actual steps involved. Avoiding this is a matter of deferring your discussion on technologies, timelines, and tactics until you have taken the opportunity to sit down and have a goal-setting session.

The primary purpose of a goal-setting discussion is to determine what constitutes success. Try to stay away from descriptions of functionality, feature lists, or comparisons with existing sites. Instead, stick to the goals of the stakeholders for the site.

Goals are:

- Clear and descriptive phrases like extend our readership, increases sales, lower our production costs, or even launch in time for the holiday season

- Not functional descriptions such as has a forum

- Measurable through use of statistics, sales numbers, or by other trackable mechanisms

- In priority order. Costs, timelines, and features can be goals, but you should identify the priorities of each, and recognize that you can't always have everything

Before deciding on the time, scope, and cost trifecta, a developer takes the client's stated goals and the available resources to produce a doable plan. It's important to include the developer at the goal-setting phase, not after all of the tactical decisions are made. Because Drupal brings a lot of tools to the table, an experienced Drupal guide can match technology choices with the stated goals. This is much more cost effective than trying to force-fit a requirement into a Drupal site. Best of all, the developer can suggest solutions that *sound* difficult and expensive but are actually quite simple for Drupal.

Acknowledge and Support Different Participants

Adding a blog to a site is a small technical feat, but generating regular and insightful blog posts can be a full-time job. If your bloggers encounter barriers or feel that they don't have adequate training and support, they may not feel confident to post new content. If fostering community was the goal you identified during your planning phase, a good Drupal execution may fail to satisfy that goal.

By contrast, the more an author or site owner understands Drupal, the more he can contribute ideas or articulate his needs in a way that works well for Drupal. Functioning is a liaison between people and technology; it's your job to help people who can contribute content understand where they fit in. Wherever possible, these people should be part of the planning, development, and post-launch strategy:

- Provide some functional demonstrations with real-world projects similar to your client's site, allowing participants to see how their needs might be translated to Drupal concepts.

- As part of the goal-setting process, consider the input of everyone who may interact with the end result.

- Create a plan that reflects the time and willingness of all participants to work on the project.

- Avoid bottlenecks by ensuring that everyone who needs to contribute can set aside the time and resources required for ongoing participation.

- If appropriate, consider including participants during the implementation process. For example, have a content manager help create new sections as part of an import process, or have content authors practice editing posts before launch.

What if this is overkill? The key to success is not making people take a class they don't want to be in, it's understanding what human resources are available and how those resources can be applied to project goals. It's just as valuable to know that there's limited time or willingness to participate in discussions, training, and ongoing content management, and there's nothing wrong with scaling back their involvement as long as that's not in conflict with stated goals.

Make Sustainable Choices

Along the way we've learned that hacking core is bad and that supporting modules with patches and feedback is good. Why spend the extra time? Because sticking to common best practices ensures that the site will work without surprises and that it can be supported by the developer, or any other qualified Drupal developer, for a long time to come.

Custom code and workarounds, while often necessary for quick delivery, add to costs and ultimately draw attention to the fact that the original developer just didn't know how to complete the project without compromising ongoing maintenance. This is partly why people blame Drupal for being inflexible and expensive to maintain.

Assuming that you are approaching this from a goal-oriented perspective, how do your technology choices affect the stated goals of the project? Perhaps a quick hack can help you launch in time for the holiday season but stymies a Drupal 8 upgrade or raises the cost of maintaining the site in the long run. It's not always the wrong choice to implement that hack! But by asking your client whether it's OK to trade short-term work for long-term return on investment, you're allowing them to help decide which is the most important.

However, before trading ongoing sustainability for short-term results, the first step is to make sure that there really is no better way. Before engaging in hackery, ask via IRC, post a forum question on drupal.org, research what you can by searching for blog posts, or consult with someone who may have more experience in the situation.

There is no reason not to avail ourselves of the abundant resources offered by the Drupal community. Learning how others do things and sharing what we learn along the way is something that helps us all do our jobs better. But bad judgment based on lack of research is useful to nobody.

Understand the Economy of Community

When a feature is missing from a module or Drupal itself, it's possible for *anyone* to support the addition of that feature. This often means paying the module maintainer to add it, which is great for Drupal and helps to guarantee that it's done on your timeline. If that's not possible, you can also make a lot of progress by providing clear documentation of your request on drupal.org, answering questions in the issue queue and testing patches to free up the maintainer's time, or contributing code of your own.

This is what makes Drupal amazing, as each small contribution affects an increasingly large group of users. If a module has 100 users, then each fix, feature, or piece of documentation can immediately impact 100 people, and, perhaps, make the module useful to 100 more. The next round of improvements is now exposed to 200 people, further expanding the pool of potential contributors. Drupal is free to download yet extremely powerful because each small effort is expanded exponentially.

Forgetting that these possibilities exist makes it seem that certain things are just broken or missing without any recourse. Browsing the issue queues throughout Drupal.org, it's common to find questions like, "When will this be ready?" or "Why won't someone fix this problem?" Ask yourself how you might respond to demands that you work on someone else's goals and schedule, without any pay, and you realize that complaining is a pretty weak mechanism for getting things done.

Whether you're expecting to use Drupal to get paid for delivering a project, or planning to rely on a Drupal site to lower costs or increase revenue, it's a cost-effective investment to support its developers and contribute to a long and healthy future.

Consider Long-term Support and Growth

As cliché as it sounds, a Drupal project launch is not the end of a development project, it's the beginning of a thriving online resource. Depending on the site's goals, there may be an active community of users to nurture, features to add, and content managers providing new information and resources. This will fail if nobody knows how to nurture a community, add a feature, or provide new resources.

To a developer who lives and breathes Drupal each day, it's a disappointing surprise when the client doesn't just pick the site up and run with it. Including an informal training session as part of the site delivery will help by making the client feel more at home and give them a safe place to ask "dumb" questions. Depending on the skills and requirements of the site contributors, a training session may last a few hours, or even a week or more. Also make sure that you've made arrangements for handling questions and additional support as new questions arise.

Ensuring Your Success

Understanding the needs of a Drupal project and approaching it from a goal-oriented perspective are the first steps toward becoming a happy Drupaler, no matter what you choose to do with it. There's nothing worse than getting caught in a project that is over-budget, over time, or impossible to deliver. Preventing this means setting aside the resources you need to plan carefully and making sure you can get help when you need it.

If you've gotten involved in the local or online Drupal community, you're already halfway there. Approaching each project with the time, thoughtful consideration, and respect for those who have gone before you will help ensure that you're moving your projects, your career, and possibly even Drupal itself forward.

Create a Process

As a Drupal professional, each project you work on builds on your expertise in harnessing Drupal's flexibility, community support, and growth for ongoing success. Documenting your findings as a well-defined process provides a repeatable plan of action that you can use to help others find their way as you introduce them to the new mindset.

Some developers define a very rigid process. Before they begin, they develop an immutable feature list and identify specific costs, check-off dates, and milestones. Before a project begins, the client has a clear understanding of exactly what will be included in the project, what it might look like, and how much it will cost. This works well for small projects because it's predictable for everyone and easier for the client to understand and buy into.

Other developers prefer a more agile process where milestones and check-in meetings are established, and the option to make changes based on new findings is always available. This process works well when there are many participants or other variables that make it difficult to predict the outcome. It's also possible to deliver a product that's better than what was imagined at the beginning. This requires a willingness to trade a clear up-front picture for the best possible outcome.

The specifics of your own process are based on how you work best, the nature of your projects, client expectations, and epiphanies you've had during your own trial and error. It doesn't matter how structured or how loose your process is as long as everyone has a clear understanding of expectations—and those expectations are being met.

It's easy to forget how confusing Drupal is when you're just starting out, but a documented process can help clients and collaborators feel like they're on solid ground, engaged in the project, and working with a clear understanding of what's next. Tips for making this work include:

- *Start and end with project goals:* Include a goal-oriented planning session at the beginning of the project, and schedule check-ins throughout the project to make sure those goals are reflected. It's also OK to re-prioritize goals—for example, to defer the launch date for a killer feature—as long as everyone agrees on the new parameters.

- *Keep your clients involved:* This is deceptively challenging because it's so easy to assume that clients know what you're talking about. Make sure there are regular meetings or check-in sessions, and, if the project is large enough, dedicate a project manager to the task of organizing these meetings. Most importantly, ensure that everyone has the proper foundation of knowledge to feel that they can make informed decisions or participate as appropriate.

- *Make sustainable choices:* When a client requests features or changes, it's easy to forget what they really *need* in the interest of chasing what they're *asking for.* If they want to make a change that will make it hard to maintain in the future, go back to the stated goals and make sure you're in alignment. If not, communicate accordingly.

- *Build in some community involvement:* If you require changes or "hacks," be sure to file issues on drupal.org so that others may benefit from your findings, and any improvements you make can find their way back into the tools. This raises your Drupal karma and supports ongoing sustainability for tools you depend on.

- *Include a post-launch plan:* If you don't want to be on the hook for ongoing support and training, make sure you're working with someone who can take on this role. If you do plan on sticking around, create a retainer agreement or maintenance plan. Think about how new technologies can benefit their goals, and consider creating a long-term upgrade strategy. Your client will appreciate the forward-thinking attitude.

Adapt and improve as you go. After each project is complete, take some time to make an honest assessment of what worked well and what could be improved next time. Involve your clients if that's appropriate, and include everyone who worked on developing the project.

Budget Your Time

Many full-time Drupal contractors and development firms find themselves raising their rates significantly after their first few Drupal projects. This doesn't mean that they're raking in cash, it means they're supporting an ongoing commitment to best practices, sustainable choices, and community participation that ensures that they're staying on the right track. As we've learned thus far, this can save a lot of client money and time, so it's actually a good investment.

This chapter also highlights other time and planning variables, such as communicating what "done" means, working with the community, and coordinating with other participants on the project. The takeaway is that you should leave plenty of room in your development schedule to "measure twice, cut once" and at least doubling the amount of time you predict for a given task.

Include learning time or community involvement time in the estimate, either by setting an hourly rate that allows you to spend less than 40 hours per week on client work or by doubling the time estimates to include these activities directly.

Leverage Existing Resources

In addition to getting your foot in the door, building ties in the Drupal community provides you with a safe environment to ask questions, see how others are doing things, and get help if you need it. There are some additional resources that you can look to when you need an extra hand.

Install Profiles and Distributions

Drupal distributions are a way to hit the ground running with common functionality that lets your new site benefit from the research and hard work of people who already understand the needs of a certain niche audience. To the extent that a distribution is well-supported, its users can also benefit from a user community of like minds, a roadmap for the future, and support resources that pertain specifically to that configuration.

   If an install profile is a good fit for the goals of your project, it may be possible to provide something better than expected at a lower cost. You can visit http://drupal.org/project/installation+profiles to begin the process of looking for a profile.

A Little Help from Your Friends

It's good to have an idea of who you can turn to when things get tricky, so keep some resources in mind from the beginning. It's often a good idea to keep some experienced developers in mind so that you can consult with them to weigh in on different architecture strategies, recommend modules, or help you avoid potential pitfalls.

   Another good source for paid support is in fostering a relationship with the maintainers of the modules or solutions you rely on. Who better to tell you the costs of adding a feature to a module than that module's author? Supporting the module maintainer also helps to secure the ongoing sustainability of the solution, which means it's more likely to be supported when you are upgrading to Drupal 8 and beyond.

   Working with an experienced developer or strategist may mean budgeting a higher rate for a small portion of the project, but it is usually well worth it. An hour's worth of insight could save thousands of dollars in workarounds and restructuring.

Building Your Drupal Career

If the rules for planning, developing, and supporting a Drupal site have changed, it's no surprise that a Drupal developer's career reflects a new approach. I have painted a picture of how well-managed Drupal projects are structured, highlighting the many roles you might fill throughout the planning, execution, community participation, and ongoing support of a Drupal project.

   A successful developer doesn't need to wear every hat, but she does need to know which roles she can excel at and when to rely on others. This means that you have the freedom to choose to do what makes you happiest and focus on that. It also means that you should be aware that you may need to fill in the gaps from time to time.

Finding Your Place

The first thing is to figure out what "making a living" would look like. If you were happy and successful beyond your wildest dreams, what would you be doing with your time in Drupal? There's a place for writers, marketers, business analysts, designers, activists, architects, coders, and trainers. Most Drupal sites, even the smallest ones, are more successful when these personalities are involved in both development and long-term maintenance.

Figuring out which roles you want to occupy will help inform your processes and identify where you might seek help and participation. For example:

- If you have a good understanding of business processes or the nuances of a specific industry, you might make a great analyst. Your job would involve developing the goals of a project and making sure that Drupal fits the bill.

- If you're great at communicating technical concepts, well-organized, and able to keep people motivated, the project manager job title may be in your future. You can help rally the project participants and make sure that everyone has what they need to keep moving ahead.

- If your strength is as a designer, you will want to consider looking for some advanced support or partnership resources with someone who is more technical. This will help you avoid the pitfalls of thinking that something will be easy and then getting caught in a project over your head.

- Similarly, approaching your projects from a more technical background may hinder your capacity to find and work with clients who require more "flair." If you find a designer you can trust, you can throw yourself into learning as much as you can about the inner workings of Drupal.

- If you've got good people skills and want to provide ongoing support, you can consider becoming a trainer or support provider.

It's also smart to think about the size of projects and the team you'd like to work with. A single Drupal expert can fill every role and launch an impressive site in no time at all. Other projects are on behalf of large organizations with many participants and resources of their own, where each function is managed by an entire department.

If you're the type of person who wants to have a lot of influence over a project, you might be happiest as an independent contractor or as part of a small team or company. If you thrive on large projects with a lot of complexity, you might find yourself fitting in as part of a larger Drupal team.

Getting Yourself Out There

Whether you're striking out on your own, on a job hunt, or staying put and ordering "Drupal rockstar" business cards, you're never on your own. The first order of business is to get involved in the community so that you have a stable foundation. You'll immediately benefit from the sage advice of people who have been there before you, and you'll begin to form a network of people you can turn to before things get challenging.

Perhaps the most important aspect of all is that you'll be putting yourself in front of potential collaborators and employers. Anyone who appreciates the successful outcome of a sustainable, community-oriented development process will be impressed that you're actively contributing to the Drupal ecosystem.

User Groups and Local Communities

Hopefully by now, you've already become part of the community at drupal.org. This is an important way to build your credibility while getting what you need from the community. If you want more hands-on assistance, participating in user groups are a good way to learn from people who want to share a discovery that might help you, or to impress people (and find work) when you have expertise of your own. In addition to training and documentation, user groups are where we all learn about the best practices you're always hearing about. You can find a local user group for your area by visiting groups.drupal.org and searching for your location or interest.

Community involvement is what you make it. If you'd like to get something different out of a group or community, consider what you can do to improve the resources:

- If the topics are too basic or not covering what you want to learn, suggest meeting topics, sprints, or additional learning groups that fit your needs better. You'll be sure to attract some like-minded people.

- If you prefer a different format for meetings, suggest an alternative format. In Minnesota, we have three monthly meetings for Drupalers: a general meeting, one for e-commerce topics, and a social happy hour at a local bar. Each of these is organized by a different person, and each attracts a different audience.

- Suggest the group to friends, associates, and other people who might not already know about it. Not everyone will be interested, but it's good to attract fresh faces and fun to hang out with people you already like.

In all cases, keep your communication open and positive and build on the existing resources. The goal should be to enhance the local community so that it better meets your needs, while still acknowledging the effort that others have invested.

Conferences and Camps

DrupalCon is very different from a technical conference where each presentation is a sales pitch from a product representative at a big company. Instead, each session you attend at DrupalCon is presented by the author of a module you depend on, a leader of the community you participate in, or a company who is helping Drupal thrive. This is an important way to keep your finger on the pulse of the Drupal community while you learn about new modules and solutions, find out what's under the hood of big Drupal sites, optimize your business, and meet new friends and collaborators. In short, it's extremely valuable to attend a conference and valuable for clients to know that you're keeping up with technology so they don't have to.

Meanwhile, the discussions and sprints that take place at DrupalCon define the ongoing direction of Drupal itself, and each attendee can choose whether to watch, learn, or get involved in helping to make positive changes to Drupal and its community. You might attend DrupalCon as a spectator, believing that you have nothing to contribute. All of a sudden, you might find yourself acting on your opinions of how something could be done better. This transition, from spectator to contributor, is how Drupal gets built.

Travel time and conference fees are often prohibitive, but fear not! There's a growing movement of local "camps" that also offer speakers, working groups, and hands-on learning opportunities. But camps are smaller and local to a particular region. Participating in a camp near your own hometown is a great way to stay in the loop, and you can often get information that's even more relevant or in-depth than what's at DrupalCon. Because Drupal is everywhere, you might also have some important module developers in attendance at a local camp.

"Think Drupal, Act Locally"

Don't forget what Drupal is for in the first place: Connecting people with a message with tools to put that message online. It's just as important to find a community that surrounds your interests beyond Drupal. For example, communities surrounding:

- Hobbies such as politics, church groups, sporting or outdoors groups, or just about any interest that strikes your fancy.

- Industry or professional focus where you've already got passion or experience. This may include non-profit causes, specific industries such as real estate or the arts, or any other professional field.

- Specific technologies that pertain to your specialty, such as graphics, social networking, database and programming technologies, ecommerce, semantic web, or content writing.

- Communities that can directly help your business, such as groups for professionals, unions, co-working facilities, or professional development.

You can find like-minded communities for just about any topic. It's fun to think about how you might apply Drupal solutions to real-world needs while expanding your professional or personal development. Best of all, you'll probably shine as the resident Drupal expert! It's a great way to build confidence and may even lead to your dream job of working with Drupal *and* a cause that's close to your heart.

It's tempting to get yourself over-committed by doing work on a volunteer basis for experience. Remember to treat every project with the same consideration for goal-oriented planning, ongoing involvement, and long-term thinking, *especially* an unpaid project that can fall off the radar because you can't sustainably provide the time. Everything you learn about planning, expectations, sustainability, and ongoing involvement is doubly true for volunteer sites.

Out on Your Own: Building a Drupal Business

Perhaps you want to parlay your Drupal chops into a career by striking out on your own and starting a Drupal business, or you may be introducing a Drupal specialty to your existing business. After finding your niche, you'll want to build a team that can help you keep things running smoothly for you and your clients.

When starting out with small projects, it may seem silly to consider the notion of building a "team" to handle the development and long-term support. One person can often handle every role in a smaller project. But it's crucial to consider that launching the site is not the end of the project but the beginning of an online Drupal presence. It will always be necessary to consider:

- Who will upgrade the site by adding new functionality or by upgrading the site to a new version?

- Who will provide content administration and long-term content control?

- Who will make sure that the content administrators have the support and training they need?

It's good to think about all of this before you even begin your first Drupal project. New Drupalers are often surprised when they can't just deliver on a project and effortlessly move onto the next paying gig. If long-term support is not in your future, consider finding someone to partner with so that you can sustainably take the load off yourself without leaving your clients hanging.

Building a Drupal Career

With so much growth and the need to specialize, now is a great time to be in the Drupal job market. After figuring out where your interests lie, you might begin finding a new Drupal job or working more Drupal into your current job responsibilities.

If you're working as one of a few Drupal developers on your company's staff, many of your job demands are the same as those of an independent contractor. You don't have to take on all of the responsibilities associated with running a business, but as the onsite Drupal guru, you may find yourself answering for the ways that Drupal does things differently. This puts you in the role of resetting assumptions, establishing goals, creating a plan, and involving people throughout the process. Make sure that you've got the time, resources, and support of your company to make informed and sustainable choices. Doing things correctly and in a way that works well for the long haul can help make you an office hero.

Alternatively, you might be looking at working as a small part of a large Drupal team, perhaps as part of a development and consulting team. Some of these companies prioritize sustainability, community, and good process, while others just want to crank out a lot of work. Part of your decision to work there will be based on whether they want to work the way you want to work, so be sure to ask about their process and decide where you fit in.

Building Drupal: Making a Living as a Contributor

The more we work with Drupal, the more we find ways that it could be better. Each new user brings a new perspective, a breadth of experience, and a new approach to solving problems they encounter along the way. The difference between a Drupal consumer and a Drupal contributor is nothing more than a willingness to share these insights, strategies, and solutions with the community at large. Sometimes a worthwhile contribution is nothing more than an insightful comment at a user group meeting. Sometimes it's a substantial rewrite to a key part of Drupal. Large or small, each change is a permanent thread in the fabric of Drupal and its community.

Contributing in this way is a rewarding way to help yourself while helping others. By solving your own problems in a public way, you gain access to new insights from people with common goals. All the while, you're building your reputation, providing ongoing sustainability for your clients, and participating in the process of making Drupal more viable to more people.

As rewarding as it is, the primary reason for *not* contributing in this way is lack of resources. Some developers have found a way to form a business model. The more we can support and identify these models, the better off we'll all be.

Benefits of "Giving Back"

The words "giving back" carry the connotation of altruism and volunteerism. It seems pretty generous to take something you've earned money to build, or could have earned money to build, and just give it away for free. In fact, that's a pretty silly business model: it's not sustainable to "give" something that has value, so referring to it that way disregards a real business case.

Doing What You Need to Do—but Better

Before skipping to the "giving away" part of the equation, think about why you might write a module in the first place. Generally, your motive is to satisfy a specific goal; whether it's performing a task more efficiently, connecting through a social network, increasing the participation of the community, or just staying online while your traffic soars. In short, your goal is not to *give something away*, the goal is to *make something better* for yourself.

Software is uniquely beautiful because once you give it away, you still have it for yourself. You don't usually benefit from hording the results of the effort you've expended to solve your own problem. After all, there's no proprietary benefit to dealing with traffic, but if someone else with the same needs can provide feedback on their own experiences, you can benefit from their insights as much as they can benefit from yours.

Participating in a Dialog

Some broader efforts, such as usability, media handling, contact management, or integrating with remote systems, require a lot of effort. When Drupal handles these things properly, it's a big win that attracts more users and will certainly help expand your business. But accomplishing any of these far-reaching efforts takes a pretty big team, which you may not have at your disposal.

The more you are able to communicate, participate, and drive an initiative that's near to your heart, the more you'll be able to influence the solutions that affect your business the most. Drupal affords every one of its users to take either an active or a passive role in this process. Each person who takes an active role, no matter how small, gets to influence the future of Drupal to suit their own goals.

Community Karma

In a relatively close-knit community like Drupal, it's possible to tell who's contributing and who's merely consuming. If a module maintainer were to follow a link to the user account attached to a support request, what would she find? A series of issue comments that say nothing more than "subscribe" or meaningful comments and helpful patches? Most maintainers respond more quickly to issues from another contributor because of the possibility that they may get further assistance or contributions from that person—or just out of simple respect.

Notoriety

We all have our vanities, and some contributors "give back" for the sole purpose of *being seen* giving back. That works too, and having your name on a well-regarded module is a great way to publicly demonstrate your Drupal skills, while attracting clients who understand the value of supporting a contributing Drupal developer.

Sustainability Counts!

If we all started thinking that "giving back" to Drupal was nothing more than a volunteer effort with no tangible benefit, we would have a difficult time prioritizing it over our jobs, families, and other obligations. It would be bankrupt for everyone to assume that Drupal is about "getting stuff for free" and not advancing our own goals forward by using and supporting a platform that will help us continue to advance our goals in the future.

There's still work to do in this arena, since it's rare for anyone to directly support a maintainer's efforts. We typically prioritize our satisfying our own needs and those of our clients, perpetuate the notion that Drupal and its modules ought to be built, fixed, and supported free of charge, and forget to recognize when applying a small amount of resources might serve a long-term goal.

The danger is creating a dependence on volunteerism. Sometimes that means that the most fruitful developers are those who have a lot of free time. For example, if a student writes a really great module during her free time, it doesn't matter that she did it without any compensation, because she was happy for the learning experience. Because she's capable of writing such an awesome module, a Drupal firm snaps her up after she graduates.

Her new employer probably *wants* her to continue working on the awesome module, but they're tasked with keeping her gainfully employed. As long as nobody is willing to fund them for the module development, they need to keep her working on deliverables for paying gigs. Thus the developer's day job is filled with client work while her free time is divided between Drupal, family, friends, and other hobbies. A crucial module loses the attention of a great developer, and that's a big problem for people who rely on that module.

As a community, it's not practical to forgo functionality provided by this developer's module, and it's impolite to write her angry e-mails insisting that she give up her family time to work on it for us. While there may be 50,000 of us depending on this module, there's currently no mechanism to request the tiny share that we could each contribute directly to sustain development. This will be a problem as long as the majority of Drupal users maintain the expectation that "someone" should fix or update the code completely free of charge.

Potential Business Models

I can paint a pretty bleak picture, but Drupal has managed to thrive over the years. This is because of the sheer leverage afforded by any effort put into Drupal. If one developer or end user invests half of what they might spend on a proprietary solution, they'll benefit significantly more than if they went with that proprietary solution.

Because of this, there are a number of indirect ways to support Drupal and open source, forming the rationale for contributing developers to help push Drupal forward for their own needs and for the rest of us.

Convincing Your Clients of the Value of Contributing

Most Drupal contributors support themselves through client development. In a most ideal scenario, that client is paying directly for the time that the developer spends on contributed code. This is in the client's best interest for all of the reasons listed as benefits of "giving back." Community contributions can make the tools you've built for them work better with less investment than having you write something proprietary.

Take, for example, a web site whose goal is to increase sales. The client pays to build a solution that provides product recommendations whenever a visitor makes a keyword search. If you introduce the idea of releasing this feature as a module, the client may express some concern over "giving away the farm,"—or putting their competitive advantage into the hands of competitors, who may use it against them.

But let's revisit the goals of the site, which are to increase sales, not to become a company that maintains software. If that module is available to others, someone on Drupal.org might suggest a fix that enhances the search algorithm. Another user might uncover and fix a security hole that puts the site's visitors at risk. The original client benefits from each of these improvements, increasing sales and consumer confidence along the way. When it comes time to upgrade to Drupal 8, there's help on developing and testing an upgrade path. Thus, the client can continually advance and gain new sales-improving features with far less effort than carrying the development load in-house.

Contrast this with a one-off module that stays proprietary. Security holes and bugs are brushed under the carpet because nobody will see them anyway, and the client is faced with paying the developer for every change and fix. The functionality is now a barrier to growth because the entire cost of its maintenance is borne by that client.

It's not always easy to make the case for having clients pay you to write open source so that they can give their secrets away, but if you started with a goals-first development process, it's possible to show a savvy client how to leverage Drupal.org to further his needs.

The "Development Plus" Model

Something that "works well enough" for the client is often cheaper than something that can be contributed and supported. In these cases, it's difficult or even senseless to try and contribute code to Drupal.org. However, after participating in several projects, a Drupal developer begins to fantasize about projects that would streamline his process, improve upon her clients' experiences with Drupal, and make it possible to do more with less in overtime. Effectively, this makes the developer the consumer, and she begins contributing code that would "scratch her own itch."

Before the CCK module existed, it was difficult for users, but relatively simple for coders, to add basic fields to an existing content type. For example, adding a subtitle to an article might have taken less than an hour. But this task became repetitive, and developers began to wish for a more automated means of performing that task. Thus, the CCK module was born.

Getting CCK from a neat idea to a viable solution took thousands of hours of development time. Even the best account manger would have a difficult time convincing a client that they should fund a thousand hours of development to allow users to add fields. Thus CCK was developed out of necessity and of developers' shared frustration with performing the same task over and over.

After this investment, CCK became a major factor in Drupal's flexibility and success as a content management system. But nobody would have predicted this, or funded the effort, without a few visionary coders who were willing to invest their time in that solution.

This story could be told many times over, and it is part of the very fabric of the Drupal we know today. In each case, the time spent on contributing to these efforts was volunteered by a developer in her spare time or by a development company that can reap the rewards of long-term improvements to Drupal itself. The takeaway is that we can create a business model by investing our own surplus resources in solutions we believe in, thus making it a more viable resource for ourselves and our future customers.

Develop a Product Offering

Install profiles are a way to begin the process of building a site based on some assumptions about how it will be used or who will be using it. For example, a blog-only install profile allows a blog-only site to get up and running quickly with common configurations for blog posts, comments, and categories.

In theory, it's possible to take this work, package it up, and provide it as a hosted service for blog sites, hosted with this platform. Tread carefully! In a competitive marketplace, the likelihood is that your install profile can be downloaded and installed more cheaply elsewhere.

The product is not the Drupal installation itself but the prepackaged knowledge, common resources, and support model that surrounds it. Approach a specific demographic that you already know well, or find a subject matter expert who already knows that market. Work to identify common needs and develop solutions that serve those needs. That solution may include an install profile or a hosted service, but the real model is probably training, community events, or developing relationships and tools that are useful to each of its participants.

It's challenging work to build a business model that competes with proprietary alternatives, but it is a rewarding way to fund new development while guaranteeing that it is useful to its benefactors.

Direct Funding

The business models described thus far paint a model where we must find indirect ways to cover the time we spend on contributing Drupal, but the most "honest" way to pay for the time we spend on open source solutions is to get paid with the express goal of funding our time working on contributions. This is challenging for a variety of reasons, but it's not impossible.

The best way to do this is to reach out to funders and grant-making organizations. Increasingly, these organizations are seeing the kinds of repetition of resources that frustrate developers. When a foundation provides resources to 100 non-profits and finds out that they've only managed to partially implement 100 copies of the same solution, they begin to realize it's a waste of effort. If they're able to see this pattern, it's possible to appeal to them with a funding proposal that outlines the breadth of impact for a common solution that serves many organizations at a time.

It may also be possible to appeal to a project's user base directly by making them aware of your ability to do work for hire. There's a strong case to be made for paying a module maintainer to fix something in the module itself, which might be equivalent to the cost of a brute-force workaround, which would otherwise need to be re-worked-around hundreds of times once again.

Setting Expectations

After determining your overall contribution goals and determining which business model might be a good fit for your work, you start to flesh out how much time you can actually spend supporting your work. Are you able to dedicate a few hours per day? A few hours per year? Are your choices strictly financial and you'd be able to make time for contribution work if someone could fund it?

It's important to include this information on the project page, by setting the "maintenance status" and providing a small description of your status in a README file, on your user profile, or on a module's description page.

For example, if you worked on a module for a client but have no intention of maintaining it beyond the project's completion, you should set the module's status as "seeking co-maintainer" or another status that indicates your intended level of involvement.

Additionally, if you're available for hire, make sure to include that information on the module's page and ensure that you're crediting anyone who has helped you get the functionality where it is. This is a useful way to garner support while recognizing those who have supported you so far.

Getting Better all the Time

Drupal powers hundreds of thousands of sites and provides thousands of developers with rewarding and productive jobs. And it only gets better: There's a new success story for every well-managed project, which helps other site owners make the jump. And each contribution, small or large, makes it easier for developers to deliver great results with Drupal.

By approaching Drupal with the right mindset, we can meet our goals by equipping the right people to wield control over the right aspects of your project. While tricky at first, Drupal's ongoing progress is attributed to a long history of light bulbs switching on over users' heads as they realize the affect they can have on their own message and online community. Stay with it, plan well, and remember what Drupal is for, and you'll be behind the next Drupal success story.

Every Drupal developer owes her career to its contributors, and every Drupal user has the potential to become the next contributor. By approaching the community with the right mindset, we can contribute to the inertia that's pushing Drupal to the next level. Just like Drupal 7 and each previous release, Drupal 8 and beyond will be greater than the sum of its parts, better than any one person could conceive of. It's a great time to be in business with Drupal!

▒ **Note** Check in at `dgd7.org/sustain` for discussion and updates on the topics in this chapter—critical, as they are, to your success and to Drupal's success.

■ ■ ■

## CHAPTER 37

Maintaining a Project

by Sam Boyer and Forest Mars

"Talk is silver, code is gold."

This principle – a slightly nicer version of *"Put up or shut up"*—has driven the Drupal community since it was barely big enough to deserve the community label. As the project has gotten bigger, the meaning of code has expanded to something more like contribution, encompassing the essential work of designers, documenters, and trainers without whom Drupal wouldn't be book-worthy. In this chapter, though, we're going to focus on that original definition: contributing code; more specifically, creating and maintaining a project on Drupal.org. We'll also talk a bit about recommended development workflows, in particular ways to leverage Drupal's chosen version control system, Git.

■ **Caution** Drupal only recently adopted Git for version control. Consequently, some of the user interface and processes discussed in this chapter may deviate from what ultimately becomes production. The inconsistencies should be minor, but we have nevertheless done our best to provide links to the relevant canonical handbook documentation. In fact there are a number of improvements to Git integration that are being rolled out as part of "Phase Next" of the migration.

What's a Drupal Project?

Drupal projects are bundles of code that can be downloaded as .zip or .tar files and installed on Drupal sites, as well as the satellite features, version control repositories, issue queues. Each project has its own project page on Drupal.org at /project/PROJECTNAME. So, for example, the token module's project page would be at drupal.org/project/token.

Drupal projects come in several different flavors:

- **Modules:** The architectural building blocks that make Drupal go. Some 85-90% of all contributed projects are modules. Their development is covered in Part 5.

- **Themes:** Front-end development, look and feel, skinning—different words with the same idea: themes are in charge of generating markup. Around 10-15% of contributed projects are themes. Theming is covered in Chapters 15 and 16.

- **Installation Profiles:** Packages of modules, themes, and initial installation logic, they are covered in detail in Chapter 34. These make up just more than 1% of contributed projects.

- **Translations:** Translations of core and/or of Drupal modules are no longer handled as projects on Drupal.org but instead through `localize.drupal.org`. The process for translations is quite different, so see there and `dgd7.org/translate` for more information on translations.

- **Theme Engines:** Theme templating engines—e.g., PHPTemplate, Smarty, PHPTAL. Fewer than 10 of these exist, and most of those have been abandoned for years. For good reason: PHPTemplate is the de facto standard theme engine. The overwhelming majority of themes are built on it. While the instructions in this chapter do apply to theme engines, making a new one is exceptionally unlikely.

The process for project creation and maintenance is almost identical for all the types of projects hosted on Drupal.org, so for simplicity's sake this chapter will refer generically to "projects." In any situation where something works differently for modules, themes, or installation profiles, we'll make a note of it.

Whatever type of project you're creating, releasing a project on d.o carries with it certain responsibilities. It's not like publishing a project to a public code repository system like GitHub—your project becomes a part of the Drupal community's offering to the entire world, and, as such, your stewardship of it reflects not only on you but on the community as a whole. If your module largely duplicates the functionality of another module, it makes finding the right tool for the job more difficult. If your project has security holes, it means more work for the already-overworked Drupal.org security team and a security advisory—which is always a little egg on the face of the community. As we'll discuss a little later, the project "sandbox" stage helps with this, but you should still keep it in mind whenever contemplating a new project you'd like to contribute to Drupal.org.

Set Up Your Drupal.org Account for Contributing

Creating a new Drupal project is a multi-step process. You'll need to agree to the conditions of having your code hosted on Drupal.org and configure your Drurpal.org account for Git access. Then you can choose a project namespace and upload your code to the project's sandbox. After you have a project sandbox you'll be able to request your project be approved to package a full release. Note that all sandbox code is associated with a specific user's account, which is slightly different from full project code, which has a maintainer, but is not subordinated to that user's account. Also there is no provision for "company" accounts, so each Drupal.org account has to be set up by/for an individual, not a group.

Once you have your Drupal.org account the first step is to log into it, and read and agree to the conditions for uploading your code. These conditions are found under your profile tab, under the Edit ➤ Git access tab (See Figure 37–1).

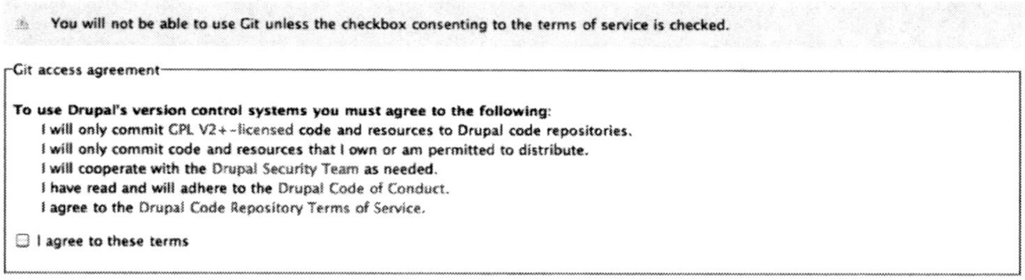

⚠ You will not be able to use Git unless the checkbox consenting to the terms of service is checked.

┌─Git access agreement───

To use Drupal's version control systems you must agree to the following:
  I will only commit GPL V2+-licensed code and resources to Drupal code repositories.
  I will only commit code and resources that I own or am permitted to distribute.
  I will cooperate with the Drupal Security Team as needed.
  I have read and will adhere to the Drupal Code of Conduct.
  I agree to the Drupal Code Repository Terms of Service.

  ☐ I agree to these terms

Figure 37–1. The conditions for uploading your code

The documents in these links lay out the Drupal community's philosophy on contributions, elaborate into greater detail on the responsibilities and expectations associated with project maintenance, and explain the legal requirements for putting code on Drupal.org.

Those legal requirements are simple, but particularly essential, so we'll paraphrase here what it means when it says that all code put on Drupal.org must be GPLv2+ compatible. In practice, that entails three conditions:

- First, if you want to include an external library with your project you can only store that code directly in your project's Git repository if it's compatibly-licensed.

- Second, the act of pushing your own otherwise-unlicensed code into a Git repository on the Drupal.org's servers has the effect of licensing that code as GPLv2. This legal agreement is packed automatically with your release

- Third, if you put someone else's incompatibly-licensed code into a Drupal.org repository, the code will be removed. People who repeatedly disregard the GPLv2 requirement may have their account suspended. This is the *only* legal requirement the community has for contributions, but it's an essential one.

Once you've agreed, by checking the box and clicking Save, you advance to the second step, creating a Git username (see Figure 37–2) Typically this will match your Drupal.org username, limited to URL-safe characters; however, that's not a requirement. Likewise you can set your password to be the same or different from your Drupal account itself.

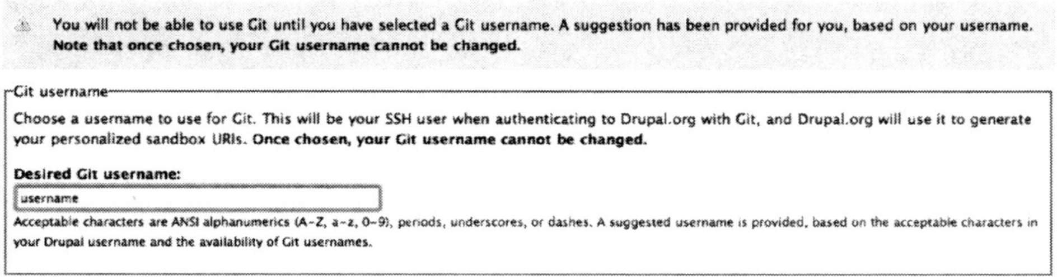

⚠ You will not be able to use Git until you have selected a Git username. A suggestion has been provided for you, based on your username. Note that once chosen, your Git username cannot be changed.

┌─Git username───
Choose a username to use for Git. This will be your SSH user when authenticating to Drupal.org with Git, and Drupal.org will use it to generate your personalized sandbox URIs. **Once chosen, your Git username cannot be changed.**

Desired Git username:
  │ username   │
Acceptable characters are ANSI alphanumerics (A–Z, a–z, 0–9), periods, underscores, or dashes. A suggested username is provided, based on the acceptable characters in your Drupal username and the availability of Git usernames.

Figure 37–2. Creating a Git username

Creating a Sandbox Project

With one-time setup steps completed, it's time to dig in and create a project—to be precise, a sandbox project. Drupal.org uses sandbox projects as a way of letting anyone contribute code to Drupal while preventing global namespace squatting and minimizing the chance of insecure (or malicious) code making its way into sites being built by unsuspecting users. There's a community approval process you'll need to go through before you can create fully functioning projects in the global namespace.

Until you have completed this community approval process, your sandbox project will differ in a few crucial ways from full projects, with the main difference being the use of a numeric value in place of the project shortname. (Project shortnames are used in the Drupal hook system to prefix functions, but this numeric substitution shouldn't cause any problems with this.)

We'll get into the details of that approval process a little later, but creating sandboxes is almost identical to creating full projects, so the instructions are pretty much interchangeable.

■ **Note** More information about how sandbox projects work can be found at `drupal.org/node/1011196`.

Head over to `drupal.org/node/add/project-project`, where you'll be presented with the project creation form.

Project type: *

○ Drupal core

○ Drupal.org projects

○ Installation profiles

○ Modules

○ Themes

○ Theme engines

Note: Translation projects have been moved and are now actively maintained at localize.drupal.org.

Modules categories:

Administration
Commerce/Advertising
Community
Content
Content Access Control
Content Construction Kit (CCK)
Content Display
Database Drivers
Developer
Drush
E-commerce
Evaluation/Rating
Event
Examples

Figure 37–3. Project categories

Status

In most cases new projects should be marked Maintenance status and Development status as Actively maintained and Under active development, respectively. Projects not intended to have a full release might also be uploaded to your Drupal.org sandbox, for example, to share code with another, similar project. Sharing your code in this manner allows you to take advantage of Drupal.org's integrated Git tools for highly collaborative code viewing and tracking.

Project Information

Your sandbox project begins its life with a number for a name: instead of your chosen name for the project, your sandbox project will use a temporary numeric name for referencing. This is used as a solution to a larger namespacing issue, but it does add a touch of complication. To work with the hook system and to prevent collisions with functions in other modules, full projects prefix their function names with the shortname of their project. Your sandbox's numeric name won't do for that; instead use a prefix that corresponds in a meaningful way to your Project title and is unique in the Drupal namespace. There's no guarantee that what you choose will still be available when you prepare to release, but, if it is, you'll save a step (see Figure 37–4).

- **Project title:** The human-readable name for the sandbox. This field can be updated.

- **Sandbox:** Until you have applied for or been granted a full Git account, sandbox will be checked by default and will be your only choice. We'll talk about this process later. Even when you do have full access it is still a good idea to start your project as a sandbox project; that way, when you do make it a full project, it already has code and is ready for use.

- **Description:** The description is the primary place for communicating the project's purpose to Drupal.org visitors. Well-written descriptions clearly express the purpose or use cases the project is intended to serve. If your project has dependencies (either external libraries or other Drupal projects), provide links. If your project is in a similar problem space as another pre-existing Drupal project, provide a link to that project, as well as an explanation of how your project differs. Of course, you might not know all this when creating a new project, especially your very first one—fear not, you can always update the description later! Once you're done, submit the form; your project page will be created, and a new Git repository will be spun up on the Drupal.org servers, ready to accept your code.

Figure 37–4. Project information

> ■ **Note** About namespaces: To determine if the function name prefix you're going to use is available, visit Drupal.org and add `project/desired_name` to the end of the URL. If you land on a project, that namespace is occupied. File not Found is an indication that the namespace may be available when you release. Keep in mind, however, that another sandbox project may have already reserved this namespace, even if it doesn't yet have a full release (and thus a project shortname).

Digging in with Git

Git is a powerful beast, and using it sometimes feels like grocery shopping in a Ferrari. We introduced its use for personal version control in Chapter 2, but that was a drive around the block and—while covering what is your most constant use of Git—didn't begin to touch on its full range of capabilities. Git can be daunting, even for people accustomed to other types of source control; it has unfamiliar names for some common actions, and it can take a while to really understand how your local repository interacts with other Git repositories (called remotes). But the Drupal community opted for it to be the version control system of choice for a reason: if you persevere, you'll find Git highly capable of managing not only your project's code but codebases for individual Drupal sites, or even large, highly complex Drupal-based systems run across server clusters and integrated with external tools and deployment strategies.

All this talk of codebases and tools and systems should not distract from what maintaining an open source free software project is all about. The real reason for using a distributed version control system such as Git is so that you can work effectively with other people to build awesome things.

The web has a nigh-bottomless supply of resources for learning Git commands—you can jump right in with the commands provided on a tab at your project's drupal.org page—but learning how Git works is invaluable for using it to maintain projects in collaboration with other people.

We'll talk about a few commands and useful techniques in the rest of this chapter, but our focus here is really on the key steps for project maintenance, those steps that help you push your code to Drupal.org and create releases. If you want to learn more, there's an appendix of Git resources at the end of this book. Keep in mind that, when browsing around the web for "git + drupal," anything written before 2011 may not be particularly helpful. Drupal was still using CVS, and much of the talk prior to the switch was focused on making Git work with CVS. And Git itself has changed just enough in recent releases that you'll want to make sure you have the most up-to-date information (and, of course, the most up-to-date version of Git).

To access that repository, you'll need to use SSH (Secure SHell), so we'll make a quick detour through getting all that set up.

Managing SSH

Drupal.org uses SSH for all authenticated communication with Git repositories, so you'll need to make sure you're set up properly with SSH. Until you set up your SSH keys you'll need to type in your password every time you interact with the server (assuming you're working from the CLI—many GUIs will store your SSH password for you). If you choose to stick with password authentication, your SSH addresses for interacting with your Drupal sandbox repositories will look something like this:

```
$ git clone dgd7@git.drupal.org:sandbox/dgd7/1041111.git
Cloning into 1041111...
dgd7@git.drupal.org's password:
```

If your password is accepted and you have access to the named project, the previous command will clone the repository to your local system (more on cloning later.) If you find passwords cumbersome or insecure, then you can opt to use key-based authentication instead, for which you will need to generate a key on your local machine and add it to your account on Drupal.org.

Once you have your public key, go to your d.o profile and click the SSH Keys tab. You'll be presented with an interface for managing your public keys. Add your key, and it'll be ready for use immediately with all git commands. With key-based authentication, you need not specify your username in your SSH commands, so the previous command becomes a bit simpler:

```
$ git clone git@git.drupal.org:sandbox/dgd7/1041111.git
Cloning into dgd7_example...
```

Because key-based SSH addresses have one less awkward variable, we're going to use them in examples throughout the chapter. If you're using username and password-based authentication, fear not—simply substitute your username for git in the examples. However, you will probably find that once you have set key-based commit authentication you will wonder why anyone still uses the more cumbersome password-based authentication.

Hack on Your Project

Now that you have a sandbox project waiting and SSH all configured, you're ready to start writing and contributing code. The first step is to get your local Git repository set up. To do that, we'll need to clone it over SSH from Drupal.org:

```
$ git clone git@git.drupal.org:sandbox/dgd7/1041111.git
Cloning into 1041111...
warning: You appear to have cloned an empty repository.
```

The warning is normal—encouraging, really, because it indicates that the repository you just cloned is brand new, freshly created, and empty. In this example you are cloning a project you've just created, so there's nothing there yet. However, you should realize that cloning a repository makes a full copy of the entire repository contents—that is, the project's entire history—and places it on your local machine. Cloning, for example, can be a bandwidth-intensive operation, especially for large projects (at the launch of Drupal 7, core's repository was around 50MB). However, having the full history is crucial to Git's decentralized, distributed functionality, so we bite the bullet on the size of the initial clone

Now that you have the repository, you can get to work adding, changing, and committing files—all of those Git basics that are covered in Chapter 2 and the Git resources listed earlier. Just as a quick recap, though, let's add and commit some files into the new repository. For brevity's sake the following example uses <?php> as a placeholder for your code:

```
$ echo 'name = "DGD7 Example Module"' > 1041111.info
$ echo '<?php>' dgd7_example.module
```

Or add these files using your graphical editor of choice. After building your code, git status should show that you have untracked files as follows:

```
$ git status
# On branch master
#
# Initial commit
#
# Untracked files:
#   (use "git add <file>..." to include in what will be committed)
#
#       dgd7_example.info
#       dgd7_example.module
nothing added to commit but untracked files present (use "git add" to track)
```

These files are currently on your working tree (i.e., working directory or working copy) only and not in your index (i.e., staging area). Next, we'll add the files to the staging area index and then we will commit them. Note that the SHA1 hash in your message will be different—the hash is computed using repository contents (which are the same) but also the time the commit was made (which is different).

```
$ git add dgd7_example.info dgd7_example.module
$ git commit -m 'Initial commit'
[master (root-commit) c8a69f9] Initial commit
 2 files changed, 2 insertions(+), 0 deletions(-)
 create mode 100644 dgd7_example.info
 create mode 100644 dgd7_example.module
```

This gets us as far as we went in Chapter 2 as all the operations so far have been local. (This is one of the most important ways Git differs from its non-DVCS predecessors: your code is stored in a local repository.) Next we're going to take the additional step of pushing this commit to a remote repository, in this case our Drupal sandbox back on d.o:

```
$ git push origin master
Counting objects: 4, done.
Delta compression using up to 2 threads.
Compressing objects: 100% (2/2), done.
Writing objects: 100% (4/4), 300 bytes, done.
Total 4 (delta 0), reused 0 (delta 0)
Unpacking objects: 100% (4/4), done.
To git@git.drupal.org:sandbox/dgd7/dgd7_example.git
 * [new branch]      master -> master
```

Congratulations—you've just put your first bit of code onto Drupal.org! Note this is just the start of your new Drupal project or projects. Drupal sandboxes are intended to be a development space where you can actively work on and commit your code. Remember to commit early and commit often. This will give your sandbox a richer history that allows the module review team to get a sense of your coding style when you apply for active status. Don't just wait until you want a full release and then upload the final version of your code! Perfection isn't prized here as much as process.

There's not a lot else to say about generic project maintaining at this point—what you do with your sandbox is really up to you. If you're just tinkering around and have no intention of ever really sharing your code with the wider world, that's fine—the only restrictions imposed on sandboxes are some size limitations, and those mostly to prevent abuse.

If you want to really share your project with the wider Drupal world, though, you'll need to take the next step and have your sandbox promoted to full project status, which is a requirement for having an official release.

From Sandboxville to Projectopolis

So you've been happily hacking away at your module (or other project) committing fast and free locally, and pushing back to Drupal.org whenever you reach a suitable point, and you're starting to think it's time your project graduated from sandbox status and joined the ranks of full, user-facing projects. Great! This is a crucial juncture in the life cycle of your project.

Once you have code in your sandbox you can then apply for permission to promote it to full status as a first-class module. This approval is required for your project to have an official release on Drupal.org. However, you only have to apply once, for the first time you wish to promote a project. Specifically, you are not applying to have a single project promoted; you are applying for yourself to be granted the role that enables you to promote your projects (using the code in your sandbox to demonstrate that you understand and it fulfills the basic requirements of Drupal). After you are granted this role the first time, you will be able to promote any of your sandbox projects when you need to, provided your code always adheres to the basic standards set forth by Drupal.org

One of the main benefits you'll get from a full release is sandbox access to Drupal's full testing environment. At the time of this writing sandbox projects aren't able to take advantage of Drupal.org's automated testing framework.

In order to ensure that developers have familiarized themselves with Drupal's coding standards and are writing secure code, the first time you wish to promote an experimental project you'll be required to apply for full Git privileges. This involves:

1. Preparing a branch for consideration.

2. Preparing your project for review.

3. Applying at `drupal.org/project/projectapplications`.

4. Participating in peer review for coding standards compliance and security considerations.

5. Being assigned the appropriate role on Drupal.org.

About Branches and Tags on Drupal.org

Branches and tags, collectively known as refs in Git and sometimes referred to as labels on Drupal.org, are a crucial building block in Git and are also an essential part of the packaging and release systems used on Drupal.org. Drupal's packaging system requires only a basic understanding of how branches and tags work (fortunately), but it's worth sticking with it beyond the basics. Git's real strength lies in its cheap branching, and so while we won't go that far into it here, you'll want to delve deeper into the developmental efficiencies Git enables in order to take advantage of Git's power. (And look forward to some of the best use cases making their way into Drupal's "Phase Next" Git rollout.)

So, what's so special about refs? First, they are used by the Drupal.org packaging and release system, and only branches and tags conforming to certain naming conventions will be approved for release. Once you grok how branching and tagging conventions work, you'll have a much better understanding of the developmental structure underlying Drupal project versions.

Preparing a Branch for Your Application

If you have a pre-existing Git repository that you're all ready to put onto d.o, all you have to do is add git.drupal.org as a new remote to the repository, then push:

```
$ git remote add origin git@git.drupal.org:project/<projectname>.git
$ git push --all origin
```

In this example we are adding it as origin, which is a default remote used by your Git repository. If you already have an origin set (for example, your main development server) chances are you already know to name the remote repository at git.drupal.org anything you like. Since Git has excellent support for tab completion, we recommend giving it the name git.drupal.org. To see what remotes your local repository is aware of, you can use cat .git/config.

After setting git.drupal.org as a remote, use git push—all to copy your complete code from your local repository into your project space on Drupal.org. Note that this will push all of the branches in your local repository.

Preparing Your Project for Review

The main part of the application process is a review of the code you have submitted to confirm that it is not a duplicate of already existing Drupal functionality and that it meets certain code and licensing requirements. These code requirements are intended to ensure that all code officially released on Drupal.org is secure, well-documented, and meets the specific coding standards set forth by Drupal's legendary collaborative development community, and that it will be free from any licensing issues that could adversely affect other Drupal users.

Coding Standards

Drupal has a very specific, detailed, and well-documented set of coding standards available at drupal.org/coding-standards. Experienced coders from other PHP frameworks or languages may disagree with some of the choices we've made, but coding standards are a crucial part of community collaboration. By adhering to coding standards, all of us can read each other's code more easily, we're saved countless hours of bickering over syntax choices or rewriting code based on varying preferences, and those who support Drupal out in the world benefit from the consistency these standards provide.

Fortunately, thanks to the Coder module (drupal.org/project/coder), adhering to Drupal coding standards is a cinch. Coder can even do a lot of the work for you, reading in what you've written and spitting out standards-compliant code. Whether you study and internalize the coding standards or clean up with Coder at the end, presenting standards-compliant code is the first step toward readying your module for the public.

Here are some examples of coding standards for Drupal. This is not an exhaustive list, but it is intended to illustrate some of the specific requirements your code will be expected to adhere to:

1. All classes should be commented.

2. All functions should be commented.

3. Simple test should be implemented (and passed!).

4. All code revisions and patches should be commented.

Security

Security issues can be harder to spot, especially for novice programmers. Coder module can be of some assistance here, too, as it will highlight certain security holes—improper escaping of database queries or user input, for example. It isn't much help with subtler issues, though, so familiarize yourself with common web application vulnerabilities (XSRF, XSS, etc.) and try to ensure your code doesn't have such problems. Novice programmers and people new to Drupal will find an excellent starting point at Drupal.org's "Writing secure code" at `drupal.org/writing-secure-code` (also see Chapter 6).

Licensing

When you originally set up your Git access you agreed to only upload GPL licensed code to your sandbox. Thus all code submitted as part of your application should already meet Drupal's licensing requirements.

Project Description

Review your project description to ensure it provides a detailed description of exactly what your project does. If your project is similar to another project on d.o. you'll want elaborate exactly how it is different, and why such functionality is being duplicated. Make sure that all data is up-to-date, clear, and proof-read before you submit your application. Don't forget to include a link to your project page, and, if your project is a theme, include a screenshot.

Applying for Access

The application itself isn't complicated: file an issue in the Drupal.org Project applications at `drupal.org/project/issues/projectapplications`.

Because the review process uses Drupal's project issue tracker, you'll need to fill out the following form fields:

- Component: "new project application" and Category: "task"

- Status: "needs review"

- Title: your project's title

- Description: your project description (as above)

Once given the sign off, you will be granted permissions both to create full projects and to promote sandbox projects to full projects. If for some reason your code is found not to meet the requirements you will be informed of the reason and given the opportunity to make the necessary fixes. While some of the reasons should be obvious, beginning Drupal developers sometimes miss less obvious, but no less impactful, requirements.

For a more exhaustive list of reasons code is typically sent back for improvement, see `drupal.org/node/539608`.

Receiving Access

Subscribe to the issue queue to receive feedback on your application and to receive notification when your access is granted. Once you have access, the interface for adding or updating a project changes. Now when you edit your project for promotion, you'll see new choices, as shown in Figure 37–5.

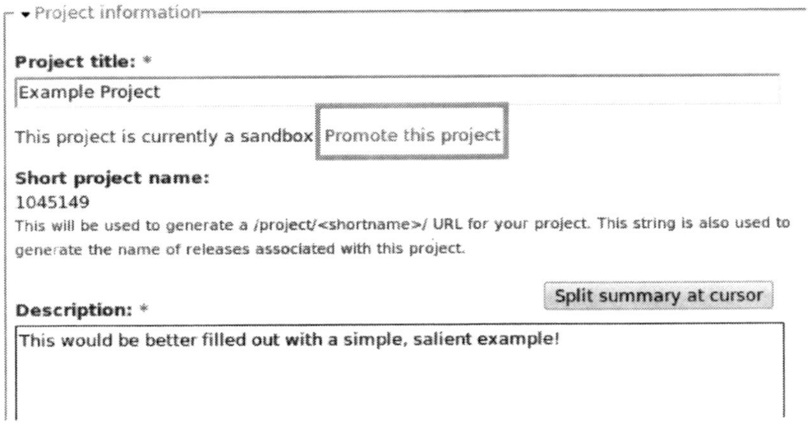

```
┌─ ▾ Project information ─────────────────────────────────────
│
│  Project title: *
│  ┌──────────────────────────────────────────────────────┐
│  │ Example Project                                       │
│  └──────────────────────────────────────────────────────┘
│  This project is currently a sandbox │ Promote this project │
│  Short project name:
│  1045149
│  This will be used to generate a /project/<shortname>/ URL for your project. This string is also used to
│  generate the name of releases associated with this project.
│
│                                            ┌─────────────────────────┐
│                                            │ Split summary at cursor │
│  Description: *                            └─────────────────────────┘
│  ┌──────────────────────────────────────────────────────┐
│  │ This would be better filled out with a simple, salient example! │
│  │                                                       │
│  │                                                       │
│  └──────────────────────────────────────────────────────┘
```

Figure 37–5. Editing your project for promotion

Summary

If you've followed the instructions outlined in this chapter you will have been able to enable Git access on your Drupal.org account, create your own project sandbox and upload code to it, and have your Drupal projects (whether you are contributing modules, themes, or documentation) promoted to a first-class Drupal release status.

■ **Note** Check out `dgd7.org/maintain` for links to resources on maintaining projects on `Drupal.org`.

■ ■ ■

## CHAPTER 38

Contributing to the Community

by Benjamin Melançon and Claudina Sarahe

"People come to me and ask how they can contribute. I always tell them to do what they want to do. If I told them what to do, then it wouldn't always be fun and it wouldn't necessarily translate into the passion that I'd like to see happen."

—Dries Buytaert, Drupal Project Lead

"A contributor is someone who has three qualities: they see something and they say, 'that's dumb,' then they say 'hey, I really wanna see that thing fixed,' and they do something about it."

—Angela Byron, Drupal 7 Maintainer

There is a common misconception that you have to be a programmer in order to contribute to Drupal. This is untrue; even those with little or no prior knowledge of code can contribute to the community in ways that will help make Drupal better. In fact, this is what happens all the time: people support the Drupal community by organizing events, answering questions, and sponsoring development sprints—all examples of vital non-code contributions that the community needs to grow. Non-code contributions, such as mentorship and writing documentation, are ideal ways to develop and grow one's skills in coding and configuring Drupal. Growing the community means, on the one hand, growing the infrastructure and number of people and, on the other, growing the capabilities of people in the community.

With this chapter, we conclude the book with a tour through the wide assortment of ways we can all make Drupal a better place to make web sites, to make a living, to make friends, and, just maybe, to make a better world.

■ **Note** This chapter might have been titled "Giving Back to the Community" except that some of those who have given the most to Drupal seem to have started giving *before* they got.

Contributing is about doing something about things that you have an interest in improving. This is the message from Dries and Angie, the two people who performed the final review and committed every improvement made to Drupal 7. Trying to contribute where it doesn't interest you is not likely to be effective. As Drupal continues to grow, so does the need for more contributors and types of contributions. It is the authors' hope that this chapter will help us all find ways we can contribute (if we aren't already), inspire us to want to contribute more, and increase our knowledge about the fuel that powers Drupal's success—the community. This chapter presents reasons to get involved and ways to make your contributions more effective. This chapter is also a way of saying thanks to those that have contributed and continue to contribute to Drupal.

Why Contribute?

There are many reasons to contribute. For the intrinsic joy of making or helping, to aid personal or professional betterment, and out of commitment to community. To the authors, contributing is about making the place where you live better. It's like changing the oil in a car; it may not immediately affect you but it will make a difference down the road not only to you but to others.

Evan Donovan (drupal.org/user/168664), one of the hundreds of contributors to Drupal 7 core, highlighted five reasons to contribute on his blog (donanvan.covblogs.com/archives/040454.html):

- It's fun to learn things.

- It's fun to solve problems.

- It's fun to help people out.

- The work you contribute back to the community can be multiplied many-fold by the others in the community. In turn, their work can provide a base for further progress.

- Sometimes, it can even be beneficial to your job prospects.

Gábor Hojtsy (drupal.org/user/4166), a major contributor to Drupal core as well as the maintainer of Drupal 7's Locale module and the entire Drupal 6 series of releases, summarized the benefits of contributing as offering the ability to:

- Work on cool technology.

- Work in an international team.

- Show off your work and talent.

- Travel.

- Make money.

Gábor, one of the first hires by Acquia (the company co-founded by Dries Buytaert eight years after he founded Drupal), views contributing to open source projects as protecting one's career:

> *If you need a good way to ensure your job security, I think this is a way. Your active work life is documented all around the Internet, you've been to conferences, established your name in the industry. When you are compared to someone who worked on a closed source legacy system and can only be believed for the pieces in his Curriculum Vitae (further details of which are under a Non-Disclosure Agreement), who is less risk to take on for a company?*

Without Contributions, There Is No Drupal

We—the authors writing, the readers reading—are here because of Drupal. Our ability to engage with Drupal (software, community events, knowledge) only exists because of all the earlier contributions of others, starting from the beginning when Dries opened his code. If no one had stepped up and contributed, there would be no Drupal.

Larry Garfield (Crell, drupal.org/user/26398), a core contributor, lead maintainer of Drupal's database layer, Senior Developer at Palantir, and Drupal Association Legal Affairs Director, uses the phrase "pay it forward" as a way to describe how free software works.

> *When you work on an open source project or release code under a Free Software license you are doing something for someone else. Someone you don't know, and who probably doesn't know you, is going to benefit from your actions. You may yourself benefit from the work you do, but so will other people that have not done anything for you. And that is the very point.*
>
> *If one person does that, the world takes advantage of them. If a thousand people do that, you get Drupal. Or Linux. Or Apache. Or Firefox. Or the KDE desktop. Or, really, all of them combined. Every one of those projects is the result of thousands of people paying it forward, to each other and to you. The net result is a robust, healthy environment of quality code and, more importantly, a culture of sharing and mutual support, even across projects.*
>
> *In my day job, I work with Drupal. I've written tons of code for Drupal, both core and contrib, as have my colleagues, and we release as much as we can back to the community. We are paying it forward to the rest of the web development world in return for the million man-hours that have already been put into building what we're leveraging for free. That is what makes open source work.*

Drupal's success is largely due to the many ways in which people can contribute without barriers. Drupal is designed to be extended; it is designed to easily allow people to contribute along the way. The modular nature of the software has been essential to the phenomenal growth of both the technology and the community. While Drupal has paved an exemplary path by putting developers' needs and happiness at the forefront of the core technological design, the success of an open source technology project is the balance of the building, maintenance, and evolution of the code and the sustained development and happiness of the community.

> *"The principles that come to mind are those of self-organization and scratching your own itch. Getting out of people's way as much as you can, and enabling people to accomplish what they are passionate about. When people can come together and take action collaboratively, impressive things can happen."*
>
> —Dries Buytaert

Taking That First Step

We can all relate to a time when it felt daunting to take that first step. You can feel like the new kid on the block when joining an already established community. The Drupal community takes care to continue to grow without any barriers to entry. Communities are often viewed as having insider groups, and to some extent this is inevitably true; the more active participants will work together more. This bonding based on related behavior and activities is common in life, but in the Drupal community it does not prevent anyone from joining. Membership in the community is defined by participation, especially contributing, and some of the many ways to contribute, open to everyone, will be covered in this chapter. Act like an insider (of whatever definition or group), and you will be an insider. Going far in Drupal is about knowing what you want and going after it. If you really want it, keep going!

The following tips apply no matter what you are contributing:

- Do not expect anything in return. A community is not a market arrangement (give X, get Y).

- Don't await the ticker-tape parade. Contributing to the community is being part of the community, not being celebrated by it.

- Have a thick skin. Don't take things personally. Katherine Senzee (ksenzee, drupal.org/user/139855) is a senior engineer who frequently helps people in IRC, writes documentation, and contributes significantly to Drupal code. She worked magic making the Overlay module for Drupal 7 core, and some insignificant author named Ben recommended disabling it in the first chapter of this book. Katherine doesn't need validation for her efforts except that people do benefit—many consider Overlay a key usability enhancement. If Katherine or the other people who make Drupal great let criticism stop them, we wouldn't have a single achievement.

Transparent Communication

Tim O'Reilly, speaking to Kent Bye, said that Drupal is one of the most important open source projects because it "has created a successful architecture of communication." A very high proportion of Drupal interaction takes place in public, primarily on IRC and in the issue queues (`drupal.org/project/issues`). In fact, it's hard to entirely avoid the issue queues, and why would you want to? Here you can see friends and co-workers disagree with each other—and people on different continents work out solutions together! Conversation also takes place in other venues, such as `groups.drupal.org`; and if a question can be conveyed in 140 characters there's always Twitter and the drupal#.

The great honesty and transparency of the Drupal project is a part of the community ethos. We learn and fail publicly. We believe it's better to do and try publicly than to aim for perfection behind closed doors. But take care to converse with civility. We all have bad and good days. We don't always get the full context of a person's day in IRC or in the issue queue Take any comment the only way it can be: as one person's perspective at one moment in time. On the other side, if you notice curt behavior, especially directed to a newcomer who has made a basic beginner mistake such as asking a question in the wrong IRC channel, do take the time to say, "Hey, I'm sorry you experienced that. This channel is not the best for your question. Let me help you in #drupal-support!"

Keeping a community happy, diverse, innovative, and active is no easy task, especially one relying on the collaborative power of individuals. The Drupal community is not perfect and we say it proudly. We learn and implement as we go along. The roads to Drupal contribution could be better marked and better-maintained. We need to get better at recognizing different kinds of contributions.

How do we remove unnecessary barriers to contributing? How do we ensure that someone putting in effort is acknowledged and supported? Do we need better tools for discussion or decision-making? These questions are a frequent matter of discussion among those who care about Drupal; in fact, working on these problems is another way of contributing to the well-being of the community. We'll look at some of these questions in the final section "Drupal as a Movement."

In the next section, we look at ways that are available to all of us to make Drupal code and the Drupal community better than ever.

Ways to Contribute

There are as many ways to contribute to Drupal as there are motivations for doing so, and all can be a rewarding experience in their own right. At the core, a contribution is made up of two components:

- *Time*, which is great, since we all have time; it's just a matter of how we use it!

- *Love*, which is usually how we decide what or where to put our time towards.

We offer you 12 ways to contribute to the community—advanced members and newcomers alike. This list is only a sampling from the growing number of ways to contribute to the welfare of the community and advancement of the code base; if you have another suggestion, please share it at `dgd7.org/suggestions`. If you write your ideas on your blog, please leave the link and a short descriptive sentence. Additionally, you have permission to use information from this book to contribute to `drupal.org` documentation.

1. Providing Non-Technical Support

A thanks or acknowledgement goes a long way. Appreciation takes many forms. If a member of the community helps you out, send them thanks on Twitter. Or make them some cookies! Those who attended Maureen Lyons' session at DrupalCon Boston 2008 will always remember getting excellent vegan brownies.

If you really like a module, theme, particular Drupal distribution, or product, acknowledge its value to your life. Christefano's love letter to the Edit Term module (`data.agaric.com/edit-term-love`) surely helped give it the karmic boost it needed to get into core.

Ryan Aslett (Mixologic, `drupal.org/user/391689`) sent the Views team love instead of bugs. Ryan created a task in the issue queue to "Keep Up the Awesome."

Every single project I work on I use Views. I never have problems with it...If the whole world understood Drupal, Views would immediately be championed as an epic work of art.

Thanks for creating/helping to maintain something positively awesome.

Fourteen other users added their praise, thanking the Views team—and thanking Mixologic for taking the time to express his gratitude publicly. The issue ended when Lynette Miles (esmerel, `drupal.org/user/164022`) changed the status to *closed (works as designed)* and wrote "Always fun to come across these ;)". (As a rule, don't misuse the issue queues for any purpose— an even better way to show support is to help out in them, see way to contribute number 7.)

You can nominate and profile people for the Drupal Community Spotlight at `drupal.org/community-spotlight.` Or post your own spotlight, as Alan Palazzolo did before contributing to the Spotlight, and Andrew Riley, Michael Anello, and Ryan Price are doing with The DrupalEasy Podcast, a weekly review of new developments and announcements in the worldwide Drupal community (`drupaleasy.com/podcast`). Don't be afraid to share your thanks publicly. Others may be having similar thoughts.

2. Sharing Everything

"If someone helps you out with an open source project, be it using it, developing for it, or even just writing about it, you can thank them personally. But the true thanks, what will really show gratitude, is paying it forward. You've just gained new knowledge and understanding. Share that knowledge and understanding with others. Help out the next person, or better yet the next people, to come after you."

—Larry Garfield (Crell)

Sharing what you have learned is one of the best ways to contribute back to the community. The process of explaining concepts and answering questions is one of the best ways to learn, too. There are a wide variety of opportunities for mentoring, teaching and learning within the Drupal community, some of which include:

- Making a presentation at your local meetup.

- Sharing your blog posts; they don't have to be Planet-worthy to share.

- Sharing incomplete code.

- Starting some documentation and letting others improve upon it.

- Allowing distribution and modification of your documentation. You can allow access to your material under whatever Creative Commons level you prefer.

Sharing is a notable aspect of the Drupal community. It doesn't have to be Drupal specific. Karen Stevenson posted her cheat sheet about the Vi editor at `lullabot.com/blog/using-vi-editor` by stating "Here is my cheat sheet, in a public place that is easy to find."

Whenever you get stuck on something, whether Git'ing your way out of a merge conflict, properly setting up Drush site aliases, configuring a module, or overriding theme functions, you're probably going to try searching for the answer. Record all the search terms you try. When you figure out how to get past the problem, or a piece of the problem, write up your notes. Put the notes up on your site in a post with all the search engine terms you tried. When the next person (anywhere in the world) has the same problem and enters the same search terms, the post you just made will come up.

Like Karen, part of the reason that Benjamin puts things online is to easily find them again. "I regularly search for answers across the whole web and find my own answers from two weeks or two years ago."

You can drop the quality filter entirely and post every investigation and half-baked idea on your own site. If you're worried that this will make you look like you don't know what you're doing, well, quite the opposite: you will be raising awareness about yourself in the Drupal community. You'll be perceived as someone who is willing to find solutions and collaborates with all, which might help you get important clients in the future. Or maybe someone will correct you. Either way, make sure your company name or `drupal.org` username and contact information are available in your posts.

■ **Note** If it's a solution that can fit anywhere in Drupal documentation pages, add it, or link your notes to the more focused writeup. Contributing to the documentation guide is advantageous because the community views it as a serious commitment to Drupal betterment. It also makes it more likely that people will help you because they know you will pay it forward.

Documentation can be as simple as a record of the things you've tried in order to get something done. You don't need to know all the answers. In fact, you can contribute by sharing incorrect information!

Contribute by Being Wrong

"I stand corrected! Thanks to the commenters for enlightening me. Drush does in fact do this."

—Ben Buckman

Drush is a powerful command line and scripting interface for Drupal, a veritable Swiss Army knife. It's designed to make common development tasks for developers and themers much easier. Expert Drupal developer Ben Buckman (drupal.org/user/342780) was looking for a way to synchronize a database between remote and local servers. He created a scripting technique because he was unable to do it with Drush. He shared his technique on his web site. Commenters pointed out that Drush could in fact synchronize databases—and do it even better.

Why is this an inspirational story? Sharing his approach led other people to share theirs. Once Ben discovered how to achieve his original goal with Drush, he updated his post and helped many others learn something new. Ben paid forward the "new knowledge and understanding" he'd gained by sharing it with others. (If you develop Drupal using live and dev sites and haven't set up Drush site aliases for syncing databases and files, see Chapter 26!)

Mentoring

You don't have to be too far along in Drupal to mentor. Beginners willing to demonstrate what they have learned are highly encouraged and welcomed into the community as the need for assisting others with the most basic tasks and concepts is so great.

Check on people you mentor frequently and help them break down tasks to make sure they are not spinning their wheels without getting traction. IBM consultant Sacha Chua recommended this in reflections on mentoring a new Drupal developer, noting "otherwise, she might get lost or stuck, because she might not yet know where things are or whether she's getting closer to an answer." Sacha's notes on work, connecting, and living an awesome life can be found at her blog sachachua.com and she shares her Drupal-related posts on Drupal Planet (drupal.org/planet).

Conversely, just telling someone what code to type without explaining the concept behind the code doesn't foster learning. Everyone learns differently. Be open to that as a mentor.

Mentoring can be informal, semi-formal as with the Drupal Dojo project, or it can be part of formal programs such as the Google Summer of Code (GSOC) or Google Code-In (GCI, drupal.org/project/issues/gci). The Drupal Open Learning Initiative (DOLI; DrupalOpenLearning.org) outlines a number of projects and on-going programs produced by and for the Drupal community.

The Drupal Dojo (DrupalDojo.com/about) is well known for the successful series of free weekly webinars. Anyone may sign up to present an educational program in the Dojo simply by adding their event to the "Building with Drupal" program lineup at groups.drupal.org/node/52023. The long-term vision includes transforming DrupalDojo.com from a virtual meeting place with program archives into a more robust Drupal Learning Resource Center that catalogs and references Drupal Learning materials. The Dojo also supports the expansion of educational programs such as regular IRC chats in the Freenode #Drupal-dojo channel, local weekly Dojo Meetings for training, and co-working sessions. As of January 2011, Drupal User Groups in Austin, Boston, and Seattle have all expanded their monthly meetings to include a weekly Drupal Dojo training or working session. The Drupal Dojo group is one of the largest groups on Groups.Drupal.org.

Drupal Learning Projects (DrupalKata.com) provides opportunities to learn by doing, under the guidance of mentors, teams, or project managers. Projects are developed in the open by following workflow that insures documentation and opportunities to generate lessons, best practices, tips and tricks, tutorials, development strategies and a host of other learning materials, all based on the lessons learned during project development. These materials are then cataloged and distributed through the Drupal Dojo.

Dojo Barn Raisings help a local non-profit by building a Drupal 7 site as an open learning project. All planning and development is completed in the open using the Drupal Kata project resources and culminates in a public barn-raising, where Drupal volunteers, mentors, and apprentices work in teams to build the site in one or two public sessions. There are observation areas for the public to watch and learn as narrators explain the work as it's completed. The Seattle Drupal User Group (groups.Drupal.com/seattle) launched another barn raising project (groups.drupal.org/node/121624) in January of 2011.

Cataloging Drupal Learning was created shortly after DrupalCon San Francisco when a group of volunteers began the process of mapping Drupal learning by developing a questionnaire that associates job responsibilities and core competencies with Drupal learning objectives. The long-term goal is to establish standards for the cataloging of all Drupal learning content from courses to learning objects (groups.drupal.org/node/15975).

Drupal Open Curriculum Project is developing a complete curriculum and course materials that anyone can use. This project offers many opportunities for individuals to get involved, regardless of experience with instructional design (gitorious.org/drupal-open-curriculum/pages/Home).

Developing a Framework for Drupal Learning is an objective of the DOLI. It hopes to bring together the wide range of experts, mentors, trainers, and educators working to develop Open Drupal Curriculum in order to define a framework for Drupal Open Learning Curriculum, including guidelines and best practices for curriculum development.

Drupal In A Day is an effort to develop shorter courses that cover Drupal for the newcomer. Learn all about Drupal in a day.

3. Answering Questions in Forums, Groups, Mailing Lists, Meetups, and IRC

"Each time you visit drupal.org take a quick look at the 'New forum topics' block. It only takes 5 minutes to help someone."

—Wim Mostrey (wmostrey, drupal.org/user/21228)

Remember when you asked a question, especially one you were timid about, and got a helpful response? Helping earns you gratitude and increases your knowledge. Fox (drupal.org/user/426416, hefox on IRC) is establishing a reputation as an "honest to goodness [Drupal] genius" by answering questions in IRC. Fox is approaching an encyclopedic knowledge of Drupal and yet still has moments of not knowing an answer: "I was curious so I searched for it."

It really is that simple: sometimes all someone really needs is for another soul to do a five second search for them instead of telling them to search on their own or read the handbook. Taking the extra 30 seconds to point them in the right direction also helps you; refining your search skills is never bad idea, especially when it comes to web development.

Angie Byron (webchick, drupal.org/user/24967) started in Drupal by answering questions, which eventually led to offers to do Drupal odd jobs for a few hundred dollars a pop. Now she's the Drupal 7 maintainer, a former Lullabot consultant and now director in the office of the CTO at Acquia, the author or *Using Drupal*, and all-around Drupal community superstar!

Chapter 9 lists places where you can get help; these are also the places where you can help others. Check in on the forums at drupal.org/forum, subscribe to some groups at groups.drupal.org, sign up for some mailing lists, go to Drupal meetups, or hang out in Drupal IRC channels.

4. Writing Documentation for Drupal.org

Perhaps the most important way to help the success of Drupal, and certainly one of the best ways to learn while doing, is to write documentation. You might build a powerful Drupal site equipped with all the bells and whistles and have it working perfectly without a single bug, but its impressiveness dims if people can't use it or continue its development. Complete documentation for people developing, administering, or simply using a Drupal site can make the difference in the success of any Drupal project.

▓ **Note** For more on documentation practices and guidelines for end users and internal production teams, see Chapter 11.

There is a terrible misconception floating around that you are not allowed to write documentation if you don't know enough about writing *or* don't know enough about Drupal. We, the authors, don't know how this came to be but it is not the case at all.

First, anything is better than nothing. It's much easier for someone else to improve the writing style or technical detail of existing documentation than it is to write it from scratch and find where it belongs. Of course, you can also be the person who improves the clarity or updates information on the existing documentation.

Second, if you're reading this book and you've made this far, we're willing to bet you can read and write—and that you have some interest in Drupal. Congratulations! We now pronounce you qualified to write Drupal documentation. There are no tests to pass when it comes to writing documentation. Just write simple, non-verbose, step-by-step instructions.

In fact, a lack of Drupal sophistication can be a distinct advantage in a documentation writer! It makes you much more likely to notice areas where users will need help, processes that make no sense, and places that beg for explanation.

Anyone with a `drupal.org` account can add and edit documentation. You can get an account at `drupal.org/user/register` and you can create documentation pages via `drupal.org/node/add/book`. Before you add a new page, do a search to make sure what you want to add doesn't already exist. You may find that a page does exist but it wasn't linked where you expected to find it. Adding links to related documentation will help others find the right page and is one of the most high-value, low-effort contributions you can make.

Some pages can only be edited by people given the "documentation" role on `drupal.org`, which lets you post content with tables and images. If you are already a regular contributor to the other documentation pages, you will probably be granted this role. More information on getting more involved with documentation can be found at `drupal.org/contribute/documentation` and `drupal.org/contribute/documentation/join`.

That's all you need to know to get started! You certainly don't have to set out with the single-minded goal of contributing to documentation to make a big impact. As you work with Drupal, improve the documentation whenever it lets you down.

▓ **Note** The people putting the most time into documentation really don't like comments on documentation pages (and in fact will probably have killed that capability by the time you read this; see `drupal.org/node/810508` for more information). If you have information to add or correct, please edit the page. If it's a change that requires discussion, file an issue about it.

---

5. Contributing Patches

Contributing patches does not necessarily mean contributing code. The novice tag (`drupal.org/patch/novice`) is a way to tag and sort core issues that are relatively simple to resolve. Just changing the wording of a comment got Benjamin listed as a code contributor to Drupal 7!

The more users get hooked on making Drupal better, the better for all. Drupal will not be able to support the growing user base if contributions do not keep pace. Currently, less than 1% of Drupal users are contributing back. That means that 99% of users benefiting from Drupal are not paying it forward. But even at that meager percentage, Drupal is able to do amazing things! The leverage of your contribution is huge.

▓ **Note** The Novice tag goes unnoticed by many, primarily by those that would be the most interested in contributing. At the time of writing, the effort to add Novice links to the set of quicklinks in Contributors blocks (mentioned in section "Reviewing the Contributions of Others") is still active at `drupal.org/node/448794`.

Another great way to start writing patches is to participate in a code or documentation sprint. These are self-organizing, informal gatherings of developers where participants work collaborative to complete code and documentation enhancements. The main Drupal Groups Events Calendar (groups.drupal.org/events) allows you to filter by event types if you aren't already a member of your closest Drupal group.

Keep an eye out for users who post topics in group forums or discussions that point back to the issue queue. These people are trying to rally troops to get something done! Documentation on creating patches with Git can be found at dgd7.org/patch. Additionally, you can find instructions for applying patches at drupal.org/patch/apply and creating patches at drupal.org/patch/create.

6. Contributing Code and Design

Contributing to Drupal by writing and maintaining projects is covered in Chapters 15 and 16 on theming, Chapters 18 to 24 on module development, and Chapter 37 on maintaining a project on drupal.org.

7. Curating Issue Queues

Another huge way to contribute to Drupal (and to the health and sanity of people writing code and documentation) is to help manage the vast number of questions, requests, and reports of problems. Every project on drupal.org has an issue queue. The goal of issue queue curation is the following:

- To close issues that aren't relevant or can't be reproduced (or understood).

- To get the right eyes on what is addressable.

- To try to fix the problem yourself!

If you are looking at an issue and it's not clear how to do any of these things or even add a useful question or clarification, simply move on to the next issue.

Authors throughout this book have encouraged you to file issues when you run into a broken part of a project (a bug) or even a missing feature. And as much as project maintainers want to hear from you, merely just adding to their pile of things to deal with is unlikely to win you many points. Daniel Kudwein (sun), a developer and designer who deals with dozens of pages of issues in his own projects' queues, has a suggestion on his user page (drupal.org/user/54136).

> *If you are asking yourself why your issue has not been resolved yet, then please have a look at my queue: drupal.org/project/user/sun. If you want me to help you, you want to help me—by testing other patches or answering support questions of other users. :)*

Pitching in by sorting through the accumulated input from the Drupal-using public is a direct way to earn the good will of a project maintainer. If it's a project that you care about, you will also benefit from increasing your own knowledge about the project's rough edges and strengths. All the while you're paying it forward.

Sun's recommendations for helping in project issue queues are summarized below:

- **Find maintainer directions.** (Not all project maintainers offer them or are as responsive as sun.)

- **Find duplicate issues.**

- Set the status of one of the issues (usually the newer or less active issue) to *closed (duplicate)*.

- Link to the open issue.

■ **Tip** You can create a link that will expand to include the title of the issue you link to by entering only the node ID in brackets, preceded by a number sign, like this: [#1207734].

- Leave a comment on the open issue inking to the issue you closed, such as "Marked [#1234578] as duplicate."

- **Find related issues.** Two issues may not be exactly the same, yet all the people involved in each should know about the other one to help each other. In *Linux Journal*'s February 2011 interview with Angela Byron, she said that she spent a lot of her time as maintainer ensuring that developers who were working on similar initiatives in core were in touch with each other.

- **Review patches.** (This is covered separately later in this chapter under "8 Reviewing Contributions of Others.")

- **Answer support requests** and close support requests (set status to *fixed*) where the original poster seems to have received the information they need.

- **Set the status of bug reports** that don't have enough explanation or detail to be reproduced to *postponed (maintainer needs more info)*.

- **Close useless bug reports.** In general, anything marked *needs more information* and without a new reply from the original poster (sometimes abbreviated "OP") for more than a week or two is not reproducible and can be marked *closed (cannot reproduce)*.

For an excellent example in community management of a project's issue queue, check out the Views Bug Squad. While some of the rules of engagement are specific to the Views module and the styles of Earl Miles (merlinofchaos, drupal.org/user/26979) and co-maintainers Daniel Wehner (dereine, drupal.org/user/99340) and Lynette Miles (esmerel, drupal.org/user/164022), most of the advice can be applied to any module, theme, or other project. In particular, see the "How to Use the Issue Queue" page (http://drupal.org/node/945492) in the Views Bug Squad Handbook (drupal.org/node/945414).

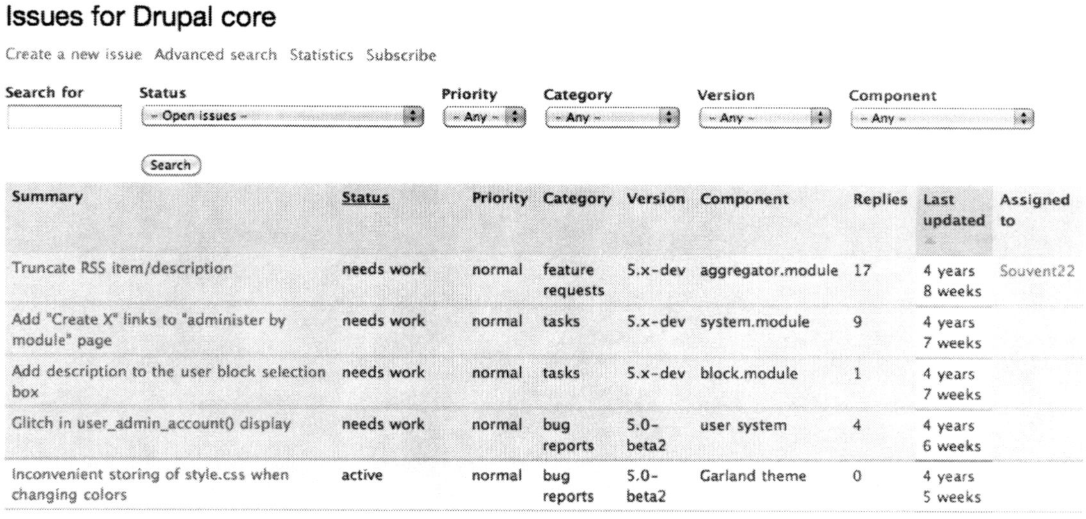

Issues for Drupal core

Create a new issue Advanced search Statistics Subscribe

Search for	Status	Priority	Category	Version	Component
	– Open issues –	– Any –	– Any –	– Any –	– Any –

(Search)

Summary	Status	Priority	Category	Version	Component	Replies	Last updated	Assigned to
Truncate RSS item/description	needs work	normal	feature requests	5.x–dev	aggregator.module	17	4 years 8 weeks	Souvent22
Add "Create X" links to "administer by module" page	needs work	normal	tasks	5.x–dev	system.module	9	4 years 7 weeks	
Add description to the user block selection box	needs work	normal	tasks	5.x–dev	block.module	1	4 years 7 weeks	
Glitch in user_admin_account() display	needs work	normal	bug reports	5.0-beta2	user system	4	4 years 6 weeks	
Inconvenient storing of style.css when changing colors	active	normal	bug reports	5.0-beta2	Garland theme	0	4 years 5 weeks	

Figure 38–1. The Drupal core issue queue, sorted by Last updated.

■ **Tip** It is a good practice to look at the oldest issues first. You can sort an issue queue by clicking on the table headers, including the "Last updated" column (see Figure 38–1). While starting from Drupal core's oldest issues may seem daunting, in some respects the oldest issues can be easier to resolve. It is also perfectly all right to work on more current issues, of course.

In her talk about the Drupal community at the Pacific Northwest Drupal Summit, Angie Byron issues a challenge to us Drupallers to answer one support question or forum request a day. The goal is about making progress, moving along steadily instead of in one giant cram session. Angie's video and slides are available at webchick.net/node/80.

8. Reviewing the Contributions of Others

OK, so every method of contributing so far has started off with a claim that it's the most important and it's a great way to learn. They really all are! And in particular there is a crying need for reviewers. Reviewing, like writing documentation, is a particularly powerful way to learn how the Drupal software and community work while getting a sneak peak at upcoming developments.

Like so much else in Drupal, reviewing centers around the issue queue. Issues ready for review are marked with the status *needs review*. To find issues for Drupal core that need review, go to drupal.org/project/issues/drupal and filter by status.

One of Drupal 7's new features is the Dashboard. You can add blocks of information (direct links to content, Drupal news, project specific issue queues) that you want to have at your fingertips. Keep current on the number of issues per queue by adding the Contributor Links block to your Dashboard (Figure 38–2).

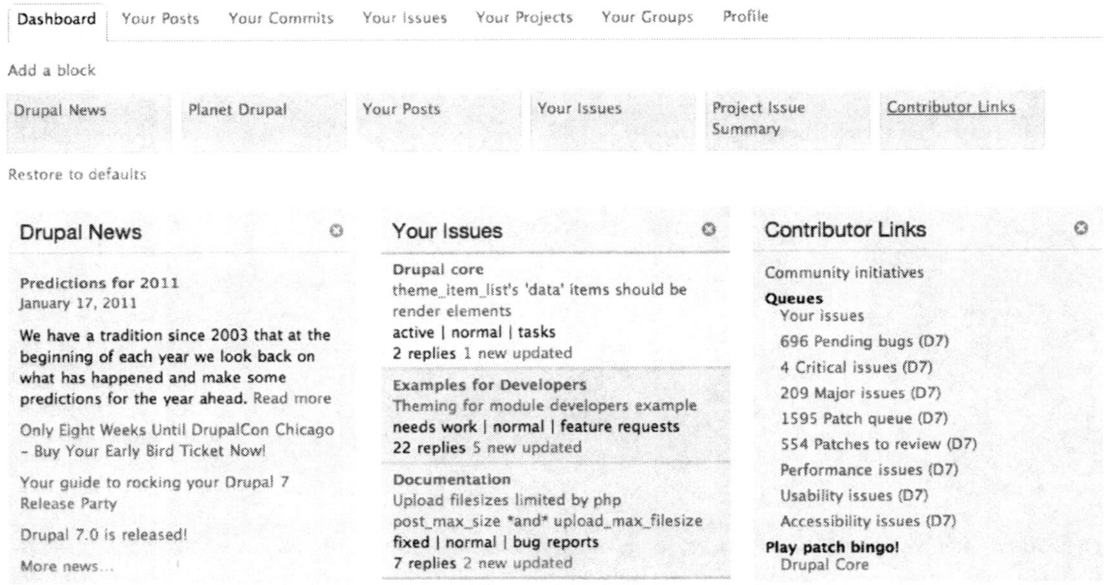

Figure 38–2. In the Contributor Links block, note the Patches to review link under Queues.

Using Dreditor to Review Patches

All the professionals and cool kids (well, a lot of them) use a Greasemonkey script called Dreditor to perform patch reviews. Dreditor stands for Drupal editor; it's script that turns your Firefox or Chrome browser into a patch reviewing machine. Created by Drupal angel Daniel Kudwein (sun), it's available at `drupal.org/project/dreditor`. To use Dreditor, simply highlight a part of code you want to comment on, type your comment in the box that appears on the left, and click Save.

■ **Note** When multiple patches are attached to an issue, review only one at a time.

Until you click Cancel, Dreditor assumes that you are you still are viewing the patch. If you try to review another patch by clicking Review, Dreditor won't bring up the new patch you want to review; instead, you continue editing the first patch.

9. Making Drupal.org Better

One of the ways to make the greatest impact on the whole Drupal community is to help improve `drupal.org`. It has gone through a major redesign in partnership with Mark Boulton Designs; all needs and goals are well-identified. The high-priority features are outlined at `drupal.org/node/1006924`. You'll notice that many sections still need to be upgraded to Drupal 7. There's no better time to be effective, to learn, and to be part of the team contributing to the Drupal project in the most direct and important way possible. Key parts of improving Drupal.org fall under the new Prarie Initiative, `groups.drupal.org/prarie-initiative`.

`Drupal.org` is the Drupal community's "online office", as Angie Byron (webchick) called it in her DrupalCon Chicago panel on Scaling the Community. Angie is following up her three-year leadership stint on Drupal 7's development by concentrating on making `drupal.org` rock ever harder! What a fantastic member of the community to get to work alongside. Get started by reading "So you want to help make Drupal.org awesome?" at `drupal.org/node/1006562`. The unstoppable Derek Wright (dww, `drupal.org/user/46549`) maintains an installation profile for creating copies of `drupal.org` on which people can do testing and development at `drupal.org/project/drupalorg_testing`.

10. Hosting and Organizing Meetups, Camps, Summits, and More

"It is fascinating to think that only a few years ago, the main DrupalCon was smaller than today's DrupalCamps. It's even more staggering when you realize that on any given weekend, there are probably several DrupalCamps happening in cities all around the world. It blows my mind. In-person meetings have been instrumental to Drupal's success and growth. If you want to grow Drupal in your area, consider to put on a DrupalCamp and to organize regular meet-ups. It is the best way to bootstrap and foster your local Drupal community."

—Dries Buytaert

The fact that we now have a half-dozen terms regularly used to describe Drupal gatherings indicates the demand for these events.

DrupalCons are multi-day conferences traditionally held twice a year (one in North America and one in Europe). DrupalCons are now reaching about 4,000 attendees. As Drupal grows, DrupalCons grow to reflect the diversity of the community attending from offering paid training to vendor booth areas. The week always culminates with a day of sprints, where people use the opportunity to work together on code and documentation. Conversations are happening in the world-wide community, particularly Asia-Oceana and Latin America, to add more DrupalCons outside North America and Europe axis.

Drupal Summits are like mini, regional DrupalCons, multi-day, multi-faceted events. Drupal Summits are a new category, and the Pacific Northwest Drupal Summit is given credit as being the first to use the term. The first Latin American Drupal Summit happened in January 2011 in Lima, Peru.

Drupal Camps are a one- or two-day event with multiple presenters that are usually held once a year per city. Camps can be organized BarCamp style (all sessions chosen on the day of the event) or the schedule may be set ahead of time. The Drupal Camp Organizing Guide can be found at `groups.drupal.org/node/10437`. There are also camps organized around a theme. Specific design-focused camps arose from people wanting to work together to improve design in Drupal. The first Design for Drupal (D4D) camp happened in Boston in 2008. Now there have been D4D camps in Boston, Los Angeles, Stanford, and Prague.

Drupal Meetups occur in cities and towns the world over. Many are held at a regular monthly time and feature lightening talks (5 to 10 minute presentations on what people are doing with Drupal) and time for attendees to ask questions and get help or advice. For information on hosting meetups, see the Local User Group Organizers group at groups.drupal.org/local-user-group-organizers, and Drupal educator Heather James' writeup of different meetup styles at acquia.com/blog/heather/what-do-you-do-your-drupal-meet.

Drupal Cafés are usually smaller gatherings than the meetups and always held where food and drink are readily available.

Drupal Dojos are smaller gatherings geared toward free, focused community learning. Austin, Boston, and Seattle hold weekly or twice monthly Drupal Dojo training/co-working sessions.

Drupal Katas are Dojo sessions focused on a particular project.

Sprints are events that result in doing, such that organizing one is a double contribution. You can have code, documentation, marketing, and planning sprints. Sprints can be open or limited to advanced levels. Decide in the beginning whether you want to teach, code, or have a hybrid, and make sure to include your plan in your announcement. Sessions are always more productive when expectations are set up front.

Drupal parties are newer entries to the scene. There were more than 300 independently-organized Drupal 7 release parties in 96 countries in early January 2011!

Drupal Dev Days (drupaldays.org), a hybrid camp-sprint-summit event, drew hundreds of developers from a dozen countries to Europe in February 2011.

The most important thing to note is that hosting and organizing is not top down. You can't organize a DrupalCon by yourself but you can certainly be part of putting one on. You can put on smaller events yourself and be the catalyst for the rest of the event types. Get creative—John Zavocki (johnvsc) began to hold drupal Play Dates randomly across New York City, and George Matthes stepped up to be a regular host.

Here are some good points and tips to keep in mind when deciding to organize, host, and plan for a sprint or camp where code work is going to be executed:

- **Find a place with stable Internet connection.** Small code sprints can even be held in people's homes.

- **Try to get veteran programmers involved** and make sure someone with commit access to the project(s) is present or available remotely.

- **Have one primary person record issues** and who is working on them. Keep notes on a Drupal wiki page or real-time collaboration document such as Google Docs or Etherpad (piratepad.net).

- **Have food available.** Everyone will eventually get hungry!

11. Money

Writing a check is a perfectly valid way to contribute and is always appreciated. If you are unsure where to contribute or don't have time to give to coding or organizing, donating money is great way to demonstrate your support. It takes money to put on events, purchase food for code sprints, and get insurance for camp attendees. The following are ways to monetarily contribute to Drupal.

Donating to the Drupal Association

The Drupal Association pays for things relating to the `drupal.org` infrastructure and works on selected other things, such as promotion of Drupal and fostering the community. It is extremely important work. Drupal has distinguished itself by providing excellent community support. As communities grow, their support requirements change. If you become a member of the Drupal Association, your membership is an annual contribution. For more information on the benefits of membership, go to `association.drupal.org/membership`. Once you are a member, you can give more at `association.drupal.org/about/donations`.

Sponsoring Events

Drupal events can always use sponsors. Drupal conferences may not have a sponsorship slot you can afford, but the nearest Drupal Camp most certainly will. (And if there aren't any Drupal Camps near you, see the section about hosting your own events!)

Sponsoring Developers

Drupal developers are in high demand, but some of those who have contributed the most are doing so on their own time. Sponsoring development by people with a good community track record is a great way to give thanks. Say there's a module that you repeatedly use, but perhaps it isn't very popular because it serves a niche purpose—but it serves it well. Check in with the maintainer(s); they might be working on their own time and could use some monetary compensation.

Scholarships are another way to sponsor developers. There's no formal process for this, but if you know someone who should be presenting at a camp or conference, you can ask if they have train or plane fare or lodging. You can usually reach out to community members through their `drupal.org` contact forms.

▓ **Tip** Get involved with ways to raise and make efficient, targeted use of funds at `groups.drupal.org/paying-plumbing`.

---

12. Making the Drupal Community Welcoming

"It's really the Drupal community and not so much the software that makes the Drupal project what it is. So fostering the Drupal community is actually more important than just managing the code base."

—Dries Buytaert

Our main challenge is keeping the community welcoming and supportive as the community scales. Drupal's Angela Byron (webchick) graced the cover of Linux Journal in 2011 for her leadership in the community and work on Drupal 7, yet her first contributions to any free software project came 10 years after she was introduced to and excited by the concept. The myth that kept her out was that you have to be Einstein smart to contribute to open source. "You don't have to be," she said. "There are a lot of smart people, but there's also everyone else contributing and sharing what they know. And that can be anything." Drupal is very, very lucky to have gotten webchick and not lost her to Linux, but how many potential awesome contributors have we (and all open source projects, and the world) lost? It is an inescapable conclusion that we're losing potential contributors because they do not have an inflated ego. We need to work to remove the false perception that you have to be some X level of smart to do Drupal and contribute to Drupal.

Studies have shown that doing something to break (or simply distract people from) a lack of confidence disproportionately and significantly helped the test scores of underperforming groups. This is called the stereotype threat, and you can help combat it simply by welcoming everyone as a contributor.

This also means we need to continue to be conscious of valuing all contributions, not only code. And just as people who come for the code stay for the community and begin to contribute in many other ways, so too people who start contributing through support, reviewing and testing, and documentation may end up making significant code contributions.

The opposite of treating everyone as a potential contributor is stereotyping anyone for any reason. Drupal IRC channels have guidelines disallowing talk that is sexist, racist, or homophobic (see drupal.org/irc/guidelines). Inappropriate comments become a problem when they are not addressed. People must speak up when they see someone undercutting another's right to equal treatment. By and large, the self-policing has worked. The advice is simple: Be sensitive to discrimination, and take action when it happens. It can mean the world to a community member to see someone step in and say "we don't do that here." Avoid a long awkward silence. Hopefully other members will back you up and soon move through the discussion.

We must ensure that our community treats everyone well. We need to be conscious of valuing all contributions and members regardless of sex, age, race, or economic background. It is impossible to remain isolated from the larger issues of economic and social disparities but we can make an effort to ensure that we avoid reproducing or compounding them within our community. Rethinking our models of collaboration, funding for low income web-projects, teaching and training are great ways to start.

Diversity makes free software more powerful. Drupal has a pretty diverse group of contributors in terms of backgrounds and countries, but traditionally, open source free software has an abysmal proportion of women participating. In fact, *less than two percent* of open source developers are women, versus 20 to 30 percent of proprietary software engineers and developers. Drupal is doing somewhat better with a 10 percent female participation rate, but there is still vast room for improvement. The DrupalChix group (groups.drupal.org/drupalchix) exists to address the underrepresentation of women in Drupal with the fortunate fact that we can do something about it. All-in-all, the Drupal community is showing excellence in keeping our environments safe and friendly to all.

Building the Movement

There is no grand plan coordinating the contributors to Drupal, which, according to Angie Byron, "gets really interesting if you're trying to take the initiative of making something happen in the community because you're trying to make a lot of individuals believe that the same thing is important. The community is founded on the concept of "do-ocracy" ... the only way things get done is if someone actually does them. It's a pretty simple concept, but there's nobody being paid to care about Drupal core, there's nobody paid to care about their modules unless they have some sort of special arrangement, so people care about stuff because they need it and they just dive in."

Amazing things have been accomplished (and amazing things are in the works) with this approach, but it's also worth noting that it is our ability to do some level of planning and coordination that makes it work. Drupal has been at its best in areas where:

- People are able to contribute without (or with easily obtained) approval.

- Tools for coordination exist and the process and authority for making decisions is clear.

Where either of these are true, such as in Drupal core and contributed projects, Drupal is often at its best. Whether ironically or fittingly, working on improving these two qualities in various places in Drupal are where you are most likely to require approval with no clear means of coordinating or making decisions (see dgd7.org/resistance).

Perhaps the most exciting thing about working on these points—how do many people work together on complex, crucial projects without structures of control or coercion, economic or otherwise?—is that they are critical, not just to Drupal's success but to making a better world.

A better world is what a surprisingly large amount of people mean when thinking about Drupal as a movement. Similarly, many people in Drupal are aware that Drupal, by giving them the ability to contribute to world-changing software and to make a living at the same time, is a unique and wonderful gift.

We share this gift each time we introduce others to Drupal but it's also possible to use our sense of community and the practices we put in place to build community beyond Drupal. This has not happened much yet, but Drupal has remarkably conscious people throughout the community. Josh Koenig (joshk, drupal.org/user/3313), founder of Chapter 3, one of the first Drupal shops, recently wrote on his blog: "We are entering a time where the potential exists for the first time to create an effective and non-oppressive set of rules that span the entire globe. Only within such a framework of global scope is a working post-industrial economy with 6 billion participants humanely possible."

Acting on this widely-shared desire for a better world in concert with the work we are doing to build a stronger Drupal community could dramatically increase our effectiveness at building both. After all, the software itself is mostly about communication and coordination, the underpinnings of all accomplishment and power. We, the people working with Drupal, have an opportunity to transform a historically temporary increase in autonomy and fair pay into crucial support of the struggle for liberty and justice for all.

The hardest work in Drupal is building the community while preserving its ethos: making it so people can contribute in every way possible and creating ways to coordinate to get great things done. This work, overlapping as it does with the pressing needs of our planet, is also the most exciting.

See you in the issue queues—and perhaps in person and in whatever else the community comes up with!

PART VIII

■■■

Appendix

Appendix A Covers the essential steps of upgrading a Drupal site from Drupal 6 to Drupal 7 and introduces its twin alternative, data migration.

Appendix B gets you started with profiling Drupal to identify, and so be able to fix, performance bottlenecks. See also Chapter 27 on scaling Drupal.

Appendix C focuses on the rendering system, or Render API, one of the major innovations in Drupal 7, and how it can benefit site builders.

Appendix D gives tips on how to approach graphical design for a site from a Drupal perspective.

Appendix E explains Drupal's accessibility enhancements and helps show you what practices to follow and what resources to use to make your site accessible to all.

Appendix F shows you how to get Drupal up and running on Windows and gets you started with Windows-based tools for working with Drupal.

Appendix G gives you a start to running Drupal on Ubuntu—including how to run Ubuntu on a virtual machine if you want to use this popular Linux variant for Drupal development.

Appendix H gets you through installing Drupal on Mac OS X.

Appendix I covers getting Drupal installed and running with a cross-platform Drupal stack installer.

And visit dgd7.org and dgd7.org/bonus for new material that supplements this book.

APPENDIX A

■ ■ ■

Upgrading a Drupal Site from 6 to 7

by Benjamin Melançon and Stefan Freudenberg with a Data Migration overview by Mike Ryan

> *"Dream. Drive. Do."*
>
> —Anjali Forber-Pratt

A cost of Drupal's continuous innovation is that upgrading a Drupal site a major version (such as Drupal 6 to Drupal 7) is usually a major deal. Drupal core promises an upgrade path for your data. It promises nothing for your code. Indeed, you can count on custom code breaking when you upgrade between major versions of Drupal. The custom code on your site that will no longer work will likely include your theme. On a complex site, you will have to replace abandoned modules or deal with new versions of modules that work somewhat differently.

For these reasons, many site owners and developers choose to add features, re-work functionality, and refresh the design as part of the upgrade. The key is to manage all these moving parts in a way that allows you to test the upgrade and new features together while bringing in new live data. You can accomplish this by capturing the configuration changes in code (along with the module and theme changes, already in code) and applying the upgrade to live data. You can also accomplish this by building a site in Drupal 7 and migrating in the content from a Drupal 6 (or Drupal 5 or 4.7 or non-Drupal) site. We focus on the upgrade approach and include an overview of data migration considerations. Many of the same principles and things to watch out for apply to both approaches.

First, however, you have to decide if you want to move your site from Drupal 6 to Drupal 7 at all. If your site is working fine and you aren't planning to make any changes, *you probably don't want to upgrade* yet. When you do have ideas that will require writing code to implement, that is a good indication it is time to upgrade. To upgrade a moderately-sized Drupal 6 site to Drupal 7, you will generally need to complete each of these broad steps:

- Update all modules to the most recent Drupal 6 release.
- Figure out which modules are available in Drupal 7.
- Replace Drupal 6 core and contrib modules with Drupal 7 counterparts.
- Run update.php.
- Use CCK's Content Migrate module to update the CCK fields.
- Reconfigure views, image style presets, content types, fields, and more, as needed.
- Update and replace custom code or abandoned modules and add features.
- Create a new Drupal 7 theme.

We aren't going to do all of that in this appendix. This book covers theming in more than 100 pages in Chapters 15 and 16 and covers site configuration and module development in numerous other chapters. This appendix will cover the upgrade-specific parts of these steps to provide a solid foundation for rebuilding a site in 7.

It's good that we'll be working on an inspirational site, that of Paralympic gold medalist Anjali Forber-Pratt, because upgrading is a lot like training. You want to set things up so that you can run the upgrade over and over until you achieve your goals. In our approach to upgrading, we will be set to follow through with a major overhaul of the site using the everything-in-code deployment approach discussed in Chapter 13. Again, this chapter won't take you through building out all the features of the new site—but the story continues at dgd7.org/anjali.

▓ **Tip** See also the steps from UPGRADE.txt under MAJOR VERSION UPGRADE. We haven't followed the steps exactly here, because Drush lets us skip a bit, but they are the community-expected practice and a good fallback if the methods here don't work. The steps may not work either, but you will be better positioned when asking for community support! Being able to clearly document and describe your issues in the Drush issue queue would also work, if following the drush site-upgrade approach. For more about seeking answers beyond the book, see Chapter 9 on getting help and getting involved.

Whatever you do, always back up your site before updating anything related to the database (as in going to update.php or introducing changes to modules that may require this). The standard "back it up!" warning goes triple when doing a major-version upgrade.

▓ **Caution** Do not attempt a major-version upgrade on a live site. Even if it has been fully tested, upgrade a copy of the site alongside the live site, and then switch from the live to the upgraded copy when it is successful. You'll have to put the live site into a read-only mode or, if it's just user posts and comments you need to worry about, you can manually bring over changes from the overlap period.

Note that some Drupal developers recommend using a build-fresh-and-migrate-content-in approach even for moderately complex sites. It's definitely an option to consider, especially for an upgrade with a major overhaul of a complex site, and so is discussed in the "Data Migration" section of this appendix. (Migration is, of course, the only option for upgrading a non-Drupal site to Drupal. For this reason, its tools are being developed at a faster pace than traditional upgrade tools.) The planning steps described here, and discussed further in that section, will be similar.

▧ **Tip** If upgrading from Drupal 5 to Drupal 7, you must upgrade to Drupal 6 first. Follow the instructions in UPGRADE.txt for Drupal 6 (which will broadly follow the steps taken in the first part of this chapter). Upgrade both core and contrib. However, **do not** bother with the fixing steps: do not upgrade your theme, do not port your custom modules, do not find replacements for contrib modules that don't have an upgrade path. Leave broken any of these parts from a 5 to 6 upgrade, proceed with the upgrade to 7, and then fix things. Alternatively, a two-version upgrade calls ever more loudly for starting fresh and using Migrate (drupal.org/project/migrate) to bring in your content, users, paths, taxonomies. (The brief overview of data migration that closes this chapter has a strong bias toward the Migrate module.) Another approach is to write your own upgrade module to use Drupal's APIs to make the leap; see quicksketch.org/node/5739.

The most important point of this appendix is to do everything and anything you do to upgrade your site in a re-playable way.

Assess the Situation

The unfortunate truth is that improving an existing site can be more work than starting fresh, and this applies when doing an upgrade, too. Estimating the work involved is important and difficult. You can get an overview by looking at the content types and how many nodes of each there are, the core and contributed modules enabled, and number of major structural elements such as views, node queues, vocabularies, panels, etc.

For upgrading a theme, you will almost certainly have to write some code, unless you are using a theme off drupal.org uncustomized, in which case it might get upgraded for you. Theming and Drupal's default regions have changed a bit, however, and it's unlikely that even a contributed theme that is ported will function identically without some reconfiguration.

Content Overview

There are many modules and tools to help you get an overview of a site (including Nancy Wichmann's Site Documentation module at drupal.org/project/sitedoc, which does much more than just content types). You can also get a content overview of a Drupal 6 site with an SQL query like the one shown in Listing A–1.

Listing A–1. SQL Query That Counts the Number of Nodes of Each Content Type

```
mysql
mysql> USE anjali;
mysql> SELECT type, count(*) FROM node GROUP BY type;
+----------------+----------+
| type           | count(*) |
+----------------+----------+
| activitystream |      918 |
| blog           |       90 |
| event          |       83 |
| feed_ical      |        2 |
| inthenews      |        4 |
| multichoice    |        3 |
| news           |       12 |
| page           |       11 |
| photo          |       28 |
| quiz           |        1 |
| resource       |        6 |
| sponsor        |        6 |
| stat           |        8 |
| story          |        5 |
| video          |        8 |
| webform        |        1 |
+----------------+----------+
16 rows in set (0.00 sec)
```

Knowing the counts is always better than guessing or making assumptions. For example, given the above counts, if the Highlights and Statistics (stat) content type is best redone from scratch, it's not the end of the world, with 8 posts. The Twitter and Facebook status updates (activitystream) content, at 918 posts, will need to be re-imported into the new site if it can't upgrade directly.

Contributed Modules

Most of the functionality you care about on a site likely comes from contributed modules. For each module, you will first want to ask if you still want its functionality at all. If yes, you will want to check on the state of that module in Drupal 7. Is it something that has been ported already? Is it something you can port—and provide an upgrade path, if needed—yourself? (See Chapter 21 on porting modules to Drupal 7.) Is it something you will need to rely on the community to port for you? This latter option means that the schedule is not necessarily yours; in that case, you will probably want to try to find a maintainer or other contributor whom you can sponsor to do the port.

The first step is knowing what modules you have. Again, this can be done with an SQL query.

```
mysql> SELECT name FROM system WHERE status=1 and type='module';
```

Or it can also be done with Drush.

```
drush pm-list --pipe --type=module --status=enabled --no-core > modules.txt
```

Remember, you are investigating your Drupal 6 site to get a plan for upgrading to 7. If you followed best practices, you would already have a spreadsheet of each module installed on your site and its purpose, but if you didn't follow best practices (or are taking over someone else's Drupal 6 site), you need to figure this out. For a complex site that may not have followed best development practice (and few have), a module being *enabled* does not necessarily mean it is *in use*.

Make a spreadsheet starting with this list of modules names and add columns for Purpose, Want to keep, and D7 status. An early version of this spreadsheet assessing the Drupal 6 version of anjaliforberpratt.com/ can be found at dgd7.org/220; a version from the end of the process is on that resource page also.

In general, the goal is not usually to make an identical site in the next version of Drupal but to make a site that reaches all of its (revised) objectives and carries forward the content, paths, and users. This means that you should not automatically include every previously used module you can find available for the new version of Drupal. Instead, modules should be evaluated against their purpose in the old site and the purpose on the new site, taking into account if the purpose is different or if the best way to achieve a purpose has changed.

▓ **Tip** A great project by Daniel Kudwien (sun) provides modules to help upgrade Drupal sites: drupal.org/project/upgrade_status. The first module, Upgrade Status, gives the availability in the next version of Drupal of the modules you have installed on your site now. The second module, Upgrade Assist, runs you through all the preparation steps (taking your contributed modules into account). Use the 6.x version for upgrading your 6.x site to Drupal 7!

Create a Plan

Once you know the situation, compare what you want with what you have, and prepare a plan to get there. For complex projects, you may want to put in an intermediate phase where you replace the site—on production—with a Drupal 7 version that does not yet implement all the features you envision.

The start of the book and Chapter 10 (on Planning and Project Management) are good overview resources. Tune in to dgd7.org/anjali to look at the planning documents used in the upgrade process.

Run the Upgrade (Again and Again)

The key concept of this section is to set up your upgrade process so that you can try it as many times as you need to, with changes to your Drupal 7 module selection and custom code each time, to have a working site at the end.

▓ **Note** The final section of this appendix, "Data Migration," takes a similar approach to repeatedly bringing data in, but separates it from (and makes unnecessary) any upgrade.

Preparation

Before beginning anything, update the Drupal 6 installation you wish to upgrade to the latest security and bugfix of Drupal 6 (see Chapter 7), and then update all upgrade-bound contributed modules to their latest stable release.

Anything that you can clean up on the live site will help you a lot. An unused content type (zero nodes of that type)? Delete it. A module that's not used or is really only for site-building use? Disable and possibly uninstall it. The less your upgrade script has to clean up the live site, the easier your life will be. On Anjali's site, Nodequeue module was unused and About This Node module (about_this_node) was for site building only. Both could be disabled on the production site without any adverse effect (in fact, disabling unnecessary modules means the live Drupal 6 site consumes less resources and may gain slightly snappier performance).

Drush Aliases for All Sites Involved in the Upgrade

If you think there's only one site involved in the upgrade, you missed Chapter 13. There's the live Drupal 6 site you don't want to do anything on directly. There's at least one local Drupal 6 site that's a copy of the live one (for development and testing things like disabling those unused modules, as in the previous section). There's probably a test or stage Drupal 6 site for letting people who aren't able to look over your shoulder at your computer vet changes to the site. Then there is, of course, at least one local development Drupal 7 site. And there should be a test or stage Drupal 7 site, too. And when you finally go live, there's a production Drupal 7 site up at the same time as the production Drupal 6 site, and you make the switch on your web server.

Managing all these sites and moving databases and files can be quite easy if you set up aliases for them in Drush, as described in Chapter 26 and shown in Listing A–2.

Listing A–2. Drush Aliases File for anjaliforberpratt.com with Test and Local Aliases Added for the 7 Version

```php
<?php
/**
 * @file
 * Drush aliases file.  See drush/examples/example.aliases.drushrc.php.
 *
 * Copy the database from production to development:
 * drush sql-sync @anjali.prod @anjali.dev --structure-tables-key=common
 *
 * Copy the database from production to testing:
 * drush sql-sync @anjali.prod @anjali.test --structure-tables-key=common
 *
 * Copy the database from testing to production (as for first launch):
 */
$aliases['prod'] = array(
  'remote-host' => 'sojourner.mayfirst.org',
  'remote-user' => 'anjaliforberpratt',
  'root' => '/var/local/drupal/anjali/web',
  'uri' => 'anjaliforberpratt.com',
);
$aliases['test'] = array(
  'remote-host' => 'simone.mayfirst.org',
  'remote-user' => 'ben',
  'root' => '/var/local/drupal/anjali/web',
  'uri' => 'anjali.agariclabs.org',
);
$aliases['test7'] = array(
  'remote-host' => 'simone.mayfirst.org',
  'remote-user' => 'ben',
```

```
  'root' => '/var/local/drupal/anjali7',
  'uri' => 'anjali7.agariclabs.org',
);
$aliases['dev'] = array(
  'root' => '/home/ben/code/anjali/web',
  'uri' => 'anjali.localhost',
);
$aliases['dev7'] = array(
  'root' => '/home/ben/code/anjali7/web',
  'uri' => 'anjali7.localhost',
);
```

Setting up these Drush aliases makes working with the old and new sites much easier.

DRUSH MAGIC

There is a nearly all-Drush approach to site upgrades. Greg Anderson reworked the `drush site-upgrade` command with additional capabilities such as automatic non-core module disabling and a theme-reset to garland. It also deals with changing dependencies, such as views-7.x requiring CTools while views-6.x does not, a common cause of surprising and mysterious fatal errors on the upgraded site. For many sites, the site upgrade can be a matter of the following steps:

1. Define an alias for your new d7 site (as above).

2. Run the command `drush site-upgrade @anjali.dev7`.

3. Wait 15 minutes or more for it to complete.

4. Test and re-theme your site.

5. Repeat as needed.

It is the repeat-as-needed step that gets tricky. By the time you read this, the command in the form `drush site-upgrade @anjali.dev7` (run from the Drupal 6 dev copy of live) will probably work for you for both the initial upgrade and re-testing it, but this appendix shows a stepped approach that works now.

A Middle Way

Drush's `site-upgrade` command will do everything for you, but for a complex site where the goal is to have every element of the upgrade committed to version control such that the code is perfect for your new Drupal 7 site and every single database change to get it there is encoded in an update hook, it's doing too much. Therefore, this appendix takes something of a middle ground approach between manual and pure Drush automation. You will soon see why the Drush `site-upgrade` command is far preferable if it will support your use case and workflow.

Starting the 7 Code Base

Even the Drush command moves you to a new site. For your version control, you could start a new branch in your repository or start a fresh repository for your Drupal 7 site, which is also just fine and probably cleaner and better (see Listing A–3).

Listing A–3. Starting the Upgrade with a New Drupal 7 Project

```
mkdir ~/code/anjali7
cd ~/code/anjali7
drush -y dl --drupal-project-rename=web
mkdir web/sites/all/modules/contrib
mkdir web/sites/default/files
mkdir private_files
sudo chown -R :www-data web/sites/default
sudo chmod -R g+w web/sites/default
sudo chown -R :www-data private_files
sudo chmod -R g+w private_files
git init
git add .
git commit -m "Drupal base."
cp web/sites/default/default.settings.php web/sites/default/settings.php
```

▓ **Tip** These commands can be saved in a shell script (this was taken from the author's) or you can use Drubuntu's `drubuntu-site-add` Drush command. Not shown above is copying over a .gitignore file which will exclude `settings.php` and the files directories from version control, copying over a model Rakefile (for deployment) and calling a script that creates a fresh database; see `dgd7.org/218` for the link to the script and its dependencies.

A database for the site above needs to be created (and `settings.php` set to look at it). Use PHPMyAdmin or another tool on your system or see the scripts at dgd7.org/218. The drush `site-upgrade` command will look for and download all copies of Drupal 7 modules it can find, automatically.

▓ **Caution** Make sure your database is clean! If a Drupal 7 table somehow gets created in your local development Drupal 6 source site, it will stay there and break your upgrades. If you do not wipe your destination Drupal 7 site's database before trying again, it will break the upgrade. *The drush sql-sync command does not delete tables; it only replaces the contents of tables it is bringing in.* Therefore, it's imperative that you drop and recreate the database or specifically wipe all tables before bringing new data in, as shown in Listing A–4.

*Listing A–4. Drop All Database Tables and Fetch the Latest Database from Production. Do **Not** Run This Command on Your Live Server.*

```
mysql -BNe "show tables" anjali | awk '{print "drop table " $1 ";"}' | mysql anjali
drush sql-sync @anjali.prod @anjali.dev
```

You do not need to put the load on your site of fetching a fresh database every time you test the upgrade; the previous steps only need to be performed every so often, when you want to make sure your upgrade still works with the latest site content.

To test an upgrade, delete any data in the target (Drupal 7) site's database. Then go to the root directory of the local Drupal 6 site, which is now a freshly-made copy of the production site you wish to upgrade, and run the upgrade (see the command-line steps in Listing A–5).

▒ **Note** For the `drush site-upgrade` command to work, the anjali7 database user needs the ability to create databases or you need to pass in the username and password of a database user that does in the command with the flags `--db-su` and `--db-su-pw`. Or you can add database switch user username and password to your **~/.drush/drushrc.php**. Working with this file is described in Chapter 26's section "Going In-Depth with Drush Configuration Options and Aliases," and the two lines you can add are

```
$options['db-su'] = 'root';
$options['db-su-pw'] = 'rootpass';
```

(with 'root' and 'rootpass' replaced with the username and password of a privileged database user).

Listing A–5. Delete all Tables in the Destination Database and Run the Upgrade.

```
mysql -BNe "show tables" anjali7 | awk '{print "drop table " $1 ";"}' | mysql anjali7
cd ~/code/anjali/web
drush site-upgrade @anjali.dev7
```

Using Drush gets you out of having to set `$update_free_access = TRUE;` in `settings.php`. It also avoids "Maximum execution time of 30 seconds exceeded" for which you often have to increase `max_execution_time` in `php.ini`. You don't get the reassuring pulsing blue progress bar, but if you can trust that Drupal and Drush are working away silently, you can stop staring at the command line waiting for the prompt to come back, and go blend an energy smoothie to prepare you for the work that will come next. The upgrade process will occasionally print messages to your screen but it will take a long time, so don't stare at it—do something productive!

▒ **Note** Views has a new dependency in CTools, so you'll need to download it (`site-upgrade` will take care of it for you). This does not enable CTools, though, so the upgrade will run through (update runs for all present and installed modules even if they are not enabled), but trying to use the site will fail until CTools is enabled. At the time of writing, a bug between Views and Drupal core also required applying a patch, found by searching online and `drupal.org` for the error dumped on the screen (remember to develop with all error reporting enabled; see Chapter 18 or `dgd7.org/err`). You shouldn't see that particular problem, but expect to be searching the web and issue queues for error messages to see if other people have come up with solutions for the problems you run into when upgrading.

The development version of the Hashcash module for Drupal 7 is preventing login to the upgraded site, so disable it with Drush (`drush -y dis hashcash`).

Capturing Additional Upgrade Steps in Update Hooks

That part was supposed to be easy, but often isn't. Now comes the fun part. Once you can run update.php on your Drupal 6 database surrounded by Drupal 7 code and come out with a somewhat working site on the other end, you can proceed to make it an awesome working site.

If no one will be adding content for the days, weeks, or months it'll take to upgrade the site, then great—just click around, and when you've finished rebuilding your site in Drupal 7, replace the old Drupal 6 one. If there will be new posts, comments, or other content and user changes on the live site, or you will be working with a team and you want to do it right, take the time (and trouble) to capture every configuration change in code. This approach is discussed in Chapter 13 in the section on Deployment.

Optional: Begin the Custom Upgrade Functions from the Drupal 7 Version of the Site's Glue Code Module

The custom update functions need to go in a custom module. Enabling this module can be scripted or done manually—or you can try the approach here.

In a perhaps foolhardy attempt to run everything with one extended database update, I am using an existing, enabled custom module to start things off by enabling a custom upgrade module. Even though the custom module will have the same name as it did on the Drupal 6 site (anjali), it need not have any connection to it, and you can start off fresh. Instead of putting all the upgrade code in this module, which you'll likely want to keep around, it can call a separate upgrade module. It begins by listing this upgrade module as a dependency, as shown in Listing A–6.

Listing A–6. Glue Code Module .info File Listing the Dedicated Upgrade Module as a Dependency

```
name = AnjaliFP.com glue code
description = Site-specific custom code for AnjaliForberPratt.com
core = 7.x
dependencies[] = anjaliup
```

Next, modules still need a .module file, even if it's blank, so create that as shown in Listing A–7.

Listing A–7. Empty .module File for the Glue Code Module

```
<?php
/**
 * @file
 * Custom code for AnjaliForberPratt.com.
 */
```

Now you get to where the action is—a .install file, shown in Listing A–8, which takes care of most of the upgrade work you will do.

Listing A–8. A .install File That Enables a Dedicated Upgrade Module

```
<?php
/**
 * @file
 * Install, update, and uninstall functions for the Anjali glue code module.
```

```
*/

/**
 * Enable the Anjaliup module to do 6.x to 7.x-specific site-building.
 */
function anjali_update_7001() {
  module_enable(array('anjaliup'));
}
```

The idea with this is that once the upgrade code is in place, you can run `drush updatedb` and 90 minutes later, you have an upgraded site! (Times will vary; it took 90 minutes for this site on an Ubuntu virtual machine on a somewhat overtaxed laptop.) The following is the ideal approach, which is used by `drush site-upgrade`:

- Turn off non-essential modules in a temporary site on the Drupal 6 (source site) codebase.

- Upgrade just core in a temporary site in the Drupal 7 (destination site).

- Then do the full upgrade.

This is the approach achieved for rerunning the upgrade (in an automatic mode requiring no responses to prompts) with two Drush commands in the section "Rerun the Upgrade."

Creating an Upgrade Module

Ideally, anything that has to do with building the Drupal 7 site can go in normal site-specific modules or Feature modules (discussed briefly in the next section).

It is highly recommended that you use a core theme that has both a Drupal 6 and Drupal 7 version for going through the upgrade, and this means Garland. After the upgrade, to focus on the site structure, content, and functionality, and not the design, you can switch to Stark. Ultimately, you will change this code to instead enable the custom theme you build for this site. But until you get to the point of testing the theme against the rest of the upgrade and functionality you add, you can capture in code the act of changing to the bare-bones Stark theme, as shown in Listing A–9.

Listing A–9. Checking the Presence and Status of Themes in the System Table

```
drush sqlc
SELECT name, status FROM system WHERE type='theme';
```

In this case the news is good: only Drupal 7 themes are listed; there are no leftover entries in the table from Drupal 6. To put your upgrade in code and test incremental updates, you can do the same thing modules do to upgrade: implement hook_update_N() for the running of update code, where the *N* stands for a number in the series of updates; see Listing A–10.

Listing A–10. Change to the Stark Theme and Set Seven as the Administration Theme

```
/**
 * Enable and set the Stark theme and set Seven as admin theme.
 *
 * Queries adapted from system.admin.inc system_theme_default() and friends.
 *
 * Note:  The Drupal 6 themes do not exist in the system table; they have been
 * cleaned up by Drupal's upgrade so we do not have to delete them ourselves.
 */
```

```
function anjaliup_update_7003() {
  $theme = 'stark';
  // Disable Garland.
  theme_disable(array('garland'));
  // Enable our chosen theme.
  theme_enable(array($theme));
  variable_set('theme_default', $theme);
  variable_set('admin_theme', 'seven');
}
```

This is function anjaliup_update_7003() because you happen to place it to run after two clean-up functions, below. Removing Unused Modules from Code and Database. Using this upgrade approach, you can delete unwanted Drupal 6 modules from code easily and they won't bother you anymore. To give your Drupal 7 site a clean start without ghosts of modules, you can clean up the database as well.

Rather than trying to run an uninstall process while the site is still in Drupal 6, you can delete traces of unwanted modules from the database yourselves. (Plus, many modules don't remove all their traces at uninstall.) There are three places modules usually store information in the database: their own tables, the variable table, and the system table.

To see what there is to be culled, you can look at the database. On the command line, Drush can connect you to your test site's database automatically when run from within the site root (saving the trouble both of looking up credentials and typing a USE databasename step). The following SELECT statement returns every module in the system table with its status (0 for disabled, 1 for enabled) and schema version:

```
drush sqlc
SELECT name, status, schema_version FROM system WHERE type='module';
```

You can see the results—254 modules, many dating back to the Drupal 5 version of this site (read: ancient history)—at dgd7.org/270. Only the modules with schema versions in the 7000s or zero are genuinely present and potentially working.

■ **Tip** The Enabled Modules module (drupal.org/project/enabled_modules), maintained by the fabulous Julian Granger-Bevan, will show you all this information in an even easier to digest format— plus let you know if the code base for a module in the database is missing.

To delete rows from a table, you want to use the db_delete() statement provided by Drupal's Database API, as shown in Listing A–11.

Listing A–11. Delete a Row for a No-Longer-Present Module from the {system} Table

```
/**
 * Remove all traces of unwanted Drupal 6 (and earlier) modules.
 */
function anjaliup_update_7001() {
  // Delete Devel module from the {system} table.
  db_delete('system')->condition('name', 'devel')->execute();
}
```

■ **Note** Update functions don't run when you install a module (enable it for the first time). In order to have the upgrade, you embed in these functions to run when this module is enabled, and you have to call all the update hook implementations from the install hook implementation. That's not the way to use `hook_install()` and `hook_update_N()` in an ordinary module, but a dedicated upgrade module is not ordinary. This is shown in Listing A–17.

Looking through the list of tables (with the query `SHOW TABLES;` when using the Drupal 7 site database) shows more things you will want to delete: tables associated with defunct modules. Leftover tables shouldn't affect site performance at all, but they can waste a lot of developer time when trying to debug something and there are database tables that have nothing to do with anything anymore lying around. One module that shouldn't show up anywhere on a production site nor in the production site's database is the Devel module. It would uninstall itself properly, but it isn't even part of the Drupal 6 site's codebase anymore, and it makes a lot more sense to code a few cleanup commands yourself then to download the module just to uninstall it.

Let's therefore add another line to the update hook for removing obsolete database information. This line will delete the entire devel_queries table and is shown in Listing A–12.

Listing A–12. Add a Line to Drop the Devel Module's devel_queries Table from the Database

```
/**
 * Remove all traces of unwanted Drupal 6 (and earlier) modules.
 */
function anjaliup_update_7001() {
// ...
  db_drop_table('devel_queries');
}
```

(The function for dropping tables was found in function `drupal_uninstall_schema()` in `includes/common.inc` by searching Drupal's code for 'uninstall_schema'. I happened to remember 'uninstall_schema' from when it had to be called explicitly in Drupal 6. Drupal 7 takes care of this call for you, but a search for 'drop_table' would have found the `db_drop_table()` function too!)

The last place to look for left-over module data is the variable table. Anjali's site, which started as Drupal 5, moved to Drupal 6, and now is moving to Drupal 7, has 1,059 rows in the variable table—all of them aren't used, and chasing down every unused one is not the best use of time. However, it makes sense to clean up a module's variable table entries as you remove its other outcroppings. Listing A–13 shows how to delete any variable with a name beginning with 'hashcash', as the Hashcash module doesn't clean up after itself fully.

Modules that have multiple variables usually clean up after themselves by deleting all variables "like" the start of the module name. Be aware that this could mean deleting variables for the wrong module. When cleaning up a site yourself you can check for this and make sure, for example, that deleting variables used by Context module (`context`) doesn't also wipe out the variables used by the completely unrelated Contextual Administration module (`context_admin`).

Listing A–13. Delete All Variables Matching a Pattern

```
db_delete('variable')->condition('name', 'hashcash%', 'LIKE')->execute();
```

▨ **Tip** If the Drupal database query you're just written is inexplicably not working, make sure you have the ->execute() method attached!

Realizing that each of these actions—deleting system table entries, dropping tables, and deleting variables—will have to be done multiple times each, you can automate it with the aid of Drupal Database API's "or condition" chained together repeatedly as many times as you need to use it; see Listing A–14.

Listing A–14. Database Cleanup Update Function in anjaliup.install Refactored to Facilitate Code Reuse

```
/**
 * Remove all traces of unwanted modules from Drupal 6 (and earlier).
 */
function anjaliup_update_7001() {
  // Delete old, not even present modules from the {system} table.
  $missing = array(
    // Site builder modules should not be in the production database.
    'devel',
    'devel_themer',
    'enabled_modules',
  );
  $or = db_or();
  foreach ($missing as $name) {
    $or->condition('name', $name);
  }
  db_delete('system')->condition($or)->execute();

  // Drop tables which are no longer used.
  $tables = array(
    'devel_queries',
    'devel_times',
  );
  foreach ($tables as $table) {
    db_drop_table($table);
  }

  $variable = array(
    'devel%',
    'hashcash%',
  );
  $or = db_or();
  foreach($variables as $variable) {
    $or->condition('name', $variable, 'LIKE');
  }
  db_delete('variable')->condition($or)->execute();
}
```

To drop multiple tables, you simple rerun the db_drop_table() command in a foreach loop. Nothing too interesting there. The db_delete() statements, however, are pretty cool. You can first build a chain of or condition methods building on the result of a db_or() function. Then this set of conditions can be handed into the condition method of a single db_delete() statement.

Modules that have working uninstall functions can be uninstalled by the drush site-upgrade function before they ever touch the Drupal 7 site. That's how the Hashcash module's table and entry in the {system} table get deleted, as you'll see in the section "Rerunning the Upgrade," but it failed to clean up its variable, so you do that here. (Incidentally, although we decided against continuing to use it for this site for now, is actually pretty cool and worth checking out in Drupal 7.)

Enabling Modules in Code

You already saw how to do this in the update function in the custom module the site inherited from its Drupal 6 edition, which was used to enable the dedicated upgrade module, but see Listing A–15 anyway.

Listing A–15. Enable a Given Array of Modules

```
/**
 * Enable modules which the site needs.
 */
function anjaliup_update_7002() {
  $modules = array(
    'ctools',  // now handled by drush site-upgrade, according to Moshe.
    'content_migrate',
    'contextual',
    'file',
    'image',
    'link',
    'pathauto',
    'rdf',
    'shortcut',
    'token',
    'toolbar',
    'views',
  );
  module_enable($modules);
}
```

Disabling Modules in Code

It won't be often, but you may want to disable a core module that upgraded well (or, later in your development, after the upgrade, you may replace one contrib module with another). In this case, you can programmatically disable a module (or multiple at once, as the function module_disable() takes an array); see Listing A–16.

Listing A–16. Disabling Two Core Modules That Won't Be Used in Drupal 7

```
/**
 * Disable core modules we no longer want to use.
 */
function anjali_update_7002() {
  $modules = array(
    'tracker',
    'trigger',
```

```
  );
  module_disable($modules);
}
```

Disabling, rather than uninstalling, preserves their data; your upgrade code can use the data if desired and then uninstall the modules with the function `drupal_uninstall_modules()`, which can be used exactly the same as `module_disable()`— by handing in an array of module system names.

Automating the Fields Upgrade

The move of CCK to core as Fields makes this upgrade more complicated, and by default not at all automatic. A special module within the CCK module, Content Migrate, is used to help upgrade Drupal 6 CCK fields to Drupal 7 fields.

If you don't need to script your upgrade (as for a simple site without many live content updates), you can visit `admin/structure/content_migrate` and migrate the fields like a regular person. To run this upgrade from code, you need to find the code that this module uses to do the migration.

Chapter 18, on making modules, discussed finding code related to a given functionality by investigating the page that contain that functionality and built the X-ray module (`drupal.org/project/xray`) in part to help that investigation. Another great way to find API functions is through Drush commands for modules that provide them. Content Migrate provides a content-migrate-fields Drush command that calls two more of its Drush commands: `content-migrate-field-structure` and `content-migrate-field-data`. These are defined in the file `cck/content_migrate/includes/content_migrate.drush.inc` and turn out to be thin wrappers around `_content_migrate_batch_process_create_fields()` and `_content_migrate_batch_process_migrate_data()`, which you can use in your update hook. (Alternatively, running some or all of an upgrade as a bash or Drush script also counts as putting it in code and could use the Drush commands directly.)

Either Content Migrate's Drush command or its administration page can provide you with the machine names and the types of the fields available for upgrading (and a trial run with one of these methods is recommended to prove it works before trying to build it into code!).

To upgrade file and image fields, you need to enable the core file and image modules first. Even though a Drupal 6 site has contrib counterparts (filefield and imagefield), Drupal will not know to turn on file and image. These must be enabled before CCK's `content_migrate` can run for files and images. We already did this in the update 7002; given that all the updates will be run again together we can add the modules we need enabled, starting with Content Migrate itself; see Listing A–17.

Listing A–17. Upgrading Fields from within hook_update_N() Functions

```
/**
 * Enable modules which the site needs.
 */
function anjaliup_update_7002() {
  $modules = array(
// Existing code not shown due to space considerations.
    'content_migrate',
    'file',
    'image',
    'link',
  );
  module_enable($modules);
}

/**
```

```
 * Upgrade fields.
 */
function anjaliup_update_7003() {
  $fields = array(
    'field_description',
    'field_event_date',
    'field_gcal_status',
    'field_link',
    'field_location',
    'field_stat',
    'field_year',
    'field_file',
    'field_image',
    'field_sponsor_logo',
  );

  module_load_include('inc', 'content_migrate', 'includes/content_migrate.admin');

  // First upgrade the structure for each field (this is the drush approach).
  $context = array();
  foreach ($fields as $field_name) {
    _content_migrate_batch_process_create_fields($field_name, $context);
  }

  // Then migrate the data for each field.
  $context = array(
    'sandbox' => array(),
  );
  foreach ($fields as $field_name) {
    _content_migrate_batch_process_migrate_data($field_name, $context);
  }
}
```

Now a major step in the upgrade of most any Drupal site from Drupal 6 to Drupal 7 is fully provided through re-playable code. Rerun the upgrade any time you want to test your upgrade process against live data. How to do this is covered next.

Rerunning the Upgrade

Every time you want to test the upgrade code you are writing, rerun the upgrade. Remember, this wipes out any configuration or content you have done on your local upgraded site unless that configuration and content has been exported to code.

First is the hack of calling all the update functions from the enable function. Aside from creating a Drush upgrade script rather than an upgrade module, one way to avoid this particular hack would be to install an empty module with the same name as the upgrade module on Drupal 6 first, so that the update hooks would run with the upgrade. However, calling each update function explicitly works for me. Having them as hook_update_N() functions makes it easy to test the new pieces of the upgrade you add: simply go to update.php (or use the command drush updatedb) and it will run any hook_update_N() functions that you have added that have a higher *N* than the last one run; the code in Listing A–18 is to run all update hooks for the upgrade module when it is enabled for the first time during upgrade by calling them from its implementation of hook_install().

Listing A–18. Run all Update Hooks for the Upgrade Module

```
function anjaliup_install() {
  // Remove all traces of unwanted modules from Drupal 6 and earlier.
  anjaliup_update_7001();

  // Disable core modules we no longer want to use.
  anjaliup_update_7002();

  // Enable and set the Stark theme and set Seven as admin theme.
  anjaliup_update_7003();

  // Enable essential modules.
  anjaliup_update_7004();

  // Upgrade fields.
  anjaliup_update_7005();

  // Enable feature modules.
  anjaliup_update_7006();
}
```

Now you're ready to rerun the upgrade from the top. At the time of this writing, drush site-upgrade (sup) is very good about allowing you to use an existing Drupal core installation and not re-downloading it (which is particularly great if you have replaced it with Pressflow, for instance). It's not so good, at the time of this writing, at running the modules upgrades without over-prompting you for input.

Listing A–19. Rerun the Site Upgrade Without Downloading Core or Contributed Modules, After

Uninstalling Modules You Want to Leave Behind in Drupal 6.

```
drush site-upgrade @anjali.dev7 --reuse --core-only --uninstall=hashcash,ping
drush @anjali.dev7 site-upgrade-modules
```

The commands in Listing A–19 could be put together in a shell script or a Drush script (see Chapter 26). Indeed, the entire site upgrade could be made a Drush script rather than a series of update hooks; use the approach you are more comfortable with. Ordinarily site-upgrade-modules can take a list of modules to enable, but you can just as easily add any modules you want in your update hook.

As usual, don't wait around. Move on to another task. Depending on your computer and your site, this task can take more than an hour. (One of the advantages to the migration approach to upgrading sites, described later in this chapter, is that it is a natural fit for the concept of continuous or incremental migration, so that even a busy site can be brought up-to-date, switched over, and any final content brought in— for a minimum of time, even no time at all, when visitors' ability to contribute to the site is disabled.)

Some things will fail. The point of putting everything into code you can replay is so that you can fix any failures and keep building on top of a solid foundation, even as new content gets added to the live site.

That's enough about cleanup. Time to build some new things for the new site!

Create a Feature

Make your re-build and enhance steps replayable by building an upgrade Features module or set of Features modules. A set of Features modules is recommended because by separating functionality into different Features, you may be able to build something you or others can use on other sites.

When undertaking a major upgrade, you will inevitably also want to take the opportunity to change some things about the way the site works. Resist, as much as possible, adding major new features to the site you are upgrading. However, if reproducing the way the site currently works will take some effort *and* you want to change the way it works, then plan out your new feature, encapsulate it as a Feature module, and make it part of the upgrade.

■ **Note** Everything exportable by Features can be exported without Features. For key modules, like Views, Features is simply using built-in export capability. You can put everything in code yourself; Features provides a convenient consistent interface and tools around this process.

The Features module allows you to export the following components which exist in Drupal core: Fields, Text formats, Image styles, Menus, individual Menu links, Content types, Taxonomy vocabularies (not the terms in them), Permissions, and Roles. Other modules that work with it then allow you to export the elements of the site they provide; prominent examples include the Views or Nodequeue modules. Additional modules extend Features to export other things, such as the Strongarm module (drupal.org/project/strongarm), which allows you to export variables (which include much of what you might touch in the Configuration section of your site's administration pages).

Consider Creating a Base Feature Module

The ideal for Features development is that each Feature be standalone, that nearly any site can get the Features module and its dependencies and be up and running with the functionality bundled together by that Feature. When using Features to capture the configuration for a specific site into code, such complete separation is not practical. Instead, certain elements that cross several Features of your site, such as taxonomy vocabularies and the fields that hold them, can be exported to a base Feature which you then can have other Features require. Creating a base feature works just like creating any feature and is described briefly next. (Once you have a base Feature, you can add it as a Dependencies component for another Feature.)

Building a Feature Module

As a major purpose of Features is to capture in code configuration done through the user interface, so it is natural to create a feature through the user interface also. It is also possible to build a feature with Drush by giving a feature name and a space-separated list of component names to the command drush features-export, but as there can be hundreds of components available, it is easier to identify the components you want to use through the Features user interface.

First, of course, you need to build your site's functionality to your liking. You might create or edit a content type, create a new type of vocabulary, and very likely make or modify a listing page with Views, as described in Chapter 3. In the code shown in this chapter, the Views module is enabled, but not Views user interface, as we don't want it enabled on the production site at all. Enable Views UI locally (with drush en views_ui), and build out your view, as well as any other structure and configuration to achieve a particular feature for your site.

■ **Tip** Record each act of configuration so that you can use Features to export that configuration to code in the next step—or to know when Features *doesn't* necessarily provide a way to export that configuration (thereby requiring that you find a helper module that does or code it yourself). Resources at dgd7.org/anjali follow on this appendix—and book—with every tool and trick ultimately needed to upgrade and build out anjalifp.com.

Navigate to Administration ➤ Structure ➤ Features ➤ Create Feature (admin/structure/features/create). Give your Feature a name (such as News), a machine name (such as anjali_news), and a description (such as "Original news and in-the-news content types and listings").

There's no need to put in a Version string because this is not for public release and it will have a Git hash each time you commit it to code anyway, and you could tag versions of the site with Git.

Go to the Edit components section and begin adding the components for this Feature. Select Content types and add relevant ones that exist from the Drupal 6 site or that you created in the previous step. For example, checkmark "In the news" and "News" content types (note that it may take a moment to process adding these). Fields associated with each content type will be included in your Feature automatically.

Then select another type of component, such as Views, and add the one you just worked on. Keep doing this until you've set to export everything you did to fix or add the most recent functionality to the site. Click Download feature and save it into your sites/all/modules/custom directory. (Many people have a features directory in modules, but as Features modules can be either contrib or custom, it makes sense to treat them as one or the other, like any other module.)

Don't worry about making your Feature complete and perfect the first time. You will be able to tweak and re-export the Feature as many times as you need to.

■ **Tip** You may want to install Diff module, which is required to see the difference between the site's current configuration and a Feature. The Diff module is also useful for administrators to see differences between versions of text content. Get it with drush dl diff and enable with drush -y en diff. Make it a permanent part of your site by committing it with Git, such as git add sites/all/modules/contrib/diff and git commit -m "Diff module for helping show differences between features and content."

Adding Feature Modules to the Automatic Upgrade

You've now encapsulated significant configuration into code, but you need to automate these steps. Again, this can be very easily scripted with Drush with the command drush en *featurename*, as either Drush commands in a bash script or a proper Drush script, but let's stick with the hook_update_N() approach here, as shown in Listing A–20.

Listing A–20. Enable the Feature Modules That Contain Your Site's Features

```
/**
 * Enable feature modules.
 */
function anjaliup_update_7007() {
  $install = array(
    'anjali_base',
    'anjali_news',
  );
  features_install_modules($install);
}
```

As you create more Feature modules, add them to this function (and call this function from your hook_install(), and they will be put into action in the course of the upgrade.

Features modules are a best practice of development whether you are upgrading a site or not, so you may well be developing Features modules for a site you build fresh in Drupal 7 for the purpose of migrating content in, also. Also, no matter the approach you take, a custom site will require a custom theme built in Drupal 7. See Chapters 15 and 16 for that.

Data Migration

Suppose you plan to move an existing web site from another CMS to Drupal. You want to preserve all the articles, comments, and user accounts while making the transition as smooth as possible. Fortunately, Drupal 7 makes migrating the data from other systems simpler than previous versions.

Another CMS may have different sets of fields on their users, comments, and content than those you see in core Drupal, but with the new Field API, corresponding fields can easily be added to all Drupal core objects. If the source has kinds of objects that don't match cleanly with those core Drupal objects, appropriate Drupal entities can be defined to hold them. (See Chapter 24 for creating a new entity.)

The new Database API (DBTNG) makes it easier to migrate data directly from different database engines. Static caching in previous Drupal versions made bulk operations (such as creating or deleting thousands of nodes) vulnerable to memory exhaustion. The new drupal_static() helper function for static caching allows recovery of memory from static caches, so many more items can be processed in a single batch.

What issues will you face? You'll find that data migration is not a one-time event, but an ongoing development process evolving symbiotically alongside site-building.

Managing the Process

It might seem that the most natural approach to data migration is to fully design the new site, define the objects (nodes, users, etc.) comprising the site, then work out how to migrate the data into the presumably optimal design. You can't be tempted to put off beginning migration work, though, for several very good reasons.

1. Migration development forces you to get your hands dirty with the legacy data, which inevitably leads to discoveries that influence the design, such as inconsistencies in the data, forgotten tables, obscure features only available through an XML feed, etc.

■ **Gotcha** The first time that stakeholders see the migrated data in context, they will wonder why some significant feature isn't present. It will be because they took it so much for granted they didn't explicitly ask for it. The earlier this happens in the development process, the better.

2. The sooner the target site can be at least partly populated with real legacy data and made visible to stakeholders, the better. Manufactured sample data always looks exactly like you expect it— legacy data won't.

3. Migration is the canary in the coal mine of performance. When developing web site functionality, viewing and creating nodes one at a time, a tenth of a second wasted in an inefficient node hook doesn't even register (until formal load testing is done, which is typically late in the development process). When those tenths are multiplied by thousands of nodes when running a migration, however, the pain is felt immediately and assuaged quickly.

Data migration will be an iterative process. You'll start migrating as soon as you have access to the legacy data and some content types to migrate into, and repeatedly rollback and reimport as the both the migration and the site-building develop.

■ **Caution** Web development environments are generally configured based on typical assumptions for serving web pages—the database server is optimized for reading, not for writing, and memory may be limited. **Data migration has different requirements**. On a migration project of any significant size, you'll be creating and deleting nodes and users in batches of thousands, if not millions. To do this without waiting overnight (or over a weekend) for a full-fledged test run to complete, you will need plenty of memory (configure PHP's memory_limit to 512MB if possible), fast disks on the database server, and a wide pipe to the legacy data.

Understanding the Legacy Data

It's critical to understand the data on the old site. It's good to have documentation, but recognize that the actual data may have drifted from the documented schema and usage. You can't take anything you're told about the data for granted—you must analyze the data thoroughly. It's essential to query ALL the data to be migrated (don't just take samples). You're sure to discover that the field you were told contains only five possible values has—for 11 articles out of 58,281—some other value. You will become adept at GROUP BY and subqueries as you analyze the legacy data to within an inch of its life. You'll identify "required" fields that aren't actually used (or always have the value "6") or fields that contain values that are outside of the documented range. Work closely with the site builders to figure out what fields need multiple values, what are required and what are optional, and what the defaults should be when legacy data is absent.

As a first step, create shared Google spreadsheets from the source tables. There should be columns for the legacy field name, the disposition (destination Drupal field name or DNM for "Do Not Migrate"), a description of their meaning, and any special handling if migrating the data isn't a simple one-to-one copy. Meet with the experts on the legacy data and go through the spreadsheets, table-by-table and field-by-field, to identify an initial set of field mappings. But you don't need to have every mapping fully fleshed out at this point. It's one thing to sit in a meeting and make decisions about the content types and fields that will compose your new Drupal site. It's quite another to see how they work in practice. By performing migrations into a staging environment visible across the project—starting as soon as possible after the first node types are defined and rerunning with each significant stage of development—you can get continuous feedback and refinement of both the site-building and migration processes.

■ **Tip** Migrate early and often.

Specific Sticking Points

Certain problems crop up repeatedly in data migration and are worth looking out for from the start.

- *Dates*: Differences in date handling between database engines; timezones.

- *Files*: How will the files be served on the Drupal site (directly from the Drupal files directory, from a separate file server, etc.)? How will the files get copied from the old system? Will it be done within the content migration process or on the side (e.g., via rsync)? Can the legacy file directory be mounted on the migration system?

- *Paths*: Will the primary path aliases on the Drupal site be different from the original? If so, will you use pathauto to generate a new path structure? In this case, you need a means to permanent redirect to the new paths. If you want to preserve the same path structure, then you need to migrate the paths.

- *Character sets*: So, you run your first migration, and apostrophes are showing up in Drupal as garbage characters. Extended characters get mucked up. What to do? The problem is different character sets on the different databases, by converting the wayward characters or aligning the database character sets.

- *Performance*: We'll say it again: Migration is the canary in the coal mine of performance. You'll need to instrument your code using the Drupal Timer API. In particular, using `timer_start()` and `timer_stop()` calls (api.drupal.org/timer_start, api.drupal.org/timer_stop) in any core function containing "invoke" (a hook invocation) will be very helpful. Static caching can be a big help; if the migration code needs to do frequent lookups, cache the results using `drupal_static()`, so your cached data can be flushed if memory becomes tight.

Initial Analysis

For the initial analysis:

- Set up spreadsheets.

- Review among legacy experts, site-builders, and migrators.

- Analyze the information. Look for discrepancies, outliers. Find min/max values for everything.

- Take a census. How many articles have related articles? What's the maximum number of related articles for one article?

■ **Note** The Migrate module can help with self-documentation to surfaces issues so they're visible to all. You can then do things such as link mappings to an issue-tracking system.

Iterate

Build migration processes. Run them. Work with site-builders: do you need another field? Does a field defined as singular need to be multiple? Why are articles importing at a rate of only 100/minute? Modify and rerun.

■ **Note** Migrate module maintains map tables between source and destination keys, which supports rolling back.

Show

Let all site builders see the migrated data. Let them show the stakeholders.

Audit

Compare source and destination data. Migrate module's map tables can be used for auditing.

Time

How long does it take to migrate all data? Where are the bottlenecks?

Launch Day

By now, you know how long a full migration will take. Unless the volume of data being migrated is quite small, you don't want to wait until the last minute to actually begin migrating it.

Continuous migration is the solution. Doing a full migration of your data from scratch will likely take many hours. If possible, you want to do a bulk migration a couple of days before, and have a process for incrementally migrating changes as they occur those last couple of days so that the day is in sync when you're ready to throw the switch. To do this, you need a reliable means of detecting changes; the old system needs to support a trustworthy "last modified" timestamp on all items being migrated or a transaction log. Note that typically deletions are harder to detect (but fortunately, typically web content is not actually deleted, but marked disabled/cancelled). Compare to database replication, to set expectations modestly. You're not going to achieve perfect, immediate synchronization; you want to minimize the window between beginning pre-migration and the final switchover (and re-audit after).

Summary

Upgrading a site is one of Drupal's pain points, but Drupal's continuous gains in allowing configuration to be captured in code make the experience more enjoyable and reliable. As migration tools also continue to make dramatic improvements, upgrading may become a special case of migration. In both cases, the key is to start early and be able to bring in live data into your site build on a regular basis.

■ **Tip** Follow along at `dgd7.org/anjali` for the unfolding story of upgrading and rebuilding `anjaliforberpratt.com` for the amazing person of the same name. In addition to covering more details about upgrading, the development of Anjali Forber-Pratt's site provides a case-specific reprise of much of the Definitive Guide to Drupal 7.

APPENDIX B

■■■

Profiling Drupal and Optimizing Performance

by Nathaniel Catchpole and Stefan Freudenberg

You don't usually need to worry about performance when developing Drupal sites and modules; instead, you should focus on clean, functional design and readability of your code. However, if your site experiences more traffic than usual or it somehow feels slow, there are ways to analyze and improve the situation.

User-Perceived Performance

When it comes to web sites, the perceived performance is key to user acceptance. In the words of Roy T. Fielding, a central figure in defining the modern web's architecture, user-perceived performance "is measured in terms of its impact on the user in front of an application. [...] The primary measures for user-perceived performance are latency and completion time."[1]

- **Latency** is the time between initiating a request on the client side and the first indication of a response.

- **Completion time** is the amount of time it takes for the complete request to be fulfilled.

Short latency is preferred for web browsers as they are capable of rendering the received content incrementally. The browser starts loading additional assets like images and JavaScript while parsing the incoming markup and can start rendering the page before images have finished loading. Latency is affected by the time a server needs to generate and send a response.

What Makes a Web Site Slow?

There are many reasons why a web site slows down over time; your aim should be to find the most important bottlenecks. Happily, Drupal is able to help out in common situations.

---

[1] Roy Thomas Fielding, "Architectural Styles and the Design of Network-based Software Architectures," www.ics.uci.edu/~fielding/pubs/dissertation/top.htm, 2000.

First, you need to have a look under the skin of your beautifully designed site. Firebug allows you to analyze the bits and bytes coming from the server after hitting the return button. Look at Firebug's network tab in Figure B–1; the first row shows the request to the page you are currently viewing, and the rows below it are all additional requests automatically fired by the browser to retrieve CSS, JavaScript, images, and other resources. Hovering over a row shows a detailed breakdown of time spent on DNS lookup, connecting to the server, sending the request, waiting for the first indication of response, and receiving the data. In Figure B–1, latency is the time between "Started" and the end of "Waiting." If that time is long, you either have a slow network connection or the server spends too much time generating the page (more on this later).

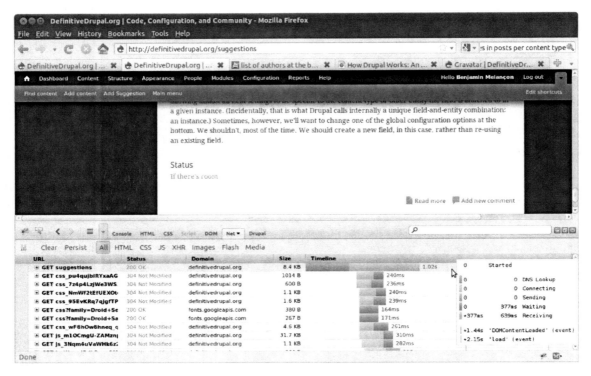

Figure B–1. *Firebug net summary*

Remember that rendering can start before all resources are fetched. Basically, it starts where Firebug shows the blue bar in the network timeline, which marks the point in time when the markup is completely parsed. You want this to be as close as possible to the time when your browser received the markup. Luckily, there are free tools that might give you some clues in case it is not. YSlow, a Firebug plug-in created by the engineers at Yahoo and available at developer.yahoo.com/yslow, can rate your site in different categories ranging from the number of HTTP requests to web server configuration options (see Figure B–2).

Figure B–2. YSlow grade

There's a wealth of information that can't be explained fully in this chapter, but here's what can be improved using vanilla Drupal: if YSlow gives you a bad grade in "Make fewer HTTP requests," enable "Aggregate and compress CSS files" and "Aggregate JavaScript files" on the performance screen (navigate to Configuration ➤ Development ➤ Performance in the administrative UI). JavaScript can't be automatically minified by Drupal, so these options make Drupal produce a few minified CSS files and a couple JavaScript files from all the CSS and JavaScript files provided by modules and your theme (and there can be dozens of each). Setting these options will earn you a better grade on the Minify CSS and JavaScript test. To learn more about these concepts, follow the Read more links to the YSlow documentation.

■ **Note** Drupal does not aggregate CSS and JavaScript into one file each for a couple reasons. Primarily, this is because some files need to be included on all pages while some only need to be included on certain pages. This is an intentional change from Drupal 6, when you would see only one file per page, but might end up with a different huge aggregated file as you navigated to different pages. Now you will end up with more than two CSS files per page (aggregated every page and aggregated page specific) because Drupal creates aggregation files that respect the order in which CSS files are loaded, and divides its aggregation into groups to reduce the likelihood of requiring a different split and a new aggregation because of the addition of a conditional style. For JavaScript, header and footer output is aggregated separately, of course. To get maximum performance, you are free to change how Drupal aggregates with hook_css_alter() and hook_js_alter(). See also www.metaltoad.com/blog/drupal-7-taking-control-css-and-js-aggregation.

Another suggested technique is compressing page components with gzip on the server before transmitting them. This reduces download time at the expense of some overhead on the client side caused by the need to unzip the received data. Enable "Compress cached pages" *only* if your web server is not configured to deliver compressed HTML. Apache's mod_deflate can also be configured to compress dynamic *and* static content on the fly.

Real Performance

After reading all about speeding up transmission and rendering of content, you—if a PHP developer—are probably eagerly waiting for the server-related stuff where you can thrive. The Drupal and PHP developer communities have already produced many solutions for situations of high CPU usage, a very common issue for successful Drupal sites.

Page and Block Level Caching

In Chapter 5 of his dissertation[2], Fielding describes the architectural constraints of Internet applications. "Cache constraints require that the data within a response to a request be implicitly or explicitly labeled as cacheable or non-cacheable." Drupal has improved on meeting that requirement over the last development cycle and can now provide the correct HTTP headers to support caching reverse-proxies like Varnish. Note that it still features a built-in page cache solution for those who don't have access to that kind of additional resources. In many cases, the workload of a busy server can be reduced significantly by turning on page caching or adding an intermediary cache. This is especially true if the bulk of the traffic comes from anonymous visitors. Page caching can be controlled in the Development section of the administration interface (see Figure B–3).

---

[2] Roy Thomas Fielding, "Architectural Styles and the Design of Network-based Software Architectures," www.ics.uci.edu/~fielding/pubs/dissertation/rest_arch_style.htm, 2000.

CACHING

☑ Cache pages for anonymous users

☑ Cache blocks

Minimum cache lifetime

| <none> ▾ |

Cached pages will not be re-created until at least this much time has elapsed.

Expiration of cached pages

| <none> ▾ |

The maximum time an external cache can use an old version of a page.

Figure B–3. *Cache settings*

Page caching is not an option, though, for logged in users because Drupal pages contain elements that are customized to individual visitors, such as a display of their user name or their level of permissions. It still makes sense to cache the results of resource-intensive algorithms and database queries using Drupal's simple yet powerful cache API described in Chapter 27. Drupal blocks can be cached by means of the block API, which leverages the cache API. But how do you know what needs to be cached on a complex site? The first rule is: don't guess! Find out in a systematic way using adequate tools.

Profiling Drupal, a Primer

After identifying a slow page on a Drupal site, a common approach is to look at the devel query log to identify slow queries on that page. However, what do you do if devel says the following:

```
"Executed 39 queries in 9.66 ms. Queries exceeding 5 ms are highlighted. Page execution time
was 210.19 ms"
```

This means that 200ms of the page generation was spent doing things in PHP, not in database queries. Drupal itself doesn't offer any clues for breaking down that 200ms, so you should consider using a code profiler. The two most common profilers used with PHP are xdebug and xhprof.

- xdebug is currently easier to install and is often enabled on local development environments already (http://xdebug.org).

- xhprof has lower overhead when enabled or profiling, plus it offers easy access to memory usage per function (https://github.com/facebook/xhprof).

For this example, we'll use xdebug and webgrind—a free web-based GUI for examining the callgrind data available from https://github.com/jokkedk/webgrind that should work on any server with xdebug and PHP (i.e., any server that can profile a Drupal site). Note that the same information can be gained using xhprof and its own web-based GUI. You'll need to install xdebug and webgrind if you haven't already; see their web sites for documentation.

The page we'll profile is admin/configs; slow performance on this page is very unlikely to be the cause of overall site slowness, but it's a page you are likely to visit thousands of times as a Drupal user, so it makes sense for it to load reasonably quickly. For this example, I downloaded Drupal 7.0, copied the profiles/standard to profiles/foo, did a find and replace for function names, and installed using the foo profile.

Now, disable devel module and set xdebug.profiler_enable_trigger=1 in php.ini, then request the page again your browser using admin/config?XDEBUG_PROFILE=1.

If everything is set up correctly, you should see a cachegrind.out file listed in webgrind, the output of which should look like Figure B–4.

Figure B–4. Webgrind view of a profile produced by xdebug

You can see that webgrind reports 715 different functions called in 436 milliseconds (1 runs, 85 shown). Note that there is significant overhead to profiling with xdebug, so a page taking 436 milliseconds during profiling when devel just said 210ms isn't unusual.

It helps if you understand the table headings.

- **Function** is the function that was called.

- **Invocation count** is the number of times that function was called during the request.

- **Total self cost** is the time spent within that function, not including any functions it calls.

- **Total inclusive cost** is the time spent inside the function, including any functions it calls and any functions called from those functions, etc.

The default sort in webgrind is by "self" cost. At the top is drupal_load() and it takes 9.59% of the request by itself and 12% including child functions. However, the page won't load at all if modules aren't loaded, so it's unlikely this is going to be easily optimized; also, 12% of the request leaves 88% unaccounted for.

However, just below that, file_scan_directory() takes 9.21% of the request itself and 46.64% including child functions. 46% of this request is a full 200ms, so this could be the culprit!

The first thing to do after finding a likely culprit is to profile the page a second time. Often slow operations like file system scans in Drupal are cached, and if a page is slow even on a cache miss, it's usually best to optimize the uncached functions first by improving algorithms or adding caching.

In this case, though, repeated profiling of the page always shows file_scan_directory() and it's consistently just under 50% of the whole request. Note that file_scan_directory() is a low-level function, called by 18 different functions in Drupal 7 core, so it's now time to look at the function detail to see where it's being called from (see Figure B–5).

Figure B–5. Webgrind displaying a call hierarchy

From here, you can follow the chain upwards: drupal_system_listing() is called by drupal_required_modules(), which is called by install_profile_info(), which is called by system_requirements(). Note that drupal_required_modules() also calls drupal_parse_info_file() 47 times, taking 88ms on this request.

At this point, it's time to open up your favorite editor to see why we're calling install_profile_info() from system_requirements(). Here's the relevant code for Drupal 7.0:

```
// Display the currently active install profile, if the site
// is not running the default install profile.
$profile = drupal_get_profile();
if ($profile != 'standard') {
  $info = install_profile_info($profile);
  $requirements['install_profile'] = array(
    'title' => $t('Install profile'),
    'value' => $t('%profile_name (%profile-%version)', array(
      %profile_name' => $info['name'],
      %profile' => $profile,
      %version' => $info['version']
  )),
    'severity' => REQUIREMENT_INFO,
    'weight' => -9
  );
}
```

So in this case, we're scanning directories and parsing the install files of 47 different modules to get the name and version of the currently installed profile. Seems a bit of a waste, doesn't it!

Since this is a real performance issue in Drupal 7.0, it also has a real issue in the issue queue. Go to drupal.org/node/1014130 to see how it might be fixed.

Slow Database Queries

Second rule: unless you are particularly concerned about improving a limited part of your code, look at the big picture. More often than not, a high server load is caused by heavy database usage. Not all queries to the database are equal, however, and some will take much more time and resources than others. But you need to identify the troublesome queries in order to deal with them. If you are using MariaDB/MySQL or PostgreSQL, you can use the database server's slow query logging facility to write queries to a file that run for more than a configurable amount of time or that don't use indexes properly. Still, you need a statistics tool that tells you how often a slow query is executed in a given period of time and how much time it is consuming over all. It won't help much to optimize an especially slow query that is only run during cron executions and isn't affecting visitors at all (or only marginally). We've been using mk-query-digest from the Maatkit tools (www.maatkit.org) for some time now.

Table B–1 shows a typical slow query summary produced by mk-query-digest. The header shows some overall numbers and the time range, and the profile part lists the slow queries by response time. Each query listed in the ranking is shown in detail. If you want to know which part of Drupal is firing the query, you can use the devel module, which can log all queries executed and display them along with the containing function. For an in-depth explanation, check out www.maatkit.org/wp-content/uploads/2010/03/query-analysis-with-mk-query-digest.pdf.

Table B–1. *A Typical Slow Query Summary Produced by mk-query-digest*

2s user time, 940ms system time, 21.97M rss, 64.80M vsz

Current date: Tue Jan 11 22:19:46 2011

Files: STDIN

Overall: 13.26k total, 219 unique, 0.15 QPS, 0.04x concurrency

# Query	total	min	Max	Avg	95%	stddev	Median
# Exec time	3768s	0	32s	284ms	0	2s	0
# Lock time	6s	0	1s	452us	0	21ms	0
# Rows sent	2.95M	0	916.40k	233.14	49.17	8.95k	0
# Rows exam	32.10M	0	916.40k	2.48k	6.96k	13.48k	4.96
# Time range	2011-01-10 06:27:47 to 2011-01-11 06:26:33						
# bytes	1.65M	22	23.81k	130.66	329.68	459.90	107.34

Profile

# Rank	Query ID	Response time		Calls	R/Cal	Item
# 1	0x5C504BFA0C055D3C	2822.0000	74.9%	414	6.8164	SELECT comments users
# 2	0x140613D48BD6C7C6	234.0000	6.2%	41	5.7073	SELECT comments
# 3	0xBB641C051DF3EC05	209.0000	5.5%	35	5.9714	SELECT comments
# 4	0xD782E6FD765926FF	99.0000	2.6%	18	5.5000	SELECT comments
# 5	0x67A347A2812914DF	90.0000	2.4%	906	0.0993	SELECT session

This kind of analysis gives a site-wide performance assessment; by addressing those queries, the server load can be reduced considerable in many cases, thereby enabling the server to handle much more traffic.

Even if everything is configured perfectly and caches are used to the utmost extent, traffic may grow and outpower even the best server. Don't worry—Drupal has options if your main bottleneck is the database. If you have many SELECT queries splitting the load over two or more servers, using replication can improve the situation. Typically, you would set up separate servers dedicated to running a database. Setting up database replication is beyond the scope of this book but there is excellent documentation available for MySQL at dev.mysql.com/doc/refman/5.1/en/replication-howto.html and PostgreSQL at www.slony.info/documentation/2.0/tutorial.html. In order to make Drupal use one or more slaves, you have to add database configurations to your settings.php, as shown in this example:

```
$databases['default']['slave'] = array(
 'driver' => 'mysql',
 'database' => 'dgd7',
 'username' => 'root',
 'password' => 'AY7qiKol',
 'host' => 'localhost',
 'prefix' => '',
 );
```

Replication support also makes sure queries are intelligently split between master and slave databases. When you have just edited a node, the next query that will fetch data to view your changes will be sent to the master because the slaves might have stale data.

Summary

While there are many ways to improve the speed of pages of your Drupal site, there's no one-size-fits-all solution. Tuning your server only makes sense if there's really a bottleneck on that end. Always try to identify the bottleneck causing the biggest impact. And last but not least, the easiest way to a smooth-running site is a simple design: don't overload your site with features (the warning sign is a growing number of modules). More resources as authors or readers come up with them will be posted at dgd7.org/profile to help keep you up to speed.

■ ■ ■

Page Rendering and Altering

by Károly Négyesi

One of the fundamental changes in Drupal 7 is how the HTML appearing in the browser is assembled. For example, in previous Drupal versions, the content of a block was returned as an HTML string. Then, the theme_block() function put this HTML in a template together with the subject, returned a somewhat bigger HTML string, and concatenating several of these together yielded the HTML for one region.

In Drupal 7, on the other hand, the content of the block is returned as an array from the block callback. Then it gets put inside an array and so on. The end result is a gigantic, multi-dimensional array fed to the drupal_render() function, which ultimately produces the HTML string the browser gets. But before it does this it allows us to interact with the whole content of the page in much richer ways than we could when it was just strings passed around.

Let's review this huge page array for the default home page with every block disabled first. Later we will walk the code flow to see how it's assembled.

To see the page array I installed the Devel module to get the pretty printed arrays, as shown in Figure C–1.

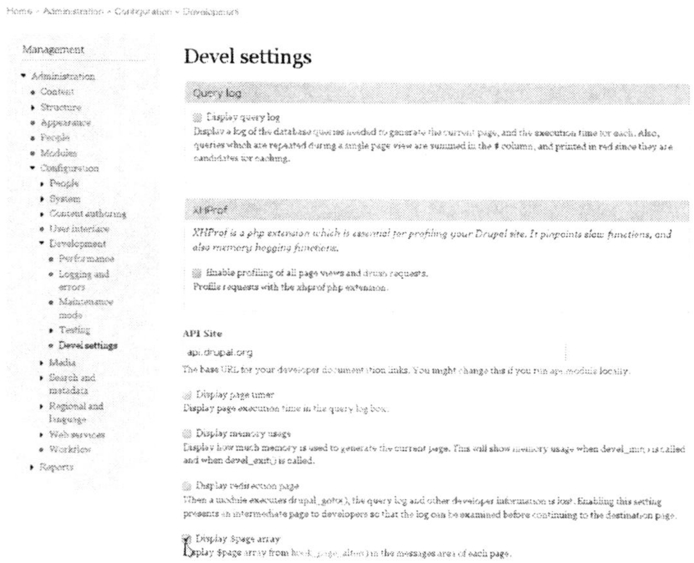

Figure C–1. *Enabling Devel module's "Display $page array" option to see how the page looks to hook_form_alter()*

Next, disable every block (aside from Management, which is not accessible for anonymous), as shown in Figure C–2.

■ **Note** After disabling all blocks, you will need to use the path 'user' to log back into your Drupal site.

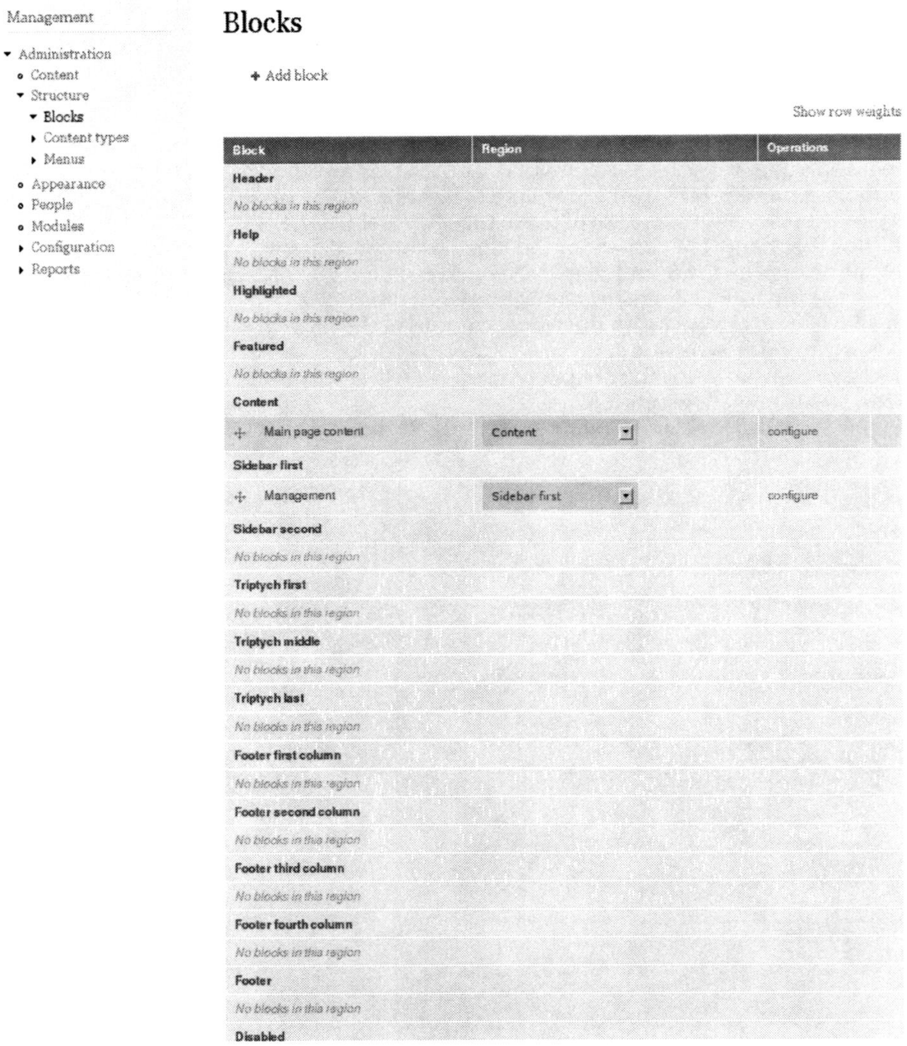

Management

- ▼ Administration
  - ○ Content
  - ▼ Structure
    - ▼ Blocks
      - ▶ Content types
      - ▶ Menus
  - ○ Appearance
  - ○ People
  - ○ Modules
  - ▶ Configuration
  - ▶ Reports

Blocks

+ Add block

Show row weights

Block	Region	Operations
Header		
No blocks in this region		
Help		
No blocks in this region		
Highlighted		
No blocks in this region		
Featured		
No blocks in this region		
Content		
⊹ Main page content	Content ▼	configure
Sidebar first		
⊹ Management	Sidebar first ▼	configure
Sidebar second		
No blocks in this region		
Triptych first		
No blocks in this region		
Triptych middle		
No blocks in this region		
Triptych last		
No blocks in this region		
Footer first column		
No blocks in this region		
Footer second column		
No blocks in this region		
Footer third column		
No blocks in this region		
Footer fourth column		
No blocks in this region		
Footer		
No blocks in this region		
Disabled		

Figure C–2. The blocks administration page

After this preparation we can finally take our first look at a really bare bones page and its page array, as shown in Figure C–3.

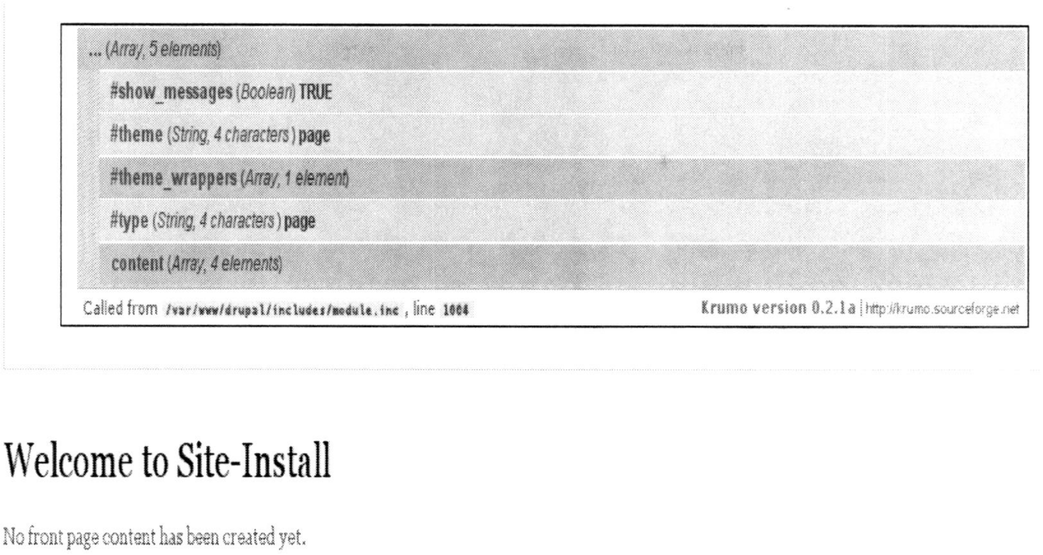

... (*Array, 5 elements*)

#show_messages (*Boolean*) **TRUE**

#theme (*String, 4 characters*) **page**

#theme_wrappers (*Array, 1 element*)

#type (*String, 4 characters*) **page**

content (*Array, 4 elements*)

Called from **/var/www/drupal/includes/module.inc** , line **1006**   **Krumo version 0.2.1a** | http://krumo.sourceforge.net

Welcome to Site-Install

No front page content has been created yet.

Figure C–3. Page array as displayed by Devel module for a page with no content or sidebar blocks— the bare minimum

The structure of the array may be familiar to you from looking at form arrays: there are properties marked with the # sign and then the children, in this case the only child is content. One property I would like to draw your attention to is the element #type, which is page, meaning that the children of this element will be themed by the page template (see Chapters 15 and 16, on Theming). Let's peek into the content, as shown in Figure C–4.

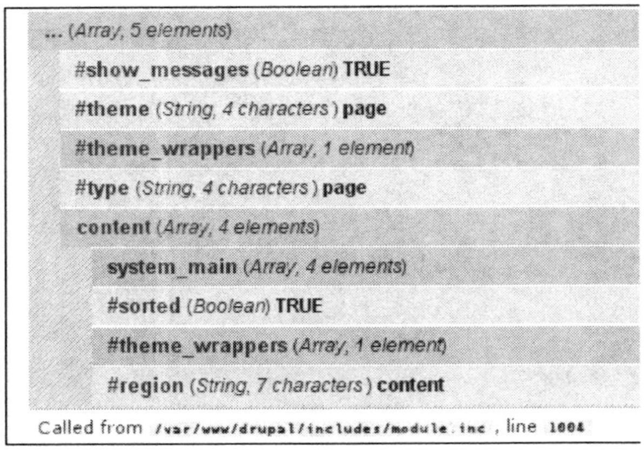

```
... (Array, 5 elements)
    #show_messages (Boolean) TRUE
    #theme (String, 4 characters) page
    #theme_wrappers (Array, 1 element)
    #type (String, 4 characters) page
    content (Array, 4 elements)
        system_main (Array, 4 elements)
        #sorted (Boolean) TRUE
        #theme_wrappers (Array, 1 element)
        #region (String, 7 characters) content
Called from /var/www/drupal/includes/module.inc , line 1004
```

Figure C–4. *Inside the* content *child of the page array*

It's the same again: more properties and one child element—let's open that child, system_main, and hopefully we find something useful in there, in Figure C–5.

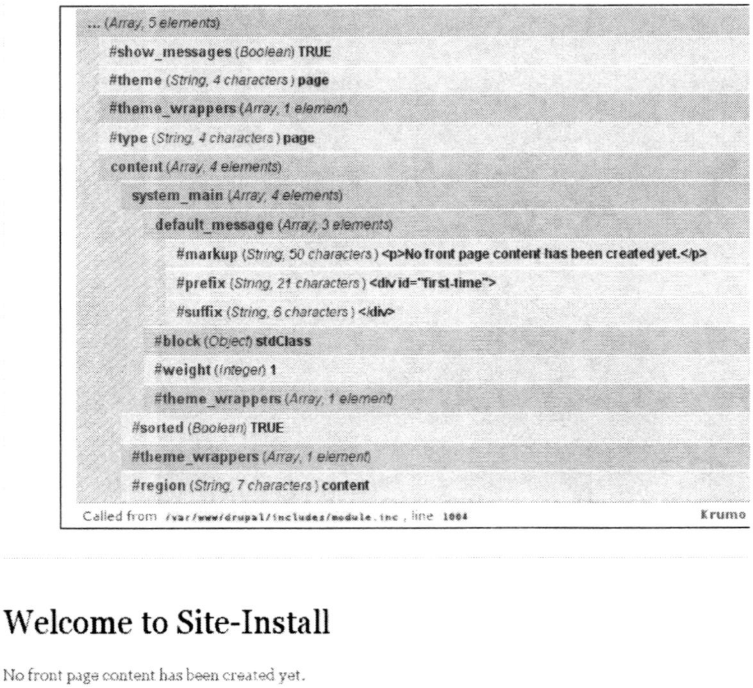

```
... (Array, 5 elements)
    #show_messages (Boolean) TRUE
    #theme (String, 4 characters) page
    #theme_wrappers (Array, 1 element)
    #type (String, 4 characters) page
    content (Array, 4 elements)
        system_main (Array, 4 elements)
            default_message (Array, 3 elements)
                #markup (String, 50 characters) <p>No front page content has been created yet.</p>
                #prefix (String, 21 characters) <div id="first-time">
                #suffix (String, 6 characters) </div>
            #block (Object) stdClass
            #weight (integer) 1
            #theme_wrappers (Array, 1 element)
        #sorted (Boolean) TRUE
        #theme_wrappers (Array, 1 element)
        #region (String, 7 characters) content
Called from /var/www/drupal/includes/module.inc , line 1004          Krumo
```

Welcome to Site-Install

No front page content has been created yet.

Figure C–5. *Drilling down through child render elements* content *and* system_main *to* default_message

Well, no such luck, so we opened its child element, the default_message array, too. And there it ends: we see the message "No front page content has been created yet." in the #markup property. Although there is no #type property here, that just means the #type is markup, meaning the HTML equivalent of this element is simply contents of the #markup property.

The only thing left closed is the #theme_wrappers arrays, so let's look into them (see Figure C–6).

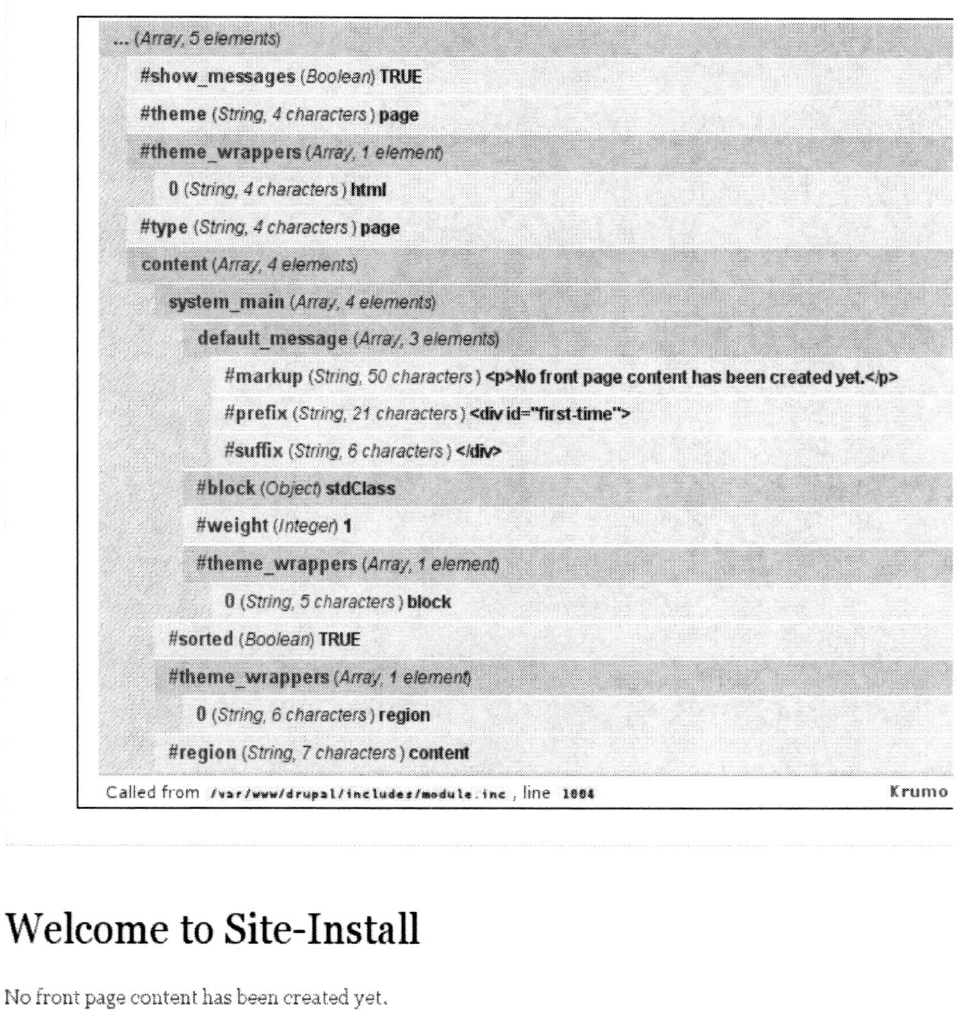

... (Array, 5 elements)

#show_messages (*Boolean*) **TRUE**

#theme (*String, 4 characters*) **page**

#theme_wrappers (*Array, 1 element*)

    0 (*String, 4 characters*) **html**

#type (*String, 4 characters*) **page**

content (*Array, 4 elements*)

    system_main (*Array, 4 elements*)

        default_message (*Array, 3 elements*)

            #markup (*String, 50 characters*) **<p>No front page content has been created yet.</p>**

            #prefix (*String, 21 characters*) **<div id="first-time">**

            #suffix (*String, 6 characters*) **</div>**

        #block (*Object*) **stdClass**

        #weight (*Integer*) **1**

        #theme_wrappers (*Array, 1 element*)

            0 (*String, 5 characters*) **block**

    #sorted (*Boolean*) **TRUE**

    #theme_wrappers (*Array, 1 element*)

        0 (*String, 6 characters*) **region**

    #region (*String, 7 characters*) **content**

Called from **/var/www/drupal/includes/module.inc** , line **1004**   **Krumo**

Welcome to Site-Install

No front page content has been created yet.

Figure C–6. *Most basic page array with every element and property expanded*

If you start from the message you see how it's wrapped first in a block theme wrapper, then in a region theme wrapper, then in a page, and then finally in the html theme wrapper. Now that we have seen such a page array in its entirety, let's see the actual code flow—and the places where we can intervene.

Step 1: The Router Item

After Drupal has been bootstrapped, the last thing index.php does is call menu_execute_active_handler(). This retrieves the router item from the menu_router based on the current path. There is an important chance here to intervene, hook_menu_item_alter(). This allows you to change anything about the menu item, such as changing the access callback based on the IP of the current user. You could relax some access control for people logging in from the office. Or you might want to provide access to only those who have used a path alias for a node and not to those who have used node/[nid]. Such can be used to implement simple token-based access by creating a random path alias and sending it to the user.

Once the access control has passed, the menu system will call the page callback, which puts together the main content. hook_menu_item_alter() can be useful to change which page callback is fired. For example, the router system only allows per node page callbacks or a single one for every node. But, you might want a different page per node type. Or if you run the Organic Groups module (drupal.org/project/og), then entirely different pages might be necessary for different groups. All this becomes possible through hook_menu_item_alter().

Step 2: The Page Callback Is Fired

Almost the whole book is basically about what this can do. The page callback might load entities, view them, and create lists, tables, etc., but at the end of the day it just returns a renderable array. For example, the default home page returns this:

```
$build['default_message'] = array(
    '#markup' => "<p>No front page content has been created yet.</p>",
    '#prefix' => '<div id="first-time">',
    '#suffix' => '</div>',
);
```

We have seen this before, haven't we?

Step 3: The Delivery Callback

Now you are back in menu_execute_active_handler(). The next callback to fire is the delivery callback, which defaults to drupal_deliver_html_page(). As the name suggests, by default you are delivering the page callback results in HTML.

■ **Note** The strict use of the term "page callback result" is important because "page" contains the return of page callback, the blocks, and everything else (as we will soon see).

You could deliver in JSON or deliver parts of the page callback results in JSON. Core does not use this capability a lot, but overlay has an interesting case. When a form submit instructs Drupal to close the overlay on the next page, it's faster to display just the styles and scripts to close the overlay instead of displaying the whole page needlessly. So here's a delivery callback to display nothing:

```
function overlay_deliver_empty_page() {
  $empty_page = '<html><head><title></title>' . drupal_get_css() . drupal_get_js() .
'</head><body class="overlay"></body></html>';
  print $empty_page;
  drupal_exit();
}
```

You can use hook_menu_item_alter() to change the delivery callback—you have already seen how altering the access or the page callback can be useful, now you see the usefulness of altering the delivery callback.

Let's presume that drupal_deliver_html_page() was chosen (that's the case almost always anyway) and let's check what that function does. It handles page not found or access denied cases, and, most importantly, it calls drupal_render_page().

Step 4: drupal_render_page()

The name is very deceiving: this function does a lot more than merely render the page. Remember, so far you only have the page callback result, not the whole page—so this function builds the page. With just a little exaggeration, all that's fun and powerful in Drupal 7 is fired from this function. (The field API is powerful but tedious.)

First, hook_page_build() is called, which allows other modules to add to the page array—because here you build that. Your modules can add to the page array, also. Second, hook_page_alter() is fired.

Step 5. hook_page_alter()

This is the hammer that makes all problems look like a nail. If you have ever seen a "dynamic hammer," some special forces use for breaching a door, well this is it.

For example, if you want to move the node links into a block called "Article tools," then it's next to impossible in Drupal 6. The links are bolted to the node, and it's a lot easier to write code that re-displays the links in a block than it is to move them. Of course this is a lot of code to duplicate and might cause expensive operations to repeat. In Drupal 7 we have an excellent hammer to drive that bolt out, and we can just move the link without much ado. Most of the example actually will be making sure the result looks like a block (note that this example only works if you have a region called sidebar_first like the default theme Bartik does):

```
function dgd7_page_alter(&$page) {
  if ($node = menu_get_object()) {
    // Create an HTML string out of the links so it can be checked for emptiness
    $links = drupal_render($page['content']['system_main']['nodes'][$node->nid]['links']);
    // Remove from the original place.
    unset($page['content']['system_main']['nodes'][$node->nid]['links']);
    // The rest of this code puts $links in a block if it's not empty.
    if ($links) {
      $page['sidebar_first']['dgd7_tools']['#markup'] = $links;
      $page['sidebar_first']['dgd7_tools']['#block'] = (object) array(
        'module' => 'dgd7',
        'delta' => 'dgd7_tools',
        'subject' => t('Article tools'),
        'region' => 'sidebar_first',
      );
```

```
        $page['sidebar_first']['dgd7_tools']['#theme_wrappers'][] = 'block';
      }
    }
}
```

Another example is changing fixed lists in Drupal core. Let's say you wanted to insert an advertisement or public service announcement into the middle of an aggregator items list or the comments of a node. This is quite tricky in previous versions of Drupal—you would probably need to display the ad from a template, which counts how many times the comment or the item was displayed—but in Drupal 7 it's again just trivial: you put it in place and that's it:

```
function dgd7_page_alter(&$page) {
  if ($node = menu_get_object()) {
    $comments = &$page['content']['system_main']['nodes'][$node->nid]['comments']['comments'];
    $comments['ad'] = dgd7_get_ad();
    // The first comment weight is 0, the second is 1, go between them.
    unset($comments['#sorted']);
    $comments['ad']['#weight'] = 0.5;
  }
}

function dgd7_get_ad() {
  return array('#markup' => t('Hello I am an ad!'));
}
```

And so we finally arrived to the point where the page array has been completed: it has started life as the page callback result, got additional pieces like blocks in hook_page_build(), and got the details put in place by hook_page_alter(). With all this said and done, you have an array that is ready to be rendered, and so drupal_render() is called. This is where the array will turn into HTML.

Step 6. drupal_render()

This is a recursive function called on every child of the page array. So you start with running drupal_render($page), then continue with drupal_render($page['content']), then with drupal_render($page['content']['system_main']), and finally with drupal_render($page['content']['system_main']['default_message']). If there would be siblings, the siblings are called first before the children (this is called breadth-first traversal of the page tree).

Let's just focus on one call of drupal_render(). First there is an access check. Every small or big piece can have access control in Drupal 7. Then the cache is checked. Again, no matter how small or big the part of the page you are looking at, the HTML string resulting from the rendering of it can be cached easily. To utilize this, the #cache argument needs to be set. This is an associative array, the keys will be familiar if you are familiar with cache_set: key, bin, expire (while cache_set takes a data argument as well, that's obviously the HTML string itself). So for example:

```
$element['#cache']  = array(
  'cid' => 'foo:bar',
  'bin' => 'cache_something',
  'expire" => 900,
);
```

Now, creating the cache id (cid) from multiple parts is quite common—even this small example contained 'foo:bar'. Instead of specifying the cid key directly, you can supply an array of keys instead:

```
$element['#cache']  = array(
  'keys' => array('foo', 'bar'),
  'bin' => 'cache_something',
  'expire' => 900,
);
```

The advantage of course is the easier manipulation of keys in hook_page_alter(). Finally, you can set a 'granularity,' which is a binary combination (Why not an array? Good question! We will fix that in Drupal 8) of flags: DRUPAL_CACHE_PER_ROLE, DRUPAL_CACHE_PER_USER, DRUPAL_CACHE_PER_PAGE. For example:

```
$element['#cache']  = array(
  'keys' => array('foo', 'bar'),
  'granularity' => DRUPAL_CACHE_PER_ROLE | DRUPAL_CACHE_PER_PAGE,
  'bin' => 'cache_something',
  'expire' => 900,
);
```

This means the element is different per role and per page—but it's not different for every user, which means that the cache table is not bloated much and the chance for a miss is much higher.

If you had a cache miss, then you come to the array of #pre_render functions. It is a similar array of callbacks like form #process callbacks.

One possible scalability tactic is to work as little as possible while creating the page and instead move the costly work into #pre_render and also the previously described caching possibility. This is particularly useful for complicated queries. It's so useful that there is a helper function for this called drupal_render_cache_by_query(). This functions sets up #cache based on the query and #pre_render properties for you. Here is a slightly simplified example from forum.module:

```
function forum_block_view($delta = '') {
  $title = t('Active forum topics');
  $query = db_select('forum_index', 'f')
    ->fields('f')
    ->addTag('node_access')
    ->orderBy('f.last_comment_timestamp', 'DESC')
    ->range(0, variable_get('forum_block_num_active', '5'));
  $block['subject'] = $title;
  // Cache based on the altered query. Enables us to cache with node access enabled.
  $block['content'] = drupal_render_cache_by_query($query, 'forum_block_view');
  $block['content']['#access'] = user_access('access content');
  return $block;
}

function forum_block_view_pre_render($elements) {
  $result = $elements['#query']->execute();
  if ($node_title_list = node_title_list($result)) {
      $elements['forum_list'] = $node_title_list;
      $elements['forum_more'] = array('#theme' => 'more_link', '#url' => 'forum', '#title'
=> t('Read the latest forum topics.'));
  }
  return $elements;
}
```

See how the query is only executed in the pre_render? Remember, #pre_render only fires after caching, so this means the query will not be sent to the database unless there is a cache miss. You can do this with any DBTNG query.

The next steps will actually create HTML, with the results saved in $element['#children']. If #theme is defined, then that's the function that will produce HTML. Next up, if $element['#children'] is empty, then you iterate the actual children of the element—remember, child keys do not start with # – call drupal_render() on them and append the result to $element['#children']. Next the #theme_wrapper theme hooks—if there are any—get a chance to wrap the element into HTML. It's most likely those also change $element['#children'].

You are almost done! You have the children of the element finally in an HTML form in $element['#children']. Next, #post_render functions fire; typically these are used to do some sort of string filtering on the resulting HTML.

The almost last step is to add any JS and CSS required for the element by processing #states and #attached. The #attached property allows you to add libraries, JS, and CSS to a render array, and it's explained in the doxygen of drupal_process_attached() (which you can see at api.drupal.org/drupal_process_attached).

Finally, #prefix and #suffix are prefixed and appended to $element['#children'], and this is the return value of drupal_render(). Also, this is what gets stored in the render cache.

To sum up, for every child of an element passed into drupal_render(), either the function defined in #theme or a recursive call to drupal_render() turns it into HTML. This is how an entire Drupal page can be one large renderable array that you can modify, before rendering, with hook_page_alter().

▒ **Tip** For more resources on page rendering and altering, including an effort led by Bryan Hirsch to fully document the Render API, visit dgd7.org/render.

APPENDIX D

■ ■ ■

Visual Design for Drupal

by Dani Nordin

Visual design plays a vital role in any successful web site project. Like many content management systems, however, Drupal presents many challenges to designers who aren't used to working with it. This appendix gives a bit of background on creating visual design for Drupal, and it offers some helpful tips for making your life easier as a Drupal designer.

Why Designers Should Work with Drupal

Drupal started its life as a developer-centered community, and in many ways it can still be viewed that way. Over the last couple of years, however, the Drupal community has seen a renaissance of designers, user experience professionals, and other creatives who have worked hard to improve the experience of designers in the Drupal community.

- All over the world, Drupal designers and themers are getting together for Drupal Camps devoted to the challenges of designing for Drupal.

- Online, there is an active design4drupal community on groups.drupal.org (groups.drupal.org/design-drupal) that discusses these issues.

- Drupal themers, such as Robert Christensen of Mustardseed Media (mustardseedmedia.com/podcast), and Emma Jane Hogbin of Design to Theme (www.designtotheme.com/) develop useful content meant to help Drupal designers understand how to turn their designs into Drupal themes.

- Since 2009, the Design and Usability track for the annual Drupalcon has grown significantly, and independent Birds of a Feather (BoF) discussions have brought designers and themers together to talk about the challenges of designing for Drupal.

In addition to all these efforts from the community at large, the development of Drupal 7, and the redesign of Drupal.org, represents an important step forward in bringing designers into Drupal. Enhancements in the administrative interface, the HTML output, and the ease of overriding CSS output, along with more steps toward creating semantic code with Views (a long-standing problem for Drupal designers) with Views 3's incorporation of some of the Semantic Views (drupal.org/project/semanticviews) module have made Drupal 7 the most designer-friendly release yet.

Designing for Drupal: What It Means

One of the biggest differences between designing for Drupal and designing for Flash, straight HTML or even a blog system like WordPress is this: **visual design must always come toward the END of the project life cycle.** For web designers not accustomed to designing for content management systems, this can be a huge hurdle to jump.

In reality, once you get used to how Drupal works, it's much easier to understand how to design for it. If you're already used to working in HTML and CSS (where components of the page are broken into page divisions, for example), you're already halfway into understanding design for Drupal. The primary challenge that Drupal poses is that you, the designer, aren't generating the HTML. Drupal is. Thus, the first challenge to creating visual design for Drupal is understanding, and finding ways to manage, the HTML that Drupal is spitting out.

Anatomy of a Drupal Page

On most sites, the pages that Drupal creates are generated from a combination of any number of different areas. This is one of the things that makes Drupal so powerful, but it also adds a layer of complexity when it comes to visual design. For example, Figure D–1 shows a sample page from a Drupal site that I created.

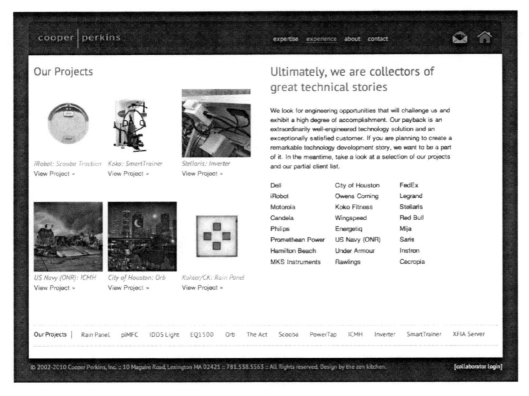

Figure D–1. The Experience page on Cooperperkins.com

If you were creating this straight in markup, it might look something like this:

```
<html>
<head>
        <title>Cooper Perkins :: Experience</title>
</head>

<div id="header">
                <div id="logo"><a href="index.html" title="Cooper Perkins Home">
<img src="/logo.gif" alt="Cooper Perkins Logo" /> </a>
        </div>
<ul id="navigation">
        <li><a href="expertise.html">expertise</a></li>
        <li><a href="experience.html" class="active">experience</a></li>
        <li><a href="expertise.html">about</a></li>
        <li><a href="contact.html">contact</a></li>
</ul>
</div>

<div id="middle">
        <div id="projects">
        <h2>Our projects</h2>
```

And so on. But when you look under the hood at the code that Drupal generates, you see something much different (see Figure D–2).

Figure D–2. *Inspecting the code under the hood. The highlighted text represents the image of the Scooba in the upper left. NOTE: This site was built in Drupal 6.*

This is because Drupal is creating this page by pulling content from different areas of the site's underlying database. Thus, the first step in designing for Drupal is understanding:

- Where information is being pulled from to create your page.

- How much of that you can control.

- What Drupal actually calls each bit of information so it can be styled.

For example, on this site, information is being pulled from the following areas (see Figure D–3):

- "Our Projects" section: pulled from a view called "projects" and a block called "project list."

- "Our Projects" menu: pulled from the "projects" view and a block called "project menu."

- Page text and headline: pulled from the node itself.

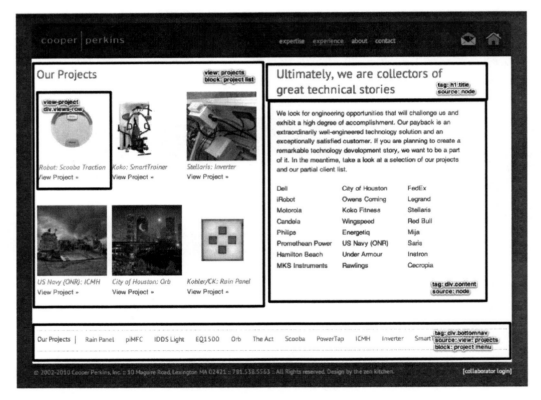

Figure D–3. *An overview of where the content is being pulled from*

The important thing to note about the structure of these pages, as it relates to design, is that for many Drupal pages, the layout of the page actually depends on the way that Drupal is configured. This adds a certain layer of complexity to the visual design, but once you understand more about how Drupal works, it's easier to create dynamic and functional layouts that are also visually effective. See Figures D–4 and D–5 for examples.

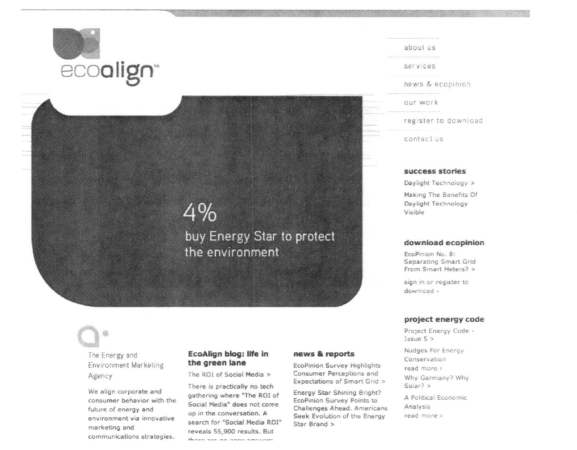

Figure D–4. *The EcoAlign site, designed by Claudio Vera of Studio Module (studiomodule.com), uses a dynamic Flash header and unique shapes to add visual interest and create a distinctly "non-Drupally" feel.*

Figure D–5. The Stoltze Design team worked extensively with developers to push the boundaries of Drupal design, focusing on bold, dynamic imagery.

Design from the Content Out

As mentioned in the Introduction (How Drupal Works), Drupal works by sorting your content into distinct Nodes based in different Content Types and displaying those nodes via pages, blocks, and views (see Figure D–6).

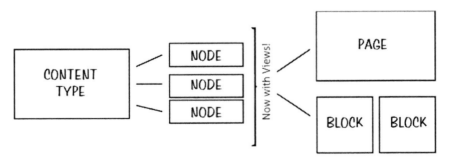

Figure D–6. A rendering of how Drupal works

This is one of the key reasons why content strategy, and understanding the content that is going *into* your site, is a vital component of any Drupal project. This is also one of the reasons visual design is best completed toward the end of the project; as the site's content changes, so does the design.

Making Your Life Easier As a Drupal Designer

Jacine Luisi (twitter: `@jacine`), of Gravitek Labs (`graviteklabs.com`), is a front-end developer who specializes in theming for enterprise-level Drupal sites. In addition to writing the Theming chapter in this book, she is the creator of the Sky theme (a gridded, HTML5-ready base theme for Drupal—`drupal.org/project/sky`), the Skinr project, which allows themers to create customized CSS styles that are re-usable within the administrative interface (`drupal.org/project/skinr`), and was a major contributor to Bartik, the default theme in Drupal 7. Together, we've compiled some advice for visual designers to help you make your life easier as you work with Drupal.

Remember—The Purpose of Design Is Communication

Watch out for areas in your design that aren't clear to the user—particularly areas such as navigation, featured content areas, or lists. Remember that the purpose of design is communication—not showing off how "cool" you can make things look.

Understand Site Architecture and Content Strategy

The importance of understanding the underlying content architecture of a Drupal project cannot be understated. When designing in Drupal, make sure that you understand how the site's content will flow from section to section, and build your site's design *around* the structure of the content, not the other way around.

Choose Fonts Wisely

Some designers love to use unique fonts (non-websafe fonts) throughout every area of their site. We suggest limiting this to titles and feature sections and against CSS using background images for titles, especially for global sites. This is important not only for usability but for page loading time. As Drupal depends on being able to change content dynamically, using CSS background images for titles makes it difficult for site maintainers to make needed changes. Additionally, these images can cause accessibility problems for screen readers or the visually impaired.

If you do want to use non-standard web fonts, consider using fonts licensed for @font-face, the CSS3 designation that allows browsers to render fonts in web-safe formats. Check out `www.css3.info/preview/web-fonts-with-font-face` for more information on using @font-face. Font hosting services like Typekit (`typekit.com`) and FontDeck (`fontdeck.com`) make it easy to include @font-face-ready fonts on your Drupal site, and sites like FontSquirrel (`fontsquirrel.com`) offer free @font-face-ready fonts, and functionality that will generate the @font-face styles for you.

Clearly Review the Requirements and Outline the Intended Functionality of Special Features

We've seen designers sneak in AJAX or jQuery functionality, above and beyond the site plan, claiming "that's what it was always supposed to do." Sometimes it's not a big deal, other times it can't be done by the themer and a developer needs to get involved. This causes project management and budget issues, which are especially problematic when they happen last minute.

Design for the Entire User Experience

Designing in Drupal isn't just about dressing up content; users of your Drupal site will also have to contend with 404 pages, search pages, and user login screens, not to mention form validation. Making sure that these components integrate with your overall site design is an essential part of making sure that your site's users have the best possible experience.

What follows is a brief (and by no means exhaustive) list of areas to consider when designing your Drupal sites, in addition to the standard considerations for each content type:

- User login/registration screens

- 404 and 403 pages

- Site breadcrumbs and navigation menus

- Special tags, such as `<blockquote>` and `<code>`

- Form elements

- Table layouts

- User profiles

- The site login block

- Site messages, such as form validation or error messages

- Taxonomy pages (i.e., lists of content based on category or tag)

- Social areas of the site, such as Groups pages (if applicable)

Nica Lorber of San Francisco's Chapter Three wrote a fantastic post (chapterthree.com/blog/nica_lorber/design_drupal_template_approach) outlining a templated approach to Drupal design that accounts for many of the Drupal default behaviors, to prevent things from being overlooked during the visual design process. In addition, Nica offered Chapter Three's template as a Fireworks .PNG file with layers, which can help make the design process much easier.

HTML5 in Drupal

While there is an effort to make Drupal 8 HTML5-native (see drupal.org/node/963832), the specification and its adoption were not ready in time for Drupal 7. However, there is a strong effort happening in the community to make Drupal ready for HTML5 right now. This effort is aligned with its own Drupal User Group (groups.drupal.org/html5), IRC room (#drupal-html5), and Twitter account (@drupalhtml5), along with several Drupal base themes on Drupal.org.

For more about HTML5 in Drupal, progress and initiative should be kept up to date at drupal.org/html5.

How You Can Get Involved

While the Drupal community has come a long way in the past couple of years (and Drupal creator Dries Buytaert has been heard many times saying that the community needs more designers), the community still needs designers to make their voices heard. Want to get involved? Check out a Drupal Design Camp in your area. Suggest Design sessions for upcoming Drupal Camps and DrupalCon. Start a Drupal Designers group in your area. Write blog posts on the challenges of designing for Drupal and help other designers get over the hurdles you've had to face.

Whatever you do to get involved, **the Drupal community needs your voice**. So get out there and be heard. Come by dgd7.org/design for these links (and more) and to stay up on reader- and author-contributed resources.

APPENDIX E

■■■

Accessibility

by Mike Gifford

Drupal 7 has made a huge leap towards universal accessibility thanks to the contributions of almost 400 people over the last three years. Drupal 7 core is one of the most accessible content management systems/platforms available today. Both public and administration pages have been reviewed for accessibility problems, and many barriers to participation have been eliminated. Drupal's modular structure uses APIs and hooks to make core functions available to themes and modules, which means that many of the enhancements in core will be inherited when developers are customizing sites. Unfortunately, this does not mean that every site developed with it will be accessible.

Recent Enhancements

The Forms API has seen a great many enhancements to ensure that interactive elements of a site are as accessible as possible, including the following:

- Skip navigation has been brought into all core themes, and there are default approaches to dealing with hidden, invisible, and visible display settings on focus elements.

- There are improvements in providing sufficient color contrast and intensity for people with low vision. In addition, images have been added to system messages to provide additional visual cues for all users.

- Likewise, there have been enhancements to the password management system to encourage everyone to have good passwords, including a progress bar that uses WAI-ARIA to alert screen readers about the level of security. (For more on WAI-ARIA, see the "Bring in WAI-ARIA" section in this appendix.)

- In most cases, drag-and-drop interfaces present barriers for blind users. To address this, drag-and-drop re-ordering can now be disabled by the user as required.

- Alerts have been added for some of the interactive elements that are added by jQuery. A screen reader user is now informed of the short list provided by auto-complete.

- Drupal core can now be both installed and administered by blind and/or keyboard-only users. The web site's content can also be viewed effectively by more people with disabilities.

What Are the Standards?

The World Wide Web Consortium (W3C)'s Web Accessibility Initiative (WAI) has been leading the development of international standards for accessible technologies. In the United States, the national standard is Section 508; however, it's being revised and will likely reflect Web Content Accessibility Guidelines (WCAG) 2.0.

Drupal is global community, and therefore we chose to test against WCAG 2.0. We also used some of the draft Accessible Rich Internet Applications (ARIA) Suite options, which allow screen readers to receive alerts when content changes dynamically.

Released at the end of 2008, WCAG 2.0 has broadened its scope from the web and aims to be technology-neutral. Rather than focusing narrowly on HTML, these guidelines offer the more general requirement that a site should be perceivable, operable, understandable, and robust (POUR). There are a number of techniques defined within these guidelines to help ensure that a site does not present barriers to its users.

As we begin to expect more dynamic, interactive web behavior delivered to a wider range of devices, it becomes increasingly important to have a generic set of guidelines that are flexible. This is why in WCAG 2.0 was built around the POUR principles, which essentially ask you:

- Can all users perceive your content? Simple things like testing color contrast and providing alternative text and captions for images and non-textual content can help with this.

- Can everyone operate your site? The tools people can now use to interact with web sites range from a mouth stick and head pointer to specialized software, keyboards, and screen readers.

- Is your site understandable? Does the user interface operate in a predictable manner? Are there ways for users to quickly identify their mistakes and correct them?

- How robust is your site? Is it future-compatible and based on open standards? What existing technology will you support and use for testing?

Who Benefits?

Yes, blind people will benefit if accessibility best practices are followed, but you already knew that. They represent a minuscule sub-section of the population, and they're just one group of users with disabilities to consider. In a 2005 survey conducted in the U.S. by the Survey for Income and Program Participation (SIPP), it was estimated that there were 54.4 million people with disabilities.

The classic icon for accessibility is the wheelchair, but when using the Internet, many people who use wheelchairs are in no way disadvantaged. The above estimate of people with disabilities includes people with mobility impairments but probably doesn't include those who are colorblind or dyslexic. We can only get rough estimates for the number of people with the latter two afflictions, but it's a significant portion of the population—and a somewhat invisible one as it's not possible to tell at a glance if someone is dyslexic.

The enhancements in Drupal 7 aren't just going to benefit those we readily recognize as being disabled. Most countries are facing a rapidly aging population; this means an increase in users who have problems with their vision, fine motor control, and hearing. By developing for the more demanding requirements for accessibility, we are able to ultimately find solutions that improve everyone's user experience.

Accessibility issues will affect everyone, even if only temporarily. As we age, our bodies and our minds change in ways that make technology harder to use and accessible design more important. And as we collectively live longer, the number of people who will benefit from accessibility enhancements grows. Accessibility issues are ultimately ones that are about our humanity.

It's the Law

There is a good chance that you are living in a country that has signed the United Nations Convention on the Rights of Persons with Disabilities. This convention is a commitment to allow inclusive participation by all. Furthermore, many countries have or are developing their own legislation for accessibility. In the USA, the Americans with Disabilities Act has shown leadership by recognizing the right for people with disabilities to live life independently and participate fully in all aspects of life. Australia, Belgium, Canada, Denmark, Finland, France, Germany, Hong Kong, India, Ireland, Israel, Italy, Japan, Korea, the Netherlands, New Zealand, Portugal, Spain, Switzerland, and the United Kingdom also have laws governing accessibility and information communications technologies.

Accessibility is becoming a legal requirement, and organizations need to be aware of this. In fact, government agencies and for-profit companies have been sued because their sites presented barriers to disabled people. This doesn't happen often, but both Target and the International Olympic Committee have been successfully sued for failing to implement accessible web sites.

Nine Ways to Make Your Site Accessible

Drupal 7 provides you with a solid framework to build a very accessible web site, but it isn't enough to ensure that your site is accessible. The implementation of contributed themes and modules can easily set up barriers for your users. The structure of user-generated content and the implementation of image fields can create further barriers.

There is a lot that could be written on this, but we'll be limiting this to the basics of choosing good modules and themes. We will take a look at color and contrast, as this is one aspect of accessible design that is often overlooked. We'll then look at how to set up automated testing and do your own simulation. Finally, we'll look at how to keep your site current regarding new standards to ensure that it stays accessible to everyone.

Accessible Modules

Drupal modules range in complexity and reliability. Drupal Core's hooks can be called from modules and themes, which can alter much of Drupal's core functionality. This means that if a module isn't developed with accessibility in mind it can degrade the accessibility of your site. You can search for accessibility issues for modules within the issue queue to see if there are any known issues with the modules you are installing (see `drupal.org/project/issues/search/?issue_tags=accessibility`).

If you run into an accessibility issue that isn't listed in an issue queue, please add a bug report to the issue queue so that it can be addressed. It is only through actions like this that we can improve Drupal's thousands of modules and themes, and develop best practices for accessibility.

The goal of the Accessible Helper module (`drupal.org/project/accessible`) is to make it easier for your site to be accessible. There are also sub-modules that allow you to easily implement improvements in accessibility for your site's theme, modules, and content.

Theming Your Site

There are good contributed base themes like AdaptiveTheme, Genesis, and Zen that work well for Drupal 7 and have been tested for accessibility. Starting with a solid base framework will help make sure your theme is accessible.

When developing your theme, don't forget to add alt tags to all of your images. Meaning is often conveyed to users visually through images, and it's important to take the time to think how to express that to someone who may not be able to see them. Using automated testing tools (discussed later) is a great way to catch missing alt tags for images.

The Drupal guide to theming accessible sites (drupal.org/node/506866) is quite good, and there are many ways to make the job of producing an accessible web site easier. Using CSS3, you can now provide some of the same effects you previously needed to use images for, such as rounded corners and great 3D effects. The CSS border-radius property and proprietary extensions for Webkit and Mozilla allows you to add depth to objects. Eliminating images makes web pages more accessible, faster, and easier to maintain.

Be very cautious of the use of the CSS display:none property, as screen readers interpret it literally. When an item is styled with display:none, it's invisible to screen readers as well as on-screen displays. Make sure that any lists of links (like a menu) has a header (usually an H2). If it needs to be hidden from sighted users, use the new Drupal CSS class .element-invisible.

Developing to a standard will save time and money over the life of the project. Ensuring that your theme validates against W3C guidelines will ensure that your site is future compatible and also that it will present well for a broad range of browsers. Using free tools like the W3C's (validator.w3.org) or Validator.nu (validator.nu) will help you find problems in your CSS and HTML.

Contrast and Color

Understanding the many different ways people see the world will improve your ability to design for them. The Drupal docs have some great resources about the use of color and the need for proper color contrast; see drupal.org/node/464500.

Many sites don't provide enough text contrast for the content to be easily read by all users. There are simple tools to ensure that your site provides enough contrast for low vision users, such as webaim.org/resources/contrastchecker.

Color is often used to convey meaning to users, but not everyone can differentiate between all colors. Eight percent of the male population has trouble seeing color. If you want to communicate important messages to your users, use color along with position, proximity, and graphical elements like icons. This extra attention to clarity will also help people with learning and cognitive disabilities decipher and navigate your site.

Automated Testing

Once you have done all this, the next step is to use automated testing tools to evaluate what you might have missed. WebAim's WAVE (wave.webaim.org) is a great tool for testing sites for known barriers. They offer a Firefox toolbar that is especially handy for determining the impact on interactive pages that require a user to be logged in. The Functional Accessibility Evaluator (fae.cita.uiuc.edu) evaluates a single web page and offers additional features after you register. Tools like the Mozilla Firebug Ainspector (code.google.com/p/ainspector/) can extend the popular Firebug tool to allow you to produce reports on accessibility.

There are a number of tools that can help you get a better sense of how others are perceiving your web site. Google's search bot remains the largest, richest, blind web user, so the more you provide semantic information for your content, the better your SEO is likely to be—and also your accessibility.

Although screen readers don't work in the same way, it's worth checking out a site in Lynx to get a sense of how it's viewed in plain text; see en.wikipedia.org/wiki/Lynx_(web_browser).

Simulation

It's also good to unplug your mouse and try to navigate around your site. The core themes and the ones suggested previously have an option to skip past or straight to the navigation links in a site. This allows keyboard-only users to navigate your site more easily. For more information, see the AIM site (webaim.org/techniques/keyboard/).

The most powerful, and arguably the most popular, screen reader is JAWS; however, other free screen readers are quickly picking up in popularity. Anyone using a modern Apple computer, iPad, or iPhone has VoiceOver built right into it. Windows users can download the free software application NVDA (www.nvda-project.org), and Linux users can use ORCA (live.gnome.org/Orca).

A sighted person can learn to navigate a site using a screen reader, but it is just an approximation of what a blind user would experience. Even someone who is recently blind will navigate a web site differently than someone who was born blind. A web developer will learn a great deal in navigating their own web site using a screen reader, but they bring with them the visual knowledge about how the information architecture works. To really understand how to best facilitate blind users' (or any disabled users') navigation of your site, it's always good to encourage feedback from people who have those disabilities themselves.

Bring in WAI-ARIA

Some elements of the Accessible Rich Internet Applications (WAI-ARIA) standard were brought into Drupal 7 core. WAI-ARIA is still a draft document so its use was limited. It was added in places where there was no other way to communicate to a screen reader an important piece of information. WAI-ARIA can offer more tools for adding semantic information to your site.

WAI-ARIA landmark roles define keywords for specific blocks of HTML to convey more meaning to screen readers. Landmarks allow a web developer to divide up a web page to make their content easier to navigate. The Juice Studio Firefox plug-in offers support in identifying the landmark roles that are defined in your site (juicystudio.com/article/examining-wai-aria-document-andmark-roles.php).

Drupal 7 and jQuery provide many interactive elements. The more dynamic elements are used, the more important it will be to add support for ARIA's live regions so that their messages can be effectively communicated back to the screen reader. By being able to define the importance of the interactive element as "polite, "assertive," or "rude," a screen reader can be instructed to either interrupt the existing text it is reading or wait until it's finished.

Maintenance is Critical

People often approach accessibility guidelines as another thing to simply check off and be done with. Ultimately, though, this isn't a very useful practice. What's really needed is a code of practice rather than a list of checkboxes.

WCAG 2.0 provides an important set of success criteria for accessibility, but this is only so useful in isolation. Having a perfectly accessible web site (WCAG 2.0 AAA) just is not attainable in anything but the very simplest site. Sites should attempt to achieve as many success criteria as they can, but it's important to schedule regular reviews for ongoing enhancement and to make sure that the publishing practices of the site continue to create accessible content.

Drupal is a powerful framework, and any user-generated content is likely to be a source of accessibility problems. Modules like HTML Purifier (drupal.org/project/htmlpurifier) can help ensure that all xHTML is valid. Other modules, such as the Accessible Content module (drupal.org/node/394252), offer specific accessibility enhancements to Drupal core.

Schedule Regular Reviews of New and Old Pages

Commonly accessed pages should be regularly reviewed by automated testing tools, and a structure of regular randomized tests will help keep your site as accessible as possible. Ideally, a large site would bring in a focus group periodically to provide feedback. Ongoing evaluation is the only means by which a site can be perpetually upgraded to reflect the changing technology and behavior of its users.

When testing, be strategic about your process. Working with Drupal 7, you can reduce your testing workload by eliminating some of the unknowns. After that, it's a matter of picking a few strategic pages to test representative functionality.

Get Expert Feedback

Consider bringing in an accessibility professional to assist you in improving your site. Best practices in delivering accessible content are changing constantly, as are the software and hardware that disabled people use to access your site. As new standards are developed and adopted, best practices need to be reconsidered to ensure that the content is being effectively displayed.

Bringing in an external person or team to review your site and look for enhancements can be well worth the investment. They will know how to look for and eliminate common barriers that an automated testing tool won't be able to detect. Also, consider hiring someone with a disability to do this review; we all learn to use technology in different ways, and the experience of disability is something that can't be fully simulated.

If you have a question, you can post it to the Accessibility Group (groups.drupal.org/accessibility) and you can read the documentation about Drupal's Accessibility initiatives at drupal.org/about/accessibility.

▓ **Tip** For all these links and resources, and more as we find them, visit dgd7.org/access.

■■■

Windows Development Environment

by Brian Travis

For those developers who spend most of their coding time with Microsoft development tools, the world of Linux/Unix is a scary place. In this chapter, I will cover various tools and configurations that make Drupal a friendly place for developers who prefer Windows.

There are systems out there that can make your Windows environment look like Linux. Cygwin comes to mind. But I, and a lot of Windows developers that I know, are not looking for that. People who develop on Windows are comfortable in their environment and don't want their beloved environment to look like Linux. They want to be able to use the tools they feel comfortable with and still get the benefits of the hard work done by the open-source community.

Windows developers have the same desires to give back to the community as the Linux-focused crowd, but the Windows zeitgeist is mostly fee for service. By showing the Windows developers that there's a community of openness and sharing in the Drupal world, they might have that incentive to give back and will expand the community as a whole.

So if you're a Windows developer, welcome to the wonderful world of Drupal!

If you prefer Linux, have some empathy for your brothers and sisters who prefer Windows. Don't discount them or force Linux on them. Rather, show them how they can live in their world and still be a part of a larger world of open-source developers.

I think Drupal 7 could be a way to introduce a massive group of really smart people into a mature open-source environment that they long for.

LAMP to WISP

As you probably know, Drupal is written for the so-called LAMP stack, "Linux/Apache/MySQL/PHP." While it is possible to substitute Windows for Linux, it is a bit more difficult to substitute IIS for Apache, and even harder to substitute SQL Server for MySQL. And don't even think about replacing PHP with C# or Visual Basic.

There are three different paths you can take to do your development in a Windows environment:

- Use a basic LAMP stack, substituting Windows for Linux. This is probably the most common approach Windows programmers take to getting their Drupal system up and running. This is commonly called a "WAMP stack."

- Start with the WAMP stack, but switch out Apache and use Internet Information Server (IIS) as the web server. This has the unfortunate acronym "WIMP" but is used in places where IIS is the preferred web server.

- Go all the way and replace IIS for Apache and Microsoft SQL Server for MySQL. This is called "WISP" and is made possible by the new database abstraction layer built into Drupal 7.

I'll cover the first configuration in this appendix. In my book, *Pro Drupal 7 for Windows Developers*, you can find more information about getting Drupal running on IIS and SQL Server.

I've been using Windows 7 running under VMWare, and so the screen shots and tools will be for that platform. Adjust for your system.

Visual Studio

For my money, Visual Studio is the perfect development environment. Visual Studio, along with .NET reflection-based IntelliSense, fits my development habits like a glove; I can't imagine coding without it.

There are other development environments available for the Windows developer. Many of these, including Eclipse and NetBeans, were ported from the Linux environment and have a definite Linux feel to them. I tried these environments and, while they certainly have a richness about them, I found that none of them was as intuitive and easy to set up and use as Visual Studio. The problem was that Microsoft doesn't support PHP.

And then I discovered VS.Php from JCX Software (http://jcxsoftware.com/vs.php). They sell a plug-in for Visual Studio that provides the same kind of environment for PHP as you would expect out of the Microsoft-supported languages C# and Visual Basic. VS.Php is less than a hundred dollars and can be used with the free Visual Studio shell.

VS.Php has all the goodness you would expect out of an add-in to Visual Studio. In addition to syntax coloring, you also get breakpoints, step-debugging, variable interrogation, and IntelliSense.

If you want to develop for Drupal (or any other PHP-based framework), then using VS.Php is a no-brainer. I'll be using this add-in to demonstrate the Windows-based Drupal environments.

After installing VS.Php into your existing Visual Studio environment, or creating a new implementation of the Visual Studio shell with VS.Php, you'll need to load a WAMP stack.

WAMP Stack

If you are using the VS.Php Visual Studio add-in, you've already got an instance of Apache, since VS.Php adds that on install. VS.Php also loads PHP. You don't, however, have a database instance. For a WAMP-based installation of Drupal, you'll need MySQL.

There are several freely available WAMP tools out there. I prefer WampServer (http://wampserver.com), but you can use any other that you might already have installed or prefer for some reason.

Actually, all you need in addition to VS.Php is MySQL. You can install that by itself, but without a stand-alone Apache instance and PHP interpreter you will always have to go through Visual Studio to see your site. By having a full WAMP stack available, you can access your site without loading Visual Studio.

■ **Tip** By having a stand-alone WAMP server in addition to VS.Php, you can access your site simultaneously with Visual Studio/VS.Php and outside. This is handy, for example, if you want to test how a site would look in different browsers or even using different users logged on.

First, get the WampServer bits and start the installation. The version current as I write this is 2.1. Download the bits as shown in Figure F–1.

DOWNLOAD WampServer 2.1e (32 bits) (december 27 2010)	DOWNLOAD WampServer 2.1d (64 bits) (december 27 2010)
Apache 2.2.17	Apache 2.2.17
Php 5.3.5	Php 5.3.4
Mysql 5.5.8	Mysql 5.1.53
PhpMyadmin 3.2.0.1	PhpMyadmin 3.2.0.1
SQLBuddy 1.3.2	SQLBuddy 1.3.2
XDebug 2.1.0-5.3	XDebug 2.1.0-5.3
webGrind 1.0	webGrind 1.0
XDC 1.5	XDC 1.5
taille: 36Mo	**taille: 36Mo**

Figure F–1. WampServer bits from wampserver.com

When you install, you will be asked where to put the bits. It's probably best for now to take the default, which is c:\wamp, as shown in Figure F–2.

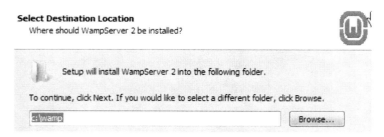

Figure F–2. Location of the WAMP bits

WAMP requires some administration privileges. Starting the WAMP server will probably require you to accept the UAC screen (see Figure F–3).

Figure F–3. *UAC for WampServer Manager*

■ **Tip** If you have Skype, you'll want to turn it off, as users have reported problems installing WampServer with Skype running. Skype uses port 80 (HTTP) as an alternative for incoming connections. If you want to use WAMP and Skype together, go into the Tools ➤ Options ➤ Advanced Connection panel in Skype and deselect the option "Use 80 and 443 as alternatives for incoming connections".

To make sure everything has been loaded properly, go to a web browser and access http://localhost. You should see the WampServer happy screen, as shown in Figure F–4.

This tells you that everything has been loaded, and it gives you the current versions loaded. If you have a problem, check to see if the WampManager icon is in the tool tray and that it is green. If it is not, then something in the stack didn't start.

The most common cause of this problem is that Apache didn't start. The most common reason for Apache not starting is that you have something else controlling port 80. The most common application that controls port 80 is Microsoft IIS.

If you have this problem, you can check to see who is sitting on port 80 by asking WampServer. Clicking on the icon will give you the WampServer control panel, as shown in Figure F–5.

Figure F–4. *The WampServer default happy screen*

Figure F–5. *The WampServer control panel*

On the Apache submenu, there is a selection to "Test Port 80" (see Figure F–6).

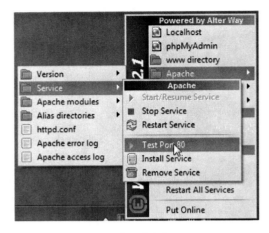

Figure F–6. *Testing the HTTP port*

This will bring up a command window so you can see who is using that port, as shown in Figure F–7.

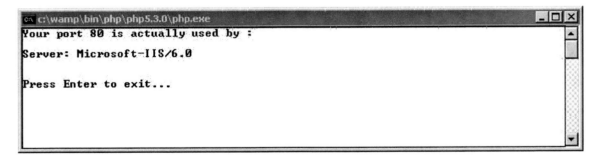

Figure F–7. *IIS is using port 80*

If you want to fix this, you'll need to turn off IIS: go to Computer Management. I usually get there by typing iis in the Search programs and files area of the Start menu. This will bring up the IIS control panel. On Windows 7 it looks like the screen shown in Figure F–8.

Figure F–8. *IIS in Windows 7*

Here we can see that, indeed, IIS is using port 80. Clicking Stop should release that port so Apache can use it. It is possible to run Apache on a different port, but I would not recommend it, especially while you are possibly learning a new environment.

Drupal Bits

Now that your WAMP environment is set up, it's time to load the Drupal 7 core code. The most direct way is to go to `http://drupal.org/project/drupal`. There you can see all of the currently supported versions, both in `.tar.gz` and `.zip` formats. For Windows users, the `.zip` format is probably the easiest (see Figure F–9).

Downloads

Recommended releases

Version	Downloads	Date	Links
7.0	tar.gz (2.6 MB) | zip (3.05 MB)	2011-Jan-05	Notes
6.20	tar.gz (1.05 MB) | zip (1.23 MB)	2010-Dec-15	Notes

Figure F–9. *Current Drupal distribution on drupal.org*

Windows Explorer will open the `.zip` file, as shown in Figure F–10.

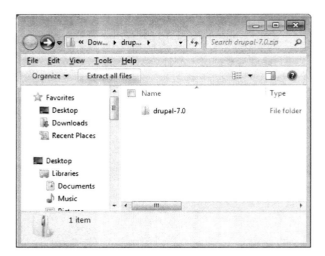

Figure F–10. *The Drupal distribution as a* `.zip` *file*

Extract the folder into a convenient location. I use `c:\wamp\www\drupal-7.0`, but you can put it wherever it feels good to you (see Figure F–11). You'll need to reference this directory in the next step.

Extract Compressed (Zipped) Folders

Select a Destination and Extract Files

Files will be extracted to this folder:

`c:\wamp\www`   Browse...

☑ Show extracted files

60 Seconds remaining

Copying 1,107 items (10.4 MB)

from **drupal-7.0.zip** (C...\drupal-7.0.zip) to **www** (C:\wamp\www)
About 60 Seconds remaining

⌄ More details   Cancel

Next   Cancel

Figure F–11. *Extracting the* `.zip` *file*

Now you'll need to tell Apache where to find Drupal. This is done by using Apache's configuration file, `httpd.conf`. WampServer provides a convenient method to edit the file from the WampServer Manager application, as shown in Figure F–12.

Figure F–12. Editing Apache's configuration file

This will bring up Notepad and allow you to edit the configuration file (see Figure F–13).

Figure F–13. Setting Apache's directories to point to Drupal

There are two lines that you need to update in this file. One is DocumentRoot and the other is <Directory>. Set these both to the directory where you extracted the Drupal programs.

To do this, simply search for the two strings, one at a time:

1. Edit…Find…DocumentRoot

2. Change the quoted value to your directory. Mine looks like this:
   DocumentRoot "c:/wamp/www/drupal-7.0/"

3. Edit…Find…<Directory

4. Change the quoted value to your directory again. Mine looks like this:
   <Directory "c:/wamp/www/drupal-7.0/">

■ **Caution** There might be more than one entry starting with <Directory. Be sure to modify the one that has an attribute. Also be careful to properly quote the value. This is an XML document and is very sensitive to the XML well-formedness constraints.

Once this is done, save the file and restart Apache to read the edited file (see Figure F–14).

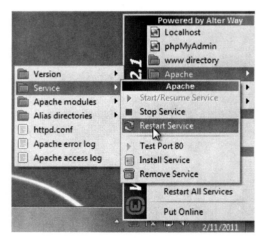

Figure F–14. Restarting Apache

■ **Note** If your service doesn't restart, the most likely culprit is a misplaced quote or angle bracket in your configuration file. As I mentioned before, the XML parts of this configuration file are pretty sensitive to syntax. Just open the file again and check to see if everything looks right.

Once this is done, go to `http://localhost` again to see if everything is configured correctly. If so, you should get the Drupal installation screen (see Figure F–15).

Figure F–15. The Drupal installation screen

From here, configuring Drupal is the same as under a typical LAMP installation. See Chapter 1 for information about how to configure a standard Drupal installation.

VS.Php

Once you have your WAMP stack running, it's time to load Visual Studio and the VS.Php add-on, if that's the development environment you have chosen.

I use Visual Studio 2010, but VS.Php supports older versions of Visual Studio as well. Plus, there is a distribution of VS.Php that has the free Visual Studio shell in case you don't have a full license of Visual Studio installed. I'll cover that version in this section.

Get the VS.Php bits from `http://www.jcxsoftware.com/download.php`. If you are using the free Visual Studio shell, you'll want to get the Web installer (see Figure F–16).

Figure F–16. *VS.Php installer site*

If the installer doesn't detect Visual Studio on your machine, it will offer to install the shell, as shown in Figure F–17.

Figure F–17. *Installing the free Visual Studio shell*

This is by far the cheapest way to get started with Drupal on Windows. As of this writing, VS.Php is a free 30-day evaluation.

■ **Tip** If you elect to install the Visual Studio Shell from the VS.Php installer, you may get a request for a restart. When you come back up, you'll have to start the VS.Php installer again.

The VS.Php installation is pretty straightforward. It's probably safe to take the defaults for now. You should end up with the happy screen shown in Figure F–18.

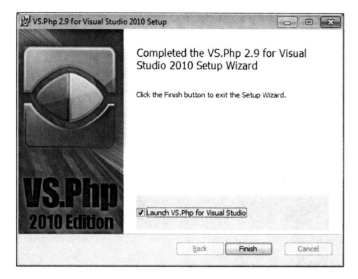

Figure F–18. *VS.Php happy screen*

Once VS.Php is installed, you can start VS.Php, which will start Visual Studio and then add itself to the development environment. Now we need to tell VS.Php about the Drupal code. From Visual Studio, select File ➤ New ➤ Php Project from Existing Code.... You will probably get the nag screen for the 30-day trial. After that, you will see a wizard that prompts you for the location of the PHP code (see Figure F–19).

Figure F–19. *New project from existing PHP code*

You can pick PHP version 5.2 or 5.3; both are supported by Drupal 7.

Since you have a new language, you'll want to tell Visual Studio how to handle the source code. The settings that follow are compatible with Drupal's code formatting conventions. In Visual Studio, go to Tools ➤ Options, and then expand to Text Editor ➤ PHP ➤ Tabs (see Figure F–20).

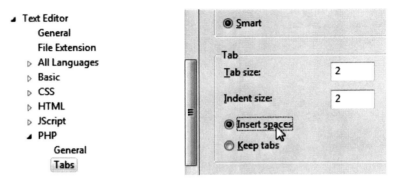

Figure F–20. *Making sure tabs are consistent with Drupal tab rules*

Drupal's code formatting conventions require two spaces for indents and that the spaces should be kept instead of inserting the tab character. Now let's tell Visual Studio that there are some additional file extensions that it should know are PHP code files. That is found under File Extensions on the same screen (see Figure F–21).

Figure F–21. *Adding filename extensions*

Add the .info and .module extensions and click OK.

■ **Note** Coding standards for the Drupal community are consolidated in a single link, drupal.org/coding-standards. As a new Drupal programmer, it would be a good idea for you to familiarize yourself with the standards so as to not be labeled a noob.

Now let's try to run the code from within Visual Studio. Set a breakpoint at line 21 of index.php, as shown in Figure F–22.

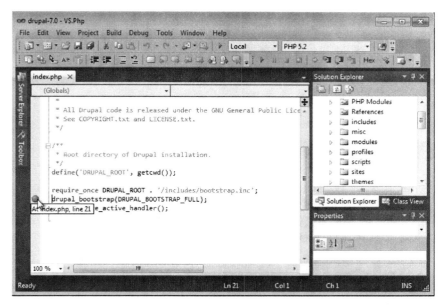

Figure F–22. Setting a breakpoint in PHP

Now press F5 to debug. You might get an error indicating a problem with starting the web server. Just dismiss this and try debugging again. Once things start loading, you might get the screen shown in Figure F–23.

Figure F–23. Configuration error

There are two things to check to resolve this:

- It could be because the WampServer is not running. Remember that you had to reboot to load Visual Studio. Just start WampServer again and try to debug.

- There is a directive in the .htaccess file that is not recognized by the Apache engine. Open the .htaccess file, which is in the same directory as your base Drupal install, and comment the line that has the word Order in it (see Figure F–24).

```
.htaccess* ✕  index.php
    #
    # Apache/PHP/Drupal settings:
    #

    # Protect files and directories from prying eyes.
    <FilesMatch "\.(engine|inc|info|install|make|module|profile|·
      #Order allow,deny
    </FilesMatch>
```

Figure F–24. Correcting the .htaccess file

Putting a hash (#) in front of the line makes it a comment.

▓ **Tip** VS.Php keeps its own set of log files. In Windows 7, the error log is found at C:\Users\{your user name}\AppData\Roaming\Jcx.Software\VS.Php\Apache2\drupal-7.0\logs.

Save the file and press F5 again to debug. If everything goes right, Visual Studio should stop at the breakpoint you set in index.php. From there, you can step through the code, interrogate variables, check the call stack, and anything else you can do with your favorite .NET language (see Figure F–25).

Figure F–25. *VS.Php turns Visual Studio into a PHP debugging environment*

phpMyAdmin and MySQL Connector

As I mentioned before, MySQL comes packaged with WampServer. MySQL comes with a tool that will allow you to manage your database server. You can create and delete databases, create and query tables, and manage users and permissions. This tool is called phpMyAdmin and is available from the WampServer console (see Figure F–26).

Figure F–26. *Accessing phpMyAdmin*

This launches your default browser and presents your MySQL database, as shown in Figure F–27.

Figure F–27. phpMyAdmin screen

If you would rather use Visual Studio to manage your database server, you can install the MySQL Connector for .NET, which is available for free at http://dev.mysql.com/downloads/connector/net. This will install itself into Visual Studio and give you the same kind of functionality you are accustomed to with the Visual Studio Server Explorer (see Figure F–28).

Figure F–28. MySQL Connector for Visual Studio

At this point, you are ready to start the learning process. Step through the code, interrogate variables, and watch how the database interacts with the code. I find this the best, fastest way to learn a new environment. And all from the comfort of your favorite Windows development environment.

In the next section, we will install a tool that has become indispensible to many Drupal developers. That tool is Drush.

Drush

Drush, the "Drupal shell," is covered in Chapters 2 and 26. Drush is a set of PHP programs that will make your Drupal development experience a lot easier. Drush requires several Linux–y tools to run. On a Linux machine, these are probably already there and all you need to do is to download the Drush code.

Unfortunately, the standard Windows machine doesn't have all of those tools, so you'll need to install them on your machine. This is sort of a hassle, but I guarantee you, if you spend a few minutes now getting this environment set up, you will save far more time as you start developing your Drupal applications in a Windows environment.

Installing Drush for Windows

Here is a procedure for getting those tools loaded and running.

First, download the Drush bits at `http://drupal.org/project/drush`. Grab the latest version (see Figure F–29).

Downloads

Recommended releases

Version	Downloads	Date	Links
All-versions-4.0	tar.gz (237.84 KB) | zip (277.95 KB)	2011-Jan-07	Notes
All-versions-3.3	tar.gz (170.79 KB)	2010-Aug-10	Notes

Figure F–29. Download the Drush bits

Unzip the files into a convenient directory. I use `c:\drush`. We'll add that to our environment path a little later.

Now, we need to get the Drush prerequisites. These are all open-source tools, and they each have Windows binaries with an installer. The download page for first one, `libarchive`, is shown in Figure F–30. It is located at `http://gnuwin32.sourceforge.net/packages/libarchive.htm`.

Download

If you download the Setup program of the package, any requirements for running applications, such as dynamic link libraries (DLL's) from the dependencies as listed below under Requirements, are already included. If you download the package as Zip files, then you must download and install the dependencies zip file yourself. Developer files (header files and libraries) from other packages are however not included; so if you wish to develop your own applications, you must separately install the required packages.

Description	Download	Size	Last change	Md5sum
• Complete package, except sources	Setup	1140310	27 June 2008	73e612405a10f690beffa8033a76cd46
• Sources	Setup	856349	27 June 2008	6b22d9e7e503b1bc1da79eccdf004eef
• Binaries	Zip	263534	27 June 2008	f2bd5a4ee39d9fc64b456d516f90afad
• Developer files	Zip	37691	27 June 2008	63f6e778ea3e8ef7fe198c08197d855c
• Documentation	Zip	717837	3 February 2008	f776dae5e66a25e69652be39c9a63bbd
• Sources	Zip	1399362	27 June 2008	63f0bbda21069c456a62f518fb2220d6
• Dependencies	Zip	73020	31 March 2008	737a54c70e4a42923f6707321c6a6aa6
• Original source	http://people.freebsd.org/~kientzle/libarchive/src/libarchive-2.4.12.tar.gz			

***Figure F–30.** Download page for an open source tool*

Grab whatever flavor you want. I usually just download the Setup program for the complete package. Run the setup program and take the defaults (see Figure F–31). This will install your program but won't make changes to the path. We'll deal with that in a moment.

***Figure F–31.** Setup program for open source tools*

You'll need a total of four GNU packages to make Drush work:

- http://gnuwin32.sourceforge.net/packages/libarchive.htm

- http://gnuwin32.sourceforge.net/packages/gzip.htm

- http://gnuwin32.sourceforge.net/packages/wget.htm

- http://gnuwin32.sourceforge.net/packages/gtar.htm

Now we need to set the PATH environment variable to include the Drush, PHP, and binaries installed. To do this, you need to get to the Environment Variables screen. This is different depending on your OS. Right-click Computer and select Properties. Click Advanced system settings and then Environment Variables…. You will see the screen shown in Figure F–32.

Figure F–32. Environment variables dialog

Under User variables, click New…, and you will see the New User Variable window, shown in Figure F–33.

Figure F–33. User variable dialog

Enter path in the variable name and the new directories in the Variable value field. Be sure to include the path to a compatible version of PHP, since Drush will be using that. I used C:\drush\;C:\Program Files\GnuWin32\bin\, but your system might be different.

The semicolon separates the paths. Paths are those to where the following files are located: php.exe, drush.bat, and the tar/gzip/wget binaries.

If you have a command prompt window open already, you'll need to close it and open another one in order for it to read the new path.

Running Drush

Now let's test to see if we were successful in installing Drush and its prerequisites. Using a command prompt window, change to the directory just above the "modules" and "themes" directories. Mine is C:\wamp\www\drupal-7.0\sites\all\.

Type drush at the command prompt. You'll get a nice long list of the wonderful things you can do, as shown in Figure F–34.

Figure F–34. Drush help screen

▪ **Note** I have gotten a message on some machines indicating that a particular DLL is missing.

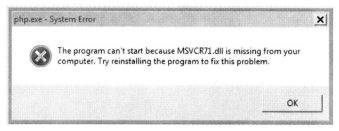

I don't know exactly why this happens, but you can download the DLL at www.dll-files.com/dllindex/dll-files.shtml?msvcr71.

If this works for you, you have just made your Drupal experience a lot more productive. Drush helps you do a lot of things that would otherwise require a lot of mousing around.

Drush knows where the Drupal projects are out in the 'tubes. It also knows the database location and login information by reading the settings.php file created by the installer. Because of this, it can perform these administrative tasks without requiring the GUI. That means, of course, that anyone who has access to Drush and your directory structure can do the same thing. Standard security precautions are applicable.

Summary

Drupal was originally designed to run under the LAMP stack. Much progress has been made in the standardization of the code to make it possible to move beyond that particular technology stack. With Drupal 7, it is possible to use different web servers and databases. In this appendix, we did just that, replacing the "L" in LAMP, Linux, with Windows. To learn more about working with Drupal on Windows, check out http://drupalforwindows.com and check out my book, *Pro Drupal 7 for Windows Developers*. There is also a Drupal group dedicated to Windows developers and administrators. It is http://groups.drupal.org/drupal-windows.

I expect that there will be a lot of demand for Drupal running under Windows with the WISP stack, and that a Windows-focused community will appear and champion this platform to make Drupal even more popular than it already is.

■ ■ ■

Installing Drupal on Ubuntu

by Benjamin Melançon

Developing your sites in a Linux environment means that the norm for all the tools you use will be that they are open source free software, like Drupal itself. More important to you, perhaps, the server, programming language, and database that Drupal relies upon are easier to set up and keep running on Linux.

I highly recommend that you develop web sites within a Linux environment for one additional reason: your Drupal sites are likely to be hosted on a server running on Linux. While all varieties of GNU-Linux are heartily endorsed, if you're running any version other than the popular Ubuntu, I will assume you already know what you are doing. This appendix will focus on setting up Drupal in Ubuntu.

■ **Tip** If you aren't running Linux and don't want to switch your main operating system yet for the sake of developing on or simply running local web sites, you can run Linux in a virtual machine.

The most important quality to have going into setting up your development environment is patience. It takes some time up front to get things working, but it will save you lots of time down the road.

Running Ubuntu on Windows or Mac OS X

To use Linux on a computer that is running another operating system—when you have a Mac OS X or Windows personal computer—you can run Linux very effectively in a virtual machine (VM). VMs have become quite good in recent years.

Download the VM of your choice. The open source VirtualBox is free for Windows or Mac (see virtualbox.org). The proprietary VMWare (including VMWare Fusion for running Linux on Mac OS X) is pretty affordable.

Also download the disk image for a current Ubuntu version (go to ubuntu.com/download and choose Download and install).

Once both the VM software and the Ubuntu disk image have downloaded to your computer, follow the instructions for your VM for installing an operating system. The most important thing is telling the VM where your disk image is on your computer (and it needs to stay at this location). Accepting the defaults for other configuration will work.

▪ **Note** If using VirtualBox, instead of downloading the Ubuntu disk image, you can get Ubuntu set up for Drupal development already on a VirtualBox appliance: `drupal.org/project/quickstart`. Quickstart gives you an environment similar to Drubuntu, described in the following section, but it is not compatible with Drubuntu—you have to pick one or the other.

Customizing Ubuntu for Drupal Development with Drubuntu

Drubuntu sets up a Drupal development environment for a single developer, with the LAMP stack (Linux, Apache, MySQL, PHP), Eclipse integrated development environment, Firefox developer tools, Git, Drush, and more. Drubuntu also includes its own Drush scripts for adding and removing your local sites.

▪ **Tip** The area of Ubuntu-based environments set up for Drupal development is rapidly improving. See `dgd7.org/ubuntu` for the latest recommendations.

Get the current instructions for installing Drubuntu from its project page at `drupal.org/project/drubuntu`. It has a way to bootstrap its own installation without even downloading first, by grabbing the drubuntu-bootstrap.sh shell script out of the repository directly. You can of course download Drubuntu from its project page (`./drubuntu/drubuntu-bootstrap.sh`) and run it, also.

Enter your password and type **y** for yes as requested (it will often say you may need to enter your password when you won't) and be patient while it installs a hefty development environment, including many things you will use every day.

Creating a Root MySQL Password

One thing Drubuntu does not set up for you that you can do to make your development environment a more convenient place to work is setting a MySQL root password.

```
mysqladmin -u root password YourPassword
```

Then add that password to a MySQL configuration file, so you never have to enter it. Open or create the file with a text editor such as Vim.

```
vi ~/.my.cnf
```

Give it these contents:

```
[client]
user=root
pass=YourPassword
```

Installing Drupal

Drubuntu's great value is in installing LAMP, Git, Drush, and other tools for you. You don't have to use its special tools (such as the drubuntu-site-add Drush command), and in fact you will not do so here. Someone is sure to put together the ultimate start a new site Drush command, and most developers have their own shell scripts—but these often tie into repositories or server practices that are not generalized. You can check out examples of helper shell scripts for many things, including setting up a new site like Listing G–1 shows with one command, at dgd7.org/sh.

When everything related to a project is in one place, it is easy to put in version control together (see Chapter 2). Therefore, I recommend you create a folder to be a project folder and put Drupal in a subfolder of that (for instance, called drupal or web). Having a project folder above the web root allows you to keep materials together with the project that should not be in the public web root (which is what the directory where Drupal's index.php is). It is good practice to create a directory for the project (in this case, **dgd7**) and put Drupal core into the web root (**dgd7/web**) in a sub-directory that I'll refer to as the Drupal root directory.

After placing a copy of Drupal core there, go to your Drupal root directory and create a copy of the sites/default/default.settings.php file, renaming it to sites/default/settings.php while making the copy, and change the permissions of the files directories to make them writable.

Listing G–1. Non-Drush command line steps to download Drupal and prepare it for running the web installer. Change drupal-7.1 to the current stable release of Drupal; for instance, drupal-7.4.

```
wget http://ftp.drupal.org/files/projects/drupal-7.1.tar.gz
tar -xzf drupal-7.1.tar.gz
mkdir -p ~/code/dgd7
mv drupal-7.1 ~/dgd7/web
cd ~/code/dgd7/web
cp sites/default/default.settings.php sites/default/settings.php
chmod -R o+w sites/default
```

▪ **Tip** Those first five steps can be done even more quickly with Drush: cd ~/code; mkdir dgd7; cd dgd7; drush dl drupal --drupal-project-rename=web; cd web.

Drubuntu sets up Apache to automatically serve up any directory placed in the ~/workspace directory as a web site. That is, if you create a directory ~/workspace/dgd7 and put an index.html file in there, you can go to dgd7.localhost in your browser and you will see that index.html file as a web page. Because Drupal is running out of a subdirectory of its project directory, put the full project directory in your own ~/code directory and create a *symlink* targeting the project's web root from the workspace directory, like so:

```
ln -s /home/ben/code/dgd7/web /home/ben/workspace/dgd7
```

When creating test sites that are not going to become projects (or if not following this approach of having a project repository that includes the web root as a subdirectory) you can create projects directly in Drubuntu's workspace directory and skip the symlink step.

Creating the Database

Drupal stores information in a database. All the information about your site is stored in this database, neatly divided up into different tables based on the type of information, such as posts, comments, and users. Creating a MySQL (see Listing G–2) or MariaDB database for your new Drupal web site to use is fast and easy using the command line, but you can also use an application or a web application such as phpMyAdmin. If using phpMyAdmin, you can quickly create a database and a user at the same time by going to Privileges ➤ Add a new User, and under "Database for User" select "Create database with same name and grant all privileges".

Listing G–2. Command line instructions to create a database in MySQL. If you haven't created a .my.cnf file as described in "Creating a Root MySQL Password," the first line will have to be mysql -u root -p password.

```
$ mysql
mysql> CREATE DATABASE database;
mysql> GRANT ALL PRIVILEGES ON database.* TO "username"@"localhost" IDENTIFIED BY "password";
mysql> FLUSH PRIVILEGES;
mysql> EXIT;
```

Fill in your own values for the parts in italics. For the database name, you can keep it simple and call it dgd7, and to keep it really easy call your database user dgd7, too. Hostname in this case will be localhost, and because security is not an issue on your own computer go ahead and make the password dgd7, too.

■ **Tip** See dgd7.org/sh for shell scripts to automate the creation of the database and everything else I just covered. When installing one site it doesn't matter much, but when you do a lot, the time adds up, and it helps to get in the habit of creating new test sites.

Drupal's Automatic Installer

Now load up your Drupal root directory in your browser. The exact address will be different depending on your local hosting environment. Usually it's localhost/drupal or similar. You'll automatically be redirected to the install.php and Drupal's automatic installer.

On the first page you choose the installation profile you want to use; unless you have downloaded a contributed one from Drupal.org or created one of your own, you likely want to use the Standard profile, as Minimal is really minimal. Click through the Choose language page, unless you want to first download a non-English translation, to get to the Set up database page. Here, you probably want to leave "Database type" as the default "MySQL, MariaDB, or equivalent" and enter under Database name, user, and password the values you provided in creating the database. Submit the form and Drupal will install itself! When it is done, you will be able fill in some basic site details along with creating a username and e-mail address with credentials suitable for the administrative user account (see Figure G–1).

Figure G–1. Drupal's site configuration page for site name and the first, privileged user, after installing a site

Congratulations! You now have an empty Drupal site. There is no content yet, and Drupal 7 is nice enough to tell you that there is no front page content. Front page content means (sensibly) content that is marked as "promoted to front page." Head to Chapter 1 to build out a new site.

■ **Note** For more information and, in particular, a better description and new recommendations based on reader feedback, visit dgd7.org/ubuntu.

APPENDIX H

■ ■ ■

Mac OSX Installation

by Dani Nordin

To set up a Drupal environment on a Mac platform using MAMP, start by downloading the free version of MAMP at `mamp.info` (left icon, see Figure H–1). Once the file has downloaded, unzip it, and click on the unzipped file to launch the installer.

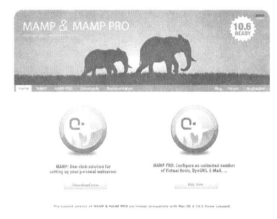

Figure H–1. Screenshot of `mamp.info`. You want the icon on the left.

MAMP basically turns a folder in your computer into a miniature development server; as a result, all sites that you develop locally will essentially be subfolders of that main folder. It's important to make sure you set the location of the main folder to something that makes sense for your file system and to back up that folder regularly.

To start up MAMP, perform the following steps:

1. Press the MAMP icon in your dock. This will start up the MySQL server and PHP.

2. Ignore the browser window that it opens up and press back to the MAMP screen (see Figure H–2).

Figure H–2. The MAMP home screen

3. Press the Preferences button, and go to the Apache Tab. Set the document root (referred to as the "web root" going forward) to something that makes sense for your file system.

Figure H–3. Setting up a default document root for MAMP

As you can see from Figure H–3, I set my main folder inside a Dropbox. Dropbox, available at getdropbox.com, allows you to store up to 2GB of data for free, and all data is synced over the Web with every change. If you don't have a ton of large files to store, Dropbox is an easy way to keep your data available to you no matter what machine you're on.

Downloading Drupal Core File

Next, download the Drupal core installation file from http://drupal.org/project/drupal (or drupal.org/start). Extract the file into the document root that you set up earlier in MAMP and change the name of the extracted folder to DGD7 or something similar.

Command-line Fu

Here are the command-line steps to download Drupal and prepare it for running the web installer. Change drupal-7.0 in the code to the number of the current stable release of Drupal 7, which you can find at http://drupal.org/project/drupal. Better yet, copy the link from the site before starting!

■ **Note** Do this from your web root. Comments surrounded by ** describe what's actually happening.

```
wget http://ftp.drupal.org/files/projects/drupal-7.0.tar.gz
        **downloads the file from  the provided link**
tar -xzf drupal-7.0.tar.gz
        **extracts it from the compressed file**
mkdir ~/dgd7
        **makes a new directory called dgd7**
mv drupal-7.0 ~/dgd7/web
        **moves the Drupal folder into the dgd7 directory**
cd ~/dgd7/web
        **navigates to the new directory**
```

Creating the Database

In order to install Drupal, you need to create a database on your local MySQL server. You can create a database using phpMyAdmin, which is free and available at phpmyadmin.net. Alternately, Navicat, a paid software available at navicat.com, is one of the easiest ways I've found to deal with databases. Although the premium software is on the pricey side (and you'll need it for copying or syncing databases on multiple servers—important when it's time to launch), you can download a free version called Navicat Lite at navicat.com/en/download/download.html that's available for both Windows and Mac. You can also download Navicat as a free trial for 30 days.

For the purposes of this demonstration, I'll use Navicat Premium, but the process in Navicat Lite is basically the same.

1. Open Navicat and select Connection ➤ New Connection ➤ MySQL.

2. Create your settings as follows: Your hostname is *localhost*, and your username and password will both be *root*. The port, if you've left your MAMP default as is, will likely be *8888*. In mine, it's been changed to 8889 (see Figure H–4).

Figure H–4. Connection settings for Navicat

3. Once you've created the connection, open the connection by double-clicking its name in the left column. Right-click on the connection name and select Create New Database from the menu. Name the database *dgd7*.

That's it. Done. See how easy it was?

Command-line Steps for Creating the Database

Here are the command-line instructions to create a MySQL database. Comments surrounded by ** explain what is happening. Remember that you're going to do this in the web root using Terminal.

```
$ mysql -u root -p
        **logs into the web root**

mysql> CREATE DATABASE dgd7;
        **creates a database called "dgd7"**
mysql> GRANT ALL PRIVILEGES ON database.* TO "username"@"localhost" IDENTIFIED BY
 "password";

        **does exactly what it says it's doing**
mysql> FLUSH PRIVILEGES;
        **so does this**
mysql> EXIT;
        **and this**
```

You will need to fill in your own values for the parts in italics. For root, use your database's admin username (typically, root). (In some setups, the root password will be blank by default.) For the database name, you can keep it simple and call it dgd7. To keep things really easy, call your database user dgd7, too. The hostname in this case will be localhost and because security is not an issue on your own computer, go ahead and make the password dgd7, too.

Starting the Install: Now the Fun Starts

Now that you've created your database, go to localhost:8888/dgd7 in your browser. This should take you to localhost:8888/dgd7/install.php. Choose the standard installation profile for now; it will take care of some basic configurations for you (see Figure H–5). On the next page, select English as the installation language. If you need to install it in another language, there's a handy link on that screen that will show you how to do so.

Select an installation profile

● Standard
Install with commonly used features pre-configured.

○ Minimal
Start with only a few modules enabled.

▶ **Choose profile**

Choose language

Verify requirements

Set up database

Install profile

Configure site

Finished

[Save and continue]

Figure H–5. The Drupal install screen

Now it's time to use the database information you just created. On the screen that follows, enter the values that you provided when you created the database.

Submit the form. Drupal will install itself within a couple of minutes. When the installer finishes, you'll be able to fill in some basic site details along with a username and e-mail address for the administrative user account (see Figures H–6 and H–7).

Figure H–6. *Setting up site defaults*

Database configuration

Database type *

◉ MySQL, MariaDB, or equivalent

○ PostgreSQL

○ SQLite

The type of database your Drupal data will be stored in.

Database name *

dqd7

The name of the database your Drupal data will be stored in. It must exist on your server before Drupal can be installed.

Database username *

root

Database password

••••

▸ ADVANCED OPTIONS

Save and continue

✓ Choose profile

✓ Choose language

✓ Verify requirements

▸ **Set up database**

Install profile

Configure site

Finished

Figure H–7. Database settings

■ **Caution** The first user created in the installation process is given permission to do everything on the site—forever. Therefore, it is strongly advised to never use this user as your own personal account. Rather, use it as a "superuser" or administrator account and give it a strong password. The site might be just on your computer now, but when you move it online, you'll need to preserve the user accounts. Drupal requires all e-mail addresses for site users to be unique, so if you only have one e-mail address, it makes sense to create a second e-mail account, like admin.user@gmail.com, that you use specifically for the superuser account.

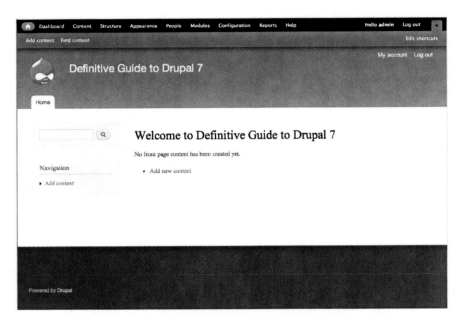

Figure H–8. *Your new home page, including the Drupal administration menu*

Congratulations! You now have an empty Drupal site, ready for content (see Figure H–8). Head to Chapter 1 to build out a new site.

■ **Tip** For reader notes about installing Drupal on Mac OS X, visit dgd7.org/mac.

■ ■ ■

Setting Up a Drupal Environment with the Acquia Dev Desktop

by Ed Carlevale

The Dev Desktop app from Acquia has many virtues. Download the installer (see Figure I–1) and within 10 minutes you will have the server, database, and your first Drupal site up and running. Access to phpMyAdmin is a click away. Create as many fresh installations as you want. Clone a site by dumping the database and importing the sql file into a new installation. Elegant, easy, and powerful.

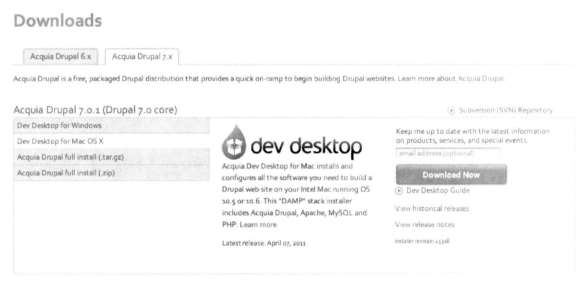

Figure I–1. Drupal stack installer from Acquia

■ **Note** The Dev Desktop is available for both Mac and Windows. I've only used the Mac version, and have found it to be a thing of beauty. The Drupal 6 version for Windows was said to be a bit quirky, though those issues may have been addressed in the Drupal 7 version.

Installation

Download the Dev Desktop as a disk image file from Acquia's web site (`acquia.com/downloads`).

Click the file to expand the disk image and open the installer.

Double-click the icon to launch the installation process.

The installer will walk you through a series of screens for the file locations, port settings, and default site settings (see Figure I–2). The default settings are what you want. The Drupal site settings are used for the first site you create, but you can modify the settings for any subsites or imported sites that you create.

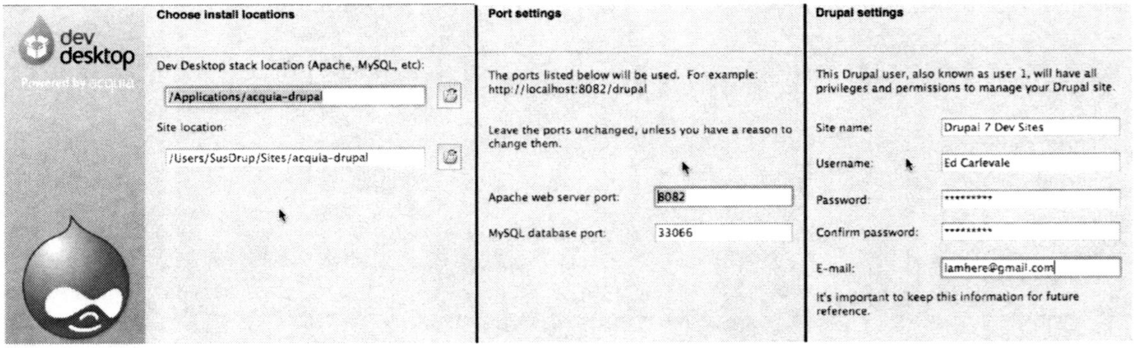

Figure I–2. Default settings for the Dev Desktop installation

■ **Note** You can set up multiple copies of the Dev Desktop (on your hard drive, a portable hard drive, Dropbox, etc). Simply repeat the installation process and modify the settings accordingly. For the port settings, increment the default settings (8082, 8083, etc.).

When the installation process has completed, the installer requests permission to create your first web site. Click yes. This will launch the Dev Desktop's Control Panel (see Figure I–3) and open a new browser window showing the Welcome screen of your new web site (see Figure I–4). Log in using the Username and Password you provided during the setup.

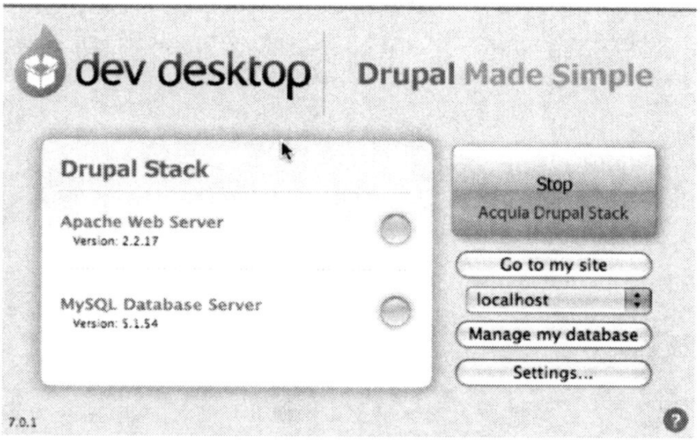

Figure I–3. *Dev Desktop's Control Panel*

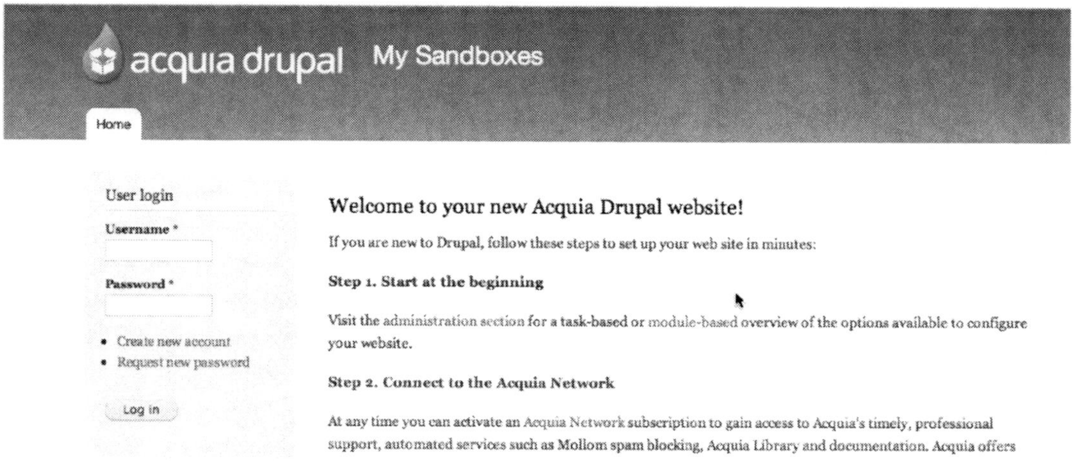

Figure I–4. *Login screen for stack installer's first web site*

Taking It Further

The real power of the Dev Desktop has to do with how easy it is to create more sites. You have two options:

1. Create subsites off your main installation—or multisites, to use Drupal terminology. A subsite creates a new database but uses the files and modules of your original installation.

2. Create a new, stand-alone Drupal 7 installation. This is ideal for use with installation profiles.

The first is quick, the second is powerful. Win, win.

It all happens from the Dev Desktop's Control Panel, which will become your best friend from here on out. From here you can open phpMyAdmin, navigate to any of the sites that you've created, or create new sites (see Figure I–5).

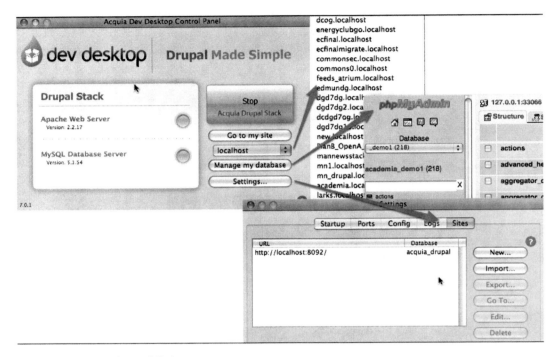

Figure I–5. *Control Panel links*

Creating a Subsite

To create a subsite of your current installation, start from your Control Panel and go to Settings ➤ Sites ➤ New. This opens up the form shown in Figure I–6. Fill in a site name. The database and subserver fill in automatically, and the other settings draw on the defaults that you provided during the installation process. Click OK. In a minute or so the new site is created. Click the Go To button to open the site in a new browser window.

More information on multisites is available from Drupal's online documentation (drupal.org/node/53705).

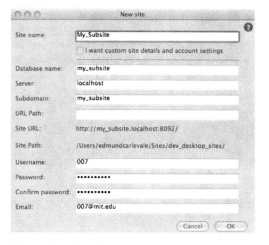

Figure I–6. Creating a subsite

■ **Note** With the Drupal 6 version of the Dev Desktop, some contributed modules were moved from their default location (/sites/all/modules) to a folder within the core modules folder (modules/acquia), thus complicating module updates. For the Drupal 7 version, some contributed modules are placed within the Profiles folder (see Figure I-7), but the new Automatic Update functionality handles updates efficiently and unobtrusively behind the scenes.

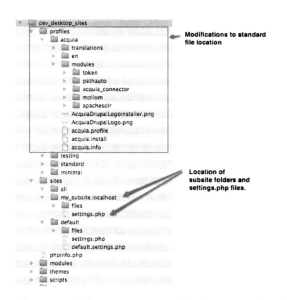

Figure I–7. Directory structure for the Dev Desktop's main Drupal installation and associated subsites

Importing Sites

The Import option is ideal for using with installation profiles. Simply download the install file and unzip it to a convenient folder, keeping it outside of the folder that stores the Dev Desktop's main Drupal installation. Then, navigate to Settings ➤ Sites ➤ Import (see Figure I–8).

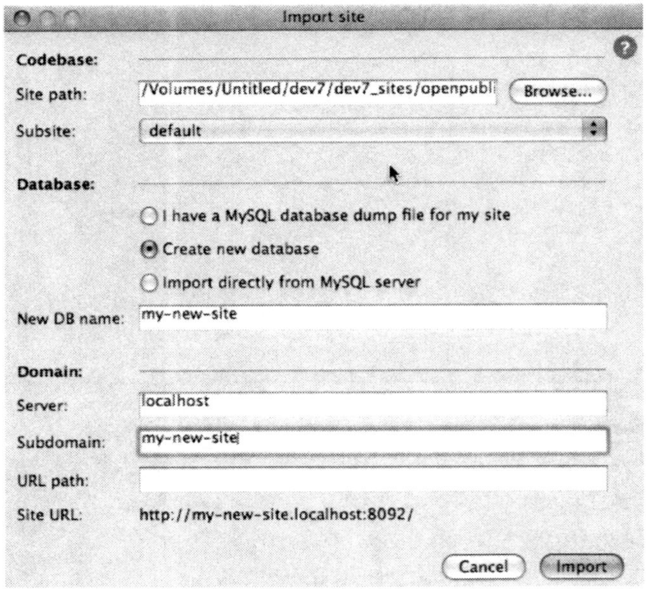

Figure I–8. Importing a new Drupal installation

For more information on installation profiles, see Chapter 38. Head to Chapter 1 to build out a new site.

▓ **Note** For updates and discussion on running Drupal with Acquia's Dev Desktop, see dgd7.org/stack. And of course, for corrections and new material related to this book as a whole, check out dgd7.org/updates.

Index

■■■

▓ A

◼ E

▒ G

▓ O

▉ U

CPSIA information can be obtained at www.ICGtesting.com
Printed in the USA
LVOW130950091011

249708LV00002B/1/P